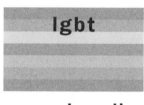

**encyclopedia
of**
lesbian, gay,
bisexual, and
transgender
**history
in america**

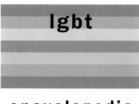

# lgbt

## encyclopedia of
lesbian, gay, bisexual, and transgender **history in america**

MARC STEIN
**editor in chief**

1

**Actors to Gyms**

**CHARLES SCRIBNER'S SONS®**

**THOMSON**
———————
**GALE**

New York • Detroit • San Diego • San Francisco • Cleveland • New Haven, Conn. • Waterville, Maine • London • Munich

# Encyclopedia of Lesbian, Gay, Bisexual, and Transgender History in America

Marc Stein, *Editor in Chief*

© 2004 by Charles Scribner's Sons
Charles Scribner's Sons is an imprint of The Gale Group, Inc., a division of Thomson Learning, Inc.

Charles Scribner's Sons® and Thomson Learning™ are trademarks used herein under license.

For more information, contact
Charles Scribner's Sons
An imprint of The Gale Group
300 Park Avenue South
New York, NY 10010

For permission to use material from this product, submit your request via Web at http://www.gale-edit.com/permissions, or you may download our Permissions Request form and submit your request by fax or mail to:

*Permissions Department*
The Gale Group, Inc.
27500 Drake Rd.
Farmington Hills, MI 48331-3535

Permissions Hotline:
248-699-8006 or 800-877-4253, ext. 8006
Fax: 248-699-8074 or 800-762-4058

**LIBRARY OF CONGRESS CATALOGING-IN-PUBLICATION DATA**

Encyclopedia of lesbian, gay, bisexual, and transgender history in America / Marc Stein, editor in chief.
    p. cm.
Includes bibliographical references and index.
    ISBN 0-684-31261-1 (hardcover set: alk. paper) — ISBN 0-684-31262-X (v. 1) — ISBN 0-684-31263-8 (v. 2) — ISBN 0-684-31264-6 (v. 3)
    1. Homosexuality—United States—History—Encyclopedias. 2. Gays—United States—History—Encyclopedias. 3. Bisexuals—United States—History—Encyclopedias. 4. Transsexuals—United States—History—Encyclopedias. I. Stein, Marc. II. Title.
    HQ76.3.U5E53 2003
    306.76'6'097303—dc22

                                                                    ##########

This title is also available as an e-book.
ISBN 0-684-31427-4 (set)
Contact your Gale sales representative for ordering information

Printed in United States of America
10 9 8 7 6 5 4 3 2

## editorial and production staff

**Project Editors**
Ken Mondschein
Anthony Aiello   Sarah Feehan

**Assistant Editors**
Elizabeth Merrick   Brad Morgan   Lisa Vecchione

**Editorial Assistants**
Birgit Danielmeyer   Erika Iverson   Rosie McCobb   Laurel Rose Webb

**Manuscript Editors**
Mary Flower   Gretchen Gordon   Michael Grosberg   Irene Kleeberg   Michael Levine
Katherine M. Moreau

Jonathan G. Aretakis   Robert A. Arlt   Patti Brecht   Anthony Coulter   Kae Denino
Sarabeth Fields   Amanda Kirk   Ourania Papacharalambous   Diana Seneschal

**Additional Editing**
Louise Ketz, Ketz Agency, Inc.
Richard Rothschild, Print Matters, Inc.
Neil Schlager, Schlager Group, Inc.:
Janet Bale   Judson Knight   Marcia Merryman Means

**Proofreaders**
Deidre Menchaca   Laura Specht Patchkofsky

**SGML Coding**
Sagar Krishnaraj

**Indexing**
Coughlin Indexing Services, Inc:
Jennifer Burton   Nedalina (Dina) Dineva   Marianna Wackerman

**Design**
Michelle DiMercurio

**Photo Research and Captions**
Melanie Somjen Frazer   Marybeth Kavanagh   Richard B. Slovak

**Imaging**
Barbara J. Yarrow
Lezlie Light   Kelly A. Quin

# contents

Contents

encyclopedia of lesbian, gay, bisexual, and transgender **history in america**

Contents

Contents

Contents

# preface

The *Encyclopedia of Lesbian, Gay, Bisexual, and Transgender History in America* (*ELGBT*) is the product of eighteen months of concentrated labor by hundreds of researchers and editors, but in a larger sense it has been made possible by more than fifty years of activism and more than thirty years of scholarship in the United States. Without the campaigns for equality, freedom, justice, and liberation waged by lesbian, gay, bisexual, and transgender (LGBT) activists since the 1950s and without the growth of LGBT studies since the 1970s, this encyclopedia would never have been imagined, much less published. Intended for use by the general public, including students, teachers, and other researchers, the encyclopedia draws on the expertise of scholars in virtually all humanities and social science disciplines and various interdisciplinary fields. Reflecting the field of LGBT studies as a whole, the volumes showcase the work of community-based researchers and academics based in colleges and universities. The result is a unique and up-to-date resource that we hope will make a lasting contribution to the pursuit of knowledge about central aspects of U.S. history, culture, politics, and society.

The *Oxford English Dictionary* offers three definitions of the term *encyclopedia*:

1.  The circle of learning; a general course of instruction.

2.  A literary work containing extensive information on all branches of knowledge.

3.  An elaborate and exhaustive repertory of information on all the branches of some particular art or department of knowledge.

From its earliest usage, the term *encyclopedia* has referred to means and methods of satisfying desires for knowledge. As many of the entries in *ELGBT* make clear, however, desires have changed dramatically over the course of history, as have ideas about and responses to them and attitudes about whose desires should be recognized and fulfilled and who should recognize and fulfill them. Circles of learning in the past may have had homoerotic and gender-crossing dimensions, but for centuries encyclopedias have offered a general course of instruction in how to hate, despise, loathe, pathologize, control, erase, and eradicate sexualities and genders viewed as transgressive. In recent decades, encyclopedias have generally ignored such subjects or have treated them as scientific, medical, biological, and psychological matters, not historical ones. Even today most encyclopedias fail to treat LGBT topics adequately or relegate such subjects to the margins. *ELGBT* brings together and focuses on different kinds of knowledge about sexualities and genders, critical but not hateful, analytic but not pathologizing, interpretive but not objectifying.

## Putting Together the Encyclopedia

Work on *ELGBT* began in the spring of 2002 with the appointment of the editor-in-chief and the editorial board, which brought together scholars in African American studies, American studies, Asian American and Pacific Islander studies, cultural studies, ethnic studies, gender studies, history, history of science, legal studies, LGBT studies, literature, sexuality studies, urban studies, and women's studies, as well as an expert in LGBT libraries and archives. For guidance in additional areas (including art history, musicology, Latina/o studies, Native American studies, religious studies, and sociology), the editorial board consulted with experts in other fields.

As work began on developing the list of more than 500 entry subjects, the editorial board engaged in extensive discussion of critical terms and parameters, a difficult task given the complex, contentious, and controversial nature of LGBT studies. At a very early stage, we decided to have the encyclopedia focus on *lesbian, gay, bisexual,* and *transgender* subjects. As many of the entries make evident, the language used to describe sexualities and genders has changed over the course of U.S. history, and this language has reflected and produced changing meanings and practices. The terms *sodomy* and *queer*, for example, have meant different things in different contexts, and the words *homosexuality* and *heterosexuality* were not even invented until the late nineteenth century, when scientific authorities attempted to impose order on a complicated and colorful cast of characters that used very different terms to describe themselves. Although it is sometimes tempting to equate the phenomena that today are designated by the terms *lesbian, gay, bisexual,* and *transgender* with what have been called by other names in the past and in distinct cultural contexts, we believe that more can be learned by exploring how these phenomena are both similar and different from one another. *ELGBT*, then, is an LGBT encyclopedia, but one that explores same-sex sexual and cross-gender phenomena that were not necessarily called LGBT in their own time and place.

Most people working in LGBT studies today seem to agree that out of the universe of same-sex sexual and cross-gender desires and acts that have existed across U.S. history, there emerged in the late nineteenth century new identities, communities, and cultures based on those desires and acts and in the mid-twentieth century new political movements organized to defend those identities, communities, and cultures. The terms *lesbian, gay, bisexual,* and *transgender* acquired their present meanings in the context of this history. We acknowledge that selecting four key terms out of the much larger group of words that have been used to name non-normative sexualities and genders runs the risk of excluding other important terms; marginalizing related practices, identities, and cultures; and decentering sexual and gender phenomena that existed before these terms were invented or acquired their current meaning. We believe, however, that the terms *lesbian, gay, bisexual,* and *transgender*, if used carefully and consciously, can be used analytically to refer to a broad range of same-sex sexual and cross-gender desires, acts, identities, communities, cultures, and movements.

The decision to produce an *LGBT* encyclopedia left unanswered questions about how the terms *lesbian, gay, bisexual,* and *transgender* should be used in individual entries. Many contributors are specialists in one, two, or three, but not necessarily all four, of the areas designated by the encyclopedia's four key terms. One of the things that is unique about *ELGBT* is that it brings together knowledge about these four areas and we encouraged all contributors, if necessary and relevant, to stretch beyond their research expertise to cover all four. While in some cases individual entries do not do so (reflecting in many cases the parameters of the particular subject or the state of knowledge in the field), the encyclopedia as a whole does.

There was considerable discussion on the editorial board and in the editing process about whether certain phenomena should be labeled gay; lesbian and gay; lesbian, gay, and bisexual; or lesbian, gay, bisexual, and transgender. For example, the homophile movement of the 1950s and 1960s consisted for the most part of exclusively female organizations and predominantly male ones. Should the predominantly male ones be described as gay or lesbian and gay? Does it matter that the term *gay* was often used for both women and men in this period? Should the movement be characterized as LGB if it did not generally discuss bisexuality but if it sometimes did and if it included people who behaved bisexually? And should it be called an LGBT movement if it generally distanced itself from cross-gender phenomena but if sometimes it did not and if some transgender people, activities, and arguments were part of the movement? Our inclination was to have the entries discuss such matters as openly and directly as possible and, where relevant, to err on the side of inclusive language, but readers should be aware that these are contested issues and the entries are not necessarily consistent in this regard.

Although *ELGBT* does not invoke the term *queer* in its title, many of the entries do. In the last fifteen years, many LGBT people have reclaimed the historically pejorative term *queer*, using it in a variety of ways. Some use *queer* as a synonym for lesbian and gay, LGB, LGBT, or a longer list of non-dominant genders and sexualities. Others use it in a more historically specific sense, referencing early twentieth-century and late twentieth-century figures who called themselves queer. Still others define queers as those who embrace dissident and militant gender and sexual politics, implicitly or explicitly suggesting that conservative LGBT people are not queer and that dissident non-LGBT people are. The term *queer* has also been used to refer to those who reject gender and sexual categories and those who are opposed to models of coherent and stable identities (which again can exclude some LGBT people and include some non-LGBT people). And finally, queer has been used as a way of referencing the process of challenging the dominant (as in calls for queering the state, queering politics, queering culture, etc.). We have not attempted to impose one definition of *queer* on all of the encyclopedia entries; usage and context generally make evident the meaning. Because the term remains highly controversial; because the encyclopedia discusses LGBT people who were not necessarily dissidents, militants, and challengers and those who did not necessarily reject coherent and stable identities; because the term *queer* often promotes celebratory rather than critical perspectives on LGBT cultures; and because many LGBT people are offended by the term *queer* (even though we are not), we think it appropriate to not call this an encyclopedia of *queer* history (even though we think the *ELGBT* is pretty queer, at least in the sense of departing from dominant norms of what counts as history).

The other key terms invoked in the encyclopedia's title are *History* and *America*. *ELGBT* covers more than 400 years of historical developments, and in some of the entries dealing with Native American topics an even longer period. Challenging the myth that sexualities and genders are unchanging, static, and fixed aspects of human nature, the encyclopedia demonstrates that they are historical phenomena, changing over time in complex ways. Working against the belief that LGBT identities, communities, cultures, and movements only emerged after the New York City Stonewall Riots of 1969 (when LGBT patrons of the Stonewall Inn and other city residents rioted after a police raid), the encyclopedia shows that they have a much longer history. And debunking the view that same-sex sexual and cross-gender desires and acts from pre-twentieth century worlds are not recoverable, the encyclopedia makes clear that they have been recovered. We have placed more emphasis than some readers might expect on pre-1969 developments; this reflects our conviction that ignorance about pre-1969 LGBT history is widespread and damaging, that post-1969 history can best be understood through extensive investigation of pre-1969 worlds, that other resources are available for helping readers learn about LGBT life in the post-1969 world, and that exploring sexualities and genders in the distant past can help us imagine better sexual and gender worlds for the future.

*ELGBT* focuses on the history of the United States and its predecessor colonies and cultures. In common speech today, *America* is an ambiguous term that sometimes refers to the entirety of South, Central, and North America and sometimes refers to the United States only. Many U.S. Americans appropriate the term *America* and *American* for themselves in part as a shorthand for a country that has a long name, in part because the adjectival form of *the United States of America* would yield the exceedingly awkward *United States of American*, and in part because U.S. Americans have a long history of imperialistically imagining themselves as having a manifest destiny to rule the hemisphere. Scribners has a set of encyclopedias on various topics *in America* and this encyclopedia, like the others in the Scribner series, focuses on the United States and the colonies and cultures that existed on lands now claimed by the United States. Other encyclopedias have made important contributions by examining LGBT histories and cultures on a global level; *ELGBT* provides a much more in-depth look at the United States specifically.

The editorial board initially worked with thirteen general subject areas that were identified as central in LGBT studies today: people; politics; culture and the arts; academic disciplines and fields; identities, communities, and cultures; geographies; law and public policy; economics and labor; sex, sexuality, intimacy, and relationships; religion and spirituality; language, symbols, signs, and concepts; social life, issues, and institutions; and social, cultural, and political processes. The two largest categories, people and politics, were broken down further into subcategories. For people, the subcategories were artists; athletes; colonial and other historical figures; movement activists; writers; political, educational, reform, and religious figures; scientists, sexologists, and social scientists. For politics, the subcategories were LGBT movement events, LGBT movement organizations; LGBT movements; LGBT publishing, publications, and presses; scandals, sex panics, and witchhunts; and social movements and political parties. Many of the more than 500 entry subjects selected could easily fit into multiple categories and subcategories.

Readers should note that we made the decision to not put "LGBT" before most entry titles, so, for example, the entry "Businesses" covers LGBT businesses, and the entry "Bookstores" covers LGBT bookstores. On the list of biographical entries, readers may also want to note that we included various figures who resided in the United States for some significant period of time but who were not necessarily U.S. citizens by birth or naturalization; but we excluded figures (such as Michel Foucault, Radclyffe Hall, and Oscar Wilde) who influenced and even visited the United States but who were not U.S. Americans in any significant sense of the term. We made the additional decision, for reasons discussed above, to include on the list of biographical and organizational entries only those individuals and groups that made noteworthy contributions before the mid-1980s. Significant individuals and organizations from the last twenty years are discussed in various topical entries. In some cases (such as Actors and Actresses, and Icons), we decided that many relevant individuals could be discussed in thematic rather than biographical entries. Some biographical entries discuss fairly obscure figures from the pre-twentieth century world. Our decision to include these reflects our desire to cover significant pre-twentieth century ground. Also, to the extent that *ELGBT* is designed to reflect the current state of knowledge, if there has been significant scholarly work on an ordinary person from the seventeenth, eighteenth, or nineteenth centuries, we are convinced that a biographical entry is merited. Many of the biographical entries (including all of the ones covering the pre-twentieth century world) discuss figures who did not necessarily call themselves or think of themselves as lesbian, gay, bisexual, or transgender; they have been included because their actions (for example, sex acts documented in court records) or their words (for example, romantic letters) have contributed to a scholarly consensus that sees them as part of LGBT history. Ultimately, selecting more than 250 individuals for biographical entries is highly subjective. We canvassed a large group of scholars for input and chose individuals on the basis of their historical contributions and the current state of knowledge.

## Using the Encyclopedia

*ELGBT* has been designed for use by a variety of types of readers. A list of entry terms can be found on page vii; a topical listing is provided on page 321. A chronology of major developments, prepared by Brett Beemyn with relevant entries highlighted in boldface or cross-referenced, can be found on page xxiii; we hope this resource will function as a chronological index for the encyclopedia.

Entries are then organized alphabetically, with relevant bibliographic references and cross-referenced items provided at the end of each entry for those who wish to explore subjects more in depth. Where we think it likely that readers may look up a term or concept that we have covered elsewhere, we provide relevant cross-references.

After the entries, in the third volume, we include a directory of LGBT libraries and archives throughout the United States and Canada, prepared by the Lesbian and Gay Archives Roundtable of the Society of American Archivists (LAGAR); a directory of contributors, their primary institutional affiliations, and the entries they prepared; and a comprehensive index.

## Acknowledgments

This encyclopedia is the product of the collective efforts of hundreds of contributors, who not only produced outstanding entries but offered invaluable suggestions for additional writers, bibliographic references, and visual images. For their help in particular subject areas, the editorial board especially would like to thank Laura Briggs, Suzanne Cusick, Maureen Fitzgerald, Judith Halberstam, Joanne Meyerowitz, Jorge Olivares, Judith Peraino, Horacio Roque Ramirez, Christopher Reed, Yolanda Retter, Will Roscoe, Susan Stryker, Verta Taylor, Pam Thoma, Jonathan Warren, Walter Williams, and Judy Wu. At Scribners, Frank Menchaca, John Fitzpatrick, and Nathalie Duval had the courage and vision to initiate this project; Anthony Aiello, Sarah Feehan, and especially Ken Mondschein guided it to completion; and dozens of editorial and production staff helped in countless ways. Lisa Duggan and John D'Emilio played central roles in launching this encyclopedia; Lisa (in the historical introduction), Brett Beemyn (in the chronology), and Brenda Marston and Deborah Richards (in the directory of LGBT archives) made crucial contributions. Members of the editorial board received major support from Maureen Fitzgerald, Ken Foster, Stephanie Gilmore, and Verta Taylor, as did I from Julie Land and Jorge Olivares. The board, consisting of Brenda Marston, Leisa Meyer, Robert Reid-Pharr, Leila Rupp, and Nayan Shah, spent hundreds and hundreds of hours developing the list of entry terms, suggesting and contacting contributors, editing entries, and participating in major decisions; I am deeply grateful for their commitment, dedication, patience, and high standards, as I am to everyone who contributed to the success of this project.

**Marc Stein**
**York University**
**September, 2003**

## historical introduction

Researching, writing, teaching, and publishing about histories of sexual and gender minorities, or sexually dissenting populations, is a contentious enterprise. Like all intellectual projects, this work is imbued with the dreams, fears, animosities, and unselfconscious assumptions of its constituencies—the academics, activists, writers, readers, and students who create and support it. The work is received by multiple broader publics with the same delight and curiosity, contempt and dismissal, or indifference with which these constituencies are met. In other words, LGBT and queer historians labor within a highly politicized field of debate; they not only write history, they make history.

The very names for sexually dissenting populations, practices, subcultures, or identities change historically, reflecting the shifting and clashing conceptions of religious groups, scientific studies, cultural sites, and social movements. Lesbian and gay history, in particular, first developed as a field of study in the 1970s, alongside the explosion of gay liberation and lesbian feminism in the United States (bisexual, transgender, and queer histories are later developments). History projects and community archives, slide shows, and lectures appeared in U.S. cities as integrated parts of larger social movements. The founding of the Lesbian Herstory Archives in 1973, and the publication of Jonathan Ned Katz's pioneering collection of documents *Gay American History* in 1976 (N.Y.: Crowell), were the achievements of social movement activists. They were political acts, and major lesbian and gay community events.

As the field of lesbian and gay history expanded, and intersected with work in lesbian and gay studies more generally, universities and colleges began to absorb, reflect, collect, and generate research projects, courses, archives, and publications alongside community and social movement institutions. Whether academic and activist institutions cooperated or conflicted as lesbian and gay histories proliferated, the field remained deeply embedded within sexual political debates. Differences of race, class, gender, nationality, and religion generated sharp critiques of existing historical narratives, and inspired new research. By the 1980s, floods of new publications reflected the influence of women of color feminism, black lesbianism, sex radicalism, and debates over identity politics. Activist writers— including Barbara Smith, Cherríe Moraga, Amber Hollibaugh, Allen Bérubé, and many others—continually called for new critical histories to expand the basis for lesbian and gay politics. The "sex wars" and the AIDS pandemic also shifted the historical questions and political investments of historians dramatically.

By the 1990s, "lesbian and gay" began to appear too narrow for framing the parameters of research and writing on histories of sexual dissent. The histories of drag queens and kings, bisexuals, sadomasochists and sex workers, and of transgendered and transsexual populations required a more expansive frame reflecting the vast historical and contemporary array of terms, identities, and communities for dissent from sexual and gender normativity. The wide cross-cultural variation in the basic organization as well as categorization of sexual and gender differences, in relation to racial, class, religious and regional differences, also pressured the simple phrase "lesbian and gay" to the breaking point. The designations "LGBT" (lesbian, gay, bisexual, and transgender) and "queer" both developed as strategies for encompassing this heterogeneity, and avoiding any presentist or ethnocentric foreclosure. These strategies have come under various critical pressures as well—neither can adequately designate the range of categories, concepts, and terms for sexual differences. Culturally and historically specific terms, such as "sodomite," "trade," or "two-spirit," in use among Native Americans, constantly fracture the generalizing power of any universalizing designation.

The *Encyclopedia of Lesbian, Gay, Bisexual, and Transgender History in America* reflects these historical layers and political debates in what is now generally called LGBT or queer history. There are entries written by groundbreaking activist intellectuals with careers beginning as early as the 1970s: Tee Corinne ("Visual Art: Painting, Drawing, and Sculpture, 1969–Present," and other entries), Joan Nestle ("Hampton, Mabel"), Karla Jay ("Literature: 1890–1969"), and Jeff Escoffier ("Businesses") among them. There are entries providing histories of significant activist institutions, figures, events, and publications as well, including Angela Bowen's "Combahee River Collective," Alice Echols's "Radicalesbians," Richard Burns's "Community Centers," Kimberly Springer's "Smith, Barbara" and Jane Gerhard's "Millett, Kate." There are entries on aspects of and issues surrounding the 1980s "sex wars" by some of the major protagonists in those debates: Patrick Califia ("Sadomasochism, Sadists, and Masochists"), Gayle Rubin ("Samois"), and Michael Bronski ("Pornography"). The impact of AIDS and AIDS activism is represented in a range of entries, including "AIDS and People with AIDS," "AIDS Coalition to Unleash Power (ACT UP)," and "AIDS Service Organizations." There are entries written by the pioneering generation of LGBTQ academic historians John D'Emilio ("National Gay and Lesbian Task Force (NGLTF)" and "Rustin, Bayard"), Estelle Freedman (on "Van Waters, Miriam"), and Blanche Wiesen Cook (on "Roosevelt, Eleanor, and Lorena Hickock"), as well as pioneering literary scholars such as Lillian Faderman ("Romantic Friendship and Boston Marriage" and "Foster, Jeannette"), and anthropologists including Walter Williams and Evelyn Blackwood ("Two-Spirit Males" and "Two-Spirit Females," respectively). The geographical listings reflect the uneven pattern of community studies that began appearing during the 1980s, as well as the major sites of LGBTQ population and activism. These entries center primarily on cities including Buffalo, New York City, San Francisco, Philadelphia, Los Angeles and West Hollywood, Boston, and Chicago because these have been the geographical scale for study as well as organization. There are, as well, entries covering vexing longtime disputes, such as "Monogamy and Nonmonogamy," the activity of LGBTQ figures in a variety of political movements, including "Anarchism, Socialism, and Communism," and the impact of LGBTQ scholarship in a wide range of academic and research fields, from "Psychology, Psychiatry, Psychoanalysis, and Sexology" to "Cultural Studies and Cultural Theory."

Among the most exciting features of the wide-ranging expertise and research represented in this encyclopedia is the work of younger scholars and activist intellectuals who are challenging the received wisdom of the field of LGBTQ history, in the engaged political spirit of their elders. Entries on race, ethnicity, and religion, and on the fields of study associated with these historical differences, reflect new research and critical approaches expanding the field since the 1990s. John Howard's entry "Mississippi" reflects his critique of both the framing of LGBTQ community studies as urban studies, and his complicating intervention in the story of the emergence of identity, community, and queer politics in the twentieth century. Susan Stryker's entries "Erickson, Reed" and "Rivera, Sylvia" represent her own activist historical scholarship within the context of an emerging transgender politics. And Roderick Ferguson's "African American Studies" pulls together the history of black LGBTQ intellectual interventions since the 1970s to offer a challenging call for an expanding queer critique of the epistemological and normative basis for Western "civilization" itself.

All together, the entries contained in this encyclopedia offer a bracing, engaging, provocative tour of U.S. history and culture from multiple, overlapping, sometimes conflicting, but always informative perspectives. The collective queer eye on the past that you will find in the following pages directs your vision toward an in-progress portrait of history writing as history making—with that eye always trained on generating more.

**Lisa Duggan**
**New York University**
**September, 2003**

# a chronology of U.S. lesbian, gay, bisexual, and transgender history

The chronology below documents the pervasiveness of LGBT issues, struggles, and contributions since the beginnings of U.S. society, from the time of the first European invasions of North American territory, to surges in visibility in the late 1960s, to the gains and new obstacles experienced in the twenty-first century.

Terms appearing in bold indicate they are entry titles (though in some instances are in abbreviated form). Other cross-references appear in bold following most chronicled events.

## Fifteenth and Sixteenth Centuries

Various **Native American** groups accept same-sex sexual practices and treat with respect males who take on traditional female roles and females who take on traditional male roles. (*See also* **Native American Religion and Spirituality; Two-Spirit Females; Two-Spirit Males.**)

Many British, Dutch, French, and Spanish colonial invaders disapprove of and attack **Native American** gender and sexual practices and identities, while also taking Native land, spreading disease among Native Americans, and disrupting Native cultural practices. Despite attempts to destroy Native traditions, gender diversity remains an important part of many Native American cultures through the nineteenth century. (*See also* **Colonial America; Colonialism and Imperialism.**)

Some free and enslaved Africans in the New World and some British, Dutch, French, and Spanish colonial invaders engage in same-sex sexual activities. High male-to-female sex ratios in some colonies and African and European cultural traditions contribute to these practices. (*See* **African Americans; Colonial America; Interracial and Interethnic Sex and Relationships; Slavery and Emancipation.**)

White colonists are both attracted to and repulsed by Africans and Native Americans of the same sex. Some white men rape and commit other acts of sexual violence toward African and Native American men. (*See* **Colonial America; Interracial and Interethnic Sex and Relationships; Race and Racism; Slavery and Emancipation.**)

**1566** Spanish military authorities in Florida execute a French interpreter named Guillermo, who lives with a local Native American man and is accused of being a "great Sodomite." (*See* **Interracial and Interethnic Sex and Relationships; Sodomy, Buggery, Crimes against Nature, Disorderly Conduct, and Lewd and Lascivious Law and Policy.**)

## Seventeenth Century

At least nineteen men are prosecuted and five are executed for sodomy (anal sex) from the early seventeenth century to the mid-eighteenth century. Many more individuals are charged with lesser offenses or are not prosecuted because a sodomy conviction requires penetration and allegations generally have to be substantiated by at least two independent witnesses. (*See* **Colonial America; Sodomy, Buggery, Crimes**

**against Nature, Disorderly Conduct, and Lewd and Lascivious Law and Policy.**)

Only a few women in the American colonies are charged with engaging in same-sex sexual acts. Perhaps reflecting how women's sexuality is often taken less seriously than men's, the punishment is less severe than the death penalty for male same-sex sex. (*See* **Colonial America; Sodomy, Buggery, Crimes against Nature, Disorderly Conduct, and Lewd and Lascivious Law and Policy.**)

Throughout the era of slavery, white men continue to rape and commit other acts of sexual violence toward enslaved African American men. (*See* **African Americans; Interracial and Inter-ethnic Sex and Relationships; Race and Racism; Slavery and Emancipation.**)

**1610**   The Virginia Colony passes the first law against sodomy in the American colonies. Like the English "buggery" statute on which it is based, the law makes sodomy a capital offense. Other colonies enact similar legislation in the decades that follow. (*See* **Sodomy, Buggery, Crimes against Nature, Disorderly Conduct, and Lewd and Lascivious Behavior.**)

**1624**   Hanged for making sexual advances toward his indentured steward, ship captain Richard Cornish of the Virginia Colony becomes the first person known to have been executed for sodomy in the British colonies in America. (*See* **Colonial America; Sodomy, Buggery, Crimes against Nature, Disorderly Conduct, and Lewd and Lascivious Law and Policy.**)

**1629**   On the long voyage across the Atlantic Ocean, "5 beastly Sodomitical boys" are discovered on an English ship. Upon arrival in Massachusetts, they are sent back to England, along with colony representatives to explain their crime to English authorities. (*See* **Colonial America; Sodomy, Buggery, Crimes against Nature, Disorderly Conduct, and Lewd and Lascivious Law and Policy.**)

In Plymouth, Virginia, **Thomasine/Thomas Hall**, who claims to be both a man and a woman, is brought to court to determine her/his "true" gender. The colony's governor agrees with Hall and requires her/him to wear items of clothing associated with both men and women. (*See also* **Transsexuals, Transvestites, Transgender People, and Cross-Dressers.**)

**1642**   In the first documented case of a woman prosecuted for same-sex sexual relations, Elizabeth Johnson, a servant in the Massachusetts Bay Colony, is found guilty of "unseemly practices betwixt her and another maid" and severely whipped. (*See* **Colonial America; Sodomy, Buggery, Crimes against Nature, Disorderly Conduct, and Lewd and Lascivious Law and Policy.**)

William Bradford describes an outbreak of sodomy and other sex offenses in the Plymouth Colony. (*See also* **Sodomy, Buggery, Crimes against Nature, Disorderly Conduct, and Lewd and Lascivious Behavior.**)

**1646**   Convicted of a second sodomy offense, Jan Creoli, a "negro" in the New Netherland Colony, is executed by being choked and then "tied to a stake, and faggots piled around him" and set afire. (*See also* **Colonial America; Interracial and Inter-ethnic Sex and Relationships; Sodomy, Buggery, Crimes against Nature, Disorderly Conduct, and Lewd and Lascivious Law and Policy.**)

**1649**   In Plymouth, Massachusetts, two married women, Mary Hammon and Sara Norman, are accused of "lewd behavior each with [the] other upon a bed." Perhaps because Hammon is only 15 years old, the charges against her are dropped. Slightly older, Norman is required to confess her "unchaste behavior" publicly. (*See* **Sodomy, Buggery, Crimes against Nature, Disorderly Conduct, and Lewd and Lascivious Behavior.**)

**1652**   Joseph Davis of New Hampshire is fined and made to admit his guilt to the community for "putting on women's apparel." (*See* **Transsexuals, Transvestites, Transgender People, and Cross-Dressers.**)

**1653**   The Reverend **Michael Wigglesworth**, a Puritan divine, writes in his diary about being tormented by feelings of affection and lust for the male students he tutors at Harvard University. (*See also* **Colonial America; Protestants and Protestantism.**)

**1655**   The New Haven Colony becomes the only American colony to enact a sodomy law that explicitly criminalizes sexual acts between women, an offense which is made punishable by death. (*See* **Colonial America; Sodomy, Buggery, Crimes against Nature, Disorderly Conduct, and Lewd and Lascivious Law and Policy.**)

**1677** **Nicholas Sension**, a prosperous resident of Connecticut, is convicted of attempted sodomy. Even though he had long made sexual advances, often violent, toward his male servants, Sension receives a light sentence, perhaps reflecting his social position or the community's ambivalence about the sodomy law. (*See also* **Colonial America.**)

Twenty-one-year-old Dorothy Hoyt of Massachusetts is ordered to be severely whipped for dressing as a man, unless her father pays a fine on her behalf. (The final outcome of the sentence remains unknown.) (*See* **Transsexuals, Transvestites, Transgender People, and Cross-Dressers.**)

**1682** Reflecting the Quaker values of its founders, Pennsylvania becomes the first American colony to make sodomy a non-capital offense. But to conform with English law, the death penalty is reinstated for African Americans in 1700 and for whites in 1718. (See also **Sodomy, Buggery, Crimes against Nature, Disorderly Conduct, and Lewd and Lascivious Law and Policy.**)

## Eighteenth Century

Prosecutions for sodomy decline during the century, as courts are relied on less and less for the regulation of sexuality. (*See* **Colonial America.**)

Between the signing of the U.S. Declaration of Independence in 1776 and the end of the century, four northern states (Pennsylvania, New Jersey, New York, and Rhode Island) abolish the death penalty for sodomy and "crimes against nature." (*See* **Sodomy, Buggery, Crimes against Nature, Disorderly Conduct, and Lewd and Lascivious Behavior.**)

**1707** Reports circulate that Lord Edward Hyde Cornbury, the royal governor of New York and New Jersey, dresses as a woman. (*See* **Colonial America.**)

**1743** The execution of an Irish doctor in Georgia is the last known capital conviction for sodomy in the U.S. (*See* **Sodomy, Buggery, Crimes against Nature, Disorderly Conduct, and Lewd and Lascivious Behavior.**)

**1756** In Connecticut, Stephen Gorton, a married Baptist minister, is dismissed from his position for "unchaste behavior with his fellow men when in bed with them." After Gorton publicly confesses to his sins, he is reinstated by his congregation. (*See* **Colonial America.**)

**1778** At Valley Forge, Pennsylvania, Lieutenant Frederick Gotthold Enslin is court-martialed after being found in bed with another soldier, making him the first known person discharged from the U.S. military for attempted sodomy. (*See* **Sodomy, Buggery, Crimes against Nature, Disorderly Conduct, and Lewd and Lascivious Behavior.**)

**1782** **Deborah Samson** of Massachusetts dresses as a man and serves in the Continental army during the waning days of the Revolutionary War.

## 1800–1865

Seven more states abolish the death penalty for sodomy, but some do so only for free persons. Two states, North Carolina and South Carolina, continue to regard sodomy as a capital offense. (*See* **Policing and Police; Sodomy, Buggery, Crimes against Nature, Disorderly Conduct, and Lewd and Lascivious Behavior.**)

Industrialization, urbanization, immigration, and migration create increased possibilities for men and women to live apart from their families of origin and to form intimate same-sex bonds with non-family members. (*See* **Capitalism and Industrialization; Migration, Immigration, and Diaspora.**)

Intimate, affectionate, romantic, and sometimes erotic friendships between women and between men develop in the context of the ideologies and practices of separate spheres for women and men. Examples include **Susan B. Anthony** and Elizabeth Cady Stanton, **Charlotte Cushman** and various women, **Emily Dickinson** and Susan Gilbert Dickinson, **Margaret Fuller** and Caroline Sturgis, **James Henry Hammond** and Thomas Jefferson Withers, **Rebecca Primus and Addie Brown**, and **Walt Whitman** and various men. (*See also* **Friendship; Romantic Friendship and Boston Marriage; Smashes and Chumming.**)

Intimate female friendships and relationships play a vital role in the early years of women's colleges and in the development of the U.S. women's movement. (*See* **Anthony, Susan B.; Colleges and Universities; Thomas, M. Carey; Woolley, Mary, and Jeanette Marks.**)

Homoerotic friendships and relationships, often involving the crossing of race and class boundaries, emerge as significant themes in the fictional and nonfictional works of a number of male writers, including James Fenimore Cooper, Richard

Henry Dana, Henry Wadsworth Longfellow, Henry David Thoreau, Herman Melville, and the authors of the Davy Crockett almanacs. (*See* **Literature**.)

Various female-bodied individuals cross-dress or live as men, including **Mary Walker** and Calamity Jane.

The cross-dressing of characters in Catharine Maria Sedgwick's *Hope Leslie* (1827) and Theodore Winthrop's *Cecil Dreeme* (1861) initiates a transgender tradition in U.S. literature. (*See* **Literature**.)

Same-sex sexual activity flourishes in predominantly male environments in the United States: cowboy and mining cultures, Chinese American bachelor societies, the military, and the Western frontier. (*See* **Asian Americans and Pacific Islanders; San Francisco; Situational Homosexuality**.)

Reflecting the gender diversity of many Native American cultures, female-bodied individuals such as **Pi'tamakan** (Piegan), **Qánqon-Kámek-Klaúla** (Kutenai), and **Woman Chief** (Crow) adopt and are accepted for their cross-gender identities. (*See also* **Native Americans; Two-Spirit Females; Two-Spirit Males**.)

**1826** Thomas Jefferson Withers writes to **James Henry Hammond** and openly refers to their past sexual relationship—one of the few surviving first-hand accounts of male same-sex sexuality from the early nineteenth century.

**1848** The Gold Rush brings many migrants to **San Francisco**, including a number of same-sex couples.

**1852** **Charlotte Cushman**, an actress famous for playing male roles on stage, moves to Rome, Italy, and becomes part of a circle of expatriate lesbian artists that includes sculptors Mary Edmonia Lewis, Harriet Hosmer, Emma Stebbins, and Anne Whitney. (*See also* **Visual Art**.)

**1855** **Walt Whitman** publishes the first edition of *Leaves of Grass*, which includes his paean to masculine and feminine bodies, "Song of Myself." Five years later, Whitman adds his homoerotic "Calamus" poems to the collection. (*See also* **Literature**.)

**1859** **Rebecca Primus and Addie Brown** begin a nine-year correspondence. Brown's preserved letters document a relationship between two African American women that is both intensely emotional and explicitly sexual.

**1861** Hundreds of biological women cross-dress as men to serve in the Civil War. At the same time, many male soldiers form intimate, romantic, and erotic bonds with each other. (*See* **Transsexuals, Transvestites, Transgendered People, and Cross-Dressers; War**.)

Harriet Jacobs's slave narrative mentions a white, male slaveholder who forces one of his male slaves to submit to "the strangest freaks of despotism," which Jacobs finds to be "of a nature too filthy to be repeated." (*See* **African Americans; Literature; Interracial and Interethnic Sex and Relationships; Slavery and Emancipation**.)

## 1866–1890

The last two of the original 13 states that regarded sodomy as a capital offense, North Carolina and South Carolina, abolish the death penalty for sodomy. The punishment for sodomy remains severe, though, and beginning in the late nineteenth century, states revise their sodomy laws to include oral sex. (*See* **Sodomy, Buggery, Crimes against Nature, Disorderly Conduct, and Lewd and Lascivious Law and Policy**.)

Women's colleges, including Vassar (1865), Smith (1872), Wellesley (1875), and Bryn Mawr (1886), are established. Among their students, teachers, and benefactors are many women who formed **romantic friendships and Boston marriages**, such as **Jane Addams, M. Carey Thomas, Katharine Lee Bates, Mary Woolley and Jeanette Marks**, and **Sarah Orne Jewett**. (*See also* **Colleges and Universities; Smashes and Chumming**.)

Intimate friendships and relationships between men and between women play a central role in the development of sex-segregated social reform campaigns: the Young Men's Christian Association, the temperance movement, and the settlement house movement. (*See* **Jane Addams; Romantic Friendship and Boston Marriage; Frances Willard**.)

A number of writers, including **Sarah Orne Jewett, Katharine Lee Bates, Charles Warren Stoddard**, and Bayard Taylor, depict romantic friendships in their work. (Bates, who wrote *America the Beautiful*, would finalize this poem in 1913.) (*See also* **Literature**.)

In the 1880s, red light districts in large cities such as Boston, Chicago, Denver, Los Angeles, New Orleans, Philadelphia, and San Francisco begin to feature businesses, especially bars, that cater to LGBT customers. (*See* **Businesses; Capitalism and Industrialization.**)

Following the lead of European sexologists, the U.S. medical profession begins to view same-sex desire as a symptom of "inversion" or "contrary sexual feeling," believing that individuals who express sexual feelings for someone of the same sex have the psyche of the "opposite" sex. (*See* **Medicine, Medicalization, and the Medical Model; Psychology, Psychiatry, Psychoanalysis, and Sexology.**)

Two-spirit and apparently two-spirit individuals from various Native American societies, including **Hastíín Klah** (Navajo), **Lozen** (Apache), **Masahai Amatkwisai** (Mohave), and **Osh-Tisch** (Crow), achieve notoriety within and beyond their cultures. (*See also* **Native Americans; Two-Spirit Females; Two-Spirit Males.**)

In the 1870s, **Jeanne Bonnet** is arrested more than twenty times in San Francisco for wearing traditionally male attire and is killed apparently for convincing prostitutes to leave their pimps.

**1866** **Horatio Alger** is dismissed from his ministerial post in Massachusetts after being charged with "unnatural familiarity" with two teenage boys.

**Frances Thompson**, a black freedwoman, testifies to a congressional committee about being raped by white men during the Memphis riots. Her testimony is later discredited when it is discovered that she is biologically male. (*See also* **Interracial and Interethnic Sex and Relationships.**)

**1869** Harlem's Hamilton Lodge sponsors its first drag ball. By the end of the nineteenth century, drag balls are held in many large U.S. cities, reflecting and adding to the growing visibility of LGBT communities. (*See also* **Drag Queens and Kings; Transsexuals, Transvestites, Transgender People, and Cross-Dressers.**)

**1878** "Mrs. Nash," a woman who had been a company laundress for George Custer's Seventh Cavalry and who had married a succession of soldiers, is discovered upon her death to have been born male-bodied.

**1879** Pennsylvania becomes the first state to amend its sodomy statute to include women and men

receiving or giving oral sex. (*See* **Sodomy, Buggery, Crimes against Nature, Disorderly Conduct, and Lewd and Lascivious Law and Policy.**)

**Frances Willard** assumes the presidency of the Women's Christian Temperance Union and becomes arguably the most powerful woman in the United States for the next decade. Her tremendous success is made possible in part by her professional and personal relationship with another movement activist, Anna Adams Gordon.

**1883** The term "lesbian" is reportedly used for the first time in a U.S. medical journal in an article about Joseph Lobdell (born **Lucy Ann Lobdell**), a female-bodied individual who lives as a man.

**1885** U.S. realist painter **Thomas Eakins**, renowned for his images of male nudes, completes his homoerotic painting *The Swimming Hole*, which depicts the artist watching a group of nude young men.

**1886** **We'Wha**, a Zuni Indian from New Mexico who had assumed a transgendered role socially sanctioned in her culture, tours Washington, D.C., where she meets and mingles with leading government officials, including President Grover Cleveland—none of whom recognize that she had been born male-bodied.

**1889** **Jane Addams** and her partner Ellen Gates Starr open Hull House, the first U.S. settlement house, in Chicago. For the rest of her life, Addams works to improve the lives of the poor and is active in the suffrage and pacifist movements, along with her subsequent partner, Mary Rozet Smith.

## 1890s

The steady growth of a commercialized leisure culture in the United States facilitates LGBT identity and community formation in cities across the country, as saloons, dance halls, cafeterias, restaurants, and other nightspots become centers of LGBT social life. (*See* **Capitalism and Industrialization.**)

Same-sex desire begins to be viewed as the defining feature of a new category, "homosexuality," rather than as a characteristic of gender inversion. (*See* **Medicine, Medicalization, and the Medical Model; Psychology, Psychiatry, Psychoanalysis, and Sexology.**)

With intimate same-sex relationships beginning to be defined as a type of perversion, **romantic**

**friendships and Boston marriages** are increasingly seen as suspect and deviant.

Like earlier women's rights leaders, **Anna Howard Shaw** devotes herself to women in her personal as well as political life. (*See also* **Anthony, Susan B.; Feminism.**)

**1890** Four years after **Emily Dickinson's** death, the bulk of her poetry is published, including many passionate and romantic poems to her sister-in-law, Susan Gilbert Dickinson.

**1891** **Alice Austen** begins to include lesbian-coded images in her photographs.

**1892** Writing in a Chicago medical journal, James G. Kiernan refers to "homosexuals," the earliest known use of the term in a U.S. publication. (*See* **Psychology, Psychiatry, Psychoanalysis, and Sexology.**)

**Charlotte Perkins Gilman** writes her most well-known work, *The Yellow Wallpaper*, based on her unhappy marriage. Gilman seems to have found more satisfaction in her relationships with women.

**Alice Mitchell** murders Freda Ward in Memphis, Tennessee, after their plans to elope, with Mitchell dressing as a man, fall through. The subsequent trial becomes a national media sensation and results in Mitchell being committed to an insane asylum. (*See also* **Memphis.**)

**1895** The Mitchell case inspires a number of novels and stories about evil, violent lesbians and the unhealthiness of female-female relationships, including Mary Wilkins Freeman's "The Long Arm," Mary Hatch's *The Strange Disappearance of Eugene Comstock*, and John Carhart's *Norma Trist; or Pure Carbon: A Story of the Inversion of the Sexes.*

The trial of Oscar Wilde for "gross indecency between males" raises the U.S. public's awareness of homosexuality. Sentenced to two years' hard labor, Wilde's punishment causes many LGBT people to fear a similar fate.

## 1900s

**1901** **Murray Hall**, a member of New York City's Tammany Hall political machine, is discovered, at his death, to have been born female-bodied. Tragically, he dies from breast cancer, for which he had avoided medical treatment due to a fear of having his secret revealed.

**1902** In one of the earliest surviving accounts of surgery to alter sex in the United States, Earl Lind convinces a physician to castrate him so that he could be less like a man. (*See* **Transsexuals, Transvestites, Transgender People, and Cross-Dressers.**)

**1908** **Edward Prime Stevenson** (under the pseudonym Xavier Mayne) publishes *The Intersexes: A History of Similisexualism as a Problem in Social Life*, the first major study of homosexuality in the United States.

**1909** U.S. expatriate **Natalie Barney** begins a literary salon in her Paris home. Candid about her own lesbianism, Barney's gatherings bring together many leading LGB writers and artists, including **Djuna Barnes**, **Romaine Brooks**, **Truman Capote**, Colette, André Gide, and **Gertrude Stein**. (*See also* **Literature.**)

In his only U.S. visit, Sigmund Freud gives a series of public lectures at Clark University in Worcester, Massachusetts. His psychoanalytic theories have a tremendous influence on how the U.S. medical profession and society in general view homosexuality. (*See* **Psychology, Psychiatry, Psychoanalysis, and Sexology.**)

## 1910s

**Bathhouses** become popular sites for sex between men, with some baths developing a reputation for allowing and even protecting same-sex sexual activities. But with their increasing prominence in homosexual culture, bathhouses also begin to be targeted by the police. Raids on baths become commonplace by the 1920s.

**Willa Cather, Gertrude Stein,** and Amy Lowell publish works that include what many contemporary critics read as masked representations of same-sex desire.

**Romaine Brooks** begins to paint life-sized female nudes and portraits of lesbians cross-dressed, including paintings of her partner **Natalie Barney** and some of her and Barney's other lovers. (*See also* **Visual Art.**)

Female impersonators such as **Ray Bourbon** and **Julian Eltinge** achieve popular and critical acclaim in Vaudeville and then in films. (*See also* **Transsexuals, Transvestites, Transgender People, and Cross-Dressers.**)

**1912** **Marie Jenney Howe** founds Heterodoxy, a social club of many of the era's leading female activists, intellectuals, and artists. A number of members, including Charlotte Perkins Gilman and Mabel Dodge, have intimate relationships with other women.

**1914** *Florida Enchantment*, one of Hollywood's first full-length silent films, features cross-dressing and same-sex relationships in a spoof on sexual roles. (See **Film and Video; Florida.**)

In November, police in Long Beach, California, arrest fifty men for "deviant sexual behavior," raising awareness of the growing gay subculture in the **Los Angeles** area.

**1915** On a U.S. lecture tour, **Emma Goldman** defends homosexuality, as well as birth control, women's rights, and anarchism. (*See also* **Anarchism, Socialism, and Communism.**)

**1916** **Angelina Weld Grimké's** *Rachel*, a play about a woman who rejects marriage and motherhood, becomes the first drama by a black woman to be professionally staged. In her own life, Grimké apparently forswears intimate relationships after being spurned by both women and men.

Writing under the initials **H.D.**, Hilda Doolittle publishes her first collection of poetry. While her poems often address her relationships with men, her posthumously published novels offer fictional portraits of her love affairs with women.

**1917** Although the military makes sodomy grounds for dismissal prior to the U.S. entry into the war, many gay and bisexual men serve in World War I. (*See* **Government and Military Witchhunts; War.**)

**Alan Hart** convinces doctors to give him a hysterectomy and, as a man, has a successful career as a novelist and radiologist. Other female-bodied individuals at this time live as men without surgery, including Jack Bee "**Babe Bean**" Garland. (*See also* **San Francisco.**)

**1919** The navy assigns sailors to have sex with other men as part of an investigation into homosexuality at the naval training station in Newport, Rhode Island. The undercover operation results in the arrest of twenty sailors and sixteen nonmilitary personnel, but also leads to a Congressional investigation into the navy's methods for addressing homosexuality. Assistant Secretary of the Navy Franklin D. Roosevelt later disavows all

knowledge. (*See* **Government and Military Witchhunts; Military.**)

**1920s**

**New York City's** Greenwich Village and Times Square, **Chicago's** Near North Side, and **San Francisco's** North Beach begin to develop reputations as LGB neighborhoods.

With Prohibition, the number of places where LGBT people can socialize proliferate, as it becomes much more difficult for authorities to regulate the underground leisure economy. (*See* **Bars, Clubs, and Restaurants; Liquor Control Law and Policy.**)

The Harlem Renaissance sees a flourishing of literary and artistic works by African Americans, many of whom are LGB, including writers **Wallace Thurman**, **Richard Bruce Nugent**, **Angelina Weld Grimké**, **Countee Cullen**, **Claude McKay**, and possibly **Langston Hughes**; blues singers **Bessie Smith**, **Ma Rainey**, **Alberta Hunter**, **Ethel Waters**, and **Gladys Bentley**; and patrons **Alain Locke** and **A'Lelia Walker**.

With a "pansy craze" sweeping **New York City**, homosexual life achieves unprecedented visibility, becoming the subject of newspaper stories, Broadway shows, songs, films, and books.

In response to Broadway plays with LGB characters, including *God of Vengeance*, *The Drag*, and *The Captive*, the New York legislature bans the presentation of "sex perversion" on stages throughout the state. (*See* **Censorship, Obscenity, and Pornography Law and Policy; Theater and Performance.**)

**Harry Benjamin** first administers hormones to treat a sex-change patient.

**1920** In *A Few Figs from Thistles*, openly bisexual poet **Edna St. Vincent Millay** writes of women who freely explore their sexuality.

The military classifies sodomy, including both oral and anal sex, as a crime under military law and routinely begins to give less than honorable discharges to suspected homosexuals. (*See* **Military Law and Policy; War.**)

**William Tilden** becomes the first U.S. man to win a Wimbledon tennis championship and is the number-one-ranked tennis player in the world throughout the 1920s. Despite being considered the greatest tennis player of his time, he is later excluded from tournaments because of his homosexuality. (*See also* **Sports**.)

**1922** **Carl Van Vechten** publishes his first novel, *Peter Whiffle*. In his seven novels, as in his life, he celebrates New York City's LGB cultures of the 1920s.

**1923** Partners Tracy Mygatt and Frances Witherspoon help found the War Resisters League. (*See* **Antiwar, Pacifist, and Peace Movements**.)

**Elsa Gidlow**'s *On a Grey Thread*, a collection of poetry celebrating same-sex love, is published.

**1924** **J. Edgar Hoover** becomes the director of the Federal Bureau of Investigation. Notorious for persecuting LGB government employees during the 1950s, Hoover is also known to have had a more than 40-year relationship with a male FBI agent.

**The Society for Human Rights**, the first known male homophile organization in the United States, is chartered in Chicago, led by **Henry Gerber**. The group disbands less than a year later, after the police arrest the group's leaders and Gerber is fired from his job for being gay.

**1925** **Aaron Copland**'s *Symphony for Organ and Orchestra* premieres and establishes his reputation as a composer. Among his many successful works is the opera *The Tender Land*, a collaboration with his then-romantic partner Erik Johns.

**1926** **Richard Bruce Nugent** publishes "Smoke, Lilies and Jade," the first work of African American fiction to have same-sex sexuality as its central theme, in *Fire!! A Quarterly Devoted to the Younger Negro Artists*.

**1927** **Dorothy Arzner** makes her directorial debut. The only known lesbian studio director during Hollywood's Golden Age (1930s–1950s), her films have been noted for their representation of women's communities, critique of heterosexuality, and femme/butch coding.

**1928** **Ma Rainey** records "Prove It on Me Blues," a song which boasts of her relationships with other women.

Radclyffe Hall's *The Well of Loneliness* is published in the United States and becomes an immediate best-seller, despite (and perhaps because of) attempts to have it banned for being obscene. (*See* **Censorship, Obscenity, and Pornography Law and Policy**.)

**Margaret Mead** writes *Coming of Age in Samoa*. Mead and her sometime romantic partner **Ruth Benedict** are among the first anthropologists to demonstrate that same-sex sexuality is not a deviant behavior but a universal practice.

**1929** Sociologist **Katharine Bement Davis** publishes the findings of research showing that same-sex sexuality is widespread among white, college-educated single women in the United States. (See also **Psychology, Psychiatry, Psychoanalysis, and Sexology**.)

**1930s**

A working-class lesbian culture based around **femme and butch** identities begins to develop in bars, clubs, and **house parties** in many U.S. cities. (*See also* **Bars, Clubs, and Restaurants**.)

The U.S. press begins to report on "sex change" operations performed primarily in Europe. (*See* **Transsexuals, Transvestites, Transgender People, and Cross-Dressers**.)

A sex crime panic sweeps the United States and leads to the passage of state laws allowing for the involuntary confinement and treatment of "sexual psychopaths." Although sensational media accounts of sexual assaults against children fuel the panic, adult gay and bisexual men who have consensual relationships with other adult men often become the focus of campaigns against sex criminals and constitute a significant portion of those institutionalized. (*See* **Sex Panics; Sexual Psychopath Law and Policy**.)

Mary Casal's *The Stone Wall* (1930), Vida Dutton Scudder's *On Journey* (1937), and Diana Frederics's *Diana* (1939) are published works that have female protagonists who love other women.

**Alice Dunbar-Nelson** chronicles her relationships with other married, black middle-class women in her diaries.

**1930** Under pressure from Catholic clergy and other moral crusaders, the Hollywood movie industry introduces what becomes known as the Hays Code to censor depictions of sex and "sex perversion" in films. Adherence to the Code becomes mandatory four years later, and it remains in effect until the early 1960s. Representations of homosexuality and cross-dressing do not completely disappear from movies during this time, as shown by films like *Morocco* (1930), *Queen*

*Christina* (1933), *Sylvia Scarlett* (1936), and *Bringing Up Baby* (1938), but such images have to be more coded. (*See* **Censorship, Obscenity, and Pornography Law and Policy; Film and Video.**)

In response to several exhibitors refusing to show his homoerotic painting *Distinguished Air*, **Charles Demuth**, one of the first U.S. modernist painters, creates even more forthright depictions of same-sex sexual desire. (*See* **Visual Art.**)

**1931** **Blair Niles**'s *Strange Brother*, one of the earliest U.S. novels to feature an openly gay protagonist, describes LGBT life during the Harlem Renaissance.

**1932** **Mildred Ella "Babe" Didrikson** sets three Olympic records in track and field. She is recognized as the greatest all-around female athlete of her time, but is also regularly criticized for being unwomanly, leading Didrikson to try to be more feminine and to hide her relationship with a female partner. (*See also* **Sports.**)

**1933** During the early years of Franklin Delano Roosevelt's presidency, **Eleanor Roosevelt** has a romantic affair with journalist Lorena Hickok.

**Charles Henri Ford** and Parker Tyler's *The Young and Evil* is published in France. Copies bound for the United States are repeatedly seized by customs officials because of the novel's frank depictions of homosexuality. (*See also* **Literature.**)

**1934** **Paul Cadmus's** painting *The Fleet's In!*, which had been commissioned as part of the Public Works of Art Project, is pulled from an exhibit at the Corcoran Gallery in Washington, D.C., because of its homoerotic subtext. (*See* **Visual Art.**)

Lillian Hellman's *The Children's Hour*, a play about two schoolteachers accused of being lesbians by one of their students, opens on Broadway to rave reviews and runs for nearly 700 performances. (*See* **Performance, Theater, and Dance Studies.**)

Composer-lyricist **Cole Porter** codes gay sexual references into his play *Anything Goes* and later *Kiss Me Kate* (1948).

**1936** Mona's, one of the first specifically lesbian bars in the United States, opens in **San Francisco**.

**Djuna Barnes**'s modernist lesbian novel *Nightwood* is published.

**1937** Hugh Hampton Young describes cases of U.S. doctors performing surgeries on patients with "ambiguous genitalia," the first detailed report on the medical treatment of **intersexuals** in the United States.

**1939** The Jewel Box Revue, the longest-running touring drag show in the United States, begins at the Club Jewel Box in Miami and enjoys success through the 1960s. (*See* **Florida.**)

**Billy Strayhorn**, one of the few openly LGBT musicians in jazz, becomes an arranger for Duke Ellington's band and writes such musical standards as "Take the A Train," "Satin Doll," and "Lush Life."

**Christopher Isherwood** and **W. H. Auden** immigrate to the United States and become widely acclaimed for their deeply personal stories and poetry, respectively.

## 1940s

Drag balls in **New York City** and **Chicago** attract 2,000–3,000 people and remain extremely popular through the 1950s. (*See* **Drag Queens and Kings.**)

Many lesbian and bisexual women writers, including **Elizabeth Bishop**, **Jane Bowles**, **Carson McCullers**, Muriel Rukeyser, and May Swenson, encode expressions of same-sex desire in their work.

**Margaret Chung**, the first U.S.-born woman physician of Chinese descent, becomes famous to more than a thousand U.S. servicemen as "Mother Chung." Much less well-known are her intimate relationships with poet **Elsa Gidlow** and entertainer Sophie Tucker.

**1941** During World War II, psychiatrists screen inductees for homosexuality and reject an estimated 4,000–5,000 men. Few women are excluded from the Women's Army Corps on grounds of lesbianism, but occasional witchhunts lead to the discharges of servicewomen. The fact that a vast force has to be quickly assembled means that lesbians, gay men, and bisexuals who want to serve typically have little difficulty entering and remaining in the military. (*See* **Government and Military Witchhunts; Military Law and Policy.**)

By uprooting millions of young women and men and often placing them in non-familial, sex-segregated environments, World War II fosters the process of LGBT identity formation and the development of LGBT communities. More than at any previous time, those attracted to people of the same sex have opportunities to find each other and to socialize publicly together. (*See* **Military; War.**)

**George Henry**'s two-volume *Sex Variants: A Study of Homosexual Patterns* is published. Although Henry's study pathologizes homosexuality, it also includes extensive statements by the LGB participants themselves, providing a rare glimpse into LGB life during the 1930s. (*See also* **Psychology, Psychiatry, Psychoanalysis, and Sexology.**)

**1943** Undersecretary of State and close Roosevelt advisor **Sumner Welles** is forced to resign after reports that he propositioned other men can no longer be suppressed.

**1945** Following the success of *The Glass Menagerie* on Broadway, **Tennessee Williams** becomes the most well-known playwright in the United States. His homosexuality is "an open secret," but that does not prevent plays such as *A Streetcar Named Desire* (1947) and *Cat on a Hot Tin Roof* (1955) from achieving widespread acclaim.

**1947** Under the name **Lisa Ben** (an anagram of "lesbian"), Edith Eyde begins producing *Vice Versa*, the first known U.S. lesbian publication, in Los Angeles. Because it is a typewritten, carbon-copied newsletter, she is only able to create twelve copies of each issue, but through readers passing it along to others, hundreds of women see *Vice Versa*. (*See also* **Homophile Press.**)

**1948** Alfred C. Kinsey's *Sexual Behavior in the Human Male* is published and, along with *Sexual Behavior in the Human Female* (1953), has a major impact on the ways that Americans view sexuality. His studies awaken the public and other researchers to the prevalence of same-sex sexuality and challenge the perception that homosexuality is pathological. (*See* **Psychology, Psychiatry, Psychoanalysis, and Sexology.**)

**Gore Vidal**'s *The City and the Pillar* becomes the first best-selling U.S. novel to have gay men as its main characters. (*See also* **Literature.**)

**1949** The term "transsexualism" begins to enter the medical literature in the United States to describe individuals who desire to change their biological sex. The concept is popularized by **Harry Benjamin**, who, with the help of **Louise Law-**rence, becomes the country's foremost expert on transvestism and transsexuality. (*See also* **Transsexuals, Transvestites, Transgender People, and Cross-Dressers.**)

A Defense Department memorandum requires the military services to seek out and promptly remove all "known homosexuals." Between 2,000–3,000 personnel are discharged each year during the 1950s. (*See* **Government and Military Witchhunts; Military Law and Policy.**)

## 1950s

Across the country, vice squads are established to harass and arrest men in parks and other cruising areas and police raids on LGBT bars increase substantially.

Hundreds of cheap paperback "pulp" novels are published with LGB themes. Among the most popular are works by Marijane Meaker (under the pen name Vin Packer), **Patricia Highsmith** (Claire Morgan), **Ann Bannon, Valerie Taylor, James Barr Fugate**), and Lonnie Coleman. (*See also* **Literature; Pulp Fiction: Gay; Pulp Fiction: Lesbian.**)

In **San Francisco**, the **Beats** emerge as a counter-force to the post-war white, middle-class ethic of conformity and compulsory heterosexuality. Some members of the Beat generation are gay or bisexual, including **Allen Ginsberg, William Burroughs,** Jack Kerouac, Robert Duncan, and Jack Spicer, and see same-sex sexuality as a form of rebellion against the heterosexual norm.

More than a hundred **physique magazines** are published for a largely gay male audience, led by **Robert Mizer**'s *Physique Pictorial*. (*See also* **Pornography.**)

The growing visibility of gay men in modern dance is reflected in the establishment of dance companies by choreographers **Alvin Ailey, Merce Cunningham, Robert Joffrey** and Gerald Arpino, and Paul Taylor. (*See also* **Dance.**)

**Leonard Bernstein** becomes a leading U.S. composer with his operas *Trouble in Tahiti* (1952) and *Candide* (1956) and the score for the musical *West Side Story* (1957).

Post-modernist painters and partners **Jasper Johns** and **Robert Rauschenberg** pioneer the use of everyday objects and recognizable imagery, including gay representations.

**1950** The disclosure that a number of State Department employees have been fired on suspicions of homosexuality is seized upon by right-wing ideologues in Congress, most notably Senator Joseph McCarthy, to stir up paranoia that "sex perverts" are rampant in the national government. The witchhunts that follow result in the dismissal of thousands of allegedly LGB federal workers. (*See* **Government and Military Witchhunts.**)

A Senate subcommittee issues a report justifying the exclusion of "homosexuals and other sex perverts" from federal employment. (*See* **Government and Military Witchhunts.**)

**Harry Hay** proposes the creation of a homophile organization in Los Angeles. The **Mattachine Society** is formed the following year, with Hay, Rudi Gernreich, Bob Hull, and Chuck Rowland among its leaders. Other Mattachine groups are subsequently established in Boston, Chicago, Denver, Detroit, New York City, Philadelphia, and Washington, D.C. (See also **Homophile Movement.**)

**1951** *The Homosexual in America* by **Donald Webster Cory** (Edward Sagarin), the first widely read insider account of LGBT life in the United States, is published. Arguing that homosexuals are a minority group deserving of equal rights, the book has a significant influence on the thinking of the early homophile movement.

**1952** **Christine Jorgensen** becomes an international celebrity when news of her "sex change" reaches the U.S. press. While often the subject of ridicule in the mainstream media, Jorgensen serves as an inspiration and role model for many transsexuals. (*See also* **Transsexuals, Transvestites, Transgender People, and Cross-Dressers.**)

Homosexuality is listed as a mental illness in the first edition of the American Psychiatric Association's *Diagnostic and Statistical Manual of Mental Disorders.* (*See* **Psychology, Psychiatry, Psychoanalysis, and Sexology.**)

Under a provision of the Walter-McCarren Act, individuals who are "afflicted with psychopathic personality"—a phrase generally understood to include homosexuals—are barred from migrating to the United States. Congress amends the law in 1965 to list "sexual deviation" specifically as grounds for exclusion. (*See* **Migration, Immigration, and Diaspora.**)

**1953** In January, *ONE* magazine, the first national LGB periodical, begins publishing in Los Angeles. The magazine's founders, many of whom are Mattachine Society members dissatisfied with the group's direction, include Martin Block, Dale Jennings, **Dorr Legg** (Bill Lambert), and Don Slater. (*See also* **Homophile Press.**)

President Dwight Eisenhower issues an executive order directing federal agencies to screen employees for "sexual perversion." Thousands of suspected lesbians, gay men, and bisexuals lose their jobs and many others quit before they can be targeted and dismissed. (*See* **Military Law and Policy.**)

**1954** Challenging psychiatric thinking on homosexuality, a study by **Evelyn Hooker** finds no differences in psychological well-being between homosexual and heterosexual men who are not in clinical treatment. (*See also* **Psychology, Psychiatry, Psychoanalysis, and Sexology.**)

**1955** In January, the **Mattachine Society** begins publishing the *Mattachine Review* to disseminate news articles and political commentaries on homosexuality. (*See also* **Homophile Press.**)

The **Daughters of Bilitis**, the first lesbian organization in the United States, is formed in **San Francisco**, led by **Phyllis Lyon and Del Martin**. At various times during the 1950s and 1960s, other Daughters of Bilitis groups exist in Boston, Chicago, Cleveland, Denver, Detroit, Los Angeles, New Orleans, New York City, Philadelphia, San Diego, and Portland, Oregon. (*See also* **Homophile Movement.**)

**Allen Ginsberg** gives his first public reading of *Howl*, a poem extolling the joys of same-sex sexuality. Two years later, Beat poet Lawrence Ferlinghetti is arrested and acquitted on obscenity charges for selling Ginsberg's *Howl and Other Poems* in his **San Francisco** bookstore.

**1956** **James Baldwin** becomes one of the first U.S. writers to provide a realistic depiction of the lives of gay and bisexual men and helps foster a post–Harlem Renaissance black LGBT literary tradition with *Giovanni's Room* and later *Another Country* (1962).

Members of the **ONE Institute** begin offering homophile studies classes, creating the first organized LGBT studies program in the United States. (*See also* **Homophile Movement.**)

In October, the **Daughters of Bilitis** begin publishing the *Ladder*, the first widely distributed lesbian periodical. It is named *Ladder* because the group envisions its newsletter as a means by which lesbians can climb out of the depths of self- and social hatred. (*See also* **Homophile Press.**)

**1958** The Supreme Court unanimously overrules lower court decisions that had found an issue of *ONE* magazine obscene, thereby making distribution easier for LGBT periodicals. (*See also* **Censorship, Obscenity, and Pornography Law and Policy; Homophile Press; Pornography.**)

**Barbara Gittings** founds the Daughters of Bilitis–New York, the first lesbian organization in the eastern United States. (*See also* **Homophile Movement.**)

**Truman Capote** becomes one of the most visible gay men in the United States with the publication of his highly acclaimed novel *Breakfast at Tiffany's.*

## 1960s

Although members of the **Daughters of Bilitis** are predominantly white, a number of black lesbians and bisexual women become involved in or support the group, including **Anita Cornwell, Ernestine Eckstein, Cleo Glenn,** and **Lorraine Hansberry.**

Toward the end of the decade, disco originates in New York City clubs frequented by black gay and bisexual men. The sound migrates to mostly white gay and bisexual men's clubs in the early 1970s. (*See* **Music.**)

**Andy Warhol** helps pioneer Pop Art with his campy images of commercial mass culture.

**1960** **Virginia Prince** begins publishing *Transvestia*, the first cross-dressing magazine in the United States. (*See also* **Transgender Organizations and Periodicals.**)

**1961** Illinois becomes the first state to repeal its sodomy law. (*See* **Sodomy, Buggery, Crimes against Nature, Disorderly Conduct, and Lewd and Lascivious Law and Policy.**)

Drag performer **José Sarria** becomes the first openly LGBT candidate for elected office in the United States when he runs for a seat on the **San Francisco** Board of Supervisors. Although he loses, he receives 6,000 votes and raises consciousness of LGBT issues. (*See also* **Electoral Politics.**)

**1962** The Supreme Court rules in *Manual Enterprises v. Day* that male physique magazines have to be treated the same as sexually explicit material targeting a heterosexual audience. (*See* **Censorship, Obscenity, and Pornography Law and Policy; Pornography.**)

**1963** **Bayard Rustin** organizes the March on Washington for Jobs and Freedom, one of the critical events of the black civil rights struggle. However, because Rustin is known to be gay, he is often forced to take a behind-the-scenes role in the movement.

**John Rechy** writes *City of Night*, a pioneering novel depicting Latino gay life.

**1964** The **Janus Society** in Philadelphia begins publishing *Drum* magazine, the first explicitly gay publication to include homoerotic photography, edited by **Clark Polak.** (*See also* **Homophile Movement; Homophile Press.**)

In what is believed to be the first public demonstration for LGB rights, a handful of homophile activists, including **Craig Rodwell** and **Randy Wicker,** protest the military's exclusion of LGB people at the Whitehall Induction Center in New York City on 19 September. (*See also* **Demonstrations, Actions, and Zaps; Homophile Movement.**)

Female-to-male transsexual and philanthropist **Reed Erickson** establishes the **Erickson Educational Foundation** to fund trans organizations and research on transsexuality.

In June, *Life* magazine features a cover story entitled "Homosexuality in America," the first in-depth examination of the topic by a major U.S. magazine.

In **San Francisco**, police raid a New Year's Ball sponsored by the Council on Religion and the Homosexual, arresting four people. At their trial, the judge orders the jury to find them not guilty, marking a major turning point for LGBT rights in the city.

**1965** On 4 July, homophile activists in the Mattachine Society, Daughters of Bilitis, and Janus Society picket at **Philadelphia**'s Independence Hall, the first of five Annual Reminder demonstrations. By protesting at the site where the Declaration of Independence was signed and on the event's anniversary, the demonstrators seek to call attention to the lack of democratic rights for LGB people. (*See also* **Homophile Movement**; **Pride Marches and Parades**.)

The Mattachine Society of **Washington, D.C.,** organizes a series of pickets of government institutions that discriminate against LGB people: the White House, Pentagon, State Department, and Civil Service Commission. (*See also* **Homophile Movement**.)

After three teenagers conduct a sit-in at Dewey's restaurant in **Philadelphia** to protest the denial of service to apparent LGBT people, the **Janus Society** organizes a five-day picket that culminates in another sit-in.

In *Griswold v. Connecticut*, the Supreme Court strikes down state laws that prohibit the use of birth control by married couples. The decision paves the way for the widespread availability and acceptance of contraceptives and, by recognizing an individual's constitutional right to privacy, serves as the basis for future LGBT rights decisions. (*See* **Sodomy, Buggery, Crimes against Nature, Disorderly Conduct, and Lewd and Lascivious Law and Policy; Privacy and Privacy Rights**.)

**1966** In August, a police raid at Compton's Cafeteria, a gathering place for drag queens and transsexuals in **San Francisco**'s Tenderloin District, leads to a riot by patrons tired of constant police harassment.

New York City Mayor John Lindsay initiates a large-scale effort to remove gay and bisexual men from the streets of Times Square and Greenwich Village.

In **San Francisco**, the **Society for Individual Rights** opens the first LGB community center in the United States. (*See also* **Homophile Movement**.)

Members of the New York City chapter of the Mattachine Society hold a "sip-in" at Greenwich Village bars to draw attention to state liquor commission policies that prevent known homosexuals from being served alcohol. (*See* **Homophile Movement; Liquor Control Law and Policy**.)

**1967** Hundreds rally in Los Angeles to protest attacks on gay bars by the police that leave a number of patrons badly injured and result in more than a dozen arrests.

COG (Conversion Our Goal or Change: Our Goal) is founded in **San Francisco**, becoming the world's first formal organization for transsexuals. Along with other trans groups formed in the late 1960s and early 1970s, COG helps transsexuals gain access to sex reassignment surgery and increases public awareness of transsexuality. (*See also* **Transgender Organizations and Periodicals; Transsexuals, Transvestites, Transgender People, and Cross-Dressers**.)

The Supreme Court upholds a law allowing for nonresidents to be excluded and deported from the United States if they are found to be homosexual. (*See* **Immigration, Asylum, and Deportation Law and Policy**.)

The New Jersey Supreme Court rejects the state's policy of revoking the liquor licenses of bars that allow "apparent homosexuals" to gather on their premises. (*See* **Liquor Control Law and Policy**.)

The Student Homophile League, the first student homophile organization, is chartered at Columbia University. Chapters are formed at Cornell University and New York University the following year and at the Massachusetts Institute of Technology in 1969. (*See* **Colleges and Universities**.)

In New York City, **Craig Rodwell** opens the Oscar Wilde Memorial Bookshop, which advertises itself as the world's first lesbian and gay **bookstore**.

*CBS Reports* airs a special episode titled "The Homosexuals." Although it perpetuates many homophobic stereotypes, the show exposes a large segment of the U.S. population to open lesbians and gay men for the first time. (*See* **Television**.)

**1968** Partners Bill Rand and Dick Michaels begin publishing the ***Advocate***, the best-selling U.S. LGB magazine, in Los Angeles.

Inspired by the Black Power movement and its celebration of black culture, the North American Conference of Homophile Organizations adopts the slogan "Gay Is Good." (*See* **Homophile Movement**.)

With its portrayal of openly gay men, Mart Crowley's *Boys in the Band* marks a turning point in LGBT theater. (*See* **Performance, Theater, and Dance Studies**.)

After being excommunicated from the Church of God for being gay, **Troy Perry** begins the Metropolitan Community Church in his Los Angeles living room. By 2002, the church had over 40,000 members and 300 congregations in nineteen countries. (*See also* **Churches, Temples, and Religious Groups.**)

In perhaps the first student LGBT rights demonstration, a group of Columbia University students protest a medical forum on homosexuality.

**1969** On 28 June, a routine police raid on the Stonewall Inn, a gay bar in New York City's Greenwich Village, sparks several nights of rioting. Widely considered to be the symbolic beginning of the modern LGBT rights movement, "Stonewall," as it becomes known, inspires the creation of LGBT organizations throughout the country. (*See* **Stonewall Riots.**)

In the aftermath of the Stonewall Riots, LGBT activists in New York City form the first **Gay Liberation Front**. Many members are also involved in the Black Power, feminist, and anti–Vietnam War movements and see LGBT rights as part of a larger movement to transform society. (*See also* **Gay Liberation.**)

Red Butterfly, a cell of the **Gay Liberation Front**, is organized with the goal of applying Marxism to the struggle for LGBT liberation. (See also **Anarchism, Socialism, and Communism.**)

In December, a number of **Gay Liberation Front** members who are dissatisfied with its lack of structure and multiple issue politics, including Jim Owles, Marty Robinson, and Arthur Evans, form the **Gay Activists Alliance**. With its focus solely on LGB equal rights, the group represents a return to the politics of the homophile movement, but it maintains the more confrontational tactics of the Gay Liberation Front.

Shameless Hussy Press, the first feminist publishing house in the United States, is founded in Oakland, California. Other early feminist and lesbian publishers include Daughters Press, The Feminist Press, and Naiad Press.

## 1970s

The growing lesbian feminist movement creates separate lesbian spaces and challenges both sexism in the LGBT rights movement and homophobia in the women's movement. (*See* **Lesbian Feminism.**)

The gains made by LGBT activists, along with more liberal sexual attitudes, lead to the prolifer-

ation of LGBT community institutions. Instead of a handful of bars that may not be owned and managed by LGBT people, cities begin to have multiple LGBT-run bars, as well as LGBT restaurants, clubs, bookstores, coffeehouses, and community centers. (*See* **Businesses.**)

Glossy magazines with explicit sexual content and full male nudity, including *Blueboy, Mandate, Honcho, Numbers, Drummer,* and *Bunkhouse,* begin to be published. (*See* **Pornography.**)

**1970** In New York City, **Sylvia Rivera** and Marsha P. Johnson found Street Transvestite Action Revolutionaries and open STAR House to provide a safe shelter for young transsexuals. (*See also* **Transgender Organizations and Periodicals.**)

In June, an estimated 10,000 people attend the first Christopher Street Liberation Day parade, celebrating the one-year anniversary of the Stonewall Riots. Marches also occur in Chicago, San Francisco, and Los Angeles. By the mid 1970s, LGBT pride celebrations are held in cities across the United States. (*See* **Pride Marches and Parades.**)

LGB activists protesting the inclusion of homosexuality in the American Psychiatric Association's *Diagnostic and Statistical Manual of Mental Disorders* disrupt the group's meeting in **San Francisco.** (*See also* **Medicine, Medicalization, and the Medical Model; Psychology, Psychiatry, Psychoanalysis, and Sexology.**)

Responding to comments by National Organization for Women President Betty Friedan that lesbians threaten to undermine the struggle for women's equality, a group of lesbians calling themselves the "lavender menace" take over the stage at the Congress to Unite Women on 1 May. The congress subsequently adopts a set of resolutions recognizing lesbianism as a women's rights issue. (*See* **Lesbian Feminism.**)

**Radicalesbians** circulates its groundbreaking statement "The Woman-Identified Woman," which argues that lesbianism is central to women's liberation and is primarily a political choice rather than a sexual orientation. (*See also* **Lesbian Feminism.**)

In an open letter entitled "Good-Bye, My Alienated Brothers," **Del Martin** states that she is devoting herself exclusively to feminist and lesbian feminist organizing and will no longer work in LGBT groups because of rampant sexism among gay men. Many other lesbians who are involved in the gay liberation movement do likewise. (*See also* **Feminism**; **Lesbian Feminism**.)

Huey Newton issues a statement calling for members of the Black Panther Party to form coalitions with gay liberation and women's liberation groups based on shared experiences of oppression and common revolutionary goals. A number of LGB activists subsequently attend the Black Panther's Revolutionary People's Constitutional Convention in Philadelphia.

Angela Keyes Douglas founds Transsexual Action Organization in southern California. The group engages in street-level protests and, at its height, has a thousand members in eight U.S. cities and three other countries. (*See* **Transgender Organizations and Periodicals**.)

**Kate Millett** comes out publicly as bisexual, becoming one of the first feminist leaders to acknowledge being LGBT. (*See also* **Bisexuality, Bisexuals, and Bisexual Movements**.)

The first feminist bookstore, Amazon Books, opens in Minneapolis; it is followed by **bookstores** in Ann Arbor, Atlanta, Tucson, and Cambridge, Massachusetts.

**Carl Wittman's** "A Gay Manifesto" is published and becomes a central ideological statement of the **gay liberation** movement.

**1971** The **Furies**, one of the most influential lesbian feminist groups, forms as a residential, publishing, and political collective in Washington, D.C., with Ginny Berson, Joan Biren, **Rita Mae Brown**, Charlotte Bunch, and Coletta Reid among its members. (*See also* **Publishers**.)

The Eulenspiegel Society, the oldest BDSM (Bondage and Discipline, Dominance and Submission, Sadism and Masochism) education and support group in the United States, is founded in New York City. (*See also* **Sadomasochism, Sadists, and Masochists**.)

The University of Michigan becomes the first college to hire staff to provide support services to its LGBT students. (*See* **Colleges and Universities**.)

What was by 2003 the oldest black LGBT organization in the country, the African Ancestral Lesbians United for Societal Change, begins as the Black Lesbian Caucus of the New York chapter of the Gay Activists Alliance. (*See* **African American LGBTQ Organizations and Periodicals**.)

**1972** East Lansing, Michigan, becomes the first city in the United States to pass a law banning discrimination on the basis of sexual orientation. (*See* **Anti-Discrimination Law and Policy**.)

The first openly bisexual organization in the United States, the National Bisexual Liberation Group, is founded in New York City. (*See* **Bisexuality, Bisexuals, and Bisexual Movements**.)

A group of lesbian, gay, and bisexual Jews in Los Angeles found the first LGBT synagogue, Beth Chayim Chadashim or the House of New Life. Two years later, it is accepted into the Union of American Hebrew Congregations. (*See* **Churches, Temples, and Religious Groups**; **Jews and Judaism**.)

The International Gay and Lesbian Archives, the first known LGBT archives in the United States, is created by **Jim Kepner** in Hollywood, California. (*See also* **History Projects, Libraries, and Archives**.)

The United Church of Christ becomes the first mainline denomination in the United States to ordain openly LGBT people. (*See* **Protestants and Protestantism**.)

Larry Townsend's *The Leatherman's Handbook*, a groundbreaking guide to the gay and bisexual leather S/M community, is published. (*See* **Leather Sex and Sexuality**; **Sadomasochism, Sadists, and Masochists**.)

**1973** Several national LGBT organizations are founded in New York City over the course of the year: the **National Lesbian and Gay Task Force** (then the National Gay Task Force), the **Lambda Legal Defense** and Education Fund, and **Parents, Families, and Friends of Lesbians and Gays**. All assume leading roles in the struggle for LGBT rights.

The **Lesbian Herstory Archives**, the world's largest and oldest lesbian archive, is founded in New York City by Joan Nestle and Deborah Edel. Opening in 1976 in the Manhattan apartment of its co-founders, the archive relocates to its own building in Brooklyn in 1992. (*See also* **History Projects, Libraries, and Archives**.)

Protests from LGB activists and supportive mental health professionals lead the American

Psychiatric Association's board of trustees to remove homosexuality from its list of mental disorders. The decision is affirmed the following year by a vote of the membership. (*See* **Medicine, Medicalization, and the Medical Model; Psychology, Psychiatry, Psychoanalysis, and Sexology.**)

*Gay Community News*, considered by some the newspaper of record for the LGBT movement, begins publishing in Boston.

**Olivia Records**, the most successful and influential women's music label, is established in Washington, D.C., by former members of the **Furies** and local musicians. (*See also* **Music.**)

**Rita Mae Brown**'s coming out story *Rubyfruit Jungle* is published and becomes one of the most widely read lesbian novels of the twentieth century. (*See* **Literature.**)

**1974** The National Women's Music Festival, the longest-running women's music event, is first held in Champaign-Urbana, Illinois. The largest and most well-known festival, the Michigan Womyn's Music Festival, begins two years later. (*See* **Music: Women's Festivals.**)

In April, Kathy Kozachenko wins a seat on the Ann Arbor City Council, becoming the first openly LGBT person to be elected to public office. Seven months later, **Elaine Noble** becomes the first openly LGBT person to win a seat in a state legislature when she is elected to the Massachusetts House of Representatives. (*See also* **Electoral Politics.**)

*Lesbian Connection*, the longest-running lesbian publication, is founded as a way for lesbians to network with each other.

The first bill banning discrimination based on sexual orientation is introduced in Congress, though it is not passed. (*See* **Anti-Discrimination Law and Policy.**)

**1975** **Barbara Cameron** (Hunkpapa Lakota) and **Randy Burns** (Northern Paiute) start Gay American Indians in San Francisco to address the discrimination faced by LGBT **Native Americans** within the predominantly white lesbian and gay movement and Christianized Native communities.

Minneapolis becomes the first municipality in the United States to outlaw discrimination on the basis of gender identity or expression. (*See* **Anti-Discrimination Law and Policy.**)

The U.S. Civil Service Commission revises its regulations to remove the ban on lesbians, gay men, and bisexuals in civilian federal government jobs. (*See* **Employment Law and Policy; Government and Military Witchhunts.**)

*Drummer* magazine, the first national leather and S/M publication, begins publishing in San Francisco. (*See* **Leather Sex and Sexuality.**)

**1976** **Renée Richards** is barred from competing in a women's tennis tournament. Her subsequent legal battle establishes the right of transsexuals to be recognized in their new identity after sex reassignment.

**1977** The **Combahee River Collective**, a Boston-based black feminist support and activist organization, publishes its influential "Black Feminist Statement." Written by a core group that includes sisters Beverly and **Barbara Smith** and Demita Frazier, the statement speaks to the importance of addressing the simultaneous, interlocking systems of racism, sexism, heterosexism, and classism. (*See also* **Lesbian Feminism.**)

Anita Bryant, a former beauty queen and bornagain Christian, leads a successful effort to overturn an ordinance in Dade County, Florida, barring discrimination on the basis of sexual orientation. Her "Save Our Children" campaign sparks a wave of violence against LGB people and the repeal of LGB rights laws in Wichita, Kansas; Eugene, Oregon; and St. Paul, Minnesota. (*See also* **Florida; New Right.**)

**Harvey Milk** is elected to the **San Francisco** Board of Supervisors, becoming the first openly LGBT elected official of a large U.S. city. (*See also* **Electoral Politics.**)

In San Francisco, Frameline produces the country's first lesbian and gay film festival. As of 2003, approximately 150 LGBT **film and video festivals** exist worldwide.

The Warehouse, a Chicago dance club, opens and gives rise to house music. By the 1980s, house becomes popular in black LGBT clubs across the country, especially in New York City, Detroit, and Washington, D.C. (*See* **Music.**)

The Rainbow Alliance of the Deaf is founded at a national conference in Fort Lauderdale, Florida. In 2003, more than twenty chapters existed across North America. (*See* **Disability, Disabled People, and Disability Movements.**)

Adrienne Rich, perhaps the most widely read openly lesbian poet, publishes her groundbreaking collection of lesbian love poetry, "Twenty-One Love Poems."

**1978** California voters decisively reject Proposition 6, an initiative sponsored by state Senator John Briggs that would have barred lesbians, gay men, bisexuals, and anyone supporting "a homosexual lifestyle" from teaching in the state's public schools. (*See* **Education Law and Policy**; **New Right.**)

On 27 November, former **San Francisco** Supervisor Dan White kills Harvey Milk and Mayor George Moscone. That night, more than 25,000 San Franciscans march in a silent candlelit procession to City Hall.

The National Coalition of Black Gays (subsequently renamed the National Coalition of Black Lesbians and Gays) is established. By the mid 1980s, chapters exist in cities across the country, including groups in Chicago, Minneapolis, New Orleans, San Francisco, and Washington, D.C. (*See* **African American LGBTQ Organizations and Periodicals.**)

The rainbow flag, designed by **San Francisco** artist Gilbert Baker, is unveiled at the city's annual Gay Freedom Day Parade.

**1979** On 21 May, a **San Francisco** jury from which LGBT people had been excluded finds Dan White guilty of manslaughter rather than murder in the shooting deaths of **Harvey Milk** and George Moscone. Following the verdict, several thousand people march to City Hall, where the crowd barricades members of the Board of Supervisors in the building and fights with the police, many of whom had openly supported White during the trial. Scores of protesters and police officers are injured in what becomes known as the White Night Riots.

Marking the tenth anniversary of the Stonewall Riots, the First National March on Washington for Lesbian and Gay Rights on 14 October attracts more than 100,000 people from the United States and ten other countries. The event features the first National Third World Gay and Lesbian Conference, which is attended by hundreds of people of color, who stage their own march that joins up with the main march. (*See* **Marches on Washington.**)

The first **Radical Faeries** gathering is held in Arizona, organized by **Harry Hay**, Don Kilhefner, and Mitch Walker.

The first LGBT group at a historically black college or university, Howard University's Lambda Student Alliance, is officially recognized by the school, but only after the students threaten to bring a lawsuit if the school rejected it. (*See* **Colleges and Universities.**)

Physicians and therapists form the Harry Benjamin International Gender Dysphoria Association and create standards for the diagnosis and treatment of transsexuals. (*See* **Transsexuals, Transvestites, Transgender People, and Cross-Dressers.**)

The first LGBT Asian Pacific American (APA) organization in the United States, Boston Asian Gay Men and Lesbians (known today as Queer Asian Pacific Alliance of New England/Boston), is formed to challenge the invisibility of LGBT Asian Pacific Americans within LGBT and APA communities. (*See* **Asian American LGBTQ Organizations and Periodicals.**)

**1980s**

Groundbreaking works by writers such as **Barbara Smith**, **Cherríe Moraga**, **Gloria Anzaldúa**, **Beth Brant**, **Pat Parker**, **Chrystos**, **Audre Lorde**, and **Merle Woo** bring greater attention to the experiences of lesbians of color and challenge the predominantly white lesbian feminist movement to fight all systems of oppression.

Doctors diagnose what becomes known as **AIDS**, and infections rise at an alarming rate among gay and bisexual men, especially gay and bisexual African Americans and Latinos. The government's slow response to the epidemic prompts LGBT people to establish the **AIDS Coalition to Unleash Power** and **AIDS service organizations**.

The deaths of leading dancers and choreographers from AIDS in the 1980s and 1990s, including **Alvin Ailey**, **Michael Bennett**, **Robert Joffrey**, Rudolf Nureyev, Edward Stierle, and **Arnie Zane**, devastate the dance community and lead many choreographers and performance artists to become more openly political in their work. (*See also* **Dance.**)

**Keith Haring's** simple yet sophisticated cartoonish figures go from public art to pop culture iconography to symbols of political and social movements, particularly AIDS awareness campaigns after the artist's death from the disease.

Combining punk music and militant LGBT politics, queercore originates in Canada and soon achieves popularity in the United States with bands such as Pansy Division, Tribe 8, and The Butchies. (*See* **Music.**)

**1980** The American Psychiatric Association adds "transsexualism" to its third edition of the *Diagnostic and Statistical Manual of Mental Disorders*. Despite opposition from many transsexuals, who resented having to be diagnosed as sick and deviant in order to gain medical assistance, the classification has remained, although it is renamed "gender identity disorders" in subsequent editions. (*See* **Psychology, Psychiatry, Psychoanalysis, and Sexology.**)

The Womyn's Braille Press is created by six feminist activists in Minneapolis-St. Paul to make lesbian and feminist literature available to women who are blind or otherwise unable to read printed material. (*See* **Disability, Disabled People, and Disability Movements.**)

**Black and White Men Together** is established in San Francisco. Twenty years later, the organization had more than thirty chapters, some under the name Men of All Colors Together or People of All Colors Together.

The **Human Rights Campaign**, known as the Human Rights Campaign Fund until 1995, is founded in Washington, D.C., as the first national lesbian and gay political action committee. In 2003, it was the largest lesbian and gay rights organization in the country, with over one hundred staff and a budget of more than $20 million.

**Melvin Boozer** is nominated for Vice President of the United States and addresses the Democratic National Convention, becoming the first leader of a LGBT organization to speak at a national political convention.

**1981** In June, the Centers for Disease Control and Prevention report on five gay men in Los Angeles who have contracted a rare form of pneumonia through a weakened immune system. Because the first cases seem to be limited to gay men, the medical establishment initially refers to the syndrome as Gay-Related Immune Deficiency. (*See* **AIDS and People with AIDS.**)

**Barbara Smith** and **Audre Lorde** establish Kitchen Table: Women of Color Press, the first publishing house owned and operated by women of color.

**Samois**, a lesbian-feminist sadomasochist group in San Francisco, edits *Coming to Power*, one of the first books to give a voice to S/M lesbians and to counter cultural feminist claims that S/M perpetuates violence and the oppression of women. (*See also* **Sadomasochism, Sadists, and Masochists.**)

Tennis superstars **Billie Jean King** and **Martina Navratilova** are outed as lesbians. (*See also* **Sports.**)

**1982** Wisconsin becomes the first state to pass civil rights protections for lesbians, gay men, and bisexuals. (*See* **Anti-Discrimination Law and Policy.**)

Meeting at the home of playwright **Larry Kramer** in New York City, a group of men establish the Gay Men's Health Crisis to address the impact of AIDS on their community. (*See also* **AIDS Service Organizations.**)

The first Gay Games is held in San Francisco. Created by former Olympian **Tom Waddell**, it becomes the largest LGBT athletic event in the world, with thousands of participants every four years. (*See also* **Sports.**)

In one of the most contentious moments in the "**Sex Wars,**" cultural feminists and lesbian sex radicals confront each other at the Ninth Scholar and Feminist Conference at Barnard College. (*See also* **Lesbian Feminism.**)

*Torch Song Trilogy* by **Harvey Fierstein** becomes one of the longest-running Broadway shows and wins a Tony Award for best play.

Women's One World (or WOW) Café opens in New York City. As of 2003, it was the oldest continuing performance venue dedicated to promoting lesbian feminist work. (*See* **Performance, Theater, and Dance Studies.**)

**1983** Massachusetts Representative Gerry Studds becomes the first member of Congress to come out as gay. (*See* **Electoral Politics.**)

**1984** Scientists in France and the United States discover that **AIDS** is caused by a retrovirus, Human Immunodeficiency Virus (HIV).

The lesbian sex magazine *On Our Backs* premieres and helps usher in a boom in lesbian erotica. (*See* **Pornography.**)

The Harvey Milk High School, the first and largest accredited public school for LGBT youth, is founded in New York City by the Hetrick-Martin Institute, with the support of the city's board of education. In 2003, the school received its own building, enabling about 100 students to enroll. (*See* **Youth and Youth Groups.**)

**1985** Gospel singer Carl Bean begins a Bible study group in his Los Angeles home to provide support to other black LGBT Christians. The overwhelming response leads Bean to establish the Unity Fellowship Church Movement. By 2003, Unity Fellowship churches existed in thirteen U.S. cities. (*See* **Churches, Temples, and Religious Groups.**)

During an AIDS candlelight vigil in San Francisco, Cleve Jones conceives of what becomes the **AIDS Memorial Quilt.** The Quilt is first unveiled at the March on Washington for Lesbian and Gay Rights in 1987. At this time, it consists of 1,920 panels and is larger than a football field. By 2003, the quilt had more than 50,000 panels.

The first International Conference on **AIDS** is held in Atlanta.

Actor Rock Hudson discloses that he has **AIDS**, leading many Americans, including President Ronald Reagan, to talk about AIDS for the first time.

In response to homophobic coverage of the AIDS crisis in the mainstream media, the **Gay and Lesbian Alliance Against Defamation** is established.

**1986** FTM International, the largest and longest-running organization for transmen, is founded in San Francisco by **Lou Sullivan.** (*See also* **Transgender Organizations and Periodicals.**)

In *Bowers v. Hardwick*, the Supreme Court upholds Georgia's sodomy law by a 5-4 ruling. The decision is subsequently used to justify discrimination against lesbians, gay men, and bisexuals in employment, housing, immigration, and child custody cases. (*See* **Sodomy, Buggery, Crimes against Nature, Disorderly Conduct, and Lewd and Lascivious Law and Policy.**)

**Joseph Beam**'s *In the Life: A Black Gay Anthology*, the first widely released book about black gay and bisexual men, is published.

**1987** On 11 October, more than half a million people participate in the second national March on Washington for Lesbian and Gay Rights. Meetings at the march lead to the formation of National Latina/o Lesbian and Gay Activists (later renamed the National Latina/o Lesbian, Gay, Bisexual, and Transgender Organization) and the Asian Pacific Lesbian Network (which subsequently becomes the Asian and Pacific Islander Lesbian and Bisexual Women and Transgender Network). The march also sees the first national gathering of bisexual activists. (*See* **Marches on Washington.**)

Two days following the March on Washington, approximately 800 people are arrested in front of the Supreme Court in the largest civil disobedience action ever held in support of LGBT rights.

The Massachusetts-based International Foundation for Gender Education is founded and begins publishing *Transgender Tapestry*. (*See* **Transgender Organizations and Periodicals.**)

The **AIDS Coalition to Unleash Power** (ACT UP) is formed in New York City, and locally autonomous chapters quickly spread across the country. More than 80 ACT UP organizations exist over the course of the early and mid 1990s. Its largest demonstrations are protests at the Food and Drug Administration and the National Institutes of Health in Maryland over their slow responses to the AIDS crisis and at St. Patrick's Cathedral in New York City over the Roman Catholic Church's opposition to safer sex education.

The Food and Drug Administration approves AZT as the first drug to treat **AIDS.**

Congress adds HIV/AIDS to the list of diseases for which people can be prevented from entering the United States. (*See* **Immigration, Asylum, and Deportation Law and Policy.**)

Representative **Barney Frank** of Massachusetts comes out, becoming the second openly LGBT member of Congress. (*See also* **Electoral Politics.**)

**1988** The Gay and Lesbian Arabic Society is established in Washington, D.C. A year later, the Arab Lesbian and Bisexual Women's Network is formed in Berkeley, California. (*See* **Arab Americans; Muslims and Islam.**)

The National Black Lesbian and Gay Leadership Forum is founded in Los Angeles by Phill Wilson and Ruth Waters. (*See* **African American LGBTQ Organizations and Periodicals.**)

The first book by and about LGBT Native Americans, *Living the Spirit: A Gay American Indian Anthology*, is published. (*See* **Native American LGBTQ Organizations and Publications.**)

A retrospective exhibit of photographs by **Robert Mapplethorpe** is canceled by the Corcoran Gallery in Washington, D.C., because of homoerotic and sadomasochistic images. A subsequent attempt to hold the show at the Contemporary Arts Center in Cincinnati is shut down by the police. The center becomes the first museum in U.S. history to be charged with obscenity; its director is later acquitted. (*See* **Visual Art.**)

11 October, the anniversary of the second national March on Washington for Lesbian and Gay Rights, begins to be marked as National Coming Out Day.

The World Health Organization designates 1 December 1as World AIDS Day.

**1989** LGBT students and heterosexual allies in private Massachusetts high schools establish the first Gay-Straight Alliances. Groups are subsequently formed at more than 1,600 high schools and junior highs across the country. (*See* **Youth and Youth Groups.**)

The City College of San Francisco creates the first Lesbian, Gay, and Bisexual Studies department. (*See* **Colleges and Universities.**)

Reminiscent of the 1901 death of **Murray Hall**, jazz musician **Billy Tipton**, who lived as a man throughout his adult life, dies and is discovered to have been born female-bodied.

Massachusetts becomes the second state to pass civil rights protections for lesbians, gay men, and bisexuals. (*See* **Anti-Discrimination Law and Policy.**)

## 1990s

Nine states enact laws that ban discrimination on the basis of sexual orientation: Hawaii (1991), Connecticut (1991), New Jersey (1992), Vermont (1992), California (1992), Minnesota (1993), Rhode Island (1995), New Hampshire (1997), and Nevada (1999). (*See* **Anti-Discrimination Law and Policy.**)

Transgender people become more visible with the formation of the American Educational Gender Information Service; It's Time, America!; Transsexual Menace; and the National Transgender Advocacy Coalition. An increasing number of books by and about transpeople, most notably Leslie Feinberg's *Stone Butch Blues* (1993) and *Transgender Warriors* (1996), Kate Bornstein's *Gender Outlaw* (1994), and Riki Anne Wilchins's *Read My Lips* (1997), also draw attention to transgender experiences and help educate others about their lives. (*See* **Transgender Organizations and Periodicals.**)

Independent feature films, including Jennie Livingston's *Paris Is Burning* (1990), Todd Haynes's *Poison* (1991), Tom Kalin's *Swoon* (1992), Gregg Araki's *The Living End* (1992), and Rose Troche's *Go Fish* (1994), give rise to what becomes known as the New Queer Cinema and provide a greater level of visibility and success for LGBT filmmakers. (*See* **Film and Video.**)

Filmmakers, writers, and artists, including **Marlon Riggs**, **Essex Hemphill**, Michelle Parkerson, Assotto Saint, and Cheryl Dunye, fuel a second black LGBT renaissance.

Building on the writing of **Cherríe Moraga** and **Gloria Anzaldúa**, Carla Trujillo's *Chicana Lesbians: The Girls Our Mothers Warned Us About* (1991) and Juanita Ramos's *Compañeras: Latina Lesbians* (1994) make important contributions to Latina/o studies and lesbian studies. (*See also* **Latina and Latino Studies.**)

**African American** gay and bisexual writers are especially hard hit by **AIDS**. Among those who die in the epidemic are **Joseph Beam**, Steven Corbin, Melvin Dixon, Craig Harris, **Essex Hemphill**, **Marlon Riggs**, Assotto Saint, and Donald W. Woods.

Lesbian and bisexual women musicians, including Melissa Etheridge, Ani DiFranco, the Indigo Girls, and k.d. lang, come out and continue to be popular with both heterosexual and LGBT audiences. (*See* **Music: Popular.**)

LGB characters on **television** become more frequent and less stereotypical with the debut of shows such as *Spin City*, *Ellen*, and *Will and Grace*.

A number of current and former professional athletes come out as LGB, including baseball players Glenn Burke and Billy Bean, diver Greg Louganis, golfers Muffin Spencer-Devlin and Patty Sheehan, mountain biker Missy Giove, and figure skater Rudy Galindo. (*See* **Sports.**)

**Queer theory** emerges as an effort to analyze sexuality and gender by bringing together elements of feminist theory, LGBT studies, and poststructuralism.

The "outing" of closeted pop culture celebrities and Washington, D.C., officials by LGBT activists prompts a number of public figures (including David Geffen, Barry Diller, Jim Kolbe, and Steve Gunderson) to acknowledge their same-sex sexuality, but the practice also generates controversy in some LGBT communities. (*See* **Coming Out and Outing.**)

**1990** At the first National Bisexual Conference in San Francisco, the groundwork is laid for the establishment of the first national bisexual organization, BiNet USA. (*See* **Bisexuality, Bisexuals, and Bisexual Movements.**)

The direct action group **Queer Nation** holds its first meeting in New York City. By the following year, 60 chapters have been formed across North America.

Congress passes the Americans with Disabilities Act, which prohibits discrimination in employment on the basis of a person's disability, including AIDS. (*See* **Disability, Disabled People, and Disability Movements.**)

The Ryan White Emergency Care Act dramatically increases AIDS funding to state governments and **AIDS service organizations**.

The term "two-spirit" is coined at the third Native American/First Nations Gay and Lesbian Conference to describe contemporary Native LGBT people and individuals who assumed a cross-gendered role in many Native cultures in the past. (*See* **Native American LGBTQ Organizations and Publications; Two-Spirit Females; Two-Spirit Males.**)

Seeking to end the mistreatment of LGBT and questioning (sexually uncertain) youth, the **Gay, Lesbian, and Straight Education Network** is founded in Boston and quickly develops into one of the country's largest LGBT organizations, with offices in New York City, San Francisco, and Washington, D.C., and over eighty local chapters.

The National Endowment for the Arts rescinds grants to four performance artists whose work deals with sex and gender politics, three of whom are LGBT: Holly Hughes, Tim Miller, and John Fleck.

**1991** The first Black Lesbian and Gay Pride celebration is held in Washington, D.C. In 2003, Black Pride events were held in twenty cities. (*See* **African American LGBTQ Organizations and Periodicals.**)

*Anything That Moves,* the first bisexual magazine in the United States, begins publishing in San Francisco. (*See* **Bisexuality, Bisexuals, and Bisexual Movements.**)

An appeals court in Minnesota awards guardianship of Sharon Kowalski to her partner Karen Thompson, ending a legal battle that began after a 1983 car accident severely injured Kowalski. (*See* **Disability, Disabled People, and Disability Movements.**)

The LGBT Victory Fund is created to support LGBT candidates for elected office. (See **Electoral Politics.**)

Sherry Harris is elected to Seattle's City Council, becoming the first openly LGBT African American to be voted into office. (*See* **Electoral Politics.**)

The **Center for Lesbian and Gay Studies (CLAGS)**, the first university-based LGBT research center in the United States, is founded at the City University of New York. (*See also* **LGBTQ Studies.**)

After the organizers of the New York City St. Patrick's Day Parade refuse the Irish Lesbian and Gay Organization permission to march, the Ancient Order of Hibernians (an Irish-American fraternal organization) agrees to have an LGB contingent march as its guest.

**1992** The **Lesbian Avengers** is formed in New York City to increase lesbian visibility and challenge queer assimilation. In 2000, there were approximately fifty-five U.S. chapters.

Statewide ballot initiatives in Colorado and Oregon seek to prevent municipalities from enacting or enforcing laws that ban discrimination on the basis of sexual orientation. The Oregon measure is narrowly rejected by voters, but Colorado's Amendment 2 is approved. (*See* **Anti-Discrimination Law and Policy; Federal Law and Policy.**)

**1993** On 25 April, nearly one million people attend the March on Washington for Lesbian, Gay, and Bi Equal Rights and Liberation, the largest demonstration in U.S. history to that time. In addition to the march, participants take part in more than 250 related events, including conferences, protests, congressional lobbying, parties, readings, and a mass wedding ceremony. (*See* **Marches on Washington.**)

President Bill Clinton goes back on a campaign promise to lift the ban on lesbians, gay men, and bisexuals serving in the armed forces. Instead, he institutes the "don't ask/don't tell" policy, which allows the military to discharge only openly LGB individuals. While seemingly designed to improve the lives of LGB servicemembers, discharges actually increase during the 1990s. (*See* **Federal Law and Policy; Military Law and Policy.**)

The murder of Nebraska teen Brandon Teena raises awareness of hate crimes against transpeople. The 1999 Academy-Award winning film about his life and death, *Boys Don't Cry*, brings further attention to anti-transgender violence.

The Intersex Society of North America is founded by Cheryl Chase to raise awareness about intersex people and to advocate for an end to medically unnecessary intersex surgeries. (*See* **Intersexuals and Intersexed People.**)

Tony Kushner's *Angels in America*, a play about the lives of gay men affected by AIDS, opens on Broadway and wins two Tony Awards for best drama and a Pulitzer Prize. (*See* **Performance, Theater, and Dance Studies.**)

Minnesota becomes the first state to outlaw discrimination on the basis of gender identity or expression. As of 2003, four states, nine counties, and 50 cities had enacted similar laws. (*See* **Anti-Discrimination Law and Policy.**)

Massachusetts becomes the first state to prohibit discrimination in its public schools on the basis of sexual orientation. A decade later, six states have laws protecting the rights of lesbian, gay, and bisexual students and three have such laws protecting transgender students. (*See* **Education Law and Policy.**)

"Camp Trans" is organized outside the Michigan Womyn's Music Festival to protest the festival's exclusion of transsexuals through its "womyn-born-womyn only" policy. (*See* **Transgender Organizations and Periodicals.**)

**1995**  The Food and Drug Administration approves the use of the first protease inhibitor to treat **AIDS.** The development of this class of drugs makes multiple drug therapies possible, dramatically improving the health of many people living with HIV and AIDS in the United States.

In response to criticism over White House security guards wearing rubber gloves during a visit of LGB elected officials, President Bill Clinton names the first White House liaison to LGBT communities.

**1996**  The Supreme Court rules in *Romer v. Evans* that Colorado's law preventing municipalities from enacting or enforcing statutes that ban discrimination on the basis of sexual orientation is unconstitutional, holding that it violates the equal protection clause of the Fourteenth Amendment. (*See* **Anti-Discrimination Law and Policy; Federal Law and Policy.**)

The University of Iowa becomes the first college to add gender identity to its campus nondiscrimination policy.

Wisconsin high school student Jamie Nabozny is awarded nearly one million dollars in a lawsuit stemming from the failure of teachers and administrators in his school district to prevent the constant harassment and violence he experienced for being gay. (*See* **Education Law and Policy.**)

A Hawaii trial court rules that the state has no "compelling interest" in banning same-sex marriages. But before the state Supreme Court can issue a final disposition in the case, Hawaii voters approve a measure blocking same-sex marriages. (*See* **Family Issues; Family Law and Policy.**)

Prompted by the Hawaii court decision, Congress overwhelmingly passes and President Bill Clinton signs the Defense of Marriage Act, which gives states the right to refuse to recognize same-sex marriages that might become legal in other states and denies numerous federal benefits to same-sex couples. (*See* **Family Issues; Family Law and Policy.**)

**1997**  *Ellen* becomes the first network primetime **television** show to feature an LGBT lead character, but is canceled at the end of the season.

Maine passes a law banning discrimination on the basis of sexual orientation, but it is repealed by a ballot initiative the following year. (*See* **Anti-Discrimination Law and Policy.**)

**1998** The brutal murder of University of Wyoming student Matthew Shepard receives unprecedented media coverage and leads to worldwide protests and stepped up efforts to include LGBT people in hate crimes legislation.

At the First International Retreat for GLBT Muslims in Boston, participants found Al-Fatiha. Within five years, U.S. chapters are formed in Atlanta, Houston, Los Angeles, Philadelphia, New York City, San Diego, San Francisco, and Washington, D.C. (*See* **Muslims and Islam.**)

Wisconsin Representative Tammy Baldwin becomes the first out lesbian member of Congress and the first person elected to federal office who is open about being LGBT from the outset of campaigning. (*See* **Electoral Politics.**)

President Bill Clinton issues an executive order prohibiting discrimination on the basis of sexual orientation in civilian federal employment. (*See* **Anti-Discrimination Law and Policy; Federal Law and Policy.**)

The Supreme Court decides in *Bragdon v. Abbott* that individuals who are HIV-positive but asymptomatic are protected under the Americans with Disabilities Act. (*See* **Disability, Disabled People, and Disability Movements.**)

*Will and Grace*, the first primetime network **television** series with a gay male lead character, premieres and becomes one of the most popular shows.

**1999** The first Transgender Day of Remembrance is held in San Francisco to memorialize those who are killed because of anti-transgender hatred or prejudice. In 2002, the day was marked in approximately 70 communities across the United States. (*See* **Transgender Organizations and Periodicals.**)

Contrary to established case law, a Texas appellate court negates Christie Littleton's marriage to her husband because she was born male-bodied. The decision and a similar ruling from the Kansas Supreme Court are a setback for transgender rights.

## 2000s

Three more states enact laws that ban discrimination on the basis of sexual orientation: Maryland (2001), New York (2002), and New Mexico (2003). (*See* **Anti-Discrimination Law and Policy.**)

Joining Minnesota, three states outlaw discrimination on the basis of gender identity or expression: Rhode Island (2001), New Mexico (2003), and California (2003). (*See* **Anti-Discrimination Law and Policy.**)

Reality **television** shows, including *Survivor, Big Brother, The Amazing Race, The Real World*, and *Queer Eye for the Straight Guy*, often feature LGB people and become extremely popular with both LGB and heterosexual audiences.

**2000** Vermont enacts the first statewide civil union law, enabling same-sex couples to have access to state benefits previously available only to married heterosexual couples in such areas as insurance, taxation, inheritance, workers' compensation, and medical coverage. (*See* **Family Issues.**)

Approximately 200,000 people attend the Millennium March on Washington for Equality. A number of groups and individuals boycott the event because of concerns about how it is organized and what it seeks to achieve. (*See* **Marches on Washington.**)

**2001** In the aftermath of the September 11 attacks, individuals who are or are perceived as Muslim or **Arab American**, including a number of LGBT people, are harassed and physically assaulted. Despite support from some predominantly white LGBT groups, the heightened anti-Arab and anti-Muslim sentiment further isolates LGBT Arab Americans. (*See also* **Muslims and Islam; Race and Racism.**)

Two days after the September 11 attacks, Jerry Falwell and Pat Robertson blame LGBT people, along with pagans, feminists, and abortion providers, for the tragedy, calling it "God's judgment on America." (*See* **New Right.**)

The Patriot Act expands the powers of the federal government to spy on individuals and to monitor and infiltrate organizations, posing a threat not just to Muslims, but also to militant LGBT activists whom conservatives can label "terrorists."

The short-lived drama *The Education of Max Bickford* becomes the first network **television** series to feature a regular transgender character.

**2003** A Florida judge rules in a groundbreaking case that Michael Kantaras, a transgender man, is legally male and was legally married to his former wife. He is awarded primary custody of the couple's two children. (*See* **Transsexuals, Transvestites, Transgender People, and Cross-Dressers.**)

Twenty-one organizations serving LGBT communities endorse a statement opposing the second war with Iraq, including the Audre Lorde Project, the National Youth Advocacy Coalition, Pride at Work, and Southerners on New Ground.

In a landmark decision, the Supreme Court in *Lawrence v. Texas* rules that sodomy laws violate the constitutional right to privacy, thereby reversing *Bowers v. Hardwick* and voiding the sodomy laws that still existed in 13 states. (*See* **Sodomy, Buggery, Crimes against Nature, Disorderly Conduct, and Lewd and Lascivious Law and Policy.**)

In response to the Supreme Court's recognition of the privacy rights of LGB people, President George W. Bush endorses a constitutional amendment banning same-sex marriages.

To address the needs of transgender students, Wesleyan University creates a gender-free residence hall floor, where the students are assigned a roommate without consideration of gender and have unisex bathrooms. (*See* **Colleges and Universities.**)

The Reverend Gene Robinson is elected and confirmed as bishop of New Hampshire, becoming the first openly LGBT bishop in the Episcopal Church. (*See* **Protestants and Protestantism.**)

Brett Beemyn

**lgbt**

**encyclopedia
of**
lesbian, gay,
bisexual, and
transgender
**history
in america**

abcdefghijklmnopqrstuvwxyz

# A

# ACTORS AND ACTRESSES

## Gender and Sexuality as Performance

Until recently, homosexual and bisexual actors and actresses—both now commonly designated "actors"—were forced to hide their sexuality from the public and often from their employers and colleagues as well. However, considerable evidence suggests that the acting profession itself has long been unusually attractive and relatively receptive to LGBT people, who may have first found safe havens from homophobia in the creative communities of their school drama clubs. For professional actors, both the theater and film worlds have sustained informal circles of LGBT artists that serve as support networks and meeting grounds for creative collaborations as well as romantic liaisons. Recently, queer theorists have argued that gender itself is always a performance, and so the long-standing theatrical practices of cross-dressing and (its gay underground form) drag have come to represent only the most emphatic forms of gender play that otherwise characterize the behavioral acts signifying gender and sexual identities in everyday life. Perhaps because LGBT people have often had to conform by performing the straight roles society expects them to fulfill, the role-playing that is the actor's craft begins early, or at least develops from a life that frequently demands the adoption of a public mask. More recently, uncloseted LGBT actors have finally been able to "play themselves," representing the diversity of LGBT identities and experiences on stage and screen in works often created for them by openly LGBT writers and directors.

## Recovering and Identifying LGBT Actors

Although recent film and theater historians have recovered a remarkable history of LGBT actors, it remains difficult and controversial to retroactively identify and thereby "out" earlier performers in terms of current contexts and definitions. The private lives of public figures were once more persistently hidden from audiences who, it was assumed, idealized film and stage stars as models of heterosexual masculinity and femininity (although comic actors could more often challenge normative gender and sexual traits since their lack of conventional masculine or feminine attributes was often central to their characters). Moreover, as many critics have argued, definitions of homosexuality and lesbianism are historical constructions, and current understandings of what defines a person as LGBT can only be applied to past lives with great caution.

But even if we cannot always know which actors were—or even now are—LGBT, this lack of certainty does not reduce the significance of many actors for LGBT audiences. One might then identify four categories of actors with relevance to LGBT culture: (1) actors known to be LGBT, through convincing evidence, from self-identification to accumulated confirmation from reliable sources; (2) actors presumed, often only through rumor or suggestion, to be LGBT, or to have at least enjoyed occasional same-sex experiences; (3) ostensibly straight actors who have, to positive or negative effect, played significant LGBT roles; and (4) ostensibly straight actors who have been especially popular among, or played a notable part in the cultural life of, LGBT fans. Choosing representative figures for each category—such as Rock Hudson (1), Jodie Foster (2), Tom Hanks (3), and Judy Garland (4)—suggests something of the range of ways in which diverse actors may interact with LGBT culture. And off the mainstream stage and screen, a distinctive series of performers, from female impersonators to queer performance artists, have radically extended the once limited boundaries of LGBT acting.

## LGBT Actors on the American Stage

Historians of European theatrical traditions—long restricted by law or convention to male performers—have often noted the suspicion of sexual "deviance" attributed to actors, and antitheatrical Puritans in early America also raised questions about the troubling fact that many actors remained happily unmarried. The development of a theatrical star system in the early nineteenth century, however, drew attention to performers who were unique and often socially unconventional: fans allowed, indeed expected, such celebrities to lead atypical lives even if the explicit details of their sexual affairs remained discreet. Recent biographical studies of leading nineteenth-century theatrical figures such as Edwin Forrest (famous for playing the Roman slave Spartacus), Charlotte Cushman (most notable for her cross-dressed "breeches" roles, including Romeo, and for her legion of female fans), and Adah Isaacs Menken (notorious for her "nude" ride strapped to a horse in *Mazeppa*) have convincingly uncovered and respectfully treated the same-sex experiences that animated both the private lives and public careers of such stars. By the early twentieth century popular theatrical forms such as musical comedy, vaudeville, and the minstrel show regularly highlighted female and male impersonators, including Julian Eltinge, Bothwell Browne, "boy" impersonator Ella Wesner, and Francis Leon, a specialist in blackface "wench" roles. After World War I a number of prominent lesbian performers, such as Alla Nazimova, cross-dressing Elsie Janis, Eva Le Gallienne, and Tallulah Bankhead, were visible on Broadway and in musical comedies. In short, both the legitimate and popular theater commonly included actors flamboyantly "performing" gender dramatically and comically, in ways that suggestively challenged its presumed biological certainty offstage. Many of these actors also led unconventional, if semisecret, private lives, enjoying long-term romances as well as brief affairs with (often equally famous) partners of both or their own sexes.

Although legitimate theater became increasingly tolerant of gay playwrights (most prominently Tennessee Williams) and gay characters after World War II, LGBT actors necessarily remained closeted during this espe-cially homophobic period, when homosexuality was conflated with communism, even if some actors were willing to reveal their own sexual identities among their peers. Prominent LGBT performers of the Cold War era include Owen Dodson (eventually more active as an innovative director), (perhaps) the musical star Mary Martin, and Sandy Dennis, the winner of two Tony awards and an Oscar in the 1960s. While the increased visibility of gay playwrights and characters on stage did not necessarily allow more openly LGBT actors (at least in starring roles), the post-Stonewall development of a range of explicitly LGBT performers and theatrical companies would soon radically revise the practices and possibilities of LGBT acting.

## LGBT Actors in Hollywood

Although early cinema drew on prior theatrical traditions, it quickly developed new performance styles suitable for the camera, and within its first decades the film industry established its own star system to promote the public's fascination with "picture personalities" and, eventually, movie stars. Unsurprisingly, some of these actors also led the unconventional sexual lives of their theatrical predecessors and peers, though the early film industry, desperate to establish its legitimacy among middle-class patrons, was even more concerned than the theatrical world to obscure the private lives of its players from public scrutiny. Eventually, the off-screen lives of the stars would emerge through studio-regulated gossip and the new fan magazines, but a number of prominent (and usually heterosexual) star scandals in the late 1920s led to Hollywood's self-imposed Production Code in 1930, which banned the explicit display of homosexuality on screen (until a slight revision in 1961), while the studios policed their players with new "morality clauses" added to their binding contracts.

As with theater history, the history of LGBT Hollywood is still being recovered and written, and must also depend on rumors and personal accounts that, even when plausible or convincing, can probably never be verified. For every Hollywood actor, such as early male leads J. Warren Kerrigan, William Haines, and Roman Novarro, or the vamp Alla Nazimova, whose homosexuality, lesbianism, or bisexuality now appears evident, many more remain the subject of speculation. In such cases, the contemporary desire to locate and celebrate past role models must be balanced against respect for the wishes and economic necessity of those figures to have guarded their private lives. Rumors about the lesbian affairs of Greta Garbo, Marlene Dietrich, and Joan Crawford, for example, or the early gay affairs of male leads such as Cary

**GLAAD Special Honorees.**
Whoopi Goldberg (right)
poses with musician Melissa
Etheridge (center) and her
then-partner, Julie Cypher, at
the 10th annual Gay and
Lesbian Alliance Against
Defamation Media Awards
Gala in Los Angeles on 17
April 1999. [**AP Photo/Victoria
Arocho**]

Grant and Gary Cooper, have circulated for decades, but may always remain difficult to confirm: such uncertainty hardly counters the fascination and admiration such figures have persistently generated among LGBT viewers. In the face of official silence, gossip about stars, critics have argued, has played a necessary role in LGBT culture whether or not the rumors are verifiable.

Although the Production Code attempted to ban suggestions of homosexuality in films, a number of gay character actors, including Edward Everett Horton and Franklin Pangborn, while embodying "sissy" and "pansy" stereotypes, kept queer characters on screen throughout the 1930s. Later, gay actors such as Clifton Webb and Monty Woolley played cultured, prissy queens in more prominent and dramatic roles. Lesbian character actors working in Hollywood included comic Patsy Kelly, Marjorie Main (best known as "Ma Kettle" in a popular series of comedies), British import Judith Anderson, and Agnes Moorehead, introduced into films via Orson Welles's Mercury Theater troupe.

Curiously, gay actors again assumed lead roles in Hollywood following World War II, ironically during one of the nation's and the film industry's most conservative eras: while masculine icons such as Rock Hudson and Tyrone Power attracted large female followings, sensitive

young men such as James Dean, Montgomery Clift, and Sal Mineo (all known or widely rumored to be gay or bisexual) projected an ambiguity more in line with the findings of the controversial Kinsey report on male sexuality (and its famous scale of varying homosexual activity) published in 1948. Often gay or bisexual young actors, including John Dall and Farley Granger (co-stars of Hitchcock's 1948 *Rope*), and Anthony Perkins (in Hitchcock's 1960 *Psycho*), played the implicitly gay and psychotic figures common to the last era to largely understand homosexuality as a psychological "problem." However, the 1955 arrest of boy-next-door star Tab Hunter at a gay party challenged the era's conventional assumptions linking homosexuality and neurosis. Although in retrospect Rock Hudson's gayness may appear to have been evident, the eventual public revelation that the virile, muscular Hudson was a gay man (despite a brief, studio-imposed marriage to his agent's secretary in 1955) forced a large number of the American public, who had never suspected Hudson's homosexuality, to drastically reevaluate their trust in Hollywood's representations of normative sexuality, and to perhaps finally abandon the lingering stereotype of gay men as sissies. After Hudson, it seemed, the public might believe that any actor could be gay—or, more tentatively, that being gay would not ruin a career.

Beginning in the late 1960s LGBT characters have been prominently, if often sensationally and even offensively, included in many popular films and television programs, although as with post–World War II theater, these gay roles have frequently been assumed by reassuringly straight actors. Straight actors who play gay characters are typically praised for their courage and daring, whereas actors who are openly gay or lesbian are rarely cast in straight roles, usually on the facile assumption that public knowledge of their sexuality will undermine their ability to convince audiences. Nevertheless, in recent years a number of film and television actors have sustained careers while affirming themselves to be gay or lesbian, including Rosie O'Donnell, Wilson Cruz (notable as a gay teen on *My So-Called Life*), Tom Hulce (Mozart in 1984's *Amadeus*), Michael Jeter, Amanda Bearse, Alexis Arquette, outrageous comic Lea DeLaria, Mitchell Anderson (on *Party of Five*), and Dan Butler (ironically playing *Frasier's* most aggressively straight character). Other popular television actors have come out in retirement or after their "media prime," including Raymond Burr (*Perry Mason*), Dick Sargent (*Bewitched*), Nancy Kulp (*The Beverly Hillbillies*), and Paul Lynde (perhaps American cinema's queerest patriarch in the 1963 film *Bye Bye Birdie*).

## LGBT and Queer Performance after Stonewall

Post-Stonewall liberation was accompanied by a remarkable flowering of openly LGBT experimentation in theater and performance, including the work appearing through such venues as Joe Cino's legendary Caffe Cino, Doric Wilson's theater company The Other Side of Silence, and Charles Ludlam's Ridiculous Theatrical Company. The avant-garde film pioneer Jack Smith staged a series of campy and challenging one-man performances in New York City lofts, while a younger generation included outrageous drag-donning actor-playwrights Charles Busch and Harvey Fierstein (soon the winner of a Tony award for his *Torch Song Trilogy*) and the lesbian performers associated with the WOW Café, including Peggy Shaw, Lois Weaver, Holly Hughes, and Carmelita Tropicana (Alina Troyano), as well as the influential troupe Five Lesbian Brothers and the queer African American performance groups Pomo Afro Homos and Four Big Girls. Many of these performers were among the first artists lost to AIDS, while others would become central to the development of "new queer performance" often involving the delivery of searing or hilarious monologues. Other key queer performance artists include Tim Miller, Ron Vawter, Kate Bornstein, and Susan Miller. At the same time, the "new queer cinema" (although more frequently celebrated for its directors than actors) and the numerous forms of guerrilla and street theater enacted by prominent AIDS activist groups such as ACT UP and Queer Nation also extended queer performance into new and often risky cultural spaces.

Clearly, it is now possible for some LGBT actors (often moving between theater, film, and television) such as Nathan Lane, Lily Tomlin, and Harvey Fierstein, to proudly or subtly acknowledge their sexual identities and also thrive professionally. However, many well-known actors still remain closeted in order to obtain diverse roles, and some of the most prominent gay characters in recent films (*Philadelphia*) and television programs (*Will and Grace*) have been played by—the resulting press reassures nervous viewers—straight actors. In 1990 conservative politicians loudly attacked the National Endowment for the Arts for funding LGBT performance artists including Holly Hughes and Tim Miller, and unusual attention was given in 1997 to the coming out of both comic Ellen DeGeneres and her character on a prime-time sitcom, a network television program that was thereafter deemed "too gay" and canceled. Although it now seems evident that LGBT actors have been consistently vital to the history of American theater and cinema, their open visibility remains frustratingly partial and persistently contested.

## Queer Reception

Recovering the history of LGBT actors and supporting current LGBT performers have been important tasks for queer audiences, scholars, and critics. As cultural analysts have emphasized, however, LGBT reception is not necessarily limited by the biographical "facts" that are known or unknown about specific stars. Dramatic Hollywood divas such as Bette Davis, Joan Crawford, Judy Garland, and Barbra Streisand, among others, have played prominent roles in gay camp as figures for both drag imitation and personal admiration and emulation. Notably independent film icons such as Garbo, Dietrich, Katharine Hepburn, and Jodie Foster have played similar, if less campy, functions for many lesbian fans. Film scholar Michael De Angelis has persuasively demonstrated how gay fans have responded in complex ways to stars whose sexuality remains ambiguous (James Dean and Keanu Reeves) and even to a star who has seemed blatantly homophobic (Mel Gibson). As public figures and objects of fantasy, actors are therefore available to be actively recoded as well as queerly decoded by LGBT fans. It is certainly valuable for LGBT spectators to know that many of the figures on stage and screen, past and present, share their sexual orientation, but the significance actors have had and continue to have in LGBT culture and imaginations occupies a wider territory.

## Bibliography

Barrios, Richard. *Screened Out: Playing Gay in Hollywood from Edison to Stonewall.* New York: Routledge, 2003.

De Angelis, Michael. *Gay Fandom and Crossover Stardom: James Dean, Mel Gibson, and Keanu Reeves.* Durham, N.C.: Duke University Press, 2001.

Ehrenstein, David. *Open Secret: Gay Hollywood 1928-2000.* New York: Perennial, 2000.

Ferris, Lesley, ed. *Crossing the Stage: Controversies on Cross-Dressing.* New York: Routledge, 1993.

Hadleigh, Boze. *Conversations with My Elders.* New York: St. Martin's Press, 1986.

———. *Hollywood Lesbians.* New York: Barricade Books, 1994.

Hatch, James V. *Sorrow Is the Only Faithful One: The Life of Owen Dodson.* Urbana: University of Illinois Press, 1993.

Mann, William J. *Behind the Screen: How Gays and Lesbians Shaped Hollywood 1910–1969.* New York: Viking, 2001.

———. *Wisecracker: The Life and Times of William Haines, Hollywood's First Openly Gay Star.* New York: Viking, 1998.

Marra, Kim, and Robert A. Schanke, eds. *Staging Desire: Queer Readings of American Theater History.* Ann Arbor: University of Michigan Press, 2002.

McLellan, Diana. *The Girls: Sappho Goes to Hollywood.* New York: LA Weekly Books for St. Martins Griffin, 2000.

Merrill, Lisa. *When Romeo Was a Woman: Charlotte Cushman and Her Circle of Female Spectators.* Ann Arbor: University of Michigan Press, 1999.

Mullenix, Elizabeth Reitz. *Wearing the Breeches: Gender on the Antebellum Stage.* New York: St. Martin's Press, 2000.

Schanke, Robert A. *Shattered Applause: The Lives of Eva Le Gallienne.* Carbondale and Edwardsville: Southern Illinois University Press, 1992.

Schanke, Roberta A., and Kim Marra, eds. *Passing Performances: Queer Readings of Leading Players in American Theater History.* Ann Arbor: University of Michigan Press, 1998.

Senelick, Laurence, ed. *Gender in Performance: The Presentation of Difference in the Performing Arts.* Hanover, N.H.: University Press of New England, 1992.

Solomon, Alisa, and Framji Minwalla, eds. *The Queerest Art: Essays on Lesbian and Gay Theater.* New York: New York University Press, 2002.

Weiss, Andrea. *Vampires and Violets: Lesbians in Film.* New York: Penguin, 1993.

**Corey K. Creekmur**

*See also* CRISP, QUENTIN; CUSHMAN, CHARLOTTE; EICHELBERGER, ETHYL; ELTINGE, JULIAN; FIERSTEIN, HARVEY; FILM AND VIDEO; ICONS; MUSIC: BROADWAY AND MUSICAL THEATER; SÁNCHEZ; LUIS RAFAEL; TELEVISION; THEATER AND PERFORMANCE.

# ADDAMS, Jane (b. 6 September 1860; d. 21 May 1935), social worker and reformer.

The cofounder of Chicago's Hull House settlement, Jane Addams's status as one of the most admired reformers of the Progressive Era helped to keep her same-sex romantic relationships hidden from public view.

Born Laura Jane Addams in Cedarville, Illinois, the future reformer was among the first generation of college-educated women in the United States. She became friends with Ellen Gates Starr while attending Rockford Female Seminary in Rockford, Illinois. Upon graduation in 1881 from Rockford, Addams spent the next few years struggling personally and professionally in a society that had little use for highly educated women. To ease her mind and find a direction for her life, she traveled throughout Europe with Starr. The two women, who developed a romantic friendship, visited London's premier settlement house, Toynbee Hall, in 1888. They decided to bridge the gap between the rich and the poor in America by duplicating the ideals that had led to Toynbee Hall's establishment.

Addams and Starr opened Hull House in Chicago in 1889. The settlement house became Addams's home for the remainder of her life. Designed initially to allow wealthy women to better the plight of the poor by sharing their knowledge of literature and art, Hull House quickly shifted its priorities and evolved into a provider of social services and an employer of women eager to find some socially worthwhile use for their intellect. The many activities held at the settlement house, including kindergarten classes, boys' and girls' clubs, theater workshops, music schools, language classes, reading groups, college extension courses, and a labor museum, were all designed to foster cooperation among people.

Addams believed that Americans enjoyed political democracy in the form of the ballot, but that the system created artificial barriers between groups which made it impossible for true social democracy to take place. This type of isolationism encouraged individuals to focus on the narrow agendas of their particular social groups rather than working for the good of all. Hull House attempted to break down the wall between the rich and the poor, thereby bettering the lives of both.

Much of Addams's compassion centered on city children. Nearly every major piece of social legislation or civic initiative having to do with the well-being of children dating from this time had its genesis at Hull House. The list is impressive: the settlement offered the first studies in Chicago of truancy, typhoid fever, cocaine, children's reading, newsboys, infant mortality, and

**Jane Addams.** The pioneer social worker and reformer —and the first American woman to receive the Nobel Peace Prize—stands at left with Hull House colleagues Julia Lathrop and Mary McDowell. [corbis]

midwifery. Firmly believing that the city should be a place of peace and beauty for all citizens, Addams also initiated investigations that led to the creation of the first model tenement code and the first factory laws in Illinois.

All these acts of goodness made Addams into a heroine and distracted her attentions away from Starr. The independent Starr clashed with Addams over the direction of Hull House. Addams devoted her energies to administering the settlement house, whereas the more aggressive Starr joined picket lines and espoused militant socialism. Mary Rozet Smith proved to be a more tractable partner. Uncritical and supportive of Addams, the wealthy Smith had joined Hull House in 1890 because it offered more excitement than did Chicago high society. She replaced Starr in Addams's affections by about 1895.

Addams and Starr had a long-term monogamous relationship, but whether their relationship included a sexual component is unknown. They may have had a Boston marriage, a common arrangement among woman-identified women that involved a sharing of lives

and resources but not necessarily sex. However, Addams's letters show an intensely romantic relationship, and the couple commonly wired ahead to hotels to make sure that they could share a double bed. Contemporaries also regarded them as a couple.

Addams may have been able to avoid the label of deviant because of her status as one of the most widely admired women of her day. As an upper-class woman who devoted her life to helping others in socially acceptable ways, Addams posed no threat to the social order. One biographer declared that she was too much of a saint to become involved in a romance with anyone. The antilesbian notion that great women do not engage in lesbian relationships and that therefore Addams could not have been a lesbian may have led to the conscious decision on the part of many, including members of the media, not to pry into the details of her private life.

From 1914 until her death from abdominal cancer in 1935, internationalism and pacifism, rather than Hull House, dominated Addams's life. She served as a vice president of the National American Woman Suffrage Association and headed the Woman's Peace Party. When Addams broke with most Progressives by opposing U.S. entry into World War I, she experienced ostracism for the first time. However, her reputation revived, and in 1931 Addams became the first American woman to win the Nobel Peace Prize.

**Bibliography**

Davis, Allen F. *American Heroine: The Life and Legend of Jane Addams.* Chicago: Ivan R. Dee, 2000.

Elshtain, Jean Bethke. *Jane Addams and the Dream of American Democracy: A Life.* New York: Basic Books, 2002.

Rupp, Leila J. *A Desired Past: A Short History of Same-Sex Love in America.* Chicago: University of Chicago Press, 1999.

**Caryn E. Neumann**

*See also* ANTIWAR, PACIFIST, AND PEACE MOVEMENTS; FEMINISM; ROMANTIC FRIENDSHIP AND BOSTON MARRIAGE; SAME-SEX INSTITUTIONS; SMASHES AND CHUMMING.

**ADOPTION.** see FAMILY ISSUES.

# ADVERTISING

The history of advertising and marketing to LGB people can be divided into five periods: underground, 1900 to 1941; development of an LGB community, 1941 to 1969; the Stonewall Riots and going public, 1969 to 1984; AIDS and retrenchment, 1984 to 1992; and the "gay '90s" and beyond.

## Underground, 1900–1941

The beginnings of what developed into advertising directed to the LGB community can be traced back to the beginning of the twentieth century. In *Gay New York* (1994), George Chauncey discusses the rise of underground gay communities in urban areas between 1890 and 1940. One of the characteristics of these early gay communities was the use of codes based on clothing, nonverbal behavior, and speech as means for identifying members of the gay community that allowed them to remain anonymous to nonmembers. Coded images can be found in the advertising illustrations of J. C. Leyendecker. In his early-twentieth-century illustrations for an advertising campaign for Arrow shirts, he used his lover, Charles Beach, as the model for the Arrow Collar Man. Leyendecker's homoerotic advertising illustrations were also used to sell products such as Ivory soap and Gillette razor blades. One Ivory soap ad from a 1917 issue of *National Geographic Magazine*, for example, depicted a locker-room scene after an athletic contest with two clothed males waiting to shower and four nude males who are showering or drying off after showering. While there was no overt marketing directed to gay men, the images certainly could be interpreted as homoerotic by gay consumers.

## Development of an LGB Community, 1941–1969

World War II brought men and women from all geographic regions together in close living quarters where LGB people were able to find others like themselves, even though it was not acceptable to be openly lesbian or gay. Some advertisements from the war years featured soldiers in all-male environments enjoying recreation. Fieldcrest Cannon Corporation, for example, ran ads for Cannon towels in *Life* magazine that showed soldiers bathing in a jungle setting or in an abandoned canoe in a Buna village with the villagers looking on. In the latter ad, one soldier is posing with a palm branch barely covering his nude body. The focus of these ads was on the value of Cannon towels to soldiers, but the images were homoerotic enough to allow for an alternate interpretation by a gay man. After the war, ads continued to appear that had hidden, or, as Michael Wilke has labeled them, "gay-vague" themes. One example was a 1958 Smirnoff vodka ad in *Esquire* magazine that showed two men close together with the text, "Mixed or straight, it leaves you breathless!"

*ONE* magazine (1953–1970), an early and successful Los Angeles–based gay magazine, carried a self-promotional ad and two others in its first issue, but the ads (for a bookstore and a design center) were included at no cost to the businesses. In the October 1954 issue, however, the first paid ad to appear in a LGB publication ran inside the back cover. It was an ad for men's night clothing by WIN-MOR of California. The ad contained images of two men, one in a nightshirt and the other in a pajama outfit. There also was a drawing of underwear, but not on a model. The nightshirt was described as an "answer" to the "gay 90's nightshirt" and carried the tagline, "They used flannel—we use nylon and satin." The underwear was described as "in satin studded with rhinestone." The Los Angeles postmaster refused to mail the magazine because he considered its contents, especially an article on gay marriage and another on lesbians, "obscene." ONE Inc. fought the ruling through the court system, until in 1958 the U.S. Supreme Court ruled in *ONE Inc. v. Oleson* that materials could not be considered obscene simply because they contained gay content. This decision paved the way for the further development of the LGBT press and LGBT advertising. In 1967 the first issue of the *Los Angeles Advocate* (later known as the *Advocate)* carried ads worth twenty-seven dollars, but only twelve dollars were ever collected. Within a year, each issue ran ads bringing in several hundred dollars. These ads were mainly from mail-order businesses selling homoerotic books and films or from local bars and restaurants with large LGB clienteles.

Classified personal ads also were a major feature of gay periodicals, especially of male magazines such as *Drum* (1964–1969), which took an aggressive, openly gay posture by using homoerotic images, nudity, and clearly gay-oriented personal ads. It also carried ads for mail-order sex businesses. Even the less blatant and aggressive *Advocate* ran a personal ads column (Trader Dick) with ads coded in jargon unique to the gay community. In *Unspeakable* (1995), a history of the gay and lesbian press, Roger Streitmatter discusses ads with coded messages like, "Are you getting your share?," "MEXICAN HOUSE-BOYS. Live-in type," and "Turn On, Tune In, Turn Over." Most of the advertising in the gay, San Francisco–based *Citizens News* and *Cruise News* was self-promotional, urging readers to buy the erotic publications of their owner, Guy Strait. Much the same can be said for advertisements in other gay publications.

## Stonewall and Going Public, 1969–1984

The 1969 Stonewall Riots marked a turning point in LGBT community development by ushering in a time of mass-based grassroots activism with the goal of obtaining civil rights for LGBT people. The events of the LGBT movement became newsworthy in the mainstream press and entertainment industry as the presence of an LGBT community became more and more obvious. A 1971 episode of the television series *All in the Family*, for example, was about the lead character Archie Bunker's encounter with a gay football player, and in 1972 ABC aired *That Certain Summer*, a made-for-TV movie about a gay father coming out to his son.

In the early 1970s companies such as Budget Rent-a-Car began to advertise in the *Advocate*, but it was not until 1979, when Carillon Importers ran an ad in the *Advocate* for Absolut vodka, that national advertisers began to view the gay press as a viable vehicle for reaching a significant market. Rivendell Marketing, formed in 1979, became the first company whose primary marketing effort was directed toward LGB consumers.

Not all the developments were focused on the traditional media and advertising. Continuing a trend begun in the 1960s, LGB publications included many ads for LGB bars, bathhouses, bookstores, telephone sex, resorts and vacations, and LGB-owned businesses. The *Advocate* was a leader in the use of small, classified-style ads for LGB businesses, but many other publications followed its lead with a mix of advertising that promoted banks, autos, alcoholic beverages, pharmaceuticals, airlines, films, music, bars, gyms, and escort services. While lesbian periodicals had more difficulty attracting advertisers, these ads helped make possible the development of a large network of LGBT newspapers and magazines.

## AIDS and Retrenchment, 1984–1992

While some companies continued to advertise to LGBT consumers during the early 1980s, marketing and ad placement was limited to the LGBT press. Most companies were unwilling or hesitant to place gay-oriented ads in the mainstream press for fear that it would lead to a backlash from non-LGBT consumers and negatively affect sales. While companies marketing products like Calvin Klein clothing and Marlboro cigarettes continued to place "gay vague" ads in the LGBT press, the advent of AIDS led to a major hiatus for LGBT-oriented ads, and those ads that did make reference to LGBT themes tended to be negative. Most images of gay men were stereotyped and often gay men were the brunt of humor or a joke. For example, Fred, a character in a 1984 Dunkin' Donuts ad, dressed in drag as a cover for spying on the competition. A 1987 ad for Kellogg's Nut N' Honey cereal showed cowboys sitting around the campfire. When the cook announced "Nut N' Honey," he was misunderstood to say, "Nothing honey." Assuming a sexual connotation, the

cowboys drew their guns in a stereotyped response toward homosexual advances.

Ads for specific LGBT-oriented businesses and products continued to be a dominant part of gay publications with the significant addition of AIDS-related pharmaceutical ads. There also was an increase in lesbian-oriented ads as the feminist and lesbian feminist community gained greater national visibility. Many of these ads continued to focus on vacation and resort destinations.

## "Gay '90s" and Beyond

The U.S. presidential campaign leading up to the election of Bill Clinton in 1992 marked a renewed emphasis on civil rights for LGB people. The news media refocused the national discussion from AIDS to LGB civil rights issues such as gays in the military. The LGBT press exploded with the introduction of gay male publications like *Genre* and *Out*, lesbian publications such as *Deneuve* (later known as *Curve*) and *Girlfriends*, and publications directed toward specific consumer audiences, including youth *(XY)* and HIV positive people *(POZ)*. Advertisers became bolder in presenting gay men and, much more infrequently, lesbians in ads that were based on less stereotypical roles. A 1994 IKEA ad, for example, featured two men shopping together for furniture. This groundbreaking ad emphasized that the two men were a couple shopping for home furnishings. Other openly gay-oriented ads were developed for AT&T, Banana Republic, GAP, Abercrombie and Fitch, and Calvin Klein.

Television introduced more gay men and lesbians in leading and supporting roles, including Ellen DeGeneres, who "came out" in a heavily publicized 1997 episode of *Ellen*. There was a significant controversy, including proposed boycotts, that caused some companies who regularly sponsored the series to pull their ads from the controversial episode, but other regular sponsors chose to continue their sponsorship and new ones came in to fill the empty spots. ABC did not continue *Ellen* in the lineup for the next programming season because of lower viewer ratings following the episode when she "came out."

Obtaining program sponsors did not present a problem for new network television shows such as NBC's *Will and Grace* and Showtime's *Queer as Folk*, which featured gay men and lesbians in leading roles in programs whose focus was LGB issues. The groundswell of LGB-positive advertising and marketing did not mean, however, that all images were positive. There continue to be ads in both print and broadcast media that focus on negative stereotypes of LGBT people, portraying them as flamers, cross-dressers, and even pedophiles.

The Internet became a major factor in the growth of advertising in general, but more especially of LGBT-oriented advertising and marketing. The Internet provided a unique medium for the development of national and international LGBT online communities. It also provided a direct means of marketing to them. One significant development in the mid-1990s was the creation of the Commercial Closet Association by Michael Wilke, a journalist working for *Advertising Age*. In 2001 the online CommercialCloset.com Web site was created to educate advertising agencies, marketers, and the general public about how LGBT people are represented in print ads and commercials. CommercialCloset.com includes an archive of historic LGBT-themed ads as well as current LGBT-themed advertising, news, and editorials about LGBT-themed advertising. Ads are evaluated as "gay positive," "gay neutral," "gay negative," or "gay vague." Companies or organizations that often sponsor "gay positive" ads include Abercrombie and Fitch, the American Civil Liberties Union, Benetton, Miller Brewing, and Daimler-Chrysler. Anheuser-Busch and Cadbury-Schweppes, among others, have sponsored "gay negative" ads, and some companies sponsor ads that could fall into several of the categories based on interpretation. Therefore, it is not always clear what companies are LGBT friendly.

## Bibliography

Chauncey, George. *Gay New York: Gender, Urban Culture, and the Makings of the Gay Male World, 1890–1940.* New York: Basic Books, 1994.

Gross, Larry P. *Up from Invisibility: Lesbians, Gay Men, and the Media in America.* New York: Columbia University Press, 2001.

Lukenbill, Grant. *Untold Millions: Secret Truths about Marketing to Gay and Lesbian Consumers.* New York: Harrington Park Press, 1999.

Streitmatter, Rodger. *Unspeakable: The Rise of the Gay and Lesbian Press in America.* Boston: Faber and Faber, 1995.

Wardlow, Daniel L. *Gays, Lesbians, and Consumer Behavior: Theory, Practice, and Research Issues in Marketing.* New York: Haworth Press, 1996.

**Edward H. Sewell Jr.**

***See also*** ADVOCATE; BUSINESSES; CAPITALISM AND INDUSTRIALIZATION; *GAY COMMUNITY NEWS*; NEWSPAPERS AND MAGAZINES; TELEVISION; WARHOL, ANDY; WEBER, BRUCE.

# ADVOCATE

The *Advocate* is one of the most widely read, most commercially successful gay and lesbian news magazines in the world. It is a glossy, full-color, biweekly modeled after such mainstream weeklies as *Time* and *Newsweek*. In some ways, the *Advocate* has become the U.S. gay community's periodical of record, one of the first sources researchers consult for a quick sense of what happened in a particular month and year in the post–Stonewall Riots era. It is the flagship title of Liberation Publications, a media group that publishes the magazines *Out, HIV Plus*, and *Out and About*. Liberation Publications also owns Alyson Publications, which for many years was the largest independent publisher devoted to LGBT-relevant books.

The *Advocate*'s focus and tone have changed many times. It began in 1967 as the *Los Angeles Advocate*, the newsletter of Personal Rights in Defense and Education (PRIDE), a local gay rights organization. The couple who edited PRIDE's newsletter, Dick Michaels and Bill Rand, had been politicized by police raids on local gay bars. Early issues, which were run off secretly on equipment owned by ABC-TV, where Rand worked, focused on police harassment. Issues sold for a quarter apiece in Los Angeles bars. In 1968, Michaels and Rand bought the publication from PRIDE for a dollar and turned it into a monthly independent periodical. It mixed news and features with photographs of half-naked men (often next to stories of political importance, to draw attention to those items) and a celebratory sense of sexual liberationism. In 1969, in a bid to professionalize the news operations, they hired Rob Cole of the *Dallas Times Herald* as news editor. Around the same time, the periodical adopted a full-size newspaper format. The geographic focus of stories was broadened and distribution nationalized. Accordingly, the publication's name was shortened to the *Advocate*.

During the early 1970s, the *Advocate* occupied a middle ground, stylistically and politically, between the conservatism of the old homophile periodicals and what Rodger Streitmatter has called the "wild and wooly" colorful publications of the new gay liberation movement. It devoted much space to the street activism of gay liberation groups, and clearly believed that those organizations were the backbone of the fight for LGBT equality.

That editorial stance changed suddenly and radically in 1974, when self-styled "practicing capitalist" David Goodstein bought the paper. A firm believer in quiet, behind-the-scenes negotiating, Goodstein considered disruptive protests and sit-ins counterproductive. On several occasions, he branded the most visible gay liberation activists as "neurotics" whose visibility needed to be curtailed or eliminated. That included several longtime writers for the *Advocate*, who were deemed too far left of center to continue contributing to the publication. During Goodstein's more than ten years as editor of the

*Advocate,* political coverage continued, but massive protests by gay liberationists received little attention. During his years, the *Advocate* added columns about lifestyle issues—travel, entertainment, and so on. Longtime writers and subscribers who were used to the paper's old grassroots, movement-based philosophy were shocked by the fact that Goodstein was running the *Advocate* like a business, with an eye on profits. However, the *Advocate* attracted a broad range of readers who could relate to its new, more mainstream tone.

The *Advocate* had always focused more on gay men than on women, but this became explicit in the cover photographs of the 1980s. Rather than running pictures of people in the news or photographs of news events themselves, the *Advocate* ran photographs of muscular, often shirtless male models with props and sets that evoked the news story in question. This would continue until around 1990, several years after Goodstein's death. The magazine's "classifieds" section, which mixed advertisements with soft-porn photographs, was eventually spun off into two new magazines from Liberation Publications: *Advocate Classifieds* and the glossy, full-color erotic magazine *AdvocateMEN.* The latter title eventually had its own spinoff, *Freshmen.*

In 1990 the word "lesbian" was added to the cover of the *Advocate* alongside the word "gay," and the beefcake photographs were largely supplanted with pictures of straight politicians and celebrities or—less often—with photographs of lesbians and gay men in the news. In 1992 the magazine underwent a radical redesign. Several longtime features—including all of the *Advocate*'s comic strips—were dropped. During the 1990s the *Advocate* increasingly strove to be seen as a serious, *Time*-style news magazine. In 1996, Judy Wieder became the first woman to serve as the *Advocate*'s editor in chief, and she continued the magazine's move toward balance between content about men and women. By the early twenty-first century, the magazine was moving toward cover photographs of openly gay people.

In the late 1990s and early 2000s, Liberation Publications began acquiring other properties and companies and turning itself into the media group it has become. As part of the makeover, it sold off or discontinued its erotic titles, bought Alyson Publications, and—most controversially—bought the rival magazine *Out.* In 2000 the recent purchase of *Out* and talk of a planned merger with Internet giant PlanetOut raised some concerns that editorial control of LGBT news sources was increasingly concentrated in the hands of a few very large corporations. However, the PlanetOut merger was can-celed shortly after it was announced. Whatever controversies it may have sparked, the *Advocate* remains one of the preeminent and most durable media brands in lesbian and gay America.

**Bibliography**

Bull, Chris. *Witness to Revolution: The Advocate Reports on Gay and Lesbian Politics, 1967–1998.* Los Angeles: Alyson, 1999.

Marcus, Eric. *Making Gay History: The Half-Century Fight for Lesbian and Gay Equal Rights.* New York: Perennial, 2002.

Streitmatter, Rodger. *Unspeakable: The Rise of the Gay and Lesbian Press in America.* Boston: Faber and Faber, 1995.

Thompson, Mark, ed. *Long Road to Freedom: The Advocate History of the Gay and Lesbian Movement.* New York: St. Martin's Press, 1994.

Tobin, Kay, and Randy Wicker. *The Gay Crusaders.* 1972. Reprint, New York: Arno Press, 1975.

**Steven Capsuto**

*See also* GOODSTEIN, DAVID; KEPNER, JAMES; KOPAY, DAVID; NEWSPAPERS AND MAGAZINES; PRESTON, JOHN.

# AFRICAN AMERICANS

African American LGBT cultures have developed in dialogue with the larger African American cultures and LGBT cultures of which they are a part, simultaneously engaging in internal dialogues across boundaries of class, color, gender, gender identity, language, religion, and sexuality. Forced to confront the racism and class oppression of Euro-American society and Euro-American LGBT cultures, African American LGBT people have also struggled against homophobia, transphobia, and heterosexism in African American communities. But African American LGBT life has been about more than just confrontation and struggle; it has also been about desires, pleasures, joys, and triumphs.

## Early History

Most Africans and African Americans who lived in North America before the 1860s had themselves been enslaved in Africa or were the descendants of those who had been enslaved. Free populations of blacks existed within the United States and its predecessor colonies and some blacks lived within Native American cultures. But until emancipation in the 1860s the vast majority lived as slaves in the American South.

Research on diverse sexual and gender traditions in Africa (for example, by Cary Alan Johnson and Gloria Wekker in Constantine-Simms) suggests that many

Africans may have brought with them to the "new world" ideas, both positive and negative, about same-sex sexualities and cross-gender behaviors. But little research has been conducted on what happened to these ideas and their associated practices in the context of enslavement and slavery in North America. From Jonathan Ned Katz's work, we know that in 1646 Dutch authorities in the New Netherland Colony (which later became New York) convicted Jan Creoli, "a negro," of sodomy with Manuel Congo, a ten-year-old boy (whose name suggests that he was also black). This apparently was Creoli's second offense; he was sentenced to death and Congo was flogged (1976; pp. 35–36). (A second black man, "Mingo, alias Cocke Negro," may have been executed for "forcible buggery" in Massachusetts in 1712; see Katz, 1983; pp. 127–128.) We also know from Katz's work that Pennsylvania's 1700 sodomy law made sodomy a capital crime for blacks but not whites and that Virginia's 1800 sodomy law removed the death penalty for free persons but not slaves. Same-sex sexual behaviors among African Americans have been documented for other slave societies in the Americas, and there is no reason to think that they did not occur in the colonies that eventually became the United States. In these colonies, high male-to-female sex ratios among slaves in the early decades of slavery (and in local contexts later) may have created conditions conducive to what has been described as situational homosexuality.

In the search for evidence of same-sex sexual acts and cross-gender behaviors in the era of slavery, some have found suggestive a passage in Harriet Jacobs's 1861 autobiography that refers to a white slaveowner who committed on his black male slave the "strangest freaks of despotism" that were "of a nature too filthy to be repeated" (p. 192). There are also countless examples, in fictional texts, nonfictional texts, and visual images, of white males gazing homoerotically at black male bodies and white females gazing homoerotically at black female bodies. These may reveal less about the sexual cultures of Africans and African Americans than about the deployment of sexuality in systems of racial control and racial violence. Yet the work of Charles Clifton (in Constantine-Simms) on slave narratives by Henry Bibb, Frederick Douglass, and Olaudah Equiano demonstrates that these texts can be explored in pursuit of knowledge about African and African American same-sex sexualities as well.

Evidence of female same-sex sexual and cross-gender behaviors in the era of slavery is perhaps even more scarce than it is for men, especially for the early years, though Cheryl Clarke provides a helpful analytic framework for pursuing this topic (in Moraga and Anzaldúa). Historical research on slave runaways suggests that some women cross-dressed as men as part of their strategies for escaping slavery; dressing as boys or men functioned not only as a disguise but also as a means of escaping notice in contexts where it was more rare for black women than for black men to be on the road. John Weiss has uncovered evidence from 1828 of a slave woman named Minty who had two last names, Gurry from her husband and Caden from the "negro woman" with whom she had "formed an intimacy" (cited in Rupp, p. 42). Karen Hansen discusses the case of two free black women, Addie Brown and Rebecca Primus, who wrote affectionate, loving, romantic, and erotic letters to one another in the 1850s and 1860s. Bonds of sisterhood among black women and brotherhood among black men have been documented for the era of slavery, as have practices that transgressed normative gender roles. But greater knowledge about the extent to which sisterhood and brotherhood were sexualized and the extent to which gender-crossing reflected desires to live as the "other" sex awaits further research.

## From Emancipation to the Twentieth Century

African American slaves freed themselves and were freed by the Union Army and the U.S. government in the crucible of the Civil War (1861–65). Most scholars now agree that the Reconstruction period (1863–1877) was one of great promise, hope, and advance for African Americans but that the so-called Redemption of southern state governments by white supremacists, a process that culminated in 1877, was profoundly destructive. In the late nineteenth century, the vast majority of blacks lived as sharecroppers in the American South, vulnerable to racist violence, economic exploitation, and Jim Crow segregation. Though many have explored African American family and gender developments in these years, these are rarely examined in relation to LGBT phenomena.

Exemplifying some of the dynamics of Reconstruction and Redemption, Frances Thompson, a black freedwoman raped by white men during the Memphis riot of 1866 testified about that rape in a congressional investigation later that year; but in 1876 she found herself discredited, excoriated, arrested, and put on a chain gang when she was revealed to be biologically male. As Hannah Rosen's account documents, she died a short time later. Lynching, like rape, functioned as a tool of racial and sexual control, and many scholars have been struck by the homoerotic sadism that is evident in accounts of the lynching of black men by white men. Sexualized racial control also operated through more conventional legal channels: Katz reports that of the 63 prisoners reported incarcerated for crimes against nature in the 1880 U.S. Census, 32 were men of color in the South. In 1890, of the 224 incarcerated for crimes against nature, 76 were black. And referencing an episode that hints at white fascination with black sexual crime, Lisa Duggan shares an 1892 Memphis newspaper account of the stabbing of 17-year-old Eleanora Richardson, a "mulatto," by Emma Williams, a 23-year-old "black" woman who was described as having a "paroxysm of jealousy resulting from an unnatural passion" (cited in Duggan, p. 139).

As Duggan has argued, media stories like this one became sexological case studies in the late nineteenth and early twentieth centuries, and these stories and studies were invariably racialized. Havelock Ellis's 1915 edition of *Sexual Inversion*, for example, included an account supplied by a Chicago doctor of the "Tiller sisters," two "quintroons." According to Ellis, one was an "invert" who was "sexually attracted to the other" and shot dead the latter's beau (cited in Duggan, p. 174). Siobhan Somerville argues that the very creation of new sexological categories (which attempted to classify bodies as homosexuals, inverteds, and heterosexuals) was influenced by projects of scientific racism, which attempted to draw strict lines and establish rigid hierarchies between black and white bodies. As Somerville points out, discourses of race perversion and sexual perversion came together in scientific work such as Margaret Otis's 1913 study, which analyzed interracial relationships between black and white girls in reform schools and schools for delinquents and argued that "the difference in color . . . takes the place of difference in sex" (cited in Somerville, p. 34). Estelle Freedman's work shows that this was just the beginning of a long tradition of criminological, psychological, and administrative interest in (and condemnation of) sex between "masculine" and "aggressive" black women and "feminine" and "normal" white women (p. 424). Jennifer Terry's work demonstrates that racist and racialized sexological projects continued to focus attention on black queer bodies through much of the twentieth century.

Many studies have now shown that police narratives, media stories, and sexological studies in this period were responding to the growth of LGBT cultures. Even when the voices of black LGBT people cannot be accessed directly in these types of texts (and sometimes, as Terry shows, they can be), they can be reclaimed by reading dominant cultural texts against the grain. When this is done, it becomes clear that something dramatic occurred in African American LGBT history in the late nineteenth century. Instead of isolated accounts of individuals and couples, we now find abundant evidence of collective cul-

tures, African American and interracial. And as many scholars have argued, the context for this transformation among blacks was not just the general developments associated with capitalism, industrialization, and immigration but also the specific circumstances of the Great Migration, in which millions of African Americans moved from the rural South to the urban North. These circumstances culminated in the Harlem Renaissance of the 1920s, the best-documented period in black LGBT history.

Evidence of the emergence of collective black LGBT cultures can be found as early as the late nineteenth century. In 1892, Dr. Irving Rosse published work about a "band of negro men" who were "androgynous" and engaged in "phallic worship" in Washington, D.C. Rosse also mentioned the arrests of eighteen "moral hermaphrodites" in Lafayette Square; a majority, he claimed, were black (in Katz, 1983, pp. 233–234). In 1893, Dr. Charles Hughes wrote about "an organization of colored erotopaths" in Washington, D.C. According to Hughes, at "an annual convocation of negro men called the drag dance," men "deport[ed] themselves as women" and a "lecherous gang of sexual perverts and phallic fornicators" gazed upon a "naked queen." A "similar organization," he claimed, had been "suppressed" by the New York City police (in Katz, 1976, p. 77). In 1907 Hughes expressed concern about "male Negroes masquerading in women's garb and carousing and dancing with white men" in St. Louis (in Katz, 1976, p. 75). Such accounts, hostile though they might be, make one thing abundantly clear: in cities across the country, black LGBT people were coming together.

### The Harlem Renaissance

By the Roaring Twenties, black LGBT urban cultures had become extraordinarily complex, dynamic, and vibrant. From the works of Hazel Carby, George Chauncey, Angela Davis, Ann DuCille, Eric Garber, Gloria Hull, Kevin Mumford, and Siobhan Somerville, among others, a portrait has emerged of what Harlem Renaissance writer Langston Hughes famously called "a spectacle in color" (in Garber, p. 324). According to Garber, during the Renaissance, "black lesbians and gay men were meeting each other on street corners, socializing in cabarets and rent parties, and worshiping in church on Sundays, creating a language, a social structure, and a complex network of institution. Some were discreet about their sexual identities; others openly expressed their personal feelings. The community they built attracted white homosexuals as well as black, creating friendships between people of disparate ethnic and economic backgrounds and building alliances for progressive social change" (pp. 318–319). Among the African American LGBT cast of Harlem Renaissance characters were artists Richmond Barthe and Richard Bruce Nugent; blues singers Gladys Bentley, Alberta Hunter, Ma Rainey, Bessie Smith, and Ethel Waters; dancers Josephine Baker and Mabel Hampton; social hosts Alexander Gumby and A'Lelia Walker; and writers and editors Countee Cullen, Angelina Weld Grimké, Langston Hughes, Nella Larsen, Alain Locke, Claude McKay, Blair Niles, and Wallace Thurman. This collection of leading lights made its mark on black culture, on LGBT culture, and on American culture. As Garber's comment indicates, however, the Harlem Renaissance consisted of more than just the triumphs of a set of notable African American LGBT cultural figures. Garber's, Chauncey's, and Mumford's work explores the geography of everyday black LGBT life during the 1920s, taking readers through extraordinarily popular drag balls (including the famous Hamilton Lodge Ball), rent parties, cabarets, saloons, speakeasies, nightclubs, black-and-tan clubs, parks, streets, and brothels.

There remains much more work to do on the black LGBT dimensions of the Jazz Age. Much of the scholarship thus far has concentrated on New York and Chicago; even the name given to the Harlem Renaissance era seems to discourage research on anything other than New York and so we know little about black LGBT developments in other cities, much less in non-urban areas, during the 1920s. There are many hints about the state of relationships between lesbians and gay men in this context, but thus far this subject has not been examined in depth. Nor do we know much about the similarities and differences between the gendered sexual systems of whites and the gendered sexual systems of blacks. One topic of significant debate has been the level of general black community acceptance of LGBT sexualities and genders and the integration of black LGBT and black straight cultures. While some have pointed to the sexual and gender conservatism of black communities, others have pointed to their liberalism on LGBT matters. Closely related to this discussion has been another one that focuses on class relations and class differences within African American communities. Carby, Chauncey, and others have pointed to the sexual and gender conservatism of many middle class black writers, church leaders, and journalists, which perhaps culminated in Reverend Adam Clayton Powell's sensational 1929 attack on homosexuality in African American religious and secular worlds. Given the centrality of the black church in black communities, further research will be necessary to more fully explore the links between black religious history and the history of black LGBT cultures. And more research of the sort done by David Serlin on Gladys Bentley will be necessary before we understand what happened to the LGBT protagonists of the Harlem Renaissance after it collapsed in the Great Depression of the 1930s.

## From the 1930s through the 1960s

The period from the 1930s through the 1960s was marked by major transformations in African American life, yet the United States remained a society of marked by racial, class, gender, and sexual inequality. Historians of the period generally emphasize the economic hard times experienced by blacks during the Great Depression; the mixed record of U.S. President Franklin Roosevelt's New Deal on race matters; the role of blacks in segregated military and industrial contexts during the Second World War; the ongoing experiences of disenfranchisement, segregation, and housing and employment discrimination after the war; and the civil rights and black power movements of the 1950s and 1960s.

Historians of black LGBT life have explored various social, cultural, and political developments during these years. In the realm of social history, Brett Beemyn's work on Washington, D.C., Allen Drexel's on Chicago (in Beemyn), John Howard's on Mississippi, Elizabeth Kennedy and Madeline Davis's on Buffalo, Marc Stein's on Philadelphia, and Rochella Thorpe's on Detroit have traced the conceptual and physical geographies of African American LGBT worlds. From their research we know that distinct black LGBT bars, clubs, and restaurants were established in this period; black LGBT people socialized in straight-dominated black and white-dominated LGBT spaces as well; they confronted homophobia and transphobia in the former and racism in the latter; drag balls, drag parades, and house parties, and femme/butch roles were important elements of black LGBT social life; and black LGBT people lived in both white-dominated LGBT neighborhoods and in straight-dominated black neighborhoods. Tim Retzloff's work on Detroit's flamboyant Prophet Jones, John D'Emilio's on civil rights leader Bayard Rustin, Howard's on Mississippi, and Stein's on Philadelphia provide insights about homophobia and homophilia in black church and religious life. Allan Bérubé's and Leisa Meyer's books contain evidence of black LGBT experiences during World War II, and Jennifer Terry's analysis of racialized sexological discourse allows constrained access to the voices of ordinary black LGBT people in this period. In certain respects LGBT social life may have challenged racial boundaries and hierarchies in this era, but for the most part it did not, and African American LGBT enclaves

**Civil Rights Unity.** Young African Americans at the 1972 Christopher Street West Parade in New York City hold signs protesting anti-gay laws. [Cathy Cade]

on Mississippi investigates links, real and imagined, between sexual dissidence and racial dissidence in the Deep South during the civil rights era. New work on Pauli Murray focuses attention on her activities in the civil rights, women's, and other movements (as well as her lesbianism and transgenderism). Anita Cornwell's and Audre Lorde's autobiographical writings provide uniquely helpful perspectives on the experiences of black LGBT people in black, women's, and LGBT movements. While Reid-Pharr analyzes the gender and sexual politics of black nationalists such as Eldridge Cleaver, Stein provides an in-depth look at how those politics played out at the Black Panther Party's Revolutionary People's Constitutional Convention in 1970. Much of this work documents the struggles faced by black LGBT activists in civil rights and black nationalist movements. While working to secure racial justice, these activists were forced to confront the gender and sexual conservatism of white and black movements and communities.

Meanwhile, although the homophile movement of the 1950s and 1960s is often seen as a white movement (and it certainly was dominated by whites), recent scholarship has highlighted the activities of black homophile activists, including Hansberry (who had work published in the lesbian periodical the *Ladder*), Cleo Glenn (who served as the president of the national lesbian organization Daughters of Bilitis), and Ernestine Eckstein (who marched in homophile demonstrations and was featured on the cover of the *Ladder*). There has also been significant work exploring the influences of the civil rights movement on the homophile movement, which appropriated its rhetoric and tactics and which analogized sexual and racial experiences in ways that often offended African Americans and ignored ongoing problems of racism in American society.

Much of this work not only documents the important roles that black LGBT people played in black, feminist, and LGBT movements in the 1950s and 1960s, but, in highlighting the failures of these movements to address the specific needs and concerns of black LGBT people, also helps set the context for the emergence of black LGBT movements in the late twentieth century.

developed primarily in relation to the problems and possibilities of African American worlds.

In the realm of cultural history, many Harlem Renaissance figures remained active in this period, negotiating their changing circumstances in complex and divergent ways. Along with these figures, dancer Alvin Ailey and writers James Baldwin, Samuel Delaney, Lorraine Hansberry, and Audre Lorde are among the black LGBT cultural workers who have received the most scholarly attention for this period. Recent works by Dwight McBride and Robert Reid-Pharr on Baldwin are particularly helpful in this area.

Countless black LGBT people, including some of the cultural figures discussed above also participated in some of the most important political movements of the 1950s and 1960s, and some had leadership roles. D'Emilio's biography of Rustin explores not only Rustin's centrality to the civil rights movement and not only the uses of gender and sexuality by both proponents and opponents of civil rights, but also larger intersections between sexuality and politics in the post-World War II era. Howard's book

## Developments since the 1960s

The extraordinary complexity of African American LGBT cultures in the post-1960s era makes it difficult to choose which elements to highlight. Three of the most notable developments have been the emergence and growth of autonomous African American LGBT organizations, institutions, and periodicals; the emergence and growth of new black queer intellectual traditions; and the emergence and growth of a new wave of black LGBT writers, artists, filmmakers, and cultural icons. In each of these areas, African American LGBT people have taken the lead in arguing and demonstrating that race, class, gender, sexuality, and other axes of difference and power in the United States are inextricably intertwined; that they intersect and overlap in ways that make it impossible to prioritize one over the others; and that intellectual work, creative art, and political action will suffer to the extent that these insights are ignored.

In the post-1960s era, African American LGBT bodies, desires, acts, identities, and cultures continue to be used by others in projects of race, class, gender, and sexual definition, differentiation, and control. Robert Mapplethorpe's erotic photographs of black men and Jennie Livingston's film *Paris is Burning* exemplify some of the dynamics of the interracial gaze. Public debates about the sexualities and genders of musical performer Little Richard, television newscaster Max Robinson, basketball player Dennis Rodman, celebrity singer RuPaul, and disco singer Sylvester make evident that dominant norms and values (in straight black, straight white, and LGBT white communities) are often defined in relation to queer black bodies. The appropriation of black gay disco culture by whites and straights illustrates larger processes associated with racialized and sexualized post-industrial capitalism. Debates about the misogyny and homophobia of some elements of black rap and hip-hop cultures reveal much about constructions of black masculinity and femininity. Ongoing discussions about the pathologies and the powers of the black family imagine black LGBT people as part of the problem, not part of the solution.

While black LGBT people have continued to experience racism, class oppression, sexism, homophobia, and transphobia in the various communities in which they live, they have also confronted a major new scourge in the last twenty years. HIV/AIDS has devastated black LGBT communities in particularly intense ways. In response, black, LGBT, and black LGBT communities have marshaled tremendous resources in struggles against government indifference, scientific neglect, and corporate profiteering. At the same time, the dynamics of HIV/AIDS in black communities have contributed to significant new discussions about distinctions between sexual cultures, sexual identities, and sexual acts, —discussions that have the potential for queering the United States in new ways. When HIV/AIDS educators target "men who have sex with men" rather than "gay men," they signal their understanding that there are communities, including black communities, that are not organized on the basis of the dominant U.S. models of sexual and gender identities (LGBT or straight). Recent discussions of black "down low" cultures also signal this understanding. As these discussions continue and link up with related conversations about distinctive gender and sexual cultures among Latinos/as, Asian Americans and Pacific Islanders, Native Americans, working class people, people with disabilities, and youth, African Americans are once again contributing to the growth of sexual and gender possibilities in the United States.

## Bibliography

Beam, Joseph, ed. *In the Life.* Boston: Alyson, 1986.

Beemyn, Brett, ed. *Creating a Place for Ourselves.* New York: Routledge, 1997.

Bérubé, Allan. *Coming Out Under Fire.* New York: Free Press, 1990.

Black, Allida M., ed. *Modern American Queer History.* Philadelphia: Temple University Press, 2001.

Bleys, Rudi C. *The Geography of Perversion.* New York: New York University Press, 1995.

Carby, Hazel. *Reconstructing Womanhood.* New York: Oxford University Press, 1987.

Chauncey, George. *Gay New York.* New York: Basic, 1994.

Cohen, Cathy. *The Boundaries of Blackness.* Chicago: University of Chicago Press, 1999.

Cornwell, Anita. *Black Lesbian in White America.* Tallahassee, FL. Naiad Press, 1983.

Davis, Angela Y. *Blues Legacies and Black Feminism.* New York: Vintage Books, 1999.

D'Emilio, John. *Lost Prophet: The Life and Times of Bayard Rustin.* New York: Free Press, 2003.

DuCille, Ann. *The Coupling Convention.* New York: Oxford University Press, 1993.

Duggan, Lisa. *Sapphic Slashers.* Durham: Duke University Press, 2000.

Freedman, Estelle B. "The Prison Lesbian: Race, Class, and the Construction of the Aggressive Female Homosexual, 1915–1965." *Feminist Studies* 22, no. 2 (Summer 1996): 397–423.

Garber, Eric. "A Spectacle in Color: The Lesbian and Gay Subculture of Jazz Age Harlem." In *Hidden from History.* Edited by Martin Bauml Duberman et al. New York: New American Library, 1989.

Hansen, Karen V. 'No Kisses Is like Youres.' *Gender and History* 7 (August 1995): 153–182.

Harper, Phillip Brian. *Are We Not Men?* New York: Oxford University Press, 1996.

Hemphill, Essex, ed. *Brother to Brother: New Writings by Black Gay Men.* Boston: Alyson, 1991.

hooks, bell. *Talking Back.* Boston: South End Press, 1989.

Howard, John. *Men like That.* Chicago: University of Chicago Press, 1999.

Hull, Gloria T., Patricia Bell Scott, and Barbara Smith. *All the Women are White, All the Blacks are Men, but Some of Us Are Brave.* New York: The Feminist Press, 1982.

Hull, Gloria. *Color, Sex, and Poetry.* Bloomington: Indiana University Press, 1987.

Jacobs, Harriet. *Incidents in the Life of a Slave Girl.* 1861. Edited by Jean Fagan Yellin. Cambridge: Harvard University Press, 1987.

Katz, Jonathan Ned. *Gay American History.* New York: Crowell, 1976.

———. *Gay/Lesbian Almanac.* New York: Harper, 1983.

Kennedy, Elizabeth Lapovsky, and Madeline D. Davis. *Boots of Leather, Slippers of Gold.* New York: Routledge, 1993.

Lorde, Audre. *Sister Outsider.* Trumansburg, N.Y.: Crossing Press, 1984.

Lorde, Audre. *Zami.* Freedom, Calif.: Crossing Press, 1982.

McBride, Dwight, ed. *James Baldwin Now.* New York: New York University Press, 1999.

McKinley, C. E., and L. J. Delaney, eds., *Afrekete: An Anthology of Black Lesbian Writing.* New York: Doubleday, 1995.

Meyer, Leisa D. *Creating G. I. Jane.* New York: Columbia University Press, 1996.

Moraga, Cherríe, and Gloria Anzaldúa. *This Bridge Called My Back.* New York: Kitchen Table, 1981.

Mumford, Kevin J. *Interzones.* New York: Columbia University Press, 1997.

Reid-Pharr, Robert. *Black Gay Man.* New York: New York University Press, 2001.

Retzloff, Tim. "Seer or Queer?: Postwar Fascination with Detroit's Prophet Jones." *GLQ* 8 (2002): 271–296.

Rosen, Hannah. "'Not That Sort of Women': Race, Gender, and Sexual Violence during the Memphis Riot of 1866." In *Sex, Love, Race.* Edited by Martha Hodes. New York: New York University Press, 1999.

Rupp, Leila J. *A Desired Past.* Chicago: University of Chicago Press, 1999.

Serlin, David. *Replaceable You: Engineering the American Body after World War II.* Chicago: University of Chicago Press, forthcoming.

Smith, Barbara, ed. *Homegirls.* New York: Kitchen Table, 1986.

Somerville, Siobhan. *Queering the Color Line.* Durham: Duke University Press, 2000.

Stein, Marc. *City of Sisterly and Brotherly Loves.* Chicago: University of Chicago Press, 2000.

Terry, Jennifer. *An American Obsession.* Chicago: University of Chicago Press, 1999.

Thorpe, Rochella. "A House Where Queers Go." In *Inventing Lesbian Cultures in America.* Edited by Ellen Lewin. Boston: Beacon, 1996.

Weiss, John McNish. "The Corps of Colonial Marines." *Immigrants and Minorities* 5:2 (1996): 80–90.

**Marc Stein**

*See also* AILEY, ALVIN; AFRICAN AMERICAN RELIGION AND SPIRITUALITY; AFRICAN AMERICAN STUDIES; AFRICAN AMERICAN LGBTQ ORGANIZATIONS AND PERIODICALS; BAKER, JOSEPHINE; BALDWIN, JAMES; BEAM, JOSEPH; BENTLEY, GLADYS; BLACK AND WHITE MEN TOGETHER; BOOZER, MEL; COMBAHEE RIVER COLLECTIVE; CORNWELL, ANITA; CULLEN, COUNTEE; DELANY, SAMUEL; DUNBAR-NELSON, ALICE; ECKSTEIN, ERNESTINE; GLENN, CLEO; GRIMKÉ, ANGELINA WELD; HAMPTON, MABEL; HANSBERRY, LORRAINE; HEMPHILL, ESSEX; HUGHES, LANGSTON; HUNTER, ALBERTA; JACKSON, DELORES; JONES, BILL T. AND ARNIE ZANE; JONES, PROPHET; LOCKE, ALAIN; LORDE, AUDRE; MCKAY, CLAUDE; MIGRATION, IMMIGRATION, AND DIASPORA; MUSLIMS AND ISLAM; NEW LEFT AND STUDENT MOVEMENTS; NILES, BLAIR; NUGENT, BRUCE; PARKER, RICHARD PAT; RACE AND RACISM; RAINEY, MA; RIGGS, MARLON; SHOCKLEY, ANN ALLEN; SLAVERY AND EMANCIPATION; SMITH, BARBARA; SMITH, BESSIE; STRAYHORN, BILLY; PRIMUS, REBECCA, AND ADDIE BROWN; RUSTIN, BAYARD; THOMPSON, FRANCES; THIRD WORLD GAY REVOLUTION; THURMAN, WALLACE; WALKER, A'LELIA; WATERS, ETHEL.

# AFRICAN AMERICAN LGBTQ ORGANIZATIONS AND PERIODICALS

Throughout much of their respective and intersecting histories, blacks and queers in the United States have tried to create independent institutions. Two things motivated them: they wanted to create a haven from the social forces that oppressed and devalued them, and they wished to create spaces that allowed them to commune with others like themselves and develop distinctive social identities and cultures. Within these two traditions black queer communities emerged.

Earlier in the twentieth century, black queers were limited in their ability to carve out spaces for themselves. They participated in drag balls that were controlled by black heterosexuals, and they frequented bars whose clientele was mostly either straight blacks or queer whites. Later, when their sexual and racial counterparts began to organize politically and protest the social forces that kept them in a subordinate role, they participated as marginalized others in the white-dominated LGBT movement and the straight-dominated black movement. Many black queers found these groups to be either hostile to their presence or culturally alienating. Because of this, during the 1970s growing numbers of black queers created spaces that affirmed both their racial and sexual identities. One way they did this was to develop social and political organizations.

## Organizational Beginnings

The earliest black queer groups were caucuses within the white queer groups that proliferated in the aftermath of the 1969 Stonewall riots in New York. The Third World Gay Revolution and the Black Lesbian Caucus in New York, as well as the Black Gay Caucus in Detroit, were among those that tried to carve out their own spaces and assert their own political agenda amidst the chorus of voices agitating for social change. At their meetings, black queers rapped about their lives, networked, and found lovers. In addition, they tried to understand the multiple forms of oppression they faced and articulate their vision of a liberated future that included them. While they sometimes railed against those who sought to render them invisible, black queers were also eager to incorporate into their own agenda the lessons learned from other social movements.

The collective feelings of empowerment many developed in these groups were short-lived, however. The groups were usually small and had problems maintaining membership. Many met in spaces that were dominated and controlled by whites, which provoked anxiety among those who rarely socialized in white America. Interpersonal conflicts and disputes over group direction took their toll, too. They were also victims of larger forces beyond their control. The country's mood grew more conservative, and the growing emphasis among white queers on single-issue reformist politics often meant that the multiple oppressions many black queers faced were not addressed. The number and visibility of black queer groups declined for a while. However, beginning in the mid-1970s, they reemerged.

Black queer women led the charge. Salsa Soul Sisters began as the Black Lesbian Caucus of the Gay Activists Alliance in New York in 1971. These black and Latina women reorganized several times after that. Through continued networking, they were able to arrive at a core membership, organizational structure, and agenda that worked by 1975. Like their earlier counterparts, Salsa Soul Sisters focused on providing spaces where members could network, discuss their lives, and become empowered. The group also published a newsletter and sponsored social events. Salsa Soul Sisters managed to survive and prosper by continually adapting to the needs of its changing core members. By the 1990s the members had transformed themselves into African Ancestral Lesbians United for Societal Change. As of 2003, they remain the oldest black queer organization in the country.

## High Tide

During the 1980s black queer groups proliferated, partly in response to the AIDS crisis. Some combined the social functions previous groups emphasized with political activism. There was often tension in some groups between those who favored one over the other. The groups were either co- or single-gender, and they were often located in cities with large black queer populations. Washington, D.C., New York, and California had a disproportionate number of them. By the early 1990s one black queer magazine listed almost 200 groups. Increasingly, the types of groups became more diverse. There were those that focused on health/HIV/AIDS, interracialism, Afrocentrism, and spirituality, among others. However, some elements of black queer America continued to be underrepresented, most notably bisexual and transgender men and women.

Most of these groups have been grassroots efforts to provide social, cultural, economic, spiritual, or political support and empowerment to local black queer communities. Although financial difficulties, lack of support, and internal conflicts led to the quick demise of some groups, others became influential and have had a lasting impact on the communities they serve. Prominent examples include the Minority AIDS Project in Los Angeles and Gay Men of African Descent (GMAD) in New York. Perhaps because of the difficulties in developing and sustaining programming on a weekly or monthly basis, since the late 1980s many groups have only held annual or special events, such as the Nia Collective's annual retreats in Los Angeles for black lesbians.

In the late 1970s national groups emerged. They fostered and provided networking opportunities for local groups and leaders, helped set the political agenda for and advocated the interests of black queers, and helped build bridges between black queers and the larger racial and sexual communities of which they are a part. The first of these, what became known as the National Coalition of Black Lesbians and Gays, was established in 1978 in Washington, D.C. A year later the coalition hosted the National Third World Lesbian and Gay Conference, which was held in conjunction with the first March on Washington for Lesbian and Gay Rights. Financial difficulties and conflicts over direction led to the coalition's demise in the early 1990s, but other groups followed its example. The National Black Lesbian and Gay Leadership Forum, founded in Los Angeles in 1988 by Phill Wilson and Ruth Waters, holds annual conferences and retreats. At their peak in the early 1990s these conferences attracted more than one thousand participants and well-known figures such as Jesse Jackson, Natalie Cole, bell hooks, and Cornel West. Like the coalition, the Leadership Forum has battled financial difficulties and conflicts over leadership direction.

Although the National Coalition of Black Lesbians and Gays and the Leadership Forum attempted to be broad-based national organizations, others have been more focused. The Black Men's (and Women's) Xchange, founded in Los Angeles in 1989 by Cleo Manago, is dedicated to serving and promoting Afrocentric homosexualities and transgenderisms. Within a few years, it established chapters in more than half a dozen cities, including Denver, Chicago, and Atlanta. The Xchange's numbers have since dwindled, but it continues to be influential in California. The Unity Fellowship Church Movement (UFCM), founded in Los Angeles in 1985 by Bishop Carl Bean, is an attempt to provide a safe space for queer black Christians to develop a spirituality that both affirms their sexuality and is rooted in black religious culture. It currently has churches in fifteen cities, including New York, Washington, D.C., and Detroit.

The International Federation of Black Prides (IFBP) and the Zuna Institute represent two recent attempts at national organizing. The federation was created in 2000 to promote and help coordinate the growing number of annual Black Pride events across the country. This celebration of black queerness began in Washington, D.C., in 1991, and the movement has since spread to at least sixteen other cities. The Zuna Institute, founded in 1999, is the first major attempt to establish a national organization to promote the interests of black queer women and provide networking opportunities for local groups and leaders. Their accomplishments include successful conferences in Atlanta (2001) and Los Angeles (2003).

## Issues and Conflicts

A central conflict among the leaders of black queer organizations has been who will serve as the chief representative of black queers. Related to this have been the organizations' relationships with white queers and heterosexual blacks. Some, such as Manago, have been critical of groups that have close connections to white queer communities. He believes that groups like the Leadership Forum do not in fact represent those black queers whose social and political ties lie primarily with black America. According to Manago and other Afrocentrists, those belonging to groups like the Leadership Forum spend their lives in mostly white queer worlds, and group members have little connection to, and do not value, black communities and culture.

Another central tension within many of these groups has been the conflict between the desire to fight for inclusion within black heterosexual and white queer communities, while asserting differences from these same communities. This tension has manifested itself in several ways. On the one hand, black queers have shown their unity with the larger queer and black communities by participating in events and institutions sponsored by those groups, creating and maintaining relationships with community leaders, and fighting for inclusion by challenging various forms of racism, sexism, and heterosexism. On the other hand, black queers have asserted their uniqueness within black communities by becoming more visible as queers and by creating institutions that reflect positive ideas about their sexuality and gender personas. In addition, many Afrocentrists and cultural pluralists have distinguished themselves from white queers by choosing names for their groups that reflect their African or black American heritage, such as Nia Collective, Adodi, and Ujima. Afrocentrists have also led the way in creating sexual identities ("same-gender-loving" and "adodi") and symbols (the "Bawabu") that do not reflect white conceptions ("gay/lesbian/queer") and symbols (pink triangles and rainbow flags). Some of their attempts to appropriate African ideas, however, have been problematic. For example, advocates claim that "adodi" is Yoruba for "a man who loves another man," and the "Bawabu" is Swahili for "gatekeeper," a mediator between men and women, as well as between the material and spiritual worlds. Although homosexuality and transgenderism existed in many pre-colonial African cultures, and African conceptions of them were often different from those developed by white queers in the United States and Western Europe, academic research does not substantiate the aforementioned claims.

## Black Queer Periodicals

Since the late 1960s there has been an explosion in the number of periodicals that serve queer communities. The *Advocate* and *Gay Community News* have been among the more influential publications. Whether they offered a glimpse into consumer lifestyles, social and cultural criticism, or community news and events, they connected queer communities, both nationally and internationally. When blacks flipped through the pages of many of these periodicals, however, they often found representations of their lives and communities missing. This was also the case when they read popular black publications such as *Essence* or *Ebony*. To correct this, black queers both fought for greater diversity within white queer and black heterosexual periodicals and created their own.

**Black Queer Leader.** Phill Wilson, cofounder of the National Black Lesbian and Gay Leadership Forum, is accompanied by activist and author Torie Osborn. [AP/Wide World Photos]

Among the early periodicals published by and for blacks "in the life" were *Blacklight* and included *Moja = Gay and Black.* Both began publishing in the late 1970s. Most of these early efforts focused on men. In the early 1980s black women produced several of their own periodicals, including *Onyx* and *Azalea.* The number of black queer periodicals grew dramatically during the 1980s and 1990s. By 1991 one survey listed more than twenty. Most focused on specific aspects of black queer life, such as women's culture, the arts, popular culture, Afrocentrism, interracialism, politics, and erotica.

The late 1980s saw the arrival of the first black queer publication to become a major national presence: *BLK,* a newsmagazine founded by Alan Bell in 1988. More so than the others before it, *BLK* tried to be a general chronicler of life in black queer America. It was able to create a national collective awareness of community and culture building through its news stories, interviews with black queer leaders, advertisements, reviews, gossip columns, and features. It was one of several publications founded by Bell during the 1980s and early 1990s.

Los Angeles, the San Francisco Bay Area, Chicago, New York, and Washington, D.C., emerged as the centers of this publishing boom. Most black queer periodicals

had relatively short lives, lasting only a year or two, and had frequent difficulties adhering to a regular publishing schedule. Limited personnel, finances, circulation, and distribution areas hampered them. Nonetheless, several managed to stay afloat at least five years, including *BLK, Venus,* and *SBC.* At their peak, they could be found in queer and mainstream bookstores across the country, as well as on the Internet. Collectively, these periodicals allowed black queers to learn about and network with each other across the African diaspora. Although the periodicals were in some ways a unifying force, they also reflected community divisions. Gender continued to be one of these divisions. For example, although *BLK* claimed to represent men and women, some female readers wrote letters of complaint alleging its lack of coverage of women's issues. New magazines such as *Aché* tried to correct this imbalance.

Primary community affiliation (queer integrationist vs. same-gender-loving Afrocentric) was another division. Some accused black queer publications such as *BLK* of being ideologically and financially beholden to white queers and those blacks who had established their primary social and political relationships with them. In response, several Afrocentric periodicals that reflected African and black American cultural values and traditions were initiated. The most prominent was Stanley Bennett Clay's *SBC*, founded in 1992. Touted as the "Africentric Homosexual Magazine" of record, it promoted the lives and politics of same-gender-loving folks in the African diaspora—and castigated those blacks whose minds they believed had been colonized by whites.

Despite the divisions these newspapers and magazines continue to function as an important glue that connects black queers and their communities. They also serve as a resource for, and a challenge to, those white queer and heterosexual black periodicals that continue to exclude or provide limited coverage of black queer life.

### In Conclusion

Black queer groups and periodicals face many challenges. There is the struggle simply to survive, along with the conflicts over how to define themselves and relate both to each other and to their racial and sexual counterparts. Despite these problems, though, these groups and periodicals have been, and continue to be, central to building a cohesive black queer community and forcing the rest of society to rethink the links between race, gender, and sexuality.

### Bibliography

"Black Prides Form New Organization." *Venus* 6, no. 4 (Winter 2000): 14.

Chauncey, George. *Gay New York: Gender, Urban Culture, & the Making of the Gay Male World 1890–1940.* New York: Basic Books, 1994.

Christopher, Rodney. "Becoming a Movement: The Growth of Group Consciousness in Black Gay Men and Lesbian Women." *BLK* 3, no. 1 (January 1991): 15–16.

Clay, Stanley Bennett. "Bishop Carl Bean: I Speak to My Ancestors." *SBC* 1, no. 3 (September/October 1992): 28–30.

Clay, Stanley Bennett. "The Forum Is . . . The Forum Ain't." *SBC* 5, no. 3 (March/April 1996): 22.

Davis, Lester. "Black Pride Goes National and Internat'l." *Blacklines* (July 1999). Available from http://www.suba.com/~outlines.

Duberman, Martin. *Stonewall.* New York: Dutton, 1993.

Gale, Leland. "The Bawabu: A Symbol of Black-on-Black Same-Gender Love." *SBC* 8, no. 6 (December 1999): 15.

Haile, Mark. "Pressing Issues: A Quick History and Survey of Current Black Lesbian and Gay Periodicals." *BLK* 3, no. 8 (August 1991): 15–19.

Jordan, L. Lloyd. "Black Gay vs. Gay Black." *BLK* 2, no. 6 (June 1990): 25–30.

Manago, Cleo. "The Various Colors & Sexualities of White Supremacy." *SBC* 5, no. 3 (March/April 1996): 20–21.

Quamina, Alvan. "An Open Call to the Community: Restructuring the National Black Lesbian and Gay Leadership Forum." *SBC* 9, no. 1 (Spring 2000): 20–21.

Streitmatter, Rodger. *Unspeakable: The Rise of the Gay and Lesbian Press in America.* Boston: Faber and Faber, 1995.

**Gregory Conerly**

*See also* AFRICAN AMERICAN RELIGION AND SPIRITUALITY; ATLANTA; BEAM, JOSEPH; BLACK AND WHITE MEN TOGETHER (BWMT); BOOZER, MEL; COMBAHEE RIVER COLLECTIVE; HEMPHILL, ESSEX; JACKSON, DELORES; LORDE, AUDRE; RIGGS, MARLON; SMITH, BARBARA; THIRD WORLD GAY REVOLUTION.

# AFRICAN AMERICAN RELIGION AND SPIRITUALITY

African Americans are increasingly practicing a wide range of religions, including Islam, Judaism, Buddhism, and African-based religions. These traditions offer a variety of responses to LGBT issues, ranging from rigid condemnation in Islam to room for gender transgression in Haitian Vodou. Some people simultaneously practice more than one religion or move between religions. There is fluidity of religious practice within African American communities and especially among LGBT people. However, notwithstanding increased religious diversity and the particular impact of Islam, African American religion and spirituality have been grounded historically in Christianity and the black Christian church.

### The Black Church

The descriptor "black church" refers to a historically diverse and complex network of denominations, including those linked to Baptist, Methodist, and Pentecostal traditions. C. Eric Lincoln and Lawrence H. Mamiya in *The Black Church in the African American Experience* (p. 8) describe the church as the cultural womb of the African American community. The church serves as a foundation for the community's value system and has a history of involvement in community mobilization, especially as it relates to survival and unity in the face of ongoing problems of racism and economic disadvantage.

Whatever its social commitments, the black church has historically maintained either complete silence around, or open hostility toward, LGBT people and their concerns. Aside from the ubiquitous sentiment of "love the sinner, hate the sin" expressed by more liberal denominations, and outright condemnation from the more conservative, it is difficult to find public church discourse on the topic. Documented examples demonstrate a generally negative attitude. In 1951, U.S. Representative Adam Clayton Powell Jr., stridently attacked so-called sexual perverts in the black church, demanding action to check and correct "swishy boys," "swaggering girls," and "degenerate" male clergy (Stein, p. 130). Prophet Jones, the successful and flamboyant Michigan preacher popular with some segments of the African American community in the 1940s and 1950s, lost his stature and garnered moral censure from other members of the community after he was arrested in 1956 for an "indecent act" with an undercover policeman (Retzloff, p. 282). In 1959, a south Philadelphia minister arrested for propositioning two youth reportedly "asked Christ to 'smite these persons who claim a man of God is queer'" (Stein, pp. 122, 130). In the 1950s and 1960s, African American ministers in the civil rights movement responded negatively when organizer Bayard Rustin's homosexuality came to public light.

When the HIV/AIDS epidemic tore down the closet door in the early 1980s, the black church had to face the fact that many choir leaders and choristers were gay men. The prevailing response was one of shock, disdain, and disbelief toward the many members of its flock who were diagnosed with HIV/AIDS. Ironically, the homophobic and AIDS-phobic reactions against ministers suspected of being gay, and against LGBT members of choirs and congregations, attest to the fact that LGBT people have long used the church as a place for social, cultural, and political networking. Many oral histories involving black LGBT people suggest that LGBT partners and friends were often found through church activities. The sustained HIV/AIDS epidemic and its impact on black communities continue to force recognition of LGBT presence, even as the demographic of people living with the virus expands beyond gay men. It becomes increasingly difficult for the church to deny that many people "singing in the choir" have been and continue to be LGBT.

The tragedy for LGBT members of the black church is that many who were previously major players in their religious communities were forced to retreat from their communities and from their circles of support. Others chose to endure what Peter Gomes in *The Good Book* (p. 164) describes as "theological thuggery" in order to have this needed church experience. For many, separation from the support and nurturing of the church community seems the more devastating option. Often, LGBT people vacillate between leaving the church and staying involved.

One such person, Godfrey Easter, in *Love Lifted Me in Spite of the Church*, details his struggle with his conflicting sexuality and church socialization, as well as his search for inner peace. Throughout the book, he discusses his battles against the programming of shame and unworthiness instilled in him by his church experience as a gay man. Easter's account is not an isolated story. LGBT presence remains a source of conflict within the African American Christian community. Many churches sustain their judgment that those gay members of the community previously held in high esteem are no longer worthy of singing the praises of "the Lord."

## Organizing

Meanwhile, a determined push for critical self-reflection and re-evaluation is also emerging at several levels. In academia, the ethicist Marcia Y. Riggs and the theologian Kelly Brown Douglas both have taken on the topic of homosexuality in the context of theorizing sexuality and power more broadly. Riggs, in *Plenty Good Room*, critiques heterosexual patriarchal privilege as a strategy in her pursuit of sexual-gender justice in the black church. Douglas identifies homophobia as a sin and a betrayal of black faith (*Sexuality and the Black Church*, p. 126).

LGBT people in African American communities have long been activists, artists, musicians, and social critics subverting heteronormative culture. At the grassroots level, direct responses to the black church's silence and animosity grew in the early 1980s. Lavender Light: The Black and People of All Colors Lesbian and Gay Gospel Choir was founded in New York City in 1985. In the early twenty-first century, this choir continued to keep alive the black gospel music tradition in an environment supportive of LGBT people. Lavender Light featured a special ministry to black lesbians and gays, who have historically been pressured by their communities to choose between their blackness and their gayness.

Negotiating this tension between aspects of identity has also sparked what to date is the only systematic, open, and affirming church movement within the African American community. In the 1980s, Carl Bean, a young gay gospel singer in Newark, New Jersey, observed the pain and shame pervasive in the black LGBT community and felt called to minister to this need. In Los Angeles in 1985, he founded the first church of what in five years would become a national phenomenon, the Unity Fellowship Church Movement (UFCM). Structured around the motto "God Is Love and Love Is for Everyone," UFCM is a nondenominational religious organization that teaches liberation theology and advocates gender equality; openness to and celebration of LGBT and intersexed identity; and commitment to people of color in a transnational perspective.

By the early twenty-first century, the movement consisted of fifteen churches located throughout the country. At least three service organizations had also evolved from the UFCM. Founded in 1985 in Los Angeles, the Minority Aids Project (MAP) was the first community-based HIV/AIDS organization established and managed by and for people of color in the United States. The Carl Bean HIV/AIDS House, also located in Los Angeles, while not a part of the UFCM, was named in honor of Bean. Loving in Truth, established later, was an HIV/AIDS outreach center founded by Reverend Elder Jacquelyn Holland, pastor of Liberation in Truth UFC of Newark and one of the first woman ministers in the movement. Some other churches, including the historic Riverside Church in New York City and Grace Baptist Church in Chicago, have also developed strong statements of openness and commitment to LGBT people. These and other churches and organizations are working to promote more fully inclusive religious and spiritual traditions in the United States.

## Bibliography

D'Emilio, John. "Homophobia and the Trajectory of Postwar American Radicalism: The Case of Bayard Rustin." *Radical History Review* 62 (spring 1995): 80–103.

Douglas, Kelly Brown. *Sexuality and the Black Church: A Womanist Perspective.* Maryknoll, N.Y.: Orbis Books, 1999.

Easter, K. Godfrey. *Love Lifted Me in Spite of the Church.* Federal Way, Wash.: LLM Publishing, 2002.

Gomes, Peter J. *The Good Book: Reading the Bible with Mind and Heart.* New York: Avon Books, 1996.

Lincoln, C. Eric, and Lawrence H. Mamiya. *The Black Church in the African American Experience.* Durham, N.C.: Duke University Press, 1990.

Retzloff, Tim. "'Seer or Queer?': Postwar Fascination with Detroit's Prophet Jones." *GLQ: A Journal of Lesbian and Gay Studies* 8, no. 3 (2002): 271–296.

Riggs, Marcia Y. *Plenty Good Room: Women versus Male Power in the Black Church.* Cleveland, Ohio: Pilgrim Press, 2003.

Stein, Marc. *City of Sisterly and Brotherly Loves: Lesbian and Gay Philadelphia, 1945–1972.* Chicago: University of Chicago Press, 2000.

**Aryana Bates and Audrey M. Skeete**

**See also** AFRICAN AMERICANS; AFRICAN AMERICAN LGBTQ ORGANIZATIONS AND PERIODICALS; AFRICAN AMERICAN STUDIES; CHURCHES, TEMPLES AND RELIGIOUS GROUPS; JONES, PROPHET; JACKSON, DELORES, PROTESTANTS AND PROTESTANTISM.

# AFRICAN AMERICAN STUDIES

To paraphrase the Trinidadian intellectual C. L. R. James (1993), African American studies is a critique of Western civilization. James defines Western civilization as a racial project constituted through the intersecting histories of European slavery, imperialism, and colonization. For James, the hidden history of Western nations lies within the racist systems of exploitation that account for the wealth and prowess of those nations. We may locate much of the work of African American queer intellectuals within this formulation of African American studies as well.

Rather than presume a coherent field of African American queer studies, it is perhaps preferable to use the term African American queer intellectuals to underline a diversity of thought and practices responding to the intertwining racial, gender, sexual and class oppressions of Western civilization. Black queer intellectuals have pointed to the ways in which Western civilization is not simply a geographic terrain but a set of ideological maneuvers that pathologize racial, gender, sexual, ethnic, and class differences and conceal the ways in which the social world is constituted out of these overlapping and intersecting differences. In general, black queer intellectuals theorize such intersections as a way to critique monolithic interpretations of blackness, womanhood, and queerness—interpretations promoted by the dominant social movements representing African Americans, women, and queers, which often imagine that all blacks are male and straight, all women are white and straight, and all queers are white and male. These paradigms often lead to the very exclusions that helped to define Western civilization.

As Western civilization idealizes citizenship and family through whiteness, patriarchy, and heterosexuality, black queer intellectuals have extended African American studies by illustrating how Western civilization as a racial project receives much of its thrust from heterosexist and patriarchal oppression. For example, when blacks are identified as failing to conform to dominant white paradigms of sex, gender, and sexuality, racist projects draw power from sexism and heterosexism. Black queer intellectuals have also tried to suggest modes of practice that do not succumb to the forms of gender, racial, sexual, and class inequality promoted by Western civilization.

## Early Development

African American studies departments and programs emerged from the student protests of the late 1960s. At San Francisco State University, students struck from 1968 to 1969 and demanded the establishment of a Division of Ethnic Studies, which would be comprised of black, Asian American, Chicano, and Native American Studies departments. In this context, the members of San Francisco State's Black Student Union drafted "The Justification for

Black Studies." As outlined by this document, African American studies would "oppose the 'Liberal-Fascist' ideology rampant on campus whereby college administrations have attempted to pacify Black Student Union demands for systematic curriculum by offering one or two courses in Black history and literature." In addition, Black studies would "reinforce the position that Black people in Africa and the Diaspora have the right to democratic rights, Self-determination and Liberation" and "oppose the dominant ideology of capitalism, world imperialism, and white supremacy" (p. 7). As this suggests, the early architects of African American studies departments and programs engaged Western civilization as an academic, political, institutional, and cultural project, compelling African American studies to intervene in a variety of locations.

Many of the originators of African American studies hailed from black nationalist organizations like the Black Panther Party. Such organizations addressed Western civilization as a constellation of political, economic, and academic institutions that fostered white and Western supremacy. These organizations claimed to speak on behalf of the interests of all blacks, but the heterosexist and patriarchal nature of black nationalist groups soon exposed the limits of such claims. Discussing those limits, Angela Y. Davis states, "It was the inability to address questions of gender and sexuality that also led inevitably to the demise of many organizations." Addressing the ways that black nationalist organizations defined political liberation in terms of heterosexuality and patriarchy, Davis goes on to argue, "These notions of struggle depended on the subordination of women, both ideologically and in practice. The women were responsible for a vastly disproportionate amount of work in a struggle constructed as one for the freedom of 'the Black man'"(Lowe and Lloyd, 1997, pp. 305–306).

As black women were regulated within black nationalist organizations that imagined liberation through and for black men, black women were also excluded and subordinated within the emerging women's movement as it imagined feminist liberation through and for white middle-class women. In fact, Anita Cornwell, an early black lesbian participant in the women's movement, recounts the racism she found among feminists in her book *Black Lesbian in White America*. The routine nature of racism within feminist organizations led Cornwell to argue, "Fear of encountering racism seems to be one of the main reasons that so many Black womyn refuse to join the Womyn's movement" (Cornwell, 1983, p. 12).

Black feminist and particularly black lesbian feminist organizations arose out of the limitations of black nationalist organizations and movements as well as the failures of the women's and labor movements. Black feminists in general and black lesbian feminists in particular critically integrated parts of black nationalism, civil rights, the women's movement, and the labor movement, while expelling other parts. We can see black feminism's critical retrieval of black revolutionary nationalism in the first black feminist anthology, *The Black Woman*, published in 1970 and edited by Toni Cade Bambara, then an associate with the African American studies think tank Institute of the Black World. In one of the anthology's essays, entitled "Double Jeopardy: To Be Black and Female," black feminist and former civil rights activist Frances Beale insisted on the simultaneity of racism and capitalism but complicated that intersection by arguing,

> The racist, chauvinistic, and manipulative use of Black workers and women, especially Black women, has been a severe cancer on the American labor scene. It therefore becomes essential for those who understand the workings of capitalism and imperialism to realize that the exploitation of Black people and women works to everyone's disadvantage and that the liberation of these two groups is a steppingstone to the liberation of all oppressed people in this country and around the world (Beale, 1970, p. 95).

Under the leadership of black feminist intellectuals marginalized by the sexism of black nationalist organizations, critique of Western civilization was reorganized to accommodate analyses of racism's convergence with patriarchy.

Out of this feminist interrogation of racism, patriarchy, and imperialism—and because of the oppressions specific to black queer women within existing social movements and the larger society—black lesbian feminists extended black nationalist and black feminist critiques of Western civilization to theorize and combat heterosexist oppression. Perhaps the most famous black lesbian feminist organization, the Combahee River Collective—a group "actively committed to struggling against racial, sexual, heterosexual, and class oppression"— worked to develop an "integrated analysis and practice based upon the fact that the major systems of oppression are interlocking." The organization was founded in 1974 in Boston by women who had been involved in civil rights and black nationalist organizations. Discussing black feminism's general emergence out of the margins of black political organizations, the women's movement, and the New Left, the Collective stated, "It was our experience and disillusionment within these liberation movements, as well as experience on the periphery of the white male left, that led to the need to develop a politics that was anti-racist, unlike those of white women, and anti-sexist, unlike those of Black and white men" (Combahee River Collective, 1983, p. 272). The Collective extended African American studies' historic interrogation of Western civilization as an imperialistic enterprise, arguing:

> We realize that the liberation of all oppressed peoples necessitates the destruction of the political-economic systems of capitalism and imperialism as well as patriarchy. We are socialists because we believe that work must be organized for the collective benefit of those who do the work and create the products, and not for the profit of the bosses. Material resources must be equally distributed among those who create these resources. We are not convinced, however, that a socialist revolution that is not also a feminist and anti-racist revolution will guarantee our liberation. . . . We need to articulate the real class situation of persons who are not merely raceless, sexless workers, but for whom racial and sexual oppression are significant determinants in their working/economic lives (pp. 275–276).

The Collective worked against the presumption that oppressions could be understood singularly and combated individually. Indeed, theorizing oppressions as simultaneous necessitated multiple and diverse forms of political action.

The Combahee River Collective and other black lesbian feminist organizations inspired a wide range of cultural, theoretical, and political interventions in African American studies, each of which advanced the argument that differences and systems of oppression were braided rather than separate. For instance, black lesbian feminist writer Audre Lorde addressed the ways in which Western civilization proposes differences as pathological and discrete rather than potentially affirming and overlapping. In *The Black Unicorn,* Lorde used poetry to contest the women's movement's singular interpretation of womanhood in terms of gender and its implicit definition of womanhood through whiteness, heterosexuality, and class privilege. In the poem entitled "A Woman Speaks," Lorde writes, "I have been woman/ for a long time/ beware my smile/ I am treacherous with old magic/ and the noon's new fury/ with all your wide futures/ promised/ I am/ woman/ and not white" (Lorde, p. 5). And in an essay entitled "Age, Race, Class, and Sex: Women Redefining Difference," Lorde addresses the ways in which a single-issue politics arises out of the history of Western thought and impairs possibilities for coalition building:

> Much of Western European history conditions us to see human differences in simplistic opposition to each other: dominant/subordinate, good/bad, up/down, superior/inferior . . .

> Certainly there are very real differences between us of race, age, and sex. But it is not those differences between us that are separating us. It is rather our refusal to recognize those differences, and to examine the distortions which result from misnaming them and their effects upon human behavior and expectation (Lorde, 1984, p. 115).

For Lorde, part of black lesbian feminism's task was to interrogate the ways in which differences of race, gender, sexuality, and class have been distorted and how those distortions have found shelter in social movements. Lorde's use of both poetry and criticism to address the gender, sexual, class, and racial norms of Western civilization was typical of many black lesbian feminists. For these scholars, activists, and artists, criticism and art converged as black queer women critiqued the exploitations of Western civilization and constructed a social movement that could redeploy differences of race, gender, sexuality, and class in liberating ways.

Attempting to excavate the ideological bases of exploitation, black lesbian feminist Cheryl Clarke wrote her classic essay "Lesbianism: An Act of Resistance," in which Clarke locates the history of Western slavery within the history of heterosexism and patriarchy. Discussing the identity formation of white slave masters, Clarke writes, "The white man learned, within the structure of heterosexual monogamy and under the system of patriarchy, to relate to black people—slave or free—as a man relates to a woman, viz. as property, as a sexual commodity, as a servant, as a source of free or cheap labor, and as an innately inferior being" (Clarke, p. 131). In a sense, Clarke was rearticulating James's earlier formulation of slavery as the foundation of Western civilization by pointing to the ways in which that foundation was also gendered and eroticized.

Critical endeavors such as these eventually coalesced into demands for a reinvented African American studies. For instance, in 1982 Gloria T. Hull, Patricia Bell Scott, and Barbara Smith published the anthology *All the Women Are White, All the Blacks Are Men, But Some of Us Are Brave: Black Women's Studies.* In their introduction, Hull and Smith located the emergence of black women's studies within the general development of black feminism, arguing that "[the] inception of Black women's studies can be directly traced to three significant political movements of the twentieth century. These are the struggles for Black liberation and women's liberation . . . and the more recent Black feminist movement" (Hull et al., p. xx). Like the work of many black feminists, the volume conceptualized black women's studies as a critical engagement that would address black communities as sexually diverse entities. In a section entitled "Visions and Recommendations," they proposed "[the] eradication of antifeminism and homophobia in the Black community and particularly among Black women academics" (p. xxiv). In 1983, the first black lesbian feminist anthology, *Home Girls: A Black Feminist Anthology*, was published with Smith as the editor. *Home Girls* compiled artistic and theoretical writings centered around issues of identity, welfare, nuclear disarmament, migration, coalition, homophobia, racism, imperialism, labor activism, environmentalism, police brutality, et cetera. The volume advanced black lesbian feminist criticism by illuminating the ways in which black feminism did not represent a single-issue politics but boasted a wide and impressive array of concerns.

During this period, the HIV/AIDS pandemic began to disproportionately affect African Americans, particularly black gay men. In addition, the Ronald Reagan administration exacerbated these effects by underfunding efforts to combat the disease. At the same time, traditional black political and community institutions were turning a blind eye to black queers afflicted with the disease (Cohen, p. 88). In response, black queer men developed critical intellectual and artistic formations. The interventions offered by black queer men began as a simultaneous critique of racism among white gay communities and institutions as well as homophobia in black communities. As black lesbian feminists had pointed to the ways in which the women's movement implicitly racialized the category "woman" as white, black queer men pointed to the ways in which the category "gay" was similarly constructed. For instance, in 1986 black queer writer Joseph Beam published the anthology *In the Life: A Black Gay Anthology*, in which he argued, "We ain't family. Very clearly, gay male means: white, middle-class, youthful, nautilized, and probably butch; there is no room for Black gay men within the confines of this gay pentagon" (Beam, pp. 14–15).

The 1980s witnessed a surge of artistic and critical work by black gay men with journals such as *Blacklight*, *Habari-Daftari*, *Yemonja*, *Black/Out*, *BLK*, *Moja: Black and Gay*, *BGM*, *Pyramid Periodical*, and *The Real Read*. In 1989, Marlon Riggs released his experimental documentary *Tongues Untied*, which dramatized the specificity of black queer male existence and the ways in which it overlapped but departed from white gay male and black straight male cultures. Later on Beam conceived of another anthology that would have to be edited by black

queer poet and activist Essex Hemphill because of Beam's death in 1988 from AIDS. That volume was *Brother to Brother: New Writings by Black Gay Men* (1991). In his introduction, Hemphill situated the critical and artistic endeavors of black queer men within the efforts paved by black lesbian feminists. He argued, "What black women, especially out black lesbians, bravely did was break the silence surrounding their experience. No longer would black men, as the sole interpreters of race and culture, presume to speak for (or ignore) women's experiences. . . . As a result of their courage, black women also inspired many of the black gay men writing today to seek our own voices so we can tell our truths" (Hemphill, p. xvii). The artistic and critical work of this volume's contributors was part of the organizing endeavors of such groups as Gay Men of African Descent, Adodi, Unity, and Black Gay Men. These projects help reconceptualize African American studies by pointing to the ways in which disease was becoming the context and justification for pathologizing homosexual difference and for enacting new forms of social inequalities that made health a racialized, classed, gendered, and eroticized issue.

As black lesbian feminism reimagined the past by reformulating slavery, black queer male writings necessitated historiographic innovations as well. For instance, Black British filmmaker Isaac Julien's experimental film *Looking for Langston* reimagined Hughes's participation in the Harlem Renaissance, marking that participation as a queer one and evoking that history as part of the genealogy of contemporary black queer male identity. *Looking for Langston* pressured scholars to consider the homoerotic and queer foundations of the Harlem Renaissance, challenging the notion that African American intellectual history could simply be regarded as uniformly heterosexual. We may locate white queer intellectual Eric Garber's classic essay "A Spectacle of Color: The Lesbian and Gay Subculture of Jazz Age Harlem" within this critical moment of black queer male intellectual production. As a part of this moment, gay black male writers worked to refashion African American intellectual traditions by denoting that tradition through black queer male figures like Richard Bruce Nugent, James Baldwin, Claude McKay, and Samuel R. Delany.

As slavery and imperialism laid the foundation for Western civilization, they also accounted for the ethnic and national heterogeneity of African American studies in general and black queer intellectual practice in particular. Slavery ensured that anti-black racism was more than an American concern, producing aggrieved black cultures throughout Europe, Africa, the Caribbean, North America, and South America. Black queer intellectuals emerged from these various cultures and infused African

American studies with a heterogeneity that frustrated attempts to narrow the discipline to one geographic terrain. The presence of black British intellectuals like Isaac Julien and Kobena Mercer and Afro-Caribbean writers like Lorde and Michelle Cliff, for instance, question the often-presumed geopolitical unity of blackness and American culture. Such intellectuals tied the racial dynamics in the United States to the gendered and sexual processes of racial exploitation in the Caribbean and Britain, for instance.

Imagining Western civilization as a gendered and eroticized racial project, black queer intellectuals have extended and challenged received notions of liberation and inherited paradigms within African American studies. These intellectuals have worked to extend African American studies' interrogation of racial and class exploitation so that the discipline can also account for the gendered and eroticized nature of those oppressions. The work of earlier intellectuals and activists has inspired more recent work among such scholars as Jennifer Devere Brody, Cathy Cohen, Dwight McBride, Phillip Brian Harper, Sharon Holland, Kevin Mumford, and Robert Reid-Phar. These scholars examined topics ranging from the writers and artists of the Harlem Renaissance, interracialism in twentieth-century urban sexual cultures, the racial and sexual politics around HIV/AIDS intervention, death as an everpresent component of people who live within the margins of race, gender, and sexuality, as well as critical analyses of black queer male identity. The history of black queer intellectual formations has also instructed non-black queer intellectuals as well. In addition to the late Eric Garber's work, Siobhan Somerville's *Queering the Color Line: Race and the Invention of Homosexuality in American Culture* extends the foundations laid by black queer intellectuals as her text interrogates the intersections of race, gender, and sexuality in sexological discourse. Queer studies and intellectuals have attempted to maneuver African American studies so that they engage the intertwining histories of nationalism and normativity, making the critique of Western civilization and sexuality a feminist, anti-racist and queer exercise.

### Bibliography

Beale, Frances. "Double Jeopardy: To Be Black and Female." In *The Black Woman: An Anthology.* Edited by Toni Cade. New York: Signet, 1970.

Beam, Joseph. "Introduction: Leaving the Shadows Behind." In *In the Life: A Black Gay Anthology.* Edited by Joseph Beam. Boston: Alyson Publications, 1986.

Brody, Jennifer Devere and Dwight McBride, (eds.). "Plum Nelly: New Essays in Black Queer Studies," *Callaloo* 23, No. 1 (Winter 2000), 285–478.

Clarke, Cheryl. "Lesbianism: An Act of Resistance." In *This Bridge Called My Back: Writings by Radical Women of Color.* Edited by Cherríe Moraga and Gloria Anzaldúa. New York: Kitchen Table Press, 1981.

Cohen, Cathy. *The Boundaries of Blackness: AIDS and the Breakdown of Black Politics.* Chicago: University of Chicago Press, 1999.

Cornwell, Anita. *Black Lesbian in White America.* Tallahassee, Fla.: The Naiad Press, 1983.

Garber, Eric. "A Spectacle in Color: The Lesbian and Gay Subculture of Jazz Age Harlem." In *Hidden from History.* Eds. Martin Bauml Duberman, Martin Vicinus and Geroge Chauncey Jr. New York: Nal Books, 1989.

Hemphill, Essex. "Introduction." In *Brother to Brother: New Writings by Black Gay Men.* Edited by Essex Hemphill. Boston: Alyson Publications, 1991.

Holland, Sharon Patricia. *Raising the Dead: Readings of Death and (Black) Subjectivity.* Durham and London; Duke University Press, 2000.

Hull, Gloria T., Patricia Bell Scott, and Barbara Smith. *All the Women Are White, All the Blacks Are Men, But Some of Us Are Brave: Black Women's Studies.* New York: The Feminist Press, 1982.

Interview with Lisa Lowe. "Angela Davis: Reflections on Race, Class, and Gender in the USA." In *The Politics of Culture in the Shadow of Capital.* Edited by Lisa Lowe and David Lloyd. Durham and New York: Duke University Press, 1997.

James, C. L. R. "Black Studies and the Contemporary Student." In *The C. L. R. James Reader.* Edited by Anna Grimshaw. Oxford and Cambridge: Blackwell, 1993.

Lorde, Audre. *The Black Unicorn: Poems.* New York: Norton, 1978.

———. *Sister Outsider: Essays and Speeches.* Trumansburg, N.Y.: Crossing Press, 1984.

Marable, Manning. "Introduction: Black Studies and the Racial Mountain." In *Dispatches from the Ebony Tower: Intellectuals Confront the African American Experience.* Edited by Manning Marable. New York: Columbia University Press, 2000.

Mumford, Kevin. Interzones: Black White Sex Districts in Chicago and New York in Early Twentieth Century. New York: Columbia University Press, 1997.

Phillip, Brian. *Are We Not Men: Masculine Anxiety and the Problem of African American Identity.* Oxford: Oxford University Press, 1998.

Reid-Pharr, Robert. *Black Gay Man: Essays.* New York, New York: New York University Press, 2001.

**Roderick A. Ferguson**

*See also* AFRICAN AMERICANS; AFRICAN AMERICAN LGBTQ ORGANIZATIONS AND PERIODICALS; AFRICAN AMERICAN RELIGION AND SPIRITUALITY; BEAM, JOSEPH; CLEO GLENN; COMBAHEE RIVER COLLECTIVE; HARLEM RENAISSANCE; HANSBERRY, LORRAINE; LORDE, AUDRE; SMITH, BARBARA.

# AIDS AND PEOPLE WITH AIDS

The Acquired Immune Deficiency Syndrome (AIDS) has fundamentally changed many aspects of life in the United States since doctors diagnosed the first cases in the early 1980s. This has been most true for the gay community, which has had to cope with the fact that, at least initially, the overwhelming majority of documented cases of AIDS in the United States were among men who have sex with men. The disease forced gay men in the U. S. to reevaluate sexual practices and mores, and drastically changed the medical system and the political landscape to deal with the effects of the AIDS epidemic in America, and in turn, the world. As the AIDS epidemic has evolved over the last two and a half decades, it has increasingly affected many different groups within the LGBT community, particularly gay men and lesbians of color, transgender people, and gay and lesbian intravenous drug users. The effect of this transformation on already diverse communities has proven that AIDS was, and continues to be, more than a medical crisis. It is in fact a political crisis that requires a political solution, a chant made popular by the activist group ACT UP at rallies in the late 1980s and early 1990s.

## Early Epidemiology

In June 1981, the Centers for Disease Control's *Morbidity and Mortality Weekly Report (MMWR)* reported on a strange disease infecting five gay men in Los Angeles, California. This illness weakened the men's immune system so severely that they contracted *Pneumocystis carinii* pneumonia (PCP), a form of pneumonia that was exceptionally rare in healthy young people. Each of the five men also was infected with cytomegalovirus (CMV), a virus related to herpes. A month later, another article appeared in the *MMWR* detailing similarly surprising cases of gay men with PCP in New York City. The report also told of twenty-six men who had been diagnosed with Kaposi's sarcoma, a kind of cancer that until that time had been diagnosed only in older men of European and African descent. In addition to voicing a fear that these men represented the first cases of a new disease, both articles expressed the idea that the disorders were probably related to "some aspect of homosexual lifestyle."

These first reports of what health care providers and government scientists initially called Gay-Related Immune Deficiency (GRID) profoundly shaped both the course of the new epidemic as well as the diverse responses that emerged to deal with it. Even when public health officials, at the behest of gay activists, created the term "Acquired Immunodefiency Syndrome" and its acronym AIDS in July 1982, most people continued to consider AIDS to be a gay disease, which effectively meant that being gay caused a man to get sick.

While the idea that AIDS was a gay disease continued to gather steam, as early as December 1981 public health officials reported immune disorders in heterosexual intravenous drug users. Not long after these initial reports, studies showed that a significant number, about 22 percent, of all people with the disease were heterosexual. It soon became apparent that children born to women with AIDS were also at risk of contracting the disease. In 1982, public health officials reported a statistically significant number of Haitians with immune disorders. Within a few months of that documentation, the first case of immune disorders also appeared in a hemophiliac, and by 1983 twenty-one U.S. hemophiliacs had been diagnosed with AIDS.

To account for the different groups of people who seemed especially at risk for contracting what appeared to be AIDS, epidemiologists categorized these new cases as belonging to one of the "four H" groups—homosexuals, Haitians, heroin users, and hemophiliacs. Almost immediately, the emerging public face of AIDS was linked to certain kinds of people instead of to certain kinds of behaviors. Public health officials regularly talked about the likelihood that a member of a risk group would be infected with AIDS, but rarely seemed interested in detailing how a person's behavior, whether sexual or not, made him or her more likely to become infected. This construction had major implications for how the epidemic would be reported and understood from then on.

## Initial Search for Causes

**Medical.** As soon as the first reports of a new disease affecting gay men appeared in the mainstream medical press, the gay press began an effort to translate this scientific discovery into language its readership could understand. Journalists struggled to comprehend a disease that they realized could be used against the community, contributing to a wide-ranging speculative conversation about "lifestyle" and illness. The *New York Native,* New York City's biweekly gay newspaper, was one of the first to report on the new medical condition. In fact, only ten days after the June 1981 *MMWR* article on the "gay" cancer, the *Native* published its first reports written by the medical adviser Dr. Lawrence Mass. Theories about what caused the disease appeared in numerous forms. Initially, some scientists and gay men hypothesized that recreational drugs played a key role. In this theory, gay men's use of poppers, a chemical inhalant that enhanced sexual arousal, threatened the immune system to such an extent that it caused illness. Facetiously, although with a modicum of fear, the *Native*'s Dr. Mass wrote in a 1982 article entitled "The Epidemic Continues" that other factors "might touch on being gay and living in New York. On the superficial basis of numbers alone, of course, wearing handkerchiefed Levi's and having Judy Garland records in one's collection might also seem risky" (p. 1). Another prominent physician, Dr. Joseph Sonnabend, argued that the disease was not caused by an infectious agent, but rather was the culmination of an overloaded immune system produced by consistent exposure to various sexually transmitted diseases. Sonnabend was one of the first in the gay community to connect AIDS to the sexual revolution, though he tried to resist being labeled moralistic or antisex. As these competing theories circulated throughout the gay community, epidemiologists at the U. S. Centers for Disease Control studied people who displayed the new illness. Throughout 1981 and 1982, a team of scientists and doctors analyzed reported cases to try to determine whether the illness was caused by an infectious agent or by environmental factors as had been the case in the 1976 outbreak of Legionnaires' disease, caused by a bacteria circulating in a hotel's air conditioning system. By 1982, scientists began to collect enough evidence to confirm that AIDS was probably caused by an infectious agent, even though the actual agent remained unidentified. At the same time, these scientists tried to document how this agent spread between people. Almost immediately they began to define the disease as infectious and not contagious. This was an important distinction because it suggested that AIDS could not be spread through casual contact. Instead, early investigations indicated that sexual practices produced conditions that made transmission possible.

**Geographical.** At the same time as scientists looked for the medical cause of AIDS, epidemiologists sought to understand the etiology of the syndrome. Following this lead, journalists began to investigate the question of where the disease came from. Because Haitians were deemed a high-risk group, public health officials focused on the role of the Caribbean island's culture in the spread of the disease. Relying on what were in fact racist assumptions, some argued that supposed voodoo practices involving animal blood put Haitians uniquely at risk for contracting AIDS. This posed a danger to the United States because the island was known as a favorite destination for gay male tourists who would return to the United States after having frequented infected male prostitutes in Haiti. This epidemiological model effectively stigmatized and marked Haitians as an AIDS threat, even though little, if any, scientific evidence could link Haiti or Haitians with AIDS. People interested in documenting the geographical origins of AIDS also turned their attention to the African

continent, another area where early AIDS cases were identified. In the early 1980s cases of an illness that had a similar presentation to AIDS appeared in several African countries. This epidemiology, when coupled with the long held belief that most infectious diseases had origins in the third world, telescoped media attention and public health studies on Africa. *Newsweek* carried one of the first cover stories on AIDS to run in a national magazine in July 1983. In it a French epidemiologist suggested that AIDS came from Equatorial Africa, while another doctor who specialized in the study of tropical disease thought that Cuban soldiers returning from military duty in Angola brought AIDS to Cuba and then to the Cuban community in Miami. Some of these hypotheses were fleeting, particularly because the investigators lacked sufficient evidence to substantiate their claims. The underlying impulse to study the origins of AIDS in Africa, however, remained strong, effectively solidifying the connection between AIDS and Africa in the popular imagination.

### Early Community-Based Response

The focus on where AIDS originated was, for many dealing with the consequences of the epidemic in their daily lives, the wrong approach in confronting the disease. Across the nation, gay men without any formal medical training attempted to address a general lack of knowledge and the growing discrimination and fear of AIDS by organizing community-based responses to the epidemic. They did this in three distinct ways: first by trying to imagine new communal practices, both sexual and social, to confront AIDS; second by creating networks to provide services for people with AIDS; and third by launching criticisms of various segments of society from the federal government to the gay community itself for failing to address the epidemic.

Some of the first lay people to discuss AIDS in print, Michael Callen and Richard Berkowitz, suggested that in the age of AIDS gay individuals had a responsibility to change their sexual behavior and embrace an ethic of caring. In 1983 Callen and Berkowitz, two gay men living with AIDS in New York City, published *How to Have Sex in an Epidemic*. The book represented an attempt to provide a manifesto for how the gay community should respond to AIDS, including the first description of "safe sex" as a form of AIDS prevention. In this book, Callen and Berkowitz critiqued the proliferation of commercialized sexuality that had become central to gay life in the aftermath of the sexual revolution of the 1960s and '70s. They argued that the effects of AIDS would not end the struggle for gay liberation, as many in the popular press claimed, but rather had the potential to resuscitate the most progressive and anticapitalist aspects of the movement.

Still, some people in the gay community believed that too little was being done to stem the tide of the AIDS epidemic. The most vociferous member of this group was Larry Kramer, a New York playwright and novelist. In numerous articles written over the course of the first decade of the epidemic, Kramer criticized the mainstream media for failing to report on AIDS, the gay community for ignoring the extent of AIDS, the federal government for removing the social service safety net for people with AIDS, and the New York City municipal government, particularly Mayor Ed Koch, for refusing to meet with AIDS activists. While Kramer was one of the founding members of the Gay Men's Health Crisis (GMHC) and AIDS Coalition to Unleash Power (ACT UP), his stinging prose left many people unwilling or unable to hear his arguments, and foreshadowed major divisions within the gay community over the need to eliminate or at least drastically change sexual practices that put people at risk for contracting HIV/AIDS.

Other gays and lesbians began to devise a system for helping people directly affected by AIDS in conjunction with the effort to create material that would be used as AIDS prevention within the gay community. In 1983 at the Second Annual AIDS Forum held in Denver, attendees formed the People with AIDS Coalition. The group's members, all of whom had AIDS, fought to resist the idea, propagated by the media, that they were victims of AIDS, powerless to deal with the effects of the disease. The Coalition built on models for establishing gay-positive health institutions first suggested by the Women's Health Movement of the 1970s. In keeping with this model, they wanted to be known as People with AIDS (PWAs) who could live with AIDS if society in general and the health profession in particular treated them with respect. The group encouraged all people with AIDS to come together and resist the isolation that accompanied illness.

Women participating in the AIDS Forum informally created the Women's AIDS Network (WAN) at the same time. It took a few months for the group to take hold, but by 1984 women in San Francisco came together to help provide services for women affected by AIDS as well as women who provided services to people with AIDS. The creation of WAN highlighted the important role women played in early community organizing. In some cities, lesbians donated blood in honor of gay men who were prohibited from making such donations, calling themselves "Blood Sisters," while in other places women volunteers provided a backbone for the new community-based organizations set up to address the AIDS crisis. Women,

**Spreading the Word.** Activism by ACT UP and other groups, such as this protest dramatizing the wide-ranging targets of AIDS, helped to raise public consciousness about the breadth of the illness, and governmental neglect of it. [Patsy Lynch]

both straight and lesbian, recognized that their history of activism could provide gay men with a powerful example of what a social movement should look like.

Women's roles as AIDS activists have often overshadowed the existence of women living with AIDS. This has been especially true for lesbians with HIV/AIDS, a group that has been all but ignored by public health officials and many gay men's AIDS organizations, both of which groups seemed unable to understand how lesbians could be at risk. It was not until 1992 that the Lesbian AIDS Project (LAP) opened at GMHC with the express purpose of designing prevention material and caring for lesbians. LAP not only created public health campaigns that eroticized the use of latex barriers for women who have sex with women, but also focused attention on the particular needs of lesbians who were sex workers and IV drug users.

### Initial Governmental Responses

Much of the initial work done within gay communities highlighted the blatant inaction of the federal govern-

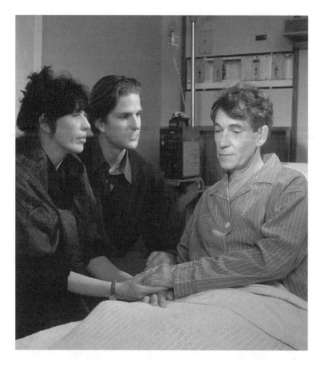

***And the Band Played On.*** Lily Tomlin, Matthew Modine (center), and Ian McKellen appear in a still from the 1993 TV movie, based on Randy Shilts's 1987 best-selling book about the start of the AIDS crisis and the inadequate responses of the LGBT community, researchers, and the nation at large. [Janet Van Ham]

ment in the first years of the AIDS epidemic. The minimal response was made possible because the first cases of AIDS were documented at the same time that the Reagan administration sought to drastically cut expenditure on social services in general and the public health apparatus in particular. This meant that fewer funds were available to study the AIDS epidemic at precisely the moment when study was most needed. In 1985, less than 1 percent of the Public Health Service's budget was spent on AIDS. In addition to the lack of funds, the election of Ronald Reagan in 1980 signaled the growing strength of conservatism in America, a political ideology whose followers believed that homosexuality had no place in U.S. society. When the federal government did initiate action to address AIDS, it focused more on identifying and isolating people with AIDS than on providing services to them.

To fill the hole created by the lack of federal expenditures, municipal governments, in particular those in New York City and San Francisco, had little choice but to deal with the growing number of AIDS cases themselves. Each municipality, however, responded differently. At the behest of the sizable and organized gay voting block in San Francisco, the municipal government dedicated more

funding and attention to AIDS than any other city in America, and significantly more money per person with AIDS than the government of New York City. In 1982, the San Francisco Department of Public Health requested $180,000 to provide funding for AIDS programs and soon thereafter created the AIDS Activities Office to coordinate the services designed for people with AIDS in San Francisco. This signaled the first steps toward instituting an integrated model for helping people with AIDS, including providing city-sponsored mental health services and creating a dedicated hospital ward for people with AIDS at San Francisco General Hospital.

In New York City the government response looked quite different. While New York had significantly more cases of AIDS than any other city, the city's gay community was not, at least initially, as organized as it was on the West Coast, and therefore was less effective in getting the government to take action. In 1983, the New York City Health Department established a formal AIDS surveillance program, but did not create the Office of Gay and Lesbian Health until several years later. The Office did not have the same kind of authority as the AIDS Office in San Francisco, leaving the bulk of the responsibility to the gay community itself.

## Scientific Breakthroughs

In May 1984, two groups of scientists—one in the United States, the other in France—completed studies that connected a then unnamed and unique retrovirus with AIDS. In practice this meant that scientists had isolated the entity that caused AIDS. The French scientists, headed by Luc Montagnier of the Pasteur Institute, named the virus lymphadenopathy-associated virus (LAV), while the American scientists, headed by Robert Gallo of the National Cancer Institute at the National Institutes of Health, named it human T-cell leukemia virus type III (HTLV-III). While the virus was not renamed human immunodeficiency virus (HIV) until 1986, by 1984 it was clear that the virus was not spread through casual contact. All of the groups involved with tracing the epidemiology of AIDS, from public health officials to gay activists continued to vociferously argue that the illness was spread only sexually and through the exchange of blood products.

Once scientists identified the virus that causes AIDS, testing for the presence of that virus not only became possible, it became a central piece of the federal government's AIDS policy. As early as 1986, the federal government called for a national testing strategy that would allow the government to document who, in fact, was HIV-positive. Many gay groups and AIDS service organizations discouraged testing because they feared how the results would be used. They saw testing as a first step in surveillance that would encourage a kind of organized discrimination. These groups reasoned that testing could not be the only strategy for dealing with AIDS, particularly because the will to provide treatment for those who tested positive was not nearly as strong as was the interest in identifying them.

### Increasing Public Awareness

At the same time that the HIV test became a tool to identify people with AIDS, several events brought the AIDS epidemic into sharp relief in the public imagination. In 1985, the famous 1950s heartthrob and actor Rock Hudson disclosed that he had AIDS. The media frenzy surrounding this announcement was tremendous, but highlighted the continued discrimination faced by gay people in America. Although he divulged he had AIDS, Hudson never came out as a gay man. Nonetheless, Hudson's disclosure forced many Americans to think about AIDS as part of their lives. President Reagan mentioned AIDS in public for the first time when learning of Hudson's status.

In 1987, St. Martin's Press published Randy Shilts's *And the Band Played On,* arguably the most popular book on AIDS ever written. A Book-of-the-Month Club selection in its first month on the market, *And the Band* was an instant best-seller. The exposé documented the fundamental failures of both the state and the gay community in early responses to the AIDS epidemic. In fact, Shilts argued that gay men, particularly in their refusal to change sexual behavior, were to blame for the AIDS crisis. Because of this accusation, many of his contemporaries called Shilts a self-hating gay man and argued that his writing would do little to help the gay community cope with AIDS. In spite of this, over 200,000 copies of the book were sold, and people read it as a history of the first decade of the AIDS epidemic.

As Shilts's book hit the shelves, a group of men in San Francisco came together to document the experiences and lives of people who had died from AIDS by designing and sewing quilt panels dedicated to loved ones. The project had been conceived two years earlier by the San Francisco activist Cleve Jones when he asked people to hold placards with names of people with AIDS at a rally. The resulting quilt not only served to memorialize the dead, it also used a classic American art form, which in turn made the quilt, and the epidemic it represented, significant to people who seemed to have no gay affiliation.

### AIDS Service Organizations

As public awareness of the AIDS epidemic grew, community organizing to deal with both the effects of the disease

**Rock Hudson.** The death in 1985 of this actor of the 1950s and 1960s jolted mainstream America, since he was one of the first celebrities—and one whose sexual orientation had not been widely known—to die as a result of AIDS. [corbis]

and the prevention of it expanded as well in the form of AIDS service organizations (ASOs). ASOs produced systems to deal with the lack of state-sponsored initiatives. Many initially relied on volunteers, but as the organizations grew they increasingly hired professional staff to address the needs of people with and without AIDS.

In 1982, five gay men met at the writer Larry Kramer's New York City apartment and formed the Gay Men's Health Crisis (GMHC). In San Francisco, a similar group was born. First called the Kaposi's Sarcoma (KS) Research and Education Foundation, it soon became the San Francisco AIDS Foundation (SFAF). Across the country, gay men and lesbians led the movement to create ASOs in cities with significant numbers of people with AIDS. From Los Angeles to Boston and Houston to Chicago, organizations developed to provide treatment and prevention services for city residents. These ASOs created and distributed safe sex material and developed other AIDS prevention campaigns to help contain the spread of AIDS. Organizations such as GMHC in New

York and the Shanti Project in San Francisco also designed services to help care for people with AIDS. Whether in the form of a "buddy" system, which paired a volunteer with a person sick from AIDS, or by delivering food to housebound people, these ASOs gave invaluable support to their clients.

### Racial Disparities

While AIDS service organizations created a broad safety net for some people living with AIDS and designed AIDS prevention materials for various groups, the disparities in infection rates between whites and people of color continued to grow. By 1986, African Americans and Latinos accounted for 25 percent and 14 percent of reported AIDS cases respectively, but only 11.7 percent and 6.4 percent of the total population. Seven years later the numbers showed even greater inequality. In 1993, the CDC showed that 66 percent of the more than 106,000 reported cases that year occurred among African Americans, and 32 percent occurred among Hispanics.

But these disproportionate statistics did not manifest themselves in policies that effectively addressed the racial disparity. While overwhelmingly white ASOs, and to a lesser extent state and federal governments, attempted to deal with how communities of color were affected by AIDS, the strategies emerged in an environment where conversations about race were ever present, but solutions to the problems created by racism remained few and far between. This led gays and lesbians of color to form organizations to deal with the inequality accentuated by the AIDS crisis. In 1983, activists in San Francisco created the Third World AIDS Advisory Taskforce. The taskforce began with the express purpose of documenting how communities of color experienced AIDS as well as how the membership, made up exclusively of people of color, could help ASOs design culturally relevant prevention and treatment services. In New York City, black gay men led the charge to create the Minority Taskforce on AIDS in 1986. On the national level, the National Minority AIDS Council emerged as an organization dedicated to helping grassroots organizations in communities of color expand.

### Activism

As the epidemic continued to expand and the government failed to respond, activist groups dedicated to finding political solutions to the epidemic began to emerge. The best example of this activist impulse was the AIDS Coalition to Unleash Power (ACT UP). ACT UP grew out of a series of community meetings held at New York City's Gay and Lesbian Community Center in Greenwich Village in the spring of 1987, rooted in a history of gay and lesbian activism in the city. The group believed that the only way to end the AIDS crisis was to initiate direct action against federal and local governments as well as industrial giants such as pharmaceutical companies. Some of the group's first protests, especially those directed at the obvious markers of global capitalism like the New York Stock Exchange, linked the AIDS crisis to economic and political inequalities. Using powerful imagery to argue that homophobia and racism were responsible for AIDS, ACT UP prided itself on deploying advertisements to make its anticapitalist message appealing. The Gran Fury collective of ACT UP created the slogan "Silence = Death," and soon the words appeared on T-shirts and posters across the country. ACT UP reinvigorated a protest style from the 1960s and 1970s in an attempt to produce the conditions for getting "drugs into bodies," a slogan that symbolized the work of the group. But real battles within the membership about how ACT UP would deal with the relationship between AIDS, racism, and sexism presented a serious challenge to the group.

### Artistic Production

Part and parcel with activist responses to the AIDS epidemic, artists working in various media, used art as both a form of protest and a way to deal with the harsh realities of the epidemic. In 1990, the playwright Tony Kushner wrote *Angels in America: A Gay Fantasia on National Themes*, a play that sardonically and acerbically chronicled the lives of men dealing with the effects of AIDS. The play ran on Broadway and won both a Tony Award for best play and a Pulitzer Prize for best drama. While some art created to confront AIDS received public acclaim, other artists did not have their work embraced by heterosexual America. Activist filmmakers Marlon Riggs and David Wojnarowicz, who were both HIV-positive, produced documentaries that portrayed the experiences of people with AIDS. Riggs's 1991 film, *Tongues Untied*, documented what it was like to be black and gay in America. The film, roundly praised by critics, sparked a major controversy when it aired on public television. The conservative activist Pat Buchanan vilified the film and its maker and used it to argue for defunding the National Endowment for the Arts. Dancers and choreographers such as Alvin Ailey and Bill T. Jones created pieces dedicated to documenting the lives of people with AIDS, and visual artist Keith Haring painted huge public murals designed to fight AIDS. Haring died of AIDS in 1990, but his legacy of activist art continues to be felt today. Within a decade of the first cases of AIDS, the epidemic trans-

**Arthur Ashe.** The first African American male tennis star— shown with his wife, Jeanie, and their five-year-old daughter, Camera, at the Arthur Ashe AIDS Tennis Challenge in New York on 30 August 1992—was as eloquently outspoken about AIDS, which he contracted during surgery, as he was about sports and racial issues, until his death in 1993. [AP Photo/Malcolm Clarke]

formed the art world by infusing it with a new political purpose and taking the lives of numerous artists.

## The AIDS Epidemic in the Twenty-First Century

While there is widespread hope for a cure for AIDS, U.S. and worldwide statistics show a devastating pandemic in full swing. Led by the gay and lesbian community, the United States now has a system in place for dealing with the effects of the AIDS epidemic in the twenty-first century. The advent of protease inhibitors, or "the cocktail," as many people have began to call the drug regime, has effectively prolonged the lives of many people with HIV/AIDS. While these new treatments have made it possible for many in the West to live healthy lives, no system is yet in place to disseminate the drugs to people who cannot afford them, whether they live in the United States or on the African continent. This inequity is most noticeable when the needs of men and women of color are considered. Recent statistics indicate that 70 percent of new male infections will be men of color, most of whom will be men who have sex with other men. The racial disparities are more severe in the case of women, where over 80 percent of new infections will be among women of color. When looking at the international scope of the epidemic, the statistics are truly alarming: an estimated 42 million people are living with HIV/AIDS. The current strategy of AIDS researchers and activists is to attack the disease in all its manifestations as a medical, social, political, and economic phenomenon.

## Bibliography

ACT UP/NY Women and AIDS Book Group. *Women, AIDS, and Activism.* Boston: South End, 1990.

Altman, Dennis. *AIDS in the Mind of America: The Social, Political, and Psychological Impact of a New Epidemic.* Garden City, N.Y.: Anchor, 1986.

Andriote, John-Manuel. *Victory Deferred: How AIDS Changed Gay Life in America.* Chicago: University of Chicago, 1999.

Bayer, Ronald. *Private Acts, Social Consequences: AIDS and the Politics of Public Health.* New York: Free Press, 1989.

Cohen, Cathy. *The Boundaries of Blackness: AIDS and the Breakdown of Black Politics.* Chicago: University of Chicago, 1999.

Crimp, Douglas, ed. *AIDS: Cultural Analysis, Cultural Activism.* Cambridge, Mass.: MIT, 1988.

Epstein, Steven. *Impure Science: AIDS, Activism, and the Politics of Knowledge.* Berkeley: University of California, 1996.

Fee, Elizabeth, and Nancy Kreiger. "Understanding AIDS: Historical Interpretations and the Limits of Biomedical Individualism." *American Journal of Public Health* 83, no. 10 (1993): 1477–1486.

Grmek, Mirko. *History of AIDS: Emergence and Origin of a Modern Pandemic.* Translated by Russell C. Maulitz and Jacalyn Duffin. Princeton, N.J.: Princeton University, 1990.

Hammonds, Evelynn. "Missing Persons: African American Women, AIDS and the History of Disease." *Radical America* 24, no. 2 (1990): 7–23.

Kramer, Larry. *Reports from the Holocaust: The Story of an AIDS Activist.* New York: St. Martin's, 1994.

Patton, Cindy. *Inventing AIDS.* New York: Routledge, 1990.

Rofes, Eric. *Reviving the Tribe: Regenerating Gay Men's Sexuality and Culture in the Ongoing Epidemic.* New York: Haworth, 1996.

Shilts, Randy. *And the Band Played On: Politics, People, and the AIDS Epidemic.* New York: St. Martin's, 1987.

Treichler, Paula. *How to Have Theory in an Epidemic: Cultural Chronicles of AIDS.* Durham, N.C.: Duke, 1999.

Watney, Simon. *Practices of Freedom: Selected Writings on HIV/AIDS.* Durham, N.C.: Duke, 1994.

**Jennifer Brier**

**See also** AIDS COALITION TO UNLEASH POWER (ACT UP); AIDS MEMORIAL QUILT—NAMES PROJECT; AIDS SERVICE ORGANIZATIONS; AILEY, ALVIN; AMERICAN CIVIL LIBERTIES UNION (ACLU); ARCHITECTURE; ARENAS, REINALDO; BEAM, JOSEPH; BENNETT, MICHAEL; DISABILITY, DISABLED PEOPLE, AND DISABILITY MOVEMENTS; EICHELBERGER, ETHYL; FASHION, STYLE, AND CLOTHING; GAY AND LESBIAN ALLIANCE AGAINST DEFAMATION (GLAAD); HARING, KEITH; IMMIGRATION, ASYLUM, AND DEPORTATION LAW AND POLICY; ISLAS, ARTURO; JONES, BILL T., AND ARNIE ZANE; KRAMER, LARRY; KUSHNER, TONY; KUROMIYA, KYOSHI; LIBERACE; MAPPLETHORPE, ROBERT; MAUPIN, ARMISTEAD; MONETTE, PAUL; MUSIC: CLASSICAL; NATIVE AMERICAN LGBTQ ORGANIZATIONS AND PUBLICATIONS; POLITICAL SCIENCE; PRESTON, JOHN; PUERTO RICO; RIGGS, MARLON; REYES, RODRIGO; RUSSO, VITO; SAFER SEX; SEXUALLY TRANSMITTED DISEASES; SULLIVAN, LOU; TELEVISION; WADELL, TOM; WITTMAN, CARL; WOJNAROWICZ, DAVID.

# AIDS COALITION TO UNLEASH POWER (ACT UP)

An organization committed to using confrontational street activism to fight the AIDS crisis, ACT UP was formed in March 1987 out of the gay community in New York City. It quickly spread across the United States and strongly influenced the AIDS activist scene into the early-to-mid-1990s. Over the course of its life, there were over eighty loosely networked, locally autonomous chapters in the United States and more than thirty in Europe, Canada, and Australia. (Not all affiliated chapters adopted the ACT UP name. Groups like OUT [Oppression under Target] in Washington, D.C., Boston's MASS ACT OUT, and GUTS [Gay Urban Truth Squad] in Dallas were part of the ACT UP network.) ACT UP was most notable for its raucous demonstrations; direct action and civil disobedience campaigns; die-ins and other forms of street theater; eye-catching and pointed graphics; and in-your-face, sex-radical, and queer-positive sexual politics.

## The Rise of Confrontational AIDS Activism

During the early and mid-1980s, as AIDS cases and deaths from AIDS-related complications skyrocketed in gay communities across the United States, government bodies largely ignored the crisis or proposed measures designed to isolate and punish rather than assist people with AIDS (PWAs) and people perceived to be at risk. Right-wing politicians and pundits used AIDS to forward their homophobic agendas, citing the epidemic as proof that homosexuality was perverse, abnormal, and sinful. With the goal of fighting both AIDS itself and the homophobia linked to the crisis, AIDS activists across the United States angrily took to the streets to demand an adequate and compassionate response from government, the scientific-medical establishment, insurance and pharmaceutical companies, the communications media, and other institutions.

The turn in the late 1980s to confrontational AIDS activism was in marked contrast to the forms of AIDS activism that prevailed in LGBT communities during the early and mid-1980s, which revolved around the vital work of caretaking, establishing and staffing AIDS service organizations, and lobbying for AIDS funding. The beginnings of a shift to more confrontational activism occurred in late 1985 when two gay men with AIDS chained themselves to the door of San Francisco's old Federal Office Building to protest the federal government's negligent response to the crisis and to demand greater federal funding to fight AIDS. Around the same time, activists in New York City formed the Gay and Lesbian Anti-Defamation League (which later became the Gay and Lesbian Alliance Against Defamation, or GLAAD), and in December 1985 eight hundred people demonstrated against the *New York Post*'s sensationalized AIDS coverage. A conjunction of developments in mid-1986—most notably the U.S. Supreme Court's *Bowers v. Hardwick* decision upholding Georgia's anti-sodomy statute, but also growing calls in state legislatures around the country for mandatory testing for HIV and for quarantine measures, along with ever-increasing deaths in a context of little government assistance—animated a more decisive and far-reaching turn toward angry, defiant activism, which fueled the emergence of ACT UP.

Numerous grassroots AIDS activist groups—precursors to ACT UP chapters—formed on the heels of the *Hardwick* decision. In September 1986, Citizens for Medical Justice (CMJ), a San Francisco–based group of lesbians and gay men, took over California governor George Deukmejian's office to protest his AIDS policies. (CMJ later changed its name to AIDS Action Pledge and then to ACT UP-San Francisco.) In the summer of 1986,

**ACT UP.** The war against AIDS takes to the streets in one of this activist organization's typical in-your-face demonstrations, to pressure government agencies and the health-care industry into responding more quickly and effectively to the spreading epidemic during the late 1980s and early 1990s.

some lesbians and gay men left GLAAD and formed the Lavender Hill Mob, a lesbian and gay direct action group; many of their zaps focused on AIDS and included a theatrical disruption of a Centers for Disease Control (CDC) conference on mandatory HIV testing in February 1987. In late 1986 and early 1987, a group of gay activist artists plastered lower Manhattan with posters that had a pink triangle above the words "SILENCE=DEATH," implicitly comparing the AIDS crisis to the Nazi Holocaust. Text at the bottom of the poster encouraged lesbians and gay men to "turn anger, fear, grief into action," reflecting and reinforcing a newly emerging emotional and political sensibility.

The founding meeting of ACT UP was on 12 March 1987 in New York City. Two nights earlier, playwright Larry Kramer had given a powerful, emotional, political speech about the AIDS crisis at the Lesbian and Gay Community Center. During discussion after Kramer's speech, the excited crowd of approximately two hundred mostly white gay men decided to meet again to form an AIDS activist organization. Groups already involved in confrontational street activism, like the Silence=Death Project and the Lavender Hill Mob, attended Kramer's speech and the founding ACT UP meeting two nights later; the Silence=Death Project contributed its subsequently famous graphic to the burgeoning movement. Two weeks later, on 24 March 1987, ACT UP held its first demonstration, targeting the Food and Drug Administration's (FDA) sluggish drug approval process as well as the profiteering of pharmaceutical companies. Hundreds of AIDS activists tied up traffic on Wall Street for several hours and seventeen were arrested. When the FDA announced just weeks later that it would shorten its drug approval process by two years, CBS News anchor Dan Rather credited ACT UP. Throughout 1987, street AIDS activist groups continued to sprout up around the country, a process that greatly accelerated after the October 1987 March on Washington for Lesbian and Gay Rights.

## Actions and Victories

As a national organization that thrived into the mid-1990s, ACT UP inserted itself into every aspect of the AIDS epidemic. Driven by a sense of urgency to save lives and community institutions and by a belief that direct action was the best way to achieve these goals, ACT UP embraced a model of grassroots activism that, rather than demanding ideological agreement among all members and chapters, undertook any tactical battle that might help save lives, as long as there was enough support within the organization to sustain such a battle. ACT UP also avoided rallies with long-winded speeches, favoring demonstrations that included multiple affinity groups engaging in theatrical, humorous, sexy, daring, and often illegal actions. Different caucuses and committees within ACT UP—including caucuses of people of color, women, and people with immune system disorders (PISD) and committees like New York's Treatment and Data Committee (which focused on AIDS drugs) and Majority Action Committee (which focused on AIDS issues of concern to people of color)—initiated many of ACT UP's actions.

Over the course of its life and with differing emphases within and across chapters, ACT UP focused on a plethora of issues and engaged in hundreds of protest actions. Memorable actions included a daylong shutdown of the Food and Drug Administration (FDA) in October 1988 to demand an expedited drug approval process; a takeover of the opening ceremonies of the Fifth International Conference on AIDS in Montreal in June 1989 to demand fundamental revisions in drug-testing procedures; a massive Stop the Church demonstration at St. Patrick's Cathedral in New York City in December 1989 to protest the Catholic Church's opposition to safe-sex education and to abortion; a national demonstration in Chicago in April 1990 that focused on the failings of the public health system and demanded national health insurance (and included the first national ACT UP conference on AIDS and people of color); a storming of the National Institutes of Health in May 1990 to demand more research on AIDS treatments and the inclusion of women and people of color in clinical trials; two demonstrations in 1990 at the CDC to demand that it alter its definition of AIDS to include the infections commonly affecting HIV-positive women and poor people; and numerous political funerals, beginning with an action in October 1992 where people threw the ashes of those who had died of AIDS-related complications onto the White House lawn. Other actions addressed issues like holistic and alternative treatments, safe-sex education, needle exchange programs, housing for PWAs, increased AIDS budgets, safe-sex information and AIDS drugs for prisoners, social security benefits, media coverage of AIDS, AIDS drug prices, and more.

ACT UP had numerous victories. Sometimes working alone and sometimes in coalition with other groups, ACT UP successfully:

- obtained increased government funding for AIDS research, services, and education;

- pressured the FDA to expedite the drug approval process and to expand access to drugs;

- forced pharmaceutical companies to lower prices of their AIDS drugs;

- pressured insurance companies to reimburse for experimental AIDS therapies not yet approved by the FDA;

- argued that PWAs should be consulted about, and that their expertise should inform, AIDS drug trial designs;

- pressured researchers to include women and people of color in clinical trials;

- demanded that the CDC expand the definition of AIDS to include infections and diseases commonly occurring in HIV-infected women and poor people; and

- prevented the passage and won the repeal of many pieces of repressive AIDS legislation.

ACT UP's numerous interventions translated into many additional concrete victories and, more generally, posed a challenge to conventional and widespread understandings of AIDS, homosexuality, and sexuality.

## ACT UP and the Birth of "Queer"

In addition to its many significant victories for PWAs, ACT UP also gave birth to a new queer era in which anger, defiant street activism, and sex-radical politics became normative and valued among lesbians, gay men, and other sexual and gender minorities, many of whom now called themselves "queer." ACT UP queers proudly embraced LGBT sexual difference and disavowed LGBT shame and the desire for acceptance by a society that, as the AIDS crisis was demonstrating, saw queers as better off dead.

With its queer-positive and sexually explicit images and rhetoric, ACT UP catapulted queer sexuality into the public realm in a manner that furnished a powerful response to the strongly sex-negative and homophobic early years of the AIDS crisis. ACT UP-New York's artist

## lesbian participation in act up

Why did lesbians participate in ACT UP? Why did they engage in activism around an ostensibly gay male issue that seemingly was not directly affecting lesbians? The question is not only academic; it was asked of ACT UP lesbians by other lesbians who were concerned that lesbians' limited time, energy, and resources were being diverted to male issues. They worried that the focus on AIDS was sidelining activism on issues like lesbian and gay civil rights, anti-LGBT violence, child adoption laws, lesbian health concerns like breast cancer, and lesbian and gay youth suicide. Their concerns derived in part from shifts in focus and resources that existing lesbian and gay organizations were undertaking in order to address the growing AIDS crisis. Some lesbians also wondered if gay men would be there for lesbians if the latter were facing a similar crisis. While lesbians in ACT UP sometimes had similar concerns, they tended to disagree with the premise that AIDS was a male issue. AIDS was certainly disproportionately killing gay and bisexual men and it was not posing anywhere near the same health threat to the vast majority of lesbians. But ACT UP lesbians tended to see AIDS as an issue affecting the entire lesbian, gay, queer world, in addition to other communities, and thus of concern to themselves as lesbians.

Lesbians got involved in AIDS activism from the earliest days of the epidemic, and similar reasons propelled many lesbians into ACT UP. Some lesbians joined ACT UP because they had friends who were dying, but AIDS was directly affecting lesbians in other ways as well. In the early days of the epidemic, lesbians were frequently constructed by the media and the religious right as AIDS carriers, along with gay men; as well, lesbians, like gay men, were one of the groups being targeted by the right wing more generally. They understood that the right wing was using AIDS to forward its homophobic agenda, they recognized that as individuals and as a community they were under attack, and many thus experienced the fight against the AIDS crisis as a battle for their own interests and lives. Many lesbians who got involved in ACT UP had long histories of involvement in other social movements—for example, the reproductive health movement, the peace movement, the anti-military intervention movement, and others—and their work in ACT UP was the first time many of them had a chance to engage in activism that would have such a direct effect on their own lives as lesbians. Lesbians also got involved because they saw how AIDS was dangerously intersecting with other social problems such as sexism and racism, and they wanted to broaden the AIDS agenda accordingly.

As well, a number of ACT UP lesbians identified as sex radicals—feminists who thought sexual politics should be informed by the pleasures and diversity of female sexuality and not simply by the dangers that women face in the sexual realm. Given dominant constructions of AIDS that disparaged gay male sexuality, ACT UP as an organization recognized the necessity of tying the fight against AIDS to the fight for sexual freedom, and that made ACT UP a political home for many lesbian sex radicals.

As in other organizations, lesbians had to contend with the sexism present in ACT UP, and it was often a rocky and contentious road. But the reasons that drew many lesbians to ACT UP encouraged many to stay; they saw ACT UP as the place to engage in confrontational street activism to fight AIDS, to fight the right wing, to fight the oppression of queers and other marginalized groups, to fight for sexual liberation, and to fight for their own liberation.

---

collaborative group Gran Fury produced LGBT-positive, sex-positive images, including its "Kissing Doesn't Kill" AIDS education poster that showed three kissing couples (one gay male, one lesbian, and one heterosexual). A bestselling ACT UP–Chicago Women's Caucus T-shirt, worn by ACT UP men as well as women, showed two women engaged in oral sex with text that read "Power Breakfast." ACT UP's meetings and actions were also vibrant cruising sites and spaces for non-normative gender and sexual expression.

ACT UP's queer sensibility and politics challenged mainstream lesbian and gay communities' more narrow identity politics and rights-based political agenda. As a movement that encouraged non-normative sexual and gender expression and that elaborated a challenge to essentialist ideas of sexual identity, ACT UP might also be credited with inspiring the birth of queer theory.

### The Decline of ACT UP

Although a few individual chapters continued to exist, ACT UP declined as a national organization in the mid-1990s—prior to the advent in 1995 and 1996 of a new generation of anti-HIV drugs called protease inhibitors that have successfully prolonged the lives of many PWAs in the United States. Reasons for ACT UP's decline are multiple, but three of the most important were

(1) heightened conflicts and declining solidarity within ACT UP; (2) a growing despondency within ACT UP due to the accumulated losses, the continuing deaths, and the lack of effective treatments; and (3) waning support for ACT UP from the broader mainstream lesbian and gay community.

In the early 1990s, internal conflicts in many ACT UP chapters began to fracture the organization. By then, a few ACT UP activists had gained access to the top AIDS science researchers and government institutions against which ACT UP had previously protested. At the same time there was a growing sense that the epidemic was increasingly affecting people of color and women. There were subsequently heated conflicts within the organization about who and what ACT UP should be fighting for and about how to deal with a system that was beginning to respond to (only) some of ACT UP's demands. Some angrily argued that those who had gained access were sell-outs and that these (mostly) white gay men were racist and sexist and only concerned about getting drug treatments into their bodies, even as the epidemic exploded in other communities. The treatment activists in turn angrily argued that their critics—perceived to be mostly HIV-negative, white lesbians—were "politically correct" leftists who had gotten off the AIDS track and were trying to build a broad social justice movement on the backs of gay, white, male PWAs. As the internal conflicts became increasingly heated, the feelings of solidarity that had previously suffused ACT UP were decimated. The internal conflicts and shifting feelings of solidarity prompted dramatic splits and departures in a few ACT UP chapters during the years from 1990 through 1992, but perhaps more devastating to the organization was the steady exodus of many individual members who were disheartened by the newly antagonistic atmosphere.

By this time, many in ACT UP had also begun to feel a profound despair as the tide of deaths continued unabated. By 1991, over 100,000 people had died from AIDS-related complications in the United States, and at least two-thirds of them were gay and bisexual men. Despite ACT UP's tremendous victories, it could not stop the deaths of either its own members or anyone else. A study released in 1993 that denied the efficacy of the standard treatment—AZT in combination with other drugs—increased the hopelessness felt by many in ACT UP. The accumulated deaths and dashed hopes took their emotional toll, making it difficult for ACT UP to continue as a viable, vibrant organization. The growing despondency also might help to explain the intensity of the internal conflicts.

Simultaneous with the conflicts and emotional shifts within ACT UP was a decline in lesbian and gay community support for the organization. In some ways prompted by ACT UP's propulsion of queer into the public realm, the late 1980s and early 1990s saw the beginnings of a cultural and political opening toward lesbians and gay men. Many corporations began advertising to gays, Hollywood paid more attention to LGBT themes, and U.S. presidential candidate Bill Clinton vowed to appoint openly LGBT people to his administration and to lift the ban on LGBTs in the military. Once seen as necessary and heroic, ACT UP's angry, confrontational street activism, in-your-face sex radicalism, and queer sensibility were increasingly viewed by more mainstream lesbian and gay individuals, leaders, and institutions as unnecessary, overwrought, irresponsible, and dangerous to the project of access and assimilation. ACT UP, now constructed as a threat to what was hailed as imminent social acceptance, lost much of its community support and was eventually eclipsed by campaigns to lift the ban on LGBTs in the military and to legalize LGBT marriage.

Despite its decline, ACT UP's legacy persists. Groups that grew out of ACT UP, including Housing Works and Treatment Action Group (TAG), continue to do important AIDS work. ACT UP has also been credited with providing inspiration for and helping to shape the emergent global justice movement. As well, ACT UP's confrontational style and sex-positive politics persisted as historical memories that informed the next generation of activists fighting for queer and transgender liberation, even in the face of the larger mainstreaming of the lesbian and gay movement.

## Bibliography

ACTUP/NY Women and AIDS Book Group. *Women, AIDS, and Activism.* Boston: South End Press, 1990.

Black, Kate. *Fighting for Life: Lesbians in ACT UP.* MA thesis, Department of Sociology, University of Kentucky, 1996.

Crimp, Douglas. *Melancholia and Moralism: Essays on AIDS and Queer Politics.* Cambridge, Mass.: MIT Press, 2002.

Crimp, Douglas, with Adam Rolston. *AIDS Demo Graphics.* Seattle, Wash.: Bay Press, 1990.

Edwards, Jeffrey. "AIDS, Race, and the Rise and Decline of a Militant Oppositional Lesbian and Gay Politics in the U.S." *New Political Science* 22 (2000): 485–506.

Epstein, Steven. *Impure Science: AIDS, Activism, and the Politics of Knowledge.* Berkeley: University of California Press, 1996.

Gamson, Josh. "Silence, Death, and the Invisible Enemy: AIDS Activism and Social Movement 'Newness.'" *Social Problems* 36 (1989): 351–367.

Kramer, Larry. *Reports from the Holocaust: The Making of an AIDS Activist.* New York: St. Martin's Press, 1989.

Patten, Mary. "The Thrill Is Gone: An ACT UP Post-Mortem (Confessions of a Former AIDS Activist)." In *The Passionate Camera.* Edited by Deborah Bright. New York: Routledge, 1998.

Patton, Cindy. *Inventing AIDS.* New York: Routledge, 1990.

Shepard, Benjamin, and Ronald Hayduk. *From ACT UP to the WTO: Urban Protest and Community Building in the Era of Globalization.* London: Verso, 2002.

Stockdill, Brett. *Activism against AIDS: At the Intersections of Sexuality, Race, Gender and Class.* Boulder, Colo.: Lynne Rienner Publishers, 2003.

Stoller, Nancy E. *Lessons from the Damned: Queers, Whores, and Junkies Respond to AIDS.* New York: Routledge, 1998.

**Deborah B. Gould**

**See also** AIDS AND PEOPLE WITH AIDS; AIDS SERVICE ORGANIZATIONS; ANTIWAR, PACIFIST, AND PEACE MOVEMENTS; COMMUNITY CENTERS; GAY AND LESBIAN ALLIANCE AGAINST DEFAMATION; HARING, KEITH; HEALTH AND HEALTH CARE LAW AND POLICY; KRAMER, LARRY; QUEER NATION; RUSSO, VITO; SEXUALLY TRANSMITTED DISEASES.

**AIDS Memorial Quilt.** Thousands of individual panels—bearing thousands of memorialized names—are placed on the Mall in Washington, D.C., stretching for blocks from the Capitol. [Paul Margolies]

# AIDS MEMORIAL QUILT— NAMES PROJECT

The AIDS Memorial Quilt, which has been viewed by over fourteen million people since 1987, is the world's best-known memorial honoring the lives of people who have died of AIDS.

The AIDS Quilt emerged in San Francisco in the mid-1980s as a form of both political protest and private grief. In November 1985, in the early years of the AIDS epidemic, political activist Cleve Jones urged participants at a lesbian and gay protest march in San Francisco to carry placards bearing the names of people they knew who had died of AIDS. During the demonstration, protestors posted the placards on the walls of the San Francisco Federal Building; according to Jones, the image reminded him of a patchwork quilt. A little over a year later, in grief over the death of a close friend, Jones sewed a small quilt as a personal memorial.

Soon thereafter, these public and private impulses coalesced in the specific form of the NAMES Project AIDS Memorial Quilt. Jones was already a veteran of San Francisco gay politics: he had worked as an assistant to openly gay City Supervisor Harvey Milk in the 1970s and served as a liaison between the city government and the lesbian and gay community. When the AIDS epidemic struck, Jones wanted to create a memorial that could pro-vide emotional strength and also mobilize political activism. But although Jones's leadership was instrumental in getting the project off the ground, it was the efforts of dozens of volunteers working in a sparsely furnished San Francisco storefront that made the AIDS Memorial Quilt a reality.

The Quilt is a profoundly inclusive memorial. No panel is rejected, so long as it meets the Quilt's basic size specifications—three feet by six feet. Some panels resemble traditional cloth quilts and include only a person's name and birth and death dates, but the Quilt is most memorable for its astonishing diversity. Individuals are memorialized with objects ranging from everyday items such as car keys and favorite albums to family photographs and even cremation ashes. Anyone can make a panel; while most are submitted by friends or family members after a person's death, many are made by strangers working in collective quilting circles or by people with AIDS themselves. By 2003, more than 84,000 names have been memorialized in the Quilt's 44,000 panels. Individual panels are sewn together in blocks of eight that can be attached or detached from each other, allowing portions of the Quilt to be exhibited in different locations at the same time. Public displays begin with an elaborate unfolding ceremony and the reading of names of people memorialized on the Quilt. Local volunteers coordinate the ceremony and offer education and emotional support to viewers.

The Quilt was conceived to assist in mourning, to educate people about AIDS, to humanize an epidemic too often described solely through statistics, and to raise funds for local AIDS organizations in the cities where it is displayed. The Quilt has also served a political function, although activists and scholars have disagreed about that function. The Quilt's first significant public display took place in October 1987, when 1,920 panels were displayed on the Mall in Washington, D.C., as part of the National March on Washington for Lesbian and Gay Rights. Similar displays took place in Washington in 1988, 1989, 1992, and 1996. Spread out between the nation's leading political memorials, the Quilt challenged the exclusion of people with AIDS from the nation's attention. Jones and other leaders of the NAMES Project aimed to place the epidemic within the conservative vocabulary of Reagan-era politics. They sought to show that AIDS was, in Jones's words, "a very American epidemic," in the hopes of prompting a response from the Reagan Administration, which continued to ignore the AIDS crisis. Some have interpreted this as a necessary tactic, arguing that AIDS could not be defeated without support from all Americans. Others—including many people of color with AIDS—have questioned whether efforts to appeal to "mainstream" America would backfire, either by erasing the distinctive aspects of the gay community out of which the NAMES Project grew, or by allowing most Americans to see people with AIDS only as victims.

The Quilt has also had an uneasy relationship with more explicitly political organizations. The NAMES Project does not participate in explicit political organizing, and the organization owes much of its success to its deliberately non-confrontational manner. The Quilt faced strong criticism for this approach from radical activist groups like ACT UP, which considered its emphasis on mourning insufficiently militant. Likewise, although most panels on the Quilt commemorate the lives of gay men, the organization has always acknowledged the epidemic's broad demographics and has sought a constituency that includes all people affected by AIDS. "The NAMES Project is not a gay organization," Jones noted as early as 1988, prompting strong criticism from more outspoken groups like Queer Nation. Quilt defenders, however, have argued that mourning is itself a political act in

the midst of the highly politicized AIDS epidemic, have insisted that it is impossible to view the Quilt without appreciating the special catastrophe experienced by gay men, and have suggested that viewing the Quilt could mobilize further political action.

Since the mid-1990s, though the AIDS epidemic continues to spiral out of control around the world, many people with AIDS in the United States have achieved breakthroughs in recognition and treatment. As a result, the AIDS Quilt operates in an environment different from the one in which it was conceived and begun. Political opposition to AIDS has lessened; conservative politician Newt Gingrich and even Miss America Erika Harold have appeared at Quilt displays, raising doubts about the continued political edge that the Quilt once claimed. NAMES Project founder Cleve Jones stepped down from his position at the helm of the organization in 1997. Like many other U.S. AIDS organizations, the NAMES Project has suffered substantial declines in donations at the same time that it must confront a global crisis. The organization continues to include new panels into the Quilt and is dedicated to incorporating worldwide traditions of quilting to face an ongoing epidemic.

### Bibliography

Brown, Joe, ed. *A Promise to Remember: The NAMES Project Book of Letters.* New York: Avon Books, 1992.

Capozzola, Christopher. "A Very American Epidemic: Memory Politics and Identity Politics in the AIDS Memorial Quilt, 1985–1993." *Radical History Review* no. 82 (Winter 2002): 91–109.

Jones, Cleve, with Jeff Dawson. *Stitching a Revolution: The Making of an Activist.* San Francisco: HarperSanFrancisco, 2000.

NAMES Project Website. "The AIDS Memorial Quilt." Available from http://www.aidsquilt.org

Ruskin, Cindy. *The Quilt: Stories from the NAMES Project.* New York: Pocket Books, 1988.

Sturken, Marita. *Tangled Memories: The Vietnam War, the AIDS Epidemic, and the Politics of Remembering.* Berkeley: University of California Press, 1997.

**Christopher Capozzola**

*See also* AIDS AND PEOPLE WITH AIDS; AIDS COALITION TO UNLEASH POWER (ACT UP); AIDS SERVICE ORGANIZATIONS; MARCHES ON WASHINGTON; MILK, HARVEY; QUEER NATION.

# AIDS SERVICE ORGANIZATIONS

AIDS service organizations (ASOs) emerged in the early 1980s to deal with the effects of AIDS on the LGBT community. Concerned LGBT people began a process of creating their own institutions to confront the AIDS crisis. In almost every case, these first ASOs shared a similar profile, initially employing a large number of gay white men who had professional experience and using volunteers, both women and men, to supplement paid staff. The ASOs sought funding from private sources to supplement scant resources provided by the federal and state governments. With small staffs and some initial funding, most ASOs developed "buddy" systems that paired volunteers with clients to help them cope with the effects of AIDS; established AIDS hotlines staffed by volunteers; and implemented education campaigns to try to prevent the spread of the disease. Most ASOs viewed AIDS as the primary, and in some cases the only, problem that needed to be addressed in the lives of people with AIDS. Although these services were invaluable to one segment of the LGBT community, they did not necessarily address the needs of everyone, particularly women and people of color, for whom AIDS was only one of many crises.

### New York City and the Gay Men's Health Crisis

In January 1982 a group of men met at playwright Larry Kramer's apartment with the intention of creating an organization to deal with the impact of AIDS on gay men. They named the organization the Gay Men's Health Crisis (GMHC). Among the attendees at that first meeting were Lawrence Mass, the medical reporter for the LGB biweekly newspaper the *New York Native*, writers Edmund White and Nathan Fain, as well as Paul Popham, the man who would become the first leader of GMHC even though he was not at the time out as a gay man.

GMHC developed programs to address both the physical and psychological needs of people with AIDS, including the first "buddy" system that furnished homebound people with volunteer attendants who could help with daily life tasks as well as navigate the social service system. To finance this service and support early scientific efforts to find a cure, GMHC raised funds through private donations. As early as 1983, GMHC held events in New York's nightclubs and even at Madison Square Garden to collect money from its mostly gay supporters.

The overall effectiveness of GMHC has been a topic of debate among scholars of AIDS. While many have argued that GMHC created both a much needed safety net for people with AIDS and a new social environment for many in the gay community, others have focused on GMHC's failure to address the experiences of New York City's gay people of color and economically disenfranchised gays. Some scholars have concluded that GMHC's early impulse to professionalize its staff and rely on private funding prevented the organization from embracing a more expansive vision of how to cope with the AIDS epidemic.

### The San Francisco Model: The San Francisco AIDS Foundation and the Shanti Project

Gay people in San Francisco, California, were quick to form ASOs as well, but unlike GMHC, Bay Area ASOs did so within a more extensive municipal support system. Led by an organized gay political bloc that had effectively lobbied the city to provide resources to the gay community, early ASOs such as the Kaposi's Sarcoma Research and Education Foundation, established in 1982, offered a wide range of services to people with AIDS. Renamed the San Francisco AIDS Foundation (SFAF) in 1983, the group focused on creating definitive information and awareness campaigns to teach the public how AIDS spread and how people, particularly men who had sex with men, could protect themselves. SFAF used marketing techniques borrowed from the world of advertising and public relations and built alliances with gay business owners in San Francisco to help deliver their message.

At the same time as SFAF was providing AIDS services, the Shanti Project encouraged the formation of AIDS support groups and created the first housing and material support program in the nation for people with AIDS. Helen Schietinger, a nurse who had worked closely with people with AIDS in a San Francisco clinic, served as the program's first director.

### Community-Based Organizations, Women, and Communities of Color

By 1983 a diverse array of community-based organizations (CBOs) emerged in San Francisco and other major cities to address some of the ASOs' inadequacies in dealing with the needs of women and people of color. Although the CBOs relied on volunteer labor as did most ASOs, they differed in their focus and their politics, recognizing the needs of underserved groups and advocating for change in the ASOs and with the government. CBO members firmly believed that only political solutions could fully confront the problems created by the AIDS epidemic.

In 1983 two advocacy groups, the Women's AIDS Network (WAN) and the Third World AIDS Advisory Task Force (TWAATF), emerged to deal with underrepresented communities. WAN, a national network that began by providing women employed by ASOs with a space to discuss their needs as providers, soon found itself advocating for women with AIDS. In a similar vein, TWAATF's membership, which was mostly activists of

**Riding to Fight AIDS.**
Bicyclists raising money for HIV and AIDS service organizations in North Carolina and Washington, D.C., depart from Raleigh, North Carolina, on 21 June 2001, for the 330-mile ride to the nation's capital. [AP Photo/Karen Tam]

color, many of whom were gay men who worked in the city's growing AIDS service institutions, prided itself on its broad political interpretation of the AIDS crisis. Its members not only actively participated in prevention strategies designed specifically to address the needs of people of color, they also called for universal health care and the need to protect the rights of immigrants with AIDS.

As the decade wore on, more lesbians and gay men of color lobbied for inclusion in the provision of AIDS services. Gil Gerard, executive director of the National Coalition of Black Lesbians and Gays (NCBLG), was at the forefront of this fight, as was Reggie Williams of Black and White Men Together (BWMT). In 1988 the Centers for Disease Control (CDC) awarded a contract to the AIDS Taskforce of BWMT San Francisco to create culturally sensitive AIDS prevention materials for gay men of color. Resource disparities continued to affect how services reached people of color, however. In 1988, when over half of New York City's AIDS cases were people of color, GMHC had a budget of $10 million and a staff of seventy-five, while the Minority AIDS Taskforce had a budget of $1 million and a staff of eight.

### ASOs outside New York and San Francisco

Major ASOs also emerged in other U.S. cities. In 1982 the AIDS Foundation Houston opened with virtually no funding from the government, supported almost exclusively by private donations and a foundation. The same year the AIDS Project Los Angeles (APLA) began as a hot-line located in the gay and lesbian community center. The Whitman-Walker Clinic, a gay health clinic in Washington, D.C., created its first AIDS program in September 1983, providing services for the District's residents, a majority of whom came from communities of color. A few years later, in 1985, the AIDS Foundation of Chicago began, quickly becoming the largest agency of its kind in the Midwest.

### AIDS Service as Big Business

In 1985 the National AIDS Network (NAN) formed with the intention of helping ASOs manage resources and share information. This impulse to create a coordinated and more professional effort to fight AIDS marks what some authors have called the emergence of an AIDS industry, with the simultaneous proliferation of AIDS service professionals who were less likely to imagine themselves as progressive activists struggling against the powers that be.

In 1990 the passage of the Ryan White Emergency Care Act (CARE Act), a federally funded AIDS initiative, completed what many saw as the transition from AIDS service as activism to AIDS service as business. Named for Ryan White, the teenage hemophiliac with AIDS who faced fierce discrimination in his hometown of Kokomo, Indiana, the CARE Act dramatically increased AIDS funding to state governments and ASOs. By the end of the first five-year funding cycle, New York and California had received more than half a billion dollars. The CARE Act also signaled attempts to "degay" the AIDS epidemic.

## Activist ASOs

Activism continued to define ASOs' work in the late 1980s, nonetheless. In June 1990 Housing Works, an ASO dedicated to providing housing and treatment for intravenous drug users, was established in New York City. Housing Works, an outgrowth of the Housing Committee of ACT UP/NY, quickly became the largest ASO in the nation controlled by people of color. Housing Works prided itself on providing services to people with AIDS whom no one else would serve, including active intravenous drug users and members of the transgender community.

Although women had played an integral part in AIDS service work from the beginning, in 1992 lesbians created the Lesbian AIDS Project (LAP) at GMHC. Led first by activist Amber Hollibaugh, LAP addressed the unique needs of lesbians with AIDS, paying attention to how lesbians of color and working-class lesbians experienced the epidemic.

The advent of protease inhibitor treatments in 1996 clearly changed the way many people with AIDS lived their lives and had major consequences for how ASOs functioned in the United States. By the late 1990s most Americans thought of AIDS as a chronic disease, making it difficult for ASOs to maintain public interest in their work as well as their funding. These shifts forced service providers to reevaluate the place of AIDS care in both the LGBT community and U.S. society. ASOs subsequently mainstreamed their work on and against the disease into a larger movement interested in the health of all Americans.

### Bibliography

Andriote, John-Manuel. *Victory Deferred: How AIDS Changed Gay Life in* America. Chicago: University of Chicago Press, 1999.

Cohen, Cathy J. *The Boundaries of Blackness: AIDS and the Breakdown of Black Politics.* Chicago: University of Chicago Press, 1999.

Hammonds, Evelynn. "Seeing AIDS: Race, Gender, and Representation." In *The Gender Politics of HIV/AIDS in Women: Perspectives on the Pandemic in the United States.* Edited by Nancy Goldstein and Jennifer L. Manlowe. New York: New York University, 1997, pp. 113–126.

Kayal, Philip M. *Bearing Witness: Gay Men's Health Crisis and the Politics of AIDS.* Boulder, Colo.: Westview Press, 1993.

Patton, Cindy. *Fatal Advice: How Safe-Sex Education Went Wrong.* Durham, N.C.: Duke University Press, 1996.

Quimby, Ernest, and Samuel Friedman. "Dynamics of Black Mobilization against AIDS in New York City." *Social Problems* 36, no. 4 (1989): 403–415.

Rofes, Eric E. *Reviving the Tribe: Regenerating Gay Men's Sexuality and Culture in the Ongoing Epidemic.* New York: Haworth Press, 1996.

**Jennifer Brier**

See also AIDS AND PEOPLE WITH AIDS; AIDS COALITION TO UNLEASH POWER (ACT UP); AIDS MEMORIAL QUILT—NAMES PROJECT; BLACK AND WHITE MEN TOGETHER (BWMT); HEALTH AND HEALTH CARE LAW AND POLICY; HEALTH, HEALTH CARE, AND HEALTH CARE CLINICS; KRAMER, LARRY; NATIVE AMERICAN LGBTQ ORGANIZATIONS AND PUBLICATIONS; REYES, RODRIGO; WHITE, EDMUND.

## AILEY, Alvin (b. 5 January 1931; d. 1 December 1989), dancer and choreographer.

Born into abject poverty in Rogers, Texas, Alvin Ailey was raised by his mother after his parents separated when he was two. He suffered a difficult, transient childhood in central Texas, until he and his mother moved to Los Angeles in 1942. By his own account, he arrived in California shy, lonely, and sensitive; the young African American man soon found solace in the fantasy worlds of theater and the movies. He also became aware of his own homosexuality during this period, and like many young gay men eager to corral the sensual impulses of the body, he turned to the study of dance. He pursued tap dancing and 1940s-style "primitive dance," but settled on "modern dance" when a high-school friend introduced him to Lester Horton's flamboyantly theatrical Hollywood studio in 1949.

Horton, an openly gay white man from Indianapolis, Indiana, had created a school and company of gay, lesbian, and straight dancers from varied ethnic backgrounds who performed his experimental choreography at concerts. Ailey responded to this vision of sexual and racial liberation, and developed a weighted and sensual performance style that suited his athletic body. He took college courses at the University of California at Los Angeles in 1949, Los Angeles City College in 1950 through 1951, and San Francisco State College in 1952, but by 1954 became a professional dancer in performances on television (*The Red Skelton Show*) and film (*Carmen Jones*).

Ailey moved to New York in December 1954 to partner Carmen de Lavallade in the Broadway production of Truman Capote's *House of Flowers*. Eager to expand professional dance opportunities for African Americans, he founded the Alvin Ailey American Dance Theater in 1958. The group began as a small repertory company devoted to both modern dance classics and new works

**Alvin Ailey American Dance Theater.** Members of the company, which the acclaimed African American dancer and choreographer founded three decades before his death of AIDS in 1989, appear onstage.

created by Ailey and other young artists. Well-received at its first performances, the company quickly became the foremost interpreter of African American experience in dance. Among Ailey's early successes, *Blues Suite* (1958), set in and around a backwoods barrelhouse, depicts the desperation and joys of life on the edge of poverty in the South. Highly theatrical and immediately accessible, the work contains elements of early-twentieth-century social dance, Horton dance technique, Jack Cole–inspired jazz dance, and ballet partnering. Ailey's *Revelations* (1960) soon became the company's signature ballet and a defining document of American concert dance. This unequivocal masterpiece depicts a broad range of black worship, including a powerful group prayer ("I've Been Buked"), a duet of trust and support between a supplicant and his guardian angel ("Fix Me, Jesus"), a baptismal ceremony in which the entire company is costumed in white ("Wade in the Water"), and a final gospel-inspired celebration ("Rocka My Soul in the Bosom of Abraham"). By 1996 *Revelations* had been seen by more than 15 million people worldwide.

Affable but closeted, Ailey gave numerous interviews throughout his career, but remained decidedly private about his personal life. He described himself as "a bachelor and a loner" to writer John Gruen and did not enjoy any sustained, long-term relationships as an adult. His choreography consistently depicted a kind of glamorous masculinity for gay audiences, as with the workingmen of *Blues Suite,* and the physically potent but chaste religious archetypes of *Revelations* and *Hermit Songs* (1961), the latter set to Leontyne Price's popular recording of Samuel Barber's song cycle. The extravagant, mod costumes and settings of Ailey's later works, including *Quintet* (1968), *Flowers* (1971), *The Mooche* (1974), and *Caverna Magica* (1986), presented a pageantry of campy excess enjoyed by gay audiences worldwide. Ailey also acknowledged homosexuality in more abstract works he choreographed for the American Ballet Theater (*The River,* 1970) and his own company (*Streams,* 1970). These dances depict an erotic intimacy between men and women in same-sex partnering framed by opposite-sex encounters.

Ailey suffered a nervous breakdown in 1980, likely provoked by pressures surrounding the administration of his large company and its affiliated school, as well as by his personal discomfort at becoming an icon for African

American artists. He recovered sufficiently to choreograph a dozen more works and receive numerous awards, including honorary doctorates in fine arts from Princeton University, Bard College, Adelphi University, and Cedar Crest College; a United Nations Peace Medal; and the Springarn Medal from the National Association for the Advancement of Colored People. In 1988 he was honored by President Ronald Reagan for a lifetime of achievement in the arts at the Kennedy Center for the Performing Arts, Washington, D.C. Ailey contracted HIV in the 1980s and died of AIDS in New York City. His company survives under the strong leadership of former principal dancer Judith Jamison and remains among the most celebrated of modern dance companies.

## Bibliography

Ailey, Alvin, with A. Peter Bailey. *Revelations: The Autobiography of Alvin Ailey.* New York: Birch Lane, 1995.

De Frantz, Thomas F. *Dancing Revelations: Alvin Ailey's Embodiment of African American Culture.* New York: Oxford University Press, 2003.

Dunning, Jennifer. *Alvin Ailey: A Life in Dance.* Reading, Mass.: Addison-Wesley, 1996.

Gruen, John. "Interview with Alvin Ailey." Interview transcript. New York: New York Public Library, 1972.

**Thomas F. DeFrantz**

*See also* DANCE.

**Edward Albee.** This American playwright's quasi-autobiographical works—most notably *Who's Afraid of Virginia Woolf* (1962)—repeatedly pushed the boundaries of modern theater since the late 1950s. [Marc Geller]

# ALBEE, Edward (b. 12 March 1928), playwright.

Born Edward Harvey but renamed Edward Franklin Albee III by his adoptive parents, the playwright was raised in Westchester County, New York. His father was the heir to the fortune of the Keith-Albee vaudeville circuit and chain of theaters. Albee never got along with his adoptive parents, preferring the company of his maternal grandmother who became a character in his early one-act plays, *The Sandbox* and *The American Dream.* After failing out of a number of private schools, Albee severed communication with his adoptive parents (he later reconciled with his mother, though she vindictively left him a minimal inheritance). His troubled relationship with his parents, particularly his mother, is central to his quasi-autobiographical works, which depict unloved sons who have in some way been purchased (*The American Dream*), died young (*A Delicate Balance*), or never actually existed at all (*Who's Afraid of Virginia Woolf*), and monstrous mothers and ineffectual fathers (*Who's Afraid of Virginia Woolf, A Delicate Balance, Three Tall Women*).

In his early twenties, Albee moved to New York City, worked at a series of odd jobs, developed friendships in New York's artistic and gay circles, and began a turbulent relationship with the composer William Flanagan. He had settled on a career as a writer, but had no particular focus. However, shortly before his thirtieth birthday, he wrote a one-act play, *The Zoo Story* (1958), that would launch his career as one of America's leading playwrights. When no one in New York would produce the short play, the Schiller Theatre in Berlin decided to perform it in German on a double bill with Samuel Beckett's *Krapp's Last Tape.* Finally the same double bill opened Off Broadway in 1960.

*The Zoo Story* depicts the Central Park confrontation of Peter, an uptight businessman who leads a conventional domestic life with his wife and daughters, and Jerry, whose chaotic, despairing existence is a sharp contrast. Jerry tells Peter a series of sagas of nonconnection, then goads Peter into killing him, thus radically changing Peter's well-ordered life. It is easy to read *The Zoo Story* as a crypto-homosexual pickup, though Albee, characteristically, does not find much joy in any human connection. In Albee's work, homosexual love is adolescent romance. Maturity is heterosexual promiscuity combined with fear of commitment or an unhappy, castrating marriage. Albee's depiction of sexuality does not change much over his career. In the 1983 one-act play *Finding the Sun*, one of the few plays he has written with gay characters, two men who had been lovers for years marry women to find the stability and social respectability they cannot attain in their own relationship. But the men can neither fully love their wives nor fully commit to each other.

In the early 1960s, Albee was hailed as the best and brightest of the younger generation of playwrights. A series of his one-acts (*The Zoo Story, The American Dream, The Death of Bessie Smith, The Sandbox*) were successfully produced Off Broadway by the team of Richard Barr and Clinton Wilder, who remained Albee's impresarios during his first productive period. Albee was the first major American playwright since Eugene O'Neill to emerge from the more adventurous Off Broadway scene. His eagerly awaited Broadway debut, with *Who's Afraid of Virginia Woolf* (1962)—a play that reminds one of O'Neill in its length (over three hours) and subject matter (illusions and a disastrous marriage), but not in its wicked sense of humor and brittle, witty dialogue—was a sensation. This long, vicious, theatrically vital duel between a college professor and his flamboyant wife elaborated themes Albee had introduced in his early, short work: the impossibility of a loving relationship and the necessity to destroy the illusions that keep one from facing the harsh truth of the meaninglessness of human existence. Some critics and directors, notably Sweden's Ingmar Bergman, saw the battling George and Martha as a crypto-gay couple and cast two men in the roles. Albee responded that if he had wanted to write a play about two men, he would have done so, but he also later admitted that some of the vituperation was inspired by arguments between him and Flanagan. There is a camp quality to the dialog that has made the play, and the bleak, miscast, humorless film made from it in 1968, an important part of pre-Stonewall gay culture.

For the next few years, Albee alternated new full-length plays with unsuccessful adaptations of prose fiction (Carson McCullers's *The Ballad of the Sad Café* [1963], James Purdy's *Malcolm* [1966], and most disastrously, Vladimir Nabokov's *Lolita* [1981]). The new plays met with varying degrees of success. Critics and audiences found *Tiny Alice* (1964) both too metaphysical and puzzling, but *A Delicate Balance* (1966) was well received, winning Albee his first Pulitzer Prize, and was successfully

revived in London and on Broadway in 1997. During the 1960s Albee, along with William Inge and Tennessee Williams, was the subject of a number of vicious homophobic attacks from the press, particularly the *New York Times*, which feared that American theater was being sullied by homosexual influences.

By the late 1960s, Albee's career seemed to be over. New plays like *The Lady from Dubuque* (1978) and *The Man Who Had Three Arms* (1982) joined the pantheon of legendary Broadway disasters. Albee spent much of his time teaching, eventually establishing a long-term relationship with the University of Houston in 1984. He never stopped writing, honing his skills on a series of short plays and finally writing the full-length *Three Tall Women* (1992), for which he received his second Pulitzer. The play is a brilliant portrait of his mother, who focuses her wrath on a gay son who sits silently by her bedside during much of the second act. Characteristically, *Three Tall Women* is firmly based in autobiography, but is stylistically experimental.

Albee's detractors criticize the chilly, intellectual quality of his work. Of all the major American playwrights, he is the one who can be most accurately labeled a modernist. He began his career as a playwright when the absurdists and continental writers like Jean Genet were being produced successfully Off Broadway. At his best, he combined the experimentation of modern British and continental playwrights with an American fascination with the family romance. Since *Three Tall Women*, Albee has completed two major full-length plays, *The Play about the Baby*, produced in London and Off Broadway in 2001, and *The Goat, or Who Is Sylvia?*, which won a Tony Award for Best Play in 2002.

**Bibliography**

Clum, John M. *Still Acting Gay: Male Homosexuality in Modern Drama*. New York: St. Martins, 2000.

Gussow, Mel. *Edward Albee: A Singular Journey*. New York: Simon and Schuster, 1999.

McCarthy, Gerry. *Edward Albee*. London: Macmillan, 1987.

Rutenberg, Michael E. *Edward Albee: Playwright in Protest*. New York: Avon, 1970.

**John M. Clum**

*See also* LITERATURE.

# ALCOHOL AND DRUGS

Alcohol and drug use has a long history in the United States. Use in LGBT communities has paralleled general

U.S. history in some ways and diverged from it in others. In both straight and LGBT communities, alcohol and other drugs are traditionally used as social lubricants, are valued as vehicles for relaxation and escape, and are offered at parties, celebrations, and special occasions. In both straight and LGBT communities, however, overuse often becomes addiction and subsequently destroys lives, contributes to domestic strife and violence, and damages communities.

LGBT communities have historically had fewer legitimate social outlets than has the heterosexual world. Especially in the early days of LGBT community development, bars often served as de facto community centers, a role more often filled in straight society by churches and civic organizations. This was particularly true in the era before the Stonewall Riots of 1969, but even in the early twenty-first century, many young LGBT people leave smaller communities for big cities and are introduced to LGBT life through bar culture. It is no coincidence that the modern LGBT movement began at a bar, the Stonewall Inn, in New York City.

### Early History
In the mid-nineteenth century, LGBT cultures began to develop in various seaport cities. Gay networks often were centered in saloons, boarding houses, and other all-male social spaces. San Francisco, which later became known internationally as a gay mecca, was 92 percent male during the gold rush and was known as "Sodom by the Sea." Alcohol abuse was rampant, and use of opiates and cocaine was common. By the late nineteenth century, most large U.S. cities had significant LGBT cultures. Bars were the central institutions of these cultures, and alcohol use was an important part of LGBT social life.

Also in the late nineteenth and early twentieth centuries, scientific and social discourses linked alcoholism and drug abuse to homosexuality. These "social ills" were all seen as the products of character flaws and as evidence of moral degeneracy, and each was seen as contributing to or causing the others. There was even a correlation made between addiction in men and femininity, which may have influenced some GBT men to use alcohol and drugs as part of a rejection of conventional heterosexual masculinity. While these views were simplistic and moralistic, the pressures of belonging to a despised minority may have led many LGBT people to seek refuge in alcohol and drugs.

The ratification of an alcohol prohibition amendment to the U.S. Constitution in 1919, and its eventual repeal in 1933, affected LGBT communities as profoundly as (or perhaps more profoundly than) they affected their heterosexual counterparts. As in straight society, Prohibition did nothing to decrease alcohol consumption in LGBT communities, but only drove it underground. In fact, some argue that LGBT bars were safer during Prohibition, since then all bars were subject, theoretically at least, to legal repression, and violating alcohol laws became popular. In many locations, however, the years after repeal witnessed an explosion in the number and variety of LGBT bars. For example, in San Francisco, the Sailor Boy Tavern, which opened in 1938 on the Embarcadero, grew out of the waterfront cruising culture. Mona's, which also opened in the years after repeal, was San Francisco's first lesbian bar.

### The Post–World War II Era
During and after World War II, alcohol consumption continued to be an important part of LGBT social life. In the 1940s, 1950s, and 1960s, for example, lesbian femme/butch culture was centered in working-class bars, and heavy drinking was common. LGBT bar culture had many positive aspects, but unfortunately many who went to the bars to find community developed serious drinking problems. Nevertheless, defense of LGBT bars became part of the LGBT political agenda in the 1950s and 1960s. In 1961, for example, the San Francisco Tavern Guild was formed by owners of LGBT bars in response to police raids and demands for protection payments.

The 1950s also witnessed the rise of the counterculture Beats, who pointedly rejected the conventions of polite society, embracing instead what they saw as the underground values of black America and jazz culture. This included drug and alcohol use, and red wine and marijuana were the substances of choice for the Beats. Many of the leading Beats, including the poet Allen Ginsberg, were gay. William S. Burroughs, another well-known gay Beat, was a lifelong drug user and heroin addict, and many of his books, from *Junky* to *Naked Lunch*, address and arguably glorify addiction.

In the late 1960s, the social revolution accelerated and counterculture activities became more popular. The drug culture of the 1960s and 1970s developed uniquely in different parts of the country, but everywhere included LGBT people. In New York City, an artistic LGBT subculture developed around Andy Warhol's Factory and influenced other LGBT communities across the United States. In these environments, cocaine, speed, and heroin were the drugs of choice. The voyeuristic Warhol trained his camera on junkies as they shot up, and followed them through their eventual decline.

The West Coast had a different aesthetic than New York and favored different drugs, but it also proved influential nationally. The drug culture of San Francisco in the 1960s and 1970s included a substantial LGBT hippie component. As San Francisco's North Beach became overrun by "squares," the Beats moved to Haight-Ashbury. Influenced by figures such as Ginsberg and Radical Faeries leader Harry Hay, gay hippies brought a unique flavor to their creative endeavors. In San Francisco, the Cockettes and the Angels of Light used prodigious quantities of psychedelic drugs and staged spectacularly epic drag extravaganzas. As Haight-Ashbury became a magnet for hard drug users and became increasingly dangerous, gay hippies went over the hill to the neighborhood that was then called Eureka Valley but soon became known as the Castro.

## Later Developments

In the 1970s and 1980s, a movement to address growing addiction issues in LGBT communities began to develop. LGBT bars, baths, clubs, and adult bookstores were filled with addicts and alcoholics. In the early days of Alcoholics Anonymous (AA), which was founded in 1935, attempts had been made to start affinity groups for LGBT alcoholics, but they proved premature and were unsuccessful. By the early 1980s, however, the time had come, and the LGBT "recovery" movement was in full operation. Many LGBT addicts and alcoholics found that the honesty necessary for successful recovery was more supported in LGBT groups. In general meetings, LGBT alcoholics and addicts often encountered homophobia and transphobia. Additionally, since newly sober people wanted to avoid the bars, the LGBT AA and Narcotics Anonymous groups became viable alternative social networks. While many people have been helped by LGBT alcohol and drug treatment programs, critics point out that when the addiction model is applied to sex itself (the approach taken by various programs attempting to help so-called sex addicts), serious questions must be raised.

*Drugs and unprotected sex.* In the early 1980s, at the beginning of the AIDS crisis, questions about disease transmission proliferated. Some theories pointed toward drug use. Eventually, the HIV virus was identified. Most medical professionals regard HIV as the direct cause of AIDS, but many also consider other factors to be contributory, and drug use was among these. Drugs such as amyl nitrate or "poppers," used to enhance sex, also suppress the immune system and are thought to make the body more susceptible to infection. Although education about poppers as a cofactor in transmission has been available since the early days of AIDS, they have continued to be

popular. Men who had sex with men and who also used intravenous drugs were the highest risk group for HIV infection in the United States. The agencies and organizations that emerged to address the growing AIDS crisis sometimes took this into account, and many established needle exchange programs that have continued to be a controversial component of prevention programs. Various efforts have also been made to educate LGBT people about how alcohol and drug use can affect decision-making about safer sex.

Another controversial component of AIDS activism is the medical marijuana movement. There is abundant evidence that marijuana eases the nausea and discomfort associated with both the symptoms of AIDS and the side effects of drugs used to treat it. In 1996, Proposition 215, the Compassionate Use Act, made medical use of marijuana legal in the state of California. The legislation continues to be challenged by the federal government in actions that attack not only the legitimacy of the particular law but also the larger issue of states' rights.

Methamphetamine, also called speed or crystal, has long been a popular and dangerous drug in LGBT communities. It induces euphoria and feelings of invulnerability, and increases sexual desire while simultaneously decreasing sexual function. Since it also lowers inhibitions and can induce psychosis, gay men who use it can be more likely to have unprotected sex, and its use is therefore considered a risk factor for HIV infection.

*"Club drugs."* In the 1990s, large "circuit" parties that moved from city to city became popular among gay men. On the circuit, many partygoers danced all night, used "club drugs," and often mixed several different kinds of drugs. The interactions of "club drugs" such as MDMA or "ecstasy," ketamine or "special K," and GBH with alcohol—and with each other—can have unpredictable results. A study by the federal Substance Abuse and Mental Health Services Administration reported that more than 70 percent of drug-related emergency room visits were the result of the combined use of drugs and alcohol.

The nonprofit organization DanceSafe is part of what has come to be called the harm reduction movement. Recognizing that abstinence is not always a viable choice, DanceSafe promotes health and safety within the rave and dance communities by testing drug samples for adulteration and providing information on how recreational drug users can reduce the risk of harm.

*A continuing problem.* Drug and alcohol use is higher among LGBT people than it is in the general population. This is especially true among young people. High school students who identify themselves as gay or lesbian have a higher incidence of substance use than their peers. Some observers think that internalized homophobia may contribute to alcohol and drug use and can also be an obstacle to recovery. Others blame social stigma and discrimination. Whatever the reasons, the results can be devastating. Depression has been linked to chemical dependency. Homeless LGBT youth often turn to prostitution to make a living and frequently trade sex for drugs. Drugs can ease the pain and loneliness of these throwaway youth, and numbness can seem to be a solution, though it is invariably temporary.

Alcohol and drug abuse is a huge and continuing problem in LGBT communities. LGBT twelve-step recovery groups continue to proliferate and to help many people in overcoming addictions. The spiritual emphasis of these programs is not for every LGBT person, however. Other programs emphasize psychotherapeutic and other models of treatment. Dual diagnosis recovery has also gained in popularity. This model of treatment acknowledges that sometimes addicts self-medicate undiagnosed mental illnesses such as bipolar disorder and clinical depression, and strives to address all of the patient's issues as part of a complete program of recovery.

## Bibliography

Brooks, Adrian. "A Tale of Two Subcultures." *Harvard Gay and Lesbian Review* 6, no. 2 (spring 1999): 30–33.

Bull, Sheana-Salyers, Patrick Piper, and Cornelius Rietmeijer. "Men Who Have Sex with Men and Also Inject Drugs." *Journal of Homosexuality* 42, no. 3 (2002): 31–51.

Higgs, David. *Queer Sites: Gay Urban History since 1600.* London: Routledge, 1999.

Keire, Mara L. "Dope Fiends and Degenerates: The Gendering of Addiction in the Early Twentieth Century." *Journal of Social History* 31, no. 4 (summer 1998): 809–822.

Kus, Robert J., ed. *Addiction and Recovery in Gay and Lesbian Persons.* New York: Haworth Press, 1995.

Kus, Robert J., and Mark A. Latcovich. "Special Interest Groups in Alcoholics Anonymous: A Focus on Gay Men's Groups." *Journal of Lesbian and Gay Social Services* 2, no. 1 (1995): 67–82.

Orenstein, Alan. "Substance Use among Gay and Lesbian Adolescents." *Journal of Homosexuality* 41, no. 2 (2001): 1–15.

Quittner, Jeremy. "All Mixed Up: Viagra, Ecstasy, Crystal, Ketamine, and Poppers Each Has Its Own Dangerous Effects. But Taken Together, They Create Drug Combinations That Can Kill." *Advocate* 838 (May 2001).

Weinberg, Thomas S. *Gay Men, Drinking and Alcoholism.* Carbondale: Southern Illinois University Press, 1994.

**Jordy Jones**

*See also* AIDS AND PEOPLE WITH AIDS; BARS, CLUBS, AND RESTAURANTS; BURROUGHS, WILLIAM S.; GINSBERG, ALLEN; HOUSE PARTIES; LIQUOR CONTROL LAW AND POLICY; PSYCHOTHERAPY, COUNSELLING, AND RECOVERY PROGRAMS; PUBLIC FESTIVALS, PARTIES, AND HOLIDAYS; RIGHTS OF ASSOCIATION AND ASSEMBLY; WARHOL, ANDY.

## ALGER, Horatio (b. 13 January 1832; d. 18 July 1899), clergyman, author, and reformer.

Horatio Alger Jr. was born in Chelsea (now Revere), Massachusetts, the son of the town's Unitarian minister and Olive Fenno Alger, daughter of a rich merchant and landowner. He graduated from Harvard in 1852 and spent the next seven years as an editor, writer, and educator before graduating from Harvard Divinity School in 1860. After spending a year in Europe, he repeatedly tried to enlist in the Union Army, but as a 5′2″, 120-pound asthmatic, he was deemed unfit. In 1864, he became minister of the First Unitarian Church of Brewster, Massachusetts.

Alger was dismissed from his post in 1866 when he was charged with engaging in sexual intimacy with a thirteen- and a fifteen-year-old boy. His punishment was forced resignation and the requirement that he leave town. He then wrote a poem, "Friar Anselmo," that described a medieval cleric who had committed an unnamed sin but expiated it through good works for the rest of his life. Alger seems to have adopted Friar Anselmo for his model, sublimating his desire for boys into writing and charity work. He moved to New York City, where the Reverend Charles Loring Brace had founded the Children's Aid Society, which was dedicated to bettering the lot of thousands of children who roamed the streets of the city. Alger threw himself into this work, raising funds for institutions such as the Five Points Mission, the YMCA, and the Newsboys' Lodging House, and arranging to place children in good homes. Joseph Seligman, a wealthy New York philanthropist, and other prominent citizens, including the father of future Supreme Court Justice Benjamin Cardozo, hired Alger to tutor their children. In his fifties and sixties, Alger brought three boys into his home and used their lives as models for novels. He seems to have successfully exorcised his sexual demons, as no hint of impropriety attached itself to him ever again.

Alger's most notable response to the plight of street children, however, was to write over one hundred novels. The most famous, *Ragged Dick; or, Street Life in New York* (1867), set the pattern for all the others. A penniless youth moves to the city to earn his fortune, only to con-

***From Farm to Fortune.*** The cover of one of Horatio Alger Jr.'s late-nineteenth-century novels of moral uplift and upward mobility. [Library of Congress]

In later years, Alger enlisted the help of Edward Stratemeyer to finish his final novels. Stratemeyer in turn created the Nancy Drew and Hardy Boys series, where young detectives preserve the moral order through intelligence and diligence. Serious writers, on the other hand, have criticized the Alger model as offering false hope. In Theodore Dreiser's *The Financier,* Frank Algernon Cooper rises through corruption, as does F. Scott Fitzgerald's *The Great Gatsby.* In Nathaniel West's *A Cool Million,* an Alger hero is torn to pieces. The character Raoul Duke in Hunter S. Thompson's *Fear and Loathing in Las Vegas* considers himself a "monster reincarnation" of Alger. Lawrence Sanders wrote two parodies for *Playboy* (April and December, 1972), whose main character, Alcock, replaces Alger in a sexual farce. In *Manchild in the Promised Land,* however, African American author Claude Brown, however, invoked Horatio Alger to show that success was still possible in mid–twentieth-century Harlem.

Alger's homosexuality was largely ignored until Gary Scharnhorst and Jack Bales published *The Lost Life of Horatio Alger, Jr.,* in 1985. Until then, even scholars relied on 1928 Herbert Mayes' *Alger: A Biography without a Hero.* Mayes fabricated an Alger diary and episodes of boozing and womanizing; in 1976, Mayes cheerfully confessed to his hoax. We can now judge Alger sympathetically as a man who, upon recognizing his attraction to adolescent boys, channeled his impulses into literature and social reform.

## Bibliography

Moon, Michael. "The Gentle Boy from the Dangerous Classes": Pederasty, Domesticity, and Capitalism in Horatio Alger." *Representations* 19 (1987): 88–110.

Nackenoff, Carol. *The Fictional Republic: Horatio Alger and American Political Discourse.* New York: Oxford University Press, 1984.

Scharnhorst, Gary, with Jack Bales. *The Lost Life of Horatio Alger, Jr.* Bloomington: Indiana University Press, 1985.

**William Pencak**

***See also*** INTERGENERATIONAL SEX AND RELATIONSHIPS; LITERATURE.

front criminals and undesirables. Thanks to hard work and a vibrant personality, he becomes the protégé of an older male who assists him in attaining middle-class respectability before becoming, in turn, a role model and friend to other youth. Two of Alger's novels—*Helen Ford* (1866) and *Tattered Tom* (1871)—substituted adolescent girls for boys but retained the same plot.

Aside from *Ragged Dick,* Alger's stories sold only moderately well during his lifetime, but into the millions early in the twentieth century. Despite his fame as creator of the "rags-to-riches" myth where a hero achieves fame and fortune thanks to effort and ability, reading any of his novels reveals that his young men require patronage to become both moderately wealthy and morally good, exactly what Alger and other reformers were doing. Nevertheless the Horatio Alger Society continues to promote the "rags-to-riches" ideal through its awards and programs.

## ALLEN, Paula Gunn (b. 24 October 1939), scholar, educator, activist, and writer.

Allen was born in Albuquerque, New Mexico, to a mother descended from Laguna Pueblo, Lakota Sioux, and Scottish forbears and a father of Lebanese descent. The third of five children, Allen grew up in Cubero, a small, multicultural, multilingual town in northern New Mexico located near the Laguna Pueblo and Acoma Pueblo reservations. After graduating from Catholic mission school in 1957, Allen attended Colorado Women's College but left in 1958 to marry her father's cousin, Eugene Hanosh. With Hanosh she had a son, Gene, and a daughter, Lauralee. She divorced in 1962 and briefly attended the University of New Mexico while working to support her children. In 1964 she married Darrel Brown, a white midwesterner, and moved to Oregon where she earned a B.A. (1966) and an M.F.A. (1968) at the University of Oregon. The marriage to Brown ended in 1971, and Allen returned to New Mexico where she completed a Ph.D. in American studies with an emphasis in Native American studies (1975). During this time she taught, published scholarly essays and her first book of poetry, married Joe Charles Allen (Cherokee), and gave birth to twin boys, Sulieman and Fuad. The loss of Fuad to sudden infant death syndrome put an irrevocable strain on Allen's third marriage, which ended in 1975. Several months later Allen came out as a lesbian; in the following decades she had several long-term relationships with women, including the well-known working-class poet, Judy Grahn. More recently, in the essay "A Mother's Story," Allen describes herself as bisexual, or "a person of gender-free sexual preference" (p. 212).

By the late 1970s, Allen had achieved significant recognition as a poet, literary scholar, and advocate of Native American studies. In 1977 she directed a Modern Language Association seminar on American Indian literatures that resulted in her edited volume *Studies in American Indian Literature* (1983), a groundbreaking collection of pedagogical and critical essays. She has taught English and Native American studies at the University of New Mexico, San Francisco State University, Fort Lewis College, Stanford University, the University of California at Berkeley, and the University of California at Los Angeles, where she retired in 1999. A prolific author, Allen has won numerous awards, including fellowships from the National Endowment for the Arts (1978) and the Ford Foundation–National Research Council (1984), a Susan Koppelman Award (1990), and the Before Columbus Foundation American Book Award (1990).

Allen has played a crucial role in redefining scholarly views of traditional and contemporary Native American sexualities. In *The Sacred Hoop* (1986) and elsewhere she challenges the erasure of American Indian lesbians and, more generally, homosexuality, from ethnographic and historical scholarship. As she explains in her 1981 essay "Beloved Women: Lesbians in American Indian Cultures" (first published in *Conditions,* revised for inclusion in *The*

## From *The Sacred Hoop* (1986)

The concepts of tribal cultures and of modern, western cultures are so dissimilar as to make ludicrous attempts to relate the long-ago women who dealt exclusively with women on sexual-emotional and spiritual bases to modern women who have in common an erotic attraction for other women.

This is not to make light of the modern lesbian but rather to convey some sense of the enormity of the cultural gulf that we must come to terms with when examining any phenomenon related to the American Indian. The modern lesbian sees herself as distinct from "society." She may be prone to believe herself somehow out of sync with "normal" women and often suffers great anguish at perceived differences. And while many modern lesbians have come to see themselves as singular but not sick, many of us are not that secure in our self-assessment. Certainly, however we come to terms with our sexuality, we are not in the position of our American Indian foresister who could find safety and security in her bond with another woman because it was perceived to be destined and nurtured by nonhuman entities, as were all Indian pursuits, and was therefore acceptable and respectable (albeit occasionally terrifying) to others in her tribe.

(*The Sacred Hoop*, p. 255)

*Sacred Hoop*), lesbians and others who transgressed binary gender systems were highly valued by many precontact tribal peoples. Allen sharply distinguishes between homosexuality in native cultures and contemporary Western practices and maintains that in many tribal cultures, LGBT people function as sacred social actors, agents of transformation who introduce alternative possibilities into existing systems of gender and sexuality. Allen's perspective offers an important critique of contemporary U.S. definitions of homosexuality that focus primarily on erotic attraction and sexual object choice.

In *The Sacred Hoop* and elsewhere, Allen attributes tribal people's widespread acceptance of homosexuality and lack of homophobia to the "spirit-centered, woman-focused worldviews" and social systems found in many indigenous cultures (p. 2). According to Allen, this profound respect for women leads to nonhierarchical, complementary gender systems, nonmonogamous family structures, and fluid sexualities. Although a few critics have claimed that Allen's provocative view lacks adequate documentation, Allen draws on her personal experiences as a Laguna woman and persuasively argues that

European colonizers and Western-trained ethnographers, influenced by patriarchal, Judeo-Christian beliefs, erased or otherwise distorted evidence of same-sex relationships and noncongruent gender norms in precontact tribal cultures.

Allen develops these woman-centered, spirit-focused themes in her poetry and fiction. Incorporating aspects of Keres, Navajo, and other Native accounts of a cosmic feminine power into her writing, she reinterprets them from a contemporary tribal-feminist perspective and develops a highly distinctive nonheterosexist mythic tradition. Her novel *The Woman Who Owned the Shadows* (1983) explores the cultural, sexual, and spiritual fragmentation experienced by those who have become disconnected from this overarching life force. As an editor and respected literary scholar, Allen has contributed greatly to the increased visibility of other lesbian, bisexual, and gay Indian writers.

## Bibliography

Allen, Paula Gunn. *Life Is a Fatal Disease*. Albuquerque N.M.: West End Press, 1997.

———. "A Mother's Story." *The Conversation Begins: Mothers and Daughters Talk about Living Feminism*. Edited by Christina Looper Baker and Christina Baker Kline. New York: Bantam, 1996.

———. *The Sacred Hoop: Recovering the Feminine in American Indian Traditions*. Boston: Beacon, 1986, 1992.

———. *The Woman Who Owned the Shadows*. San Francisco: Spinsters Ink, 1983.

Keating, AnaLouise. *Women Reading Women Writing: Self-Invention in Paula Gunn Allen, Gloria Anzaldúa, and Audre Lorde*. Philadelphia: Temple University Press, 1996.

Van Dyke, Annette. "The Journey Back to Female Roots: A Laguna Pueblo Model." In *Lesbian Texts and Contexts: Radical Revisions*. Edited by Karla Jay and Joanne Glasgow. New York: New York University Press, 1990.

**AnaLouise Keating**

*See also* GRAHN, JUDY; NATIVE AMERICAN STUDIES; TWO-SPIRIT FEMALES; TWO-SPIRIT MALES.

# AMERICAN CIVIL LIBERTIES UNION (ACLU)

The American Civil Liberties Union (ACLU) is a membership-based advocacy organization dedicated to the protection and expansion of the rights guaranteed to all United States citizens by the U.S. Constitution and its Amendments. The ACLU was founded in 1920 by Roger Baldwin, Crystal Eastman, Albert De Silver, and other activists in New York City. It had started in 1917 as the Civil Liberties Bureau, itself an offshoot of the American Union Against Militarism, established in 1914 to oppose U.S. entry into World War I and defend conscientious objectors. After the war Baldwin and Eastman agreed on the need for an ongoing organization that would challenge in a legal context the government's increasingly repressive measures, particularly against war resisters, immigrants, and labor organizers. "Our client is the Bill of Rights" is an ACLU motto. The organization prides itself on its commitment to the nonpartisan defense of civil rights and liberties, regardless of the sometimes odious nature of the client or cause.

The ACLU's first cases involved the power of local governments and federal bureaus to silence dissenting speech and writing. The group recruited volunteer lawyers to represent people who were being imprisoned or deported for speaking out on controversial issues in public gatherings or private meetings. Local branches or affiliates of the ACLU were started in major metropolitan areas—beginning in 1923 in Los Angeles—to deal with often violent reprisals against union organizers, students, and those advocating progressive political views. During the 1930s and 1940s the ACLU fought censorship, limits on speech and assembly, and, on the West Coast, the internment of Japanese Americans, a government action which the Washington and California affiliates challenged unsuccessfully all the way to the U.S. Supreme Court.

The ACLU also fought against loyalty oaths during the 1950s, despite the chill of the Cold War era, a chill that had been felt inside the organization itself even before World War II. On the heels of the Nazi-Soviet Pact of 1939, the national board of the ACLU in 1940 passed a policy measure stipulating that members of "totalitarian" groups could not serve on local or national ACLU governing bodies. Founder Roger Baldwin's close ties with members of the Roosevelt administration, the ACLU's successes in cases before the U.S. Supreme Court, and the constant barrage of criticism and charges of communist domination from right-wing pressure groups all had an impact on how the ACLU positioned itself during this period. A more centrist, and cautious, defense of civil liberties characterized the organization in the 1940s and 1950s at the national level.

Local affiliates, however, continued to adhere to the organization's founding principles. When the homophile activists of the 1950s began to organize, the ACLU was one of the first organizations to whom they turned for help. For example, San Francisco ACLU founder Ernest Besig was one of the first guest speakers invited to a

ACLU. Matthew Coles (center) became director of the American Civil Liberties Union's National Lesbian and Gay Rights Project in 1996. [AP Photo/Marta Lavandier]

Daughters of Bilitis (DOB) meeting in that city. He spoke to a small group of women at a meeting on 5 July 1956 and emphasized that only certain homosexual acts were illegal, not homosexuality per se. Besig advised the women to become well-educated about their rights and to help educate others, particularly regarding their dealings with the local police and raids on bars.

When homophile activist Vern Bullough moved to Los Angeles in 1959, he immediately joined the ACLU there and began meeting with the director of the local office, Eason Monroe, to change national ACLU policy regarding gay men and lesbians. Although ACLU leaders in a number of affiliates around the country were supportive of homophile organizing and were featured as speakers at national conferences and local meetings, the national office took a very measured approach to the issue of LGBT rights until the 1960s. The official position of the ACLU in 1957 was that there was no constitutional basis on which to challenge felony arrests for homosexual acts, but that "homosexuals, like members of other socially heretical or deviant groups, are more vulnerable than others to official persecution, denial of due process in prosecution, and entrapment." Such matters were deemed to be "of proper concern to the Union." Local laws requiring the registration of people convicted of homosexual acts were condemned as unconstitutional. The ACLU affirmed its previous policy, and that of President Eisenhower's Executive Order 10450, that the use of homosexuality as a factor in determining federal government security clearances was valid—but also

added that this applied only when there was "evidence of other acts which come within valid security criteria" (as indicated in the policy statement of the ACLU national governing board, 17 January 1957). This rather tepid statement on the rights of homosexuals was nonetheless met with thanks from many homophile activists, who interpreted it as an opening to work with the national organization.

Many of the leaders of the homophile movement were also members of their local ACLU. Some, such as Franklin Kameny in Washington, D.C., were elected to the affiliate's board of directors and helped change organizational policy at that level. These changes, in turn, helped influence the national board and in 1966 the ACLU formally endorsed the principle of LGBT rights. In 1973 the national organization formed the Sexual Privacy Project. In addition to litigation and lobbying, it began to address LGBT issues internally through education and policy debates. And at the local level, the affiliates once again led the way. The ACLU of Northern California started a gay rights chapter in 1978; one of the founders was Florence Conrad, who had been DOB's research director in the 1950s and 1960s. ACLU staff lawyers specializing in LGBT rights issues were based in the Southern California office, and handled local and national cases dealing with discrimination and the denial of basic rights.

In 1986 the ACLU established its National Lesbian and Gay Rights Project at the organization's New York headquarters with Nan Hunter as its first director. Hunter brought to the new project her experience as a reproductive rights expert and her commitment to activism and advocacy. William Rubenstein took over leadership of the project in the early 1990s and helped further establish the ACLU's organizational commitment to LGBT rights as well as AIDS-related issues. Matthew Coles became director in 1996, the same year that the ACLU won a landmark U.S. Supreme Court victory in *Romer v. Evans.* For the first time, the Court recognized the civil rights of lesbians and gay men by invalidating a Colorado constitutional amendment that prohibited state and local governments from passing LGBT rights laws. The decision was especially important in that it weakened the Court's earlier 1986 decision in *Bowers v. Hardwick,* which said that prosecution of sexual conduct between gay consenting adults was legally permissible. In 2003 the ACLU's friend of the court brief in the *Lawrence v. Texas* case challenging state sodomy statutes helped the U.S. Supreme Court construct its historic decision striking down such statutes as unconstitutional violations of the right to privacy.

Today, the Lesbian and Gay Rights Project works on issues such as discrimination against LGBT people in the workplace; marriage and custody rights; the rights of LGBT teens and young adults; criminalization of sexual expression; and freedom of association. Working closely with the ACLU's fifty-three affiliates, the Project coordinates the most extensive LGBT rights legal program in the United States.

**Bibliography**

Bullough, Vern. "Lesbianism, Homosexuality, and the American Civil Liberties Union." *Journal of Homosexuality* 13 (1986): 23 -32.

———, ed. *Before Stonewall: Activists for Gay and Lesbian Rights in Historical Context.* New York: Haworth, 2002.

Cain, Patricia A. *Rainbow Rights: The Role of Lawyers and Courts in the Lesbian and Gay Civil Rights Movement.* Boulder, Colo. Westview, 2000.

Coles, Matthew A. *Kids, Try This at Home!: A Do-It-Yourself Guide to Instituting Lesbian and Gay Civil Rights Policy.* New York: New Press, 1996.

D'Emilio, John. *Sexual Politics, Sexual Communities: The Making of a Homosexual Minority in the United States, 1940-1970.* Chicago: University of Chicago Press, 1983.

Eskridge, William N., Jr. *Gaylaw: Challenging the Apartheid of the Closet.* Cambridge, Mass.: Harvard University Press, 1999.

Hunter, Nan, Sherryl E. Michaelson, and Thomas B. Stoddard. *Rights of Lesbians, Gay Men, Bisexuals, and Transgendered People.* Carbondale, Ill.: Southern Illinois University Press. In press. Retitled 4th ed. (Previously entitled *Rights of Lesbians and Gay Men.*)

Murdoch, Joyce, and Deb Price. *Courting Justice: Gay Men and Lesbians v. the Supreme Court.* New York: Basic Books, 2001.

Rubenstein, William B. *Rights of People Who Are HIV Positive: The Authoritative ACLU Guide to the Rights of People Living with HIV Disease and AIDS.* Carbondale: Southern Illinois University Press, 1996.

Walker, Samuel. *In Defense of American Liberties: A History of the ACLU.* New York: Oxford University Press, 1990.

**Marcia M. Gallo**

**See also** AIDS AND PEOPLE WITH AIDS; CENSORSHIP, OBSCENITY, AND PORNOGRAPHY LAW AND POLICY; DISABILITY, DISABLED PEOPLE, AND DISABILITY MOVEMENTS; EMPLOYMENT LAW AND POLICY; FEDERAL LAW AND POLICY; KAMENY, FRANKLIN; PRIVACY AND PRIVACY RIGHTS.

**AMERICAN INDIANS.** see NATIVE AMERICANS.

# ANARCHISM, SOCIALISM, AND COMMUNISM

Since the late nineteenth century there have been several American Lefts, including the pre–World War I anarchists, the Debsian Socialist Party, the Communist Party of the 1930s, and the New Left of the 1960s. What binds these disparate groups together is a shared view of capitalism as an inherently oppressive and dehumanizing system. There is no agreement, however, on much beyond this point. Some on the Left seek change through electoral gains, some insist that the working class must seize state power, and some reject the use of state power entirely. The Left is deeply divided over goals and tactics.

Needless to say, there is no easy answer to the question: "What is the attitude of the Left toward homosexuality?" Each phase or grouping of the Left has had a different view on the subject. The pre–World War I Socialist Party cannot be said to have had much of an interest in the topic at all. The anarchists, in contrast, developed a broad and critical sexual politics that defended the rights of men and women to pursue their desires free of state regulation and social opprobrium. The Communist Party endorsed a rather conservative sexual politics. Nonetheless, the Communist Party played a critical, if unintentional, role in the emergence of post–War World II gay politics and community. By the time New Leftists appeared they had to fight for space with politically LGBT people. Out of the somewhat awkward meeting between these groups was born the Gay Left, a queer love child owing political and ideological allegiance to its many parents.

## Anarchists

In the years of their greatest influence, roughly 1880 to 1917, American anarchists fought for the transformation of all aspects of life, including sexuality. Anarchist sexual politics, unlike the vast majority of socialist pronouncements on the subject, were not framed by the primacy of the biological, nuclear family. Benjamin Tucker, the leading individualist anarchist of the day, wrote in his 1893 essay "State Socialism and Anarchism" that anarchists "acknowledge and defend the right of any man and woman, or any men and women, to love each other for as long or as short a time as they can, will, or may" (p. 14). Neither the state nor the church should govern the sexual and emotional choices people make. This defense of "free love" was the context in which the anarchist defense of homosexuality emerged.

When the state acted to police sexuality, the anarchists reacted strongly. The persecution of Oscar Wilde, for example, prompted swift condemnation. "The imprisonment of Wilde," wrote Tucker, "is an outrage that shows how thoroughly the doctrine of liberty is misconceived" (1895, p. 4). In the decade before World War I, the communist anarchists Emma Goldman and Alexander Berkman delivered public lectures on the subject of "homo-sexualism" (they employed a shifting sexual vocabulary). Berkman's *Prison Memoirs of an Anarchist* is one of the most interesting primary sources on turn-of-the-century homosexuality among men. The sexual politics of the American anarchists influenced some of their European comrades, such as John Henry Mackay and E. Armand, who also addressed the subject of homosexuality in their work.

The anarchists stripped the discussion of homosexuality of its moral encrustation, preferring the language of rights and rationality. John William Lloyd hoped for the day that "we shall have an American (better still an International) Institute and Society of Sexology, composed of our greatest scientists, philosophers, physicians and men and women of the finest character studying sex as fearlessly as geology, discussing it calmly as the 'Higher Criticism,' and publishing it far and wide in a paper which no Church nor State can gag" (pp. 5–6). While the sophisticated reader might be wary of Lloyd's desire to construct such a mighty node of knowledge-power, the idea of a disinterested scientific approach to the study of sex was, in its time, a powerful rebuke to those who wished to frame any analysis of homosexuality in the language of sin, degeneracy, and danger.

## Socialist Party

Founded in 1901, the Socialist Party enjoyed considerable electoral support in the years prior to World War I. The party's perennial candidate for U.S. president, Eugene Debs, won 6 percent of the national vote in 1912. A number of mayors and state and federal representatives came to office on the Socialist Party ticket. Hundreds of publications, including the *Appeal to Reason,* which in some weeks had a circulation of over a million, served the various factions and ethnic groups within the party. The Socialist Party brought together tenant farmers, native-born skilled workers, middle-class reformers, and immigrant laborers who each contributed to the formation of party discourse and policy.

The Socialist Party's sexual politics were generally conservative; the topic of homosexuality seems not to have been an issue among party members. There was considerable support for the Socialist Party among the bohemian intellectuals of Greenwich Village, but their well-documented sex radicalism did not extend far beyond heterosexual relations. Though Village radicals celebrated the writings of Edward Carpenter and Havelock Ellis, for example, they were curiously silent on these authors' discussions of homosexuality. No Socialist Party faction or conference produced a position paper on the question of homosexuality. The only sustained discussion of homosexuality—albeit a meager one—in the party press occurred during the Eulenberg scandal of 1907 to 1909. In their reporting on the case, the Socialist Party press cast homosexuality as an indication of the immoral, decadent nature of the German ruling class and by extension their American counterparts.

## Communist Party

The Socialist Party's influence was cut short by the rise of the Communist Party. Forged in the aftermath of the Russian Revolution of 1917, the Communist Party emerged as the dominant voice of the American Left and remained so through the 1950s. The peak of its influence came in the 1930s and 1940s. Like its Soviet counterparts, the Communist Party was organized around Leninist principles. Though much of the Communist Party's work was carried out on the local level, the party's structure and rules gave great power to leadership. The remnants of the Socialist Party and the anarchist movement were bitter foes of the communists, whom they saw as autocratic, bureaucratic, and opportunistic.

The Communist Party's relationship with the politics of homosexuality is contradictory and complex. Harry Hay, one of the founders of the Mattachine Society, the nation's first successful gay rights organization, was a onetime Communist Party member. Hay used the organizing skills and analytic methods he learned in the party to name and to fight the oppression of homosexuals. But, when he was active in the Communist Party, Hay had to hide the fact that he was gay; he married a fellow party member and adopted two children. In order to pursue his interest in the politics of homosexuality, Hay had to leave the party. The Communist Party had no relationship with the Mattachine Society, nor was it on friendly terms with the Daughters of Bilitis or any of the other LGB rights groups that emerged in the post–World War II decades. Ironically, shortly after he helped establish the group, Hay was purged from the Mattachine Society by a membership that looked upon his old political connections with great suspicion.

The National Union of Marine Cooks and Stewards (NUMCS) represents a major exception to the party's position on homosexuality. The NUMCS, one of the several Communist Party–led unions formed in the 1930s, represented about eight thousand maritime workers on the Pacific Coast. Union leaders actively protected the substantial number of gay men who were members from "gay baiting." They did so in order to prevent management and rival unions from attacking or drawing off its membership. But the Communist Party did not attempt to incorporate the lessons learned in the NUMCS into its broader agenda. The sexual politics of the NUMCS stopped at the water's edge. The NUMCS was ultimately crushed by the anti-Communist backlash of the 1950s. The type of progressive politics forged in the NUMCS would eventually come to characterize much of the American labor movement, but only decades after the NUMCS's collapse and forcible erasure.

## New Left

The New Left that emerged in the 1960s was so named, in part, because of its rejection of the culture and politics of the Communist Party–dominated Old Left. The politics of these young men and women was, the historian Paul Buhle writes, "definitely outside the norms of communist, socialist, of other past 'Left' movements." New Left activists "stressed human rights and visions of cultural change over the familiar [Old] Left struggles of labor and the promise of egalitarian industrial progress" (p. 545). The rather vague and sweeping goals of the New Left were in part a reflection of the lack of an organizational or even ideological center to the movement. Though some activists embraced the teachings of Mao or Lenin, most New Left activists drew on a broad spectrum of ideas and traditions—not limited to the canons of Left discourse—to shape their views.

Among those "visions of cultural change" embraced by the New Left was the forging of a new liberal sexual ethics that stressed pleasure and individual autonomy rather than reproduction, family, and obligation. In practice, however, this meant a celebration of men's unfettered access to women. It was not at all unusual, for example, to see posters stating "Girls Say Yes to Guys Who Say No" at antiwar rallies. Many women in New Left organizations did not appreciate being viewed and treated in this manner. The eruption of women's liberation in the late 1960s was in part a reaction against this phenomenon. Women's liberation, in turn, provided a venue for many women to explore their identities as lesbians. The same dynamic operated for many gay men drawn to the radicalism and promise of the New Left. Though many gay liberation groups explicitly identified themselves as being part of the New Left, they found it difficult to navigate the movement's raging heterosexist milieu. The explosive growth in gay liberation organizations in the late 1960s and early 1970s was in part a product of a migration out of New Left organizations into specifically gay-identified groups. The New Left was an important way station for many of the men and women who forged gay liberation and lesbian feminism, but their passage was not an entirely happy journey.

In the decades since the collapse of the New Left, the relationship between the Left and LGBT people has been transformed. The Democratic Socialists of America and other "mainstream" Left groups have incorporated the defense of sexual diversity into their platforms, and socialist publications such as *In These Times* and *Radical America* have provided space to LGBT rights activists. It is not at all unusual to find such people in leadership positions in Left organizations. Even some of the surviving shards of the Old Left, such as the Workers World Party (WWP), have moved to address the needs of sexual and gender minorities. Leslie Feinberg, a leading transgender rights activist, joined the WWP in 1973 and has been actively working for the party since that time. Anarchism has continued to provide a home for those interested in radical sex and gender politics. In many cities, anarchist bookstores, in keeping with their libertarian traditions, are among the few venues where the works of the North American Man/Boy Love Association and pamphlets and magazines put out by groups representing marginalized sexualities can be purchased.

Among the most interesting products of the intersection of the politics of homosexuality and socialism is the Gay Left. Although small, it has had influence far beyond its size. This is especially true in the growth of LGBT studies, which until the 1990s did not enjoy significant support in academia. The institutions and leaders of the Gay Left created the space within which LGBT studies grew during its early years. Publications such as *Body Politic, Sinister Wisdom, OUT/LOOK,* and *Gay Community News,* whose politics were definitely on the Left of the American political spectrum, all provided forums for scholarship on sexuality. Community-based working groups such as San Francisco's Lesbian and Gay History Project were put together by men and women whose political commitments were largely on the Left. They saw their work as sex radicals, socialists, and historians as part of the same project. And although it has been little recognized, much early conceptualization of the idea that sexual identity is constructed was forged by people deeply informed by the work of Left historians.

### Bibliography

Buhle, Mari Jo, Paul Buhle, and Dan Georgakas, eds. *Encyclopedia of the American Left.* 2d ed. New York: Oxford University Press, 1998.

D'Emilio, John. *Sexual Politics, Sexual Communities: The Making of a Homosexual Minority in the United States, 1940–1970.* Chicago: University of Chicago Press, 1983.

Diggins, John Patrick. *The Rise and Fall of the American Left.* New York: Norton, 1992.

Duberman, Martin. *Left Out: The Politics of Exclusion, Essays 1964–2002.* Boston: South End Press, 2002.

Gay Left Collective, ed. *Homosexuality: Power and Politics.* London: Allison and Busby, 1980.

Hekma, Gert, Harry Oosterhuis, and James Steakley, eds. *Gay Men and the Sexual History of the Political Left.* New York: Harrington Park Press, 1995.

Lloyd, John William. *The Free Comrade.* August, 1902.

Tucker, Benjamin R. *Instead of a Book: By a Man Too Busy to Write One.* New York: Benjamin R. Tucker, 1893.

———. "The Criminal Jailers of Oscar Wilde." *Liberty,* June 15, 1985.

**Terence Kissack**

*See also* ACTORS AND ACTRESSES; AFRICAN AMERICAN STUDIES; AMERICAN CIVIL LIBERTIES UNION (ACLU); ANDERSON, MARGARET, AND JANE HEAP; ANTIWAR, PACIFIST, AND PEACE MOVEMENTS; AUDEN, W.H.; COMBAHEE RIVER COLLECTIVE; CORY, DONALD WEBSTER; DIAZ COTTO, JUANITA; ERICKSON, REED; FEDERAL LAW AND POLICY; FEMINISM; GIDLOW, ELSA; GILMAN, CHARLOTTE PERKINS; GOLDMAN, EMMA; GOODMAN, PAUL; GOVERMENT AND MILITARY WITCHUNTS; HAY, HARRY; HUGHES, LANGSTON; HOOVER, J. EDGAR; KEPNER, JAMES; KUROMIYA, KYOSHI; LABOR MOVEMENTS AND LABOR UNIONS; MATTACHINE SOCIETY; MATTHIESSEN, F.O.; MCKAY, CLAUDE; MILLAY, EDNA ST. VINCENT; MURRAY, PAULI; MUSIC: CLASSICAL; NEW LEFT AND STUDENT MOVEMENTS; POLITICAL SCANDALS; POOR PEOPLE'S MOVEMENTS; RADICAL FAERIES; ROBBINS, JEROME; RUSTIN, BAYARD; SHELLEY, MARTHA; SMITH, BARBARA; THIRD WORLD GAY REVOLUTION; WITTMAN, CARL; WOO, MERLE.

## ANDERSON, Margaret (b. 24 November 1886; d. 19 October 1973), and Jane HEAP (b. 1 November 1883; d. 16 June 1964), radicals and editors.

Margaret Anderson and Jane Heap played important roles in twentieth-century international avant-garde movements as coeditors of the radical journal the *Little Review* (1914–1929). Born in the Midwest—Anderson in Indianapolis, Indiana, and Heap in Topeka, Kansas—both women traveled to Chicago in the early 1900s. Anderson worked sporadically as a book reviewer, while Heap studied at the Chicago Art Institute and worked as an actor and set designer in Maurice Browne's Little Theater.

In 1914 Anderson founded the *Little Review,* dedicating the early years of the magazine to a wide variety of literary and political movements. Anderson published the early poetry of T. S. Eliot, William Butler Yeats, H.D. (Hilda Doolittle), and Amy Lowell and wrote editorials supporting experimental literature, the labor movement, and feminism.

Part of Anderson's radicalism sprang from her self-identification as a lesbian. In 1915 she wrote a *Little Review* editorial analyzing a speech made by Edith Ellis, wife of the famous British sexologist Havelock Ellis, which—in Anderson's view—made insufficient reference to the prejudices in American society toward inversion. In *Gay/Lesbian Almanac: A New Documentary History,* Jonathan Ned Katz has identified Anderson's editorial as the first radical defense of homosexuals published by a lesbian in the United States. Anderson also used the *Little Review* as a platform for other revolutionary political ideas, including anarchism. Her enthusiastic support of Emma Goldman cost her financial backing in the first year of the magazine.

Anderson and Heap met in 1916 in the Fine Arts Building, where the *Little Review* was published. Impressed by Heap's background in art and theater, her acerbic wit, and her dry humor, Anderson convinced her to write for the journal. It was the beginning of a tumultuous partnership. The two women were a study in contrasts. Anderson was full of optimism and energy, Heap prone to depression and pessimism. Anderson was beautiful and feminine, attracting much male attention, while Heap was described by many contemporaries as "mannish." Heap was a cross-dresser by the time she met Anderson.

In 1917 Anderson and Heap moved the *Little Review* to New York City. During the next few years they published work by Djuna Barnes, Hart Crane, Mina Loy, Dorothy Richardson, and William Carlos Williams. Ezra Pound, based in London, became the journal's foreign editor and sent the two editors the work of Ford Madox Ford, Wyndham Lewis, and James Joyce. Anderson and Heap were the first to publish Joyce's 1922 novel *Ulysses*, which they serialized in the *Little Review* between 1918 and 1920. After several issues were confiscated and burned by the post office in New York City, the two women were tried for obscenity, found guilty, and fined one hundred dollars. *Ulysses* was not published in the United States again until the 1930s. After the trial, Anderson and Heap left for Paris, where they became familiar figures in international bohemian circles during the interwar period.

The year 1924 was a major turning point in the lives of both Anderson and Heap. They were introduced to the philosophy of the Armenian mystic George Gurdjieff, an event that was to radically transform their views on both life and art. Anderson and Heap studied at Gurdjieff's Institute for the Harmonious Development of Man in Fontainebleau, France, on and off during the 1920s. Their relationship came to an end when Anderson became involved with the French opera star Georgette Leblanc and left Heap with the primary responsibility for the *Little Review* from 1924 to 1929.

The magazine became bolder and increasingly more avant-garde as Heap published articles on surrealism, constructivism, modern architecture, and machine age aesthetics. More interested in the visual arts than Anderson, Heap published reproductions of the works of Frank Stella, Fernand Léger, Joan Miró, and Constantin Brancusi. During the 1920s Heap traveled frequently between Paris and New York, managing the Little Review Gallery, procuring foreign art for exhibitions, and staging ambitious projects such as the International Theatre Exposition (1926) and the Machine Age Exposition (1927), both in New York City. Concentrating increasingly on their spiritual studies, Anderson and Heap reunited to edit the last issue of the *Little Review* in 1929.

Under Gurdjieff's direction, Heap moved in the late 1930s to London, where she taught his ideas to small numbers of followers. Revered as a teacher, she continued the groups during the blitz in World War II and later escorted her pupils to France for meetings with Gurdjieff. She died in 1964 from complications of diabetes and is buried in East Finchley, London.

Anderson spent the majority of her post–*Little Review* years writing three autobiographies—*My Thirty Years' War* (1930), *The Fiery Fountains* (1951), and *The Strange Necessity* (1969)—as well as editing *The Little Review Anthology* (1953, 1969) and writing a book on her spiritual beliefs, *The Unknowable Gurdjieff* (1962). She unsuccessfully attempted to get a lesbian novel, *Forbidden Fires*, published in the 1950s; it was eventually published by Naiad Press in 1996. Anderson died of heart failure in 1973 and is buried next to Georgette Leblanc in the Notre Dame des Anges Cemetery at Le Cannet, France.

### Bibliography

Baggett, Holly. "Aloof from Natural Laws: Margaret C. Anderson and the *Little Review*: 1914–1929." Ph.D. diss., University of Delaware, 1992.

Baggett, Holly, ed. *Dear Tiny Heart: The Letters of Jane Heap and Florence Reynolds.* New York: New York University Press, 2000.

Bryer, Jackson. "A Trial Track for Racers: Margaret C. Anderson and the *Little Review*." Ph.D. diss., University of Wisconsin–Milwaukee, 1964.

Katz, Jonathan. *Gay/Lesbian Almanac: A New Documentary History.* New York: Harper and Row, 1983.

**Holly A. Baggett**

*See also* ANARCHISM, COMMUNISM, AND SOCIALISM; GOLDMAN, EMMA.

# ANDROGYNY

"Androgyny" (from the Greek roots "andro" for man and "gyn" for woman) can refer to either a person who appears to combine masculine and feminine or male and female traits or a person whose gender or sex is difficult to determine. It has also been a euphemism for and a concept linked with homosexuality, bisexuality, transsexuality, and intersexed conditions.

For the period before the late nineteenth century, Native American *berdaches* (or two-spirit people), passing women and men, cross-dressing performers, and intersexed people can be conceptualized as androgynous, but ideas about androgyny were transformed with the rise of sexual science in the nineteenth century. In the late nineteenth and early twentieth centuries, European sexologists such as Havelock Ellis and Karl Heinrich Ulrichs believed that homosexuality was rooted in gender abnormality. A man who felt sexual desire or romantic love for another man must, they assumed, have a physical or psychological feminine or female component. A woman who felt sexual desire or romantic love for another woman must incorporate masculinity or maleness in her body or mind. They therefore often referred to such men and women as inverts. Magnus Hirschfeld later agitated for the decriminalization of sodomy on the grounds that people should not be punished for inborn traits. Hirschfeld and his allies hoped that the larger society would accept homosexuality if it could be interpreted as the coming together of male and female states of being. Early American sexual scientists, most of whom were critical of both androgyny and homosexuality, were profoundly influenced by their European counterparts.

These conceptions of homosexual desire were popular in sexual and gender minority communities as well and are acutely described in Radclyffe Hall's scandalous lesbian novel *The Well of Loneliness*, declared obscene in Great Britain in 1928, in which the "invert" gives up her ostensibly normal female partner to a man who can offer her marriage and children. Hall vividly depicts the suffering of Stephen, a character modern readers would label a butch lesbian, who assumes that her lover will experience no disjunction at being with a man rather than a female invert. There were also fictional depictions of male inverts doomed to loneliness because the "real men" their feminine natures were attracted to could never reciprocate their affection. For two inverts to fall in love or have sex would be an aberration. Among the early- and mid-twentieth-century androgynous figures analyzed by American LGBT historians and anthropologists, perhaps the best known are the fairies and pansies explored by George Chauncey in *Gay New York* (1994) and the butches and studs examined by Elizabeth Kennedy and Madeline Davis in *Boots of Leather* (1993).

A great deal of the research on sexual and gender variation from the 1880s until the 1970s focused on searching for physiological or psychiatric confirmation of this paradigm. And, in fact, the idea that homosexuality is synonymous with gender nonconformity continues to crop up in social science research, as does the concomitant notion that transsexuals are actually homosexuals who cannot accept their same-sex desires. LGBT studies scholars, however, have focused on examining the worlds made by those who transgressed sexual and gender norms. In their works androgyny often figures centrally, even when it is not named as such.

### Lesbian Feminism and Gay Liberation

As the LGB movements of the latter half of the twentieth century developed, LGB people challenged the root of the heterosexual paradigm—the notion that all eroticism must derive from the pairing of the masculine and the feminine. Gay fiction during and after World War II shifted to focus on masculine-masculine pairings rather than masculine-feminine ones. In the 1970s, gay men in

**Androgyny.** In this fashion show androgyny is reflected both in the fashion and the model. [AP/Wide World Photos]

urban America developed a masculine look that was so pervasive it was satirically labeled "the Castro clone" or the "Christopher Street clone" style. Gay masculinity was also celebrated in pornography and in leather communities. In the 1970s, lesbian feminists eschewed femme/butch roles, in part to establish a lifestyle in which women loving women could create a unique Amazonian culture that could not be labeled "imitation heterosexuality." Androgyny became a universal expectation among lesbian feminists, rather than the exclusive territory of self-identified butches. While these trends opened up new possibilities for LGB people, they also moved drag queens, effeminate gay men, femme/butch lesbians, leatherdykes, and transsexuals to the fringes.

From the 1960s on, however, the women's movement was ground zero for deconstructing masculine and feminine sex roles. By changing what was acceptable public and private behavior for women, late-twentieth-century feminists hoped to raise the status of women in employment, education, sports, the arts, religion, and virtually every other arena. For some feminists, androgyny became an ideal in which women would take on the best aspects of what were traditionally assumed to be male emotions, activities, and dress. For some, appropriating aspects of male sexuality such as engaging in casual sex also became an ideal. It was argued that men, in turn, would be healthier if they could develop ostensibly womanly traits like empathy with others, verbal expression of emotions, nurturance of children, cooperative rather than competitive attitudes toward others, and aversion to physical conflict. The androgynous ideal of feminists was attacked by conservatives, who demonized it as leading to the political or even physical castration of men, pacifism and weakness, destruction of motherhood and the family, the end of fashion and beauty, and a dead-end of ugly uniformity and asexuality. While androgyny remained popular among some segments of LGBT and straight communities, it did not become the dominant ideal.

## Bisexuality and Transsexuality

Bisexual writers and commentators often point out that some of the ancestral figures revered in the gay community were actually androgynous bisexuals, such as some of the members of the Bloomsbury Group. In the United States, androgyny can be seen in Walt Whitman's eroticizing of nature and his similarly sensual love of both men and women, in the relentlessly androgynous intelligence of Gertrude Stein, in Bessie Smith singing about wearing a coat and tie, and in the androgynous gay boys described by James Baldwin.

Transactivists have been similarly concerned about LGB people who lay claim to androgynous transgendered people. These activists were especially angered when initial coverage of the murder of Brandon Teena, a genetic female who dressed and lived as a man, was covered by a lesbian journalist, Donna Minkowitz, whose articles in the *Village Voice* referred to Teena as a gay woman. Not wishing to be victimized in this manner and seeking to minimize discrimination, many transmen and transwomen are more interested in conforming to conventional sex roles and see androgyny as an undesirable state of limbo they are forced to endure before they can live fully in their gender of preference. Kate Bornstein's book *Sexual Outlaw*, however, has spearheaded a drive among some transpeople to live between or without gender and to embrace androgyny as a celebratory sex toy.

## Spirituality

Some gay men have rejected the masculine bias of their culture's discourse of sexuality and spirituality. Groups like the Radical Faeries draw inspiration from ancient mythology, specifically from the ecstatic worship of the gender-ambiguous god Dionysus. Some gay people of color were already familiar with the dual gendered *orisha* in religions of the African diaspora. Harry Hay, one of the founders of the homophile movement and the Faeries, criticized the separation of the male and female in monotheistic religions and pointed out that in less homophobic and patriarchal cultures androgyny was a sign of divinity or spirituality. Hay urged other gay men to develop the unique spiritual knowledge they possessed by virtue of their androgyny.

The work of psychologist Carl Jung is often cited in support of the benefits of androgyny. Jung posited the existence of a female archetype, or anima, within the male psyche and a male counterpart, or animus, within the female psyche, and believed that these cross-gender components of the personality were essential to personal growth. Today, it should be recognized that androgyny is a quality independent of sexual orientation or even gender identity.

Queer people (and others) have yet to exhaust the revolutionary potential of androgyny; the demarcations of social sex roles continue to place glass ceilings upon our understanding of ourselves. While it is certainly safer to be visibly androgynous in 2003 than it was in the 1950s, it still takes a brave and rebellious spirit to live as a manly woman, a womanly man, or a third-gender person.

## Bibliography

Bell, Quentin. *Bloomsbury Recalled*. New York: Columbia University Press, 1995.

Bornstein, Kate. *Gender Outlaw: On Men, Women, and the Rest of Us*. New York and London: Routledge, 1994.

Califia, Pat. *Sex Changes: The Politics of Transgenderism*. San Francisco: Cleis Press, 1997.

Chauncey, George. *Gay New York: Gender, Urban Culture, and the Makings of the Gay Male World*. New York: Basic, 1994.

Cline, Sally. *Radclyffe Hall: A Woman Called John*. New York: Overlook Press, 1998.

Conner, Randy P. *Blossom of Bone: Reclaiming the Connection between Homoeroticism and the Sacred*. San Francisco: HarperSanFrancisco, 1993.

Heilbrun, Carolyn G. *Toward a Recognition of Androgyny*. New York and London: W. W. Norton and Company, 1964.

Kennedy, Elizabeth Lapovsky, and Madeline D. Davis. *Boots of Leather, Slippers of Gold: The History of a Lesbian Community*. New York: Routledge, 1993.

**Patrick Califia**

See also BISEXUALITY, BISEXUALS, AND BISEXUAL MOVEMENTS; GENDER AND SEX; TWO-SPIRIT FEMALES; TWO-SPIRIT MALES.

## ANGER, Kenneth (b. 3 February 1927), filmmaker.

Kenneth Anger was born in Santa Monica, California, and grew up fascinated by the glamour and dark excesses of the studios and their stars. His *Hollywood Babylon* books and many of his films tell us as much. Anger's early Hollywood-infused avant-garde short films contain leather and sequins, motorcycles and makeup, rock and classical music. Taken as a group, these films are also a testament to the filmmaker's queeny-butch sensibilities. Anger's *Fireworks* (1947), along with Jean Genet's *Un Chant d'Amour* (1950), Jean Cocteau's *Orphée* (1949/ 1950), and Gregory Markopoulos's *Psyche* (1947–1948), *Lysis* (1948), and *Charmides* (1948), marks the beginning of an established gay underground and art cinema after the one-off 1930 American film *Lot in Sodom* (Melville Webber and James Sibley Watson). With their combination of queer sex, glamour, and camp, the Anger films between 1947 and 1953 helped set the stage for "second-wave" gay American avant-garde filmmakers like Jack Smith and Andy Warhol.

Legend has it that Anger made *Fireworks*, his first important film, in his parent's middle-class home while they were away for the weekend. The resulting symbolic melodrama concerns a young man (played by Anger) cruising rough trade and finding what he desires in a sailor who is both brutal and tender, devil and angel. Anger's next film, *Puce Moment* (1948), is the femme to *Fireworks*'s butch. Shimmering dresses are flung at the camera as a diva tries to decide what to wear to walk her dogs. That's about it—but it's funny and mesmerizing.

Moving to Paris a few years later—supposedly encouraged by a fan letter from Cocteau—Anger worked on projects with the French artist. His next solo films continue the nightmarishly dreamy tone of *Fireworks*, and, as with *Puce Moment*, they are, in part, tributes to silent films. The magic lantern and Melies-inspired *Rabbit's Moon* (1950) features a Pierrot figure who inhabits a blue-tinted forest, while *Eaux d'Artifice* (1953) finds a lavishly dressed woman (or is it?) wandering through an enchanted green-tinted garden filled with fountains as Vivaldi plays in the background. In typical Anger style, the latter is a beautifully shot period film that is also, symbolically and outrageously, about urophilia.

Following these "French" works, Anger—temporarily back in Los Angeles—completed *Inauguration of the Pleasure Dome* (1954), a film he would tinker with for more than a decade. This film is important within the filmmaker's oeuvre as the first one clearly influenced by Aleister Crowley's notions of "Magick," which center around erotically charged pagan rituals designed to conjure up spirits and forces that lead practitioners into a transcendent state. Later in his life, Anger dubbed his films from *Fireworks* on the "Magick Lantern Cycle," suggesting that viewers should consider all of these works expressions of Magick rituals. As for *Inauguration of the Pleasure Dome*, it is both campy and sensuous in its evocation of a bacchanal attended by a Magus, Pan, Hecate, Lord Shiva, and Lady Kali, among others. Anger later made two other films to complete a Crowley-inspired trilogy: *Invocation of My Demon Brother* (1969) and *Lucifer Rising* (1982). Both films feature the expected mythic figures and thematic concerns (queer sexuality, camp humor, magic, ritual, and the occult), but the former is constructed through loose, associational montages, while the latter presents a quasi-narrative in which an Egyptian god and goddess visit sacred sites before finally appearing at the Pyramids in a pink flying saucer.

Returning permanently to the United States in the early 1960s, Anger made his best-known film, *Scorpio Rising* (1962–1963), an avant-garde classic that, like *Un Chien Andalou*, can still shock and rile people, particularly with cross-cutting that draws parallels between Jesus and his disciples, queer motorcycle studs, and Nazis—and that is set to pop and rock songs of the period like "I Will Follow Him," "He's a Rebel," "Devil in Disguise," and "Wipe Out." *Kustom Kar Kommandoes* (1965–1966), which followed *Scorpio Rising*, is actually part of a larger unfinished project. But even what remains is characteristic: a well-built man in jeans and a white T-shirt cleans his car with a big powder puff to the accompaniment of the pop song "Dream Lover." It doesn't get much more butchy femme (or femmy butch) than this.

Since the mid-1980s, Anger has spent his time writing sequels to his book *Hollywood Babylon*, revising certain films, packaging his films for video release, developing new film projects (particularly one based upon Crowley's *Gnostic Mass*), and offering screening-and-lecture programs around the world.

### Bibliography

Cagle, Robert L. "Auto-Eroticism: Narcissism, Fetishism, and Consumer Culture." *Cinema Journal* 33, no. 4 (1994): 23–33.

Dyer, Richard. *Now You See It: Studies on Lesbian and Gay Film*. New York: Routledge, 1990.

Lowrey, Ed. "The Appropriation of Signs in Scorpio Rising." *Velvet Light Trap* 20 (1983): 41–47.

Murray, Raymond. *Images in the Dark: An Encyclopedia of Gay and Lesbian Film and Video.* Philadelphia: TLA, 1994.

Sitney, P. Adams. *Visionary Film: The American Avant-Garde, 1943–1978.* New York: Oxford University Press, 1979.

Suarez, Juan A. *Bike Boys, Drag Queens, and Superstars: Avant-Garde, Mass Culture, and Gay Identities in the 1960s Underground Cinema.* Bloomington: Indiana University Press, 1996.

Tinkcom, Matthew. "Scandalous!: Kenneth Anger and the Prohibitions of Hollywood History." In *Outtakes: Essays on Queer Theory and Film.* Edited by Ellis Hanson. Durham, N.C.: Duke University Press, 1999.

**Alexander Doty**

*See also* FILM AND VIDEO.

# ANTHONY, Susan

(b. 15 February 1820; d. 13 March 1906), educator, women's rights and suffrage leader.

The struggle for women's rights and woman suffrage was the focus of Susan B. Anthony's life. For half a century, she joined with Elizabeth Cady Stanton in a deep intellectual, political, and emotional partnership. As Stanton wished, Anthony's picture was placed on her casket. Anthony, who never married and urged other promising women leaders to forgo wedded life, created a family of women that included her sisters and nieces as well as a number of longtime suffrage leaders such as Rachel Avery Foster, Anna Dickinson, and Anna Howard Shaw. As she fought for new options for women, she modeled a woman-centered life surrounded by similarly independent women.

Anthony was born in western Massachusetts and raised as a Quaker, the religious heritage of her father, Daniel Anthony. While the family prospered, Anthony benefited from the Quaker ideas of sex equality and gained a relatively rigorous education. At a girls' boarding school, after a serious bout of homesickness, Anthony found that she could construct a life apart from her family. When the family fortunes declined too steeply to allow for her continued education, Anthony began a teaching career. During the years she taught, Anthony explored the world outside the Quaker community. She was courted by men but rejected all of them, while she grew as an educator and administrator.

A career in education did not provide an adequate outlet for Anthony's increasing political interests. Lecturing and activism called her, and she quit teaching when she saw that she could commit her life to the causes of temperance, abolition, dress reform, and women's rights. She sought out a meeting with Stanton, a recognized women's rights leader who had organized the 1848 Seneca Falls Convention. By this time Anthony's family had settled in the Rochester, New York, area, not far from Stanton's Seneca Falls home. Their early collaborative efforts were directed at the broad array of challenges women faced, from constraints on married women's property rights to limitations on women's education. Only after the Civil War and the splits that resulted from differing responses to the Fourteenth and Fifteenth Amendments to the U.S. Constitution did Anthony and, to a lesser extent, Stanton, narrow the focus to women's enfranchisement. At this point, Anthony demonstrated her willingness to accept alliances with racist and nativist forces to further her cause, moves that brought her criticism from other activists.

Anthony personified the movement for women's right to vote. While there were many extraordinary women leaders in the second half of the nineteenth century, and while Anthony herself would give Stanton the title of mother of the women's rights movement, Anthony kept the struggle alive. It was her life focus, and the people, mostly women, who shared a dedication to this cause were her only family. Her energetic spirit and work ethic sustained the movement, while women in the movement along with her immediate kin stepped in to provide financial support when personal and movement funds were depleted.

There was no boundary between Anthony's political and personal worlds. She argued that marriage made wealthy women into dolls and poor women into drudges, and she keenly felt, and often resented, the demands of domesticity and family that kept Stanton from giving the same energy to that cause that she, Anthony, did. Anthony had hoped that Stanton would live with her when Stanton no longer had family responsibilities, but Stanton chose her family over Anthony. Since most of Anthony's demands on other women were couched in terms of the needs of the movement, it is not clear how many of her demands on Stanton arose from her personal desires. It may be that Anthony did not or could not acknowledge her emotional needs separately.

While Stanton was her partner at a level never approached by any other woman, Anthony had remarkable bonds with other women such as her sisters, especially Mary, with whom she shared a home in the last decade of her life, and her actual as well as adopted nieces. The significance of her presence in the lives of these younger women is perhaps best illustrated by her relationship with Anna Howard Shaw. Shaw claims that during the eighteen years that she worked with Anthony,

encyclopedia of lesbian, gay, bisexual, and transgender **history in america**

**Susan B. Anthony.** An 1898 portrait of the lifelong champion of women's suffrage and women's rights.

they were rarely separated, and Shaw dedicates two chapters of her autobiography to Anthony.

Anthony worked for a society in which women had choices outside of a patriarchal heterosexuality while at the same time creating an intensely loyal and loving community of women. Though most portrayals of Anthony present her as a singular figure determinedly fighting for women, she created a cadre of activists who were inspired as much by this charismatic figure as they were by the cause to which she committed her life.

### Bibliography

Barry, Kathleen. *Susan B. Anthony: A Biography of a Singular Feminist.* New York: New York University Press, 1988.

Harper, Ida H. *The Life and Work of Susan B. Anthony, Including Public Addresses, Her Own Letters, and Many from Her Contemporaries during Fifty Years. A Story of the Evolution of the Status of Women.* 3 vols. Indianapolis: Bowen-Merrill, 1899–1908.

Shaw, Anna Howard. *The Story of a Pioneer.* New York: Harper, 1915.

**Trisha Franzen**

*See also* FEMINISM; MUSIC: OPERA; SHAW, ANNA HOWARD; SMASHES AND CHUMMING.

# ANTHROPOLOGY

Anthropology is the study of cultures or ways of life around the world. The field is distinguished by its signature text—the ethnography. An ethnography is a detailed, descriptive study of a community. Ethnographic data is gathered primarily through participant-observation or a prolonged stay in the field that involves the anthropologist living with the people he/she is studying and conducting informal interviews and observations. Ethnographies examine various aspects of culture, including religion, political organization, economic systems, kinship, and family.

## Colonial Beginnings

The study of LGBT peoples and practices in anthropology developed rather late in the history of the field. This is not because anthropologists were unconcerned with such phenomena, but rather because of the field's unique history. Unlike sociological and psychological work on sexuality and gender, anthropological study of these topics began not as a part of pre-existing disciplinary research endeavors, but in response to European imperial expansion into the New World in the seventeenth and eighteenth centuries. In fact, the origins of anthropology can be traced to the need to study non-Western societies as part of the colonization process. As instruments of colonial control, anthropology and the ethnographic recording of behavior were used to gain knowledge in order to conquer and rule over non-Western peoples.

The discipline's provenance influenced early anthropological records of sexual and gender phenomena. For example, anthropological colonial records included descriptions of gender nonconforming behavior such as the cross-dressing of Native American *berdaches* and shamans. In these cases, sexual and gender behaviors were seen as evidence of the "native's" lack of civilized comportment, which necessitated the establishment of colonial rule and encouraged religious conversion.

## Emergence of the Discipline in the Early Twentieth Century

The professionalization and emergence of anthropology as a social science discipline began in the early twentieth century, when there was a move to shape the discipline according to the tenets of the natural sciences. Information related to observable phenomena was gathered and compiled to come up with what was put forward as the complete empirical truth. This period saw a shift from the mere recording of exotic behaviors for colonial ends to the provision of data for scientific analyses that could lead to the generation of universal laws of human behavior and cultures. In *Sexual Life of Savages* (1929), the Polish anthropologist Bronislaw Malinowski led the trend for anthropologists to observe patterns and schemas in cultural behavior. In this book, about a Papua New Guinea culture, Malinowski studied sexual behavior as part of the organic functioning of society. Sexuality was studied in relation to normative modes of behavior such as courtship, marriage, and family relations.

Also in this period, fieldwork was formalized as the primary method of anthropologists. Instead of comparing and analyzing records generated by colonial officers and missionaries, anthropologists themselves traveled to far-flung places to observe culture firsthand.

## Mapping Sexual Worlds before Stonewall

The Cold War confrontation between the United States and the Soviet Union, as well as the conditions of post–World War II academic environments, influenced the rise of anthropological research projects that sought to document and compare social behavior and societies around the world. These projects were considered crucial in the introduction of modernizing or Westernizing processes. In such studies, societies were categorized according to specific characteristics that placed them in various stages of modernization.

The Human Relations Area Files (HRAF), founded in 1949 at Yale University, was one such project. Information about gender and sexual behavior in the files was fragmentary and incomplete at best. Despite this shortcoming, many anthropologists and other social scientists created typologies and categories of homosexual behavior based on regional and national locations.

*Patterns of Sexual Behavior* (1951), written by Clellan Ford and Frank Beach, was one such heroic attempt to come up with a comprehensive analysis. Utilizing HRAF data, they catalogued and categorized various sexual behaviors and included a significant section on homosexuality, in which they grouped societies according to those that approved of homosexuality and those that proscribed it. Basically, their analysis showed that in most of the 200 societies surveyed, homosexuality was practiced, and in at least two-thirds, homosexuality was considered normal or acceptable. Ford and Beach also suggested that male homosexuality was more prevalent than female homosexuality. Interestingly, they combined this survey with comparative cases among subhuman primates and other mammals, concluding that there was a natural, or biological, tendency for this kind of "inversion."

The sexual patterns and schemas proposed by various researchers during this period were never neutral and were always ordered around Western forms and types as the ideal end-point of hierarchical typologies. Non-Western sexual behaviors were seen as premodern antecedents of modern Western sexual formations.

While sex research during the 1950s and 1960s was often linked with the dominant figure of the sexologist Alfred C. Kinsey and his team, in the nonclinical social sciences, the stigma theory proposed by Erving Goffman held sway. In his 1963 work *Stigma,* Goffman suggested that people dissimulate and hide behind facades in everyday life. He further asserted that people with "spoiled" identities or those labeled "deviant" attempt to manage these conditions through various strategies in daily encounters. Although Goffman never explicitly focused on homosexuality, his ideas provided the framework for many post-Stonewall anthropological studies.

## The Emergence of LGBT Anthropology

The Stonewall Riots in 1969, the removal of homosexuality from the standard list of mental illnesses by the American Psychiatric Association in 1973, and the slow but eventual establishment of LGBT and queer studies in academia precipitated a noticeable shift in anthropological research on LGBT issues. One difference between anthropology and other disciplines in the social sciences and humanities is that anthropology focuses more attention on non-Western perspectives. LGBT anthropology provided a critique of existing categories and concepts such as homosexuality through the study of non-Western, non–Euro-American, and nondominant cultures, which did not necessarily find these categories and concepts useful or meaningful. This, in turn, challenged previously held assumptions about marginalized groups of "deviant" people in American communities. Homosexuality was increasingly seen as a historically and culturally specific phenomenon that arose in Euro-American societies in the late nineteenth century and was identified as neither a universal source for identity formation nor a ubiquitous basis for social stigma or discrimination. For example, anthropologists suggested that, unlike the situation in dominant European and American cultures today, in many societies, sexual object choice (choice about whether to have sex with people of the same sex or the other sex) was not the all-encompassing foundation for determining gender and sexual identities.

Laud Humphreys's controversial *Tearoom Trade* (1970) was the first intensive ethnographic study of covert homosexual practices in the United States. Humphrey chronicled the intricacies of behavior in a men's public toilet and the sexual and social interaction that occurred therein. Taking a different approach, Esther Newton's pioneering 1972 book *Mother Camp,* about female impersonators in several American cities, was not a simple description of these men's lives. Rather, Newton, through her use of stigma theory, questioned foundational precepts and categories by provocatively suggesting that gender is a fiction or a performance. Gender, she argued, is constituted through a series of performative scripts from which people enact and improvise their roles in everyday life. Newton's study provided the impetus and propelling force in mobilizing debates in contemporary feminist and transgender studies. In 1980, Kenneth Read provided a compelling ethnography of a gay bar called the Columbia, combining symbolic analyses with stigma theory to delineate what he called "homosexual styles." Following Goffman's scheme, Read suggested that homosexuality was a genre with multiple styles of expression.

Elizabeth Kennedy and Madeline Davis's influential study of working-class butch/femme lesbians in Buffalo, New York, *Boots of Leather, Slippers of Gold: The History of a Lesbian Community* (1993), took a diachronic view of race, class, and gender components in lesbian bar culture. Utilizing life-history narratives of European American, African American, and Native American lesbians, the authors, whose work was first published in the 1970s, wove together stories that reveal how historical conditions, race, class, and gender played roles in the development of a lesbian community in upstate New York from the early years of the twentieth century.

Humphrey, Read, Newton, Kennedy, and Davis were concerned with specific geographic sites that homosexuals frequented. In a radical departure from these approaches, Gilbert Herdt, the editor of *Ritualized Homosexuality in Melanesia* (1986), considered homosexuality not only as a practice in a specific social site, but also as a constitutive element in the socially prescribed process of a boy's development. Studying the Sambia, a group in highland Papua New Guinea, Herdt asserted that homosexuality was part of ritualized practices in the transition from Sambian boyhood to manhood. Homosexual practices between Sambian boys and men were episodic, and early homosexual interactions in childhood led to exclusive heterosexuality in adulthood.

## Class, Race, Gender, and Space

The tendency to focus on the cultural particularities of homosexual persons and behaviors led to more studies where homosexuality was subjected to further classification and where gay and lesbian identities were shown to be gaining ground in various societies. Differences

between and among homosexual practices were primarily attributed to geographic place. However, in many cases, these works constructed homosexuality, homosexuals, gays, and lesbians in monolithic and unproblematic terms and did not consider influences and interaction between and across politically demarcated national, regional, or cultural borders. More importantly, in most cases, these works did not consider how, even within a specific geographic location, cultural background, race, class, age, gender, and other factors all influence how people behave and identify.

At the same time, the idea that having same-sex sexual partners necessitated a gay or lesbian identity was increasingly questioned. The AIDS pandemic in the 1980s brought this problem to the forefront when health officials were faced with the disjunction between behavior and identity. Many women and men did not identify as gay or lesbian, even after admitting to having had sex with members of their own sex, and so could not effectively be reached through informational campaigns that targeted people who identified as gay or lesbian. Eventually, LGBT anthropological research began to consider how race, class, and ethnic cleavages exist in LGBT culture and how LGBT culture itself contains a plurality of practices and identities.

Evelyn Blackwood's important 1986 volume *The Many Faces of Homosexuality* explores various dimensions and "faces" of homosexuality by providing a more critical cross-cultural array of cases from China to Native American societies. Blackwood's book veers away from the uncritical classificatory schemes still prevalent in the field by confronting head-on the existence of multiple contexts for what is considered "homosexual."

United States–focused LGBT anthropology also exhibited a growing sensitivity to racial, class, and ethnic differences. The broad and wide-ranging body of research on Native American *berdaches* and two-spirit people is a crucial intervention that has helped to create a more complicated view of homosexuality. The pioneering works of William Roscoe (*The Zuni Man-Woman,* 1991) and Walter Williams (*The Spirit and the Flesh,* 1992), together with such works as a collection by Jacobs, Thomas, and Lang (*Two Spirit People,* 1997), demonstrate how gender-crossing and sexual practices among Native Americans are not local expressions of modern gay and lesbian identities. Instead, these works portray the complicated links between these practices and the fraught histories and cultures of Native Americans.

Gilbert Herdt's edited volume on American gay culture *Gay Culture in America* (1992) and Stephen Murray's book *American Gay* (1996) also were responses to the growing effort to dislodge the monolithic idea of American gay culture as primarily white and middle class. Both books attempted to seriously consider the particular contexts and conditions that confront American gay men, including AIDS, suburban life, and racial tensions.

William Hawkeswood's research on black gay men in the Harlem district of New York City, *One of the Children* (1996), is the first full-length ethnographic study of a nonwhite American gay community. His subjects were primarily African American men who lived and socialized in their own community. Among these men, race and sexuality are identities that are negotiated with the realities of living in what was then an economically deprived and crime-ridden area in New York City and at the same time a center for African American cultural life. For this group of men, being black took precedence over being gay, illustrating how identities are differentially valued, maintained, and transformed in various communities.

In addition to considering a broader context for queer cultures and identities, LGBT anthropology moved from a preoccupation with gay bars and other public institutions to the examination of the domestic sphere. Kath Weston's now-classic study *Families We Choose* (1991) demonstrated the creative ways in which gays and lesbians from various ethnic and racial backgrounds recast and refigure kin and family relationships. Ellen Lewin responded to the dearth in anthropological study of lesbians with two works, a sole-authored book on lesbian mothers, *Lesbian Mothers* (1993), and an edited volume on lesbian culture in the United States, *Inventing Lesbian Cultures in America* (1996). In *Lesbian Mothers,* Lewin focused on the role of motherhood by comparing groups of lesbian and heterosexual mothers. She argued that, despite obvious structural differences, both groups shared common pools of meanings and practices. At the same time, Lewin suggested that motherhood should not be seen as a unitary phenomenon but as a dynamic source of strategies that shape and maintain domestic practices and identities.

Transgender issues have slowly become part of LGBT anthropology. While the history of gender nonconforming persons such as the Native American *berdache* and the Filipino *bantut* have been part of the cross-cultural data in LGBT anthropology, it was only in the 1990s that political and cultural debates about transgenderism began to widen the scope and range of the phenomena included within the categories under discussion. David Valentine's work on the transgender communities in New York City is not just an attempt to add transgender to the LGB triad,

but rather to critically examine the cultural, political, economic, and social conditions that make this category possible—or impossible—to maintain on both a scholarly and political level.

## Institutionalization of LGBT Anthropology

Within the anthropology profession, LGBT anthropology gained an institutional home in the Society of Lesbian and Gay Anthropologists (SOLGA). The history of the organization can be traced to 1978, when some members of the American Anthropological Association (AAA), the national professional organization of anthropologists in the United States, met as the Anthropology Research Group on Homosexuality during the association's annual meeting in Los Angeles. Before this historic first meeting, there had been other organizing efforts, including academic panels on homosexuality and resolutions on research and training in LGBT studies during the AAA meetings.

In 1987, the Anthropology Research Group on Homosexuality was renamed the Society of Lesbian and Gay Anthropologists to reflect the political, social, and academic concerns of its constituents. While LGBT anthropological scholarship has flourished since the 1980s and 1990s, numerous problems still exist, including discrimination against LGBT students and faculty and the lack of opportunities for scholars doing LGBT research. In response to these issues, the AAA created the Commission on Lesbian, Gay, Bisexual and Transgendered Issues in Anthropology (COLGBTIA) in 1993 to document past and continuing discriminatory practices in the profession and to suggest future actions to improve conditions for LGBT scholars.

## Toward a Global LGBT Anthropology

Anthropology, together with other humanities and social science disciplines, is today confronted with the processes of globalization. While traditional anthropology initially focused on the image and idea of the stranded, nonmobile native other, it has become clear that with the rise of immigration, the rapid movement of transnational capital, and new communication and transportation technologies, ideas, cultures, and people are no longer bound to specific geographic places. Colonialism and transnationalism form the backdrop for an LGBT anthropology that is increasingly global.

Most LGBT anthropological works now acknowledge that LGBT identities and practices are not spreading in a uniform and equal way in various parts of the world. For example, Martin F. Manalansan IV's work on Filipino gay immigrant men's deployment of Stonewall Riots tropes suggests that the world is not witnessing a progressive linear transformation that culminates in modern gay and gender identities. New works demonstrate how various groups, including immigrants of color, formerly colonized peoples, and migrant laborers, are negotiating new practices and identities that depart from hegemonic Western LGBT identities and practices.

Elizabeth Povinelli and George Chauncey have emphasized that, while studies of globalization in general have focused on the study of circuits or flows of information, practices, and peoples, the task of LGBT research should be to explore how various peoples are confronting these received images, ideas, and identities. Don Kulick illustrates how cultural, historical, and economic conditions affect the formation of queer identities, activism, and communities among Brazilian gay men and transgender sex workers. The case studies of Deborah Amory, Lisa Rofel, and Rosalind Morris in Tanzania, China, and Thailand are responding to the call to meticulously document and analyze the uneven and contradictory relationship between the forces of transnational media-borne queer ideas and practices and local negotiations. In the realm of language, Andrew Wong and Quing Zhang's research on Chinese *tongzhi* discourse illustrates the mobility of identity and language in a transnational context. These studies are part of the growing body of research in LGBT anthropology that engages with the travails of queers in a globalizing world.

## Bibliography

Amory, Deborah P. "Mashoga, Mabasha, and Magai: 'Homosexuality' on the East African Coast." In *Boy-Wives and Female Husbands: Studies in African Homosexualities*. Edited by Stephen O. Murray and Will Roscoe. New York: Palgrave, 1998.

Blackwood, Evelyn, ed. *The Many Faces of Homosexuality: Anthropological Approaches to Homosexual Behavior*. New York: Harrington Park Press, 1986.

Ford, Clellan, and Frank A. Beach. *Patterns of Sexual Behavior*. New York: Harper, 1951.

Goffman, Erving. *Stigma: Notes on the Management of Spoiled Identity*. Englewood Cliffs, N.J.: Prentice-Hall, 1963.

Hawkeswood, William. *One of the Children: Gay Black Men in Harlem*. Berkeley: University of California Press, 1996.

Herdt, Gilbert H., ed. *Ritualized Homosexuality in Melanesia*. Berkeley: University of California Press, 1986.

———. *Gay Culture in America: Essays from the Field*. Boston: Beacon Press, 1992.

Humphreys, Laud. *Tearoom Trade: Impersonal Sex in Public Places*. Chicago: Aldine, 1970.

Jacobs, Sue-Ellen, Wesley Thomas, and Sabine Lang, eds. *Two Spirit People: Native American Gender Identity, Sexuality, and Spirituality*. Urbana: University of Illinois Press, 1997.

Kennedy, Elizabeth Lapovsky, and Madeline D. Davis. *Boots of Leather, Slippers of Gold: The History of a Lesbian Community*. New York: Routledge, 1993.

Kulick, Don. *Travesti: Sex, Gender, and Culture among Brazilian Transgendered Prostitutes*. Chicago: University of Chicago Press, 1998.

Lewin, Ellen. *Lesbian Mothers: Accounts of Gender in American Culture*. Ithaca, N.Y.: Cornell University Press, 1993.

———, ed. *Inventing Lesbian Cultures in America*. Boston: Beacon Press, 1996.

Malinowski, Bronislaw. *Sexual Life of Savages in North-western Melanesia*. New York: Routledge, 1929.

Manalansan, Martin F., IV. "In the Shadows of Stonewall: Examining Gay Transnational Politics and the Diasporic Dilemma." *GLQ* 2, no. 4 (1995): 425–438.

Morris, Rosalind C. "Educating Desire: Thailand, Transnationalism and Transgression." *Social Text* 52–53 (1998): 53–79.

Murray, David. "Between a Rock and a Hard Place: The Power and Powerlessness of Transnational Narratives among Gay Martinican Men." *American Anthropologist* 102, no. 2 (2000): 261–270.

Murray, Stephen O. *American Gay*. Chicago: University of Chicago Press, 1996.

Newton, Esther. *Mother Camp: Female Impersonators in America*. Chicago: University of Chicago Press, 1979.

Povinelli, Elizabeth A., and George Chauncey. "Thinking Sexuality Transnationally: An Introduction." *GLQ* 5, no. 4 (1999): 439–450.

Read, Kenneth. *Other Voices: The Style of a Male Homosexual Tavern*. Novato, Calif.: Chandler and Sharp, 1980.

Rofel, Lisa. "Qualities of Desire: Imagining Gay Identities in China." *GLQ* 5, no. 4 (1999): 451–474.

Roscoe, William. *The Zuni Man-Woman*. Albuquerque: University of New Mexico Press, 1991.

Society of Lesbian and Gay Anthropologists (SOLGA). "A Brief History of the Society of Lesbian and Gay Anthropologists." Available from http://homepage.mac.com/ctgrant/solga/history.html

Valentine, David. "'We Are Not about Gender.' The Uses of Transgender." In *Out in Theory: The Emergence of Lesbian and Gay Anthropology*. Edited by Ellen Lewin and William Leap. Urbana: University of Illinois Press, 2002, 222–245.

Weston, Kath. *Families We Choose: Lesbians, Gays and Kinship*. New York: Columbia University Press, 1991.

Williams, Walter. *The Spirit and the Flesh: Sexual Diversity in American Indian Culture*. Boston: Beacon Press, 1992.

Wong, Andrew, and Qing Zhang. "The Linguistic Construction of the Tongzhi Community." *Journal of Linguistic Anthropology* 10, no. 2 (2001): 248–278.

**Martin F. Manalansan IV**

*See also* BENEDICT, RUTH; KINSEY, ALFRED C.; MEAD, MARGARET; RACE AND RACISM.

# ANTIDISCRIMINATION LAW AND POLICY

### Local and State Nondiscrimination Laws

In March 1972, East Lansing, Michigan, became the first political jurisdiction in the United States to pass a law banning discrimination on the basis of sexual orientation. A year earlier, New York City had considered an LGB rights law but failed to pass it. In 1982, Wisconsin became the first state to pass a sexual orientation nondiscrimination law. By 2003, more than two hundred cities, towns, and counties in the United States had sexual orientation nondiscrimination laws, along with fourteen states plus the District of Columbia. The states are Wisconsin (1982); Massachusetts (1989); Connecticut and Hawaii (1991); California, New Jersey, and Vermont (1992); Minnesota (1993); Rhode Island (1995); New Hampshire (1997); Nevada (1999); Maryland (2001); New York (2002); and New Mexico (2003). Of the fourteen states that have passed these laws, seven are in the Northeast, two in the upper Midwest, four in the West, and one in the upper South. Most of these states, though not all, voted Democratic in the U.S. presidential elections of 1992, 1996, and 2000. Maine twice passed a state nondiscrimination bill, in 1997 and 2000, but both laws were repealed by ballot measures shortly following the state legislature's passage of the laws. Nine states specifically banned sexual orientation discrimination in public sector employment: Colorado, Delaware, Illinois, Indiana, Montana, New Mexico, New York, Pennsylvania, and Washington. Minneapolis, Minnesota, was the first town, city, or county to pass a nondiscrimination law inclusive of people who are gender variant or transgender. The 1974 ordinance defined "affectional preference" as "having or projecting a self-image not associated with one's biological maleness or femaleness." In 1993, Minnesota became the first state to outlaw discrimination on the basis of gender identity, doing so when it also outlawed anti-LGB discrimination. By 2003, four states—including Rhode Island (2001), New Mexico (2003), and California (2003)—and about fifty municipal governments banned anti-transgender discrimination. The years 2002–2003 were a particularly busy period for transgender-inclusive legislation, with Boston, New York City, Chicago, Philadelphia, and numerous other cities and towns passing gender-identity nondiscrimination laws. The question of whether to include "gender identity or expression" along with sexual orientation in statewide nondiscrimination bills has emerged as a divisive issue. Maryland and New York passed laws covering LGB, but not transgender people in 2001 and 2003, respectively. Supporters of transgender-inclusive bills claimed that Minnesota's and New Mexico's passage of such laws proves that including transgender people need not "kill" a bill. Opponents said that New York's Sexual Orientation Nondiscrimination Act, introduced in the 1970s, was on the verge of passing and that adding "gender identity" at the eleventh hour would have delayed nondiscrimination protection for thousands of LGB people across the state. A bill to ban anti-transgender discrimination was introduced in the New York State Assembly in 2003.

Sexual orientation laws protect everyone against discrimination on the basis of sexual orientation, whether heterosexual, homosexual, or bisexual. Transgender-inclusive laws protect people on the basis of real or perceived gender identity or expression. Most of these laws cover discrimination in employment (in both the public and private sectors), housing, and public accommodations. Anti-LGBT discrimination is widespread. A 1998 study of more than five hundred members of three national LGBT rights organizations found that one in three had experienced discrimination. A study conducted in Philadelphia in 2000 found that 30 percent of LGBT respondents had experienced discrimination, and a 2001 New York State study found that half of 1,800 LGBT respondents had encountered discrimination or hostility in a public setting. A 1997 U.S. General Accounting Office report found that all nine states that had passed sexual orientation nondiscrimination laws had reported sexual orientation discrimination cases every year since the passage of the law, although the numbers were small (no more than two hundred cases per year per state).

### Federal Nondiscrimination Policy

In 1975, Congresswoman Bella Abzug of New York first introduced the federal LGB civil rights bill, which would have expanded the Civil Rights Act of 1964 to include sexual orientation. Later, Paul Tsongas and John Kerry, both of Massachusetts, sponsored the bill in the Senate. This bill was comprehensive and would have outlawed discrimination in employment, housing, and public accommodations, as the Civil Rights Act had done on the basis of race, color, national origin, and other characteristics. In 1994, after nearly two decades of frustration over lack of passage of the LGB rights bill, activists shifted strategy and promoted the Employment Nondiscrimination Act (ENDA), a bill that covered only employment and exempted small businesses. ENDA just barely failed to pass the U.S. Senate in 1996 on a 50–49 vote, and it has never passed the House.

In the late 1990s, the LGBT movement split over ENDA's failure to include gender identity in its nondiscrimination language. The National Gay and Lesbian Task Force; Parents, Family, and Friends of Lesbians and Gays; the National Organization for Women; and other groups pushed for the expansion of ENDA to cover gender identity. Other groups and leaders have promoted a dual-track approach, urging that ENDA remain unchanged and instead suggesting a separate gender-identity nondiscrimination bill or a second, transgender-inclusive ENDA.

U.S. President Bill Clinton issued Executive Order 13087 in May 1998, which banned discrimination in federal civilian employment on the basis of sexual orientation. In the second presidential debate in October 2000, Texas governor George W. Bush expressed opposition to what he called "special rights" or "special protective status" for gays and lesbians, using the rhetoric of the anti-LGBT right wing. While Clinton and Vice President Al Gore supported ENDA, Bush expressed his opposition to it, yet he did not revoke the nondiscrimination executive order issued by Clinton in 1998 when he became president, and the order still bans sexual orientation–based discrimination in federal civilian employment.

## Housing

Access to a place to live is an important human right, but same-sex couples and LGBT people are vulnerable to housing discrimination. When couples search for apartments or homes together, they may be easily identifiable as gay or lesbian. Few states ban sexual orientation–based discrimination in housing; those that do are California, Connecticut, New York, New Mexico, Maryland, Massachusetts, Minnesota, New Hampshire, New Jersey, Rhode Island, Vermont, and Wisconsin, along with the District of Columbia. In many cases, LGBT families have little or no remedy when they are denied a home because of their sexual orientation or marital status. In addition, LGBT families are unable to qualify as a "family" when applying for public housing, which decreases their likelihood of being able to access public housing. Federal fair housing laws do not protect LGBT people from discrimination.

In 1977, the Department of Housing and Urban Development (HUD) attempted to adopt an expansive definition of family that would have encompassed same-sex couples, but Congress eliminated this provision. In the 1989 case of *Braschi v. Stahl Associates,* a New York court ruled that a gay man whose partner had died of AIDS had the right to stay in his rent-controlled apartment, under state protections against the sudden eviction of family members following the death of the person who

had signed the lease. Under the Clinton administration, HUD policy was not to discriminate on the basis of sexual orientation. It remained unclear whether that continued to be the policy under the Bush administration. Low-income and elderly LGBT people are particularly in need of affordable housing and especially vulnerable to discrimination.

## Backlash: Anti-LGBT Initiatives

The first of more than a hundred anti-LGBT ballot initiatives in the last three decades of the twentieth century sought and achieved the repeal of a sexual orientation nondiscrimination ordinance in Boulder, Colorado, in 1974. Anita Bryant's successful "Save Our Children" campaign, which repealed Dade County, Florida's sexual orientation nondiscrimination law in 1977, was the second anti-LGBT ballot measure but the first to reach national prominence. It led to a wave of anti-LGBT measures, many involving the repeal of LGB rights laws, in the late 1970s. A second wave of ballot measures seeking to repeal sexual orientation nondiscrimination laws swept the country in the early 1990s, in part in reaction to the widespread passage of LGB rights laws at the local and state levels. The citizens of Colorado passed Amendment 2 in November 1992 by a 53 to 46 percent margin. This measure repealed existing local and state laws or policies protecting "homosexual, lesbian, or bisexual" people against discrimination and prohibited the future adoption or enforcement of "any [such] law or policy." A year later, the voters of Cincinnati, Ohio, Lewiston, Maine, and dozens of municipalities in Oregon passed similar ballot questions.

In 1996, in *Romer v. Evans,* the U.S. Supreme Court struck down Colorado's Amendment 2, ruling that it violated the Constitution's guarantee of equal protection of the laws and that it was motivated not by any rational state interest but solely by "animus" toward LGB people. Despite this ruling, the U.S Supreme Court declined to review another federal court's ruling upholding Cincinnati's law, which was modeled on the Colorado measure. Cincinnati's repeal of and prohibition of LGB rights laws still stands, making the actual impact of *Romer v. Evans* unclear. Narrower ballot measures repealing existing nondiscrimination laws have passed in Maine (1995, 1998, and 2000) and in several municipalities around the country. In the late 1990s, anti-LGBT activists broadened their scope beyond repealing nondiscrimination laws, also attacking same-sex marriage, other forms of partner recognition, antihomophobia initiatives in public schools, and sex education. LGBT and progressive straight activists may have turned the corner in 2001 and 2002, when, for the first time, they won a majority of anti-LGBT ballot measure campaigns. This included the successful defense of Dade County's sexual orientation nondiscrimination law in September 2002 and of an LGBT nondiscrimination law in Tacoma, Washington, in November 2002. On-the-ground training and capacity-building support from the National Gay and Lesbian Task Force, as well as the leadership and hard work of local activists, played a key role in this shift.

## Faith-Based Initiative and Discrimination in Employment and Service Provision

The Faith-Based Initiative, issued as an executive order by President Bush in December 2002, authorizes the transfer of federal funds to religious institutions to pay for the delivery of a wide range of social services. This executive order represents a significant step toward privatization and desecularization of the social service infrastructure in the United States. Under the House of Representatives Faith-Based Initiative bill passed in 2001 (H.R.7), institutions receiving such funding were explicitly allowed to discriminate on the basis of religious affiliation. While the Senate bill (S.1924) removed this explicit authorization of discrimination, its silence on the issue may have been interpreted by the Justice Department as authorizing such discrimination. Bush issued his executive order after the Democratic-controlled Senate failed to pass the bill. Religious discrimination often serves as a proxy for race, gender, and sexual orientation discrimination. Under the faith-based initiative, LGBT people could be discriminated against in hiring and in the provision of services, and religious organizations could justify it as essential to maintaining the "religious character" of a program. Although guidelines issued by Bush as he signed the executive order urged compliance with local and state nondiscrimination laws, these laws all exempt religious organizations.

Under experiments with public funding of religious social service providers, people have lost or been denied social service jobs in Kentucky and Georgia. Two were fired because they were lesbians, and one was denied a job because he was Jewish. (After being asked to provide the name of his minister on a job application, this man was told, "We don't hire people of your faith.") A federal court ruled that the firing by the state-funded Kentucky Baptist Homes for Children of a Kentucky lesbian counselor due to her sexual orientation did not violate any laws or constitutional principles.

## Strong Majority Support for Nondiscrimination Laws

At the dawn of the twenty-first century, some 103 million Americans (more than one third of the country's population) lived in cities, counties, or states that outlawed sexual orientation discrimination; in 1990, less than 20 million did. Three states and more than fifty municipalities also have passed transgender nondiscrimination laws. This expansion of nondiscrimination laws has resulted from the hard work of thousands of grassroots activists and from the increased support of the general public for such laws. In the last decade of the twentieth century, strong majorities emerged in public opinion polls in support of sexual orientation nondiscrimination laws with respect to employment. In the 2000 National Election Study, a majority of Republicans (55.6 percent) advocated sexual orientation nondiscrimination laws, as did two thirds of independents and three fourths of Democrats. Three in five Americans endorsed transgender nondiscrimination laws, according to a September 2002 Human Rights Campaign poll. In short, LGBT nondiscrimination laws enjoy strong majority support and city, county, and state governments all over the country are leading the way in passing laws to mandate equal treatment.

## Bibliography

Cahill, Sean, Mitra Ellen, and Sarah Tobias. *Family Policy: Issues Affecting Gay, Lesbian, Bisexual, and Transgender Families.* New York: Policy Institute of the National Gay and Lesbian Task Force, 2003.

Keen, Lisa, and Suzanne B. Goldberg. *Strangers to the Law: Gay People on Trial.* Ann Arbor: University of Michigan Press, 1998.

U.S. General Accounting Office. *Sexual-Orientation-Based Employment Discrimination: States' Experience with Statutory Prohibitions,* GAO/OGC-98-7R. Washington, D.C. 23 October 1997.

Vaid, Urvashi. *Virtual Equality: The Mainstreaming of Gay and Lesbian Liberation.* New York: Anchor Books, 1995.

Van der Meide, Wayne. *Legislating Equality: A Review of Laws Affecting Gay, Lesbian, Bisexual, and Transgendered People in the United States.* New York: Policy Institute of the National Gay and Lesbian Task Force, 2000.

Yang, Alan S. *The 2000 National Election Study and Gay and Lesbian Rights: Support for Equality Grows.* New York: Policy Institute of the National Gay and Lesbian Task Force, 2001.

**Sean Cahill**

*See also* ATLANTA; BOSTON; BOY SCOUTS AND GIRL SCOUTS; COLORADO; DISCRIMINATION; EDUCATION LAW AND POLICY; EMPLOYMENT LAW AND POLICY; FAMILY LAW AND POLICY; FEDERAL LAW AND POLICY; HATE CRIMES LAW AND POLICY; HEALTH AND HEALTH CARE LAW AND POLICY; KAMENY, FRANKLIN; LIQUOR CONTROL LAW AND POLICY; MILITARY LAW AND POLICY; NATIONAL GAY AND LESBIAN TASK FORCE (NGLTF); PRIVACY AND PRIVACY RIGHTS; RIGHTS OF ASSOCIATION AND ASSEMBLY; TRANSGENDER AND GENDER IMPERSONATION LAW AND POLICY.

# ANTI-SEMITISM

Anti-Semitism is generally understood to refer to negative or stereotyped ideas about and hostile behavior toward Jews. It should be distinguished from anti-Judaism, which refers specifically to negative attitudes toward Judaism as a religious system, and anti-Zionism, which is strong antipathy to the existence of the state of Israel. Anti-Semitism could refer to hatred of Semitic peoples in general and so include antipathy toward any group that comes from or resides in the Middle East, but it has been associated primarily with hatred toward Jewish people, without reference to geographic location or national origin. The term "anti-Semitism" was coined in the nineteenth century by scholars who accepted the newly theorized, biologically based racial divisions among humankind. While the biological basis for considering Jews to be Semites is no longer taken seriously, the term has retained its importance as a social category, analogous with terms like racism and homophobia. The analogy between anti-Semitism and homophobia, and the fact that there are many LGBT people who also identify as Jews, makes anti-Semitism an important category for the LGBT community.

## Anti-Semitic Stereotypes

The most virulent anti-Semitic stereotypes common in Europe in the nineteenth century depicted Jews as gender inverts. Jewish men were viewed as weak and Jewish women as overbearing and strong. In cartoons, Jewish men were often caricatured with breasts, and anti-Semitic literature suggested that they menstruated. Jewish women were shown as masculine, large, and hairy creatures who were dominating, often depicted bestride men in sexualized poses. In these ways Jews were assumed to be sexual inverts, and so connected to the stereotypes of masculine women and feminine men that were the hallmark of homosexual "deviance" during this period.

## Magnus Hirschfeld and Charlotte Wolff

The Nazis developed the connection between the experiences of Jews and male homosexuals by persecuting both groups. For example, one of the leaders of the sexology movement, Magnus Hirschfeld, was persecuted by the Nazis as a Jew and as a homosexual. His Institute for Sexual Science in Berlin was shut down by the Nazis in 1933, and he died in exile. Charlotte Wolff was another sex researcher who went into exile from Nazi Germany. She left in 1933 after she lost her job in a family planning clinic because Jews were forbidden to serve as doctors. She narrowly escaped arrest by the Gestapo the week

before she planned to leave, taken in by the authorities not because of her Jewish identity, but because she dressed in male attire and was presumed to be a woman impersonating a man. She was saved by one of the arresting officers, whose wife had been Wolff's patient. In the 1970s Wolff returned to Germany and spoke to the nascent lesbian movement about the connections she saw between anti-Semitism and the oppression of "sexual deviants" in Nazi Germany. The experiences of Hirschfeld and Wolff are emblematic of the way anti-Semitism and homophobia can be linked.

## Connecting Anti-Semitism and Homophobia

From the start of the homophile movement in the 1950s, LGBT people in general and Jews in the LGBT community in particular have been aware of the links between the institutional discrimination encountered by both Jews and LGBT people. As they understood the connections, both Jews and LGBT people were the subject of stereotyping based on gender nonconformity and sexual "deviance" as well as Nazi persecution. Members of both groups have felt the need to hide their identities to avoid being the victims of hatred or assault, the loss of jobs, or the respect of people around them. These parallels have created bonds between Jews and LGBT people, but also friction. Many Jews are quite sensitive about the suffering the Jewish people experienced during the Holocaust, and are not always pleased when the LGBT community compares the suffering of its members to that of the Jews under the Nazi regime. Some Jews are uncomfortable with any comparison between Jewish suffering in the Holocaust and the suffering of others. Some are simply homophobic and recoil at any comparison between Jews and gay men. To be sure, gay men in Germany were sent to concentration camps and died there in large numbers, and homosexuality was forbidden by law and subject to severe punishment. But many Jews believe that this is not comparable to the Nazi persecution of Jews, the event that defined the term "genocide." Hitler destroyed two-thirds of Europe's Jewish population and most of its culture and institutions. The notion that the pink triangle worn by homosexual men in concentration camps could rival the yellow star Jews were forced to wear under the Nazis distressed some LGBT Jews. Others appreciated the analogy and fashioned a pink triangle on top of a yellow star to suggest their approval of the connections and similarities. The Holocaust Memorial Museum in Washington, D.C., has led the way in bringing both experiences to public attention and making clear the similarities of oppression while highlighting the difference in terms of the magnitude of suffering.

While Jewish concerns with the comparison have focused primarily on misuse of the Holocaust, the LGBT community also has not always welcomed the comparison of homophobia and anti-Semitism. Many in the LGBT community see anti-Semitism as an issue of the past, as it appears to most people outside the Jewish community to have almost disappeared since the 1970s. Parts of the LGBT community have appeared insensitive to the ways in which invisibility functions to silence Jews as well as LGBT people in society and to how anti-Israel sentiment affects the Jewish community. These misunderstandings have led to some friction between LGBT Jews and the greater LGBT community.

## The Metropolitan Community Church

At the beginnings of the gay liberation and lesbian feminist movements in the 1960s, religion in general was not held in high regard. Many people who associated with these movements initially believed that they could and should leave their ethnic and religious identities behind. In addition, LGBT people suffered terrible oppression in their churches and synagogues, and religious institutions were (and in many instances still are) the central institutional symbol of LGBT oppression. While the antagonistic relationship with organized religion was prevalent, many LGBT people worked to reconcile their deeply held religious beliefs with their sexual orientation. Some brought those elements together in the Universal Fellowship of Metropolitan Community Churches (MCC), founded in 1968 by the Reverend Troy Perry. In the early years, Jews became involved in MCC as the only place to turn where they could have a spiritual connection and be open about their sexuality. But it soon became clear that MCC was a Christian space; Jews felt unwelcome and uncomfortable, and invisible as Jews. This led to the founding of synagogues that later federated as the World Congress of LGBT Jews.

## Lesbians in the Women's Movement

Jewish women were present in large numbers during the early years of the lesbian feminist movement. Many of them, while not religious, soon discovered that they were uncomfortable with the absence of any mention or understanding of their Jewish roots or identity in the face of the universalizing tendencies of the majority Christian culture. They also expressed concern about anti-Judaism within the feminist movement, where the Hebrew Bible was being blamed for the birth of patriarchy. When they raised the issues of anti-Judaism or Jewish invisibility, they were often met with hostility and outrage. This isolation within the feminist movement was the leading impetus for the publication in 1982 of the anthology *Nice*

*Jewish Girls: A Lesbian Anthology* and of a second volume in 1986 titled *The Tribe of Dina*. The books condemned the invisibility of Jews in the lesbian feminist movement and were attempts to correct it by discussing Jewish lesbian experience. The essays argued that feminists trivialized Jewish experience and used stereotypes of "pushy" and "aggressive" Jews to silence Jewish women in the movement. These works made feminist and lesbian groups aware of the irony of permitting Jews to remain invisible in a movement whose very purpose was to support the visibility of LGBT people. They also paved the way for dialogue about connections among issues of racism, homophobia, and anti-Semitism as, for example, portrayed in the book of essays *Yours in Struggle: Three Feminist Perspectives on Anti-Semitism and Racism* (1984). They also raised the consciousness of the Jewish community about LGBT Jews.

Much of the anti-Semitism faced by Jews in the early years of the gay liberation and feminist movements has ceased. Jews, however, still experience invisibility and occasional hostility in the LGBT movement, especially in conservative enclaves.

### Bibliography

Alpert, Rebecca T. *Like Bread on the Seder Plate: Jewish Lesbians and the Transformation of Tradition.* New York: Columbia University Press, 1997.

Beck, Evelyn Torton, ed. *Nice Jewish Girls: A Lesbian Anthology.* Watertown, Mass.: Persephone Press, 1982.

Bulkin, Elly, Minnie Bruce Pratt, and Barbara Smith. *Yours in Struggle: Three Feminist Perspectives on Anti-Semitism and Racism.* New York: Long Haul Press, 1984.

Cooper, Aaron. "No Longer Invisible: Gay and Lesbian Jews Build a Movement." In *Homosexuality and Religion.* Edited by Richard Hasbany. New York: Harrington Park Press, 1989.

Gilman, Sander L. *The Jew's Body.* New York: Routledge, 1991.

Kantrowitz, Melanie Kaye, and Irena Klepfisz, eds. *Tribe of Dina: A Jewish Women's Anthology.* Montpelier, Vt.: Sinister Wisdom Books, 1986.

**Rebecca T. Alpert**

*See also* ARAB AMERICANS; GINSBERG, ALLEN; JEWS AND JUDAISM; LESBIAN FEMINISM; MUSLIMS AND ISLAM; RACE AND RACISM.

# ANTIWAR, PACIFIST, AND PEACE MOVEMENTS

U.S. lesbians and gay men have long claimed leadership roles in the quest for peace. Their open participation in antiwar movements has been contested at times through the course of the twentieth century, however, and lesbians and gay men themselves have debated whether or not their cause should be bound up in the struggle against war and militarism.

In the aftermath of World War I, Tracy Mygatt and Frances Witherspoon helped launch the War Resisters League (WRL) in 1923. Typical of romantic friendships between upper-class women of their era, Mygatt and Witherspoon lived and worked together for sixty-five years (1908–1973), sharing their passion for peace. During World War II, even as the mass mobilizations and demobilizations of millions of men and women proved critical to the growth of urban lesbian and gay communities, thousands of men went to prison rather than accept induction into the armed forces. These draft resisters included several gay men who emerged as preeminent postwar pacifists, most notably Bayard Rustin. The African American activist better known as Dr. Martin Luther King, Jr.'s advisor and as the organizer of the 1963 civil rights march on Washington, D.C., Rustin worked for the Christian-pacifist Fellowship of Reconciliation (FOR) through the 1940s and early 1950s.

When Rustin lost his position with FOR following his 1953 arrest by Pasadena, California, vice squad officers on charges of lewdness and vagrancy, the secular, socialist-pacifist WRL hired Rustin. He remained with the organization for more than a decade. Rustin also helped launch the influential journal *Liberation,* which advocated economic and social justice through nonviolent revolution. *Liberation* featured writings by other LGB pacifists, including David McReynolds, Barbara Deming, and Paul Goodman. Synthesizing the philosophies of Karl Marx and Mohatmas Gandhi, McReynolds worked for nearly forty years as a WRL organizer (1960–1999)—and as an openly gay man for almost that entire time.

The escalation of the Vietnam War in the 1960s prompted diverse reactions among U.S. lesbians and gay men. Many homophile activists, some of whom served in the armed forces during World War II, contrasted their service to the nation with what they perceived as the cowardice of antiwar protestors, and urged the government to lift the military ban on homosexuals. However, many younger gays and lesbians joined their heterosexual counterparts protesting the war, even as they often suffered the heterosexist prejudices and presumptions of their comrades in the movement.

Greg Calvert, who served as the National Secretary of Students for a Democratic Society (SDS), the largest white student organization of the 1960s, reported the extensive harassment he received as a somewhat openly bisexual man in the New Left. The gay-baiting accelerated as SDS leaders began advocating violent means to end the Vietnam War and U.S. imperialism in general, eventually driving Calvert out of SDS altogether. From there he turned to organizing active-duty servicemen in Texas and Massachusetts against the war, and later joined the antinuclear and Central American solidarity movements. Calvert's story was repeated throughout the New Left, as heterosexual men mocked their rivals as homosexuals, bragged about their prowess with women, and joked about pretending to be gay to avoid the draft, partly to deflect the condemnation of those who equated their opposition to the war with insufficient masculinity.

Following the Stonewall rebellion of 1969, gay and lesbian New Leftists organized Gay Liberation Front (GLF) groups across the United States. In taking that name, GLF paid homage to the National Liberation Front of South Vietnam, the insurgency more commonly known as the Vietcong. Activists such as the former SDS leader in Philadelphia, Kyoshi Kuromiya, led GLF contingents marching at antiwar demonstrations in the early 1970s. However, many lesbians in GLF quickly grew frustrated by the sexism of their gay male comrades and left to establish lesbian feminist organizations, whereas new groups like the Gay Activists Alliance criticized GLF's efforts to fuse gay liberation with antiwar, antiracist, and anticapitalist politics.

Throughout the 1970s and 1980s, lesbians and gay men openly participated in a wide range of peace protests. They joined solidarity movements opposed to U.S. policies toward Chile, El Salvador, and Nicaragua; campaigned against nuclear weapons; and worked to end Washington's support for the apartheid regime in South Africa. Lesbian feminists played an especially significant role in leading these movements, taking part in feminist peace encampments at the Seneca Army Depot in upstate New York and at the Savannah River weapons-grade plutonium processing facility in Barnwell, South Carolina. As young lesbians looked to foremothers such as Barbara Deming for theoretical and personal inspiration, veteran 1960s activists such as Leslie Cagan and Mandy Carter built careers organizing others around peace, feminist, and lesbian/gay issues. Cagan, previously a participant in the 1967 Pentagon demonstrations, early Cuban solidarity projects, and 1970s feminist organizing, coordinated the 12 June 1982 Central Park rally for nuclear disarmament, which was attended by a million people. Cagan did so despite the discomfort of some rally sponsors at having a lesbian in such a visible position.

In early 1991 AIDS Coalition to Unleash Power (ACT UP) and Queer Nation chapters took to the streets to join demonstrations against the first Persian Gulf War. In New York, ACT UP members interrupted the *CBS Evening News* show hosted by Dan Rather, shouting, "Fight AIDS not Arabs!" In San Francisco, queer protestors chanted, "Fags suck dick, Dykes lick labia, U.S. out of Saudi Arabia!" As Operation Desert Shield segued into Desert Storm, the National Gay and Lesbian Task Force (NGLTF) condemned the war. Some community members questioned whether organizations dedicated to LGBT rights should speak out on foreign policy. However, NGLTF argued that its mission of social justice required the group to address the broad consequences of the war, including its impact on lesbian and gay servicepersons and the associated deep financial cuts to healthcare services and AIDS research.

This debate continued through the 1990s as U.S. troops saw action in Somalia, Haiti, Kosovo, Afghanistan, and elsewhere. Late in 2002, with the second Persian Gulf War looming, NGLTF, the Metropolitan Community Church, the International Gay and Lesbian Human Rights Commission, and numerous smaller LGBT organizations joined with a broad coalition of social, racial, economic, and environmental justice groups to oppose a unilateral invasion of Iraq. Simultaneously, the gay Log Cabin Republicans endorsed the Bush administration's campaign against Saddam Hussein's alleged weapons of mass destruction program. In doing so, they demonstrated that the relationship between U.S. LGBT and antiwar movements would remain contested for the foreseeable future.

## Bibliography

Calvert, Gregory Nevala. *Democracy from the Heart: Spiritual Values, Decentralism, and Democratic Idealism in the Movement of the 1960s.* Eugene, Ore.: Communitas Press, 1991.

D'Emilio, John. *Lost Prophet: Bayard Rustin and the Quest for Peace and Justice in America.* New York: The Free Press, 2003.

Deming, Barbara. *We Are All Part of One Another: A Barbara Deming Reader.* Edited by Jane Meyerding. Philadelphia: New Society Publishers, 1984.

Early, Frances H. *A World without War: How U.S. Feminists and Pacifists Resisted World War I.* Syracuse, N.Y.: Syracuse University Press, 1997.

Jay, Karla, and Allen Young, eds. *Out of the Closets: Voices of Gay Liberation.* New York: New York University Press, 1992.

McReynolds, David. *We Have Been Invaded by the 21st Century.* New York: Praeger, 1970.

Spatt, Mindy. "Gay and Lesbian Experiences and Sensibilities in the Antiwar Movement." In *Cultural Politics and Social Movements.* Edited by Marcy Darnovsky, Barbara Epstein, and Richard Flacks. Philadelphia: Temple University Press, 1995.

Suran, Justin David. "Coming Out against the War: Antimilitarism and the Politicization of Homosexuality in the Era of Vietnam." *American Quarterly* 55, no. 3 (Sept. 2001): 452–488.

Teal, Donn. *The Gay Militants: How Gay Liberation Began in America, 1969–1971.* New York: Stein and Day, 1971.

**Ian Lekus**

*See also* ADDAMS, JANE; AIDS COALITION TO UNLEASH POWER (ACT UP); ANARCHISM, SOCIALISM, AND COMMUNISM; BACA, JUDY; GAY LIBERATION FRONT; GILMAN, CHARLOTTE H.; GINSBERG, ALLEN; GOODMAN, PAUL; ISHERWOOD, CHRISTOPHER; KEPNER, JAMES; KUROMIYA, KYOSHI; MILITARY; NATIONAL GAY AND LESBIAN TASK FORCE (NGLTF); NEW LEFT AND STUDENT MOVEMENTS; RICH, ADRIENNE; RUSTIN, BAYARD; WAR; WITTMAN, CARL.

## ANZALDÚA, Gloria (b. 26 September 1942), writer.

Born into a sharecropping–field-worker family in south Texas, Gloria Anzaldúa has produced work that critiques the multiple forms of violence against which women of color and border dwellers struggle in south Texas and elsewhere in the United States. As a woman of color publishing in Anglo feminist circles (a term broadly used in Chicana feminist writings in the 1970s and 1980s) and as a Latina who became widely read throughout liberal arts classrooms in the United States, she was pivotal in breaking through various barriers. Equally important, her collaborative work served as a bridge to spur dialogue among women, especially queer women of color and Anglo feminists. In the twenty-first century, much of her writing became controversial, as women from a number of communities interpreted and claimed her work for their own purposes.

Anzaldúa grew up in south Texas. Her father died when she was fourteen, making it necessary for her to work in the fields throughout high school. While a student at Pan American University, she was still working in the fields, and attributed the intersecting experiences of farm worker meetings, La Raza Unida Party conferences, and feminist consciousness raising to forming her early mestiza consciousness. She earned her B.A. in English, art, and secondary education from Pan American University, went on to earn an M.A. in English and education from the University of Texas, and then supported herself through teaching, while writing and producing a number of important works.

A prolific writer, speaker, poet, and theorist, Anzaldúa's most widely read works are *This Bridge Called My*

Back: Writings by Radical Women of Color (1981), edited with queer Chicana poet and playwright Cherríe Moraga; This Bridge We Call Home: Radical Visions for Transformations (2002), edited with AnaLouise Keating; and Borderlands/La Frontera: The New Mestiza (1987). These works were part of a larger genre utilized by women of color in the 1980s that used anger and rage to challenge and transform colonialism. Other works of this genre, with which Anzaldúa was in dialogue, include Cherríe Moraga's Loving in the War Years: Lo que nunca pasó por sus labios (1983), Audre Lorde's Zami: A New Spelling of My Name (1982), and Barbara Smith's black feminist anthology, Home Girls (1983). Such works were a product of a larger dialogue among women of color as they worked in multiple women's, workers', lesbians', and nationalist movements but found no place where they, as queer women of color, could fully empower themselves.

When This Bridge Called My Back was first published, it produced a flurry of responses among white women and women of color. In the 1990s, Anglo feminists were struggling to broaden their vision of feminism; This Bridge Called My Back is one of the texts that caused Anglo Feminists to attempt to be more inclusive of other voices. For many women of color, the text voiced struggles too long silenced or marginalized by Anglo feminists. For white women, it provided a bridge over which they could begin to struggle and grapple with concepts of multiple identities and the problems of colonial feminism. The book quickly became a textbook for many women's studies courses. In 1986 This Bridge Called My Back won the Before Columbus Foundation American Book Award, and shortly thereafter the Astrea Lesbian Writers Fund also awarded Anzaldúa the 1992 Sappho Award of Distinction.

Anzaldúa's first monograph, Borderlands, met a similar reception. Because of its accessibility, Borderlands was often utilized by Anglo feminists, both in their classrooms and to inform their own scholarly work. Unfortunately, the scholarship sometimes failed to move beyond gestures of tokenism or, worse, became yet another instance of appropriation. While some white readers criticized Anzaldúa's anger, the text broke down barriers both in the classroom and in the world of publishing. At a number of levels, it was revolutionary: it utilized code-switching between English and Spanish; it called attention to the many ways that structural oppressions intersect at the border and on the bodies of women of color, particularly Chicana lesbians; and it opened up a national dialogue on the importance of borderlands. Borderlands was chosen as one of the "38 Best Books of 1987" by Library Journal. By the time of its reprinting in 1999, it was a nationally recognized text, assigned in many literature, women's

studies and ethnic studies courses throughout the nation. The popularity of the text gave rise to new challenges; with so many critics interpreting the work, it became (along with Cherríe Moraga's Loving in the War Years) one of the most appropriated Chicana lesbian texts of the twentieth century. Eventually Donna Haraway's "A Cyborg Manifesto" became the most commonly cited work that attempted to integrate mestiza theory, but in reality appropriated and distorted Chicana texts instead.

Other writings and anthologies by Anzaldúa attracted less attention. Yet all of her texts, including her children's literature, challenge her readers to look deeper, to search beneath anti-immigrant, antiwoman, antiqueer, and antimestiza mythologies to find deeper truths, power struggles, and opportunities for liberation. Likewise, in both her formal essays and in her interviews, she continues to challenge readers to "queer the world" and not to think of queerness in sexual terms alone, but instead to use queerness to disrupt the status quo, those social systems that continue to inflict violence upon borderlands and upon the bodies of queer women of color.

## Bibliography

Aigner-Varoz, Erika. "Metaphors of a Mestiza Consciousness: Anzaldúa's Borderlands/La Frontera." MELUS 25, no. 2 (Summer 2000): 46–62.

Anzaldúa, Gloria. Borderlands/La Frontera: The New Mestiza. San Francisco: aunt lute books, 1987.

———. Prietita and the Ghost Woman. San Francisco: Children's Books Press/Libros Para Niños, 1995.

Anzaldúa, Gloria, ed. Making Face, Making Soul: Haciendo Caras. San Francisco: aunt lute books, 1990.

Anzaldúa, Gloria, with AnaLouise Keating, eds. Interviews/ Entrevistas. New York: Routledge, 2000.

Anzaldúa, Gloria and Cherríe Moraga, eds. This Bridge Called My Back: Writings By Radical Women of Color. New York: Kitchen Table: Women of Color Press, 1984.

Folkes, Diane L. "Moving from Feminist Identity Politics to Coalition Politics through a Feminist Materialist Standpoint of Intersubjectivity in Gloria Anzaldúa's Borderlands/La Frontera: The New Mestiza," Hypatia 12, no. 2 (Spring 1997): 105–124.

Hernández, Monica. "With Heart in Hand/Con Corazón en la Mano: An Interview with Gloria Anzaldúa." Color Lines 2, no. 3 (1999): 29–31.

Moya, Paula M. L. "Postmodernism, "Realism," and the Politics of Identity: Cherríe Moraga and Chicana Feminism." In Feminist Genealogies, Colonial Legacies, Democratic Futures. Edited by M. Jacqui Alexander and Chandra Talpade Mohanty. New York: Routledge, 1997.

Rueman, Ann. "Coming into Play: An Interview with Gloria Anzaldúa," MELUS 25, no. 2 (Summer 2000): 4–45.

**Linda Heidenreich**

See also LITERATURE; MORAGA, CHERRÍE; RADICAL SPIRITUALITY AND NEW AGE RELIGION.

# ARAB AMERICANS

A diverse ethnic group, Arab Americans or their ancestors have emigrated from Arab countries in Southwest Asia and North Africa; some are people of mixed ethnic heritage. Emigration patterns vary among Arab Americans, in part due to the different political, social, and economic histories of Arab countries.

Sexual and gender transgressions (queerness) in Arab American contexts include dating, extramarital sex and premarital sex, homosexuality, ethnic and religious exogamy, and pregnancy outside of marriage. These behaviors are understood to be defiant according to a set of sexualized and gendered norms that define Arab culture in Arab American communities. The importance of sexual transgression in Arab American communities can be understood in terms of the role that Arab women's sexuality plays in defining Arab culture. Arab women living in the United States feel pressure to maintain their Arab culture as they are understood to be the conveyors of culture. One of the strongest ways that culture is viewed as being maintained is through the continuation of behaviors that are part of the honor complex such as modesty in clothing (i.e., no shorts or mini-skirts), abstaining from talking with males other than family members, living in the parents' home until marriage, not staying out late at night, and remaining a virgin until marriage. According to Nadine Naber in her 2001 work *Arab San Francisco,* the "cult of true Arab culture" is a discourse that distinguishes the self from the other by regulating subjectivities, social practices, and behaviors, and that thereby serves to control Arab American bodies, behavior, appearance, and sexual relations.

Arab Americans also regulate sexuality through welcoming or denying belonging and membership in the imagined Arab American community. Sexual transgression could result in a range of responses including familial or community ties being severed. Related to this is the identification by family and community of the transgressor as American, rather than Arab. These varied forms of separation from family and community have the potential to result in an emotional, social, or economic loss to the transgressor and thus serve as a way to maintain control over sexuality.

## Organizations

Although there have always been Arab Americans who have transgressed sexual and gender boundaries, the communal identities and histories of LGBT Arab Americans were largely undocumented until the 1980s. During the late 1980s, formal organizational structures for Arab American lesbians and gays began to emerge as part of a larger movement of lesbian and gay people of color in the United States who organized to create visible structures of support. The first Arab American lesbian organization, the Arab Lesbian Network, was formed in Berkeley, California, in May 1989 by Huda Jadallah. There were five women at the first gathering. The Arab Lesbian Network changed its name (to Arab Lesbian and Bisexual Women's Network) in the course of its development to include bisexual women. Another group, the Arab Lesbian, Gay, and Bisexual Network, which included gay men, also formed.

At the same time that the Arab Lesbian Network was founded on the West Coast, the Gay and Lesbian Arabic Society (GLAS) was established on the East Coast. GLAS was founded by Ramzi Zakharia in Washington, D.C., and, while its membership was mostly male, several women have joined the group. In 1991 GLAS formed a Los Angeles branch that existed until 1994. In 1996, a New York City branch of GLAS was founded, and as of 2002 it is the most active GLAS chapter.

Also in New York City, the Lesbian Arab Network (LAN) held its first meeting on 10 June 1990 at the Lesbian and Gay Community Services Center. A social support group, LAN consisted of seven members, and although it officially ended in 1991, many women continued to be active in other groups. In April 1997, twelve lesbian and bisexual women of Arab and Iranian descent and their partners held a meeting at the Astraea National Lesbian Action Foundation in New York. They formed a group for Arab and Iranian lesbian, bisexual, and transgender women, which was later named Assal (the word for honey in both Arabic and Farsi). The organization grew in size to include over thirty women who traced all or part of their cultural and ethnic identity to Egypt, Iran, Jordan, Lebanon, Morocco, Palestine, or Sudan. The mission of Assal East Coast is to provide a forum for social connection, political activism, and community building. The group's members endeavor to empower themselves, reach out to others, create a presence in the queer movement, and foster acceptance in Arab and Iranian communities.

## The Internet

In the mid- to late 1990s the Internet became a major organizing tool for LGBT Arab Americans. Via Internet lists and websites, queer Arab organizing accelerated at a fast pace. The Internet fostered the growth of both local and international networking among Arab queers. It enabled communities that had been separated by geographical distance to become connected on a regular basis, thus creating not only networks of individuals but also networks of communities. Arab Americans created and participated in both local and international cyber groups. In some cases the groups were cyber groups only and in other cases the groups held regular gatherings in addition to their cyber contact.

In March 1996 Katherine Sherif formed the first Arab lesbian, bisexual, and transgender women's e-mail list. Although the members of the list group are mainly from the United States, there are also members from other countries. The women from the list hold an annual gathering that provides a space for people who have been connecting via the Internet to meet in person. The first gathering was held in 1997 at the Marin Headlands in California. In 1998 and 1999 the gatherings were held in the Catskills in New York. There was no gathering in the year 2000, and in 2001 the gathering was held in Healdsburg, California. In 2002 the gathering was held in the Wisconsin Dells.

Southwest Asian and North African Bay Area Queers (SWANABAQ) is a support group and discussion forum for lesbian, gay, bisexual, transgender, and intersex people (people born with an anatomy that is not standard for males or females). The group includes Afghans, Arabs, Armenians, Assyrians, Berbers, Cypriots, Kurds, Persians, and Turks living in Northern California. SWANABAQ was founded by Heba Nimr, Laura Farha, and Bassam Kassab in November 2000. As of October 2002, there were 183 e-mail list members. They have regular gatherings and parties; thirty people marched in the 2002 San Francisco Pride Parade.

Karama, the New England Lavender Society, is a support group of LGBT Arabs, Persians, and Turks. Based in Boston, the group has members from six states in the northeast. The word *karama* means dignity in Arabic and the organization was founded in January 1999 by Bassam Kassab. As of October 2002, Karama had thirty-five members. They have monthly gatherings, book readings, and lectures. Thirteen people marched with a float in the Boston Pride Parade in 1999.

Additional Internet sites for queer Arabs include GLAS-NYC, GLAS-LA, and Queer Arabs (another cyber group also formed by Sherif that is open to anyone). *Bint el Nas* is an e-zine by and about queer Arab women that is executive produced by the mujadarra grrls. (*Mujadarra* is a traditional Arabic dish made of lentils and rice. The group chose this word because it reflects the nourishing traditions of their ethnic heritage. "Grrls" represents the influence of late 20th century urban U.S. culture on their lives.) Sehakia and Lazeezat are other websites that are for Arab lesbians (including but not limited to Arab Americans).

## Politics

While queer Arab American communities often come together (either in person or on the Internet) as a social network, they also often participate in political activism. Queer Arab Americans express their politics through various means and deal with a range of political issues, from creating queer Arab American visibility within Arab communities and other queer communities to addressing feminist issues to speaking out in solidarity with Arabs around the world who are affected by U.S. foreign policy. These political acts, include marches, protests, educational forums and conferences. The first Gulf War against Iraq in the early 1990s can be seen as a particularly potent moment in the history of queer Arab Americans as they bonded together for social support as Arabs in the United States. As a community they came together to respond politically, holding educational teach-ins and fundraisers in order to send money to Iraqi war survivors in need. Although the impact on queer Arab Americans of the post 9/11 "war on terrorism" is strong, only time will tell the full effect it has on these communities. Many queer Arab Americans have been actively protesting the "war on terrorism" and racial profiling, others have kept a low profile, perhaps out of fear of visibility at a time when being queer and Arab can leave one feeling particularly vulnerable.

## We Exist

Queer Arab Americans are active members of queer communities, Arab communities, and many other communities that reflect who they are as individuals. They come from many walks of life. They are rich, homeless, working class, and middle class. They include lawyers, hairdressers, grocery store owners, temporary workers, and school teachers; they live in big metropolitan cities and in small towns. Very few have children. Their existence and the changing nature and development of their communities is testimony to the fact that Arab Americans cannot be stereotyped as a monolithic group of people, with similar sexualities, families, and lives. In the words of Lina Baroudi, from the 2002 film, *I Exist: Voices from the Lesbian and Gay Middle Eastern Community in the U.S.*: "My being queer is defined by being Arab and my being Arab is defined by my being queer. They exist together, otherwise they cannot exist at all and I know they do, because I exist."

## Bibliography

Baroudi, Lina. *I Exist: Voices from the Lesbian and Gay Middle Eastern Community in the U.S.* A film produced by Peter Barbosa and Garrett Lenoir. San Francisco: EyeBite Productions, 2002.

Massad, Joseph. "Re-Orienting Desire: The Gay International and the Arab World." *Public Culture* 14, no. 2 (2002): 361–385.

Naber, Nadine. "Arab San Francisco: On Gender, Cultural Citizenship and Belonging." Ph.D. dissertation, University of California at Davis, 2002.

**Huda Jadallah**

*See also* ALLEN, PAULA GUNN; ANTI-SEMITISM; MIGRATION, IMMIGRATION, AND DIASPORA; MUSLIMS AND ISLAM; RACE AND RACISM.

# ARCHITECTURE

In 1994, around the time of the twenty-fifth anniversary of the Stonewall uprising, a number of exhibitions, public lectures, and publications came together in New York City to promote the importance of a queer public memory of persons and places. The New York Public Library mounted the exhibit "Becoming Visible." "Windows on Gay Life," a series of installations organized by the National Museum and Archive of Lesbian and Gay Culture, appeared in storefront windows along Christopher Street. "Design Legacies," partly sponsored by the Design Industries Foundation Fighting AIDS, addressed the contributions of architects and designers who had died of AIDS. The Organization of Lesbian and Gay Architects and Designers (OLGAD) published a guide to lesbian and gay New York historical landmarks. The book, *Gay New York,* inspired a history walk focused on LGBT experiences. *In Their Footsteps: Six Walks through New York's Gay and Lesbian History* included the former sites of various LGBT political organizations' headquarters.

Articles and lectures about the queer sexual history of public sites such as bathhouses, rest areas, and piers became popular. OLGAD sponsored the first international conference for queer architecture and design practitioners, entitled "Design Pride '94." Professional organizations such as the Association of Collegiate Schools of Architecture, the National Trust for Historic Preservation, and the Society of Architectural Historians began to regard queer scholarship as part of their heritage. Around this time, Stephen Glassman, a gay architect in Baltimore, helped revise the American Institute of Architects (AIA) Code of Ethics to rule out workplace discrimination based on sexual orientation. He also helped lead the AIA to include sexuality issues as part of the annual AIA national conference on diversity.

This outpouring of information on and interpretations of a queer architectural past and the fight to develop a hospitable future continue to influence LGBT designers. People coming into the field realize the rich history—of persons and places—that came before them. The knowledge that prominent architect Philip Johnson is gay, for example, can encourage a gay student to learn more about Johnson's practice. Learning about the underground and hidden sites of sexual play can influence a designer to think differently about the circulation paths and overlooks found in nightclubs and restaurants.

Space plays a role in the construction of sexual identities. Single sex institutions such as YMCAs, prisons, and schools allow for experiences that help shape sexual choices. These places, where same-sex bonding is encouraged, also contain sites, such as communal showers, where the nude body is visible. By seeing another, a person can test and communicate his or her interests. Bathrooms, which are single-sex and clearly defined, provide private opportunities for the exchange of glances and touching. Bars, which in the past often did not allow visible signs of LGBT presence in the community, are now active participants in the streetscape. The city of Chicago even marks the LGBT neighborhood with rainbow pylons. As a result, people in several urban areas feel freer to express their affections in public.

Architecture, which organizes activities spatially, has historically served to put into built form exclusionary relations of power based on class, race, gender, and sexuality. In the Jim Crow era, people of color were excluded from certain facilities in order to divide the races. In offices, secretaries, often women, were put on display in open spaces while their bosses worked in private spaces of their own. LGBT employees were forced to keep their desks free of personal items such as photos or symbols in order to keep their sexuality hidden from their coworkers. Openly LGBT people were made to feel unwelcome in public. Their safe havens became the often unsafe, abandoned, or destitute nighttime areas. Housing was designed for married, heterosexual couples and their children. It was considered a waste for a single man or woman to own a house on his or her own.

Since buildings support the social purposes they serve, a wider range of open voices can introduce new narratives into architectural actions. The built environment becomes an influence and inspiration. By studying how the construction of space provides the locations where experiences take place, by analyzing what is visible and who is allowed to look, and by outlining the boundaries defined by regulations and culture, designers come to understand that spatial hierarchies inform the relationship of one individual to another. Designers use this knowledge to put change into practice. By identifying and reclaiming the architectural contributions of queer men and women, the profession opens itself up to more diverse interpretations and to an expanding group of practitioners.

## LGBT Architects

What follows is a discussion of some of the LGBT architects who influenced and, in many cases, continue to influence the field as a whole. With the exception of Ashbee, they are all American. While many of these architects were not open about their sexuality, scholars have begun to read through papers and letters trying to find tangible evidence for what others have intuited or implied.

Louis H. Sullivan (1856–1924) was an intuitive architect who followed his own ideas. While the nature of his sexuality is not known definitively, there is a good deal of evidence—both personal and architectural—that suggests he was gay. In his writing and designs, Sullivan fought against tradition and helped create a modern language for tall office buildings. His celebrated phrase, "Form ever follows function," led to efficient structures covered with decorative skin. He drew inspiration from nature and cycles of growth.

Charles Robert Ashbee (1863–1942) was twenty-five years old when he established the Guild and School of Handicraft in Britain to set a high standard of craftsmanship and protect the status of the craftsman. The London-based guild specialized in metalwork, furniture, and bookmaking. A member of the Arts and Crafts movement, Ashbee offered complete house design, from exterior shell to interior decoration and furniture design.

Ralph Adams Cram (1863–1942) moved to Boston from New Hampshire in 1881. The book *Boston Bohemia* describes the creation of a gay subculture at the end of the nineteenth century with Cram at its center. This community of artists and writers fought against convention by challenging Victorian bourgeois ideals and pushing forward modernism. Cram, who understood the importance of cultural symbols, created designs that mixed the erotic, artistic, aesthetic, and religious.

Julia Morgan (1872–1957) came of age as women were becoming more empowered in U.S. society. She was the first woman to study architecture at Paris's École des Beaux Arts and to be registered as an architect in the state of California. In her practice, she was less concerned with creating a name for herself than with remaining sensitive to the needs of her buildings' users. Hired by many women's organizations, she designed houses, schools, and churches around Berkeley. She also worked with William Randolph Hearst; the most famous result is his grand estate, Hearst Castle, which is located in the small town of San Simeon, California.

Geoffrey Scott (1884–1929), an architect and writer, is best known for the book *Architecture of Humanism*, first published in 1914. This distills the principles of the Roman architect Vitruvius down to the three essentials of good architecture: Commodity, Firmness, and Delight. Scott also argued that to be appropriate, design must always take the human body into consideration.

Eleanor Raymond (1887–1989), an architect with innovative ideas, was never able to break into the mainstream of design. Exploring new technologies and materials, she built several "firsts" in New England, including an International Style home and a prefabricated plywood dwelling. She also worked with Dr. Maria Telkes of the Massachusetts Institute of Technology to use solar power for environmentally sound heating systems.

Bruce Alonzo Goff (1904–1982) became a champion of individual expression and promoted his sometimes eccentric beliefs while chairman of the School of Architecture at the University of Oklahoma. Goff's complex, amorphous enclosures rely on the geometry of simple shapes and the unusual use of everyday materials. His Seabee Chapel in California is made from Quonset huts, while Bavinger House in Oklahoma uses oil well drilling pipes, and Price House in Oklahoma includes walls of coal and glass and ceilings of goose feathers.

Philip Cortelyou Johnson (1906–present) helped curate the influential exhibit "International Style: Architecture since 1922" at the Museum of Modern Art in New York in 1932; this presented European architecture focused on functional structure and simple aesthetics rather than traditional forms and ornament. As an architect, he became well known in 1949 for his own home in New Canaan, Connecticut, an open glass-box house interrupted by minimal plumbing walls. After introducing architectural elements from the past into his work, Johnson became a leading proponent of corporate postmodernism. While criticized as someone more interested in a building's outward appearance than in ideology or social purpose, Johnson continues to evolve and has perhaps the most famous face in architecture. Though it was not until his eighties that Johnson publicly came out, he has always lived a fairly open life with his partner, David Whitney.

**Drager House.** This 1994 modernist building, set into a hillside in Berkeley, California, was designed by Franklin D. Israel. [**ESTO Photographics**]

Paul Rudolph (1918–1997) rebelled against the simple, functional forms of modernism. His lively, adventurous buildings have labyrinthine plans, multifaceted facades, and textured materials. The bold, expressive style he promoted became known as brutalism. In his government, commercial, and residential buildings, light enters the interior at a variety of angles and directions, staircases wind through the space creating overlooks and terraces, and reinforced concrete surfaces are animated with striations.

Charles Willard Moore (1925–1993) was a teacher at several influential universities including Princeton, Yale, the University of California at Los Angeles, the University of California at Berkeley, and the University of Texas (Austin). One of the creators of architectural postmodernism, he promoted the playful and colorful interplay of classical elements. He incorporated ordinary materials, was influenced by the vernacular, and designed with a sense of theatricality. His memorable designs make a place identifiable and acknowledge the people who use the buildings.

Alan J. Buchsbaum (1935–1987) developed a style known as "high tech." His informality and use of off-the-shelf industrial materials helped create the look of lofts in New York City. A favorite among celebrities, his interiors were unpretentious and adventurous, mixing together pop art and more conservative styles, color and texture, and fixed and temporary elements. He died of complications from AIDS.

Robert A. M. Stern (b. 1939) is admired by clients for his stylish nostalgia and criticized by academics for his cynical revivalism. He has worked on planning studies for public spaces such as Times Square and Celebration, Florida; served on the board of corporations such as Disney; and designed tableware, furniture, and textiles. His built projects include museums, office buildings, and a number of residences, many influenced by eighteenth-century estates.

Rodolfo Machado (b. 1942) and Jorge Silvetti (b. 1941) are partners in their architectural and private lives. Their projects, which rely on both fantasy and experience, are tactile and exaggerated, confrontational and hopeful. They question cultural forms while creating beautiful alternatives. Diverse in scale, these projects show that the architects are comfortable designing pavilions, residences, and public buildings, as well as handling urban design plans. The firm is dedicated to envisioning a meaningful architecture in the public realm.

Franklin D. Israel (1945–1996), while born in Brooklyn, came to Los Angeles to practice. His work reflects the fragile balance and cultural context of the city. Designing sculptural and innovative residences and offices for Hollywood stars and top executives, he challenged the banality and regularity of modern structures. His contemporary approach encompassed fragmentation, juxtaposition, and heterogeneity, mirroring the multiplicity and clashing elements of a twenty-first century city. His career ended early due to AIDS.

Mark Robbins (b. 1956) produces architectural works that examine the social and political aspects of living in the built environment. His installations ask viewers to explore the public and institutional contexts that help shape our surroundings. Often shown in galleries or designed as site-specific projects, Robbins's works also reveal how the body and its representations intersect with the ordering of space. In recent photographic collages, Robbins relates our obsession with body culture to interior design and the urban context.

Joel Sanders (b. 1958) questions the norms of society by creating innovative, fluid environments for a changing culture. He examines how new forms of domesticity can make room for contemporary life, encouraging alternative forms of interaction. He also designs flexible, multipurpose spaces with high-tech possibilities. *Stud:*

*Architectures of Masculinity*, which he edited, explores the relation between space and male identity.

## Claiming a Queer Space

How do we interpret spaces that are layered with LGBT history? How do queer neighborhoods turn sites of commerce and social life into rich cultural and historical experiences? How do we build for diverse interests and perspectives?

LGBT people appropriate and transform the sites around them and are themselves appropriated and transformed by their sites. They play a role in designing and shaping the urban, suburban, and rural landscape, and landscape plays a role in designing and shaping them. The assertion of sexual identity in public spaces and activist resistance to discriminatory zoning policies have something to say about the social dimensions of architecture. If space has function and meaning, then marking or claiming a place contributes to self- and social acceptance.

While it is hard to read built form, some openly LGBT architects offer alternative approaches that challenge conventional notions. They blur distinctions and push supposed limits. Their sexuality is one of the many facets that factor into their imagining or reimagining of our built environment.

## Bibliography

Betsky, Aaron. *Queer Space: Architecture and Same Sex Desire*. New York: Morrow, 1997.

Chauncey, George. *Gay New York: Gender, Urban Culture, and the Making of the Gay Male World, 1890–1940*. New York: Basic Books, 1994.

Hurewitz, Daniel. *In Their Footsteps: Six Walks through New York's Gay and Lesbian History*. New York: Footsteps, 1994.

Ingram, Gordon Brent, Anne-Marie Bouthillette, and Yolanda Retter, eds. *Queers in Space: Communities, Public Places, Sites of Resistance*. Seattle, Wash.: Bay Press, 1997.

Leap, William L., ed. *Public Sex, Gay Space*. New York: Columbia University Press, 1999.

Martinac, Paula. *The Queerest Places: A National Guide to Gay and Lesbian Historic Sites*. New York: Holt, 1997.

Sanders, Joel, ed. *Stud: Architectures of Masculinity*. New York: Princeton Architectural Press, 1996.

Shand-Tucci, Douglass. *Boston Bohemia, 1881–1900: Ralph Adams Cram: Life and Architecture*. Amherst: University of Massachusetts Press, 1995.

Schulze, Franz. *Philip Johnson: Life and Work*. New York: Knopf, 1994.

Twombly, Robert. *Louis Sullivan: His Life and Work*. New York: Viking, 1986.

**Ira Tattelman**

*See also* GHETTOS AND NEIGHBORHOODS; SAME SEX INSTITUTIONS; URBAN, SUBURBAN, AND RURAL GEOGRAPHIES.

# ARENAS, Reinaldo (b. 16 July 1943; d. 7 December 1990), writer.

Perhaps the best-known gay Cuban writer in the twentieth century, Reinaldo Arenas was born in the countryside, near the city of Holguín, in Cuba's Oriente province. The son of unmarried peasant parents, Arenas was raised by his mother and maternal grandparents. Early on in life, Arenas discovered the joys of sex (with girls, boys, uncles, farm animals, and trees) and writing (his juvenilia include soap opera-inspired novels). In 1958, he joined Fidel Castro's guerrillas, who were fighting against dictator Fulgencio Batista. With the triumph of the revolution in 1959, he was awarded a scholarship to attend a provincial polytechnic institute and later, in 1962, the University of Havana.

In the nation's capital, Arenas won a storytelling competition, a recognition that secured him a job at the National Library. He then wrote his first novel, the prize-winning *Celestino antes del alba* (1967; *Singing from the Well* [1987]), the only one of his many books to be published in Cuba. Arenas soon experienced the revolution's oppressive measures in matters sexual and cultural. He began to be the object of constant harassment for his openly gay sexuality and for his smuggling of manuscripts out of Cuba—most notably, his second novel, *El mundo alucinante* (1969; *The Ill-Fated Peregrinations of Fray Servando* [1987]). Undaunted, Arenas continued to write incessantly, having to write again several manuscripts each time the secret police confiscated the original copies. Between 1974 and 1976, he was imprisoned for a year and a half on trumped-up charges of molesting a minor.

Despite Cuba's efforts to silence Arenas, he was immediately recognized, upon the publication abroad of *El mundo alucinante*, as a major voice in Latin American letters. In 1980, he engineered a way to leave the island in the midst of the confusion of the Mariel boatlift as one of the thousands of gays the Cuban authorities literally shipped to the United States among 125,000 "undesirables." Arenas settled in New York City, where, after struggling with AIDS, he committed suicide in 1990.

During the ten years that he lived in the United States, Arenas rewrote lost and confiscated manuscripts and penned new works. In his structurally unconventional, defiantly carnivalesque, and stylistically brilliant writings, Arenas challenges the repressive power of institutions (e.g., the state, the family) that limit political, artistic, and sexual expression. Castro and the "mother" figure, who for Arenas personify the oppression against which citizens and sons must fight or face "castration," are two of the dominant figures in the Cuban's fictions. In his works, Arenas situates same-sex eroticism within a broader array of transgressions, including nonmarital, orgiastic, intergenerational, and incestuous sexualities. A prolific author who wrote in all literary genres, Arenas was best known during his lifetime as a novelist.

Of Arenas's nine novels, *El mundo alucinante* is his masterpiece. A fictionalized biography of a rebellious eighteenth-century Mexican friar, it has been interpreted as both Arenas's spiritual autobiography and an allegory of Cuba's repressive regime. *Celestino antes del alba, El palacio de las blanquísimas mofetas* (1980; *The Palace of the White Skunks* [1990]), *Otra vez el mar* (1982; *Farewell to the Sea* [1986]), *El color del verano* (1991; *The Color of Summer* [2000]), and *El asalto* (1991; *The Assault* [1994]) constitute a five-novel cycle. As they delineate the portrait of a gay artist, these novels also narrate what Arenas calls "a secret history of Cuba." *Arturo, la estrella más brillante* (1984; *Arturo, The Brightest Star*, included in *Old Rosa: A Novel in Two Stories* [1989]) tells the story of a gay man in one of Cuba's labor camps to which, between 1965 and 1967, men suspected of "improper conduct" were sent for rehabilitation. Of these seven novels, only *El color del verano* was written entirely in the United States, as were his other two novels: *La Loma del Ángel* (1987; [*Graveyard of the Angels* (1987)]), a parodic rewriting of Cirilo Villaverde's novel *Cecilia Valdés* (1882); and *El portero* (1989; *The Doorman* [1991]), a fable set in New York City that re-creates the painful experiences of a life in exile with Arenas's characteristic humor.

In August 1990, four months before committing suicide, Arenas completed his autobiography, *Antes que anochezca (Before Night Falls)*. Published posthumously in 1992 and immediately translated into other languages, Arenas's lyrical, nostalgic, humorous, irreverent, and sexually explicit autobiography became a commercial and critical success. The *New York Times Book Review* not only pictured Arenas on its cover, but also hailed the memoir as one of the best books of 1993. With an introduction, which addresses the author's sufferings from AIDS and the book's genesis (Arenas composed it on his deathbed), *Antes que anochezca* proceeds chronologically, starting with Arenas's childhood and adolescence in eastern Cuba, followed by his Havana years, and ends with his exile in the United States. Politics, literature, and sex, the three constants in Arenas's life, take up most of the book's pages. Although the story of the persecuted dissident writer captivates many readers, the story of the sexual outlaw has earned Arenas's autobiography a distinctive place in the Latin American canon. By most accounts, *Antes que anochezca* is the first openly gay autobiography written by a Latin American writer—a writer who, for instance, had no qualms about telling his readers that he regularly had young men queue up outside of his room waiting for their turns to penetrate him anally; that he actively sought sex with "real men" (not other gay men); and that by the age of twenty-five he had had sex with some five thousand men. In the United States, where he found sexual reciprocity to be the norm among gay-identified men, Arenas longed for the gender-differentiated sex of his Cuban years.

Dissatisfied with the ghettoization of North American gay culture and alienated from the Cuban American community because of its materialism, anti-intellectualism, and machismo, Arenas did not feel at home in the United States. Ironically, Arenas, still considered a persona non grata in his native Cuba, has secured a place in the hearts and minds of many U.S. Americans, though perhaps less for his books than for Julian Schnabel's film adaptation of his autobiography in the highly acclaimed *Before Night Falls* (2000).

**Bibliography**

Arenas, Reinaldo. *Before Night Falls.* Trans. Dolores M. Koch. New York: Viking, 1993.

*Before Night Falls.* Director, Julian Schnabel. Fine Line Features, 2000.

Epps, Brad. "Proper Conduct: Reinaldo Arenas, Fidel Castro, and the Politics of Homosexuality." *Journal of the History of Sexuality* 6 (1995): 231–83.

González Echevarría, Roberto. "An Outcast of the Island." *New York Times Book Review* 24 October 1993: 1, 32–33.

Olivares, Jorge. "A Twice-Told Tail: Reinaldo Arenas's 'El Cometa Halley.'" *Publications of the Modern Language Association of America* 117 (2002): 1188–1206.

Ríos Ávila, Rubén. "Caribbean Dislocations: Arenas and Ramos Otero in New York." In *Hispanisms and Homosexualities,* edited by Sylvia Molloy and Robert McKee Irwin. Durham: Duke University Press, 1998.

Santí, Enrico Mario. "The Life and Times of Reinaldo Arenas." *Michigan Quarterly Review* 23 (1984): 227–36.

Soto, Francisco. *Reinaldo Arenas.* New York: Twayne, 1998.

**Jorge Olivares**

# ART HISTORY

Stereotypes of the effeminate male connoisseur and the bossy old-maidish museum guide have long linked art history to homosexuality. Though oversimplified and pejorative, these stereotypes—like most—contain a kernel of truth, for the history and practice of art history are fundamentally linked to sexual and gender identity. More positive views of the links between art history and minority sexual and gender identities are products of the feminist and LGBT movements of the late twentieth century, which turned many pejorative stereotypes into affirmations of identity.

The origin of art history as a field of study (as it evolved from collections of biographies or treatises on technique published by artists) is generally credited to the detailed analyses of the stylistic evolution of classical sculpture by the eighteenth-century German scholar Johann Joachim Winckelmann (1717–1768). A subsequent important step in art history's development was the nineteenth-century invention of handbooks on artists and iconography intended for tourists and museum goers; these were the first art history books written in English and the first intended for a broad audience. Both of these formative stages in the development of art history may be linked to the history of sexual identity.

The influence of Winckelmann's homosexuality on his scholarship has been recognized since at least the Victorian era, when the English historian Walter Pater (1839-1894) described him as a prototype for the Aesthete, an individual in whom artistic sensibility and transgressive sex/gender identity fused. "That his affinity with Hellenism was not merely intellectual, that the subtler threads of temperament were interwoven in it, is proved by his romantic, fervent friendships with young men," Pater asserted (p. 191). More recently, the art historian Whitney Davis, in his pioneering 1994 anthology on lesbian and gay art history, analyzed Winckelmann's influential methodology as an androgynous fusion "of subjective, feminized 'witness' and objective, masculinized 'allusion,'" which expresses "Winckelmann's homosexuality (or homotextuality)" (p. 151). Davis is critical of art history's subsequent efforts to deny its feminized emotional and erotic aspects, often by relegating them to supposedly less objective practices under the rubrics of art criticism or art appreciation.

A similar reevaluation of the sex/gender dynamics of art history's development derives from feminist investigations of once popular but now ignored Victorian art handbooks, most of which were written by women. Foremost among these authors was the American Anna Jameson (1794–1860). Briefly married, Jameson supported herself through her writing and was passionately committed to feminist campaigns for equality of education and opportunity. She assisted and promoted female artists and actresses, including those in her community of expatriate women in Rome, where Jameson's rigorous museum tours were both admired and mocked by visiting male intellectuals (writer Nathaniel Hawthorne described her in his Notes on Travel as "a very sensible old lady" who assumed her auditors did not know "one single simplest thing about art"). Although shifting standards of acceptable physical intimacy among women preclude a simplistic application of current notions of sexual identity to these women, this community was at least protolesbian. Jameson's women-centered approach found groundbreaking expression in the chapter "Thoughts on Female Artists" from her 1834 Visits and Sketches at Home and Abroad. Jameson here proposed ideas later developed by feminists of the 1970s concerning the reevaluation of aesthetic characteristics conventionally belittled as feminine, among them patient attention to craft and a female sensibility that Jameson described as "a power, felt rather than perceived, and kept subordinate to the sentiment of grace" (quoted in Holcomb, p. 20).

Winckelmann's sensuality, Pater's Aestheticism, and Jameson's feminism all exemplify what might be called the "queer" origins of art history. However, the stigma attached to these associations between art history and homosexuality has made the profession reluctant to analyze—or even acknowledge—visual expressions of homosexuality. Before the mid-1980s, the only sustained analysis of art's relationship to homosexuality was James Saslow's thoughtful reviews and art historical essays in the Advocate. Saslow in 1978 also contributed to a pioneering anthology on gay and lesbian culture a biting critique of the institutional forces that prompted museums and universities to obscure artists' sexual orientation, contrasting these to the small commercial galleries willing to promote openly gay contemporary artists to gay consumers.

Feminist collectives in the late 1970s offered another pioneering venue for the identification and analysis of art about sexual orientation. Small exhibitions in New York in 1978 and Los Angeles in 1979 featured art by self-identified lesbians. In 1982, when the New Museum in New York mounted Extended Sensibilities, the first exhibition to focus on gay and lesbian artists, the art press reacted skeptically to the show's premise that a "sensibility" connected to sexual orientation united the work (these shows are analyzed in Harmony Hammond's Lesbian Art in America and short essays by the organizers appear in Nayland Blake et al.'s In a Different Light).

The first effort at a comprehensive study of modern art in relation to homosexuality was not published until 1986, and then by an author, Emmanuel Cooper, unaffiliated with a museum or university, and through a commercial press. The first effort at a global survey of the topic was Saslow's 1999 *Pictures and Passions,* also published by a commercial press.

These survey texts display the strengths and weaknesses of the genre. Produced quickly, widely available, and covering a great deal of material, they in some instances oversimplify complex issues. More scholarly study of homosexuality has come slowly to art history. Again, Saslow was a leader. His 1986 *Ganymede in the Renaissance* meticulously documents the importance of homosexuality in the careers of some of the most famous artists in history. Other scholars who make sophisticated use of visual sources to understand the history of homosexuality include John R. Clarke on ancient Rome, Abigail Solomon-Godeau on eighteenth-century France, and Gary P. Leupp on Tokugawa Japan. It is worth noting, however, that Leupp is a cultural—not an art—historian, for art history has been especially reluctant to address issues dealing with homosexuality before the nineteenth century and outside European and Euro-American cultures. One often cited reason is concern over the distortions inherent in applying contemporary categories of identity to other times and places. This caution seems to affect studies of homosexuality disproportionately, however, when logically it ought to apply equally to other historically fluid forms of identity, such as nationality. The slow growth in the study of homosexuality's relation to art history also reflects continuing institutional imperatives to orient the discipline toward uncritical "appreciation" of sanctioned aesthetic experiences and away from topics perceived as controversial, such as sexual identity.

Although these imperatives have sometimes succumbed to challenges from feminist and LGBT activists, since the 1980s a political backlash against reform movements of the previous decades combined with anxieties about AIDS has strengthened the repression of art and strategies of interpretation dealing with homosexuality. Debates sensationalized by local and national politicians focused on museums that hosted a retrospective exhibition of Robert Mapplethorpe's photography between 1988 and 1990, culminating in the much publicized criminal trial of the director of the Contemporary Arts Center in Cincinnati, Ohio, on charges of distributing obscene images. Although the trial ended in an acquittal, the defense's argument that the extraordinary abstract beauty of Mapplethorpe's photographs justified their erotic subject matter did not encourage other museums to exhibit art dealing explicitly with sexuality. During the debates, right-wing politicians led by Senator Jesse Helms enacted

legislation prohibiting federal funding for any exhibition of "obscene or indecent" art, defined broadly and vaguely to include depictions of "homoeroticism" (documents from these debates are anthologized in *Culture Wars,* edited by Richard Bolton).

In this cultural climate, subsequent major museum shows with supposedly comprehensive catalogs devoted to artists such as Andy Warhol, Robert Rauschenberg, and Thomas Eakins ignored the homoerotic elements in these artists' works and lives. The Guggenheim Museum canceled an essay it commissioned from the eminent art historian Thomas Crow for the catalog of its 1997 Rauschenberg retrospective when the artist objected to the author's acknowledgment of his "intimate" relationship with Jasper Johns (the essay was eventually published in *Artforum* in September 1997). As mainstream a source as the *New York Times* even commented on the omission of any reference to sexual identity in exhibitions on the work of Warhol and Eakins. Art historians associated with small gay-identified art institutions such as the Queer Cultural Center in San Francisco reported active interference by galleries and journalists in their efforts to curate and publicize exhibitions dealing with homosexuality (the May 1998 and October 2002 newsletters of the Gay and Lesbian Caucus of the College Art Association report on such censorship issues).

Debates over the relevance of homosexuality to art history have been especially bitter in relationship to the art of Rauschenberg and Johns. The veil of secrecy that surrounded public discussion of their relationship as a couple was pierced by Kenneth Silver. His essay "Modes of Disclosure," although not published until 1992, broke ground in lecture versions delivered in 1986 and 1988, he elucidated Johns's and (to a lesser extent) Rauschenberg's art as an expression of the condition of secrecy imposed on homosexuals. Arguments that both the "closet" and the AIDS epidemic were formative to Johns's art were developed in Jill Johnston's *Jasper Johns: Privileged Information.* Jonathan Katz's "The Art of the Code" developed a complementary analysis in relation to Rauschenberg, and his "Passive Resistance" proffered persuasive arguments for why art dealing with secrecy should have become the paradigm for avant-garde American culture in the 1950s.

Johns and his allies among high-profile art historians have actively discouraged and denigrated such scholarship. Johns refused to allow the reproduction of his art in Johnston's book, and when powerful Museum of Modern Art chief curator Kirk Varnedoe collaborated with Johns on a major retrospective of the artist's work in 1996, he gave an interview attacking those who "read explicit homosexual content" in Johns's art as "ghettoising or narrowing the list of meanings in the work," and then refused to elaborate on how strategies of coding constitute "explicit homosexual content" or how adding new interpretations of art can narrow its meaning (Kaufmann, pp. 16–17).

Similarly, a gratuitous final footnote in Rosalind Krauss's essay, written in collaboration with Rauschenberg for the Guggenheim's catalog, belittles Katz for elucidating "themes of gay subculture" in the art, although her own conclusion that Rauschenberg's work offers a "message of uncertainty, slippage, of unreadability and fragmentation" (Krauss p. 223, no. 60) is quite close to the analysis of both Katz and Silver, who see this "message"—not specific iconographic details—as reflecting the condition of homosexual identity. The persistence of homophobia is evident in these panic-stricken defensive and illogical reactions by famous artists and influential scholars to thoughtful analysis of the links between homosexuality and art history.

This context renders all the more important recent groundbreaking art historical scholarship on the relationship between modern (and postmodern) American art and homosexuality. Martin A. Berger, Whitney Davis, and Jonathan Weinberg, all very sensitive to changing cultural perceptions of same-sex eroticism, have traced manifestations of homosexual identity in late-nineteenth- and early-twentieth-century American art. In addition to Katz, Johnston, and Silver, Ann Eden Gibson and Richard Meyer have focused on art from the mid-twentieth century. Gibson has documented how sexuality (along with race and gender) marginalized certain artists within the Abstract Expressionist movement during the 1950s, while the others have analyzed how the dynamics of sexual secrecy and censorship affected some of the best-known art from that period. Curators Trevor Fairbrother and Thomas Sokolowski have played an especially crucial role in guiding some museums and galleries toward thoughtful display and scholarship on art that engages sexual identity. Thomas Waugh, traversing the lines that conventionally divide art from commercial photography, has traced the development of a male homoerotic aesthetic among photographers. Erica Rand has explored the implications of lesbian perspectives on the production of and reaction to a wide range of popular visual culture. Exploring fields that art historians have traditionally neglected, the artist Harmony Hammond has published useful surveys of U.S. lesbian and homosexual artists in the American Southwest.

## Bibliography

Berger, Martin A. *Man Made: Thomas Eakins and the Construction of Gilded Age Manhood.* Berkeley: University of California Press, 2000.

Blake, Nayland, Lawrence Rinder, and Amy Scholder, eds. *In a Different Light: Visual Culture, Sexual Identity, Queer Practice.* San Francisco: City Lights Books, 1995.

Bolton, Richard, ed. *Culture Wars: Documents from the Recent Controversies in the Arts.* New York: New Press, 1992.

Clarke, John R. *Looking at Lovemaking: Constructions of Sexuality in Roman Art, 100 B.C.–A.D. 250.* Berkeley: University of California Press, 1998.

Cotter, Holland. "Everything about Warhol but the Sex." *New York Times,* 14 July 2002.

Crow, Thomas. "This is Now: Becoming Robert Rauschenberg." *Artforum* September 1997: 95–100, 139–152.

Davis, Whitney. "Erotic Revision in Thomas Eakins's Narratives of Male Nudity." *Art History* 17 (September 1994): 301–341.

———. "Winckelmann Divided: Mourning the Death of Art History." In *Gay and Lesbian Studies in Art History,* pp. 141-159. Edited by Whitney Davis. New York: Haworth Press, 1994.

Davis, Whitney, ed. *Gay and Lesbian Studies in Art History.* New York: Haworth Press, 1994.

Fairbrother, Trevor. "Tomorrow's Man." In *"Success Is a Job in New York": The Early Art and Business of Andy Warhol,* pp. 55–74. Edited by Donna M. DeSalvo. New York: Grey Art Gallery, 1989.

Gay and Lesbian Caucus of the College Art Association Newsletter (now Queer Caucus for Art Newsletter). Queer Caucus for Art of the College Art Association. http://forums.nyu.edu; keyword "queerart."

———. *John Singer Sargent: The Sensualist.* Seattle: Seattle Art Museum, 2000.

Gibson, Ann Eden. *Abstract Expressionism: Other Politics.* New Haven, Conn.: Yale University Press, 1997.

———. *Lesbian Art in America: A Contemporary History.* New York: Rizzoli, 2000.

Holcomb, Adele M. "Anna Jameson on Women Artists." *Woman's Art Journal* 8, no. 2 (Fall–Winter 1987): 15–24.

Johnston, Jill. *Jasper Johns: Privileged Information.* London: Thames and Hudson, 1996.

Katz, Jonathan. "The Art of Code: Jasper Johns and Robert Rauschenberg." In *Significant Others: Creativity and Intimate Partnership.* Edited by Whitney Chadwick and Isabelle de Courtivron, pp. 189–207. London: Thames and Hudson, 1993.

———. "Passive Resistance: On the Success of Queer Artists in Cold War American Art." *Image* (Winter 1996): 119–142.

———. "Dismembership: Jasper Johns and the Body Politic." In *Performing the Body/Performing the Text,* pp. 170–185.

Edited by Amelia Jones and Andrew Stephenson. London: Routledge, 1999.

Kaufman, Jason Edward. "Jasper Johns: More than the Slayer of Abstract Expressionist Giants." *Art Newspaper*, Oct. 1996, pp. 16–17.

Krauss, Rosalind. "Rauschenberg and Performance, 1963–67: a 'Poetry of Infinite Possibilities'" in *Robert Rauschenberg: A Retrospective* (Walter Hopps and Susan Davidson, editors.) New York: Guggenheim Museum, 1999.

Leupp, Gary P. *Male Colors: The Construction of Homosexuality in Tokugawa Japan.* Berkeley: University of California Press, 1995.

Meyer, Richard. *Outlaw Representation: Censorship and Homosexuality in Twentieth-Century American Art.* New York: Oxford University Press, 2002.

Pater, Walter. "Winckelmann." In *Studies in the History of the Renaissance.* London: Macmillan, 1873.

Rand, Erica. *Barbie's Queer Accessories.* Durham, N.C.: Duke University Press, 1995.

Saslow, James. *Ganymede in the Renaissance: Homosexuality in Art and Society.* New Haven, Conn.: Yale University Press, 1986.

———. "Closets in the Museum: Homophobia and Art History." In *Lavender Culture.* Edited by Karla Jay and Allen Young. New York: New York University Press, 1994.

———. *Pictures and Passions: A History of Homosexuality in the Visual Arts.* New York: Viking, 1999.

Silver, Kenneth E. "Modes of Disclosure: The Construction of Gay Identity and the Rise of Pop Art." In *Hand-Painted Pop*, pp. 178–203. Edited by Russell Ferguson. Los Angeles: Museum of Contemporary Art, 1992.

Sokolowski, Thomas. *Rosalind Solomon: Portraits in the Time of AIDS.* New York: New York University, 1988.

Solomon-Godeau, Abigail. *Male Trouble: A Crisis in Representation.* London: Thames and Hudson, 1997.

Thomas, Clara. *Love and Work Enough: The Life of Anna Jameson.* 2nd ed. Toronto: University of Toronto Press, 1978.

Waller, Susan. "The Artist, the Writer, and the Queen: Hosmer, Jameson, and Zenobia," *Woman's Art Journal* 4, no. 1 (Spring–Summer 1983): 21–28.

Waugh, Thomas. *Hard to Imagine: Gay Male Eroticism in Photography and Film, from Their Beginnings to Stonewall.* New York: Columbia University Press, 1996.

Weinberg, Jonathan. *Speaking for Vice: Homosexuality in the Art of Charles Demuth, Marsden Hartley, and the First American Avant-Garde.* New Haven, Conn.: Yale University Press, 1993.

**Christopher Reed**

*See also* ADVOCATE; CLOSET; EAKINS, THOMAS; JOHNS, JASPER; MAPPLETHORPE, ROBERT; NEW RIGHT; RAUSCHENBERG, ROBERT; VISUAL ART; WARHOL, ANDY.

# ARZNER, Dorothy (b. 3 January 1897; d. 1 October 1979), filmmaker.

Dorothy Arzner is the only known lesbian to have directed Hollywood studio films during the so-called Golden Age (1920s–1950s). She lived with her partner, the dancer Marion Morgan, from 1930 to 1971. Beginning as a scriptwriter (*The Red Kimono*, 1925) and editor (*Blood and Sand*, 1922; *The Covered Wagon*, 1923; *Old Ironsides*, 1926), Arzner made her directorial debut with *Fashions for Women* (1927) for Paramount, where she would shoot her first ten films, from 1927 to 1932. *Fashions for Women*, with Esther Ralston, was also the first of many films for which Arzner was entrusted with building up or bolstering a female star; eventually she would attempt to do so for Esther Ralston, Clara Bow, Katharine Hepburn, Anna Sten, Rosalind Russell, and Maureen O'Hara.

In every case except Hepburn in *Christopher Strong* (1933) (and, perhaps, Russell in *Craig's Wife* [1936]) Arzner was the offscreen butch to the star's onscreen femme—and there are publicity stills to prove it. Interestingly, Arzner publicly proclaimed that she identified not with Hepburn's aviator character, Cynthia Darrington, but rather with the title character, an upper-class Englishman torn between love for his wife (Billie Burke) and desire for Cynthia. But then, it makes sense that faced with a heterosexual romantic triangle story, a lesbian might position herself as the person caught between two women as striking as Hepburn and Burke.

Rediscovered in the 1970s, largely for post-Paramount films like *Christopher Strong, Craig's Wife,* and *Dance, Girl, Dance* (1940), Arzner's work has since become Exhibit A for the case that "women's discourses" and "women's voices" can be articulated within classical film narrative codes and conventions. Judith Mayne was the first critic to consider how Arzner's lesbianism might have inflected the female discourses in her films. In general, Mayne, and other critics who followed, investigated Arzner's films along three sometimes overlapping lines: class and the representation of women's communities, the critique of heterosexuality, and femme/butch (and other lesbian) coding.

Among the most prominent Arzner films in the first category are *The Wild Party* (1929), *Working Girls* (1931), *Nana* (1934), and *Dance, Girl, Dance*. With the exception of *The Wild Party*, which concerns women at college, these films focus upon working women who bond while struggling with their place within capitalist patriarchy. *Merrily We Go to Hell* (1932), *Christopher Strong*, and *Craig's Wife*, Arzner's most powerful and complex examinations of male-female love and sex, suggest that straight men and women are better off on their own, by and large; *Merrily We Go to Hell* ends with a husband substituting for a dead child, *Christopher Strong* with the suicide of a pregnant Cynthia, and *Craig's Wife* with a dedicated housewife left alone in her home.

Reflecting some of the coding of the publicity stills of the director and her female stars, films like *Christopher Strong, Craig's Wife,* and *Dance, Girl, Dance* contain visually and narratively charged pairs of women: Hepburn and Helen Chandler, Hepburn and Billie Burke (*Christopher Strong*); Russell and Dorothy Wilson, Russell and Burke (*Craig's Wife*); Maureen O'Hara and Maria Ouspenskaya, Ouspenskaya and Lucille Ball (*Dance, Girl, Dance*). While not explicitly named as lesbian (how could they be?), these couples nonetheless provide many sapphic, or queer, pleasures for appropriately positioned viewers.

But femme/butch coding isn't the only way Arzner's films queerly eroticize the space around women characters. In *The Wild Party,* Clara Bow's character says of her female roommate, "You see, I love her too"—and to her roommate's boyfriend, no less. *Christopher Strong* inscribes a potential lesbian narrative and spectator position by having an adoring female fan ask Cynthia for an autograph at a party. Earlier in the same film, Arzner has Cynthia comfort the daughter of her lover by embracing her on a sofa in such a way that it initially looks as if the two are about to share a romantic kiss. In *Dance, Girl, Dance* Arzner strikingly represents lesbian voyeurism by cutting from a shot of Ouspenskaya's character secretly looking at O'Hara's character dancing to then show O'Hara directly from Ouspenskaya's point of view.

Arzner never considered her work self-consciously feminist—let alone lesbian—and she seemed to resist later attempts to understand her work as such. Despite this, her films, and the director herself, have become central to feminist and lesbian film histories.

**Bibliography**

Cook, Pam. "Approaching the Work of Dorothy Arzner." In *Feminism and Film Theory.* Edited by Constance Penley. New York: Routledge, 1988.

Doty, Alexander. *Making Things Perfectly Queer: Interpreting Mass Culture.* Minneapolis: University of Minnesota Press, 1993.

Johnson, Claire. "Dorothy Arzner: Critical Strategies." In *Feminism and Film Theory.* Edited by Constance Penley. New York: Routledge, 1988.

Mayne, Judith. *The Woman at the Keyhole: Feminism and Women's Cinema.* Bloomington: Indiana University Press, 1990.

**Dorothy Arzner.** The films of Arzner—a female director in the Hollywood studio system of the late 1920s to mid-1940s—have been reexamined since the 1970s in light of her lesbianism and the rise of feminist perspectives. [Otto Dyar © Hulton-Deutsch Collection/CORBIS]

———. "Lesbian Looks: Dorothy Arzner and Female Authorship." In *How Do I Look? Queer Film and Video.* Edited by Bad Object-Choices. Seattle: Bay Press, 1991.

———. *Directed by Dorothy Arzner.* Bloomington: Indiana University Press, 1994.

Suter, Jacqueline. "Feminist Discourse in *Christopher Strong.*" In *Feminism and Film Theory.* Edited by Constance Penley. New York and London: Routledge, 1988.

**Alexander Doty**

*See also* FILM AND VIDEO.

# ASIAN AMERICANS AND PACIFIC ISLANDERS

Asian Americans and Pacific Islanders are people of Asian or Pacific Islander descent who were born in or immigrated to the United States. As a term, "Asian American" only came into popular usage in the 1960s; for much of Asian American history, Asians in the United States were considered by mainstream society to be sojourners or visitors, even if they were born in America.

## Early History

The first U.S. immigrants from Asia were Chinese, recruited in large numbers to work on the railroads in the mid-nineteenth century. They were followed by many Japanese and Filipino immigrants, as well as smaller numbers of other groups. Because of immigration and citizenship restrictions (culminating in the Chinese Exclusion Act of 1882, the Gentlemen's Agreement of 1907–1908, the "Barred Zone Act" of 1917, and court rulings and laws that prevented Asian Americans from becoming naturalized U.S. citizens) and periodic anti-Asian pogroms around the country, many Asian Americans congregated in ethnic enclaves such as Chinatowns (especially in San Francisco, Chicago, Los Angeles, and New York). They also participated in migrant labor networks in rural regions of the U.S. West. For many decades, the number of Asian men outnumbered women many times over, resulting in what historians have termed "bachelor societies."

Queer historians such as Jennifer Ting and Nayan Shah now view these bachelor societies as fostering same-sex cultures that challenged heteronormative values and enabled the beginnings of a sort of queer domestic life. Ting's analysis of "deviant heterosexuality" (1995) explores the female prostitution and male gambling and vice cultures of Chinese bachelor societies. Shah (2001) details living arrangements in San Francisco's bachelor society that encouraged sexual diversity among men and women. His analysis of "queer domesticity" illuminates the homoerotics and gender and sexual transgressions of male bathhouses, female-headed households, and interracial social spaces such as opium dens. Similar formations of queer gender and sexuality have shaped the lives of migrant laborers from Japan, the Philippines, and India. Judy Tzu-Chun Wu has explored the transgressive life of Dr. Margaret Chung, believed to be the first American-born Chinese American woman physician. She was well known as an advocate for China during its war against Imperial Japan during the 1930s and 1940s. Wu's historical research (through letters written by Chung to her lovers) has uncovered Chung's homoerotic relationships with white women, though she never identified as lesbian. Chung's life offers a tantalizing glimpse of the strategies of survival and transgression across race and gender boundaries engaged in by Asian American LGBT people in the period before and during World War II.

## From World War II to Gay Liberation

Although Filipino sailors had a long history of service as U.S. colonial subjects in the U.S. Navy and merchant marine, the vast mobilization of World War II brought thousands of Chinese American, Japanese American, Filipino American, and South Asian American men and smaller numbers of women into the U.S. military and wartime manufacturing industries, facilitating their participation in wartime LGBT cultures. Demobilization after the war enabled Asian American soldiers, sailors, and civilians, and Japanese American internees to migrate to city centers far removed from their families and natal communities. Many lived lives of gender and sexual nonconformity.

The personal history of Kiyoshi Kuromiya strikingly illustrates a remarkable experience of Asian American queer migration and queer possibility. Born in the Heart Mountain relocation camp, one of several internment camps for Japanese Americans during World War II, Kuromiya grew up in Los Angeles and later moved to Philadelphia. He was openly gay even in his teenage years in the 1950s, when he would pick up older men for sex. In the 1960s, he was active in the civil rights, student, and antiwar movements. Later, he was the one Asian featured in Arthur Dong's 1995 documentary *Out Rage '69*, which highlighted LGBT activists from the period before the Stonewall Riots of 1969. In the early 1970s, he was a pioneer in the early gay liberation movement, leading the Gay Liberation Front of Philadelphia and speaking as an openly gay delegate at the Black Panthers' Revolutionary People's Constitutional Convention in 1970. After collaborating with Buckminster Fuller on the book *Critical Path* (1981) as well as other titles, he became an AIDS activist, founding the Critical Path AIDS Project. Kuromiya served on a National Institutes of Health panel on alternative therapies and was an advocate of the medical use of marijuana. In 1996 he fought for the right to disseminate sex education information to youth when he became a plaintiff in an American Civil Liberties Union case challenging the Communications Decency Act. He was the lead plaintiff the next year in another federal case (*Kuromiya et al. v. United States*) that sought to legalize medical marijuana. He succumbed to AIDS in 2000 in Philadelphia.

Kuromiya came of age during a period when it was difficult for LGBT people to be open about their sexual desires. Those who were willing to be more open were valued by the homophile movement as public marchers, educational speakers, and contributors to movement publications. In June 1964, the *Ladder*, a monthly produced by the Daughters of Bilitis, published a letter, "Isolation in Indonesia," from a young Djakarta woman, identified as G van B. Later revealed to be Ger van Bram, the woman was featured on the cover of the November 1964 issue of the *Ladder*, arguably the first Asian on the cover of any queer magazine. The curious lesbian who a few months earlier had admitted that she did not know anything about "homophilism" was now a full-fledged *Ladder* contributor from Asia, proclaiming herself to be "gay" and that she and her lesbian lover and another friend would not care who found out about them.

The homophile movement of the 1950s and 1960s soon gave way to a new, more radical movement. The Stonewall Riots of June 1969 sparked the beginning of the gay liberation movement in the United States. Within a few years, Gay Liberation Fronts (GLFs, modeled in name after the National Liberation Front fighting against U.S. forces in Vietnam) were founded in many cities and on many campuses. The gay liberation movement emerged out of the turmoil of multiple radical movements. People of color were marching in the streets, as were women in the emerging women's liberation movement. The Yellow Power movement was in full swing, taking its cue from the Black Power movement, which endorsed the idea that "black is beautiful." Contributing to Yellow Power was the fact that, in the mid-1960s, the Asian American population began to grow dramatically, as immigration restrictions dating from the late nineteenth and early twentieth centuries were lifted. Asian Americans took to the streets and college campuses, proclaiming pride in their identity while engaging in the struggle against racism. Most early Asian American LGBT activists came to LGBT activism after having been involved in one or more other movements before "coming out." Many were inspired to seek a radical restructuring of society, not just reformist social change. As they gradually "came out" about their sexualities, these early activists questioned why they had to hide their sexual identities and why Asian American movements refused to acknowledge their LGBT existence. Meanwhile, LGBT and women's liberation movements seemed to cater more to white aspirations than to those of people of color. These early activists would, in time, become strong voices of a still nascent Asian American LGBT movement.

## Organizing in the 1970s

In the 1970s, LGBT Asian Americans and Pacific Islanders began to organize their own distinct movement. The first nationally circulated Asian American periodical was *Bridge* magazine, published out of New York's Chinatown. Dan Tsang's essay "Gay Awareness," published in 1975 in *Bridge,* eventually came to be known as the first gay Asian American manifesto, helping to mobilize LGBT people of Asian heritage to attend the first National March for Lesbian and Gay Rights (held on 14 October 1979) in Washington, D.C. That essay described the

dilemma faced by progressive LGBT people of color who experienced homophobia, often in silence, within the social change movements in which they participated. Recognizing "the depth of homosexual oppression, even that emanating from sisters and brothers in the Third World movement," "Gay Awareness" called on its readers to come out as gay:

> In opting for gay liberation, we strike a blow against sexism, machismo and political repression. Coming out as both Asian and as gay enables us to relate better and more honestly with our yellow sisters and brothers. It liberates us from one of the major obstacles in the Asian American struggle: the alienation of Asians from other Asians. No longer will Asians who meet on the street avert their eyes: we shall embrace each other with joy. Let us get rid of pretense, and live honestly. Gay sisters and brothers, unite in the struggle. (pp. 44-45)

The 1979 March on Washington was the first time LGBT Asians anywhere marched publicly as a group. Participants began in the black neighborhoods of Washington, D.C., then marched through Chinatown, carrying a large banner proclaiming, "We're Asian, Gay & Proud," and eventually joined up with other marchers in a Third World contingent, led by Native Americans, to end up at the Washington Monument.

The previous day (13 October), Tana Loy, a Chinese American lesbian, had addressed participants at the first National Third World Lesbian and Gay Conference at Howard University. Her speech, titled "Who's the Barbarian?," referenced an imperialist America. Describing Asians as alienated from each other, Loy called the conference "history making" because "we Asians, gay Asians—and that means Chinese, Japanese, Filipino, Indonesian, Vietnamese, whether we're from Guam, Korea, Malaysia, whether we're Indian, whether we're Pakistani—have for the first time, for many of us, with open hearts and minds, run toward each other" (p. 15).

That radical theme was echoed the next day at the Washington Monument. Among the rally speakers was Michiyo Fukaya (Margaret Cornell), a Japanese European lesbian selected by the dozen or so people who had participated in an Asian caucus, called the Lesbian and Gay Asian Collective, at the Third World conference that weekend. Fukaya, a poet from Vermont, electrified the crowd of 100,000 when she spoke about the agonies of "living in Asian America," which she described as "a statement of our experiences and a statement of racism in America." In blunt language, she proclaimed, "We are called the model minority, the quiet, passive exotic erotics. . . . But we are not." She talked about shared oppressions, suggesting that white gays and lesbians should begin addressing their white privilege. She also called for Asians to come out, despite their fears of deportation and their fears about family and community rejection. Fukaya implored the crowd: "We need to come out of the closet for not to do so would be living a lie."

Another early pioneer was Chinese American poet Kitty Tsui, an immigrant from Hong Kong via England who fell in love with another Chinese American woman in 1975 in San Francisco and came out almost immediately to everyone she knew. Initially, she was shunned by her family and her movement friends. Joining Tsui as another early activist was Chinese Korean American lesbian Merle Woo, a university lecturer and socialist who successfully fought the University of California system for the right to remain a faculty member.

## Developments in the 1980s and 1990s

The 1993 March on Washington for Lesbian, Gay, and Bisexual Rights and Liberation (25 April) brought the largest Asian LGBT turnout to date to the nation's capital. Asian lesbians were, if anything, more visible than Asian gay males on the Washington Mall, with provocative signs that proclaimed their right to engage in same-sex sex.

One participant in the 1993 march was Eric Estuar Reyes, a self-described queer activist, who had read Fukaya's moving speech at the 1979 march. He later wrote (1996) that while he acknowledged Fukaya's clarion call for Asians to end invisibility by "coming out," he also questioned the efficacy of national marches. Instead, he thought that queer activists should focus on creating sufficient local space to meet local needs.

## Coalition Building

One of these local struggles involved protests in 1991 over the theatrical production of *Miss Saigon* on Broadway. Gay Asian and Pacific Islander Men of New York and Asian Lesbians of the East Coast (ALOEC) formed coalitions with other people of color, LGBT, and women's groups to protest sexism and racism in the portrayals of Asians in the musical. The protests also exposed a rift within the LGBT community, because they were also aimed at the Lambda Legal Defense and Education Fund and the New York City Gay Community Center, established LGBT groups that were using the musical as a fund-raiser. Other examples of coalition building involved actions taken together with people of color immigrant groups to fight anti-immigrant state legislation such as California's Proposition 209 in 1996. Asian LGBT people also joined others to protest cutbacks of AIDS funding that threatened AIDS support groups for people of color. While Asian American and Pacific Islander LGBT people built coalitions with other groups, they also struggled to deal with internal divisions within their communities.

It would be wrong to view Asian American queers as one homogenous group. Sex, gender, sexuality, age, class, ethnicity, immigration status, country of origin, and date of arrival in the United States all conspired in different ways to disrupt any presumed cohesion. While many Asian American queers sought refuge in same-sex, same-race, or same-ethnicity groups, others sought friendships and relationships across racial and ethnic lines. As is the case with other minority groups, queer Asians soon developed their own terms to deal with such phenomena, using such terms as "snow queen" (to describe an Asian exclusively attracted to whites), "rice queen" (a white exclusively attracted to an Asian), and "sticky rice" (an Asian attracted to another Asian). The terms reveal the extent to which race and racism continue to mark all discourses and relationships in America.

## Queer Asians and Pacific Islanders

Influenced by queer theory, by the 1990s many activists began using the term "queer" to describe themselves. Adopting this terminology suggested that people were free to move among, and adopt, more fluid sexual and gender identities. No longer was sexual and gender identity viewed as necessarily fixed. It became more of a choice, rather than something dictated by birth. The very concept of "Asian" itself also came under scrutiny, as more and more ethnicities laid claim to the term or rejected it.

Meanwhile, the growing visibility of Pacific Islanders among the Asian American sexual body politic raised interesting challenges to the way in which Asians in the United States had constructed sexual and gender identities. Lisa Kahaleole Chang Hall and J. Kehaulani Kauanui (1996) have observed that the "struggle for decolonization and the reclamation of traditional practices" have resulted in a "more complex view of Pacific sexuality than has previously existed" (p.116). For example, the word *m~hā*, thought to refer to a male homosexual, is actually a term for a homosexual of either gender who adopts the opposite gender role. They point to the growing movement for Hawaiian sovereignty and the Hawaii Supreme Court decisions recognizing same-sex marriage as raising the profile of nationalism and sexuality issues in the region. They also note that LGB Hawaiians in the early 1990s joined together in a group, Na Mamo o Manoa, to oppose the "appropriation of and erasure of indigenous culture and history by both white gays and some sovereignty leaders" (p. 117). Carolina E. Robertson (2002), in her essay on the *m~hā*, suggests that, given our tendency to assign a "polarized identity" (male or female) to individuals, we may not be able to understand the gender variation implied by the term *m~hā*. This is a limitation of English, she asserts. "In Hawaiian, by contrast, there are not female/male adjectives or articles, and proper names are also androgynous." To Hawaiians, the "notion of gendered polarity or opposition is foreign" (p. 266, n. 2).

The advent of the Internet and its wide proliferation by the 1990s freed those seeking to make contact from being limited to face-to-face encounters. Suddenly, all sorts of subgroups and sexual tastes proliferated, and Asian and Pacific Islander queer networking took a quantum leap forward. The 2000 U.S. census also revealed the statistical breakdown of unmarried Asians and Pacific Islanders households with domestic partners of the same gender, taking "coming out" to another level. There were about seventeen thousand unmarried same-sex households involving at least one Asian partner and two thousand involving at least one Hawaiian or Pacific Islander partner. The dilemma facing queer Asian Americans and Pacific Islanders in the future is how—and whether—to fit a U.S.-based queer agenda within a rapidly changing global system that is more and more interconnected. As national boundaries become increasingly irrelevant, local conditions continue to dictate whether and where this queer agenda will take root.

**Asian American LGBT Activism.** Demonstrators in California carry signs protesting anti-Asian discrimination in gay bars, exemplifying some of the complexities in ongoing struggles for rights related to race and sexual orientation. [Rink Foto]

## Bibliography

Eng, David L., and Alice Y. Hom, eds. *Q&A: Queer in Asian America.* Philadelphia: Temple University Press, 1998.

Cornell, Margaret (Michiyo Fukaya). "Living in Asian America: An Asian American Lesbian's Address Before the Washington Monument." *Gay Insurgent: A Gay Left Journal,* no. 6 (Summer 1980): 16.

Hall, Lisa Kahaleole Chang, and J. Kehaulani Kauanui. "Same-Sex Sexuality in Pacific Literature." In *Asian American Sexualities: Dimensions of the Gay and Lesbian Experience.* Edited by Russell Leong. Los Angeles: UCLA Asian American Studies Center Press, 1996.

Hutchins, Loraine, and Lani Kaahumanu, eds. *Bi Any Other Name: Bisexual People Speak Out.* Boston: Alyson Publications, 1991.

Lai, Eric Yo Ping. "Queer APA Households by the Numbers." In *The New Face of Asian Pacific America: Numbers, Diversity, and Change in the 21st Century.* Edited by Eric Yo Ping Lai and Dennis Arguelles. San Francisco: Asian Week, 2003.

Leong, Russell, ed. *Asian American Sexualities: Dimensions of the Gay and Lesbian Experience.* New York: Routledge, 1996.

Loy, Tana. "Who's the Barbarian? An Asian American Lesbian Speaks Before the Third World Conference." *Gay Insurgent: A Gay Left Journal,* no. 6 (Summer 1980): 15.

Masequesmay, Gina. *Becoming Queer and Vietnamese American: Negotiating Multiple Identities in an Ethnic Support Group of Lesbians, Bisexual Women, and Female-to-Male Transgenders.* Ph.D. diss., University of California at Los Angeles, 2001.

Ordona, Trinity Ann. *Coming Out Together: An Ethnohistory of the Asian and Pacific Islander Queer Women's and Transgendered People's Movement of San Francisco (California).* Ph.D. diss., University of California at Santa Cruz, 2001.

Ratti, Rakesh, ed. *A Lotus of Another Color: An Unfolding of the South Asian Gay and Lesbian Experience.* Boston: Alyson, 1993.

Reyes, Eric Estuar. "Strategies for Queer Asian and Pacific Islander Spaces." In *Asian American Sexualities: Dimensions of the Gay and Lesbian Experience.* Edited by Russell Leong. Los Angeles: UCLA Asian American Studies Center Press, 1996.

Robertson, Carolina E. "The M~hā of Hawai'i." In *Pacific Diaspora: Island Peoples in the United States and Across the Pacific.* Edited by Paul Spickard, Joanne L. Rondilla, and Debbie Hippolite Wright. Honolulu: University of Hawai'i Press, 2002.

Shah, Nayan. "Perversity, Contamination, and the Dangers of Queer Domesticity." In his *Contagious Divides: Epidemics and Race in San Francisco's Chinatown.* Berkeley: University of California Press, 2001.

Ting, Jennifer. "Bachelor Society: Deviant Heterosexuality and Asian American Historiography." In *Privileging Positions: The Sites of Asian American Studies.* Edited by Gary Y. Okihiro et al. Pullman: Washington State University Press, 1995.

Tsang, Chun-Tuen Daniel. "Gay Awareness." *Bridge: Asian American Perspective* 3, no. 4 (February 1975): 44–45.

Tsang, Daniel C. "Breaking the Silence: The Emergence of the Lesbian and Gay Asian Press in North America." In *Bearing Dreams, Shaping Visions: Asian Pacific American Perspectives.* Edited by Linda A. Revilla et al. Pullman: Washington State University Press, 1993.

———. "Losing Its Soul? Reflections on Gay and Asian Activism." In *Legacy to Liberation: Politics and Culture of Revolutionary Asian/Pacific America.* Edited by Fred Ho. Brooklyn, N.Y.: Big Red Media, 2000.

———. "Slicing Silence: Asian Progressives Come Out." In *Asian Americans: The Movement and the Moment.* Edited by Steve Louie and Glenn K. Omatsu. Los Angeles: UCLA Asian American Studies Center Press, 2001.

———. "The Good Fight: Kiyoshi Kuromiya." *Nikkei Heritage* 14, no. 3 (Summer 2002).

Tsui, Kitty. *Words of a Woman Who Breathes Fire.* San Francisco: Spinsters, 1983.

Van B[ram], G[er]. "Notes from Abroad: Isolation in Indonesia." *Ladder* 8, no. 9 (June 1964): 9–11.

Wat, Eric. *The Making of a Gay Asian Community: An Oral History of Pre-AIDS Los Angeles.* Lanham, Md.: Rowman and Littlefield, 2002.

Woo, Merle. "Three Decades of Class Struggle on Campus." In *Legacy to Liberation: Politics and Culture of Revolutionary Asian/Pacific America.* Edited by Fred Ho. Brooklyn, N.Y.: Big Red Media, 2000.

Wu, Judy Tzu-Chun. "Was Mom Chung a 'Sister Lesbian'? Asian American Gender Experimentation and Interracial Homoeroticism." *Journal of Women's History* 13, no. 1 (Spring 2001): 58–82.

**Daniel C. Tsang**

**See also** ARAB AMERICANS; ASIAN AMERICAN AND PACIFIC ISLANDER STUDIES; ASIAN AMERICAN LGBTQ ORGANIZATIONS AND PERIODICALS; BUDDHISTS AND BUDDHISM; CHUA, SIONG-HUAT; CHUNG, MARGARET; FUKAYA, MICHIYO; HINDUS AND HINDUISM; KIM, WILLYCE; KUROMIYA, KYOSHI; MIGRATION, IMMIGRATION, AND DIASPORA; MUSLIMS AND ISLAM; NODA, BARBARA; RACE AND RACISM; TSANG, DANIEL; TSUI, KITTY; WOO, MERLE.

# ASIAN AMERICAN AND PACIFIC ISLANDER STUDIES

Asian American and Pacific Islander studies emerged out of the 1968 to 1969 student strikes for ethnic studies courses and programs at San Francisco State University and the University of California, Berkeley. These grassroots community protests were part of the emerging Asian American movement. The original mission of Asian American studies was to empower students, reform higher education, uncover the hidden histories of oppressed peoples, and join in community struggles.

LGBT studies also emerged out of the social movements of the 1960s (in particular, the June 1969 Stonewall Riots in New York City and the gay liberation movement), but for several decades, the two disciplines grew separately. Their trajectories initially shot past each other, despite the fact that both were born in activism and were engaged in similar missions. For many years, Asian American studies did not pay attention to LGBT issues. Even when the roles of women and gender in Asian America came to be considered appropriate subjects and objects of study, Asian American LGBT issues were scarcely noticed or recognized.

## Years of Silence

One marker of the state of Asian American studies is the work presented at the annual conferences of the Association for Asian American Studies (AAAS), which formed in 1979. In published proceedings from the conferences held from 1987 to 1993, there were no LGBT-related papers until the 1990 conference, when there was one. Thus, for its first decade, LGBT Asian American scholarship was effectively silenced in the association.

Another marker is the annual selected bibliography series that has appeared in the leading journal in the field, *Amerasia Journal.* In these comprehensive compilations of scholarly and nonacademic output, the absence of written material about LGBT issues in the 1970s and 1980s is striking. When the bibliography did begin to include some LGBT research in the 1990s, the material was initially subsumed under categories such as "Identity and Assimilation," as with the 1994 work by Glenn Omatsu. In 1996, however, the *Amerasia Journal* bibliography placed LGBT research within the category "Gender and Sexuality."

The silencing of work related to Asian American LGBT experience extended to other disciplines. *Amerasia Journal* editor Russell Leong, in an introduction to his 1996 anthology, *Asian American Sexualities*, suggests one reason. North American studies on sexuality and gender have largely excluded racial minorities in their discussions. As racial, sexual, and gender "others," Asian Americans and Pacific Islanders who are sexual and gender nonconformists have been met with "silence or token inclusion at best" (p. 3).

## Silence Broken

In the 1990s, the academic silence within Asian American studies began to be broken. The first appearance of an AAAS conference paper with gay or lesbian in the title, Daniel C. Tsang's "Breaking the Silence," on the topic of the gay and lesbian Asian press, was presented at the 1990 AAAS conference in Santa Barbara, California. Its inclusion in the conference proceedings prompted coeditor Linda A. Revilla to remark that the paper "reminds us that there are marginalized groups within the Asian Pacific American community whom we still fail to acknowledge" (p. 63).

LGB Asian writing soon began to proliferate. At least half a dozen Asian American bisexuals contributed to *Bi Any Other Name,* an anthology that came out in 1991. The *Journal of Homosexuality* published a dialogue between Alice Y. Hom and Ming Yuen S. Ma on lesbian and gay writing in 1993. Also in 1993, the *Asian/Pacific American Journal* published a special issue, "Witness Aloud: Lesbian, Gay, and Bisexual Asian/Pacific American Writings." And in 1994, a Canadian small press, Sister Vision Press, published *The Very Inside,* an anthology of Asian lesbian writing from North America. Also in 1994, the *Amerasia Journal* published a special issue on "Asian American Sexualities," which was later expanded into a book edited by Leong.

## Conference Breakthrough in 1993

In 1993, the AAAS conference acknowledged the contribution of its queer membership at the annual meeting held at Cornell University in Ithaca, New York. Writing about that development, Dorothy Fujita-Rony, in her introduction to the "Sexuality and Queer Studies" section of the conference proceedings, called it "historic" because, in addition to the by-then "usual scattering of papers concerning sexuality," the conference organizers "deliberately positioned sexuality as a central topic in a conference 'mega-session' " (pp. 245–249). She called it a "new cultural moment" signifying the "arrival of a generation of Asian American studies people whose coming-of-age has been informed by the AIDS crisis, as well as by a greater 'acceptance' of gay and lesbian issues." Fujita-Rony also noted the "relative youth of the participants in the sexuality mega-session" and the "general absence of senior people." This she attributed to the lack of "out"

senior professors, which showed "the difficulties of being gay, lesbian, bisexual or transgender in our supposed 'home' of Asian American studies." The bulk of the contributors included in this section were graduate students, with only one paper from a professor, reflecting the "cutting edge" nature of this research. Fujita-Rony also observed that two queer studies panels were presented at the conference. Yet there still existed a "perennial" problem with Asian American studies: an "insufficient representation of all Asian Pacific groups." She pointed out that "South Asians are again little mentioned, as are Pacific Islanders. Bisexuals, transgenders and heterosexual women are also not focused upon." Southeast Asians were also underrepresented. Nevertheless, Fujita-Rony concluded, taken together, the papers in the section "offer not only valuable documentation, but also new theoretical advances for Asian American studies."

By the late 1990s, academic conferences were organized specifically on the topic of Asian American sexualities. On 26 April 1997, California State University's Asian American Studies Department, together with the university's Center for Sex Research, UCLA's Department of Psychiatry, and the Gay Vietnamese Alliance, sponsored "CrossTalk: Asian and Pacific American Sensuality and Sexuality." On 16 November 2002, a successor conference, CrossTalk II, was held at the same university. An updated bibliography on the topic was compiled and edited by Eric Uba, revising an earlier compilation distributed at CrossTalk 1997. Another conference, at Arizona State University in Tempe on 29 January and 9 April 1999, hosted by the Asian Pacific American Studies Program around the theme "Asian Pacific American Genders and Sexualities," showed the growing importance of gender and sexuality studies within the field.

## Theoretical Challenges

In the same volume of conference papers that emerged from the 1993 AAAS Conference, sociologist Dana Y. Takagi, who from 2002 to 2003 would preside over the association as its first openly lesbian leader, discussed the theoretical attraction postmodernism offered to Asian American studies. Asian American studies, she argued, had thus far failed to take advantage of postmodern theories to challenge and advance the field so that Asian Americanists could become central to any theoretical debate and not remain at its periphery.

Takagi expanded that analysis to explicitly address the state of Asian American studies in relation to queer and sexuality studies in another essay, "Maiden Voyage: Excursion into Sexuality and Identity Politics," which first appeared in a 1994 *Amerasia Journal* special issue and was subsequently included in a 1996 expanded anthology, *Asian American Sexualities,* edited by Leong. Takagi argues that Asian American studies cannot just respond by treating sexual identities like other ethnic identities. She deliberately uses the plural form, sexualities, to reference a variety of sexual identities, all in flux and impermanent. Incorporating sexualities into the field can transform the way we think about how scholars have traditionally researched and taught Asian American studies. The "inscription of non-straight sexualities in Asian American history immediately casts theoretical doubt about how to do it," offering the opportunity for "rethinking and reevaluating notions of identity that have been used for the most part unproblematically and uncritically in Asian American Studies" (1996, p. 22). Nor is it sufficient to just add sexual identity to the field, since "identities, whether sourced from sexual desire, racial origins, languages of gender, or class roots, are simply not additive" (p. 23).

Historian Jennifer Ting, who in a paper at the 1993 AAAS conference called on fellow Asian American scholars to place sexuality at the "conceptual center" of Asian American studies (1995), elaborated on this call in the February 1999 inaugural issue of the AAAS publication, *Journal of Asian American Studies.* She urged fellow scholars to rethink the role sexuality plays in Asian American studies, utilizing the perspectives of "feminists, queer studies scholars, and historians of sexuality" (1998, p. 65). Ting argued that it is not enough to just write about "same-sex activity, sexual identities, and lesbian, gay, and bisexual people" (p. 79). This does not necessarily challenge what she calls "heteronormativity" in the field. Instead:

> [t]o understand that heteronormativity, we must have writing about sexuality as a discourse of power whose effects and operations are not limited to the constitution of sexual identities alone. . . . It is indeed time to think about sexuality, the structures and relations of power that produce it, the categories it enables or prevents from forming, and the logics and narratives that inscribe it in the heart of our field.

In 2001, David L. Eng took the analysis further, suggesting that, instead of bemoaning the end of a class-based politics rooted in cultural nationalism, scholars of Asian American studies should see that queerness has become one of the contemporary sites of progressive politics. Eng calls this a phenomenon of "queerness and diaspora" in Asian American studies:

> If earlier Asian American cultural nationalist projects were built on the political strategy of claiming home and the nation-state through the domestic

and the heterosexual, a new political project of thinking about this concept in Asian American studies today would seem to center around queerness and diaspora—its rethinking of home and nation-state around across multiple identity formations and numerous locations 'out here' and 'over there.'

Eng also suggests a shift from the politics of cultural nationalism to that of transnational culturalism (pp. 219–220).

In 1996, Lisa Kahaleole Chang Hall and J. Kauanui warned about lumping together different people with different colonial histories under the rubric of "Asian Pacific," given that many "Asian Pacific" groups are seeking self-determination from American domination and control. Given different conceptions of "homosexuality" or even "sexuality" in the region, they remind us of the danger of imposing Western terminology that does not capture the cultural meanings that are at play. They also warn of the problem of denying indigenous people agency: "Though there is a rich history of same-sex sexual relations and cross-gendered roles in the Pacific, the vast majority of literature focusing on Pacific peoples is anthropological in nature and written by outsiders to the culture described. A preoccupation with 'sexual deviance' is a recurrent theme" (p. 115).

## Queering the Field

One of the most exciting aspects of the new scholarship has been the intriguing and challenging questions it raises about Asian American and Pacific Islander studies. Ting's research uncovered a heterosexual bias in literary and historical texts, especially those relating to the bachelor society discussed in much early Asian American history. In 1995, analyzing two historiographically important texts, Ting found that these works construct the pre–World War II Chinese bachelor society in Chinatown as one marked by "deviant heterosexuality." In 2001, historian Nayan Shah advanced the concept of "queer domesticity" to analyze the social dynamics of the bachelor society in San Francisco's Chinatown in the early twentieth century. He argued that the heterosexual norms that underlay previous research (and public health practice) distorted and masked much of what could arguably have been going on among Chinese men living together or among the less-numerous women labeled "prostitutes," who also lived together.

Martin Manalansan, whose 1994 research into the Filipino queer community offered documentation of resilience and resistance as well as linguistic creativity, has argued that Asian American ethnographies can fruitfully benefit from postmodern analyses. In his introduction to a 2000 compilation of ethnographic research, Manalansan argued that Asian American studies has often neglected such analyses, and that ethnographies enable research that is not only multisided, but also looks at the subjective and nonsubjective barriers to travel (nonmovement). The essays in his book "attempt to build, question, and contest the idea of Asian America as a space as well as a moment within the (trans)national imaginary" (p. 1). Manalansan concludes, "A critical ethnography of Asian America enables multiple strategies and readings that are productive and expressive of political struggles, cultural critiques, and social change" (p. 11). In 1997, Gayatri Gopinath argued that work on gender and nationalism paid little attention "to the production and deployment of nonheteronormative, or 'queer,' sexuality within colonial, anticolonial nationalist, and contemporary nationalist discourses. . . . By failing to examine the existence and workings of alterior sexualities within dominant nationalisms, such analyses leave intact hegemonic constructions of the nation as essentially heterosexual" (pp. 468–469). Gopinath's research on South Asian diasporic cultural productions and texts looked at how these cultural producers reposition the home and the nation as a "site of nonheteronormative desire and pleasure in a nostalgic diasporic imaginary" (p. 485).

## The Future

It could very well be that from the ashes of the old Asian American movement and the old Asian American and Pacific Islander studies will emerge a new interdisciplinary field that confronts the theoretical challenges involved when researchers address queer sexualities and challenge heteronormativity. Queer studies and cultural studies have already had a major impact on Asian American studies. Productive cross-pollination of the disciplines of literary criticism, cultural studies, history, and anthropology is already evident in the publication of anthologies such as those edited by David Eng and Alice Hom (1998), by Quang Bao and Hanya Yanagihara (2000), and in scholarly output, as more and more scholars in Asian American and Pacific Islander studies research queer topics.

### Bibliography

Bao, Quang, and Hanya Yanagihara, eds. *Take Out: Queer Writing from Asian Pacific America.* New York: Asian American Writers' Workshop, 2000.

Chin, Justin, et al., eds. "Witness Aloud: Lesbian, Gay and Bisexual Asian American/Pacific Writings." *Asian/Pacific American Journal* 2, no. 1 (1993).

Chung, C., et al., eds. *Between the Lines: An Anthology by Pacific/Asian Lesbians of Santa Cruz, California.* Santa Cruz: Dancing Bird Press, 1987.

Eng, David L. "Epilogue: Out Here and Over There. Queerness and Diaspora in Asian American Studies." In *Racial Castration: Managing Masculinity in Asian America.* Durham, N.C.: Duke University Press, 2001.

Eng, David L., and Alice Y. Hom, eds. *Q&A: Queer in Asian America.* Philadelphia: Temple University Press, 1998.

Eng, David L., and Candace Fujikane. "Asian American Gay and Lesbian Literatures." In *The Gay and Lesbian Literary Heritage.* Edited by Claude J. Summers. New York: Holt, 1995.

Espiritu, Yen Le, et al., comp. *Amerasia Journal: Thirtieth Anniversary Cumulative Index, 1971–2001.* Los Angeles: UCLA Asian American Studies Center, 2002.

Fujita-Rony, Dorothy. "Part Three—Sexuality and Queer Studies: Introduction." In *Privileging Positions: The Sites of Asian American Studies.* Edited by Gary Y. Okihiro et al. Pullman: Washington State University Press, 1995.

Gopinath, Gyatri. "Nostalgia, Desire, Diaspora: South Asian Sexualities in Motion." *Positions* 5, no. 2 (fall 1997): 467–489.

Hall, Lisa Kahaleole Chang, and J. Kehaulani Kauanui, "Same-Sex Sexuality in Pacific Literature." In *Asian American Sexualities: Dimensions of the Gay and Lesbian Experience.* Edited by Russell Leong. Los Angeles: UCLA Asian American Studies Center Press, 1996.

Him-Ling, Sharon, ed. *The Very Inside: An Anthology of Writing by Asian and Pacific Islander Lesbian and Bisexual Women.* Toronto: Sister Vision Press, 1994.

Hom, Alice Y., and Ming-Yuen S. Ma. "Premature Gestures: A Speculative Dialogue on Asian Pacific Islander Lesbian and Gay Writing." *Journal of Homosexuality* 26, nos. 2–3 (1993): 21–51.

Hutchins, Loraine, and Lani Kaahumanu, eds. *Bi Any Other Name: Bisexual People Speak Out.* Boston: Alyson, 1991.

Lee, Marjorie, and Raul Ebio. "1996 Annual Selected Bibliography." *Amerasia Journal* 22, no. 3 (1996): 185–235.

Leong, Russell, ed. *Asian American Sexualities: Dimensions of the Gay and Lesbian Experience.* New York: Routledge, 1996.

Manalansan, Martin F., IV. "(Dis)Orienting the Body: Locating Symbolic Resistance among Filipino Gay Men." *Positions* 2, no. 1 (spring 1994): 73–90.

———. "Introduction: The Ethnography of Asian America. Notes toward a Thick Description." In *Cultural Compass: Ethnographic Explorations of Asian America.* Edited by Martin F. Manalansan IV. Philadelphia: Temple University Press, 2000.

Masequesmay, Gina. "Becoming Queer and Vietnamese American: Negotiating Multiple Identities in an Ethnic Support Group of Lesbians, Bisexual Women, and Female-to-Male Transgenders." Ph.D diss. University of California, Los Angeles, 2001.

Nakayama, Thomas K., ed. *Asian Pacific American Genders and Sexualities.* Tempe: Asian American Faculty and Staff Association, Arizona State University, 1999.

Okihiro, Gary Y., et al. *Privileging Positions: The Sites of Asian American Studies.* Pullman: Washington State University Press, 1995.

Omatsu, Glenn. "1994 Annual Selected Bibliography: Asian American Studies and the Crisis of Practice." *Amerasia Journal* 20, no. 3 (1994): 119–210.

Ordona, Trinity Ann. "Coming Out Together: An Ethnohistory of the Asian and Pacific Islander Queer Women's and Transgendered People's Movement of San Francisco (California)." Ph.D diss. University of California, Santa Cruz, 2001.

Ratti, Rakesh, ed. *A Lotus of Another Color: An Unfolding of the South Asian Gay and Lesbian Experience.* Boston: Alyson, 1993.

Revilla, Linda A., et al., eds. *Bearing Dreams, Shaping Visions: Asian Pacific American Perspectives.* Pullman: Washington State University Press, 1993.

Robertson, Carolina E. "The Mahu of Hawai'i." In *Pacific Disapora: Island Peoples in the United States and across the Pacific.* Edited by Paul Spickard, Joanne L. Rondilla, and Debbie Hippolite Wright. Honolulu: University of Hawaii Press, 2002.

Shah, Nayan. "Perversity, Contamination, and the Dangers of Queer Domesticity." In *Contagious Divides: Epidemics and Race in San Francisco's Chinatown.* Berkeley: University of California Press, 2001.

Takagi, Dana Y. "Maiden Voyage: Excursions into Sexuality and Identity Politics in Asian America." In *Asian American Sexualities: Dimensions of the Gay and Lesbian Experience.* Edited by Russell Leong. Los Angeles: UCLA Asian American Studies Center Press, 1996.

———. "Postmodernism from the Edge: Asian American Identities." In *Privileging Positions: The Sites of Asian American Studies.* Edited by Gary Y. Okihiro et al. Pullman: Washington State University Press, 1995.

Ting, Jennifer. "Bachelor Society: Deviant Heterosexuality and Asian American Historiography." In *Privileging Positions: The Sites of Asian American Studies.* Edited by Gary Y. Okihiro, et al. Pullman: Washington State University Press, 1995.

———. "The Power of Sexuality." *Journal of Asian American Studies* 1, no. 1 (February 1999): 65–82.

Tsang, Daniel C. "Breaking the Silence: The Emergence of the Lesbian and Gay Asian Press in North America." In *Bearing Dreams, Shaping Visions: Asian Pacific American Perspectives.* Edited by Linda A. Revilla et al. Pullman: Washington State University Press, 1993.

Uba, Eric, et al. *CrossTalk Updated Bibliography on Asian Pacific Islander American Sensuality and Sexuality.* Northridge, Calif.: Asian American Studies Department, California State University, 2002.

Wat, Eric. *The Making of a Gay Asian Community: An Oral History of Pre-AIDS Los Angeles.* Lanham, Md.: Rowman and Littlefield, 2002.

**Daniel C. Tsang**

*See also* ASIAN AMERICANS AND PACIFIC ISLANDERS; ASIAN AMERICAN LGBTQ ORGANIZATIONS AND PERIODICALS.

# ASIAN AMERICAN LGBTQ ORGANIZATIONS AND PERIODICALS

Asian and Pacific Americans (APAs) constitute a diverse population of people who trace their heritage to dozens of nations and cultures throughout Asia and the Pacific Islands. Yet in the United States, APAs are often lumped together, despite the cultural differences and even political tensions that have historically existed among ethnic groups. While some APAs have responded to this essentialization by emphasizing the differences among APAs, others have called on APAs to coalesce, recognizing that the racisms targeting various ethnic groups intersect and overlap in significant ways. This paradoxical response of emphasizing both differences and sameness has characterized APA community building and activist movements since the "Asian American" racial identity first emerged in the 1960s.

A similar paradoxical movement has characterized the histories of APAs who identify as LGBT, intersexed, questioning, or queer (QAPAs). QAPAs often experience different forms of oppression within their various communities. This includes not only anti-APA racism and heterosexism/homophobia within mainstream U.S. society, but also racism within LGBTQ communities and heterosexism within APA communities. In response, QAPAs have created and participated in a variety of organizations to address their unique experiences and needs, some that distinguish between QAPA subgroups and some that bring all QAPAs together.

## Emergence of QAPA Organizations

QAPA activists had been involved in a range of antioppressive organizations (socialist, feminist, LGBT rights, and civil rights) throughout the 1960s and 1970s, but often felt frustrated by the heterosexism, Eurocentrism, and other forms of oppression that prevented these organizations from addressing the experiences and needs of QAPAs. Both building on and troubling these other movements, QAPAs began meeting separately in the late 1970s, and in the summer of 1979 they formed the first QAPA organization in U.S. history: Boston Asian Gay Men and Lesbians (BAGMAL), later renamed Alliance of Massachusetts Asian Lesbians and Gay Men (AMALGAM), and then again renamed Queer Asian Pacific

Alliance of New England and Boston (QAPA). The changes in the name of this organization reflected its evolving mission statement, which expanded to address a wider range of queer and APA identities while maintaining one of its initial goals of addressing the invisibility of QAPAs within LGBT and APA communities. In the fall of 1979, QAPAs from BAGMAL and across the United States and Canada formed the Lesbian and Gay Asian Collective in Washington, D.C., at the first National Third World Lesbian and Gay Conference, which coincided with the first Gay and Lesbian March on Washington. The collective was not an ongoing organization, but it did present a rare opportunity to meet other QAPA activists, many of whom went on to form organizations across North America, such as Asian Lesbians of the East Coast (ALOEC) in New York City in 1983.

In 1980 the West Coast saw the emergence of its first QAPA organization, Asian Pacific Lesbians and Gays (APLG) in Los Angeles. The group eventually changed its name to Asian Pacific Gays and Friends (APGF) to acknowledge that its membership had become primarily male and was open to non-APAs. In 1983 Asian Pacific Lesbians and Friends (APLF) emerged in Los Angeles as a breakaway group from APLG. Some women wanted a group separate from the male-dominated APLG, which was sometimes critiqued as sexist and as primarily a dating service for QAPA men. Throughout the 1980s, similar breakaway groups began forming in other cities as women responded to the tendencies of QAPA organizations to overlook the experiences and needs of QAPA women. Such was the case in San Francisco, where Asian Women, eventually renamed Asian Pacific Sisters (APS), formed in 1984 as an alternative to the Association of Lesbian and Gay Asians (ALGA), formed in 1981. Breakaway groups also began forming for other subpopulations of QAPAs (including ethnic groups, younger and older people, transgenders, and men) throughout the 1980s and 1990s.

For example, although APLG was critiqued for being male-dominated, some QAPA men in Los Angeles followed their sisters by forming a breakaway QAPA men's group in 1984, one not open to non-APAs, called Gay Asian Rap (GARP), later renamed Gay Asian Pacific Support Network (GAPSN). Other groups began forming specifically for QAPA men across the United States. Gay Asian Pacific Alliance (GAPA) formed in 1988 in San Francisco as an outgrowth of the Asian Gay Men's Support Group at Berkeley's Pacific Center (an LGBTQ community center), partly in response to the growing AIDS epidemic and partly to create an alternative to the social group Pacific Friends, open to both APA and non-APA

men. Gay Asian and Pacific Islander Men of New York (GAPIMNY) formed in 1990 in New York City, the culmination of discussions first begun in retreats for QAPAs held in 1988. Gay Asians and Pacific Islanders of Chicago (GAPIC) formed in 1994, Asian and Pacific Islander Queers United for Action (AQUA) formed in Washington, D.C., in 1997, and Queer and Asian (Q'n'A) formed in Seattle, Washington, in the 1990s. In these groups, discussions in meetings often focused on the participants' experiences with racism, heterosexism, and other forms of oppression in their families, communities, and other activist organizations. The groups often struggled to find a balance between being both a support group and an advocacy group; and they often succeeded in joining with women's groups to bring greater visibility to QAPAs in mainstream LGBT and APA events (such as pride marches and cultural celebrations).

## Women's Organizing

In 1977, Asian American Feminists began meeting in the San Francisco Bay Area as a support group for APA women that grew out of the women's movement consciousness-raising groups. The group was not specifically for QAPA women and only lasted for two years, but—predominantly consisting of QAPA women—it set the stage for QAPA women's organizing. Beginning in the early 1980s and into the 1990s, regional organizations specifically for QAPA women began emerging, including the Asian Lesbian and Bisexual Alliance (ALBA) in Seattle; DC Asian Lesbians in Washington, D.C. (later renamed Asian Pacific Islander Queer Sisters, APIQS); Los Angeles Asian Pacific Islander Sisters (LAAPIS); Pacifica Asian Lesbians Networking (PALS) in Chicago; and the Asian Pacific Islander Lesbian Bisexual Transgendered Network (APLBTN) in Atlanta.

Many of these organizations coalesced into a national network of organizations to address QAPA women's issues. In 1987 the Asian Pacific Lesbian Network (later renamed the national Asian and Pacific Islander Lesbian and Bisexual Women and Transgender Network, APLBTN) emerged after members of QAPA groups across the United States formed an APA contingent in the second National March on Washington for Lesbian and Gay Rights. The planning for such a network had begun earlier that year when QAPA women gathered in the first West Coast Asian Pacific Lesbian retreat, called "Coming Out and Community Together," in Sonoma, California, as well as in the first Asian Pacific Gay and Lesbian conference, called "Breaking the Silence, Beginning the Dialog," in San Francisco. The formation of APLBTN led to many more national and regional gatherings for QAPA women, including the First National Asian Pacific Lesbian retreat, called "Coming Together, Moving Forward," in Santa Cruz, California, in 1989; the first West Coast APLBTN retreat, "Moving beyond Visibility," in Santa Cruz in 1993; the first Midwest Asian Pacific Islander Lesbian Bisexual Transgender Retreat in Minneapolis, Minnesota, in 1995; and the Second National APLBTN Conference in Los Angeles in 1998. APLBTN increased the visibility of QAPA women and women's issues in LGBT pride marches and at various activist conferences, and spearheaded the Asian and Pacific Islander Lesbian, Bisexual, Transgender, and Queer Task Force, which offered testimonies and recommendations for the Presidential Advisory Commission on Asian Americans and Pacific Islanders in 2000.

In the 1990s, QAPA women's organizations continued to emerge, especially organizations for subgroups of women. In 1991, Older Asian Sisters in Solidarity (OASIS) formed in San Francisco as a social group for women over thirty-five years of age. In 1994, Kilawin Kolektibo formed in New York City as a networking and support group for LBT Filipinas. Khuli Zaban formed in Chicago in 1995 for South and West Asian Women Who Love Women. O Moi also formed in 1995 as a support network for Vietnamese lesbians, bisexual women, and transgenders in Los Angeles and in Orange County, California. The San Francisco Bay area saw the emergence of several more ethnic-specific women's groups, including Mandarin Asian Pacific Lesbian Bisexual Network (MAPLBN), which in 1999 produced the booklet, "Beloved Daughter," to help Chinese and Chinese American families communicate about sexual orientation; and Ligaya Ng Kababaihan, a queer Filipina organization that formed in 2000. The San Francisco Bay area also saw the emergence of a new coalition of women's organizations, API Queer Women's Coalition, which in 1999 consisted of more than twenty groups.

As was the case with other QAPA groups, women's organizations were formed, at least in part, because of the recognition that certain needs were not being met by other LGBT, APA, or QAPA organizations, including needs of women who are older, of marginalized ethnic groups, and of groups with different language backgrounds.

### Differences among QAPAs

The increased number of QAPA organizations that emerged throughout the 1980s and especially the 1990s reflected the diversity of interests and needs among QAPAs. One type of group was organizations for distinct ethnic groups (especially ethnic groups that had histori-

cally been marginalized within APA communities). They emerged as early as 1986, when *Trikone*, a newsletter for LGBTs of South Asian descent published in Palo Alto, California, inspired chapters called Trikone to form around the world, beginning in the San Francisco Bay area that same year. In the 1990s many more organizations emerged. Some sprang up in response to controversies, such as Kambal sa Lusog, an organization for GLB Filipinos and Filipinas in New York City, which formed in 1991 in response to a controversy about the racist and gendered undertones of the Broadway show *Miss Saigon;* the formation of the group was also spurred by the inadequate responses of other activist organizations to the controversy. Other organizations formed as people with shared ethnic backgrounds found a kinship not apparent in other organizations. They included Barangay, a group for LGBT Filipinos and Filipinas in Los Angeles that began hosting social and rap sessions in 1990 and was officially established in 1996; Khush-DC, formed in 1994 to serve the South Asian LGBTQ communities in Washington, D.C.; the Malaysian Gay and Lesbian Club, formed in San Francisco in 1995; the China Rainbow Association, formed in Los Angeles in 1996; Iban/Queer Koreans of New York, formed in 1997; and Gay Polynesians Alliance/California (GPAC, later renamed United Territories of Polynesian Islanders Alliance, UTOPIA), formed in San Francisco in 1998 and Hawaii in 1999 to support Polynesian LGBTs. Other organizations included Chingusai-Chicago, for LGBTs of Korean descent; Na Mamo o Hawai'i, for LGBTs of Hawaiian and Pacific Islander descent; and, for LGBTs of South Asian descent, the Massachusetts Area South Asian Lambda Association (MASALA), Sangat-Chicago, and South Asian Lesbian and Gay Association of New York (SALGA-NYC).

A second type of QAPA group to emerge consisted of organizations for QAPA children, teenagers, and young adults, which formed across the United States on university campuses and in community organizations. In 1993 students at the University of California at Berkeley formed CAL-B-GAY (Cal Asian Lesbian, Bisexual, and Gay Alliances You-nited (later renamed CalQ&A, or Cal Queer and Asian), only a few years after students at the University of California at Los Angeles formed Mahu. Other campuses with QAPA student organizations active in the early 2000s were Mothra at the University of Michigan at Ann Arbor and Trikone-Tejas at the University of Texas at Austin. Of course, not all young people were in college or even of college age. In the 1990s community centers and organizations began creating support and social groups for a wider range of QAPA young people. In San Francisco in 1991, young people formed FABRIC (Fresh Asians Becoming Real in the Community), which dissolved in 1995 when one of the APA community health organizations formed another group, AQUA (Asian and Pacific Islander, Queer and Questioning, 25 and Under, All Together). Both groups were created, in part, to reach QAPA youth who did not feel that the more established community LGBT youth group was responsive to APA youth. A few years later, QUACK (Queer Asian and Pacific Islander Chicks) formed as a breakaway from AQUA, which was often seen as male dominated. Other cities with organizations for QAPA young people that emerged in the 1990s included Atlanta, with its PAY (Pride for Asian Youth) Program, and Boston, with its A Slice of Rice group.

A third category of groups formed throughout the 1980s and 1990s in response to the growing AIDS epidemic, sometimes emerging from early QAPA organizations. In 1986 in San Francisco, an Asian AIDS task force was created to conduct a needs assessment and raise funds for what was to become the first program to address AIDS among APAs. The task force became the Asian Pacific AIDS Coalition, of which GAPA became a member in 1987. That year GAPA created the Community HIV Project (GCHP), which was the first U.S. gay-identified APA HIV/AIDS program. Also that year in San Francisco, the Asian American Recovery Services created the Asian AIDS Project to provide health education to APAs (the Asian AIDS Project merged with GCHP in 1997 to become the Asian and Pacific Islander Wellness Center). A similar development took place in Los Angeles in 1987 when the Asian Pacific AIDS Intervention Team developed out of APLG. AIDS-related organizations emerged in the Midwest and on the East Coast several years later: the Asian and Pacific Islander Coalition on HIV/AIDS in New York City in 1989; the Asian American AIDS Foundation in Chicago in 1992; and AIDS Services in Asian Communities (ASIAC) in Philadelphia in 1995. Organizations also emerged for specific populations of QAPAs, including the Filipino Task Force on AIDS and the Southeast Asian Transgender AIDS Prevention Program, both in San Francisco.

The fourth type of QAPA organizations consisted of groups created less for support or advocacy and more for non-APA people (typically men) who wanted to interact with QAPAs. Such organizations included chapters of the Long Yang Club, an international network of chapters first formed in London in 1983 but with chapters throughout the United States. A similar but more loosely affiliated network of groups was Asians and Friends, first formed in 1984, which had organizations across the

United States and took on a different name in some places (for example, San Francisco's Pacific Friends). Other regional organizations for APAs and non-APAs included Atlanta's Oriental Express (renamed Asian Express and Friends), New York City's Asian Pacific Alliance of New York, Orange County Asian Pacific Crossroads in California, Texas's Dragonflies of Dallas, and San Francisco's Gay Asian Multicultural Exchange. Many of these groups belonged to the International Friendship Alliance, which hosted International Friendship Weekend retreats annually beginning in 1990.

Fifth, some organizations consisted of and spoke to APAs who were not necessarily LGBT about QAPA people and issues. For example, in 1994 the Japanese American Citizen's League (JACL)—a national civil rights organization—created an Asian Pacific Islander Lambda chapter to help address LGBT-related issues among APAs. In 1995 the San Francisco chapter of PFLAG (Parents, Families, and Friends of Lesbians and Gays) created the API-PFLAG Family Project (later called API Family Pride); it produced a video documentary to help APA families discuss sexual orientation, and in the years following, created a network for APA parents and families to support one another. In the mid-1990s parents and families created another API-PFLAG in Los Angeles with support from GAPSN. These organizations formed in response to the recognition that existing APA and LGBTQ organizations needed to do more to address sexual and racial differences among their constituencies. In 1999, Al and Jane Nakatani, parents of two QAPAs, created Honor Thy Children, an educational organization that promoted the acceptance of human diversity among all children, including QAPAs.

**Tensions and Evolutions**

The preceding lists of QAPA organizations are not exhaustive. In 2003 other organizations were active (including South Bay Queer and Asian, SBQA, a social group in northern California, and Asian Pacific Islanders for Human Rights, APIHR, an advocacy group in southern California), and of those that have since dissolved, some did not leave records or archives, perhaps because of lack of time and resources, perhaps for fear of safety and loss of privacy, and perhaps because the organization did not last for very long. Over the past decades, many organizations have struggled to exist as members tried to find the time to bring leadership and energy into them and their initiatives and to cope with disagreements between one another over the groups' missions and scopes. For example, LGBT Asians and Asian Americans existed in Madison, Wisconsin, for barely two years, from

1997 to 1999. Debates over who could join (non-APAs? transgenders?) and the mission of the group (to provide a space for QAPAs to form a community or to create opportunities for singles to meet and date) ended with many members choosing to leave the organization. By 1999 the added difficulty of finding members to plan gatherings and maintain the mailing list resulted in the dissolution of the organization. It was not surprising that such debates existed. No single organization can meet all the interests and needs of a group of people. Furthermore, the very act of creating an organization often involves only certain voices making decisions about who is in, who is out, and what issues are and are not going to be addressed. The difficulty of creating an organization in an inclusive way helped to derail discussions about forming a national network of QAPA activists that took place in 2000 and 2001 on NQAPA (National Queer Asian Pacific Americans), an e-mail discussion list for QAPAs. In 2003 activists were continuing to meet informally to strategize a new national movement.

## Bibliography

Eng, David L., and Alice Y Hom, eds. *Q & A: Queer in Asian America.* Philadelphia: Temple University Press, 1998.

Kumashiro, Kevin K. *Restoried Selves: Autobiographies of Queer Asian/Pacific American Activists.* Binghamton, N.Y.: Harrington Park Press, 2003.

Leong, Russell, ed. *Asian American Sexualities: Dimensions of the Gay and Lesbian Experience.* New York: Routledge, 1996.

Lim-Hing, Sharon, ed. *The Very Inside: An Anthology of Writings by Asian and Pacific Islander Lesbian and Bisexual Women.* Toronto: Sister Vision Press, 1994.

Matzner, Andrew, ed. *'O Au No Keia: Voices from Hawai'i's Mahu and Transgender Communities.* Xlibris Corporation, 2001.

Ratti, Rakesh, ed. *A Lotus of Another Color: An Unfolding of the South Asian Gay and Lesbian Experience.* Boston, Mass.: Alyson Publications, 1993.

Varney, Joan Ariki. "Undressing the Normal: Community Efforts for Queer Asian and Asian American Youth." In *Troubling Intersections of Race and Sexuality: Queer Students of Color and Anti-Oppressive Education.* Edited by Kevin K. Kumashiro. Lanham, Md.: Rowman and Littlefield, 2001.

Wat, Eric C. *The Making of a Gay Asian Community: An Oral History of Pre-AIDS Los Angeles.* Lanham, Md.: Rowman and Littlefield, 2002.

**Kevin K. Kumashiro**

*See also* CHUA, SIONG-HUAT; FUKAYA, MICHIYO; KIM, WILLYCE; TSANG, DANIEL; TSUI, KITTY; WOO, MERLE.

# ATKINSON, Ti-Grace (b. 1939), activist and author.

Ti-Grace Atkinson was born in Baton Rouge, Louisiana, to a wealthy Republican family. In 1956, at the age of seventeen, she married her high school boyfriend. Atkinson attended the University of Pennsylvania and completed a bachelors degree in fine arts in 1964. While living in Philadelphia, Atkinson helped with the founding of the Institute of Contemporary Art and wrote for *Art News.* In 1961 she divorced her husband. Atkinson moved to New York City in the mid-1960s and enrolled in a Ph.D. program in political philosophy at Columbia University. There, she became part of a politically savvy and activist community of students. As with many women of her generation, she read French philosopher Simone de Beauvoir's *The Second Sex* (1949) and was deeply moved by it. In 1965 Atkinson wrote de Beauvoir, who suggested that she contact Betty Friedan.

With few feminist organizations in existence, Atkinson joined the National Organization for Women (NOW) in 1967. Founder Betty Friedan quickly recognized Atkinson's talents and propelled her into a leadership role. In 1967 Atkinson was elected president of NOW New York, the largest and most dynamic branch of the organization.

Almost immediately, Atkinson advocated positions that were far more controversial than NOW was willing to support, particularly on matters such as abortion rights, lesbianism, and marriage. Informed by the Students for a Democratic Society and its commitment to participatory democracy, Atkinson proposed that NOW no longer elect officers but assign tasks by lottery. This, she proposed, would allow the membership to shape the organization and enable individual women to learn important leadership skills as they rotated through staff positions. When the board of directors of both NOW's national board and the New York City chapter turned down her proposal in 1968, Atkinson resigned.

Upon leaving, Atkinson formed a much more radical group, named the October 17 Movement for the date of her break from NOW. Initially small, the group gained members as radical feminism in New York City rapidly expanded. In June 1969 the group renamed itself The Feminists and began to generate new theories of women's oppression. Deeply informed by Valerie Solanas's view of marriage as incompatible with feminism and sex as oppressive for women, Atkinson soon became the group's dominant voice. The New Left's tradition of political theater and direct action also shaped Atkinson's politics. On 23 September 1969 five members of The Feminists charged New York City's Marriage License Bureau officials with fraud before moving on to confront the city's mayor as "an official representative of male society" whose support of marriage kept women psychologically damaged. So critical of marriage was the group that it allowed only one-third of its members to be married or living with a man. Eventually, all married members of the group dropped out. Atkinson, who argued that romantic heterosexual love was the psychological internalization of oppression, refused to be seen in public with a man.

Viewing themselves as the vanguard of the women's movement, The Feminists put a premium on discipline and commitment. The group demanded full attendance at weekly meetings. Tasks were decided through lottery, and women with specific skills, like writing, were encouraged not to put their name in the lottery pool for jobs that utilized those skills. Speaking discs, in the form of poker chips or slips of paper, were passed out at the beginning of each meeting to ensure that no one dominated and the group remain leaderless. The Feminists rejected consciousness-raising as a distracting technique that obscured the need for action. Group members also viewed heterosexual sex as the primary method through which women internalized and naturalized patriarchal oppression.

In 1970 Atkinson herself left the group over the restrictions it placed on her speaking to the press. She had been designated the group's spokesperson by *Newsweek* magazine early that year and was riding a wave of notoriety for her good looks, her outspoken views, and her high profile in New York City. Walter Cronkite interviewed Atkinson after she participated in the 19 March 1970 feminist takeover of the *Ladies Home Journal*. She also garnered media attention when she appeared on 17 December 1970 at a press conference to defend feminist Kate Millett, who had been outed as a lesbian by *Time* magazine in November 1970. In 1974 Atkinson's extensive writings and political speeches appeared as a collection entitled *Amazon Odyssey,* which secured her place as a major theoretician of lesbian feminism.

In 1975 Atkinson participated in a new feminist summer institute, Sagaris, at Goddard College in Plainfield, Vermont, but broke with it once the Ms. Foundation became a sponsor. Rumors about *Ms.* magazine editor Gloria Steinem's involvement with the Central Intelligence Agency had undermined Steinem's credibility among some radical women, including Atkinson, who had long struggled with government informers infiltrating their political organizations. As of 2003 Atkinson lived in New York City and remained politically active in feminist causes.

## Bibliography

Atkinson, Ti-Grace. *Amazon Odyssey: The First Collection of Writings by the Political Pioneer of the Women's Movement.* New York: Links Books, 1974.

Echols, Alice. *Daring to be Bad: Radical Feminism in America, 1967–1975.* Minneapolis: University of Minnesota Press, 1989.

Jay, Karla. *Tales of the Lavender Menace: A Memoir of Liberation.* New York: Basic Books, 1999.

Rosen, Ruth. *The World Split Open: How the Modern Women's Movement Changed America.* New York: Viking, 2000.

Wandersee, Winifred. *On the Move: American Women in the 1970s.* Boston: Twayne, 1988.

**Jane Gerhard**

*See also* FEMINISM; LESBIAN FEMINISM; MILLET, KATE; RADICALESBIANS; SOLANAS, VALERIE.

# ATLANTA

Atlanta's LGBT community is large, well organized, and politically powerful. Census data from 2000 showed that Atlanta has the sixth-largest percentage of same-sex households among U.S. cities with populations over 100,000. The president of the Atlanta city council, Cathy Woolard, is a lesbian, and the city made history in 2000 by electing the first openly LGBT state legislator in the South, State Representative Karla Drenner. Three municipalities in the Atlanta metro area—the cities of Atlanta, Decatur, and Pine Lake—have nondiscrimination ordinances that include sexual orientation and gender identity/expression. Atlanta's annual Pride celebration draws more than 300,000 people each year from throughout the South, and two other annual events, Black Gay Pride and the transgender conference Southern Comfort, also draw large crowds.

Atlanta, located in the heart of the Bible Belt South, was not always this hospitable to its LGBT residents. Little is known about the history of LGBT life in Atlanta before World War II; same-sex sexual relations and gender nonconformity apparently were clandestine and discreet enough to remain largely outside the public's consciousness. However, in Atlanta, as in other cities across the United States, the war marked a turning point.

As the work of historian Allan Bérubé and others has demonstrated, World War II itself created the conditions under which a homosexual consciousness and culture could develop in the United States. After the war, thousands of newly self-identified gay men and lesbians flocked to the relative safety and anonymity of the nation's cities. Atlanta, as the most populous urban area in the South, was the destination of many Southerners from small towns and rural areas. Although this increase in the numbers and visibility of LGBT people was a step forward, it had an unintended consequence: LGBT people faced extremely oppressive conditions from the postwar period well into the 1960s.

John Howard has documented the oppression gay white men faced in Atlanta during the 1940s and 1950s. He notes that Atlanta was no different from other cities during this period in its heightened surveillance of public spaces and its harsh punishment of men caught engaging in same-sex sexual relations or cross-dressing, or even possessing printed material with homosexual content. However, Howard argues that two factors distinguished (and may still distinguish) the experiences of gays in Atlanta from those of gays in other parts of the country: the significance of religion in the lives of those on either side of the crackdown on gay activity, and racial segregation, which ensured that the public spaces where white men risked prosecution by coming together for sexual activity were not open to African American men.

By the time of New York City's Stonewall Riots in June 1969, Atlanta had a thriving if still largely underground white gay community, with a few bars and many social networks, but no public organizations. LGBT African Americans maintained social networks and gathered in after-hours clubs, which generally were restaurants that operated as gay bars after their regular hours. Billy Jones, who entertained crowds at the Joy Lounge as "Phyllis Killer" beginning in 1967, remembers the pre-Stonewall years as a time of constant police harassment and frequent raids on bars. As in the rest of the country, this situation began to change after Stonewall.

The 1970s in Atlanta are significant for the intensity and radical nature of LGBT political activity that occurred as the gay liberation movement gained momentum. As was the case nationally, most of the city's early lesbian and gay activists were leftists, many of whom had been active in the civil rights, antiwar, and student movements. Atlanta's first Pride celebration was held in June 1970; its initial gay and lesbian organization, a local chapter of the Gay Liberation Front (GLF), was founded in 1971. The city's first lesbian and gay political action committee, First Tuesday, formed in 1977 and launched candidate forums the same year. In 1978 Atlanta had its biggest Pride event yet: more than two thousand people marched and demonstrated at Atlanta's World Congress Center to protest Anita Bryant's keynote address to the Southern Baptist Convention.

Atlanta was also one of several U.S. cities that had an organized lesbian-feminist community during the 1970s. From the beginning, some Atlanta lesbians had felt marginalized within the gay liberation movement, and in 1972 they elected to work separately and formed their own organization, the Atlanta Lesbian Feminist Alliance (ALFA). ALFA rented a house in Little Five Points, an Atlanta neighborhood in the heart of the city, and maintained it as a women-only space. The organization also fielded an openly lesbian softball team in Atlanta's city league beginning in 1974. Its newsletter, *Atalanta*, kept lesbians throughout the Southeast in touch with the lesbian-feminist movement, and its lending library made available a plethora of printed material produced by women-owned presses and publishing houses. The feminist bookstore Charis Books and More opened in Little Five Points in 1974 and was another source of the written material that became so important to the feminist and lesbian-feminist movements.

Before 1980, no organization specifically for African American LGBT people is known to have existed in Atlanta, but that year an organization called the Gay Atlanta Minorities Association (GAMA) held a discussion session entitled "Black Lesbian/Gay/Transperson Survival in the 1980s" during Pride week. In addition to GAMA, a group for black lesbians, Sisters, existed for a time during the 1980s, and in 1987 the African-American Lesbian and Gay Alliance (AALGA) was founded. As of 2003, a number of organizations specifically for African Americans and other people of color exist in Atlanta, and large Black Gay Pride celebration is held every Labor Day weekend. Moreover, the LGBT community as a whole has benefited from political alliances with the city's African American leaders beginning with the man elected in 1974 as the city's first African American mayor, Maynard Jackson.

One of the events for which LGBT Atlanta is most famous took place in 1981, when Michael Hardwick was arrested for having sex with another man in his own home. The case eventually made its way to the U.S. Supreme Court, which in 1986 issued its infamous ruling, *Bowers v. Hardwick*, upholding Georgia's sodomy law and asserting that the right to privacy does not extend to private, adult, consensual same-sex sexual activity. Georgia's sodomy law remained in force until the state Supreme Court struck it down in 1998.

Atlanta's hosting of the 1996 Olympics led to two additional events for which the city's LGBT community is known nationally. The first involved Cobb County, a suburb just north of Atlanta whose county commission had passed an ordinance in 1993 condemning homosexuality. When Cobb County was later announced as the site of the Olympic volleyball competition, activist Pat Hussein and others formed Olympics Out of Cobb and organized protests that eventually led the Atlanta Committee for the Olympic Games to relocate the competition to another county. While this was cause for celebration, the second Olympics related event was not: a local lesbian bar called the Otherside was bombed early in 1997, presumably by the same person who had bombed Centennial Olympic Park in Atlanta during the games. Right-wing terrorist Eric Rudolph was later charged in connection with both bombings; he evaded capture until being apprehended in North Carolina in 2003.

As of the early twenty-first century, Atlanta's LGBT community continues to grow in numbers and influence. According to many, the next step is to extend this power and influence to the small towns and rural areas that make up most of the state of Georgia. With a track record of success, Atlanta's LGBT leaders are confident enough to take on the task.

## Bibliography

Bérubé, Allan. *Coming Out under Fire: The History of Gay Men and Women in World War II.* New York: Free Press, 1990.

Brown, Laura. "From Stonewall to Piedmont Park: Three Decades of Atlanta's Gay History." *Southern Voice,* 24 June 1999, 1, 32–33.

Chesnut, Saralyn, and Amanda C. Gable. "'Women Ran It': Charis Books and More and Atlanta's Lesbian-Feminist Community, 1971–1981." In *Carryin' On in the Lesbian and Gay South.* Edited by John Howard. New York: NYU Press, 1997.

D'Emilio, John. *Sexual Politics, Sexual Communities: The Making of a Homosexual Minority in the United States, 1940–1970.* Chicago: University of Chicago Press, 1983.

Fraker, Debbie. "Atlanta Lesbian and Gay Activists: Fighting so Others Can Come Out." *Southern Voice,* Special Pride Supplement, 20 June 1991.

Hayward, Dave, and Cal Gough. "Twenty Years of Atlanta Lesbian and Gay History: A Timeline." *Southern Voice,* Special Pride Supplement, 20 June 1991.

Howard, John. "The Library, the Park, and the Pervert: Public Space and Homosexual Encounter in Post-World War II Atlanta." In *Carryin' On in the Lesbian and Gay South.* Edited by John Howard. New York: NYU Press, 1997.

———. *Men Like That: A Southern Queer History.* Chicago: University of Chicago Press, 1999.

Sager, Brendan. "Atlanta No. 6 in Households with Same-Sex Couples." *Atlanta Journal-Constitution,* 13 March 2003.

**Saralyn Chesnut**

*See also* AFRICAN AMERICAN LGBTQ ORGANIZATIONS AND PERIODICALS; ANTI-DISCRIMINATION LAW AND POLICY; BOOKSTORES; ELECTORAL POLITICS; GAY LIBERATION FRONT; LESBIAN FEMINISM; PRIDE MARCHES AND PARADES; SODOMY, BUGGERY, CRIMES AGAINST NATURE, DISORDERLY CONDUCT, AND LEWD AND LASCIVIOUS LAW AND POLICY; SPORTS; STATE, LOCAL, AND MUNICIPAL LAW AND POLICY; VIOLENCE.

## AUDEN, W. H. (b. 21 February 1907; d. 28 September 1973), poet, playwright.

Wystan Hugh Auden was born in York, England, the third son of George Auden and Constance Bicknell. His father was a doctor; his mother, a cultured woman whose appreciation of music Auden inherited, was responsible for his upbringing in the Anglican Church, a religion that he rejected in his youth and then returned to in his middle years. It was a happy household. The parents Auden later characterized as admirable and lovable raised their children to be voracious readers and connoisseurs of the arts. For example, Constance taught young Wystan the words to the love duet from Wagner's *Tristan and Isolde.* Auden also read countless science fiction and fantasy books. Still, he fancied that, one day, he might become something practical, a mining engineer.

This sort of cultured and intellectual upbringing was likely to reveal itself at school, and so it did. By the time he was eight and attending St. Edmund's boarding school in Surrey, Auden had developed a reputation for preternatural self-possession and insight. His classmates nicknamed him Witty, although it was surely his mature knowledge of matters sexual, gleaned from his father's anatomical manuals, rather than his propensity to recite verse that most astonished his young friends. It was there, at St. Edmunds, that Auden met Christopher Isherwood, then thirteen, and the two launched a friendship that would endure for the rest of their lives.

In 1925 Auden entered Christ's Church, Oxford University, where he studied music, biology, and, nominally at first, English. It was at Christ's Church that he began the personal transformation that would make him into a poet. The reputation for erudition he had earned at St. Edmunds continued. He was known as an able conversationalist, although in truth he tended to pontificate and harangue, rather than converse. Politically, his sympathies ran toward socialism, but despite his attempts to abandon the Anglican faith, he never indulged in the rejection of bourgeois values that led so many of his friends to turn on their parents. From his professors and tutors, especially J. R. R. Tolkien, he learned to appreciate Old English verse. He became a close friend of Cecil Day-

Lewis, Stephen Spender, and John Betjeman, and wrote frequently, developing the ability to critically appraise his own work. In time Auden was confident enough to initiate a regular correspondence with T. S. Eliot, then reading manuscripts for the publisher Faber and Faber. Eliot found his efforts immature but intriguing, and encouraged him to continue his development as a writer.

Only later, in 1928, was the course of Auden's life set when his first collection of poetry was published—privately, by Spender. In 1930, after Auden had taken a post at Larchfield Academy, Scotland, Eliot at last accepted for publication a collection of his work. It was called *Poems,* although most of the volume was taken up by a play. By 1935 his lyrics had begun to bring him fame. That same year, despite having been openly gay for some time (at least among his family and closest acquaintances—he had grown too reserved to be flamboyant about anything), Auden took a wife, Erika, the daughter of the well-known writer Thomas Mann. He did so at the urging of Isherwood, who had been asked to marry Erika first, and then only so that she might obtain British citizenship. It was a marriage in name only, and while the two maintained an amicable relationship, their personal encounters were at best infrequent.

For the rest of his life, Auden remained extremely active, rarely in one place for very long and always working. He served in the Spanish Civil War. Besides producing his own work, he wrote plays with Isherwood and collaborated with Igor Stravinsky, Benjamin Britten, and Chester Kallman, his partner for thirty-five years. With Isherwood, he traveled to China and then, in 1939, to the United States, where he taught at the New School of Social Research in New York City, Swarthmore College in Pennsylvania, and Bennington College in Vermont. He edited a selection of poems by Lord Alfred Tennyson for a New York publisher, but raised some eyebrows when in his introduction he opined that Tennyson was the "stupidest" English poet. (Eliot famously replied that if Auden had been a better scholar he could have thought of many stupider.) In 1946, having fallen in love with New York, he became a U.S. citizen.

Although the various wars and tragedies of the twentieth century altered his politics and led him back to the religion of his youth, Auden's poetry continued in the style he had developed at Christ's College: ordinary language employed in elaborate structures of verse. He wrote about change and people and places and death, treating even this last subject with his customary wit and good humor, even as he neared the end of his own life. As a result of this light-heartedness, some critics considered his work too vulgar for serious contemplation.

Auden died of a heart attack in Vienna on 28 September 1973. His fanciful suggestion that he be roasted and eaten as a final act of communion with his friends was politely elided. Another of his requests, however, was honored: the music of Wagner created the backdrop for his funeral.

## Bibliography

Bloom, Harold, ed. *W. H. Auden.* New York: Chelsea House, 1986.

Carpenter, Humphrey. *W. H. Auden: A Biography.* Boston: Houghton Mifflin, 1981.

Johnson, Wendell Stacy. *W. H. Auden.* New York: Continuum, 1990.

Osborne, Charles. *W. H. Auden: The Life of a Poet.* New York: Harcourt Brace Jovanovich, 1979.

**Laura M. Miller**

***See also*** ISHERWOOD, CHRISTOPHER; MCCULLERS, CARSON; MUSIC: OPERA; RICH, ADRIENNE; ROBBINS, JEROME.

## AUSTEN, Alice (b. 17 March 1866; d. 9 June 1952), photographer.

Active from the 1880s to the 1930s, Alice Austen was the first lesbian photographer known to have included lesbian indicators within her images.

Austen was born as Elizabeth Alice Munn on Staten Island in New York City to Alice Cornell Austen and Edward Stopford Munn, an Englishman who deserted his family before she was born. Austen's mother returned to her parents' Staten Island house, called Clear Comfort, and abandoned the use of the name Munn for herself and young Alice.

Austen was an adored only child in a household that included her mother, grandparents, an aunt, two uncles, and maids. She began learning photography in 1876 at age ten, when a seafaring uncle taught her to use a box camera and glass negatives. By age eighteen, her photographic equipment weighed fifty pounds. An upstairs storage closet in Clear Comfort became her tiny darkroom. There was no running water inside, so she washed her negatives and prints out-of-doors using a hand pump.

Austen often included herself in photographs by using a pneumatic cable to release the camera's shutter by remote control. Her favorite subjects were her home, family, friends, and neighbors. Her photographs of mothers and their children are more realistic than those of most of her contemporaries. They were also unusual in picturing women engaged in gymnastic exercise, swimming, and riding bicycles.

In 1890, when she was close to twenty-five years of age, Austen began photographically pushing the boundaries of decorum. In one picture, two women raise long skirts above their knees as if dancing, showing a then-shocking amount of black-stockinged leg. Elsewhere, four women pretend to drink alcoholic beverages. In another, Austen and two friends dress in male clothing complemented by fake mustaches, cigarettes, and an umbrella handle positioned as an erect penis.

Several photographs from 1891 indicate that Austen knew she was attracted to women and sought ways to visualize that attraction. In some pictures, one woman possessively clasps another's leg. Austen's arms encircle a woman's waist in a photograph of paired female couples embracing. She also photographed herself and another woman standing in front of a bed, pretending to light fake cigarettes. Their long hair is unbound; they wear only slips, stockings, shoes, and masks. In the late 1890s she began to record images of her new lover, Gertrude Amelia Tate, with whom she would remain for the next half century. The early pictures show the vivaciousness of Tate, a dancing teacher five years younger than Austen.

Austen also photographed Manhattan's newly arrived immigrants, including newsgirls, ragpickers, peddlers, bootblacks, and street cleaners. Fifty of these photographs were published as "Street Types of New York" in 1896. In the 1890s she began photographing the federal quarantine facilities on Hoffman and Swinburn Islands (off the eastern shore of Staten Island) for the U.S. Public Health Service on a semiofficial basis. She continued this project on her own until 1910. Some of these pictures were exhibited in Buffalo, New York, at the Pan-American Exposition of 1901.

Austen lost her independent income from investments in the stock market crash of 1929. Not understanding the seriousness of the situation, she mortgaged Clear Comfort—which she had inherited—and took a planned trip to Europe with Tate. After their return, they attempted to cope financially by taking in boarders, running a tearoom, and selling off household items. Tate taught ballroom dancing and deportment. Austen could seldom afford to make new photographs.

In 1945 Tate and the seventy-nine-year-old Austen, who was crippled by arthritis, were evicted from Clear Comfort because they could not keep up with mortgage payments. Approximately 5,500 glass-plate negatives were lost, but 3,500 were rescued from the house by a quick-thinking volunteer from the Staten Island Historical Society.

Tate took care of Austen in a small apartment on Staten Island until 1949, when Austen was moved into a nursing home. In 1950, her funds depleted, Austen was admitted to the Staten Island Farm Colony, a home for paupers.

In 1951 a Manhattan editor, Oliver Ormerod Jensen, became aware of her photographs. He arranged for the publication of some in his own 1952 book, *The Revolt of American Women: A Pictorial History of the Century of Change from Bloomers to Bikinis*, and the sale of publication rights to others to *Life* and *Holiday* magazines. With the money thus earned, she was moved into a comfortable residence for the last year of her life. Dead at age eighty-six, Austen was buried in the family plot in the Moravian Cemetery on Staten Island. Tate lived with relatives for another decade. Red tape and expense prevented her burial beside Austen as both had wished. Clear Comfort, purchased by the Staten Island Historical Society, became the Alice Austen House Museum and Garden.

## Bibliography

Jensen, Oliver Ormerod. *The Revolt of American Women: A Pictorial History of the Century of Change from Bloomers to Bikinis, From Feminism to Freud*. New York: Harcourt, 1952.

Novotny, Ann. *Alice's World: The Life and Photography of an American Original: Alice Austen, 1866–1952*. Old Greenwich, Conn.: Chatham Press, 1976.

———. "Alice Austen's World." In *Heresies: A Feminist Publication on Art and Politics* 1, no. 3 (Fall 1977): 27–33.

Rist, Darrell Yates. "Alice Austen House: A Gay Haven on Staten Island Is Reclaimed." *The Advocate*, no. 438 (21 January 1986): 38–39.

**Tee A. Corinne**

*See also* VISUAL ART.

# B

**BACA, Judy** (b. 20 September 1946), artist, activist. Judith Baca was born into a woman-centered, Spanish-speaking family in Huntington Park, California. When her family moved to Pacoima, Judy was not yet fluent in English, so to keep her occupied, her teacher gave her art materials to work with during class. Her interest in art developed and she went on to study art at California State University in Northridge. After her grandmother questioned the usefulness of her art, Judy had an epiphany: she realized that her art had to "be connected with something that had meaning or purpose beyond self-gratification . . . [so that it] could speak to the people I cared most about, my family and community."

Baca went on to teach art at her alma mater, Bishop Alemany High School, but was fired in 1970 along with other activists for her opposition to the Vietnam War. She then found employment with Los Angeles's Cultural Affairs Division, where she organized a group of gang members and community youth from Hollenbeck Park to design and paint a mural. The success of this radical project led her in 1974 to found the Los Angeles Citywide Mural Project, which over a ten-year period created more than four hundred murals using the talent of over two thousand multicultural participants.

In an interview with Yleana Martinez, Baca stated, "I believe that taking art to the people is a political act" (Martinez, p. 36). This perspective is reflected in the work of the Social and Public Art Resource Center (SPARC), founded by Baca, printmaker Christina Schlesinger, and filmmaker Donna Deitch in Venice, California, in 1976.

The SPARC Website explains that the organization is "a multi-ethnic arts center that produces, distributes, preserves and documents community based public art works. SPARC espouses public art as an organizing tool for addressing social issues, fostering cross-cultural understanding and promoting civic dialogue. . . . Over the last twenty-five years SPARC has created murals in almost every ethnic community in Los Angeles." SPARC houses a collection of sixty thousand slides of public art from around the world.

In the mid-1970s Baca discovered the work of Mexican muralists Diego Rivera, David Siqueiros, and José Clemente Orozco and traveled to Mexico to study materials and techniques at Siqueiros's studio. Upon returning, she embarked on what was to become one of her best-known projects, the *Great Wall of Los Angeles.* This collective endeavor is a half-mile-long narrative mural painted on the walls of the Tujunga Wash Canal, in the San Fernando Valley west of Los Angeles. Baca supervised teams of young artists who researched, envisioned, and painted images of the multicultural history of the Los Angeles area from prehistoric times to the 1950s.

In 1984, as part of the Los Angeles Olympic festivities, Baca was one of ten local artists chosen to create murals along the Los Angeles freeways. Her mural, *Hitting the Wall,* celebrated the sports successes of women of color. Three years later Baca began working on *World Wall: A Vision of the Future without Fear,* a project that depicts global awareness, peace, cooperation, and the futility of war. Baca recalls that in planning the project, "It was not imagining destruction that was so hard for us but rather imagining peace." The portable mural is made up of seven ten-by-thirty-foot panels painted by Baca and arranged in a semicircle. Additional panels will be painted by artists in other countries and arranged in an outer circle.

A SPARC project that expands concepts of mural art at the beginning of the twenty-first century is the Digital Mural Lab, which makes use of the latest technology to create a "new form of muralism." In partnership with the University of California at Los Angeles's César Chávez Center, the Lab uses state-of-the-art digital technology to challenge widely held conceptions about the limits of mural art. Digital imaging is flexible and allows a new generation of muralists to apply images onto aluminum panels, a medium that deteriorates more slowly than conventional surfaces and is less expensive. One of the Digital Mural Lab's most prominent projects revolves around the mural *America Tropical*, painted in Los Angeles by Siqueiros in 1932. The work, an allegory depicting U.S. imperialism in Latin America, was considered politically unacceptable by city leaders and was immediately whitewashed. It has been restored, and to accompany its permanent exhibition at the Getty Museum students at the Digital Lab, working with community members, created three new murals that contrast Siqueiros's vision with visions of Los Angeles at the end of the twentieth century.

Baca has been SPARC's artistic director since 1976 and since 1996 she has also been a full professor of art at the University of California at Los Angeles. Her awards include an Arts Award from Hispanic Women, City of San Francisco (1986); a Rockefeller Fellowship (1991); and a Creative Vision Award from the Liberty Hill Foundation (2001). Her work appears in *Dialectics of Isolation: An Exhibition of Third World Women Artists of the United States* (1980) and in the exhibition catalog *Saber es Poder/ Interventions* (1994). Her experiences as a developing artist and public art activist are described in interviews with Diane Neumaier and Amalia Mesa-Bains, among others. While Baca identifies as lesbian, she has not focused politically on this part of her life. Like a number of activists and artists of color working in culture-specific environments, rather than underscore this part of her life, she has chosen to integrate it into the rest of her personal, political, and cultural identity.

## Bibliography

Baca, Judith. Interview by Amalia Mesa-Bains. Archives of American Art, Smithsonian Institution, 1986.

———. "Our People Are the Internal Exiles." Interview by Diane Neumaier. In *Making Face, Making Soul/Haciendo Caras: Creative and Critical Perspectives by Women of Color.* Edited by Gloria Anzaldúa. San Francisco: Aunt Lute Foundation, 1990.

Martinez, Yleana "Judy Baca." In *Notable Hispanic Women.* Edited by D. Telgen and J. Kamp. Detroit, Mich.: Gale Research, 1993.

**Yolanda Retter Vargas**

*See also* VISUAL ART

# BAKER, Josephine (b. 3 June 1906; d. 12 April 1975), dancer, singer, and activist.

Born Freda Josephine McDonald to African American parents Caroline McDonald and Edward Carson in St. Louis, Missouri, she spent her childhood years with her three younger siblings in St. Louis working odd jobs. At age seven she went to work as a domestic servant and was often mistreated.

Baker's first marriage, at age thirteen to Willie Wells, was short lived. By the early 1920s Baker was performing in melodramas, dancing in choruses, and touring with the Theater Owners' Booking Association. In 1921 Baker was married again, this time to William "Billy" Howard Baker. Baker toured with the Sissle and Blake vaudeville group of traveling performers. While touring, Baker had a string of male and female lovers, including vaudevillians Clara Smith and Evelyn "Little Shep" Sheppard. Racial segregation restricted where entertainers could stay while traveling; performer Maude Russell recalls that women often shared boardinghouse rooms while on the road, which possibly enabled romantic and sexual encounters to occur.

In 1925 Baker was living in Harlem, in New York City, and performing at the Plantation Club, when she was offered a contract to perform at Paris's Théâtre des Champs-Élysées in the new show the Revue Nègre. At first Baker refused to dance topless in her feature number "Danse Sauvage" (the wild dance); later she conceded to the French acceptance of female nudity. Baker's frenetic and angular dancing, coupled with her ragged costume and heavy makeup, garnered ambiguous reactions from the audience: some thought it sexy and sensual; others found it to be obscene and irritating. The show was a success, illustrating the popularity and fetishization of what Parisians believed to be African art.

The popularity of the Revue Nègre prompted the director of the Folies-Bergère to approach Baker to star in his new show. Baker's fame continued to grow with her popular "Banana Dance," which she performed in a skirt that was fashioned out of bananas. Her manager,

**Josephine Baker.** An international star, especially beloved in France, this sensual dancer and singer was also a lifelong crusader against discrimination. [AP/Wide World Photos]

Giuseppe "Pepito" Abatino, subsequently encouraged her to leave her contract at the Folies-Bergère and open her own club, Chez Joséphine. While continuing to work as a dancer, Baker recorded over 230 songs between 1926 and 1975, which she sang in English, French, German, Italian, Portuguese, and Spanish.

Just before World War II, Baker married Jean Lion, though they became legally separated by the start of the war. Their interracial marriage increased their visibility as targets: she as a black woman; he as white and Jewish. Baker participated in the French resistance during the war and was awarded the Croix de Guerre for her secret intelligence work and propaganda efforts. During the occupation, Baker entertained troops in Europe and North Africa and was made a sublieutenant of the Women's Auxiliary of the Free French Air Force. Baker believed her work during World War II was part of the greater struggle against racism. In 1961 she was awarded the Légion d'Honneur for her service to France. Baker openly discussed the discrimination she faced while touring in the United States, and she preferred to perform abroad where she was valued as an African American artist. She wore her Free French Air Force uniform when she spoke at the 1963 March on Washington to illustrate the links between the fight against fascism in Europe and the fight against racism in the United States.

In 1947, Baker married Joseph "Jo" Jean Étienne Bouillon, and beginning in 1954 she and Bouillon began to adopt children from various countries to fulfill Baker's longtime desire for children. Eventually Baker and Bouillon adopted twelve young orphans and one young teenager whose family was still alive. Baker's goal was to create a brotherhood of races; she named her brood the "Rainbow Tribe" and stirred up controversy with whites and blacks alike. By the end of her marriage to Bouillon in the late 1950s, it was rumored that each of them brought home same-sex lovers. In her later years her children filled her life. The immense cost of providing for such a large family led Baker to come out of retirement several times.

When she died in 1975, twenty thousand people spilled out into the street at her state funeral at the Church of the Madeleine in Paris. Royalty, government officials, celebrities, and family crowded inside. Floral arrangements in the forms of a cross, a Star of David, and a heart were placed alongside a wreath from the president of the French republic. Josephine Baker, an African American expatriate, was buried as a French hero.

### Bibliography

Baker, Jean-Claude, and Chris Chase. *Josephine: The Hungry Heart.* New York: Random House, 1993.

Baker, Josephine, and Jo Bouillon. *Josephine.* Translated by Mariana Fitzpatrick. New York: Harper and Row, 1976.

Rose, Phyllis. *Jazz Cleopatra: Josephine Baker in Her Time.* New York: Doubleday, 1989.

**Anne Collinson**

## BAKER, S. Josephine (b. 15 November 1873; d. 22 February 1945), physician, public health and child welfare advocate.

Sara Josephine Baker laid the foundations of public health and child welfare in New York City in the early twentieth century. Under her visionary leadership, the New York City Health Department developed a Division of Child Hygiene (later a bureau) that worked to reduce infant mortality rates and emphasize preventative medicine. These two avenues of medical care were the focus of Baker's professional life as she sought to improve the lives of women and children.

Born in 1873 to Quaker parents in Poughkeepsie, New York, Baker vowed to make it up to her father for having been born a girl and so grew up as a tomboy. Her father, Orlando Daniel Mosher Baker, was a renowned lawyer, and her mother, Jenny Brown, was one of Vassar College's first graduates. Baker herself planned on attending Vassar until tragedy struck her family when her younger brother and father died suddenly when she was sixteen. This, combined with the poor health of her older sister, changed her financial prospects dramatically. She elected to attend the Women's Medical College of the New York Infirmary for Women and Children, founded and operated by Drs. Elizabeth and Emily Blackwell, respectively, and graduated second in her class in 1898.

Baker established in 1908 and subsequently oversaw the Division of Child Hygiene, within which she developed several pilot programs aimed at reducing infant mortality rates. Through education programs that targeted mothers, home care visits from nurses, improved training of midwives, and aid for young girls ("little mothers") who were caring for their younger siblings, Baker sought to help mothers and children. She was dedicated to the training and licensing of midwives. While other welfare advocates condemned outright the phenomenon of "little mothers," Baker sought to improve their lot by providing training and education through the "Little Mothers' League." She chose to begin the programs on New York City's Lower East Side, which had high incidences of infant mortality; under Baker's direction these rates dropped significantly. Other local heath departments reproduced Baker's ideas and her programs were eventually adopted by the U.S. Children's Bureau in 1912. Baker promised to retire when there were offices of child hygiene in every U.S. state. After this goal was achieved, she left professional medicine at age fifty. During her career she helped found the Babies Welfare Association (1911), reorganized into the Children's Welfare Federation of New York in 1912; the American Child Hygiene Association; and the College Women's Equal Suffrage League. She served as the U.S. representative to the League of Nations Health Committee from 1922 to 1924 and toured the Soviet Union in 1934 to examine its centralized and comprehensive child welfare system. Her work as an activist, advocate, and consultant in the field of preventative medicine thus continued long after her retirement.

Baker surrounded herself with women for intellectual and emotional support. Baker and her longtime partner, novelist Ida Wylie, were members of a group of women known as Heterodoxy. The group met biweekly over lunch to engage in discussions with other freethinking women, many of whom self-identified as lesbian or bisexual.

Baker, who faced obstacles in her profession caused by sexism, styled herself after the independent and strong-willed character Jo March in Louisa May Alcott's novel *Little Women* (1868–1869). As a physician in tenements and flophouses she had to deal both with drunks and with the tough political men of Tammany Hall. Baker adopted a male style of dress, wearing tailored suits and neckties, possibly to allow her to pass more easily in a male-dominated profession.

After Baker's retirement, she and Wylie moved to New Jersey, where they shared a house with another physician, Louise Pearce. Neighbors referred to them as "the girls" and the three lived together until their deaths: Baker's in 1945 and Wylie's and Pearce's in 1959.

### Bibliography

Baker, Josephine S. *Fighting for Life.* New York: Macmillan, 1939.

Berson, Robin Kadison. *Marching to a Different Drummer: Unrecognized Heroes of American History.* Westport, Conn.: Greenwood Press, 1994.

Hansen, Bert. "Public Careers and Private Sexuality: Some Gay and Lesbian Lives in the History of Medicine and Public Health." *American Journal of Public Health* 92, no. 1 (January 2002): 36–44.

**Anne Collinson**

*See also* HOWE, MARIE JENNEY.

# BALDWIN, James (b. 2 August 1924; d. 28 November 1987), writer.

Baldwin was born in Harlem in New York City. The illegitimate son of a domestic worker, he never knew his own father and was brought up in poverty. When Baldwin was three, his mother married a factory worker. His stepfather was also an evangelical preacher who demanded rigorous religious behavior from his nine children. Shortly after he graduated from high school in 1942, Baldwin had to find work in order to help support his brothers and sisters. Taking a job in a defense plant in New Jersey, he was confronted with racism, discrimination, and segregation. These experiences were followed by his stepfather's death in a mental hospital in 1943, after which Baldwin determined to become a writer.

He moved to Greenwich Village and began a novel. However, although he was awarded the 1945 Eugene F. Saxton Fellowship, which gave him financial freedom, Baldwin was unable to complete this work. Increasingly stifled by the social restrictions of the United States, he moved to Paris in 1948, using funds from another fellowship to pay his passage.

Baldwin was one of the most important, and one of the least understood, writers of his generation. Beginning with one of his earliest essays, "The Preservation of Innocence," which appeared in the magazine *Zero* in 1949, he elaborated over the course of his career as a writer an unusually complex understanding of identity, one that puzzled many readers, even those who admired him. In this essay, which examined the homophobia of American society, Baldwin protested what he believed was the one-dimensional representation of homosexuals in American fiction and asserted, somewhat controversially, that it was "quite impossible to write a worthwhile novel about a Jew or a Gentile or a Homosexual, for people refuse, unhappily, to function in so neat and one-dimensional a fashion" (p. 22). For Baldwin, categories of identity such as race, class, and sexuality could not be understood apart from each other, but rather needed to be analyzed in relation to other crosscutting axes of subordination and difference. Thus, homosexuals were never just homosexuals. They also had a race, a class, and a gender, a combination of identities that writers of gay and lesbian fiction tended to overlook in their attempts to expose homosexual oppression. By contrast, Baldwin attempted to show how individuals disabled by one set of oppressions (homophobia and classism, for example) could be empowered by another (racism and sexism, for example). For this reason, his work challenged the organization of identity in the period following World War II, which depended on the binary oppositions white/black, male/female, and straight/gay.

Even more unsettling for many readers was Baldwin's understanding of sexuality. For Baldwin, sexuality constituted a mobile, permeable terrain that could not be easily contained by the fixed boundaries of a stable identity. Especially in his novels, identity, desire, and practice do not always line up neatly and frequently shift. For example, in what is arguably his best novel, *Another Country* (1962), the black male Rufus has an affair with the white male Eric as well as with the white female Leona; Eric has an affair with the frustrated straight housewife Cass while waiting for his gay French lover Yves to join him in New York; during his affair with Cass, he also has sex with the straight Italian American Vivaldo, who is the lover of Rufus's sister, Ida. In other words, the sexual complications multiply as the novel progresses, suggesting that sexuality has the potential to disrupt, if not overturn, identity.

Baldwin's understanding of sexuality seems to have been rooted in his own experience as a man who was both African American and gay, forms of identity that in the 1950s and 1960s were thought to be contradictory. Near

**James Baldwin.** This post–World War II expatriate writer explored the complexities of identity, race, and sexuality, but his increasing focus on the latter turned critical acclaim to hostility among some of his readers. [AP/Wide World Photos]

the end of his life, he confessed to the gay African American novelist Randall Kenan, who was writing a biography of him, that when he immigrated to Paris, "I no longer felt I knew who I really was, whether I was really black or white, really male or female, really talented or a fraud, really strong or merely stubborn" (Kenan, p. 56). Baldwin's lack of racial and gendered belonging was compounded by the controversy surrounding his homosexuality, which, for many blacks and whites, meant that he could not speak authoritatively about African American experience, despite the enormous pressure placed on him by the media to do so.

Beginning with the controversial novel *Giovanni's Room* (1955), which centers on David, a Euro-American struggling to come to terms with his homosexuality while living as an expatriate in Paris, Baldwin's emphasis on the fluidity of sexuality increasingly provoked a hostile reaction from critics, who accused him of squandering his talents. Although not especially scandalized by the novel's homosexual themes, they took Baldwin to task for abandoning the theme of race, which had been central to his first novel, *Go Tell It on the Mountain,* a thinly disguised autobiographical account of his experience growing up in Harlem, published in 1953. Such commentators completely overlooked Baldwin's trenchant analysis in *Giovanni's Room* of the "whiteness" of the category of the homosexual as it was constructed in the 1950s.

These criticisms reached a crescendo in 1962, with the publication of *Another Country,* which, more elaborately than any of Baldwin's previous novels, explored the multiplicity of identity. For many critics, the novel's focus on the fluidity of sexuality undercut its exploration of the racial and class antagonisms that defined American society, and they failed to see how, for Baldwin, such antagonisms were intimately related to social conflicts rooted in gender and sexuality. Reaction to *Another Country* in the Black Power movement was especially hostile. Some Black Panthers used the novel's sexual politics to undermine Baldwin's authority as one of the nation's most eloquent and persuasive advocates for racial justice—consolidated with the publication in 1963 of the best-selling *Fire Next Time,* Baldwin's extended essay on race relations. They began to call him "Martin Luther Queen," an epithet directed not only at Baldwin's homosexuality, but also at what they perceived to be his lack of political radicalism.

However, it is precisely because Baldwin insisted on exploring the complexity of identity that he is such an important writer. His refusal to be pigeonholed exclusively as an African American or a gay writer, however harmful to his reputation, enabled him to achieve unusual insight into the formation, expression, and operation of a variety of modes of social difference.

Although Baldwin remained prolific until his death, producing such important books as *Blues for Mister Charlie* (1964), *If Beale Street Could Talk* (1972), and *The Devil Finds Work* (1976), these works were dismissed by critics as evidence of his declining powers as a writer, and they have only recently begun to attract the critical attention they deserve. Although Baldwin spent much of his life in Europe, he also spent long periods in New York City and never relinquished his United States citizenship. He spent his latter years in Saint Paul-de-Vence on the French Riviera, where he died of stomach cancer.

### Bibliography

Baldwin, James. "The Preservation of Innocence." *Zero* 1 (1949): 11–23.

Campbell, James. *Talking at the Gates: A Life of James Baldwin.* New York: Penguin, 1992.

Corber, Robert J. *Homosexuality in Cold War America: Resistance and the Crisis of Masculinity.* Durham, N.C.: Duke University Press, 1997.

Kenan, Randall. "James Baldwin." In *Lives of Notable Gay Men and Lesbians.* Edited by Martin B. Duberman. New York: Chelsea House, 1994.

McBride, Dwight A., ed. *James Baldwin Now.* New York: New York University Press, 1999.

Robert J. Corber

See also LITERATURE; PULP FICTION: GAY; SÁNCHEZ, LUIS RAFAEL.

## BANNON, Ann (b. 15 September 1932), writer.

Ann Bannon is the pseudonym for the best-selling author of the Beebo Brinker series of five lesbian romance novels, published between 1957 and 1962. She was born and raised in Hinsdale, Illinois, the eldest of five siblings. The family experienced financial difficulties, and Bannon bore much of the responsibility for raising her four half-brothers. Growing up, she found comfort in writing fantasies. Bannon continued to live at home until 1954, when she graduated Phi Beta Kappa with a B.A. in French from the University of Illinois. That same year she married an engineer and changed her surname from Thayer, that of her stepfather, to her husband's. Her husband's work took them to Maryland, New Jersey, Long Island, New York, Philadelphia, California, and Washington, D.C.

Bannon's first trip to Greenwich Village, in search of lesbian culture, took place in 1955. She was guided by Vin Packer (Marijane Meaker), author of the phenomenally successful *Spring Fire* (1952). Both *Spring Fire* and Radclyffe Hall's *The Well of Loneliness* (originally published in 1928 and later as a pulp romance in 1951) had inspired Bannon to create her own romances, peopled with characters she invented in part from living persons, in part from iconic figures, and in part from characters she wished she knew. By 1956, soon after completing her first lesbian romance novel, *Odd Girl Out* (1957), Bannon and her husband were living in Sierra Madre, California. The novel became the second best-selling title for Fawcett Gold Medal in 1957. Its unexpected commercial success, and the success of other lesbian pulp romances, identified another sizable reading audience besides the male soft porn market: lesbians.

By 1959, the year Bannon's second and third novels— *I Am a Woman* and *Women in the Shadows*—were published, the couple's two daughters had been born. In 1960 she published *Journey to a Woman* and *The Marriage.* The latter explored heterosexual incest, not lesbian relationships. Bannon's fifth and final lesbian narrative—*Beebo Brinker* (1962)—provided the name for her well-known series. After 1962 Bannon produced no further lesbian romances, and her subsequent writing, consistent with her career as a linguistics professor, was academic.

Bannon began work on her M.A. in English at California State University, Sacramento (CSUS) between 1967 and 1969. In 1975 she received her Ph.D. in linguistics from Stanford University. One of her academic specialties was seventeenth-century English literature. She wrote her dissertation on the use of seductive language in Edmund Wilson's short story "The Princess with the Golden Hair." For nearly twenty-four years, until her retirement in 1997, she taught undergraduate and graduate courses in linguistics at CSUS. She chaired the Liberal Studies Program and was Associate Dean for Curriculum in the School of Arts and Sciences, and later served as Associate Dean for Budget and Curriculum in the College of Arts and Sciences.

Bannon and her husband divorced in 1981. In an interview she characterized the marriage as the last Victorian marriage of the twentieth century. Throughout the marriage, as she has stated in many interviews published in LGBT presses and journals from the time of her divorce to the present, her own imagination sustained her. She created characters in her novels that provided her with an intellectual and emotional connection to lesbians across the United States, especially butch personalities like Beebo. Beebo was inspired by her grandfather, the Statue of Liberty, and the ship *Queen Mary*—all of which represented protective but exciting and invincible power for her. Bannon stated in a recent lecture that even the femme actress Venus Bogardus, Beebo's love interest in *Beebo Brinker*, is a composite of various historical figures: Marilyn Monroe, Grace Kelly, and Ingrid Bergman. Combining ordinary figures—those in her daily life and those encountered during her frequent visits to Greenwich Village—and iconic figures like Monroe, Kelly, and Bergman, led to the compelling characters in Bannon's novels. They are dramatic, colorful, and yet realistic within the terms of post-World War II America. She prefaces the Cleis Press reprint of *Beebo Brinker* (2001) with these words: "They [the books] speak truly of that time and place as I knew it. . . . And if Beebo is really *there* for some of you—and Laura and Beth and the others—it's because I stayed close to what felt real and right."

Indeed, Beebo, Laura, Beth, and Jack Mann appear throughout most of the series, developing individually and in relationship to each other as the series progresses. These varied characters provided a familial presence for lesbian readers, many of whom were severely closeted in small towns. The figures were equally important to urban lesbians who, though they could gather in bars, nonetheless suffered from police brutality, social alienation, and

the consequences of national paranoia over homosexuality and communism that 1950s McCarthyism produced. As one of the most popular lesbian pulp authors, Bannon not only mitigated her own isolation and that of her readers, but also powerfully influenced lesbian culture in America. Her novels taught readers that they were not alone in desiring other women, that they could enjoy and celebrate their sexuality, and that they were not immoral, insane, or criminal human beings. Through her publisher, Bannon received numerous letters, her readers' thanks for providing positive images of lesbian lives.

Bannon's novels provide a valuable historical glimpse into the 1950s and 1960s and continue to delight present-day audiences with their tenderness, drama, and vitality. In 2000 the Board of Supervisors of San Francisco awarded her a Certificate of Honor, hailing Bannon as someone who "expanded a genre which voiced lesbian experiences at a time when explicit lesbian subject matter was silenced by government and communities." Perhaps the greatest tribute to the importance of her work has been its frequent republication. After the series' initial release by Fawcett (1957–1962), it appeared again through Arno Press/New York Times (1975), Naiad Press (1986), Quality Paperback Book Club (1995), and, most recently, Cleis Press (2001–2003).

Bannon is an articulate, energetic, and engaging lecturer, much in demand by audiences across the nation. She has appeared in two documentary films: *Before Stonewall: The Making of a Gay and Lesbian Community* and *Forbidden Love: The Unashamed Stories of Lesbian Lives* and was interviewed by Terry Gross on National Public Radio in 1999.

## Bibliography

Bannon, Ann. For publication history and selected citations to articles, interviews, and essays related to Bannon, see Bannon's web site: www.annbannon.com or Jaye Zimet's *Strange Sisters.*

*Before Stonewall: The Making of a Gay and Lesbian Community.* Directed by Greta Schiller, Robert Rosenberg, and John Scagliotti. Produced by the Center for the Study of Filmed History, 1984.

*Forbidden Love: The Unashamed Stories of Lesbian Lives.* Directed by Aerlyn Weissman and Lynne Fernie. Produced by National Film Board of Canada, 1992.

Hall, Radclyffe. *The Well of Loneliness.* New York: Covici Friede, 1928. Reprint, New York: Permabooks, 1951.

Packer, Vin. *Spring Fire.* New York: Fawcett Gold Medal, 1952.

Zimet, Jaye. *Strange Sisters: The Art of Lesbian Pulp Fiction 1949–1969.* New York: Viking Studio, 1999.

**Mary Elliott**

*See also* LITERATURE; PULP FICTION: GAY; PULP FICTION: LESBIAN.

# BARBER, Samuel (b. 10 March 1910; d. 23 January 1981) and Gian Carlo MENOTTI (b. 7 July 1911), composers.

Gian Carlo Menotti and Samuel Barber met in 1928 while students at Philadelphia's Curtis Institute. Menotti was fresh from Italy and Barber hailed from a musical Philadelphia family—his aunt, contralto Louise Homer, was a star at the Metropolitan Opera, and his uncle, Sidney Homer, was a composer. Barber and Menotti quickly formed an intense, sustained personal and professional bond.

Barber and Menotti differed in career trajectory and artistic range. An excellent baritone and competent conductor, Barber was a major figure by the 1930s, adept at securing financial and artistic patronage from figures such as conductor Arturo Toscanini. Barber's *Symphony No. 1* (1936), *Essay for Orchestra* (1937), and other works quickly gained an audience. He composed and won recognition in nearly every genre—orchestral, chamber, ballet, choral, song, and opera—although selectively in most. His *Adagio for Strings* (1938) became "America's national funeral music," as his friend Charles Turner calls it (Heyman, p. 173): heard when great figures such as presidents Franklin D. Roosevelt and John F. Kennedy died, and after disasters such as the September 11, 2001, attacks on the World Trade Center and the Pentagon. It has also been used in Hollywood film scores and—in countless arrangements, by Barber and others—recorded and performed perhaps more than any other "serious" American music. Barber also collaborated with celebrated women, such as choreographer Martha Graham, cellist Zara Nelsova, and singers Eleanor Steber and Leontyne Price.

Although Menotti composed in many genres, his fame rested on his small-scale, highly dramatic operas, such as *The Medium* (1946), *The Telephone* (1947), and *The Consul* (1950). Some of his works were staged on Broadway, and in 1954, he won a Pulitzer Prize for *The Consul*. He also created the Christmas piece *Amahl and the Night Visitors* (1951), which premiered on nationwide television. Often dismissed by critics as warmed-over Puccini but easily performed by smaller companies, these operas were the first written by an American composer to find an enduring audience after George Gershwin's earlier attempt, *Porgy and Bess*.

Menotti and Barber were among the many composers who contributed to a vibrant queer presence in mid-century American arts. Whereas Aaron Copland and Virgil Thomson drew on French modernism, Barber and Menotti sought inspiration from Central Europe and Italy, where they often lived, studied, composed, and performed. Their lyrical styles were often criticized after World War II as romantic and backward compared to serial and other modernist idioms. But Barber drew on modernism—serialism, jazz, and the blues—adeptly, though briefly, and often wrote gnarly, percussive music. Menotti and Barber additionally borrowed from a wide range of source materials; Barber's included ancient Irish texts, philosopher Søren Kierkegaard, and writer James Agee. Though Copland focused on American texts and musical idioms and was more commonly identified as an "American composer," Barber also composed major Americana, such as *Knoxville: Summer of 1915* (1948). Among musical historians, Menotti and Barber are now viewed not as reactionaries but as cosmopolitan modernists who, like other gay artists of the period, gave modernism accessible, popular expression.

Some observers during Barber and Menotti's heyday noted that most gay composers embraced tonal lyricism and rejected serial modernism, and some complained bitterly that "sissified" composers dominated American music—a charge to which gay magazines gleefully pled guilty. Though subject to post–World War II queer-bashing that centered on an imagined arts "homintern" (an international queer conspiracy akin to the communist version), composers were less vulnerable than playwrights (such as Tennessee Williams), whose texts, staged characters, and more easily identifiable politics offered readier targets. Cultural associations between musicality and homosexuality also protected composers, even as they invited snickering; that many composers were gay was unsurprising. Above all, composers, gay or otherwise, asserted an American presence within classical music just as imperial ambitions for American culture made them valuable as emblems of American superiority over the Soviet Union—or, alternatively, they served as symbols of the hope that cultural exchange might thaw the Cold War. And with gay composers so dominant, who else could represent American vitality? Hence, Barber journeyed to Moscow and chatted with Soviet Premier Nikita Khrushchev in 1962. By then he and Copland were regarded as America's leading composers.

Barber, whose music gained high-profile performances, received numerous commissions and prizes, including Pulitzers for his opera *Vanessa* (1958), with a libretto by Menotti, and for his *Piano Concerto* (1962). He was also featured at America's most glamorous and imperial endeavor in high culture, New York City's newly cre-

**Samuel Barber.** One of the leading American composers of classical music in the twentieth century, including his 1938 *Adagio for Strings,* though some modernists criticized his compositions for their lyricism and accessibility.

ated Lincoln Center complex. There his career faltered, however, as many critics harshly judged *Antony and Cleopatra* (1966), which premiered at the new Metropolitan Opera House in September 1966.

The opera's celebrated failure, attributed variously to Barber, a disastrous production by Franco Zeffirelli (also the librettist), and technical troubles in the brand-new opera house, darkened Barber's life. So too did growing difficulties with Menotti (the far more exuberant partner), aging, alcohol, changing artistic tastes, a waning cultural Cold War, and gay and lesbian politics, which viewed figures such as Barber as decidedly "closeted." Released in 1966, the *Paris Diary* of younger composer Ned Rorem noted Barber's observations on gay sex in Italy along with other gossip, infuriating, Rorem later claimed, Barber and others. But Barber had no illusions that he was known as anything but gay—instead, he was probably furious at the manner of Rorem's revelations. He and Menotti had long moved in semipublic circles of gay artists and mentored many younger composers. Their relationship and shared home in Mt. Kisco, New York, had been widely publicized, albeit in the coded terms of

an "open secret." They themselves satirized secrecy in their biting chamber opera *A Hand of Bridge* (1959): one character imagines "every day another version of every known perversion" and knowingly refers to the secrets hidden in books by Havelock Ellis. Moreover, the "closet," a metaphor invented in the late 1960s, poorly fits figures like Barber and Menotti, for whom homosexuality was so entwined personally, culturally, and professionally with musicality as to be fundamental to their identities, if rarely to their specific creative intentions.

Despite all the gossip and negative speculation after *Antony*'s failure, Barber continued to create new works, including the dark, inventive piece *The Lovers* (1971), set to the poems of Pablo Neruda. But, always a procrastinator, he produced less and seemed more out of fashion. He did not live long enough to witness the 1980s surge of recordings and performances of music by lyrical modernists, the popularity of works such as his *Violin Concerto* (1939), and revivals of his operas. After Barber's death, Menotti continued to compose and direct. He became the driving force behind the Spoleto Festival, which he founded in 1958, lived his later years in Scotland, and declared his wish to be buried beside Barber.

## Bibliography

Ardoin, John. *The Stages of Menotti.* Garden City, N.Y.: Doubleday, 1985.

Gruen, John. *Menotti: A Biography.* New York: Macmillan, 1978.

Heyman, Barbara B. *Samuel Barber: The Composer and His Music.* New York: Oxford University Press, 1992.

Hubbs, Nadine. *Composing Oneself: Gay Modernists, American Music, and National Identity.* Berkeley: University of California Press, 2004.

**Michael Sherry**

**See also** MUSIC: CLASSICAL; MUSIC: OPERA; ROREM, NED.

# BARNES, Djuna (b. 12 June 1892; d. 19 June 1982), writer.

Djuna Chappell Barnes was born in Cornwall-on-Hudson, New York, the second of five children of Wald Barnes and Elizabeth Chappell. Life in the unorthodox Barnes household, headed by Zadel Turner Barnes, Djuna's paternal grandmother, featured agricultural tasks, spiritualist activities, and a kind of home schooling that left the children well-read in the classics. Barnes was raised in an atmosphere in which free love was openly espoused by her father and grandmother. A particularly painful expression of this attitude occurred after Zadel Barnes invited Fanny Faulkner Clark into the Barnes household when Djuna was five years of age: the newcomer soon became her father's mistress. In the years that followed, both Djuna's mother and Clark bore Barnes seven more children.

Before Elizabeth Chappell and Wald Barnes were divorced in 1912 and her father married his mistress, eighteen-year-old Djuna was married off to fifty-two-year-old Percy Faulkner, Clark's brother, in an unofficial family ceremony. After two months, Djuna returned to the Long Island farm where her family now lived. Two years later she and her brothers departed with their mother after her parents' marriage dissolved. Biographer Phillip Herring reports that in later life Barnes accused her father of "conspiring to take her virginity by bringing in a neighbor—also three times her age" (p. 63). Several critics, citing explicitly sexual drawings in Djuna's correspondence with Zadel, have also suggested that Barnes was sexually molested by her grandmother. In any case, it is clear that Barnes emerged from her unconventional childhood and adolescence with complicated and conflicted feelings.

After a short stay with her mother and a brief period of enrollment at the Pratt Institute in Brooklyn, Barnes moved to Greenwich Village, where she continued her work as a journalist for the *Brooklyn Daily Eagle* and attended the Art Students League of New York. In 1915 she published her first poetry chapbook. Entitled *The Book of Repulsive Women: Eight Rhythms and Five Drawings*, the collection, inspired by the nineteenth-century decadent movement, features eight poems depicting lesbian life and five illustrations in the style of Aubrey Beardsley. During this period, Barnes also contributed plays to the Provincetown Players and expanded her journalistic career. When *McCall's* magazine sent her to Paris in 1921 to serve as an overseas correspondent, she began an extended period as an expatriate.

Although Barnes was romantically involved with both men and women throughout much of her life, her eight-year relationship with American silverpoint artist Thelma Wood, whom she met in Paris during her first year abroad, was arguably the most significant of the writer's life. Memorialized in the 1937 novel *Nightwood*, the period of Barnes's and Wood's tortured involvement also witnessed the publication of several key works by Barnes, including *A Book*, her first collection of short stories, printed in 1923. The year 1928 marked the appearance of Barnes's first novel, *Ryder*, a Rabelaisian family saga—with a sharp feminist critique—that briefly

became a bestseller. In contrast, Barnes's second novel of 1928, a spoof on the circle surrounding U.S. lesbian expatriate Natalie Clifford Barney, was only privately printed and distributed, although it was warmly received by its immediate audience, the participants in Barney's salon and their friends.

After her separation from Wood in 1929, Barnes returned to New York the following year; she nonetheless traveled frequently to Europe and elsewhere during the ensuing decade. While some suggest she may have begun work on *Nightwood* as early as 1927, critics agree that she only turned to the novel in earnest in the early 1930s, drawing on the friendship and support of such benefactors as Peggy Guggenheim. After several publishers rejected the novel, writer and friend Emily Coleman gave the sprawling manuscript to T. S. Eliot, who agreed to publish a version of the work so heavily edited (by many people, including Barnes herself) that approximately 670 pages were reduced to 212. The actual plot of the novel may be further condensed, Carolyn Allen suggests, since "the outlines of the original story take only ten pages of narration" (p. 25). Yet even in its attenuated version, *Nightwood* is a modernist classic, viewed by Barnes as her most significant artistic achievement.

In 1940 Barnes moved to a studio apartment in Greenwich Village where she lived for the next forty-two years. During this period her artistic productivity diminished, although in 1958 she published *The Antiphon*, an autobiographically based verse play. A bestiary entitled *Creatures in an Alphabet* was brought out the year she died.

## Bibliography

Allen, Carolyn. *Following Djuna: Women Lovers and the Erotics of Loss: Theories of Representation and Difference.* Bloomington: Indiana University Press, 1996.

Broe, Mary Lynn, ed. *Silence and Power: A Reevaluation of Djuna Barnes.* Carbondale: Southern Illinois University Press, 1991.

Herring, Phillip F. *Djuna: The Life and Work of Djuna Barnes.* New York: Viking, 1995.

**Anne Charles**

***See also*** BARNEY, NATALIE; FORD, CHARLES HENRI; LITERATURE.

## BARNEY, Natalie (b. 31 October 1876; d. 2 February 1972), literary salon hostess, writer.

Natalie Clifford Barney, the hostess of a salon on the Left Bank in Paris, was a literary landmark and one of the most celebrated and candid lesbians of her time. Born into wealth and privilege in 1876 in Dayton, Ohio, she received her earliest instruction from a French governess and then attended boarding school at Les Ruches in Fountainebleau, where she was educated in the arts of a French finishing school. At Les Ruches, Barney mastered the French language, her preferred language of artistic expression, and the forms and conventions of French poetry that heavily influenced her own. Barney used her affluence to stage elaborate seductions, establish a salon, as well as an *Academie des femmes*, and to cultivate her well-feted charm and talent.

The eldest daughter of the bohemian painter Alice Pike and socialite Albert Clifford Barney, Natalie made her debut in society in Washington, D.C., at the age of eighteen. Her introduction into Washington society provided her with numerous courtiers and she even went so far as to become engaged to several of them. Barney had discovered at an early age that she was only attracted to her own sex, though until the death of her father she had to be discreet about her liaisons with women, and so found her engagements to be quite useful in deflecting her father's suspicions about her sexual orientation. This tactic succeeded until 1900, when Barney published her first volume of poetry, *Quelques portraits-sonnets de femmes*, inspired by her love affairs. This book reportedly enraged her father to the point that he purchased all available copies and even the typesetting plates. Barney's renown as a seducer of women crystalized soon after her arrival in Paris, when one of the most infamous and celebrated of the courtesans of the belle époque, Liane de Pougy, published in 1901, with Barney's help, the story of her seduction by Barney in a thinly veiled novel, *Idylle Saphique*. It was a best-seller, and the first of a number of novels about Barney's many love affairs with women, including Colette and the tragic poet Renée Vivien, with whom she traveled in 1904 to the island of Lesbos intending to establish a "Sapphic school of poetry," though it never materialized. Her longest and arguably most significant relationship was with the painter Romaine Brooks.

Moving to Paris at the turn of the century, Barney immersed herself in the cultural vitality that is Paris, cultivating enduring friendships with numerous male literati such as Remy Gourmont, Ezra Pound, and Andre Gide, to whom she turned for literary advice, though that advice was seldom taken. Perhaps more significant to Barney's life and work than any of these male literati, at least symbolically, was the figure of the fin-de-siècle dandies, most specifically that of Oscar Wilde (whom she met when she was six years old). Many of Barney's biographers note that Barney modeled her life after that of Wilde. In an ironic twist, she was even engaged for a short while to Wilde's lover, Lord Alfred Douglas, and also had an affair and close friendship with Wilde's niece, Dolly Wilde. Believing that art and life were inextricably bound, Barney set about constructing a life that would itself be a work of art, and to become a dandy of sorts. In one such manifestation, Barney adopted the alternative identity or persona, replete with costume, of "the page," both in her poetry and in her romances, and later that of "the Amazon."

Barney's home, which she rented at 20 rue Jacob on the Left Bank, was the site of the famous salon established by her in 1909. For over sixty years she brought together French, English, and American writers, intellectuals, and artists. Through the salon, Barney introduced women writers and their work to each other and to the larger public. During these years, Barney continued to write novels, poems, plays, memoirs, essays, and epigrams. Her literary salon is often acknowledged as the most important of the twentieth century and attracted some of the greatest figures of art and literature, including Isadora Duncan, Gertrude Stein, and Truman Capote.

Biographers of Barney have generally placed greater emphasis on her romantic adventures than on her writing. Only since the middle 1990s have scholars situated Barney's work within the modernist movement, of which she was very much a part. By the end of her life, she had become one of the most famous salon hostesses in Paris as well as a noted and prolific writer.

## Bibliography

Benstock, Shari. *Women of the Left Bank: Paris, 1900–1940.* Austin: University of Texas Press, 1986.

Elliott, Bridget, and Jo-Ann Wallace. *Women Artists and Writers: Modernist (Im)positionings.* London: Routledge, 1994.

Jay, Karla. *The Amazon and the Page: Natalie Clifford Barney and Renee Vivien.* Bloomington: Indiana University Press, 1988.

Rodriguez, Suzanne. *Wild Heart, a Life: Natalie Clifford Barney's Journey from Victorian America to Belle Epoque Paris.* New York: Ecco, 2002.

**Nichole Suzanne Prescott**

*See also* BARNES, DJUNA; BROOKS, ROMAINE; CAPOTE, TRUMAN; LITERATURE; MUSIC: CLASSICAL; STEIN, GERTRUDE, AND ALICE B. TOKLAS.

**BARR, JAMES.** see FUGATE, JAMES BARR.

# BARS, CLUBS, AND RESTAURANTS

No matter how many battles between local police forces and LGBT bar, club, and restaurant patrons were waged in the years before 1969, the Stonewall rebellion refuses to relinquish its paramount place in the queer American historical imagination. According to legend, in the early hours of 28 June 1969 patrons of the Stonewall Inn spontaneously responded to the latest police raid with violence. Bar patrons and the New York City police waged war for several days and nights and, as news of the riot spread across the country, LGBT people everywhere shook off years of complacency and decided that they, too, would fight back. Though scholars have debunked the myth that LGBT people were complacent before 1969 and that the Stonewall rebellion was singularly responsible for launching the gay liberation movement, its unwavering popularity highlights how bars and other commercial spaces have been essential in the history of LGBT communities and cultures.

The story of the Stonewall rebellion also reveals some of the less positive aspects of LGBT history. Some versions credit the initial call to arms to a lesbian, others to a young transgender Latina. Whether or not either account is true, gender, sex, class, race, and ethnicity have long divided queer communities. LGBT people have come together and remained apart in bars, clubs, and restaurants, producing and reproducing everyday practices of sexism, racism, and class oppression that characterize American society as a whole.

## From the 1890s to the 1930s

Beginning in the late nineteenth century, the steady growth of commercialized pleasure and leisure culture in the United States expanded the range of social, gender, and sexual possibilities in urban America and created new opportunities for gender and sexual outsiders. Privately owned commercial spaces facilitated LGBT identity and community formation in cities and towns throughout the United States. Taverns, saloons, dance halls, and other nightspots whose owners were either indifferent toward or tolerant of "fairies," mannish women, and their partners served as centers of queer social life, which often overlapped substantially with straight culture and vice culture. LGBT patrons spilled out into local restaurants, cafeterias, and coffeehouses, creating small, tenuously held enclaves that would later come to be known as gay ghettos and later still as gay villages. Secured by local, usually working-class patrons, these enclaves attracted larger numbers of middle-class visitors and "tourists" at night and on weekends.

Finding such places was no easy task, but in the 1920s and 1930s it was not as difficult as one might think. New York City's Times Square and Greenwich Village, Chicago's South Side, and San Francisco's North Beach neighborhoods, for example, were home to visible LGBT residents whose outrageous styles and physical displays of affection added color to scandal sheet reports on the urban demimonde. Most people learned about "gay society" by word of mouth, but popular restaurant and nightlife guidebooks listed establishments known for their queer clientele, often drawing special attention to popular show clubs where drag queens regularly performed. One of New York City's best-known establishments was the Black Rabbit, while San Francisco's included Finocchio's and Mona's. According to George Chauncey's *Gay New York* (1994), Prohibition (1920–1933) aided the proliferation of LGBT drinking establishments. With much of urban nightlife forced underground, it became more difficult for city officials to regulate commercial leisure culture. Systems of police payoffs and the control of many illegal speakeasies by crime syndicates provided a protective shield around LGBT and straight bars alike. Because LGBT people were denied the constitutional right to congregate in public places, those found in LGBT hangouts could be charged with a variety of offenses. Owners and managers of many LGBT establishments were willing to pay police protection money to keep local law enforcement officers at bay. In predominantly African American neighborhoods such as New York City's Harlem, speakeasies were permitted to flourish with little police or political interference. Though largely a heterosexual scene, Harlem's speakeasies featured African American and European American LGBT subcultures as well. Harlem's clubs were among the few places where leading blues performers like Gladys Bentley could sing openly about being a "bulldagger."

Few cities were able to sustain a public queer life of comparable size and complexity (New York and San Francisco featured dozens of popular LGBT establishments), but by the 1920s most had bars, cafeterias, and restaurants that served as meeting and cruising places for local and out-of-town gay men, with lesbians often sharing the space with them. For example, from 1925, Washington, D.C.'s Allies Inn was well-known as a gay-friendly restaurant, and in Seattle, the Casino Pool Room was a popular gay gathering place in the 1930s. Neither started out as gay, but both proved to be tolerant of homosexual clientele over time. In most larger cities and many smaller ones, LGBT bars, clubs, and restaurants were differentiated by class, race, and gender, with some establishments attracting predominantly or exclusively white middle-class men, while others attracted predominantly or exclusively African American, female, or working-class clientele, and still others featured multicultural, mixed-sex, and cross-class patronage. Particularly in regions of the country marked by legal and extralegal racial segregation, access to LGBT commercial establishments was restricted.

After Prohibition ended and the power to regulate liquor was restored to state authorities, keeping the culture of alcohol consumption clean was a priority for local officials and applications for liquor licenses for establishments known to cater to LGBT people were frequently refused. The end of Prohibition also coincided with the start of the Great Depression, and as is often the case in times of economic strain, those who lived outside of the mainstream were cast as a public menace, putting such establishments under greater scrutiny. Consequently, police payoffs did not end with Prohibition but continued to operate as one of the few means available to keep and protect LGBT patrons. In some places, however, LGBT commercial establishments proliferated after the end of Prohibition. While Chauncey's work on New York City suggests that LGBT bars went into a period of decline in the 1930s, Nan Alamilla Boyd has shown in *Wide-Open Town* (2003) that in San Francisco, where liquor was regulated primarily by tax authorities and where organized crime was less powerful, the number of LGBT nightclubs and drinking establishments increased.

## The 1940s, 1950s, and 1960s

In 1925 Eva Kotchever opened "Eve's Hangout," a Greenwich Village speakeasy that was patronized by lesbians as well as heterosexuals, and after Prohibition Mona Hood attracted a substantial lesbian clientele to Mona's on San Francisco's Temple Hill. Not until the 1940s, however, did a distinct lesbian bar culture largely independent of gay men and heterosexuals take shape. As Elizabeth Lapovsky Kennedy and Madeline D. Davis have shown in *Boots of Leather, Slippers of Gold* (1993), this occurred not only in larger cities but also in smaller ones such as Buffalo. During World War II, an abundance of well-paying factory jobs, the absence of men, and a growing acceptance of women traveling out for a night of fun unescorted by men enabled lesbians to secure public places and a public presence, sometimes in conjunction with gay men and sometimes independently. Though lesbian bars have never existed in great number and gay male bars were much more numerous during and after World War II, dime-store pulp fiction novels, churned out by the hundreds of thousands, provided detailed descriptions of the bars and their patrons to isolated and curious women

across the country. By the early 1960s, there were multiple published gay guides that included dozens of lesbian establishments among the hundreds of LGBT bars, clubs, and restaurants listed for various locations in the United States.

Working-class butches made lesbian public space visible, and as Joan Nestle has eloquently explained in *A Restricted Country* (1987), working-class femmes carried the sexual charge that made the sparks fly. But heavy alcohol consumption, combined with the introduction of drugs in the 1950s and 1960s and the constant threat of the Saturday night butch brawl made these public spaces unpalatable for many women, and especially for middle-class lesbians. The Daughters of Bilitis, a lesbian organization founded in the 1950s, worked to create social alternatives to the bar scene, demonstrating in the process that public commercial spaces were central institutions for many American queers.

In the 1950s and 1960s nothing made LGBT bars, clubs, and restaurants more inhospitable than local police and vice squads. From coffeehouses in Philadelphia to nightclubs in Houston, LGBT hangouts became featured targets of local morality campaigns. This was the era of the mass arrest, when bars were regularly raided and patrons corralled into paddy wagons (vehicles named in the context of anti-Irish prejudice). Some were booked and charged, others simply held for a few hours and released. Women were sexually and physically assaulted by the police and by other inmates, as were men. Police blotters in local newspapers sometimes listed those caught in raids on LGBT establishments, and employers and families were sometimes informed. Some committed suicide as a result of the public shame and humiliation of being exposed as queer. Not surprisingly, fear of arrest was enough to keep many away from the bars, and local police forces used this to their advantage. Parking a cruiser outside a known "homosexual haunt" was often enough to turn most people away.

Crime syndicates continued to own many of the bars and clubs appropriated by LGBT people. Independent owners often held properties as investments only, and LGBT people were most able to make a spot their own when either the management was LGBT friendly or the establishment was on the verge of bankruptcy. Occasionally, individual bar owners became intimately involved in the day-to-day operation of their establishments, and these owners fought some of the first legal battles for LGBT rights. In 1951 the owner of San Francisco's famous Black Cat hired a civil rights lawyer who successfully argued before the California Supreme Court that no state law prohibited gay men and lesbians from being served alcohol in a public establishment. Seven years later the two Canadian owners of a Seattle bar won a landmark court case that barred police harassment of their clientele. In 1967 a New Jersey Supreme Court case financed by homophile groups extended protection to all lesbians and gays in that state's bars. These rulings did not, however, prevent the police from laying charges on bar, club, and restaurant patrons for sexual solicitation, sodomy, and other crimes.

Battles between bar owners and police in the post–World War II era gave birth to the Tavern Guild, a coalition of San Francisco LGBT bars formed in 1962. The Guild retained a lawyer and bail bondsman for anyone arrested in or near an LGBT bar, and it published a brochure on how to deal with being arrested or harassed by the police. Similar organizations subsequently formed in other American cities and continue to exist in the twenty-first century, though many LGBT bar, club, and restaurant owners have not been willing to engage in political activism or legal advocacy. In other contexts, LGBT people in the pre-Stonewall era organized to fight against discrimination, harassment, and violence in bars, clubs, and restaurants. According to Marc Stein's *City of Sisterly and Brotherly Love* (2000), mistreatment of LGBT people in Philadelphia led to a sit-in at Dewey's restaurant in 1965 and homophile confrontations with police after a raid on the lesbian bar Rusty's in 1968. Susan Stryker has documented a riot precipitated by anti-trans practices at Compton's cafeteria in San Francisco's Tenderloin in 1966.

Racial segregation continued to define the organization of queer social life in this period. European Americans often remember LGBT bars and clubs as racially mixed, but blacks and other nonwhites recall an active culture of exclusion. For example, race, class, and gender privilege enabled white gay men to dominate Washington, D.C.'s post–World War II sexual geography, a finding supported by similar studies of other U.S. cities. As Brett Beemyn argues in *Creating a Place for Ourselves* (1997), both blacks and whites regularly crossed gender and class lines, but racial borders were rarely traversed. For example, it was not unusual for white bars to maintain unwritten quotas for nonwhites, and many actively barred admission to nonwhite groups by demanding a variety of different identification cards. Certain bars, such as Washington's Cozy Corner, became known as places where white and African American men sought out one another as sexual partners, but more generally the two groups remained highly segregated. Similar studies of lesbians in Detroit and Buffalo show that African American

women overcame their exclusion from predominantly white lesbian bars by creating their own social venues in private homes. Admission was frequently charged, and while news of these gatherings spread primarily by word of mouth, they were not limited to closed groups of friends. Thus, argues Rochella Thorpe in her "A House Where Queers Go," (1986), "private" parties should be considered a vital part of public LGBT culture, giving rise to distinctive identities and communities.

## After "Liberation"

Battles won by gay liberationists and lesbian feminists, in combination with the more liberal sexual attitudes of the 1970s, paved the way for an explosion of LGBT culture and community and with it a dramatic expansion of the number and types of LGBT commercial establishments. After the 1960s, LGBT people were much more likely to be the owners and managers of LGBT bars, clubs, and restaurants, and LGBT neighborhoods were much more likely to sustain multiple bars, clubs, and restaurants, each catering to distinct clientele. In general, police repression appears to have declined after 1970, but LGBT bars, clubs, and restaurants remain vulnerable in various ways. In 1972, for example, two Philadelphia gay bars burned down under "mysterious circumstances" and in 1979 a gay bar in St. Louis, Missouri, was firebombed during the anti-LGBT "Save Our Children" campaign. While "respectable" establishments have been generally safe from official repression, bars and clubs that allow or encourage sex on the premises continue to be targeted.

Raced, classed, and gendered patterns of social interaction have remained embedded in old and new commercial spaces and activists have at times picketed LGBT commercial establishments for racist and sexist practices, but the last several decades have been marked by increased diversity in types of LGBT bars, clubs, and restaurants. Bars that have appealed to different populations of gay men in the post-Stonewall era range from piano bars, dance clubs, circuit party clubs, country western bars, and discotheques to neighborhood, cruise, hustler, leather, sadomasochism, drag, and bear bars. In the 1970s lesbian commercial establishments also diversified; the lesbian feminist movement contributed to the creation of feminist coffeehouses and restaurants; and lesbian patronage of some predominantly gay establishments (including leather bars) increased. At the same time, lesbian feminist criticisms of butch-femme culture, the increased availability of social, athletic, and political alternatives, and a variety of other factors contributed to what some perceived to be a decline in lesbian bars, many of which were forced to close in the 1980s and 1990s. In the last decade, one noticeable trend has been the creation of weekly, monthly, or occasional lesbian events in gay bars and other commercial spaces where gay girls, lipstick lesbians, dykes, femmes, drag kings, genderfuckers, and other parts of the lesbian community gather.

LGBT people of color have patronized white-dominated and multicultural establishments while also creating commercial cultures in which distinct LGBT communities of color congregate. African American LGBT bars and clubs have existed for nearly one hundred years, while their Asian American and Latina/Latino counterparts have existed for at least several decades (and it seems likely that historians will document earlier establishments as well). In the 1970s African American LGBT people contributed greatly to the LGBT disco scene; today many large U.S. cities feature multiple bars and clubs dominated by African American LGBT people. In the 1990s queer Latina/Latino clubs sprung up across the United States, from New York City's La Casita to San Francisco's Esta Noche. One of the best-known Asian American LGBT clubs is San Francisco's dance bar N'Touch. Transgendered people have played vital social, sexual, and entertainment roles in LGBT bars, clubs, and restaurants for more than one hundred years and they continue to be welcomed in some establishments, but they are also excluded from and ostracized within others. Mixed LGBT bars such as 'Bout Time in Austin, Texas, are considered hospitable to transgender people, but many others are not.

Some commentators have predicted the future decline of LGBT bars, clubs, and restaurants as more LGBT people become parents, as LGBT baby boomers age, as more LGBT people move to the suburbs, and as LGBT people win greater acceptance in mainstream society. While some LGBT commercial establishments, including LGBT bookstores and lesbian bars, have suffered in recent years, others show no signs of decreasing in social, economic, and cultural importance.

**Bibliography**

Beemyn, Brett, ed. *Creating a Place for Ourselves: Lesbian, Gay, and Bisexual Community Histories.* New York: Routledge, 1997.

Boyd, Nan Alamilla. *Wide-Open Town: A History of Queer San Francisco to 1965.* Berkeley: University of California Press, 2003.

Chauncey, George. *Gay New York: Gender, Urban Culture, and the Makings of the Gay Male World, 1890–1940.* New York: Basic Books, 1994.

D'Emilio, John. *Sexual Politics, Sexual Communities: The Making of a Homosexual Minority in the United States, 1940–1970.* 2d ed. Chicago: University of Chicago Press, 1998.

Garber, Eric. "A Spectacle in Color: The Lesbian and Gay Subculture of Jazz Age Harlem." In *Hidden from History: Reclaiming the Gay and Lesbian Past.* Edited by Martin Bauml Duberman, Martha Vicinus, and George Chauncey Jr. New York,: NAL, 1989.

Kennedy, Elizabeth Lapovsky, and Madeline D. Davis. *Boots of Leather, Slippers of Gold: The History of a Lesbian Community.* New York: Routledge, 1993.

Nestle, Joan. *A Restricted Country.* Ithaca, N.Y.: Firebrand Books, 1987.

Stein, Marc. *City of Sisterly and Brotherly Loves: Lesbian and Gay Philadelphia, 1945–1972.* Chicago: University of Chicago Press, 2000.

Thorpe, Rochella. "'A House Where Queers Go': African-American Lesbian Nightlife in Detroit, 1940–1975." In *Inventing Lesbian Cultures in America.* Edited by Ellen Lewin. Boston: Beacon Press, 1996.

**Elise Chenier**

*See also* ALCOHOL AND DRUGS; BUSINESSES; DRAG QUEENS AND KINGS; FEMMES AND BUTCHES; LIQUOR CONTROL LAW AND POLICY; RIGHTS OF ASSOCIATION AND ASSEMBLY; STONEWALL RIOTS.

# BATES, Katharine Lee (b. 12 August 1859; d. 28 March 1929), poet, author, and educator.

Katharine Lee Bates is perhaps best known as the author of the poem "America the Beautiful" (1895), which was later set to music. She was inspired to write the poem while enjoying the view from Pikes Peak in Colorado. Filled with female imagery, "America the Beautiful" symbolized for many the positive and idealistic aspects of America. A movement to adopt the song as the U.S. national anthem was defeated in 1931 when the U.S. Congress chose "The Star-Spangled Banner."

Born in Falmouth, Massachusetts, Katharine was the daughter of William Bates, a Congregationalist minister, and Cornelia Frances Lee Bates, a graduate of Mount Holyoke. Bates's parents valued education, and Katharine was the brightest of their four children. Bates received an excellent education at a time when higher education for women was uncommon. Graduating from Wellesley College in 1880, Bates later attended Oxford University in preparation for her master of arts degree.

Founded in 1875, Wellesley College was for women only. Henry Durant, Wellesley's founder, firmly believed in women's abilities, and he hired only female faculty for his women's college. In 1886 Bates was hired at Wellesley and later became head of the English Department. Besides writing poetry, Bates authored textbooks, travel books, and children's books. Among her many publications are

*The College Beautiful and Other Poems* (1887), *The English Religious Drama* (1893), *The Pilgrim Ship* (1926), and *America the Beautiful and Other Poems* (1911).

It was at Wellesley that Bates met Katharine Coman, a professor of history and political economy. Coman reorganized the department of economics while at Wellesley and was a published author in her own right. A social activist, Coman helped found settlement houses and assisted African Americans, immigrants, and farmers. Bates and Coman began their relationship in 1890 and lived together until Coman's death in 1915.

Bates and Coman's relationship typifies the type of female relationships embraced by upper-class and academic America during the nineteenth century. What were called romantic friendships or Boston marriages were considered quite normal and even necessary for women. Close, personal, romantic relationships between women were seen as a way to bolster their roles as wives and mothers. The notion of two women having sex in such a relationship was not acknowledged and generally dismissed by nineteenth-century society. (The term "lesbian" was not used until the late nineteenth century.) Other women in Boston marriages who were friends of Bates and Coman include Vida Scudder—another member of the Wellesley English Department—and Florence Converse, and Jeanette Marks and Mary Emma Woolley. Because so many Wellesley faculty, like Bates and Coman, were in Boston marriages, the relationships were referred to as "Wellesley marriages" at the college.

There is no doubt that Bates and Coman were dedicated to one another spiritually, psychologically, and emotionally. Bates's sonnets celebrated their love and life together, and many of Bates's letters attest to her intense love of Coman. In one childhood diary entry, Bates admitted to liking women better than men and liking women with full figures better than lean women.

Bates retired from teaching in 1925 and became a professor emeritus. She died in Wellesley, Massachusetts, in 1929. Her *Yellow Clover: A Book of Remembrance* (1922), a memorial book of forty-seven sonnets, was dedicated to Coman and privately published after Bates's death.

Bates and women like her have been reclaimed by lesbian feminists from the pages of history. As a consequence, she has come to be seen as a forebearer of modern LGBT identity.

### Bibliography

Katharine Lee Bates Papers. Wellesley College Archives, Margaret Clapp Library. Wellesley, Massachusetts.

Bates, Katharine Lee. *Yellow Clover: A Book of Remembrance.* New York: Dutton, 1922.

Burgess, Dorothy. *Dream and Deed: The Story of Katharine Lee Bates.* Norman: University of Oklahoma Press, 1952.

Faderman, Lillian. *Surpassing the Love of Men: Romantic Friendship and Love between Women from the Renaissance to the Present.* New York: Morrow, 2001.

History Project, comp. *Improper Bostonians: Lesbian and Gay History from the Puritans to Playland.* Boston: Beacon Press, 1998.

Schwarz, Judith. "Yellow Clover: Katharine Lee Bates and Katharine Coman." *Frontiers* 4, no. 1 (Spring 1979): 59–67.

**Michael W. Handis**

*See also* COLLEGES AND UNIVERSITIES; LITERATURE; ROMANTIC FRIENDSHIP AND BOSTON MARRIAGE; WOOLLEY, MARY, AND JEANETTE MARKS.

# BATHHOUSES

In a 2002 episode of the popular television program *Will and Grace*, the character Jack falls asleep and dreams that he has died and gone to heaven, only to encounter Cher, played by the performer herself. Shaking with anticipation, he asks her, "Are you God?" The pop diva's pithy reply? "It depends at what bathhouse you pray at." Cher's playful comment is an inside joke that conjures up the heyday of bathhouse culture during the 1970s, when popular gay icons like Bette Midler, Barry Manilow, and the Village People performed at gay bathhouses in New York and San Francisco. But as Cher's witty reference suggests, bathhouses continue to occupy an important place in the gay male imagination even into the twenty-first century.

Unlike other commercial establishments, such as bars, bookstores, gyms, and restaurants, that cater to a predominately gay male clientele, bathhouses remained contested sites within LGBT politics and urban politics more broadly. While some constituencies celebrated gay bathhouses as institutions for sexual freedom and liberation from monogamy, others saw them as breeding grounds for promiscuity and sexually transmitted diseases and as anathema to public health concerns and an LGBT political agenda centered on the domestic family unit. What is less well-known is that bathhouses have a rich and distinguished history that predates the sexual liberation movements of the 1960s, when bathhouses became distinct institutions in urban centers with large gay populations. (Although women who are sexually attracted to other women have no doubt discovered each other at bathhouses and other public settings, bathhouses that cater to a specifically lesbian population in North

America are a phenomenon that did not begin until relatively late in the twentieth century.)

## Historical Context

Historically, the terms "bathhouses" and "baths" cover a wide range of different types of facilities for the purposes of public bathing and personal hygiene. In the United States, the emergence of bathhouses was closely linked to the influx of immigrants to large American cities in the nineteenth and early twentieth centuries. For example, immigrants from Eastern Europe, Scandinavia, and the Middle East brought different public bathing traditions to the United States. Typically, these included some combination of dry heat rooms; saunas; "sweat lodges"; swimming pools; rooms for depilation, exfoliation, and massage; showers; and communal recreation halls.

At the same time that immigrants were establishing their own traditional baths, many social reformers concerned about the poverty, overcrowding, sanitation, and nutrition problems perceived as endemic to immigrant groups turned their attention to the lack of adequate bathing facilities for the poor. By the late nineteenth century, following the establishment of a public bath by the New York Association for the Improvement of the Condition of the Poor in 1852, free municipal baths, swimming pools, and showers for the residents of cities such as Boston, Chicago, Detroit, New York, Philadelphia, and San Francisco were considered politically and morally necessary for urban populations. Bathhouses, reformers hoped, would not only help to contain disease and improve public hygiene but also instill democratic and community values. By the 1890s, citizens in large and small cities around the United States could choose from a variety of both public and commercial establishments for the purposes of bathing: from municipal baths and public beaches to bathhouses run by ethnic and working-men's associations, to elite institutions with exclusive memberships.

## The Emergence of the Bathhouse Culture

For many, bathhouses were social institutions that provided spaces to relax, discuss current events, spend time with old friends, and meet new ones. For example, an Italian immigrant in 1920s Brooklyn, New York, who lived in a "cold-water flat" could have a hot shower and catch up on the latest gossip from his native village for five cents. Bathhouses were homosocial environments—that is, gender-segregated spaces—as was customary in traditional societies. A single bathhouse may have served both male and female customers, but such facilities were always kept apart and often included separate entrances.

For most of the twentieth century, bathhouses were among the few places that remained homosocial even as many other public and commercial facilities, such as beaches and dance halls, were becoming increasingly heterosocial.

For some, the gender-segregated space of the bathhouse created the social conditions for homosexual contact and, to some degree, homosexual community. Although same-sex sexual contact between women no doubt occurred within bathhouses, nineteenth- and early-twentieth-century gender roles for women required them to maintain a self-conscious modesty and self-regulating propriety about their bodies that would have made public sexual contact extremely difficult. By contrast, many men might have experienced the freedom with their bodies in the bathhouses as an extension of the male privilege that they already held in other gender-segregated spaces such as fraternal organizations, schools, military barracks, prisons, and ships at sea. The homosocial space of the bathhouses provided an opportunity for men who were sexually attracted to other men to find one another. This was true not only for men who were gay-identified but also for others interested in same-sex sex. In the 1910s and 1920s, same-sex sexual contact among men was common within bathhouse culture and enabled many men to pursue their pleasures removed from the compulsory heterosexual demands of the straight world. Baths were, by their very nature, intimate spaces that created numerous opportunities for male bonding, and they encouraged and even demanded public displays of nudity that held the potential to be erotically charged.

Bathhouse owners often ignored the homosexual activities that took place in their establishments, while others cultivated commercial relationships with their gay clientele. But as certain baths became known for allowing and even protecting homosexual activity, local police forces, mobilized by antivice groups, began to conduct raids. In 1916, for example, thirty-seven patrons and employees of New York's Ariston baths were arrested; twenty-five of them were found guilty of lewd behavior and sent to prison. Raids on bathhouses in the 1920s and 1930s, like raids on LGB bars in the 1950s and 1960s, occurred frequently during local elections, as homosexual sex was an easy target for city officials and police chiefs looking to make a display of saving the public from vice and crime.

Although many men seeking male sexual attention within bathhouse culture faced hostility, criminal conviction, and violence, some bathhouses, such as the Everard Baths in New York, formed part of an extended network of commercial establishments that, while not specifically

**Bathhouses.** *Men in Hot Baths,* by the early-nineteenth-century artist John Augustus Atkinson. [Historical Picture Archive/corbis]

gay, gained a national and international reputation for sustaining and to some degree even celebrating sexual and social interaction among men. As George Chauncey (1994) argues, "While the baths attracted men in the first instance because of the sexual possibilities they offered—and, indeed, fostered a distinctive sexual culture—they encouraged the cultivation of broader social ties as well" (p. 208).

## The Gay Bathhouse Comes of Age

During World War II, soldiers and sailors who were on temporary shore leave in port cities like Los Angeles, New York, and San Francisco frequented bathhouses and commercial places that had well-known reputations as being friendly to homosexuals. Municipal authorities and government officials often turned a blind eye toward such activities, since they did not appear to conflict with the military's antiprostitution campaigns or larger public health campaigns against sexually transmitted diseases such as syphilis and gonorrhea. As Allan Bérubé (1990) notes, many servicemen who discovered the joys provided by bathhouses and other gay-friendly commercial establishments during their visits to San Francisco and New York also chose to make those cities their home after the war.

The 1950s inaugurated a new era of crackdowns on homosexual activity in bathhouses, this time emboldened by a concurrent federal mandate to purge suspected homosexuals from workplaces. Newspapers regularly published the names of those caught in police raids, con-

tributing to a state of panic among those who frequented the baths for sexual contact and community. Although such a politically conservative environment could have led to a decline in bathhouse popularity, the large number of bathhouses that allowed homosexual activity in the 1950s and 1960s is corroborated by the memoirs of many gay men. For the African American writer Samuel Delany (1988), who describes gay bathhouse culture as anything but repressive, the resilience of the bathhouse as a community forum mirrored the resilience of homosexuals even in a time of crisis and adversity. And as many accounts suggest, bathhouses remained popular not only among men who identified as gay but also among men who identified as straight but engaged in same-sex sexual activities.

The sexual liberation movements of the late 1960s and 1970s, which ushered in a new era of open promiscuity, sexual experimentation, and gender role-playing, helped to give shape to the culture of the modern bathhouse. A chain called Club Baths, which turned the bathhouse idea into a kind of brand-name commercial franchise, appeared around the United States in the early 1970s at about the same time that heterosexual and bisexual swingers discovered the joys of adult-themed clubs like Plato's Retreat in New York. The new baths were clean, spacious, and modernized with the latest in audio and video entertainment. In cities like San Francisco and New York, the bathhouse achieved its most spectacular incarnation when it expanded beyond the traditional bath to include gyms, bars, restaurants, theaters, discotheques, and clothing boutiques and helped catalyze the careers of performers like Bette Midler. Many baths also served as community health clinics, providing information and checkups for sexually transmitted diseases.

Although police raids on baths declined significantly during the 1970s, the steady growth of moral and social conservatism meant that bathhouses—and the liberal sexual culture that they symbolized—remained vulnerable targets. In February 1981, police in Toronto, Canada, raided the city's six gay bathhouses and arrested more than three hundred men, many of whom were forced to line up wearing only their towels and handcuffs. The following day, three thousand demonstrators descended on the Ontario Parliament. Later, a city-sponsored investigation condemned the police actions. (Vocal protests also occurred after a police raid on a lesbian bathhouse in Toronto in 2000.)

## Baths in the Age of AIDS

A bitterly contested phase in the history of bathhouses occurred during the last two decades of the twentieth century with the arrival of AIDS in the early 1980s and its attendant sexual and moral panics. In contrast to the political action of Toronto's gay leaders, many gay leaders in the United States used their political clout to challenge the rights of other gay people to enjoy public sex in bathhouses, sex clubs, parks, and beaches. Public debate erupted over whether to close down gay bathhouses.

While many championed bathhouses as symbols of gay civil rights, others believed that closing them down could help stem the spread of HIV infection. Many prominent gay public figures and self-appointed community spokespersons, such as Larry Kramer and Randy Shilts, created a backlash against bathhouses by promoting the notion that there was a link between rising HIV transmission rates and the promiscuous behavior that occurred in commercial sex establishments. In November 1985, officials in New York forced the closure of the Mineshaft, a popular gay bar with a backroom; shortly thereafter, the city closed down the St. Mark's Baths, which had served the gay community for decades. Many of San Francisco's bathhouses had closed by the late 1980s, although in important respects they have been replaced—as in other cities—by sex clubs. These clubs retain many of the features of bathhouse culture but have none of the amenities, such as steam rooms and pools, that made bathhouses so attractive to generations of gay men.

In the mid-1990s, debates about public sex erupted yet again when New York City Mayor Rudolph Giuliani initiated a campaign to crack down on commercial sex establishments in Manhattan. Like the gay spokespersons in the mid-1980s who encouraged the closing of gay bathhouses, a number of LGB journalists vitalized Giuliani's campaign by arguing that commercial sex establishments were responsible for rising HIV infections and poor LGB public relations. In 1995, several grassroots organizations—namely Gay and Lesbian AIDS Prevention Activists and AIDS Prevention Action League—emerged to undermine the perception that public sex was equivalent to unsafe sex and to reinterpret commercial sex establishments as instrumental in providing HIV-AIDS education and prevention, particularly to men who have sex with men who do not identify as gay. Despite such efforts, Giuliani's campaign succeeded in displacing more than one hundred businesses, which moved from Manhattan to New York City's outer boroughs, bringing to light changing relationships between public health, urban space, city politics, and sexual communities.

## Bibliography

Bayer, Ronald. *Private Acts, Social Consequences: AIDS and the Politics of Public Health.* New York: Free Press, 1989.

Bérubé, Allan. "The History of Gay Bathhouses." *Coming Up!* (December 1984): 15–19.

———. *Coming Out under Fire: The History of Gay Men and Women in World War Two.* New York: Free Press, 1990.

Chauncey, George. *Gay New York: Gender, Urban Culture, and the Making of the Gay Male World, 1890–1940.* New York: Basic Books, 1994.

Dangerous Bedfellows, eds. *Policing Public Sex: Queer Politics and the Future of AIDS Activism.* Boston: South End Press, 1996.

Delaney, Samuel R.. *The Motion of Light in Water.* New York: Arbor House, 1988.

Ingram, Gordon Brent, Anne-Marie Bouthillette, and Yolanda Retter, eds. *Queers in Space: Communities, Public Places, Sites of Resistance.* Seattle: Bay Press, 1997.

Leap, William L., ed. *Public Sex/Gay Space.* New York: Columbia University Press, 1999.

**David Serlin**

**See also** AIDS AND PEOPLE WITH AIDS; BUSINESSES; HEALTH AND HEALTH CARE LAW AND POLICY; KRAMER, LARRY; PUBLIC SEX; SEX CLUBS; SEXUALLY TRANSMITTED DISEASES.

# BEAM, Joseph (b. 30 December 1954; d. 27 December 1988), writer, editor, activist.

Joseph Beam was a major African American gay activist and an influential writer and editor in the 1980s, publishing poetry, fiction, and personal essays that described the life experiences of black gay men in America. Beam was perhaps most famous for collecting several dozen black gay voices in a groundbreaking anthology, *In the Life* (1986). In addition to serving as a contact and editor for hundreds of black gay writers, Beam edited the community journal *Black/Out*, helped to resurrect the National Coalition of Black Gays, and served in the leadership of the Gay and Lesbian Task Force of the American Friends Service Committee and the National Coalition of Black Lesbians and Gays. Before his death from complications related to HIV in 1988, he was busily organizing a major creative anthology that he planned to call "Brother to Brother."

Beam was born in Philadelphia, the only child of Sun and Dorothy Beam. He attended a Catholic preparatory school and high school and matriculated at Franklin College, a small Baptist liberal arts college in Indiana. In most of his school settings, he was one of only a few black students. An apparently outgoing young man, he decided to pursue degrees in radio programming and journalism. One of his formative political experiences was in the Black Student Union at Franklin. After graduating in 1976 with a B.A. degree, he was admitted to a master's degree program in communications and worked odd jobs in the Midwest, living in Iowa for a time. Given the small amount of available information about Beam, it is difficult to say when he decided to "come out" as a gay man. But by 1980 he had returned to Philadelphia and was working in the city's main LGBT bookstore, Giovanni's Room. As an initiate to the gay literary community, he met many writers who appeared in the store and were published widely in both local and national LGBT publications. Dissatisfied with the absence of black gay men in most LGBT literature, Beam decided to put out a call for writings on black gay identity. He then published them in *In the Life*. According to one source, the book was ignored by African American critics but hailed as a milestone in the LGB community.

Beam believed in producing accessible publications for the community and in the crucial role of the anthology for building a social movement. Two of his most famous statements are, "I cannot go home as who I am" and "Black men loving Black men is the revolutionary act of the eighties." The great success of Beam's first anthology inspired him to plan for a second book. The distance that his work covered—from a provocative exploration of desire and multiple identity to the affirmation of friendship among black gay men—presciently plotted a powerful trajectory in black culture into the 1990s.

Beam died three days before his thirty-fourth birthday. His influential anthology *Brother to Brother* was completed and then published in 1991, thanks to the efforts of Essex Hemphill and Beam's mother.

### Bibliography

Beam, Joseph. Papers, New York Public Library. Collection description by Steven Fuller.

Beam, Joseph. *In the Life: A Black Gay Anthology.* Boston: Alyson, 1986

Brinkley, Sidney. "A Remembrance of Joseph Beam." Available from Blacklightonline.com.

Hemphill, Essex, ed. *Brother to Brother: New Writings by Gay Black Men.* Boston: Alyson, 1991.

**Kevin Mumford**

*See also* LITERATURE.

## BEAN, Babe (b. 9 December 1869; d. 18 September 1936), writer.

Babe Bean, born Elvira Virginia Mugarrieta and also known as Jack Bee Garland, lived life as a male, enjoying the freedom of travel and job opportunities accorded to men at that time in the United States.

Raised in the Russian Hill section of San Francisco, Bean came from an upper-class family. Her father, José Marcos Mugarrieta, had served as the Mexican consul in the city from 1857 to 1863, whereas her mother, Eliza Alice Denny Garland, was the daughter of former U.S. Congressman and Louisiana Supreme Court Justice Rice Garland. At some point in her childhood, the tomboyish Mugarrieta frightened her parents with her rebellious ways and was sent to a convent. To escape the nuns and see the world, at the age of fifteen she married her brother's best friend, possibly named Bean. Within a few months, the couple divorced, and Mugarrieta adopted a male name to match his male attire. He maintained contact with his family throughout his life.

Now known as Babe Bean, he passed for a man in hobo camps, in the mountains, and on city streets. Male attire protected Bean from sexual assault and allowed him entry into all-male settings. It also offered him the opportunity to engage in same-sex relationships, but there is no evidence that he ever did so.

During the summer of 1897 the police in Stockton, California, received reports of a young woman posing as a man. They spent two weeks trying to track down the wrongdoer and finally apprehended Bean in August. His clothing of a large hat, a boy's long suit jacket with padded shoulders, long vest, tie, and oversized shoes disguised the curves and build of a woman approximately 5 feet tall and weighing 104 pounds. A high-pitched voice would have further ruined the illusion, but Bean claimed to be mute as the result of an accident. (He would suddenly regain his voice in 1898 when he needed to call for help following a carriage accident.)

Bean willingly provided the details of his personal life, including his past, to the police and also newspaper reporters soon aware of the arrest of this unusual person. Not long thereafter the police released him. Bean remained in Stockton, but never hid, never stopped wearing male clothing, and never again experienced arrest.

Bean's ability to escape imprisonment might be attributable to his class background. Other transgender women, notably Jeanne Bonnet, suffered considerable police harassment and spent many days behind bars for donning the clothing of the opposite sex. Bean's ease with the authorities, literacy, and material possessions all spoke to respectability, although his dress did not. He stated to reporters that he wore male clothing because "it is my only protection. I do it because I am all alone" (Sullivan, p. 46). This declaration may have combined with other factors to transform Bean from a dangerous deviant into a sympathetic character.

Bean became a local celebrity, with contemporary newspaper accounts indicating that the people of Stockton regarded him affectionately. The local bachelor club named him an honorary member, all the more interesting because Bean presented himself as a gay man, with his effeminate manner and lack of interest in women, and the Stockton *Evening Mail* hired him as a reporter. Called "Jack" by his neighbors, he lived happily on a houseboat on McLeod's Lake until the Spanish-American War.

Determined to experience conflict from a man's point of view, Bean secured passage in 1899 on the troop transport *City of Para* to Manila, in the Philippines. He worked as a field hospital aide and a freelance newspaper correspondent before returning to the port of San Francisco.

Bean again took up residence in the Bay Area and briefly resumed wearing women's clothing. He discovered that the attire still limited his freedom to roam at night and donned a man's suit once more. In 1903 San Francisco passed an ordinance banning its citizens from wearing opposite-sex apparel, and Bean soon feared arrest. He adopted his mother's maiden name, becoming Jack Bee Garland, and then faded from view.

Garland died of generalized peritonitis following the perforation of a peptic ulcer. He had been suffering from abdominal pains for some time but, like many transgender people, feared that a physician would expose his secret. He collapsed on a sidewalk and later died in a hospital. Predictably, the medical examiner performing an autopsy, in undressing the body, discovered Garland's sex and publicized his findings. Garland's sister claimed the remains amid a swirl of publicity and buried her sister in an unmarked grave of the Mugarrieta family plot at Cypress Lawn Cemetery in Colma, California, just south of San Francisco.

### Bibliography

Rupp, Leila J. *A Desired Past: A Short History of Same-Sex Love in America.* Chicago: University of Chicago Press, 1999.

San Francisco Lesbian and Gay History Project. "'She Even Chewed Tobacco': A Pictorial Narrative of Passing Women in America." In *Hidden from History: Reclaiming the Gay and Lesbian Past.* Edited by Martin Bauml Duberman, Martha Vicinus, and George Chauncey, Jr. New York: NAL Books, 1989.

Sullivan, Louis. *From Female to Male: The Life of Jack Bee Garland.* Boston: Alyson, 1990.

**Caryn E. Neumann**

*See also* BONNET, JEANNE; FEMMES AND BUTCHES; TRANSSEXUALS, TRANSVESTITES, TRANSGENDER PEOPLE, AND CROSS-DRESSERS.

# BEARS

In the middle 1980s gay men began self-identifying as bears—a term that had long been in popular use in the gay community to describe with fondness burly, bearded, and often affectionate men. Several factors coincided to transform this informal moniker into a new means of self-identification; coming out as bears led to the creation of a bear community and subsequently to a broad dispersal of this ideal beyond its original predominantly gay, white American, male subculture.

Drawing upon a range of commercial images, and totemic and populist interpretations of ursine qualities, the first generation of bears self-identified as naturally masculine men, who either did not fit in or did not identify with or participate in gay male communities. This backlash to the predominant commercially propagated and peer-dictated ideal of the youthful, smooth-skinned, muscle-toned ephebe, or the "California surfer boy," began to effect a deeper transformation. Self-identifying bears found each other primarily through online bulletin

*Bear.* The cover of the magazine's fifteenth issue, from 1991; the line at the top promotes "Masculinity . . . without the trappings." [Courtesy of the Bear History Project Archives, a project of the Nashoba Research Institute, Inc.]

board services and *Bear* magazine, founded in San Francisco by Richard Bulger, whose editorial program promoted mutual sexual attraction among men who fetishize masculine gender markers: beards, body hair, the male "beer belly," and blue-collar male attire.

Meanwhile, urban enclaves of traumatized survivors of the AIDS pandemic emerged—or "came out of hibernation"—in the middle 1980s. In San Francisco, the commercial leather scene had all but collapsed and the "Castro clone" (the mustached and muscled gay type linked with San Francisco's preeminent gay neighborhood) had become identified with "AIDS victim," leaving a cultural vacuum that bears quickly filled. Clone-era survivors were now older, and thus more mature physically. Extra body weight was fetishized as healthy, and therefore a sign of beauty. At the same time, the collective experience of care giving for people with AIDS reawakened a vision of Walt Whitman's "dear love of comrades"—a desire for gentle, affectionate, nurturing, and democratic male relationships. Rejecting the old clone-era values, early bears embraced a self-concept based on a mix of

physical characteristics and a warm, nurturing temperament. Inclusivity and lack of attitude became the distinguishing ideals of the emergent community.

The rise of bear networks on the Internet and bear print publications, intersecting with aspects of gay community unique to San Francisco, led to the establishment of San Francisco as a bear mecca and a nearly instantaneous global propagation of self-identifying bears, bear clubs, bear publications, and bear events. The rise of this global/local nexus contributed to localized variations in bear self-definition, while reproducing the look of American bears. The global bear community is possibly the first queer community to be created primarily through the Internet.

In the first quarter century of bear identity, three successive generations appeared. First-generation bears emerged as a divergent group of men over thirty-five; some embraced bears as an attitude, while many self-identified with the naturally masculine look of bears. Generation-X bears emerged in the 1990s, making room for themselves as twenty-somethings, bringing a stronger sense of bear pride and focusing more on organizing. In larger communities with bear clubs, Gen-X bear clubs were often created to accommodate younger men. In the 2000s Third Generation Bears (3GBs) have begun to make their presence known. First-wave beardom—notably the gay white male bear look—eventually became the established culture. As the slogans of democratic inclusivity faded, diverse elements increasingly asserted their presence among the bear tribe. African American bears had been a small, nearly invisible presence from the start. Asian American bears have become more vocal. Both transbear and lesbian bear (ursulina) identities emerged in the 2000s. Bear Youth and 3GBs have created a public space for people under eighteen years of age who identify as bears.

Bear community and culture emerged in the 1980s. Communication was key. Early bear Internet bulletin boards gave way to a plethora of online mailing lists and websites. The grassroots community standards—the "Bear Mailing List" and the *Resources for Bears* website—were both founded by Bob Donahue. Along with Jeff Stoner, Donahue developed a Natural Bears Classification System (or "bear codes"), borrowed from the star and galaxy classification system. It has become the standard shorthand of self-descriptors. Lastly, a growing catalog of classification by totemic animals has added to both the confusion and expansion of "bears" and includes cubs, otters, wolves, and others, which correspond to body type and temperament. The bear look, as embodied in the bear icon Jack Radcliffe (a porn model for *Bear* magazine), has been complemented by the development of a bear commercial market niche, selling porn magazines, casual attire, jewelry, and other "bearaphernalia." Bears have rallied around a range of bear flags, though the brown-black-white stripes of the International Bear Brotherhood Flag, developed by Craig Byrnes, is nearly universally embraced.

Social activities arose in sexual spaces, such as bear-friendly bars (notably San Francisco's Lone Star Saloon), bear social clubs (sometimes organized as charitable non-profit corporations), and regional weekend gatherings often organized around beauty competitions. The seminal model has been the annual International Bear Rendezvous in San Francisco. The pinnacle of bear society consists of "A-list bears" and a bear circuit society, both paralleling the circuit boy culture of the 1990s and 2000s.

Bear culture developed a historical dimension in 1993 with the founding of the Bear History Project by Les Wright, and early results led to the publication of the *Bear Book* (the "bible" of bear culture, akin to Larry Townsend's seminal *Leatherman's Handbook* in the 1960s), *Bear Book II* (2000), and a four-installation series of *Bear Icons and Beyond* art exhibitions in the Northeast (in New York, Boston, Provincetown, and Washington, D.C.), which presented a diverse range of representational and nonrepresentational art work manifesting or expressing bear ideals, values, and sensibilities. In keeping with the diffusion of bear iconography into broader society, leading artists have begun to embrace bear-themed or bear-inspired art, either without prior knowledge of the Bear Icons project or, as in the case of the rise of queer theory, in spite of the knowledge of the groundbreaking grassroots efforts that led to the acceptability of such artistic production.

Bears, as both a distinct social identity and subculture within the LGBT community in the U.S., began as a series of localized responses during a period of historical transformation (the impact of AIDS on the gay male community, the shrinking of the leather and S/M communities, the end of the "Castro clone" fashion and lifestyle). The initial basic bear tenet of social "inclusivity," to be welcoming of any and all bears and their admirers, was quickly supplanted by sexual objectification and self-commodification through the rise of bear clubs and commercial venues. Through the rise of the Internet and cyberculture, bear identity and culture proliferated on the international stage as rapidly as it took shape in the U.S. Within a quarter century, bears had become quickly iden-

tifiable by the burly, bearded look, as well as a remarkably amicable social disposition. The comment most frequently heard when describing them remains, "Bears are so friendly!"

## Bibliography

Kampf, Ray. *The Bear Handbook: A Comprehensive Guide for Those Who Are Husky, Hairy, and Homosexual and Those Who Love 'Em*. New York: Harrington Park Press, 2000.

Suresha, Ron Jackson. *Bears on Bears: Interviews and Discussions*. Los Angeles: Alyson, 2002.

Wright, Les, ed. *The Bear Book: Readings in the History and Evolution of a Gay Male Subculture*. New York: Harrington Park Press, 1997.

Wright, Les, ed. *The Bear Book II: Further Readings in the History and Evolution of a Gay Male Subculture*. New York: Harrington Park Press, 2001.

**Les Wright**

# BEATS

Referring to the post–World War I era's "lost generation," (a phrase coined by Gertrude Stein) and its bohemian lifestyle and rejection of mainstream materialism, Jack Kerouac said to John Clellon Holmes: "Ah, this is nothing but a beat generation." It was 1948. By 1952 and the publication of Holmes's "This Is the Beat Generation" in the *New York Times Magazine*, "beat" became the term that defined a subculture, which in its disillusionment with mainstream morality, determined to defy it by establishing new aesthetic standards. Against a backdrop of events surrounding the Cold War, U.S. Senator Joseph McCarthy's investigations of what he called "un-American activities," the emergence of the hydrogen bomb, the Cuban revolution led by Fidel Castro, and what many sensed as a growing complacency within the American mainstream, Kerouac's term "beat" described "a swinging group of new American men" who possessed "wild self-believing individuality" (Charters, *Beat Down to Your Soul*, p. xv). For Kerouac and others associated with the Beat Generation, the term "beat" was not fixed; rather, they understood it as a vision, one that signaled a "kind of weariness with all the forms, all the conventions of the world" (Campbell, pp. 27, 29), and instead imagined what Lucien Carr referred to as a "New Vision." That new vision contained three basic tenets: "Naked self-expression is the seed of creativity; The artist's consciousness is expanded by derangement of the senses; and, Art eludes conventional morality." Eluding conventional morality—and by extension, rigid notions of heterosexuality—Beat art was understood as inseparable from Beat lives. In his

"Essentials of Spontaneous Prose" (1957), Kerouac, for example, describes his writing method as "in accordance (as from center to periphery) with laws of orgasm . . . 'beclouding of consciousness.' Come from within, out—to relaxed and said" (*Portable Beat Reader*, p. 58). His prose style, best known from *On the Road* (1957) and *The Subterraneans* (1958), celebrates an improvisational structure and feeling he associates with jazz and sexual climax. Orgasm was as crucial to Kerouac's daily life as it was to his writing: not only did he celebrate the controversial psychoanalyst Wilhelm Reich's claim that a fully realized orgasm could produce a healing energy—an "orgone"—but he also carefully maintained a "sex list" that recorded the frequency of his sexual encounters with women as well as with men such as Neal Cassady (Dean Moriarty in *On the Road)* and Gore Vidal (Arial Lavalina in *The Subterraneans)*. Sex, for Kerouac, was an aesthetic and an everyday practice.

In 1948, the year Kerouac uttered the word "beat," Ginsberg underwent Reichian therapy and admitted his sexual preference for men. Ginsberg, like Kerouac, had had an affair with Neal Cassady. While reading the manuscript of Kerouac's *Visions of Cody* (1972), Ginsberg referred to it as *Visions of Neal*. In 1945, while a student at Columbia University, Ginsberg was expelled from his dormitory for obscenity and for being caught naked in bed with Kerouac. In a 1958 poem to his father, "Don't Grow Old," Ginsberg describes the scene: "A look startled his face. 'You mean you like to take men's penises in your mouth?'" Later in his controversial poem "HOWL for Carl Solomon" (1956), sexual freedom as a requirement for Beat art is readily apparent: "who howled on their knees in the subway and were dragged off the / roof waving genitals and manuscripts, / who let themselves be fucked in the ass by saintly motorcyclists, and / screamed with joy" (ll. 90–93). Ginsberg wrote the poem while living in Berkeley with his lover, Peter Orlovsky. He had met Orlovsky in San Francisco in 1954 just as he was ending his relationships with Sheila Williams Boucher, a singer and a mother of a young son, and William S. Burroughs, author of *Junky* (1977) and *The Naked Lunch* (1959). While living with Boucher and her son, Ginsberg passed as a heterosexual even as he maintained a long-distance romantic correspondence with Burroughs and entertained occasional visits from Cassady. Burroughs and Ginsberg had begun their affair in New York in 1953, at a time when Ginsberg was maintaining a full social and writing schedule. Burroughs's attraction to Ginsberg grew, and he hoped that their sexual relationship would grow into something extraordinary. He wanted to possess Ginsberg and also be possessed by him. In *Junky,*

Burroughs writes, "What I look for in any relationship is contact on the nonverbal level of intuition and feeling, that is, telepathic contact" (Schumacher, p. 157). As much as the major Beat figures have been understood to have shared aesthetic and intellectual consciousness, they also shared bodies.

While the Beats portrayed themselves and lived as a "swinging group [of] new American men," the women who associated with them generally remained behind the scenes. As girlfriends, wives and mothers, they served as supporters of the Beat Generation's notable men (who included Lawrence Ferlinghetti, Bob Kaufman, Ted Joans, LeRoi Jones [Amiri Baraka], Philip Lamantia, Michael McClure, and Gary Snyder). Even as many Beat men endorsed a woman's right to an abortion as well as social equality for African Americans and for homosexuals, many critics viewed Beat men as insensitive to women and to feminist concerns. However, in spite of their minority position, Beat women such as Carolyn Cassady, Diane DiPrima, Hettie Jones, and Lenore Kandel contributed important writings to the Beat canon. For example, in response to Gary Snyder's declaration, "The female is fertile, and discipline / (*contra naturam*) only / confuses her," DiPrima produced the poem "The Practice of Magical Evocation," noting "the female is ductile" (*Portable Beat Reader*, p. 361). And, like Ginsberg's "HOWL," Kandel's *The Love Book* (1966) was challenged in a San Francisco court as obscene and pornographic.

## Bibliography

Charters, Ann, ed. *Beat Down to Your Soul.* New York: Penguin, 2001.

———. *The Portable Beat Reader.* New York: Penguin Books, 1992.

Campbell, James. *This Is The Beat Generation.* Berkeley; Los Angeles; London: University of California Press, 1999.

Knight, Brenda. *Women of the Beat Generation.* Berkeley, Calif.: Conari Press, 1996.

Schumacher, Michael. *Dharma Lion: A Biography of Allen Ginsberg.* New York: St. Martin's Press, 1992.

**Shelly Eversley**

*See also* BURROUGHS, WILLIAM S.; GINSBERG, ALLEN; LITERATURE; NEW YORK CITY; SAN FRANCISCO; VIDAL, GORE.

# BEN, Lisa (b. 1921), editor, writer, and singer.

"Lisa Ben" (an anagram for "lesbian") was the pseudonym of Edith Eyde, the founder, editor, and chief writer of *Vice Versa*, the first magazine in the United States to be devoted to a lesbian readership. Eyde grew up in rural northern California, attended college for two years, and was then forced by her family to go to business school in order to develop secretarial skills. In 1945, shortly after World War II ended, she moved to Los Angeles to escape an uncomfortable parental relationship. There, for the first time, she became acquainted with a lesbian community, through which she was introduced to softball (which she claimed to loathe) and lesbian bars.

Eyde took a job as a secretary at RKO Studio for a minor executive who told her he had little work to give her, but that she must never knit or read on the job and must always "look busy." It was then that she conceived of the idea for *Vice Versa,* and during her abundant free time at RKO she typed the magazine, using one of the studio's office typewriters. Eyde named the magazine *Vice Versa,* she recalled in a 1990s interview with Eric Marcus for his *Making History,* "because in those days our kind of life was considered a vice. It was the opposite of lives that were being lived—supposedly—and understood and approved by society" (p. 8).

Nine issues appeared, from June 1947 to February 1948. In those pre–mimeograph machine days, Eyde typed the entire issue of each magazine twice, making four or five copies every time. Thus her press run was limited always to ten to twelve copies. The format was typing-paper size, 8.5 by 11 inches. The magazine ceased publication when Eyde lost her RKO job and became a secretary for a firm where she had less leisure time and privacy.

Eyde distributed *Vice Versa* by mailing it to acquaintances from her office (with no return address) and handing it directly to patrons of the If Club, considered by many to be Los Angeles's first lesbian bar. She asked readers not to throw the magazine away, but rather to pass it on to other acquaintances when they finished reading. It is estimated that each issue thus had a readership of dozens and even hundreds. In the second issue, Eyde implored readers to keep the magazine "just between us girls" (though in some issues a heterosexual male friend of Eyde's was a contributor of letters and short articles).

Though the magazine was necessarily amateurish in its production values, it was truly remarkable as an energetic celebration of lesbian life in hostile times. Eyde was able to convince a few acquaintances to contribute articles to the magazine, but most of the work was her own, including book and movie reviews, short stories, editorials, and poetry. Eyde has claimed that she was not very political when she founded *Vice Versa,* that her true

motive for establishing the magazine (in addition to the need to "look busy") was that she was very lonely and hoped that *Vice Versa* would bring her new friends. But the magazine's contents belie her claims to be apolitical. Much of her writing anticipated the tone and message of gay liberation and lesbian-feminism by more than two decades. In a September 1947 issue, she declared:

> In these days of frozen foods, . . . compact apartments, modern innovations, and female independence, there is no reason why a woman should have to look to a man for food and shelter in return for raising his children and keeping his house in order unless she really wants to. . . . Never before have circumstance and conditions been so suitable for those of lesbian tendencies. (Ben, p. 5)

In a February 1948 article she angrily stated, "I for one consider myself neither an error of nature nor some sort of psychological freak. . . . Is it not possible that we are just as natural and normal by our standards as so called 'normals' are by theirs?" In several articles she condemned the "vicious propaganda" against homosexuals and cried out against "convention" that forced homosexuals "to live a life of deceit and subterfuge."

None of Eyde's writing in *Vice Versa* was signed. She adopted "Lisa Ben" as a pseudonym only in the 1950s, when several pieces from *Vice Versa* were reprinted in the *Ladder* (the second periodical in America to be aimed at a lesbian readership). Eyde wrote original pieces for the *Ladder* as well during the 1950s. In those years she also garnered considerable attention in Los Angeles LGB bars as an entertainer, writing and singing lesbian parodies of popular songs, with lyrics such as "I'm gonna sit right down and write my butch a letter, And ask her won't she please turn femme for me." In 1960 Los Angeles Daughters of Bilitis, a chapter of the national lesbian organization, released a recording of her songs, dubbing her "the first gay folk singer."

**Bibliography**

Ben, Lisa. *Vice Versa* (September 1947): 5.

Katz, Jonathan Ned. *Gay/Lesbian Almanac: A New Documentary.* New York: Harper and Row, 1983.

Marcus, Eric. *Making History: The Struggle for Gay and Lesbian Equal Rights, 1945–1990, An Oral History.* New York: Harper Collins, 1992.

Streitmatter, Rodger. *Unspeakable: The Rise of the Gay and Lesbian Press in America.* Boston: Faber and Faber, 1995.

**Lillian Faderman**

*See also* COMEDY AND HUMOR; DAUGHTERS OF BILITIS; HOMOPHILE PRESS; *LADDER.*

# BENEDICT, Ruth (b. 5 June 1887; d. 17 September 1948), anthropologist.

Ruth Fulton was born in New York City to a physician father who died before her second birthday and a librarian mother who never recovered from the loss of her husband. As a result of a childhood illness, Fulton was partially deaf. She and her younger sister, Margery, both attended St. Margaret's Academy in Buffalo, New York, and then Vassar College. After graduation, Fulton worked as a social worker in Buffalo and then taught in Los Angeles while living with her sister and brother-in-law. Hoping to "cure" her restlessness, she married Stanley Benedict, a biochemist and friend of a college classmate. During World War I, Benedict wrote a biography of Mary Wollstonecraft and worked on (but never finished) biographies of Margaret Fuller and Olive Schreiner.

In 1919 she enrolled at the New School for Social Research in New York City. Her mentors, Elsie Clews Parsons and Alexander Goldenweiser, urged her to enter the Ph.D. program in anthropology at Columbia University and study with Franz Boas, the most influential North American anthropologist of the time. She became his assistant and "right hand." Her 1923 library research dissertation mapped guardian spirit quests in Native North American cultures. Her first fieldwork (in 1922) was with Serrano Indians in California. She published poetry under the pseudonym Anne Singleton and made a number of relatively brief fieldwork visits to work with Pueblo informants (Zuni and Cochiti) in New Mexico after completing her dissertation.

Although her collections of Pueblo folklore are known to specialists, *Patterns of Culture,* Benedict's book characterizing Zuni as "Apollonian" in contrast to the "Dionysian" Kwagiutl studied by Boas and the "treacherous" Dobu studied by Reo Fortune made her famous. It introduced to a general audience the reduction of a culture to a single type of personality. *Patterns of Culture* also included references to different conceptions of homosexuality (pp. 262–265).

Benedict's alienation from U.S. society and cultural expectations led her to reformulate concepts of normality and abnormality and she looked with favor on the acceptance and respect accorded to the *berdache*—a category she saw as providing a niche in Native American cultures for homosexuals, though doing gender-typed work not of one's natal gender is the most recurrently observed feature of the role that some recent writers call "two-spirit."

Benedict remained at Columbia as a part-time teacher during the 1920s and later as an assistant and associate professor. Noted for a lack of sympathy for male students, she had a coterie of younger women around her, including her most famous student, Margaret Mead, with whom she was sexually, intellectually, and politically involved during the last two decades of her life. Both had relationships with other women as well, and Mead with several men, including Reo Fortune and two other husbands. Near the end of her life, Benedict settled happily into living with psychologist Ruth Valentine.

Aiming to contribute to the waging of psychological war and to provide simple introductions to the lifeways of U.S. wartime enemies and those societies then ruled by the Axis powers, Mead and Benedict pioneered "the study of culture at a distance" during World War II. They and their assistants interviewed persons in New York who had been raised in cultures that were of strategic interest to the U.S. war effort and that were likely to be occupied after the war. Benedict wrote about Rumanian and Thai culture, as well as her famous discussion, in *The Chrysanthemum and the Sword* (1946), of militarism and aestheticism in the Japanese "national character."

With funding from the U.S. Navy, Benedict directed a large project on diverse cultures at the start of the Cold War. She was planning large-scale comparisons of contemporary cultures when she died in New York City on 17 September 1948, a month before she would have delivered a presidential address to the American Anthropological Association annual meeting. (She had been elected president of the national association before Columbia promoted her to the rank of full professor.) Although maintaining a liberal belief in human malleability and tolerance for difference, Benedict did not develop a more complex model for change, and only touched on other cultures accepting what her culture characterized as "deviates" in gender and/or sexuality.

## Bibliography

Benedict, Ruth F. *Patterns of Culture.* Boston: Houghton, 1934.

———. *The Chrysanthemum and the Sword.* Boston: Houghton, 1946.

Caffrey, Margaret. *Ruth Benedict: Stranger in This Land.* Austin: University of Texas Press, 1989.

Lapsley, Hilary. *Margaret Mead and Ruth Benedict: The Kinship of Women.* Amherst: University of Massachusetts Press, 1999.

Modell, Judith Schachter. *Ruth Benedict: Patterns of a Life.* Philadelphia: University of Pennsylvania Press, 1983.

Young, Virginia. *Beyond Cultural Relativism: Ruth Benedict's Later Work.* Lincoln: University of Nebraska Press, 2004.

**Stephen O. Murray**

*See also* ANTHROPOLOGY; MEAD, MARGARET.

# BENJAMIN, Harry (b. 12 January 1885; d. 24 August 1986), endocrinologist, expert on transsexuality, advocate for transsexuals.

Born in Berlin, Harry Benjamin studied medicine at the Universities of Rostock, Berlin, and Tübingen, graduating in 1912. He first came to the United States in 1913 to work with a doctor who claimed, incorrectly, to have found a cure for tuberculosis. Eventually, Benjamin established himself as a key proponent of experimental attempts to rejuvenate the elderly. In the 1920s he publicized the allegedly rejuvenating vasoligation technique, a ligation of the vas deferens (spermatic duct) similar to vasectomy, of Austrian physiologist Eugen Steinach. Later he treated elderly patients with the administration of sex hormones.

From the 1920s on, Benjamin also worked to introduce his American colleagues to European sexual science. In 1930 he helped arrange the visit to the United States of the renowned German sexologist Magnus Hirschfeld, and in 1932 he failed in his attempt to bring to Chicago the conference of the World League for Sexual Reform, founded in 1928 by Hirschfeld and other sexologists. Benjamin was an open supporter of sexual freedom, a stance that placed him outside the mainstream of American medicine. In the 1930s he argued publicly for the decriminalization of homosexuality and also promoted the legalization of prostitution. He expressed contempt for what he saw as prudery and hypocrisy, and he befriended sex reformers and sex researchers, including Robert Latou Dickinson and Alfred Kinsey.

Benjamin first offered hormonal treatments for cross-gender identification in the 1930s, when he treated a male-to-female cross-dresser with an estrogenic extract, and he first advocated transsexual surgery in 1949, when Kinsey referred to him a patient who desperately desired operations to change the bodily characteristics of sex. However, it was not until the early 1950s, after the international media blitz concerning male-to-female Christine Jorgensen, that Benjamin earned his reputation as the foremost expert on transsexuality in the United States. In 1953 he published "Tranvestism and Transsexualism" in the *International Journal of Sexology,* the first of his many articles on the subject, and in 1966 he published *The Transsexual Phenomenon,* the book that solidified his place at the center of the field.

Throughout his career, Benjamin placed little faith in psychotherapeutic treatments. He believed that cross-gender identification had somatic causes, and he disagreed openly with the psychiatrists and psychotherapists who cast transsexuality as a mental illness. In his lectures, articles, and book, Benjamin distinguished transsexuality from homosexuality and transvestism. He constructed a spectrum of cross-gender behavior and identification that ran from occasional cross-dressing to intense transsexuality. Although he could find no physical markers of transsexuality, he speculated about genetic or hormonal causes.

By the 1960s, hundreds of transsexual patients had found their way into Benjamin's care at his offices in New York City and San Francisco. He was a benevolent paternalist who went out of his way to advise, correspond with, and treat his patients and also to help them find surgeons in the United States and abroad. In return, many of his patients expressed their appreciation for his concern, his Old World charm, and the nonjudgmental way in which he accepted their unconventional desires. In 1964 one such patient, Reed Erickson, a wealthy female-to-male transsexual, provided funds that allowed Benjamin and some colleagues to launch a formal research program, the Harry Benjamin Foundation, which was replaced in 1969 by the Harry Benjamin Research Project and a few years later by the Benjamin Gender Identity Research Foundation. In his private practice and research projects, Benjamin worked with a number of other doctors and scientists, including Leo Wollman, Charles Ihlenfeld, Robert Laidlaw, and Wardell Pomeroy.

Aside from gerontology and transsexuality, Benjamin had other areas of interest. He wrote several articles on prostitution and co-authored with Robert E. L. Masters the book *Prostitution and Morality,* published in 1964. From 1954 to 1982 he served on the board of consultants to *Sexology,* a popular magazine on the science of sex, and in 1957 he helped found the Society for the Scientific Study of Sex.

Benjamin retired in the mid-1970s, but he continued to meet with and advise physicians and therapists. In 1979 a group of physicians, therapists, and researchers who worked with transsexuals formed a professional organization that they named, in his honor, the Harry Benjamin International Gender Dysphoria Association, which became best known as the organization that establishes the professional standards of care for the treatment of transsexuals. In the 1980s Benjamin's vision deteriorated and he rarely left his home. He died in his sleep in 1986 at the age of 101, survived by his wife Greta, known as Gretchen.

## Bibliography

Buckley, Tom. "Transsexuality Expert, 90, Recalls 'Maverick' Career," *New York Times,* 11 January 1975.

Harry Benjamin Collection. The Kinsey Institute for Research in Sex, Gender, and Reproduction, Indiana University, Bloomington, Ind.

Meyerowitz, Joanne. *How Sex Changed: A History of Transsexuality in the United States.* Cambridge, Mass.: Harvard University Press, 2002.

**Joanne Meyerowitz**

**See also** ERICKSON EDUCATIONAL FOUNDATION; ERICKSON, REED; INTERSEXUALS AND INTERSEXED PEOPLE; LAWRENCE, LOUISE; PSYCHOLOGY, PSYCHIATRY, PSYCHOANALYSIS, AND SEXOLOGY; RICHARDS, RENÉE; TRANSGENDER ORGANIZATIONS AND PERIODICALS; TRANSSEXUALS, TRANSVESTITES, TRANSGENDER PEOPLE, AND CROSS-DRESSERS.

# BENNETT, Michael (8 April 1943; 2 July 1987), dancer, choreographer, and director.

Born Michael Bennett DiFiglia in Buffalo, New York, one of two sons to a machinist father and a secretary mother, Bennett began dance lessons at the age of 3. He became proficient in tap and jazz dance and before finishing high school joined an international tour of *West Side Story* in the role of Baby John, directed by Jerome Robbins. Upon returning to New York he achieved success in the dance ensemble of several Broadway shows, including *Subways Are For Sleeping* (1961), *Here's Love* (1963), and *Bajour* (1964). Ambitious and highly motivated to achieve his own distinctive success, he choreographed his first professional musicals, *A Joyful Noise* (1966) and *Henry, Sweet Henry* (1967) before he was twenty-five years old. Both of these musicals flopped, but Bennett received critical acclaim for his efforts, and the first of several Tony Award nominations for his choreography. Bennett's efforts subsequently moved steadily toward commercial success, as in his choreography for Neil Simon's *Promises, Promises* (1968), Andre Previn and Alan Jay Lerner's *Coco* (1970), Stephen Sondheim and George Furth's *Company* (1970), and Sondheim's *Follies* (1971) which Bennett co-directed with theatrical veteran Hal Prince. For *Follies*, Bennett won two Tonys, one for direction and one for choreography.

Bennett's most important work, *A Chorus Line*, opened at the Newman Theater at the New York Public Theater in May 1975 and moved to Broadway in July of that year. Universally hailed as a landmark of musical theater craft, the work resulted from more than a year of development in which dancers discussed their personal histories in tape-recorded sessions which were then adapted into songs, monologues, and dance sequences coordinated by Bennett and his collaborators. The resulting "backstage musical" chronicled the lives of seventeen Broadway dancers during a grueling audition. The show welded confessional stories of childhood fantasies, dysfunctional family life, sexual identity confusion, and professional disappointments to a carefully coordinated structure of costume, lighting, musical score, staging, and humorous dialogue. Widely celebrated as the ultimate Broadway musical, *A Chorus Line* ran 6,137 performances before it closed 28 April 1990 and garnered many awards, including the Pulitzer Prize, the New York Drama Critics Circle Award, and the Tony Award for best musical.

Himself bisexual, Bennett's work consistently broached sexuality to appeal to lesbian, gay, and bisexual audiences. *A Chorus Line* included frank discussions of sexuality by several gay characters and offered an array of coming out stories within the supportive social environment of entertainment professionals. Bennett's next Broadway hit, *Dreamgirls* (1981), chronicled the rise of an African American girl-group from amateur talent shows to international stardom. Set in the 1960s and 1970s, *Dreamgirls* featured fantastical glamorous imagery admired by some LGBT audiences, including exquisite costumes and production numbers reminiscent of Hollywood film musicals of the 1940s. Bennett's unproduced musical *Scandal* (1984) explored a woman's sexual adventures in Europe and included a "ménage-à-trois ballet" as well as a lesbian sex fantasy sequence.

Bennett formed Plum Productions to oversee his business interests in 1971. Clearly interested in the well-being of the New York dance and musical theater communities, in 1977 he used profits from his successes to purchase a building at 890 Broadway in New York and converted the space into a premiere dance rehearsal site. Although he directed some nonmusical plays, including George Furth's *Twigs* (1971) and Neil Simon's *God's Favorite* (1974), he achieved greater renown as choreographer and "show doctor" for other people's projects, including Cy Coleman and Dorothy Fields' *Seesaw* (1973), the musical that made Tommy Tune a Broadway star.

Provocative, acerbic, and emotionally manipulative, Bennett enjoyed no long-term intimate relationships and remained closeted to those he did not know well. According to associates, his brief marriage to Donna McKechnie, a star dancer with whom he worked in *Promises, Promises*, intended to offer him entry to a heterosexual world of entertainment industry power-brokers; their union lasted from 4 December 1976 until their divorce in 1978.

Known as the "king of backstage musicals," Bennett also developed *Ballroom* (1978), which was a commercial and critical disappointment, and *Chess* (1986), but was forced to withdraw from the latter as his health declined. Bennett moved to Tucson, Arizona, in 1986, and died there of AIDS-related cancer in 1987. The next year, he was elected to the Theater Hall of Fame. His legacy to the world of musical theater was to celebrate craftsmanship that knits plot, character, music, stage design, and dance into a seamless whole, fully equipped with emotional highs and lows best suited to the theatrical moment.

## Bibliography

Gerard, Jeremy. "Michael Bennett, Theatrical Innovator, Dies at 44." *New York Times* 3 July 1987.

Mandelbaum, Ken. A Chorus Line *and the Musicals of Michael Bennett.* New York: St. Martin's Press, 1989.

**Thomas F. DeFrantz**

*See also* DANCE.

# BENTLEY, Gladys (b. 12 August 1907; d. 18 January 1960), entertainer, songwriter.

Gladys Bentley was born in Pennsylvania to a Trinidadian mother and an African American father. Although little is known about Bentley's early life, in 1923, at the age of sixteen, she left Philadelphia and migrated to Harlem, the center of black cultural life in New York City during a period of enormous creative outpouring known as the Harlem Renaissance. Harlem in the 1920s boasted a large number of African American writers and performers—including such figures as Countee Cullen, Langston Hughes, Nella Larsen, Moms Mabley, Bruce Nugent, Ma Rainey, Bessie Smith, and Wallace Thurman—who were known within private circles as lesbian, gay, or bisexual. This combination of creative ferment and sexual diversity, as well as a familiar mixing of black American and Caribbean cultures, was attractive and liberating for Bentley, a heavyset young woman with a penchant for wearing men's clothes.

During the mid-1920s, the height of the Jazz Age, Bentley turned her talents at piano playing and blues singing into an appealing nightclub act. As "Fatso" Bentley, she began making appearances at restaurants, bars, and cabarets located on Harlem's "Jungle Alley," the block of 133rd Street between Lenox and Seventh Avenues. In her public appearances, she performed her own songs as well as bawdy versions of popular songs of the day while wearing her trademark white tuxedo and top hat and flirting suggestively with female audience members. Assuming the role of a butch daddy, for example, she proudly disclosed the details of her wedding ceremony,

held in Atlantic City, at which she married her white girlfriend. In 1928, at the age of twenty-one, she began recording many of her own compositions—including such classics as "How Much Can I Stand?"—though none of these gave evidence of the persona that Bentley cultivated in live shows. Bentley became a darling of gossip columnists and was regularly sought out by white bohemians who went "slumming" uptown. Bentley's onstage antics were memorialized by contemporary writers in works of fiction such as Blair Niles's exploration of homosexual subculture, *Strange Brother* (1931), and Clement Wood's study of interracial romance, *Deep River* (1934), as well as in nonfiction works like Carl Van Vechten's *Parties: Scenes From Contemporary New York Life* (1930) and Langston Hughes's autobiographical *The Big Sea* (1940).

Bentley achieved great wealth and notoriety, but several factors conspired to change her fortunes. Although she was a resident performer at popular gay venues like Harry Hansberry's Clam House and the Ubangi Club through the mid-1930s, the ravages of the Great Depression and the loss of Harlem's prominence as a tourist destination encouraged entertainers such as Bentley to consider other options. In 1937, Bentley moved to California with her mother and purchased a small bungalow in a middle-class black neighborhood in downtown Los Angeles. Performing at both upscale West Coast supper clubs and at local lesbian and gay cabarets, she remained a strong draw for black audiences and gay audiences alike. A December 1942 advertisement for Mona's Club 440, a lesbian cabaret in San Francisco where Bentley appeared, promotes her as "America's greatest sepia piano artist" and the "brown bomber of sophisticated songs." She also recorded her own songs, such as "Gladys Isn't Gratis Any More," and performed them regularly at Hollywood clubs such as the Rose Room. In the late 1950s, she appeared on Groucho Marx's television show *You Bet Your Life* alongside an adolescent Candice Bergen.

Historians champion Gladys Bentley as an African American lesbian who chose to live her life daringly ahead of her time. But despite her carefully cultivated reputation as a blues-singing bulldagger, in the last years of her life she completely disavowed her own past. In August 1952, *Ebony* magazine published an essay by Bentley titled "I Am a Woman Again," in which the author described how under the guidance of a gynecologist she had taken estrogen treatments to cure her homosexuality. Her gynecologist believed that a depressed estrogen supply had prevented her from accepting her gender role as a feminine heterosexual woman. Photographed wearing pearls while cooking dinner and making the bed, Bentley described a blissful marriage to a newspaper columnist, J. T. Gibson, who later denied that the two had ever wed. Bentley married a cook named Charles Roberts in 1953, but the two eventually divorced. In her remaining years, Bentley became an active member of the Los Angeles–based ministry Temple of Love in Christ, Inc. Bentley was studying to become an ordained minister when she died in a flu epidemic on 18 January 1960.

## Bibliography

Garber, Eric. "A Spectacle in Color: The Lesbian and Gay Subculture of Jazz Age Harlem." In *Hidden From History: Reclaiming the Gay and Lesbian Past.* Edited by Martin Duberman, Martha Vicinus, and George Chauncey, Jr. New York: New American Library, 1989.

———. "Gladys Bentley: The Bulldagger Who Sang the Blues." *Out/Look* 1 (Spring 1988): 52–61.

Mitchell, Carmen. "Creations of Fantasies/Constructions of Identities: The Oppositional Lives of Gladys Bentley." In *The Greatest Taboo: Homosexuality in Black Communities.* Edited by Delroy Constantine-Simms. Los Angeles: Alyson, 2001.

Serlin, David. "Gladys Bentley and the Cadillac of Hormones." In *Replaceable You: Engineering the American Body after World War Two.* Chicago: University of Chicago Press, 2004.

**David Serlin**

*See also* COMEDY AND HUMOR; FEMMES AND BUTCHES; HARLEM RENAISSANCE; HUGHES, LANGSTON; MUSIC: POPULAR; NILES, BLAIR; TRANSSEXUALS, TRANSVESTITES, TRANSGENDER PEOPLE, AND CROSS-DRESSERS; VAN VECHTEN, CARL.

**BERDACHE.** see NATIVE AMERICANS; TWO-SPIRIT FEMALES; TWO-SPIRIT MALES.

## BERNSTEIN, Leonard (b. 25 August 1918; d. 14 October 1990), composer, conductor, pianist.

Leonard Bernstein was the twentieth century's most protean figure in American music, although George Gershwin offered precedent. Bernstein excelled as pianist, "serious" composer, Broadway composer, conductor, television star (especially conducting his Young People's Concerts), teacher, writer, and more. He moved restlessly among those roles, to his own frustration and that of observers who lamented his failure to settle on one. His longest-held major position was as the New York Philharmonic's music director, a post he held from 1958 to 1969. His huge talents were both blessing and curse, giving him enormous range but fostering chaotic movement within it. Successful from the start as a Harvard University undergraduate, he repeatedly triumphed and teetered on collapse, successfully reinventing himself each time.

That was true as well of his personal life. He married the Chilean actress Felicia Montealegre (who died in 1978) in 1951 and was the father of three children. But he was conflicted about his Boston Jewish family (even late in life he carried on in agony about his businessman father), the married life he chose, and his passions for other men, which began early and persisted. He was too self-dramatizing to hide those passions forever; the kisses he planted on other men at the Kennedy Center premier of his *Mass* in 1971 incited the tape-recorded private fury of President Richard Nixon. He was already anathema to the White House for his leftist politics; his patronizing glibness often irritated his allies as well. In the 1970s he fashioned himself a champion of "coming out" and gay rights, yet another role for him, though it never eclipsed his artistic career. His flamboyant public style, media savvy, good looks, tall tales about himself, affairs with men and women, and immersion in a glittering world of celebrity—"Glitter and be gay" is the appropriate line from his opera *Candide* (1956)—made him source and object of recurrent gossip, and in turn an elusive figure for reliable biography.

Like most queer composers of his generation, Bernstein rarely set forth identifiable gay content, which in any event is often less a creator's intention than a listener's perception in response to a combination of music, performance, text, audience, and historical circumstance. The Broadway musical *West Side Story* (1957) told no gay love tale but appealed to gay audiences, in part for its jazzy, energized male dance routines and perhaps its—and Bernstein's—emotive flair. He was also a savage critic of conformity in his operas *Candide, Trouble in Tahiti* (1952), and its follow-up, *A Quiet Place* (1983).

Bernstein created a large and varied output despite the much-publicized dramas about his inconstant attention to composing. He became famous for his score (and some lyrics) for the musical *West Side Story,* a collaboration with other Jewish gay artists (Arthur Laurents, Stephen Sondheim, and Jerome Robbins). He produced compelling, popular scores for ballet (*Fancy Free,* 1944), an earlier musical (*On the Town,* 1944), and Hollywood film (*On the Waterfront,* 1954). *Candide* slowly gained acceptance; its overture became a ubiquitous performance and recording piece. He produced a virtual violin concerto (*Serenade,* 1954), symphonies (including *The Age of Anxiety,* 1949), the choral piece *Chichester Psalms* (1965), the controversial *Mass* (1971), the disastrous bicentennial musical *1600 Pennsylvania Avenue* (1976), and other works.

**Leonard Bernstein.** The legendary composer and conductor, famous as well for championing Gustav Mahler's music, exuberantly leads the Boston Symphony into the climax of Mahler's Symphony no. 2 in C Minor (*Resurrection*) at the Tanglewood Music Festival in Massachusetts in July 1970—a performance that earned the maestro an eleven-minute ovation. [Bettmann/corbis]

Bernstein promoted other American composers, but his restless eclecticism made his own musical pedigree indistinct. Compared to Aaron Copland and Virgil Thomson, he drew less on musical modernism and created no "school" of American composing. He was more influential with protégés like conductor Michael Tilson Thomas. Although he composed Americana, he looked forward to postmodernist styles and back to Gustav Mahler, whose music he championed. He did, however, have a trademark sound, which mixed soaring lyricism, aching nostalgia, dark religiosity, bitter lament, emphatic rhythm, and vivid orchestration. A consummate performer himself, he had a keen, if sometimes overwrought, feel for performance—for what worked on stage. As conductor for recordings, he was enormously prolific in a wide range of music.

Once a brash young man of American music, Bernstein carried off his final reinvention as an old master of the European classics and tutor to post-Holocaust central Europe's fallen gentiles as well as a frequent conductor of the Israel Philharmonic. Mahler seemed to inspire his most grand (or grandiose) compositions and conducting, and he carried Mahler's cause to Vienna and Berlin, harnessing the gifted but skeptical orchestras there to his passions, and finally to freedom and European unity. His conducting of Beethoven's *Ninth Symphony* in Berlin in December 1989 after the Berlin Wall's demise was the biggest cultural moment of the Cold War's end.

Already in ill health, he spent his last days in New York City.

**Bibliography**

Burton, Humphrey. *Leonard Bernstein.* Boston: Faber and Faber, 1994.

Secrest, Meryle. *Leonard Bernstein: A Life.* New York: Knopf, 1994.

**Michael Sherry**

*See also* CAGE, JOHN; MUSIC: BROADWAY AND MUSICAL THEATER; MUSIC: CLASSICAL; MUSIC: OPERA; SONDHEIM, STEPHEN.

# BIOLOGY AND ZOOLOGY

The homosexual animal body has been an object of considerable social anxiety, inspiring a long history of scientific effort to discover what, if anything, makes this body biologically different from the heterosexual animal body. Similarly, intersexuality, bisexuality, transgenderism, and transsexuality have been labeled aberrant, leading biologists and zoologists toward extraordinary explanatory efforts. In these scientific projects, the "normal" body— the heterosexual and unambiguously sexed and gendered body—generally does not arouse a similar need for special investigation, except insofar as it provides the baseline or default against which sexual and gender variance can be measured.

Biological and zoological arguments have been used to both support and oppose LGBT interests. Advocates of LGBT rights, for example, often emphasize that if LGBT people are biologically "born" as such, then anti-LGBT discrimination, intolerance, and inequality are unjustified. Transsexual advocates have depended upon biological research to secure sex change operations. At the same time, anti-LGBT activists sometimes suggest that if there is a biological basis for sexual and gender variance, perhaps LGBT people can be cured. And, they say, just because LGBT behaviors can be found in nonhuman populations does not mean that such behaviors are acceptable among humans. These types of arguments suggest that biological and zoological research will not yield definitive answers about the acceptability and desirability of LGBT identities and behaviors.

## Queer Animals: Zoological Studies

The problems faced by biological and zoological studies of sex and gender variance are numerous. Defining basic terms such as "homosexuality," "lesbian," "gay," "heterosexual," "bisexual," "transgender," "mixed gender," and "transsexual" is extraordinarily complicated. In animal behavior studies, for example, "homosexuality" has been assessed on the basis of courtship, affection, pair-bonding, coparenting, genital pleasure, and sexual acts. In contrast, in human studies there are an assortment of scales and diagnostic techniques used to measure and identify sexual and gender behaviors, desires, fantasies, identifications, identities, bonds, relationships, and other variables. Questions of frequency and stability complicate matters, as do issues surrounding translatability and comparability, both within the same species and across different species (and, in humans, across cultural groups). Additionally, anthropomorphic tendencies can lead researchers to apply culturally specific human categories such as "lesbian," "gay," "bisexual," "transgender," and "transsexual" when analyzing animals. At the same time, in some contexts there have been persistent homophobic and transphobic tendencies to overlook, discount, erase, and ignore LGBT behaviors and characteristics in animal studies.

Nonetheless, zoological research on a wide variety of animals over the course of the last one hundred years reveals the undeniable prevalence of homosexual, bisexual, and transgender behaviors. In addition, nature supplies many examples of intersexed animal bodies, as well as many examples of invertebrate species (including species of slugs, worms, and fish) that are hermaphroditic (with individual animals functioning simultaneously as

female and male). Parthenogenic species, including a number of fish, lizards, insects, and other invertebrates, reproduce solely through the female body. Animal behaviors can be classified as transgender (where the animal "mimics" the other sex behaviorally, visually, or chemically) and transsexual (where, for example, invertebrates such as shrimp, oysters, sow bugs, and fish are capable of physically becoming the other sex, in which case the reproductive organs undergo a complete sex change). Females that turn into males undergo "protogynous sex change" and males that turn into females undergo a "protandrous sex change."

Bruce Bagemihl has identified more than 450 kinds of animals in which homosexual behavior occurs. While this is only a fraction of animal species worldwide, Bagemihl estimates that in species that have at least some form of same-sex courtship, sexual, and/or pair-bonding activities, about 20 percent of these intraspecies interactions are homosexual. In many of these studies, the assessment of "homosexual" behavior presumes a sexually dimorphic heterosexual mating pattern as the norm. In species in which elements of normative mating behavior occur between animals of the same sex, many researchers identify the behavior as "homosexual"; examples include an array of same-sex mounting, submission, and penetration behaviors, along with oral sex and masturbation. Many primates closely related to humans demonstrate homosexual "exuberance"—examples include bonobos or pygmy chimpanzees, common chimpanzees, gorillas, orangutans, white-handed gibbons, hanuman langurs, leaf monkeys, and a variety of macaques, baboons, and new world monkeys, as well as numerous marine and hoofed animals and many varieties of birds.

## The Argument from Nature

The attempt to establish the existence of homosexual, bisexual, and transgender behaviors in the animal world has often been designed to counter the traditional argument from nature used to pathologize human sex and gender variance. The argument from nature holds that there are two and only two kinds of human bodies (male and female) and that nature has "designed" male and female bodies to have sex with each other. Nature demonstrates this, it is argued, in the creation of sexually reproducing species comprised of two sexes that display dimorphic characteristics and behaviors organized by complementary genital and gonadal structures designed for intercoital mating. Bodies that fail to fit into this scheme are viewed as errors of nature, pathological aberrations, or congenital misfits. And so LGBT behaviors are regarded as "unnatural." Studies on a wide variety of animal species, however, have demonstrated an observable fluidity of sexualities, sexes, and sex-dimorphic behaviors and displays, a diversity of erotic and affectionate pleasures, and a variety of reproductive, pair-bonding, and parenting strategies and styles. These studies suggest that arguments from nature are highly selective, producing evidence that affirms both the plethora of heterosexualities and sex dimorphisms in nature as well as the exuberance of nature's sexual and morphic queerness.

Arguments from nature are also often flawed because they fail to take into account the evolution of vertebrate species, producing brains of increased complexity that make possible more flexibility in behavioral responses and expanded capacity for culturally mediated sentient and sense-making behaviors. In other words, arguments from nature often ignore nature's evolution. Using non-human animal behaviors as a basis for making claims about human behaviors not only assumes that human behaviors are the inevitable evolutionary consequence of ancestral evolutionary genetics but also overlooks the plasticity enabled by human culture, history, language, and memory. Recent sociobiological theory, however, has rejuvenated the traditional argument from nature in its appeal to invertebrate studies as a basis for understanding human social behaviors—appealing ultimately to a kind of atavistic, if not mythic, notion of psycho-physical memory that tethers the human body to strictly prescriptive (and often ethnocentric, patriarchal, and parochial) sexual and gender norms. Attempting to understand all human behaviors as products of the body's natural desire to reproduce its genes, sociobiological approaches and other arguments from nature fail in multiple ways to account for the complexity of human culture.

## Biological and Biomedical Research

Since the late nineteenth century, the existence of sexual and gender variance has inspired a great deal of biological and biomedical research in the United States. In the late nineteenth and early twentieth centuries, most of this research was conducted within the frameworks of psychoanalysis, psychology, and sexology, and much of it was influenced by Darwinian, social Darwinian, and eugenic theories. These theories set the stage for a decidedly empiricist and positivist turn toward the body as a source of explanation for social and cultural phenomena. Utilizing advances made in biological theory and research technology, biology and biomedical science probed the body's genitals, hormones, genes, neural tissues, and general morphology for clues about the causes of sexual and gender diversity. This turning to the body accompanied the ascendance of specialization in biological and biomedical sciences; interest in the cellular, genetic, and bio-chemical bases of life; and the emergence of biomedical models of the body.

Two conflicts can be seen in this research. The first was between researchers who aimed to identify constitutional pathology in the "deviant body" and those who posited a continuum of benign variance. The latter group was part of a scientific tradition that runs from German sexologist Magnus Hirschfield through U.S. sexologist Alfred Kinsey. The second conflict addressed the question of how much the human body and its biological constitution contribute to "deviant behavior." This question was framed by the nature/nurture controversies in the middle of the twentieth century, the social constructionist/biological determinist debates of the 1970s, and the conflicts between cultural studies discourse theorists and endocrine-neural-genetics researchers in the late twentieth and early twenty-first centuries.

Biological, zoological, and biomedical research in the first half of the twentieth century generally aimed to make the body a source of explanation, establishing sex and gender variance as an immutable, genetic, and isolatable trait of particular types of bodies. Even after the American Psychiatric Association declassified homosexuality as a mental illness in the 1970s, which many took to be a sign of the rejection of biological pathology models, the biological sciences maintained interest in identifying the biological basis of genders and sexualities they defined as "different." The cause of sexual and gender variance was thought to reside and persist in the body, whether that variance was seen as benign or perverted. These biological studies have been troubled by a set of research issues: incomplete replication and verification of experimental results; lack of clarity on the causes inferred from the research; omission of confounding variables and possible cofactors; problems related to how subject groups and their controls are gathered, evaluated, and compared; and lack of consensus on definitions and interpretations.

Most research on the biological causes of sexual and gender variance has fit within two frameworks—either morphological, endocrine, and physiological, or neuro-anatomical and genetic. Morphological research has aimed to establish measures of variance in deviant bodies. This approach was used, for example, in the New York Sex Variant Study (1935–1941), which investigated the bodies of forty lesbian women and forty gay men for signs of ambiguous genitalia or cross-gendered anatomical features. Often based on models of a continuum of bodies, these studies frequently relied on an intersexual matrix, searching for anatomical signs of abnormal or "in-between" bodies to explain sexual and gender variance. For example, deviations in the size or shape of the clitoris or labia majora in lesbian women were noted.

A second type of research has been based on endocrine and physiological frameworks. The speculation that sexual and gender variance may be a function of glandular secretions dates back to nineteenth-century sexology and studies in the 1920s that developed in the context of new research about the endocrine system and the hormonal regulation of the body. The 1960s ushered in a flood of studies on the effects of castration and the administration of cross-sex hormones on the mating behaviors of rats. These studies resulted in contradictory findings. As Ruth Blier concluded: "Estrogens do not necessarily determine typical female mating behaviors and may, in fact, abolish them and enhance male mating behaviors; conversely, androgens do not necessarily determine male mating behaviors or inhibit female behaviors, but may instead abolish male and enhance female mating behaviors" (p. 174). Later studies that attempted to find higher levels of testosterone in lesbians or lower levels in gay men were inconclusive.

Also in the 1960s, gender identity research projects originating with Robert Stoller, John Money, and Anke Ehrhardt entered the nature versus nurture fray with their work on human gender identity formation and gender variance. The hormonal prenatal and postnatal environments became a main focus of concern in research involving genetic females born with congenital virilization, genetic males born with testicular feminization, and genetic males born with a five-alpha reductase deficiency who purportedly experienced transsexual conversion at puberty. Critics have raised questions about the background assumptions of these studies, the measures used for gender behavioral units, and confounding factors contributing to the results and their interpretations.

A third type of research has relied on neuroanatomical and genetic frameworks. The notion that sexual and gender variance may be an inherited trait has been put forward in various twin studies since the 1950s. In the 1970s, a considerable number of brain studies singled out an area of the brain—a cluster of nodes in the anterior hypothalamus—that seemed to play a role in animal sexual orientation. In human studies, Simon LeVay (1991) located a difference in one of the interstitial anterior hypothalamic nodes that seems to be correlated with gay male sexual orientation. In the 1990s the body's prenatal neural tissues also became an object of sex variance inquiry. The link to prenatal neural development and genetic markers was posited in Dean Hamer's work

(1993) on the Xq28 gene sequence found on the X chromosome. This appears to be a gene sequence more commonly shared by gay brothers than gay and heterosexual brothers. LeVay's and Hamer's research connects a possible genetic marker on the X chromosome with a prenatal neural formation in the nodes of the anterior hypothalamus that may affect the endocrine system and have subsequent effects on gay male sexual orientation. In this view, the body provides both the cause and the effect of sex variant desire. These results are controversial and tentative, and while they clearly fit within a biological and zoological framework, they raise the question that haunts the heteronormative narrative of evolution: Why would a trait that does not foster its own reproduction in the affected organism persist?

## Bioevolutionary Frameworks and Freedoms

In 1959, evolutionary biologist George Hutchinson noted that homosexuality appears to be a biological constant in nature, which means that it must have some evolutionary value. In 1975, sociobiologist E. O Wilson offered the kinship hypothesis, which argued that homosexual animals provide evolutionary utility by assisting their breeding kin in the care of their young. Attempts to account for the constancy of sexual variance in animal populations assumes that heterosexual mating is the end-all aim of animal life and that homosexually inclined animals never breed. These assumptions and others can be called into question by noting the widespread phenomenon of nonreproductive and alternative heterosexualities in animal life and the plethora of animal behaviors, including widespread bisexuality, that do not revolve exclusively around reproduction or care for kindred offspring. Homosexual and bisexual animal behaviors, like many other animal behaviors, suggest that pleasure may be a motivating force and that heterosexual mating may be more an incidental consequence than an overriding goal.

The pursuit of animal pleasures in the play of animal bodies seems a relentless and restless piece of nature that may or may not be contained by empirical measures of sexual behavioral units, by causal determinants in molecular or cellular matter, or by grand narratives of reproductive imperatives. When biology and zoology approach sex and gender variance, researchers may have to simply observe nature's incautious resources of animal invention and joy. As Bagemihl has noted, regarding biofunctional explanations of same-sex animal kissing (such as the deep tongue kissing among bonobos): "'The kiss' is a perfect symbol of the limitations of biological reductionism—

for even if its origins can ultimately be traced to such functional considerations, something ineffable still remains in the gesture each time it is performed, something that continues to transcend its biological 'purpose,' and evade 'explanation'" (p. 212).

**Bibliography**

Bagemihl, Bruce. *Biological Exuberance: Animal Homosexuality and Natural Diversity.* New York: St. Martin's Press, 1999.

Bleir, Ruth. *Sex and Gender: A Critique of Biology and Its Theories on Women.* New York: Pergamon Press, 1984.

Brookey, Robert Alan. *Reinventing the Male Homosexual: The Rhetoric and Power of the Gay Gene.* Bloomington: Indiana University Press, 2002

De Cecco, J. P., and D. A. Parker, eds. *Sex, Cells, and Same-Sex Desire: The Biology of Sexual Preference.* New York: Haworth Press, 1995.

Fausto-Sterling, Anne, P. Gowaty, and M. Zuk. "Evolutionary Psychology and Darwinian Feminism," *Feminist Studies* 23: 403–417.

Hamer, D. H., S. Hu, V. L. Magnuson, and A. M. L. Pattatucci. "The Linkage Between DNA Markers on the X Chromosome and Male Sexual Orientation." *Science* 261 (1993): 321–327.

Hutchinson, George Evelyn. "A Speculative Consideration on Certain Possible Forms of Sexual Selection in Man." *American Naturalist* 93 (1959): 81–91.

LeVay, Simon. "A Difference in Hypothalamic Structure Between Heterosexual and Homosexual Men." *Science* 253 (1991): 1034–1037.

Meyerowitz, Joanne. *How Sex Changed: A History of Transsexuality in the United States.* Cambridge, Mass.: Harvard University Press, 2002.

Money, John, and Anke A. Ehrhardt. *Man and Woman, Boy and Girl: The Differentiation and Dimorphism of Gender Identity from Conception to Maturity.* Baltimore: Johns Hopkins University Press, 1972.

Stein, Edward. *The Mismeasure of Desire: The Science, Theory and Ethics of Sexual Orientation.* New York: Oxford University Press, 1999.

Stoller, Robert. *Sex and Gender: On the Development of Masculinity and Femininity.* New York: Science House, 1968.

Terry, Jennifer. *An American Obsession: Science, Medicine, and Homosexuality in Modern Society.* Chicago: University of Chicago, 1999.

Wilson, E. O. *Sociobiology: The New Synthesis.* Cambridge, Mass.: Harvard University Press, 1975.

———. *On Human Nature.* Cambridge, Mass.: Harvard University Press, 1978.

**Jacqueline N. Zita**

*See also* MEDICINE, MEDICALIZATION, AND THE MEDICAL MODEL; PSYCHOLOGY, PSYCHIATRY, PSYCHOANALYSIS, AND SEXOLOGY.

# BISEXUALITY, BISEXUALS, AND BISEXUAL MOVEMENTS

Individuals who are sexually attracted to both women and men frequent the annals of history, but the use of the term "bisexuality" to describe this phenomenon began only in the early 1900s. Previously, the field of sexology had typically categorized such individuals as "psychosexual hermaphrodites," believing that a "bisexual" not only desired both males and females, but was both male and female. The new meaning of "bisexuality" reflected the influence of Sigmund Freud, who argued that everyone possessed an innate bisexual disposition that would diverge into either heterosexuality or homosexuality by early childhood. Although Freud's conceptualization helped naturalize bisexuality in popular discourse, he assumed that a normal course of development would lead to a heterosexual object-choice.

The landmark research of Alfred Kinsey and his colleagues in the late 1940s and early 1950s added further weight to the "naturalness" of bisexuality. Finding that 28 percent of women and 46 percent of men had responded erotically to or were sexually active with both women and men, Kinsey's studies awakened the U.S. public to the prevalence of sexual variation and proved to many bisexuals that they were not alone. Although researchers have since challenged his methodology and data, Kinsey's conception of human sexual behavior as existing on a continuum from heterosexuality to homosexuality, rather than fitting within a hetero/homosexual dichotomy, has had a lasting influence on how sexuality is perceived.

## Early Bisexual Communities

At the time of Kinsey's research, most bisexuals did not visibly differentiate themselves from either heterosexuals or from lesbians and gay men. Recognizing the risks for anyone known to be involved in same-sex sexual relationships, some bisexuals, like some lesbians and gay men, passed as heterosexual; they kept their interest in people of the same sex hidden while emphasizing their attraction to people of another sex, often through marriage. Given their bisexuality, however, these were more than marriages of convenience, and in some cases, the spouses knew of their partners' attraction to members of the same sex. Other bisexuals joined lesbians and gay men in creating same-sex social networks and group institutions such as bars, private parties, and cruising locations in cities across the United States during the early and mid-twentieth century. By establishing spaces where they could find emotional support, make friends, and meet potential partners, lesbians, gay men, and bisexuals forged cultures that enabled them to develop a positive self-identity and a sense of community membership.

Whereas predominantly bisexual communities have rarely received much attention, bisexuality was a critical element in two influential circles of writers and artists that developed in the early twentieth century. London's Bloomsbury group, which defined English modernism and postimpressionism from the 1900s through the 1920s, consisted primarily of bisexuals, including writers Virginia Woolf and Lytton Strachey, painters Duncan Grant and Dora Carrington, and economist John Maynard Keynes. In the United States, the Harlem Renaissance of the 1920s ushered in a renewed sense of race consciousness and led to a boom in the production of black literary and artistic works, many created by bisexuals. For singers Bessie Smith and Ma Rainey, and writers Wallace Thurman, Richard Bruce Nugent, Angelina Weld Grimké, Countee Cullen, Claude McKay, and possibly Langston Hughes, being attracted to both women and men frequently had as much of an impact on their lives as being African American.

### Bisexuality and the Homophile Movement

Bisexuals played a central role in founding early homophile political groups, although many were not vocal about their bisexuality, either because they did not feel the need to assert a separate bisexual identity or because they feared being rejected after finally finding a place where they could belong. The first known male homophile organization in the United States, Chicago's Society for Human Rights, denied membership to bisexuals when it was chartered in 1924, as it was believed that they would be less committed to the cause. As a consequence, the vice president of the group, who was married, had to keep his bisexuality a secret from other members.

Bisexual women and men subsequently took part in the Mattachine Society, the Daughters of Bilitis, and other homophile organizations founded in the 1950s and 1960s. The first LGBT college group, Columbia University's Student Homophile League, was established by Stephen Donaldson (né Robert Martin), an openly bisexual student, in 1966 and recognized by the university the following year. With his support, other campuses soon created similar groups, laying the groundwork for the development of the gay liberation movement in the late 1960s and early 1970s. But despite their involvement in the homophile movement, bisexuals were not always accepted even though many of the people who sought the assistance of homophile organizations were ostensibly bisexual. Throughout the 1960s, bisexuality was rarely mentioned in homophile publications such as the *Ladder*

and the *Mattachine Review* or discussed in group meetings; bisexuals became an absent presence, except when their visibility made denial impossible. For example, other homophile activists thought "it was a scandal" when Donaldson and Martha Shelley, a principal organizer of the New York City Daughters of Bilitis and later a founder of the Gay Liberation Front, began a long-running affair. "[B]ut at the same time, because the two of us were so blatant and out there in public being pro gay," Shelley remembers, "they certainly couldn't afford to throw us out" (Donaldson, p. 33).

### Bisexuality and the LGBT and Sexual Liberation Movements

In contrast, bisexuality was often accepted and, at times, celebrated in the LGBT and sexual liberation movements of the early 1970s. Both radical LGBT groups such as the Gay Liberation Front and organizations that consisted mainly of heterosexually identified "swingers" such as the Sexual Freedom League encouraged sexual fluidity and experimentation, believing that people should be free to love regardless of gender. "For gay liberation there was no 'normal' or 'perverse' sexuality, only a world of sexual possibilities. ... Once everyone was free to express her or his latent sexualities, boundaries between the homosexual and the heterosexual should fade into irrelevance and false partitions in the flow of desire give way to personal fulfillment" (Adam, p. 78).

But this utopian vision of sexual freedom did little to provide a space for bisexuality in the present, and even gay liberationists who were bisexual often felt compelled to come out as gay in order to challenge compulsory heterosexuality and avoid charges that they were trying "to escape the greater stigma of homosexuality" (Angelides, p. 128). According to Carl Wittman's "A Gay Manifesto," one of the movement's most widely circulated statements of principles, "[t]he reason so few of us are bisexual is because society made such a big stink about homosexuality that we got forced into seeing ourselves as either straight or non-straight. ... We'll be gay until everyone has forgotten that it's an issue. Then we'll begin to be complete" (p. 381).

### The Emergence of Early Bisexual Groups

By the early 1970s, many bisexuals were tired of waiting to be whole people. Influenced by gay liberation politics, the civil rights movement feminist movements, and more liberal social attitudes toward sex, they began to come out publicly and establish their own organizations. The National Bisexual Liberation Group and Bi Forum were formed in New York City in the early 1970s and the San

Francisco Bisexual Center opened its doors in 1976. Early bisexual groups also developed in Los Angeles, Chicago, Detroit, Minneapolis, and Washington, D.C.

Contributing to the increased visibility of bisexuals were a spate of articles in popular magazines in the mid-1970s that proclaimed bisexuality as a fashionable new sexual trend that "everybody does now." With titles such as "Bisexual Life-Style Appears to Be Spreading and Not Necessarily Among 'Swingers'" (*New York Times*), "The New Bisexuals" (*Time*), "Bisexual Chic: Anything Goes" (*Newsweek*), and "Bisexuality: The Newest Sex-Style" (*Cosmopolitan*), these stories focused on the growing number of bi-identified celebrities including David Bowie, Mick Jagger, Kate Millett, and Joan Baez, and the gender-bending club scene in major U.S. cities. The articles ignored the rise of bisexual political activism, but in discussing the psychological, social, and cultural dimensions of bisexuality, this unprecedented national press coverage undoubtedly led some readers to recognize that they too were bisexual. Some of the first popular books on bisexuality were also published at this time, including Bernhardt J. Hurwood's *The Bisexuals* (1974), Julius Fast and Hal Wells's *Bisexual Living* (1975), Janet Bode's *View from Another Closet: Exploring Bisexuality in Women* (1976), and Fred (Fritz) Klein's *The Bisexual Option: A Concept of One-Hundred Percent Intimacy* (1978).

## The 1980s

Many of the early bisexual groups were run by and for married men, and all had disbanded by the mid–1980s, as AIDS began to affect bisexual men. Many bisexual male leaders became involved in AIDS activism, while a new generation of bisexual men largely stayed away from the movement as the mainstream media began to blame bisexual men for the spread of HIV to the heterosexual population through infecting their unsuspecting female partners. Magazines marketed to young, heterosexual women led the way in popularizing the stereotype of the deceitful, diseased bisexual man, with stories such as "The Risky Business of Bisexual Love" (*Cosmopolitan*) and "The Secret Life of Bisexual Husbands" (*Redbook*), but newspapers and television talk shows also helped turn bisexual men into what a *Newsweek* article described as "the ultimate pariahs" (Rodríguez Rust, 2000).

As bisexual men were leaving the movement and the first wave of bisexual organizations was folding, bisexual women were starting to found their own groups to support each other and to counter the hostility they increasingly received from many lesbian communities. Most had been active themselves in lesbian groups until lesbian separatism and a dichotomous view of sexuality became more entrenched in the late 1970s. Rather than being a woman-loving woman, a "lesbian" often began to be defined as a woman who did not have sex with men, forcing lesbians who sometimes had relationships with men to hide their sexual attraction, a situation that reminded them of the isolation and silencing they had experienced before coming out as lesbians. In subsequently identifying as bisexuals, they reclaimed pride in their sexuality and began to organize politically—methods that they had learned, ironically, from their involvement in the lesbian-feminist movement.

Although the women who emerged as leaders during the second wave of bisexual organizing rejected an exclusive lesbian politic, they remained committed to feminism, women's culture, and women-only spaces. As a result, feminist principles were central to the bisexual women's groups formed in the 1980s: the Boston Bisexual Women's Network (1983), the Chicago Action Bi-Women (1983), and the Seattle Bisexual Women's Network (1986). These organizations not only provided support and social opportunities, but also engaged in political activism and, in the case of the Boston and Seattle groups, published newsletters that reached bisexual women across the country.

The 1980s also saw the formation of mixed-gender bisexual political groups in San Francisco, Philadelphia, and Boston and the creation of the first regional bisexual organization, the East Coast Bisexual Network. The San Francisco group, the Bay Area Bisexual Network, produced the first national bisexual magazine, *Anything That Moves: Beyond the Myths of Bisexuality*, from 1991 through 2000. The East Coast Bisexual Network, which has since changed its name to the Bisexual Resource Center, serves as a national clearinghouse for bisexual material and publishes the Bisexual Resource Guide, an international listing of bisexual and bi-inclusive groups.

## Toward a National Bisexual Movement

A national bisexual movement began to take shape when a call for a bisexual contingent for the 1987 March on Washington for Lesbian and Gay Rights brought together seventy-five activists from around the country and laid the groundwork for the establishment of the North American Bisexual Network. The movement took further shape at the first national bisexual conference, held in San Francisco in 1990. The following year, the group's name was changed to BiNet U.S.A.

During the 1990s, BiNet fought biphobia in the popular press and increased the visibility of bisexuals, with members appearing on television talk shows and being quoted in mainstream and lesbian and gay newspapers and magazines. The organization also educated national lesbian and gay groups about the importance of using bi-inclusive language and recognizing the involvement of bisexuals in what was more appropriately called the lesbian, gay, bisexual, and transgender rights movement. One major victory was convincing lesbian and gay organizers to include bisexuals by name in the 1993 March on Washington and subsequently to have an openly bisexual speaker as part of the rally afterward. This was the first time that bisexuals had been acknowledged in a national political action (although lesbian and gay leaders would agree to add only the word "bi" to the march title, fearing that the word "bisexual" would overly sexualize the event). Another important success was the inclusion by the National Gay and Lesbian Task Force of bisexuals and transgender people in its mission statement and work. In 1997 it elected a self-identified bisexual to its board of directors—the first out bisexual to serve on the board of a national LGBT group.

The bisexual movement has also made significant progress on the local level. In the 1990s, the number of bisexual organizations in the United States grew tremendously, from several dozen groups established primarily on the coasts to more than three hundred located in every region of the country. As a result, bisexuals have created supportive communities throughout the United States, not just in major cities or at traditionally liberal universities. At the same time, the names and charters of many local lesbian and gay organizations, newspapers, and conferences have been changed to include bisexuals, as more bi-identified individuals have come out and, mirroring the national political scene, sought to have their involvement recognized. Many groups formed in the 1990s simply referred to themselves as "queer" in order to be inclusive of bisexuals and transgender people and often to challenge heteronormativity.

### The 1990s and Beyond

During this period, bisexuals began to make greater inroads into academia and literature. The first course on bisexuality was taught at the University of California at Berkeley in 1990, followed by courses at the Massachusetts Institute of Technology and Tufts University. These classes were accompanied by a boom in the number of books by and about bisexuality, especially anthologies of personal narratives and texts focusing on the experiences of bisexual women. Among the most influential works were Loraine Hutchins and Lani Kaahumanu's *Bi Any Other Name: Bisexual People Speak Out* (1991), Elizabeth Reba Weise's *Closer to Home: Bisexuality and Feminism*

(1992), the Bisexual Anthology Collective's *Plural Desires: Writing Bisexual Women's Realities* (1995), Naomi Tucker's *Bisexual Politics: Theories, Queries, and Visions* (1995), and Paula C. Rust's *Bisexuality and the Challenge to Lesbian Politics: Sex, Loyalty, and Revolution* (1995).

Bisexuality also received renewed attention in the mainstream press in the 1990s when bisexuality was characterized as a "new sexual identity" that would forever change how people view sexuality. "Unlike the 1970s, when popular magazines described bisexuality as a trendy sexual behavior that heterosexuals—and sometimes lesbians and gay men—were enjoying in increasing numbers, or the 1980s, when they described bisexuals as threats to the health of the nation, in the 1990s bisexuality was portrayed as a revolution not in sexual behavior but in the conceptualization of sexuality" (Rodríguez Rust, p. 545). As with the bisexual media moment of the early 1970s, the rediscovery of bisexuality partly reflected the visibility of a new generation of bisexual musicians and actors, including Ani Difranco, Jill Sobule, Michael Stipe, Sophie B. Hawkins, Me'Shell Ndege'Ocello, and Sandra Bernhard.

Because of the sustained prominence of bisexuals and bisexual groups and the inclusion of bisexuals in many formerly "lesbian and gay" campus and community organizations over the past decade, people growing up in the early twenty-first century generally have a much greater awareness of bisexuality than did previous generations. As a result, more youth today openly identify as bisexual when they first begin to acknowledge their sexuality, and do not feel compelled to come out as lesbian or gay or to emphasize heterosexual relationships, as did many of their predecessors.

**Bibliography**

Adam, Barry D. *The Rise of a Gay and Lesbian Movement.* Boston: Twayne Publishers, 1987.

Angelides, Steven. *A History of Bisexuality.* Chicago: University of Chicago Press, 2001.

Beemyn, Brett. "The New Negro Renaissance, A Bisexual Renaissance: The Lives and Works of Angelina Weld Grimké and Richard Bruce Nugent." In *Modern American Queer History.* Edited by Allida M. Black. Philadelphia: Temple University Press, 2001.

Donaldson, Stephen. "The Bisexual Movement's Beginnings in the 70s: A Personal Retrospective." In *Bisexual Politics: Theories, Queries, and Visions.* Edited by Naomi Tucker. Binghamton, N.Y.: Harrington Park Press, 1995.

Raymond, Dannielle, and Liz A. Highleyman. "Brief Timeline of Bisexual Activism in the United States." In *Bisexual Politics: Theories, Queries, and Visions.* Edited by Naomi Tucker. Binghamton, N.Y.: Harrington Park Press, 1995.

Rodríguez Rust, Paula C. *Bisexuality in the United States: A Social Science Reader.* New York: Columbia University Press, 2000.

Storr, Merl, ed. *Bisexuality: A Critical Reader.* New York: Routledge, 1999.

Udis-Kessler, Amanda. "Identity/Politics: A History of the Bisexual Movement." In *Bisexual Politics: Theories, Queries, and Visions.* Edited by Naomi Tucker. Binghamton, N.Y.: Harrington Park Press, 1995

Wittman, Carl. "A Gay Manifesto." In *We Are Everywhere: A Historical Sourcebook of Gay and Lesbian Politics.* Edited by Mark Blasius and Shane Phelan. New York: Routledge, 1997.

**Brett Beemyn**

*See also* ALLEN, PAULA GUNN; BENNETT, MICHAEL; CHEEVER, JOHN; CLASSICAL STUDIES;COLLEGES AND UNIVERSITIES, COMING OUT AND OUTING; CUKOR, GEORGE; CULTURAL STUDIES AND CULURAL THEORY; DANCE; DUNBAR-NELSON, ALICE; FEMMES AND BUTCHES; FEMINISM; GAY LIBERATION; GRIMKÉ, ANGELINA WELD; H.D.; HARLEM RENAISSANCE; HOMOPHILE MOVEMENT; LITERATURE; MCCULLERS, CARSON; MCKAY, CLAUDE; MEDICINE, MEDICALIZATION, AND THE MEDICAL MODEL; MILLETT, KATE; KING, BILLIE JEAN; KINSEY, ALFRED C.; PIÑERO, MIGUEL; PROSTITUTION, HUSTLING, AND SEX WORK; PSYCHOLOGY, PSYCHIATRY, PSYCHOANALYSIS, AND SEXOLOGY; PSYCHOTHERAPY, COUNSELING, AND RECOVERY PROGRAMS; QUEER THEORY AND QUEER STUDIES; RAINEY, MA; SEX ACTS; SHELLEY, MARTHA; SITUATIONAL HOMOSEXUALITY; SMITH, BESSIE; SOCIOLOGY; STEREOTYPES; TELEVISION; VISUAL ART; WITTMAN, CARL; YOURCENAR, MARGUERITE.

# BISHOP, Elizabeth (b. 8 February 1911; d. 6 October 1979), poet, translator, and author.

One of the greatest U.S. poets of the twentieth century, Elizabeth Bishop is respected and admired for writing verse that is technically precise and lush with vivid natural imagery. Her poems are contemplative and mysterious. Beneath their carefully crafted obscurity and cool detachment lie intense emotional undercurrents that intimate the great losses she endured during her life.

Bishop fell in love with many women and had numerous lesbian relationships. She shunned the public life, however, and was understandably secretive about her lesbianism at a time when homosexuality was considered a medical disorder and a cause for persecution. Lesbian and gay literary scholars find Bishop especially intriguing because her art resonates with same-sex desire underneath an obsessive determination to keep her lesbianism in the closet. The elusive, lapidary quality of her poems attests to her fear of exposure as a lesbian and her guilt and shame for the terrible losses she suffered.

Bishop was born in Worcester, Massachusetts. Her father, a wealthy businessman, died of Bright's disease when she was eight months old. Her mother, distraught from her husband's sudden death, lapsed into depression and mental illness. When Bishop was five years old, her mother was diagnosed as permanently insane and was hospitalized in a public sanatorium. Bishop never saw her mother again after her institutionalization. Amid the loving care of her maternal family in Great Village, Nova Scotia, she thrived until her affluent paternal grandparents took her away to live with them in Worcester, Massachusetts. There she became extremely ill with nervous ailments, asthma, and implacable loneliness. Her paternal grandparents gave her up to her mother's sister in Boston with whom she remained throughout her adolescence.

Bishop attended Vassar College, where she studied literature and established a campus literary magazine. In her senior year she met the poet Marianne Moore, and the two began a friendship that lasted for much of Bishop's life. Under Moore's mentorship, Bishop published her first book of poems, *North and South* (1946), the first of her five volumes of poetry. She earned numerous prizes, fellowships, and honors for her work. She won the Pulitzer Prize for *Poems: North and South—A Cold Spring* (1956); the National Book Award for *Questions of Travel* (1965); and the National Book Critics Circle Award for *Geography III* (1976). Although remarkably successful with her career, Bishop endured much unhappiness, and she continued to suffer from asthma and incapacitating depression, turning to alcohol to assuage her physical pain and the ordeal of separation and loneliness.

Supported by wealth from her father's family, Bishop traveled extensively in Europe and the U.S. eastern seaboard. She owned a home in Key West, Florida, and lived there in the company of other women from 1936 to 1945. Yet it was a trip to South America that changed her life forever. In 1951 she won a fellowship that took her to Brazil. In Rio de Janeiro she met and fell in love with Lota de Macedo Soares, an architect, who nursed Bishop back to health after she became violently ill from eating the Brazilian cashew fruit. Bishop remained in Brazil living with Soares for the next fifteen years, writing much poetry and prose, including the translation of a journal by a young woman, *The Diary of Helena Morley* (1957).

Racial relations in Brazil affected Bishop profoundly. She praised the country for what she believed was its progressive antiracism, and published articles for Brazilian papers that voiced her dismay and condemnation of racial injustice and oppression in the United States. She

**Elizabeth Bishop.** The critically acclaimed but reticent American poet in 1956, shortly after being awarded an international prize for literature. [Library of Congress]

wrote about race relations in her poetry, especially in her last book *Geography III,* whose poems describe an American child's disturbing encounter with photos of nude African women in *National Geographic* ("In the Waiting Room"), interracial love between two men ("Crusoe in England"), and the Western media's dehumanizing portrayal of black natives ("12 O'Clock News").

Bishop's relationship with Soares ended tragically when the two of them both suffered mental breakdowns in Brazil. After hospitalization, Bishop left for New York and Soares later joined her. In the United States, Soares continued to suffer depression, and she committed suicide, overdosing on tranquilizers while Bishop slept next to her. The death of her lover devastated Bishop for the remainder of her life. Amid this time of unhappiness, however, her reputation as a poet excelled, and she went on to write and publish until her death by cerebral aneurysm while teaching at Harvard.

During the rise of the feminist movement in the 1960s and 1970s, Bishop refused to be included in anthologies of women's writing because she objected to a patriarchal literary tradition that neglected and devalued the poetry and prose of women as "women's writing." Although she never revealed her lesbianism to the public, Bishop completed a fascinating oeuvre that includes such queer themes as gender inversion, transvestitism, same-sex desire, and interracial eroticism.

### Bibliography

Fountain, Gary. "'Closets, Closets, and More Closets' Elizabeth Bishop's Lesbianism." In *Queer Representations: Reading Lives, Reading Cultures. A Center for Lesbian and Gay Studies Book.* Edited by Martin Duberman. New York; London: New York University Press, 1997, 247–257.

Millier, Brett C. *Elizabeth Bishop: Life and the Memory of It.* Berkeley: University of California Press, 1993.

Oliveira, Carmen L. *Rare and Commonplace Flowers: The Story of Elizabeth Bishop and Lota de Macedo Soares.* Translated by Neil K. Besner. New Brunswick, N.J.; London: Rutgers University Press, 2002.

**Jeffrey Santa Ana**

*See also* LITERATURE

# BLACK AND WHITE MEN TOGETHER (BWMT)

Black and White Men Together is a social and political group established in 1980 in San Francisco. Its principal founder, Michael Smith, had two main motivations for launching the organization. One was his sexual attraction to black men (Smith was white). As was the case in the United States generally, those who wanted to cross racial lines for sexual or social interaction sometimes faced disapproval or hostility within queer male communities. In this climate, there were few public places where such people could comfortably interact. Smith's second motivation was related to other forms of racism he saw. Few queer male bars and other businesses employed people of color, and some used practices like carding (requiring particular forms of identification for admission) to discourage nonwhite patronage. In the queer media, there were few representations of people of color, and queer publications often ran "whites only" employment and housing ads.

To change this, Smith sought out fellow interracialists by placing ads in the *Advocate* newsmagazine. By the summer of 1980, chapters of Black and White Men Together had formed in San Francisco, New York, Boston, and Chicago. A year later chapters from across the country met in San Francisco and formed what would become the National Association of Black and White Men

Together (BWMT). Twenty years later the organization boasted more than thirty chapters. Together, they have provided safe meeting spaces, networking opportunities, and other resources for those interested in cross-cultural interaction.

Antiracism and other forms of social activism have been an important part of BWMT's agenda, especially at the national level. To ensure that whites do not dominate leadership positions, the group's charter mandates multicultural parity at all levels, and special efforts have been made to recruit and train nonwhites for leadership roles. As a result, several people of color, including John Teamer and Phill Wilson, have become influential members. Some chapters have been particularly active in countering racism, especially within queer male communities. For example, the New York City and Los Angeles chapters have conducted sting operations in conjunction with other antiracism groups. They targeted clubs that were suspected of restricting the number of nonwhites they admitted. Clubs that discriminated were picketed, sued, or served with formal complaints. Nationally, BWMT has held antiracism workshops and consciousness-raising sessions at its annual conventions. In 1996 the organization created the Multiracial/Multicultural Institute to develop antiracism educational programming. To address the lack of attention given to HIV/AIDS among people of color, BWMT created the Task Force on AIDS Prevention.

Although the national organization has retained its original title, some chapters have changed their names to Men of All Colors Together or People of All Colors Together to reflect a broader multicultural vision. The name changes have been controversial. When the New York City chapter decided to become Men of All Colors Together and proposed at the 1987 convention that the national organization do the same, many, including founder Michael Smith, were bitterly opposed to what they saw as a shift away from the group's original focus. This did not, however, stop several chapters from following New York City's lead.

Some people, especially more Afrocentrically inclined blacks like Cleo Manago, have been critical of BWMT. They have accused it of being nothing more than a sex club that promotes racist forms of interracial desire. That is, white members were thought to want only blacks who fit certain stereotypes (hypermasculine, wildly passionate, and well endowed) or to want blacks only in certain contexts (for casual sex or in relationships where the white partner is socially or economically dominant). Blacks, especially if they had an exclusive sexual interest in whites or socialized primarily in white queer commu-

nities, were seen as hating themselves and their race. Some have also accused the group of imposing what they see as white cultural values, practices, and political agendas on individuals, groups, and businesses that claim to serve black queer communities. Among those believed to have been affected are *BLK* magazine and the Black Lesbian and Gay Leadership Forum. Finally, critics of BWMT have claimed that its programming has only reached blacks who socialize primarily within white-dominated queer communities, who supposedly constitute a minority of blacks who are "in the life."

Group members have often found themselves on the defensive, trying to explain their mission and to break down stereotypes. In part, this reflects the fact that cross-cultural interaction is still often stigmatized in America. Nevertheless, BWMT remains an important organization committed to integrating queer America.

## Bibliography

Banneker, Revon Kyle. "Rev. Carl Bean." *BLK*, July 1989, 8–17.

Bell, Alan. "Cleo Manago." *BLK*, March 1990, 7–18.

Jordan, L. Lloyd. "Black Gay vs. Gay Black." *BLK*, June 1990, 25–30.

Manago, Cleo. "The Various Colors and Sexualities of White Supremacy." *SBC*, March–April 1996, 20–21.

"Multiracial/Multicultural Institute." Available from http://www.nabwmt.com.

Smith, Michael J., ed. *Black Men/White Men: A Gay Anthology.* San Francisco: Gay Sunshine Press, 1983.

**Gregory Conerly**

*See also* AFRICAN AMERICANS; AIDS SERVICE ORGANIZATIONS; INTERRACIAL AND INTERETHNIC SEX AND RELATIONSHIPS; RACE AND RACISM.

# BONNET, Jeanne (b. 1849; d. 14 September 1876), frog catcher, thief.

The life of Jeanne Bonnet, a female-to-male transgender criminal in late-nineteenth-century San Francisco who led a gang of former prostitutes turned thieves, illustrates the harassments and dangers facing working-class women who dressed in male attire.

Born in Paris in 1849, Bonnet moved some time later to the booming city of San Francisco to work with his family as part of the French Theatrical Troupe. As a youth, he began to get into trouble with the law. His exact crimes are unknown, but he may have been a petty thief. The city fathers committed Bonnet to the Industrial School, which served as San Francisco's first reformatory.

Upon his release around 1870, Bonnet put his light fingers to use catching frogs in the marshes of San Mateo County for the dinner plates of Bay Area residents. He received the nickname the "Little Frog Catcher," presumably for his petite build. Bonnet abandoned this line of work after a few years.

By this point, Bonnet had gained considerable notoriety among the people of San Francisco as a cross-dresser. While in his mid-teens, he concluded that he hated having the body of a woman. As a young adult, Bonnet wore shortly cropped hair, spoke with a deep-pitched voice, and always dressed in a boy's suit. The police arrested him more than twenty times for wearing the attire of the opposite sex. Each arrest resulted in a fine, which Bonnet consistently refused to pay. He frequently served time in jail.

A small frame may have made it difficult for Bonnet to disguise his sex, but he appears to have also refused to hide. Displaying a macho streak, he challenged the police to continue to arrest him by stating publicly that he would never abandon male clothing.

Bonnet's class status and criminal history may have played a role in his inability to evade police harassment. Other transgender women, notably fellow Californian Babe Bean, a contemporary, also had repeated encounters with the police. Bean eluded arrest because of his respectability, but Bonnet's background meant that he could not escape more significant trouble.

Bonnet began visiting brothels about 1875. Of the three types of brothels that could be found in San Francisco, parlor houses offered the most refined entertainment as well as the youngest and prettiest prostitutes. Bonnet became a frequent customer of these establishments. Madame Johanna Werner's brothel, locally famous for the peep show performances of three French girls known as the Three Lively Fleas, was a particularly favorite stop for the French immigrant.

In 1876, having dropped frog catching as livelihood, Bonnet resumed his old habit of thievery. This time he organized and led an all-female gang of about a dozen young shoplifters and petty thieves. Headquartered in a shack south of Market Street on an unfrequented part of the waterfront, the gang consisted of former prostitutes. When they abandoned prostitution, these women had also abandoned all sexual dealings with men.

Bonnet had vowed to rescue as many women from prostitution as possible, but in doing so he took income away from the brothel owners as well as from the boyfriends who had once lived off the prostitutes. While women who labored in the brothels known as cribs and cow-yards made comparatively little money, the prostitutes who worked in the higher-class parlor houses could earn a considerable annual sum. As a habitué of parlor houses, Bonnet presumably chose most of his gang members from this elite group.

One of the gangsters was fellow French immigrant Blanche Buneau. Bonnet's close friend and presumed lover, Buneau had come to San Francisco from Paris in 1875 with Arthur Deneve. She had supported Deneve with her earnings as a prostitute until Bonnet persuaded her to adopt the healthier occupation of a thief.

Deneve and other pimps repeatedly threatened and attacked Bonnet for interfering with their livelihoods by stealing away their women. On 14 September 1876, Bonnet went to his room at the San Miguel Saloon, about four miles outside of San Francisco. He expected to spend the night with Buneau. Bonnet smoked a pipe, drank a glass of cognac, and removed his suit and hat in preparation for bed. A shot crashed through the glass of the window and entered his heart. He died immediately. The killing was never solved, though not for a lack of suspects. While Bonnet's death robbed San Francisco of one of its more colorful citizens, the murder also served to emphasize the violence directed at working-class transgender women.

## Bibliography

Asbury, Herbert. *The Barbary Coast: An Informal History of the San Francisco Underworld.* New York: Knopf, 1933.

Rupp, Leila J. *A Desired Past: A Short History of Same-Sex Love in America.* Chicago: University of Chicago Press, 1999.

San Francisco Lesbian and Gay History Project. "'She Even Chewed Tobacco': A Pictorial Narrative of Passing Women in America." In *Hidden from History: Reclaiming the Gay and Lesbian Past.* Edited by Martin Duberman, Martha Vicinus, and George Chauncey, Jr. New York: Penguin, 1989.

**Caryn E. Neumann**

*See also* BEAN, BABE; PROSTITUTION, HUSTLING, AND SEX WORK; TRANSSEXUALS, TRANSVESTITES, TRANSGENDER PEOPLE, AND CROSS-DRESSERS.

# BOOKSTORES

Books by and about LGBT people are indispensable sources of information, validation, and growth for LGBT individuals and their communities. The same is true of LGBT bookstores, which made large numbers of LGBT books available for the first time in "regular" bookstores rather than in adult bookstores or on the drugstore racks on which pulp paperbacks were sold. LGBT bookstores typically do more than sell books; they are de facto community centers, queer spaces where a person can meet others like him or herself, find information about local LGBT events and organizations, and attend book signings and other cultural programs.

## 1940s–1960s: The Way Is Prepared

The earliest LGBT bookstores in the United States opened in the late 1960s and early 1970s in the wake of gains made by the homophile movement, and, just as significantly, a proliferation of published works by and about LGBT people that had begun in the 1940s. The earliest of these were literary novels by gay male authors including Gore Vidal, James Baldwin, and Truman Capote. However, during the Cold War era, LGBT-themed literary works like these hardly reached a wide audience. Libraries refused to buy them, bookstores refused to stock them, and LGBT people outside urban areas were largely unaware of their existence. Obscenity laws presented another problem, as they allowed for the arrest and prosecution of publishers and sellers of LGBT-themed books.

The post–World War II era was also the era of paperback "pulp" novels, cheap to produce as well as to buy, and sold not in bookstores but on racks in drugstores, dime stores, and bus stations. Many of these novels were about "social problems" of the day, including homosexuality. As Michael Bronski and Ian Young have pointed out, the pulps first provided many Americans—including LGBT Americans—with information about LGBT life. A third category of books with LGBT content arose after a series of legal decisions in the years from 1959 to 1966 eviscerated existing obscenity laws, clearing the way for the publication of works with sexually explicit content, many of which were aimed at the gay male consumer. These gay erotic novels were sold not on drugstore racks but in adult bookstores and other venues, and they were widely read.

## 1967–1980s: The Time Is Right

By the late 1960s, a LGBT readership had developed, a body of work with LGBT themes existed (although much of it was deemed of little or no literary merit), obscenity laws were no longer an obstacle, and the sexual revolution had begun. It was in this climate that, in 1967, owner-operator Craig Rodwell opened the first LGBT bookstore in the United States. Rodwell named his New York City store the Oscar Wilde Memorial Bookshop and identified it as a queer space by placing in its window a "Gay Is

Good" sticker underneath a sign that read "A Bookshop for the Homophile Movement." From the bookstore's original location on Mercer Street (it later moved to Christopher Street in Greenwich Village), Rodwell organized a march in June 1970 to commemorate the first anniversary of the Stonewall Riots, giving birth to the annual LGBT pride celebrations that now take place nationwide.

The gay liberation and lesbian feminist movements that arose in the wake of the Stonewall Riots opened a broader political, cultural, and social space in which LGBT bookstores could develop and operate. Inspired by Rodwell's success with Oscar Wilde, gay men opened bookstores in Philadelphia (Jay's Place, 1969, Giovanni's Room, 1973), Washington, D.C. (Lambda Rising, 1974), Los Angeles (A Different Light, 1979), and other cities across the country. Although these early bookstores catered primarily to gay men (and lesbians routinely registered complaints about this fact), lesbians were at the same time entering the bookselling business via a separate path. Beginning in the early 1970s, the second-wave women's movement gave rise to the development of feminist bookstores, the majority of which were owned and operated by lesbian feminists. Like LGBT bookstores, feminist bookstores have always been vital parts of the feminist and lesbian communities in which they are located. The first such bookstore, Amazon Bookstore Cooperative, opened in Minneapolis, Minnesota, in 1970. It was followed in quick succession by Common Language in Ann Arbor, Michigan, in 1972; and New Words in Cambridge, Massachusetts, Antigone in Tucson, Arizona, in 1973; and Charis Books and More in Atlanta, Georgia, in 1974.

## 1980s and After: The Price of Success?

Since the 1970s, LGBT bookstores have continued to proliferate; by 1999 more than ninety were in existence nationwide. And as mainstream publishers noted the demand for books aimed at the LGBT consumer, more and more such books were published. A Different Light Bookstore in New York City, for example, stocked about 5,000 LGBT titles in the early 1980s; by the end of the 1990s, the number of titles had grown to over 23,000, according to the former owner, Norman Laurila.

Today, LGBT bookstores have become to some extent victims of their own success. Having demonstrated that there is a market for LGBT books, some stores have lost market share and seen their prices undercut by bookstore chains such as Barnes and Noble that can sell at discounts and invest large sums in advertising. Online sellers such as Amazon.com also sell LGBT books at prices that independent, locally owned stores cannot match. To counter this threat, some LGBT bookstores depend on sales of videos, CDs, rainbow flags and bumper stickers, and jewelry in addition to books. Some owners have used funds from other enterprises or stores to subsidize their bookstores or have branched out into Internet sales. Others, like the lesbian-feminist bookstore Charis Books in Atlanta, have nonprofit arms that raise funds to subsidize their bookselling.

Still, several venerable LGBT bookstores have closed their doors in recent years; A Different Light in New York and Different Drummer Books in Laguna Beach, California closed in 2001 and 2002, respectively, and the Oscar Wilde Bookstore was slated to close in early 2003 before Deacon Maccubin, owner of Lambda Rising in Washington, D.C., agreed to buy it and keep it open. New Words in Cambridge also closed its doors in 2002, reopening in 2003 as the Non-Profit Center for New Words.

Whether or not the number of LGBT bookstores in the United States is currently declining, one thing is clear: these stores remain vital to LGBT people and communities. Although chain and online bookstores have some advantages—they allow someone who is not openly LGBT to purchase LGBT books anonymously, for example—they are neither queer spaces nor community resources. Moreover, their staff usually lack expertise in LGBT books and are less helpful with difficult-to-find books and magazines. For all these reasons, it is likely that as long as there are LGBT people and LGBT books, there will be LGBT bookstores.

### Bibliography

Bronski, Michael. "Fictions about Pulp." *Gay and Lesbian Review Worldwide* 8, no. 6 (November–December 2001): 18–20.

Bronski, Michael. "The Paradox of Gay Publishing." *Publisher's Weekly* 249, No. 34 (26 August 2002): 27–31.

Chesnut, Saralyn, and Amanda C. Gable. "'Women Ran It': Charis Books and More and Atlanta's Lesbian-Feminist Community, 1971–1981." In *Carryin' On in the Lesbian and Gay South.* Edited by John Howard. New York: New York University Press, 1997.

High, John. "A New Dawn at A Different Light." *Publisher's Weekly* 248, No.7 (12 February 2001): 91-92.

Stein, Marc. *City of Sisterly and Brotherly Loves: Lesbian and Gay Philadelphia, 1945-1972.* Chicago: University Of Chicago Press, 2000.

Rosen, Judith. "My Sister's Next Wave." *Publisher's Weekly* 249, No. 46 (18 November 2002): 24.

Santora, Mark. "Plot Twist for a Gay Bookstore: The Last Chapter Actually Isn't." *New York Times,* 4 February 2003, B3.

Young, Ian. "How Gay Paperbacks Changed America." *Gay and Lesbian Review Worldwide* 8, no. 6 (November–December 2001): 14–17.

Saralyn Chesnut

*See also* BUSINESSES; CENSORSHIP, OBSCENITY, AND PORNOGRAPHY LAW AND POLICY; RODWELL, CRAIG; PORNOGRAPHY; PRIDE MARCHES AND PARADES; PULP FICTION: GAY; PULP FICTION: LESBIAN.

## BOOZER, Melvin (b. 1945; d. 6 March 1987), activist.

Melvin Boozer grew up and spent most of his life in Washington, D.C. The second oldest of three siblings, he was raised by his mother and stepfather. After graduating from Dunbar High School in 1963, he went to Dartmouth College on a scholarship. His social consciousness was awakened there and he became politically active, especially in the antiwar movement. After graduating with a sociology degree in 1967, Boozer spent several years in Brazil working for the Peace Corps. While there, he began to act on the homosexual desires of which he had been aware since childhood.

When Boozer returned to the United States, he did graduate work at Oberlin College and Yale University. While at Yale, he began to explore Greenwich Village's queer community, though he still dated women. He also became active in Yale's queer political scene.

A teaching job at the University of Maryland took Boozer back to Washington in the mid-1970s. There he also became involved in the local Gay Activists Alliance (GAA). Many of his family and friends, however, were still unaware that he was gay. That changed in 1979, when his election as president of the local GAA, as well as his participation in the first lesbian and gay March on Washington, put him in the media spotlight. He was featured in the *Washington Post* and several local television shows.

Nationally, Boozer was probably best known for his efforts to increase awareness of queer issues within the Democratic Party. His greatest success occurred when he participated in the 1980 Democratic National Convention in New York City. As part of the Gay and Lesbian Caucus, he helped fight for changes in the party's charter and platform that included civil rights protections based on sexual orientation. The Caucus then organized to have Boozer become a nominee for vice president. They did so not because they thought he had a chance of being elected to the party's ticket with President Jimmy Carter, but because it would mean he would have the chance to address the convention and confront the party's reluctance to deal with sexuality as a human rights issue. Through the Caucus's efforts, Boozer became the first openly gay candidate for the vice-presidential nomination. In his 14 August address to the convention, he helped cement the place of homosexual rights on the national political stage. He said,

> I know what it means to be called a nigger. And I know what it means to be called a faggot, and I understand the difference in the marrow of my bones. And I can sum up that difference in one word: none. Bigotry is bigotry. Discrimination is discrimination. It hurts just as much. It dishonors our way of life just as much, and it betrays a common lack of understanding, fairness and compassion just as much. (Boozer, p. 6)

Until his death, Boozer continued to play a role in national politics, most notably as the head of the National Gay and Lesbian Task Force's Washington office in the early 1980s and through his involvement in Jesse Jackson's 1984 presidential campaign. He was most active, however, in the Washington local political scene. Between 1979 and 1981 he served as president of the area's GAA. In 1982, he helped found the mostly black and queer Langston Hughes–Eleanor Roosevelt Democratic Club. Through these groups he worked on a number of issues, including improving relations between queers and local police, protesting discrimination in government institutions, and working with politicians like the Washington mayor, Marion Barry.

Boozer's involvement in the Hughes–Roosevelt Club reflected a shift in his political ideals. Until that point, he had been guided by an integrationist vision. This led him to work within established political groups, whether it was mostly white queer groups or traditional parties. He encouraged black queers to do the same, so that they could become more visible and help shape the political agenda of white queer communities. Some black queers, however, were critical of Boozer. They claimed that white queers were using him and that he had become alienated from other blacks. The new Democratic Club allowed Boozer to work more closely with black queers while still maintaining his integrationist focus.

Melvin Boozer died in 1987 of an AIDS-related illness. His life and work have been recognized in several ways. He was honored in 1987 by the city of Washington; he has two panels on the AIDS Quilt; and in 1988 a coalition of local AIDS organizations named their group the Melvin Boozer Leadership Roundtable.

## Bibliography

Boozer, Melvin. "Text of Mel Boozer's Convention Speech." *Washington Blade*, 21 August 1980.

Brinkley, Sidney. "Interview with Melvin Boozer." *Blacklight Online* 2, no. 2. Available from http://www.blacklightonline.com.

Leavitt, Don. "Coming Out to an Entire City." *Washington Blade*, 25 October 1979.

Morgan, Thomas. "A Black Gay Leader Speaks Out." *Washington Post*, 13 October 1979.

Pearson, Richard. "Homosexual Rights Activist Melvin Boozer Dies at 41." *Washington Post*, 10 March 1987.

**Gregory Conerly**

*See also* DEMOCRATIC PARTY; ELECTORAL POLITICS; GAY ACTIVISTS ALLIANCE; NATIONAL GAY AND LESBIAN TASK FORCE.

# BOSTON

Boston's European colonial founders lived in a world circumscribed by political and religious attempts to regulate behavior that did not conform to the Puritan belief system. Same-sex sexual acts were regarded as sins, as were sexual relations between a woman and a man outside of marriage. Such transgressions were punishable by fines, whipping, and standing in the pillory.

## The Colonial Setting

Puritan settlers established the town of Boston in 1630. The native population called the area Shawmut. The belief systems of Puritans and Native Americans were antithetical. Some local Native American men, including those from tribes related to the Wampanoag and the Iroquois, dressed, worked, and spoke as women and may have been shamans or spiritual leaders. Native Americans lived in close proximity to colonists, but when colonists were not successful in converting natives to Christianity, they pushed the natives into outlying areas of the Massachusetts Bay Colony. By the end of the seventeenth century, the region's native population had been decimated by disease, slavery, and war.

At the same time, Boston's Puritan leaders were devising laws to govern their colony by combining elements of British common law with Old Testament law. The 1649 Province Laws of Massachusetts classified sodomy as a capital crime. Unless the defendant in such cases pled guilty, there had to be at least two witnesses to the act, an important modification of English law. Few individuals were successfully prosecuted for sodomy in Boston and its surrounding towns. More commonly, men and women were prosecuted for lewd and lascivious acts or unnatural behaviors. In 1649, Sarah Norman was brought before the Court in New Plymouth Colony "for misdemeanor and lude behavior with Mary Hammon uppon a bed, with divers lasivious speeches by her allso spoken." In another case that came before the same court in 1649, Richard Berry accused Teage Jones of sodomy. Berry later testified that he had made a false accusation and was sentenced "to be whipte at the poste." Three years later both men "and others with them" were ordered to "part theire uncivell living together" (*The History Project,* 18–20). Some Puritan leaders, including Michael Wigglesworth (1631–1705) and Thomas Shepard (1605–1649), wrote of lustful feelings toward male students. Wigglesworth kept a diary in which he recorded his feelings. Shepard wrote about "secret Whoredom, Self-pollution, and speculative Wantonness, men with men or woman with woman" (quoted in Godbeer, p. 264).

Colonial leaders also attempted to control nonnormative gender practices. Following the prosecution of several women for wearing men's clothing, the Massachusetts General Court enacted a law in 1695 prohibiting the wearing of the apparel of the opposite sex. By the early nineteenth century, appearing in public in masquerade (hiding or altering one's appearance) was also against the law. (Some of these laws continued to be enforced into the 1960s.) Some Boston women may have chosen to disguise themselves as men in order to work in male occupations or join the army. Ann Bailey enlisted in the Boston Regiment of the Continental Army in February 1777 under the alias of Samuel Gay. She was quickly discovered to be female, and for wearing male apparel was arrested and charged with fraud. Deborah Samson, alias Robert Shurtleff, joined the Continental Army in 1782 and served until 1783, when she was discharged honorably.

## Transformations: The Late Eighteenth and Nineteenth Centuries

By the middle of the eighteenth century, Boston had grown significantly as a seaport with a population of over seventeen thousand. The North End and West End (Beacon Hill) were inhabited by the town's small African American population as well as by white poor and working-class residents. Both areas were viewed by law enforcement and the growing middle classes as centers of brothels and dens of vice. Two incidents involving same-sex sexual behaviors among members of Boston's elite, however, achieved notoriety. In 1760, future U.S. President John Adams wrote in his diary of a deacon who was "discovered to have been the most salacious, ram-

pant, Stallion, in the Universe . . . , lodging with this and that Boy and Attempting at least the crime of Buggery." In 1771 Adams was the defense attorney in *John Gray* v. *Lendall Pitts.* Pitts had mistaken Gray for a woman, and when he learned of his error gave Pitts a beating. A witness testified, "I saw him dressed in women's cloaths. I saw a couple of young gentlemen gallanting him. Pitts was one. . . . They appeared to be very loving, she rather coy. I called out to Pitts. . . . He turned a deaf Ear. He came back and said he had a very clever Girl, and went to her again" (Wroth and Zobel, eds. p. 157–161.). While these kinds of incidents did have legal repercussions, there was a level of tolerance of such behaviors that would change drastically in the nineteenth century.

Some middle- and upper-class men in this period adopted a style of colorful and expensive European dress. Portrayed in the popular press as dandies and macaronis, they wore foppish clothes, copied the effeminate styles of English and Parisian fops, and influenced later U.S. and British decadents and aesthetes such as Oscar Wilde. At the same time, a growing middle class allowed more men the freedom to remain unmarried, and bachelorhood became less peculiar. Bachelorhood even attained a level of public acceptance with the publication in Boston of the *Bachelors' Journal* (1828).

Though such behaviors were indulged in by only a small number of men, the trend reflected economic transformations that also contributed to the emergence of more clearly defined separate spheres for women and men. Middle-class men's lives were spent primarily in the political and mercantile milieu, all-male surroundings, while middle-class women typically spent their lives in a more private world, away from their fathers, brothers, and husbands. In this context, intense same-sex friendships became the norm for both men and women. The Boston Transcendentalist authors, including Ralph Waldo Emerson, Louisa May Alcott, Margaret Fuller, and Henry David Thoreau, wrote about their passionate same-sex feelings. Walt Whitman visited Boston in 1860, a few years after publication of the homoerotic *Leaves of Grass,* and received an enthusiastic reception. Later in the century, however, several Boston Brahmins pronounced Whitman's work "obscene" (*The History Project,* p. 50).

Middle-class women tended to their children and households and spent their leisure time with female relatives and women friends. While it is not known to what extent these friendships were sexual, we have considerable evidence that male and female couples expressed their deep and passionate feelings for each other and remained close throughout their lives. Some women, most notably the actor Charlotte Cushman and her circle of "emanci-

**Impuritan Thought.** John O'Brien's cartoon humorously touches on censorious attitudes that persisted in Boston long after the colonial era of stocks (a probably unwelcome form of bondage). [**The New Yorker**]

pated females," which included the sculptors Harriet Hosmer and Edmonia Lewis, had the economic independence to live in Europe, where they had the freedom to work as artists and live with other women. Other female couples lived in fashionable Back Bay or Beacon Hill. Long-term same-sex intimate relationships became known as "Boston marriages." Some examples were the relationships of Annie Adams Fields and the writer Sarah Orne Jewett; the sculptor Anne Whitney and the painter Abby Adeline Manning; and the poet Amy Lowell and the actress Ada Dwyer Russell.

Meanwhile, in male universities such as Harvard, popular theater groups, including the Hasty Pudding Club, often featured female impersonation. Women who attended women's colleges such as Simmons, Mount Holyoke, Wellesley, and Smith commonly formed romantic friendships with classmates and enjoyed satiric masquerading as men, even performing mock weddings.

The nineteenth century closed with the privileged classes enjoying a certain range of lifestyle choices. An important shift, however, took place before the turn of the twentieth century. In 1805 the state's General Court had amended the law against sodomy, abolishing the death penalty and substituting the sentence of ten years imprisonment. In 1887 legislation was enacted against "unnatural lewd and lascivious acts," with one section declaring that "it was not necessary to list what these acts were." This law was used to arrest and prosecute prostitutes as well as individuals involved in same-sex consen-

sual sex. The law also expanded the state's earlier sodomy statute by including oral along with anal sex.

In the years after passage of the law, the number of arrests for unnatural lewd and lascivious acts rose considerably. Many of those arrested lived in rooming houses in the South End or Beacon Hill and worked as clerks; others were cooks, housecleaners, teachers, hairdressers, musicians, or college students. Ten percent of all arrests in Boston for unnatural acts between 1889 and 1899 were women. In many cases, Boston police entered residences, usually without a warrant, upon observing an unusual number of men entering a building or hearing from informants (such as operatives of the Watch and Ward Society, an anti-vice organization). The police also entrapped men in subway and department store bathrooms and hid in areas of the Public Gardens where they believed that immoral and lewd acts occurred.

By the early twentieth century, middle- and upperclass women such as Eleanora Sears could wear malestyled suits in public without fear of arrest. Poor and working-class women who cross-dressed, however, were subject to arrest. A number of women who passed as men were discovered when they were reported to law enforcement officials by landlords or coworkers or when they had a medical emergency. Some of these women were committed to institutions such as the Boston Psychiatric Hospital. Ethel Kimball, who went by the name James Hathaway and who wed Louise Aechtler in Boston in 1921, was unmasked while attempting to buy a car a year after the wedding. Hathaway was charged with falsification of a marriage license. Aechtler claimed that she had been unaware of Hathaway's true identity.

## The Early Twentieth Century

By the turn of the twentieth century, the medical profession in general and psychiatrists in particular increasingly regarded same-sex sexual acts as symptoms of pathological and deviant conditions. In 1898 *The Boston Medical and Surgical Journal* published an essay by a Massachusetts doctor who recommended that "inverts" in whom homosexuality was innate should be sent to mental hospitals, while "perverts" who demonstrated these tendencies should be imprisoned for the protection of society: "There is a community not far removed . . . , men of perverted tendencies, men known to each other as such, bound by ties of secrecy and fear and held together by mutual attraction. . . . To themselves they draw boys and young men over whom they have the same jealous bickerings and heart burnings that attend the triumphs of a local belle" (*History Project,* p. 102).

Not all physicians, however, shared these views. The German physician Magnus Hirschfeld, the leader of the first homosexual emancipation organization, published a letter he had received in 1908 from an anonymous Boston correspondent: "And how many homosexuals I've come to know! Boston, this good old Puritan city, has them by the hundreds. The largest percentage, in my experience, comes from the Yankees of Massachusetts and Maine, or from New Hampshire; French Canadians are also well represented. Here, as in Germany, homosexuality extends throughout all classes, from the slums of the North End to the highly fashionable Back Bay. Reliable homosexuals have told me names that reach into the highest circles of Boston." This letter is not only an evocative description of life in Boston; it is also one of the earliest examples of the written use of the term "homosexual" (*History Project,* pp. 101–102).

In the early part of the twentieth century, elite men could still engage in same-sex social and sexual encounters in their own homes or in private men's clubs located in Back Bay and Beacon Hill. Working-class men interested in same-sex encounters frequented more public areas, such as the theaters, bars, and restaurants centered in Scollay Square and the South Cove (now Chinatown). They drew on a code of words and signs to communicate with other gay men. Working-class lesbians in Boston frequented neighborhood bars, taverns, and social clubs, while middle- and working-class women alike attended private parties, which offered some protection from police raids and harassment from straight men.

By the 1920s Boston had several establishments that were known to be frequented by both gay men and lesbians. These included several speakeasies, such as the Brick Oven Tea Room, the Joy Barn, and the March Hare, all located on Beacon Hill. The Scollay Square area, adjacent to Beacon Hill, was another gathering place for LGBT people and a rendezvous point for sailors on shore leave who were seeking male sex partners. Several cheap hotels in the area provided rooms for rent by the hour. After Prohibition was repealed in 1933, more establishments began to attract a partially gay clientele. In Scollay Square the bar at the Crawford House was a popular gay venue, as was the nearby Pen and Pencil. Playland, which opened in 1938 in Chinatown, was the first bar in Boston whose customers were predominantly gay. By the late 1950s, Sporters on Beacon Hill had become a predominantly gay bar. Lesbians frequented Cavana's in the South End, the Empty Barrel in Bay Village, and Phil Harris's, later renamed the Punch Bowl, in Park Square.

In middle- and upper-class environments such as single-sex colleges and universities, women and men continued to form close intimate friendships and sexual relationships. In the spring of 1920, as a result of the suicide of a Harvard student in nearby Cambridge, evidence was presented to the university administration that there was a group of homosexuals on campus. A secret tribunal called "The Court" interrogated the students and faculty whose names were linked to this gay subculture. By the end of the "trial," fourteen men (eight undergraduates, one graduate student, a teacher, and four men not connected to Harvard) had been found guilty. All were told to leave the university and Cambridge. While a few of the students were allowed to re-enroll after a year or two, others were never reinstated, and all nine students as well as the teacher had permanent comments placed in their alumni files that indicated that they had committed an act or acts of moral turpitude (Paley).

## The Late Twentieth Century: LGBT Movements

In the 1950s, LGBT Bostonians began to organize politically and advocate LGBT rights in public. Boston's earliest and most notable openly gay man, Prescott Townsend (1894–1973), was born into a Boston Brahmin family and lived most of his life as a bohemian on Beacon Hill, where he was active in local theater productions. In the 1950s, Townsend participated in radio talk shows advocating change in the Massachusetts same-sex sex laws and he lobbied state legislators to repeal laws pertaining to chastity, morality, and good order. In the early 1960s he founded the Demophile Society (a homophile group) and several years later he organized a Boston chapter of the New York Mattachine Society. The chapter lasted only a few years before a split occurred, after which several members formed the Homophile Union of Boston (HUB) in 1969.

In the late 1960s, a new group of Boston LGBT activists, many of them veterans of the anti–Vietnam War and civil rights movements, established some of the first gay liberation groups in the country. While the 1969 Stonewall Riots in New York galvanized national LGBT activism, a generation of LGBT activists had already begun to lay the foundation for the organization and institution building of the 1970s. In Boston, a chapter of the national Daughters of Bilitis (DOB), a lesbian group, was founded in 1969 and is now the only chapter of DOB still in existence. By 1970, the Student Homophile League had chapters at several local colleges and universities in the Boston area.

At the National Mobilization Against the War demonstration on Boston Common, held on 15 April 1970, the Gay Liberation Front carried a banner reading: "BRING THE BOYS HOME NOW, Gay Liberation Front," causing some consternation among both bystanders and fellow marchers. In June 1970, Boston held its first Gay Liberation Week, consisting of a series of lectures and discussions culminating in a "Love In" on the Cambridge Common. In the early twenty-first century, the Lesbian, Gay, Bisexual and Transgender Pride parade is an annual event that attracts over 120,000 people.

By the mid-1970s Boston's LGBT community had created a significant number of organizations, support groups, and institutions. LGBT activists continued to work toward the repeal of the state's sodomy and unnatural acts laws. In 2002 the Massachusetts Supreme Judicial Court ruled that the state's sodomy statutes could not be enforced unless the individuals engaged in the acts had known that they could be seen by others. The June 2003 decision of the U.S. Supreme Court in *Lawrence* v. *Texas* may have nullified the Massachusetts sodomy laws. In 1989 Massachusetts became the second state in the country to pass laws prohibiting discrimination on the basis of sexual preference in insurance, credit, and employment. In the mid-1980s, Boston adopted a domestic partnership ordinance. Under this law, a city employee could officially declare a "domestic partnership" and qualify for family employee benefits for the partner, including medical coverage. In 2000, however, the Massachusetts Supreme Judicial Court, ruling that only the state legislature had jurisdiction over medical coverage, struck down the law. In 2002, Boston passed legislation prohibiting discrimination against transgender people in employment, housing, and credit.

While efforts to change anti-LGBT laws continue to be a focus of many LGBT people, activists have organized around other issues, too. In March 1971 over one hundred women took over a former knitting factory in Cambridge that was owned by Harvard University. The women occupied the building for ten days to protest Harvard's control over local housing and real estate. For many, the event was an exhilarating and defining moment in their developing identities as lesbians. Inspired by the takeover, women went on to raise the funds necessary to purchase a building for the creation of a permanent women's center. The Women's Center in Central Square, Cambridge, is the oldest continuously operating center for women in the United States and continues to have a strong lesbian presence.

Lesbian activists also opened a women's health clinic, a bookstore, a credit union, a restaurant, all-women bars, and a Boston women's monthly newspaper, *Sojourner*, which survived until 2002. The Combahee River Collective, a black lesbian-feminist group, was formed in 1974 and became active in the black, lesbian, and feminist communities in Boston for several years. Its members wrote the "Combahee River Collective Statement," which offers an important analysis of the position and role of black feminists and black lesbian feminists in the struggle for liberation. Lesbians and gay men worked together to publish *Gay Community News* (1973–1998), a national weekly newspaper that published news and articles on a range of often controversial issues. Other groups that started in this period and which still exist today include the Fenway Community Health Center; Boston Area Gay and Lesbian Youth (BAGLY), and SpeakOut (formerly the Lesbian and Gay Speakers Bureau).

Organizations that have had a significant impact locally and nationally include Gay and Lesbian Advocates and Defenders (GLAD). GLAD had its roots in the 1978 sex scandals that took place in the Boston area. There were two incidents: one involved the arrest of over a hundred men in the Boston Public Library rest rooms and another, the arrest of over two dozen men in Revere (a small city near Boston) for alleged involvement with young and underage boys. The Boston/Boise defense committee was formed. Later that year, a Boston conference concerning these arrests led to the formation of the North American Man-Boy Love Association (NAMBLA). The group continues to be a controversial element in the LGBT movement. Also that year, in November, GLAD was founded by attorneys and others to defend these men. A major focus for GLAD is currently the struggle for full LGBT civil rights, and its recent work has been centered on the issue of civil marriage.

In the early 1970s Boston's unofficial LGBT community center was located at the Charles Street Meeting House on Beacon Hill. Many LGBT groups were organized and held their first meetings there before renting space in commercial buildings. Later several LGBT groups, including Glad Day Bookshop, found space in Boston's central business district at 22 Bromfield Street. *Gay Community News* (*GCN*) also rented offices in this building, and *GCN* was the first home for the Black Gay Men's Caucus, the Committee for Gay Youth, Boston Asian Gay Men and Lesbians (one of the first LGBT Asian groups in the country, founded in 1979), and the Boston Area Lesbian and Gay History Project, which began meeting in February 1980. One of the earliest groups to respond to the needs of the transsexual community was Gender Identity Service (GIS), which opened its offices in April 1974. GIS's counseling and medical services were later incorporated into programs at the Fenway Community Health Center.

In 1974 Boston was the first city in the country to elect an "out" LGBT person to a state legislature. Elaine Noble, a professor of communications at Emerson College, successfully ran for state representative on a platform that promised to expand local neighborhood services for her Fenway district, which had a large population of elderly residents on fixed incomes, students, and LGBT residents. Her election as the first out lesbian in the Massachusetts House was largely won by the enormous efforts of the LGBT community. Noble's LGBT support had eroded by 1978, when she was considering a run against State Senator Barney Frank (first elected in 1972). Frank had proven his support for LGBT rights. In the end, Noble declined to run and Frank emerged victorious. Two years later, Frank was elected to the U.S. House of Representatives and in 1987 he came out as gay. In 1983, David Scondras was the first openly gay man to be elected to Boston's City Council.

The beginning of the AIDS epidemic in the early 1980s was devastating to LGBT communities and changed the focus of LGBT activism. Organizations were created to meet the needs of people with HIV/AIDS. The AIDS Action Committee was established in 1983 as part of the Fenway Community Health Center and became a separate organization in 1986. One of the oldest and largest AIDS organizations in the United States, the committee has been a leader in the battle for condom distribution, intravenous needle exchange programs, and an end to discrimination against people with HIV/AIDS. In the first decade of the epidemic LGBT people in Boston were often targeted for bashing and other forms of harassment. Some Boston City Councilors proposed a

quarantine of people with AIDS and many called for the registration of anyone diagnosed as HIV positive. After more than a decade of resistance from many public officials, Boston began to take major steps in responding to HIV and AIDS. In 2002, for example, the city instituted a program to provide clean needles to all who requested them.

As the AIDS epidemic continued to incapacitate and kill larger and larger numbers of people, some activists began to call for more militant and confrontational tactics. In 1987, following the October LGB March on Washington, activists in Boston and other parts of Massachusetts formed MASS ACT OUT. The specific focus of the group was to fight homophobia and to protest society's response to the AIDS crisis. In 1988 Boston ACT UP (AIDS Coalition to Unleash Power), Boston PWA (People With AIDS), and the Women and AIDS Network were also established. In the several years that MASS ACT OUT and Boston ACT UP existed, they initiated scores of demonstrations and acts of civil disobedience at federal, state, and local medical institutions, health care agencies, pharmaceutical companies, and government offices.

Boston's LGBT residents are spread throughout the city and can be found in large numbers in Jamaica Plain, Fenway, Roslindale, Dorchester, Allston, and Brighton. No area of Boston, however, has the population or the wealth of the LGBT community of the South End. The South End's squares and townhouses reflect an earlier era of affluence, but in the 1960s and 1970s its residents were predominantly poor, immigrants, and people of color. In the early 1970s, LGBT people, primarily white men, began to move into this neighborhood in larger numbers because of the beauty of its architecture, its affordability, and its proximity to downtown Boston. Over time, the South End became one of the most economically and ethnically diverse neighborhoods of Boston and an important enclave of the LGBT community, with a gentrified population of predominantly white gay men owning real estate and businesses.

The 1980s was a period of advances for LGBT people in Boston, but it was a time of backlash, too. In 1985, Governor Michael Dukakis, considered a progressive, instructed the state Department of Social Services to remove two young boys from their foster home for no reason other than the fact that the foster parents were a gay male couple. The boys were subsequently placed in six different foster homes. Dukakis's actions were viewed by LGBT communities as consciously homophobic. At the time, the governor was campaigning to be the Democratic candidate for U.S. president, and as he traveled around the country, LGBT people and their allies met him wherever he went, vociferously chanting the slogan, "Foster Equality."

The LGBT communities of Boston have made great strides in the past decade. In the early 1990s the Lesbian and Gay Pride Committee added Bisexual and Transgender to their name. In 1994 the state legislature enacted legislation prohibiting discrimination against the state's lesbian and gay students. Dozens of school districts around the state have started LGBT-and-Allies groups on their campuses.

Several new issues have begun to concern many in Boston's LGBT communities. These include designing and implementing programs and services to meet the needs of a growing number of older (sixty-five and over) LGBT people as well as a growing population of young (under twenty-five) LGBT people. Violence against LGBT people in Boston continues to be a serious concern. Until full and complete civil rights for all people are achieved in Boston and the United States, LGBT people will be vulnerable to attacks.

The history of LGBT communities in Boston is the history of Boston itself. It may even be seen as the history of the United States. Key themes include cultural encounters and cultural conflicts; oppression and resistance; and intersections of sex, gender, sexuality, ethnicity, race, religion, and class. The persistent struggle for LGBT equality in Boston reflects the hope and idealism of a city founded on a commitment to freedom and of a country founded on principles of revolution.

**Bibliography**

Godbeer, Richard. *Sexual Revolution in Early America*. Baltimore: Johns Hopkins Press, 2002.

Wroth, L. Kinvin, and Hiller B. Zobel, eds. *Legal Papers of John Adams*. 3 vols. Cambridge, Mass.: Belknap Press, 1965.

**Libby Bouvier**

*See also* ANTIDISCRIMINATION LAW AND POLICY; CHEEVER, JOHN; CHUA, SIONG-HUAT; COLLEGES AND UNIVERSITIES; COLONIAL AMERICA; COMBAHEE RIVER COLLECTIVE; CUSHMAN, CHARLOTTE; DALY, MARY; DUNBAR-NELSON, ALICE; FULLER, MARGARET; FRANK, BARNEY; GAY COMMUNITY NEWS; JEWETT, SARAH ORNE; KLUMPKE, ANNA; NATIVE AMERICANS; NOBLE, ELAINE; RESORTS; ROMANTIC FRIENDSHIP AND BOSTON MARRIAGE; SAMSON, DEBORAH; SODOMY, BUGGERY, CRIMES AGAINST NATURE, DISORDERLY CONDUCT, AND LEWD AND LASCIVIOUS LAW AND POLICY; WALSH, FRANK; WHITMAN, WALT; WIGGLESWORTH, MICHAEL.

**BOSTON MARRIAGE.** see ROMANTIC FRIENDSHIP AND BOSTON MARRIAGE.

# BOURBON, Ray (Rae) (b. 11 August 1892?; d. 20 July 1971), entertainer.

Comic and female impersonator Ray (Rae) Bourbon had a sixty-year career in a marginal profession not known for its longevity. To keep afloat, Bourbon negotiated a shifting terrain of social attitudes and law enforcement with regard to homosexuality, gender transgression, and race.

Bourbon was most likely born on 11 August 1892. As he told it, he was the illegitimate son of European royalty and an expatriate from the U.S. More likely, he came from mixed Irish-Mexican heritage; he may have been the son of Frank T. Waddell and a woman named Elizabeth. Bourbon was raised by foster parents near the Texas-Mexico border.

From the late 1910s through the 1920s, Bourbon worked in and out of drag in vaudeville and silent movies. By the late 1920s, the rise of tourist clubs with exclusively female impersonation entertainment provided Bourbon with another venue. In the 1930s, Bourbon often played as a "pansy performer"—wearing a tuxedo but retaining his flamboyance and shrieking wit. In the middle 1930s Bourbon stopped appearing in drag, although he still performed cross-gender comedic pantomimes and monologues.

During the 1930s and 1940s, Bourbon could usually find work in Los Angeles. Celebrities like Errol Flynn, Bob Hope, Dorothy Lamour, and Joan Crawford flocked to his shows at Club Rendezvous in Hollywood. Although at the height of his fame, Bourbon continued (as he would throughout life) to fight personal demons, including heavy drinking and a nasty temper. When drunk he could not manage the breakneck pace and improvisation for which audiences loved him. His comedy would also sometimes stumble outside the semilegal bounds it was forced to inhabit. In March 1937, for example, an intoxicated Bourbon was arrested for simulating the use of toilet paper onstage. Bourbon's bitchy and self-aggrandizing personality provided him with a shrewd instinct for exploiting those around him and a defense against an industry and society that only marginally valued his talent. Unfortunately, Bourbon's behavior also rendered him incapable of long-term intimacy and often blurred his sense of fairness and truth.

In 1940, after a European tour, Bourbon went back into drag, playing a grand dame with a filthy mouth. As he grew older, Bourbon's material increasingly began to assert gender ambiguity as a personal right. His most "legitimate" work as an entertainer came from 1944 to 1950, playing swishy parts in Mae West's tours of *Catherine Was Great* and *Diamond Lil.* This did not lead to lasting employability. Like so many impersonators, Bourbon struggled for a respectability made elusive by the desires he publicly expressed, the way he expressed them, and the gender identities he took on both onstage and off.

Throughout the next fifteen years, Bourbon performed in small nightclubs, bringing a powerful, unnerving queer comic presence into communities across the country. Bourbon also reached audiences through "blue" recordings. From the early 1930s onward Bourbon had augmented his stage income by recording and selling dozens of party records. By the middle 1940s distribution of the records warranted mentions in the *San Francisco Chronicle* and *Variety*. In the late 1950s, Bourbon put out ten full-length albums with names such as *Around the World in 80 Ways;* these became the performer's most popular records.

In September 1955, Bourbon reportedly had a sex change, changing, as one routine goes, from "R-A-Y" to "R-A-E." Perhaps attempting to capitalize on the media spotlight Christine Jorgensen faced following her highly publicized 1952 and 1954 sex reassignment surgeries, Bourbon incorporated the transformation into his act. It is difficult to determine the extent to which the sex change did or did not occur. Bourbon's own gender ambiguity and lack of autobiographical documentation leave unclear the performer's motives for claiming to have undergone such a procedure.

From the late 1950s on, Bourbon lived and performed within a blend of self-professed male, female, and transgendered identities. During a time when society demanded gender/sex/sexuality congruity as a qualification for Americanism, Bourbon's performance was radical and subversive. By the end of the 1950s, Bourbon had been banned outright from the nightclubs of Seattle and Los Angeles, where the performer was arrested for impersonating a woman. On the other hand, in Miami, cops threw Bourbon in jail on the charge of impersonating a man. By the 1960s, Bourbon enjoyed the privileges of neither of the two "legitimate" sexes. As an itinerant single older person, Bourbon experienced ever-greater vulnerability and eccentricity. In the early 1960s, Rae contacted the FBI on several occasions, fearing assassination at the hand of Soviet spies. To some extent, such anxiety was justified—during these years, Bourbon was robbed, beaten, and shot.

In 1966 Bourbon wrote and starred in *Daddy Was a Lady*, a semiautobiographical musical comedy, in Colorado. Bourbon negotiated a deal to have the show move to New York City, but it fell through when he refused to cut the show's bawdy elements. Still, Bourbon worked when possible and gained comfort from the stray dogs and cats s/he would pick up on the roadside and nurture back to health. By the middle 1960s, Bourbon carted around dozens of animals in a ramshackle trailer hitched on the back of whatever jalopy s/he was driving (and living in). In 1967 Bourbon was forced to board the animals after the car s/he had been driving caught fire outside Big Spring, Texas, and was destroyed. Months later, the man who boarded and then sold the performer's animals to a Dallas medical lab was murdered. While two young hustlers were found guilty of the actual crime, police accused Bourbon of masterminding it. In 1970 Bourbon was convicted of conspiracy to murder and received a life sentence.

On 20 July 1971, Bourbon died in Big Spring State Hospital from heart failure complicated by leukemia. He is buried in Woodlawn Park in Miami. In recent years, Bourbon has enjoyed a small renaissance of popularity. The old recordings garner high prices in online auctions, and the performer appears in a host of the most popular LGBT histories of the twentieth century. He is also the subject of a Web site developed by filmmaker and Bourbonaholic Randy Riddle.

### Bibliography

Riddle, Randy. *Don't Call Me Madame: The Sad and Crazy Life of Ray Bourbon.* Http://www.coolcatdaddy/bourbon.html.

Romesburg, Don. "Ray Bourbon: A Queer Biography." Master's thesis, University of Colorado, Boulder, 2000.

**Don Romesburg**

*See also* COMEDY AND HUMOR; TRANSSEXUALS, TRANSVESTITES, TRANSGENDER PEOPLE, AND CROSS-DRESSERS.

# BOWLES, Paul (b. 30 December 1910; d. 18 November 1999), author and composer, and Jane BOWLES, (b. 22 February 1917; d. 4 May 1973), author.

In 1937, Jane Auer and Paul Bowles met in New York City. She was talented, energetic, and determined to become a writer. He was an accomplished composer known both for his Broadway scores (he wrote for Orson Welles in the 1930s and later for Tennessee Williams and others) and for chamber music and art songs influenced by his mentors Aaron Copland and Virgil Thomas. Jane and Paul's artistic affinity quickly developed into an emotionally complex relationship, and the two were married in 1938. They led separate sexual lives—Jane with women, Paul with men—and they often maintained separate residences, but over the ensuing thirty-five years they wrote their signature stories and novels in each other's shadows.

Of the two, Jane was more outspoken about homosexuality, both in her personal life and in her writing. Born in New York City, she frequented the Greenwich Village lesbian bar scene as a young woman, and sexual orientation emerged as an important facet of her personal identity. Her letters, published as *Out in the World: The Selected Letters of Jane Bowles 1935–1970* (1985), speak to some dimensions of her love affairs. Her relationship with Paul Bowles and with women friends and lovers informed her fiction, and she had a precise talent for writing psychologically dense dialogues, sharpened by undercurrents of desire, anxiety, and despair.

Jane Bowles established her reputation for writing highly stylized and idiosyncratic yet sharp and compelling fiction with the novel *Two Serious Ladies* (1943). The title characters, Christina Goering and Mrs. Copperfield, through extraordinarily creative methods seek autonomy and purpose in lives painfully circumscribed by bourgeois conventions. Goering, a wealthy spinster, decisively renounces wealth and comfort by devoting herself to sexual and alcoholic debauchery. The middle-class and seemingly weak-willed Mrs. Copperfield, while traveling in Central America, casually leaves her husband for Pacifica, a local prostitute. These characters became archetypes for the roles, power struggles, decisions, and indecisions Jane Bowles explored further in her 1953 play *In the Summer House* and in several of the short stories reprinted in *My Sister's Hand in Mine: An Expanded Edition of the Collected Works of Jane Bowles* (1978). Relations between women in Jane Bowles's fiction are rarely romantic and even less so heroic. They are instead characterized by pain and conflict, and are often torn apart by competing urges for independence or attachment, adventure or security, genius or passivity.

Jane and Paul Bowles traveled in Mexico and Central America shortly after their marriage in 1938, and in 1947 they took up residence in Tangier, Morocco. Her novel *Two Serious Ladies* as well as short stories such as "A Day in the Country," "A Guatemalan Idyll," and "East Side: North Africa" bear the mark of Jane Bowles's years abroad. Central American and Moroccan characters appear in her fiction as especially strong and sexually self-assured women, often in sharp contrast to wealthy white American characters.

This fascination with differences marked by race, nationality, class, and social standing is even more pro-

**Paul Bowles.** The expatriate writer and composer speaks into a tape recorder in his home in Tangier, Morocco, in 1969, four years before the death of his wife, Jane. [Shepard Sherbell/corbis]

nounced in the writing of Paul Bowles. He traveled extensively in North Africa and Europe before the couple's marriage, and afterward toured South and Southeast Asia. His most esteemed novel, *The Sheltering Sky* (1949), follows an American couple, Port and Kit, as they journey recklessly into the Algerian Sahara. Port pays for his naive pursuit of colonial nostalgia with death from typhoid, and in shock Kit abandons herself to the leader of a passing caravan. Kept as a mistress in the man's desert village, unable to communicate, Kit loses contact with reason. She eventually returns to the West, but without redemption or triumph. The violent death of Western naïveté, romanticism, and rationality in the face of a non-Western "other" became the hallmark of Paul Bowles's fiction.

In addition to *The Sheltering Sky*, Paul Bowles wrote the novels *Let It Come Down* (1952) and *The Spider's House* (1955), both set in Morocco, and *Up Above the World* (1966), set in Central America; he was a masterful writer of short stories, many of which were also set in exotic locales where he either lived or traveled. His wanderlust emerged at an early age. In his first year of college, Paul Bowles left abruptly for Europe, where he met Gertrude Stein and Alice B. Toklas. They urged him to visit Tangier, and he returned there to live from 1947 until his death in 1999. During the 1950s and early 1960s, Paul and Jane Bowles were the most prominent of Tangier's literary expatriates, which included William Burroughs, Alfred Chester, Joe Orton, Jean Genet, and dozens of other residents and tourists.

Paul Bowles's writing career began in the early years of his marriage to Jane, as he admired her work and helped edit her novel. During the 1950s his energies shifted away from musical composition, while he concentrated on both his fiction and on caring for Jane, who suffered from alcoholism and other illnesses, culminating in a stroke in 1957. Her work had declined during her residence in Tangier, and after the stroke, reading and writing became painfully difficult. She died in 1973.

Paul Bowles found little time to write during Jane's illness, but occupied himself with a new project: translating stories told to him in Maghrebi Arabic, most notably by Larbi Layachi and Mohammed Mrabet. He also translated the early works of Mohamed Choukri. Several of these books explore sexual relations between young Moroccan men and their wealthy American and European patrons. Bowles's translations are more frank in this respect than most of his fiction, which approaches male-male sexuality through displacement and disguise. A notable exception is the short story "Pages from Cold Point" (1947), in which a son seduces his father. Paul Bowles guarded his privacy tightly, but in the final years of his life he began to speak on the record about homosexuality and about some dimensions of his sexual life. His fiction, like that of Jane Bowles, is centrally concerned with both conscious and unconscious same-sex desire, and both Jane and Paul Bowles crafted elliptical representations of non-normative sexuality. They wrote literature of enduring consequence.

### Bibliography

Caponi, Gena Dagel. *Paul Bowles: Romantic Savage.* Carbondale: Southern Illinois University Press, 1994.

Dillon, Millicent. *A Little Original Sin: The Life and Work of Jane Bowles.* New York: Holt, Rinehart, and Winston, 1981.

Mullins, Greg. *Colonial Affairs: Bowles, Burroughs, and Chester Write Tangier.* Madison: University of Wisconsin Press, 2002.

Skerl, Jennie. *A Tawdry Place of Salvation: The Art of Jane Bowles.* Carbondale: Southern Illinois University Press, 1997.

**Greg Mullins**

*See also* FORD, CHARLES HENRI; MUSIC: OPERA.

# BOY SCOUTS AND GIRL SCOUTS

From their early-twentieth-century inceptions, the Boy Scouts and Girl Scouts of America have dealt differently with issues relating to homosexuality. In the 1980s and 1990s, this came to a head as the Girl Scouts made formal gestures toward inclusion while the Boy Scouts moved to exclude all gay people.

## Boy Scouts of America

The Boy Scouts of America (BSA), incorporated by William Boyce in 1910, brought together features of General Robert Baden-Powell's military-style Scouting program in England and a more nature-oriented "Boy Scouts" group led by Ernest Thompson Seton in the United States. As part of the "muscular Christianity" movement, the BSA sought to strengthen boys' masculinity by toughening their moral and physical fiber. Movement leaders believed that discipline, the outdoors, and a code of honor would counter the demoralizing and effeminizing perils of modern urban life. Like the Young Men's Christian Association and the burgeoning high school athletics programs of the same era, the Boy Scouts saw the adult-supervised youth group as a vehicle for socializing boys toward a combination of self-assurance, obedience, and civic duty. The BSA provided activities to manage the budding sexuality and homosocial sentiments of pubertal boyhood. To counter both "morbidly selfish" masturbation and "effeminate" homosexuality, the BSA contrived to "short circuit" the sex impulse by sublimating sexual urges into camping, athletic play, arts, and crafts.

Within the BSA, adult men were expected to ensure that the proper balance was struck to steer preadolescent and adolescent Scouts toward a moral, masculine, and heterosexual adulthood. Yet organizers worried that the scoutmasters and troop leaders themselves could potentially corrupt young boys. In 1911, the BSA created a centralized system of "red tab files" on men who had been rejected from scouting. Alongside those ousted for drunkenness, criminal background, or pedophilia were those suspected of homosexuality and those who displayed too much effeminacy. Beginning with Baden-Powell, adults involved with scouting frequently celebrated the attractive, robust innocence of boyhood and boys' bodies. But the romantic language of intergenerational, homosocial affection—commonplace in the nineteenth century—was, by the early twentieth century, burdened by homosexual implications. Like Baden-Powell's warnings against British Scout leaders letting their "sentimentalism" toward boy charges become excessive, Judge A. B. Cohn, the Scout Commissioner of Toledo, Ohio, in the 1920s, lamented that too often a man is admitted who "calls his scouts 'dear' and 'paws' them" (Macleod, p. 208).

## Girl Scouts of America

Since the formation of the Girl Scouts of America (GSA) in 1912, women and girls have been drawn to the organization's homosociality, and discrete lesbians have found some acceptance. Many involved in the GSA (reincorporated as GSUSA in the 1950s) have also enjoyed a degree of freedom from traditionally feminine constraints in dress, behavior, and attitude. Unlike the Camp Fire Girls, who utilized the "Indian maiden" archetype to steer girls toward domesticity and femininity, the GSA adapted the military aesthetic of the BSA. Girl Scouts donned khaki uniforms, sold war bonds, marched in drill formations, and hiked on rugged outdoor adventures. Much to the chagrin of the BSA, which upheld the Camp Fire Girls as its ideal gender compliment, early GSA literature defended the tomboy as healthy and natural. Still, the GSA awarded many badges for traditionally feminine activities, such as nursing and laundering.

The GSA also countered the transgressive potential of extreme tomboyism. The historian Leslie Paris, writing about summer camps for girls during the years between World War I and World War II, suggests that the cross-gendered play and assumption of masculine nicknames at Girl Scout camps was clearly bounded as "fantasy." Moreover, throughout the 1920s and 1930s, GSA and girls' camping industry literature addressed the "problem" of same-sex crushes. The sex-segregated institution fostered intense friendships between girls. Scout leaders closely monitored such friendships to prevent them from becoming sexual. Nonetheless, GSA camp settings continued to provide many girls with opportunities to bunk in or snuggle with their summer crushes.

## The Golden Age of Scouting

The 1950s and 1960s are called the "golden age" of scouting because the baby boom led to a surge in membership. The Cub Scouts exploded from around 750,000 members in 1949 to 1.6 million in 1956, while the GSA went from 1.8 million in 1950 to 4 million in 1960. The same era saw a surge in nationalism related to the cold war, a rise in church attendance, increases in antihomosexual persecution, and the assertion of polarized gender ideals. In this period of "civil religion," when Americanism was more explicitly conflated with Judeo-Christianity, the Religious Awards Program of the BSA provided incentive for strengthening ties between troops and churches. The BSA

continued to conflate religion, nation, and heterosexuality into the next century as its leadership came to be increasingly dominated by conservative Mormon, Catholic, and evangelical men. Meanwhile, the BSA explicitly policed homosexuality. During the 1960s, it regularly shared information from its "red tab files" with the Federal Bureau of Investigation.

Within the GSA, the quiet celebration of gender diversity among women and girls, like the willingness to include discrete lesbians, continued. Many baby-boom lesbians have fond memories of camping, crushes, gender bending, and the butch women who participated in the GSA. Nancy Manahan's anthology *On My Honor: Lesbians Reflect on Their Scouting Experience* (1997) speaks to the role that the GSA's all-female environments, strong women, and celebration of nature may have had in that generation's development of lesbian-feminist ideals. Lesbian activist and scholar Margaret Cruikshank recalled butch troop leaders, tough talk, and gender bending at Camp Olcott, Minnesota, in the late 1950s and early 1960s, where she was both a camper and then a counselor. Still, antilesbian witch hunts did periodically occur and the standards of tolerance varied widely from community to community. Cruikshank explained, "No one said a word about being gay; it was still a taboo topic, and scouts was the perfect cover" (Cruikshank, "One Entry Point to Lesbian Nation," in Manahan, pp. 40–44).

## Membership Criteria and Controversy

Since the 1970s, self-identified gay people have insisted that their openness should not preclude scouting participation. In 1980 a Berkeley, California, Eagle Scout, Timothy Curran, was profiled in a local newspaper article about gay teens; Curran was taking a male date to his senior prom. The Mount Diablo Council of the BSA consequently withdrew his membership. With the backing of the American Civil Liberties Union and LGBT political and civil liberties organizations, Curran fought back in court, asserting that the BSA, as an organization subject to state civil rights law, did not have the right to discriminate against him. The case sparked a series of debates about the right of the BSA to define its membership criteria and the vague legal place that the BSA, as a semi-public institution, held in U.S. society.

In both the Curran case and later the New Jersey case of James Dale, a gay Eagle Scout and assistant scoutmaster, the BSA argued that as a private organization it had the right to exclude whomever it wanted, whether it be atheists, females, or gay people. BSA legal opponents maintained that its status as a private club was and is questionable. While BSA had no formal ties with the fed-

**Steven Cozza.** Scouting for All, founded by this California (and heterosexual) teenager, promotes tolerance rather than the antigay policy of the Boy Scouts of America. [AP/Wide World Photos]

eral government (aside from a congressional charter that enabled its founding), it enjoys special access to many public accommodations, from parks to schools. In 2001, for example, the annual Boy Scout Jamboree, bringing troops from around the country together, secured $5 million in state and federal funds. Throughout the 1990s, numerous communities with antidiscrimination policies covering sexual orientation, such as San Francisco, Chicago, and Tucson, ended the BSA's free use of public space.

In 1990, James Dale, a scoutmaster who was expelled after a local college newspaper mentioned he was co-president of a gay and lesbian organization on campus, sued on the grounds that the BSA was basically a public accommodation, like a hotel or restaurant, rather than a private club. A year later, Tim Curran lost his case in California, when that state's Superior Court ruled that the BSA's freedom of association superceded the state's antidiscrimination law. Emboldened by its victory, the BSA aggressively silenced dissent through the 1990s. In

1992, a San Jose, California, troop that adopted a resolution renouncing the antigay policy had its charter revoked, and the BSA purged Dave Rice, a sixty-nine-year-old northern Californian with fifty-nine years of Scout involvement, for participating in the anti-exclusion efforts. When Unitarian Universalist churches, which sponsored troops across the country, refused to verse boys in the belief that homosexuality was immoral, the BSA revoked the churches' privilege to give Scouts religious and ethics badges.

BSA justification for the exclusion of homosexuals rests on the section of the Scout's Oath that calls on Scouts to be "morally straight" and "clean in word and deed" (Mechling, pp. 220–221). Until the late 1970s, the eight editions of the Boy Scout handbook that had appeared since 1910 made no reference to sexuality in relation to being "morally straight." The 1979 edition, however, defined being "morally straight" through adolescent boys' responsible handling of their capacity to procreate, explaining, "When you live up to the trust of fatherhood your sex life will fit into God's wonderful plan of creation" (Mechling, pp. 220–221).

In the 1990s, protest against the BSA for its stand on homosexuality became more vocal. In July 1991, a group calling itself "Queer Scouts" staged a kiss-in at the San Francisco regional BSA headquarters. LGBT groups across the nation pressured governments, businesses, and United Way chapters to refuse the BSA any support on the grounds of their own antidiscrimination policies. In 1999, an aspiring Eagle Scout named Steven Cozza, a heterosexual teenager in Petaluma, California, founded Scouting for All, a group that appeals to basic scouting values such as tolerance and justice as a critique of the BSA's antigay policy.

Meanwhile, in 1998, New Jersey's high court had ruled in favor of James Dale, and Judge James M. Harbey stated, "There is absolutely no evidence before us, empirical or otherwise, supporting a conclusion that a gay Scoutmaster, solely because he is a homosexual, does not possess the strength of character necessary to properly care for or to impart B.S.A. humanitarian ideals to the young boys in his charge" (Mechling, p. 212). But in 1999 the case went to the U.S. Supreme Court, and on 28 June 2000, the Court ruled 5–4 in favor of the BSA, affirming its right as a private group to free association.

Scouting for All subsequently coordinated a National Day of Protest, 21 August 2000, when small demonstrations in thirty-six cities around the United States voiced disapproval. Some Eagle Scouts turned in their badges, and former Eagle Scout Steven Spielberg left the BSA advisory board. The Union of American Hebrew Congregations called for synagogues and congregants to pull out of the BSA. Over 4,500 schools have ended their preferential status for the BSA (meaning that BSA chapters have lost access to meeting space), and corporations from Wells Fargo to Levi Strauss and the pharmacy chain CVS have severed all ties (meaning that BSA has lost financial support).

By contrast, the GSA has formalized its unstated positions of both tolerance and discretion. In 1980, the GSA adopted a "don't ask, don't tell" position, explaining that "personal lifestyle or sexual orientation . . . are private matters for girls and their families to address" (Manahan, p. 7). In practice, this sanctions public declarations of heterosexuality and requires silence around issues of homosexuality. The GSUSA provides materials on heterosexual dating and sex, and Girl Scouts and leaders socialize alongside male partners. Few Scouts or leaders would feel comfortable openly integrating same-sex partners into GSUSA culture. Because the organization's position is not policy, local councils create their own standards, so only the most progressive communities have truly open troops. Nevertheless, the GSUSA's relative tolerance of homosexuality and religious diversity has provoked the ire of conservative Christians. In 1995, a group of evangelical women began the American Heritage Girls as an exclusionary alternative to the GSUSA, although by 2002 the group had attracted few more than a thousand members.

As the BSA increasingly has become entrenched in its exclusion and the GSUSA gradually has become more open, membership in the BSA has dropped by an average of 4 percent nationally from 2000 to 2001. GSUSA membership, by contrast, has boomed, rising to a twenty-year high in 2000.

## Bibliography

Boyle, Patrick. *Scout's Honor: Sexual Abuse in America's Most Trusted Institution.* Rocklin, Calif.: Prima, 1994.

Macleod, David L. *Building Character in the American Boy: The Boy Scouts, YMCA, and Their Forerunners, 1870–1920.* Madison: University of Wisconsin Press, 1983.

Manahan, Nancy, ed. *On My Honor: Lesbians Reflect on Their Scouting Experience.* Northboro, Mass.: Madwoman Press, 1997.

Mechling, Jay. *On My Honor: Boy Scouts and the Making of American Youth.* Chicago: University of Chicago Press, 2001.

Paris, Leslie. "The Adventures of Peanut and Bo: Summer Camps and Early-Twentieth-Century American Girlhood." *Journal of Women's History* 12, no. 4 (2001): 47–76.

**Don Romesburg**

*See also* ANTIDISCRIMINATION LAW AND POLICY; HOMOEROTICISM AND HOMOSOCIALITY; INTERGENERATIONAL SEX AND RELATIONSHIPS; LAMBDA LEGAL DEFENSE; SAME-SEX INSTITUTIONS.

# BOYCOTTS

A long-standing tool for promoting social change, boycotts involve a deliberate refusal to buy from an objectionable business or from businesses in a targeted location. On one level, such actions have the potential to deprive businesses of sales revenue, putting economic pressure on firms to change policies. Boycotts also generate bad publicity for the company concerned, creating another powerful motivation for the company to change. Many social change movements, including those involving unions, environmentalists, and LGBT activists, have used boycotts to protest objectionable policies and practices.

The LGBT movement has used the boycott as a primary weapon in the movement's economic arsenal. Since the point of boycotts is to withhold consumer spending rather than to take a perceptible action, organizations or individuals calling for boycotts must make special efforts to render the boycott visible, using the news media and more noticeable means, such as pickets, to enlist supporters and put clear pressure on the target entity. Because of the substantial resources needed to conduct a successful boycott, boycotts have tended to be used to punish particularly egregious antigay acts, not simply everyday disparities in treatment, such as unequal benefits packages. The most prominent and successful LGBT boycotts since 1970 have targeted Coors Brewing, the state of Colorado, Cracker Barrel Old Country Store restaurants, and United Airlines.

## An Early Coalition against Coors

In *The Mayor of Castro Street* (1982), Randy Shilts recounts the gay boycott against Coors beer that catapulted Harvey Milk into politics. Union and gay activists came together to protest anti-union and antigay actions by Coors Brewing Company. Milk and others canvassed gay bars in San Francisco in the 1970s to convince gay bar patrons to boycott Coors. (This alliance between the Brotherhood of Teamsters and gay activists helped Milk win election to the city's Board of Supervisors in 1977.)

Eventually Coors rescinded its objectionable policies, leading to an apparent (although to many, invisible) end to the boycott. In the 1990s the company even began marketing directly to the LGB community, offered domestic partner benefits to its workers' same-sex partners, made financial contributions to gay organizations, and hired a liaison to the gay community. Nevertheless, some gay activists continue to promote a boycott of Coors since Coors family members provide financial support to the Castle Rock Foundation, which in turn funds conservative organizations with antigay agendas, such as the Heritage Foundation.

### Taking on Cracker Barrel and Colorado in the Early 1990s

In 1991 Cracker Barrel Old Country Store Inc. implemented a new policy of dismissing gay employees by firing eleven people in Georgia. Those fired quickly found out that they had no legal recourse, so activists set up local pickets and announced a nationwide boycott of the chain. The company rescinded the antigay policy but refused to rehire the workers or add to its nondiscrimination policy a ban on discrimination based on sexual orientation. The boycott continued through the 1990s, fueled by attention from the National Gay and Lesbian Task Force.

In December 2002 the company finally announced that it would change its policies to prohibit discrimination based on sexual orientation. The policy change was motivated not by the economic effects of the boycott, which were not evident in the company's strong profit performance through the 1990s, but by the efforts of shareholders of CBRL Group Inc., the parent company of the restaurant chain. Led by the New York City Employees' Retirement System and other socially responsible investors, shareholder activists had spent a decade garnering majority support for the nondiscrimination policy. The company changed the policy only after shareholders had voted for the change in November 2002.

A second important boycott in the 1990s targeted not a single business but the state of Colorado. Boycotters wanted to punish the state's voters, who in 1992 enacted Amendment 2, a state constitutional provision that forbade laws against antigay discrimination. The boycott generated as much debate within the LGBT community as the referendum did in Colorado. Some activists argued that the boycott was too broad in its effects and would hurt gay and gay-friendly businesses as well as the antigay forces. Those supporting the boycott acknowledged that impact but believed that it would be immoral and strategically unwise to fail to take action against the state.

With widespread media attention and the cooperation of large organizations, the boycott appeared to deprive the state of $100 million in canceled conventions as well as $20 million in meetings and business relocations. Antigay organizations such as the Southern Baptist Convention claimed to have replaced some of that lost business, however. As always, identifying a net impact of the boycott in actual dollar terms is difficult, especially since Colorado's economy grew at roughly the same rate during the boycott as it had right before the boycott (good snowfalls and a papal visit probably helped).

In Romer v. Evans (1996), a different set of voters—the justices of the U.S. Supreme Court—voted six to three that Amendment 2 violated the U.S. Constitution. That ended the boycott and, for the time being, the debate. Once again the boycott itself could not be considered decisive in changing the state's law.

### Uniting against United Airlines

In 1997 San Francisco implemented the Equal Benefits Ordinance, which required city contractors to offer equal benefits to spouses and domestic partners of employees. United Airlines, a city contractor, refused to comply and led other airlines (through the Air Transport Association) in filing a lawsuit that challenged the law. The San Francisco activist group Equal Benefits Associates and the Human Rights Campaign announced a nationwide boycott of United. When it became clear that the courts would not back up most of the airlines' arguments, United announced in 1999 that it would extend benefits to domestic partners, ending the boycott.

### Antigay Groups Turning the Tables

Gay activists have no monopolistic claim on boycotts, of course. Perhaps the best-known gay-related boycott in the 1990s was the announcement of the Southern Baptist Convention in 1997 that they wanted members to boycott theme parks and other entertainment products made by Disney. In the Baptist view, Disney's production of the television show *Ellen* and objectionable movies, its policy of offering domestic partner benefits, and even its allowing Gay Day at Disneyworld all constituted assaults on Baptist religious principles that required action. Beyond the publicity surrounding the boycott, no effect on Disney's economic performance was evident. The company's performance, and especially revenues generated by the theme parks, remained strong. Nor did the boycott generate enough public relations pressure on Disney to intimidate the company—the company has not rescinded any of the pro-gay policies to which the Baptists objected.

### Economic Success or Political Excess?

The history of boycotts in the gay movement provides little evidence that boycotters marshal enough consumer clout to cause obvious economic pain for the target. In all the cases discussed here, bad public relations and other political or legal tools appear to have been more directly effective in changing policies and practices. Boycotts also suffer from a lack of clear leadership, since political groups tend to be organized more around electoral or legislative issues. Who gets to start and stop boycotts? So far no national organization has emerged to provide widely accepted leadership on consumer actions.

Boycotts, however, are likely to continue as a tool for LGBT activists. They offer a clear action for ordinary activists and allies to take in response to an antigay outrage. Perhaps most importantly, boycotts provide an opportunity for education through public relations efforts that are directed at getting consumers to change their spending decisions, and that education can have much more far-reaching effects.

### Bibliography

Badgett, M. V. Lee. *Money, Myths, and Change: The Economic Lives of Lesbians and Gay Men.* Chicago: University of Chicago Press, 2001.

Coors Boycott Committee. Available from www.coorsboycott.org.

Shilts, Randy. *The Mayor of Castro Street: The Life and Times of Harvey Milk.* New York: St. Martin's Press, 1982.

**M. V. Lee Badgett**

*See also* ADVERTISING; BUSINESSES; CAPITALISM AND INDUSTRIALIZATION; COLORADO; EMPLOYMENT AND OCCUPATIONS; HUMAN RIGHTS CAMPAIGN; LABOR MOVEMENTS AND LABOR UNIONS; MILK, HARVEY; NATIONAL GAY AND LESBIAN TASK FORCE (NGLTF).

# BRANT, Beth E. (b. May 6, 1941), writer.

Beth Brant (Degonwadonti) is a Mohawk (Kanienke'haka) lesbian writer of the Bay of Quinte Mohawk, from the Tyendinaga Mohawk Reserve in Ontario, Canada. In addition to working as an editor, speaker, and lecturer, Brant has written poetry, short stories, and essays. She frequently emphasizes that she writes out of a deep commitment to her own people, to indigenous peoples generally, and to promote healing from the traumas inflicted by racism and colonization. She has brought her whole self to her work, including her life and experiences as a lesbian, her past as an abused spouse, and her mixed heritage as the daughter of a Mohawk father and a Scots-Irish mother. She has published three books of short stories and essays, as well as three edited anthologies.

Born in Detroit, Michigan, in 1941, Brant grew up in the city while maintaining a strong connection to her father's Tyendinaga Mohawk community and to her Detroit-based paternal grandparents, from whom she learned traditional stories and the Mohawk language. She became pregnant at age seventeen and left high school to marry, eventually bearing and raising three daughters. After leaving her abusive fourteen-year marriage in 1973, Brant became active in the feminist movement and then came out as a lesbian. She met her partner, Denise Dorsz, in 1976 and the two have been together for more than two decades.

In the first years after her divorce, Brant supported herself and her daughters by working as a salesclerk, waitress, and cleaning woman. She began writing at the age of forty after an encounter with an eagle while driving through Mohawk territory. The eagle flew in front of the car in which Brant was driving with Dorsz, then landed on a nearby tree. Stopping the car, Brant exchanged a long gaze with the bird, experiencing the interaction as a communication that she was meant to become a writer. She began writing upon returning home.

Beth Brant is a gifted writer and her work achieved almost immediate recognition. She published work the same year she began writing and has published regularly since. In 1983 editors Adrienne Rich and Michelle Cliff of the lesbian periodical *Sinister Wisdom* asked Brant to edit a collection of writings by Native American women. This project, titled *A Gathering of Spirit* (1988), was initially published in 1984 as a special issue of *Sinister Wisdom* and has been reissued as a book several times. It was the first anthology of Native women's writing edited by a Native American woman and has had enormous influence.

In 1985 Brant published *Mohawk Trail,* a mix of poems, short stories, and creative nonfiction. A second book of stories, *Food and Spirits,* appeared in 1991. Her fiction is powerful, evocative, and sometimes autobiographical, exploring themes of racism, colonialism, abuse, survival, love, friendship, community, and the experience of being Native and of finding one's way home. Brant's volume of essays, *Writing as Witness: Essays and Talk,* was published in 1994. These essays cover a range of subjects relating to the writer's craft and its meaning. In 2003 Brant was working on a second collection of essays, called *Testimony from the Faithful.*

Brant has also pursued oral history and a second editing project. *I'll Sing 'Til the Day I Die: Conversations with Tyendinaga Elders,* a series of largely autobiographical stories told by elders of the Tyendinaga Mohawk

Territory, was published in 1995. This project has preserved the knowledge and wisdom of the community's elders and made a significant scholarly contribution to the growing literature on Aboriginal oral history. A year later she and Sandra Laronde published their co-edited issue of the annual journal *Native Women in the Arts*, titled *Sweetgrass Grows All Around Her*

Brant has played a momentous role as one of the first Native lesbian writers in North America, one who insists on the centrality of both her lesbian and her Native identities, as well as the importance of her roles as mother and grandmother. She had few role models when she began writing and has devoted considerable effort to nurturing Native women writers who have come after her. At the same time, her work is frequently taken up in university classes, where it offers students opportunities to engage with issues of colonialism, racism, sexism, homophobia, and the survival of Aboriginal peoples. As a speaker and lecturer, Brant has continued to address such themes in many venues. She has declared more than once that her writing is a gift, or a "giveaway," an act of giving to her communities. Few who have read her beautiful, potent, courageous works would disagree.

## Bibliography

"Beth Brant." Gale Group, Inc. Available from http://wwwnativepubs.com.

Disch, Jackie L. "Beth E. Brant (Degonwadonti)." Department of English, University of Minnesota. Available from http://voices.cla.umn.edu.

Kobayashi, Tamai. "The Work of Beth Brant." Available from www.angelfire.com.

**Robin Jarvis Brownlie**

# BREWSTER, Lee (b. 27 April 1943; d. 19 June 2000), activist, publisher, entrepreneur.

Lee Greer Brewster was best known as the proprietor of Lee's Mardi Gras Boutique in New York's Greenwich Village, which catered to a diverse transgender clientele that ranged from the most outrageous urban gay drag stars to the most closeted heterosexual cross-dressers in small-town America. Brewster also helped establish the Queens Liberation Front in the aftermath of the 1969 Stonewall Riots and published the influential *Drag* magazine between 1971 and 1980.

The son of a miner, Brewster was born in a log cabin in Honacker, Virginia, and raised in the Appalachian coal region. He worked as a file clerk in the fingerprint section of the Federal Bureau of Investigation during the 1960s, but was fired for being gay. Upon moving to Manhattan soon thereafter, Brewster became involved in the New York chapter of the Mattachine Society. He organized well-attended fundraiser drag balls for the organization, but he quickly became disillusioned with Mattachine's censorious attitude toward drag. Acting independently, from 1969 to 1973 Brewster began giving drag balls at the Diplomat Hotel on 43rd Street; these became so fashionable that they were attended by celebrities like Jacqueline Suzanne, Carol Channing, and Shirley MacLaine.

Galvanized by the role militant street queens had played in the rioting in Greenwich Village that followed the police raid on the Stonewall Inn in June 1969, and offended by the antidrag sensibilities of the homophile, gay liberation, and lesbian feminist movements, Brewster founded an organization originally known as Queens, and later as the Queens Liberation Front (QLF), on Halloween 1969. The purpose of the QLF was "to legalize the right to dress in the attire of the opposite sex in public without fear of arrest or police harassment" (Nichols). The QLF succeeded in overturning municipal ordinances in New York that made cross-dressing illegal. Members worked within the broader gay and lesbian movements to ensure that drag interests remained visible in the annual Stonewall commemoration events and participated in statewide marches and rallies on behalf of legal reforms related to sexual freedom. Brewster was quoted in the *New York Times* as saying: "We fought for our rights as people. Under our civil rights component, the Queens Liberation Front became the first transvestite organization to parade and protest in New York City. We legalized the wearing of 'drag' in New York City bars and cabarets. No longer could a club be closed, or patrons arrested just because there was a cross-dresser present" (Martin). Brewster announced the launch of Lee's Mardi Gras Boutique the same Halloween night he founded the QLF in 1969. In the years ahead, profits from the business would support Brewster's political activism as well as provide for his livelihood. The boutique began as a mail-order business, but enough customers started knocking on Brewster's Hell's Kitchen apartment door that he opened a store at a nearby location. The boutique moved several times before it grew to fill five thousand square feet of loft space on the third floor of 400 W. 14th Street. It was reputedly the first business to cater explicitly to cross-dressers, stocking everything from dimestore-quality cosmetics to sequined gowns costing thousands of dollars. Brewster carefully protected the anonymity of his customer base, many of whom were conservative businessmen, but he also served as drag maven to the stars.

Lady Bunny, founder of the Labor Day cross-dressing festival Wigstock, was a regular patron. Brewster also consulted on and provided costumes for such big-screen movie productions as *Priscilla, Queen of the Desert*; *Tootsie*; *The Bird Cage*; and *To Wong Foo, With Love, Julie Newmar*.

In addition to selling clothing, Lee's Mardi Gras Boutique carried thousands of transgender-related book and magazine titles, making it one of the foremost informational resources on a topic that remains difficult to access. Brewster also self-published *Drag* magazine. Originally titled *Drag Queens*, the periodical initially served both to publicize the political activism of the QLF and to advertise Brewster's boutique and his drag balls. It grew in scope throughout the early 1970s, reporting regularly on transgender legal and political news from throughout the United States and becoming one of the most significant early publications of the transgender movement.

Brewster cut a flamboyant figure throughout his life, never relinquishing his fondness for white stiletto heels, form-fitting gowns, silver-sequined maxi coats, and lush false eyelashes. In the style of old school theatrical female impersonators, he preferred the title "Mr." and never tried to pass as a woman. He died of cancer at age fifty-seven in New York City.

### Bibliography

Martin, Douglas. "Lee Brewster, 57, Proponent of Men Who Dress as Women." *New York Times*, 24 May 2000.

Nichols, Jack. "Lee Brewster Dies at 57—Pioneering Transvestite Activist." Available from http://gaytoday.badpuppy.com/garchive/events/052500ev.htm

**Susan Stryker**

See also BUSINESSES; MATTACHINE SOCIETY; TRANS ORGANIZATIONS AND PERIODICALS; TRANSSEXUALS, TRANSVESTITES, TRANSGENDER PEOPLE, AND CROSS-DRESSERS.

## BROOKS, Romaine (b. 1 May 1874; d. 7 December 1970), artist.

Painting in the early decades of the twentieth century, Romaine Brooks—working against art fashion but in synchronization with younger lesbian contemporaries Gluck (Hannah Gluckstein) and Berenice Abbott—created a lesbian visual iconography.

Born Beatrice Romaine Goddard in Rome, Italy, Brooks was the youngest of three children of wealthy American parents, Ella Waterman and Major Harry Goddard of Philadelphia, who separated before her birth. She endured an unstable childhood that included abandonment, boarding schools in the United States and Europe, and long periods with her emotionally disturbed mother and older brother. Brooks studied art at the Scuola Nazionale in Rome (1896) and at the Académie Colarossi in Paris (around 1899). Her primary subject was single-figure portraiture; most of her paintings were of women. After her mother's death in 1902, Brooks inherited the family fortune and then briefly married pianist (and homosexual) John Ellingham Brooks. Her first one-person exhibition of paintings was at the prestigious Galeries Durand-Ruel in 1910. Other exhibitions followed through the middle 1930s.

In 1910 Brooks became emotionally involved with the pro-fascist Italian poet Gabriele D'Annunzio, whom she would paint twice, in 1912 and 1916. Around the same time Brooks became lovers with the Russian Jewish Ballet Russe dancer, Ida Rubinstein, with whom D'Annunzio was also enamored. Rubinstein inspired numerous paintings and photographs, including two formal portraits (1912 and 1917) and the allegorical *La France Croisée* (*The Cross of France*, 1914). Rubenstein's fragile, androgynous, emaciated body appears in four paintings of nudes: *Le Trajet* (*The Crossing*, around 1911); *Spring* (around 1912); *La Venus Triste* (*The Weeping Venus*, 1916–1917); and *L'Archer Masque* (*The Masked Archer*, 1910–1911), which caricatures the Rubinstein-D'Annunzio romance.

The great love of Romaine Brooks's life was Natalie Clifford Barney, whom she met around 1915, early in World War I. Their nonmonogamous relationship lasted over fifty years. Brooks painted Barney in 1920 and some of Barney's other lovers such as bisexual American artist and designer Eyre de Lanux, who appeared in *Chasseresse* (*The Huntress*, also called *Boréal*) in 1920 and *Elisabeth de Gramont, Duchesse de Clermont-Tonnerre*, around 1924.

Another of Brooks's lovers was pianist Renata Borgatti, whom Brooks painted in *Renata Borgatti au Piano* (1920). Both Brooks and Borgatti were satirized (Brooks as Olimpia Leigh) in Compton Mackenzie's novel *Extraordinary Women* (1928); in Radclyffe Hall's first novel, *The Forge* (1924), artist Venetia Ford is a fictionalized portrait of Brooks—one that Brooks hated.

*Peter, A Young English Girl* (1923–1924), one of Brooks's last paintings, was of the lesbian English Jewish painter Gluck. At least two other subjects, Jean Cocteau and Carl Van Vechten, were gay or bisexual men.

***Self-Portrait.*** A painting by, and of, the early twentieth-century artist Romaine Brooks. [**Smithsonian Institution**]

In 1925, after two decades of sustained artistic output, Romaine Brooks, at fifty years of age, virtually ceased painting, creating only three more works on canvas during the rest of her lifetime. Five years later, in 1930, she began writing her unpublished memoirs, "No Pleasant Memories." At the same time, she made a series of small continuous-line drawings based on dreams and the traumas of her childhood. Although the symbolist-inflected imagery and later realism of her paintings grew less fashionable as the twentieth century wore on, her drawings gained recognition through association with the theories of Sigmund Freud and Carl Jung. One hundred and one drawings were exhibited at Galerie Th. Briant in Paris in 1931. Fifty were in a show at the Arts Club of Chicago in 1935.

Brooks and Barney lived together in Florence, Italy, during World War II—one of the few times during which they shared a home. In 1967 Brooks moved to Nice, France, where she spent the final three years of her life.

If Brooks painted still lifes or landscapes, none remain. Her images appear most queer, in the modern sense of that word, in her paintings of lesbian women in tailored garb: *Renata Borgatti au Piano; Una, Lady Troubridge* (1924) (of Radclyffe Hall's lover); *Peter, a Young English Girl;* and the 1923 *Self-Portrait* in top hat and dark jacket. These paintings project a sense of merged dichotomies that resonate well with the postmodern interest in gender mobility.

Brooks began donating her paintings, drawings, and scrapbooks to the Smithsonian Institution's National Collection of Fine Arts in 1966. The three paintings she kept longest were *The Cross of France;* the large portrait of Ida Rubinstein; and *Peter, A Young English Girl.* She lived to age ninety-six and died in Nice in 1970. Two exhibitions of her work—the first in almost four decades—were held in 1971 at the National Collection of Fine Arts in Washington, D.C., and the Whitney Museum of American Art in New York City.

### Bibliography

Breeskin, Adelyn D. *Romaine Brooks.* 2d ed. Washington, D.C.: National Museum of American Art-Smithsonian Institution Press, 1986.

Chadwick, Whitney. *Amazons in the Drawing Room: The Art of Romaine Brooks.* Berkeley: University of California Press, 2000.

Secrest, Meryle. *Between Me and Life: A Biography of Romaine Brooks.* Garden City, N.Y.: Doubleday, 1974.

**Tee A. Corinne**

***See also*** BARNEY, NATALIE; VISUAL ART.

**BROWN, ADDIE.** see PRIMUS, REBECCA, AND ADDIE BROWN.

# BROWN, Rita Mae (b. 28 November 1944), writer, activist.

Rita Mae Brown was born in Hanover, Pennsylvania, and adopted by Ralph and Julia Brown. When she was eleven years old, her family moved to Fort Lauderdale, Florida, where she grew up and attended high school. In 1964 Brown lost her scholarship at the University of Florida for participating in the civil rights movement and being open about her sexuality. Brown then hitchhiked to New York City where she lived, for a time, in an abandoned car, became more involved in political activities, and commenced what would be a prolific writing career. Brown received a bachelor's degree in English and Classics from New York University in 1968, a certificate in cinematography from the New York School of the Visual Arts in 1968, and a doctorate in English and political science from the Institute for Policy Studies in 1976. She has written more than twenty-six novels, twenty-three screenplays for film and television, and three poetry collections in addition to many other works. Brown resides on a farm outside of Charlottesville, Virginia, where she continues to write and publish.

From 1967 to 1977 Brown was active in a series of second wave feminist organizations and projects, generating controversy and contradictions wherever she went. Sexual orientation was a dividing point on more than one occasion for Brown, who describes herself as "pansexual." Although a founding member of the National Organization of Women (NOW) and among the earliest members of the socialist feminist Redstockings, she left NOW in 1970 and later left the Redstockings in protest over their homophobia. Already a longtime activist for gay and lesbian rights, Brown next became interested in separatist experiments. She was a founding member of the Furies, a Washington, D.C., lesbian commune, and of Sagaris College, with its woman-centered curriculum. As a member of the Radicalesbians, Brown co-wrote the famous 1970 manifesto of lesbian separatism, "Woman Identified Woman," and in her essays she has frequently theorized lesbianism in essentialist and determinist terms. Yet Brown has also often expressed impatience with identity politics and resisted the divisions they impose. Indeed, from the very start of her political life, Brown has been remarkably clear about the need for building coalitions across cultural differences and has focused her efforts and analyses on the interconnections among differing forms of oppression.

Brown's writing career has been extraordinary for both the rate and variety of its output. She is best known for her semiautobiographical novel, *Rubyfruit Jungle* (1973), which follows its bisexual heroine, Molly Bolt, as she comes of age in Florida, moves to New York City, and rises to prominence as a filmmaker. The novel is often criticized for its undeveloped characters (Molly, most particularly) and polemical voice. Yet others defend *Rubyfruit* for its humor and social satire and for its massive, international impact as an unabashed celebration of lesbian identity. Initially published by Daughter's Press, the novel was picked up in 1977 by Bantam (which has published most of Brown's work since) and helped create an upsurge of lesbian publishing. Yet *Rubyfruit* represents just a small fraction of Brown's writing and only one of her many genres. Her first book was a collection of feminist poetry entitled *The Hand That Cradles the Rock* (1971), and she has published two poetry collections since, *Songs to a Handsome Woman* (1973) and *Poems of Rita Mae Brown* (1987). Brown has written more than twenty-three scripts for television and film, two of

**Rita Mae Brown.** The eclectic novelist, poet, screenwriter, activist, and self-described "pansexual," best known for her influential and popular 1973 novel *Rubyfruit Jungle,* has advocated both lesbian separatism and coalition building across cultural divides to combat oppression. [AP/**Wide World Photos**]

which—*I Love Liberty* (1982) and *The Long Hot Summer* (1985)—received Emmy nominations. She has also published a memoir, a writer's manual, a cookbook, and a translation of six medieval Latin plays.

Brown's 1976 essay collection, *A Plain Brown Rapper,* offers the writer's stance on a range of issues from separatism to film criticism and demonstrates a certain degree of anti-intellectualism. Brown, who tends to identify academics with masculine authoritarianism, adopts a pointedly informal style, emphasizing personal experience over abstract analysis. In the more than twenty-five novels she has written since *Rubyfruit,* Brown has addressed lesbian and gay themes with decreasing frequency. In fact, the bulk of Brown's output has been devoted to the best-selling Mrs. Murphy mystery series that began publishing in 1990. Given that this series is billed as cowritten with her cat, Sneaky Pie Brown, and centers on the adventures of a cat-dog-human sleuthing trio, it is perhaps not surprising that many of Brown's old readers lament what they perceive as the loss of her radical sensibility. Other readers, however, point out that Brown continues to demonstrate her gift for social critique and satirical humor, as well as her intolerance for bigotry in any form.

## Bibliography

Chew, Martha. "Rita Mae Brown: Feminist Theorist and Southern Novelist." *Southern Quarterly* 22, no. 1 (Fall 1903): 61 80.

Fishbein, Leslie. "Rubyfruit Jungle: Lesbianism, Feminism, and Narcissism." *International Journal of Women's Studies* 7, no. 2 (March–April 1984): 155–159.

Ward, Carol M. *Rita Mae Brown.* New York: Twayne, 1993.

**Katherine Adams**

*See also* COMEDY AND HUMOR; FURIES; LITERATURE; RADICALESBIANS; SHELLEY, MARTHA.

# BUDDHISTS AND BUDDHISM

Buddhism, a religion that began in the Indian subcontinent and is practiced widely today in Asia, has no official teaching on sexuality and no mechanism to impose a teaching on all Buddhists, so Buddhists are free to interpret the tradition as they wish and act as they think best. However, most forms of Buddhism regard desire, especially sexual desire, as the cause of continual rebirth in this world of suffering and recommend celibacy where possible. Homosexuality, as merely one form of sexual desire, is not prominently discussed. In the monastic regulations it is condemned along with all other forms of sexual activity, including autoeroticism. The Five Precepts taken by lay practitioners include a vow to abstain from "sexual misconduct," a vague term usually taken to mean adultery but occasionally broadened to include homosexuality. Many Buddhist teachers from Asia claim that homosexuality does not exist in their countries and so they have no opinion on it. The XIV Dalai Lama was neutral on the subject until he found authoritative texts of his lineage prohibiting it.

Although Buddhism does not have anything comparable to the natural law that some Christians find in the Bible, homosexuality is occasionally identified by Buddhists as a defect. It may be said to be the fruiting of unfortunate karma from a previous life or the seed of an unfortunate rebirth. In some ancient Indian texts, medical reasons are given as the cause of homosexuality. For example, a *pandaka* is an individual with some sort of sexual dysfunction, said to be the result of coitus with the woman on top. *Pandaka* is sometimes translated as "eunuch" but more likely means "an effeminate male."

Traditional Buddhism is organized around temples staffed by monastics. In the United States, immigrants from Buddhist countries in Asia often use the temple as a social and cultural center and their Buddhism is typically conservative. Americans not of Asian descent who find Buddhism attractive have established centers for study and meditation, which may be associated with a traditional Buddhist lineage and may have a monastic as resident teacher, but the majority of members are laypeople. The operation of the centers is usually democratic and seeks to respond to the needs of the lay clientele. It is in this context that LGBT Buddhists have been recognized.

## Independent LGBT Buddhist Groups

The formation of LGBT groups of Buddhist practitioners in the United States was more or less contemporaneous with the beginning of the AIDS epidemic. The spectacle of gay men meeting premature deaths in great numbers was a reminder of mortality to survivors, who looked for spiritual alternatives to the bar and party scene. Buddhism was seen as less homophobic than Christianity. LGBT Buddhist groups were begun in many cities, particularly San Francisco. The leading figure of the early LGBT Buddhist movement was Issan (1933–1990). Born Tommy Dorsey in Santa Barbara, California, he became what he called "a crazy drag-queen junkie" (Schneider, p. 76) in New York, Chicago, and San Francisco, where, via the hippie scene, he met Shunryu Suzuki, founder of the San Francisco Zen Center. Dorsey was impressed, began practicing Zen, and joined the Gay Buddhist Club that had formed in the Castro district. (Zen, a Japanese form of Buddhism imported from China, emphasizes sitting meditation practice.) The club became the Hartford Street Zen Center (HSZC) and established itself as the unofficial LGBT branch of the San Francisco Zen Center, with Issan as its Abbot from 1989 until shortly before his death. HSZC gave birth to Maitri, a hospice for AIDS patients, which is now a separate entity, while HSZC continues to hold regular meetings for Zen and to provide space for other Buddhist groups.

In 1991 the Gay Buddhist Fraternity was founded in San Francisco as an independent society for LGBT Buddhists. It later changed its name to the Gay Buddhist Fellowship (GBF). Typically, only men attend, although it is officially open to men and women, and a woman often gives the Dharma talk (the English-language term for a Buddhist sermon). GBF is very loosely organized, with no formal membership, and a group of GBF members who wanted more structure broke off to form the Gay Men's Buddhist Sangha (GMBS). Lesbians organized separately as the Dharma Sisters and, across the bay in Oakland, the

East Bay Lesbian Sangha. In 2003, Ji-Sing Norman Eng, a disciple of outspoken LGBT supporter Thich Nhat Hanh, was appointed as Minister of Buddhist Spirituality to the Metropolitan Community Church of San Francisco. Eng heads Q-Sangha, an authorized Thich Nhat Hanh meditation group that holds regular meetings attended by both men and women for meditation, chanting, and the study of Buddhism within a Christian context.

## Mainstream LGBT Buddhism

Stimulated by these independent groups, many established Buddhist centers are developing programs specifically for LGBT practitioners. The oldest of these programs appears to be the LGBT retreats led by Eric Kolvig and Arinna Weisman at Spirit Rock Meditation Center in Woodacre, California, which is the West Coast branch of the Insight Meditation Center of Barre, Massachusetts. Similar programs have been sponsored by the Zen Center of Los Angeles and Zen Mountain Monastery in Mount Tremper, New York. In 1994 there were reports that San Francisco Zen Center had a climate of "don't ask, don't tell" in regard to its LGBT members, but by 2003, LGBT persons appeared to have gained open acceptance.

A mainstream Buddhist group that explicitly and vigorously supports its LGBT members is Soka Gakkai International (SGI), a lay organization that traces its roots back to the Japanese reformer Nichiren (1222–1282). When SGI-USA, then known as Nichiren Shoshu of America, first came to the United States, it retained many Japanese customs, including sitting on the floor, and negatively hallucinating the presence of LGBT members (a negative hallucination is said to occur when someone does *not* see something that everyone else sees). In 1991 there was a major disagreement between SGI and its much smaller clerical parent group, resulting in mutual decrees of excommunication. Freed from Japanese control, SGI-USA adapted to American culture, in part by establishing LGBT groups in which LGBT persons are encouraged to see their LGBT orientation as their Buddha Nature and to nurture it. Racial and sexual-gender diversity is prominent at the meetings.

By the early 2000s, the future for LGBT Buddhists in America was bright. The independent LGBT groups were well established, and their influence on mainstream Buddhist centers showed signs of increasing.

### Bibliography

Cabezón, José. "Homosexuality and Buddhism." In *Homosexuality and World Religions.* Edited by Arlene Swidler. Valley Forge, Penn.: Trinity Press International, 1993.

Corless, Roger. "Coming Out in the Sangha: Queer Community in American Buddhism." In *The Faces of Buddhism in America.* Edited by Charles S. Prebish and Kenneth K. Tanaka. Berkeley: University of California Press, 1998.

———. "Gay Buddhist Fellowship." In *Engaged Buddhism in the West.* Edited by Christopher S. Queen. Boston: Wisdom Publications, 2000.

Leyland, Winston, ed. *Queer Dharma: Voices of Gay Buddhists.* Volume 1. San Francisco: Gay Sunshine Press, 1998.

———. *Queer Dharma: Voices of Gay Buddhists.* Volume 2. San Francisco: Gay Sunshine Press, 2000.

Schneider, David. *Street Zen: The Life and Work of Issan Dorsey.* Boston and London: Shambhala, 1993.

**Roger Corless**

*See also* CAGE, JOHN; CHURCHES, TEMPLES, AND RELIGIOUS GROUPS; GINSBERG, ALLEN.

# BUFFALO

A small and fragmented gay and lesbian community first emerged in the 1930s in Buffalo, a midsized industrial city on the shores of Lake Erie in upstate New York. By 1950, when Buffalo reached its peak population of 580,132, this community, which was built around bars, had grown significantly, leading to the development of distinct gay and lesbian identities and a visible lesbian and gay presence. Years before lesbians and gay men established their first political organization in Buffalo in 1969, they had forged a community.

## Historiography

The historians Elizabeth Lapovsky Kennedy and Madeline D. Davis provide a glimpse into the development of Buffalo's working-class lesbian community in their valuable *Boots of Leather, Slippers of Gold* (1993), which draws on oral histories from women involved in this community from the 1930s to the 1960s. Their social history provides an important perspective for understanding the development of LGBT consciousness, community, and politics in twentieth-century America. Kennedy and Davis assert that working-class lesbian women, through the femme-butch roles they developed, created a "culture of resistance" that played the most important role in the emergence of both the homophile and gay liberation movements, not only in Buffalo but elsewhere in the United States.

This interpretation challenges the view presented by Lillian Faderman in *Odd Girls and Twilight Lovers,* her 1991 survey of twentieth-century lesbian history in the United States. Faderman sees femme-butch identities as constricting and conservative, imitations of working-class heterosexual gender roles, often imposed on lesbians rather than freely chosen, and she describes bar life as oppressive and limiting. Faderman attributes much more historical importance in the creation of gay and lesbian political consciousness to the middle-class women who were involved in homophile organizations such as the Daughters of Bilitis and the Mattachine Society in the 1950s and 1960s and those who participated in the gay liberation and lesbian feminist movements of the late 1960s and 1970s. Leslie Feinberg's *Stone Butch Blues* (1993), a fictionalized account of her life in the Buffalo femme-butch community in the 1960s and 1970s, describes the conflicts between working-class lesbians and lesbian feminists and also discusses transgender individuals in Buffalo's gay and lesbian community.

## Lesbian and Gay Life in the 1930 and 1940s

According to Kennedy and Davis, a small gay and lesbian community had emerged in Buffalo by the 1930s, but it was fragmented and difficult to find. There were a few bars where gay men and lesbians could congregate during the decade. In 1932 they could go to Galante's, a downtown gay and lesbian speakeasy located behind City Hall. Galante's was frequently raided and it closed shortly after the end of Prohibition. Another mixed gay and lesbian bar, the Hillside, located far from downtown, operated for a year in the late 1930s. On Saturday nights Eddie's, a straight bar, allowed lesbians to use its back room. In the 1930s and 1940s, lesbians also went to the entertainment bars on Michigan Avenue in the black section of Buffalo. Most lesbian socializing, however, took place at private parties, especially during the period in the mid-1930s when the city had no gay or lesbian bars.

Buffalo's gay and lesbian community expanded and became much more visible in the 1940s. The city's industries thrived during World War II and its population increased. Gay bars, located mostly in the downtown red light district, proliferated. While lesbians and gay men mixed at Ralph Martin's, a large, popular bar open throughout the decade, they also socialized in separate public spaces. In addition to bars, gay men met each other and made sexual contacts at parks and beaches, areas that were far too dangerous for lesbians. Lesbians, whose social life was built around private parties as well as bars, could go to Winters, a small downtown lesbian bar owned by two black women. Discreet, well-dressed lesbians mixed with showgirls at Eddie Ryan's Niagara Hotel. Several bars catered to gay men. Those who wished to be discreet went to Down's, while working-class men and sailors frequented Polish John's and the Shamrock. Many other gay bars opened during the decade, and black entertainment bars and other straight bars also drew gay men and lesbians. George Chauncey points out in *Gay New York* (1994) that the New York State Liquor Authority labeled the mere presence of gay men and lesbians in bars as disorderly conduct and thus made it illegal to serve them. But there were only a few bar raids in Buffalo in the 1940s. This was most likely due to payoffs to the notably corrupt city police by the owners of lesbian and gay bars.

Because of the dramatic social changes brought about by World War II, lesbians were able to develop a common culture and public community in Buffalo. The more visible lesbian and gay bars of the 1940s made lesbians aware of others like them. High-paying industrial jobs not only gave lesbians more discretionary income, but also allowed them, for the first time, to wear pants in public without drawing notice. This permitted many lesbians to display openly a masculine style of dress. The smaller number of men in the city during the war made it safer for women to walk the streets, and since so many women were socializing with one another, camouflaged the social activities of lesbians. But there were constraints on lesbian life as well. Because many working-class lesbians lived with their parents and held jobs they could lose if their sexuality was revealed, they sharply divided their public and private lives. While socializing in the bars on weekends, lesbians could openly appear as butch. But at home and at work, they were usually discreet. For this reason, lesbians in this period often used gay men for cover in social situations.

The social life of white working-class lesbians moved to the public world of bars in the 1940s. The same was not generally true for black lesbians or white lesbians from other classes. Black lesbians lacked the necessary anonymity to support their own lesbian bar. They socialized primarily at elaborate, weekend-long house parties organized by black femmes. Some black lesbians went to Buffalo's white gay and lesbian bars, but these bars were not integrated until the next decade. Most middle-class white lesbians avoided bars because they feared losing their jobs if their lesbianism became known. Most wealthier lesbians, while more open about their sexuality, did not feel safe entering the tough neighborhoods where lesbian and gay bars were located. Unlike gay men, lesbians in Buffalo rarely socialized across class lines.

## Building a Femme-Butch Community in the 1950s

The working-class women who frequented gay and lesbian bars built a lesbian community and developed a lesbian culture through the femme-butch roles that organized their relationships. These roles also expanded the lesbian community by making lesbians visible to women attracted to women and to others. In the 1950s and the early 1960s, butches were the dominant figures in the lesbian community. But the intensified political attacks on homosexuals in this period, combined with a cultural emphasis on rigid gender roles and the nuclear family, led to increased harassment of those who rejected gender and sexual norms. Butches confronted this homophobia by taking on a more open and aggressive stance than they had in the 1940s.

By the 1950s many butches no longer divided their private and public lives. They dressed in male clothes all the time, which narrowed their job options. Butches worked in factories or gay bars, drove cabs, or, in some cases, pimped for femme prostitutes. By the late 1950s, the masculine dress and tough demeanor of butches made it difficult for many of them to work at all. Increasingly, they spent their days and evenings in gay and lesbian bars. Femmes were more able to hold down jobs and worked as clerical workers, waitresses, and prostitutes.

Lesbian relationships were structured by the femme-butch dynamic. Femme-butch couples were more likely than they had been in the 1930s and 1940s to live together. Because butches were underemployed, they were often supported by their femmes. Femmes also did most of the housework. A strict gender division marked their sexual relationships. Butches initiated lovemaking but rejected sexual reciprocity. By the late 1950s, the "stone butch," a woman who never allowed herself to be touched, became the sexual norm for butch women. Butches were often controlling and possessive of their femmes, and jealousy and violence, fueled by drinking in the bars, often wracked their relationships. While butches generally had friendships with other butches, femmes were more isolated.

Through their visible and defiant public stance, butches expanded the lesbian community in the 1950s. They were more welcoming of newcomers; older butches would educate younger lesbians about the sexual behavior and appearance necessary to establish a butch identity. Butches now fought openly when harassed on the street or in the bars, thus defending public space for lesbians. By the 1950s, Buffalo's gay and lesbian bars were clustered in a few dangerous blocks of downtown that had become known as the homosexual section. Two bars were popular among lesbians in the 1950s. Upwardly mobile working-class lesbians holding white-collar jobs went to the Carousel, a popular mixed lesbian and gay bar open from the late 1940s to the early 1960s. This group of lesbians,

unlike tough bar lesbians, still separated their public and private lives and continued to socialize with gay men. Tough lesbians hung out at Bingo's, a lesbian bar, or at rough bars that catered to prostitutes and pimps. While lesbians sometimes went to gay male bars, which included Johnny's Club Sixty-Eight and the Oasis in the gay downtown area, and the elite Five O'Clock Club, which was located in a nicer neighborhood, they were no longer welcome because the violent bar fights among tough lesbians brought trouble. Due to police payoffs, there were no police raids or arrests in Buffalo's gay bars in the 1950s.

Buffalo's tough bar lesbians racially integrated their community in the 1950s. While ethnic divisions among lesbians were rare and Native American women had socialized with white lesbians, Buffalo's lesbian bars became substantially desegregated in the 1950s. Bar lesbians built friendships across racial lines, but black lesbians continued to lead a mostly autonomous social life built around house parties and bars. Buffalo's black population had more than doubled in the 1940s, which allowed black lesbians the anonymity to patronize two racially mixed lesbian bars, the Five Five Seven and the Two Seventeen, which opened in the black section of Buffalo in the 1950s. Black lesbians also created the Royal L's in the mid-1960s, the first social organization for lesbians in the city. While the lesbian bar community became integrated in the 1950s, racism continued to mark the actions of the Buffalo police, who harassed black lesbian house parties and were much more likely to arrest black lesbians for disorderly conduct.

Violence marked the life of tough bar lesbians in the 1950s. Butches expanded lesbian territory by fighting men who attacked them on the streets and in bars. Femmes, who often worked as prostitutes in the 1950s and 1960s, also had to confront a great deal of street violence. In the homophobic climate of the 1950s, it was the tough bar lesbians who expanded the lesbian community and made it increasingly visible. Middle-class lesbians avoided the bars and remained closeted for fear of losing their jobs, while upwardly mobile white-collar workers continued to divide their private and public lives to maintain family connections and jobs. Kennedy and Davis assert that the femme-butch culture and violent resistance of these working-class lesbians in cities throughout America played a crucial role in fomenting the gay and lesbian liberation movement.

## Political Activism in the 1960s and 1970s

Working-class tough lesbians, along with gay men, founded the first gay and lesbian political organization in

Buffalo, the Mattachine Society of the Niagara Frontier, in 1969. They had been politicized by the police crackdowns on gay and lesbian bars and increased harassment of gay and lesbian bar patrons that occurred in the 1960s. Nelson Rockefeller, who became the governor of New York in 1959, launched an antivice campaign targeted at ending police corruption that led to the closing of gay and lesbian bars in the early 1960s. Bar owners could no longer make the police payoffs that had kept them in business. For a time in the 1960s, there were no gay or lesbian bars in Buffalo, and those that opened did not stay in business for long. Feinberg, in *Stone Butch Blues*, describes in graphic detail the violence that tough butches and femmes, as well as drag queens, faced at the hands of the Buffalo police in the 1960s when they were captured in bar raids. This increasingly hostile climate, together with the fledgling gay liberation movement launched by the Stonewall Riots, led lesbians and gay men to organize a chapter of the Mattachine Society in 1969 after they heard a talk by Franklin Kameny, the president of the Washington, D.C., Mattachine Society.

While working-class white and black lesbians were instrumental in founding the Mattachine Society of the Niagara Frontier, they were quickly marginalized by both the gay and women's liberation organizations that multiplied in Buffalo in the 1970s. Kennedy and Davis point out that bar lesbians did not share the gay liberation movement's interest in analyzing gay and lesbian oppression and were uncomfortable discussing their sexuality with the media. Nor did they find a place with lesbian feminists in the women's liberation movement. As Lillian Faderman describes in *Odd Girls and Twilight Lovers* (1991), lesbian feminists criticized femme-butch roles as imitations of heterosexual gender roles. Feinberg relates how young, middle-class lesbian feminists took over the lesbian bars in Buffalo, as they did in other cities. Just as femme-butch roles had been mandatory for women involved in the lesbian community from the 1940s through the 1960s, now these roles precluded many lesbians from participating in the community.

Feinberg poignantly describes how the lesbian-feminist labeling of butches as imitation men and the destruction of their bar-based social life combined with the destruction of Buffalo's industrial base in the early 1970s to lead some butches to pass as men. Some took male sex hormones and a few also had sex-change operations in order to find factory jobs in the increasingly bleak economic climate.

Gay and women's liberation groups proliferated in Buffalo from the late 1960s through the mid-1970s. A Buffalo chapter of the Radicalesbians and a Gay Men's Liberation Front were founded in 1969. The following year, the latter group added women and became the Gay Liberation Front. On 14 March 1971, hundreds of gay and lesbian activists from Buffalo participated in a gay and lesbian rights march in Albany, the first such march on a state capital. Members of the Mattachine Society of the Niagara Frontier and Buffalo Women's Liberation were among the nearly three thousand protesters who called for repeal of state laws against cross-dressing and sodomy. The Mattachine Society of the Niagara Frontier published a monthly newsletter called the *Fifth Freedom* from 1971 until 1983. The Sisters of Sappho met at the Buffalo Women's Center, which was located at 499 Franklin Street, held Saturday dances, and in 1977 published the *Lavender Grapevine Newsletter*. A women's self-help clinic also was located at the Women's Center. Buffalo's first gay and lesbian community center opened in the 1970s above a tire store on Main Street. For the most part, however, Buffalo gay men and lesbians socialized separately in the 1970s.

Buffalo's LGBT community has continued to grow and become more visible since the late 1970s. Yet in the 1990s the number of lesbian and gay bars was about the same as in the 1940s. This reminds us that it was the lesbian and gay patrons of those bars who, long before Stonewall, began to develop a gay and lesbian culture and community in Buffalo and in other cities around the nation.

## Bibliography

D'Emilio, John. *Sexual Politics, Sexual Communities: The Making of a Homosexual Minority in the United States, 1940–1970*. Chicago: University of Chicago Press, 1983.

Empire State Pride Agenda. "Sexual Orientation Non-Discrimination Act Chronology." Available from http://www.espany.org/sonda/SONDAChronology.PDF.

Faderman, Lillian. *Odd Girls and Twilight Lovers: A History of Lesbian Life in Twentieth-Century America*. New York: Columbia University Press, 1991.

Feinberg, Leslie. *Stone Butch Blues*. Ithaca, N.Y.: Firebrand Press, 1993.

"Historical Timeline of Buffalo's Gay, Lesbian, Bisexual, Transgender Movement." Available from http://www.infotrue.com/ubtimeline.html.

Katz, Jonathan Ned. *Gay American History: Lesbian and Gay Men in the U.S.A., a Documentary History*. Rev. ed. New York: Meridian, 1992.

Kennedy, Elizabeth Lapovsky, and Madeline D. Davis. *Boots of Leather, Slippers of Gold: The History of a Lesbian Community*. New York: Routledge, 1993.

Klose, Craig. "Gay History in Buffalo." Available from http://www.pridebuffalo.org/gay_history.htm.

Landman, Rick. "Personal Story of How the GLF in Buffalo Got Started." Available from http://www.infotrue.com/ubglf.html.

**Lynn Gorchov**

*See also* BENNETT, MICHAEL; FEMMES AND BUTCHES.

## BURNS, Randy (b. mid-twentieth century), activist, writer.

A Northern Paiute, Burns is a member of the Pyramid Lake Indian tribe, located primarily in Nevada. While a student at San Francisco State University (SFSU), Burns attempted to recruit Native American students to come to SFSU. While still in college, Burns came out as a gay activist during an interview for the *Nevada State Journal.* He has subsequently been interviewed by a variety of West Coast LGBT journals and newspapers. He has written various essays and introductions to books, among them *Living the Spirit: A Gay American Indian Anthology* and *Third and Fourth Genders in Native North Americans.* Burns has served with a variety of San Francisco government advisory groups and social programs. A member of the People of Color AIDS and the Human Rights Commission, Burns has served as an election official for more than two decades. He volunteers his time with numerous nonprofit organizations and programs focused on Native Americans in the San Francisco area.

Burns found that LGBT Native Americans continue to be ostracized or even bashed for their sexual orientation. Historically, every member of a Native American tribe had a specific role to play; no one was shunned for being different. People with ambiguous sexual or gender orientations were no different. Sometimes called "Two-Spirit People," these men and women served in a variety of roles, including leaders, shamans, healers, and—in the case of women—warriors. Viewed as both male and female, *berdache* (transvestites) were said to have links with the spiritual world and therefore were able to mediate between that world and the physical one.

With the conquest of the Americas by Europeans, an attempt was made to "civilize" Native Americans and make them like Europeans. Cultural assimilation was imposed; Judeo-Christian values—including taboos against homosexuality—became the emblem of "civilization." Traditional Native American religions and rituals were repressed, and—completely misconstruing who the *berdache* were and devaluing the functions that they played in Native American society—Europeans linked the *berdache* to the sins of sodomy and homosexuality. As a result, the *berdache* suffered severe persecution. Many

Native American apologists, in an attempt to mitigate the European attack on Native American culture and identity, diminished the role of the *berdache* in tribal life and ceremonies, some even suggesting that *berdache* were outcasts and scorned by their communities. Although Native American cultures resisted the assimilating influences, the role the *berdache* played in many societies was inarguably diminished.

Having seen violence committed by Native Americans against their LGBT brethren, Burns sought to remind Native Americans of the *berdache* heritage and to show people that LGBT Native Americans deserve cultural respect based on history. He cofounded Gay American Indians (GAI) with the late Barbara Cameron of the Lakota tribe in San Francisco in July 1975. In Burns's view, modern LGBT Native Americans are the direct descendants of the historic *berdache;* it is their duty to fulfill the roles the *berdache* once played in the traditions of their tribes.

By the end of the twentieth century, GAI had grown to more than six hundred members and spawned other LGBT American Indian groups in San Diego, Toronto, and New York City. GAI has documented *berdache* roles in more than 130 Native American tribes. Burns's own Northern Paiute has traditional *berdache* roles: *tuva'sa* (male) and *moroni noho* (female).

Burns has been given numerous awards over the years, including the Pioneer Award from the San Francisco Gay and Lesbian History Society in 2002. Until recently, Burns worked as a nurse assistant at San Francisco General Hospital.

### Bibliography

KQED Public TV and Radio. "Local Heroes: Randy Burns." http://www.kqed.org/topics/history/heritage/lgbt/heroes-rburns.jsp.

Roscoe, Will. "Bibliography of *Berdache* and Alternative Gender Roles among the North American Indians." *Journal of Homosexuality* 14, no. 3–4 (1987): 81–171.

———. "Living the Tradition: Gay American Indians." In *Gay Spirit: Myth and Meaning.* Edited by Mark Thompson. New York: St. Martin's Press, 1987.

———. *Changing Ones: Third and Fourth Genders in Native North America.* New York: St. Martin's Press, 1998.

Roscoe, Will, ed., and Gay American Indians, comp. *Living the Spirit: A Gay American Indian Anthology.* New York: St. Martin's Press, 1988.

Trexler, Richard C. *Sex and Conquest: Gendered Violence, Political Order, and the European Conquest of the Americas.* Ithaca, N.Y.: Cornell University Press, 1995.

**Michael W. Handis**

*See also* NATIVE AMERICAN LGBTQ ORGANIZATIONS AND PUBLICATIONS; NATIVE AMERICAN STUDIES.

# BURROUGHS, William S.
(b. 5 February 1914; d. 2 August 1997), author.

Muse of the Beats, godfather of punk, icon of counterculture, William Seward Burroughs was also a devoted homosexual, drug addict, firearm enthusiast, libertarian, and contentious man of letters. His cultural critique influenced successive generations of writers, musicians, and artists who rebelled against bourgeois aspirations and social norms.

Burroughs was born into a stiflingly conventional upper-middle-class family in St. Louis, Missouri. He was educated at private schools (including a ranch school at Los Alamos, New Mexico) and at Harvard University, and haphazardly pursued graduate studies in Vienna and Mexico City. In the mid-1940s he befriended street criminals and sex workers in New York City. His circle included hustler and fellow addict Herbert Huncke, who introduced him to morphine, and his common-law wife Joan Vollmer, who introduced him to Jack Kerouac and Allen Ginsberg. Burroughs's friendship with Ginsberg would prove crucial to his literary career. Over the next several years, Burroughs resided with Vollmer in New York, Texas, and Louisiana, narrowly escaping from various encounters with the police. He fled Mexico City in 1951 after accidentally shooting and killing Vollmer in a drunken game of William Tell, and traveled to Colombia and Ecuador in search of the hallucinogenic drug yage. Burroughs wrote about these experiences in *Junkie: Confessions of an Unredeemed Drug Addict* (1953), which Ginsberg edited and persuaded Ace Books to publish, and in *The Yage Letters* (1963), which includes the correspondence between Burroughs and Ginsberg during this period. The unexpurgated *Junky* appeared in print in 1977, and in 1986 his other manuscript from this era, which focused on sex, was published as *Queer*.

In his early work Burroughs developed conventional narratives based on life experiences. His writing changed markedly after 1953, when he moved to Tangier, Morocco. At the time, Tangier had unusual political status as an "international zone," separate from the rest of Morocco and governed by a coalition of colonial powers. Opiates and sex were easy to find and cheap to purchase, and Burroughs dedicated himself to both pursuits. Whether inspired by opiate highs or nightmarish withdrawals, Burroughs wrote hundreds of pages of surreal, paranoid, satiric, grotesque, and comic prose during this

**William S. Burroughs.** The eclectically unconventional icon of counterculture is perhaps best known for his unconstrained 1959 novel, *The Naked Lunch*—and for the scope of his influence on other outsiders and rebels since then. [AP/Wide World Photos]

period. Ginsberg and Kerouac arrived in Tangier to help Burroughs sort through the material and fashion a book, first published as *The Naked Lunch* in Paris in 1959.

The formal qualities of this book, a pastiche of fragmented and nonlinear episodes, marked it as a signal text of postmodern literature; both its style and substance were Burroughs's specific responses to the pressures he experienced as a queer drug user on the run from U.S. social mores and vice laws, and living in what he called the "Interzone." He struggled with social conditioning that instilled both guilt about his sexual desires and fear of male effeminacy, and in Tangier he proactively pursued sex, drug use, and writing as a means to move beyond such conditioning. Burroughs developed a theory that language acts upon people the way a virus attacks an organism, and conditions thought and behavior the way opiates overwhelm addicts. *The Naked Lunch* was his first attempt to strike back at language by refusing to adhere to the constraints of narrative coherence, rationality, literary and social conventions, and unified consciousness. In 1958 he moved to Paris and then London in 1960, where he attempted to push this approach even further with *The Soft Machine* (1961), *The Ticket That Exploded* (1962), and *Nova Express* (1964), for which he literally cut up pages of text and experimented with random juxtapositions, aiming to redefine literature and authorship. Burroughs's theory of language anticipated Michel Foucault's explanation of how power is exercised through discourse, and his "cut-up" novels attempted a mode of deconstruction before Jacques Derrida introduced that concept.

Burroughs resumed writing narrative with the novel *The Wild Boys* (1971), and returned to the United States in 1974. His next novels were *Cities of the Red Night* (1981), *The Place of Dead Roads* (1984), and *The Western Lands* (1987). Pornography, sexual fantasy, sadomasochism, fetishism, adolescence, violence, masculinity, and racialized sexuality continued to exert considerable influence on his literary imagination. He settled in Lawrence, Kansas, where he wrote, took up painting, and pursued various projects, including acting for director Gus Van Sant. His impact on rock music was decisive; he collaborated with or influenced Tom Waits, Kurt Cobain, Patti Smith, Lou Reed, the Rolling Stones, U2, and others. During the last forty years of the twentieth century, Burroughs became an icon of underground arts and radical cultural critique. Through his fiction, essays, and interviews, as well as through the deliberate circulation of his image (gravelly voice and signature fedora and dark suit), Burroughs celebrated the political loners, sexual outsiders, and agents provocateurs of American society.

### Bibliography

Morgan, Ted. *Literary Outlaw: The Life and Times of William S. Burroughs.* New York: Henry Holt, 1988.

Mullins, Greg. *Colonial Affairs: Bowles, Burroughs, and Chester Write Tangier.* Madison: University of Wisconsin Press, 2002.

Russell, Jaime. *Queer Burroughs.* New York: Palgrave, 2001.

**Greg Mullins**

***See also*** BEATS; GINSBERG, ALLEN; LITERATURE.

# BUSINESSES

The development of LGBT communities after the Stonewall Riots of 1969 spurred the growth of commercial institutions to serve and reach those communities. Compared to what came later, relatively few businesses or other economic institutions catering to sexual and gender minorities existed before 1969. Such businesses were usually marginal and often illegal, operating under "black market" conditions. The LGBT community mostly consisted largely of informal networks of friends who socialized in private homes, at cruising sites, and in LGBT bars. After Stonewall, the number of businesses grew rapidly and provided an increasingly wide range of goods and services—although growth took place unevenly between various segments of LGBT communities, who were differentiated by gender, race, class, and erotic preferences.

## LGBT Businesses before Stonewall

Before Stonewall, the large but relatively invisible character of the LGBT population made it difficult for LGBT businesses to emerge. The necessary secretiveness of much of LGBT life limited the information necessary for economic markets to operate efficiently and for businesses successfully to identify and reach their customers. The desire to avoid public identification often meant that LGBT bars, bathhouses, bookstores, and other businesses, especially those that catered to middle-class clientele, sought to be as inconspicuous as possible—their outside appearances were often muted, their signs cryptic or insignificant. Bouncers often "screened" customers in order to minimize the intrusions of hostile outsiders or undercover police. These businesses often were located in neighborhoods that were segregated from everyday business and residential activities—for example, in industrial areas, in red light districts, or on isolated roads in rural areas. In addition, the prevalence of secrecy frequently encouraged different forms of "extortion" in LGBT economic life, ranging from crude efforts at blackmail to the refined "protection" provided by LGBT bar payoffs to police and organized crime.

The business and economic life of LGBT people developed sporadically and unevenly before 1969. Nevertheless, starting approximately in the 1880s, the center of gay communal life, and therefore of its economic life as well, was the drinking institution, whether it was bar, saloon, or dance hall. Public bathhouses, a staple of immigrant urban communities living in tenement housing without running water, also served gay and bisexual men. These commercial venues provided institutional contexts for homosexual and transgender socializing, sexual activity, and the establishment of relationships. LGBT people also congregated in certain urban neighborhoods where there were rooming houses, female boardinghouses, and low-cost hotels.

In *Gay New York* (1994), George Chauncey shows that in the late nineteenth and early twentieth centuries "fairy resorts" in specific city districts (including Times Square) often served as centers of social life for both neighborhood men and homosexuals from other areas of the city. Some male homosexuals earned income from prostitution and from live performances in sex and drag shows. LGBT people gathered together in cafeterias, coffee shops, and restaurants. In the 1920s and 1930s, Greenwich Village and Harlem showed more visible signs of the presence of LGBT communities—speakeasies, bars, social clubs, theaters, drag balls, and nightclubs that catered to homosexual and transgender clientele. These were well known among the public; in fact, straight tourists came to see the fairies and other oddities.

New York was not alone. From as early as the 1880s, red-light districts in large cities like Chicago, Boston, New Orleans, Philadelphia, Denver, Los Angeles, and San Francisco, with their concentrations of prostitutes, burlesque theaters, peep shows, and stores selling erotic literature, erotic apparel, and other sexual merchandise, featured enclaves of businesses, especially bars, that catered to LGBT customers. The number of these businesses appears to have grown significantly during World War II, although they catered more to men than to women before, during, and after the war. In part this was due to men's higher incomes and their greater presence in public space.

After World War II, concentrations of LGBT people in certain neighborhoods of larger cities, such as New York, Los Angeles, Chicago, Philadelphia, and Washington, D.C., helped support increased LGBT business development. Bars, clubs, restaurants, and coffeehouses continued to be the most significant commercial establishments serving LGBT communities in both large and smaller cities. Despite their economic significance, however, they provided few jobs and little income to LGBT people and therefore did little to develop a more diversified LGBT commercial sector.

Gay or lesbian bars were rarely owned by gay men or lesbians, although the pattern of bar ownership varied from one region or city to the next. In the Northeast, bars were often owned and controlled by organized crime, "the Mafia," while in cities like San Francisco, perhaps 25 to 30 percent of the gay bars in the mid-1960s were owned, according to Bob Damron (founder of *Damron's Travel Guides*), by gay men or lesbians. The Tavern Guild, an association of LGBT owners of LGBT bars was founded in San Francisco in 1962, was the first LGBT business association in the United States. The Stonewall Inn in New York, one of the most famous businesses in LGBT history and the site of the 1969 police raid and riots that launched the gay liberation movement, was owned by three small-time Mafia figures. Through the

1950s and early 1960s, it had been a local Greenwich Village bar. In 1966 three young men associated with the Genovese crime family, "Mario," Zucchi, and "Fat Tony" Lauria, opened the Stonewall Inn as a gay club. Lauria was not known to be gay when he and his partners opened the Stonewall; soon after, however, he began to have sex with men. In most cities, the profits and income generated by LGBT customers went to straight owners and was never reinvested in LGBT communities.

Bars both helped and hurt LGBT people economically. Although bars were often raided, they afforded their customers some protection against entrapment, physical assault, and blackmail. In many cities, owners paid the police and organized crime for "protection," which reduced the risks of police raids and criminal violence. However, owners justified charging extra for drinks, food, and other refreshments, to recover the costs of payoffs.

LGBT business development was encouraged by the emergence of homophile organizations and publications in the 1950s and 1960s. LGBT publications of various types were among the first and most important ways that LGBT people were able to communicate with one another outside of face-to-face relationships. Periodicals such as *ONE*, published by ONE Inc.; the *Mattachine Review*, published by the Mattachine Society; the *Ladder*, published by the Daughters of Bilitis; and *Drum*, published by the Janus Society, carried small-scale advertising for various types of businesses. Their notices of books and mail-order advertisements, for example, helped to develop niche markets for LGBT people. Cultural goods, clothing, and erotic literature were also marketed to the LGBT community through these publications. Meanwhile, homophile activists created a set of publishing and distribution companies, some of them quite large, oriented to the LGBT market. These included Pan-Graphic Press, founded by Hal Call and Donald Lucas in San Francisco; Guild Press, founded by H. Lynn Womack in Washington, D.C.; and Trojan Book Service, founded by Clark Polak in Philadelphia.

Several of these operations functioned primarily as mail-order businesses, which were able to reach a self-selected LGBT market. One mail-order business that emerged in this period was able to adapt itself and survive after Stonewall, producing the *Damron Travel Guide*. In 1964, businessman Bob Damron published a small book listing all of the LGBT bars that he encountered on his extensive travels in the United States. He claimed to have visited each bar personally and briefly characterized it. At the beginning of the twenty-first century, the company was still operating and publishing men's and women's travel guides, maps, and city guidebooks.

Another early gay mail-order business was the publication and distribution of male nude and erotic photographs (both individually and in magazines). Guild Press and Trojan Book Service specialized in these types of business activities. Almost everyone who published or distributed these publications faced arrest or persecution at one time or another. Even *ONE,* a somewhat staid homophile periodical, was declared obscene and banned from the mails by the U.S. Post Office, merely because it was a homosexual publication. It won a landmark 1958 decision in the U.S. Supreme Court, which recognized its redeeming cultural value. Bob Mizer, the founder of the Athletic Model Guild, served a short term in jail in 1954, but afterward protected his business by marketing erotic photographs in the guise of "artistically" posed seminude male models. Magazines such as *Physique Artistry, Grecian Guild Pictorial, MANual,* and *Trim* also published photographs of semiclad and nude male models. The many court battles of the 1950s and 1960s that focused on obscenity gradually made possible more explicit representations.

Bookstores also played a significant role in the pre-Stonewall period. Before Stonewall, calling a bookstore "gay" usually implied that it sold pornography. But Craig Rodwell, who founded New York's Oscar Wilde Memorial Bookshop in 1967, decided to sell only real "literature."

Meanwhile, many LGBT professionals, including physicians, dentists, psychologists, and lawyers, were self-employed and operated businesses that, to some degree, served LGBT people. In addition, certain occupations were defined in the pre-Stonewall era as stereotypically gay or lesbian. Male interior decorators, hairdressers, librarians, and nurses and female gym teachers are among the most prominent examples. In part because of the stereotypes, some LGBT people were attracted to these occupations, which seemed to offer a safe haven.

## After Stonewall, 1969–1989

After the Stonewall Riots, LGBT economic life changed dramatically. The politics of visibility, based on the gay liberation principle that enjoined homosexuals to "come out of the closet," established the basis for political organizing and community building, but it also had economic consequences—helping to create a visible population of LGBT consumers. Many small businesses, including nonprofit spin-offs from LGBT organizations, such as bookstores, publications, coffeehouses, bathhouses, and counseling services, opened to serve LGBT customers and clients.

Businesses that provided cultural goods, including newspapers, music recordings, books, magazines, pornography, and erotica, found profitable niches very quickly. The *Advocate* (published by Liberation Publications) started out as a local Los Angeles newspaper in 1967 and became a national publication after Stonewall. Bookstores specializing in gay, lesbian, and women's literature opened in many large and medium-sized cities across the country. For example, in Philadelphia, Jay's Place opened as a "homophile" bookstore in 1970, and in Washington, D.C., Lambda Rising Bookstore, which opened in 1970 as a "head shop" (for psychedelic and drug paraphernalia), soon transformed itself into a gay bookstore.

In the 1980s and early 1990s, *Publishers Weekly* and other book trade publications announced the "gay publishing boom." Mainstream publishers together with newly founded gay, feminist, and lesbian presses published an unprecedented number of books on LGBT topics. By 1991, there were more than four hundred gay and lesbian publishers of books, magazines, and newspapers. Alyson Books in Boston became a leading lesbian and gay publishing house in the 1980s. Initially the offshoot of a bookstore and a book and magazine distributor, it was purchased by Liberation Publications in 1995.

The new visibility of LGBT communities in the years after Stonewall attracted large numbers of sexual and gender minorities to large and medium-sized cities, with significant economic ramifications. San Francisco, Los Angeles, Chicago, and New York became "gay meccas" with large and diversified communities. Between the early 1970s and the early 1980s, thousands of LGBT people migrated from suburbs, towns, and small cities to these urban meccas and to regional centers like Houston, New Orleans, Atlanta, St. Louis, Philadelphia, and Boston. By 1993, Overlooked Opinions, an LGB marketing research firm, claimed that 45 percent of lesbians and 53 percent of gay men lived in urban areas. Many of these gay men and, to a lesser extent, lesbians moved into comfortable and inexpensive neighborhoods, where they purchased houses and apartment buildings, renovated them, and started businesses to support the process of gentrification. Among these businesses were real estate brokers, housewares companies, hardware stores, contractors, and providers of financial services.

The growth of LGB-owned small businesses was reflected in political developments. In 1976, for example, Harvey Milk, the owner of a camera shop on Castro Street in San Francisco, was elected to the city's Board of Supervisors. His election represented, in part, the consolidation of the Castro district as an LGBT neighborhood (through the process of gentrification during the 1970s) and was financed in part by many small business owners in the community.

**LGBT Businesswoman.** Judy Dlugacz owns a lesbian travel agency, Olivia, an offshoot of the music business, Olivia Records, that she cofounded two decades earlier. [Jill Posener]

The economic development that took place in this era was not equitably balanced between lesbians and gay men. Generally, lesbians had fewer economic resources at their disposal than gay men did. Lesbians and gay men also often specialized in different kinds of businesses and lived in different neighborhoods. Lesbian community-building and economic development reflected different needs and agendas. In the mid- to late 1970s lesbians entered a separatist phase, partly in their effort to build women's communities and partly because gay men were no less chauvinist than straight men. During the 1970s many businesses founded by lesbians were inspired by the vision of developing goods and services that would uniquely satisfy the needs of lesbians. There was a desire also to establish lesbian workplaces based on lesbian-feminist principles. One of the most successful of lesbian businesses was Olivia Records, founded in 1973 by a group including singers Meg Christian and Cris Williamson. In the 1990s, Olivia evolved into Olivia Cruises and Resorts when founder Judy Dlugacz organized a concert at sea. The challenge of starting a lesbian-owned business organized around lesbian-feminist business principles is explored by Kathy Weston and Lisa Rofel in their 1997 essay on Amazon Auto Repair. They found that workplace stresses could not always be easily dealt with within a lesbian feminist context, and eventually Amazon underwent a crippling and debilitating strike

by its employees. While the business survived the strike, the shared lesbianism of owners and workers did not facilitate the resolution of workplace conflict.

One of the thriving businesses that emerged from its early origins as an underground business was the production and distribution of gay pornography. During the 1900s, the gay pornography industry experienced a boom when video production became cheaper, VCRs allowed for porn videos to be viewed privately at home, and, in response to the AIDS epidemic, many gay men turned to viewing pornography as a substitute for casual sex. Some companies, such as San Francisco's Falcon Studios, were extremely successful. Falcon's founder, Chuck Holmes, funded many LGBT political campaigns and charities and donated more than one million dollars to San Francisco's Lesbian, Gay, Bisexual, and Transgender Community Center, which has been renamed in his honor.

The AIDS epidemic, in addition to the grief engendered by the loss of life, has also imposed a huge economic burden on LGBT communities, and on society as a whole. Individuals who developed more advanced HIV-related illnesses often lost income through the loss of full-time jobs or through a necessary reduction in work hours. Moreover, they have experienced massive increases in healthcare expenses. The AIDS epidemic has also drained economic resources from LGBT communities more generally. The mobilization of LGBT communities to provide support for people with AIDS and the creation of institutions for education, care, and research about AIDS have diverted resources from other activities such as non-AIDS-related education, leisure, investment in small businesses and careers, and real estate improvement. In the years between 1985 and 1995, probably the largest economic institutions in many LGBT communities were nonprofit AIDS organizations, such as Gay Men's Health Crisis in New York City and the San Francisco AIDS Foundation, and LGBT community centers, such as the Los Angeles Gay and Lesbian Community Services Center, which provided social services for people with HIV and AIDS.

The development of LGBT communities is the result of a simultaneous process of cultural identification and economic development. Identification as LGBT is built on cultural reinforcements such as LGBT popular culture, consumer goods specifically developed for LGBT people, residence in LGBT neighborhoods, and participation in LGBT activities, such as lesbian softball teams or gay choirs. In the early days of LGBT liberation, the community's small businesses supplied LGBT cultural and consumer needs in the form of commodities and encouraged community leaders to think of the LGBT community as an "ethnic group." In this respect, LGBT people have followed in the footsteps of the Irish, Italians, Jews, Poles, and Scandinavians in the United States—the construction of communities and the development of political machines and economic resources eventually leading to the achievement of "assimilation." LGBT people have also followed in the footsteps of other groups by developing businesses that serve a growing and increasingly diverse population. There are now businesses that cater to the needs and interests of African American, Latino, and Asian American LGBT communities.

## The LGBT Marketing Moment, 1990–2000

In the early 1990s, the gay and lesbian market emerged as a major consumer market, one worth "untold millions," according to business writer Grant Lukenbill (1995). Large companies like AT&T, Miller Beer, Continental Airlines, and Calvin Klein developed marketing campaigns that explicitly targeted gay and lesbian communities. A growing number of mainstream companies advertised in gay magazines, sponsored TV shows with gay and lesbian characters, and customized their products and services for lesbian and gay men's needs.

Studies by market research firms projected lucrative LGBT market segments. According to data from Overlooked Opinions, the average household income for lesbians in 1992 was $45,827; for gay men it was $51,325. In comparison, the 1990 average household income in the United States was $36,520. One newsletter, *Affluent Marketers Alert,* estimated that gay men spend two out of every three "queer dollars". Other aspects of lesbian and gay lifestyles are revealed by the fact that more than 80 percent of gay men dine out more than five times per month. Lesbians who own their homes make up 43 percent of the lesbian community; gay male homeowners represent 48 percent of their community. Together, lesbians and gay men took more than 162 million trips in 1991.

Amy Gluckman and Betsey Reed (1997) have argued that the gay marketing moment obscures the economic disparities caused by race, class, and gender differences in the gay community. Unfortunately, as Gluckman and Reed point out, the LGBT marketing bonanza has encouraged corporations to cultivate a narrow definition of gay identity (white, male, affluent) as a marketing tool. In addition, while mainstream corporations provide some consumer benefits and spend more money in LGBT communities than previously, the LGBT market effort of mainstream corporate America has led to increased competition with existing LGBT businesses (driving some of them out of business). This means that most LGBT dollars continue to end up in the coffers of "straight" businesses.

The flourishing economic and commercial life of LGBT communities also has given rise to the mistaken belief that all gay men and lesbians are more affluent than heterosexuals are, that they are more engaged in conspicuous consumption, and that they enjoy a more self-indulgent lifestyle. But in fact, LGBT people continued to endure economic discrimination on many different levels (for example, lack of access to tax and inheritance benefits for married couples, prejudice in hirings, denials of promotions and salary increases, and restrictions on healthcare). Despite these many challenges, the market process continues to play an important role—both negative and positive—in the development of LGBT communities.

## Bibliography

Achilles, Nancy. "The Development of the Homosexual Bar as an Institution." In *Sexual Deviance.* Edited by John H. Gagnon and William Simon. New York: Harper and Row, 1967.

Badgett, M. V. Lee. *Money, Myths, and Change: The Economic Lives of Lesbians and Gay Men.* Chicago: University of Chicago Press, 2001.

Baker, Dan. "A History in Ads: The Growth of the Gay and Lesbian Market." In *Homo Economics: Capitalism, Community, and Lesbian and Gay Life.* Edited by Amy Gluckman and Betsey Reed. New York: Routledge, 1997.

Bemym, Brett, ed. *Creating a Place for Ourselves: Lesbian, Gay, and Bisexual Community Histories.* New York: Routledge, 1997.

Chasin, Alexandra. *Selling Out: The Gay and Lesbian Movement Goes to Market.* New York: St. Martin's, 2000.

Chauncey, George. *Gay New York: Gender, Urban Culture, and the Making of the Gay Male World, 1890–1940.* New York: Basic Books, 1994.

Escoffier, Jeffrey. "Stigmas, Work Environment, and Economic Discrimination against Homosexuals." *Homosexual Counseling Journal* 2, no. 1 (January 1975): 8–17.

———. "The Political Economy of the Closet: Notes toward an Economic History of Gay and Lesbian Life before Stonewall." In *Homo Economics: Capitalism, Community, and Lesbian and Gay Life.* Edited by Amy Gluckman and Betsey Reed. New York: Routledge, 1997.

Friedman, Mack. *Strapped for Cash: A History of American Hustler Culture.* Los Angeles: Alyson Books, 2003.

Gluckman, Amy, and Betsey Reed, eds. *Homo Economics: Capitalism, Community, and Lesbian and Gay Life.* New York: Routledge, 1997.

Goffman, Erving. *Stigma: Notes on the Management of Spoiled Identity.* Englewood Cliffs, N.J.: Prentice-Hall, 1963.

Harry, Joseph, and William B. DeVall. "Urbanization and the Development of Homosexual Communities." In their *The Social Organization of Gay Males.* New York: Praeger, 1978.

Kennedy, Elizabeth Lapovsky, and Madeline D. Davis, *Boots of Leather, Slippers of Gold: The History of a Lesbian Community.* New York: Routledge, 1993.

Knopp, Lawrence. "Some Theoretical Implications of Gay Involvement in an Urban Land Market." *Political Geographical Quarterly* 9, no. 4 (October 1990).

Levine, Martin P. "Gay Ghetto." In *Gay Men: The Sociology of Male Homosexuality*. Edited by Martin P. Levine. New York: Harper and Row, 1979

Lezneff, Maurice, and William A. Westley. "The Homosexual Community." *Social Problems* 3 (1956).

Light, Ivan, and Stavros Karageorgis. "The Ethnic Economy." In *The Handbook of Economic Sociology*. Edited by Neil J. Smelser and Richard Swedberg. Princeton, N.J.: Princeton University Press and Russell Sage Foundation, 1994.

Luckinbill, Grant. *Untold Millions: Positioning Your Business for the Lesbian and Gay Consumer Revolution*. New York: Harper Business, 1995.

Lynch, Frederick R. "Nonghetto Gays: An Ethnography of Suburban Homosexuals." In *Gay Culture in America: Essays from the Field*. Edited by Gilbert Herdt. Boston: Beacon Press, 1992.

Mumford, Kevin. *Interzones: Black/White Sex Districts in Chicago and New York in the Early Twentieth-Century*. New York: Columbia University Press, 1997.

Philipson, Tomas J., and Richard A. Posner. *Private Choices and Public Health: The AIDS Epidemic in Economic Perspective*. Cambridge, Mass.: Harvard University Press, 1993.

Singer, Bennett L., and David Deschamps, eds. *Gay and Lesbian Stats: A Pocket Guide of Facts and Figures*. New York: New Press, 1994.

Stein, Marc. *City of Sisterly and Brotherly Loves: Lesbian and Gay Philadelphia, 1945–1972*. Chicago: University of Chicago Press, 2000.

Stigler, George. "The Economics of Information." *Journal of Political Economy* 69 (1961).

Stryker, Susan, and Jim Van Buskirk. *Gay by the Bay: A History of Queer Culture in the San Francisco Bay Area*. San Francisco. Chronicle Books, 1996.

Wardlow, Daniel L. *Gays, Lesbians, and Consumer Behavior: Theory, Practice and Research Issues in Marketing*. New York: Harrington Park Press, 1996.

Weston, Kathy, and Lisa B. Rofel. "Sexuality, Class, and Conflict in a Lesbian Workplace." In *Homo Economics: Capitalism, Community, and Lesbian and Gay Life*. Edited by Amy Gluckman and Betsey Reed. New York: Routledge, 1997.

**Jeffrey Escoffier**

*See also* BARS, CLUBS, AND RESTAURANTS; BATHHOUSES; BOOKSTORES; CAPITALISM AND INDUSTRIALIZATION; CORDOVA, JEANNE; CROSS-CLASS SEX AND RELATIONSHIPS; FURIES; GRAHN, JUDY; GYMS, FITNESS CLUBS, AND HEALTH CLUBS; NEWSPAPERS AND MAGAZINES; OLIVIA RECORDS; POLAK, CLARK; PUBLISHERS; RESORTS; RODWELL, CRAIG; SEX CLUBS; WICKER, RANDOLFE; WOMACK, H. LYNN.

**BUTCHES AND FEMMES.** see FEMMES AND BUTCHES.

# C

## CADMUS, Paul (b. 17 December 1904; d. 12 December 1999), artist.

The son of two artists, Paul Cadmus was born in New York City in 1904. He showed creative promise from an early age and had a sketch published in the *New York Herald Tribune* at the age of nine. Cadmus later studied at the National Academy of Design and worked for several years as a graphic artist and lay-out designer for an advertising agency in New York. From the early 1930s to his death in 1999, Cadmus produced a remarkable body of paintings, prints, and drawings. His debut painting, a raucous scene of sailors on shore leave titled *The Fleet's In!* (1934), was confiscated by federal officials just before its intended display at The Corcoran Gallery of Art in Washington, D.C., in 1934. This act of censorship, undertaken at the behest of the U.S. Navy, sparked a media sensation, with scores of newspapers and national magazines running articles on the episode, many accompanied by a reproduction of the work. While the navy successfully removed *The Fleet's In!* from public exhibition, it unwittingly insinuated the picture into the powerful flow of mass culture. As Harry Salpeter reported in *Esquire* (July 1937, p. 106), "for every individual who might have seen the original at the Corcoran, at least one thousand saw it in black and white reproduction."

This episode might have provided a moment of mere (and fleeting) notoriety to the artist. Instead, Cadmus followed up *The Fleet's In!* with a string of ambitious paintings that were widely reviewed and exhibited. These paintings furnish a vivid, if broadly comic, account of period life in New York City, of half-clad men in the locker room of the Young Men's Christian Association, of rough-and-tumble bathers on Coney Island, and of revelers in a hotel room on New Year's Eve. By his own account, Cadmus's conception of the human form was inspired by Italian Renaissance artists such as Luca Signorelli, Andrea Mantenga, and Marcantanio Raimondi, artists who were themselves reclaiming the classical forms and themes of antiquity. Yet Cadmus's work was never a simple borrowing of Old Master sources. Instead Cadmus fused Renaissance forms with contemporary social satire, all the while emphasizing the sexual energies and overtight clothing of the figures (especially the male figures) that formed his primary pictorial focus.

Cadmus's first one-man show (at the Midtown Galleries in 1937) attracted some seven thousand visitors, and broke attendance records at the venue. All the works on display were sold. In a *New York Times* (27 March 1937, p. 12) review of the show, Edward Jewell praised "this very gifted young American [for his] splendid draftsmanship, so lusty and firm yet so full of unforced subtlety, and his quite as splendid design," while a notice in the *Art Digest* (1 April 1937, p. 17) celebrated "the rare ability of this thirty-two-year-old who promises to play a dominant role in the growing art of this country."

This prophecy would remain unfulfilled because Cadmus's career was eclipsed by the rise of abstract expressionism and the preeminence of modernist art and criticism following World War II. So far out of favor would the artist fall by the 1960s that his name all but disappeared from the *Art Index* during that period. Yet critical attention should not be confused with creative

*Horseplay.* This 1935 painting by Paul Cadmus is one of the artist's many ambitious works blending Renaissance forms, contemporary social satire, and homoeroticism. [Sandra Paci, D.C. Moore]

productivity. Cadmus produced some of his most accomplished work, including some of his most ambitious and painstaking egg tempera paintings, during periods of relative obscurity.

Beginning in the late 1970s, scholarly and curatorial interest in the artist underwent a gradual renaissance, one that included a doctoral dissertation and popular monograph on the artist as well as the first, full-scale retrospective of his career. Even before art historians had completed the initial scholarship on Cadmus, however, the gay male community began to reclaim the artist as a significant figure within its own, largely unwritten, history. As early as 1976, gay newspapers and magazines were casting Cadmus as an artistic pioneer whose homoerotic works had laid the foundation for those of later gay painters and photographers such as David Hockney, Robert Mapplethorpe, and Tom of Finland. Such articles were part of a wider, post-Stonewall effort to retrieve forgotten or overlooked gay and lesbian lives from the historical record. Since then, Cadmus's reputation has been enhanced by the field of lesbian and gay studies and by the serious attention paid to the social history and visual representation of homosexuality.

The male nude, always at the center of Cadmus's creative vision, emerged in his later years as the artist's primary subject. Throughout much of his late work, Cadmus focused on the beloved form of his life partner and longtime model, Jon Anderson. In 1998 Cadmus was honored with a lifetime achievement award from the College Art Association, the largest organization of artists and art historians in the United States. Cadmus continued working and exhibiting to the time he died in 1999 at the age of ninety-four.

"I believe," Cadmus wrote in his 1937 *Credo,* "that art is not only more true but also more living and vital if it derives its immediate inspiration and its outward form from contemporary life." The outward forms of contemporary life that inspired Cadmus were often highly charged moments of social and sexual interaction. Through the combination of seemingly incompatible pictorial modes—of the classical and the contemporary, of the carnal and the carnivalesque—Cadmus wrought an utterly original vision of the human body and the volatile forces of desire that swirl around it.

## Bibliography

Anonymous. "Cadmus, Satirist of Modern Civilization." *Art Digest,* 1 April 1937, p. 17.

Cadmus, Paul. "Credo" (1937 broadside). Reprinted in *Paul Cadmus,* by Lincoln Kirstein, 142. Petaluma, Cal.: Pomegranate Art Books, 1992.

Jewell, Edward Alden. "Cadmus Canvases Hung at Midtown." *New York Times,* 27 March 1937, p. 12.

Kirstein, Lincoln. *Paul Cadmus.* Petaluma, Cal.: Pomegranate Art Books, 1992.

Salpeter, Harry. "Paul Cadmus: Enfant Terrible." *Esquire,* July 1937: 105–111.

**Richard Meyer**

*See also* VISUAL ART.

# CAGE, John (b. 5 September 1912; d. 12 August 1992), composer, author.

Valedictorian at Los Angeles High School, Cage dropped out of Pomona College in 1930 to travel in Europe and study music and architecture. He studied music in New York with Henry Cowell and in Los Angeles with Arnold Schoenberg, the latter having agreed to take him on as a pupil even though Cage could not pay his high fee. Cage claimed to have no feeling for harmony, and Schoenberg told him he would never be able to write music as a result: "You'll come to a wall and you won't be able to get through"; to which Cage responded, "I'll beat my head against that wall" ("Autobiographical Statement"). Much of Cage's life was spent creating an alternative musical language that rejected harmony.

In 1935 Cage married Xenia Andreevna Kashevaroff, the artistic daughter of an Alaskan priest—they were divorced in 1945—although he had previously had homosexual experiences, notably with Don Sample, an American artist with whom he had traveled in Europe. In 1937 Cage moved to Seattle, where he worked as both piano accompanist and composer for the Cornish School, an avant-garde dance academy. There, in 1938, he met his lifelong partner and artistic collaborator, Merce Cunningham (b. 1919). They began working together in 1942 and continued to do so until Cage's death, for the most part with the dance company Cunningham founded at Black Mountain College, North Carolina, in 1953, which still bears his name and performs under his direction. Cunningham's conception of dance—in which performers do not dance "to" music (which they sometimes do not hear until the live performance) and either improvise much of their work or assume different roles based on chance procedures—corresponded well to Cage's vision of music.

Cage's music was greatly influenced by his study of artists Marcel Duchamp and Robert Rauschenberg. Just as Duchamp believed that art could not be separated from life, and anything could be art, Cage did not believe music could be divorced from sound, or even noise— "everything we do is music." He noted: "Noises escape power, that is, the laws of counterpoint and harmony.... My idea is that there should be no more prisons" (Katz, "John Cage's Queer Silence"). He invented an instrument, the prepared piano, in which objects are placed between the strings on a soundboard to create a variety of sounds. Cage's equivalent of Duchamp's upside-down bicycle wheel and Rauschenberg's *White Paintings* was his *4'33"* (1952), a composition in which a pianist sits at a keyboard and does nothing for that length of time. The "music" consists of whatever sounds emerge from the audience. It was followed in 1962 by *0'00"*, subtitled "solo to be performed in any way by anyone."

Cage's aesthetic relied heavily on Zen Buddhism, which had convinced him that the purpose of music "is to sober and quiet the mind, thus making it susceptible to divine influences" (Katz), as opposed to the Western notion that music must follow a specific path and communicate particular meanings. He also relied on the principles of the *I Ching,* an ancient Chinese system of predicting the future, to dictate the chance arrangement of fragments in the manner of a collage. Jonathan Katz has argued effectively that by rejecting psychoanalysis and Western philosophy in favor of Zen's acceptance of the world as it is—thus refusing to contest a homophobic and conservative society—Cage was able to focus his energies on liberating music rather than on self-destructive introspection and protest. Cage believed social protest was more likely to lead to a backlash than produce desirable change, but his inclusion of silence in music could in part be seen as an affirmation of that which was silenced in society—homosexuals and others who did not conform to the mainstream—while his emphasis on chance and "noise" offered access to a wider world than the predetermined music of traditional composers.

Cage expanded the notion of what a musical "instrument" was in works such as *Imaginary Landscape No. 4* (1951), in which twelve radios "performed" whatever was being broadcast, and *Cartridge Music* (1960), in which he amplified the sounds of ordinary household items. Using chance procedures, he combined snippets of music by celebrated composers of the past with other sounds in *HPSCHD* (1969), for several harpsichords, tapes, and "other sounds"—creating the musical equivalent of the large-scale "happenings" of the era. He later turned to setting works by Henry David Thoreau and James Joyce to music, as with, for example, *Roratorio, an Irish Circus on Finnegan's Wake.*

Throughout his career, Cage associated with and was admired by visual artists and intellectuals such as Jasper Johns, Robert Motherwell, and Buckminster Fuller—but in the music world, it was only in middle age that he achieved recognition outside of a small circle of musical mavericks. In the 1950s he was championed by European avant-garde composers such as Luciano Berio and Karlheinz Stockhausen, and this led gradually to (at least partial) mainstream acceptance. In 1962 Leonard Bernstein and the New York Philharmonic first performed a Cage work. Cage later worked with Pierre Boulez at the Institute for the Research and Coordination of Acoustical Music (IRCAM) in Paris, gave the Charles Eliot Norton lectures at Harvard University, and held numerous visiting professorships. He also wrote many works on aesthetics and philosophy as well as poetry, although not on homosexual subjects. Cage neither flaunted nor hid his sexuality, but his close artistic and personal relationship with Merce Cunningham and his dance troupe subtly proclaimed his affirmation of a queer world.

## Bibliography

Cage, John. "An Autobiographical Statement." Available from http://www/newalbion.com/artists/cage/autobiog.html.

Katz, Jonathan. "John Cage's Queer Silence or How to Avoid Making Matters Worse." Available from http://www.queerculturalcenter.org/Pages/KatzPages/KatzWorse.html.

Perloff, Marjorie, and Charles Junkerman, eds. *John Cage: Composed in America*. Chicago: University of Chicago, 1994.

**William Pencak**

**See also** BERNSTEIN, LEONARD; CUNNINGHAM, MERCE; JOHNS, JASPER; MUSIC: CLASSICAL; RAUSCHENBERG, ROBERT.

## CALL, Hal (b. 20 September 1917; d. 18 December 2000), publisher and activist.

Born in Trenton, Missouri, Harold (Hal) Leland Call moved to San Francisco in 1952 and shortly thereafter became one of the most important and controversial figures in the homophile movement. Prior to living in San Francisco, Call attended the University of Missouri, where he earned a degree in journalism. Upon graduation, he took a job with the *Kansas City Star*. While on a business trip to Chicago, Call was arrested on a morals charge and, like many men of his generation, found his life changed even though the case ultimately was dismissed.

Call's rather checkered reputation stems from his contentious personality and from his participation in the so-called conservative takeover of the Mattachine Foundation and the subsequent formation of the Mattachine Society in 1953. Although there were other political and ideological elements to the change, Call thought new leadership was necessary because of the reluctance of the founders to present themselves and their agenda publicly. Upon assuming a leadership role in 1953, Call became one of the first American homosexuals to proclaim his sexuality publicly while fighting for homosexual civil rights.

Although Call can accurately be labeled an activist, his activism was not in the tradition of protest and resistance of Rosa Parks or Emma Goldman. Rather, he sought change through educating the public and directly influencing decision makers. His activism was liberal, but not radical, as he advocated "evolution, not revolution" throughout his public career.

With the emergence of the Mattachine Society, Call immediately began pressing his agenda, which included establishing a publications chapter in San Francisco. From this base of operations, society members led by Call and Donald S. Lucas started publishing the *Mattachine Review* in February 1955; during its eleven years in print, the review was one of the most respected and widely read publications of the homophile press. Publishing the *Mattachine Review* was the most public and well-documented of the society's education-oriented activities. Call and the other leaders also spent a good deal of time working with professionals who were sympathetic to the cause of homosexual civil rights. To that end, Call built productive relationships with sexologist Alfred Kinsey and psychologist Evelyn Hooker as well as with assorted lawyers, clergy, politicians, journalists, medical doctors, sociologists, business owners, and law enforcement personnel. These relationships in turn helped make the society a recognized authority on homosexuality as well as other variant gender and sexual behaviors. In part because of Call's efforts, experts started seeking the advice and assistance of the society by the late 1950s, thus enabling homosexuals themselves to make an important contribution to the growing discourse on homosexuality.

In 1954, Call and Lucas pioneered the practice of combining activism with commerce when they founded Pan-Graphic Press to print the review and what they thought were quality works of fiction and nonfiction that represented homosexuality in an enlightened, objective, and nonsensationalistic manner. Over the next twelve years, Pan-Graphic Press also published the *Dorian Book Review Quarterly* (a combination anticensorship journal and mail-order catalog) and *Town Talk* (one of the first gay publications to contain advertising and to be distributed free in gay bars).

Call's writings published in the *Mattachine Review* in the mid-1960s reveal that, although he experienced his greatest successes with the society at that time, he also was beginning to see that organization fall apart. Extensive media coverage of the organization, which included a 1964 *Life* magazine spread, meant worldwide recognition but also countless requests for information and help. Simultaneously, new and more specialized organizations formed in San Francisco (a few, such as the Council on Religion and the Homosexual, Call helped to found) and started to take over some of the functions of the society as well as draw away monetary and volunteer resources.

By the end of 1967, the society had moved from the offices it had occupied since 1954 into a space that was less of an office and counseling center and more of a sex shop and bookstore, and Donald Lucas, Call's business partner, moved on to other professional activities. It was around this time that the society really ceased to function as an activist, social service, and publishing organization.

The end of the society, however, did not mark the end of Call's career. In 1967 he founded the Adonis bookstore in San Francisco, which preceded the opening of the Oscar Wilde bookstore in New York City and thus was probably the nation's first gay bookstore. Adonis continued to operate throughout the 1960s and 1970s. In the late 1960s, Call and his associates began presenting pornographic films privately to audiences and soon thereafter opened a public pornographic theater, the Circle J, which continues to operate.

## Bibliography

Boyd, Nan Alamilla. *Wide-Open Town: A History of Queer San Francisco to 1965*. Berkeley: University of California Press, 2003.

D'Emilio, John. *Sexual Politics, Sexual Communities: The Making of a Homosexual Minority in the United States, 1940–1970*, 2d ed. Chicago: University of Chicago Press, 1998.

Marcus, Eric. *Making History: The Struggle for Gay and Lesbian Equal Rights, 1945–1990*. New York: HarperCollins, 1992. A collection of edited oral history interviews, including a particularly candid one with Call.

Meeker, Martin. "Behind the Mask of Respectability: Reconsidering the Mattachine Society and Male Homophile Practice, 1950s and 1960s." *Journal of the History of Sexuality* 10, no. 1 (2001): 78–116.

Sears, James. *Behind the Mask of the Mattachine: The Early Movement for Homosexual Emancipation, the Hal Call Chronicles*. Binghamton, N.Y.: Haworth, 2003.

Steitmatter, Rodger. *Unspeakable: The Rise of the Gay and Lesbian Press in America*. Boston: Faber and Faber, 1995.

**Martin Meeker**

*See also* HOMOPHILE MOVEMENT; MATTACHINE REVIEW; MATTACHINE SOCIETY.

# CAMERON, Barbara (b.22 May 1954; d. 12 February 2002), activist, writer.

Barbara Cameron was born in North Dakota and raised by her grandparents on the Standing Rock Reservation. She once described herself as "Lakota patriot, Hukpapa born with a caul" (Moraga and Anzaldúa, p. 246), referring to a thin, veil-like piece of skin that covers the face of a newborn and is considered a sign that the child is special. After high school Cameron studied photography and film at the American Indian Art Institute in Santa Fe, New Mexico, and later moved to San Francisco where she worked at the American Indian Center. In July 1975 a small group that included Cameron and Randy Burns founded Gay American Indians (GAI), of which Cameron and Burns became co-leaders. In an interview with Dean Gengle, Cameron notes, "We [are] first and foremost a group for each other; bringing together Gay Indians is our most important current task" (Katz, p. 333). In its early years GAI sent speakers to Indian gatherings, where they faced homophobic resistance. When they sent speakers to white-dominated LGTB gatherings, they met resistance based on racism and on stereotypes associated with the activism of the American Indian Movement.

According to writer Kelly Cogswell, Cameron refused "to be queer in one corner of her life, and native in another." Like many lesbians of color, Cameron struggled at the intersection of oppressions, being subject to racism from white gays and lesbians, sexism from males, homophobia from native people, classism from the privileged, and lateral prejudice from other people of color. In "Gee, You Don't Seem Like an Indian from the Reservation," she writes about trying to maintain the "uneasy balance" between the white and Indian worlds. Lifelong negative experiences with racism left a psychological and spiritual imprint on her: "Because of experiencing racial violence, I sometimes panic when I'm the only non-white in a roomful of whites" (Moraga and Anzaldúa, p. 47).

Cameron also struggled with sexism in the native community. In an interview from the 1970s she noted, "The heavy male trip [in GAI] does bother me somewhat. We are trying to reach more lesbian Indians." But Cameron focused on the larger goal: "For now, it's important that Indians know there are gay Indians, [of] both sexes" (Katz, p. 334). Cameron was also concerned about lateral prejudice between people of color, using as an example the dynamics at the Third World Gay Conference held near Howard University just prior to the First Gay March on Washington in October 1979. On that historic occasion, African Americans and Latinos were in the numerical majority and did not take the meaning and consequences of this into consideration. Indians and Asian Pacific Islanders felt left out. Cameron recalled that the Indian group "didn't spend much time in workshops conducted by other third world people because of feeling unwelcome at the conference and demoralized by having an invisible presence. What's worse than being invisible among your own kind?" she asked (Moraga and Anzaldúa, p. 50).

In 1988 Cameron attended the Democratic National Convention as a Jesse Jackson delegate. She also served on the San Francisco Human Rights Commission and the Commission on the Status of Women, and worked with the international indigenous AIDS network and on a project to improve conditions for women in Nicaragua. Cameron died prematurely, at the age of forty-seven. She is survived by her partner of twenty years, Linda Boyd, and their son, Rhys.

### Bibliography

Cameron, Barbara. "Gee, You Don't Look Like an Indian from the Reservation." In *This Bridge Called My Back: Writings by Radical Women of Color.* Edited by Cherie Moraga and Gloria Anzaldúa. New York: Kitchen Table, 1983.

Cogswell, Kelly. "Remembering Barbara Cameron." *The Gully,* March 13, 2003. Available from http://www.thegully.com/essays/gaymundo/020313_barbara_cameron.html.

Gengle, Dean. "Gay American Indians, G.A.I." In *Gay American History: Lesbians and Gay Men in the U.S.A.* Edited by Jonathan Katz. New York: Crowell, 1976.

**Yolanda Retter Vargas**

*See also* NATIVE AMERICAN LGBTQ ORGANIZATIONS AND PERIODICALS; NATIVE AMERICAN STUDIES.

# CAMP

Despite critics' warnings about the pitfalls of trying to define "camp," a 1999 collection of essays on the subject, edited by Fabio Cleto, contains a bibliography of well over a thousand entries. Ever since Susan Sontag's "Notes on Camp" (1964) first introduced the topic to the mainstream, many have argued about where the word came from and when it first acquired its particular meaning. Still, most of the debates have focused on what qualifies as camp. How does camp overlap with, yet exceed, irony, parody, theatricality, burlesque, masquerade, kitsch, humor, and the carnivalesque? Is camp inherent in certain objects, or is it something an artist-performer intends (or must necessarily not intend)? Is camp in the eye of the beholder? More telling, perhaps, are the debates over who has the privilege to confer such meaning, and from what position they speak. Variously described as a (gay) sensibility, an aesthetic, a taste, a style, and a queer signifying practice, critics often go wrong by failing to historicize camp and look at how it functions differently according to time and place. If it is impossible to generalize about what camp means, we can ask why we have so much invested in these questions. What a discussion of camp therefore provides us with is a historical debate about LGBT and queer representation.

## Camp Beginnings

Part of the problem with searching for the origins of camp relates to whether we are looking for the word and its first usages or the appearance of the aesthetic and practice itself. Sontag has said that camp had its origins in the Gothic novels and chinoiserie of the eighteenth century or even earlier in mannerist art, yet others would dismiss such examples. Although Oscar Wilde (to whom Sontag dedicated her "Notes") is surely associated with what we have come to know as camp, the word does not appear to have been a part of his lexicon. A number of critics argue that the English word "camp" comes from the French *se camper,* meaning "to take a stand," "to flaunt," or "to pose," and it is the latter that turns up in one of Wilde's more famous epigrams (from his play *An Ideal Husband,* 1895): "To be natural is such a very difficult pose to keep up." This type of camp ethos destabilizes the "natural" and is connected to aestheticism, with which camp is often equated. Moe Meyer (1994), however, has argued that the aestheticism and by extension the dandyism of Victorian England have only come to be associated with homosexuality because Wilde infused a homoeroticism into these modes. Moreover, it was the very spectacle of the Wilde sodomy trials in 1895 that solidified the connections between camp and a particular image of the upper-class, white, male homosexual constructed at the end of the nineteenth century.

## Camp Coding

If the Wilde trials do not actually suggest that there is something inherently gay about camp or its practitioners, they do remind us of what lay in store for those who were "out" or "outed" regarding their sexuality. In his examination of camp in early-twentieth-century New York City (1994), George Chauncey argues that being out had little to do with telling heterosexuals of one's proclivities. What mattered instead was whether one identified oneself to like-minded individuals, and camp was central to this practice. Camp during this period was very much about coding, hidden meanings, and double entendre (which we can also see later in the work of Tennessee Williams, Noël Coward, and Liberace). If most writers on the subject note the connection between camp and playing with gender roles, the early camp practice of replacing "he" with "she" to confound suspicious peers and colleagues is simply one practical manifestation of this affinity. It would be misleading, though, to see camp as simply a means of upholding the closet, since, as Chauncey tells us, camp and the use of "gay argot" allowed gay men, who were used to being excluded, to finally be insiders by reading themselves into mainstream culture. These acts of appropriation helped to transform a "straight" space into a gay one, argues Chauncey, whether it be a Judy Garland concert or a respected newspaper or magazine that contained coded personal ads from men seeking out other men.

## Popularizing Camp

If this image of camp is essentially a political (or proto-political) one about gay survival in a homophobic world, it goes against Sontag's argument that camp is "disengaged, depoliticized—or at least apolitical" (p. 277), because, for her, it is both "frivolous" and narcissistic. Sontag's position is worth exploring in detail, since it was her "Notes on Camp" that influenced the way mainstream America came to view camp and thus fueled much of the debate that followed within gay circles. For Sontag, camp is a mode of aestheticism, a way of seeing the world in terms of artifice and style, of taking pleasure in a so-called failed seriousness. To camp it up—and thereby draw attention to the performer of camp, rather than its perceiver—is, for Sontag, the "vulgar" form. This hierarchy she sets up between "deliberate" (camping it up) and "naïve" (failed seriousness) is merely one of many binary distinctions critics would make. Ten years earlier Christopher Isherwood, in his novel *The World in the Evening* (1954; one of the first literary discussions of the subject), distinguishes between "high" and "low" camp (citing baroque art or the ballet versus bad drag); still others, including Moe Meyer, talk about Camp versus camp, or queer versus Pop camp. The problem with such formulae is deciding where to place the work of Andy Warhol, for example (or even that of John Waters and Divine, with their "trash" camp). While clearly concerned with a Pop Art aesthetic, Warhol's work is, according to Matthew Tinkcom, a form of "gay labor," since it articulates a gay ironic response to capitalist production, particularly the way Warhol turned marginal figures into "stars" in his factory.

Another aspect of Sontag's essay that has proven irksome for some critics concerns her discussion of the relationship between camp and homosexuality. Leaving the topic until the end of the piece, she tells us that, although "homosexuals have been its vanguard, Camp taste is much more than homosexual taste. . . . One feels that if homosexuals hadn't more or less invented Camp, someone else would" (pp. 290–291). Sontag argues that camp is apolitical, yet by telling us it is also a "solvent of morality" (p. 290) that has allowed gays to assimilate into the mainstream, camp does indeed appear to be a political act. David Bergman, by contrast, argues it was the civil rights action taken by gays and lesbians, and not their aesthetic sense, that was used to fight for equality and inclusion.

## Camp and Gay Sensibility

Picking up on Sontag's observation that camp is a sensibility, Jack Babuscio politicized this idea by labeling it a specifically gay sensibility. While some saw this classification as essentialist, it is worth noting that Babuscio considered this sensibility a particular response to oppression, one that would change according to context. However, is that response automatic or universal? We might also ask if this logic implies that camp would cease to exist in a world where queers were no longer oppressed. Many have argued that camp is in fact retrograde, especially since the Stonewall Riots, that it merely reconfirms one's marginal status, and that it is ultimately debilitating, nostalgic, and a reflection of self-hatred. Mart Crowley's *The Boys in the Band* (play, 1968; film, 1970) is often invoked as the perfect illustration. Babuscio and Esther Newton both disagree with the position that camp is simply a form of internalized homophobia, but do so from a different stance. If Babuscio emphasizes the mechanics of camp, identifying its four basic features as irony, aestheticism, theatricality, and humor, Newton, in *Mother Camp* (1972), provides a sociological model by exploring the lived experience of drag queens. Highlighting the way camp theatricalizes stigma, Newton speaks of camp as a survivalist discourse and thus presents us with an ethnicity model, leading subsequent critics to compare it to black "soul."

## Queer Camp

If camp can potentially denaturalize gender, it is because it exposes the incongruity between sex and gender, often through exaggerated performances of masculinity and femininity. Incongruity is a central feature of camp for both Babuscio and Newton, and many others have also noted that camp often works by highlighting discrepancies between form and content, expected and actual response (for example, tears versus laughter), imagined and real or historical situations. Moreover, these critics note, camp reminds us of the absurdities of living a double life and how gay love is itself thought to be incongruous and unnatural. If camp thus affirms identity amidst a hostile world, queer theorists challenge the very notion of a stable and knowable self. Judith Butler, whose work has been instrumental in contemporary formulations of camp, looks at the way identity and gender are performative, whereby acts, gestures, and other discursive means create the illusion of an essence or identity. Camp, as drag, is not simply an imitation of fixed ideas about male and female, but instead draws attention—through theatricality—to the concept of gender as a sustained and repeated performance. "In a sense it renders gender a question of aesthetics," says Jonathan Dollimore (p. 311).

Camp drag therefore reveals the "radical contingency" of heterosexuality itself, according to Butler, since compulsory heterosexuality depends on stable, universal, and timeless notions of what it means to be a real man or woman. In foregrounding the politics of representation, camp is used to scrutinize the process by which heterosexuality is produced and maintained through popular culture and imagery. In taking a social constructionist approach to the notion of identity, a queer articulation of camp challenges the supposed universality of a subject that is typically assumed to be straight, white, and male. By doing so, it also exposes "gay sensibility" as an ahistorical concept that does not necessarily have meaning for all LGBT people. Yet, by celebrating drag and "genderfuck" and reveling in the theatricality and play of identity, queer camp often upsets those who desire assimilation for gays and lesbians, especially at the expense of others they label as "too queer."

## Women and Camp

Given camp's potential to subvert and disrupt a naturalized vision of gender that has been used to control and oppress women in particular, why, we might ask, has camp (and drag) been seen as misogynist? Carole-Anne Tyler reminds us that every instance of drag must be read "symptomatically." Daniel Harris has argued that, because of assimilation and corporatization, gay culture is losing its once-radical edge manifested in camp. Whereas camp was once about the admiration a gay male spectatorship had for the gutsy screen personae of women like Bette Davis, that reverence has since turned to ridicule. A case in point, Harris observes, would be "Joan Crawford clobbering [her daughter] Christina with a can of bathroom cleanser" (p. 22). If Gloria Swanson, Tallulah Bankhead, Greta Garbo, Judy Garland, Elizabeth Taylor, and Carmen Miranda are classic camp icons, Caryl Flinn has argued that camp is troubling in its fascination with waste, decay, and the out-of-date, particularly in relation to women's (aging) bodies. But according to Pamela Robertson, in her discussion of feminist camp, too many treatises on the subject have explained it as a one-way process of gay men imitating or borrowing from women, and not how women themselves have used camp and taken on gay-inflected personae. The figures she has in mind include Mae West, Marlene Dietrich, and even Madonna. (One might add Camille Paglia, Fran Lebowitz, and Sandra Bernhardt to this list.) If Tennessee Williams's heroines have often been read as camp hysterics, as has Martha in Edward Albee's *Who's Afraid of Virginia Woolf* (play, 1962; film, 1966), a character like Blanche Deveraux, from television's *The Golden Girls,* is a far more self-conscious agent of camp posturing.

Recent feminist and queer work has looked at the politics of representation of lesbian camp, which we see in the growing interest in drag king performances. While early butch-fem culture could not be designated camp, according to Elizabeth Lapovsky Kennedy and Madeline Davis (and Esther Newton) because it was never ironic, Judith Halberstam has shown how nonwhite and working-class masculinities are currently more susceptible to parody because white masculinity presents itself as nonimitative. Halberstam also documents the different histories of cross-dressing and male performance that have existed in white and black women's communities, noting the presence of people like Ma Rainey or Gladys Bentley in the latter. Where critics such as Sue-Ellen Case conceive of lesbian camp as a potential challenge to the realism associated with gender and sexual identities, others like Kate Davy maintain that the histories and politics of performing masculinity and femininity are substantially different; for Davy, camp is always a gay male phenomenon that offers lesbians little opportunity to be agents in the production of their own visibility. Negotiating a type of compromise, Robertson suggests that camp allows women to play with their images, with watching and being watched, while remaining conscious of the power such images wield over their lives, and that therefore camp blurs the distinction between production and reception.

## Camp and Race

If camp's gender politics will forever remain suspect for some critics, its racial politics are also worth interrogating. The paucity of critical work on the subject is itself disconcerting, because it suggests that the discourse and theory around camp have focused on white gay men, even though others have engaged in practices we might label camp. In addition, while gender drag may indeed be subversive, racial drag is far more troubling. Does camp play a role in the way blackface, early cinematic representations of African Americans, and "negrophilia" (such as lawn jockeys) become subjects of parody in Spike Lee's *Bamboozled* (2000)? David Henry Hwang clearly uses camp humor in his 1988 play *M. Butterfly* (all but lacking in the 1993 film adaptation by David Cronenberg) to undermine the assumptions that Western men have about Asian women, reminding audiences that a discussion of gender is always also about race. The film documentary *Paris Is Burning* (1990), Jennie Livingston's examination of the African American and Latino drag ball scene in New York City, is one example that forces us to rethink the racial implications and executions of camp (as do performers like RuPaul or Pomo Afro Homos). The goal of a number of the younger characters who are transitioning from male to female is to "pass," and hence they would not want their "performances" labeled camp, nor do they see irony or humor in their situations. Some of the practices documented in the film, however, such as "reading," "shade," or "voguing," have elements of camp about them, making viewers aware of how humor has functioned as a subversive and survivalist discourse in queer and black communities. When the final credits are rolling, for instance, we see one queen doing an over-the-top rendition of Patti Labelle's "Somewhere Over the Rainbow." The kind of homage to both black and gay culture in such an act complicates our traditional understanding of appropriation in a film that exposes and perhaps itself participates in the fetishization and commodification of black culture.

## AIDS Camp

An interesting way to talk about the presence of camp today and what we might expect from it in the future is to examine camp aesthetics and performances in relation to the AIDS epidemic. Although the initial pairing would appear indecorous to some, we do not have to look very far to note the camp sensibility in works such as Tony Kushner's *Angels in America* (1993–1994), Paul Rudnick's *Jeffrey* (1993), several plays by Terrence McNally, and in the stand-up routine "AIDS—God, I Hope I Never Get That Again!" by the comic Steve Moore. No less obvious are some of the tactics deployed by ACT UP, and later by Queer Nation, to emphasize queerness and the politics of visibility. If camp, because of its attention to surface and style, can destabilize rigid notions of identity, one could clearly see the benefits of upsetting the powerful associations between gay identity and HIV/AIDS. Since mainstream AIDS narratives have merely reinforced and naturalized the tragic story of the lonely, guilt-ridden, and promiscuous homosexual, camp agency can call such images into question, which is what we see in the black humor 'zine *Diseased Pariah News,* for example. If headlines like "Hey kids! Want to win fabulous prizes? Just guess Tommy's December T-cell count" or "Darn, Our Centerfold Is Sick!" may strike one as glib, *DPN*'s well-known parody "AIDS Barbie" provides a radical critique of the AIDS industry by telling us that while Barbie is a registered trademark of Mattel, AIDS is a trademark of Burroughs Wellcome (now the drug company Glaxo-SmithKline), the manufacturers of AZT. For a time, it was costing people with HIV/AIDS around $10,000 a year, making it the highest-priced drug in U.S. history. Others, like David Feinberg, who died from AIDS-related illness in 1994, displayed a similar camp ethos in pieces such as "Etiquette for the HIV-Antibody-Positive," where he gives Miss Manners–type advice like "Avoid bleeding in pub-

lic," and "Be sure to inform each and every sexual partner of your antibody status. If shy and not given to easy verbalizing, consider the compassionate suggestions of William F. Buckley Jr.: a tasteful tattoo on the hindquarters" (pp. 57–58). Where a writer like Edmund White dismisses camp humor as inappropriate to the occasion, and critics like David Román see it as a form of denial, a desire for a time before the epidemic, Feinberg shows us the way in which camp works by, in Babuscio's words, "discovering the worthiness in a thing or person that is supposedly without value" (p. 48). For Scott Long, "Camp assaults a society that presumes it knows what is serious and what is not" (p. 54), and thus it can challenge the complacency and apathy surrounding a crisis so many refused to take seriously. If camp is to have meaning as well as political efficacy in the delineation of queer life and death, it must, in a very camplike maneuver, change its style and harness different, though not entirely new, strategies and guises. In order to resist normality itself, camp must therefore continue to frustrate those who try to write about it and those who practice or experience the pleasures and subversive power of its various (re)incarnations.

## Bibliography

Babuscio, Jack. "Camp and the Gay Sensibility." In *Gays and Film.* Edited by Richard Dyer. London: British Film Institute, 1977.

Bergman, David, ed. *Camp Grounds: Style and Homosexuality.* Amherst: University of Massachusetts Press, 1993.

Butler, Judith. *Gender Trouble: Feminism and the Subversion of Identity.* New York: Routledge, 1990.

Chauncey, George. *Gay New York: Gender, Urban Culture, and the Makings of the Gay Male World, 1890–1940.* New York: Basic Books, 1994.

Cleto, Fabio, ed. *Camp: Queer Aesthetics and the Performing Subject: A Reader.* Ann Arbor: University of Michigan Press, 1999.

Dollimore, Jonathan. *Sexual Dissidence: Augustine to Wilde, Freud to Foucault.* New York: Oxford University Press, 1991.

Feinberg, David B. *Queer and Loathing: Rants and Raves of a Raging AIDS Clone.* Harmondsworth, U.K.: Penguin, 1994.

Halberstam, Judith. *Female Masculinity.* Durham, N.C.: Duke University Press, 1998.

Harris, Daniel. *The Rise and Fall of Gay Culture.* New York: Hyperion, 1997.

Long, Scott. "Useful Laughter: Camp and Seriousness." *Southwest Review* 74 (1989): 53–70.

Meyer, Moe, ed. *The Politics and Poetics of Camp.* New York: Routledge, 1994.

Newton, Esther. *Mother Camp: Female Impersonators in America.* Englewood Cliffs, N.J.: Prentice-Hall, 1972.

Sontag, Susan. "Notes on 'Camp.'" *Partisan Review* 31 (1964): 515–530. Reprinted in *Against Interpretation, and Other Essays.* New York: Farrar, Straus, 1966.

White, Edmund. "Esthetics and Loss." *Artforum* 25, no. 5 (January 1987): 68–71.

**Scott Rayter**

See also ALBEE, EDWARD; DRAG QUEENS AND KINGS; ICONS; LIBERACE; MA; WARHOL, ANDY; WATERS, JOHN.

# CAPITALISM AND INDUSTRIALIZATION

Capitalism and industrialization had a major impact on the emergence and development of LGBT cultures and identities in the United States. While there is general agreement on this point among historians and other scholars, there is debate about exactly what this entails and what the relationship is between capitalism, industrialization, and queer histories.

Capitalist social relations are based on the exploitation of the working class and the private ownership of the means of production. In capitalism profit comes from the surplus value created by workers during the process of production. Surplus value is the difference between the wages paid to workers and the value of the commodities that they produce. This is realized as profit when the commodities are sold. Capitalism emerged prior to industrialization but took over social relations more generally when it developed into its industrial form, which was based on the intensification of the rate of exploitation of workers through the subordination of workers to new forms of technology, factory production, and "scientific" management. Industrial capitalism was also characterized by increased urbanization and the development of bureaucratic state agencies and professional disciplines that emerged in response to new "social problems," including those related to gender and sexuality.

## Capitalist Social Relations and Social Space

Three major social processes were involved in the emergence in the late nineteenth century of the "homosexual" and the "lesbian" which in turn set the stage for the emergence of the "heterosexual." These are the opening up of new social spaces in capitalist societies, the activity and resistance of those who came to be called queer, and the responses of the police and scientific disciplines to new LGBT cultures. The emergence and development of capitalist social relations and wage labor opened up social spaces beyond the family and household economy, which

made possible the emergence of LGBT erotic networks and cultures. John D'Emilio was the first to make visible this crucial process. Although he referred to wage-labor as free labor, he suggested that LGBT identities emerged from capitalism in spontaneous and linear ways, and neglected to examine the roles of state authority and LGBT resistance in this dynamic historical process. D'Emilio established a critical foundation for further analysis.

The transition to capitalist relations, which occurred fairly rapidly in some parts of the northern and eastern United States in the late eighteenth and early nineteenth centuries, began to remove much of the laboring population from ownership and control over the means of production, including the land. This process also increasingly separated "productive" labor from "reproductive" labor and other aspects of the household "economy," which had a major impact on gender relations. These trends were complicated by the white settler–colonizer character of the U.S. social formation. As indigenous people were killed and marginalized, more land was opened in the American West for "settlement" and capitalist social relations expanded. Slavery in the South, while not itself capitalist, supported the country's capitalist development and shaped the development of capitalist social relations by ensuring that they were intensely racialized. These social changes integrated and transformed previous forms of labor, gender, and sexual regulation imported from England and other European countries.

A crucial part of this was the transformation of family/household and sex/gender relations. Market processes developed unevenly but began to provide for meeting more daily needs outside of the household economy. The separation of "work" from the household economy meant that men employed in wage labor could now live outside of or on the fringes of the family/household system, earning wages and living in nonfamily households, including boardinghouses. Over time, more and more of these men could eat in taverns and restaurants and rent rooms in inns, hostels, and hotels. Only the wealthy could afford meals and rooms at first, but these later became available to working-class men with pay in their pockets. Later, smaller numbers of working-class women could also live more independently. Some people were beginning to transgress and live beyond social and familial norms. This created the spaces in which LGBT networks and cultures began to emerge in the late nineteenth century.

Several types of social space were opened up outside of family/household networks. These included "work" space (as wage-labor became separated from household labor), "recreational" space (including bars and clubs where those with discretionary income could go after work), and "private" space (where men and women could have intimate same-sex liaisons). For many men, private space for same-sex encounters was difficult to obtain. Men who were married and lived at home, younger men who did not have their own rooms, and other men whose situations did not permit them to bring home the men they met had to develop creative ways to meet and have sex. Women searching for same-sex liaisons may have had similar difficulties, although ironically the "separate spheres" for middle-class white women and men that developed alongside capitalist social relations allowed women's erotic friendships to flourish in the nineteenth century.

Same-sex erotic networks emerged within the limits of these social spaces. Some men, given the constraints placed on "private" space, found ways to meet and have sex in "public" spaces such as parks, streets, washrooms, and other cruising spots. They also frequented new types of commercial establishments, including bars, clubs, dance halls, amusement parks, and other commercialized amusements that became known as places where same-sex liaisons could be pursued. These men and smaller numbers of women handled the problem of their lack of "private" space in an innovative fashion that helped form LGBT erotic cultures and social communities.

All of these social transformations had complicated class, gender, and race dimensions, affecting the middle and working class, men and women, and whites and people of color in distinct ways. As George Chauncey has argued, for late nineteenth- and early twentieth-century New York, middle-class and working-class male sexual cultures differed, with the former more readily accepting the notion of distinct homosexual and heterosexual identities and the latter more interested in classifying men as "masculine" or "feminine," with sex between "normal" men and "fairies" considered acceptable in a variety of contexts. Over time, middle-class gay men developed sexual cultures that were more "private," while working-class gay men developed sexual cultures that were more "public." Meanwhile, as Lisa Duggan has argued, while many middle-class women pursued erotic relationships in their distinct "private" sphere, some working-class women passed in public as men, in part to create opportunities for same-sex liaisons. In the early twentieth century, as Elizabeth Kennedy and Madeline Davis have shown, middle-class lesbian social life developed in private homes while working-class butch and fem lesbians created vibrant sexual cultures in semi-public bars.

Capitalist social development also had distinct effects on people of color. As capitalism encouraged the expansion of U.S. territorial control over North America in the nineteenth century, Native American *berdache* and two-spirit traditions were suppressed. When the North defeated the slave South in the Civil War (1861–1865), "emancipated" African Americans faced new sexual possibilities. By the late nineteenth and early twentieth centuries, the Great Migration of African Americans from the agricultural South to the industrial North was influencing the development of distinct African American LGBT cultures. In this same period, capitalist needs for workers to exploit, combined with racist fears about reproduction among nonwhites, contributed to the immigration of large numbers of Asian men who created unique same-sex cultures in the American West.

## Resistance and Regulation

As much of the preceding discussion suggests, LGBT people played active roles in these processes and were not simply passive objects. And their complex resistances and accommodations were not only integral features of the formation of LGBT cultures but also influenced the development of capitalism itself. E. P. Thompson pointed out in his history of the making of the English working class that the working class was present at and participated in its own making. In similar fashion, LGBT people were present at and participated in the making of queer identifications, cultures, and communities. People both actively seized social spaces that capitalist social relations opened up and resisted attempts to clamp down on the cultures and networks that formed in these spaces. As Chauncey and others have pointed out, while "scientific experts" may have invented the terms "homosexuality" and "heterosexuality" in the late nineteenth century, the subjects of their case studies had already invented themselves. And while middle-class moralists may have attempted to regulate working-class LGBT cultures, their efforts invariably failed. Nevertheless, the regime of sexual regulation that accompanied the rise of capitalism and industrialization did police the social spaces that queer networks and cultures seized, defining "deviant" and "normal" genders and sexualities in the process. In *The History of Sexuality,* Michel Foucault emphasizes the creation of the "homosexual" through the medical, psychological, and sexological labelling of what had previously been called the "sodomite." As various scholars have emphasized, these types of scientific and social scientific "experts" played complex, semi-autonomous roles in capitalist transformations in the late nineteenth and early twentieth centuries, generally supporting the further development of capitalist social, gender, and sexual relations.

Foucault does not, however, emphasize that this classification was developed in response to the new queer cultures that had seized social spaces in large urban centers in Europe and North America in the nineteenth and early twentieth centuries. Contrary to Foucault's suggestion, the homosexual did not spring fully formed from medical, sexological, or psychological discourse. Popular LGBT cultures were not simply "reverse discourses" formed within and against ruling discourses of sexual pathology and deviance; they were forms of social life that developed within social spaces that had been seized. Out of this interaction between the opening of new social spaces, sexual regulation, gender policing, and queer resistance, LGBT cultures emerged and developed.

Dominant discourses and practices regulated and policed sexualities and genders not only by pathologizing LGBT cultures but also by inventing new norms. At the same moment in the late nineteenth century when scientific experts created the new category "homosexuality," they created the new category "heterosexuality." Heterosexual hegemony emerged as heterosexuality was constructed as "normal," "natural," and "healthy," while LGBT sexualities and genders were constructed as "sick," "criminal," and "abnormal." Over time, heterosexuality became central to capitalist social relations, playing important roles in advertising, marketing, tourism, leisure culture, consumer culture, popular culture, social policy, and family policy.

### The Limitations of Political Economy

The formation of LGBT and non-LGBT experiences and categories were based in the transformation of the social relations of production, reproduction, gender, and sexuality that occurred over the last three centuries. It would be a mistake, however, to see this transformation as simply reflecting in direct, causal, and linear ways the development of a new capitalist mode of production, particularly if this definition of capitalism is reduced to the economic domain alone. This is a common misreading of the Marxist critique of political economy, which unfortunately marks many works in queer theory.

In investigating relationships between capitalism and queer cultures, economic determinism—the view that there is a direct cause and effect relationship between capitalist economic relations and noneconomic relations—should be avoided. Capitalist social relations are also not simply "economic" in character; they are profoundly social, moral, cultural, and political. Sexuality and gender as social practices cannot simply be reduced to an "effect" of the economy or to narrow notions of class. We need a more historically and socially specific

approach and a wider notion of class as embodying all of social life, including erotic and gender relations. In this broader conception, struggles over sexual and gender relations have been central aspects of class struggles, and vice versa. Class struggles are fought not only at the point of production in the factory, office, and other type of workplace but also in relation to community, moral, sexual, gender, and race relations. For example, in the social purity movement of the late nineteenth and early twentieth centuries, struggles against the "social evils" of prostitution, "self-abuse," and "perversion" were central aspects of class struggles and played critical roles in dividing the working class into "respectable" and "nonrespectable" sections. Struggles over what people do with their bodies have continued to be important dimensions of class struggle.

### The Return of Class

Capitalist social relations both opened up and constrained LGBT possibilities. For example, while capitalism helped create the social space for institutions such as LGBT bars, restaurants, newspapers, bookstores, and other businesses, it also established the mechanisms for regulating and policing those institutions. While capitalism helped create new possibilities for bodily pleasure, it also insisted on disciplining the body for work and later for consumption and "leisure." Capitalists may now market cars, alcohol, clothing, vacations, books, and other consumer goods to LGBT people, but in doing so they transform and limit what it means to be LGBT and they oppress and exploit LGBT people who cannot afford these commodities. LGBT critics of capitalism also argue that, to the extent that capitalism is based on class exploitation and promotes class, race, gender, and sexual oppression, it lies at the roots of the oppression of LGBT people as well.

While LGBT critics of capitalism have existed since the emergence of Queer movements and the U.S. LGBT movement was founded by anticapitalists who created the initial homophile movement, only in the late 1960s and early 1970s did large numbers of U.S. LGBT activists adopt anti-capitalist politics. They did this in the context of the radical gay liberation and lesbian feminist movements, when a variety of social movements in the United States were challenging capitalist, patriarchal, and racist social relations. Within a few years, however, anticapitalist politics became less prominent in LGBT communities and movements as more moderate currents came to the fore. In the early twenty-first century, they survive in various LGBT social, cultural, and political locations in the United States, including labor unions, anti-globalization movements, anti-poverty and antiracist organizing, and academic institutions.

## Bibliography

Louise Adams, Mary. *The Trouble With Normal: Postwar Youth and the Construction of Heterosexuality.* Toronto: University of Toronto Press, 1997.

Chauncey, George, Jr. "From Sexual Inversion to Homosexuality: Medicine and the Changing Conceptualization of Female Deviance." *Salmagundi* (Fall 1982/Winter 1983): 144–145.

———. *Gay New York, Gender, Urban Culture, and the Making of the Gay Male World, 1890–1940.* New York: Basic Books, 1994.

D'Emilio, John. "Capitalism and Gay Identity." In *Powers of Desire, The Politics of Sexuality.* Edited by Ann Snitow, Christine Stansell, and Sharon Thompson. New York: Monthly Review Press, 1983.

———. *Making Trouble: Essays on Gay History, Politics, and the University.* New York: Routledge, 1992.

Duggan, Lisa. *Sapphic Slashers: Sex, Violence, and American Modernity.* Durham, N.C.: Duke University Press, 2000.

Ebert, Teresa L. *Ludic Feminism and After: Postmodernism, Desire, and Labor in Late Capitalism.* Ann Arbor: University of Michigan Press, 1996.

Faderman, Lillian. *Surpassing the Love of Men: Romantic Friendship and Love Between Women from the Renaissance to the Present.* New York: Williaɴ Morrow, 1981.

Hennessy, Rosemary. *Profit and Pleasure: Sexual Identities in Late Capitalism.* New York and London: Routledge, 2000.

Katz, Jonathan Ned. *The Invention of Heterosexuality.* Foreword by Guy Vidal. New York: Dutton Book, 1995.

Kennedy, Elizabeth Laporsky, and Madeline D. Davis. *Boots of Leather, Slippers of Gold: The History of a Lesbian Community.* New York: Routledge, 1993.

Kinsman, Gary. *The Regulation of Desire.* Montreal: Black Rose, 1996.

Simmons, Christina. "Companionate Marriage and the Lesbian Threat." *Frontiers: A Journal of Women's Studies* 4, no. 3 (Fall 1979): 54–59.

Foucault, Michel. *The History of Sexuality. Vol. 1, An Introduction.* New York: Vintage, 1980.

Freedman, Estelle. "Separatism as Strategy: Female Institution Building and American Feminism, 1970–1930." *Feminist Studies* 5, no. 3 (Fall 1979): 512–529.

Morton, Donald, ed. *The Material Queer.* Boulder, Colo.: Westview Press, 1996.

Smith-Rosenberg, Carroll. "The Female World of Love and Ritual: Relations Between Women in Nineteenth-Century America." In her *Disorderly Conflict: Visions of Gender in Victorian America.* New York: Knopf, 1985.

Thompson, E. P. *The Making of the English Working Class.* New York: Vintage, 1966.

**Gary Kinsman**

*See also* ADVERTISING; BUSINESSES; BOYCOTTS; CLASS AND CLASS OPPRESSION; CROSS-CLASS SEX AND RELATIONSHIPS; EMPLOYMENT AND OCCUPATIONS; MIGRATION, IMMIGRATION, AND DIASPORA; POOR PEOPLE'S MOVEMENTS.

# CAPOTE, Truman (b. 30 September 1924; d. 25 August 1984), writer.

Truman Capote is a very controversial figure, both as an author and as a celebrity who moved among the rich and famous and who often appeared on television interview shows from the late 1960s onward. Capote published his major works before 1969, and he was not associated with gay liberation. He did, however, refer to his same-sex sexual experiences on television and in print, as when in the 1979 essay "Nocturnal Turnings, or How Siamese Twins Have Sex," he declares himself a homosexual and a genius, as well as an alcoholic and drug addict. The alcohol and drug abuse Capote alludes to aggravated the writer's block he began to experience in the 1970s and ultimately led to his early death.

Capote was born in New Orleans, and his unhappily married parents sent him in 1927 to live in rural Alabama with relatives, including Miss Sook Faulk, whom he later portrayed in three famous holiday stories. His parents divorced in 1931, and when his mother married Joseph Garcia Capote in 1939 Truman was sent off to a series of boarding schools. In 1942 he began to work for *The New Yorker;* in 1946 he became involved with Newton Arvin, the famous literary scholar, who wrote on Melville and Hawthorne. From 1948 onward Capote was based mostly in and around New York City and Long Island. His partner was Jack Dunphy, who survived him. The later years of his life were devoted to writing, travel, and mixing with high society.

Capote seldom wrote about homosexuality, and his output for a writing career of forty years was small. He published two novels, *Other Voices, Other Rooms* (1948) and *The Grass Harp* (1951) as well as a collection of nine stories, *A Tree of Night and Other Stories* (1949) before he was thirty years old. In mid-career he turned out *Breakfast at Tiffany's* (1958), a volume including that novella and three stories. *In Cold Blood* (1966), which he called a nonfiction novel, was his last and greatest triumph. It is the story of the brutal murder of the four members of the Clutter family in Holcomb, Kansas, in November 1959. When asked, Capote denied that the murderers, Perry Smith and Dick Hickock, were sexually attracted to each other.

**Truman Capote.** A portrait of the artist—Southern writer and self-promoting celebrity—as a young man. [Library of Congress]

Of Capote's novels only *Other Voices, Other Rooms* deals directly with male homosexuality, as does one story, "A Diamond Guitar" (1950), from *Breakfast at Tiffany's,* and the television film *The Glass House.* The latter two have prison settings. Capote never wrote about fulfilling relations between adult men or depicted sex scenes between adult men in his fiction. Indeed, he did not write about romance or sex between adult heterosexuals either. His fictional world, often set in the 1930s, concentrated on depictions of the grotesque, often through the viewpoints of teenage boys.

In *Other Voices, Other Rooms,* Capote shows skill in his use of symbols and his depiction of semiconscious states. *Other Voices, Other Rooms* combines the sexual oddity of Faulkner's Southern Gothic *Sanctuary* with the decaying family mansion of Poe's "The Fall of the House of Usher" and the possibly haunted house of James's "The Turn of the Screw." Joel Knox, a boy from New Orleans, comes to the rural South during the Great Depression to live in a decaying mansion inhabited by his father, whom he has not previously known. Joel does not meet his father at first, but eventually finds that his parent is a paralytic who communicates his needs by tossing red tennis balls from his bed. Joel becomes fascinated by his decadent, lazy, artistic, sometimes cross-dressing cousin,

Randolph, who, he discovers, has physically wounded his bed-ridden father. After an unsuccessful attempt to run away, Joel decides to stay with Randolph at Scully's Landing. It is unclear if Randolph and the underage Joel will become lovers, although it is a distinct possibility. The novel asks us to look at Joel's maturation and acceptance of himself as a sexual outsider without regard to moral systems.

Whereas some gay critics have championed *Other Voices, Other Rooms* as a liberating, queer, and/or camp adaptation of the Southern Gothic, others have seen it as almost exactly the opposite: another contribution to the literature presenting male homosexuals as grotesques. The plot of *Other Voices, Other Rooms* is still so troubling that when the novel was filmed in 1997 by David Rock-savage (with David Speck as Joel and Lothaire Bluteau as Cousin Randolph), its ending was completely changed, so that Joel runs away from his cousin, recognizing that he must flee the decadence Randolph represents.

**Bibliography**

Christensen, Peter G. "Major Works and Themes." In *The Critical Response to Truman Capote.* Edited by Joseph J. Waldmeir and John C. Waldmeir. Westport, Conn.: Greenwood Press, 1999.

———. "Truman Capote." In *Contemporary Gay American Novelists: A Bio-Bibliographical Sourcebook*. Edited by Emmanuel S. Nelson. Westport, Conn.: Greenwood Press, 1993.

Clarke, Gerald. *Capote*. New York: Ballantine, 1988.

Mitchell-Peters, Brian. "Camping the Gothic: Que(e)ring Sexuality in Truman Capote's *Other Voices, Other Rooms*." *Journal of Homosexuality* 39, no. 1 (2000). 107–138.

Plimpton, George. *Truman Capote: In Which Various Friends, Enemies, Acquaintances, and Detractors Recall His Turbulent Career*. New York: Nan A. Talese, Doubleday, 1997.

Sarotte, Georges Michel. *Like a Brother, Like a Lover: Male Homosexuality in the American Novel and Theater from Herman Melville to James Baldwin*. Garden City, NY: Doubleday/Anchor, 1978.

**Peter G. Christensen**

***See also*** BARNEY, NATALIE; LITERATURE.

## CARSON, Rachel (b. 27 May 1907; d. 14 April 1964), writer, environmentalist.

Rachel Louise Carson, born the third child of struggling parents, was much younger than her siblings, and had a close (later, often difficult) relationship with her mother. The two spent many hours reading and exploring the environment surrounding their Pennsylvania farm. These early experiences laid the groundwork for Carson's eventual and unusual success as a gifted scientist and talented writer; her career eventually culminated in the book widely claimed as the birth of the modern environmental movement: *Silent Spring* (1962).

Carson began her postsecondary education at the Pennsylvania College for Women in 1925. At the end of her sophomore year, she added to her English major a minor in science—eventually switching to biology—inspired by Mary Scott Skinker, Carson's earliest biological mentor. When Skinker left to complete her doctorate at Johns Hopkins University, Carson wanted to follow immediately but finances prevented her. Carson began postgraduate studies at Johns Hopkins on full scholarship in 1929, beginning a lifelong love for the ocean and spending the summer at Woods Hole Marine Biological Laboratory. Carson's experience at Johns Hopkins revealed a pattern that would continue throughout her early career. On one hand, she was a passionate biologist, eventually completing her master's thesis (on catfish urinary systems) in 1932. On the other, she was an unmarried woman with increasing financial responsibilities to her family in the middle of the Great Depression.

Carson was unable to continue doctoral work and instead wrote the federal civil service examinations in 1935. In the absence of full-time employment she turned back to writing. A contract with the Bureau of Fisheries gave her the chance to write a radio program on marine life, and she transformed her research into a series of feature articles for the *Baltimore Sun*. Carson was eventually hired at the Bureau of Fisheries in 1936. Despite the death of her older sister—and Carson's subsequent responsibility for two nieces—she also continued to write, publishing "Undersea" in *The Atlantic* (1937). As she rose in the ranks of the civil service, she worked on the manuscript of *Under the Sea Wind* (1941). Partly because of the U.S. entry into World War II, the book received little popular attention, although it was praised by both literary and scientific critics.

Carson's second book, *The Sea Around Us* (1951), was more widely appreciated, and the book immediately became a bestseller, spurring the republication of *Under the Sea Wind*, allowing her to quit Fisheries and, later, to write *The Edge of the Sea* (1955). Carson was catapulted from public service into public life. Although male reviewers consistently questioned the ability of a woman to write such knowledgeable books, Carson won numerous prizes for both literature and science. In Carson's lectures during this period, she began to articulate an environmental ethic that called people to consider the consequences of human interference with ecological systems, contrasting the wonders of natural cycles with the arrogance of human intervention.

With newfound economic security, Carson bought a small property on the Maine coast for her family, which now included her great-nephew Roger (for whom Carson became sole parent in 1957). Shortly after moving there in 1953, she met Dorothy and Stan Freeman. Although Carson had many intense friendships with women, including Skinker and literary agent Marie Rodell, she found in Dorothy a kindred spirit. Their friendship bloomed intensely and quickly; although they lived most of their lives apart due to family obligations, they developed an extraordinary and passionate correspondence. As Rachel wrote to Dorothy in 1957, "what I feel most clearly is that we must never again for a moment forget what a precious possession we have in our love and understanding, and in that constant and sometimes almost puzzling longing to share with each other every thought and experience" (Freeman, p. 224).

Although long concerned with pesticide spraying, Carson began to think seriously about writing on the subject in 1957. The topic was politically charged; local residents concerned with aerial spraying were beginning to make contact with researchers who were investigating declining wildlife populations. Despite her failing health (she had surgery for breast cancer in 1960 but the cancer continued to metastasize), Carson pushed ahead with the monumental task of composing the strongest argument possible against pesticide overuse, which she knew would be attacked by the chemical industry. Carson was right—industry response was swift, and once again Carson's gender was used to undermine her research—but public reaction was overwhelmingly in her favor. On top of the direct influence of *Silent Spring* on policy regulating pesticides, the book made widely available a lucid critique of unquestioned technological progress that remains a central narrative for environmental politics.

### Bibliography

Brooks, Paul. *Rachel Carson: The Writer at Work*. San Francisco: Sierra Club Books, 1989.

Freeman, Martha, ed. *Always, Rachel: The Letters of Rachel Carson and Dorothy Freeman, 1952–1964*. Boston: Beacon Press, 1994.

Lear, Linda. *Rachel Carson: Witness For Nature*. New York: Henry Holt, 1997.

**Catriona Sandilands**

*See also* ENVIRONMENTAL AND ECOLOGY MOVEMENTS.

# CATHER, Willa (b. 7 December 1873; d. 24 April 1947), journalist, poet, novelist.

Willa Cather (originally Wilella) was born in Back Creek, Virginia, but when she was nine years old her family abruptly moved to a farm in Webster County, Nebraska, where Willa's grandfather had already settled. After a year and a half on the frontier, the Cathers moved nearby to the town of Red Cloud, probably because Willa's mother, Virginia, was dissatisfied with frontier life. Willa remained in Red Cloud until she graduated from high school in 1890, when she moved to Lincoln to attend the University of Nebraska. After graduating from college in 1895, Cather worked in Pittsburgh as an editor and schoolteacher. In 1906 Cather assumed an editorial position at *McClure's* magazine in New York City where she lived until the end of her life.

At age fourteen, Cather rejected normative feminine behavior and publicly assumed a male identity, renaming herself William Cather Jr., or M.D., which signified what was, during her teenage years, her intended profession. Despite Virginia's desire to see her daughter inaugurated into "proper" womanhood, and likely because of the draining effects of rugged, small-town Nebraska life (Virginia was often ill), she did not condemn her daughter's transformation. Cather cut her hair short—a buzz cut—and donned boyish clothing. Her transgendering may have been sparked by her assumption of male roles in plays such as *Beauty and the Beast;* regardless, she did, during some formative years of personal development, live publicly as "William."

The first woman about whom Cather felt passionately was Louise Pound, a classmate at the University of Nebraska. Cather had left Red Cloud for the university when she was sixteen, but had to take preparatory classes before matriculating as a freshman. She began her first university year by taking premedical courses, but after receiving accolades for her campus publications, Cather turned her attention to writing. She attended and reviewed plays and operas, where she met Pound, who was from an affluent family and was an accomplished sportswoman. For a short time, Cather and Pound co-edited a college literary publication but, as her letters to Pound show, Cather was experiencing youthful, smothering passion towards her friend, and Pound gradually withdrew from the relationship.

After graduating from college, *Home Monthly,* a Pittsburgh magazine, offered Cather an assistant editorship, and in Pittsburgh she formed a long-lasting, intimate relationship with another wealthy, beautiful woman named Isabelle McClung. McClung lived with her parents, and in 1901 Cather moved in with the family. Isabelle created space in the large house for Cather to write, and from there she penned her only book of poetry, *April Twilights* (1903), and assembled her first book of short stories, *The Troll Garden* (1905). Their intimacy lasted for seventeen years, and with Isabelle providing emotional and physical support, Cather also wrote her first novel, *Alexander's Bridge* (1912), several short stories, and large portions of *The Song of the Lark* (1915) and *O Pioneers!* (1913). Their relationship ended when, granting her father's dying wish, McClung married. Although the newlyweds attempted to make room for Cather, the rift caused by McClung's marriage was irreparable.

While in Pittsburgh, Cather's short stories caught the attention of S. S. McClure of *McClure's* magazine. He hired Cather as editor of the magazine and played a key role in the publication of *The Troll Garden*. In 1906 Cather moved to Washington Square in New York City to assume her duties, bringing with her to the magazine Edith Lewis, an acquaintance from her university days. At first Lewis was a helpful friend. Cather made frequent trips to visit McClung, and although Cather and Lewis took an apartment together in 1908, Cather still traveled without Lewis. But by 1913 Cather and Lewis had become interdependent; they cohabitated, bought furniture, and

**Willa Cather.** The early-twentieth-century writer is critically acclaimed primarily for several regional and autobiographical novels, including *O Pioneers!*, *My Ántonia*, and *Death Comes for the Archbishop*. [AP/Wide World Photos]

threw dinner parties. Cather and Lewis remained intimate companions until the end of Cather's life.

While Cather was at *McClure's*, she encountered a figure who became a mentor by introducing Cather to literature by women who could provide Cather a female literary inheritance. Cather was on assignment in Boston in 1898 when she was introduced to Sarah Orne Jewett. With her partner, Annie Fields, Jewett presented to Cather an example of a long-term, same-sex relationship. Jewett's attention to regional dialects, her austere rather than sentimental content, and her connections between characters and the land influenced Cather's approach to fiction, but she diverged from Jewett in that she rarely depicted same-sex love. While some literary critics assert that Cather simply was not concerned with portrayals of homosexuality, others theorize that her transgender experience, coupled with society's aversion to homosexuality, compelled her to infuse male characters with her own desires. Thus, in *My Ántonia* (1918), perhaps her most widely read novel, Jim Burden's love for Ántonia is believable because of Cather's own sexual desire for women. Cather's better-known novels deal with two

major themes. The regional novels, usually set in Nebraska or the Southwest, include *My Ántonia, The Professor's House* (1925), *Death Comes for the Archbishop* (1927), and *O Pioneers!* The autobiographical novels (although all are, to some extent) include *The Song of the Lark* and *Sapphira and the Slave Girl* (1940). Cather died of a brain hemorrhage in 1947, and was buried in Jaffrey, New Hampshire, a rural retreat where with Lewis she spent many summers composing literature. Edith Lewis is buried next to her.

**Bibliography**

Lee, Hermione. *Willa Cather: A Life Saved Up.* London: Virago, 1989.

O'Brien, Sharon. *Willa Cather: The Emerging Voice.* New York: Oxford University Press, 1987.

**Michael H. Berglund**

*See also* JEWETT, SARAH ORNE; LITERATURE; MUSIC: OPERA; WHITMAN, WALT.

# CATHOLICS AND CATHOLICISM

The history of Catholicism and same-sex desire is fraught with both controversy and change. Given the Catholic reliance upon church history as a source of models for the present, the political implications of that history guarantee that no single narrative will be agreed upon any time soon, if ever. Part of the difficulty in determining what is sometimes termed "gay and lesbian history" in the Catholic church lies in the extensive debate over what it means to be "gay," "lesbian," and so on. In most contemporary Western cultures, these terms indicate a fundamental, intrinsic, and unalterable aspect of one's identity. However, in other cultures and other periods of Western history, gender-crossing and same-sex love or desire have carried very different connotations. What does one make, then, of fervent professions of love between two nuns, a bonding ceremony designed for two men, or even the ongoing use of long, flowing ritual robes by Catholic priests and officials? To arguments that the relationships represent only friendship and the robes an honored tradition, one can protest that the same interpretation would not be applied were the relationship to involve a monk and a nun or were the robes less of a tradition. Yet to the suggestion that these cases constitute evidence of homosexuality or transgenderism in church history, one must respond by asking what, exactly, defines those terms. However, since official versions of Catholic history still assert that it contains no examples of gender-crossing or same-sex desire save as objects of excoriation, it is worthwhile to focus briefly here on new versions that tell a different story.

In 1980, historian John Boswell sent shock waves through the Catholic world with the publication of *Christianity, Social Tolerance, and Homosexuality*. This book argued, contrary to official Catholic teachings, that homosexuals had always been present in the church. Moreover, Boswell suggested, they had been present as priests, nuns, and monks, as well as laypeople, and at certain times (especially in the twelfth century) they had been fairly widely tolerated. Boswell followed this book with a second in 1994 that argued for the existence of a ritual for same-sex unions in early and medieval Christianity. Following Boswell's lead have been such historians as E. Ann Matter, Judith C. Brown, and Bernadette J. Brooten, who have unearthed evidence of passionate, intimate relationships between women in Christian history, and Mark D. Jordan, who has devoted two books to exploring the construction of the category of "sodomy" in Catholic doctrine.

Jordan's second book on this topic, *The Silence of Sodom*, also levels a devastating critique of the Catholic church as an institution that fosters an intensely homosocial and homoerotic environment and yet harshly condemns the homosexuals in its midst. Jordan argues that the term "sodomy" only came to refer specifically to same-sex eroticism in the eighteenth century, a development that was echoed and exacerbated by the advent of the term "homosexual" in nineteenth-century European culture. Despite the Roman Catholic Church's increasing anxiety about "sodomy" and "homosexuality," however, it was not until the mid-twentieth century that the growing visibility of gays and lesbians led the church to make an increasing number of formal (and condemnatory) statements on the issue.

### Official Catholicism Today

In 1975, the Congregation for the Doctrine of the Faith, the official doctrinal branch of the Roman Catholic Church, issued its first statement on contemporary gays and lesbians (bisexuals and transgender people continue to be nearly invisible in official Catholic discourse). The *Declaration Regarding Certain Questions of Sexual Ethics* addressed several ways in which Catholic sexual norms had been challenged by the social changes of the past decade and a half. As part of this discussion, the declaration asserted that same-sex eroticism was "disordered" and thus immoral; furthermore, it opened up the possibility of distinguishing between "curable" (sometimes termed "temporary") and "incurable" (or "permanent") "homosexuals."

Later statements confirmed and further developed the church's teachings on contemporary homosexuality. The *Letter to All Catholic Bishops on the Pastoral Care of Homosexual Persons*, released in 1986, reaffirmed that some people might be "incurable homosexuals" (a concession to the increasing evidence for genetic factors in sexual orientation). However, it strongly asserted that any organization or individual who supported the gathering of groups of homosexuals—whether for support, activism, social contact, or any other purpose—was encouraging "sinful" behavior unless the group adhered strictly to official Catholic doctrine. The letter also contained a particularly disturbing passage on antigay/lesbian violence: while decrying such attacks, it also characterized them as an unsurprising result of the increasing social acceptance of "homosexual association."

The 1997 American bishops' letter, *Always Our Children* (revised in a conservative direction in 1998), softened this rhetoric considerably without fundamentally changing its message. While confirming once again the "disordered" nature of homosexuality, the letter does at least encourage parents not to reject children who come out to them, and it gently warns that reparative therapy may not be as effective as its advocates promise. This is a far cry, however, from the message that many LGBT and queer Catholics—and their allies—believe the church is called to affirm. With the official hierarchy determined to condemn them, lay and religious queer Catholics and their allies have persisted instead in writing their own texts, sometimes at the risk of being silenced (ordered to desist from discussing a particular topic) or excommunicated.

### Queer and Allied Voices in Catholicism

Contemporary queer and allied voices in Catholicism have surfaced in two major and usually interconnected areas: theology and gay and lesbian ministries. Members of religious orders who contribute to either area run the risk of being silenced; however, they continue to stand up to this challenge and often find ways to work around the church's restrictions.

One of the first Catholic theologians to write openly on the topic of gay and lesbian theology was former Jesuit John J. McNeill, who was silenced in the 1970s and dismissed from the Society of Jesus in 1988 because of his ministry with gay men and lesbians. McNeill's first book, *The Church and the Homosexual*, was in fact one of the earliest works of gay/lesbian Christian theology, and it has proved to be long-lived and immensely influential both within and outside Catholicism. Starting from the powerful assumption that all people are created and loved by God, McNeill sets out to prove his assertion through a critical examination of each biblical text used to attack gays and lesbians.

Since McNeill's early work was published, a number of other Catholic theologians have begun to write on questions pertaining to LGBT people. Many, including McNeill himself, have also put their ideas into practice in the form of affirming ministries for sexual and gender minorities and their families. Some, such as feminist liberation theologian Mary Hunt, have seen their work as existing in a broader context of liberatory theologies and activism; Hunt cofounded the Women's Alliance for Theology, Ethics, and Ritual (WATER) after working as a human rights advocate in Argentina. Others, such as Sister Jeannine Gramick and Father Robert Nugent, have focused their theology and ministry more specifically on lesbian and gay Catholics. Gramick and Nugent founded New Ways Ministry in 1977 after successfully organizing workshops for Catholic gays and lesbians in Washington, D.C., for several years. In 1984, both were ordered by the Vatican to sever their ties with the organization; they did so on a formal level but continued their work in other ways, and New Ways Ministry continued to thrive. In July 1999, Nugent and Gramick faced another setback in their work: the Vatican ordered them to cease all ministry to gays and lesbians because, it contended, they had failed to follow official Catholic teachings on the matter. In May 2000, both were officially silenced on LGBT issues, and were ordered not to comment publicly on even the process of their own silencing.

In spite of the Vatican's explicit condemnations of affirming gay/lesbian outreach ministries, a number of such ministries have continued (albeit sometimes cautiously) since then. Certain parishes support queer-positive ministries—although it must be noted that others run programs that are intended to assist gays and lesbians in "becoming" heterosexual or committing to lives of celibacy. The organization known as Courage is one example of the latter. Especially in heavily gay neighborhoods, however, gay men and sometimes lesbians have made it increasingly clear that they expect to attend Mass without condemnation, and for the most part their parish priests have complied; some have gone further by implementing support groups for their queer parishioners. Even a small number of dioceses and archdioceses have implemented surprisingly supportive programs, often lay-led in order to afford them greater autonomy. In some cases, these support groups may be sapping strength from Dignity (the LGBT Catholic organization) as they draw back into the church Catholics who seek no more radical goal than to be accepted as "out" gay men and lesbians.

## Dignity

Begun in 1969, Dignity was only the second religious organization founded specifically to serve gay men and lesbians (and, later, bisexuals and transgender people). It was started under official church auspices by Father Patrick Nidorf of San Diego, California. Shortly thereafter, however, the Los Angeles archbishop ordered Nidorf to give up his role in the organization and Dignity became lay-led. As with diocesan ministries, this was advantageous because it allowed the group to become increasingly activist; during its early years, however, Dignity served primarily as a safe space in which gay and lesbian Catholics could gather to worship. As the organization spread rapidly around the United States and eventually into Canada as well, Dignity chapters rented meeting space from local parishes, brought in sympathetic priests (often gay themselves), and held Masses in which gay men and lesbians could openly participate.

While the promulgation of the 1986 letter caused this situation to change drastically, the church's increasingly vociferous rejection of Dignity sparked a movement within the group toward advocating broader and more radical change in Catholicism. Not only did Dignity begin to include bisexuals and transgender people, but it also became a strong advocate of women's ordination.

## Bisexuals, Transgender People, and Women

Not everyone benefits from outreach programs or from Dignity, however. In 2002, for example, most church outreach is directed only at gay men and lesbians. Bisexuals who have explored the more welcoming parishes occasionally report that even gays and lesbians sometimes view them as having the "option" of being in a heterosexual marriage—which they are expected, therefore, to choose. Moreover, transgender issues have rarely been addressed at all within the church. Dignity has attempted to remedy that situation by broadening its official purview to include bisexuals and transgendered people, but it still struggles—not only with this issue, but like the church, with gender as well. Leonard Norman Primiano reported in 1993, for instance, that far fewer women than men attended the meetings of Dignity in Philadelphia, and that women generally perceived the organization as being overwhelmingly dominated by men and by gay male culture.

## The Sex Scandals

In 2001, the Catholic Church in the United States was rocked by accusations that a number of its priests had sexually abused young boys and girls in past decades; this turn of events had unfortunate repercussions for gays in the church and for the church's discussions of homosexuality. In understanding the reactions to these accusations, however, it is important to keep several things in mind. First, for over a century, non-Catholics in the United States have entertained lurid fantasies about the adverse effects on priests (not nuns, interestingly enough) of "enforced" celibacy. Prior to the mid-twentieth century, these fantasies involved the ravishing of young female parishioners; more recently, they have shifted to focus suspicion on the "vulnerability" of altar boys. Second, for at least the same amount of time, nonqueer people have persisted in associating male homosexuality with pedophilia—despite a vast array of statistics that leave no doubt that the majority of pedophiles are heterosexual. Third, given its increasing agitation over the presence and visibility of queer folk and their allies within its domain, the Catholic Church has found it all too easy to deflect attention from its own failures through what Jordan calls "hysterical rhetoric" about homosexuality. Although it is doubtful that the church will carry out its threats to purge all gay men from its ranks (if only because it would be left with a severe shortage of clergy), the sex scandals have further complicated an issue already fraught with tension.

## Looking to the Future

Academic observers of the Catholic church often comment on its impressive ability to encompass cultural and theological diversity. While serious ideological conflict often ruptures Protestant denominations, Catholicism has repeatedly demonstrated an ability to survive such conflicts with a minimum of schism. In part, this is the result of strict hierarchical control; however, it also indicates that the church is capable of including opposing points of view (if not embracing them), and that it sometimes is even fundamentally altered by them. This is already the case with the issue of homosexuality, as LGBT Catholics continue to attend Mass and to identify as Catholic in defiance of official doctrine, and as increasing numbers of heterosexual, nontransgendered Catholics come to reject the idea that homosexuality is "intrinsically disordered." Whether this will eventually lead to alterations in official church doctrine is as difficult to predict as the question of whether women will be ordained as priests; while positive strides have been made over the past several decades, the church is still far from full inclusion of LGBT people. In the meantime, however, queer Catholics and their allies persist in defying Vatican authority by claiming the religion as their own and demanding their rightful place in it.

### Bibliography

Boswell, John. *Christianity, Social Tolerance, and Homosexuality: Gay People in Western Europe from the Beginning of the Christian Era to the Fourteenth Century.* Chicago: University of Chicago Press, 1980.

———. *Same-Sex Unions in Premodern Europe.* New York: Vintage, 1994.

Brooten, Bernadette J. *Love Between Women: Early Christian Responses to Female Homoeroticism.* Chicago: University of Chicago Press, 1996.

Brown, Judith C. *Immodest Acts: The Life of a Lesbian Nun in Renaissance Italy.* New York: Oxford, 1986.

Gramick, Jeannine and Robert Nugent, eds. *Voices of Hope: A Collection of Positive Catholic Writings on Gay and Lesbian Issues.* New York: Center for Homophobia Education, 1995.

Hunt, Mary. *Fierce Tenderness: A Feminist Theology of Friendship.* New York: Crossroad, 1991.

Jordan, Mark D. *The Silence of Sodom: Homosexuality in Modern Catholicism.* Chicago: University of Chicago Press, 2000.

Matter, E. Ann. "My Sister, My Spouse: Woman-Identified Women in Medieval Christianity." *Journal of Feminist Studies in Religion* 2, no. 2 (1986): 81–93.

Primiano, Leonard Norman. "Intrinsically Catholic: Vernacular Religion and Philadelphia's 'Dignity.'" Ph.D. diss., University of Pennsylvania, 1993.

**Melissa M. Wilcox**

***See also*** CHURCHES, TEMPLES, AND RELIGIOUS GROUPS; DALY, MARY.

# CENSORSHIP, OBSCENITY, AND PORNOGRAPHY LAW AND POLICY

A confusing set of legal and extra-legal mechanisms for regulating obscenity in the United States has shaped the history of censorship of LGBT representations. Local, state, and federal statutes making the possession or distribution of obscenity a crime coexist with municipal licensing powers, industrial self-regulation, and surveillance and boycotts from quasi-official and self-styled "citizen" groups. Since the early twentieth century, all these weapons have been brought to bear against media that reveal the existence of homosexual desire. Probably the most notorious was the so-called Comstock Act (1873), a federal law that prohibited the mailing of "obscene," "lewd," or "indecent" publications and articles, as well as information on contraception and contraceptive devices. Its passage prompted the enactment of "little Comstock" laws in many states, which went further in criminalizing the possession or distribution of such materials. For many years the definition of the obscene was governed by a legal standard known as the Hicklin rule, established in Great Britain in 1868 and endorsed by U.S. courts in 1879, which established as the test for obscenity "whether the tendency of the matter charged . . . is to deprave or corrupt those whose minds are open to such immoral influences, and into whose hands a publication of this sort may fall." Under this rule, courts might find a work obscene on the grounds that a single word or picture might harm the most "vulnerable viewer," to use historian Francis Couvares's phrase.

## Popular Entertainment and Censorship Strategies

Until the early twentieth century, criminal obscenity statutes were the primary means of suppressing those representations of homosexual desire that might circulate in illicit photographs or classical pornography. "Scientific" descriptions of the invert sometimes were targeted, but generally such materials reached a relatively small audience and were of less concern to officials. In the early decades of the new century, however, portrayals of homosexuality moved into popular entertainment, occasioning the development of new censorship strategies. The appearance of "sissy" characters in motion pictures prompted the National Board of Review of Motion Pictures, a "voluntary" censorship board that worked in cooperation with moviemakers, to issue in 1916 rules barring the "comedy presentation of the sexual pervert." Subsequent self-regulation codes enacted in the 1920s perpetuated this injunction, but enforcement was lax, and effeminate men (and, occasionally, mannish women) surfaced in films until the Catholic Church's pressures on the motion picture industry resulted in a stronger Motion Picture Code in 1934. Even then, while the portrayal of so-called sexual perversion was prohibited, male effeminacy continued to be played for laughs, although the hint of homosexual desire was harder to detect.

Before and after 1934, the real impact of movie censorship was to mute positive discussions of homosexuality while facilitating negative portrayals. Sympathetic portrayals of lesbianism were excised from *Maedchen in Uniform* (1932) when it was distributed in the United States; in contrast, *Suddenly Last Summer* (1959) implied homosexuality, but since it suggested "the horrors of such a lifestyle," the film was approved by the Code Authority and the Catholic Legion of Decency. In the 1950s, even as various court rulings that movies were entitled to First Amendment protection weakened the Code, it continued to prohibit portrayals of homosexuality while abandoning bans on interracial sex and prostitution. Not until the

1960s would Hollywood address homosexuality more directly, and even then most treatments remained rather negative.

The legitimate theater followed a similar trajectory. Soon after representations of male homosexuality and lesbianism appeared on stage in the 1920s, such portrayals were officially prohibited by the Wales Padlock law of 1927, but their interdiction was only partially successful. On Broadway, it was lesbian characters who first drew attention. In 1923 *God of Vengeance*, Yiddish playwright Sholem Asch's moralistic tale about prostitution, became the first play ever to be found obscene under New York's obscenity statutes. Prosecutors focused on a love scene between two women to obtain the conviction. By 1927 state officials passed the Wales Padlock Act in response to the production of *The Captive*, a play about the tragedy of lesbianism, and the impending opening of Mae West's "homosexual comedy-drama" *The Drag*. This law established that a play could be found obscene on the basis of isolated passages rather than the production as a whole (as was beginning to be the case for books); that a theater in which an obscene play was performed could be padlocked for up to a year; and that, significantly, no portrayal of "sex degeneracy or perversion" was permitted on the stage. Although the law did not completely suppress all such portrayals—for instance, Lillian Hellman's *The Children's Hour* had a successful run on Broadway in 1933—its terms made the production of any plays with an LGBT theme much more difficult. In 1928, for example, New York officials harassed Mae West into closing *The Pleasure Man*, a play showcasing "female impersonators." In 1944 the producers of *Trio*, another play about a lesbian relationship, blamed the Wales Act for their difficulty in finding a theater where they could stage the drama. After the play opened, New York's license commissioner revoked the theater's license, under pressure from anti-obscenity activists. However, the public outrage that followed his action suggested the erosion of the social consensus that was the underpinning of the Wales Act—that homosexuality was itself obscene. The law remained on the books until the 1960s, but no other plays were closed for their portrayals of homosexuality after this incident.

By the 1920s and 1930s the portrayal of homosexuality also surfaced in American print, mainly in homophobic sociological "studies" and novels, but also in more sympathetic treatments by LGBT authors. The former were largely ignored by government officials. Efforts to suppress the latter had uneven results. A growing consensus in favor of "freedom of speech" for literature had made it increasingly difficult to ban "serious" books on the basis of existing obscenity statutes by this time, although there remained notable local exceptions. Other strategies, such as customs regulation, were sometimes more successful. The British edition of Radclyffe Hall's *The Well of Loneliness*, for example, was originally banned by the U.S. Customs Bureau after its suppression in England. But when a New York court failed to uphold criminal charges against the book's U.S. publisher, the Customs Bureau lifted the ban; the book went on to become a national bestseller. On the other hand, the Customs Bureau did successfully exclude Parker Tyler and Charles Henri Ford's less staid novel about Greenwich Village gay life, *The Young and the Evil* (1933), which had been published in France.

### The 1950s: Backlash and Increasing Permissiveness

Not until the 1950s did a LGBT print culture flourish in the United States. Its emergence prompted both backlash and, finally, legal recognition that portrayals of homosexuality were not obscene per se. As U.S. LGBT communities grew after World War II, they sustained a wide variety of media; censorship was one strategy among many for policing LGBT life during the Cold War. For example, lesbian pulp novels, widely available in supermarkets and drugstores, attracted some attention from anti-obscenity activists but were mostly not targeted by government officials, perhaps because they generally offered a dreary vision of lesbian life, at least on the surface. The publishers of male physique magazines and homophile periodicals, however, were harassed by postal officials and police. Even "serious" literature, when it contained explicit descriptions of LGBT sex, was targeted in the late 1950s. In 1957 San Francisco bookstore owner and publisher Lawrence Ferlinghetti was arrested, but later acquitted, for distributing Allen Ginsberg's poem *Howl*. Several years later William Burroughs's ambisexual and pornographic novel *Naked Lunch* was the subject of both a postal ban and an obscenity prosecution in Boston, but it, too, was exonerated. These failed censorship efforts helped to publicize Beat culture and change the nature of the publishing industry within the United States. As Norman Mailer observed, after Burroughs's novel was cleared of obscenity charges, "American publishers were pretty much willing to print anything" (de Grazia, p. 395).

By the late 1950s the U.S. Supreme Court had redefined the nation's obscenity laws. In its landmark 1957 case, *Roth v. United States,* the Court replaced the Hicklin rule's emphasis on the vulnerable viewer with a new test: whether "to the average person, applying contemporary community standards, the dominant theme of the material taken as a whole appeals to prurient interest." This new standard was used by the Court to justify greater tolerance of LGBT publications in two important cases: *One, Inc. v. Oleson* (1958), which overturned the Los Angeles postmaster's decision to exclude a homophile magazine from the mails, and *Manual Enterprises, Inc. v. Day* (1962), reversing a similar effort by Virginia postal officials to censor three physique magazines published by H. Lynn Womack. Womack's magazines had been under scrutiny by postal authorities around the country; in a notorious 1960 case, Smith College professor Newton Arvin and several of his friends were convicted of possessing such magazines and other homoerotic material and sharing them with others. Although the Supreme Court justices disagreed about the reasons for exonerating the magazines, their decision in *Manual* was interpreted by publishers to mean a new tolerance for LGBT expression, and both the physique magazines and publications such as Clark Polak's *Drum* began to feature greater sexual explicitness. Legal harassment of these print sources did not end for several more years, but the LGBT press of the post-Stonewall era was made possible by the reform of the obscenity regime that began in the late 1950s.

### After Stonewall

The last three decades of the twentieth century bore witness to a series of "culture wars" in which pornography and homosexuality were central. As obscenity jurisprudence came to sanction a wider range of representations and the pornography industry expanded, movements on both the left and right seized on controlling pornography as a cure for the nation's ills. The "feminist sex wars" of the 1980s and 1990s proved especially divisive, as feminists disagreed over whether pornography was violence against women, or a means to sexual pleasure of which women had historically been deprived. Lesbian sexual practices were hotly contested within these debates, sometimes resulting in censorship within the feminist community; for example, in the mid-1980s some feminist bookstores refused to sell *Coming to Power*, a collection of essays and stories about lesbian sadomasochism published by the San Francisco group Samois.

The feminist antipornography movement emerged within the context of a conservative response to the social changes of the 1960s and 1970s, and feminists sometimes collaborated with right-wing activists on the issue of pornography. Andrea Dworkin and Catherine MacKinnon, for example, cooperated with the Reagan administration's Meese Commission on Pornography, and allied with social conservatives to pass local ordinances defining pornography as a form of sex discrimination. Although in the United States such ordinances were ruled unconstitutional, Dworkin and MacKinnon's theoretical argument against pornography was cited in 1992 by the Supreme Court of Canada in a decision upholding that nation's obscenity law. The Canadian law was quickly used to prohibit the circulation of an American lesbian magazine, *Bad Attitude*, suggesting to many the dangers of such an alliance.

In the meantime, conservative and Christian activists, emboldened by the Meese Commission's support of antipornography efforts, turned their attention to LGBT representation, particularly in the area of visual and performance art. Reflecting the difficulty in obtaining criminal convictions on obscenity charges, however, they increasingly focused on the question of federal funding. For example, the 1990 trial of Dennis Barrie, the former director of Cincinnati's Contemporary Arts Center, for authorizing an exhibit of Robert Mapplethorpe photographs resulted in an acquittal. But U.S. Senator Jesse Helms successfully manipulated the controversy to impose on the National Endowment of the Arts (NEA) a "decency clause," requiring that the NEA consider "general standards of decency and respect for the diverse beliefs and values of the American public" when awarding funds. Although this language was much less specific than the original "Helms Amendment," which would have prohibited funding for depictions of "sadomasochism, homoeroticism, the exploitation of children, or individuals engaged in sex acts," its impact was quickly felt by LGBT artists. While the decency clause was being debated, then NEA Chairman John Frohnmeyer had revoked performance grants to four artists (Karen Finley, John Fleck, Holly Hughes, and Tim Miller), three of who were openly gay or lesbian. The "NEA Four" sued, but in 1998 the U.S. Supreme Court ruled that the NEA's decency clause was constitutional. Similar opposition to LGBT free speech was behind conservative activists' efforts to remove the books *Heather Has Two Mommies* and *Daddy's Roommate* from school libraries across the nation. Thus, at the turn of the twenty-first century, debates about censorship had broadened to include questions about access to funding and to public space. Nonetheless, as was the case one hundred years earlier, it was the increasing visibility of homosexuality in national life that gave rise to many censorship efforts.

## Bibliography

Barrios, Richard. *Screened Out: Playing Gay in Hollywood from Edison to Stonewall.* New York: Routledge, 2003.

Caught Looking Collective. *Caught Looking: Feminism, Pornography, and Censorship.* Seattle: Real Comet Press, 1988.

Chauncey, George. *Gay New York: Gender, Urban Culture, and the Making of the Gay Male World, 1890–1940.* New York: Basic Books, 1994.

Curtin, Kaier. *"We Can Always Call Them Bulgarians": The Emergence of Lesbians and Gay Men on the American Stage.* Boston: Alyson Publications, 1987.

de Grazia, Edward. *Girls Lean Back Everywhere: The Law of Obscenity and the Assault on Genius.* New York: Vintage Books, 1993.

Duggan, Lisa, and Nan D. Hunter. *Sex Wars: Sexual Dissent and Political Culture.* New York: Routledge, 1995.

Friedman, Andrea. *Prurient Interests: Gender, Democracy, and Obscenity in New York City, 1909–1945.* New York: Columbia University Press, 2000.

Meyer, Richard. *Outlaw Representation: Censorship and Homosexuality in Twentieth-Century American Art.* New York: Oxford University Press, 2002.

Russo, Vito. *The Celluloid Closet: Homosexuality in the Movies.* New York: Harper & Row, 1981.

Stein, Marc. *City of Sisterly and Brotherly Loves: Lesbian and Gay Philadelphia, 1945–1972.* Chicago: University of Chicago Press, 2000.

Waugh, Thomas. *Hard to Imagine: Gay Male Eroticism in Photography and Film from Their Beginnings to Stonewall.* New York: Columbia University Press, 1996.

Werth, Barry. *The Scarlet Professor: Newton Arvin: A Literary Life Shattered by Scandal.* New York: Anchor Books, 2001.

**Andrea Friedman**

*See also* BOOKSTORES; DRUM; FILM AND VIDEO; FORD, CHARLES HENRI; GINSBURG, ALLEN; HOMOPHILE PRESS; LITERATURE; MAPPLETHORPE, ROBERT; MIZER, ROBERT; NEWSPAPERS AND MAGAZINES; *ONE*; PHYSIQUE MAGAZINES AND PHOTOGRAPHS; POLAK, CLARK; PORNOGRAPHY; PUBLISHERS; PULP FICTION: GAY; RIGGS, MARLON; SAN FRANCISCO; SEX WARS; THEATER AND PERFORMANCE; WOMACK, H. LYNN.

# THE CENTER FOR LESBIAN AND GAY STUDIES (CLAGS)

The Center for Lesbian and Gay Studies (CLAGS) was the first university-based research center in the United States whose mission centered on lesbian and gay studies. Since its formal establishment in 1991 at the Graduate Center of the City University of New York (CUNY), CLAGS has sought to advance inquiry on LGBT topics by bringing together scholars, activists, artists, and writers from the New York region, the United States, and increasingly from other countries. First conceived in historian Martin Duberman's New York City living room in 1986, the Center developed initially into a primarily regional center for community- and university-based scholars and researchers in New York. In recent years, CLAGS has expanded its national and international profile through increased public programming, competitive fellowships and awards, a publication series, and efforts to build international links between scholars in queer studies.

One of twenty-eight research institutes at CUNY, the Center was one of the earliest and most prominent symbols of the institutionalization of lesbian and gay studies in the 1990s. In this period, many colleges and universities began to establish interdisciplinary programs or concentrations in lesbian and gay studies; a few have even begun to advertise academic positions for scholars in these fields. Duberman, the founder of CLAGS, was an early and vocal advocate of this trend. Duberman was a prizewinning professor of United States history at Princeton University when he became increasingly drawn to the social movements of the late 1960s and early 1970s. By 1972, his growing involvement in the gay liberation movement led him to "come out" in print, an action that at the time earned him scorn from some of his colleagues in the academic world. Soon afterward, Duberman helped found the Gay Academic Union and became involved in efforts to make it possible for other scholars to engage in research and teaching on LGBT history and life. He ultimately left Princeton and joined the faculty at CUNY. Duberman was succeeded as Executive Director by Jill Dolan in 1996 and Alisa Solomon in 1999.

### CLAGS and the Academy

The Center's institutional base, the City University of New York, is the nation's largest urban public university. CUNY traditionally educated many first-generation college students; with the establishment of the Graduate Center in 1961, it also began to provide doctoral training to graduate students. Many faculty hold joint appointments both at the Graduate Center, located in midtown Manhattan, and at one of the university's nineteen teaching colleges, located throughout the city's five boroughs.

Unlike many university-based research institutes, CLAGS has an explicit mission of connecting academic scholarship with struggles for social change. The Center fuses the tradition of queer studies scholars who are self-consciously engaged in community movements for social change with the benefits of a permanent institutional location within a major university. After helping to institutionalize the field of lesbian and gay studies in the early 1990s, CLAGS increasingly sought to encourage and support inquiry on the intersections between gender, sexuality, class, race, and gender identity. Many scholars

affiliated with CLAGS remain involved in queer activism both within and outside the academy.

Among the Center's most visible early activities was its public programming, which brought together speakers on queer studies from various colleges and universities, mainly in the New York area, who might otherwise have remained isolated in their home departments. Many of these talks and panel discussions were collected in two volumes, *A Queer World* and *Queer Representations,* both edited by Duberman and published by New York University (NYU) Press in 1997. The Center subsequently created an academic book series, *Sexual Cultures,* also published by NYU Press and edited by José Esteban Muñoz and Ann Pellegrini. Monthly colloquia have given scholars the opportunity to present and discuss works in progress. The Center now grants several annual fellowships and awards both to CUNY graduate students and to scholars from across the United States who have pursued research on queer topics. In recent years, the Seminars in the City program has sponsored month-long seminars for the general public on such topics as queer Latina and Latino literature and Homo Economics. Recent major programs and conferences sponsored by the Center have addressed transgender law and identity, sexuality in the African diaspora, disability studies, and electoral politics.

The Center also sponsors an annual David Kessler Lecture in lesbian and gay studies, which honors the work of a scholar who has made special contributions to the development of lesbian and gay studies. Past Kessler Lecture honorees have included Barbara Smith, Cherrie Moraga, Samuel Delany, Judith Butler, Joan Nestle, John D'Emilio, and Esther Newton.

### Bibliography

Duberman, Martin, ed. *A Queer World: A Center for Lesbian and Gay Studies Reader.* New York: New York University Press, 1997.

Duberman, Martin, ed. *Queer Representations: Reading Lives, Reading Cultures.* New York: New York University Press, 1997.

CLAGS website: http://www.clag.org

**Timothy Stewart-Winter**

*See also* COLLEGES AND UNIVERSITIES; LGBTQ STUDIES; QUEER THEORY AND QUEER STUDIES.

## CHAMBERS, Jane (b. 27 March 1937; d. 15 February 1983), playwright.

Jane Chambers was the first openly lesbian playwright to portray openly lesbian relationships within a realist playwriting genre. Using a linear plot style and the traditional structures of a well-made play, Chambers situated herself within the conventions of mainstream theater. While her form may have been familiar, her content disrupted the roles women had previously played on the American stage. In this sense she served feminism, placing women in unconventional relationships, as well as gay and lesbian liberation, by creating public representations of lesbian love and identity at the very time that the lesbian and gay movement was struggling for early visibility.

Chambers was born in Columbia, South Carolina, but for most of her early years she lived in Orlando, Florida. Beginning at the precocious age of eight, Chambers wrote such novelty radio scripts as *Girl Scout Time* and *Hi Time* and hosted a talk radio show for kids, *Let's Listen,* as well as a Sunday series entitled *Youth Pops a Question.* After attending Rollins College in Winter Park, Florida, for a year, the nineteen-year-old Chambers moved to Los Angeles to study at the Pasadena Playhouse. Chambers wished to study writing and directing. At the time, however, women were only allowed to study acting, so in 1957 Chambers relocated to New York City. Remaining on the East Coast, she obtained a B.A. degree at Goddard College in 1971. In 1968, while at Goddard, she met Beth Allen, who became her partner and manager and remained so until Chambers's death.

As the women's liberation movement was experiencing a second wave in the 1970s, Chambers became involved in the women's theater collectives that were becoming popular on the East Coast. She founded Corpswoman Theatre (1971) and Women's Interart Theatre (1972), organizations with publicly feminist, though not necessarily queer, political aims. Shortly thereafter, Chambers's play *A Late Snow* was produced in 1974 by New York City's Playwrights Horizons, a popular venue for new work. The play focuses on Ellie, a young, lesbian professor, and is set in what will become Chambers's signature pastoral environment, where the lesbians go to escape the cultural restraints of the city. *A Late Snow* marked a shift in American theater history, in which an openly lesbian playwright debuted a realist drama in which lesbianism is merely one of her characters' complex identities and just another way of loving. Optioned for an Off-Broadway run, *A Late Snow* did not attract the necessary funding due to its controversial subject matter, and the production was never realized. (The same was true for Chambers's play *The Common Garden Variety* [1976], which was workshopped at the Mark Taper Forum in Los Angeles but failed to open.) As Lil says in *Last Summer at Bluefish Cove* (1980), "We're sur-

vivors. We straddle both worlds and try to keep our balance" (p. 61). Perhaps her best-known work, *Bluefish Cove* marked a great victory for Chambers, as well as for gay and lesbian theater history, as it received an overwhelmingly positive reception in the summer of 1980. The play focuses on a lesbian summer community on Long Island where Eva, who has just left her husband of twelve years, and Lil, a single lesbian dying of cancer, fall in love. Around the same time, Chambers discovered that she herself had a terminal brain tumor.

Chambers continued to be prolific, writing *My Blue Heaven* (1981) and *The Quintessential Image* (1983). In these works, her main characters confront and challenge the notion that lesbian-identified artists must commit autobiographical erasure to enter mainstream media. These plays, in fact, came at the very time that Chambers herself was charting this course from the margins to the mainstream, with, in 1983, a production of *Kudzu* in a pre-Broadway workshop. During a *Kudzu* rehearsal, however, Chambers suffered a stroke that left her paralyzed on one side of her body. Still, after surgery, a determined Chambers held a production meeting in the hospital.

Chambers has been memorialized by the Women and Theatre Program of the Association for Theatre in Higher Education (ATHE), which created the Jane Chambers Playwriting Award for emerging playwrights. Chambers's final piece of writing was an unpublished letter written to the lesbian community that brought her tremendous support as she faced her death: "To My Friends at Foot of the Mountain: I feel sure that this committed family of lesbians was not simply going to let me die, that they had removed all the terror and anger from me and all that was left for me to do was heal. We can do that for each other. We can heal by loving, we certainly proved that."

## Bibliography

Chambers, Jane. *Last Summer at Bluefish Cove: A Play in Two Acts.* New York: JH Press, 1982.

Curb, Rosemary Keefe, ed. *Amazon All Stars: Thirteen Lesbian Plays with Essays and Commentary.* New York: Applause Books, 1996.

Curtin, Kaier. *We Can Always Call Them Bulgarians: The Emergence of Lesbians and Gay Men on the American Stage.* Boston: Alyson, 1987.

Dolan, Jill. *Presence and Desire: Essays on Gender, Sexuality, Performance.* Ann Arbor: University of Michigan Press, 1993.

**Jaclyn Iris Pryor**

***See also*** LITERATURE; THEATER AND PERFORMANCE.

# CHEEVER, John (b. 27 May 1912; d. 18 June 1982), novelist, short-story writer.

John Cheever wasn't planned, as his parents sometimes remarked. His brother, Fred, a figure so important in his fiction, was nearly seven years older; despite this—and despite the reputed appearance of the local abortionist at the Cheever's supper table—John Cheever was born in Quincy, Massachusetts, a seaside village. His mother, Mary Devereaux, was ten years younger than her husband, Frederick Lincoln, but whereas he was an affable storyteller and something of a drunk, Mary was strong-willed, sometimes cruel. When Frederick lost his shoe factory following the stock market crash of 1929, Mary started her own business and preserved the family. Cheever would, in later years, come to both resent and admire her powerful presence; she was a woman whose dominating personality could easily slide into petty tyranny and bullying.

Mary was not, in any event, very impressed with her son's performance in school. Although skilled at telling tales—something recognized even by his grammar school teachers—Cheever was a failure as a student. Math seems to have been beyond him, and his attempts at Latin and French were equally disastrous. Some of his lowest marks were in English. He enrolled at Thayer Academy, a tony institution in South Braintree, but was asked to leave because of his poor performance. He then attended the somewhat humbler Quincy High School before being given a second chance at Thayer on a probationary basis; his performance did not improve, and he soon flunked out. A story based on this experience, "Expelled," was accepted for publication in the October 1930 issue of the New Republic. Cheever was just eighteen years old at the time.

Finished with formal education, Cheever undertook a walking tour of Germany with his brother, then moved with him to Boston, where the two planned to buy a house together. The relationship was a troubled one, however. The brothers had grown too close, "morbidly close." Cheever would recall, hinting, as he sometimes did, at the incestuous nature of their relationship. This bond, like that with his mother and father, formed the basis of much of Cheever's most important later work, particularly the stories "Late Gathering" (1931) and "The Brothers" (1937), as well as many of his personal problems. Later, living in Greenwich Village in New York City, Cheever became acquainted with e. e. cummings, James Agee, Edmund Wilson, and Sherwood Anderson. He wrote literary reviews for Malcolm Cowley at the New Republic and novel synopses for MGM, all the while struggling to find his own voice as a writer.

In 1941 he married Mary Winternitz, whom he had met on a visit to his agent's office. World War II began soon after he was married, and Cheever was determined to enlist. While his unit was preparing for a confrontation with German troops in North Africa, he received news that Random House planned to publish his first collection of stories, The Way Some People Live (1943). It was a turning point in his life. He began writing more and more, submitting his stories to the New Republic and the New Yorker, among many other publications.

Perhaps his most famous collection, and certainly the one that most clearly demonstrated his style, The Enormous Radio, and Other Stories, appeared in 1953. His subjects were family—very often his own, and very often only thinly veiled, though he disliked the idea of fiction as disguised autobiography—and the nature of relationships, but the tone was lofty, imbuing ordinary events with an almost mythic quality. When he started work on his first novel, The Wapshot Chronicle, he again turned to this theme, as well as to the theme of confusion over sexual identity, something else that would recur throughout much of his subsequent fiction. In 1958 he was awarded the National Book Award for this novel.

But all was not well. Like his father, Cheever had always been a heavy drinker, and one who prided himself on it, but Cheever's steady drinking degenerated into alcoholism. His tortured relationship with his brother, his troubled family life, and his somewhat formless bisexuality began to take their toll. Cheever started to drink earlier in the day, and soon he was drinking before noon to stave off tremors. He regularly made scenes at parties and when dining with friends. He carried on adulterous affairs with both men and women.

Though Cheever maintained that the greatest part of his sexual activity was heterosexual, it was surely his homosexual impulses that brought him the most frustration. In public, Cheever played the quintessential husband and family man, but in private, his feelings were conflicted, even tormented. "At my back I hear the word 'homosexual' and it seems to split my world in two," he wrote in his journals. "It is ignorance, our ignorance of one another, that creates this terrifying erotic chaos." Driven by his urges, Cheever made repeated visits to the men's room at Grand Central Station, where he observed and engaged in group masturbation sessions. He dated a number of younger men, only to fret incessantly about the difference in their ages. Following the cool critical reception of his darkly existential novel Bullet Park (1969), matters grew even worse.

It was a moment of crisis, but one that inspired Cheever to accept a teaching position at Sing Sing prison and begin collecting details for his novel *Falconer* (1977), maybe his most successful. In it, Zeke Farragut, confined in Falconer Prison for murdering his brother, carries on an affair with Jody, a fellow inmate. Far from the comical sexual uncertainty of Coverly Wapshot in *The Wapshot Chronicle*, or the outsize stereotypes of homosexuality in some of Cheever's earlier stories, the passions described in *Falconer* are transforming and ultimately redemptive. It was while he was at work on *Falconer*, too, that his wife Mary and brother Fred persuaded him at last to enter rehab. Cheever never drank again.

Perhaps more at peace with himself than he had ever been, Cheever was soon able to resume the earlier, almost hectic pace of his writing. *Falconer* brought him great financial and critical success. In 1979 Cheever received the Pulitzer Prize in literature and the National Book Critics Circle Award for a collected volume, *The Stories of John Cheever*. It was a vindication of his life's work and, in a way, of his troubled life.

Cheever developed cancer and died a quiet death at home, surrounded by his family.

### Bibliography

Cheever, John. *The Journals of John Cheever*. New York: Knopf, 1991.

Donaldson, Scott. *John Cheever: A Biography*. New York: Random House, 1988.

Meanor, Patrick. *John Cheever Revisited*. New York: Twayne, 1995.

Waldeland, Lynne. *John Cheever*. Boston: Twayne, 1979.

**Laura M. Miller**

# CHICAGO

The first recorded example of homosexual behavior in the region that would become Chicago dates back to the late seventeenth century. Jesuit priest and explorer Jacques Marquette observed several unmarried Native American men of the Illinois nation wearing the attire of their tribe's women. He noted the unusual manner in which they lived but also observed that, despite their seemingly low status, these men seemed to be highly sought advisers among the Illinois leaders. Several years later, explorer and trader Pierre Liette noted similar men that populated the nearby Miami nation. He wrote that the men had no interest in bows and arrows and that, among them, "the sin of sodomy prevails" (Katz, p. 288).

Following the exploration of men like Marquette and Liette, well over a century passed before the tiny settlement of Chicago attracted any type of migrant population that would rival that of the Native Americans. The small trading post established by Jean Baptiste Point duSable in 1779 only became a city in 1837. Its explosive growth did not begin to occur until the development of the railroads in the 1850s, at which point Chicago rapidly became a center of transportation, commerce, and industry. Large numbers of immigrants soon learned that Chicago, Illinois, was the destination for economic opportunity and personal freedom.

As the city's population increased dramatically in the late nineteenth century, officials attempted to assert some control over vice activity among its citizens. Following the Great Chicago Fire in 1871, a district known as the Levee was established just south of downtown. The Levee was the city's attempt to contain vice activity within one area and it was the location of some of the earliest reports of an active LGBT subculture. The Levee was home to titillating nightclubs like the lesbian-themed Sappho Club and provided ample business opportunities for scores of prostitutes, both female and male.

### "Social Evil"

By 1889, Chicago physician G. Frank Lydston was writing of a sizable homosexual subculture that he had investigated. He referred to the gay men he observed as "sexual perverts" and noted that they liked to congregate together in search of their sexual conquests. The doctor's contempt aside, he was correct in reporting that there were a significant number of homosexuals in Chicago. What was unclear, however, was how prevalent homosexuality was in the various classes of Chicago society. It was thought to be a problem of the lower socioeconomic class, but that thinking was to change.

For working-class gays living in crowded apartments and boarding houses, finding privacy for sexual encounters was difficult. Consequently, they used the city's open spaces for sex more than other groups did, putting them at greater risk for arrest and prosecution. Their journey through the judicial system gave city officials some idea as to the extent of homosexual behavior among the working poor, but little was known about the middle and upper classes.

In 1910, Mayor Fred A. Busse, at the prodding of city religious leaders, commissioned a study to investigate the homosexual problem. The report, "The Social Evil of Chicago," was released in 1911. Investigators claimed that numerous homosexuals, estimated at some 20,000, could be found in all strata of Chicago society. Furthermore, they concluded, there was little that could be done to control the sexual underground.

In the late 1800s and early 1900s, while most homosexual activity was part of the sexual underground, a few people dared to discuss same-sex love in a public forum. Henry Blake Fuller, a Chicago author and playwright, wrote one of America's first homosexual themed plays, *At St. Judas,* in 1896. Another Chicagoan, Margaret Anderson, editor of the influential *Little Review,* had the audacity to write an editorial in March 1915, advocating the idea of homosexual rights.

### "Age of the Pansy"

As Chicago experienced the one-two punch of Prohibition and the Jazz Age, opportunities for social interaction among the city's LGBT population became more abundant. Some African American jazz clubs on the city's South Side featured unprecedented diversity, crossing class, racial, and gender lines. One club, the Cabin Inn, even allowed same-sex dancing. Cross-dressing in public also became more pronounced and by the mid-1920s drag balls were beginning to be held.

This period has been referred to by some historians as the "Age of the Pansy." Gay men were perceived to be easily identifiable by their effeminate manner. The belief that gay men were harmless pansies gave homosexual men new freedom to become tentative participants in the public sphere. In Chicago, gays became more visible, claiming neighborhoods of their own. Towertown on the near northside became a popular neighborhood for gay men. Restaurants like Thompsons became gay haunts and clubs like Diamond Lil's and the Bally Hoo Cafe made little secret that they welcomed those who were "in the life."

The idea of a gay community, however minuscule, belonged to the more affluent homosexuals in Chicago. The sexual life of working-class gays often continued to be relegated to public spaces, like parks and beaches, and they ran the risk of being arrested for, among other things, sodomy. In 1924, Chicago postman Henry Gerber tried to strike a blow for all LGBT people by forming the Society for Human Rights. He envisioned the society successfully lobbying Illinois to repeal its antisodomy law. His dream was short lived, however, as his organization collapsed following a police raid on his apartment in 1925.

The visibility of LGBT people continued to grow in the 1930s. Sociology researchers at the University of Chicago found extensive LGBT social networks that often

centered on private parties. Lesbians and gay men also co-opted public areas. Michigan Avenue, particularly around the Wrigley Building, was a popular place for the under-thirty crowd to gather. Public drag balls, held on Halloween and New Year's Eve, became big events and offered social opportunities for homosexuals, transgender people, and even adventurous heterosexuals. Some of the biggest costume balls were held at the Coliseum Annex, located south of the Loop.

### Weekend Pass

The late 1930s began to see a change in the urban LGBT culture. Public anxiety began to fixate upon the homosexual. A series of sensationalized crimes grabbed the nation's attention, with press accounts often alluding to motives rooted in the "perverted" gay underworld. Foreshadowing of this sex crimes panic occurred in Chicago in 1924, when friends Nathan Leopold and Richard Loeb were convicted of the thrill killing of a fourteen-year-old boy. In the decade that followed, the idea of the harmless "pansy" began to crumble.

With America's entry into World War II in 1941 and the subsequent large infusion of military personnel into the city, Chicago officials felt pressured to crack down on gay activity. Police raids on LGBT clubs occurred more frequently. Arrests increased at popular gay cruising grounds like Lincoln Park and Oak Street Beach. Despite the crackdown, gay men and lesbians serving in the military still found opportunities to sample the gay life in Chicago.

On a weekend pass, LGBT service people would make their way to the Town and Country Lounge in the Palmer House Hotel. There were also several bathhouses that served as rendezvous points for gay men. In addition to frequenting public parks, gay servicemen also had liaisons in movie theater balconies, Young Men's Christian Associations, and public restrooms, which were referred to as "tearooms" in gay circles.

The 1940s and 1950s also saw the increasing popularity of drag balls in Chicago. First staged on the city's South Side in the 1920s, drag balls began as a social outlet for African American LGBT people. In 1935, Alfred Finnie organized a drag ball in the basement of a tavern at 38th Street and Michigan Avenue. Held several times throughout the year, Finnie's Balls—as they came to be known—were large public affairs by the late 1940s. Held at locations like the Pershing Ballroom and, for the most part, free from police harassment, Finnie's Balls became quasi-society events covered in magazines like *Ebony* and *Jet.*

## City Menace

The perception of the homosexual as a "menace," which had begun in the late 1930s, flourished by the early 1950s. With the publishing of Alfred Kinsey's landmark study in 1948, which estimated that 37 percent of all adult males had had a post-adolescent homosexual experience, many Americans realized that most gays were not identifiable. In Chicago, LGBT people who ventured into the semipublic world of the gay bar risked arrest, fines, and even jail time. Local newspapers like the *Chicago Tribune* sometimes printed the names of those arrested in bar raids. For closeted homosexuals, which most were, being identified in a newspaper usually had devastating consequences.

It was in this environment of intense suppression of the homosexual identity that the beginnings of a LGB political movement began to form in Chicago. In 1953 the Chicago Mattachine Society was formed to address the problem of discrimination against homosexuals. The group was an offshoot of the Mattachine Society (originally called the Mattachine Foundation), which had been founded by Californian Harry Hay in 1950. Chicago's membership was small and most of its members were too fearful of exposure to confront discrimination aggressively, but it did serve a purpose. The society gave a few gay men and lesbians a forum to discuss the commonality of their problems. It offered a faint optimism that, in time, circumstances might improve.

LGBT literature was one bright spot during the 1950s. In 1951, Donald Webster Cory published *The Homosexual in America*, a work that argued for understanding for homosexuals, not contempt. Five years later, Chicagoan Jeanette Howard Foster, a library science teacher, published *Sex Variant Women in Literature*. Her work was the first critical study undertaken on lesbian literature. In lesbian fiction, Chicago author Valerie Taylor wrote several lesbian-themed novels in the 1950s. She was also active in the Chicago Mattachine Society and an early chapter of the homophile group Daughters of Bilitis.

## Fighting Back

In 1964, the oppression of Chicago's homosexuals reached a pinnacle. Despite the passing of the Model Penal Code by the Illinois Legislature in 1962, which repealed the state's sodomy law, persecution of homosexuals grew. In April 1964, the Fun Lounge, an after-hours gay club on the city's West Side, was raided. Police arrested 103 men and women. The names of city employees and teachers were printed in the next day's edition of the *Chicago Tribune*. Outraged at such a large-scale raid, several LGBT activists decided political organizing needed another try.

*Gay Chicago.* The cover photo of this magazine—one of several LGBT publications in Chicago since 1973—salutes Mr. Windy City of 1981.

Mattachine Midwest, founded by activists Ira Jones and Robert Basker along with civil liberties attorney Pearl Hart, held its first meeting in the downtown Midland Hotel in July 1965. The organization took up the banner of gay rights, which the previous Mattachine Society had been unable to carry for a sustained period. For the next five years, under the fiery leadership of President Jim Bradford, Mattachine Midwest engaged in a campaign to publicize and fight police harassment.

In the late 1960s, the court system began to be used to combat LGB discrimination. In 1968, the Trip—a downtown gay bar—was raided after police witnessed same-sex dancing. The bar was forced to close temporarily because its liquor license was suspended. The bar management challenged the suspension and the case was eventually appealed to the Illinois Supreme Court. The Trip won when the court ruled that the city had no right to suspend licenses when bars were contesting charges.

## Gay Liberation

New York City's Stonewall Riots in June 1969 ushered in the modern LGBT rights movement. In Chicago, college student Henry Wiemhoff was one of the first gay leaders to embrace the idea of "gay liberation." In May 1969, he helped form the group Chicago Gay Liberation at the University of Chicago. The group was determined to take a bolder approach to activism than previous homophile movement groups like ONE of Chicago and Mattachine Midwest had taken. By the following year, Chicago Gay Liberation was organizing large dances that violated the city's ordinance against same-sex slow dancing. The group also helped students at other universities begin gay liberation groups.

LGBT media became vital in providing a connection for the diverse homosexual community that was spread throughout the city. Mattachine Midwest made the first attempt to mass circulate a publication in the 1960s. The group distributed its newsletters to bookstores and LGBT bars on the city's North and South sides. In 1973, Michael Bergeron and William Kelley began the city's first gay newspaper, the *Chicago Gay Crusader*. Two years later, Grant Ford began successful publication of the weekly *GayLife* newspaper. The *Lavender Woman*, the first Chicago lesbian newspaper, began in 1971.

Police harassment of the city's homosexuals began to diminish considerably by the mid-1970s. With the decriminalization of the gay social scene, the city's gay activists began forming new organizations that represented their strategies for ending anti-LGBT discrimination. Lesbian activists began groups like the Women's Caucus and Radicalesbians. African Americans organized the Black Caucus, later known as Third World Revolutionaries. The Chicago Gay Alliance formed in 1970 to achieve LGB rights through the electoral and legislative process. The group opened the city's first LGB community center in 1971.

Cultural opportunities expanded greatly for the Chicago LGBT community in the 1970s. In 1974, author Valerie Taylor and literary activist Marie Kuda organized the first Lesbian Writer's Conference in the United States. Historian Gregory Sprague began the Chicago Gay History Project in 1978. His history collection effort became the Gerber/Hart Library and Archives in 1983.

LGBT playwrights and actors had the opportunity to showcase their work in groups like the Speak Its Name theater troupe. Gay music lovers founded the Chicago Gay Men's Chorus in 1983. In the realm of religion, groups like Dignity, Integrity, and the Metropolitan Community Church all began serving LGBT spiritual needs in the decade following Stonewall.

## AIDS and Beyond

AIDS entered Chicago's LGBT community at a slower pace than it did the populations of cities like New York and San Francisco, but its effects were no less devastating. Chicago House opened in 1985 to care for people living with AIDS. The Howard Brown Health Center, founded in 1974, became an important health resource for the LGBT community. ACT UP Chicago formed to protest the institutional homophobia that surrounded the disease.

Chicago LGBT activists continued to work in the 1980s and 1990s to pass legislation outlawing anti-LGBT discrimination. In 1988, the city council passed the Chicago Ordinance of Human Rights, making it illegal to discriminate in the areas of housing, employment, and public accommodations. The ordinance had first been introduced by Alderman Clifford Kelley in 1973. In 2002, the city council added the Gender Identity Amendment to the ordinance, protecting transgendered and gender variant individuals from discrimination.

In 1991, Chicago became the first city in the nation to establish a city-sponsored Gay and Lesbian Hall of Fame. Induction ceremonies are held each year recognizing individuals and groups that have made far-reaching contributions to Chicago's LGBT community. While once one of the most oppressive cities in America for LGBT people, today Chicago enjoys a reputation as one of the most progressive.

## Bibliography

Chauncey, George. *Gay New York: Gender, Urban Culture, and the Making of the Gay Male World.* New York: Basic Books, 1994.

D'Emilio, John. *Sexual Politics, Sexual Communities: The Making of a Homosexual Minority, 1940–1970.* Chicago: University of Chicago Press, 1983.

Drexel, Allen. "Before Paris Burned: Race, Class, and Male Homosexuality on the Chicago South Side, 1935–1960." In *Creating a Place for Ourselves: Lesbian, Gay, and Bisexual Community Histories.* Edited by Brett Beemyn. New York and London: Routledge, 1997.

Johnson, David K. "The Kids of Fairytown: Gay Male Culture on Chicago's Near North Side in the 1930s." In *Creating a Place for Ourselves: Lesbian, Gay, and Bisexual Community Histories.* Edited by Brett Beemyn. New York and London: Routledge, 1997.

Katz, Jonathan Ned. *Gay American History: Lesbians and Gay Men in the U.S.A.* rev. ed. New York: Meridian, 1992.

Kuda, Marie. "Chicago Gay and Lesbian History." *Outlines* (July 1995): 27–30.

———. "Chicago's Gay and Lesbian History from Prairie Settlement to World War II." *Outlines* (June 1994): 25–32.

Loughery, John. *The Other Side of Silence: Men's Lives and Gay Identities, A Twentieth Century History.* New York: Henry Holt and Company, 1998.

Onge, Jack. *The Gay Liberation Movement.* Chicago: Alliance Press, 1971. Available in Special Collections, Gerber/Hart Library, Chicago.

Sprague, Gregory. "Chicago's Past: A Rich Gay History." *Advocate* (18 August 1983): 28–31.

www.glhalloffame.org. Official website of Chicago's Gay and Lesbian Hall of Fame.

**John D. Poling**

*See also* ADDAMS, JANE; ANDERSON, MARGARET, AND JANE HEAP; CHICAGO SOCIETY FOR HUMAN RIGHTS; FOSTER, JEANETTE; GERBER, HENRY; GRAHN, JUDY; HART, PEARL; HOMOPHILE MOVEMENTS; HUNTER, ALBERTA; KOPAY, DAVID; MATTACHINE SOCIETY; RODWELL, CRAIG; TAYLOR, VALERIE; VAN VECHTEN, CARL.

**CHICAGO SOCIETY FOR HUMAN RIGHTS.** see SOCIETY FOR HUMAN RIGHTS.

# CHORUSES AND BANDS

Since they were first established in the 1970s, LGBT musical organizations have grown remarkably in number, size, and sophistication. Their many concerts, recordings, and events are among the most striking examples of communal expression within the gay and lesbian subculture.

Most medium and large North American cities boast gay and lesbian choruses, as do many cities in Europe and Oceania. These organizations have evolved to become much more than musical institutions. As representatives of gay and lesbian communities, they generate powerful political and social expression both for and between those communities, through texts and symbolism as well as through the sheer emotional power of music. As alternatives to a bar/club culture, they are catalysts for the creation of solidarity and commonality among individuals often marginalized by the larger society.

Lesbian musical organizations began appearing in the 1970s. The earliest of these, Women Like Me, was established by composer Roberta Kosse in 1971 in New York. In 1975, Catherine Roma founded the oldest chorus still in operation, the Anna Crusis Women's Choir, in Philadelphia. This group has since joined GALA as its senior member.

The Gotham Male Chorus was founded in New York in late 1977 by conductor Donald Rock, who wanted a chorus that would "dig music as well as each other." In 1980 this group began to include women and became the Stonewall Chorale, first of the gay and lesbian mixed-voice ensembles.

The San Francisco Gay Freedom Day Marching Band & Twirling Corps, the first such organization to declare its gay or lesbian identity by name, was founded in June 1978 by Jon Reed Sims (1947–1984) and made its first public appearance later that month at the Gay Pride Day parade. After the establishment of the Band & Twirling Corps, Sims founded in rapid succession the San Francisco Gay Men's Chorus (November 1978, at the public memorial for Harvey Milk and George Moscone), Golden Gate Performing Arts (an administrative organization, March 1979), the orchestra Lambda Pro Musica, and the San Francisco Lesbian & Gay Men's Community Chorus. He always intended to create a nationwide network of gay and lesbian instrumental and choral ensembles; the success of that network, both in his lifetime and after, remains an astonishing legacy.

Choruses were soon founded in Los Angeles (July 1979), Seattle (September 1979), and Chicago (October 1979). A 1981 national tour by the San Francisco Gay Men's Chorus instigated the founding of choruses and bands in many cities. In 1981, the Sister Singers Network was established among the women's and lesbian choruses; as of 2002 it had forty-five member choruses, and it has produced a number of regional, national, and international women's choral festivals. The first organizational meeting (June 1981, Chicago) of what later became GALA (the Gay and Lesbian Association of Choruses) followed soon after. In 1982, at the first Gay Games in San Francisco, fourteen choruses met for the First West Coast Choral Festival, which led to the establishment of the GALA Choruses Network.

The first national GALA Festival (New York, 1983) was called COAST (Come Out and Sing Together), and attracted twelve choruses with some twelve hundred members. This was followed by festivals in Minneapolis (1986), Seattle (1989), Denver (1992), Tampa (1996), and San Jose (2000), each of which has shown a steady increase both in attendance and GALA membership. In 2004 the festival will be in Montreal, the first held in Canada. Since 1995 events have also included numerous regional festivals, as well as Small Ensemble Festivals, which showcase the numerous chamber and popular ensembles that have emerged from the larger choruses.

As of 2002, GALA included 170 choruses with a total of about eight thousand individual members, including gay male, lesbian, and mixed-voice groups in North America, Europe, and Oceania. Composers commissioned by the GALA choruses have included Roger Bourland, David Conte, Janice Giteck, Libby Larsen, Holly Near, Ned Rorem, Robert Seeley, Conrad Susa, Gwyneth Walker, and Martin Wesley-Smith. Many of these commissions have been subsequently published, some of them under the auspices of GALA. Performers that have appeared with GALA's member choruses include Maya Angelou, Natalie Cole, Michael Feinstein, Jerry Hadley, Marilyn Horne, Bobby McFerrin, Bette Midler, Liza Minnelli, Mark Morris, Holly Near, Bernadette Peters, Roberta Peters, and Frederica von Stade.

In addition to the GALA choruses, at least seventy other gay and lesbian choruses exist. Although many of the choruses in the larger North American cities are large ensembles (thirty or more singers), most of the European choruses are smaller groups, often oriented toward chamber or cabaret productions. The repertoire for the lesbian and gay choruses includes the existing traditional and classical choral music for women's and men's, as well as mixed, voices, in addition to many new compositions and arrangements of popular and classical works written for the choruses.

Although they have not resulted in such a large network, instrumental ensembles such as concert and marching bands and orchestras have appeared in many cities, most notably the Bay Area Women's Philharmonic (San Francisco). Lesbian & Gay Bands of America (LGBA), which held its first meeting in Chicago in October 1982, comprised twenty-five ensembles in 2002, including bands in North America and Australia. LGBA celebrated its tenth anniversary at the Gay Games in San Francisco in 1992, and an ensemble of LGBA members performed at Clinton's Presidential Inaugural in 1993; its twentieth anniversary was celebrated in Melbourne in 2002.

Programming concerts for all of the lesbian and gay ensembles is a complex activity, since band and chorus music—especially that performed by same-sex choruses, with their more limited pitch range—is not in itself a major attraction in the contemporary marketplace. The gay and lesbian ensembles do not automatically fit the audiences for particular musical genres; most have instead chosen to target their communities, presenting cross-genre concerts in a sort of endless balancing act. Many ensembles find it useful to create traditions, such as holiday concerts or yearly productions of stage shows, in order to keep their audiences. Performances, especially at political events, often include musical works that are symbolic in some way; the impact is often not in words, however, but in the emotional effects of the music.

**Bibliography**

Attinello, Paul. "Authority and Freedom: Toward a Sociology of the Gay Choruses." In *Queering the Pitch: The New Gay and Lesbian Musicology.* Edited by Philip Brett, Elizabeth Wood, and Gary C. Thomas. New York: Routledge, 1994.

———. "Sims, John Reed." In *Baker's Biographical Dictionary of Musicians,* 8th edition. New York: Schirmer/Macmillan, 1992.

Gordon, Eric A. "GALA: The Lesbian and Gay Community of Song." *Choral Journal* 30, no. 9 (1990): 25–32.

Roma, Catherine. "Choruses, Women's." In *Lesbian Histories and Cultures: An Encyclopedia.* Edited by Bonnie Zimmerman. New York: Garland, 2000.

———. "Women's Choral Communities: Singing for our Lives." *Hotwire* 8, no. 1 (January 1992): 36.

Vukovich, Dyana. "The Anna Crusis Women's Choir. *Women and Performance: A Journal of Feminist Theory* 4, no. 1 (issue 7): 50–63.

Wise, Matthew. "Choruses and Marching Bands." In *Gay Histories and Cultures: An Encyclopedia.* Edited by George E. Haggerty. New York: Garland, 2000.

**Paul Attinello**

*See also* MUSIC: CLASSICAL.

# CHRYSTOS (b. 7 November 1946), poet, activist, writer, and artist.

Chrystos was born in San Francisco to a Menominee father and a mother of European heritage and self-identifies as an "urban Indian" and a Two-Spirit Native American. She came out in the working-class bar world of San Francisco's Haight-Ashbury district in the 1960s. Painful events and emotions Chrystos experienced during her childhood and adult life drive her sharp, unvarnished poetry: her mother's depression and abusive behavior, her father's shame about his Indian heritage, sexual abuse suffered at the hands of a relative, her own alcoholism and recovery, and her outrage at the treatment of Native Americans and women. According to one critic, "Her personal experiences are woven throughout her testimonial poetry" (Valimaa). As Chrystos herself said, "Writing has always been my blanket to pull me through."

For some, Chrystos's poetry is unsettling, but for others her work gives voice to the pain of women with no venue in which to express it. As she writes in "Bitter as the Pockmarked Street,"

This beautiful mind given to me by Creation
has never been used for more
than a few days at a time
What's the use of weeping?
What's the use of breathing?
There is no place to match my need.

A glimpse of that need is seen in "Not Editable," where she writes that success does not interest her: "I want something vastly more difficult—spiritual release, inner and world peace, a body of work I can heal through" (in Moraga and Anzaldúa, p. 225).

Some critics are drawn to the insightfulness of Chrystos's observations on historical (white male) racism, but are put off by her views on the racism of white lesbians. Barbara May refers to some of Chrystos's statements on the subject as being "at once offensive and intriguing." May also notes that Chrystos is best known for her "angry political poems and her identification with society's victims," but that it is "her erotic poems that are most original and lyrical." Such praise for Chrystos's erotic poems but dismissal of her work advocating against oppression may be viewed as a reflection of white women's ambivalence toward women of color—as acceptable partners for lovemaking but not suitable spokespersons for radical politics. Despite the wide spectrum of responses to it, Chrystos's poetry sings of the intimacy between women: "I roll in you like first snow melt shocking my blood / with this glistening new river of humming birds between us" (from "Na Natska").

Her work first appeared in *This Bridge Called My Back: Writings by Radical Women of Color* (1983) and *Living the Spirit: A Gay American Indian Anthology* (1988). Her books of poetry include *Not Vanishing* (1988), *Dream On* (1991), and *Fugitive Colors* (1995). She also coedited and authored the introduction for *Best Lesbian Erotica* (1996), and contributed to *The Prison Industrial Complex and the Global Economy* (1998). She was the recipient of a National Endowment for the Arts grant for *Dream On* and a finalist in the Audre Lorde International Poetry Competition (1994), and received the Sappho Award of Distinction from the national Astraea Lesbian Action Foundation.

Chrystos's activism has included work to free Native Americans Norma Jean Croy, who was imprisoned for nineteen years, and Leonard Peltier, who as of 2003, was still incarcerated. She has also labored tirelessly on behalf of indigenous peoples' land and treaty rights, such as those of the Dine and Mohawk nations. Since 1980, she has resided on Bainbridge Island in Washington State.

**Bibliography**

Chrystos. "Not Editable." In *This Bridge Called My Back: Writings by Radical Women of Color*. Edited by Cherríe Moraga and Gloria Anzaldúa, pp. 46–52. New York: Kitchen Table Press, 1983.

Claudia, Karen. Interview. *Off Our Backs* (March 1989): 18–19.

May, Barbara Dale. "Chrystos." In *Contemporary Lesbian Writers of the United States*. Edited by Sandra Pollack and Denise D. Knight. Westport, Conn.: Greenwood Press, 1993.

Snelling, Lieve. Interview. *The Gully* (13 March 2002). Available from http://www.thegully.com/essays/gaymundo/020313_chrystos_native_gay.html.

Vaīmaa, Virpi. "Chrystos." *Voices from the Gap*, 1997. Available from http://voices.cla.umn.edu/authors/Chrystos.html.

**Yolanda Retter**

## CHUA, Siong-huat (b. 24 October 1954; d. 15 August 1994), writer, activist.

Born and reared in Malacca, Malaysia, Siong-huat Chua became a writer and leader of sexual liberation and Asian American organizing in the United States. His father, Geok-Koon Chu, was a Malaysian fisherman and devout Buddhist; Chu-Tuan Chua, his mother, a refugee from the Japanese invasion of China, became a successful businesswoman operating beauty salons in Malaysia. From his Buddhist father he inherited a notable equanimity and pride in being Chinese, and from his mother a quest for style, change, and progress. His friend Mark Matthiessen remembered that Chua never stopped loving his family as much as they loved him, and he never stopped loving the Chinese culture he had been born into.

Schooled by Methodists in Malaysia, Chua entered the Massachusetts Institute of Technology (MIT) in 1974. His initial revulsion to some students' career orientations led him to join an Asian American Maoist study group, which sometimes criticized him for being "flippant"—a common code word for gay sensibility. Chua nevertheless retained his admiration for Mao, even after graduating in 1979 with a degree in computer studies and taking a job with the Dana Farber Cancer Institute, his employer until his death in 1994.

While a student at MIT, "SH" (as his friends called him) attended an anarchist Black Rose forum on gay male liberation, featuring the collective that published the *Fag Rag* periodical. One of the fundamentals of the collective's anarchist philosophy held that each group should organize itself around its participants' own grievances and aspirations. In that spirit, Chua not only came to play a central role in lesbian and gay groups but also reached out to other Asians by organizing the first lesbian and gay Asian group in the world.

In 1979 Chua played a central role in Boston Asian Gay Men and Lesbians (BAGMAL); the group expanded in 1988 to include all Massachusetts as the Alliance of

Massachusetts Asian Lesbians and Gay Men (AMAL-GAM). Both groups published newsletters providing outreach and education. Nusrat Retina worked with Chua to include more lesbians in AMALGAM; her presentation of Trinity Ordona's slide show showcased Asian Pacific lesbians all over the world coming out and coming together. Chua collaborated in the translation of "A Brief History of Chinese Lesbianism," an essay by Sam Sasha, published in Hong Kong. Gay liberationist and librarian Dan C. Tsang, then at Temple University Library and later at the University of California at Irvine, provided bibliographies, contacts, and friendship. Chua also joined Richard Fung and others in Toronto who presented an elegant revue in conjunction (but separate from) a 1985 international lesbian-gay studies conference. The Toronto-based group who published the magazine *CelebrAsian* sponsored the show, which provided relief from the conference debates.

Chua showed great courage in supporting causes he considered just. Even before acquiring U.S. citizenship, he marched with the Boston/Boise Committee and later the North American Man/Boy Love Association. Working with many other groups in Boston, Chua became a board member of Gay/Lesbian Advocates and Defenders (GLAD), where he helped introduce new computer technology and began in 1987 to organize forums on lesbian and gay immigrants. With *Gay Community News (GCN)*, *Fag Rag*, Glad Day Books (both in Boston and Toronto), and other groups, Chua's hours of volunteer tutoring brought expanded Internet capabilities to the lesbian-gay movement. Chua's articles often appeared in *Fag Rag* and *GCN*; his fun-loving humor and wit enlivened many meetings and informal gatherings.

His lover Duane Neeli had formerly been a lover of John Wayne Gacey, a Chicago construction contractor and serial killer who murdered his male sexual partners and buried them in his basement. Neeli lived some years with Chua in Roxbury, a once-fashionable area of Boston with abandoned nineteenth-century mansions that were reoccupied in the 1960s and eventually became a largely gay and black community. He was also a member of the Fort Hill Faggots for Freedom, a group begun in the early 1970s. Neeli eventually moved to New York City, became a pornography star, and died of a drug overdose.

Chua devoted his final years of activism to understanding and overcoming AIDS. When he received a positive diagnosis for HIV, he immediately called his mother in Malacca who told him they would fight the disease together. Victor Bloise, Chua's partner for his last eleven years, also offered love and support. Mark Matthiessen, a writer who had lived in Fort Hill, worked on *Fag Rag*, and

published in *Gay Community News*, had become a nurse specializing in AIDS treatment. As Chua's health declined, Matthiessen helped Chua visit his family in Malacca. Meanwhile, Chua studied (as a matter of life and death) recent AIDS literature, scouring learned journals as well as Chinese markets in hope of finding some herbal or other alleviation, if not a complete cure for his disease. Unfortunately, he died before the 1996 Vancouver AIDS conference, where significant advances in the fight against AIDS were announced. Shortly after Chua's death, overcome with feelings of loss and grief, Bloise took his own life.

When Chua died, Matthiessen joined a group of friends and family for a farewell tribute. At the gathering, an interview in Richard Fung's video *Fighting Chance* (1990) showed Chua speaking without apologies about his life and disease. Thus, even after death he continued through writings and video to rally support for sexual liberation and better medical treatment for himself, for all Asians, and indeed for all humans.

### Bibliography

"Siong Huat Chua, 39." *Boston Globe*, 19 (August 1994): 37.

Tsang, Daniel C. "Founder of First Gay and Lesbian Asian Group Succumbs to AIDS." *Asian Week* 3(2 September 1994): 19.

**Charles Shively**

*See also* ASIAN AMERICAN LGBTQ ORGANIZATIONS AND PERIODICALS; NORTH AMERICAN MAN/BOY LOVE ASSOCIATION (NAMBLA); TSANG, DANIEL.

**CHUMMING.** see SMASHES AND CHUMMING.

# CHUNG, Margaret
(b. 2 October 1889; d. 5 January 1959), physician.

Margaret Jessie Chung was born in Santa Barbara, California, to Wong and Minnie Chung. Her parents emigrated from China during the 1870s and converted to Christianity. Because of their poverty, the Chung family moved frequently, first to Ventura County and then to Los Angeles. Motivated by the desire to serve as a medical missionary to China, Margaret enrolled in the University of Southern California's College of Physicians and Surgeons in 1911.

In the overwhelmingly masculine and white environment of medical school, Chung experimented with her gender and cultural identities. Photographs reveal that she dressed like a man by wearing dark suits and ties and pulling or slicking her hair back. At the same time, she expressed solidarity with the few female students by helping to found a medical sorority, Nu Sigma Phi, in 1914. Chung also culturally "passed" by adopting western clothing and embracing western science. However, she gained recognition for giving lectures about China and providing health care services for Chinese people in Los Angeles. While Chung was in medical school, her mother—who played an instrumental role in supporting her professional and religious goals—passed away. In 1916 Margaret graduated and became the first known American-born Chinese female doctor.

Following graduation, Chung worked in a variety of institutions to establish her career. However, her applications to serve as a medical missionary in China were rejected by white-dominated religious organizations. Also facing difficulties in obtaining an internship in California, a state with historically intense anti-Asian sentiment, she initially worked as a surgical nurse at the Santa Fe Railroad Hospital in Los Angeles. In the fall of 1916, Chung moved to Chicago to serve as an intern at the Mary Thompson Hospital for Women and Children. In October 1917, her father died following a car accident in Pasadena because the local hospital refused to admit him on racial grounds. With the contacts that she developed among progressive female and Jewish reformers, Chung obtained a paid residency at the Illinois Juvenile Psychopathic Institute to help support her six younger siblings in California. In November 1918 Chung was granted military leave to volunteer her medical services. With the conclusion of World War I that very month, she decided to return to Los Angeles.

Back in Southern California, Chung returned to the Santa Fe, this time as a physician on the hospital staff. She also developed a private practice, attracting clients from the burgeoning Hollywood film industry. Despite her relative success, Chung decided to move to San Francisco in the early 1920s to pursue her original goal of providing medical care to people of her own ancestry. She established one of the first western medical clinics and helped found the Chinese Hospital in 1925 in San Francisco's Chinatown. As a result of tensions with her adopted community, however, most of her patients were male and non-Chinese.

The tensions arose because of the way Chung navigated sexual boundaries as well as professional ones. She remained single, an unusual choice given the gender imbalance in the Chinese American community and the existence of antimiscegenation laws. Residents in Chinatown as well as various love interests speculated about her sexual orientation. Chung developed homoerotic relationships, two of which were with white women from immigrant backgrounds: poet Elsa Gidlow and entertainer Sophie Tucker. However, Chung also distanced herself from the emerging modern lesbian identity. Instead, she evoked Victorian forms of romantic friendship to characterize her intimate relationships.

Beginning with the Japanese attack on Manchuria in 1931, Chung became an advocate of Chinese and eventually Allied war efforts. To express her dual patriotisms, she created a fictive kinship network dedicated to fighting the war: known as Mom Chung, she had over one thousand "adopted" children, most of whom were white men in the American military, political circles, and the entertainment industry. Her surrogate family was divided into three branches: the Fair-Haired Bastards for pilots, Kiwis for those who did not fly, and Golden Dolphins for submariners. Members included actor Ronald Reagan, conductor Andre Kostelanetz, aviator Amelia Earhart, and Fleet Admiral of the U.S. Navy Chester Nimitz. Chung used these contacts to recruit pilots for the Flying Tigers, the American volunteer air force in Asia, and to lobby for the creation of WAVES, the women's naval reserve, which was accomplished in 1942. Despite her efforts to open the military to women, Chung's requests to serve were repeatedly rejected. Chung maintained a medical practice until the late 1950s, though she decreased her hours during World War II and afterwards, probably due to health considerations. She eventually passed away in San Francisco in 1959 from ovarian cancer.

**Bibliography**

Margaret Chung Papers. Asian American Studies Collections. Ethnic Studies Library, University of California at Berkeley.

Rupp, Leila. *A Desired Past: A Short History of Same-Sex Love in America.* Chicago: University of Chicago Press, 1999.

Wu, Judy Tzu-Chun. "'The Ministering Angel of Chinatown': Missionary 'Uplift,' 'Modern' Medicine, and Asian American Women's Strategies of Liminality." In *Asia/Pacific Islander American Women: A Historical Anthology.* Edited by Shirley Hune and Gail Nomura. New York: New York University Press, 2003.

———. "Mom Chung of the Fair-Haired Bastards: A Thematic Biography of Dr. Margaret Chung, 1889–1959." Ph.D. diss., Stanford University, 1998.

———. "Was Mom Chung a 'Sister Lesbian'?: Asian American Gender Experimentation and Interracial Homoeroticism." *Journal of Women's History* 13:1 (Spring 2001): 58–82.

Yung, Judy. *Unbound Feet: A Social History of Chinese Women in San Francisco.* Berkeley: University of California Press, 1995.

———. *Unbound Voices: A Documentary History of Chinese Women in San Francisco.* Berkeley: University of California Press, 1999.

**Judy Tzu-Chun Wu**

# CHURCHES, TEMPLES, AND RELIGIOUS GROUPS

Religious groups serving LGBT and queer people have blossomed at an impressive rate since the late 1960s. Although individual organizations existed before that time, little evidence of them remains: they neither lasted long nor spread beyond a single congregation. In the late 1960s, however, groups of gay men and lesbians began to take religious matters into their own hands. Although many continued to struggle with religious questions about their sexual orientation, some refused to allow existing religious groups to define them and instead created their own spaces in which to be religious without fear of rejection or reprisal. The first such organization was the Metropolitan Community Church.

## The Universal Fellowship of Metropolitan Community Churches

On 6 October 1968, the Metropolitan Community Church (MCC) began in the living room of defrocked Pentecostal minister Troy Perry. Attracted by an advertisement Perry had placed in the newly founded *Advocate,* the twelve people who attended came from a wide variety of Christian backgrounds in search of a place to worship with other gays and lesbians. This desire was a powerful draw: the church outgrew Perry's house in ten weeks, and within two years the movement had spread to San Francisco, Chicago, San Diego, and Honolulu. In September 1970, representatives from these congregations met for the inaugural general conference of the Universal Fellowship of Metropolitan Community Churches (UFMCC). This rate of growth continued for more than a decade, and by 2002 the UFMCC claimed over 40,000 members and 300 congregations in nineteen countries. MCC churches exist in most major urban areas of the United States, and the Cathedral of Hope, MCC's Austin congregation, holds the distinction of being the world's only LGBT and queer megachurch.

Though the denomination was founded by a Pentecostal minister, its doctrinal range has been broad from the beginning, and this breadth has increased over the years. As a result, MCC congregations range from feminist groups using experimental liturgy to traditional Pentecostals who believe that their mission is to bring all LGBT people to Christ. Despite its size and influence, however, the UFMCC remains marginal in the context of official Christianity in the United States and worldwide: while it holds observer status in the World Council of Churches, the denomination has repeatedly been denied membership in the National Council of Churches in the United States.

## The World Congress of Gay, Lesbian, Bisexual, and Transgender Jews

In 1972, a group of lesbian, gay, and bisexual Jews began meeting at MCC-Los Angeles, initially calling themselves the Metropolitan Community Temple. Shortly after formally organizing, they selected a new name: Beth Chayim Chadashim (BCC) or the House of New Life. Like MCC, this organization grew successfully as other Jews began to hear of a congregation in which they could worship and be open about their sexual orientation. Unlike the UFMCC, however, BCC both requested and was granted membership in a mainstream organization early in its history: in 1973, the congregation applied for membership in the major organization for Reform synagogues, the Union of American Hebrew Congregations (UAHC). Acceptance was not immediate, but it came soon thereafter, in 1974.

Shortly after BCC was founded in Los Angeles, a second gay/lesbian synagogue took shape in New York: Congregation Beth Simchat Torah (CBST). The subject of anthropologist Moshe Shokeid's book, *A Gay Synagogue in New York,* CBST was founded through a series of events strikingly similar to those that produced MCC. In this case, a number of gay and lesbian Jews met in an Episcopal church in New York City. Eventually, some of the church members suggested that the Jews should have their own meeting, and a man named Jacob Gubbay advertised a "gay synagogue" in the local alternative newspaper, the *Village Voice.* Ten people showed up for the inaugural Shabbat service in the basement of the Church of the Holy Apostles, but like MCC and BCC, this group grew quickly. CBST now claims to be the largest LGBT synagogue in the world.

Others soon built on these examples both within and beyond the United States, and in 1976 an international meeting of LGBT Jews took place in Washington, D.C., sparked in part by the UN's condemnation of Zionism. After three more such meetings (two in the United States and one in Israel), the World Congress of Gay, Lesbian, Bisexual, and Transgender Jews was founded in 1980. Included in its membership in 2002 were over sixty-five organizations from such disparate areas as Hungary, the United States, Australia, Israel, and Sweden.

## Dignity, Integrity, and Other Denominational Groups

As one might expect, Protestants and Jews were not the only ones to organize religious groups supportive of LGBT people during the post-Stonewall era. In 1969, Father Patrick Nidorf organized a support group for gay and lesbian Catholics in San Diego, California. Like MCC and the synagogue movement, this group also grew rapidly as Catholics began to come out, and as those who were already out learned that there was a place in which they could be gay or lesbian and Catholic.

Named simply "Dignity," this organization faced one challenge that MCC and the synagogues did not: it functioned under the auspices of an existing religious group that did not focus its ministry on lesbians and gay men. In 1971, the Los Angeles archbishop asked Nidorf to resign from Dignity's leadership; in response, the organization turned to lay leadership and thus became less susceptible to the control of the church hierarchy. This change has served the group well as its goals have become more far-reaching: over the years, Dignity has shifted from asking solely for noncondemning inclusion to demanding full and open acceptance and equal rights in the church for transgender people and sexually active gay men, lesbians, and bisexuals. Moreover, it has become an avid proponent of women's ordination. As a result, the Roman Catholic hierarchy has pushed Dignity farther and farther away from the boundaries of "acceptable" Catholicism, even preventing parishes from renting their facilities to the group for either meetings or Mass.

Other organizations, working within more liberal or less hierarchical branches of Christianity, have had greater success in remaining integrated with their parent denominations. Usually, these groups hold meetings but not services and are attended frequently by heterosexual allies as well as LGBT Christians. Members take part in Bible study sessions, support networks, and social interaction, but they also usually attend services at their local churches. Such groups now exist with varying degrees of official recognition for nearly every major Christian denomination, ranging from Mormon (Affirmation) to evangelical (Evangelicals Concerned) to Unitarian Universalist (Interweave). Perhaps the best known, however, is Integrity, the LGBT and ally organization for Episcopalians.

Founded in Georgia in 1974 by Louie Crew, Integrity holds the distinction of being one of the few early, queer religious organizations not founded in Southern California. Though it began on the opposite coast from MCC, Dignity, and the synagogue movement, Integrity grew just as quickly as the others, expanding by 2002 to well over sixty member groups internationally. Unlike its autonomous forerunners, which use their independence to work for change on a broad level, Integrity has been influential in Episcopal policy by virtue of being an "insider" group: an organization of people who continue to belong to Episcopal parishes but who challenge those parishes as well as their archdiocesan leaders for greater

**Church Service.** Calvary Lutheran Church is the setting of the first services of the Church of Saint Sergius and Saint Bacchus. [Associated Press]

levels of inclusion. The same holds true for other, similar organizations, including (among many others) American Baptists Concerned for Sexual Minorities; the Gay, Lesbian, and Affirming Disciples Alliance; and Lutherans Concerned.

## The Unity Fellowship Church Movement

Both MCC and the synagogue movement, focused as they are on providing an open, comfortable, and safe worship space for every LGBT Christian or Jew, must by necessity encompass a wide range of religious backgrounds, doctrines, practices, and needs. Religious leaders in synagogues and churches face and often overcome great challenges in designing a worship service that includes everyone, allows space for differences in worship tastes and practices, and creates a community that goes beyond such differences. Where MCC has not been overwhelmingly successful, however, is in its inclusion of people of color. Though a few MCC churches have Spanish-language services and some congregations are widely multicultural, many African Americans choose not to attend because MCC simply does not have the feel of a black church.

In 1985 in Los Angeles, gospel singer Carl Bean decided to remedy the lack of attention given to black Christians who were LGBT or queer. He started a home Bible study group, but his flock grew rapidly and Bean soon began to hold services in Los Angeles' historic Ebony Showcase Theater. Shortly thereafter, the Unity Fellowship Church Movement (UFCM) and its major outreach program, the Minority AIDS Project, were officially founded. Both organizations eventually found a home in a historically black neighborhood of Los Angeles, and, in 2002, the UFCM buildings housed not only the church offices, the Minority AIDS Project offices, and a sanctuary seating several hundred people, but also an alternative high school program for local LGBT youth.

Bean and others began to spread the word about their movement, and similar churches opened in other cities across the United States—twelve by 2002. Now archbishop of the movement, Bean serves as both administrator and circuit preacher, spending one-half of his year visiting the various Unity Fellowship churches and the other half running the movement from its central offices in Los Angeles.

## Newer and Smaller Organizations

The oldest and largest religious organizations whose efforts focus on LGBT people are Jewish and Christian groups. However, there are also a number of LGBT and queer religious organizations that are either smaller or newer than those discussed above.

Within Christianity, some of the newer movements focus on providing welcoming church spaces for charismatic and evangelical Christians. One of these is Glory Tabernacle MCC in Long Beach, California. In other areas of the West and southwest United States, though, are scattered a handful of churches affiliated with a small organization known as Christ Chapel. This group, founded by former drag queen Michael Cole (known as "Honey Carolina" in his younger days), especially attracts LGBT people with backgrounds in the more conservative Protestant denominations.

Umbrella organizations for queer Hindus and Buddhists have been less common. Among native and immigrant practitioners of these religions, this is in part because of negative cultural attitudes toward Western forms of homosexuality. Among Western converts, on the other hand, there is a perception that sexual orientation is irrelevant to the contemplative practices of both religions—practices to which such converts are generally

most strongly drawn. However, despite the lack of a strong national group, organizations of LGBT Buddhists do exist in a number of urban areas of the United States, and gay Zen Buddhist monk Issan Tommy Dorsey (another former drag performer) is well known for founding one of the first AIDS hospices, San Francisco's Maitri Hospice, before he himself succumbed to the disease.

Finally, the late 1990s saw the beginnings of queer activism among Muslims in the formation of groups known as Al-Fatiha and Queer Jihad. To date, these organizations have operated mostly through the Internet, as online sources of support, but Al-Fatiha has also begun to hold local meetings and to organize local chapters. Given the strong and sometimes violent opposition to sexual and gender minorities in many Muslim cultures, the greater invisibility of LGBT Muslims in the United States is unsurprising. Hopefully, however, these two organizations will change that situation for the better, broadening both the acceptance of queer people in Islam and the acceptance of Islam among queer communities.

## Bibliography

Gill, Sean, ed. *The Lesbian and Gay Christian Movement: Campaigning for Justice, Truth, and Love.* London: Cassell, 1998.

Gorman, E. Michael. "A New Light on Zion: A Study of Three Homosexual Religious Congregations in Urban America." Ph.D. dissertation, University of Chicago, 1980.

Perry, Troy D., with Thomas L. P. Swicegood. *Don't Be Afraid Anymore: The Story of Reverend Troy Perry and the Metropolitan Community Churches.* New York: St. Martin's Press, 1990.

Primiano, Leonard Norman. "Intrinsically Catholic: Vernacular Religion and Philadelphia's 'Dignity.'" Ph.D. dissertation, University of Pennsylvania, 1993.

Shokeid, Moshe. *A Gay Synagogue in New York.* New York: Columbia University Press, 1995.

Thumma, Scott, and Edward Gray, eds. *Gay Religion: Innovation and Tradition in Spiritual Practice.* Walnut Creek, Calif.: Alta Mira, 2003.

Tinney, James S. "Why a Black Gay Church?" In *In the Life: A Black Gay Anthology.*, Edited by Joseph Beam. Boston: Alyson, 1986, 70–86.

Wilcox, Melissa M. *Coming Out in Christianity: Religion, Identity, and Community.* Bloomington: Indiana University Press, 2003.

**Melissa M. Wilcox**

***See also*** AFRICAN AMERICAN RELIGION AND SPIRITUALITY; ANTI-SEMITISM; BUDDHISTS AND BUDDHISM; CATHOLICS AND CATHOLICISM; DALY, MARY; HINDUS AND HINDUISM; JEWS AND JUDIASM; MUSLIMS AND ISLAM;

NATIVE AMERICAN RELIGION AND SPIRITUALITY; PERRY, TROY; PROTESTANTS AND PROTESTANTISM; RADICAL SPIRITUALITY AND NEW AGE RELIGION; WITCHES AND WICCA.

# CLASS AND CLASS OPPRESSION

Commentators have long noted the peculiar status of class consciousness, class politics, and class analysis in the United States. In a country built on myths of upward mobility, rags-to-riches fables, and legends about the land of opportunity, it has often been difficult to break through the notion that everyone in the United States is part of the expansive and expanding middle class. To be sure, there are those on the top and bottom of class hierarchies who have been conscious of their position, and there have been times when groups in the United States have developed distinct class politics. But post–World War II polls consistently reveal that the majority of Americans think of themselves as middle-class and that this perception is common to people with widely divergent incomes, jobs, and, to use the Marxist phrase, relations to the means of production. Elements of this view stretch back at least to the founding of the U.S. republic—which was based on the enfranchisement of a relatively small minority (propertied adult white males) but had an antiaristocratic rhetoric of universal democratic equality—and to the early nineteenth century, when suffrage was achieved for most adult white males.

Notwithstanding the multiple ways in which class relations and class oppression have been obfuscated and mystified in U.S. history, class dynamics have shaped sexualities and genders and, in turn, sexualities and genders have shaped class dynamics. Class has been a major category of analysis in LGBT studies, though the significance of sexuality and gender have not been as consistently recognized in scholarship on class.

## Colonial Economies

In colonial America, at least three significant economic systems (and linked systems of social relations) coexisted and interacted, each influencing and being influenced by sexual and gender systems. As Walter Williams, Will Roscoe, and Ramon Gutierrez have demonstrated, relatively egalitarian Native American economies, which were not really class systems and which generally featured distinct and valued roles for males and females, interacted with sexual and gender systems that often accepted same-sex sexual expression and cross-gender roles. A sec-

ond economic system, which was based on racialized slavery and was established most strongly (though not exclusively) in the American South, featured invariably exploitative same-sex sexual relationships between Euro-American masters and African American slaves as well as same-sex sexual relationships between slaves and between free people. A third economic system, based on Euro-American agricultural household production, was established most firmly (though again not exclusively) in the northern U.S.; it shaped and was shaped by sexual and gender systems that strongly valued cross-sex, marital, and reproductive forms of sexual expression and stigmatized all other forms of sex. Here we find generally exploitative same-sex sexual relationships between masters and servants as well as same-sex sexual relationships between servants and between free people.

In both northern and southern colonies, distinct and unequal social and economic roles for men and women contributed to distinct possibilities for transgressing sexual and gender norms. As Jonathan Ned Katz and Richard Godbeer have shown, for example, legal and other types of records suggest that female servants who worked together sometimes had sex with each other, free men sometimes were accused of sexual aggression against male servants, and women sometimes passed as men, in part for economic motives and with economic effects. Class oppression was certainly sexualized, but as historians of women, slaves, and workers have argued, sexuality could also be a terrain and a tool of resistance, power, and solidarity for the disempowered.

## From the Early Republic to the Late Nineteenth Century

Over the course of the nineteenth century, the United States invaded and appropriated more and more Native American land, putting intense pressures on Native American economies, social structures, and gender and sexual systems. Slave economies, which continued to feature exploitative same-sex sexual relationships between Euro-Americans and African Americans as well as same-sex sexual relationships between African Americans and between Euro-Americans (as documented, for example, by Martin Duberman), disappeared in northern states, expanded in southern states, and then collapsed during the Civil War of the 1860s. After the Civil War, racialized systems of agricultural sharecropping in the South replicated many, though not all, aspects of the slave society's system of gender and sexual relations, and sexuality continued to be used as a terrain and a tool of race, class, and gender struggle (as suggested in the work of Hannah Rosen).

Meanwhile, the family-based agricultural economies that were dominant in the North (and later in other parts of the country) began to be transformed by the market revolution, the spread of wage labor, and the rise of industrial capitalism. Increasingly, the owners of the means of production (capitalists, the bourgeoisie) purchased the labor of workers (the proletariat when capitalism reached its industrial stage). Bourgeois culture in this period imagined and in some respects created separate (and unequal) spheres of activity for middle-class men and women, with the former defined as the worlds of politics and work and the latter defined as the worlds of home and family (though certainly there was plenty of productive and reproductive work to do in the home).

For those included in the republic of white men, rhetorically democratic discourses of brotherly love and virtue were simultaneously homosocial and homoerotic. Although Walt Whitman pursued some of the more radical political and sexual implications of these discourses, they generally were deployed for purposes of class, race, and gender control. At the same time, homosocial discourses and practices were full of sexual possibilities. As Carroll Smith-Rosenberg and others have argued, the separate spheres of middle-class women and men created conditions that promoted intense forms of same-sex intimacy and affection that were often erotic and sexual. As scholars such as Karen Hansen have explored these spheres in greater depth, it has become clear that working-class women and men also created homosocial and homoerotic spheres of activity, often within particular ethnic and racial communities. And class lines were also crossed as middle-class whites eroticized and exoticized the bodies of their working-class counterparts and as passing women and passing men attempted to achieve economic and gender mobility.

## From the Late Nineteenth Century through the 1960s

In "Capitalism and Gay Identity," John D'Emilio argues that transformations associated with the rise of capitalism (including urbanization, immigration, the growth of wage labor, and the decline in family size) created the conditions necessary for the emergence of gay identities and communities in the late nineteenth century. As the spread of wage labor made it more possible to live in nonfamilial environments in anonymous cities, as commercialization and consumerism encouraged the development of a sphere of leisure and entertainment distinct from the worlds of family and work, and as individuals acquired greater personal autonomy, those sexually oriented to members of the same sex, many of whom also trans-

gressed dominant gender norms, began to see themselves as distinct types of people and began to form distinct sexual communities.

Various scholars have foregrounded the class aspects of this process, with most also examining intersections of class with race, gender, and sexuality. Lisa Duggan argues that modern lesbian identities emerged in the late nineteenth century as an amalgam of earlier working-class traditions of passing women and middle-class traditions of romantic friendship. Jennifer Terry and Henry Minton explore interactions between middle-class sexologists and the mostly working-class sexual and gender "deviants" whom they studied. George Chauncey suggests that working-class and middle-class men in New York who were sexually oriented to members of the same sex developed distinct sexual cultures and distinct relationships to working-class and middle-class cultures more generally. While working-class feminine fairies and pansies paired off with masculine husbands, trade, and wolves in relatively public and sexually integrated cultures, middle-class queer and gay men distanced themselves from their more public and flamboyant counterparts and developed more private and less sexually integrated social networks. Chauncey's evidence suggests that working-class and middle-class lesbians were also developing distinct sexual cultures, though more is known about this process from the work of scholars such as Eric Garber and Kevin Mumford, who have written about the Harlem Renaissance, and Judith Schwarz and Shari Benstock, who have studied lesbian bohemians, radicals, and writers.

Various scholars have examined class convergences and divergences within LGBT cultures after the 1920s, with most once again focusing attention as well on the ways in which class in the United States always intersects with race, gender, and sexuality. Elizabeth Kennedy and Madeline D. Davis's work on Buffalo analyzes bar-based working-class cultures of femmes and butches and home-based middle-class lesbian cultures. Maintaining her interest in class, Kennedy's more recent biographical work explores the role of class privilege and class discretion in the life of a bourgeois lesbian. Esther Newton's study of Cherry Grove, Fire Island, describes relations between owners, tenants, and day-trippers in this LGB resort. Brett Beemyn's work on Washington, D.C., Rochella Thorpe's work on Detroit, and Marc Stein's work on Philadelphia document the distinct class characteristics of middle-class and working-class bars and house parties. John Howard's study of Mississippi and Nan Boyd's book on San Francisco offer insights about class dynamics in these locations, and Joanne Meyerowitz's survey of transsexual history makes clear that the lives of transsexuals who could afford sex reassignment surgery were profoundly different from the lives of those who could not.

A number of these studies and others discuss the class dimensions of processes of LGBT urban neighborhood development that began before World War II and accelerated afterward. In a variety of cities, middle-class gay men (and to a lesser extent other LGBT people) began purchasing significant numbers of homes in urban neighborhoods with attractive architectural features, proximity to LGBT leisure culture, and low property values. In doing so, they often displaced poorer populations, which included poorer LGBT people, though they sometimes also created new possibilities for LGBT renters. As processes of urban gay gentrification resulted in increased property values and rents, more poor people were displaced. Eventually, however, many of these neighborhoods became newly attractive to middle-class straight white populations, resulting in the partial displacement of LGBT people. At each stage in this process, class intersected with race, gender, and sexuality to transform urban space.

In the 1950s the homophile movement was launched by anticapitalists such as Harry Hay, who had been active in the Community Party. Within a few years, however, more middle-class perspectives became dominant in groups such as the Mattachine Society, ONE, Inc., and the Daughters of Bilitis. Although all three of these groups and other homophile organizations in the 1950s and 1960s certainly had working-class members, the social uplift character of many of these groups, the strategies of gendered respectability that they championed, and the critical stances that they took toward central aspects of working-class LGBT cultures (including femme/butch roles, drag queens and cross-dressers, and public sex) marked their politics as middle-class in character. The extent of the homophile movement's conservative class politics should not be exaggerated, as homophile activists participated in predominantly working-class bar cultures, and some elements of the homophile movement were critical of homophile elitism. But on the whole the LGB movement of the 1950s and 1960s reproduced class hierarchies rather than challenging them.

## Beyond the 1960s

In the last thirty years, various LGBT scholars and activists have sought to develop anticapitalist theories and politics that would simultaneously deal with homophobia, transphobia, and heterosexism. In the 1970s the Combahee River Collective, the Furies, *Gay Community News*, the Gay Liberation Front, Radicalesbians, Red Butterfly, Gayle Rubin, Third World Gay Revolution, and Carl Wittman produced some of the most influential statements and analyses linking class oppression with the oppression of LGBT people. In the 1980s and 1990s, elements of the AIDS Coalition to Unleash Power and Queer Nation, antiglobalization queers, and various LGBT scholars and writers also embraced radical anticapitalist politics.

More commonly, however, LGBT activists have focused on reforming capitalism from within or taking steps to ameliorate its worst effects. This is the position taken, for example, by most LGBT labor and employee groups, by campaigns to secure increased state support (and fight cutbacks) for the poor and the ill, and by programs to help homeless LGBT youth, elders, sex workers, and people with AIDS. Efforts to embrace class "diversity" and to bridge class differences within LGBT communities also reflect reformist politics, aimed as they are not at revolutionizing capitalism but at making it operate more smoothly.

This is perhaps not surprising in a postindustrial era in which sexes, genders, and sexualities are increasingly commodified. Between around 1970 and the early 2000s, corporate advertising in LGB venues increased dramatically, LGB tourism exploded, commercial LGB pornography became extraordinarily lucrative, and LGB people were identified as a "lifestyle" market with significant disposable income. LGBT people who could afford it participated actively in these developments, queering them in some respects but also enjoying their benefits. In the process, they have reproduced the fiction that the United States is a classless and egalitarian society, while contributing to class inequality and class oppression.

### Bibliography

Beemyn, Brett. *Creating a Place for Ourselves.* New York: Routledge, 1997.

Boyd, Nan Alamilla. *Wide Open Town.* Berkeley: University of California Press, 2003.

Chauncey, George. *Gay New York.* New York: Basic, 1994.

D'Emilio, John. "Capitalism and Gay Identity." In *Powers of Desire.* Edited by Ann Snitow, Christine Stansell, and Sharon Thompson. New York: Monthly Review Press, 1983.

———. *Sexual Politics, Sexual Communities.* Chicago: University of Chicago Press, 1983.

Duberman, Martin, Martha Vicinus, and George Chauncey, eds. *Hidden from History.* New York: New American Library, 1989.

Garber, Eric. "A Spectacle in Color: The Lesbian and Gay Subculture of Jazz Age Harlem." In *Hidden from History.* Edited by Martin Bauml Duberman et al. New York: New American Library, 1989.

Gluckman, Amy, and Betsy Reed, eds. *Homo Economics: Capitalism, Community, and Lesbian and Gay Life.* New York: Routledge, 1997.

Godbeer, Richard. *Sexual Revolution in Early America.* Baltimore: Johns Hopkins University Press, 2002.

Gutierrez, Ramon A. *When Jesus Came, the Corn Mothers Went Away.* Stanford: Stanford University Press, 1991.

Hansen, Karen. "'No Kisses Is Like Youres'." *Gender and History* 7 (August 1995): 153–182.

Howard, John. *Men Like That.* Chicago: University of Chicago Press, 1999.

Katz, Jonathan Ned. *Gay/Lesbian Almanac.* New York: Harper and Row, 1983.

Kennedy, Elizabeth Lapovsky, and Madeline D. Davis. *Boots of Leather, Slippers of Gold.* New York: Routledge, 1993.

Lewin, Ellen, ed. *Inventing Lesbian Cultures in America.* Boston: Beacon, 1996.

Meyerowitz, Joanne. *How Sex Changed.* Cambridge, Mass.: Harvard University Press, 2002.

Mumford, Kevin J. *Interzones.* New York: Columbia University Press, 1997.

Newton, Esther. *Cherry Grove, Fire Island.* Boston: Beacon, 1993.

Raffo, Susan, ed. *Queerly Classed.* Boston: South End, 1997.

Roscoe, Will. *Changing Ones.* New York: St. Martin's, 1998.

Rosen, Hannah. "'Not That Sort of Women': Race, Gender, and Sexual Violence during the Memphis Riot of 1866." In *Sex, Love, Race.* Edited by Martha Hodes. New York: New York University Press, 1999.

Rupp, Leila J. *A Desired Past.* Chicago: University of Chicago Press, 1999.

Schwarz, Judith. *Radical Feminists of Heterodoxy.* Norwich, Vt.: New Victoria, 1986.

Smith-Rosenberg, Carroll. *Disorderly Conduct.* New York: Knopf, 1985.

Stein, Marc. *City of Sisterly and Brotherly Loves.* Chicago: University of Chicago Press, 2000.

Williams, Walter. *The Spirit and the Flesh.* Boston: Beacon, 1986.

**Marc Stein**

**See also** CAPITALISM AND INDUSTRIALIZATION; CROSS-CLASS SEX AND RELATIONSHIPS; FURIES; POOR PEOPLE'S MOVEMENTS.

# CLASSICAL STUDIES

Like almost every other area of classical studies, scholarly inquiry into ancient Mediterranean homoerotic representations and practices has an unmistakably Teutonic pedigree. It was a German scholarly journal, *Hermes,* that in 1931 published an article by the celebrated British scholar A. E. Housman explicating several passages depicting same-sex male erotic acts in the works of such classical Roman authors as Catullus, the younger Seneca, Martial, and Suetonius. Its title, "Praefanda," meaning "things that must not be uttered publicly," may allude to the description of homosexuality of Alfred, Lord Douglas (the lover of Oscar Wilde) as "the love that dare not speak its name." Housman's comments on these passages include oblique references to his own, apparently voyeuristic, engagement in homoerotic activity.

Housman had good reason to select a German outlet for this controversial essay. *Pauly-Wissowa,* the prestigious German encyclopedia of classical scholarship, contains an entry, written by Wilhelm Kroll in 1924, on "Lesbian Love." From 1926 onward, the German scholar Hans Herter issued a series of studies—culminating in *De Priapo: Religionsgeschichtliche Versuche und Vorarbeiten* 23 (1932)—on the Greco-Roman god Priapus, whom literary sources comically portray as threatening to force his huge genital organ into the bodily apertures of those (usually males) offending him. In 1927 and 1928, a German classicist named Paul Brandt (under the pseudonym Hans Licht) published a comprehensive, multivolume analysis of ancient Greek sexuality that dealt extensively with Greek male homoeroticism: *Sittengeschichte Griechenlands,* translated in 1934 as *Sexual Life in Ancient Greece.* In 1933, the year that Adolf Hitler rose to political power, another German classical scholar, Otto Kiefer, published *Kulturgeschichte Roms unter besonderer Beruecksichtigung der roemischen Sitten,* translated as *Sexual Life in Ancient Rome.*

Brandt's and Kiefer's books were soon translated into English, the latter by Gilbert Highet in the year following its publication, shortly before Highet left Oxford University in England and began an illustrious forty-year career as a Columbia University classics professor and influential public intellectual. Yet scholarly interest in ancient Greek and Roman homoeroticism, even in the Anglophone world, would not truly awaken for thirty-five years, until several studies appeared on various aspects of ancient sexuality by an East German classical scholar. This was Werner Krenkel of Rostock, who spent a year as a visiting professor at Columbia a few years before Highet's retirement in 1972. Krenkel's investigations merit recognition because they were largely conducted in a repressive intellectual environment, an atmosphere not conducive to the meticulous, responsible interpretations of classical texts that his close readings produced.

To be sure, scholarly interest in ancient Greek and Roman sexuality, particularly in its homoerotic manifestations, had been expressed in the United States by the late 1960s. Consider, for example, Jeffrey Henderson's 1972 Harvard University doctoral thesis on obscenity in the comedies of Aristophanes, which dealt extensively with the language of homosexual abuse. A revised version, published in 1975 by Yale University Press as *The Maculate Muse: Obscene Language in Attic Comedy*, cites earlier articles on Greek and Roman homo- and heteroerotic topics by American and British, as well as German, Dutch, and other continental, scholars. But a number of classicists based in the United States who were Krenkel's lifeline to the "free world"—most notably British-born John Patrick Sullivan—played a more important role in fostering and advancing research on ancient Greek and Roman sexuality. They linked Krenkel's distinctive scholarly concerns with those of other scholars, particularly those classicists investigating women and gender in classical antiquity from a feminist perspective.

In 1972, Sullivan joined with five female classicists to found the Women's Classical Caucus (WCC). Since then, panels sponsored by the WCC at the annual meeting of the American Philological Association (APA) have nurtured feminist classical scholarship in various areas, among them the study of LGBT phenomena in ancient Greece and Rome. In the spring of 1973, Sullivan devoted a special issue of the journal *Arethusa*, which he then edited, to the topic of women in antiquity (vol. 6, no. 1). Significantly, however, two of its essays focused on the topic of Greek male homoeroticism.

The first *Arethusa* essay, "Classical Greek Attitudes to Sexual Behaviour" by the renowned British classicist Kenneth J. Dover, briefly stated several of the premises expounded in Dover's monumental 1978 book *Greek Homosexuality*. Dover's major contentions have shaped the way in which classical scholars have subsequently understood ancient Greek and Roman constructions of sexuality. To quote Amy Richlin's article on "Sexuality" in the 1996 *Oxford Classical Dictionary*,

> Greeks and Romans divided sexual behavior into active/passive as well as (some say, and not) homosexual/heterosexual. The normative role for adult males was penetrative ('active'); penetrated ('passive') partners were normally women, and boys aged twelve to seventeen. Texts generally convey the experience of penetrators, and evaluate passivity negatively, at worse (oral) as contaminating; the experience of the passive has to be reconstructed (p. 1399).

In other words, "bisexuality" was normative for adult males, since the sex (and for the most part the erotic satisfaction) of the penetrated partner was not of primary concern.

Yet in some regards, the second *Arethusa* essay, "Plato: Misogynist, Paedophile, and Feminist," by Dorothea Wender, a founding member of the WCC, has proven equally influential. Explicitly feminist in its approach, it attempts to explain the inconsistency between Plato's dismissive remarks about women and his willingness to remove the limitations imposed on women by classical Athenian society. It does so by adducing his outspoken appreciation for the physical appeal of young males, concluding that he was less threatened by women's sexual power and speculating that his challenge to Athenian culture may have been connected to a sense that his sexual preferences challenged "nature." By forthrightly addressing the topic of homoerotic sexual attraction in the context of women's social circumstances, Wender's article inspired efforts by other female classicists to write frankly and directly about topics of a sexual nature, homoerotic (and hence "bisexual") activity among them.

Consider the first book-length study of women in ancient Greece and Rome, *Goddesses, Whores, Wives and Slaves: Women in Classical Antiquity* (1975), by Sarah B. Pomeroy, another feminist scholar and founding member of the WCC. It contains discussions of homoerotic relationships in Athens, among the gods, at Lesbos, in Rome, in Sparta, and in the visual arts. Significantly, Pomeroy had contributed a selected, and richly annotated, bibliography on women in antiquity to the Sullivan edition of *Arethusa* two years earlier. The sections of this bibliography on Greek and Roman erotic life (the former written by David Schaps) did not, however, refer to homoeroticism, save for when he quoted the title of a 1967 psychoanalytic article entitled "Greek Pseudo-Homosexuality and the 'Greek Miracle'" (*Symbolae Osloenses* 42, 1967, pp. 69–92). Nor, in her section on the Greek family in the bibliography, did Pomeroy's discussion of Philip Slater's *The Glory of Hera: Greek Mythology and the Greek Family* (1971) acknowledge Slater's efforts to explain Athenian male homoeroticism as a reaction to maternal behavior.

As Richlin documented in a 1991 essay about the anomalous history of scholarly work on ancient Greek and Roman sexuality, a substantial body of feminist work on Roman gender by women was produced in the decade immediately following the publication of Pomeroy's book. Much of the work sought to illuminate literary representations of homoerotic and "bisexual" conduct. One such study was a paper given at the 1975 WCC panel by Judith P. Hallett, another WCC founder. Published in 1977 in the *American Journal of Ancient History* 2 as "*Perusinae glandes* and the Changing Image of Augustus" (pp. 151–171), it examined the efforts by the future emperor Augustus to combat an effeminate and homosexually passive public image. Richlin's 1970 Yale dissertation, published in 1983 by Yale University Press as *The Garden of Priapus: Sexuality and Aggression in Roman Humor,* argued that the attitude of (homo)sexual aggressiveness attributed to the Roman god Priapus serves as a model for the genre of Roman satire and illuminates a variety of Roman cultural practices. Marilyn Skinner's 1979 "Parasites and Strange Bedfellows: A Study in Catullus' Political Imagery" (*Ramus* 8, pp. 137–152), which focused on the language of homosexual abuse in Catullus's invective poems, was the first of several articles she published on the gender politics of Rome in the late republican era.

It warrants emphasis that Hallett, Richlin, and Skinner were all untenured at the time that they presented and published these studies, and, in Hallett's case, several studies dealing with Greek and Roman female homoerotic and transgender behavior. What is more, owing to the controversial nature of their scholarly work, none was teaching in a department that offered a graduate degree in classics when, after considerable difficulties, each of them was tenured in the 1980s. By way of contrast, upon completing his Harvard doctorate in 1972, Henderson was hired at Yale. He subsequently held tenured positions in Ph.D.-granting classics departments at the University of Michigan, from 1978, the University of Southern California (USC), from 1986, and Boston University, from 1991.

Yet Henderson advised and encouraged Richlin on her Yale dissertation, and she was appointed to a tenured position at USC during the time that Henderson taught there. Consequently, Henderson differs from several male, and for the most part gay male, classicists who began to publish widely recognized scholarly studies on aspects of ancient Greek and Roman sexuality in the late 1980s and early 1990s. Admittedly, the most gifted and creative of this group, the late John Winkler, also championed Richlin and her work on sexuality when he taught alongside Henderson at Yale. But Winkler, David Halperin, and others had waited until they were safely tenured before turning their scholarly attention to ancient Greco-Roman homoeroticism.

In their work, these scholars paid homage to the pioneering studies of Michel Foucault by formulating an all-embracing "ancient Mediterranean" model of sexual behavior and representation, which not only defined sex in terms of phallic penetration and pleasure, but also made little or no distinction between homosexual and heterosexual couplings. The title of Halperin's *One Hundred Years of Homosexuality* (1990) typifies this approach in its suggestion that homosexuality, as it had been defined for the last century, did not exist in the ancient world. Like Foucault, these scholars focused almost exclusively on Greek testimony and practices, a focus that led them to shortchange Roman evidence and culture. They also tended to erase the contributions of earlier feminist research by female colleagues.

Richlin's 1991 article "Zeus and Metis: Foucault, Feminism, Classics" (*Helios* 18, pp. 160–181) compellingly narrates the circumstances prompting her to protest this tendency. She begins in 1990 with "Deciphering the Codes of Sexual Life in the Ancient Mediterranean," the first APA panel sponsored by the new Lesbian and Gay Caucus (later known as the Lambda Classical Caucus), a group founded in 1989 with strong support from the WCC. Richlin recalls that the papers of the panel, heavily indebted to the work of Foucault, "did not have much to say about previous work by women." She adds, "Much like Zeus swallowing Metis and bringing forth Athena, [Foucauldian] work reinvents what feminists have done before." Chief among the papers was Eva Keuls, *The Reign of the Phallus: Sexual Politics in Ancient Athens* (1985). "Most importantly," Richlin continues, "the speakers were also curiously silent about Roman culture, focusing mainly on Greek." She also calls attention to the short shrift given by Halperin to other works of feminist scholarship, in so doing making extensive use of material as well as literary evidence, and Hallett's 1989 "Female Homoeroticism and the Denial of Roman Reality in Latin Literature" (*Yale Journal of Criticism* 3, pp. 209–227), which analyzes the Roman literary tendency to masculinize transgender as well as female same-sex eroticism.

Richlin, Hallett, and Skinner have continued to publish and edit feminist work on Roman sexuality that primarily deals with LGBT texts and topics. In 1992, Oxford University Press issued the second edition of Richlin's *The Garden of Priapus,* as well as a collection of essays Richlin edited, *Pornography and Representation in Greece and Rome.* In 1997 Hallett and Skinner published *Roman Sexualities,* dedicated to the memory of J. P. Sullivan. The volume reprints Hallett's essay on Roman female homoeroticism and a revised version of Skinner's 1993 study on the construction of male sexuality in Catullus. It also includes essays on the impenetrable Roman male body by

Jonathan Walters, the schematization of Roman penetration practices by Holt Parker, and Ovid's transgender depiction of Sappho by Pamela Gordon.

LGBT studies critical of feminist scholarship merit attention as well. Among them are two studies of Roman homosexuality by Craig Williams. The first is a 1995 article in *Classical Quarterly* 45 (pp. 517–539), "Greek Love at Rome," responding to Ramsay MacMullen's 1982 "Roman Attitudes toward Greek Love" (*Historia* 31, 1982, pp. 484–502). The second is a 1999 book in a series edited by Halperin, *Roman Homosexuality: Ideologies of Masculinity in Classical Antiquity.* Also worth noting is Bruce Thornton's 1997 book *Eros: The Myth of Ancient Greek Sexuality,* which voices outright hostility both to Halperin's Foucauldian work and to feminist studies of ancient sexuality, arguing that the Greeks rightly held a negative view of sexual desire as dangerous, and of sexual expression as a violation of their most sacred beliefs.

Feminist perspectives, however, have informed and continue to loom large in scholarship on LGBT texts and topics in classical Greek society and Greece under the Roman Empire. Parker's 2001 article "The Myth of the Heterosexual or the Anthropology and Sexuality for Classicists" (*Arethusa* 34, no. 3, pp. 313–362) is noteworthy for situating ancient constructions of sexuality in a broader theoretical context. Other important studies include Maud Gleason's *Making Men* (1995); Jane Snyder's *Lesbian Desire in the Lyrics of Sappho* (1997); and *Rethinking Sexuality: Foucault and Classical Antiquity* (1998), a collection of essays edited by David Larmour, Paul Allen Miller, and Charles Platter.

One of the major LGBT topics and questions of interest to classical scholars is the relationship between political, economic, and literary power and male homoerotic attraction in the representation and self-representation of Marcus Aurelius and other Roman emperors. The depiction of male homoeroticism in Greek myth and the Greek and Roman moral discourse on (same-sex and opposite-sex) prostitution are also major topics. LBGT issues also figure prominently in studies of the classical tradition and the history of classical scholarship, since several of the figures most closely scrutinized were themselves homoerotically inclined: not only renowned scholars such as Housman, but also prominent and influential secondary school classics educators such as the American Edith Hamilton (whose best-selling books popularized classical mythology and the Greek legacy) and the Austrian David Oppenheim (an associate of Sigmund Freud and Alfred Adler who tragically perished at the Czechoslovakian ghetto Theresienstadt).

**Bibliography**

Gordon, P. "The Lover's Voice in Heroides 15: Or, Why Is Sappho a Man?" In *Roman Sexualities.* Edited by J. P. Hallett and M. B. Skinner. Princeton, N.J.: Princeton University Press, 1997.

Hallett, J. P. "The Women's Classical Caucus." In *Classics: A Discipline and Profession in Crisis?* Edited by P. Culham and L. Edmunds. Lanham, Md.: University Press of America, 1989.

Halperin, D. M., J. J. Winkler, and F. I. Zeitlin, eds. *Before Sexuality: The Construction of Erotic Experience in the Ancient Greek World.* Princeton, N.J.: Princeton University Press, 1990.

Housman, A. E. "Praefanda." *Hermes* 66 (1931): 402–412.

Krenkel, W. *Pompeianische Inschriften.* Leipzig, Germany: Koehler und Amelang, 1961.

———. "Mannliche Prostitution in der Antike." *Das Altertum* 24 (1978) 49–55.

———. "Pueri Meritorii." *Wissenschafliche Zeitschrift der Wilhelm-Pieck-Universität,* Rostock 28 (1979): 179–89.

———. "Fellatio and Irrumatio." *Wissenschaftliche Zeitschrift der Wilhelm-Pieck-Universität,* Rostock 29 (1980): 77–88.

Kroll, W. "Lesbische Liebe." In *Real-Encyclopedie der klassischen Altertumswissenschaft.* Edited by A. Pauly and G. Wissowa. 1924: 2100–2102.

Parker, H. "The Teratogenic Grid." In *Roman Sexualities.* Edited by J. P. Hallett and M. B. Skinner. Princeton, N.J.: Princeton University Press, 1997.

Richlin, A. E. *Pornography and Representation in Greece and Rome.* New York: Oxford University Press, 1992.

Skinner, M. B. "*Ego mulier:* The Construction of Male Sexuality in Catullus." *Helios* 20, no. 2 (1993): 107–130.

Walters, J. "Invading the Roman Body: Manliness and Impenetrability in Roman Thought." In *Roman Sexualities.* Edited by J. P. Hallett and M. B. Skinner. Princeton, N.J.: Princeton University Press, 1997.

**Judith Hallett**

# CLOSET

The image of the closet, evoking both individual secrecy and collective invisibility, is the most widely used metaphor for the oppression of LGBT people. This concept suggests that institutionalized homophobia and heterosexism cause LGBT people to adopt strategies for hiding their desires, identities, and experiences. *Out of the Closet* (1972), an anthology of radical LGBT writings, explored the impact of bias in government, health care, religion, and media. Post–Stonewall Riots activists often focused on the solution of visibility and representation, calling for LGBT people to come "out of the closets and into the streets." Although enormously influential, the concept of the closet has also been a subject of academic debate, raising questions about how effectively this concept captures diverse LGBT experiences in various historical contexts.

## Individual Closets: Secrecy and Shame

For an individual, being in the closet might mean a lack of acceptance or recognition of one's own LGBT desires, practices, or identity; failure to disclose such desires, practices, or identities to others; and feeling shame or self-hatred. Being in the closet has also been characterized as a form of passing (as heterosexual) in order to avoid identification. This experience of the closet plays an important role in many LGBT coming-out stories from the latter half of the twentieth century. In *Telling Secret Stories* (1995), the sociologist Ken Plummer argues that such a highly conventionalized narrative form articulates LGBT identity as a movement from ignorance and invisibility to knowledge and visibility. While such narratives play an important role in community building and collective identity formation, they also prescribe a normative script that may not reflect the complexities of sexual identities. Nor does the simple in-out binary accurately reflect lived experience, in which LGBT people may have varying levels of disclosure and visibility to different individuals and in different contexts.

LGBT activists have argued that individual feelings, especially those related to shame, are often a product of homophobic social structures rather than simply personal issues. Until the 1970s, the American Psychiatric Association's *Diagnostic and Statistical Manual of Mental Disorders (DSM)* listed homosexuality as a mental disorder. By targeting homophobic bias in the mental health professions, activists challenged the stigmatization of LGBT people and argued for recognition of empirical research demonstrating that homosexuality was a normal sexual variation. Despite success in removing homosexuality from the *DSM* in 1973, persistent cultural perceptions of homosexuality as deviant, shameful, or immoral create conditions that may encourage individuals to hide or feel shame about their desires, practices, and identities and thus to remain closeted.

## Institutional Closets: Criminality, Marginality, and Invisibility

As the example of the *DSM* suggests, institutional closets result from practices that privilege heteronormativity and pathologize or prohibit LGBT desires, identities, and sexual expression. Politically, laws prohibiting same-sex marriage and criminalizing sodomy created conditions of secrecy and danger. The 1986 U.S. Supreme Court deci-

sion in *Bowers v. Hardwick*, which upheld the constitutionality of a Georgia sodomy statute, demonstrated that LGBT people could not claim a fundamental right to consensual sexual activity, even in the privacy of their homes. (In 2003 this legal principle was reversed in *Lawrence v. Texas*, a decision that overturned the Texas sodomy statute.) Various religious traditions (and their modern reinterpretations or misinterpretations) condemning homosexuality played a role in creating conditions of shame and secrecy both within religious faiths and in the broader culture, as in the *Hardwick* case, which made reference to "Judaeo-Christian moral and ethical standards." Contemporary military policy, summed up as "don't ask, don't tell," creates conditions in which LGBT enlisted personnel must conceal their sexualities in order to preserve their positions. Economic structures may also play an important role in shaping visibility. In *American Homo* (1998), Jeffrey Escoffier uses the term "closet economy" to describe the period of post–World War II LGBT economic history characterized by marginal, quasi-legal sexual businesses.

Because of the equation of the closet with invisibility and oppression and coming out with visibility and liberation, media representation has been a central issue for LGBT scholarship and activism. Vito Russo's influential *The Celluloid Closet* (1987) catalogued the images of LGBT people on film, arguing that the Hollywood closet was characterized not by simple invisibility, but by a particular kind of negative visibility. Although the strict standards of the Motion Picture Production Code (also known as the Hays Code), enforced from 1934 until 1968, included prohibitions on representations of sexuality including "sex perversion," "excessive and lustful kissing," and "miscegenation," dangerous, laughable, or other negatives images of LGBT characters appeared in a range of films. More recently, debates about decency and advertisers' unwillingness to be associated with LGBT images continue to constrain media representation. Controversy in the 1990s about homosexuality on the small screen erupted around television personalities Ellen DeGeneres and Rosie O'Donnell and provoked questions about the pressures for celebrities and public figures to conceal their sexual orientations.

Educational institutions have been another central focus for debates about the closet. The ubiquity of homophobic violence at secondary schools encourages young people to conceal LGBT desires, practices, and identities and creates feelings of isolation and hopelessness, which researchers link to increased rates of suicide among LGBT youth. Teachers at elementary or secondary schools may feel pressure not to disclose their sexual orientation to protect their jobs. In 1978 community organizers worked to successfully defeat Proposition 6 in California, which would have allowed the dismissal of LGBT teachers. Despite such victories, moral clauses in some teachers' contracts create a context of vulnerability. Escoffier uses the term "ivory closet" to describe the evolution of LGBT academic programs at universities, noting that while the early researchers felt pressure to hide personal identities and avoid work on LGBT subjects, emerging distance between university-based researchers and LGBT communities may suggest a new form of closeting.

## Closets in LGBT Communities

As the example of higher education suggests, the concept of the closet has also been used to describe issues of power and visibility within LGBT communities. Here, the role of homophobia in constraining the freedom to be fully oneself serves as a metaphor for the role of other forms of discrimination affecting the complex subjectivities of LGBT people. The concept of the closet itself reflects a particular cultural understanding of sexuality that may not reflect the diverse forms of identity and sexual behavior among various racial or ethnic groups, which for example is a central issue in AIDS prevention campaigns working to reach men who have sex with men but who do not identify as gay. Nor does the concept of the closet as a form of oppression capture the diversity of reasons for adopting strategies of secrecy, dissemblance, or silence. Although remaining in the closet can be a form of protection from violence and discrimination, the intersection of identities can create unique risk for lesbians, working-class LGBT people, and LGBT people of color. Elements of identity, personal history, or experience difficult to articulate or unwelcome in hegemonic LGBT culture can create other sorts of closets around experiences of racial or class identity. For transgender people, the closet is a particularly complex concept. In some cases it may refer to claiming a different gender identity than one previously assigned. In other contexts, it may refer to visibility as a transgender person, though the concept seems ill-suited to express the varying reasons that individuals choose either to adopt a transgender identity or to remain private about prior gender identities or trans status. LGBT people of color experience important, sustaining relationships with ethnic and racial communities, even in contexts in which they employ strategic silence, and racism within LGBT communities may complicate the meaning of the closet as a condition related only to sexuality and imposed solely by heterosexism. Transgender people in particular face institutional obstacles in areas where lesbian and gay people have made some progress, such as mental health, employment, and education. Biphobia can result in the misperception that bisexual individuals are really partially closeted, assuming a sexual binary in which fully disclosed sexual orientation is ultimately either heterosexual or homophobia.

In *Feminism, the Family, and the Politics of the Closet* (2000), Cheshire Calhoun focuses on the gendered dimensions of the closet, especially the difficulties of representing lesbian concerns within feminist treatment of the category "woman." Her concept of a "gender closet" suggests that the closet may also be a gendered concept that casts feminized domestic space as necessarily oppressive.

## Historical Closets: Problematizing Progress Narratives

Historians have raised important challenges to the universal applicability of the closet by examining its role in narratives about LGBT progress. While some popular accounts of LGBT history describe a collective movement from a pre–World War II closet to post–Stonewall Riots visibility, historians demonstrate that this characterization fails to describe accurately the diverse conditions of historical periods and geographical locations. In *Gay New York* (1994), George Chauncey argues that the closet is central to myths about post–World War II LGBT history. Popular assumptions suggest that this oppressive structure shaped both individual life narratives and community histories, accurately describing LGBT life before the 1969 Stonewall Riots. In his analysis of gay men's lives in New York City, Chauncey describes three central "myths": isolation, or the notion that gay men lived solitary lives isolated from subcultural communities; invisibility, or the idea that gay men struggled to find each other; and internalization, the assumption that gay men adopted mainstream perceptions of homosexuality. He refutes this notion by describing a range of sexual subcultures, shaped by ethnicity and class, that had more public visibility from the 1890s to the 1930s than it would subsequently, when intensified policing created the modern closet, a term that dates from the 1960s.

In *Men Like That* (1999), John Howard is similarly troubled by the utility of the closet metaphor to describe LGBT history for people living outside of coastal urban centers. He suggests that rural areas are often described as a spatial closet from which LGBT subjects must escape in order to achieve self-actualization. This assumption leads to a lack of recognition of the diverse creative strategies employed by LGBT people in rural areas to realize their desires and lead meaningful lives. Howard suggests that it is precisely the association of closets with the hidden and unseen that creates the possibility to realize LGBT sexualities beyond heteronormative surveillance.

## Contemporary Relevance

Although fierce debates about the ethics of "outing" in the early 1990s suggested that closets retained an important protective power and role in the cultural invisibility of LGBT people, the status of the central metaphor remains a matter of debate. LGBT scholars offer differing perspectives on the contemporary relevance and utility of the closet. In *Beyond the Closet* (2002), the sociologist Steven Seidman uses ethnographic data to argue that the closet is no longer the dominant issue for lesbian and gay Americans. Although individuals in his study had previous experiences of hiding their sexual orientations, this necessity did not determine their current life decisions. While Seidman argues that lesbian and gay people face a continued struggle for full "sexual citizenship," the closet no longer serves as an adequate or useful metaphor for oppression.

The geographer Michael Brown's *Closet Space* (2000) offers a proactive examination of the contemporary relevance of the closet by examining both the metaphorical and material implications of this spatial metaphor. Brown's analysis of space emphasizes the importance of bodily and material context for understanding strategies of silence or evasion, which sometimes serve as tactics for resisting heteronormativity. While unmarked bars might be an example of the political economy of the closet, such locales also provide—for those who find them—an opportunity for expression of same-sex desires. Brown's postmodern empirical approach describes the space of the closet as a site of oppression and simultaneously an opportunity for desire.

To the extent that this concept shapes discourses of sexuality and culture more broadly, the closet is central to a general politics of sexual and cultural liberation. In the groundbreaking *Epistemology of the Closet* (1990), literary scholar Eve Kosofsky Sedgwick describes the closet as a "performance" based in "silence." The closet was not a preexisting location into which individuals and communities entered or were forced. Rather, it emerged from specific practices of not-knowing and not-saying. As part of a broader argument she makes about the centrality of the homosexual-heterosexual binary to Western culture, Sedgwick problematizes the notion that coming out provides an unmediated form of liberation. Coming out does not cause the closet to disappear, because it represents a form of power-knowledge central to Western conceptions of sexuality. The practices of the closet, as a response to powerful norms, have been central to the production of LGBT identity and culture. But Sedgwick does not see the closet as relevant only to LGBT people. The coding, hiding, and evasion that mark the closet influence and constrain a broad range of sexualities and identities. *Epistemology of the Closet* is a foundational text in the emergence of queer theory, exploring the ways in which LGBT identities are not necessarily inherently oppositional but do constitute an important element in the production of heteronormative binary discourses of sexuality.

Whatever its relevance to LGBT experiences, the concept of the closet has acquired great currency in American culture. The phrases "in the closet" and "closet case" function as mainstream signifiers for nondisclosure or concealment, not just in reference to sexuality, but also to a range of elements of personal identity. Although LGBT scholars and queer theorists have challenged the binary logic and normative assumptions of this concept, it remains an enormously powerful and common characterization of LGBT oppression. Contemporary scholarship works to pluralize the meaning of the closet and examine the ways in which various closets emerge or disappear in changing social contexts. Recent analysis of the globalization of American forms of LGBT identity suggest the necessity to examine how the concept of the closet might travel, and to what effects.

### Bibliography

Brown, Michael P. *Closet Space: Geographies of Metaphor from the Body to the Globe.* London and New York: Routledge, 2000.

Calhoun, Cheshire. *Feminism, the Family, and the Politics of the Closet: Lesbian and Gay Displacement.* New York: Oxford University Press, 2000.

Chauncey, George. *Gay New York: Gender, Urban Culture, and the Making of the Gay Male World, 1890–1940.* New York: Basic Books, 1994.

Escoffier, Jeffrey. *American Homo: Community and Perversity.* Berkeley: University of California Press, 1998.

Eskridge, William N., Jr., ed. *Gaylaw: Challenging the Apartheid of the Closet.* Cambridge, Mass.: Harvard University Press, 2002.

Gross, Larry P. *Contested Closets: The Politics and Ethics of Outing.* Minneapolis: University of Minnesota Press, 1993.

Halley, Janet. "The Politics of the Closet: Towards Equal Protection for Gay, Lesbian, and Bisexual Identity." In *Reclaiming Sodom.* Edited by Jonathan Goldberg. New York: Routledge, 1994.

Howard, John. *Men Like That: A Southern Queer History.* Chicago: University of Chicago Press, 1999.

Jay, Karla, and Allen Young. *Out of the Closets: Voices of Gay Liberation.* 2d ed. New York: New York University Press, 1992.

Plummer, Ken. *Telling Sexual Stories: Power, Change, and Social Worlds.* New York: Routledge, 1995.

Russo, Vito. *The Celluloid Closet: Homosexuality in the Movies.* New York: Harper and Row, 1987.

Sedgwick, Eve Kosofsky. *Epistemology of the Closet.* Berkeley: University of California Press, 1990.

Seidman, Steven. *Beyond the Closet: The Transformation of Gay and Lesbian Life.* New York: Routledge, 2002.

**Meredith Raimondo**

*See also* COMING OUT AND OUTING.

**CLUBS.** see BARS, CLUBS, AND RESTAURANTS.

# COHN, Roy (b. 20 February 1927; d. 2 August 1986),
lawyer, government official, anticommunist activist.

Roy Marcus Cohn was a zealous anticommunist, a political power broker who supported conservative causes, and a man who for decades both hid and denied his homosexuality. He was the only child of Albert Cohn, a well-connected state judge from Brooklyn, and Dora Marcus, a famously overbearing mother and the daughter of a banking family. The precocious Roy attended Columbia University and completed undergraduate and law degrees by the time he was twenty years old. In 1948, at age twenty-one, he became an assistant U.S. attorney, and for the next six years he made his national reputation by forging connections with such powerful men as U.S. attorney Irving Saypol and Walter Winchell; promoting himself aggressively; and immersing himself in the hunt for communists, which included a much-publicized role in the prosecution of Julius and Ethel Rosenberg.

Roy Cohn. Best known as the ruthless chief counsel for the 1950s anticommunist U.S. Senator Joseph McCarthy, Cohn was an ardent conservative who publicly vilified homosexuality while trying to deny his own sexual orientation throughout his life—a life cut short by AIDS. [Corbis Corporation (New York)]

Cohn is best remembered for his work as the chief counsel for the Permanent Subcommittee on Investigations of the Committee on Government Operations, headed by U.S. senator Joseph McCarthy of Wisconsin, who used the subcommittee to launch a series of anticommunist witchhunts. Cohn took the position in January 1953 and relinquished it the following year, after McCarthy had self-destructed before a national television audience. In fact, though McCarthy's committee had already begun investigating the loyalty screening procedures of the U.S. Army, it was Cohn's personal obsession with Private G. David Schine that eventually dragged the senator from Wisconsin into a political nightmare from which his career never recovered. The army accused Cohn of attempting to secure special favors for Schine—which he had indeed done—and for spurring McCarthy's investigations when his efforts failed. During the course of the hearings Joseph Welch, attorney for the army, insinuated that Cohn's interest in Schine went beyond mere friendship, at one point invoking the word "fairy" in a suggestive way that was lost on neither the millions of American viewers nor on Cohn himself.

After the dust from the Army-McCarthy hearings of 1954 had settled, Cohn went into private practice in New York City. Over the remainder of the decade, he built his reputation as a wily, ruthless attorney while also making numerous lucrative, if shady, business deals that allowed him to enjoy a lavish lifestyle in Manhattan and Greenwich, Connecticut. Cohn also drew the ire of U.S. attorneys Robert Kennedy and Robert Morgenthau, who tried unsuccessfully on three different occasions to have him indicted on charges of tax evasion, fraud, and jury tampering.

In spite of his legal troubles, the 1960s and 1970s were good to Roy Cohn. He traveled extensively and hosted elegant gatherings that attracted elite politicians, socialites, and celebrities. He became friends with Steve Rubell, co-owner of the nightclub Studio 54, which opened in Manhattan in 1977 and quickly became the epicenter of the hedonistic sex-and-drug world of the rich and fabulous. Rubell, who also hired Cohn as his lawyer, held extravagant birthday parties for Cohn at the club, and on a regular basis lined up legions of beautiful young men for sexual liaisons with him. Though Cohn's sexuality was something of an open secret among those who knew him, he had long been in the habit of making public appearances with women on his arm, and he made sure that those were the stories that made it into the gossip pages of New York City's newspapers.

The 1980s were perhaps the apotheosis of the paradoxes of Roy Cohn's life. On the one hand, he campaigned for and befriended Republican president Ronald Reagan, palled around with conservative multimillionaires Donald Trump and George Steinbrenner, and gave speeches condemning homosexuality and the movement for lesbian and gay rights. On the other hand, he was forced to deal with the reality that he was dying of AIDS—at that time still considered a gay disease in the United States. To his last breath, Cohn insisted that it was liver cancer, but his friends and companions knew the truth, which also made its way into the media coverage of his final months (during which time he was also disbarred in New York State). After Cohn's death he became a lightning rod for gay and lesbian Americans who were outraged at his brazen hypocrisy, as well as the hypocrisy of many conservatives, who could befriend a homosexual privately but continue to advocate anti-LGBT policies under the banner of "family values." In Nicholas Van Hoffman's *Citizen Cohn* and Sidney Zion's *The Autobiography of Roy Cohn*, both published in 1988; in a cable television movie; and in Tony Kushner's Pulitzer Prizewinning play, *Angels in America* (1993), Cohn was enshrined as a symbol of the self-inflicted wounds—and the greater public damage—wrought by internalized homophobia.

**Bibliography**

Von Hoffman, Nicholas. *Citizen Cohn.* New York: Doubleday, 1988.

Zion, Sidney. *The Autobiography of Roy Cohn.* Secaucus, N.J.: Lyle Stuart, 1988.

**Stacy L. Braukman**

*See also* GOVERNMENT AND MILITARY WITCHHUNTS; NEW RIGHT; POLITICAL SCANDALS.

# COLLEGES AND UNIVERSITIES

From the earliest days of American higher education, colleges and universities have played multiple roles in promoting and challenging sexual and gender norms and practices. Postsecondary institutions have reproduced dominant sexual and gender values in and out of classrooms and residences; on and off athletic fields; and inside and outside of staff, faculty, and administrative offices. LGBT students, staff, faculty, and administrators have experienced physical and psychological violence; encountered heterosexist, homophobic, and transphobic curricula; faced damaging social expectations; been isolated from other LGBT people; and dealt with anti-LGBT regulations, disciplinary actions, and hiring, promotion, and firing practices. At the same time, colleges and universities have provided LGBT individuals with opportunities to escape from unsupportive families and communities; come out as LGBT; pursue sexual and romantic encounters and relationships; find safety, comfort, friendship, love, and eros; and learn critical lessons about surviving and thriving as LGBT people.

As in society at large, the history of LGBT people in the academy reflects a legacy of invisibility, discrimination, and maltreatment, followed in more recent times by movement toward understanding, acceptance, and full participation. Over the last three decades, the general perception of LGBT students, staff, faculty, and administrators has progressed from unacknowledged presence, to recognition of gay men and lesbians, and more recently to greater awareness of bisexual, transgender, questioning, intersex, and other individuals whose sexual and gender identities challenge dominant paradigms. In this same period, the inclusion of sexual orientation and gender identity–expression language in college and university nondiscrimination statements; the establishment of LGBT academic and nonacademic programs; the formal recognition and support of LGBT student, alumni, faculty, and employee groups; and other changes in college and university policies and practices have contributed to an improved campus climate for all.

## Diversity

Surveying LGBT college and university history in the United States is difficult, in part because of the great diversity of institutional types. From all-male preserves staffed by and serving a relatively homogenous population of elite white Christian men, colleges and universities have evolved to incorporate an increasingly broad spectrum of individuals and groups. LGBT experiences in postsecondary institutions may vary according to whether a school is predominantly or exclusively female, male, coeducational, European American, African American, Native American, or multicultural as well as other organizational factors. Secular institutions differ from those affiliated with religious groups (such as the Catholic Church), and LGBT experiences in the latter may vary greatly based on the denomination's attitudes and practices concerning LGBT issues. Public colleges and universities tend to be more directly affected by the actions of politicians who allocate funding and unions that represent employees, while private institutions tend to be more heavily influenced by the views of alumni donors and religious sponsors.

LGBT experiences may also differ based on whether an institution is considered academically elite or nonelite; whether students live on or off campus; and whether the school is a community college, four-year liberal arts college, major research university with undergraduate, graduate, and professional students, or specialized academy or institute. In all settings, LGBT student, staff, faculty, and administrative experiences are additionally shaped by the characteristics of the individuals who inhabit them. LGBT people of color; those from nondominant ethnic, class, and religious backgrounds; international students and scholars; graduate and older students; individuals with children; people with disabilities; and members of other special populations all confront distinct challenges and possibilities.

## History

Records of same-sex lust, desire, attraction, affection, and intimacy in American colleges and universities stretch back more than three hundred years to the diary entries of Michael Wigglesworth at Harvard College. Autobiographical texts by, biographical works about, and oral histories of various nineteenth- and twentieth-century LGBT people (including Daniel Webster at Dartmouth College, M. Carey Thomas at Bryn Mawr College, Gertrude Stein at Johns Hopkins University, Harry Hay at Stanford University, and Audre Lorde at Hunter College and Columbia University) are filled with accounts of same-sex attractions, encounters, and relationships among college and university students, faculty, and administrators.

While substantial evidence suggests significant levels of acceptance of same-sex intimacy in colleges and universities in the nineteenth century, that began to change around the turn of the twentieth century, in the same period when scientific discourse classifying homosexuality as a mental illness became increasingly influential. In the late 1800s and early 1900s, growing concern over intense involvements—known popularly as crushes and smashes—between students and between faculty at women's colleges led to disciplinary action and dismissal. In 1920 a secret investigation resulted in a purge of eight male Harvard College undergraduates, a graduate student, and one instructor for homosexual acts and fraternization. (Uncovered by a student reporter in 2002, the story prompted a statement of regret from the Harvard

president.) After World War II scrutiny increased, with institutional and state authorities eyeing same-sex relationships involving both students and faculty with greater suspicion in the context of the Cold War. The University of Florida fired sixteen faculty and staff in 1958 and 1959 after a state legislative committee focused its attention on alleged homosexuals. At Smith College in 1960, three gay men were dismissed from the faculty after their conviction (later reversed on appeal) on pornography charges stemming from the private sharing of homoerotic photographs. In this same period, colleges and universities increasingly took pains, through standard academic courses and special family and marriage classes, to teach students how to conform to dominant sex, gender, and sexual norms.

Simultaneously, institutions were sponsoring and promoting groundbreaking research on LGBT issues. While the University of Pennsylvania was home to the anti-LGB scholarship of psychiatrist Samuel Hadden in the 1950s and 1960s and Temple University sponsored the electroshock aversive conditioning therapy of Joseph Wolpe in the 1960s, the University of Chicago supported progressive LGBT sociological research in the 1920s and 1930s, Indiana University was home to the pioneering work of sexologist Alfred Kinsey in the 1940s and 1950s, the University of California at Los Angeles sponsored Evelyn Hooker's gay-affirming psychological research in the 1950s and 1960s, and the Johns Hopkins University was the site of John Money's research on transsexuals in the 1960s and 1970s. The balance of college- and university-based research was anti-LGBT before the Stonewall Riots of 1969. Afterward, however, significant foundations were established for the development of LGBT studies.

## LGBT Studies

While academic research on LGBT topics began over a century ago and some of this research made its way into college and university classrooms in the pre-Stonewall era, the last thirty years have witnessed major developments. Courses in LGBT studies began to appear in the 1970s. In 1973 the Gay Academic Union was established and held its first conference in New York City, with three hundred attendees and daylong panels on Scholarship and the Gay Experience and Coming Out in the University. The nation's first LGBT faculty group, the Union sought to eliminate discrimination against women and LGB people, supported faculty members in coming out, and advocated LGB studies. LGBT caucuses now exist in many academic professional organizations, including the Modern Language Association and the American Psychological Association.

In 1989 the City College of San Francisco (CCSF) became the first institution in the United States to form a gay and lesbian studies department and to offer a degree in the field. At present, CCSF still proudly claims to have the only department of gay, lesbian, and bisexual studies in the country. A small but growing number of institutions offer concentrations, minors, majors, and certificates in LGBT and queer studies, often under the rubric of women's studies or gender and sexuality studies. Historically, efforts by individual faculty members to include LGBT content in their courses or to offer LGBT-specific classes have at times been accepted and encouraged, and at other times have caused uproar. Currently, numerous courses on LGBT topics exist at both the undergraduate and graduate levels. To support this blossoming field of study, library resources have grown exponentially; the University of Chicago's massive *Guide to Gay and Lesbian Resources* expanded by 60 percent between its 1998 and 2002 editions, reflecting both escalating demand for LGBT-related works and their burgeoning supply. University scholars working and publishing in LGBT studies find support from various centers, institutes, and programs, such as the Center for Lesbian and Gay Studies (CLAGS) at the City University of New York, the first university-based research center devoted to gay and lesbian studies.

## Students

In the last three decades, developments on college and university campuses, from admissions to commencement, have transformed LGBT student life. Increasingly in the last decade, admissions offices are considering the needs of LGBT students in their recruitment efforts. For example, in the last two years, as part of Boston's Gay/Straight Youth Pride celebration, an admissions fair for LGBT students has been held, drawing representatives from nearly 100 local and regional colleges and universities. LGBT applicants now routinely review ranking guides that rate campuses as LGBT friendly or not, and some institutions directly address LGBT issues in their admissions materials and Web sites. Other colleges and universities are recognizing the implications of coming out for financially dependent students and providing assistance when family support is curtailed. The Frank-Tremblay Safe College Scholarship at Bridgewater State College in Massachusetts, for example, offers aid to LGBT students who experience financial hardship due to their sexual orientation or gender identity. Scholarships for LGBT students and allies are also available from organizations including the Astraea Lesbian Action Foundation, the Point Foundation, and the International Foundation for Gender Education.

Single-sex colleges and universities have faced unique student admissions and retention issues. These institutions, and especially all-female schools, experience special challenges resulting from factors such as the perceived larger presence of LGB students; homophobic attitudes about women's and men's colleges; and the needs of transgender students who may or may not wish to transition during their school years. As president of Smith College from 1975 to 1985, Jill Ker Conway confronted head-on the homophobic stereotypes of women's colleges by vigorously challenging those who repeatedly asked her to fix what they perceived as a lesbian problem on campus. Since the late 1990s, all-female institutions have been rethinking core definitions of sex and gender as they contemplate what to do when a student admitted as female no longer identifies as such and how best to serve students who do not wish to be classified as female or male.

Once admitted, LGBT students confront unique housing issues. Residential housing on virtually all campuses is organized with non-LGBT students in mind. Same-sex roommate matching is nearly universal and single-sex halls and dormitories remain common. For LGBT students, such housing arrangements can be appealing, but also problematic. Some schools have developed special interest LGBT housing, such as the 2 in 20 Floor inaugurated in 1992 at the University of Massachusetts at Amherst, which offers safe living spaces for LGBT students and those interested in LGBT issues. The availability of safe housing options for transgender students on a case-by-case basis is a more recent development, though by no means widespread. In 2003 Wesleyan University announced that it would establish a gender-blind floor for students who choose not to be classified according to sex for purposes of on-campus housing; it is believed to be the first U.S. higher education institution to create such a residence. Provisions for same-sex couples to live together in campus housing and to serve as residence hall staff exist on some campuses, sometimes with the requirement that the couple be registered domestic partners.

Much of the educational process occurs outside of classrooms and residence halls, and extracurricular organizations are an important way for LGBT students to create and maintain a sense of community. Depending on institutional size and other factors, there may be one campus LGBT group, none, or many. For some, the focus is social: establishing a safe space to meet others; discussing sexual and gender identity issues; and organizing campus events. For others, the agenda is political: raising awareness of LGBT issues on campus; providing educational programs; lobbying for changes to university policies; and aligning with other social justice groups. The first LGB student organization in the United States, the Student Homophile League, was launched at Columbia University in 1966–1967; soon thereafter, LGB groups were founded at New York University and Stanford University. In 2003 hundreds exist nationwide, sometimes recognized and supported by their colleges and universities and sometimes not. Fair treatment for LGBT student groups at institutions such as Georgetown University and Texas A & M University resulted only after legal action. Gay-straight alliances (GSAs) such as the Allies of Boston College, officially recognized in 2003, often exist alongside LGBT organizations.

Campus LGBT activism commonly includes the celebration of National Coming Out Day (11 October), the organization of a spring LGBT awareness period (known at some institutions as Gaypril), and participation in LGBT pride marches in June. Begun in 1996 at the University of Virginia and now coordinated by GLSEN (Gay Lesbian Straight Education Network) and the United States Students Association, the annual National Day of Silence involved students at four hundred colleges and universities in April 2003. A youth-run project to protest the historical silencing of LGBT people and to raise awareness of LGBT concerns, the National Day of Silence encourages student participants and allies in middle schools, high schools, colleges, and universities to take a daylong vow of silence, wearing pins or distributing cards to explain their reasons for not speaking; the quiet is often supplemented by educational activities and breaking the silence celebrations. Activist LGBT groups also typically pursue issues such as the presence on campus of Reserve Officers' Training Corps (ROTC) programs and U.S. armed forces recruiters in light of military policies that discriminate against LGB people; anti-LGB policies regarding blood donations; problems with HIV/AIDS, counseling, and health services; hate speech; the absence of LGBT studies courses; and other social justice concerns.

Athletics are a major extracurricular activity on many campuses. While the National Collegiate Athletic Association (NCAA) includes sexual orientation in its nondiscrimination policy, many consider athletics to be the last closet on campus and the number of collegiate athletes who are out as LGBT remains small, especially at Division I institutions. Phenomena such as homophobic recruiting practices, lesbian baiting of female student athletes and coaches, anti-LGBT harassment, and worse persist, despite efforts by students, coaches, athletic directors, universities, the NCAA, and other organizations working to address issues of homophobia and transphobia in sports.

Sororities and fraternities also deserve mention. Often the hub of the campus social world, the Greek system has substantial effects on key components of undergraduate life. Sheila James Kuehl, who became the first openly lesbian or gay member of the California state legislature in 1995, was dismissed from her sorority at the University of California at Los Angeles (UCLA) in 1959 after letters from her girlfriend were discovered; she later became an alumna advisor to a lesbian sorority at UCLA. The Lambda 10 Project National Clearinghouse for Gay, Lesbian, and Bisexual Fraternal and Sorority Issues works with national organizations and campus chapters to help them become more inclusive. A small number of LGBT fraternities and sororities, including Delta Lambda Phi and Lambda Delta Lambda, have been established.

## Commencement and Alumni Affairs

The end of the academic year is a time of traditions and adaptations. Various institutions have featured LGBT commencement speakers and awarded LGBT academic, leadership, and other types of prizes. At some schools, lavender graduation ceremonies are held to recognize the unique contributions that LGBT students have made to their colleges and universities, to celebrate their academic and extracurricular achievements with family and friends, and to affirm their place in higher education.

LGBT graduates of many institutions have formed alumni groups, either within or outside of official alumni associations. Whether in the context of alumni groups or not, alumni involvement has been critical in creating safe and welcoming campuses for LGBT students, staff, faculty, and administrators. By supporting current students via mentoring and professional networking and by providing targeted financial contributions to colleges and universities, LGBT alumni affect the student body and the institution as a whole. In 2000, two University of Pennsylvania graduates gave $2 million to fund the renovation of the Penn LGBT center, the country's first dedicated, on-campus building serving as a community center for sexual and gender minorities. At Yale University, the Larry Kramer Initiative for Lesbian and Gay Studies was established in 2001 as a five-year program to fund conferences, speakers, visiting fellows, and scholars; coordinate LGBT studies; and sponsor student and faculty research. The initiative honors Kramer—a Yale alumnus, writer, and AIDS activist—and was inaugurated by the $1 million gift of his brother Arthur, also a Yale graduate. LGBT alumni groups are increasingly common and active participants in college and university life, fostering institutional loyalty and building community.

## Faculty, Staff, and Administration

LGBT faculty, staff, and administrators have concerns both similar to and distinct from those of students and alumni. They, too, have struggled for recognition and equal treatment, but with additional concerns such as hiring, promotion, tenure, job security, and salaries; parental, medical, and caregiving leave; partner hiring; and domestic partner benefits (in such areas as health insurance and health care, facilities access, and tuition waivers). In many locations, colleges and universities are among the largest local employers, playing important roles in setting standards for employment nondiscrimination policies. Currently, over 250 higher education institutions include sexual orientation in their nondiscrimination policies, and a small but growing number incorporate gender identity-expression nondiscrimination language as well. Perceptions of a lavender ceiling exist in academe, and progress has been uneven. Various LGBT disciplinary and professional associations, including groups affiliated with the American Anthropological Association and the American Historical Association, have documented significant patterns of discrimination that affect both those who identify as LGBT and those who research LGBT topics.

Along with faculty, student affairs staff have played multiple roles in dealing with LGBT issues on campus. Often serving as key allies of LGBT students, student affairs professionals have helped to establish a growing number of campus LGBT centers with funded staff positions and dedicated resources. Over one hundred such centers exist at present, and among the most recent institutions to create a coordinator of LGBTQ community resources position is Georgetown University. The National Consortium of Directors of LGBT Resources in Higher Education maintains a Web site to gather national data, monitor campus climates, share best practices, and act as an information clearinghouse. Both the National Association of Student Personnel Administrators and the American College Personnel Association have committees that work proactively on behalf of LGBT issues. Orientation programming focused on sexual and gender identity, safe zone and ally programs, LGBT-sensitive health services, professional and peer counseling, and specialized mentoring programs are increasingly in place to demonstrate institutional commitment to LGBT members of campus communities.

At the top of the academic ladder, Charles Middleton of Roosevelt University received national attention in 2002 as the first openly gay president of a major U.S. university. Other college and university presidents, provosts, and deans are known to be LGB, with varying degrees of openness about their LGB identities.

## Future Tasks

As in many areas of American society, there is much to be done to make colleges and universities truly safe and nurturing places for LGBT individuals, whether students, alumni, administrators, faculty, staff, family members, or guests. The needs of transgender individuals are only beginning to be addressed on most campuses. Bisexuals are frequently marginalized, as are students of color who also identify as LGBT. The unique concerns of lesbians and gay men must be considered independently as well as together. Myriad special populations and settings require individualized attention, and recognition of the complex intersections of identities is vital to ensuring that all voices are heard. As more and more out and proud students, alumni, faculty, staff, and administrators arrive and emerge on college and university campuses and claim their right to equal treatment, the educational environment for LGBT individuals will move toward the goal of providing a place of learning, teaching, growth, and wisdom for all who enter the gates of academe.

## Bibliography

D'Emilio, John. *Making Trouble: Essays on Gay History, Politics, and the University.* New York: Routledge, 1992.

Dilley, Patrick. *Queer Man on Campus: A History of Non-Heterosexual College Men, 1945–2000.* New York: RoutledgeFalmer, 2002.

Evans, Nancy J., and Vernon A. Wall, eds. *Beyond Tolerance: Gays, Lesbians, and Bisexuals on Campus.* Alexandria, Va.: American College Personnel Association, 1991.

MacKay, Anne, ed. *Wolf Girls at Vassar: Lesbian and Gay Experiences, 1930–1990.* New York: St. Martin's Press, 1992.

McNaron, Toni A. H. *Poisoned Ivy: Lesbian and Gay Academics Confronting Homophobia.* Philadelphia: Temple University Press, 1997.

Mintz, Beth, and Esther D. Rothblum, eds. *Lesbians in Academia: Degrees of Freedom.* New York: Routledge, 1997.

Rankin, Susan R. *Campus Climate for Gay, Lesbian, Bisexual, and Transgender People: A National Perspective.* New York: National Gay and Lesbian Task Force Policy Institute, 2003.

Rhoads, Robert A. *Coming Out in College: The Struggle for a Queer Identity.* Westport, Conn.: Bergin and Garvey, 1994.

Sanlo, Ronni L., ed. *Working with Lesbian, Gay, Bisexual, and Transgender College Students: A Handbook for Faculty and Administrators.* Westport, Conn.: Greenwood Press, 1998.

Sanlo, Ronni, Sue Rankin, and Robert Schoenberg, eds. *Our Place on Campus: Lesbian, Gay, Bisexual, Transgender Services and Programs in Higher Education.* Westport, Conn.: Greenwood Press, 2002.

Shand-Tucci, Douglass. *The Crimson Letter: Harvard, Homosexuality, and the Shaping of American Culture.* New York: St. Martin's Press, 2003.

Shepard, Curtis F., Felice Yeskel, and Charles Outcalt. *Lesbian, Gay, Bisexual, and Transgender Campus Organizing: A Comprehensive Manual.* Washington, D.C.: National Gay and Lesbian Task Force, 1996.

Wall, Vernon A., and Nancy J. Evans, eds. *Toward Acceptance: Sexual Orientation Issues on Campus.* Lanham, Md.: University Press of America, 2000.

Windmeyer, Shane L., and Pamela W. Freeman, eds. *Out on Fraternity Row: Personal Accounts of Being Gay in a College Fraternity.* Los Angeles: Alyson Books, 1998.

Windmeyer, Shane L., and Pamela W. Freeman, eds. *Secret Sisters: Stories of Being Lesbian and Bisexual in a College Sorority.* Los Angeles: Alyson Books, 2000.

**Patricia M. Broderick**

***See also*** BOSTON; CENTER FOR LESBIAN AND GAY STUDIES (CLAGS); SEXUAL REVOLUTIONS; LGBTQ STUDIES; NEW LEFT AND STUDENT MOVEMENTS; QUEER THEORY AND QUEER STUDIES; RIGHTS OF ASSOCIATION AND ASSEMBLY; SMASHES AND CHUMMING; THOMAS, M. CAREY; WIGGLESWORTH, MICHAEL; WOO, MERLE; YOUTH AND YOUTH GROUPS.

# COLONIAL AMERICA

Reconstructing the sexual lives and values of North Americans in the seventeenth and eighteenth centuries is a considerable challenge, given that most people did not leave behind any account of their sexual activities or attitudes. Most surviving information either promotes official values or attacks unauthorized behavior. Yet recent historians have sought to filter out the negative rhetoric and preconceptions that framed assaults on unconventional behavior, including same-sex relations, to shed clearer light on the practices being condemned and the attitudes that they express. Scholars have also used court transcripts that record the words of those who could not write for themselves to broaden our understanding of sexual culture in colonial America.

## Native American Culture and the "Half-Man/Half-Woman"

European explorers were fascinated and appalled by Indian sexual customs. The condoning of sexual experimentation among young people prior to marriage, serial monogamy, and polygamy contrasted sharply with official European codes of conduct and served to illustrate the alleged barbarity of Native Americans. Spanish and French reports from the New World described a category of men who lived as women, dressed in female clothing, and engaged in sexual relations with other men. (In some nations, there were Indian women who assumed male clothing and roles, though this phenomenon seems to have been less widespread. Given the considerable authority exercised by women in many Native American nations, the adoption of male roles by women would not have involved the same degree of inversion of power relations as would have been the case in European society; the same would have been true of men assuming female roles.) European observers expressed amazement that Indians apparently revered men who lived as women, especially given that they made themselves sexually available to other men. That such behavior, criminalized in Europe as whoredom and sodomy, should serve as a badge of respectability among Indians exemplified for these writers the immorality and savagery of Indian culture. Europeans used the word *berdache* (an Arabic word meaning "male prostitute") to describe such men. Yet Indians often referred to them as "half-man/half-woman."

The specific characteristics and functions of the half-man/half-woman varied from nation to nation, but in general the individual combined male and female attributes, remaining anatomically male and in some nations wearing both male and female articles of clothing. Such individuals could not attain the honor associated with male-identified roles that they had forsaken, but they were esteemed for unique contributions made possible by their gender mixing. Whereas Europeans saw the *berdache* as an emblem of sin and disorder, from an Indian perspective the half-man/half-woman embodied and promoted the harmony that resulted from reconciling opposites within the physical and spiritual realms. Their composite identity as half-men/half-women enabled them to mediate between the polarities of male and female as well as between those of spirit and flesh. Boys were prompted by dreams or visions to become half-man/half-woman, made the transition through established rituals, and then assumed a prominent role within the ritual life of their communities. Some scholars have suggested that the presence of the half-man/half-woman may have worked to the advantage of other men in terms of gender politics within native communities. The incorporation of female qualities into male ceremonies without actually involving women may have appealed to Indian men who wished to symbolize the coming together of male and female without sacrificing their monopoly over certain aspects of ceremonial life. The half-man/half-woman sometimes married a man, but unless or until he did so he was sexually available to other men within his community, which would have given both married and unmarried men a sexual outlet that avoided potential conflict over access to women.

Europeans who sought to convert and "civilize" Indians insisted that setting aside native sexual traditions should play an important part in that process. Colonial leaders meanwhile sought to prevent European settlers from adopting Indian customs, sexual and otherwise. It is striking, though, that a court in Virginia charged to deal with the case of Thomas/Thomasine Hall, an anatomically male colonist who dressed sometimes as a man and sometimes as a woman, ordered that the defendant should be made to wear clothing that combined male and female components. It is tempting to wonder if the Native American half-man/half-woman tradition had any impact on this decision.

## Seventeenth-Century Virginia

Imposing on the population at large an official moral code that criminalized practices ranging from premarital sex to sodomy proved even more challenging in the New World than in the Old. Virginia, England's first permanent colony in North America, was initially an all-male colony. Though women did migrate to the Chesapeake region in subsequent years, they remained relatively few in number throughout the first half of the seventeenth century. The Chesapeake's skewed sex ratio made it extremely difficult for men to find wives and establish conventional family households. It also meant that most colonists did not have access to sexual relations with English women during the initial period of settlement; nor does there seem to have been much sexual contact with Indians. The first black laborers did not arrive until 1619. The number of blacks in Virginia remained modest until the end of the seventeenth century (in 1675 they made up just 5 percent of all non-Indian inhabitants) and the black population was at first, like the white population, predominantly male. Few scholars have been willing to ponder the sexual implications of this unusual demographic situation. Settlers often paired off to form all-male households. Some of these men may have engaged in sexual relations with each other out of desire or desperation. Some of those colonists who had male servants, black or white, working for them may have coerced them sexually. Others may have taken advantage of an unusual situation to form consensual relationships that would have been more controversial under normal circumstances. But whatever their motives, men who coupled sexually with other men are unlikely to have been anomalous in such an environment. It seems reasonable to assume that much of the sex that took place in the first few years of settlement in the south was sodomitical. That

kind of situational same-sex intimacy presumably faded as the sex ratio evened out.

When Captain Richard Cornish was prosecuted and hanged for raping his servant William Couse in 1624, the trial provoked heated controversy, in large part because the only evidence against the defendant came from Couse. This is the only sodomy trial known to have taken place in Virginia during the first phase of colonization. As women arrived in greater numbers, enabling the formation of more conventional households and marriages, the authorities may have wanted to make an example of Cornish. Those who gathered to discuss the case and attack the court may have been anxious about the vulnerability of other men, including themselves, especially if accusations of male rape were to result in conviction even without corroborative evidence. None of the reported conversations suggested any revulsion toward sodomy itself. But Virginians at the time (along with subsequent historians) were not eager to cast light on sexual relations between men in the fledgling colony.

## Seventeenth-Century New England

In sharp contrast, sodomy figured as a regular topic of public discussion further north in New England, where Puritan leaders were eager to guard colonists from sin by denouncing in sermons and other official pronouncements all illicit impulses. Colonists there were taught that God had ordained sex as an expression of loving fellowship between husband and wife; it also enabled procreation. All nonmarital sex was sinful, disorderly, and polluting. The physical body, ministers taught, played a crucial role in the drama of spiritual redemption; it was intended by God as a temple for the soul and so should be kept safe from the pollution of sin. When Puritans condemned illicit sex as "unclean," "filthy," and "defiling," they used language that underscored the need to protect their bodies from contamination for the sake of their souls.

That incorporation of sex and the body into a larger moral drama conditioned the ways in which New England ministers explained sexual urges. They evoked neither sexuality as an independent force that gave rise to erotic desire nor sexual orientation as a determinant of who was attracted to whom. They explained masturbation, premarital sex, adultery, sodomy, and bestiality just as they did any other sin, such as drunkenness or disobedience: they were all driven by the innate corruption that men and women inherited from Adam and Eve. Official teaching did not, then, conceive of sodomy as fundamentally distinct from any other manifestation of human sin. Nor did it see particular individuals as constitutionally inclined or limited to any one form of sexual offense; anyone could be tempted to commit any sin.

Yet official condemnation of illicit sex was far from indiscriminate. Ministers distinguished carefully between different kinds and degrees of offense. They classified sexual acts in terms of those involved and their relationships to each other: their marital status, sex, and species. According to New England's spiritual teachers, there was a clear distinction between illicit sex performed by a man and woman and that between either two persons of the same sex or a human being and an animal. Same-sex sodomy and bestiality disrupted the natural order and crossed scripturally ordained boundaries between sexes and species. They were thus more clearly sinful and disorderly than "uncleanness" between a man and a woman.

Puritan ministers included in their definitions of "unnatural" sex not only the coupling of "men with men" but also that of "woman with woman." Yet New England's laws against sodomy focused much more specifically on sex between men. The one exception to this was the New Haven law, which incorporated into its definition of the crime sex between women as well as between men, virginal penetration of a girl prior to puberty, and anal penetration by men of women and children, male or female. (This is the only surviving example of New England authorities, judicial or clerical, using the word "sodomy" to signify anal sex between a man and woman; there are no references in the extant sources to oral sex.) That reflected the legal system's conception of sex as a phallic act. Because lawmakers and magistrates understood sex in terms of penetration, they found it difficult to conceive of a sexual scenario that did not involve a penis along with a male to which it was attached. As a result, there was little room for the recognition or prosecution of sex between women. On only two known occasions did women appear before New England courts on charges of "lewd" behavior with each other; in neither case was their behavior categorized specifically, perhaps in large part because the magistrates were not sure how to do so.

New England courts were reluctant to convict on charges of sodomy (or other capital offenses such as adultery, rape, and bestiality) unless there was clear proof that sexual intercourse had occurred. Yet most courts had only circumstantial evidence on which to base their deliberations; witnesses may have seen the accused in compromising circumstances, but they rarely claimed to have witnessed penetration itself. When dealing with capital cases, New England courts generally insisted that the allegation be substantiated either by a confession or by at least two independent witnesses. The two-witness rule, in combination with the legal system's narrow definition of sex as an act of intercourse, made conviction extremely difficult. As a result, those accused of sodomy in seventeenth-century New England were mostly whipped or fined for either suspicious behavior or an attempted crime. Only two individuals, William Plaine and John Knight, are known to have been executed for this crime in the northern British colonies. (Jan Creoli, a black man living in New Netherland, was executed in 1646 for sodomizing a ten-year-old boy, Manuel Congo.) Not only were executions for sodomy rare in seventeenth-century New England, but prosecutions were also remarkably few in number. Throughout the colonial period, New England communities preferred to handle problematic behavior through informal channels; they resorted to ecclesiastical discipline or the legal system only when private exhortation or local and informal measures failed to resolve the situation. Though most of the surviving information about illicit sex comes from court records, colonists did not see such behavior primarily as a legal problem. Any number of local incidents and controversies involving sodomy may have escaped the record because of this preference for noninstitutional forms of social control. Addressing the situation through nonjuridical channels was, moreover, less dire than invoking capital law and so would have appealed to those who disapproved of sodomy but did not want the accused to hang. We should also bear in mind that many sexual offenses came to light because pregnancy resulted; in this respect there was less risk for men engaging in sexual relations with each other.

Some incidents relating to sodomy may not have reached court records because too few people were upset for prosecution to be worthwhile. We should beware of assuming that all colonists shared official values or abided by prescribed codes of behavior. Responses to sodomy seem to have ranged from outright condemnation to a live-and-let-live attitude that did not go so far as to condone such behavior but that did enable peaceful cohabitation, especially when the individual concerned was an otherwise valued member of the local community. Much of the time, colonists appear to have found nonsexual aspects of a person's behavior more significant in determining his or her social worth. If the individual was otherwise popular as a neighbor and as long as his sexual behavior did not outweigh his more positive attributes, then disrupting social and economic relationships in the local community may have struck the practical minded as too high a price to pay for the enforcement of moral absolutes. Difficult though it was to secure a conviction for sodomy in a New England court, the greater challenge for those who favored legal action lay in persuading their neighbors to join them in pressing charges, even against notorious individuals. The weight of unofficial opinion does not appear to have rested with those actively hostile toward sodomy.

Fragmentary evidence suggests that some New Englanders also rejected or ignored official guidelines as they sought to understand those who engaged (or tried to engage) in sodomy. Puritan theologians insisted that any individual had the potential to commit any sin, sexual or otherwise; the modern notion of sexuality as a distinct aspect of human identity that impels each man and woman toward members of the same or opposite sex had no place in their ideological framework. Yet some colonists apparently recognized in particular individuals an ongoing preference for specific kinds of sexual partner. Colonists did not go so far as to posit sexual identity as such, but they did perceive in certain individuals a persistent inclination toward sodomy that transcended the sexual acts themselves. This appears to have been the case, for example, with respect to Nicholas Sension of Connecticut.

A few scholars have argued that condemnation of sodomy in early New England was driven in large part by a profound fear of femininity and effeminization. Yet the colonists do not appear to have made any connection between sodomy and effeminacy. Such a linkage would become an important, even crucial, component of the homoerotic subculture that had emerged in London by the early eighteenth century; the inhabitants of late colonial North America read accounts of English "sodomites" who assumed a feminine persona and also of foppish men who, it was implied, might engage in sodomy. But colonial court cases and controversies involving cross-dressing (concerning, for example, Lord Edward Hyde Cornbury of New York) did not include allegations or even insinuations of same-sex intimacy. And none of the defendants in sodomy cases during the colonial period were accused of cross-dressing. Nor did Puritans see femininity as intrinsically undesirable. In certain respects their understanding of gender was remarkably fluid, so that men were expected to adopt female roles in specific contexts, just as women assumed male roles in certain circumstances: male subjects were taught to defer to their rulers as if wives obeying their husbands; godly men envisaged Christ as a husband and themselves as his bride.

## The Eighteenth Century

By the end of the colonial period, representations of sex between men in English print culture had undergone a dramatic transformation. The emergence of the sodomite as a social category—referring to a specific cadre of men with a consistent, though not necessarily exclusive, sexual interest in other men—represented a significant shift away from earlier models. Though the eighteenth-century sodomite should not be confused with the modern category of "homosexual," sodomy was now perceived as a crucial part of specific personality types, and male Londoners attracted to members of the same sex could find partners and social camaraderie in recognized gathering places, including London's "molly houses." Sodomy and effeminacy were now firmly conjoined. Readers of eighteenth-century colonial newspapers encountered items describing police raids on molly houses in London and the prosecution of those who participated in that city's sodomitical subculture. Yet surviving evidence from colonial cities in North America gives no signs of a subculture such as London offered.

In eighteenth-century New England, older religious frameworks that understood sodomy in terms of moral corruption inviting divine retribution still exerted a powerful influence. Yet there were even fewer prosecutions for sodomy in New England than in the seventeenth century. In addition to the factors that had previously discouraged formal censure of even those notorious for sodomy, three additional developments in the late colonial period militated against prosecution. First, the courts paid less and less attention to moral regulation in general as their caseloads became dominated by financial and commercial issues. This redirection of legal energies did not mean that local communities had lost interest in addressing problematic behavior informally, but it did represent a significant change in the tone of public life. At the same time, a growing preoccupation with privacy and a decline in enthusiasm for public shaming as an instrument of moral renewal made New Englanders eager to avoid formal proceedings.

An additional change linked sodomy to the growth of commercial corruption, urban development, and foreign vice. Concern about the potentially corrupting impact of economic development had been a staple of seventeenth-century Puritan writing, but anxiety relating to the moral ramifications of commercial and urban life took on new significance in the late colonial and revolutionary periods as Americans sought to distance themselves from what they depicted as a decadent metropolitan culture across the Atlantic. One case study has shown that Philadelphians were well aware of the new models for understanding same-sex intimacy that had emerged across the Atlantic, but there is no sign of these new models being adopted by or applied to Philadelphians. One likely explanation for this is that because sodomy served as a handy measure of British corruption, Americans were loathe to acknowledge its presence in their own communities. The silence of the eighteenth-century historical record thus points not to the absence of sodomy but to its implication in the project of American separation and the assertion of cultural as well as political independence.

## Friendship and Love

All of the colonies in British America criminalized same-sex sodomy. Yet in common with their contemporaries across the Atlantic, early Americans accepted and even idealized loving friendships between members of the same sex that included expressions of romantic and physical affection. Reading backward in time, we have to be very careful not to mistake same-sex affection for sexual desire. Prior to the late nineteenth century, same-sex friendships could draw from a broad spectrum of possibilities that were not yet constricted by the modern conflation of love and sex. Just as long as their expressions of love did not become explicitly sexual, members of the same sex could explore and enjoy a degree of intimacy that would later become heterodox within American society. Some of these earlier friendships between men or between women may have included a sexual element, but many (it would seem) did not. An intimate, affectionate, and avowedly loving friendship between two members of the same sex was seen as socially respectable and also quite compatible with marriage to a member of the opposite sex.

Correspondence between Puritan men was, for example, richly expressive of love and affection that was framed quite openly in romantic terms. John Winthrop's celebration of brotherly love in public addresses and private correspondence in the seventeenth century drew on his ardent reading of the biblical relationship between David and Jonathan as well as the passionate language of Canticles. Such language does not, of course, mean that Winthrop had or wanted to have sexual relations with men, but it does suggest a wide range of possibilities within early modern male friendship that emerges also from other letters written by men to men in colonial and early national America. In the eyes of persons of these eras, male intimacy could nurture and reinforce or corrupt and undermine authorized cultural endeavors, depending upon the mode of its expression. In his famous lay sermon delivered aboard the *Arbella,* John Winthrop exalted brotherly love as essential to the success of a godly commonwealth, yet the year before, "5 beastly Sodomiticall boyes" had been exposed on the *Talbot* and subsequently sent back to England for punishment

(Warner, p. 345). As scholar Michael Warner has noted in "New English Sodom," Winthrop's sermon "was thus delivered in the very space of the repudiation of sodomy, en route to the New Canaan" (p. 345). Winthrop and others may have feared sodomy as a perversion of that "brotherly affection" that would, if expressed in appropriate ways, unite and redeem New England's citizens.

Over a century later, male love had equally profound implications for early republican society. During the eighteenth century a transformation had taken place in the gendering of moral virtue: in sharp contrast to earlier representations of women as morally corrupt and untrustworthy, American writers now portrayed women as the guardians of virtue; negative characteristics previously associated with women were now transposed onto men. With republican ideology seeking to nurture civic virtue as the social and political cement that would replace loyalty to the Crown and inspire citizens to disinterested public engagement, political writers placed increasing emphasis upon the role to be played by republican wives and mothers in fostering a moral rectitude and altruistic spirit of which men were often incapable if left to their own instincts. Although postrevolutionary political discourse claimed that the ties of social affection could hold men together in civic fraternity, the nature of those ties had to be negotiated with great care, given a male propensity toward personal vice and political corruption. Late-eighteenth-century Americans worried that male rakes and profligates might corrupt other young men who kept company with them. Yet contemporaries also believed that men could influence each other in more positive directions, quelling each other's corrupt tendencies and appealing to each other's potential for virtue. The families and friends of men who engaged in loving, even romantic, relationships with other men often saw such relationships as morally, socially, and politically desirable. Loving friendship and virtue would nurture each other: both were personal and private in their origins; both had public, political, and constructive implications. Fraternal love, in conjunction with the loving influence of mothers and wives, could redeem American manhood and so sustain the republic.

Republican ideology's depiction of women as the guardians of virtue was designed to inspire and reform men through interaction between the sexes. Ironically, that ideology ended up fostering an increasingly homosocial atmosphere. Women were now taught to see themselves as fundamentally different from men and economic change reinforced that cultural message. By the early nineteenth century, men increasingly went out to work instead of laboring in the immediate vicinity of the home. Consequently, the household became more and more a feminine domain: whereas in a preindustrial economy many women had worked alongside or at least nearby their husbands, women from the upper or middling ranks of society now spent most of their time with other women, identified with each other, and sought emotional sustenance from each other. These close friendships often included tender expressions of love. As the two sexes moved apart, so both men and women increasingly turned to friends of the same sex for emotionally meaningful relationships.

### Bibliography

Blackwood, Evelyn. "Sexuality and Gender in Certain Native American Tribes: The Case of Cross-Gender Females." *Signs* 10 (1984): 27–42.

Brown, Kathleen M. "'Changed . . . into the Fashion of Man': The Politics of Sexual Difference in a Seventeenth-Century Anglo-American Settlement." *Journal of the History of Sexuality* 6 (1995): 171–193.

Foster, Thomas Alan. *Sex and the Eighteenth-Century Man: Anglo-American Discourses of Sex and Manliness in Massachusetts, 1690–1765.* Ph.D. diss., Johns Hopkins University, 2002.

Godbeer, Richard. *Sexual Revolution in Early America.* Baltimore: Johns Hopkins University Press, 2002.

———. *The Overflowing of Friendship: Love between Men in Eighteenth-Century America.* Forthcoming.

Gutiérrez, Ramón A. *When Jesus Came, the Corn Mothers Went Away: Marriage, Sexuality, and Power in New Mexico, 1500–1846.* Stanford, Calif.: Stanford University Press, 1991.

Houser, Raymond E. "The 'Berdache' and the Illinois Indian Tribe during the Last Half of the Seventeenth Century." *Ethnohistory* 37 (1990): 45–65.

Lyons, Clare A. "Mapping an Atlantic Sexual Culture: Homoeroticism in Eighteenth-Century Philadelphia." *William and Mary Quarterly* 60 (2003): 119–154.

Myles, Anne G. "Queering the Study of Early American Sexuality." *William and Mary Quarterly* 60 (2003): 199–202.

Talley, Collin L. "Gender and Male Same-Sex Erotic Behavior in British North America in the Seventeenth Century." *Journal of the History of Sexuality* 6 (1996): 385–408.

Thompson, Roger. "Attitudes towards Homosexuality in the Seventeenth-Century New England Colonies." *Journal of American Studies* 23 (1989): 27–40.

Warner, Michael. "New English Sodom." In *Queering the Renaissance.* Edited by Jonathan Goldberg. Durham, N.C.: Duke University Press, 1994.

Williams, Walter L. *The Spirit and the Flesh: Sexual Diversity in American Indian Culture.* Boston: Beacon Press, 1986.

**Richard Godbeer**

*See also* BOSTON; FRIENDSHIP; HALL, THOMAS/THOMASINE; NATIVE AMERICANS; ROMANTIC FRIENDSHIP AND BOSTON MARRIAGE; SENSION, NICHOLAS; SODOMY, BUGGERY, CRIMES AGAINST NATURE, DISORDERLY CONDUCT, AND LEWD AND LASCIVIOUS LAW AND POLICY; TRANSSEXUALS, TRANVESTITES, TRANSGENDER PEOPLE, AND CROSS-DRESSERS; TWO-SPIRIT FEMALES; TWO-SPIRIT MALES; WIGGLESWORTH, MICHAEL.

# COLORADO

Colorado became the thirty-eighth state to enter the Union in 1876. The state's history, political culture, and geography are similar to those of other Rocky Mountain states, but LGBT history in the state has been relatively unique for the region. Rapid population growth and urbanization in the state starting in the 1940s have attracted migrants from the Midwest and Southwest, many of whom differ significantly in terms of race, ethnicity, and socioeconomic status from long-time residents of the state. As has been the case in many areas of the country, these rapid changes served as a backdrop for the development of LGBT economic, social, cultural, and political institutions within the state.

### Early History

As early as the 1880s local Colorado newspapers, following a national trend, were reporting on same-sex companionships that were signs of "monstrous, unnatural affection" (Katz, pp. 150–151), but organized activity by the LGBT community only developed much later. During the 1940s LGBT bars were established in Denver along with cities on the U.S. coasts—mostly as a result of troops returning from World War II. Indeed, Denver was one of the first Mountain or Midwestern states to permit exclusively LGBT bars, and although similar bars were not established in cities such as Boulder and Colorado Springs until the 1970s, networks within these bars formed the social basis for the first LGBT political groups in Colorado. By the 1950s chapters of several national LGBT groups had formed in Denver. The Denver chapter of the Mattachine Society, for example, was founded in 1956 by Carl Harding and was large enough to support its own newsletter. Consistent with the philosophy of the national organization, the Mattachine chapter sought heterosexual allies in its fight for equality and was able to gain the support of local American Civil Liberties Union leaders and Robert Allen, the majority leader in the state house of representatives.

The Mattachine chapter convinced the national office of the Mattachine Society to hold its annual conference in Denver during September 1959, making this the first and only time a Mattachine conference was held outside of New York City or California. For the first time in any city, the group's activities received fairly positive and balanced newspaper coverage by the local media. However, the media coverage also identified chapter leaders to the Denver police force, and in October law enforcement officers searched the homes of all Mattachine leaders in the Denver area. As a result of the raids, one leader was jailed and another was fired from his job, and police seized the group's membership roster. Furthermore, the raids caused the Denver chapter to stagnate, lose membership, and ultimately disappear as a formal organization within a few years.

However, a number of LGBT activists continued working behind the scenes, and the relatively discreet ties LGBT activists established with members of the Colorado legislature in the late 1950s and throughout the 1960s paid off when the legislature repealed the state's anti-sodomy law in 1971. Additionally, although he failed, Boulder Councilman Tim Fuller attempted to add sexual orientation to the city's newly drafted human rights ordinance in 1972. For his efforts, Fuller was subjected to harassment and his house and car were vandalized.

The first social and cultural LGBT organization, the Gay, Lesbian, and Bisexual Community Services Center of Colorado, was founded in Denver in 1976. This was one of the first of a large number of LGBT community centers established around the country, and in 2003 it remained one of the ten largest such centers in the country. Like most other centers, the Denver center has served to bring LGBT people together for social, cultural, and political activities. During the 1980s smaller but similar centers, such as the Pride Center in Colorado Springs, were established in Aspen, Boulder, Fort Collins, and Lakewood.

By the late 1970s much of the focus on policy change on the part of LGBT activists was directed toward enacting new policies that would protect the civil rights of LGBT people. In Aspen, LGBT activists pushed for and passed a local ordinance that banned sexual orientation discrimination in public employment. Activists subsequently persuaded Denver's mayor to issue an executive order in 1983 that prohibited sexual orientation discrimination in public employment and housing. And although the next mayor repealed the executive order, the city council enacted a broader policy in 1990.

In the late 1980s several Colorado localities banned discrimination based on sexual orientation in public employment. Boulder enhanced its human rights ordinance to include sexual orientation in 1987 by a vote of the city council and subsequent close public vote at the

ballot box (51 to 49 percent). Boulder County followed suit later that year, and Morgan County adopted a similar policy in 1988. Fort Collins placed a proposal (Ordinance 106) on the local ballot that would extend civil rights protections to LGB people in 1988. However, the city council was unable to pass a resolution supporting passage of the ordinance, and the measure failed at the ballot box in a 57 to 43 percent vote.

Although LGBT issues were clearly being raised in select communities, statewide LGBT issues seemed to receive little notice until 1990, when Governor Roy Romer signed an executive order banning sexual orientation discrimination for state employees. At about the same time, residents of Colorado Springs began debating the adoption of a general antidiscrimination policy, and this too brought more attention to LGBT issues, even though the sexual orientation clause of the measure failed to pass with the human rights ordinance in 1991.

### The Politics of Amendment 2

By 1991 religious conservatives in Colorado were becoming increasingly disturbed by the policy victories the LGBT movement had achieved across the state. But the event that appears to have triggered the mobilization of religious conservatives was Denver's reenactment of an antidiscrimination law through its city council in October 1990. Religious conservatives quickly collected enough signatures to place a measure on the May 1991 ballot that would repeal the new city ordinance. Through the urging of LGBT activists, many social and political leaders opposed the repeal measure and it was successfully defeated 55 to 45 percent.

With a defeat in Denver and victory in Colorado Springs, religious conservatives began to assess their tactics. A number of conservative activists started meeting in Colorado Springs in 1991 and soon formed an organization called Colorado for Family Values (CFV) to sponsor a statewide ballot initiative (Amendment 2) that would repeal all sexual orientation antidiscrimination policies in the state and ban the passage of any new related policies.

Facing a well-organized and well-funded movement, LGBT groups within the state were unable to block Amendment 2 from reaching the ballot or stop its eventual passage. Hindering the efforts of LGBT activists was the fact that no statewide LGBT political group was active in Colorado. The strongest group was Denver-based Equal Protection, which had successfully defeated the attempt to repeal Denver's new gay rights ordinance. Although Equal Protection seemed the obvious choice too lead the efforts against Amendment 2, smaller LGBT groups from around the state wanted to form a broader grassroots coalition to fight the measure. Equal Protection assumed control of the campaign, but subsequent divisions hindered the efforts against Amendment 2, which passed with almost 54 percent voter support in November 1992.

Following the vote, many new LGBT groups formed and this coalition initiated a successful, but painful economic boycott of Colorado. Furthermore, LGBT legal groups successfully fought Amendment 2 in court, first gaining a state court injunction in December 1993, and eventually seeing the measure overturned by the U.S. Supreme Court in May 1996. In that case, known as *Romer v. Evans,* the Court's 6-3 decision reasoned that the law would have unconstitutionally prevented homosexuals from using the political process to achieve policy goals.

## The Aftermath of Amendment 2

Amendment 2, the subsequent boycott, and the legal proceedings surrounding both brought unprecedented attention to the Colorado LGBT movement. This attention helped to mobilize the LGBT community for political action. The group Equal Protection transformed itself in 1993 into a statewide group called Equality Colorado (later changed to Equal Rights Colorado); chapters of national LGBT groups, such as the Log Cabin Republicans and Parents, Families, and Friends of Lesbians and Gays, were established in the state; and a major new philanthropic foundation focusing on LGBT issues, the Gill Foundation, was established in 1996.

In the public policy arena, throughout the 1990s and early 2000s state and local officials in Colorado continued to debate LGBT policy proposals. A number of local governments adopted antidiscrimination policies and some, such as in Denver, also adopted policies to benefit the domestic partners of public employees. However, even as the strength of LGBT groups grew in the state, LGBT rights continued to be defeated in local ballot contests, including in Fort Collins in 1998 and Greeley in 1999, and the Colorado legislature failed to pass any significant legislation to protect the rights of LGBT citizens in the state.

By the start of the new millennium, LGBT service centers and support groups had sprung up in every corner of the state. Increasingly these organizations have begun to serve the diverse needs of the LGBT community, by focusing on, among other things, issues relating to LGBT youth, hate crime victim assistance, LGBT parenting and adoption issues, racial and ethnic diversity within the LGBT community, and the fuller inclusion of the transgender and transsexual communities.

Nonetheless, despite the fact that LGBT groups in Colorado are fairly strong relative to other states, and that the number of lesbian and gay households with committed relationships is relatively high, public support for LGBT rights is fairly low and policy protections for LGBT people are relatively weak in comparison to other states. Thus, although the LGBT movement in Colorado was transformed during the 1990s, the policy successes of the movement are still few relative to other parts of the country.

## Bibliography

Adam, Barry D. *The Rise of a Gay and Lesbian Movement.* Revised edition. New York: Twayne, 1995.

Bernstein, Mary. "Celebration and Suppression: The Strategic Uses of Identity by the Lesbian and Gay Movement." *American Journal of Sociology* 103 (1997): 531–565.

Gallagher, John, and Chris Bull. *Perfect Enemies: The Religious Right, the Gay Movement, and the Politics of the 1990s.* New York: Crown, 1996.

Gilmartin, Katie. "'The Very House of Difference': Intersection of Identities in the Life Histories of Colorado Lesbians, 1940–1965." Ph.D. dissertation, Yale University, New Haven, Conn., 1995.

Haider-Markel, Donald P. "Lesbian and Gay Politics in the States: Interest Groups, Electoral Politics, and Public Policy." In *The Politics of Gay Rights.* Edited by Craig A. Rimmerman, Kenneth D. Wald, and Clyde Wilcox. Chicago: University of Chicago Press, 2000.

Haider-Markel, Donald P., and Kenneth J. Meier. "The Politics of Gay and Lesbian Rights: Expanding the Scope of the Conflict." *Journal of Politics* 58 (1996): 352–369.

Katz, Jonathan. *Gay/Lesbian Almanac: A New Documentary.* New York: Harper and Row, 1983.

Keen, Lisa. "By the Books: D.C. Ranks Second in Survey of States Treatment of Gays." *Washington Blade,* 9 November 2001, p. 1.

Lewis, Gregory B., and Jonathan L. Edelson. "DOMA and ENDA: Congress Votes on Gay Rights." In *The Politics of Gay Rights.* Edited by Kenneth D. Wald, Craig A. Rimmerman, and Clyde Wilcox. Chicago: University of Chicago Press, 2000.

Padilla, Liz. "A Proud yet Divisive History." *Daily Camera,* 25 July 1997, p. A5.

Stroh, Tony. "Immigration Law Test: Male Couple Married outside Clerk's Office." *Daily Camera,* 22 April 1975, p. A12.

**Donald P. Haider-Markel**

*See also* BOYCOTTS; NAVRATILOVA, MARTINA.

# COMBAHEE RIVER COLLECTIVE

The Combahee River Collective (CRC), a Boston-based support and action group of black feminists, formed in 1974 after a few activists discovered one another at the first regional meeting of the National Black Feminist Organization in New York City in 1973. Its name "came from the guerrilla action conceptualized and led by Harriet Tubman on June 2, 1863 in the Port Royal region of South Carolina. This action freed more than 750 slaves and is the only military campaign in American history planned and led by a woman" (Smith, p. 272). The CRC's initiatives included consciousness-raising, the promotion of abortion rights, efforts to combat violence against women, and coalition-building around other social justice issues.

In existence from 1974 to 1980, the CRC was extremely influential in second wave feminism. The unstructured group had as many as three hundred loosely affiliated members over its lifetime. However, the central document the collective created, which is now a cornerstone of feminist theory, was written by a small core group, including Barbara Smith, considered by many to be the first black feminist literary critic; her twin sister, Beverly Smith; and Demita Frazier. Its formal title, "The Combahee River Collective Statement: A Black Feminist Statement," is often shortened to "The Combahee Statement" or "A Black Feminist Statement," while the group itself is frequently referred to as "Combahee." Striving to equalize decision making and therefore equalize power within the group, Combahee used insights (positive and negative) gained through experiences within both the civil rights and women's movements. It embraced both movements but also squarely critiqued them: the civil rights movement was fundamentally patriarchal in structure and power, and the women's movement principally driven by the concerns of white, middle-class women. In so doing, the collective established a beachhead from which to launch its bold "Statement," challenging both male domination and white supremacy.

The "Black Feminist Statement," which remains an essential theoretical text within college and university women's studies courses a quarter of a century after its initial appearance in 1978, addresses black women's distinct "quadruple vision." The authors take a sharply focused look at themselves, evaluating their own ideas and commitment to politics; their social position and condition in relation to men, both white and black; their relationship to white women in the women's movement; and the rejection they sometimes experience at the hands of nonfeminist black women who support patriarchy and discriminate against lesbians, who made up a large percentage of Combahee members and the women's movement in general.

The "simultaneity of oppression" theory, first expressed within the "Combahee River Collective Statement," has become standard shorthand for referring to a well recognized phenomenon. It addresses the experience of being black, being female, being poor, and being lesbian. It contends that black men endure racial oppression, white women endure oppression related to their gender, and lesbians endure oppression related to their sexual orientation. Black women are triply oppressed by race, sex, and class—and in the case of black lesbians, that oppression is further compounded. This theory allows any group that suffers the effects of more than one form of oppression to claim simultaneous oppression, and as a result additional kinds of oppression, such as those related to age, disability, or body size, have been taken into account. The "simultaneous oppression" theory is applied so widely now, and in so many ways, that its origin is generally unknown to the majority of its users.

The "Combahee River Collective Statement" or "Black Feminist Statement" is divided into four sections. The first, "The Genesis of Contemporary Black Feminism," begins by describing the involvement of black women, including Sojourner Truth (1797–1883) and Mary Church Terrell (1863–1954), in first wave feminism. It then discusses the role of black women within second wave feminism, addressing their involvement in other liberation movements such as the civil rights struggle, the Black Panthers, and black nationalism—and their subsequent disillusionment over their treatment within those movements. It also describes the consciousness-raising that led to black women's feminist beliefs once they began collectively analyzing sexual politics, patriarchal rule, and "feminism, the political practice that we women use to struggle against our oppression" (Hull et al., p. 15).

The second section, "What We Believe," addresses Combahee's belief that a healthy love for "ourselves, our sisters, our community . . . allows us to continue our struggle and work" (p. 16). Black women are the only ones who care enough about their own liberation to fight for it: "The most profound and potentially the most radical politics come directly out of our own oppression as opposed to working to end somebody else's oppression" (p. 16). According to Combahee, black women have always been self-sufficient, which is why nobody else has consistently worked for their freedom. The members of Combahee are socialists who believe in the distribution of material resources among those who manufacture those resources. Although they are feminists and lesbians, they reject the stance of lesbian separatism, preferring instead to work in "solidarity with progressive Black men" (p. 16). They refuse to believe in a biological determinism that causes men to be sexist, finding such a notion "a particularly dangerous and reactionary basis upon which to base a politic" (p. 17). Sexism, rather than being biologically determined, is socially learned behavior.

The third section of the Statement, "Problems in Organizing Black Feminists," addresses the obstacles Combahee faced in organizing, including the difficulty of even announcing "in certain contexts that we *are* Black feminists" (p. 18). Black women are at the bottom of the social hierarchy and would benefit from feminism, but "the reaction of Black men to feminism has been notoriously negative," and, since most black women are heterosexual, "accusations that Black feminism divides the Black struggle are powerful deterrents to the growth of an autonomous Black women's movement" (p. 19). In order to demonstrate "the reality of [their] politics to other Black women," as well as "reach other Black feminists living in isolation all over the country," the CRC stated its intention to write and to widely distribute its work, and also to continue political action in coalition with other groups.

The fourth section, "Black Feminist Issues and Practice," traces the history of the CRC and speculates on its future as a group, claiming a particular commitment to "working on those struggles in which race, sex and class are simultaneous factors in oppression" (p. 21). Expressing a belief in "collective process and a nonhierarchical distribution of power within our own group and in our vision of a revolutionary society," the authors commit themselves to "a continual examination of our politics as they develop through criticism and self-criticism as an essential aspect of our practice" (pp. 21–22).

Two years after the publication of "The Combahee River Collective Statement," the group dissolved, but its influence continues to be felt.

### Bibliography

Combahee River Collective. "A Black Feminist Statement." In *All the Women Are White, All the Blacks Are Men, but Some of Us Are Brave.* Edited by Gloria Hull, Patricia Bell Scott, and Barbara Smith. Old Westbury, N.Y.: Feminist Press, 1982.

Hull, Gloria, Patricia Bell Scott, and Barbara Smith, eds. *All the Women Are White, All the Blacks Are Men, but Some of Us Are Brave.* Old Westbury, N.Y.: Feminist Press, 1982.

Smith, Barbara, ed. *Home Girls: A Black Feminist Anthology.* New York: Kitchen Table: Women of Color Press, 1983.

Springer, Kimberly. "The Interstitial Politics of Black Feminist Organizations." *Meridians: Feminism, Race, Transnationalism* 1, no. 2 (Spring 2001): 155–191.

**Angela Bowen**

*See also* BOSTON; FEMINISM; LESBIAN FEMINISM; SMITH, BARBARA.

# COMEDY AND HUMOR

Laughter, satire, and camp have long been part of LGBT life in America. Even during the 1969 Stonewall riots—a militant, angry protest if ever there was one—several participants found time to form a kick-line and sing a satiric song to the tune of "Ta-Ra-Ra-Boom-Dee-Ay." On a more organized level, LGBT wit has been expressed over the years through both performance and printed humor.

## In Performance

LGBT comedy in America dates back to the late nineteenth century, when sexual-minority saloons and dance halls began to appear in major cities. Since then, lesbian and gay comedians, in particular, have become increasingly visible, both in "queer" venues and in the mainstream media. Openly bisexual comedians, by contrast, have attained relatively little visibility. Transgender comedy has always been visible, but in very narrow forms: typically in performances marked as gay or straight drag. Comedy performances by and about transsexual people remain practically unheard of, except at events sponsored by transgender organizations or in edgy, alternative performance spaces.

Many of the earliest sexual-minority comedians, circa 1900, were cross-dressed waiters and waitresses in LGBT-friendly saloons. They filled their downtime by entertaining customers with comic quips and songs that ranged from whimsical to raunchy. Similar acts sometimes appeared in queer friendly dance halls: either formal performances by the staff or impromptu entertainment by customers. Performers were known primarily by regulars in the places where they performed. They only reached a crossover audience when a thrill-seeking straight tourist decided to go "slumming" in disreputable night spots.

During Prohibition in the 1920s, some big-city and resort-town speakeasies with largely LGBT clientele featured overtly lesbian or gay comedians. Several comedians who honed their acts in queer-friendly 1920s speakeasies found success performing gay material in predominantly straight nightclubs. Examples included the camp comedian Jean Malin, a former drag comic who served as emcee at the Club Abbey in New York's Times Square district. Malin, who also performed in California, acknowledged his homosexuality both in his act and in interviews. Another crossover performer was the brash, tuxedoed Gladys Bentley, known for her ribald rewrites of popular songs. She performed in gay and straight venues in several cities, but apparently never recorded any of her lesbian-specific material. The popular drag comedian Ray (or Rae) Bourbon, who broke into vaudeville in the 1920s, made GBT humor a staple of his underground records for decades. On a 1940s 78 RPM disc, Bourbon boasted that despite his feminine stage persona, he was a real "man's man." "*I was in the navy!*" he proclaimed. After a coy giggle, he added: "Or vice versa."

By the mid-twentieth century, the fad of "queer" comics in straight clubs was over. To be sure, celebrity transsexual Christine Jorgensen's managers made a brief, unsuccessful attempt to turn her into a comedian, but her performances at mainstream nightclubs were quickly reworked when it became clear that spinning a joke was not her strong suit. In the 1950s and 1960s, sexual-minority comedians were mostly minor, local celebrities. Bars were a primary outlet for LGBT socializing, and so the regular entertainers at the bars were often central figures for a given city's sexual-minority community. Some of these performers are still remembered a half-century later. Examples include San Franciscan José Sarria, who mixed political humor with drag operatic satires at the legendary Black Cat Café. The writer Lisa Ben occasionally performed in Los Angeles clubs. Her act mixed serious songs with same-sex sendups of popular tunes, such as "I'm Gonna Sit Right Down and Write My Butch a Letter." Every city had its own personalities.

Such up-front comedy stood in stark contrast to the coy, semicloseted humor of certain gay male performers in the mass media in the 1960s and early 1970s. Examples include the comedian Paul Lynde, who appeared regularly on television sitcoms and the game show *Hollywood Squares*. Some comics, like Alan Sues of the television series *Laugh-In*, did play obviously gay comic roles on television, but it was comedy *about* gay people written largely *by* and *for* straight people. The mainstream visibility of Lynde and Sues—and, less often, drag performers like Michael Greer and Charles Pierce—was important. However, the necessarily reined-in material they presented on television was very different from the unapologetic LGBT comedy that they or others could practice in the era's sexual-minority venues.

Gay-themed comic theater productions, phonograph records, and films began to flourish in the 1970s, as lesbian and gay issues gained more attention in the mainstream media. Comedies such as Terrence McNally's 1984 *The Ritz* (later made into a movie) entertained gay and straight audiences alike. During the same period, gay-focused comedy records began to appear. Some were by presumably straight comedians (such as Sandy Baron's 1972 *God Save the Queens*) while others included political humor by LGBT people. Records in the latter category include the 1977 album *Out of the Closet*, coauthored by future celebrity gag writer Bruce Vilanch. The comedian Robin Tyler began including lesbian material on her albums in 1978, with the release of *Always a Bridesmaid, Never a Groom*. Humorous films also grew out of the push for LGBT equality and visibility, including such shorts as 1977's *Rollin' with Love* (with animated tennis balls acting out scenes from gay life) and *Altered Habits* (featuring the Sisters of Perpetual Indulgence) in the early eighties. The trend toward filmed LGBT comedy skyrocketed several years later, with the rise of a movement initially known as New Gay Cinema.

Mainstream comedy clubs proliferated across America in the 1970s and 1980s. At the same time, a smaller LGBT comedy scene was developing alongside it, especially in New York and San Francisco. A few pioneering comics—most notably the out-and-proud Tyler—performed gay material in predominantly straight clubs. This, however, was not yet a widespread practice. As in the past, most openly "queer" comics were performing for sexual-minority audiences. At least they had an advantage over their predecessors. By the late 1970s, there were countless sexual-minority periodicals, events, and organizations that could publicize their acts, making it easier to get gigs outside of their home cities.

By 1982, when the Valencia Rose performance space in San Francisco began holding a weekly lesbian and gay comedy night, the trend toward gay comedy performers was gaining visibility. In August 1982, the *Advocate* ran two stories, one about New York and one on San Francisco, highlighting LGB comedians such as Gothan and The Debbies, Tyler ("North America's premiere lesbian standup comic"), the drag artiste Ruby Rims, and the openly bisexual comic Jim Morris. Much of the San Francisco article focused on Valencia Rose, a proving ground for such future prominent performers as Tom Ammiano and Lea Delaria. Around the same time, a lesbian English teacher, Kate Clinton, began performing her pointedly witty political humor in clubs and theaters.

In the 1980s and 1990s, even more venues became available as LGBT organizations at colleges and universities began to sponsor conferences and awareness weeks, for which they needed speakers and performers. The singer, songwriter, and wit Lynn Lavner and the singing comedy duo of Romanovsky and Phillips made the most of the burgeoning gay and lesbian college circuit, while continuing to perform at other LGBT cultural and community events. Other performers sought still less traditional venues for gay humor. In 1988, Jaffe Cohen, Bob Smith, and Danny McWilliams combined their three standup acts into an evening-long program called Funny Gay Males, which they booked into theaters and comedy clubs around the country. There were also sketch-comedy troupes like Pomo Afro Homos, who got their start in 1991 at Josie's Cabaret and Juice Joint, a popular San Francisco club that was an unofficial successor to the Valencia Rose. In 1993, a prominent mainstream comedy club—the Comedy Store, in Los Angeles—instituted a Gay and Lesbian Comedy Night.

Since the early 1990s, it has been increasingly possible for out-and-proud comedians to appear on television and include LGBT references in their acts. In 1990, the cable television channel HA! gave the openly gay comic Frank Maya his own standup special, and the same year Jaffe Cohen made a groundbreaking appearance on the Fox network's *Comic Strip Live*, performing a routine about growing up gay. Perhaps the biggest breakthroughs in national visibility came in the early to mid-1990s. The Comedy Central cable television channel presented three annual hour-long lesbian and gay standup specials under the umbrella title *Out There* in 1993, 1994, and 1995, and HBO gave half-hour specials to Suzanne Westenhoefer and Bob Smith in 1994. As Delaria noted in advance publicity for the first *Out There* special (which she emceed), it was a nice change to see gay people telling the jokes rather than being the butt of them.

Around the mid-1990s, mainstream television programs such as the *Tonight Show* and the *Arsenio Hall Show* began to feature openly lesbian and gay comedians, who were often there to promote cable specials. Indeed, by 1994, the public visibility of "queer" comedians had grown to the point where ABC's prime-time newsmagazine show *Day One* could devote an entire report to the phenomenon. The growth of sexual-minority-specific television series, such as the public television newsmagazine *In The Life*, provided still more national (if niche market) publicity for comedians. Television visibility and news reports about that visibility boosted sales of such comedians' books and CDs, thus making LGBT standup comedy a more viable profession. Harvey Fierstein—a wit if not primarily a comedian—also became a frequent guest on "straight" talk shows, where he talked about gay issues. The film critic Frank DeCaro's snippy, campy "Out at the Movies" segment was a regular feature on Comedy Central's *The Daily Show* throughout the late 1990s.

Almost certainly, the United States' most famous out-of-the-closet comedian in the late twentieth century was Ellen DeGeneres, though her comedy was not predominantly gay-focused. She came out publicly in 1997 and began to incorporate same-sex material into her television sitcoms and, later, occasionally, into her stage act. In 2003, she became the first openly gay host of a nationally syndicated talk show. Since DeGeneres's coming out, other television sitcoms have also focused on gay leading roles. The most notable example is NBC's *Will & Grace*, which premiered in 1998 and was cocreated by a gay man and his straight male writing partner.

## Printed Humor

Cartooning and comic strips were among the earliest and most enduring forms of published LGBT humor. Satiric drawings had appeared occasionally in homophile magazines as early as the 1950s, but the first known ongoing American gay comic strip was A. Jay's spy spoof "Harry Chess, That Man from A.U.N.T.I.E." It lasted eight years, premiering in *Drum* in 1964 and moving to *Queens Quarterly* in 1969 after *Drum* folded. Joe Johnson's "Miss Thing" ran in the *Advocate* in the early 1970s, as did the work of other comic artists. *Christopher Street* magazine, which debuted in 1976, became known for its witty, *New Yorker*–esque one-panel cartoons. These were collected into paperback books with titles such as *Relax! This Book Is Only a Phase You're Going Through* (1978, edited by Charles Ortleb and Richard Fiala). A 1978 paperback also collected risqué comics from the erotic magazine *In Touch for Men*.

In 1974, the cartoonist Mary Wings issued what is generally considered the first lesbian comic book: *Come Out Comix*, which she followed in 1978 with *Dyke Shorts*. Several successful lesbian cartoonists have cited Wings as a strong influence on their work. The most widely available gay comic book series of the 1980s and 1990s was *Gay Comix*, which debuted in 1980 under the editorship of Howard Cruse (whose popular "Wendel" comic strip ran in the *Advocate* from 1983 to 1989). *Gay Comix* was not always comical—it sometimes featured more serious works by lesbian and gay graphic artists—but most issues included much humor. With the explosion of LGBT periodicals in the 1980s, sexual-minority cartoonists found a growing market for their work. Comic strips of the 1980s that appeared in national magazines or were syndicated nationally included Alison Bechdel's long-running "Dykes to Watch Out For," Gerard P. Donelan's "It's a Gay Life," N. Leigh Dunlap's "Morgan Calabrese," Eric Orner's

"The Mostly Unfabulous Social Life of Ethan Green," Rupert Kinnard's "B.B. and the Diva," and Andrea Natalie's one-panel "Stonewall Riots." Successors to these pioneering works include Joan Hilty's "Bitter Girl" and Dave Brousseau's "A Couple of Guys."

The first truly "queer" comic novel to reach the bestseller lists was probably *Myra Breckinridge*, a controversial satire about a male-to-female transsexual, written in 1968 by the "homosexualist" author Gore Vidal. However, even before then, some small publishing houses had issued limited-run humorous paperbacks aimed at gay male readers. Although not pornographic, they were often sold through sex shops and adult book stores. A typical example is Don Holliday's gay espionage parody *The Man from C.A.M.P.*, published in 1966 by the San Diego-based Corinth Publications.

In the 1970s, major publishing houses issued a growing number of witty books by and about sexual-minority people. Rita Mae Brown's *Rubyfruit Jungle*, originally published by a small feminist press in 1973, was later reissued in several editions by mainstream publishers. Armistead Maupin's San Francisco newspaper serial "Tales of the City" became a Harper & Row novel in 1978, followed by five sequels. Countless gay comic novels have been published in the United States since then.

Narrative fiction is just one outlet for comic prose. Satirical essays appeared in LGBT publications from the mid–twentieth century on. At least one such article resulted in legal action: in 1981, John Zeh, the host of a gay radio show in Cincinnati, was charged with disseminating obscene matter to juveniles when he read his listeners a comical newspaper article about sexual lubricants. A judge dismissed the case.

Gay and mainstream publishing houses alike issued gay humor books in the 1980s, most of them aimed at gay men (whom business publications were touting as a lucrative market with "disposable income"). Examples include Clark Henley's *The Butch Manual* (1982), Daniel Curzon's *The Joyful Blue Book of Gracious Gay Etiquette* (1982), and Tony Lang's *The Gay Cliché; or, How to be a Homosexual Guy and Still Maintain Some Slight Degree of Individuality* (1985). In the 1990s, when the fight for gay equality was saturating the news, publishing houses issued ever more volumes of sexual-minority humor. Many were by humorists the public knew from their radio or television appearances or their columns in LGBT periodicals. The autobiographical essays in David Sedaris's books take his gayness for granted, neither obsessing on it nor downplaying it. Yvonne Zipter's tongue-in-cheek newspaper columns were supplemented by new material for her 1995 book *Ransacking the Closet*. Books by such varied performers as the Five Lesbian Brothers, the Funny Gay Males, Scott Thompson, and Lea Delaria have appeared since the mid-1990s. The humor of numerous prominent LGBT comedians was collected in the books *Out Loud and Laughing* (1995) and *A Funny Time to Be Gay* (1997). Humorous books since the 1990s include Kevin Dilallo and Jack Krumholtz's *The Unofficial Gay Manual: Living the Lifestyle or at Least Appearing To* (1994). Helen Eisenbach's *Lesbianism Made Easy* (1996), Joel Perry's *Funny That Way: Adventures in Fabulousness* (2000), and Sedaris's *Me Talk Pretty One Day* (2000).

## Bibliography

Chauncey, George. *Gay New York: Gender, Urban Culture, and the Makings of the Gay Male World, 1890–1940*. New York: Basic Books, 1994.

Flowers, Charles, ed. *Out, Loud, and Laughing: A Collection of Gay and Lesbian Humor*. New York: Anchor Books, 1995.

Guthmann, Edward. "Humor Is Still the Best Medicine in San Francisco." *Advocate*, 19 August 1982, pp. 45–46.

Karvoski, Ed, Jr., comp. *A Funny Time to Be Gay*. New York: Fireside, 1997.

Saslow, James M. "There's Something Gay to Smile About in New York." *Advocate*, 19 August 1982, pp. 45–46.

Triptow, Robert, ed. *Gay Comics: The Smartest and Wittiest Gay and Lesbian Cartoonists*. New York: New American Library, 1989.

**Steven Capsuto**

*See also* BEN, LISA; BENTLEY, GLADYS; BOURBON, RAY (RAE); BROWN, RITA MAE; FIERSTEIN, HARVEY; JORGENSEN, CHRISTINE; MAUPIN, ARMISTEAD; MCNALLY, TERRENCE; SARRIA, JOSÉ; TELEVISION; VIDAL, GORE.

# COMICS AND COMIC BOOKS

When discussing LGBT comics, two names spring instantly to mind. One is Howard Cruse, who has had a very lengthy history in LGBT comics. Cruse had a strip in the 1970s called *Barefootz*, in which he created one of the first out gay characters in comics. Cruse founded *Gay Comix* in 1980 and was its first editor. He published a series of strips in the *Advocate* from 1983 to 1989 (with a hiatus in 1985), as well as book collections based on a character named Wendel Trupstock (and his very extended family). He is perhaps best known for his 1995 book *Stuck Rubber Baby*, which combines civil rights and gay rights content in telling the story of Toland Polk, who is living in the South as a gay white man during the 1960s. Cruse discusses race and ethnicity through varied characters, including Les Pepper, a young man trying to find the balance between religion, race, and sexuality. Cruse paved the way for many other LGBT cartoonists, such as Tim Barela, whose own continuing series, *Leonard and Larry,* begun in 1984, first appeared in *Gay Comix.*

The other "elder statesman" of LGBT comics is undoubtedly Alison Bechdel, whose strip *Dykes to Watch Out For* is perhaps the most recognized and widely read LGBT comic published today. It is currently syndicated in over seventy publications throughout North America and has been translated into dozens of languages. First published in the June 1983 issue of *WomaNews* and self-syndicated in 1985, Bechdel's strip deftly skewers world politics and simultaneously represents the diversity of queer life, including characters of nearly every ethnicity, background, class, education, and gender. She has expanded the scope of the strip far beyond its title to include a heterosexual white man and a female-to-male gay man. Bechdel has published nine collections of her work and won numerous accolades (including multiple Lambda Literary Awards for Humor and Vice Versa Awards for Excellence in the Gay and Lesbian Press). Her work is widely anthologized and has appeared in *Out, Advocate, Ms, Dyke Strippers, Gay Community News,* and *American Splendor,* to name just a few. However, many do not know that in 1988 Bechdel created a strip, *Servants to the Cause,* about the staff of a LGBT newspaper, which appeared in the *Advocate* for just under two years and is collected in the all-Bechdel issue of *Gay Comics* (#19).

## History

Arguably, LGBT characters have been in comics for as long as comics have existed, but many, like those in Alan Moore and Dave Gibbons's *Watchmen,* published in the mid-1980s, were only a backdrop to the book's primary action. During the days of comics prior to the Stonewall Riots in 1969, those portrayals were generally negative or cursory, though a cartoonist named Blade reportedly had gay pornographic material circulating in the underground during the heyday of comic books in America prior to World War II. But openly positive LGBT characters did not prominently appear in comics until after the Stonewall Riots. The effect of that event on comics (as on the rest of the homophile movement) was long lasting enough so that Andrea Natalie named a series of hers *Stonewall Riots* in 1989. LGBT comics (initially often spelled "comix" to indicate their difference from mainstream comics as well as their more adult "X" content) were first found in underground comic books. These were self-published or printed and distributed by small-press publishers, in contrast to the then-bland mass-

market comic books. In this period, many anthologies (like *Wimmin's Comix* and *All Atomic Comics)* took up political issues. It is logical that gay comix followed. Underground comix prior to 1976 had of course made mention of LGB (if not yet trans) issues, like Lee Marrs's *Pudge, Girl Blimp.* Lee Marrs helped start the Wimmin's Comix Collective, which was founded in 1972 and is widely considered the birthplace of lesbian comics.

A. Jay's character Harry Chess appeared in the gay magazine *Drum* during the mid-1960s. The first gay male comic book series, *Gay Heartthrobs,* appeared in 1976. Mary Wings (who subsequently wrote lesbian detective novels) published the first lesbian underground comic in 1973, titled simply *Come Out Comix.* She created it as a reaction to Trina Robbins's story "Sandy Comes Out" in the first issue of *Wimmin's Comix.* Robbins is one of the most widely known figures in American underground comics history, and she created the first all-women comic book, *It Ain't Me, Babe,* published by Last Gasp in 1970. The year 1976 saw the publication of Roberta Gregory's *Dynamite Damsels* (only the second openly lesbian comic book) and the outing of Headrack, a character created by gay comix pioneer Howard Cruse in *Barefootz Funnies* #2.

Roberta Gregory also found herself influenced by early issues of *Wimmin's Comix,* publishing "A Modern Romance" in #4 in 1974. Mary Wings self-published *Dyke Shorts* in 1978, and Cruse began the still-running anthology *Gay Comix* in 1980. When Cruse left after four issues, Robert Triptow took the helm until #14, when Andy Mangels stepped in. (The title changed with #15 to the more conventionally spelled *Gay Comics).* Triptow, along with Robert Sienkiewicz and Trina Robbins, edited *Strip AIDS USA* in 1988, and he published a book history of LGBT cartoonists, titled *Gay Comics,* the following year. Each year Andy Mangels organizes the *Out in Comics* panel for Comic Con International in San Diego, first published in 1999. He is a prolific cross-genre writer. Prism Comics cited him as a direct influence on its decision to found an organization to promote LGBT folks in the industry. In addition to her multiple book projects, Roberta Gregory has published more than thirty issues of her comic book *Naughty Bits* (begun in 1991) and appeared in all but six of the twenty-five issues of *Gay Comics.*

As the 1980s progressed, LGBT characters continued to appear in titles as diverse as Wendy and Richard Pini's *Elfquest* and the Hernandez brothers' *Love and Rockets* (which prominently featured a lesbian couple named Maggie and Hopey). In 1986, Leyland Publications began issuing a series of book-length anthologies called *Meatmen,* and Robert Kirby published *Curbside* in 1998, followed in 2002 by a second collection, *Curbside Boys,* with the well-known LGBT publishing house Cleis Press. Kirby also created two queer comics anthologies: *Strange-Looking Exile: The All-Cartoon Zine For Queer Dudes 'n Babes* (published by Diane DiMassa's Giant Ass Press) and *Boy Trouble* (with David Kelly). DiMassa is the creator and publisher of *Hothead Paisan: Homicidal Lesbian Terrorist,* which is often termed a "comics-zine" (because of DiMassa's choice to self-publish and distribute). Besides the first twenty issues, there are also two anthologies (and one collection of over four hundred pages) published by Cleis Press.

The 1980s also saw the rise of the HIV/AIDS pandemic. Jerry Mills, creator of the strip *Poppers* (started in 1982), penned a short history of gays in comics for the first *Meatmen* collection and printed his strip as health would allow; Mills died 28 January 1993 of complications from HIV. In 1996, DC Vertigo (a small division within a large mass-market publisher developed in order to publish comics aimed for a non-child readership) released David Wojnarowicz and James Romberger's *Seven Miles a Second,* completed after Wojnarowicz's AIDS-related death in 1992. In 2001 an autobiographical account by Judd Winick of the friendship between himself and Pedro Zamora—who died of AIDS in 1994—called *Pedro and Me* (2000) won an Outstanding Comic Award from the Gay and Lesbian Alliance Against Defamation (GLAAD) and was nominated for an Eisner Award. Winick went on to work in mainstream titles, namely DC Comics' *Green Lantern* and Marvel's *Exiles.* Angela Bocage, creator and editor of *Real Girl* (billed as a comic anthology for all genders and all orientations) has long been an outspoken AIDS activist and critic of the public health care system.

### Mass-Market Comic Books

Marvel's Northstar came out in *Alpha Flight* #106 in 1992 in the midst of an AIDS-related storyline, officially making him the first out gay superhero. He had his own four-issue spin-off series from April to July 1994, which complicates Marvel's recent claim that *The Rawhide Kid* is the first openly gay title character. There is also Go-Go Fiasco, sidekick of secret agent Angela St. Grace, in DC Vertigo's *Codename: Knockout* series, created by Robert Rodi. Prior to that, in the late 1980s, John Byrne wrote a lesbian police captain—Maggie Sawyer—into *Superman.* Image Comics' *Gen 13* series included Sarah Rainmaker, a lesbian Native American character, in 1994. LGBT characters have appeared in other prominent mass market books, including *The X-Men, X-Force, The Incredible Hulk,* and *Legion of Super-Heroes.* DC's *The Authority* included the first openly gay couple in mass-market

comics; *Green Lantern* has the out lesbian duo Lee and Li, and many have read *Batman*'s Riddler and the Joker as gay. That is not surprising, since many people—the two most widely divergent being Fredric Wertham, the Joe McCarthy of comic books during the 1950s, and more recently, cultural critic Andy Medhurst in the widely reprinted "Batman, Deviance, and Camp"—see Batman and Robin as gay and Wonder Woman as lesbian. Machinesmith (from *Daredevil*) and Pied Piper (*The Flash*) are gay. Ivan Velez Jr. worked on *Ghost Rider* for Marvel, but is better known for *Tales of the Closet. Ghost Rider* and *Captain America* included gay story arcs, and Peter David wrote a *Supergirl* story line that drew favorable response from GLAAD.

### Recent Comics

The number of LGBT independent comics since 1990 has increased rapidly, with works like Kris Dresen's *Max and Lily,* Sean Bieri's *Cool Jerk* and *Homo Gal,* and Carrie McNinch's *The Assassin and the Whiner.* In the early 1990s, Donna Barr began a series, the *Desert Peach,* detailing the life of Erwin Rommel's fictional gay brother. Also notable are strips like the long-running internationally syndicated *For Better or Worse,* by Lynn Johnston, which recently featured a gay male coming-out story, and Rupert Kinnard's characters the Brown Bomber and Diva Touché Flambé, who were the first out LGBT African American superheroes. Sick of comix pornography, a staple in some gay male comics, some LBT women began to create comix erotica for women, notably Colleen Coover's *Small Favors,* Ellen Forney's *Tomato* (which includes the bisexual character Birdie), and Molly Kiely's *Diary of A Dominatrix.*

Other notable LGBT cartoonists are Paige Braddock, Eric Orner, Jackie Urbanovic, P. Craig Russell, Jennifer Camper, and Leslie Ewing. Joan Hilty, an editor for DC Vertigo, produces a strip called *Bitter Girl* published on PlanetOut.com. Terry Moore published *Strangers in Paradise,* which featured a bisexual lead character, and Reed Waller and Kate Worley of *Omaha, The Cat Dancer* outed themselves as the first out bisexual comics creators in 1988. Like Bob Fingerman, Waller and Worley have included characters of all identities in their comics. The award-winning *Sandman* series by Neil Gaiman (which P. Craig Russell worked on for a time) has long been a prominent LGBT ally; it presented one of the first trans characters in comics—Wanda, from *A Game of You.* Trans comics are not as established as LGB comics, but they include the online comic *T-Gina* by Gina Kamentsky at T-Gina.com and Diana Green's comic strip *Tranny Towers,* which began in 1995 and ran for over a year.

**Bibliography**

"Dykes to Watch Out for—The Definitive Website. Available from http://www.dykestowatchoutfor.net.

"The Gay Comics List." Available from http://gaycomicslist .free.fr.

Medhurst, Andy. "Batman, Deviance, and Camp." In *The Many Lives of Batman: Critical Approaches to a Superhero and His Media.* Edited by Roberta E. Pearson. New York. Routledge, 1991.

Sabin, Roger. *Comics, Comix, and Graphic Novels.* London: Phaidon Press, 1996.

Warren, Roz, ed. *Dyke Strippers: Lesbian Cartoonists A to Z.* San Francisco: Cleis Press, 1995.

**Anne N. Thalheimer**

See also ADVOCATE; DRUM; NEWSPAPERS AND MAGAZINES.

# COMING OUT AND OUTING

In LGBT contexts, the term "coming out" generally refers to the process of disclosing one's identity as LGBT to one's self, to other LGBT people, and to others. "Outing" refers to the process of disclosing someone else's identity as LGBT, usually against their wishes. Although LGBT people often talk about being "out" as an all or nothing thing, in practice most LGBT people are "out" in some contexts and not in others.

## Historical Notes

According to popular myth, LGBT people did not come out until the Stonewall Riots of 1969 inspired the development of the gay liberation movement. While this may have been true of the young people who joined the LGBT movement in the 1970s, those who embraced the myth made the common mistake of conflating their personal history with their community's history. John D'Emilio was among the first to challenge this myth, arguing in his 1983 book *Sexual Politics* that lesbians and gay men were not silent, invisible, or isolated in the pre-Stonewall era. According to D'Emilio, military mobilization during World War II, which threw millions of women and men into new homosocial and nonfamilial environments, "created something of a nationwide coming out experience." (p. 24) In his 1994 book *Gay New York*, George Chauncey similarly criticized the myths of "isolation, invisibility, and internalization," but his work turns back the "coming out" clock to the late nineteenth and early twentieth centuries, when large and complex LGB urban subcultures first developed in the United States (p. 2).

Chauncey also traces the origins of the gay meanings of "coming out": "Like much of campy gay terminology, 'coming out' was an arch play on the language of women's culture—in this case the expression used to refer to the ritual of a debutante's being formally introduced to, or 'coming out' into, the society of her cultural peers." According to Chauncey, gay men first used the expression "coming out" to refer to their formal presentation at the large drag balls held in various U.S. cities in the early twentieth century. He also emphasizes that until the 1960s gay men never referred to coming out *of* "the closet," but instead referred to coming out *into* "homosexual society" or the "gay world" (p. 7).

Over the course of the twentieth century, the phrase "coming out" migrated from debutante culture to LGBT culture, but it did not stop there. In the last several decades, "coming out" has come to refer to various disclosures of secrets, so that people now "come out" about all sorts of things, including food preferences, entertainment orientations, and racial, ethnic, and religious identities. It has also come to refer to any movement from private to public. In her 1990 book *Epistemology of the Closet*, Eve Kosofsky Sedgwick argues that "the 'closet' and 'coming out' now verg[e] on all-purpose phrases for the potent crossing and recrossing of almost any political charged lines of representation." She goes on to say that "a whole cluster of the most crucial sites for the contestation of meaning in twentieth-century Western culture," including sites related to "secrecy/disclosure" and "private/public," have been influenced by gay-inflected notions of "the closet" and "coming out" (p. 71–72).

## Class, Race, Sex, Gender, Age, and Context

Various scholars have emphasized that class, race, region, sex, gender, and age have all influenced the history and politics of coming out. Chauncey argues that in early twentieth-century New York working-class gay men generally were more "out" than middle-class gay men, in part because of the more public nature of working-class leisure and entertainment culture. Elizabeth Kennedy and Madeline Davis's 1993 book on midcentury Buffalo makes a similar point about working-class and middle-class lesbians. While scholars such as Eric Garber have suggested that African American lesbians and gay men during the Harlem Renaissance could be more "out" because their community was accepting of sexual difference, others have emphasized the sexual and gender conservatism of black cultures and the resulting difficulties of coming out. Many LGBT people of color in the United States have faced unique struggles related to coming out insofar as problems of racism (for example in employment and housing) can be exacerbated by problems of homophobia and transphobia. John Howard's 1999 study of twentieth-century gay life in Mississippi, which emphasizes the feigned ignorance that often characterized treatment of sexual and gender deviance in the rural south, suggests that region also affected coming out dynamics. In the context of debates about outing and the specific case of actress/director Jodie Foster in the 1990s, C. Carr calls attention to differences between the sexes: "Anyone who thinks . . . that a lesbian can proclaim her sexuality in an industry as male-centered as Hollywood, where even straight women have trouble getting work . . . has to be out of his fucking mind" (cited in Duggan, p. 161).

Carr's point, which refers specifically to employment and professional matters, points to the importance of context when considering the history and politics of coming out. When LGBT people have come out to themselves, their senses of identity have been at stake. When they have come out to desired sexual partners, they have risked violence and rejection, but have also achieved sex, love, and friendship. The history of coming out to family members is also filled with violence and rejection (and homelessness in the case of youth), but it has also been marked by tolerance, acceptance, and, in some cases, reciprocal coming out. Coming out at work, in contexts where employment discrimination on the basis of sexual orientation and gender identity is not prohibited by law, has led to sexual harassment, employment termination, and denials of hiring and promotion, but also to increased acceptance of gender and sexual diversity. In politics, coming out has ended careers, but, as the case of U.S. Representative Barney Frank suggests, it has also sustained them.

Bisexuals, transsexuals, and transgender people have faced unique challenges and possibilities in coming out. Bisexuals often must come out about their same-sex sexual desires, identities, and experiences to straights but also about their cross-sex sexual desires, identities, and experiences to lesbians and gays. In both cases they risk rejection and court acceptance. Some transsexuals want to be "out" as transsexuals, whereas others want to "pass" as female-born women or male-born men. Some of the same dynamics operate with transgender people. Men who have passed as women and women who have passed as men have generally not wanted to be out in contexts in which they are passing, but some have been "out" to selected partners and friends, some have been forced "out," and some have been "outed" after their deaths. Masculine women and feminine men have generally been more "out" as LGBT than masculine men and feminine women have been, sometimes because of choices made about appearance and sometimes because of popular assumptions about relationships between bodies, genders, and sexualities. In short, it is difficult to make sweeping historical generalizations about the dynamics of LGBT coming out.

## Constructionism and Essentialism

Narratives of coming out, common in both fictional and nonfictional literature since the end of World War II, can be read as essentialist or constructionist. For essentialists, who believe that sexual and gender identities are biological, innate, and fixed, coming out generally represents the discovery and disclosure of an internal essence. Coming out in this sense signifies a coming to terms with an authentic, genuine, and true self. Essentialist LGB coming out narratives generally assume that one is born LGB, but that it takes some time to recognize one's birthright. These narratives usually find proof and coherence in memories of childhood characteristics, desires, and behaviors.

For constructionists, who believe that sexual and gender identities are shaped primarily by society, culture, and history, coming out narratives generally represent a decision (conscious or unconscious) to embrace an identity made available in a particular social, cultural, and historical context. Coming out in this sense involves a process of imposing coherence on what are often incoherent characteristics, desires, and behaviors. These narratives may use childhood memory elements, but they concentrate on the process of selecting and assembling these elements rather than on the "truth" of the elements themselves.

## Coming Out Before and After Stonewall

The homophile movement of the 1950s and 1960s, which consisted primarily of groups such as the Mattachine Society, ONE, Daughters of Bilitis, and the Janus Society, did not regard "coming out" as a central political strategy. In fact, one of the first controversies in the movement took place in the early 1950s, when the leaders of the Mattachine Society were criticized for not revealing their names even within the movement. According to Marc Stein's 2000 book *City of Sisterly and Brotherly Loves,* after a 1960 police raid on one of the first meetings held in the Philadelphia area to organize a local homophile group, leaders urged participants to come to subsequent meetings by reciting the children's chant, "Come out! Come out! Wherever you are!!" (p. 184). But coming out more publicly was not actively encouraged. In Philadelphia, Barbara Gittings was unusual in using her real name in the homophile movement and some local leaders were angry when the names and addresses of LGB bars and other cultural institutions were revealed in a 1963 journalistic expose on the local gay community. As Stein points out, activists came out in public at five Annual Reminder demonstrations at Philadelphia's Independence Hall on the Fourth of July from 1965 to 1969, but many of those marching in the picket lines were from New York and Washington, D.C., and thus had less to lose from local media coverage.

After Stonewall, coming out became the central political strategy of the gay liberation movement. "Out of the closets and into the streets!" was a popular slogan in the 1970s. Coming out was encouraged in part as a means of self-expression, which was in keeping with the era's countercultural emphasis on authenticity and openness and with therapeutic ideas about the damage done by secrecy. But it was also encouraged as a vehicle for promoting tolerance and acceptance. Advocates of coming out believed that if everyone who was LGB came out as such in all spheres of life, the ubiquitous presence of LGB people in every corner of the country would invariably lead to reductions in prejudice and discrimination. While excessively optimistic in important respects, polls that indicate that support for LGB rights is positively correlated with knowledge of someone who is LGB suggest that the coming out strategy was generally successful in this regard.

Many gay liberationists and lesbian feminists in the 1970s took the notion of coming out one step further. Critical of essentialist notions of sexual identity and rigid concepts of sexual categories, gay liberationists urged all people to come out as gay. Lesbian feminists, endorsing new conceptions of lesbians as "women-identified women," similarly urged all women to come out as lesbians. Although this notion of coming out did not become dominant in LGBT communities, it did encourage sexual experimentation and exploration and it remained a powerful current in radical political and academic networks. Meanwhile, beginning in the late 1980s, the more conventional notion of coming out has been promoted each year on National Coming Out Day (11 October), sponsored by the Human Rights Campaign.

## "Outing"

There is a long tradition of LGBT people being involuntarily "outed" by hostile opponents and critics. Whether outed in investigations of "gays in the military," campaigns against perverts in government, sensational stories of sex crimes, tabloid coverage of celebrities, obituaries of passing men and women, proceedings in divorce and custody cases, or police blotters in local newspapers, countless LGBT have suffered significant consequences from this type of outing.

"Outing" did not emerge as a commonly used term until the late 1980s and early 1990s, and when it did those doing the "outing" were mostly LGB themselves. In the context of the rise of the New Right, the Reagan and Bush (father and son) presidencies, and ongoing government inaction in response to the AIDS epidemic, a number of militant LGB activists associated with the AIDS Coalition to Unleash Power (ACT UP) and Queer Nation began to "out" prominent LGB people who were accused of damaging the LGB cause by remaining closeted. Led by Michelangelo Signorile, who had a column in the New York–based weekly periodical *OutWeek,* and supported by prominent gay figures such as Armistead Maupin, militant activists outed a variety of prominent figures, including Hollywood moguls Barry Diller and David Geffen; actors Jodie Foster, Sandra Bernhard, and Richard Chamberlain, musicians k.d. lang, Michelle Shocked, Leonard Bernstein, and Michael Stipe; gossip columnist Liz Smith; athlete Greg Louganis, business executive Malcolm Forbes (who had recently died), fashion designer Calvin Klein, and political figures including Assistant Secretary of Defense Pete Williams, Illinois Governor James Thompson, U.S. Representatives Steve Gunderson and Jim Kolbe, and U.S. Senator Barbara Mikulski.

Defenders of outing argued that LGB people needed positive role models; that all people should recognize the accomplishments of LGB people; that secrecy about LGB identities contributed to the notion that LGB life is shameful; that notions of privacy invariably worked against the interests of LGB people; that the media's code of silence about LGB public figures was hypocritical; and that LGB public figures should be held accountable for not acting in the community's best interests and for colluding in the oppression of LGB people and people with AIDS. Although some critics responded by defending rights of privacy, others argued that "outing" reproduced the practices of homophobes and totalitarians, emphasized that closeted figures did not make positive role models, pointed out that outing public figures did not yield positive LGB gains, and criticized the ways in which outers ignored the problems of racism and sexism encountered by LGB people of color and women. Many commentators worked to distinguish between cases in which outing was justified and cases in which it was not. By the mid-1990s, the general controversy about "outing" had died down, although it continues to be revived each time a public figure is named as LGBT against their will.

## Outing in the Late Twentieth Century

Later in the 1990s, although evidence accumulated that young people were coming out at younger and younger ages, coming out and outing were implicitly criticized by the queer turn in LGBT history, politics, and scholarship. Coming out and outing are linked to the history and politics of LGBT identities, and for queer critics of identity politics coming out and outing can seem terribly old-fashioned and retrograde. Whether they express nostalgia for the erotic possibilities of the closet or hope for the erotic promises of nonidentity-based liaisons, some queer sex radicals question the limitations imposed by coming out expectations and requirements. Scholars interested in exploring the history of queer people who crossed genders or acted on the basis of same-sex desires without adopting LGBT identities often see coming out and outing as irrelevant at best and obfuscating at worst. Educators who develop safe sex programs to reach "men who have sex with men" have recognized that there may well be more people who fit that description than there are men who come out as gay. Postmodernists and poststructuralists who are more interested in deconstructing identities than in constructing or reconstructing them can be critical of linear and teleological coming out narratives. Ironically, however, while many of these queer critics, radicals, scholars, educators, and theorists challenge the notion of coming out as LGBT, they routinely come out as queer and express the hope that others will as well.

### Bibliography

Chauncey, George. *Gay New York.* New York: Basic, 1994.

D'Emilio, John. *Sexual Politics, Sexual Communities.* Chicago: University of Chicago Press, 1998.

Gross, Larry. *Contested Closets: The Politics and Ethics of Outing.* Minneapolis: University of Minnesota Press, 1993.

Howard, John. *Men Like That.* Chicago: University of Chicago Press, 1999.

Jay, Karla, and Allen Young, eds. *Out of the Closets.* New York: Douglas, 1972.

Kennedy, Elizabeth, and Madeline D. Davis. *Boots of Leather, Slippers of Gold.* New York: Routledge, 1993.

Mohr, Richard D. *Gay Ideas: Outing and Other Controversies.* Boston: Beacon Press, 1992.

Murphy, Timothy, ed. *Gay Ethics: Controversies in Outing, Civil Rights, and Sexual Science.* Binghamton, N.Y.: Haworth Press, 1994.

Sedgwick, Eve Kosofsky. *Epistemology of the Closet.* Berkeley: University of California Press, 1990.

Stein, Marc. *City of Sisterly and Brotherly Loves: Lesbian and Gay Philadelphia, 1945–1972.* Chicago: University of Chicago Press, 2000.

**Marc Stein**

---

**See also** CLOSET; GAY LIBERATION; QUEER NATION.

**COMMUNICATIONS.** see MEDIA STUDIES AND JOURNALISM.

**COMMUNISM.** see ANARCHISM, SOCIALISM, AND COMMUNISM; GOVERNMENT AND MILITARY WITCHHUNTS

# COMMUNITY CENTERS

Safe space, a place to find friends and lovers, a place to organize and advocate—these are among the many roles the LGBT community center has played in the lives of queer folk for more than thirty years.

The country's first lesbian and gay community centers opened in 1971 on opposite coasts: one in Los Angeles, the other in Albany, New York. Each was founded on the premise that LGBT people were entitled to a place where they could congregate safely, live openly with dignity, and receive culturally appropriate services.

The concept was revolutionary. After all, it was a time when police harassment of bars frequented by LGBT people was common, nondiscrimination laws protecting LGBT people were nonexistent, positive public portrayals of LGBT people were difficult to find, and homosexuality was still classified as a mental disorder by the American Psychiatric Association. With little to affirm their existence in mainstream society—and plenty of hostility waiting to be heaped on them from religious institutions, unsupportive families, and an uneasy public—many LGBT people hid in their closets and suffered alone. LGBT community centers were among the most important spaces created to address this problem.

### The Early Years

Prior to the establishment of LGBT community centers, there were relatively limited options as far as places for LGBT people to gather. There were LGBT bars, clubs, and restaurants, most of which were not LGBT-owned. There was the occasional LGBT bookstore, church basement, or homophile movement office. There were parks, bathhouses, and other spaces where LGBT people congregated. There were private living rooms where small groups of friends and associates mingled. But there was no place for the broader LGBT community to converge, organize, socialize, or receive services specifically geared toward them.

Carrying forth the legacy of the Stonewall Riots—and the belief that queer people needed a home of their own—some LGBT activists decided it was time to fill the void by renting or acquiring real estate that would serve as a community haven.

The Los Angeles and Albany centers were the first in a long line of LGBT community centers that would eventually sprout up across the United States. In 1974 the Los Angeles Gay and Lesbian Center became the nation's first organization with the word "gay" incorporated in its name to be awarded federal 501(c)(3) tax-exempt status.

Today, nearly 140 LGBT community centers exist. Some are situated in major metropolises, others in suburban and rural settings. They range from one-room drop-in centers to multimillion-dollar social service agencies. All have provided a venue for LGBT people to break through their isolation.

## Meeting the Community's Expanding Needs

In addition to being places to converge, LGBT centers also provide services. Particularly during the early years, as LGBT communities began addressing the issue of substance abuse among LGBT people, services often focused on alcohol and drug prevention and intervention. The menu of services at many centers has grown to include programs for youth and seniors, public policy forums, cultural programming, Internet access in state-of-the-art cyber centers, HIV/AIDS prevention and education programs, coming-out support groups, and dances and summer camps for queer youth. This diverse range of offerings is reflective of the diversity of LGBT communities themselves, as well as of their development.

For example, in the 1980s, when HIV/AIDS began ravaging the gay community, many centers were at the forefront of providing services. People came to the centers for information about the then-emerging epidemic; when lovers and friends died, they came for solace and support. Those outraged by the government's response to HIV/AIDS came to their centers to organize. In fact the AIDS activist group, AIDS Coalition to Unleash Power (ACT UP), was founded at the Lesbian, Gay, Bisexual, and Transgender Community Center (then called the Lesbian and Gay Community Services Center) in New York City in March 1987.

The 1980s saw the start of the so-called lesbian and gay baby boom, and some centers launched programs geared toward queer parents or those considering parenthood. Meanwhile, people were coming out at increasingly younger ages, and centers responded with services and programs of particular interest to LGBT youth. In July 2000, for example, the San Diego Lesbian, Gay, Bisexual,

Transgender Community Center (established in 1973) opened the Hillcrest Youth Center for LGBT youth. As the transgender community became more active, organized, and visible, some centers started offering services specifically for trans people. In 1990, for example, the New York center established the Gender Identity Project to provide counseling and support services to people with transgender experience. In addition, many centers facilitate cultural celebration by hosting movie nights, art exhibits, theater outings, queer historical field trips, and more. Several centers have libraries, among them the Gay, Lesbian, and Bisexual Community Services Center of Colorado, based in Denver, and the Pride Center in New Brunswick, New Jersey.

## Serving as a Crossroads

On any given night at some centers, there might be one meeting for queer Democrats and another for gay Republicans. There might be a lesbian chorus rehearsal, a trans movie screening, and a forum on same-sex marriage rights. Queer people from different backgrounds with a variety of interests find themselves at LGBT centers because of a common bond and a desire to connect with others.

Individuals benefit, as do the LGBT groups that find affordable meeting space at their local LGBT centers. The availability of this meeting space has proven to be a powerful organizing tool. In 1985, for example, a group of New York activists angry over the *New York Post*'s media coverage of gay and AIDS issues met at the New York center to plan a demonstration, which in turn led to the founding of the Gay and Lesbian Alliance Against Defamation (GLAAD), the national LGBT media watchdog group. GLAAD is among the many organizations that have benefited from LGBT community centers—queer safe space has allowed these groups to find their distinctive voices and develop agendas that have advanced the LGBT movement as a whole.

## Community Centers Support Each Other

In July 1987 representatives from many LGBT centers gathered in Los Angeles during the annual conference of the National Lesbian and Gay Health Foundation. The meeting was a success, and representatives from each of the centers decided to meet annually at the conference. In June 1994, during the twenty-fifth anniversary celebration of the Stonewall rebellion, leaders of an estimated thirty centers came together to formalize their network, meeting at the New York center to found the National Association of Lesbian, Gay, Bisexual, and Transgender Community Centers.

The association's founding was another important step in the development of the LGBT movement, providing—for the first time—a national networking and training vehicle solely devoted to bolstering LGBT community centers. In a 2001 study the association found that there were more than 130 LGBT community centers in the United States, with centers located in 41 of the 50 states; those centers, it found, were the primary LGBT access points for organizing, services, and information. More than half the centers had annual operating budgets of less than $50,000, and 50 to 70 of the smaller centers were the only staffed LGBT organizations in their communities and the only LGBT-related listings in their local phonebooks. Of the 50 largest urban areas, 18 did not have LGBT community centers, and 10 had centers with budgets of less than $100,000.

The association facilitates the development of newly formed community centers by providing peer-based technical assistance, leadership training, and financial resources to centers in all stages of formation. It also undertakes national projects that are implemented locally, including Promote the Vote, a nonpartisan voter registration and mobilization project in which centers distribute voter registration forms at queer bars, clubs, coffeehouses, and other businesses. The outreach project, which creates a visible voting constituency, is now one of the largest LGBT voter registration programs in the United States.

## Looking Forward

The contention arises from time to time that, because LGBT people have secured more legal rights and greater social acceptance, LGBT meeting spaces are no longer necessary. Community centers definitely know otherwise. Indeed, three decades since the first LGBT community centers opened, the need for such centers is as evident as ever. The reasons they are needed are numerous:

- They provide safe, supportive meeting space for LGBT and HIV-related organizations and publicize the groups' meetings and events.

- They create and offer programs to meet the wellness, cultural, and recreational needs of LGBT people.

- They provide civic leadership in the LGBT community via public forums and by demanding government response to community needs.

- They provide a public voice for the LGBT community in the larger society.

Small or large, LGBT community centers are the places to which queer people continue to turn for sup-

port, services, recreation, and affirmation. There would be far less "community" in the LGBT community were it not for these hubs of queer life and proven catalysts for progressive social change.

**Richard D. Burns**

*See also* AIDS COALITION TO UNLEASH POWER (ACT UP); COLORADO; CORDOVA, JEANNE; GAY AND LESBIAN ALLIANCE AGAINST DEFAMATION (GLAAD); PRESTON, JOHN.

**CONSTRUCTIONISM.** see ESSENTIALISM AND CONSTRUCTIONISM.

# COPLAND, Aaron (b. 14 November 1900; d. 2 December 1990), composer.

Aaron Copland's reputation as one of his generation's leading composers of art music remains undisputed. Centenary celebrations surrounding his birth witnessed innumerable performances, colloquia, recordings, and publications and gave renewed evidence of his enduring preeminent stature in the history of American music and in music worldwide.

Having studied with Rubin Goldmark in New York City and with Nadia Boulanger in Paris, Copland went on to produce a wide range of works: from jazz-inspired compositions during the 1920s; through examples of profound simplicity and purposeful accessibility beginning in the 1930s; to contributions of a severe, complex, dissonant character at various times throughout his career, including works using serial procedures in the 1950s and afterward. He is best remembered for such populist scores as *El Salón México* (1936) and the ballets *Billy the Kid* (with Eugene Loring, choreography; 1938), *Rodeo* (with Agnes de Mille, 1942), and *Appalachian Spring* (with Martha Graham, 1944). These and several other highly influential scores reflect Copland's aim, at times, to reach as wide an audience as possible. Inspiring this objective were social, political, and economic developments of the Great Depression along with technical innovations in radio, film, and phonograph that put enlarged, mass audiences within reach of composers for the first time.

In seeking to integrate himself and his music into contemporary life, Copland succeeded like no previous composer in the classical domain. He greatly influenced the history of American concert music through his career-long efforts to establish music composition as a viable livelihood in America. His organizational efforts included co-founding and heading many organizations

**Aaron Copland.** The versatile composer (*right*) of *Fanfare for the Common Man* and other populist scores is accompanied by another hugely popular and influential (as well as discreetly gay) twentieth-century American composer, Leonard Bernstein. [Library of Congress]

designed to improve the economic and pragmatic circumstances of American composers, many of whom came to regard him as the dean of American composers. Copland indeed led in organizing concerts of new music by his confreres; in working to secure their publication, distribution, and collection of royalties; and in teaching and advising young composers at the Berkshire Music Center in Lenox, Massachusetts, and elsewhere.

Musically he influenced generations of composers from the likes of Leonard Bernstein and William Schuman in the era of World War II to composers active at the turn of the next century, including John Adams, Stephen Sondheim, and a host of film music composers calling on Copland's distinctive sound to evoke diverse aspects of the American landscape and character. In popular culture, encountering such emblems of Copland's Americana as his *Fanfare for the Common Man* (1942) and "Hoe-Down" from *Rodeo* has proved virtually unavoidable. In television commercials alone, arrangements of and derivations from his most familiar music have been used by others to sell everything from cars to ketchup.

That he identified as homosexual was something kept from the public during most of his professional life, though among his colleagues his homosexuality was widely known. Without proclaiming himself gay to the public, Copland nevertheless served as a gay role model within music circles when such models were badly needed. From Copland's maturity onward, many young gay and bisexual composers gravitated toward him for counsel, as did others. By not marrying, he abstained from posing as straight, which was somewhat daring for someone in his position of leadership and notoriety. In his private life, his amorous pursuits often entailed a series of involvements with considerably younger men, with whom Copland tended to stay on friendly terms long after the love affairs had ended.

In his own quiet, discreet way, Copland—when in his eighties—finally divulged an account of his life as a closeted homosexual. Though he never technically came out in his two-volume autobiography, *Copland* (cowritten with music historian Vivian Perlis; 1984, 1989), there as elsewhere, nevertheless treated his homosexuality as an open secret. Most readers would find it impossible to conclude from the books that he lived as anything but gay.

On the subject of expressing elements of homosexuality musically, Copland maintained a mostly ambivalent attitude. For while he often wrote of music as expressing his emotional essence and even his private thoughts, he never went so far in his voluminous output of articles, interviews, and books as to link this personal aesthetic with sexuality per se. The ambivalence is understandable given the social taboos prevailing against homosexuality, and the fact that only at the end of Copland's life did debates concerning sexuality and gender first enter mainstream music criticism and scholarship.

Arguably, the closest Copland ever came to commenting openly on his views about sexuality in a musical context occurs in his opera *The Tender Land* (1952–1954). In the early and mid-1950s, amid political difficulties climaxing in an appearance before Senator Joseph McCarthy and his Senate Permanent Subcommittee on Investigations, he composed the work to a libretto by his young friend Erik Johns (under the pseudonym Horace Everett), a dancer, painter, and eventually a designer as well, whom he had met in the late 1940s. Together he and Johns shared a love relationship that overlapped their operatic collaboration. With debates about such issues as personal acceptance and affirmation of so-called deviant identity having come to mark many musical discussions starting in the late twentieth century, owing in part to the influence of new musicological methods, some interpretations of *The Tender Land* unapologetically began viewing the opera as implicating these and other issues of sexual difference.

## Bibliography

Copland, Aaron, and Vivian Perlis. *Copland*. 2 vols. New York: St. Martin's Press, 1984, 1989.

Mathers, Daniel E. "Expanding Horizons: Sexuality and the Re-zoning of *The Tender Land*." In *Copland Connotations: Studies and Interviews*. Edited by Peter Dickinson. Woodbridge, Suffolk, U.K.: Boydell Press, 2002.

Moor, Paul. "Fanfare for an Uncommon Man: The Real Score on Composer Aaron Copland." *Advocate* (15 January 1991): 54–55.

Pollack, Howard. *Aaron Copland: The Life and Work of an Uncommon Man*. New York: Holt, 1999.

———. "The Dean of Gay American Composers." *American Music* 18 (2000): 39-49.

**Daniel E. Mathers**

*See also* BERNSTEIN, LEONARD; MUSIC: CLASSICAL; MUSIC: OPERA; SONDHEIM, STEPHEN.

# CÓRDOVA, Jeanne (b. 8 July 1948), activist and publisher.

Jeanne Córdova was born in Germany to Irish and Mexican parents and grew up as a tomboy in a family of twelve children. She and her younger brother Bill "gathered the neighborhood boys in the 'burbs of Orange Grove fifties California and galloped away the years playing Lone Ranger, hardball, and King of the Mountain" (Córdova, 1992, p. 274).

Toward the end of her teen years, Córdova spent some time as a postulant (probationary candidate) in the Order of the Immaculate Heart of Mary, an experience she later wrote about in the anthology *Lesbian Nuns: Breaking the Silence*. After Córdova chose to leave the convent, she came out publicly. She then went on to obtain a master's degree in social work from UCLA and began her activist career with the Daughters of Bilitis (DOB), for which she served as Los Angeles chapter president. The DOB chapter newsletter evolved into *The Lesbian Tide*, with Córdova serving as both editor and publisher. *The Tide* is arguably the newspaper of record for the lesbian feminist decade (1970–1980). It contained news, analysis, and discussions of social and political issues important to lesbians and women during those years. Its content also included coverage of issues that were not considered politically correct at the time, such as roles (butch vs. femme) and sadomasochism.

Córdova devoted several decades to tireless activism on behalf of lesbians, gays, and women. She was especially effective as a moving force in campaigns and projects that required considerable effort in a short period of time. In the 1970s Córdova was a key organizer of the West Coast Lesbian Conference (1973), an event held at the University of California, Los Angeles, and attended by over fifteen hundred women from twenty-six states and several countries. She also sat on the Board of the Gay Community Services Center (now the Los Angeles Gay and Lesbian Center). In 1976 she was voted off the Board because of her support for workers who alleged they had experienced sexism, racism, and manager/worker inequalities at the Center. After Córdova was dismissed and a number of workers were fired, a strike was called against the center, and an internecine struggle raged in the gay and lesbian community for several years.

While still publishing *The Tide*, Córdova was elected as a delegate to the first National Women's Conference in Houston (1977), where she was a moving force behind the passage of a lesbian affirmative action resolution. She also participated in the campaign to defeat the antigay Briggs initiative (1977–1978). This amendment would have purged LGBT teachers from public schools as well as non-LGBT teachers who supported them. In 1978 non-LGBT Californians helped defeat the initiative. This campaign brought lesbians and gay men together and formed the foundation for the resurgence of a co-gender alliance. Córdova's subsequent activism illustrates the dual commitment of some lesbians. She went on to be a key organizer of the National Lesbian Feminist Organization Conference held in Los Angeles (1978), and served as president of the Stonewall Democratic Club (1979–1981).

In the 1980s Córdova helped form the Gay and Lesbian American Caucus within the National Democratic Committee and served as a delegate to the 1980 National Democratic Convention. She was a founder of the Los Angeles Gay and Lesbian Press Association (1983) and a founding board member of Connexxus Womens' Center/Centro de Mujeres, a lesbian and women's center located in West Hollywood (1984). She also worked as media director for STOP 64, a campaign that defeated the statewide AIDS quarantine measure proposed by conservative Lyndon LaRouche (1986).

Córdova's contributions as a journalist and writer include a column on sociopolitical issues written for the *Los Angeles Free Press* (in the 1960s and 1970s); several books (*Sexism: It's a Nasty Affair*, 1976; *Kicking the Habit: A Lesbian Nun Story*, 1990); and essays and stories in a number of anthologies, including *Lesbian Girl Scouts* (1996), *Persistent Desire: A Femme-Butch Reader* (1992), *Lesbian Nuns: Breaking the Silence* (1985), and *After You're Out* (1975). During the 1980s and well into the 1990s, she turned to publishing as a form of activism. Córdova founded the Community Yellow Pages (CYP), which is now the nation's largest LGBT business directory. She also published a queer spiritual magazine, *Square Peg*.

Several years ago, Córdova sold the CYP, and now resides for most of the year in Mexico with her partner Lynne Ballen and is working on an autobiographical novel.

## Bibliography

Córdova, Jeanne. *Sexism: It's A Nasty Affair*. Spring Park, Minn.: New World, 1976.

———. *Kicking the Habit: A Lesbian Nun Story*. Los Angeles: Multiple Dimensions, 1995.

———. "Butches, Lies, and Feminism." In *The Persistent Desire: A Femme-Butch Reader*. Edited by Joan Nestle. Boston: Alyson, 1992. Also available from http://www.members.aol.com/Córdovajj.

**Yolanda Retter Vargas**

*See also* BUSINESSES; COMMUNITY SERVICES CENTERS; DAUGHTERS OF BILITIS; DEMOCRATIC PARTY; LATINA AND LATINO ORGANIZATIONS AND PERIODICALS; NEWSPAPERS AND MAGAZINES.

**CORNELL, MICHIYO.** see FUKAYA, MICHIYO.

# CORNWELL, Anita (b. 23 September 1923), writer.

Anita Cornwell was in her forties by the time second wave feminism arrived in the mid-1960s. She soon became one of the few black lesbians in the United States who were living out, speaking out, and writing out. Born in Greenwood, South Carolina, Cornwell moved to Pennsylvania at age sixteen, living first in Yeadon with her aunt, then in Philadelphia with her mother, who moved north when Anita was eighteen to be with her.

Aspiring to become a writer, Cornwell enrolled at Temple University, graduating in 1948 with a B.S. degree in journalism and the social sciences. She began writing for local weekly newspapers while working in clerical positions in city, state, and federal government agencies. All the while, Cornwell saw herself as biding her time until the journalism position that she knew she could fill came her way. When that did not happen, she answered a recruiting call in 1958 for college graduates and was selected to participate in a Ford Foundation teacher training program. The program took place over the course of the summer, and the trainees were then placed in minority schools. Cornwell studied diligently through the summer and was duly assigned to a junior high

school, but once she began teaching, she realized that she had no patience for young people who needed discipline. She realized also that the program had never provided training in how to keep order in a classroom. Appalled at the behavior of her adolescent students, she resigned after two weeks, returning to the familiar clerical work that bored her utterly. From 1958 until 1960, she was a case worker for the Pennsylvania State Department of Public Welfare, after which she never worked for wages again.

Cornwell has been a freelance writer since 1961, contributing essays, interviews, stories, reviews, commentary, articles, poetry, and plays to a variety of journals, newspapers, and magazines, including *Azalea, Black Maria, Negro Digest, Elegant Teen, Essence, Feminary, Feminist Review, Gay Alternative, Griot, Hera, Liberator, Labyrinth, Ladder, Los Angeles Free Press, Motheroot, New Directions for Women, National Leader, New York Native, Philadelphia Gay News, Phylon Welcomat,* and *WICCE.*

Cornwell's work also appears in several anthologies, including *The Lavender Herring* (1976), *Lavender Culture* (1979), *Top Ranking: An Anthology on Racism and Classism in the Lesbian Community* (1980), *For Lesbians Only* (1988), and *The Romantic* (1993). The anthology *Revolutionary Tales: African American Women's Short Stories from the First Story to the Present* (1995) republished her short story "A Sound of Crying," which had previously been published in the *Negro Digest* in 1964. Cornwell also published a young adult novel, *The Girls of Summer* (1989). *Black Lesbian in White America* (1983) is her most widely circulated work—a book of essays that includes a comprehensive interview with the black lesbian feminist poet Audre Lorde.

Asked how she managed for so long without holding a steady job, Cornwell says that she and her mother had an understanding. "She took care of me and I took care of her," she responded cryptically. Freed by her mother's support from the need to hold a job that she could lose at any moment because of her sexual orientation, Cornwell was able to write, organize, and speak up without fear. Cornwell showed her mother everything she wrote, and her mother met her girlfriends. Therefore, Cornwell could state confidently about her lesbianism, "She [Cornwell's mother] knew. Of course she knew. But we never talked about it." Cornwell was asked why not by two different interviewers a decade apart (Marc Stein on 6 October 1993 and Anita Bowen on 12 March 2003). Cornwell responded that talking about it might cause her mother to say something negative about her lesbianism that would in turn cause her to respond disrespectfully, and she wanted to retain respect for her mother while remaining true to her own feelings. Thus, they maintained a delicate balance, exercising self-discipline and respect for one another's boundaries.

### Bibliography

Stein, Marc. *City of Sisterly and Brotherly Loves: Lesbian and Gay Philadelphia, 1945–1972.* Chicago: University of Chicago Press, 2000.

**Angela Bowen**

*See also* LESBIAN FEMINISM; RADICALESBIANS.

# CORY, Donald Webster (b. 18
September 1913; d. 1986), sociologist, writer, homophile leader.

Donald Webster Cory's book, *The Homosexual in America,* was published in 1951, and it became one of the most influential works in the history of the gay rights movement. The first nonfiction, insider account of the gay American subculture by an avowed homosexual, Cory's book politicized numerous gay men and lesbians and earned him the title "father of the homophile movement." Though timid in his reliance on a pseudonym—his real name was Edward Sagarin—Cory boldly asserted that gay men and lesbians deserved civil rights as members of a large, unrecognized minority.

## Early Life

Born in 1913 to Russian Jewish parents in Schenectady, New York, Cory had scoliosis and suffered his entire life from a disfiguring hunchback. As a student at the City College of New York, he was drawn to leftist politics and joined the National Student League, a militant group that sought to build a mass student protest movement. At the age of twenty-three he married fellow radical Gertrude Liphshitz, and the couple had one child. Dropping out of college during the Great Depression, he worked in the cosmetics and fragrance industry but maintained his scholarly aspirations by writing *The Science and Art of Perfumery* (1945). Since early adolescence Sagarin had felt an attraction for other men and a deep sense of shame about that attraction. He scoured libraries to try to understand his sexual difference. During a year in France he met French author André Gide, whose spirited defense of homosexuality, *Corydon* (1920), inspired Sagarin's pseudonym. When marriage failed to dampen his homosexual desires, he sought psychoanalysis, which succeeded not in changing his orientation but in lifting his sense of guilt. By the age of thirty-seven, as he wrote *The Homosexual in America,* he had integrated his sexuality into the

rest of his life, maintaining his marriage and a "firm bond of friendship" with a man named Howard.

## The Homosexual in America

*The Homosexual in America* was part "spiritual autobiography," part sociological study of gay male life, and part civil rights manifesto. It showed the influence of Gunnar Myrdal's *The American Dilemma: The Negro Problem in Modern Democracy* (1944), a landmark study of race relations that argued that the "Negro problem" was the result of white prejudice. Despite his Freudian belief that homosexuality was caused by an unbalanced home life, and especially a strong attachment to one parent, Cory rejected the notion that homosexuality could be suppressed or cured. Asserting that societal prejudice rather than inherent deficiencies accounted for most of the problems that homosexuals experienced, Cory called on gay men and lesbians to accept themselves and stop wearing masks.

In his book Cory examined many aspects of the gay subculture, including cruising, slang, bars, social hostility, and sex crime laws. He sought to help gay people gain self-acceptance and break the embarrassed silence that often surrounded the subject. A budding sociologist, Cory understood the growing importance of minority rights and envisioned a time when homosexuals would take their place beside blacks, Jews, and others demanding equal treatment. But more so than members of other minority groups, gay men and lesbians had first to acknowledge themselves. Cory argued that gay men and lesbians hid their sexuality not merely to avoid discrimination, but to avoid facing up to their difference. "There is surely no group of such size, and yet with so few who acknowledge that they belong," Cory lamented (p. 6). He pointed out the unique conundrum facing the gay community: as members of a discriminated class, few homosexuals were willing to speak out, yet without such martyrs, society's attitudes were unlikely to change. His book hoped to place a small wedge into this vicious cycle of fear and concealment.

In 1957 *The Homosexual in America* went through its seventh printing, and in 1960 Castle Books published a second edition. Translated into several languages, the book had a tremendous impact on the nongay world by portraying homosexuals as complex human beings, not mere psychopaths or degenerates. With appendices listing fiction and nonfiction book titles on homosexuality, it served as an early resource guide. Many pioneering gay activists from the 1960s trace their involvement with the movement back to their reading of *The Homosexual in America.* Barbara Gittings contacted the publisher and met with Cory several times. Through these conversations she discovered the existence of the Daughters of Bilitis and soon founded a New York chapter. Jack Nichols passed the book around his circle of gay friends at Bethesda-Chevy Chase High School, for whom it became a sort of in-group Bible, prompting some to come out to their teachers and parents. Franklin Kameny relied on the book's arguments when he wrote his influential brief to the U.S. Supreme Court challenging the federal civil service's antigay employment policies.

## Later Betrayal

Using the large correspondence prompted by *The Homosexual in America* that he received, Cory opened the Cory Book Service, which offered gay-themed books to subscribers. He served as a contributing editor to *ONE* magazine and spoke at many homophile meetings. But as gay activists turned more militant in the 1960s, openly challenging the notion that gays and lesbians suffered from mental illness, Cory became a critic of the movement he had helped to launch. As a member of the Mattachine Society of New York, he tried to prevent 1960s militants from taking over the organization. In the introduction to the second edition of *The Homosexual in America*, he denounced what he saw as a misinterpretation on the part of some overzealous readers who believed that his call for fair treatment of gays was a denial that they were psychologically disturbed. In *The Homosexual and His Society* (1963), Cory denied the possibility of a "well-adjusted homosexual." In an introduction to Albert Ellis's *Homosexuality: Its Causes and Cures* (1965), he argued that men and women who were exclusively homosexual were compulsive and neurotic. His stance that gay men and lesbians should reorient their drives and accept their heterosexuality led movement leaders to denounce him as a traitor. He eventually resumed his formal education and received a Ph.D. in sociology from New York University in 1966. He served as a professor of sociology at City College of the City University of New York, publishing many books on the topic of homosexuality and other forms of supposed deviance under his real name, Edward Sagarin, while refusing to acknowledge the works he had produced as Donald Webster Cory. He died at age seventy-three of a heart attack.

## Bibliography

Cory, Donald Webster. *The Homosexual in America: A Subjective Approach.* New York: Greenberg, 1951.

Cory, Donald Webster, and John P. LeRoy. *The Homosexual and His Society: A View from Within.* New York: Citadel, 1963.

Duberman, Martin. "The 'Father' of the Homophile Movement." In his *Left Out: The Politics of Exclusion, Essays, 1964–1999.* New York: Basic Books, 1999.

Marotta, Toby. *The Politics of Homosexuality.* Boston: Houghton Mifflin, 1981.

**David K. Johnson**

See also GITTINGS, BARBARA, AND KAY TOBIN LAHUSEN; HOMOPHILE MOVEMENT; KAMENY, FRANKLIN; MATTACHINE SOCIETY; SOCIOLOGY.

# CRANE, Hart (b. 31 July 1899; d. 27 April 1932), poet.

Harold Hart Crane was born in Garrettsville, Ohio, and was raised in Cleveland. His mother, Grace Hart, exerted a lifelong influence on him, though their relationship was always tumultuous. Crane did not speak to his mother after 1928, but she shaped his literary legacy, not only suggesting to him in 1917 that he use his middle name—her maiden name—to sign his poems, but also preserving (and destroying) his correspondence, and even, years after his death, claiming to have channeled new poems from him in séances. Crane's father, Clarence Arthur Crane (known as C. A.), was a successful entrepreneur and the inventor of Life Savers candy. As with Grace Hart, Crane's relationship with C. A. was ambivalent since he always felt his father wanted him to join the family business rather than devote himself to poetry, but they reconciled in 1930, a few months before C. A.'s death.

In 1916, shortly after his parents filed for divorce, Crane left Cleveland for New York, telling them he planned to enroll at Columbia University. Instead, he immersed himself in the literary and bohemian activity there, absorbing with particular eagerness the currents of literary modernism available to him in small-press poetry journals like *Broom,* the *Dial,* the *Pagan,* and the *Little Review.* That year he published his first poem, "C 33," which laments Oscar Wilde's imprisonment (and whose title refers to the number of Wilde's prison cell). Money problems forced Crane to return to Cleveland late in 1919, but by then he had begun writing the poems of his adulthood, including some that would eventually appear in his first book, *White Buildings* (1926).

Crane remained in Cleveland until 1923, working in advertising firms and for his father. He found Cleveland isolated and culturally backward after New York, but his poems from this period are in fact intensely engaged with the literary and philosophical questions of the day. "For the Marriage of Faustus and Helen" (1922) stands out in Crane's work as it addresses a timely cultural issue—in this case, the prevailing sense in the United States and Western Europe that Western civilization was somehow "in decline." Crane was impatient with this idea, and "Faustus and Helen" may be read as his attempt to characterize the age in terms derived less from the aftermath of World War I than the excitement of the Jazz Age.

Back in New York from 1923 through 1925, Crane composed most of the poems that appear in *White Buildings,* including "Possessions" (1924) and "Voyages I–VI" (1926), poems recognizably addressing gay male love and sexuality. During this period Crane met Emil Opffer, a Danish merchant marine who became Crane's lover, and with whom Crane lived briefly at 110 Columbia Heights, Brooklyn, not far from the Brooklyn Bridge. The relationship and the view of New York Harbor both fed into Crane's work on a new, long poem, which would eventually become his great work, *The Bridge* (1930), a poem Crane called "a Myth of America," and which uses the Brooklyn Bridge as a figure for what could unite Americans into an ideal community of past and future brotherhood.

Though it has since been acknowledged as a major poem, *The Bridge* suffered from influential negative reviews when it was published. Allen Tate and Yvor Winters, poets and friends of Crane's, both denounced the poem in print; their assessment of the poem as fragmentary and unfocused was linked to their private belief that Crane's homosexuality prevented him from writing "mature" poems. Even skeptics acknowledged the ambitiousness of *The Bridge,* however, and in 1931 Crane was awarded a Guggenheim fellowship, which he took to Mexico.

Crane's time in Mexico in 1931 and 1932 was turbulent and exhausting: since 1927 he had been drinking heavily, and his binges in Mexico City led to more than one night in jail. He was frustrated with his inability to focus on writing, though he did produce the last great lyric of his career that year, the "Broken Tower," which Crane hoped would set him on the path of a new epic poem about Cortes and Montezuma. Instead, with the Great Depression deepening and his father's estate eaten up by creditors, Crane set sail for New York in April 1932. Though he had begun a new relationship with Peggy Cowley, the former wife of the critic Malcolm Cowley, he was overcome with despair; he leapt from the rail of the SS *Orizaba* at noon on 27 April 1932.

### Bibliography

Berthoff, Werner. *Hart Crane: A Re-introduction.* Minneapolis: University of Minnesota Press, 1989.

Hammer, Langdon. *O My Land, My Friends: The Selected Letters of Hart Crane.* New York: Four Walls Eight Windows, 1997.

Unterecker, John. *Voyager: A Life of Hart Crane.* New York: Farrar Straus and Giroux, 1969.

**Christopher Nealon**

*See also* ANDERSON, MARGARET, AND JANE HEAP; JOHNS, JASPER.

# CRIME AND CRIMINALIZATION

Sexual and gender minorities have been outlaws for most of U.S. history. Not only has the conduct of those labeled sodomites, sexual inverts, and homosexuals, traditionally violated the criminal law, but their violations have also been considered most serious. For most of U.S. history, some forms of same-sex intimacy constituted a capital crime. Once the punishment eased up, the ambit of the crime expanded, and then new crimes were added to the legal codes to target people that mainstream Americans considered a dangerous species. Such criminalization and punishment intensified to a fever pitch in the second third of the twentieth century, and was then succeeded by a rapid, albeit incomplete decriminalization.

### Early Regulation: Sodomy Laws, 1533–1880

For most of U.S. (and English) history, the most relevant regulations concerning same-sex intimacy were what are now called sodomy laws. At the behest of Henry VIII, the Reformation English Parliament of 1533 criminalized "the detestable and abominable vice of buggery committed with mankind or beast." As applied by the English courts, buggery was understood to include anal intercourse between two men or between a man and a woman, but not oral intercourse. As Jonathan Ned Katz has documented, the southern and middle colonies in seventeenth-century America generally assumed or legislated that the Act of 1533 and its death penalty applied within their jurisdictions. Without further statutory authorization, for example, Virginia in 1625 executed a ship's master for attacking and sodomizing a steward. Rather than following the 1533 act's buggery prohibition, the New England colonies legislated the biblical injunction against men "lying" with other men. The New Haven Colony in 1656 prohibited under pain of death men lying with men, women lying with women, masturbation, and any other "carnall knowledge." Masturbation and female same-sex "lying" were dropped as offenses when the Connecticut Colony was formed in 1665. Altogether there are records for at least twenty sodomy prosecutions, and four executions, during the colonial period.

Between U.S. independence and 1820, the original thirteen states all adopted laws similar to the Act of 1533 and the colonial statutes, but dropped the death penalty. New states adopted similar laws criminalizing "sodomy, or the crime against nature, with mankind or beast." None of the early statutes defined what precisely was meant by buggery or sodomy, for this remained the "unmentionable" sin against nature; U.S. courts religiously followed English authorities in the few cases where interpretation was demanded. In most of the states the sodomy statutes were interpreted to criminalize unspecified types of intercourse between men and women as well as men and men, but not between women and women. Almost all the reported cases involved males accused of anal intercourse with animals, boys, or unwilling male partners.

## Regulatory Expansion: 1880–1945

As the United States became increasingly urbanized after the Civil War, its middle class became alarmed at the growth of communities of gender "inverts" and sexual "degenerates" in large cities and grew concerned with protecting the sexuality of children. Urban police forces harassed and arrested "inverts" and "degenerates" under an ever-broadening array of municipal ordinances and state statutes. To begin with, most states between 1880 and 1921 expanded their sodomy laws (usually by legislation) to include the oral sex that lawmakers believed was the favored activity of sexual minorities. Arrests and successful prosecutions for sodomy or attempted sodomy soared in every major city. For the first time in U.S. history, women (prostitutes for the most part) were arrested for violating state sodomy prohibitions. New York City, which had prosecuted a total of twenty-two sodomy cases between 1796 and 1873, made double that number of arrests in 1900 alone. Between 1900 and 1910, its police arrested 601 people, including thirty-three women.

Other new laws enacted in this period targeted sexual or gender deviance more specifically. In 1851 Chicago adopted an ordinance making it a criminal offense for a person to appear in a public place "in a dress not belonging to his or her sex." Over the next century, dozens of municipalities and at least two states enacted similar laws against cross-dressing. Although these laws generated fewer arrests than sodomy laws did, they and more general laws against "indecent attire," "disorderly conduct," and "lewd vagrancy" were legal bases for police harassment of gender-deviant women. Almost every state and major city adopted multiple statutes giving police discretionary authority to harass and arrest "prostitutes," a term contemporaries used broadly and that included persons whose sexual preferences we would consider gay or lesbian. Among the new criminal offenses were being an "idle or dissolute" person, "lewd or lascivious speech or behavior," "indecent exposure," "lewd vagrancy," "loitering" for lewd purposes, and public "solicitation" for immoral purposes, including sodomy. Tens of thousands of female sex workers and unmarried (often lesbian) women were arrested under these laws—while thousands of gay or bisexual men were picked up as they cruised for sexual partners.

The same period saw the enactment of state laws protecting minors of both sexes against sexual interactions with adults. The most comprehensive regulatory regime was that instituted in California. Concluding that its nineteenth-century sodomy, fellatio, and seduction laws were insufficient, California created the new crimes of committing lewd acts with children (1901), sending a minor to an "immoral" place (1905), committing "degrading, lewd, immoral" practices in front of a child (1907), "contributing to the delinquency of minors" (1915), loitering in a schoolyard (1929), and molesting children (1929). The authorities in California and elsewhere applied these statutes with particular vigor against "homosexuals," a category of people society considered synonymous with child molesters.

## Kulturkampf (1946–1969) and Thermidor (1969–Present)

The half-generation after World War II witnessed a nationwide "sex panic," which swept up thousands of sexual and gender minorities in police dragnets. For most states, especially the urbanized states having noticeable gay subcultures, there was little need to add new statutory prohibitions (though most did so). The main postwar development was that more gay or bisexual men were arrested for consensual same-sex intimacy, and more lesbians, bisexual women, and transvestites were harassed and arrested for gender-deviant behavior such as cross-dressing or dancing with one another. Unprecedented investment in police stakeouts, raids, and dragnets yielded unprecedented numbers of arrests of gay people for consensual activities. Between 800 and 4,250 sexual and gender nonconformists, on average, were arrested each year for sodomy or attempted sodomy between 1946 and 1965. Between 20,800 and 79,250 gender nonconformists, on average, were arrested for lesser crimes each year.

This Kulturkampf (state-declared culture war) sent many gay people to jail, sometimes for exceedingly long periods of time. The longest sentences generally were given to men convicted of sex with children, but some men were sentenced to decades of jail time for sex with consenting adult men. Women usually did not go to jail, and when they did their sentences were short. A significant minority of those convicted of sodomy or other serious crimes were committed to state mental institutions such as California's Atascadero (the so-called Dachau for Queers). Between 1946 and 1957, twenty-nine states enacted or updated "sexual psychopath" laws which authorized indefinite hospitalization for sex offenders. Thousands of gay and bisexual men who were incarcerated in these institutions not only suffered loss of liberty, but also were subjected to medical experimentation and torture, as Katz has documented.

California's aggressive enforcement of laws criminalizing consensual same-sex intimacy appalled medical and legal professionals across the country. According to John D'Emilio, the Kulturkampf contributed to the homophile (1950s and 1960s) and then the gay and lesbian rights (1970s onward) movements. In the 1950s, law revision commissions and the American Law Institute criticized laws criminalizing consensual sodomy on the grounds that they were arbitrarily enforced, reached behavior that had no third-party harms, and undermined respect for the rule of law. Only Illinois (1961) and Connecticut (1969), however, heeded these criticisms and decriminalized consensual sodomy. Once lesbians and gay men "came out" of their "closets" in large numbers after the Stonewall Riots (1969), however, consensual sodomy laws dropped like flies in a hailstorm. By 1983, twenty-five states (representing about 60 percent of the population) had decriminalized consensual sodomy, and eleven others (about 15 percent of the population) had reduced it to a misdemeanor. The United States Supreme Court upheld the remaining state laws in *Bowers v. Hardwick* (1986), but at least ten more states and the District of Columbia decriminalized consensual sodomy between 1983 and 2003. In *Lawrence v. Texas* (2003) the Supreme Court overruled *Bowers v. Hardwick.*

Other laws aimed at the conduct of gender or sexual minorities have also disappeared. The most complete deregulation has been the victory of transgender as well as gay and lesbian people over cross-dressing laws. State and federal courts have invalidated several of them as unconstitutional, and legislatures have repealed most of the rest. It is no longer a crime in the United States to dress in the attire of the "opposite sex." Likewise, state courts and legislatures have cast skeptical eyes on vagrancy, disorderly conduct, public toilet loitering, and lewdness laws that were aimed at consensual same-sex intimacy. Few such laws remain on the statute books, but laws generally prohibiting public sexual solicitation, pay-

**Supreme Court "Injustices."** The signs indicate that this demonstration is in opposition to one of the judicial decisions, most notably *Bowers v. Hardwick* (1986), that upheld laws against sodomy. The U.S. Supreme Court overturned such legislation in *Lawrence v. Texas* (2003). [The Washington Blade]

ment for sex (including oral or anal sex), disorderly conduct, and vagrancy survive in some jurisdictions; such laws were not written to regulate private intimacy and same-sex intimacy, though they have been used in both ways. In the last generation, laws against sexual conduct with or molestation of children have expanded in detail and in penalties, but like the other surviving laws do not target homosexual activity per se. Thus, the gay or bisexual man who has sex with minors, solicits sex in public places, or engages in nonconsensual conduct is today subject to the same formal rules as straight men engaged in the same kind of activities. Discriminatory enforcement of such formally neutral laws persists in many jurisdictions, however. Even gay-friendly jurisdictions such as New York City reportedly enforce their public sex laws disproportionately against men soliciting sex from other men. While the Supreme Court's decision in *Lawrence* does not by its terms invalidate public indecency laws, it might pose problems for laws that are enforced in a clearly discriminatory manner.

In a final twist, the criminal law is now deployed for the protection of gay and lesbian people in some jurisdictions. The District of Columbia and almost half the states have laws establishing higher penalties for crimes committed against people because of their sexual orientation. The federal government collects statistics on crimes motivated by animus against sexual minorities. Ironically, a minority once the most vilified by the criminal law now finds some protection in it.

## Bibliograhy

Bérubé, Allan. *Coming Out under Fire: The History of Gay Men and Women in World War II.* New York: Free Press, 1990.

Bingham, Caroline. "Seventeenth Century Attitudes toward Deviant Sex." *Journal of Interdisciplinary History* 1 (1971): 447-468.

D'Emilio, John. *Sexual Politics, Sexual Communities: The Making of a Homosexual Minority in the United States, 1940-1970.* Chicago: University of Chicago Press, 1983.

Eskridge, William N., Jr. *Gaylaw: Challenging the Apartheid of the Closet.* Cambridge, Mass.: Harvard University Press, 1999.

Faderman, Lillian. *Odd Girls and Twilight Lovers: A History of Lesbian Life in Twentieth-Century America.* New York: Penguin, 1991.

Freedman, Estelle. "'Uncontrolled Desires': The Response to the Sexual Psychopath, 1920–1960." *Journal of American History* 74 (1987): 83–106.

Jenkins, Philip. *Moral Panic: Changing Concepts of the Child Molester in Modern America.* New Haven: Yale University Press, 1998.

Katz, Jonathan. *Gay American History: Lesbians and Gay Men in the U.S.A.* New York: Avon, 1976.

———. *Gay/Lesbian Almanac: A New Documentary.* New York: Carroll and Graf, 1983.

Kennedy, Elizabeth Lapovsky, and Madeline D. Davis. *Boots of Leather, Slippers of Gold: The History of a Lesbian Community.* New York: Routledge, 1993.

McLaren, Angus. *The Trials of Masculinity: Policing Sexual Boundaries, 1870–1930.* Chicago: Chicago University Press, 1997.

Smith-Rosenberg, Carroll. *Disorderly Conduct: Visions of Gender in Victorian America.* New York: Knopf, 1985.

**William N. Eskridge Jr.**

*See also* CENSORSHIP, OBSCENITY, AND PORNOGRAPHY LAW AND POLICY; DISCRIMINATION; FEDERAL LAW AND POLICY; HATE CRIMES LAW AND POLICY; LIQUOR CONTROL LAW AND POLICY; MILITARY LAW AND POLICY; POLICING AND POLICE; PRIVACY AND PRIVACY RIGHTS; PROSTITUTION, HUSTLING, AND SEX WORK LAW AND POLICY; RIGHTS OF ASSOCIATION AND ASSEMBLY; SEXUAL PSYCHOPATH LAW AND POLICY; SODOMY, BUGGERY, CRIMES AGAINST NATURE, DISORDERLY CONDUCT, AND LEWD AND LASCIVIOUS LAW AND POLICY; TRANSGENDER AND GENDER IMPERSONATION LAW AND POLICY.

# CRISP, Quentin (b. 25 December 1908; d. 21 November 1999), writer, actor.

Quentin Crisp was born Dennis Pratt in the London suburb of Sutton. He exhibited effeminate traits in boarding school and was frequently tormented by his fellow students. Moving to London in 1930, he determined to live openly and proudly as a homosexual, wearing eye shadow, dyeing his hair lilac, and sporting flamboyant scarves, hats, and jewelry. Since homosexuality was then a crime in England, Crisp's appearance was unique and attracted the attention of both the police and gay bashers. Although Crisp worked at a variety of jobs, including book illustration and advertising—"if at first you don't succeed, failure may be your style," he quipped—he found his permanent livelihood in 1942 as an artist's nude model, a job he performed for some thirty-five years. The only sign of his future literary genius was a comic poem, "All This and Bevin Too," a 1943 satire on excessive government red tape.

Crisp became more than a local celebrity in 1968 when he published the first of four volumes of memoirs, *The Naked Civil Servant.* Written with a lively wit that would also characterize his subsequent books, it detailed both his determination not to compromise his way of life despite loneliness and attacks, but also his shame at being homosexual, which he considered a sickness. The book was made into a BBC film starring John Hurt in 1975. Crisp, meanwhile, opened a one-man show in 1978, *An Evening with Quentin Crisp,* that he continued to perform until the end of his life. In this changing monologue, he would discourse on various topics in his inimitable "Crisperanto." One of his favorite targets was the oversexed nature of modern people: "Nothing in our culture, not even home computers, is more overrated than the epidermal felicity of two featherless bipeds in desperate concourse." It was on tour preparing to perform this play in Manchester, England, that he died.

Crisp was never happy in England. He considered the people cold and self-centered compared to the warmhearted American soldiers he met during World War II. In 1981 he moved to New York City and remained a resident alien in the United States for the rest of his life, adoring both the city and the country. He was famous not only for his appearance, but also for continuing to live in a one-room apartment at 46 East Third Street despite the opportunity to move elsewhere—his refusal to clean it was legendary, as was his saying, "Never keep a frequent and extremely amusing guest on television talk shows and lent his style to commercials for products such as Calvin Klein and Impulse perfumes. Crisp wrote film reviews for the gay magazine *Christopher Street,* which became the basis of *How to Go to the Movies* (1989), and a regular column for the gay newspaper *New York Native,* which provided the raw material for three additional autobiographies: *How to Become a Virgin* (1981), *Resident Alien: The New York Diaries* (1996), and *Dusty Answers* (which was edited for posthumous publication in the early 2000s by Richard Ward). The essence of his thought and personality is evident in *The Wit and Wisdom of Quentin Crisp* (1984), which features such gems as "Looked at from the front, a television screen appears to be a lighted rectangle full of celebrities and other disasters. Seen from behind, it is an arid waste in which, like farmers in a dust bowl, broadcasters and producers dig for something—anything—on which to feed their bleating flocks" (p. 6).

### Bibliography

Bailey, Paul, ed. *The Stately Homo: A Celebration of the Life of Quentin Crisp.* New York: Bantam Press, 2002.

Crisp, Quentin. *Archives.* Available from http://www.crisperanto.org.

———. Selected quotations available from http://www.quotationspage.com/quentin crisp.

———. *The Wit and Wisdom of Quentin Crisp.* Edited by Guy Kettelhack. New York: Harper & Row, 1984.

Fountain, Tim. *Quentin Crisp.* Carlisle, England: Absolute Classics, 2001.

**William Pencak**

*See also* ACTORS AND ACTRESSES.

**Quentin Crisp.** Noteworthy at first for defiantly living openly—and flamboyantly—as a homosexual when it was illegal in 1930s London, he achieved far wider fame in his last thirty years for his witty memoirs, one-man stage show, and television appearances. [Quentin Crisp Archive]

up with the Joneses. Drag them down to your level." He was a much seen and beloved figure in Greenwich Village, keeping his phone number listed so anyone might talk with him and conversing with strangers on an almost daily basis at the Cooper Square Diner.

During the last twenty years of his life, Crisp made numerous recordings of his own and other's works, including Oscar Wilde's *The Ballad of Reading Gaol.* He appeared in many films, notably of his own show, but also starring as Queen Elizabeth I in both Derek Jarman's *Jubilee* (1977) and Sally Potter's version of Virginia Woolf's *Orlando* (1993). (His cameo in *Fatal Attraction* [1987], starring Glenn Close and Michael Douglas, was cut.) Crisp was in addition a compelling witness to the past in the documentaries *Stonewall* (1994 for WNYC TV) and *The Celluloid Closet* (1996), the classic exposé of closeted homosexuality in the film industry. He was also

# CROSS-CLASS SEX AND RELATIONSHIPS

When in the 1930s gay writer Glenway Wescott referred in his journal to the "cult of the normal young man of the people, that is, of the lower classes" (p. 11), he reminded his readers that sex and relationships across the divides of class have been an enduring feature of LGBT history in the United States. Much of what people know about cross-class sex and relationships, however, rests on a pop psychology of questionable value. Explanations for cross-class sexual liaisons often emphasize such things as bourgeois men's class guilt, how class opposites attract, or how class difference stands in for the supposed absence of male/female difference in same-sex relationships. Historians, by contrast, generally eschew such psychological analysis in favor of tracing the specific social settings, changing historical contexts, and shifting cultural meanings in which same-sex and cross-class relations unfold.

## British Influence

Sensitivity to the theme of cross-class sex and relationships owes much to the pioneering work of British gay historians. This may be related to what is arguably the greater consciousness of class in Britain compared to the United States, and to the fact that early investigations into the British gay past emerged out of a vibrant leftist gay movement during the 1970s, in which questions of class were very much on the intellectual and political agenda. For example, in *Coming Out* (1977) and in much of his subsequent work, Jeffrey Weeks draws attention to the middle-class male homosexual's fascination with crossing the class divide, be it Oscar Wilde's preference for stable lads and laborers, Edward Carpenter's desire for the "thick-thighed, hot, coarse-fleshed young bricklayer with the strip around his waist," or E. M. Forster's urge "to love a strong young man of the lower classes and be loved by him and even hurt by him" (pp. 40–41). British homosexual scandals, such as the Cleveland Street Affair of 1889, which involved aristocrats and messenger boys, further revealed the clandestine world of cross-class sexual relations. These scandals, widely reported in the American press, defined homosexuality in the cross-class terms of aristocratic vice and working-class corruptibility.

## U.S. Cross-Class Male Relations

In the United States, sex across class lines emerged in tandem with historically changing class formations. In the colonial era, for instance, same-sex sexual relations reflected the social distinctions of wealth and economic inequalities characteristic of colonial society. In his *Gay/Lesbian Almanac*, Jonathan Ned Katz includes a case from 1637, in which a Plymouth court found John Allexander and Thomas Roberts guilty of "often spending their seed one upon the other." As Katz notes, the "class differences of the parties"—Allexander was a free man, whereas Roberts was an indentured servant—were significant enough to be recorded in the documents. Katz poses the intriguing question of "whether this intermingling of social orders, as well as of seed, lent gravity to the crime" (p. 75). Other legal records from the colonial and later periods underscore the ways in which cross-class sexual relations emerged out of and mirrored distinct social settings, such as those of master and servant, or master and apprentice.

By the nineteenth and early twentieth centuries, the consolidation of a capitalist economy and an expanding

cash nexus left an indelible mark on cross-class same-sex relations. One sees this most clearly in the forms of male prostitution in which poor and/or working-class men, often existing on the margins of market society, exchanged sex for money with men of greater financial means. But cash alone cannot account for the persistence of cross-class relations; they flourished also in part because they made sense within prevailing sex/gender systems. In *Gay New York*, George Chauncey explains how, in the first half of the twentieth century (a period in which homosexual desire was often conceived of as feminine desire), many gay men, including middle-class gay men, were attracted to masculine workingmen, particularly the aggressive masculinity of sailors, soldiers, laborers, and other men drawn from the ranks of the "rough" working class. This eroticization of class difference has been central to the gay erotic imagination throughout the twentieth century. Tom Waugh has noted that underground gay graphics from the pre-Stonewall period "appealed to an assumed middle-class fascination for the presumed exaggerated masculinity of the muscled (lumpen-) proletarian . . . certain class-colored icons, occupational types like the truck driver or the farmboy or the soldier belong to this configuration, but especially the sailors" (p. 32).

One of the dilemmas in researching this history concerns the self-perceptions of the men on the working-class end of cross-class relations. Middle-class men were more likely to leave behind diaries and journals, and these can provide an indication of their class desires. The historical self-understandings of working-class men are more difficult to discern. It would be wrong to assume, however, that workingmen's relations with middle-class men were only ever about economic necessity and/or casual sexual exchange. In the British context, James Gardiner's *A Class Apart*, a photographic record of the early-twentieth-century relationship between Montague Glover, an architect, and Ralph, his handsome, working-class lover, suggests that class difference could form the basis of a long-term, mutually dependent relationship, one that even incorporated the conscious erotic play of class indicators and fantasy.

## Meanings of Cross-Class Sex

A number of different meanings have been attributed to cross-class sex over time. A sentimental belief in the power of cross-class liaisons to bridge the chasms of class in capitalist society has been one dominant strain. Something of this can be detected in Walt Whitman's manly love of working-class comrades—from the artisans he cruised on the streets of his beloved republican

New York City to Civil War soldiers—which informed his vision of American democracy. But there are also less romantic aspects to sexually crossing the class divide. On the part of some middle-class men, as Weeks has noted, there might be a strong element of "sexual colonialism" in their relations with workingmen (p. 40). There has also often been an element of potential danger, something vividly captured in Wilde's evocative expression, "feasting with panthers." Historically, this has included theft and blackmail in which cross-class liaisons set the stage, if not for class conflict, then certainly for class antagonisms. And as Chauncey has explained about early-twentieth-century New York, many middle-class queers who combined same-sex object choice with conventionally masculine gender identity rejected the flamboyant effeminacy of the working-class fairy and, in so doing, simultaneously engaged in a profound act of class differentiation. This is a forceful reminder that if same-sex relations have sometimes facilitated the crossing of class lines, they have just as often reflected and reproduced within the gay world the class divisions within society at large.

## Lesbian Worlds

Within lesbian history, the eroticization of class appears to have been less pronounced. This is not to say that class was absent or unimportant within lesbian communities. On the contrary, as Esther Newton detailed in her history of Cherry Grove, Fire Island, rather sharp class divisions existed between the "fun gay ladies," a group of older, white lesbians with professional jobs and independent incomes, and younger, mostly Jewish and Italian-American working-class lesbians. Gender further complicated the class configuration of the community. "Unlike many Grove 'boys,'" Newton notes, "few 'ladies' admitted to being lured over class lines by sexual attraction" (p. 219). According to Newton, gay men's sexual encounters across class lines were made easier by their casual nature, while for lesbians, who tended to seek sex embedded in relationships, "cross-class eroticism would have been far more consequential than for men" (p. 219). Similarly, in their study of femme/butch lesbian culture and community in Buffalo, New York, during the 1950s and 1960s, Elizabeth Lapovsky Kennedy and Madeline D. Davis discovered a "lack of contact between different classes of lesbians" (p. 45) and a striking "lack of eroticization of class difference" (p. 65). Kennedy and Davis note that this contrasted sharply with "gay male culture, which has a long tradition of explicitly erotic cross-class socializing" (p. 43), and they suggest several possiblities for the difference. For reasons related primarily to gender and personal safety, lesbians did not have access to the same range of sexual spaces as gay men, notably the sites

of public sex that played such a crucial role in facilitating men's cross-class liaisons. By contrast, the central institution of lesbian sexual culture—the bar—tended to be marked by greater class homogeneity. In Colorado, one middle-class lesbian, a narrator in Katie Gilmartin's study of lesbian cultural spaces in mid-twentieth-century Denver, put it succinctly: "We weren't bar people." Similary, in Buffalo, upper class lesbians, who tended to socialize at private parties, rarely ventured into the city's tough lesbian bars, which attracted a decidedly working-class clientele. Kennedy and Davis also suggest that it was "perhaps the lesbian interest in relationships as well as sex that makes the eroticization of class difference less compelling" (p. 65); butch-femme relationships were organized primarily around the eroticization of the difference between masculine and feminine. Highlighting the gender and class differences between lesbian and gay male sexual cultures and relationships, Kennedy and Davis conclude about Buffalo's lesbian community that "there was not an erotic force bridging the gap between the classes" (p. 44).

## Contemporary Cross-Class Sex

If the meanings of cross-class sex and relationships have varied over time and across gender, their political import also remains ambiguous. In the early days of gay liberation in the late 1960s and early 1970s, gay men's sexual spaces, such as the bathhouses, were offered up as bastions of sexual democracy in which the distinctions of class in the outside world were supposed to be stripped away along with one's clothes. But such utopian beliefs in the redemptive powers of same-sex relations to dissolve class difference have failed to materialize; no matter what personal pleasures and meanings have been discovered from cross-class relations in the gay sites of public sex, they have done little fundamentally to alter the class—and often overlapping racial—hierarchies of the gay world. The truth is that strikingly little about cross-class sex and relationships in contemporary LGBT life is known. How, for instance, are class differences negotiated in same-sex relationships? Perhaps the lack of knowledge stems from the more general silence surrounding issues of class in contemporary LGBT politics and culture, and in society in general. Ironically, it may be that more is known about the dynamics and significance of cross-class sex and relationships in the LGBT past than in the present.

### Bibliography

Chauncey, George. *Gay New York: Gender, Urban Culture, and the Making of the Gay Male World, 1890–1940*. New York: Basic Books, 1994.

Gardiner, James. *A Class Apart: The Private Pictures of Montague Glover*. London: Serpent's Tail, 1992.

Gilmartin, Katie. " 'We Weren't Bar People': Middle-Class Lesbian Identities and Cultural Spaces." *GLQ* 3, no. 1 (1996): 1–51.

Katz, Jonathan Ned. *Gay/Lesbian Almanac: A New Documentary*. New York: Harper and Row, 1983.

Kennedy, Elizabeth Lapovsky, and Madeline D. Davis. *Boots of Leather, Slippers of Gold: The History of a Lesbian Community*. New York: Routledge, 1993.

Newton, Esther. *Cherry Grove, Fire Island: Sixty Years in America's First Gay and Lesbian Town*. New York: Beacon Press, 1993.

Waugh, Thomas. *Out/Lines: Underground Gay Graphics from before Stonewall*. Vancouver, B.C.: Arsenal Pulp Press, 2002.

Weeks, Jeffrey. *Coming Out: Homosexual Politics in Britain from the Nineteenth Century to the Present*. London: Quartet, 1977.

Wescott, Glenway. *Continual Lessons: The Journals of Glenway Wescott, 1937–1955*. Edited by Robert Phelps with Jerry Rosco. New York: Farrar Straus Giroux, 1990.

**Steven Maynard**

*See also* ALGER, HORATIO; CAPITALISM AND INDUSTRIALIZATION; CLASS AND CLASS OPPRESSION; PROSTITUTION, HUSTLING, AND SEX WORK; SENSION, NICHOLAS; TOURISM; WHITMAN, WALT.

**CROSS-DRESSERS.** see TRANSEXUALS, TRANSVESTITES, TRANSGENDER PEOPLE, AND CROSS-DRESSERS.

# CRUISING

"Cruising" refers to the practice of seeking casual sexual partners, typically in public, semipublic, or commercial spaces. Though not unique to LGBT cultures, the practice has been important to the formation of LGBT subcultures in the United States. Since publicly expressing sexual interest in a stranger could, at times, expose LGBT people to severe social and physical risks, many have used ambiguous gestures and signs to make their erotic interests apparent to those "in the know" without tipping off outsiders unfamiliar with LGBT cultural codes. Partly in response to the dangers associated with cruising in public places, LGBT people, especially gay men, have created commercial and semipublic spaces in which same-sex cruising was not just tolerated but actually affirmed.

## Urbanization, Street Culture, and the Subculture

The social history of cruising in the United States has generally been analyzed through local case studies of twentieth-century cities. In working-class subcultures of both lesbians and gay men, the practice of cruising in the early and mid-twentieth century was linked to distinct gender positions or roles that LGBT people adopted. As George Chauncey has demonstrated, gay male street culture in early twentieth-century New York City was embedded in a broader, rough-and-tumble working-class street culture, which middle-class observers regarded as a threat to bourgeois propriety. These men adopted styles of clothing, dress, and mannerism that identified them as "wolves," "trade," "fairies," and "punks," which denoted specific gender roles and represented forms of self-identification. These cultural roles helped to indicate what type of same-sex sexual interaction a man might want to pursue.

Although less is known about the history of urban cruising between women before World War II, historians have shown that women in nineteenth-century America frequently developed intensely intimate bonds that may have blurred the boundary between sexual and nonsexual practice. All-women's institutions, such as reformatories, women's colleges, and athletic and camping teams, offered women the opportunity to pursue same-sex emotional and physical intimacy outside the presence of men. This may partly explain why cruising was less prevalent between women before World War II.

## Cultural Codes and Strategies of Ambiguity

Same-sex cruising has been governed by several conditions that differentiate it from cruising in heterosexual culture. First, LGBT people have had to rely on subtle cultural codes—styles of dress and mannerisms of walking and talking—to indicate to each other their shared membership in a subculture. These codes have needed to be subtle enough not to disrupt participation in a broader society dominated by heterosexuals, yet clear enough to signal group membership to other LGBT people. Among gay men in the early twentieth century, wearing handkerchiefs or flowers could designate one's same-sex sexual interests or even a desire for specific sexual acts. LGBT people have often established distinct cruising zones in places as small as a park bench or as large as an entire urban neighborhood.

In the early twentieth century these areas frequently overlapped with urban "bohemian" subcultures or busy metropolitan theater districts. Chauncey cites Cary Grant's famous line in the 1938 film *Bringing Up Baby,* in which Grant's character declares, "I just went gay all of a sudden. I'm just sitting in the middle of Forty-second Street waiting for a bus." In New York City, Times Square, at Forty-second Street, was then the most active cruising area for "fairies"—male prostitutes with "effeminate" status who openly wore feminine garb and make-up. During the post–World War II period, despite increased police crackdowns in many cities, men continued to cruise each other in a wide variety of public spaces. Cruising became easiest in gay "ghettoes," especially in very large and complex cities.

Although it has played a different and perhaps more central role in LGBT cultures, same-sex cruising has followed patterns similar to those of cross-sex cruising. Both LGBT and straight people, for instance, use ambiguous glances to convey their interest to each other. Just as in LGBT cultures, cross-sex cruising has been linked to gendered patterns that subject "feminine" partners to the gaze, and sometimes unwanted advances, of "masculine" partners who have set the terms of courtship. Influenced by the politics of second-wave feminism, some LGBT and straight people in the 1970s began to reject these distinct roles, valuing an emotional connection over what they regarded as the gendered combination of pleasure and control embodied in the practice of cruising. Other LGBT people affirmed cruising as a valuable cultural practice and community-building tactic in a hostile world.

## Cruising and the Femme/Butch Image in Lesbian Bars

Although less is known about cruising practices between women, historians Elizabeth Lapovsky Kennedy and Madeline Davis have shown that by the 1940s working-class lesbians in Buffalo developed a bar culture in which lesbians identified themselves as either "butches" or "fems." (Kennedy and Davis found that their interview subjects preferred the use of "fems" instead of the more commonly used "femmes" because they felt that the latter had more of an upper-class connotation.) In this sexual culture, it was the responsibility of a butch not only to provide sexual pleasure to her femme, but also to take the lead role in courting, usually in a bar setting. Patterns of courtship were highly ritualized: butches would pursue femmes in bars by buying them drinks, asking for a dance, or eyeing them. Femmes, by contrast, as the objects of this cruising practice, were expected not to assert their interest in such an overt fashion. "House parties" were especially important forums for African American lesbians who sought a way to conduct a lesbian social life while remaining safely hidden within Buffalo's black community.

Marc Stein has demonstrated that in post–World War II Philadelphia, distinct lesbian and gay cruising practices overlapped in the public space of downtown Rittenhouse Square. While lesbian cruising was perhaps less visible than gay male cruising, lesbians wore masculine clothing and "DA haircuts" to signify their interest to one another as they crossed the park. Sometimes, lesbians and gay men cruised in the same spaces; other times, they did not, especially in parks where gay men had sex with each other. Although cruising is more often discussed as a gay male phenomenon, scholarship has established that lesbians do also have a long history of cruising.

## Cruising in LGBT Resorts, Beaches, and Neighborhoods

By uprooting countless women and men who joined the military or moved to cities in search of high-paying work in war industries, World War II contributed dramatically to the rise of lesbian and gay urban subcultures. Allan Bérubé describes how the routes between military bases and nearby cities became cruising grounds where civilian men could pick up uniformed men. In the post–World War II era, LGBT neighborhoods in so-called "meccas," especially San Francisco and New York, have drawn LGBT migrants and tourists from other regions. For example, many gay veterans returning from the Pacific front remained in San Francisco, where they found a relatively open community with a history of tolerance for sexual deviance.

Many same-sex institutions, such as YMCAs and all-female schools and colleges, were associated with cruising between men or between women, yet they did not offer the security of knowing that a potential partner was likely aware of or receptive to one's intentions. Specific places of employment and recreation, such as theaters, restaurants, or women's softball leagues, became known for their tolerance of same-sex cruising. LGBT enclaves in areas such as New York's Greenwich Village and Harlem, Fire Island (near New York), and Provincetown, Massachusetts, offered LGBT people relative security in pursuing partners. Esther Newton's study of Fire Island revealed that cruising between gay men took place more often on beaches and outdoor dance parties, whereas lesbians tended to hold dinners and indoor parties for the same purpose. The cruising practices of gay men and lesbians partially overlapped, sometimes amicably, at other times uncomfortably.

In the era of post-Stonewall "gay liberation," gay men in urban settings developed extensive networks of casual sex partners. Many gay men met each other in commercial spaces such as bathhouses, bars, adult bookstores, cafeterias, movie theaters, and peep shows, whose management often successfully bribed the local police to ignore their presence and where cruising was often safer than in streets or parks. Other men cruised in public parks and "tearooms" or on the beach, where the risk of a hostile response was higher.

## Cruising and the Politics of Sexual Culture

In the late 1960s and early 1970s urban gay subcultures expanded and commercialized, and cruising between gay men became more visible than in previous decades. Martin Levine has argued that gay male cruising was shaped by masculine gender norms, because men cruised in order to affirm their masculine prowess and obtain "release" from attractive sexual partners. At certain times of the day, bars, discos, cafes, and sex clubs would become "active" cruising sites. By making eye contact with a man across the room, gay men signaled their erotic interest. Depending on the location, gay men might pursue sexual contact in the space where they first cruised each other (e.g., in the back room of a bookstore or sex club), or one might invite the other home or to another locale for sex in a more "private" space.

Physique magazines and drag performances had contributed to the formation of gay communities since at least the early twentieth century, but by the mid-1970s, these communities became larger and more complex than ever before. With the rise of the so-called "clone" look, which drew on working-class male cultural styles, earlier "effeminate" styles became increasingly subordinate and stigmatized, whereas overt muscularity and masculinity were increasingly prized. Some gay activists have criticized the predominance of cruising in gay male sexual culture as a fulfillment of masculine norms of possession, domination, and objectification. Other gay men claim that the separation of sex from intimacy holds the potential of emancipation from heterosexist norms.

As they became more and more visible to straight Americans in the print media, and especially after the AIDS epidemic began in the early 1980s, LGBT cultures were often associated solely with spaces for cruising and with the seemingly endless pursuit of sexual partners. Some LGBT people sought to distance themselves from the practices of cruising and multiple partners, encouraging others to eschew anonymous sex and instead embrace monogamy along the model of heterosexual marriage. In addition, increasing acceptance of gays and lesbians in the workplace and within the judicial system made it easier for LGBT people to participate in conventional forms of family life.

In 1980 the Hollywood film *Cruising*, directed by William Friedkin and starring Al Pacino, in which the police attempt to track down a serial killer murdering men within New York City's gay bar subculture, drew mainstream attention and the anger of LGBT activists—both for its sensationalized portrayal of leather and S/M clubs, and its representation of gay men pursuing seemingly dangerous and meaningless sex. LGBT activists picketed the film and demanded a more balanced portrayal of cruising and its practice within the gay world.

Meanwhile, bitter controversy about female sexual practices in this era, known as the feminist "sex wars," tended to focus on the respective roles of pleasure and danger in shaping female sexuality. The increased politicization of sexuality led some women to criticize practices, including cruising, that involved the cultural objectification of bodies.

In the 1980s the emergence of the AIDS epidemic among homosexual men generated tremendous controversy about gay sexual practices. Conservative public commentators, including many Reagan Administration officials, blamed the virus on gay "promiscuity." Since the 1980s some gay cultural critics have argued that gay culture needs to be transformed so as to place less emphasis on casual sex. Although efforts to promote safer sex among gay men were quite successful in reducing the spread of the virus after the epidemic's first wave, casual sexual interactions are, in general, more widely accepted among gay men, even some in long-term relationships, than in the dominant heterosexual culture.

In the present as well as the past, cruising has put some LGBT people at physical risk and been used as a justification or explanation for anti-LGBT violence. Transgender people, transsexuals, men and women with gender-variant appearances, and LGBT sex workers have been especially subject to brutal physical violence. Heterosexual men have claimed that unwanted sexual advances from other men justified violent assaults against them. In 1998 the deaths of James Byrd in Jasper, Texas, and Matthew Shepard in Laramie, Wyoming, brought the issue of anti-LGBT violence to the forefront of national politics, and President Bill Clinton soon advocated the passage of federal laws specifying additional penalties for "hate crimes" against LGBT people and members of other minority groups.

That LGBT people have continued to cruise in a variety of environments, despite the dangers, suggests the importance of cruising to LGBT cultures.

## Bibliography

Bérubé, Allan. *Coming Out under Fire: The History of Gay Men and Women in World War Two.* New York: Plume, 1990.

Boyd, Nan Alamilla. "'Homos Invade S.F.!' San Francisco's History as a Wide-Open Town." In *Creating a Place for Our-*

selves: *Lesbian, Gay, and Bisexual Community Histories.* Edited by Brett Beemyn. New York: Routledge, 1997.

Chauncey, George. *Gay New York: Gender, Urban Culture, and the Makings of the Gay Male World, 1890–1940.* New York: Basic Books, 1994.

Faderman, Lillian. *Odd Girls and Twilight Lovers: A History of Lesbian Life in Twentieth-Century America.* New York: Columbia University Press, 1991.

Katz, Jonathan. *Gay American History: Lesbians and Gay Men in the U.S.A.: A Documentary Anthology.* New York: Avon, 1976.

Kennedy, Elizabeth Lapovsky, and Madeline D. Davis. *Boots of Leather, Slippers of Gold: The History of a Lesbian Community.* New York: Routledge, 1993.

Levine, Martin P. In *Gay Macho: The Life and Death of the Homosexual Clone.* Edited by Michael S. Kimmel. New York: New York University Press, 1998.

Newton, Esther. *Cherry Grove, Fire Island: Sixty Years in America's First Gay and Lesbian Town.* Boston: Beacon Press, 1993.

Stein, Marc. *City of Sisterly and Brotherly Loves: Lesbian and Gay Philadelphia, 1945–1972.* Chicago: University of Chicago Press, 2000.

**Timothy Stewart-Winter**

*See also* PUBLIC SEX; SEX CLUBS; TEAROOMS (BATHROOMS); TRICKING; URBAN, SUBURBAN, AND RURAL GEOGRAPHIES.

**George Cukor.** The director points over the head of a boyish-looking Katharine Hepburn while filming *Sylvia Scarlett* in September 1935, early in what would be a long career. [Bettmann/corbis]

# CUKOR, George (b. 7 July 1889; d. 24 January 1983), filmmaker.

One of the most prolific directors of Hollywood's so-called Golden Age (1930s–1950s), George Cukor was also one of a group of largely closeted LGB directors—including James Whale, Dorothy Arzner, Edmund Goulding, and Vincente Minnelli—who successfully worked within the studio system. Tagged early in his career as a "woman's director"—a label he would come to resent as restrictive, if not stereotypic—Cukor's rapport with stars like Greta Garbo, Katharine Hepburn, Constance Bennett, Tallulah Bankhead, Joan Crawford, Norma Shearer, Judy Holliday, and Judy Garland does reveal an empathy with women, if not with the conventionally feminine. Indeed, some of Cukor's most interesting work with women stars happens when he brings out the masculine (or the non–gender conformist) in their screen personas. Take, for example, Garbo's Marguerite Gautier in *Camille* (1937), who pursues Robert Taylor's younger pretty boy Armand, kissing him all over his face as he sits passively in a chair. Katharine Hepburn provides a masculine example as well, from her tomboyish Jo in *Little Women* (1933), to her masquerade as a young man in *Sylvia Scarlett* (1936), and her butch athleticism in *Pat and Mike* (1952).

It cannot be a mere coincidence that Cukor directed films and collaborated with many women stars dear to LGBT fans. The key performer and film in this queer context are Hepburn as Sylvia Scarlett, in which the star not only plays a teenage boy, Sylvester, for most of the running time, but kisses one woman, has another bisexual woman infatuated with him/her, and is told by a male artist, "I don't know what it is that gives me a queer feeling when I look at you." A major financial disaster in 1936, *Sylvia Scarlett* was rediscovered and hailed in the 1970s. Cukor said that the film's original reception "slowed [him] up," and that he "wasn't going to be so goddamned daring after that" (Lambert, p. 92).

Cukor's zenith as a woman's director came with *The Women* (1939), a screen version of Clare Boothe Luce's Broadway hit. The film contains alliances among women, misogyny, camp, bitchy wit, glamour, and a secondary lesbian character. Popular in its day, the film quickly became a classic gay cult film rivaled only by *The Wizard* of Oz (1939), All About Eve (1950), Sunset Boulevard (1950), and Whatever Happened to Baby Jane? (1962).

Aside from the "woman's director" label, Cukor has often been subtly patronized by critics through descriptions of his work as "theatrical" and overly concerned with style. In retrospect, it appears that his success in the 1930s was the result of being assigned a number of projects with literary prestige value like The Royal Family of Broadway (1930), Little Women, Dinner at Eight (1933), David Copperfield (1935), Romeo and Juliet (1936), Camille, and Holiday (1938). The prestige value of these films effectively counterbalanced attempts to derogatorily (ef)feminize the director and his work. This was not enough to keep him from being dismissed from Gone with the Wind (1939), however, reportedly because the star Clark Gable and the producer David O. Selznick felt he could not handle the epic aspects of the Civil War melodrama.

Not surprisingly, it is precisely for Cukor's theatrical, gender-bending, woman-centered high style that many of his films have entered LGBT cultural canons. In fact, it is a rare film by the director that is not of interest to some queer viewer by virtue of its star, subject matter, dialogue, visual style, or genre (high comedies, melodramas, and musicals were central to Cukor's output). Among Cukor's mid- and late-career films, four stand out as of particular interest to queers: the musicals A Star is Born (1954), with Judy Garland, and My Fair Lady (1964); Graham Greene's Auntie Mame–like story Travels with My Aunt (1972); and Rich and Famous (1981), a remake of Old Acquaintance (1943) that focuses upon the decades-long friendship (and professional rivalry) between two women. At the end of his career, Cukor directed his favorite star—and one with a dedicated LGBT following—Katharine Hepburn, in two television films, Love among the Ruins (1974) and The Corn Is Green (1979).

### Bibliography

Carey, Gary. Cukor and Co.: The Films of George Cukor and His Collaborators. New York: Museum of Modern Art, 1971.

Lambert, Gavin. On Cukor. New York: Putnam, 1972.

Levy, Emanuel. George Cukor: Master of Elegance. New York: Morrow, 1974.

Lippe, Richard. "Gender and Destiny: George Cukor's A Star is Born." CineAction nos. 3–4 (January 1986): 46–57.

McGilligan, Patrick. George Cukor, A Biography of the Gentleman Director, a Double Life. New York: St. Martin's Press, 1991.

**Alexander Doty**

*See also* FILM AND VIDEO.

## CULLEN, Countee (b. 30 March 1903; d. 9 January 1946), writer, teacher.

Scholars have found it difficult to learn exactly where Cullen was born or with whom he spent the earliest years of his childhood. New York City, Baltimore, and Louisville have all been suggested with varying degrees of evidence. Sometime between 1903 and 1918 he was adopted by the Reverend Frederick A. and Carolyn Belle (Mitchell) Cullen of the Salem Methodist Church in Harlem. He was their only child. Until 1918 Cullen went by the name of Countee Porter. He was Countee P. Cullen until 1921. Thereafter, he was known simply as Countee Cullen. He attended DeWitt Clinton High School in New York and earned degrees from New York University and Harvard University.

Cullen became one of the star literary figures of the Harlem Renaissance, the period in African American history roughly between 1915 (the start of the great migration of southern blacks to the North and Midwest) and 1930 (just after the start of the Great Depression) when African Americans became a major presence in U.S. urban life. Key Renaissance figures emphasized literature (although blacks made their biggest cultural impact with music, especially jazz and blues), and during this period a number of significant writers emerged, including Jean Toomer, Zora Neale Hurston, Claude McKay, Jessie Fauset, and Wallace Thurman. The work of Cullen and these other writers was largely shepherded and promoted by three powerful figures: James Weldon Johnson, field secretary of the National Association for the Advancement of Colored People; Charles S. Johnson, research director of the National Urban League; and Alain Locke, a philosophy professor at Howard University. Cullen, along with Langston Hughes, was the most talented and revered African American poet of the day. Unlike Hughes, who wrote mostly free verse highly influenced by Carl Sandburg and Walt Whitman, Cullen wrote regularly metered couplets in the style of his contemporary Edna St. Vincent Millay and in homage to his idol, John Keats. He won more literary prizes than any other black writer of the 1920s. His first two volumes of poetry, Color (1925) and Copper Sun (1927), were highly praised and enjoyed some commercial success. He eventually produced an anthology of black poetry (1927); another major book of verse, The Black Christ and Other Poems (1929); a satirical novel, One Way to Heaven (1932); a translation of The Medea (1935); and, at the end of his career when he had become a schoolteacher, several children's books. He was never to enjoy the acclaim and success with his later work that he had with his first two publications.

Many of the leading writers of the Harlem Renaissance were homosexual or bisexual: Alain Locke, Bruce

Nugent, Wallace Thurman, Langston Hughes, and Countee Cullen, to name only some of the more prominent figures. The powerful strain of homosexuality that runs through the movement might eventually lead, and to some degree has already led, to entirely fresh interpretations of the significance of the entire period and, certainly, reconsiderations of the politics of who was promoted and who was not.

Cullen's father was a transvestite and this may have had an impact on the younger Cullen. He deeply admired his father, was very close to him, and they traveled together often. In April 1928 Cullen married Yolande Du Bois, daughter of W. E. B. Du Bois, the great African American scholar and activist, in what was the most celebrated black wedding of the 1920s, but many believe that the marriage was never consummated. It barely survived its honeymoon, on which the couple was accompanied by Cullen's best man, Harold Jackman, who was also homosexual. It was reported that Cullen virtually ignored his wife during the honeymoon. (Black newspapers of the day made much sport of this.) They divorced in 1930, and Cullen remarried in 1940. He had no children.

Racial and sexual themes are very apparent in a good deal of Cullen's work, although Cullen did not consider himself a racial poet or a "black poet," in the conventional understanding of that term. His long poem, "The Black Christ," for instance, is both sexual and racial in its concerns, dealing with interracial romance and lynching. And his popular works "Yet Do I Marvel," "The Shroud of Color," "Heritage," and "Incident" all deal with racial topics, although "Heritage" betrays the sensuality of things pagan (heterosexual lovers in an African setting that seems reminiscent of India or China) that one finds in his translation of *The Medea* and, in a different way, in poems like "To a Brown Girl," where he advises a female friend to enjoy sex with a man to whom she is sexually attracted. He wrote many carpe diem poems. "Since in the end consort together/Magdalen and Mary," Cullen writes, which summarizes the essential conflict he sees in Christianity that acknowledges and denies the sensual life. Cullen usually disguised his own homosexual preoccupations in his poems as a conflict between a character's pagan (homosexual, sexually liberated) and Christian (the "sin" of sexuality and the need for redemption) inclinations. This is clearly evident in "Heritage," arguably his finest poem, he ties the conflict between the natural (African) and the artificial (the white west) with the liberation of the pagan in his pagan reality and the tragic restriction of the pagan in the Christian world.

Cullen wrote less in the 1930s, probably because he became a full-time junior high school teacher in 1932.

Among his students was James Baldwin. He tried his hand at drama, co-writing "St. Louis Woman," with Arna Bontemps, based on Bontemps's novel, *God Sends Sunday* (1931). He was frustrated by both the lack of commercial success of "St. Louis Woman" and the criticism to which it was subjected by several prominent blacks who felt this story of a black jockey and the women in his life denigrated black people. He published two children's books in 1940 and 1942 and seemed quite attracted to that genre, but garnered little of the attention and success he had in the 1920s. Cullen died of uremic poisoning on January 9, 1946, at the age of forty-two.

### Bibliography

Baker, Jr., Houston A. "A Many-Colored Coat of Dreams: The Poetry of Countee Cullen." In *Afro-American Poetics: Revisions of Harlem and the Black Aesthetic.* Madison: University of Wisconsin Press, 1988.

Early, Gerald, ed. *My Soul's High Song: The Collected Writings of Countee Cullen, Voice of the Harlem Renaissance.* New York: Doubleday, 1991.

Tuttleton, James W. "Countee Cullen at 'The Heights.'" In *The Harlem Renaissance: Reevaluations.* Edited by Amrijit Singh, William S. Shiver, and Stanley Brodwin. New York: Garland Publishing, 1989.

Wagner, Jean. *Black Poets of the United States: From Paul Laurence Dunbar to Langston Hughes.* Translated by Kenneth Douglas. Champaign-Urbana: University of Illinois Press, 1973.

**Gerald Early**

***See also*** HARLEM RENAISSANCE; HUGHES, LANGSTON; LITERATURE; WALKER, A'LELIA.

# CULTURAL STUDIES AND CULTURAL THEORY

There are many ways to study culture, depending on how the term itself is understood. For some, culture means works of literature and the arts, and cultural studies examines and interprets objects appreciated largely for their beauty. For others, culture refers not only to literature and the arts, but also to great works of philosophy, politics, and history, said to have enduring worth as "classics." In these traditional and humanistic understandings of culture, one studies literature, the arts, and the classics (taken as the creative work of exceptional individuals), for purposes of self-development or the cultivation of sensibility, taste, and wisdom. Others associate culture not with the individual but with the collective or the group, and define culture as a complex system, not as a set of specific products or objects. Among those who think of

The term "culture" originally referred to a process, to the cultivation of crops and of animals, and then by extension to the cultivation of human beings, referring not only to the cultivation of the mind, but also to the objects (art, fashion and writings, . . .) and practices involved. Sometimes interpreted narrowly to mean only artistic and intellectual activities, [culture] is often used more broadly to refer to "a whole way of life" associated with a particular group of people (Williams, p. 13).

culture as a system, there is considerable difference about how the cultural system is defined. Some think of it as a symbolic system of meanings to be read and interpreted like a text. The latter would include students of culture as diverse as the anthropologist Clifford Geertz and the poststructuralist historian Michel Foucault. Still another approach is the Marxist, one that sees culture as inseparable from the economic system of a given society. The Marxist approach takes the cultural and economic systems as sites of difference and conflict and thus, in studying culture, emphasizes political struggle between different social groups and classes.

In a broad sense, cultural studies has the capacity, as one critic has written, "to shake up, if not completely transform" more familiar forms of study and pedagogy (Taylor, p. 1). The field's capacity to disturb and transform more familiar knowledge comes from the fact that, at its best, it is basically a dehierarchizing mode of intellectual inquiry and form of pedagogy. By seriously studying popular culture (produced for and by the masses), cultural studies critiques the assumed superiority of traditional studies centered exclusively on the classics (produced for and by elites). It therefore challenges class hierarchy and dominant norms and values by critiquing privileged forms of knowledge and education. Often working within cultural studies frameworks, especially since the late 1960s, groups on the sexual and gender margins have challenged the heterosexist hierarchy of dominant sex/gender and sexual systems by developing new knowledge, logics, and theories to describe, explain, criticize, and celebrate both dominant and alternative identities, practices, and cultures.

## LGBT Cultural Studies, Historiography, and Ethnography

Cultural studies scholarship on LGBT communities creates new knowledge, in part by making neglected LGBT ways of life the objects of investigation. One strand of scholarship has been devoted to recovering the "hidden histories" of the sexual margins. This work has helped to create a sense of community and a shared past, if not a homogeneous group identity or common culture. Paralleling the recovery of hidden histories, new ethnographic work has provided detailed, substantial descriptions of previously "hidden" LGBT cultures.

In this process, the privileged place of white, middle-class lesbians and gay men has rendered them the most visible and the most-studied groups. For example, several scholars have argued that, at different historical moments, middle-class women-loving women have had a variety of ways of life. "Romantic friendships" between women flourished under the nineteenth-century American sex/gender system, which because of sharper sex segregation threw same-sex friends together more strongly. Some of these relationships, for example, the "Boston marriage," in which women lived in marriagelike relationships, enjoyed semipublic acknowledgement. Other scholars have looked beyond the white middle class to explore other cultural formations. The cultural practices of the "romantic friendship," including "exchanging pinkie rings," buying "each other violets," and reveling in the "romance of the closet" (Rupp, p. 154), were quite different from those of working class femme/butch lesbians in the bar culture of the mid-twentieth century. Different still was the lesbian-feminist culture of the 1970s, with its foregrounding of women's music, its separatist impulse, its strongly antipatriarchal stand, and its notion of the political lesbian. The bohemian culture of 1920s Harlem was a site not only of musical and literary development but also of sexual experimentation. There, with such performers as Bessie Smith, Ma Rainey, Alberta Hunter, Jackie "Moms" Mabley, and Ethel Waters, African American LGBT people achieved cultural visibility, as they did in the 1970s and later with writers such as Audre Lorde and Cheryl Clarke.

## LGBT People and Mainstream Culture

Taking their hegemonic position for granted, white, middle-class gay men have sometimes represented their lives and practices as "gay culture" in general, which some scholars have also done. A strong strand of writing has evolved around the idea of a common transhistorical, innate, gay identity, or a "distinct sensibility" (Murray, p. 192). Some have found cultural unity in the idea of a common gay vocabulary or slang. Making a larger claim, Susan Sontag, narrowing culture to the arts, in 1964 associated gay men with the camp ironic-aesthetic mode of discourse and assigned them, as a group, a leading role in mainstream culture as arbiters of style, taste, and fashion.

This tendency, which survives in early twenty-first-century writings of white, middle-class gay men who celebrate their gifts of taste, sophistication, and cosmopolitanism, aestheticizes what is fundamentally a political relation, not only between the sexual margins and the dominant culture, but also between various segments of the sexual margins with different social, political, cultural, and economic interests. What some celebrate as the special cultural role of gays (and sometimes lesbians, as in the "lesbian chic" of Hamer and Budge) is critiqued by others as ghettoization, keeping nonheterosexuals away from centers of economic, social, and political power. Nevertheless, LGBT cultural studies critics have put notable intellectual energy into alternative (queer) readings of mainstream popular culture.

Writing that homogenizes quite diverse populations is seen by many cultural studies scholars as obscuring important social and cultural differences. For example, the "fairy" culture of New York's early twentieth-century Bowery was different from the "clone" culture of the 1970s and from the internationalized circuit party culture of the 1990s. In the 1980s and early 1990s, the AIDS epidemic significantly altered LGBT cultures, bringing forth not only a new militancy about health care but also a heightened sense of community service.

Racial and ethnic differences further shatter the idea of a single gay culture. The Latin American sex/gender system (which influences Latino/Latina LGBT cultures) differs significantly from the dominant U.S. system. The former, which is shaped by a strong patriarchal family structure, foregrounds sexual aim (who penetrates/is penetrated), not the sex of one's partner. The latter foregrounds sexual object (male or female) and is shaped by a weakened family structure. The strength of Asian and Pacific American family structures, their own ethnic diversity, and the status of some as "high achieving" immigrant minorities produce differences for Asian and Pacific American LGBT cultures. While there are examples of culturally and politically prominent black gay men (including the poet Langston Hughes, the writer James Baldwin, and the civil rights activist Bayard Rustin), the legacy of slavery, the influence of the black church, and the pressures of racism and economic exploitation on the African American family have fed a "black sexual conservatism" that has made it difficult for black LGBT people to come out and created for that culture special problems in the AIDS crisis. Some of the same oppressive factors inflect LGBT cultural life in the American South.

**Bisexuals and Transgender Persons**

Since the inauguration in the 1950s, 1960s, and 1970s of the sexual liberation and LGBT movements, a complex sorting-out process has been taking place in which sexu-

Like the recovery of slave narratives and unknown women's writings, these new histories have been part of a recent "revisioning of American history" (West, p. 208) aimed at achieving greater political, social, and cultural inclusiveness.

ally marginal groups have increasingly distinguished themselves from each other. By definition, such a sorting-out process depends to a significant degree on the existence (or fiction) of stable and knowable identities that are part of distinctive, if historically changing, cultures.

To some commentators, bisexuality is a serial oscillation between specific stable identities/cultures, heterosexual and homosexual. To others, bisexuality actually "confounds the concept of sexual categories" altogether (Garber, p. 523). Some charge that bisexuals live in a politically self-serving manner, simultaneously enjoying the pleasures of homosexuality and the safety and privileges of normative heterosexual culture. Others represent bisexuality as a liberating potential in every person and, more recently, as the very embodiment of the fluidity and hybridity of the postmodern subject. Some degree of common bisexual group interest exists, and since the 1990s, cultural organizations, information networks, support groups, and publications for and about bisexuals have proliferated.

The terms "transgender" and "genderqueer" refer to different forms and degrees of cross-gender practices and identification, ranging from various levels of men who identify as feminine and women who identify as masculine to transsexuals, whose characteristic is not cross-dressing or cross-gender talk or gesture but the desire for a surgical change of their biological sex. The sexual identification of transsexuals can be heterosexual, homosexual, bisexual, or asexual, and it can change over time. While transgender people have found refuge in the alternative sexual cultures of different periods, the issues for various groups are sometimes quite different.

In the early 1950s, Christine Jorgensen (born George Jorgensen, Jr.) became the exemplary transsexual cultural icon of the United States, appearing in a nightclub act and in summer stock before straight audiences intrigued by the sex-change phenomenon. At one cultural pole was Jorgensen, who emphasized gender change and downplayed sexual issues; at the other was the transsexual heroine in Gore Vidal's novel *Myra Breckenridge* (1968), a caricature of a male-to-female transsexual overtly exercising sexual power. In lesbian or gay cultures, transgender people such as the "butch" woman or the male "queen" or "fairy" often used their cross-gender self-representation to signal homosexual availability. For them, it was same-sex sex that was at stake in terms of legality and social acceptance. For a male-to-female transsexual, who may have acted as a male homosexual before surgery but as a female heterosexual afterward, the social and cultural issues are obviously different. A physical sex change requires specialized medical knowledge and sustained clinical intervention (including hormone treatments). A legal name change requires new judicial decisions on such questions as whether biological sex is determined by chromosomes or by sex organs.

## Economics and Sexual Cultures

In the 1990s, the forces of globalization and worldwide capitalist commodification intensified, and the aesthetic (the beautiful and the pleasurable) was increasingly and more obviously absorbed into the economic (the profitable). Danae Clark ("Commodity Lesbianism"), Daniel Harris (*The Rise and Fall of Gay Culture)*, and Alexandra Chasin (*Selling Out*), among others, acknowledge that today's gay and lesbian cultures have basically been assimilated to the general commodity culture of late capitalism. Such work reveals the extent to which economic forces drive what some still represent as autonomous cultural developments and suggests how commodification "constrains political activity" (Chasin, p. 221). The globalization of capitalism has also been accompanied by the worldwide export of American gay and lesbian politics and cultural forms.

## Cultural Theory

Cultural theory takes two basic forms. The materialist approach assumes that external material forces (economic, social, cultural, and linguistic) condition and shape human subjects, identities, and cultural practices. The idealist approach assumes the reverse, that through their ideas, intentions, and cultural practices, human subjects shape external material conditions. From the outset, cultural studies was understood as a socially progressive form of knowledge production heavily indebted to Marxist materialist social theory. It critiqued class structure and class difference as major causes of social inequality and argued that dominant knowledge serves the ideological function of sustaining the class system.

Since the late 1960s, a second, poststructuralist/postmodernist version of materialist theory has developed under the influence of French intellectuals such as Derrida, Lacan, Barthes, Foucault, Irigaray, and Cixous. As of the early years of the twenty-first century, this form was the dominant influence on LGBT cultural theory and produced what is called "Queer Theory." It locates the material force producing difference and inequality not in class (or any other) structure but in the destabilizing operations of language and representation. In this view, we do not have access to reality itself (including the reality of our gender and sexual identities) but only to unreliable representations of reality. The term "queer" has come to mean the radical instability or fluidity of all identities, and for many, this reflects the subversive impact of unconscious desire.

Poststructuralist/postmodernist materialism rejects not just the Marxist emphasis on class structure as the primary cause of social inequality, but the very idea of stable structure and the reliability of our knowledge of cause and effect. Instead of situating various social differences in relation to larger determining structures, this form of cultural theory focuses on the specificity of each kind of social difference (gender, race, class, and sexuality) and the relationships between those differences.

## Sexual Identity Theory: Essentialism versus Constructionism

Idealists tend to support the view that human beings have stable identities defined by their inner essences (variously named, soul, spirit, psyche, or consciousness), which give continuity and coherence not only to their personalities but also to their social and cultural practices. Essentialist thinking about sexuality appeared in those nineteenth-century European homophile movements that saw homosexuals as a "third sex" with its own defining essence. In the twentieth-century United States, a resurgent essentialist view of homosexuality appeared in the widely reported—and controversial—work of researchers looking for another, this time physical, essence—the "gay gene." Materialists tend to support the opposing view, called constructionism, which argues that human identities are shaped and conditioned by economic forces (as in Marxist materialism) or by the forces of language and representation (as in poststructuralist/postmodernist materialism).

These opposing theoretical positions have important broad implications for cultural studies. The essentialist/idealist position tends to valorize the concept of sameness (a universal type, a cultural unity, homogeneity), whereas the constructionist/materialist position tends to valorize the notion of difference (the historical or language-produced variability of human identities, heterogeneity). Essentialism appears to emphasize individual freedom, which constructionists say is, if not illusory, at least conditional. In contrast, constructionism raises the question of determinism. To what extent, if at all, do human actors in the grip of historical conditions or the forces of language have any autonomy or capacity for self-directed political or social agency?

## Bibliography

Adam, Barry D. *The Rise of a Gay and Lesbian Movement.* Boston: Twayne, 1987.

Adam, Barry D., Jan Willem Duyvendak, and André Krouwel, eds. *The Global Emergence of Gay and Lesbian Politics.* Philadelphia, Penn.: Temple University Press, 1999.

Almaguer, Tomás. "Chicano Men: A Cartography of Homosexual Identity and Behavior." In *The Lesbian and Gay Studies Reader.* Edited by Henry Abelove, Michèle Aina Barale, and David M. Halperin. New York: Routledge, 1993.

Bell, David, and Jon Binnie. *The Sexual Citizen: Queer Politics and Beyond.* London: Polity, 2000.

Blasius, Mark, and Shane Phelan, eds. *We Are Everywhere: A Historical Sourcebook of Gay and Lesbian Politics.* New York: Routledge, 1997.

Brown, Michael P. *Replacing Citizenship: AIDS Activism and Radical Democracy.* New York: Guilford, 1997.

Burr, Chandler. *A Separate Creation: The Search for the Biological Origins of Sexual Orientation.* New York: Hyperion, 1997.

Butler, Judith. *Bodies That Matter: On the Discursive Limits of "Sex."* New York: Routledge, 1993.

Carbado, Devon W., Dwight A. McBride, and Donald Weise, eds. *Black Like Us: A Century of Lesbian, Gay and Bisexual African American Fiction.* San Francisco: Cleis Press, 2002.

Chasin, Alexandra. *Selling Out: The Gay and Lesbian Movement Goes to Market.* New York: Palgrave, 2000.

Clark, Danae. "Commodity Lesbianism." In *The Lesbian and Gay Studies Reader.* Edited by Henry Abelove, Michèle Aina Barale, and David M. Halperin. New York: Routledge, 1993.

Clifford, James. "On Collecting Art and Culture." In *The Cultural Studies Reader.* Edited by Simon During. London: Routledge, 1993.

Creekmur, Corey K., and Alexander Doty, eds. *Out in Culture: Gay, Lesbian, and Queer Essays on Popular Culture.* Durham, N.C.: Duke University Press, 1995.

Dews, Carlos L., and Carolyn Leste Law, eds. *Out in the South.* Philadelphia: Temple University Press, 2001.

Duberman, Martin, Martha Vicinus, and George Chauncey, Jr., eds. *Hidden from History: Reclaiming the Gay and Lesbian Past.* New York: Meridian, 1990.

Evans, David T. *Sexual Citizenship: The Material Construction of Sexualities.* New York: Routledge, 1993.

Foucault, Michel. *The History of Sexuality.* New York: Pantheon, 1978.

Garber, Marjorie. *Vice Versa: Bisexuality and the Eroticism of Everyday Life.* New York: Simon and Schuster, 1995.

Geertz, Clifford. *The Interpretation of Cultures; Selected Essays.* New York: Basic Books, 1973.

Hamer, Dean, and Peter Copeland. *The Science of Desire: The Search for the Gay Gene and the Biology of Behavior.* New York: Touchstone, 1996.

Hamer, Diane, and Belinda Budge, eds. *The Good, the Bad, and the Gorgeous: Popular Culture's Romance with Lesbianism.* London: Pandora, 1994.

Harris, Daniel. *The Rise and Fall of Gay Culture.* New York: Hyperion, 1997.

Hennessy, Rosemary. *Profit and Pleasure: Sexual Identities in Late Capitalism.* New York: Routledge, 2000.

Kennedy, Elizabeth Kapovsky, and Madeline D. Davis. *Boots of Leather, Slippers of Gold: The History of a Lesbian Community.* New York: Routledge, 1993.

Koestenbaum, Wayne. *Jackie under My Skin: Interpreting an Icon.* New York: Plume, 1995.

Laclau, Ernesto, and Chantal Mouffe. *Hegemony and Socialist Strategy: Towards a Radical Democratic Politics.* 2d ed. New York: Verso, 2001.

Leap, William L. *Word's Out: Gay Men's English.* Minneapolis: University of Minnesota Press, 1996.

Leong, Russell, ed. *Asian American Sexualities: Dimension of the Gay and Lesbian Experience.* New York: Routledge, 1996.

Levine, Martin P. *Gay Macho: The Life and Death of the Homosexual Clone.* New York: New York University Press, 1998.

Leyland, Winston, ed. *Gay Roots: Twenty Years of Gay Sunshine. An Anthology of Gay History, Sex, Politics, and Culture.* San Francisco: Gay Sunshine Press, 1991.

Litvak, Joseph. *Strange Gourmets: Sophistication, Theory, and the Novel.* Durham, N.C.: Duke University Press, 1997.

Meyerowitz, Joanne. *How Sex Changed: A History of Transsexuality in the United States.* Cambridge, Mass.: Harvard University Press, 2002.

Miller, D. A. *Place for Us: Essay on the Broadway Musical.* Cambridge: Harvard University Press, 1998.

Miller, Neil. *Out of the Past: Gay and Lesbian History from 1869 to the Present.* New York: Vintage, 1995.

Milner, Andrew. *Re-Imagining Cultural Studies: The Promise of Cultural Materialism.* Thousand Oaks, Calif.: Sage, 2002.

Minton, Henry L., ed. *Gay and Lesbian Studies.* New York: Haworth, 1992.

Moraga, Cherríe. "Queer Atzlán." In *The Material Queer: A LesBiGay Cultural Studies Reader.* Edited by Donald Morton. Boulder, Colo.: Westview Press, 1996.

Morton, Donald, ed. *The Material Queer: A LesBiGay Cultural Studies Reader.* Boulder, Colo.: Westview Press, 1996.

Murray, Stephen O. *American Gay.* Chicago: University of Chicago Press, 1995.

Nestle, Joan, Clare Howell, and Riki Wilchins, eds. *GenderQueer: Voices from Beyond the Sexual Binary.* Los Angeles: Alyson, 2002.

Nimmons, David. *Soul beneath the Skin: The Unseen Hearts and Habits of Gay Men.* New York: St. Martin's Press, 2002.

Norton, Rictor. *The Myth of the Modern Homosexual: Queer History and the Search for Cultural Unity.* Washington, D.C.: Cassell, 1997.

Rodgers, Bruce. *Gay Talk: A (Sometimes Outrageous) Dictionary of Gay Slang.* New York: Paragon, 1972.

Rubin, Gayle. "The Traffic in Women." In *Toward an Anthropology of Women.* Edited by Reyna R. Reiter. New York: Monthly Review Press, 1975.

Rupp, Leila J. *A Desired Past: A Short History of Same-Sex Love in America.* Chicago: University of Chicago Press, 2002.

Sontag, Susan. "Notes on Camp." In *Against Interpretation and Other Essays.* New York: Anchor, 1990.

Taylor, Alan. "The Failure of Historical Materialism: Crisis Rhetoric and Cultural Studies." Available from http://www.uta.edu/english/apt/homepage/papers/crisis.html.

West, Cornel. "The New Cultural Politics of Difference." In *The Cultural Studies Reader.* Edited by Simon During. London: Routledge, 1993.

Williams, Raymond. *Culture.* London: Fontana, 1981.

**Donald Morton**

*See also* CAPITALISM AND INDUSTRIALIZATION; ESSENTIALISM AND CONSTRUCTIONISM; FILM AND VIDEO STUDIES; LITERARY CRITICISM AND THEORY; QUEER THEORY AND QUEER STUDIES.

# CUNNINGHAM, Merce (b. 16 April 1919), choreographer, dancer.

Arguably the most influential choreographer of the twentieth century, Merce Cunningham's contributions to the world of dance have not only changed the ways in which dances appear, but have also revolutionized the ways in which they are made. After dancing for Martha Graham's company from 1939 to 1945, Cunningham proceeded to change radically the way that audiences saw modern dance. Emerging as a choreographer in the conservative political climate of the McCarthy era during the 1950s, his ardent relationship with long-term partner and collaborator John Cage existed in the shadow of his public persona, allowing his innovative choreographic techniques to be highlighted instead.

In opposition to the movement vocabulary of Graham, who used the kinetic concept of torque to symbolize a relationship to the psyche, Cunningham developed a dance technique that emphasized the body's articulate range of motion. Whereas modern dance in the early half of the twentieth century had been discussed primarily in terms of what it said or meant on a psychological level, Cunningham's movement challenged audiences and critics to consider what the movement kinetically enacted, allowing for the movement to be seen as expressive in and of itself. And though the erect spine that is characteristic of Cunningham's choreography has sometimes been compared to the aesthetic of ballet, the task-oriented, perfunctory quality that can be observed in his work negates the ballet's emphasis on virtuosity. Additionally, the sense of phrasing that both ballet and earlier modern dance choreographers had used to draw attention to a particular movement within a sequence was evened out by Cunningham so that no one movement dominated any other.

Cunningham's choreography has been characterized as technically brilliant, irreverently theatrical, and innovative in exploring the compositional tools of time and space. Early solos such as *Untitled Solo* (1953) and *Changeling* (1957) have been used to trace Cunningham's earlier association with Graham while noting the use of complex transitions and purposefully awkward movements to reject the mythic symbolism of her choreography. Ensemble works such as *Antic Meet* (1958) featured absurd uses of props and unconventional costuming. For example, a section of the choreography has Cunningham dancing with a chair strapped to his back while partnering a woman (Carolyn Brown) in an antique wedding dress. Perhaps Cunningham is most known for dances that rigorously explore compositional tools such as *Septet* (1953), *Suite for Five* (1956–1958), and *Summerspace* (1958). The majority of Cunningham's choreography can be described as most akin to these early works, challenging expectations regarding the choreographer's role in directing the audience's eye.

Perhaps most importantly, Cunningham has come to be known for his use of chance methods in making choreography. In the process of making many of his dances, Cunningham has devised charts to separate the dance material into individual components. The choreography of the dance has then been constructed through chance procedures such as flipping a coin to choose the movement vocabulary, order of movements, and spatial composition of the dance. Rather than viewing his dances as works of art, Cunningham has recast choreography as an act of solving puzzles, thereby disconnecting dance from narrative and psychological confinements. Recent scholarship has interpreted Cunningham's use of chance as a rejection of the authorship associated with the romanticized icon of the male artist. Though Cunningham has sometimes been criticized for an apolitical stance in his work, it has also been argued that by disassociating himself from the authorial role of the creator, he has effectively subverted one aspect of the myth of masculinity.

**Merce Cunningham.** The revolutionary modern choreographer is framed by other dancers.

Further, Cunningham's concentration on movement can be seen as neutralizing many of the gender politics and erotic associations connected to concert dance. It has been suggested that the nonerotic nature of his work served to deflect inquisitions regarding his own sexual orientation, thereby providing safety from the repressive sociopolitical climate during which his artistic philosophy was formed.

Throughout his career, Cunningham's radical and forward-thinking innovation has been recognized with awards such as Guggenheim Fellowships for choreography in 1954 and 1959, a MacArthur Foundation Fellowship in 1985, and the National Medal for the Arts in 1990. Cunningham has continued to be a radical force within the world of concert dance, most recently for the incorporation of computer-assisted choreography. Using LifeForms, a choreography software program, since 1989, Cunningham has continued to disassociate the role of the choreographer from the myth of artistic genius. In so doing, he has successfully brought the craft of composition into the forefront of dance making while opening new options for emerging generations of choreographers.

## Bibliography

Burt, Ramsay. *The Male Dancer: Bodies, Spectacle, Sexualities.* London and New York: Routledge, 1995.

Cunningham, Merce. *The Dancer and the Dance: Conversations with Jacqueline Lesschaeve.* New York: M. Boyars, 1985.

Foster, Susan Leigh. *Reading Dancing: Bodies and Subjects in Contemporary American Dance.* Berkeley: University of California Press, 1986.

———. "Closets Full of Dances: Modern Dance's Performance of Masculinity and Sexuality." In *Dancing Desires: Choreographing Sexualities On and Off the Stage.* Edited by Jane C. Desmond. Madison: University of Wisconsin Press, 2001.

**Peter Carpenter**

*See also* CAGE, JOHN; DANCE; JOHNS, JASPER; RAUSCHENBERG, ROBERT.

# CUSHMAN, Charlotte (b. 23 July 1816; d. 16 February 1876), actress.

Actress Charlotte Cushman was born in Boston, Massachusetts. Originally, Cushman trained for a career as an

**Charlotte Cushman.** A portrait of the internationally renowned mid-nineteenth-century actress. [Bettmann/corbis]

peculiar, rebellious, and passionate, Cushman's so-called "masculine" qualities were not merely an acceptable *violation* of gender expectations, but rather a *reinforcement* of a particular variety of national identity the British had come to expect. For Americans who still smarted under the weight of their assumed cultural inferiority when compared with the British, championing the success of one of their own took on a nationalistic fervor. Soon countless articles proclaimed the success of "Our Charlotte," as the press in the United States tended to describe her. As the first American actress to be so well received abroad, particularly in Shakespearean roles, Cushman was a source of pride to her country's people.

Following the success of her first British theater season, Cushman chose to play Romeo opposite her sister Susan in the role of Juliet. Although Cushman had played Romeo and numerous other "breeches" roles previously in the United States, anticipating objections from British audiences, she claimed publicly that she had only taken on the role of Romeo to give her sister Susan "the support I knew she required, and would never get from any gentleman that could be got to act with her." In this way Cushman represented herself as the protector of her sister's respectability, rather than as a possible transgressor of gender norms in her own right. When the Cushman sisters first performed *Romeo and Juliet* for London audiences on 29 December 1845, critics were overwhelmed. Critics from the (London) *Times*, the *Era*, and the *Britannia* found Cushman exciting and captivating as well as believable as Romeo.

Soon after, following her success in Britain, Cushman became America's most famous actress, celebrated in the press and welcomed into circles of the most notable literary, artistic, and political personages of her era in Europe and the United States. In 1845 Cushman became romantically involved with the popular English poet, journalist, and editor Eliza Cook. For years Cook celebrated the two women's relationship with poetry published in periodicals and anthologies throughout England and the United States.

Cushman's next major relationship, with novelist and translator Matilda Hays (who briefly toured as Juliet to Cushman's Romeo in the English provinces), excited the attention of Elizabeth Barrett Browning, who referred to Cushman and Hays's partnership as a "female marriage." With Hays at her side, Cushman launched a successful return tour throughout the United States. In 1852 Cushman announced her decision to retire and she, Hays, and several women friends moved to Italy. However, Cushman soon returned to the stage, performing sporadically for the next two decades while living in London and

opera singer. In 1835, however, after straining her voice while on tour in New Orleans, Cushman switched to dramatic roles and debuted as Lady Macbeth. From her earliest years on stage, Cushman provided the primary support for her mother, sister, and two brothers (her father having abandoned her mother and their four children when Cushman was in her teens). Cushman, who was five feet six inches tall, angular, and physically powerful, specialized in roles where she depicted strong female characters such as Lady Macbeth, Queen Katherine, and Meg Merrillies (in Sir Walter Scott's *Guy Mannering*) and male characters such as Romeo, Hamlet, Cardinal Wolsey, and Oberon. While working as an actress with companies in New York and Philadelphia, Cushman became romantically involved with writer Anne Hampton Brewster and artist Rosalie Sully.

In November 1844, Cushman left the United States to try her hand at performing in England. When Cushman performed for her first London audiences in February 1845, she was even more lauded than she had been at home because her "forcefulness" was seen to reflect her identity as an American. In England, to audiences for whom Americans were already regarded as

Rome. In 1856 Cushman became intimately involved with American sculptor Emma Stebbins, whom she had met in Rome. There, Cushman and Stebbins established an expatriate community of American women sculptors. Cushman later adopted her nephew Ned. His wife, Emma Crow Cushman, referred to herself as Cushman's devoted "little lover."

An astute businesswoman, Cushman earned a fortune, single-handedly supporting her family, friends, and the women with whom she shared her life.

## Bibliography

Merrill, Lisa. *When Romeo Was a Woman: Charlotte Cushman and Her Circle of Female Spectators*. Ann Arbor: University of Michigan Press, 1999.

**Lisa Merrill**

*See also* ACTORS AND ACTRESSES; THEATER AND PERFORMANCE.

**CUSTODY.** see FAMILY ISSUES.

# D

## DALY, Mary (b. 16 October 1928), philosopher.

Mary Daly was born and raised in Schenectady, New York, and graduated with a B.A. in English (1950) from the College of St. Rose in Albany. She was educated in Catholic institutions from her parochial school days through her three doctoral degrees. Her first doctorate came from the pioneering (all-female) School of Sacred Theology at St. Mary's College, Notre Dame, Indiana (1954). She then sought the highest Catholic degree in theology awarded by a pontifical faculty of sacred theology and was rejected—because of her sex—from the Catholic University of America, the only U.S. institution that offered the degree. She enrolled at Fribourg University in Switzerland, where she was awarded doctorates in theology (1963) and philosophy (1965).

In the autumn of 1965, Daly visited Rome and was caught up in the heady atmosphere of Vatican II (1962–1965), an international meeting of Catholic bishops convened to discuss the place of the church in the twentieth century. Daly, like many Catholic intellectuals of the early 1960s, believed that radical change in the church's theology and social policies was possible. In her first book, *The Church and the Second Sex* (1968), she spoke for an increasingly vocal community of Catholic feminists who sought to promote changes in the church so that its teachings on human dignity would inform its theology and policies on women. In 1966 Daly joined the theology faculty at Boston College, then a Jesuit-run all-male university. Three years later she was denied tenure, despite her prominence as a Catholic feminist and the acclaim surrounding her book. Boston College administrators reversed the decision in the summer of 1969, in the wake of highly publicized student protests.

In 1972 Daly read an interview by Ann Koedt in *Notes From the Third Year* which awakened her to her lesbian identitiy. The following year she published *Beyond God the Father*, in which she proposed the replacement of static Christian (male) God-language with dynamic terminology more compatible with the social and existential goals of sisterhood and women's self-actualization. By 1975 she was calling herself a postchristian feminist. In 1977 Daly began to identify herself as a lesbian in her public lectures, but her writings, then and decades later, rarely touch upon the personal dimension of her lesbian identity. When she addresses this topic in her autobiography, *Outercourse: The Be-Dazzling Voyage* (1992), she maintains that being a lesbian is not merely about sexual preference, lifestyle, or even community. It is about integrity, and the spiritual and cosmic power unleashed by women who fully and openly identify with women.

In 1978, with the appearance of *Gyn/Ecology: The Metaethics of Radical Feminism*, Daly made explicit what was implicit in *Beyond God the Father:* her rejection of the conventions and expectations of the academic establishment. In *Gyn/Ecology* Daly extended the scope of her critique of the institutional oppression of women beyond the Christian churches to cultural practices such as suttee, foot binding, female circumcision, Nazi medicine, and gynecology. Here and in all her subsequent books, she writes of a spiral-shaped feminist journey to the Boundary, away from the spaces colonized by the enemies of women and the natural world. During the 1970s, Daly

**Mary Daly.** The radical feminist philosopher has battled male cultural and religious domination, as well as institutional and societal oppression of women, since the mid-1960s. [AP/Wide World Photos]

began to offer women's studies courses, and by the end of the decade, she was teaching female students separately from males, a policy that elicited criticism, even from academics, and was cited by Boston College administrators as their reason for breaking Daly's contract in 1999. In May, 1979, Audre Lorde wrote Daly a letter, published later that year, to protest her treatment of non-European women in *Gyn/Ecology*. She asked Daly to pay more attention to black women, not to confine them to footnotes and negative examples, but rather, include the works and words of black women and their ancient goddess images alongside those of white women.

*Pure Lust* (1984) represents the second part of a three-stage project that Daly began with *Gyn/Ecology*: her own feminist encounter with the seven deadly sins (pride, avarice, anger, lust, gluttony, envy, and sloth), renamed the Eight Deadly Sins of the Fathers (Processions, Professions, Possession, Aggression, Obsession, Assimilation,

Elimination, and Fragmentation). Daly completed the project in a futuristic work entitled *Quintessence* (1998). This process of renaming—and reclaiming women's power to name their own reality rather than have it defined for them by male professors, clerics, and other designated male leaders—has been central to Daly's writings since *Beyond God the Father*. It became especially controversial with the appearance of *Webster's First Intergalactic Wickedary of the English Language* (1987), a collaborative work by Daly and Jane Caputi. The *Wickedary* presents three groupings (webs) of words recovered from obscurity and erasure by Daly and Caputi, words with the capacity to help women imagine and realize another kind of time and space on the Boundary, where women and other living creatures endangered by male-dominated, technology-driven societies can thrive and find peace.

Daly's autobiography, *Outercourse*, provides insight into what radical feminism means to Daly. It is a spiral-shaped journey from her graduate school days, when she first challenged and then left behind the caste system that she discovered within the teachings and institutions of the Catholic church, to her more recent commitment to biophilia, the love of life, which often requires migration to a separate space on the Boundary of a predominantly necrophilic, life-hating world.

During the early 2000s, Daly remained active on the lecture circuit and is at work on her eighth book, *Amazon Grace*.

### Bibliography

Daly, Mary. *Pure Lust: Elemental Feminist Philosophy.* Boston: Beacon, 1984.

———. *Beyond God the Father: Toward a Philosophy of Women's Liberation.* 2d ed. Boston: Beacon, 1985.

———. *The Church and the Second Sex.* 3d ed. Boston: Beacon, 1985.

———. *Gyn/Ecology: The Metaethics of Radical Feminism.* 2d ed. Boston: Beacon, 1990.

———. *Outercourse: The Be-Dazzling Voyage.* San Francisco: HarperSan Francisco, 1992.

———. *Quintessence . . . Realizing the Archaic Future: A Radical Feminist Manifesto.* Boston: Beacon, 1998.

———, and Jane Caputi. *Webster's First New Intergalactic Wickedary of the English Language.* Boston: Beacon, 1987.

Hoagland, Sarah Lucia, and Marilyn Frye, eds. *Feminist Interpretations of Mary Daly.* University Park: The Pennsylvania State University Press, 2000.

**Debra Campbell**

***See also*** CATHOLICS AND CATHOLICISM.

# DANCE

Dance scholarship exploring lesbian and gay perspectives since the middle 1990s has posited queer identity as the dark secret of dance history in the United States. Jane C. Desmond has gone so far as to assert that homophobia has directly influenced the majority of dance canon formation. Given this, attempts to explore the complexities inherent in viewing choreographies from a queer perspective have made it clear that such a project will forever be catching up to itself—attempting to re-imagine dances of the past while keeping abreast of contemporary choreographies that may be designated as queer.

Different time periods within the twentieth century have required unique strategies for LGBT people making dances on the concert stage. The emergence of homosexual identity in the earlier half of the twentieth century, for example, led some choreographers to reject homoeroticism, whereas the AIDS epidemic pushed many choreographers to create overtly political material in the face of devastating illness. Even within a given era, different artists have used different strategies. For example, comparing Judson Church choreographer James Waring's flamboyant uses of ballet and modern dance vocabularies with the minimalism of Steve Paxton can illuminate two different approaches to subverting established norms of masculinity through dance.

Contemporary dance scholarship has also remarked on the relative invisibility of lesbians on the concert stage. The reason has been seen as stemming from a variety of social and historical factors. Ironically, the dominance of female bodies on the stage often stands as an uncontested and unexamined condition in dance—while two men need only touch shoulders to evoke homoeroticism, two women in a full embrace will potentially be denied such a reading. To counter this, contemporary lesbian artists have employed different strategies in their choreographies. Whereas artists such as Julie Tolentino, Jill Togawa, and Jennifer Monson have sought to increase overt lesbian visibility, other choreographers such as Yvonne Rainer, Elizabeth Streb, and Ann Carlson have worked to change the very way that contemporary choreographies are seen. These choreographers and their gay male counterparts have worked rigorously in the latter part of the twentieth century to undermine assumptions regarding sexuality and gender on the concert stage, oftentimes radically subverting formalist concepts of space, time, and structure in the process.

## The Emergence of Ballet and Male Homosexual Identity

Les Ballets Trockadero De Monte Carlo, an all-male ballet company established in New York City in 1974, has become renowned for drag ballet performances that alternately mock and effectively utilize established ballet conventions. The critical and commercial success of Les Ballets Trockadero comes from the deliberately campy reinterpretations of famous scenes from the European ballet tradition, as well as the technical accomplishment of its corps de ballet. The overwhelmingly affectionate response to the company stands in contrast to the status of the male ballet dancer a century earlier, when he had all but disappeared from the European concert stage.

After the predominance of the travesty dancer (women performing in the roles of men) in nineteenth-century Europe, Serge Diaghilev's the Ballets Russes marked the reemergence of the male ballet dancer in Europe, due largely to the exceptional performances of dancer Vaslav Nijinsky. Touring the United States in 1916 and 1917, the Ballets Russes introduced many U.S. audience members to the male ballet dancer for the first time. Nijinsky's athletic and, as remarked by critics, effeminate performance as the Golden Slave in *Schéhérazade* (1910), as well as his subversively sensual performances in *Le Spectre de la Rose* (1910) and *L'Après-midi d'un Faune* (1912), have retrospectively been read as celebrating the subjugated position of homosexuality on the concert stage. Amidst legislative and medical efforts to patrol homosexuality in Europe and the United States in the period from 1890 to 1920, the widely celebrated physique of Nijinsky conjoined with his emotional and impassioned performance style to disturb audience assumptions of masculinity and the culturally patrolled boundaries regarding appropriate male behavior. In part due to Diaghilev and Nijinsky's homosexual relationship from 1909 to 1913, some dance scholars have argued that the Ballets Russes marks the beginning of a homosexual association with dance. Later in the century, Lincoln Kirstein and Oliver Smith would reinforce this association as gay men who opened the American Ballet Company (the forerunner to the New York City Ballet) and the Ballet Theatre (later named the American Ballet Theater), respectively.

## Modern Dance Pioneers

In 1916, shortly after Nijinsky arrived in the United States with the Ballets Russes, choreographer Ted Shawn wrote a scathing indictment of Nijinsky's effeminate performance style in the *New York Dramatic Mirror*. In opposition to Nijinsky's subversive effeminacy, Shawn created work that celebrated a masculine ideal as he attempted to disassociate effeminacy from homosexuality through the medium of modern dance. Touring as Ted Shawn and His Male Dancers from 1933 to 1940, Shawn's movement vocabulary derived more from motifs of physical labor and images of warriors than from his childhood dance training in ballet and ballroom dance styles.

In comparison to Shawn, bisexual choreographer Isadora Duncan spent a great deal of her adult life as an expatriate and expressed her disdain for modern America. Yet part of her success in Europe and the United States was the result of what dance scholar Ann Daly has described as the "Americanness" of her choreographic vision. Often hailed as one of the pioneers of American modern dance, Duncan valorized the position of the individual in a radical departure from the European ballet tradition. Simultaneously, Duncan was notorious for a string of romantic relationships, one of which was with the lesbian writer Mercede de Acosta.

Chicago-born choreographer Loie Fuller created dances known for their spectacular etherealness and their use of light, set, and costume elements. Through performances in Paris in the late nineteenth and early twentieth centuries that disregarded established dance technique and often shrouded the female body in shimmering fabric, her work confused the many critics who were unprepared to write about such a radical departure from historically established choreographic norms. Fuller began a relationship with her artistic collaborator and lifelong lover Gabrielle Sorère in 1899, established her own all-female school and company in 1908, and continued to make innovative work that challenged critics and inspired her audience members into the 1920s.

Leaving the Denishawn company in 1928 to form a company with Charles Weidman, Doris Humphrey is widely known for the innovation of "fall and recovery," a momentum-based approach to modern dance phrasing. Additionally, Humphrey was the first choreographer to write about the craft of movement composition, effectively separating the art of making dances from the art of dancing. After the disbanding of Humphrey's company in the early 1940s, she was appointed the artistic director of the José Limón Dance Company. In 1999 dance scholar Susan Leigh Foster spoke from a lesbian perspective to the Society of Dance History Scholars Conference about Humphrey's ardent relationship with Limón's wife, Pauline Lawrence. Before marrying Limón, Lawrence was the costume designer for Humphrey's company—the two met while they were both associated with Denishawn. According to Foster's controversial address, Lawrence and Humphrey remained companions for most of their lives.

### Pre-Stonewall Innovations

Dance audiences in the 1950s witnessed the emergence of a growing number of gay male choreographers in modern dance. The establishment of companies by choreographers Merce Cunningham, Paul Taylor, Robert Joffrey and Gerald Arpino (both founders of the Joffrey Ballet), and Alvin Ailey during this time can be seen as a further development of the gay male association with dance. Additionally, the growing number of gay male dancers and choreographers can be seen as related to the growing consciousness of homosexual identity in the United States. As homophile groups such as the Mattachine Society began to emerge in the 1950s, so also did a heightened display of the male dancing body. While heterosexual narratives often shrouded the homoerotic imagery of gay choreographers, as has been done in the case of Ailey's 1958 *Blues Suite,* the erotic pleasure of the male dancer nonetheless reinforced an already-growing gay fan culture in dance audiences.

This association between gay men and dance was bolstered by ballet dancer Rudolf Nureyev's international star status following his defection to the United States from the Soviet Union in 1961. Nureyev's exceptional technique and charismatic performance persona cemented a gay male association with ballet, as did the reports of Nureyev's frequent presence in gay discos and his relationship with dancer Robert Tracy. Also in the 1960s, Lar Lubovitch established his own company (1968), and the Judson Church movement began in New York City.

Extending the formalist experimentation already begun by Merce Cunningham, the Judson Church choreographers included Steve Paxton, who is credited with minimalist solos such as *Flat* (1964) that can be viewed as subverting the erotic display seen in the performances of Nureyev. The often-campy choreographies of James Waring, who also emerged through the Judson Church performances, can be seen as a counterpoint to Paxton while still rigorously examining choreographic practice at the dawn of postmodern dance. Perhaps most significantly from the Judson Church era, choreographers Meredith Monk and Lucinda Childs each created works that may be productively viewed from a lesbian perspective. As women consciously breaking choreographic convention in an era of increased consciousness surrounding lesbian identity, the way in which they have each utilized avant-garde strategies such as voice, repetition, and phrasing has often been viewed in terms of the subversion of the straight male gaze. Judson choreographer Yvonne Rainer similarly created experimental pieces such as *Trio A* (1966), which was recently revisited as part of the White Oak Dance Project in 2002. Most known for her experimental film work beginning in the early 1970s, Rainer publicly identified as a lesbian in 1993.

## Post-Stonewall Choreographies

Often hailed as the beginning of the gay rights movement, the Stonewall Riots of 1969 can perhaps better be seen as a milestone in an ongoing struggle for LGBT equality in the United States. Newly emboldened by this milestone, many already-established choreographers started to experiment with same-sex partnering as part of their repertoire. Jerome Robbins's *The Goldberg Variations* (1971) is one example; others are the establishment of Les Ballets Trockadero and the works of Broadway choreographers Michael Bennett and Tommy Tune.

In the 1980s a new wave of emerging LGBT choreographers challenged not only gender and sexuality, but also race and the very notions of established dance practice. The emergence of Elizabeth Streb's choreography, replete with movements derived more from gymnastics, circus, and boxing than modern dance, challenged gender through choreography that displayed women and men in equally athletic movement. Additionally, Streb's action-packed choreography caused audiences and choreographers alike to question their own preferences in the lyrical movement that still dominated modern dance. Also in the 1980s, Ann Carlson became known as a choreographer who worked innovatively with nondancers, live animals, and performance in nontraditional spaces. For Bill T. Jones and Arnie Zane, choreographing sexuality also explored issues of race. Jones's work has especially interrogated the connection between race and eroticism through the use of text—sometimes directly addressing, even interrogating his audience. Mark Morris utilized a modern dance vocabulary hybridized with staging conventions of ballet to subvert gender roles—these experiments were brought to fruition in *Dido and Aeneas* (1989) and *The Hard Nut* (1991). Meanwhile, in San Francisco, Joe Goode emerged as a choreographer whose work often intersected with elaborate theatricality. For Goode, Jones, and Zane, AIDS became a major influence in their choreography.

The AIDS epidemic has arguably altered the dance community and the very content of dance more than any other event in the twentieth century. The deaths of prominent dancers and choreographers such as Alvin Ailey, Michael Bennett, Robert Joffrey, Arnie Zane, Rudolf Nureyev, and Edward Stierle in the 1980s and 1990s devastated the dance community while simultaneously creating the need for an activist stance amongst many choreographers and performance artists. The widely publicized controversy surrounding *New Yorker* dance critic Arlene Croce's refusal to attend Bill T. Jones's 1994 *Still/Here*, developed through workshops with the terminally ill, highlights an example of an established choreog-

rapher creating noteworthy work in reference to the AIDS epidemic. Choreographer David Roussève has dedicated much of his choreography to the subject of AIDS as it relates to aspects of memory, grief, and identity with such works as *Urban Scenes/Creole Dreams* (1992), *The Whispers of Angels* (1995), and *Love Songs* (1998). Jones and Roussève are just two of many artists who have used the concert stage to dance passionately in the face of devastating loss, and have done so politically amidst charges of government inaction regarding the spread of AIDS.

## Lesbian Visibility on Stage

A longtime member of David Roussève's REALITY company, emerging choreographer Julie Tolentino collaborated with performance artist and AIDS activist Ron Athey on the 1996 work *Deliverance*. Her own solo creations often deal directly with AIDS and her identity as a Filipino–El Salvadorian lesbian artist. Tolentino states that one of her artistic goals is to increase lesbian visibility on and off the stage. Similarly, San Francisco choreographers Krissy Keefer and Anne Bluethenthal have collaborated to produce the first lesbian and gay dance festival in the United States, an annual event in the Bay Area since 1996. This festival has served to bring increased visibility to other lesbian choreographers in turn—perhaps most notably Jill Togawa, who as artistic director of the Purple Moon Dance Project aims to increase imagery by and for lesbians and women of color. In 1994 Togawa performed as part of a program called *Passion and Grace: A Program of International Dance,* an event organized by Stephen Brown and Paul Sutherland for the Culture Festival of Gay Games IV. Also as a part of this festival, choreographer Jennifer Monson and D. D. Dorvillier performed a piece described by *New York Times* critic Jennifer Dunning as "a combative duet in which contact improvisation met unbridled lust" (25 June 1994, sec. 1, p. 15). Though Monson has long been known as a choreographer whose work deals with the politics of sexuality, in this instance Monson and Dorvillier, perhaps aided by the context of a gay dance festival, succeeded in having their performance read in terms of lesbian eroticism and innovative choreography at the same time.

The queer context that the San Francisco Gay and Lesbian Dance Festival and the Culture Festival of the Gay Games has provided may be a productive model for more firmly establishing lesbian visibility on the concert stage. As more such environments emerge, LGBT choreographers will undoubtedly continue to subvert the ever-changing choreographic norms of dance in the United States. Dance history shows that this subversion has already begun, not only with regard to gender and sexuality, but also in terms of the very ways that dances are made and seen.

## Bibliography

Adair, Christy. *Women and Dance: Sylphs and Sirens*. London: Macmillan, 1992.

Anderson, Jack. "In the Ancient Greeks' Theatrical Tradition," *New York Times*, 24 June 1994, sec. C, p. 3.

Banes, Sally. *Terpsichore in Sneakers: Post-Modern Dance*. Hanover, N.H.: Wesleyan University Press, 1977.

Burt, Ramsay. *The Male Dancer: Bodies, Spectacle, Sexualities*. London and New York: Routledge, 1995.

Daly, Ann. *Done into Dance: Isadora Duncan in America*. Bloomington and Indianapolis: Indiana University Press, 1995.

———. "The Hybrid Yvonne Rainer: Avant-Garde Aesthete, Utopian Activist." *Chronicle of Higher Education*, 22 November 2002, sec. B, pp. 15–16.

Desmond, Jane C., ed. *Dancing Desires: Choreographing Sexualities on and off the Stage*. Madison: University of Wisconsin Press, 2001.

Dunning, Jennifer. "A Gay Evening in the Word's 2 Meanings." *New York Times*, 25 June 1994, sec. 1, p. 15.

Foster, Susan Leigh. "Narrative with a Vengeance: Doris Humphrey's *With My Red Fires*." Paper presented at the Twenty-second Annual Conference of the Society of Dance History Scholars, Albuquerque, N.M., 10–13 June 1999.

Gere, David. *How To Make Dances an Epidemic: Tracking Choreography in the Age of AIDS*. Madison: University of Wisconsin Press, 2004.

McGarry, Molly, and Fred Wasserman. *Becoming Visible: An Illustrated History of Lesbian and Gay Life in Twentieth-Century America*. New York: Penguin Studio, 1998.

Morris, Gay, ed. *Moving Words: Re-Writing Dance*. London and New York: Routledge, 1996.

Wolf, Sara. "Lesbian Choreographers Redefine Motion." *Village Voice*, 11-17 June 2003, pp. 44, 46.

**Peter Carpenter**

*See also* AIDS AND PEOPLE WITH AIDS; AILEY, ALVIN; BAKER, JOSEPHINE; BENNETT, MICHAEL; CUNNINGHAM, MERCE; JONES, BILL T., AND ARNIE ZANE; KIRSTEIN, LINCOLN; PERFORMANCE, THEATER, AND DANCE STUDIES; ROBBINS, JEROME; SHAWN, TED.

**DANCE STUDIES.** see PERFORMANCE, THEATRE, AND DANCE STUDIES.

# DAUGHTERS OF BILITIS

The Daughters of Bilitis (DOB) was the first national lesbian organization in the United States. Founded in 1955 in San Francisco, the DOB was for over twenty years an active part of the homophile movement. Its members organized local meetings, sponsored national conventions, answered thousands of letters and telephone calls, lobbied for institutional and political change, and published the *Ladder*, the first ongoing lesbian magazine, from 1956 through 1970. An organization for women only, the DOB reached women and men of all races, genders, and sexualities throughout the country and around the world, and helped change public opinion about female homosexuality.

This historic group started simply. When Phyllis Lyon and Del Martin moved to San Francisco in 1953, they found it difficult to meet other lesbians. Two years later, through a gay male friend, they met Noni Frey and were invited to join her and five other women one Friday night in September to discuss organizing a secret social group. From that discussion the DOB was born.

It was Frey who suggested the name, taken from the book *Songs of Bilitis* by the nineteenth-century French poet Pierre Louys, who claimed that Bilitis was a contemporary of the Greek poet Sappho. As Sappho was one of the few historical references to lesbianism available in the 1950s, the name "Daughters of Bilitis" simultaneously signaled to those in the know that it was a gay group. The name also shielded the group from the general public, who, as Martin noted in *Lesbian/Woman*, would not know the difference between DOB and the Daughters of the American Revolution or "a society for raising cats."

Within the first year, the original eight founders split over disagreements about DOB's purpose. Some of the women wanted it to be strictly a social group, which would hold parties and plan recreational activities for its members, while others wanted that and more. Martin and Lyon insisted that DOB could provide a place for lesbians to talk about whatever was on their minds, find support and information about homosexuality, and begin to change the isolation and fear that so many lived with on a daily basis.

During a time when gay bars were the most popular gathering places for lesbians and gay men, the DOB provided an alternative. The bars were frequently raided by the San Francisco police department's vice squad or agents of the California alcohol beverage control. The creation of a safe and welcoming space in which a lesbian could meet others like herself was the priority for the leaders of DOB. But they also wanted to change society's negative view of homosexuality and eliminate the discrimination that gay women and men faced on the job, in their communities, and at home.

One issue that DOB had to address immediately was the pervasive distrust in the middle 1950s of social change organizations in general, and a keen suspicion of those who belonged to "secret" groups in particular. When the front pages of daily newspapers featured Hollywood stars, noted authors, politicians and even military leaders being hounded in public hearings led by Wisconsin Senator Joseph McCarthy and others, it is no wonder that the average woman or man, especially one attempting to come to terms with being a "deviant" homosexual, would be wary of joining a group addressing such issues.

Coexisting with the public's suspicion of secret societies and the rabid climate of accusation in the 1950s was a passionate belief in the power of the individual, and it is this basic American belief that motivated the women of DOB. The founders of DOB were influenced by groups such as the American Civil Liberties Union (ACLU), the American Friends Service Committee (AFSC), and the National Association for the Advancement of Colored People (NAACP), and they sought to create an organization that would integrate lesbians into society. DOB worked both to raise the self-esteem and self-acceptance of individual lesbians as well as to change society's attitudes and practices. They believed that each person could make a contribution toward the empowerment of herself and others like her.

In advancing the cause of equality for lesbians and gay men, the DOB always had a close, though sometimes complicated relationship with the largely male homophile movement. They received support, shared office space, and participated in one another's meetings and conferences throughout the 1950s and 1960s. However, the women of DOB felt strongly that a woman-only organization was necessary to delineate issues like discrimination, where the problem rose both from their status as *women* in a sexist society and *lesbians* in a homophobic one. But while they often challenged misogyny within the movement, they also singled out many of the male homophile leaders as "SOBs" (Sons of Bilitis) and praised their work at DOB conventions in the 1960s.

DOB was always a tiny part of a small movement for social change. From a handful of women in San Francisco it grew to include about five hundred members in cities across the country by the late 1960s. Through its magazine, DOB reached thousands more, with roughly three thousand women (and some men) on the mailing list in 1970. However, DOB always attracted a range of women from different racial, ethnic, and economic backgrounds. Two women of color were among the group of eight lesbians who founded the organization in 1955, and in 1963 Cleo Glenn became the first African American to head a national LGBT organization when she assumed the position of DOB's national president. A DOB questionnaire in 1958 revealed that many of the early members had come from working- and middle-class backgrounds but had managed to attend college. Many worked as teachers, but there were also engineers, nurses, printers, journalists, and secretaries. DOB's emphasis on changing society's view of lesbians as sick, immoral, and criminal meant they emphasized conventional dress and appearance. Like most advocacy groups at that time—from the NAACP to Women Strike for Peace—they were very conscious of the impact of ordinary (and gender-appropriate) attire when pressing the claims of an unpopular issue or despised minority group.

## Launching the *Ladder*

By the summer of 1956, the DOB's few active members saw that they needed to expand their efforts to reach other women. Both Lyon and Martin had backgrounds in journalism from their college years. Publishing a newsletter, which would advertise their newly devised programs of private parties and public discussions, seemed like a logical next step for the new organization.

By the end of June, Lyon was named editor of the new publication, the *Ladder*, which first appeared in October of 1956. DOB member Brian O'Brien ("Bob") submitted a drawing for the first issue's cover, which featured two women at the foot of a ladder reaching up to the sky. The title reflects the thinking of the times. The magazine was intended to be a vehicle of hope and possibility, a way to make real the vision of a better future and to help the lesbian lift herself up, out of the depths of self-hatred and social stigma.

The *Ladder* made its debut as a typed, mimeographed newsletter with a homespun look, and for the first year it featured Brian's hand-drawn cover. The DOB quickly ran out of the two hundred or so copies they produced after mailing the newsletter to everyone the members knew as well as to women lawyers, doctors, and other professionals whose names were in the San Francisco telephone directory. That was the beginning of a national circulation that later included supportive professionals and the prominent Kinsey Institute for Sex Research.

Many of the women involved in the organization in this period protected themselves by using pseudonyms or "pen names" in the newsletter. From the first issue of the *Ladder* on, the leaders of the DOB sought to reassure their readers that involvement in the organization would help, not harm, them. They also appealed for financial support, in addition to original artwork, fiction, poetry,

## the purpose of the daughters of bilitis

Developed in 1956, the Statement of Purpose was printed in every issue of the organization's magazine the *Ladder* until April/May 1970.

A women's organization for the purpose of promoting the integration of the homosexual into society by:

1. Education of the variant*, with particular emphasis on the psychological, physiological and sociological aspects, to enable her to understand herself and make her adjustment to society in all its social, civic, and economic implications—this to be accomplished by establishing and maintaining as complete a library as possible of both fiction and non-fiction literature on the sex deviant theme; by sponsoring public discussions on pertinent subjects to be con-

*In 1967, "variant" was changed to "lesbian."

ducted by leading members of the legal, psychiatric, religious and other professions; by advocating a mode of behavior and dress acceptable to society.

2. Education of the public at large through acceptance first of the individual, leading to any eventual breakdown of erroneous taboos and prejudices; through public discussion meetings aforementioned; through dissemination of educational literature on the homosexual theme.

3. Participation in research projects by duly authorized and responsible psychologists, sociologists and other such experts directed towards further knowledge of the homosexual.

4. Investigation of the penal code as it pertains to the homosexual, proposal of changes to provide an equitable handling of cases involving this minority group, and promotion of these changes through due process of law in the state legislatures.

and essays. Over the years they received a wealth of responses. From one of the first "letters to the editor" published in 1957, which was written by playwright Lorraine Hansberry (as "L. N." or "L. H. N.") to numerous debuts of lesbian authors ranging from Rita Mae Brown to Marion Zimmer Bradley to Valerie Taylor, the *Ladder* was the place where lesbians could find information about homophile activities, read reviews of the growing numbers of works dealing with lesbianism and homosexuality, and find a sense of connection to other lesbians.

Over the fourteen years the *Ladder* was published by the DOB, it drew on the editorial talents of Lyon, Martin, Barbara Gittings, Helen Sandoz, and Barbara Grier. In 1970, Grier decided with then-DOB national president Rita Laporte to sever the magazine's ties to the organization and publish it independently. It lasted for two more years as a lesbian feminist magazine. As a groundbreaking publication, the *Ladder* still stands as one of the DOB's most significant contributions to the gay and lesbian rights movement.

### Chapter Organizing

Through the *Ladder,* DOB reached people throughout the United States and around the world. It helped bring together lesbians who were eager for an organizational home, and in 1958 local chapters of the DOB were started in Los Angeles and New York. Within the next dozen years, groups were also formed in Chicago, Philadelphia, New Orleans, Denver, and Houston, among other cities.

The Boston chapter, formed in 1969, still exists today as an informal social group. DOB groups were run on local volunteer labor and governed by a national board with offices in San Francisco. In addition to the *Ladder,* each chapter published a local newsletter that featured information and analysis of local activities and issues. These newsletters were often the first lesbian publications to appear in their areas, and a few, like *Lesbian Tide* in Los Angeles, went on to become national magazines.

Chapters also organized "Gab 'n' Javas," which were informal discussion groups about issues of concern to lesbians, a forerunner of the consciousness-raising groups promoted by women's liberation activists in the late 1960s and 1970s. DOB members also represented the organization in public gatherings and through media appearances, beginning in 1959 on the radio in the San Francisco Bay area and expanding throughout the 1960s and 1970s to include print and television coverage in major U. S. cities.

In the late 1950s and 1960s, DOB members participated in both their own and institutionally based research projects, working with a few psychologists and psychiatrists to gather information about lesbians who were living "normal" lives. They hoped that these efforts would challenge the prevailing view of homosexuals as "sick" and thus help advance gay rights. They also built coalitions with religious leaders to counter the notion of homosexuality as immoral, and in 1964 helped form the

Council on Religion and the Homosexual in San Francisco. On the East Coast, from 1964 on, some DOB members joined the earliest gay picket lines at Independence Hall in Philadelphia and at the White House, making visible the demand that it was discrimination, not homosexuality, which was "illegal."

Beyond U.S. borders, the *Ladder*'s reach helped extend the idea of lesbian organizing as well. In London, Esme Langley was inspired to start a DOB-type group and in 1962 began the Minorities Research Group. She also began publishing *Arena Three,* the first lesbian magazine in England. And fifteen years after the DOB was formed in the United States, Australians Marion Paull and Claudia Pearce organized a DOB chapter in Melbourne. The group, formed in January 1970, lasted for just a few years. It is recognized as Australia's "first openly homosexual political organization" (Willett, p. 37) and helped jumpstart the fledgling gay rights movement in that country.

By 1970, however, DOB as a national organization was hindered by old and new political and organizational differences. Intense disagreements over more militant strategies and direct action tactics had begun in the middle 1960s. Some DOB leaders believed primarily in research and educational activities as the way to change society while others increasingly urged the organization's involvement in public protests and demonstrations. In addition, long-simmering disputes over misogynistic attitudes and sexist behaviors in the largely male homophile movement sharpened, fueled in part by the resurgence of feminism in the middle to late 1960s. Some of DOB's long-time leaders had become involved with the re-emerging women's movement and wanted DOB to be more woman-centered and less allied with male homophile groups. Others felt strongly that DOB was still primarily a gay organization and that involvement in other issues would dilute the cause of gay rights. Also, the rapid growth of chapters in the middle to late 1960s stretched the organization's resources thin.

The breaking point came in 1970, when then-editor Barbara Grier ("Gene Damon") and national president Rita Laporte decided to publish the *Ladder* as an independent lesbian feminist review and removed the mailing list and other crucial publishing materials from DOB's headquarters in San Francisco. Without the magazine, the glue that held the organization together dissolved. The national board voted to disband rather than face an expensive and possibly disastrous legal battle over ownership of the magazine. They also agreed to continue to support local organizing, and many DOB chapters continued their work throughout the 1970s.

Despite its demise as a national organization in 1970, the DOB has had a lasting impact. As the first U. S. organization run by and for lesbians, it helped launch a revolution in American attitudes about, and openness toward, basic rights for all sexual minorities.

### Bibliography

Bullough, Vern, ed. *Before Stonewall: Activists for Gay and Lesbian Rights in Historical Context.* New York: Haworth Press, 2002.

Clendinen, Dudley, and Adam Nagourney. *Out for Good: The Struggle to Build a Gay Rights Movement in America.* New York: Simon and Schuster, 1999.

Cruikshank, Margaret, ed. *The Lesbian Path.* Tallahassee, Fla.: Naiad Press, 1981.

D'Emilio, John. *Sexual Politics, Sexual Communities: The Making of a Homosexual Minority in the United States, 1940–1970.* Chicago: University of Chicago Press, 1983.

Duberman, Martin. *Stonewall.* New York: Penguin, 1993.

Faderman, Lillian. *Odd Girls and Twilight Lovers: A History of Lesbian Life in Twentieth-Century America.* New York: Columbia University Press, 1991.

Grier, Barbara, and Coletta Reid, eds. *The Lavender Herring: Lesbian Essays from the Ladder.* Baltimore: Diana Press, 1976.

Martin, Del, and Phyllis Lyon. *Lesbian/Woman.* Volcano, Calif.: Volcano Press, 1972, rev. 1991.

Rupp, Leila. *A Desired Past: A Short History of Same-Sex Love in America.* Chicago: University of Chicago Press, 1999.

Stein, Marc. *City of Sisterly and Brotherly Loves: Making Lesbian and Gay History in Philadelphia, 1945–1972.* Chicago: University of Chicago Press, 2000.

Tobin, Kay, and Randy Wicker. *The Gay Crusaders.* New York: Paperback Library, 1972.

Willett, Graham. *Living Out Loud: A History of Gay and Lesbian Activism in Australia, 1958–1998.* St. Leonards, Australia: Allen and Unwin, 2000.

**Marcia M. Gallo**

*See also* CORDOVA, JEANNE; ECKSTEIN, ERNESTINE; GIDLOW, ELSA; GITTINGS, BARBARA, AND KAY TOBIN LAHUSEN; GLENN, CLEO; GRIER, BARBARA; HART, PEARL; HOMOPHILE MOVEMENT; HOMOPHILE MOVEMENT DEMONSTRATIONS; *LADDER*; LATINA AND LATINO ORGANIZATIONS AND PERIODICALS; LYON, PHYLLIS, AND DEL MARTIN; ONE INSTITUTE; RADICALESBIANS.

# DAVIS, Katharine Bement (b. 15 January 1860; d. 10 December 1935), social scientist, prison reformer.

A member of the first generation of American women to earn doctoral degrees in social science, Katharine Bement Davis pioneered the sexual survey a generation before

**Katharine Bement Davis.** The pre-Kinsey pioneer of the sexual survey, whose landmark study of female sexuality was published in 1929. [corbis]

Alfred Kinsey. Her landmark study, *Factors in the Sex Life of Twenty-Two Hundred Women* (1929), provided the earliest nonjudgmental account of same-sex relations among women. Davis, who neither married nor regretted her decision not to, left little record of her personal relationships.

The eldest of five children, Davis grew up in the area of upstate New York that had been a seedbed for reform since the early nineteenth century, when her grandmother advocated woman's suffrage and temperance. Her father's business reverses delayed her entrance to college by a decade, during which time she taught high school. After graduating from Vassar College in 1892, at age thirty-three, Davis taught science to girls, directed the Workingman's Model Home at the Chicago World's Fair, and served as head resident of a settlement house in Philadelphia. She returned to Chicago in 1897 and studied political economy with Thorstein Veblen and other leading social scientists at the University of Chicago, earning a Ph.D. in 1900.

Committed to applying social science to the solution of problems of poverty and delinquency, Davis accepted the position as first superintendent of the New York State Reformatory for Women at Bedford Hills. She rejected arguments that crime was hereditary, and trained women inmates for citizenship, emphasizing health care, outdoor activities, and vocational training. Davis earned a national reputation for her reforms, and John D. Rockefeller Jr., impressed by a pamphlet she wrote about prostitution, invited her to join the board of his Bureau of Social Hygiene. In 1912 the bureau opened a laboratory of social hygiene at Bedford Hills to study female crime.

Soon after Davis left the reformatory, state investigations exposed overcrowding and corruption, as well as the existence of lesbian relationships among inmates. The testimony revealed that Davis had been tolerant of these relationships, many of which were formed between black and white women. On principle she had insisted on integrated housing at the reformatory; however, after her successors blamed disciplinary problems on interracial lesbian relationships, the institution introduced segregated inmate housing.

In 1917 Davis became the general secretary of Rockefeller's Bureau of Social Hygiene and after World War I, as director, she encouraged social science research on human sexuality. In 1920 Davis began her study of female sexuality, which she published in 1929. *Factors in the Sex Life of Twenty-Two Hundred Women* analyzed replies to questionnaires that were sent to college graduates and women's club members concerning sex education, contraceptive use, masturbation, and same-sex desires and practices. Davis hoped that by studying "normal" women she would learn about sexual abnormality, but she found instead that prevailing ideas of normality had to be revised. She reported widespread same-sex desires: 28 percent of women's college graduates and 20 percent of former coeds reported intense ties with other women that included some sexual contact; equal numbers had intense emotional attachments that involved kissing and hugging. Given this extensive evidence of homoerotic desire, Davis did not consider these women deviant or "psychopathic." Rather, she wrote, measures of the education, health, mental health, and reported happiness of women who had homosexual experiences were "not significantly different from that of the entire group" (p. 261). Most of the case histories she included revealed women's comfort with same-sex relationships. Davis suggested that feelings of disapproval were "probably a reflection of public opinion as to homosexuality, especially in view of the high per cent of those who have found the relationship helpful and stimulating" (p. 255).

Despite the decline of Victorian morality by the time she published her study, Davis's views remained controversial and her publisher feared "undesirable publicity." Not entirely pleased by her research, Rockefeller dismissed her from the Bureau of Social Hygiene, just a few years before Davis planned to retire. In parting she called for further scientific study of sex as a research priority, but the bureau instead turned to crime and delinquency studies. Davis retired to California with her two unmarried sisters and died of cerebral arteriosclerosis at her Pacific Grove, California, home.

## Bibliography

Davis, Katharine Bement. *Factors in the Sex Life of Twenty-two Hundred Women.* New York: Harbor, 1929.

D'Emilio, John, and Freedman, Estelle B. *Intimate Matters: A History of Sexuality in America.* New York: Harper and Row, 1988.

Fitzpatrick, Ellen. *Endless Crusade: Women Social Scientists and Progressive Reform.* New York: Oxford University Press, 1990.

Freedman, Estelle B. *Their Sisters' Keepers: Women's Prison Reform in America, 1830–1930.* Ann Arbor: University of Michigan Press, 1981.

Lewis, W. David. "Katharine Bement Davis." In *Notable American Women.* Edited by Edward T. James. Cambridge, Mass.: Belknap Press, 1971.

**Estelle B. Freedman**

*See also* PRISONS, JAILS, AND REFORMATORIES: WOMEN'S; PSYCHOLOGY, PSYCHIATRY, PSYCHOANALYSIS, AND SEXOLOGY; SAME-SEX INSTITUTIONS.

**DEGONWADONTI.** see BRANT, BETH.

# DELANY, Samuel R. (b. 1 April 1942), writer and educator.

A major gay and African American voice in science fiction, Samuel R. Delany is among today's most interesting intellectuals. Born in Harlem in New York City into a middle-class family that lived above his father's funeral home, Delany was educated at Dalton Elementary in Manhattan and the Bronx High School of Science, after which he briefly attended City College of New York. His career as a published science fiction writer began when, following the suggestion of his then-wife Marilyn Hacker, he submitted *The Jewels of Aptor* (1962) to Ace Books. Delany has published over thirty-five books and is a multiple winner of science fiction's highest honors: the World Science Fiction Society's Hugo Award and the Science Fiction and Fantasy Writers of America's Nebula Award.

Other honors include the Pilgrim Award for excellence in science fiction scholarship, the Bill Whitehead Award for Lifetime Achievement in Gay and Lesbian Writing, and a 2002 induction into the Science Fiction Hall of Fame. Delany lives in New York City, the inspiration, topic, and setting for much of his work.

Delany's science fiction analyzes the systems of the world; it reveals social, political, economic, as well as sexual norms to be matters of convention rather than nature. In his hands, science fiction reaches its full potential as a tool for imagining the world differently. For example, in an early published short story, "Aye, and Gomorrah . . ." (1967), the surgical alteration of space travelers makes them objects of desire for certain earthbound humans. Other early works are notable for the value placed on difference, such as *The Ballad of Beta-2* (1965), *Empire Star* (1966), and *The Einstein Intersection* (1968), and representations of racial, cultural, and sexual diversity, including *Babel-17* (1966) and *Nova* (1968). These and other early works, including the trilogy collectively entitled *The Fall of the Towers* (1963, 1964, 1965), caused one critic to hail Delany as "the best science fiction writer in the world." Prior to the Stonewall Riots in 1969, Delany drafted *Equinox* (1973) and *Hogg* (1995), both pornographic novels, the latter a particularly angry one, that went unpublished for years.

Another phase of Delany's career began with *Dhalgren* (1975), a lengthy and complex million-seller that included representations of gay, straight, and group sex. A cultural concomitant to the black, women's, and gay liberation movements of its era, *Dhalgren* is set in a city that has experienced an unspecified apocalypse, creating remarkable dangers and freedoms for its inhabitants. *Trouble on Triton* (1976) critiques privileged white, male, heterosexual subjectivity, as represented by its antihero, an unhappy person in a world where difference abounds. In the *Return to Nevèrÿon* series, Delany employs science fiction's generic cousin, sword and sorcery, to explore sex and semiotics in tales loosely organized around Gorgik the Liberator's quests to abolish slavery and to engage in satisfying sexual practices, which for him necessitate the use of slave collars. The series' third volume features *The Tale of Plagues and Carnivals* (1984), where fantasy and reality converge. In the first U.S. novel about AIDS from a major U.S. press, the publication of the series' final volume was delayed by a temporary ban of Delany, and other fantasy writers addressing gay themes, by America's largest book retailer. *Stars in My Pocket Like Grains of Sand* (1984), a story of gay love in the far-off future, garnered enthusiastic reviews and confirmed Delany's eminence in science fiction. *The Motion of Light in Water: Sex and SF Writing in the East Village, 1957–1965* (1988) is a memoir that details Delany's sexual life—in an era before both the Stonewall Riots and AIDS—and the intersections of race, sexuality, and the author's identity as a writer. Other autobiographical writings include *Heavenly Breakfast: An Essay on the Winter of Love* (1979), which describes life in a commune/rock band, and later works such as "Citre et Trans" (1995), about homosexual rape in Greece, and the graphic novel *Bread and Wine* (1999), about Delany meeting his current partner of fourteen years, who had been homeless in New York City. Delany also published four volumes of science fiction criticism during the 1970s and 1980s: *The Jewel-Hinged Jaw* (1977), *The American Shore* (1978), *Starboard Wine* (1984), and *The Straits of Messina* (1989).

In the 1990s, Delany embraced modes of writing other than science fiction. *The Mad Man* (1994, revised 2002) combines satire of academia, detective fiction, and pornography to tell of a graduate student's sexual life during the emerging AIDS crisis in New York and his investigation into the death of a philosopher. The novel's very specific descriptions of particular sexual practices purposefully contrast with the generalities of early medical discourse on HIV transmission. The novella *Atlantis: Model 1924* (1995) concerns the migration of a young black man from North Carolina to New York City; it features characters based on Delany's father and aunts and uncles, and an appearance by the poet Hart Crane. Delany's reputation as a talented literary and cultural critic has been advanced by collections of written interviews (*Silent Interviews,* 1994), essays (*Longer Views,* 1996, and *Shorter Views,* 1999), letters (1984, 2000), and a study of Manhattan's pornographic theaters (*Times Square Red, Times Square Blue,* 1999).

Delany has taught in the Clarion Science Fiction and Fantasy Writers Workshop, and at the University of Massachusetts at Amherst and the State University of New York at Buffalo. In 2003, he was a professor of English and creative writing at Temple University in Philadelphia.

### Bibliography

Fox, Robert Elliot. "Samuel R. Delany: Astro Black." In *Conscientious Sorcerers: The Black Postmodernist Fiction of LeRoi Jones/Amiri Baraka, Ishmael Reed, and Samuel R. Delany.* Westport, Conn.: Greenwood Press, 1987.

Jackson, Earl, Jr. "Imagining It Otherwise: Alternative Sexualities in the Fictions of Samuel R. Delany." In *Strategies of Deviance: Studies in Gay Male Representation.* Bloomington: Indiana University Press, 1995.

Sallis, James, ed. *Ash of Stars: On the Writing of Samuel R. Delany.* Jackson: University Press of Mississippi, 1996.

**Jeffrey A. Tucker**

*See also* LITERATURE.

# DEMOCRATIC PARTY

Over time, the lesbian, gay, bisexual, and transgender movements have embraced varying approaches to political, social, and economic change. In doing so, they have used liberationist and assimilationist strategies, approaches that reflect the use of unconventional and conventional politics to foster change. A liberationist strategy typically demands that those in power allow for a new way to conceive of the world, while the assimilationist approach celebrates the "work within the system, let us in" political strategy. The use of conventional, assimilationist politics has often meant interacting with Democratic Party officials at all levels of government. The movements have received varying degrees of support from the Democratic Party over the years.

## The 1970s

The Democratic Party's 1972 National Convention in Miami was the site where lesbians and gays were first officially noticed at a national party convention, as five openly gay/lesbian delegates participated on the convention floor. Gay and lesbian delegates were invited to participate because the convention organizers wished to signal that the party was being more inclusive and also recognized the voices of gay and lesbian delegates within the Democratic Party. Jim Foster, a George McGovern delegate who was chairman of San Francisco's Society for Individual Rights, and Madeline Davis, the vice president of the Mattachine Society's Niagara Frontier in Buffalo, were given ten minutes to make a case for a gay rights plank in the Democratic Party platform on the podium. Foster informed convention delegates that "we did not come to you pleading your understanding or begging your affirming the validity to seek and maintain meaningful emotional relationships and affirming our right to participate in the life of this country on an equal basis with every citizen" (Raben, p. 281). Moments later, Madeline Davis said "I am a woman—I am a lesbian. . . . We have suffered the gamut of oppression, from being totally ignored to having our heads smashed and blood spilled in the streets. Now we are coming out of our closets and onto the convention floor to tell you, the delegates, and to tell all gay people through America, that we are here to put an end to your fears" (Clendinen and Nagourney, p. 134). For many assimilationists, Foster's and Davis's appearances represented a triumph for the young lesbian, gay, bisexual, and transgender movements. But for those who embraced a more radical, liberationist perspective, the visibility given to Foster and Davis by the McGovernites paled in the face of the gay rights plank defeat, thus raising broader strategic questions of overall movement strategy.

But movement activists did not merely look to the national Democratic Party as a vehicle for assimilation into American politics. The year 1973 witnessed a number of failed attempts by gay Democratic contenders to win elective office: Harvey Milk ran for the Board of Supervisors in San Francisco, Jim Owles sought election to a City Council seat in New York City, and Jack Baker (who had been the first gay activist elected as a student body president of a major university when University of Minnesota students elected him in 1971) unsuccessfully sought a city council seat in Minneapolis. Milk, a Castro Street camera store owner, eventually was elected to the San Francisco Board of Supervisors (the City Council) in 1977, thus becoming one of the most celebrated and high-profile gay activists in the United States. He served until November 1978, when he (along with Mayor George Moscone) was assassinated by former San Francisco supervisor Dan White. With his death, the charismatic Milk became a martyr in the larger movement, one whose contributions have been explored in books, films, and opera.

In 1974, Elaine Noble became the first openly gay or lesbian statewide political official when she won election to the Massachusetts House of Representatives as a Democrat, representing a Boston area district. In doing so, she was among the first political candidates to run as unclos eted. She later sought the Democratic nomination for the U.S. Senate in 1980, but lost to Paul Tsongas. As a veteran lesbian activist, Noble helped to open doors for other out lesbians and gays who sought access to the Democratic Party and to grassroots organizing.

Democrat Jimmy Carter's 1976 U.S. presidential campaign responded to the gradual progress that was being achieved in the broader area of lesbian and gay rights. For example, in 1975 California approved a bill that decriminalized consensual sex, a gay civil rights measure was introduced for a second time in the U.S. House of Representatives, and the United States Civil Service Commission eliminated its longstanding ban that prevented lesbians and gays from being hired for "nonmilitary federal government jobs" (Raben, p. 282). Responding to the changing nature of the times, in February 1976 Carter announced his opposition to discrimination based on sexual orientation. That position was included in the plank of the Democratic convention until June 1976, when Carter retreated by withdrawing his support for the plank and the platform committee ultimately voted for its elimination (Raben, p. 282). Carter's decision reminded lesbian and gay activists of the perils of counting on Democratic Party politicians to support potentially unpopular political decisions in the name of social justice. The Carter White House did

**Human Rights Campaign.** Executive Director Elizabeth Birch welcomes President Bill Clinton to the HRC's first National Dinner on 8 November 1997—which was picketed both by demonstrators against gay rights and by AIDS protesters pressing for better policies from the federal government. [AP Photo/Wilfredo Lee]

receive national publicity when Midge Costanza, his liaison to minority communities, invited fourteen lesbian and gay activists to the White House. Costanza's invitation provided welcome access to the White House, but reopened a longstanding debate over larger movement strategy concerning whether access to mainstream political officials leads to concrete policy accomplishments.

**The 1980s**

By 1980, however, the political and social landscape regarding lesbian and gay rights was slowly changing. National politicians from both major parties were forced to address lesbian and gay concerns. These changes were reflected in the 1980 presidential campaign between Jimmy Carter and Republican Ronald Reagan, though Reagan publicly attacked homosexuality and Carter disappointed lesbian and gay activists by announcing that his administration would not issue an executive order that would ban antilesbian and antigay federal employment discrimination. Carter also announced that he could not support a gay rights plank at the 1980 Democratic Party convention. That convention was notable for its seventy-seven lesbian and gay delegates (Raben, "Politics," p. 284). Among the delegates was Melvin Boozer, an African American delegate from the District of Columbia who formally addressed the convention from the podium and called for coalition building across race and sexual orientation divides. Boozer said, "Would you ask me how I dare to compare the civil rights struggle with the struggle for lesbian and gay rights? I know what it means to be called a nigger, and I know what it means to be called a faggot, and I understand the difference, in the marrow of my bones. And I can sum up that difference in one word: nothing. Bigotry is bigotry" (Thompson, p. 196). Boozer is historically significant as well because he became the first openly gay person to be nominated for the vice presidency of the United States.

With Ronald Reagan's 1980 election victory and the emergence of AIDS in the United States in June 1981, the political, electoral, policy, and social landscape for LGBT people shifted considerably. By 1982 and 1983, the seriousness of the AIDS epidemic threatened new-found sexual freedoms and the broader social and political gains accomplished by the movement over the past thirty years. Two congressional Democrats, in particular, played important roles in challenging the Reagan administration's desultory response to HIV/AIDS. Under the leadership of Rep. Ted Weiss (D-New York), who was chair of the Subcommittee on Human Resources and Intergovernmental Relations, and Rep. Henry Waxman (D-California), who chaired the Subcommittee on Science and Technology, Congress in 1983 investigated the U.S. Public Health Service (PHS) response to AIDS. The Weiss report highlighted AIDS funding problems in the Reagan administration and lengthy delays in research into AIDS-related drugs, as well as management problems in funding, coordination, and communication within the PHS (Panem, pp. 31–35). On the Senate side, Edward Kennedy (D-Massachusetts) consistently fought Jesse Helms's (R-North Carolina) efforts to block funding for HIV/AIDS education at a time when such education was desperately needed. The highly public, adversarial relationship between Democratic members of Congress and the Reagan administration regarding federal governmental responses to AIDS continued throughout Reagan's two-term presidency.

Representative Barney Frank (D-Massachusetts) was also a central figure in opposing the Reagan administration's conservative economic and social policies. In the summer of 1987, Frank became the second member of the United States Congress to reveal that he was gay, but the first to do so voluntarily. His fellow Massachusetts Democrat, Gerry Studds, had disclosed his sexual orientation in 1983, when confronted with the possibility of being publically outed.

## The Clinton Presidency

With Democrat Bill Clinton's election to the presidency in 1992, Frank would play an integral role in building bridges between the Clinton White House and the mainstream LGBT movements. Clinton had served notice in the campaign that if elected, he would be more supportive of lesbian and gay rights than any previous occupant of the Oval Office. On 18 May 1992, at a Los Angeles, California, AIDS benefit, Clinton enthusiastically reached out to lesbians and gays for their money and votes when he said: "I have a vision of America, and you're part of it" (Cleninden and Nagourney, p. 572). Clinton's videotaped speech was distributed to LGBT organizers throughout the United States in an effort to raise money for the Democratic Party's nominee and to heighten support for his candidacy. But this successful fundraising strategy also understandably had the further effect of raising expectations for what a Clinton White House would deliver to the LGBT movements. Indeed, Clinton had made several important promises during the campaign. He called for a Manhattan Project on AIDS, one that would lead to a significant increase in funding for AIDS research and the appointment of an AIDS czar. He promised to recognize lesbians and gays in ways that they had never been recognized by previous occupants of the Oval Office, mostly using the presidential appointment process to appoint lesbians and gays throughout the federal government. Clinton made several additional promises as well: to overturn the ban on lesbians and gays in the military, to issue an executive order that would prohibit discrimination on the basis of sexual orientation in all federal agencies, and to support a gay civil rights bill. Clinton immediately pleased his supporters in lesbian and gay communities when Roberta Achtenberg, a California lesbian, and Bob Hattoy, a gay man with AIDS, were given prominent speaking opportunities at the 1992 Democratic National Convention. Both would later receive appointments to the Clinton administration.

Once elected, Clinton's honeymoon was very short indeed. His failure to overturn the military ban on lesbians and gays through an executive order and his willingness to instead accept the "don't ask, don't tell" compromise proposal, which fell well short of his original goals, irreparably injured his relations with the larger LGBT movements. His movement supporters within the Democratic Party were deeply disappointed that he lacked the courage to follow through on his original plan, and his critics within the movements were quick to point out that Clinton's record of supporting lesbian and gay rights as governor of Arkansas was most disappointing and that his leadership failure should be no surprise. They also raised serious concerns about the larger move-

**Campaign Stop.** Protester Christina McKnight interrupts an address by U.S. Senate candidate Hillary Rodham Clinton to the Gay and Lesbian Independent Democrats in New York on 8 March 2000, demanding to know why the former first lady intended to march in the city's St. Patrick's Day Parade despite its organizers' exclusion of gay and lesbian contingents. [AP/Wide World Photos]

ment's strategy of pursuing an assimilationist strategy, one that celebrated access to power. Clinton himself encouraged the latter when he met with six lesbian and gay representatives in the Oval Office to discuss the military ban on 16 April 1993. This meeting was the first publicly announced session of lesbian and gay representatives with any president in the Oval Office.

Equally disappointing to many LGBT activists was Clinton's failure (and the failure of many Democratic Party officials) to support same-sex marriage, despite the reality that Clinton had never supported it as a presidential candidate or during his first term as president. When Clinton signed the Defense of Marriage Act (DOMA) into law on 21 September 1996, he acquiesced to his conservative Republican opponents, who had hoped to make same-sex marriage an important 1996 election-year wedge issue. The law is written to accomplish two central goals, as Mark Strasser states in *Legally Wed: Same-Sex Marriage and the Constitution*, "(1) prevent states from being forced by the Full Faith and Credit Clause to recognize same-sex marriages validly celebrated in other states, and (2) define marriages for federal purposes as the union of one man and one woman" (p. 127). Those most critical of Clinton's decision claimed that DOMA was both highly discriminatory and unnecessary, and that Clinton could have stated his opposition to same-sex marriage while vetoing DOMA. The practical reality of Clinton's decision is that battles over same-sex marriage

are now taking place at the state and local level, through both the courts, state legislatures, and, to a lesser extent, city councils. The most celebrated decision thus far was when then Vermont Governor Howard Dean signed into law the first-in-the-nation "civil unions" bill, which extended to lesbian and gay couples all the rights and benefits of marriage that are granted by Vermont state law. His decision was largely viewed as a step forward for those who support same-sex marriage, though some movement members lamented Vermont's failure to endorse marriage, per se.

In the end, the Clinton administration's policy record points out some of the pitfalls of relying almost exclusively on an insider, assimilationist strategy, one that celebrates access to power over concrete policy accomplishments. But at the same time, Clinton's eight years in office did signal some progress for the LGBT movements. Clinton's presidency helped to create a broader climate of acceptance and support for sexual diversity in the larger culture. He deserves credit for endorsing a federal bill that would have prohibited private employers from discriminating on the basis of sexual preference, the Employment Non-Discrimination Act (ENDA), an effort that was, unfortuantely, narrowly defeated. In doing so, he became the first president to publicly back lesbian and gay civil rights legislation. In addition, he created the White House liaison to the lesbian and gay community in 1995, the first time any president had established an official White

House position to work with lesbian and gay communities. And he deserves credit for using his presidential pulpit to deliver speeches that supported lesbian and gay rights and that called for more attention and resources to be devoted to HIV/AIDS education and research. But perhaps his greatest contribution has been to inspire the LGBT movements to reassess their political organizing strategies and to evaluate their interaction with the Democratic Party at all levels of government.

## Bibliography

Andriote, John-Manuel. *Victory Deferred: How AIDS Changed Gay Life in America.* Chicago: University of Chicago Press, 1999.

Cleninden, Dudley, and Adam Nagourney. *Out for Good: The Struggle to Build a Gay Rights Movement in America.* New York: Simon and Schuster, 1999.

D'Emilio, John, William B. Turner, and Urvashi Vaid, eds. *Creating Change: Sexuality, Public Policy, and Civil Rights.* New York: St. Martin's Press, 2000.

Panem, Sandra. *The AIDS Bureaucracy.* Cambridge, Mass.: Harvard University Press, 1988.

Raben, Robert. "Politics." In *St. James Press Gay and Lesbian Almanac.* Edited by Neil Schlager. Detroit, Mich.: St. James Press, 1998.

Rayside, David. *On the Fringe: Gays and Lesbians in Politics.* Ithaca, N.Y.: Cornell University Press, 1998.

Rimmerman, Craig A. *From Identity to Politics: The Lesbian and Gay Movements in the United States.* Philadelphia: Temple University Press, 2002.

Rimmerman, Craig A., ed. *Gay Rights, Military Wrongs: Political Perspectives on Lesbians and Gays in the Military.* New York: Garland, 1996.

Strasser, Mark. *Legally Wed: Same-Sex Marriage and the Constitution.* Ithaca, N.Y.: Cornell University Press, 1997.

Thompson, Mark, ed. *Long Road to Freedom: The Advocate History of the Gay and Lesbian Movement.* New York: St. Martin's Press, 1994.

Vaid, Urvashi. *Virtual Equality: The Mainstreaming of Gay and Lesbian Liberation.* New York: Anchor Books, 1995.

**Craig A. Rimmerman**

**See also** BOOZER, MEL; CAMERON, BARBARA; CORDOVA, JEANNE; ELECTORAL POLITICS; FEDERAL LAW AND POLICY; FRANK, BARNEY; HALL, MURRAY; MILK, HARVEY; NATIONAL GAY AND LESBIAN TASK FORCE (NGLTF); NOBLE, ELAINE; OWLES, JIM; REPUBLICAN PARTY; RUSTIN, BAYARD; WALSH, DAVID.

# DEMUTH, Charles (b. 8 November 1883; d. 25 October 1935), artist.

Charles Demuth was one of a small group of artists who brought European modernism to the United States during the first two decades of the twentieth century. Born to an affluent and prominent family in Lancaster, Pennsylvania, Demuth was contemptuous of his provincial hometown, but nonetheless drawn to the possibilities it offered for generating a genuinely American subject matter. On three trips to Paris between 1907 and 1921, Demuth studied the most advanced trends in painting, from postimpressionism through cubism, which he discussed with fellow artists at Gertrude Stein's famous salon on the Rue de Fleurus. Urbane and sophisticated, Demuth frequented the bohemian nightclubs and theaters of New York City and Provincetown and was part of two avant-garde circles in New York: the Dada artists associated with art patrons Walter and Louise Arensberg and Alfred Stieglitz's 291 Gallery. Despite these international experiences, after World War I Demuth chose to live and work in Lancaster, where he was cared for by his doting mother.

Demuth's art was as paradoxical as his lifestyle. His work falls into three distinct categories: watercolors, consisting of still lifes (1912–1934) and figurative scenes (1914–1920, 1930–1934); oil or tempera compositions, consisting of industrial landscapes (1920–1933); and the famous "poster portraits," which were nonfigurative homages to fellow artists (1923–1929). One might conclude that Demuth did not want to be tied to one artistic identity, but rather elected to remain artistically ambiguous, even self-contradictory. However, his varied oeuvre is united by that very quality of ambiguity, as well as a sly wit that imbued everything he created with a sense of detached irony. His best known work, *My Egypt* (1927, Whitney Museum of American Art), is a rendering in the precisionist style of a grain elevator in Lancaster, the monumentality of which is undercut by the painting's cynical title.

Elegant and aloof, Demuth was a dandy and drawn to the decadent writers of the turn of the century: J. K. Huysmans, Walter Pater, and Oscar Wilde. His figurative watercolors are arguably the American counterpart to Aubrey Beardsley's illustrations. And, like Beardsley, he was gay. Although his friends were certainly aware of—and accepting of—his sexual orientation, he lived in an age when homosexuality was illegal. And as it turned out, Demuth's personal profile happened to precisely correspond to the Freudian "explanation" of homosexuality popular during the interwar years. A frail child and diabetic adult, he was dependent his entire life on the ministrations of his overbearing, protective mother. Although in the twenty-first century there are few who subscribe to Freud's theory or accept his categorization of homosexuality as deviant or abnormal, having an explanation for his sexuality may have provided some emotional solace to a man for whom accepted avenues to love and sex were closed. Moreover, if most modernist artists at the time

**Distinguished Air.** A famously explicit 1930 watercolor by the modernist artist Charles Demuth, who absorbed European and New York influences but created his art in his Pennsylvania hometown. [Whitney Museum of American Art]

subscribed to the Freudian notion that artistic creativity is derived from the male, heterosexual sex "drive," Demuth embraced an alternate interpretation of that theory.

Perhaps in an effort to protect his friend's work from negative stereotyping, Marcel Duchamp told Demuth's biographer, Emily Farnham, that "the little perverse tendency that he had was not important in Demuth's life. . . . It had nothing to do with his art" (Farnham, 1959, p. 973). In fact, the contrary is true. In his figurative work—his depictions of cafés, vaudeville, the circus, and steam baths—as well as his illustrations for, among others, Emile Zola, Frank Wedekind, and Henry James, Demuth provided a unique visual record not only of New York bohemia from 1915 to1920, but also of its homosexual subculture. If the references to homosexual encounters in public and domestic spaces were (thinly) veiled in these works, Demuth "came out" a decade later in his watercolor *Distinguished Air* (1930, Whitney Museum of American Art), which he created in response to Robert McAlmon's story of the same name. Demuth's scene does not illustrate an episode from the author's story of a gay

American in 1920s Berlin, but rather connects a notorious modernist sculpture, Constantin Brancusi's phallic *Princess X* (1916), with the openly affectionate gay couple who admire it, and who are, in their way, equally avant-garde in their challenge to social conventions. The last of his illustrations before his death in 1935, *Distinguished Air* is also representative of the explicit homoerotic concerns in his late work. Upon his death, he willed all of his watercolors to his long-time lover from Lancaster, Robert Locher. His poster portraits went to Georgia O'Keeffe.

In the contemporary art world these poster portraits, particularly *The Figure Five in Gold* (1928, Metropolitan Museum of Art), which refers to a poem by William Carlos Williams, are admired as precursors of pop art's use of commercial signage. However, Demuth must also be acknowledged, along with the realist painter Paul Cadmus, as an artist who depicted aspects of homosexual desire at a time when such expression was truly transgressive.

**Bibliography**

Allara, Pamela Edwards. "Charles Demuth: Always a Seeker." *Arts Magazine* 50 (June 1976): 86–89.

Fahlman, Betsy. *Pennsylvania Modern: Charles Demuth of Lancaster.* Philadelphia: Philadelphia Museum of Art, 1983.

Farnham, Emily. *Charles Demuth: His Life, Psychology, and Works.* Columbus: Ohio State University Press, 1959.

———. *Charles Demuth: Behind a Laughing Mask.* Norman: University of Oklahoma Press, 1971.

Haskell, Barbara. *Charles Demuth.* New York: Whitney Museum of American Art, 1987.

Kellner, Bruce, ed. *The Letters of Charles Demuth, American Artist, 1883–1935.* Philadelphia: Temple University Press, 2000.

Weinberg, Jonathan. *Speaking for Vice: Homosexuality in the Art of Charles Demuth, Marsden Hartley, and the First American Avant-Garde.* New Haven, Conn.: Yale University Press, 1993.

**Pamela Edwards Allara**

***See also*** HARTLEY, MARSDEN; STEIN, GERTRUDE, AND ALICE B. TOKLAS; VISUAL ART.

**DEPORTATION LAW AND POLICY.** see IMMIGRATION, ASYLUM, AND DEPORTATION LAW AND POLICY

# DÍAZ-COTTO, Juanita (b. 9 February 1953), activist, writer, educator.

Juanita Díaz-Cotto (also known as Juanita Ramos) was born in Puerto Rico to working-class parents and came to the United States when she was eight years old. At eighteen she returned to her homeland and enrolled at the University of Puerto Rico, where she received a B.A. in political science. She later received a master's degree from the University of Chicago and a Ph.D. from Columbia University, both in political science. Díaz-Cotto is an indefatigable worker on behalf of progressive and LBGT causes and a long-time supporter of the Puerto Rican independence movement. In an effort to articulate her multiple identities and her focus on activism, she asks to be introduced at events as a "Black Puerto Rican lesbian feminist socialist."

In 1978 she made a decision to come out and joined the Comité Homosexual Latinoamericano. The Comité was an early LGBT Latina/o group that emphasized outreach and education about homophobia, race and ethnicity, and class oppression. Members also networked with people of color and progressive groups in Latin America. Díaz-Cotto served on both the National Planning Committee and New York Committee for the first National March on Washington for Gay and Lesbian Rights (1979). This historical event was organized at a grass-roots level, since conservative and mainstream LGBT groups and activists did not endorse the march until close to the time of the event. There were few people of color involved in the planning and Díaz-Cotto recalls that "Latino and Black people were reluctant to work in lesbian and gay organizations because of the racism and class oppression they had confronted" (Ramos, p. xiv). Díaz-Cotto decided to "stick it out" and help with plans for the march because she wanted white gays and lesbians to deal with those issues. She was one of the speakers at the rally before the march.

Díaz-Cotto also served on the Christopher Street Liberation Day Committee in New York City (working on the march and rally) and with the Coalition for Lesbian and Gay Rights, which worked for the passage of a lesbian and gay rights bill for the city (the Gay Rights Bill finally passed in 1986). In 1980 she helped organize the Women's Pentagon Action, a demonstration and teach-in, and later co-coordinated the People's and Gay and Lesbian demonstrations at the Democratic National Convention in New York City.

In the 1980s Díaz-Cotto turned her attention to issues concerning Latina lesbians. She was a founding member of Las Buenas Amigas, a political and social Latina lesbian group in New York City. She also began editing (under the pseudonym Juanita Ramos) the anthology *Compañeras: Latina Lesbians* (1987). *Compañeras,* a collection of essays, oral histories, poems, short stories, and artwork, was the first Latina lesbian anthology published in the United States. One goal of the book

was to reduce the isolation felt by this group due to "society, our families and the Church . . . constantly telling us that women who identify with other women in a sexual or loving manner are either sick, sinners or both" (Ramos, p. xiii). At the time, few Latina lesbians had been included in lesbian anthologies; *Compañeras* allowed the voices of forty-seven women from ten countries to be heard.

Díaz-Cotto is now an associate professor of sociology, women's studies, and Latin American and Caribbean-area studies at the State University of New York at Binghamton. She continues to work on behalf of social causes as a teacher, writer, speaker, workshop facilitator, and mentor. Since 1979 she has dedicated herself to working on behalf of prisoners in the United States and Latin America, and as part of that work has published *Gender, Ethnicity, and the State: Latina and Latino Prison Politics* (1996). The book examines deep-rooted dynamics in New York's penal system that keep Latina/o prisoners from empowering themselves: structural barriers imposed by the penal system, lack of social support systems, and the social, personal, and political divisions among inmates.

Díaz-Cotto also works in the medium of video. She has attended several lesbian and feminist *encuentros* (conferences or gatherings) in Latin America as a delegate and has made videos of the proceedings. Her current projects include video documentaries on Latina lesbians and on black women in Latin America and a book: *Chicanas and the Criminal Justice System in California.*

### Bibliography

Ramos, Juanita. *Compañeras: Latina Lesbians.* New York: Latina Lesbian History Project, 1987.

Retter, Yolanda. "Herstory: Juanita Ramos." *Lesbian Tide* (September 1997): 68.

**Yolanda Retter Vargas**

*See also* LATINA AND LATINO LGBTQ ORGANIZATIONS AND PERIODICALS; PUERTO RICO.

# DICKINSON, Emily (b. 10 December 1830; d. 15 May 1886), poet.

Emily Elizabeth Dickinson was born in Amherst, Massachusetts, and had one brother, Austin, and one sister, Lavinia. Emily, the elder daughter, grew up under a cloud of fear because many children of her parents' extended family had died young. Edward and Emily Norcross Dickinson tirelessly protected Emily, often keeping her in the house during harsh winter months. The Dickinsons were a deeply religious family, and Emily heard numerous preachers and sermons throughout her childhood. She attended Amherst Academy as a child and matriculated at Mount Holyoke Female Seminary. Both schools used religion as the basis for their curricula, and Emily was inundated with messages of death and eternal damnation. She noticed that often in Bible stories, women were excluded, discarded, or only peripherally active. These matters emerged in Dickinson's poetry, where she examined the problems of religion and women, as well as religion and death. At the age of eighteen, Dickinson was pulled out of school because her father discovered that she had a cough.

Soon after Dickinson left Mount Holyoke, her mother took ill, her siblings were out of the house, her best friend left town, and she was left largely alone. The simultaneity of these events propelled Dickinson to begin writing poetry, which she often inserted in letters. Despite Dickinson's chosen seclusion (some critics incorrectly posit that she was agoraphobic), she maintained contact with friends and family through letter writing. She published only seven poems in her lifetime, but after she died, Lavinia discovered about two thousand poems in various letters and documents. Known for her brevity, her syntactical obfuscation, and her unconventional punctuation—especially "dashes"—Dickinson believed that moments of intensity were best conveyed through well-chosen words. She read and was likely influenced by the Romantic ideals of Keats and the Brownings, but never expressed a theoretical approach to poetry writing. While she used conventional rhyme patterns, she also expanded notions of rhymes to include identical word rhymes, vowel rhymes, imperfect rhymes, and suspended rhymes.

Dickinson's primary contribution to poetry lies in her subject matter. Her family's religious tradition, as well as Amherst's religious culture and the influence of revivals during the Second Great Awakening, contributed to her sense of womanhood, God, and death. Dickinson's poetry contains deft irony and is full of contradictions. Where at one turn she appears respectful of religious tenets, at another she criticizes God. She wrote poems celebrating domesticity, but also excoriated a culture that offered few choices to women.

From her early years, Dickinson passionately attached herself to those whom she admired. While at Amherst and Mount Holyoke, she developed crushes on teachers (both male and female), and her attachments to female friends bordered on romance. Witnessing her parents' marriage seems to have led Dickinson to eschew heterosexual romance; she viewed her mother's yielding to a man as similar to her yielding to God, which in Dickinson's eyes meant relinquishing autonomy.

**Emily Dickinson.** A youthful-looking painting of the solitary, introspective poet, whose literary eminence emerged after her death in 1886. [**Library of Congress**]

Dickinson's passion for women most clearly emerges in her interaction with her sister-in-law, Susan Gilbert Dickinson. The two women lived next door to each other for thirty years. Dickinson wrote poems about and to Susan, many of which contain overt and covert romantic references. Historian Carroll Smith-Rosenberg has argued that the nineteenth-century ideology of separate spheres prescriptively relegated women to private, domestic space (rather than the public space inhabited by men), where women depended on each other physically and emotionally. Intimacy between men and women was severely regulated, but same-sex relations between women often went unnoticed or were seen as expressions of women's tendency toward sentimentalism.

During Austin and Susan's courtship, when Austin was away Emily often filled the role of suitor. Early in their marriage, Austin and Susan were unhappy, prompting Austin to begin an affair with Mabel Loomis Todd. In Susan, Emily found an intellectual companion who would discuss philosophy and critique her poems. Susan also provided an outlet for Emily's feelings of passion. Emily's letters to Susan include poems that celebrate

Susan's love for Emily, that compare her to Nature, and that extol the bliss of "owning" Susan. Emily's affection for women, and specifically for Susan, did not deviate from conventional nineteenth-century relations between women, but the passion and eroticism evinced by Emily for Susan, coupled with the absence of similar affection for men in her life and work, justify Emily's entry into the canon of lesbian writers.

Controversy exists over the veracity of Mabel Loomis Todd's hasty publication of Emily's poems in 1890. Todd never met Emily, and some critics believe she constructed Emily as the typical nineteenth-century woman poetess who, in the secluded domestic space, torturously scrawled away at her poems. More recently, critics such as Martha Nell Smith and Ellen Louise Hart have more closely examined Susan and Emily's passionate relationship, revealing not only the erotic, intimate exchanges between the women, but also Emily's desire for companionship and interaction with women. Emily Dickinson died before Susan, on 15 May 1886, of kidney failure.

## Bibliography

Habegger, Alfred. *My Wars Are Laid Away in Books: The Life of Emily Dickinson.* New York: Random House, 2001.

Hart, Ellen Louise, and Martha Nell Smith. *Open Me Carefully: Emily Dickinson's Intimate Letters to Susan Huntington Dickinson.* Ashfield, Mass.: Paris Press, 1998.

Sewall, Richard B. *The Life of Emily Dickinson.* 2 vols. New York: Farrar, Strauss and Giroux, 1974.

Smith-Rosenberg, Carroll. *Disorderly Conduct: Visions of Gender in Victorian America.* New York: Knopf, 1985.

**Michael H. Berglund**

*See also* LITERATURE.

# DIDRIKSON, Mildred Ella (b. 26 June 1911; d. 27 September 1956), athlete, medical humanitarian.

Mildred Ella Didrikson was born in Port Arthur, Texas, the sixth of seven children born to poor Norwegian immigrants. Her mother, Hannah Marie Olson, a shoemaker's daughter, took in laundry to support the family. Her father, Ole Senior, was a seaman turned furniture refinisher and cabinetmaker. The Didriksons' southeast Texas locale isolated them from other Norwegians, as did her father's determination to be Americanized. Yet they felt a sense of ethnic pride, and observed Norwegian cultural holidays.

Didrikson was called *Baden* (baby) even after her younger brother's birth. This became "Babe"—notwithstanding her claim that it stemmed from her Babe Ruth–like baseball skills.

In 1914 the Didriksons moved inland to Beaumont after a devastating Gulf Coast hurricane. At Magnolia Elementary, David Crockett Junior High, and Beaumont High School, Didrikson excelled in basketball, tennis, and swimming. Her parents consistently encouraged her athleticism. She was an androgynous looking boy–girl who baffled her peers, taunted her teachers, and was either adored or avoided for her self-aggrandizing bravado. Because of her rowdy, unfeminine behavior and physicality Didrikson's gender identity was a subject of open speculation.

In 1930, as a high school senior, Didrikson was scouted to play semiprofessional Industrial League basketball for the Employers Casualty Insurance Company's (ECIC) Golden Cyclones in Dallas. Her parents agreed because of her athletic excellence and the princely $75 monthly Depression-era salary she commanded. She sent home the bulk of these hefty earnings to support her family.

Didrikson led ECIC to two consecutive championships (1930 and 1931) as her team's leading scorer. She abraded her teammates and provoked cruel press speculation (circa 1932) about whether she was "Miss, Mr., or It." To challenge her and to generate publicity, ECIC entered her as a one-woman team in the 1932 Amateur Athletic Union National Track and Field championships in Evanston, Illinois; these doubled as Olympic tryouts. In one afternoon she entered eight of ten events, won six, and set four world records. This made her a national sensation. The speculation about her sexuality continued. It apexed in a vicious 1932 *Vanity Fair* article, "Honey," that labeled her a muscle moll and the premiere member of the "third sex." Surrounded by curiosity, Babe won two Olympic gold medals in Los Angeles in August 1932, as well as another for a third event, the only half-gold half-silver medal issued.

After her Olympic glory Didrikson pitched baseball with the all-male House of David team of former major leaguers. This, too, contributed to her odd status, as did arranged stunts with a middleweight boxer's brother who took a staged dive on film. She also punted for a college football team. In newspaper headlines she was greatly ridiculed and ostracized.

In the mid-1930s, under the tutelage of a Dallas golfing maven, Bertha Bowen, Didrikson undertook a deliberate and self-conscious transformation to femininity, including "appropriate" heterosexual flirtations, aspirations, and accoutrements. She feminized her public wardrobe and gestures and turned her astounding ath-

**Mildred Ella Didrikson.** Better known as Babe, the Woman Athlete of the Century won two gold medals in track and field in the 1932 Olympics but achieved her greatest fame for dominating women's golf from the mid-1930s to the mid-1950s. [Ralf-Finn Hestoft/corbis SABA]

letic prowess to "the 'ladies' game" of golf, which offered middle-class and feminine ascendance away from her working-class Amazonish exploits.

In 1937 she met George Zaharias, the professional wrestler who used the mat persona "The Crying Greek from Cripple Creek" (Colorado) at a celebrity golf match in Los Angeles. His muscularity complemented her excessively arrived-at womanliness. They wed on January 3, 1938. It was, for several years, an intimate heterosexual union. He forsook his own athletic career to manage hers and in many ways he assumed a wifely/auxiliary role.

Their marriage chronologically paralleled her rise to dominance in women's golf. Ceaseless practices, joined with her fierce determination, yielded eighty-two career and thirteen consecutive wins. She also co-founded and presided over the Ladies Professional Golf Association (LPGA) during its fledgling years.

In 1950 Didrikson met Betty Dodd, twenty years her junior, of San Antonio, Texas, at a golf tournament. Their bond was instant, intimate, and a zealously kept secret from the public. All early biographers ignored the intimacy between the two women. The three adults, Didrikson, Zaharias, and Dodd shared a residence for the last six years of Didrikson's life. There was considerable tension amongst them, but constant travel pursuing the golf tour and Zaharias's extended absences from home

ameliorated the stress. In the press Dodd was cast as Didrikson's sidekick, buddy, or golf protégée. When Didrikson became ill with her first bout of cancer in 1953, Dodd assumed the real and acceptable role of her medical caretaker. They were inseparable and lived an isolated life on the tour, which was exacerbated by Didrikson's strained relationships with the other women pros and her determination that her relationship with Dodd not be made more public. They fished, played golf and cards, made music on the guitar and harmonica and thoroughly enjoyed each other's companionship. Dodd did not emerge as an accomplished golfer until after Didrikson's demise. She accepted the role of backup helpmate graciously.

As Didrikson struggled with cancer from 1953 to 1956, she emerged as a genuine medical humanitarian. She raised funds, visited hospitalized cancer patients, and lent her name to fundraising golf tournaments. She appeared as a spokesperson for the American Cancer Society and was honored by President Dwight D. Eisenhower at the White House.

Didrikson did not choose to be an advocate for either women's sports or same-sex intimacy. In the conservative climate of the 1950s, and having suffered much from the cruelty of the press, Babe chose instead to publicly perform the role of the contented heterosexually married wife. Almost thirty years after Didrikson's death Dodd spoke of their bond, maintaining that she was empowered by her own life circumstances and, likely, ensuing cultural changes.

Didrikson's legacy is as a path-breaking athlete whose excellence and power cleared the way for generations of girls and women. She was voted Woman Athlete of the Year six times, Woman Athlete of the Half Century (1950), and Woman Athlete of the Century (2000). She was the driving force behind improving cash prizes for women golfers, helped establish the LPGA, and distinguished herself as a medical humanitarian. Her legacy to the lesbian community is more diffuse: she was an inspiration to many athletic women and/or lesbians during her lifetime who "read" her life as one they recognized. But her unwillingness to reveal her same-sex bond kept her from being an open role model. This is hardly surprising given the conservative cultural context in which she lived, her own painful history, and the homophobia that surrounded female athletes.

### Bibliography

Cayleff, Susan E. *Babe: The Life and Legend of Babe Didrikson Zaharias*. Urbana, Illinois: University of Illinois Press, 1995.

Didrikson Zaharias, Babe. *This Life I've Led: My Autobiography*. As told to Harry Paxton. New York: A.S. Barnes, 1955.

Johnson, William Oscar, and Nancy Johnson. *"Whatta-Gal": The Babe Didrikson Story*. Boston: Little, Brown, 1975.

**Susan E. Cayleff**

*See also* SPORTS.

# DISABILITY, DISABLED PEOPLE, AND DISABILITY MOVEMENTS

Every nation, every group, and every community includes a significant minority of people with physical and mental disabilities, and the LGBT community is no exception. Approximately 20 percent of the U.S. population has some type of disability, and 12 percent have a disability that is significant or severe. There are probably well over five million queers with disabilities in the United States. While LGBT people have struggled for social acceptance, self-respect, and civil rights, LGBT people with physical and mental disabilities have engaged in parallel struggles, both in society at large and within their disability communities and their queer communities.

Queer identity and disability identity have been more or less problematic at different times for different groups of people. Who is disabled, who is queer, and what difference does it make anyway?

Complicating many people's queer identity is the prevalent social denial of disabled people's basic sexuality. This denial undermines possibilities for queer friendship and romance. Further, it reinforces a presumption of incompetence and irresponsibility. For example, puritanical service delivery systems forbid sexual expression by those in their charge. People may assume that sexually active LGBT people are actually being victimized by their partners. The common perception is that disabled people shouldn't be doing, or even feeling, anything—let alone "deviant" things.

Within the LGBT community some people have preferred to keep their disabilities invisible, whenever possible, in order to try to preserve the privileges associated with nondisability, privileges such as blending in, avoiding scorn or pity, being invited to social events, and getting dates. In fact, not all disabled queers identify as "disabled." Many think of themselves instead as chronically ill, sick, frequently depressed, bothered by back pain, or similar descriptions based on symptoms, not social identity. (This article includes all such people in the "disability community.") Other disabled queers, unwilling or unable to closet their disabilities, closet their sexualities in order to survive homophobic service systems or to retain relationships with important support people.

Sometimes, however, queer identity and disability identity collide—either in an individual's experience or in issues faced by whole communities—bringing notions of ability, sexuality, and normalcy into sharp relief or conflict. These struggles have encouraged deeper discussions of diversity, inclusion, and ownership in both queer and disability communities.

## A History of Activism

Though rarely visible to the wider LGBT community or to the straight disability community, LGBT disabled people—or queer crips, as many choose to call themselves—often respond to exclusion and marginalization by taking constructive action, either individually or collectively, to improve social conditions and subvert oppressive conventions. (The term "crip," derived from "cripple," has historically referred primarily to people with physical impairments that affect walking. Recently, however, the word has been appropriated by many in the disability community as an umbrella term signifying a proud, somewhat sardonic identification.) The following are a few examples of disabled queers' organizing and activism:

- 1977: LGBT people founded Rainbow Alliance of the Deaf (RAD) and held its first national conference in Fort Lauderdale, Florida. RAD now has over twenty chapters throughout North America, and holds a national conference every other year. The Alliance promotes educational, economic, and social rights and offers social opportunities and discussions of problems and solutions.

- 1980: Six feminist activists in Minneapolis-St. Paul, Minnesota, founded Womyn's Braille Press to make lesbian and feminist literature available to women who were blind or otherwise unable to read print. Through grant-writing, grassroots fund-raising, and the enthusiastic work of founders and volunteers, Womyn's Braille Press was able to produce and circulate over eight hundred lesbian and feminist books recorded on tape and forty in Braille.

  Womyn's Braille Press also produced a quarterly newsletter, distributed in print, in Braille, and on tape, which created a sense of community among disabled women, including lesbians. Eventually funding and energy ran out, and in 1994 the Press disbanded and transferred its inventory to the Bureau of Braille and Talking Book Services in Daytona Beach, Florida, where it continues to be available to readers by request.

- 1981: Activist Connie Panzarino organized the first Disabled Lesbian Conference following the Michigan Women's Music Festival.

- 1983: Dykes, Disability & Stuff (DD&S), a quarterly grassroots newsletter featuring news, reviews, verse, essays, and art, began publication in Wisconsin. In order to meet the accessibility needs of lesbians with all types of disabilities, DD&S is available in many formats, including standard print, large print, audio cassette, Braille, DOS diskette and modem transfer.

  DD&S is an aggressive proponent of greater access to lesbian culture and community; for example, it will not accept advertisements and notices for resources or events which are not accessible to disabled people or which fail to provide access information.

- 1989: Hillary Russian, a young disabled dyke in Seattle, Washington, founded Ring of Fire: A Zine of Lesbian Sexuality. This low-budget, irreverent publication has continued to appear on an irregular basis, offering erotic and often humorous stories and cartoons about gender-bending, crip culture, living with a disability, and sex.

- 1992: Members of Deaf Counseling, Advocacy and Referral Agency obtained funding from United Way

and from the State of California to establish the Deaf Gay and Lesbian Center (DGLC). The Center serves deaf and hard of hearing LGBT communities throughout the San Francisco Bay area and fights isolation, oppression, discrimination, and inaccessibility of information through advocacy, empowerment, and communication access.

- 1997: Deaf Youth Rainbow was launched as a project of Capital Metropolitan Rainbow Alliances in the Washington, D.C., area to provide a safe, supportive, educational environment for deaf and hard-of-hearing people ages thirteen to twenty-four.

- 2002: Sharon Duchesneau and Candy McCullough, a deaf lesbian couple in Bethesda, Maryland, went public with their decision to select a deaf sperm donor in order to increase the chances that their child would be born deaf. A Washington Post Magazine article about the couple sparked a national online debate. While many people acknowledged and understood the couple's lesbian pride, many more were highly critical of their deaf pride.

- 2002: Over three hundred activists, artists, and academics came together for the first-ever Queer Disability Conference in San Francisco, California. Presentation topics included medical discrimination; being out at work about disability and sexual orientation; queer crip performance; partners and allies; queer crip sexualities; and much more. Drawing a vast range of disabilities and identities, the conference became a space for revelation, networking, conflict, and solidarity.

## Intersecting Issues, Parallel Oppressions

In addition to the many people who are both queer and disabled, some activists within both groups have pointed out the parallels and intersections in the histories of (disabled and nondisabled) LGBT people and (straight and queer) disabled people. Individuals from both groups generally come of age in isolation from others "of their kind" and come to terms with an identity not shared by their immediate families, close friends, or communities. Some families reject the queer family member (by disowning or disinheriting him/her) or the disabled family member (by sending him/her to a nursing home or other institution). Even when families accept and stand by their family member, they may not be able to nurture her/his full cultural development as a queer or disabled person. Without a ready-made community able to understand or reflect their experiences, disabled people and queer people must often embark on a quest to find support, solidarity, and mentorship.

## language, art, and literature: queer cripdom defines itself

Though often excluded or overlooked equally by mainstream, queer, and disability cultures, queer crips have insisted on fighting invisibility with truth. Becoming visible and staking out a space (or spaces) in the culture involves conjuring paintings, crafting stories, telling poems—and arguing about terminology.

Beginning in the 1970s, some well-meaning LGBT people, and some people with disabilities adopted what they thought were more positive-sounding terms for disability, including "differently-abled" and "physically challenged." However, many disability activists rejected these terms, arguing that they reflected an ableist urge to erase disability through euphemism and that they trivialized the realities of socially-constructed disablement.

Some powerful cultural work has been produced by out queer disabled writers and artists. One of the earliest and most vivid examples was Frida Kahlo, the Mexican painter (and frequent visitor to the United States) who was openly bisexual, loved to cross-dress, and had several significant disabilities which she portrayed imaginatively and sometimes brutally in her art. As a child, Kahlo developed polio, which affected her right leg and her spine. As a young woman she was seriously injured in a bus-trolley collision; a metal handrail impaled her, breaking her spinal column, pelvis, collarbone, two ribs, right leg, and foot. During her lifetime she endured numerous medical treatments and surgeries. She explored the physical and spiritual impact of these experiences in paintings such as *The Broken Column* (1944). In her art and in life, Kahlo celebrated her sexualities and her disabilities in provocative, flamboyant ways that some critics have found shocking and perverse, but which many disabled lesbians have found affirming and liberating. For

example, she had her first Mexican one-artist show in 1953 at the Galería de Arte Contemporáneo, just after a surgery to repair the fusion in her spinal column. Still recovering, and too disabled to stand, she attended the show on a stretcher.

Audre Lorde, African American lesbian poet and essayist, wrote prolifically about courage and sisterhood and always insisted on recognition and inclusion of diverse women's lives. In 1980 her book the *Cancer Journals* offered an intimate yet politically challenging account of her mastectomy. The American Library Association named it 1981's Gay Caucus Book of the Year. Lorde had a lifetime of experience in overcoming marginalization: "Growing up Fat Black Female and almost blind in America requires so much surviving that you have to learn from it or die," she wrote (p. 40). Still, nothing had prepared her for the trauma of facing cancer and surgery. She described going through the "many stages of pain, despair, fury, sadness and growth" until she came to "feel that in the process of losing a breast I had become a more whole person" (p. 55). She learned to know herself as a woman warrior, battling patriarchal culture and industrial carcinogens. Lorde rejected a prosthetic breast that was supposed to gloss over her loss so that "'nobody will know the difference.' But it is that very difference which I wish to affirm," Lorde wrote, "because I have lived it, and survived it, and wish to share that strength with other women. . . For silence and invisibility go hand in hand with powerlessness" (p. 61).

Lorenzo Wilson Milam, a radio broadcaster and author of several books, and a disability-sexuality columnist for *Independent Living* magazine, broke new ground by writing openly about his crip queer experience. Milam grew up disabled from polio, and came out as gay in college. In his 1984 autobiography, *The Cripple Liberation Front Marching Band Blues*, Milam wrote eloquently about his struggles for

---

Both disability and queerness have been pathologized in the United States. Early American notions of "normality" clearly excluded those whose bodies or minds worked differently, and those with unconventional sexualities. Intersexed people, transgender people, and people with physical and mental differences were "enfreaked" (a term used by some disability history scholars to signify the process of constructing individual or group differences into a public spectacle of abnormality) in the nineteenth-century freak shows accompanying traveling carnivals. As the medical profession grew and

gained social and intellectual influence, its definitions, diagnoses, and prescriptions shaped the dominant view of both disabled people and queer people. Both groups were seen as deviant and in need of being fixed—through cure or rehabilitation regimens aimed to restore the disabled person to able-bodied "wholeness," or through "reparative therapy" designed to turn homosexuals into heterosexuals.

The medical profession and society have sometimes blurred the lines between "defective" and "perverted" and between "queer" and "crazy." Nineteenth-century medical honesty, self-love, and acceptance as a disabled gay man. Later, in 1993, he wrote *CripZen: A Manual for Survival*, in which he offered advice and other words of wisdom. Rejecting all other labels, Milam consistently used the term "Crip"—capitalized—because, he said, "it is the only word I have found over the years that contains the pith and vigor we need to describe our condition" (p. vii).

Connie Panzarino's life embodied many of the obstacles and activism of the disability community and the lesbian community. She lived with a lifelong physical disability, spinal muscular atrophy, and became a writer, advocate, and art therapist. She was a catalyst for a strong and active community of lesbian and bisexual women with and without disabilities, participating in feminist organizing, peace work, and disability advocacy. In 1994 Panzarino wrote her autobiography, *The Me in the Mirror*, in which she described her life of activism and attacked the roots of ableism in the LGBT community.

Raymond Luczak has played a key role in the literary landscape of deaf queers, many of whom do not identify as disabled. Instead, many deaf queers align themselves with the broader Deaf-with-a-capital-"D" community, constituted by a distinct language, culture, and history. Luczak edited a 1993 anthology, *Eyes of Desire: A Deaf Gay & Lesbian Reader*. This collection of essays by deaf lesbians and gay men covers coming out, communication, culture, and much more. Luczak has also published several books of his poetry, including 1995's *St. Michael's Fall*, "an autobiographical account of a boy growing up deaf, oral, and Catholic—and discovering the forbidden fruit of American Sign Language (ASL)—in a small mining town during the 1970s."

Kenny Fries, a poet and playwright who won the Gregory Kolovakos Award for AIDS Writing for *The Healing*

*Notebooks* (1990), has contributed several important queer crip literary works. Fries' *Body, Remember: A Memoir,* published in 1997, narrates his physical and emotional life by following the map of scars on his legs. In 1996, Fries published *Anesthesia,* a meditation on his experiences as a gay, disabled, Jewish man and "how oppression and loss affect language, memory and desire."

Introducing dozens of disabled lesbians' voices, some familiar and some previously unheard, were two anthologies—*Pushing the Limits: Disabled Dykes Produce Culture,* edited by Shelley Tremain, published in 1996; and 1999's *Restricted Access: Lesbians on Disability,* edited by Victoria A. Brownworth and Susan Raffo. These volumes presented a racially diverse group of North American writers and poets who, as Tremain writes, "push the limits of who counts as a dyke, what constitutes 'lesbian experience,' who engages in female same-sex erotic activity, and how" (p. 21). Deaf Chicana lesbian activist Dragonsani Renteria, for example, writes in her poem "Rejection" about the judgments she faces from the different communities to which she wants to belong. "I am rejected and oppressed, / Even by those who cry out readily / Against rejection, oppression, and discrimination. / When," she demands, "will it end?" (p. 131).

Eli Clare has emerged as one of the most powerful recent crip queer literary voices. Merging analyses grounded in disability rights, tranny activism, environmentalism, and class awareness, Clare's 1999 book *Exile and Pride* sheds light on a tangle of overlapping and sometimes conflicting identities and issues. "Queer and cripple are cousins," Clare writes. "Words to shock, words to infuse with pride and self-love, words to resist internalized hatred, words to help forge a politics. They have a gladly chosen—queer by many gay/lesbian/bi/trans people, cripple, or crip, by many disabled people" (p. 70).

---

practitioners applied arbitrary psychiatric labels, such as "hysteria" and "neurasthenia," to women who challenged patriarchal gender roles by, among other audacities, loving other women. For many years homosexuality was labeled a mental illness, making it a form of disability. The American Psychiatric Association withdrew that designation in 1973 and condemned the practice of "reparative therapy" in 2000. But even now many LGBT teenagers are committed to psychiatric facilities and subjected to aversive treatments; by one estimate 300,000 adolescents, including many queer youth, are currently living in such facilities.

Throughout U.S. history, both queer people and disabled people have frequently been stigmatized, ostracized, and targeted for violence, both official and random. For example, during the twentieth century thirty-three states enacted laws allowing the forced sterilization of marginalized groups such as those labeled (in the words of Oregon's law) "feeble-minded, insane, epileptic, habitual criminals, moral degenerates and sexual perverts," including homosexuals. In all, more than sixty thousand people underwent involuntary castrations, tubal ligations, and hysterectomies. In December 2002, advocates for disability rights and for lesbian and gay rights received a public apology from Oregon Governor John Kitzhaber for that state's role in forcibly sterilizing 2,600 people. California and Virginia have also apologized to both groups for similar policies.

Queer people and disabled people, like other minority groups, face many other hazards of marginalization, including hate violence, discrimination, and a culture suffused with negative and inaccurate stereotypes. Yet queer people and disabled people have historically been left out of civil rights laws and hate crimes laws enacted at federal, state, and local levels to offer protection to racial, religious, and other minority groups. During the 1990s and early 2000s some states and cities debated and in some cases passed amendments to add LGBT people and disabled people to existing bias crime laws or nondiscrimination ordinances or new statutes that included LGBT people and disabled people among others.

### Sharon Kowalski: Double Discrimination Sparks Activism

The issues of disability and sexuality came together in dramatic and public ways in the Sharon Kowalski case. Kowalski was a college professor in St. Cloud, Minnesota, and a closeted lesbian living in a committed, four-year relationship with Karen Thompson when, in 1983, she sustained serious injuries in a car accident. She emerged from a coma with significant physical and cognitive disabilities. When Donald and Della Kowalski learned about the nature of Thompson's relationship with their daughter, they attempted to bar her from visiting her partner. Had the couple been heterosexual and married, Thompson would have been the next of kin, with the right to make decisions about Kowalski's placement and treatment. For a lesbian couple, no such rights existed. Had Kowalski been nondisabled, she never would have been stripped of her autonomy and liberty by being institutionalized and ignored. In an effort to stay involved in Kowalski's life and her rehabilitation process, Thompson filed for guardianship; the Kowalskis counter filed. An out-of-court settlement was reached which appointed Donald Kowalski his daughter's guardian but also protected Thompson's right to visit and to have input into medical care decisions. Soon, however, a court granted Donald Kowalski guardianship with unlimited powers. He used this power to ban not only Thompson but also other friends and advocates from visiting his daughter, and he had her transferred to a nursing home far from St. Cloud. Over the next six years, the parties returned to court several more times. Thompson's claims were supported by the American Civil Liberties Union, the Lambda Legal Defense Fund, and other LGBT rights

groups, as well as by some disability groups. The two communities framed the issues somewhat differently: LGBT advocates focused on the need for recognition of same-sex partnerships, while disability advocates focused on disabled people's need to have self-determination and alternatives to independent living.

This case galvanized activists from two communities that had rarely cooperated. "National Free Sharon Kowalski Day" on August 7, 1988, brought together thousands of people in twenty-one cities to express support and concern for the issues raised by this case. Thompson became a popular speaker at LGBT rights events. In 1988, a competency hearing determined that Kowalski could in fact communicate. In August 1992 Thompson was finally given guardianship of Kowalski, and in April 1993 Kowalski moved back home with her partner. As of this writing, Kowalski continues to live with Thompson and another woman, supported by them and, after intensive advocacy to secure adequate support services, by state-funded assistance.

### Positive, Disabled: The (Incomplete) Transformation of AIDS from Medical Crisis to Disability Rights Issue

The AIDS epidemic had a major impact on the LGBT community, killing thousands of gay men and sparking activist groups to demand treatments and cures. As time went on, AIDS cases continued to increase, but drug regimens prolonged the lives of many people with the disease. While many advocates stayed focused on the goal of curing AIDS, some others expanded their agenda to address issues facing people living with AIDS such as job discrimination, housing discrimination, inadequate community-based support services, other issues that are, essentially, disability issues.

This new recognition of AIDS as a disabling condition led to tentative coalitions between AIDS activist groups and disability rights organizations. These coalitions proved durable, and important in the development of civil-rights laws. During Congressional debates over the 1987 Civil Rights Restoration Act and the 1988 Fair Housing Amendments Act, attempts were made to exclude people with "contagious diseases," including HIV. These attacks were successfully defeated. Before the U.S. Senate began consideration of the Americans with Disabilities Act (ADA) in 1990, over fifty organizations representing AIDS, disability, civil rights, and religious groups sent letters to every Senator urging that the ADA protect "people with AIDS and HIV infection." Since the ADA was enacted, a number of HIV-positive people have used it to assert their rights to equal treatment in employ-

**Pas de Deux.** A wheelchair is incorporated into this expressive performance. [Brenda Prager]

ment, state and local services, and public accommodations. In 1998, the U.S. Supreme Court ruled that asymptomatic HIV is a disability under the ADA.

### Help and Independence: Meeting Disabled Queers' Support Needs

Some people with AIDS and other disabilities need varying degrees of support services, including personal assistance with daily living, nursing care, and/or housekeeping assistance. As currently configured in the United States, support services for disabled people are often inadequate and/or confining. Services are not available to all the people who need them, but are restricted to those who meet eligibility requirements based on geographical area, income, age, diagnosis, and other factors. Private health insurance rarely pays for long-term care, especially in-home care. And publicly-funded programs, such as Medicaid and Medicare are more likely to fund such services in nursing homes and other large congregate-care facilities, rather than in the individual's own home, despite the U.S. Supreme Court's 1998 Olmstead decision which declared unnecessary segregation a form of discrimination, and ordered states to provide support services in the "most integrated setting" possible for the individual.

For disabled LGBT people, support services can be even more problematic. When LGBT people have to rely on social programs, which may be heterosexist in structure, policy, and practice, they may experience homophobic attitudes from staff, isolation from peers, even violence. In one study, more than half of the nursing home social workers surveyed said their staff was intoler-

ant or condemning of homosexual activity between residents. A transgender person with a non-congruent body may face judgment, taunting, or cruelty from health care workers providing intimate personal assistance, such as dressing and bathing. Fearing such treatment, some people may forgo the help they need, thus jeopardizing their health, rather than deal with potential providers' insensitivity and ridicule. Experts say this homophobia may reflect larger sexphobia within assisted and congregate living situations, particularly in nursing homes. Researchers report a high degree of discomfort on the part of nursing home staff regarding residents' sexual expression.

Compounding the problem of obtaining adequate personal assistance is the lack of social support and recognition for LGBT families. Family members are an important source of care for disabled and older people, yet LGBT people are less likely than other elders to have a spouse or children and more likely to live alone. While 31 percent of American elders live alone, some studies suggest that as many as 65 to 75 percent of older lesbians and gay men live alone.

The Policy Institute of the National Gay and Lesbian Task Force Foundation (2000) has identified additional barriers to care giving for LGBT people who are older and/or disabled. These include:

- discriminatory health care plans that deny same-sex partners access to coverage that might pay for caregiving needs, as well as loss of health care benefits following loss of employment due to discrimination;

- exclusion from financial support and incentives provided by government support strategies for caregiving, such as the Family and Medical Leave Act of 1993;

- loss of potential caregivers within the gay community, due to the large number of deaths from AIDS;

- pervasive negative attitudes, particularly within the gay male population, against older and disabled people who need caregiving services;

- health care providers' lack of cooperation (for example, unwillingness to share information) with caregivers who are not immediate family members, or who do not fit into the heterosexual definition of "family."

Some LGBT advocates have proposed the establishment of gay or gay-friendly nursing homes in order to meet the needs of aging and disabled queers. Most disability rights activists in the community reject this argument, arguing that institutions of any orientation inevitably segregate and deprive people of their liberty.

A number of LGBT people with disabilities are active in American Disabled for Attendant Programs Today (ADAPT), a grassroots movement demanding a nationwide system of in-home support services for all who need them in order to live independently. ADAPT activists emphasize the importance of consumer-responsive services to enable people to enjoy self-determination, including the right to live with whomever one chooses, and to select one's own helpers—both crucial considerations for LGBT disabled people who need personal assistance. While not a queer organizations, ADAPT's diversity has always included LGBT members.

### Who Belongs Here?: Access and Inclusion in Queer Communities

Inclusiveness and solidarity were high ideals of the early lesbian and gay rights movement. Influenced by feminism, African American civil rights, and other liberation movements, LGBT groups generally placed a high premium on trying to be sensitive to issues of race, ethnicity, class, and ability. But as equality politics replaced liberation politics, the assimilation of LGBT people into straight society required greater conformity. As disabled writer and editor Victoria Brownworth has written, "The political desire to present to straight society a community 'deserving' of heterosexual privilege, a community that is comprised of straight-seeming, monied, middle-class and otherwise 'normal' queers, looms large on the mainstream political agenda as a polemic that argues 'We are no different from you' is emphasized. . . . Inclusion often

depends on the loudness of voice, the cohesion, solidarity, and access of a particular minority within a collective minority. Disabled queers, who have always skirted the margins of queer community, have become virtually invisible" (p. xii-xiii).

This tension between inclusiveness and mainstreaming has played out in countless queer spaces—gay bars, LGBT community centers, women's music festivals, queer studies conferences, and many more. Demands for access have been met, variously, by guilt, bafflement, intransigence, genuine effort, productive change—and often, a combination of these.

Despite decades of calls for inclusiveness, many queers and queer communities remain either hostile or indifferent to disabled people. In 2000, the magazine the *Advocate* conducted a poll, asking readers: "Do you think people with disabilities are treated fairly within the gay and lesbian community?" 56 percent answered "No," while 22 percent answered "Yes," and 21 percent answered "Undecided." If that poll were conducted among disabled queers exclusively, the "Yes" vote might have been much higher.

Nevertheless, queer crips persist in being present in all of their diversity. As one disabled lesbian said, "We cannot be compartmentalized people. I had to integrate everything. I am a person who happens to be a lesbian, who happens to have a disability, but most importantly, I am a whole person" (Brownworth and Raffo, p. 30).

### Make Love, Not Barriers: Access to Sex

Sexuality is one element binding together various queer communities. Dating, dancing, clubbing, coupling, flirting, and having sex are, for many people, important aspects of the queer experience. Disabled people are no different in having a whole range of sexual desires. Yet barriers and stereotypes often inhibit the expression and enactment of these desires. LGBT meeting places may have steps or inaccessible bathrooms that prevent wheelchair users from entering (despite the access requirements in the Americans with Disabilities Act). Social groups may shun people with mental illnesses, cognitive disabilities, blindness, or obvious impairments. Public transportation may be insufficiently accessible to enable people with all kinds of disabilities to attend gatherings. All of these barriers can make it difficult for disabled queers to meet potential partners.

Even more limiting, for some, are the prevalent cultural messages—false impressions that disabled people are childlike, asexual, damaged, undesirable. Disabled queers often have to negotiate other people's awkward, negative, or simply clueless reactions in order to establish relationships that might lead to romance and/or sex.

Many queer crips have responded by rejecting ableist definitions of sexual beauty and activity, offering more diverse and liberating possibilities for connection, attraction, and fulfillment. For example, lesbian writer and activist Connie Panzarino, whose extremely limited mobility made it difficult for her to be physically active during sex, candidly describes her many relationships with women. Writes Panzarino: "I learned to use my mouth, my breath and my creative voice to accompany my lover touching herself." (pp. 235–236). Eli Clare, a disability/transgender/queer activist and writer, has called for a proud reassertion of sexual expression by LGBT people with disabilities. "I say it's time for us to talk sex, be sex, wear sex, relish our sex, both the sex we do have and the sex we want to be having," wrote Clare in 2002. "I say it's time for some queer disability erotica, time for an anthology of crip smut, queer style" (Queer Disability Conference keynote).

## Bibliography

Brownworth, Victoria A., and Raffo, Susan, eds. *Restricted Access: Lesbians on Disability.* Seattle: Seal Press, 1999.

Clare, Eli. *Exile and Pride.* Boston: South End Press, 1999.

———. "Sex, Celebration, and Justice." Available from http://www.disabledwomen.net/queer/paper_clare.html.

Fries, Kenny. *Body, Remember: A Memoir.* New York: Dutton, 1997.

———. *Anesthesia.* Louisville, KY: Advocado Press, 1996.

Lorde, Audre. *The Cancer Journals.* San Francisco: Aunt Lute, 1980.

Luczak, Raymond, ed. *Eyes of Desire: A Deaf Gay & Lesbian Reader.* Los Angeles: Alyson Publications, 1993.

Luczak, Raymond. *St. Michael's Fall.* Rochester, N.Y.: Deaf Life Press, 1995.

Milam, Lorenzo Wilson. *The Cripple Liberation Front Marching Band Blues.* San Diego: Mho & Mho Works, 1984.

———. *CripZen: A Manual for Survival.* San Diego: Mho & Mho Works, 1993.

Panzarino, Connie. *The Me in the Mirror.* Seattle: Seal Press, 1994.

Tremain, Shelley, ed. *Pushing the Limits: Disabled Dykes Produce Culture.* Toronto: Women's Press, 1996.

**Laura Hershey**

*See also* AIDS AND PEOPLE WITH AIDS; AMERICAN CIVIL LIBERTIES UNION (ACLU); DISCRIMINATION; KLUMPKE, ANNA; LAMBDA LEGAL DEFENSE; LORDE, AUDRE; MEDICINE, MEDICALIZATION, AND THE MEDICAL MODEL; NATIONAL GAY AND LESBIAN TASK FORCE (NGLTF).

# DISCRIMINATION

Like racial and ethnic minorities and women, LGBT people historically have been subject to public and private prejudice, discrimination, harassment, and violence in the United States. The term "prejudice," linked to the notion of prejudgment, generally refers to negative attitudes and ideas about social groups. "Discrimination" sometimes refers to neutral processes of differentiating, distinguishing, and making distinctions between social groups, but when used in relation to race, class, gender, and sexuality it generally refers to the unequal treatment of social groups (usually but not necessarily because of prejudice).

Sexual and gender prejudice have been widespread in the United States since the colonial era and large segments of American society historically have felt strong antipathy toward LGBT people. In the last few decades, there has been a significant shift in public attitudes that has partially mitigated this historical opprobrium. Notwithstanding this shift, however, discrimination against LGBT people remains commonplace, and transgender people in particular continue to be the targets of intense discrimination. LGBT people face significant problems related to discrimination in adoption, custody, and foster care; education; employment; family law; health care; housing; inheritance; law enforcement; marriage; the military; religion; social services; and tax policy.

Historians have noted that overt and systematic discrimination against LGBT people did not begin in earnest until economic and social changes in the late nineteenth century permitted the development of LGBT identities. Although same-sex sex and relationships have been documented throughout history, before the late nineteenth century the concept of sexual orientation (whether heterosexual or homosexual) as a defining characteristic of a person's identity did not exist. With the industrial revolution, the resulting transition from an agrarian to an urban society, and mass migration and immigration, men and women began to have increased opportunities to form relationships and communities outside of traditional heterosexual and reproductive marriages. It therefore was not until the early twentieth century that a significant number of men and women began to self-identify as LGB, which in turn led to the development of LGB communities in large urban areas. While there was certainly discrimination against transgressive sexual and gender desires and acts in earlier periods, only after large numbers of people began to self-identify as LGB did discrimination against LGB people become a significant problem.

**Discrimination in Scouting.** James Dale (left), with one of his lawyers from the Lambda Legal Defense and Education Fund, challenged his 1990 ouster as an assistant scoutmaster; however, the U.S. Supreme Court decided in 2003 that as a private organization, the Boy Scouts of America could discriminate against homosexuals. [AP/Wide World Photos]

## Legal Discrimination

Discrimination against LGB people historically has been embodied in and justified by sodomy laws, which criminalized first anal and then oral sex. While some sodomy laws specifically targeted same-sex sexual activity, generally such laws applied to cross-sex sex as well. As William Eskridge has most comprehensively demonstrated, however, facially neutral laws against sodomy, buggery, crimes against nature, lewd and lascivious conduct, disorderly conduct, cross-dressing, public indecency, loitering, solicitation, and vagrancy have often been used primarily against LGB people. Most notably, the U.S. Supreme Court reasoned in the landmark case *Bowers v. Hardwick* (1986) that Georgia's facially neutral sodomy law, which prohibited oral and anal sex for both same-sex and cross-sex couples, reflected the "presumed belief of a majority of the electorate in Georgia that homosexual sodomy is immoral and unacceptable" (478 U.S. at 196). Only in the 2003 case of *Lawrence v. Texas* did the Supreme Court reverse its judgment in *Bowers*. At the time, four states

specifically prohibited same-sex sexual activity, while nine states had facially neutral sodomy laws that were often enforced in discriminatory ways.

A wide variety of other laws have explicitly discriminated against LGBT people or have been applied and enforced in discriminatory ways. Marriage laws, for example, not only discriminate against LGBT people as far as marriage itself is concerned, but also result in discrimination in a variety of other contexts. Until recently this discrimination arose from the way marriage laws, which generally did not reference gender or sexual orientation, were applied. Since the early 1990s, however, various states have passed laws that prohibit same-sex marriage more explicitly. Discrimination against LGBT people in marriage law continues to lead to discrimination in tax law, inheritance rights, hospital visitation rights, medical decision-making rights, employee benefits, and so on. Military policies also have traditionally prohibited sexual misconduct of various kinds, but starting in the World War Two era the military began targeting LGB conduct and speech more directly. After World War Two, the federal government and many state governments passed explicitly discriminatory policies against employing LGB people in government jobs. Facially neutral immigration laws that excluded people with "psychopathic personalities" and indeterminate sentencing laws for sexual psychopaths were passed in the early and mid-twentieth century, but enforcement disproportionately and oftentimes primarily affected LGBT people. In the second half of the twentieth century some states passed laws that discriminated openly against LGB people in adoption, custody, and foster care cases, but more generally public officials have discriminated in these cases by interpreting policies about fit and unfit parents and the best interests of the child in discriminatory ways.

Similarly, disorderly conduct and obscenity laws have usually been written in facially neutral ways, but enforcement has often discriminated against LGBT bars, clubs, parks, magazines, books, plays, and films. Until a set of court rulings in the second half of the twentieth century, activities that would not lead to arrests in straight bars (drinking, talking, touching, kissing, cross-dressing) frequently led to arrests in LGBT bars. Disorderly conduct and similar types of laws continue to be applied in discriminatory ways when LGBT people walk hand in hand on public streets, socialize together in public parks and beaches, and cruise, court, flirt, kiss, or express affection in public. Insofar as the Supreme Court's 2003 decision in *Lawrence* was based on doctrines of privacy, discrimination against LGBT people for public behavior will likely remain legal in the majority of states.

Discriminatory laws have influenced and been influenced by various forms of social discrimination. Historical case studies of Buffalo, Cherry Grove (on New York's Fire Island), Mississippi, New York, and Philadelphia, research by legal scholars, and scholarship on the media have documented countless examples of landlords who refused to rent to LGBT people; employers who discriminated in the hiring, promoting, and firing of LGBT workers; businesses that discriminated against LGBT consumers; magazines and newspapers that refused to accept LGBT advertising; radio and television stations that discriminated against LGBT access to the public airwaves; and "private" and religious organizations such as the Boy Scouts and the Catholic Church that discriminated openly against LGBT people. Except in jurisdictions where laws have been passed prohibiting discrimination on the basis of sexual orientation and gender identity, discrimination against LGBT people remained legal. And even in these jurisdictions, institutions that had been exempted (such as religious institutions) continued to discriminate legally against LGBT people.

## Reacting to Discrimination

LGBT people have challenged discrimination in everyday life and, since the 1950s, in organized political movements. Successes in the 1950s and 1960s in specific areas (most notably in the enforcement of obscenity laws, laws affecting LGBT bars, and laws concerning sexual psychopaths) culminated in the 1970s in the passage of local (and in the 1980s, state) laws prohibiting discrimination based on sexual orientation. As of 2003, fourteen states and the District of Columbia, as well as a large number of municipalities, have enacted statutes that expressly prohibit discrimination on the basis of sexual orientation, generally in employment, housing, and public accommodations. Many private employers, and a more limited number of state and local agencies, also have adopted policies against discrimination based on sexual orientation and have begun to offer domestic partner benefits to their LGB employees.

Although no comprehensive federal antidiscrimination statute has been enacted to protect LGBT people, the U.S. Congress has passed hate crimes laws that require the collection of national statistics regarding crimes that manifest evidence of prejudice based on, among other things, sexual orientation. The majority of states and the District of Columbia have enacted similar hate crimes laws that increase penalties for violence motivated by anti-LGB hate. In 1998 U.S. President Bill Clinton issued an executive order that established a uniform policy pro-

hibiting discrimination based on sexual orientation in all federal employment.

Significant strides also have been made to reduce discrimination in the realm of family law. An increasing number of states no longer consider LGB identity as incompatible with parenthood, both for biological and adoptive children. In response to a ruling of the Vermont Supreme Court in 1999, the legislature in that state became the first to grant same-sex couples rights similar to marriage through the enactment of a civil union statute. While not granting the same level of substantive rights, other jurisdictions have established domestic partnership registries through which same-sex couples can publicly state their commitment to one another and gain some of the rights and benefits previously reserved only for married couples.

While LGB people in recent years have been able to secure certain protections against discrimination, as of 2003, transgender people remain vulnerable. Only four states have enacted statutory prohibitions of discrimination based on gender identity or expression, and only six states have included gender identity or expression within their hate crimes laws. Early discrimination against transgender people was generally embodied in municipal prohibitions on gender-nonconforming dress, which made it illegal to appear in attire not of one's sex. Such laws fell into disfavor, however, by the 1970s, as courts invalidated them as unconstitutional. Nonetheless, the general stigma against transgender people has continued into the present, resulting in abnormally high levels of violence, harassment, and discrimination. Transsexuals, in particular, have faced legal difficulties in a number of states when they attempt to change the sex listed on their birth certificates and other public records after sex reassignment surgery. In states that do not permit such records to be corrected to reflect a person's current sex, individuals have been precluded from marrying someone of their same biological birth sex, since such marriages would constitute same-sex marriages. Courts similarly have relied on such restrictions to deny transsexuals parental rights and to prohibit the distribution of property during inheritance proceedings.

Thus, despite the enactment of antidiscrimination and hate crimes statutes, violence and harassment against LGBT people as a group remains common in many areas of the United States, particularly for LGBT youth. As of 2003, the number of reported hate crimes against LGBT people continues to increase rather than decrease and LGBT people continue to experience discrimination in multiple sectors. The belief that LGBT people are inherently immoral, sinful, diseased, ill, criminal, perverted, and deviant remains common and many continue to express a deep and visceral antipathy that is often used to justify discrimination against LGBT people.

## Bibliography

Badgett, M. V. Lee. *Money, Myths, and Change: The Economic Lives of Lesbians and Gay Men.* Chicago: University of Chicago Press, 2001.

*Bowers v. Hardwick,* 487 U.S. 186 (1986).

Cain, Patricia A. "Litigating for Lesbian and Gay Rights: A Legal History." *Virginia Law Review* 79 (1993): 1551–1641.

D'Emilio, John. *Sexual Politics, Sexual Communities: The Making of a Homosexual Minority in the United States, 1940–1970.* 2d ed. Chicago: University of Chicago Press, 1998.

D'Emilio, John, and Estelle B. Freedman. *Intimate Matters: A History of Sexuality in America.* 2d ed. Chicago: University of Chicago Press, 1997.

Duberman, Martin D., Martha Vicinus, and George Chauncey Jr., eds. *Hidden from History: Reclaiming the Gay and Lesbian Past.* New York: New American Library, 1989.

Eskridge, William. *Gaylaw: Challenging the Apartheid of the Closet.* Cambridge, Mass.: Harvard University Press, 1999.

Faderman, Lillian. *Odd Girls and Twilight Lovers: A History of Lesbian Life in Twentieth-Century America.* New York: Columbia University Press, 1991.

Gonsiorek, John C., and James D. Weinrich, eds. *Homosexuality: Research Implications for Public Policy.* Newbury Park, Calif.: Sage, 1991.

Herek, Gregory M. "The Psychology of Sexual Prejudice." *Current Directions in Psychological Science* 9 (2000): 19–22.

Herek, Gregory M., and Kevin T. Berrill, eds. *Hate Crimes: Confronting Violence against Lesbians and Gay Men.* Newbury Park, Calif.: Sage, 1992.

Katz, Jonathan Ned. *Gay American History: Lesbians and Gay Men in the U.S.A.* New York: Plume, 1992.

*Lawrence v. Texas,* 123 S.Ct. 2472, nos. 02–102 (26 June 2003).

Namaste, Viviane K. *Invisible Lives: The Erasure of Transsexual and Transgendered People.* Chicago: University of Chicago Press, 2000.

Rimmerman, Craig A., Kenneth D. Walk, and Clyde Wilcox, eds. *The Politics of Gay Rights.* Chicago: University of Chicago Press, 2000.

Rubenstein, William B. *Cases and Materials on Sexual Orientation and the Law.* St. Paul, Minn.: West, 1996.

**W. Mason Emnett**

**See also** ANTI-DISCRIMINATION LAW AND POLICY; CRIME AND CRIMINALIZATION; EMPLOYMENT LAW AND POLICY; FAMILY LAW AND POLICY; FEDERAL LAW AND POLICY; HATE CRIMES LAW AND POLICY; HEALTH AND HEALTH CARE LAW AND POLICY; IMMIGRATION, ASYLUM, AND DEPORTATION LAW AND POLICY; MILITARY LAW AND POLICY; POLICING AND POLICE; PRIVACY AND PRIVACY RIGHTS; SEXUAL PSYCHOPATH LAW AND POLICY; SODOMY, BUGGERY, CRIMES AGAINST NATURE, DISORDERLY CONDUCT, AND LEWD AND LASCIVIOUS LAW AND POLICY; TRANSGENDER LAW AND POLICY.

**DOMESTIC PARTNERSHIP.** see FAMILY ISSUES.

**DOOLITTLE, HILDA.** see H.D.

**DOWN LOW.** see AFRICAN AMERICANS.

# DRAG QUEENS AND KINGS

Drag queens and drag kings are gay men and lesbian women who cross-dress and perform femininity, masculinity, something in between, or some combination thereof. Drag queens have long been part of gay life and gay communities, but drag kings are a relatively recent phenomenon, emerging in the 1990s out of feminism and influenced by queer theory. To different degrees each are subject to controversies over whether they challenge or underscore traditional understandings of gender or sexuality.

Not all men who dress as women are drag queens. Other categories include transvestites or cross-dressers, generally straight men who wear women's clothing for erotic reasons; preoperative male-to-female transsexuals; and transgender people who display and embrace a gender identity at odds with their biological sex, but who do not intend to undergo surgery to change their sex. Drag queens, in contrast, are gay men who dress and perform as—but do not usually want to be—women or have women's bodies (although some drag performers are "tittie queens" who acquire breasts through either hormones or implants). Within the category of drag queen, there are further distinctions based on performance style. Esther Newton, in her classic study of drag in the 1960s, distinguished between "stage impersonators," talented performers who sang in their own voices, and "street impersonators," more marginal drag queens who lip-synched their numbers. One basic distinction is between "female impersonators," who generally do celebrity impersonation and keep the illusion of being women, and drag queens who regularly break the illusion by, for example, speaking in their male voices, referring to themselves as men, or discussing their tucked penises.

## History

The term "drag" in the sense of men wearing women's clothing dates back to the mid- or late nineteenth cen-

**All Dressed Up.** A drag queen, adorned with wig, fur, and heavy makeup, cheers beside a gay couple. [Corbis Corporation (New York)]

tury. Theater historian Laurence Senelick traces the origins of the term to criminal slang meaning "slowed down," from the "drag" of a carriage that was used as a brake, and then applied the term to the effects of long skirts trailing on the ground. "Queen," originally "quean," is a much older term, originally meaning "whore" and used in late-seventeenth-century England to refer to "mollies," the term for effeminate sodomitical men. The terms "drag" and "queen" seem to have joined no earlier than the 1930s. The first usage in print anyone has found to date is 1941. The meaning was clearly a gay man dressed as a woman for purposes of entertainment.

Drag as we know it today had its origins in the mid-nineteenth century, when glamorous female impersonators first appeared on stage. A half century earlier, the only men who wore women's clothes on stage were "dame comedians," who burlesqued old women for a laugh. Such portrayals evolved into glamour drag via all-male school theatricals, the circus, and minstrel shows. But in addition to these respectable origins, female impersonation on stage had connections to the subculture of cross-dressing men looking for male sex partners. By the 1920s, with the advent of Prohibition, speakeasies began introducing drag to mixed audiences of middle- and working-class patrons—and in Harlem, to white and African American patrons. This was also the high point of public drag balls, where men might use the cover of masquerade to dress in women's clothing and dance with other men and where straight people came to gape. In part because of the popularity of the balls, and in part out of club owners' desperation to attract business as the Depression thinned the crowds of paying customers, New York's Times Square experienced a "pansy craze" in the early 1930s as night spots featuring female impersonators became all the rage. But then the repeal of Prohibition, and the end of its flouting of law-abiding, middle-class codes of behavior, also meant an end of the speakeasy life that had brought drag out of the subculture. The creation of a liquor control board, in New York as well as other states, gave the government more leverage than ever over drinking establishments, leading to a ban on homosexual behavior in reputable bars and clubs and, ironically, fostering the growth of exclusively gay bars.

During the Second World War, drag found a surprising home when soldier drag queens, both African American and white, put on elaborate shows to entertain their buddies. And drag survived the postwar crackdown on gay culture, in part by catering to straight audiences. In San Francisco, where the tourist industry touted the city's reputation for sexual license, gay men and lesbians mingled with heterosexual tourists at the drag shows at Mona's and Finocchio's. The Jewel Box Revue, although born in a Miami gay bar in 1939, also aimed at a straight audience. With a cross-dressed female performer and an ethnically mixed cast unusual for the time, the troupe toured the country for thirty years.

Despite the persistence of such clubs, the postwar environment took its toll on drag performances. In a number of cities, wearing drag on the street was illegal, so female impersonators had to carry cabaret cards to prove that they were performers. Only on Halloween could men get away with dressing in drag, so traditional drag balls, like the African American–sponsored events in Chicago, continued to flourish throughout the 1950s. As the clubs where drag queens performed suffered financially, they began to substitute recorded music and lip-synching, opening stages to a less trained and more marginal group of performers. At the same time, the increasing viability and public awareness of transsexuality cast drag in a new and more deviant light.

As drag changed in dramatic and less dramatic ways up to the explosion of gay and lesbian activism in the 1970s, two things remained constant: drag both built community among gay and lesbian people and challenged, more or less politely, the dominant gender-divided and heterosexual order. José Sarria, who performed in drag at the Black Cat in San Francisco and ran for city supervisor in 1961 as part of the struggle against police harassment of gay bars, formed the Imperial Court System in 1965, arguably the first drag queen movement organization. The court system (now known as the International Court System, with chapters scattered over the western part of the country) raises money for the LGBT community (and other charitable purposes) through drag shows, but more importantly provides a "family" and respect for drag queens, the heart of the court.

If drag historically has created community, it has also always carried the possibility of challenge. Even the tourist shows at Finocchio's or the Jewel Box Revue had a potentially political edge. Comic routines called attention to the illusion of femaleness, and even traditional female impersonation worked to arouse sexual desire in straight male audience members. The role of drag queens in the resistance that followed the raid on the Stonewall Inn in 1969 is well known. In the years that followed, groups such as Street Transvestites Action Revolutionaries (founded by Sylvia Rivera, a heroine of the Stonewall Riots) and Flaming Faggots, along with men who identified as "radical fairies" and "effeminists," and butch women, challenged gender conformity within the movement. But such gender revolutionaries fought an uphill battle with gay liberationists and radical feminists who tended to dismiss drag as politically incorrect. Not until the 1980s, when groups such as the Sisters of Perpetual Indulgence and Church Ladies for Choice took up comic drag in a serious political struggle with the religious right,

did transgender presentation again play a more central role in the movement.

Nevertheless, drag queen performances, especially the more "in-your-face" political variety in which there is no pretense to being women and a great deal of direct discussion of gay life, sexuality, and gender-crossing, can be seen as an effective strategy of the LGBT movement. Drag shows at the 801 Cabaret in Key West, Florida, for example, explicitly challenge audiences composed of heterosexual as well as gay, lesbian, and bisexual people to confront the question of what makes a man a man and what makes a woman a woman, as well as to experience desires seemingly at odds with their own sexual identities.

## Drag in the Twenty-First Century

Drag in the early twenty-first century has taken on a wide variety of forms, but all of them are foreshadowed in drag history. Contemporary drag includes talented artists who impersonate female icons or create their own personae; street queens who live a marginal life; professional and amateur drag queens who lip-synch and adopt a range of styles, from female impersonation to campy drag to voguing, a competition developed in black and Latino clubs in which men dress and move in order to pass as women, businessmen, or other figures that they are not; movement activists who adopt drag for explicitly political purposes; and mainstream celebrities such as RuPaul and Lady Chablis, who began their careers like other drag queens but became famous. Perhaps nothing illustrates the rags-to-riches possibilities of drag so much as the fortunes of Wigstock, the Labor Day drag festival in New York City that began in 1984 with an impromptu performance by tired drag queens as they left a club at the end of the night and grew over the years into an international extravaganza attracting tens of thousands of spectators and official recognition from the city.

What is relatively new is the emergence of a drag king culture in the United States and abroad. There were successful male impersonators beginning in the 1930s, including Gladys Bentley, the tuxedo-clad Harlem performer, Storme DeLaverié, who emceed the Jewel Box Revue, and the "boys" at Mona's in San Francisco. Drag kings also in some sense follow in the traditions of various forms of female masculinity, from butches to transgender and gender-crossing women. But in other ways drag kings are a late twentieth-century development. Drag kings are women who perform masculinity, although drag king groups also include "bio-queens," women who perform femininity or sometimes femininity as performed by drag queens, and "trans kings," transgender individuals who go on stage as drag kings. Like drag queens, who sometimes identify as transgender or who acquire breasts or go on to become transsexuals, for some drag kings performance paves the way to identifying as transgender, transsexual, or intersexual.

Like the political "in-your-face" version of drag queen styles, drag king performances tend to be very explicitly political. But they go even further, representing an enactment of feminist and queer theory critiques of masculinity and engaging with such issues as incest, rape, sadomasochism, and hate crimes, although some numbers are simply humorous and fun. Drag king troupes and individual performers come together at an annual conference, the International Drag King Extravaganza, held in Columbus, Ohio, since 1999, where, in addition to attending academic sessions and performances, those interested can learn how to apply facial hair, bind their breasts, "pack" (wear a dildo or in some other way create a penis), and move like men. There is also a drag king e-mail distribution list.

The major scholarly critique of drag queens—that they are more gender-conservatives than gender-revolutionaries—has not extended to drag kings, although there are no doubt some who would see them as aping traditional masculinity. Gender theorists have been very interested in cross-dressing and transgender performances for what they reveal about the social construction and performativity of gender and sexuality. Some in LGBT communities, however, are critical of both drag queens and drag kings for calling attention to gender transgression and thus undermining the argument—a cornerstone of the struggle for LGBT civil rights—that LGBT people are just like heterosexuals.

What is clear from the history of drag is that it has long served a community-building function, since drag shows and drag balls were places where women and men with same-sex desires knew they could meet others with the same interests. At the same time, drag as a theatrical spectacle has also attracted the attention of straight onlookers, especially in tourist destinations, thus educating people who might otherwise never be exposed to LGBT culture. Drag king performances tend to be less available to mainstream audiences, although popular media have begun to give some attention to drag kings. In contrast to mainstream media representation of drag, performances by small-town drag queens and theoretically sophisticated drag kings that go on all across the country are much more central to community-building and the potential troubling of gender and sexuality.

**Josephine and Daphne.** Tony Curtis (left) and Jack Lemmon find a different way to hide from gangsters in *Some Like It Hot,* Billy Wilder's daring 1959 film comedy. [Getty Images]

## Bibliography

Brubach, Holly, and Michael James O'Brien. *Girlfriend: Men, Women, and Drag.* New York: Random House, 1999.

Butler, Judith. *Gender Trouble: Feminism and the Subversion of Identity.* New York: Routledge, 1990.

Dolan, Jill. "Gender Impersonation Onstage: Destroying or Maintaining the Mirror of Gender Roles?" *Women and Performance: A Journal of Feminist Theory* 2 (1995): 5–11.

Garber, Marjorie. *Vested Interests: Cross-Dressing and Cultural Anxiety.* New York: Routledge, 1992.

Halberstam, Judith. *Female Masculinity.* Durham, N.C.: Duke University Press, 1998.

Muñoz, José Esteban. *Disidentifications: Queers of Color and the Performance of Politics.* Minneapolis: University of Minnesota Press, 1999.

Newton, Esther. *Mother Camp: Female Impersonators in America.* Chicago: University of Chicago Press, 1972.

Paulson, Don, with Roger Simpson. *An Evening at the Garden of Allah: A Gay Cabaret in Seattle.* New York: Columbia University Press, 1996.

Rupp, Leila J., and Verta Taylor. *Drag Queens at the 801 Cabaret.* Chicago: University of Chicago Press, 2003.

Schacht, Steven P. "Four Renditions of Doing Female Drag: Feminine Appearing Conceptual Variations of a Masculine Theme." *Gendered Sexualities* 6 (2002): 157–80.

Schacht, Steven P. "The Multiple Genders of the Court: Issues of Identity and Performance in a Drag Setting." In *Feminism and Men: Reconstructing Gender Relations*. Edited by Steven P. Schacht and Doris W. Ewing. New York: New York University Press, 1998.

Senelick, Laurence. *The Changing Room: Sex, Drag and Theatre.* New York: Routledge, 2000.

Shapiro, Eve. "The Dynamics of Gender, Sexual, and Political Consciousness in Drag Kinging." Dissertation in progress, University of California, Santa Barbara.

Tewksbury, Rick. "Men Performing as Women: Explorations in the World of Female Impersonators." *Sociological Spectrum* 13 (1993): 465–486.

Tewksbury, Rick. "Gender Construction and the Female Impersonator: The Process of Transforming 'He' to 'She.'" *Deviant Behavior: An Interdisciplinary Journal* 15 (1994): 27–43.

Troka, Donna Jean, Kathleen LeBesro, and Jean Bobby Noble. "The Drag King Anthology." *Journal of Homosexuality* 43 (2002).

Volcano, Del LaGrace, and Judith "Jack" Halberstam. *The Drag King Book.* London: The Serpent's Tail, 1999.

**Verta Taylor, Leila J. Rupp**

**See also** BENTLEY, GLADYS; EICHELBERGER, ETHYL; FEMMES AND BUTCHES; GENDER AND SEX; RIVERA, SYLVIA; SARRIA, JOSÉ; STONEWALL RIOTS; TRANSGENDER ORGANIZATIONS AND PERIODICALS; TRANSGENDER AND GENDER IMPERSONATION LAW AND POLICY; TRANSSEXUALS, TRANSVESTITES, TRANSGENDER PEOPLE, AND CROSS-DRESSERS.

**DRUGS.** see ALCOHOL AND DRUGS.

# *DRUM*

Founded and edited by Clark Polak and published by Philadelphia's Janus Society, a homophile organization, *Drum* was the most widely circulating homophile magazine in the United States during much of the 1960s. Breaking from earlier homophile publications in its explicitly "queer" agenda, *Drum*, which was published from 1964 to 1969, can also be seen as a precursor to later gay magazines in its mix of humor, politics, and sexuality. Polak was a longtime figure in the Philadelphia area homophile movement, though he alienated the more mainstream elements there by espousing a broader perspective that focused as much on sexual rights as civil rights. A typical issue of *Drum* was thirty-five to forty pages. The covers invariably featured a photograph of a shirtless, good-looking white male, usually in his twenties. Many articles were reprints of works on gay-themed topics, including some

on psychological issues, such as articles by Albert Ellis, the leader of the rational-emotive school of psychology. Much attention was paid to the debate over whether or not homosexuals were "sick." Fiction was included in every issue. Articles dealing with censorship, which invariably argued for expansion of free speech and freedom of the press, were another constant. Such a perspective is no surprise in an era that saw confiscation and censorship of even marginally explicit materials, including *Drum* itself. Most amazingly, one of Polak's editorials praises Barry Goldwater, the 1964 Republican candidate for U.S. president, because of Goldwater's libertarianism.

And for the time, the photographs were explicit, especially for a magazine that was largely distributed through the mail. The work of one of the best-known gay photographers of the 1960s, Mel Roberts, as well as that of Troy Saxon, was often included. Both continue to have an audience among collectors. By early-twenty-first-century standards, the photographs would be considered soft-core, but they were far more explicit than anything that appeared in homophile publications such as the *Mattachine Review, ONE,* or the *Ladder.*

Perhaps *Drum*'s greatest contribution was providing an outlet for gay humor: little published work at the time captured this element of gay sensibility. Much of *Drum*'s humor consisted of parodies of popular ads of the time— the Jolly Green Giant and Tareyton cigarettes ads, for example—that formed the basis of the feature "Gay Moments in Advertising." Literature was also parodied. All these parodies supported a way of seeing gayness in the larger world, making the gay perspective seem more reasonable and building up group coherence. The Batman and Robin cartoons still resonate with gay men. Other cartoons, including the long-running series "Harry Chess," took note of the fantasies and foibles of gay life and its stereotypical characters.

Other features were news items, often excerpted from the mainstream press, dealing with gay issues or sexuality in general. Many were notices of research findings. Announcements from the Guild Book Service, a distributor of gay-related novels and nonfiction, were also common. Occasionally, a national directory of homophile organizations was included. Letters were usually laudatory, commending *Drum* for its liberationist stance and some encouraged even more risks. Some of them have a "canned" quality that makes them seem like in-house panegyrics.

*Drum* began ostensibly as a continuation of the Janus Society's newsletter. It was controversial even before its first issue. The initial advertising for it, which appeared in other homophile publications, proposed "news for 'fairies' and fiction for 'perverts.' " The *Mattachine Review,* the *Ladder,* and *ONE* sought to display an image that would be acceptable to a larger audience. Unlike earlier homophile publications, however, *Drum* was unapologetic in its use of sexuality. The name "Drum" itself was meant to bring to mind the famous quote by Thoreau, who referred to those who march to a different drummer. From the beginning, Polak wanted the magazine to be a gay equivalent of *Playboy* by encouraging freedom from confining forms of sexuality and release from the stifling repression of bourgeois society. More importantly, he wanted it to provide a balanced look at sexuality. His intention for *Drum* was made clear in its subtitle, "sex in perspective."

If these factors were not enough to make *Drum* controversial in the mid-1960s, there was also the fact that it was also completely geared to men. Polak was already unpopular with lesbians after defeating a lesbian candidate to become president of the Janus Society; *Drum* made him even less popular. Leaders of other homophile organizations were also concerned that the magazine could be of little use or even damaging to the larger movement because of its radical sexual politics.

*Drum*'s greatest troubles came from law enforcement officials. The Philadelphia region was already primed for 1960 surveillance since a major police raid on the homophile movement had taken place there in 1960. Beginning in the 1960s, the post office, in loose coordination with other federal agencies, kept tabs on *Drum.* Mostly surveillance consisted of lower-level bureaucrats' examination of issues for salacious content. Most disturbingly, however, is the reality that the magazine's readers across the country were also being watched. Polak knew all of this and responded with pugnacity by publishing combative articles like "I was a Homosexual for the FBI." Nevertheless, Polak did remove his parody "Tropic of Crabs" on the advice of lawyers who thought it might lead to obscenity charges.

After 1966, *Drum* was published less frequently. Nevertheless, by 1968 it was selling over fifteen thousand copies. Clearly, Polak's formula worked. Critics accurately point out *Drum*'s lack of women, which is curious since the Janus Society included lesbians as well as gay men; this omission possibly reflects Polak's misogyny. Lesbians, naturally, became increasingly disenchanted with Janus and Polak, and focused on other organizations. Polak himself became the target of censors for his other business activities, including peep shows and book services, which involved far more explicit materials than *Drum.* In 1969, Polak was arrested and convicted for selling obscene publications. These publications took so much of his energy that he ceased publishing *Drum.* The Janus Society (though it was in such disarray by this point that to what extent it was really a distinct organization in any meaningful way remains unclear) published a follow-up magazine called *PACE!,* which only lasted for two issues.

It is a mistake to think of *Drum* merely as a period piece. Polak's unapologetic openness about sexual freedom, his clever use of humor, and his mixing of various materials presaged later gay publications. The importance of gay periodicals is not well researched, but it is clear that *Drum* was the first to offer such a mélange. Before it, most were either coyly sexual and disguised as fitness publications or limited by a particular political perspective that bordered on the monotonous. *Drum* still seems quite contemporary though its thirty-one issues date from over thirty-five years ago.

## Bibliography

Stein, Marc. *City of Sisterly and Brotherly Loves: Lesbian and Gay Philadelphia, 1945–1972.* Chicago: University of Chicago Press, 2000.

**David Azzolina**

*See also* CENSORSHIP, OBSCENITY, AND PORNOGRAPHY LAW AND POLICY; HOMOPHILE PRESS; JANUS SOCIETY; PHYSIQUE MAGAZINES AND PHOTOGRAPHS; POLAK, CLARK.

# DUNBAR-NELSON, Alice (b. 19 July 1875; d. 18 September 1935) writer, activist.

Alice Dunbar-Nelson, an African American bisexual political activist and Harlem Renaissance participant, is best known for her distinguished career as a poet and a writer of short stories.

Born Alice Ruth Moore in New Orleans on 19 July 1875 to seaman Joseph Moore and seamstress Patricia Wright Moore, her fair coloring and auburn hair gave evidence of her mixed racial background. Dunbar-Nelson proved to be a brilliant and precocious child. At the age of fifteen, she began a two-year training program at Straight College, later Dillard University, in New Orleans and graduated in 1892. With degree in hand, she began a teaching career and taught elementary school in New Orleans until 1896. This experience may have encouraged the no-nonsense, forceful attitude she would display throughout the remainder of her life.

When her family decided to join the great migration of blacks for the greater opportunities and possibilities of the North, Dunbar-Nelson left the Crescent City for the Boston area. By this time she had already established her credentials as an African American literary talent. Her first published work, *Violets and Other Tales* (1895), gathered poems and sketches about life in Louisiana and Mississippi. Publicity about the collection led her to Paul Laurence Dunbar, an African American poet of considerable note. Dunbar saw a picture of the beautiful Alice in a Boston-area periodical and began corresponding with her. After two years of writing, the couple met in 1897 and married a year later amid false fears that Alice had become pregnant. The match became one of the most celebrated of the day.

Dunbar-Nelson continued to pursue her literary ambitions through these years, aided by criticism from her husband. *The Goodness of St. Rocque and Other Stories* (1898) exploited New Orleans color in tales of Creole history and culture. The limited options accorded women became a major theme in her stories, perhaps because as a married woman she was not permitted by school boards to teach and she had to write as a means of livelihood.

Unfortunately, marital difficulties soon appeared. The bride's family, less than thrilled by the groom's courtship approach, financial prospects, and dark skin color, never fully supported the marriage. Dunbar also had a problem with alcohol that contributed mightily to the turbulence of the relationship. One day in 1902, Dunbar beat his wife and spread a scandalous story about her. A woman of this era, especially an African American one, could not tolerate an assault upon her character if she hoped to remain in good social standing. Although Dunbar-Nelson seemed most outraged about the slander, her great fear of another beating at her husband's hands also led to her decision to leave him. Both strong willed, they never reconciled and never divorced.

Upon the death of her husband in 1906, Dunbar-Nelson delighted in the stature she received as the widow of a great man. This esteem may have prevented her from achieving recognition for her own literary accomplishments. Lost in the shadow of Dunbar, she never published another major literary work, although she edited a number of anthologies. To make ends meet, Dunbar-Nelson began teaching English at all-black Howard High School in Wilmington, Delaware, in 1902. Edwina B. Kruse, the mixed-heritage Puerto Rican and German principal of the school, became her lover. "Ned" paid Dunbar-

Nelson's expenses, helped her family financially, wrote passionate letters, and displayed a jealous side. The relationship lost strength by 1908, apparently because Dunbar-Nelson had met the man who would become her second husband. She embarked on a very brief marriage to Arthur Callis in 1910.

Dunbar-Nelson lost her teaching job in 1920 when a new principal used Dunbar's political activities to fire her (she had agitated for equal pay for African Americans and against lynching). Active in the black clubwoman's movement, she moved among exclusively female political and literary networks and may have met her subsequent female lovers through these connections.

Dunbar-Nelson wrote lesbian-themed poems but destroyed them along with many of her other papers before her death. However, her diary, spanning the years 1921 to 1931, did not get tossed into the flames. In its pages, Dunbar-Nelson used coded references to recount her affairs with Fay Jackson Robinson and Helene London. She also included lines from the lost poems.

Dunbar-Nelson married African American journalist Robert Nelson in 1916 and this marriage proved both lasting and happy. Nelson decoded the poorly concealed diary passages and, although upset at his wife's extramarital activity, tolerated her affairs. The couple published the *Wilmington Advocate* but struggled to maintain a steady income. Dunbar-Nelson died in Philadelphia on 18 September 1935 of a heart ailment, and was survived by Nelson.

## Bibliography

Alexander, Eleanor. *Lyrics of Sunshine and Shadow: The Tragic Courtship and Marriage of Paul Laurence Dunbar and Alice Ruth Moore, A History of Love and Violence Among the African American Elite.* New York: New York University Press, 2001.

Hull, Gloria T. *Color, Sex, and Poetry: Three Women Writers of the Harlem Renaissance.* Bloomington: Indiana University Press, 1987.

Hull, Gloria T., ed. *Give Us Each Day: The Diary of Alice Dunbar-Nelson.* New York: Norton, 1984.

Hull, Gloria T., ed. *The Works of Alice Dunbar-Nelson.* New York: Oxford University Press, 1988.

**Caryn E. Neumann**

*See also* HARLEM RENAISSANCE.

# E

## EAKINS, Thomas (b. 25 July 1844; d. 25 June 1916) artist, photographer, teacher.

Thomas Eakins was the foremost American realist artist of the late nineteenth century, producing an acclaimed body of oil-painted portraits and genre scenes, sculptures, and photographs. Eakins's place in the history of American art was only recognized after his death, having gone largely unappreciated by critics during his lifetime. He was born in Philadelphia, trained at the Pennsylvania Academy of Fine Arts, and studied human anatomy at Jefferson Medical College. He also studied at the École des Beaux-Arts, Paris, from 1866–1869. Eakins established himself as a portrait painter in Philadelphia with friends and family serving as subjects. His portraits sensitively captured the psychological state as well as the outer appearance of his subjects. One of his more famous sitters was Walt Whitman, considered by many to be America's greatest poet, and renowned today for his candid poetic expressions of same-sex desire. From 1875 to 1886 Eakins taught at the Philadelphia Academy for Fine Arts but his insistence that all students work with nude models ultimately led to his dismissal.

Eakins's genre paintings focused on sports and outdoor life, manifesting a broadly felt artistic shift toward depicting everyday life. Although Eakins is not known to have been homosexual, many of these works resonate with historians of gender and sexuality because they indicate an aesthetic preoccupation with the nude male figure and reflect late-Victorian anxieties about masculinity. Preeminent in this vein is Eakins's monumental canvas *The Swimming Hole* (1885, Amon Carter Museum), which depicts a group of nude male youths on a summer swim. Scholars have detected homoerotic valences in the painting's formal similarities to Classical Greek sculptural forms, in the central prominence of one youth's bare posterior, and in the curious juxtaposition of one boy's groin reflected on the surface of the water next to the head of (what turns out to be a self-portrait of) the artist. *The Swimming Hole* is all the more suggestive when compared to a series of photographs Eakins made of the actual site featuring him and his male students swimming in the nude. This was not an uncommon practice well into the twentieth century but suggests a casual physical intimacy between men that would now be routinely open to charges of homosexuality and/or sexual impropriety.

In a series of paintings devoted to the new fad for boxing, Eakins captured the sexual frisson in American men's appreciation of the bloody sport. The spectacularized body of nearly-nude working-class pugilists in such works as *Salutat* (1998, Phillips Academy) allowed male spectators to participate in a seemingly-authentic form of masculinity unencumbered by the social restraints of bourgeois propriety and modern civilization. In their simultaneous identification with, and objectification of, the athletic male body, a widely diverse group of men found shelter under a common definition of masculinity grounded in an essential male body. It is this revelation of the formative workings of hegemonic masculinity that queer scholars have found so provocative in Eakins's imagery.

A similar dynamic is at work in a thematic series of paintings focused on sculling, a fixture of elite British and

**Thomas Eakins.** A portrait of the prominent nineteenth-century American artist, c. 1889, by Susan Macdowell Eakins, his wife and fellow painter. [Philadelphia Museum of Art/corbis]

triumph of modern medicine—namely the introduction of ether anesthetics—the painting's composition also recalls a panopticon, the model prison first described by Jeremy Bentham and made famous by French philosopher Michel Foucault through his widely-read book *Discipline and Punish: The Birth of the Prison.* Eakins's implicit understanding of the way panoptic spaces structure power relations thematizes the professionalization and masculinization of medical expertise in the late-nineteenth century, a process that would have profoundly deleterious effects for LGB people when doctors pathologized same-sex desire in the twentieth century.

**Bibliography**

Davis, Whitney. "Erotic Revision in Thomas Eakins's Narratives of Male Nudity." *Art History* 13, no. 3 (September 1994): 301–41.

Hatt, Michael. "The Male Body in Another Frame: Thomas Eakins's 'The Swimming Hole as a Homoerotic Image.'" In *Journal of the Philosophy of the Visual Arts: The Body.* London: The Academy Group, 1993.

Hatt, Michael. "Muscles, Morals, Mind: The Male Body in Thomas Eakins' *Salutat.*" In *The Body Imaged.* Kathleen Adler and Marcia Pointon, eds. Cambridge, U.K.: Cambridge University Press, 1993.

**Michael J. Murphy**

*See also* ART HISTORY; VISUAL ART; WHITMAN, WALT.

American prep schools and universities. These pictures celebrate a proper form of middle-class sport, which eschewed the blunt force of boxing in favor of the instrumental and intellectual effort of rowing, a sport dependent on precise, almost mechanical, physical effort and mental discipline. Anticipating the twentieth-century's veneration of managers, experts, and professionals, Eakins's rowing pictures speak to those values crucial to bourgeois manliness in an era of managerial capitalism: repetitious, divided labor; subordination of self to a larger organization; elevation of mental over physical labor. Eakins undertook an appropriately technical, scientific process in the production of the paintings, with elaborate preparatory drawings and oil studies reminiscent of architectural blueprints.

Eakins's understanding of the intersections of social authority, male gender, and emergent cultures of expertise was exhibited in his ambitious group portrait *The Gross Clinic* (1875, Philadelphia Museum of Art). It depicts the famed anatomy professor, Dr. Samuel D. Gross, lecturing while working on a gangrenous limb at the center of a brightly-lit operating theater, surrounded by a class of eager young medical students. A tribute to the

# ECKSTEIN, Ernestine (b. 1941–?),
activist.

In October 1965, a small group of lesbians and gay men picketed the White House to protest government discrimination against homosexuals. Among them was Ernestine Eckstein, a twenty-four-year-old African American woman who had been active in the civil rights movement since her college days. In a photograph taken that day, she carries a sign reading "Denial of Equality of Opportunity Is Immoral." An earlier picket at the White House had occurred in April of the same year. Similar demonstrations had taken place since July 1965 at Independence Hall in Philadelphia, and they continued every 4 July for the rest of the decade. Eckstein joined some of these protests as well. She was among a handful of people in the 1960s who were willing to take visible public action to advance social justice for gay men and lesbians. Although we know very little about her today, in the 1960s she was a pioneering homophile activist whose commitment to civil rights for black Americans complemented her belief in lesbian and gay liberation. She is also an example of the ways in which homosexual women and men revealed their homosexuality in public when doing so could be dangerous.

Born in 1941, Eckstein arrived in New York City in 1963, having graduated from Indiana University in Bloomington, where she had majored in journalism and also studied government and Russian. In New York, she found employment as a social worker and found herself attracted to her female roommate. After a brief period of soul-searching, she accepted herself as a lesbian and sought an organization to join. At Indiana University, Eckstein had assumed leadership roles within the campus chapter of the National Association for the Advancement of Colored People (NAACP). Within two years of her arrival in New York, she joined not only the activist Congress of Racial Equality (CORE), but the two local homophile organizations, Mattachine Society and the Daughters of Bilitis (DOB). She became vice president of the New York chapter of DOB in 1966.

Eckstein applied lessons learned in the civil rights movement and urged the homophile organizations to give more emphasis to legal strategies. "My feeling is that there are certain broad, general problems that we all have as homosexuals, across the board so to speak, and we should concentrate on those—the discrimination by the government in employment and military service, the laws used against homosexuals, the rejection by the churches" (Gittings, p. 10). Although her tenure as a homophile leader was brief, through her activism Eckstein helped to create positive social change in each of these areas.

Although Eckstein allowed herself to be photographed on the picket line and profiled on the cover of the lesbian magazine the *Ladder* (June 1966), she did not use her real surname. Like many lesbians and gay men who lived in fear of losing their livelihoods and their families if they were known to be homosexual, Eckstein opted for the protection of a pseudonym. In this way, she balanced her desire for political visibility with personal caution. Millions of gay men and lesbians in the 1960s struggled with the very real effects of repression. Some, like Eckstein, were as active and open about their sexuality as they felt they could be for a few years, and then decided to step out of the limelight.

Eckstein left New York and relocated to the San Francisco Bay area in the 1970s. There she joined Black Women Organizing for Action (BWOA). A colleague learned that Eckstein was a lesbian and suggested that she contact Phyllis Lyon and Del Martin. However, she dropped out of sight and has not been located by scholars. What we know of her now comes from an interview conducted in 1966 by

Barbara Gittings, editor of the *Ladder,* and printed in the June issue. In it, Eckstein discusses her commitment to equality and integration and draws some rough parallels between the black civil rights and the homophile movements. "The homosexual has to call attention to the fact that he's been unjustly acted upon. This is what the Negro did," she said. "Demonstrations, as far as I'm concerned, are one of the very first steps toward changing society" (pp. 8, 11).

**Bibliography**

Gittings, Barbara. "Interview with Ernestine." *The Ladder: A Lesbian Review* (June 1966): 4–11.

Stein, Marc. *City of Sisterly and Brotherly Loves: Making Lesbian and Gay History in Philadelphia, 1945–1972.* Chicago: University of Chicago Press, 2000.

**Marcia M. Gallo**

*See also* DAUGHTERS OF BILITIS; GITTINGS, BARBARA, AND KAY TOBIN LAHUSEN; HOMOPHILE MOVEMENT; *LADDER*; MATTACHINE SOCIETY.

# ECONOMICS

The discipline of economics discovered LGBT people in the 1990s. In 1992 a panel of four economists introduced economic and policy issues related to LGB lives at the annual meeting of the American Economic Association. Since then, a growing number of economists have contributed theoretical and empirical insights into various aspects of LGB economic life, including employment issues, family issues, identity development, and economic history. Although economics was perhaps the last social science discipline to take on topics related to sexual orientation, the discipline's relative prominence in public policy debates makes economists' entry into the field of LGBT studies particularly important. And yet the fact that the landmark 1997 book *Homo Economics,* edited by Amy Gluckman and Betsy Reed, included only seven self-identified economists among its twenty-one contributors suggests that the discipline's attention to economic issues for LGBT people is still thin compared to the interest in such topics. There has never, however, been a formal LGBT group within the American Economic Association, and the informal one is no longer active as of 2003.

For the most part, economists have relied on the existing theoretical lenses that were originally developed to analyze other family, employment, and historical issues. For at least the last fifty years, economists have explored the economic organization of families as well as the causes and consequences of employment discrimination based on race and sex. This work provided theories and methods to apply to the economics of sexual orientation.

Beyond family and employment issues, however, economists have been unprepared to take on other important topics. In particular, neither mainstream nor feminist economists who have studied the gendered nature of economic processes and outcomes have transcended binary notions of gender, a situation that has prevented serious consideration of transgender issues. The prominence of economist Deirdre McCloskey and her memoir of her "crossing" from being Donald to being Deirdre may encourage economists to think more productively about the economic implications of a broader understanding of gender, but no economists have yet addressed issues related to the lives of contemporary transgender people.

## Family Economics

Economists' interest in the family stems from the family's central role in the consumption of goods and services in a market economy, in the supply of labor to the market, in the labor expended within the home, and in the reproduction of human beings. One enduring goal in economists' theorizing has been to explain the sexual division of labor, an inherently heterosexist concept denoting the tendency within heterosexual family units for women to be responsible for child rearing and household production, while men are more likely to be breadwinners working outside of the home. In the context of existing theory, two primary levels of economic interest in LGB people's families have emerged since the early 1990s. One aspect concerns simply the well-being of those families and their larger contributions to the economy, which is important for policy purposes and for a larger recognition of the existence of LGB families. A second aspect focuses on how economists might fruitfully contrast the experiences of LGB and heterosexual families for insight into the sources of the sexual division of labor.

Several economists have analyzed 1990 census data on same-sex couples to develop a snapshot of their economic well-being, as measured primarily by the household's income. The strong impact of gender on income—that is, the fact that men earn significantly more than do women—had led some commentators to refer to a hierarchy of household incomes. Marieka Klawitter and Victor Flatt's 1998 analysis of the census data show that two male partners have higher incomes than a married man and woman, and both of those kinds of couples have higher incomes than do two female partners. However, the gender advantage goes away for male couples when

the researchers use statistical procedures to take into account other differences between couples that lead to different incomes, such as age, education level, and place of residence. After taking those factors into account, married couples top the economic ladder; they are followed by gay male couples, with lesbians still occupying the bottom rung.

Economists have also used census data and historical accounts of the family relationships of LGB people to offer insight into theories of what members of families do, particularly asking why men and women end up doing very different kinds of economic tasks. Some economists believe that couples divide up the time spent on household and labor market activities so as to maximize their efficiency. To summarize a complicated story, these economists argue that women's ability to breastfeed makes them more efficient child-care providers than men, and that men's earnings advantage in the labor market makes them more efficient breadwinners, hence the observed sexual division of labor as family members specialize in the tasks that they do best. Other economists (along with some sociologists and psychologists) argue instead that women and men are assigned to different family roles by strong social rules, or gender norms. Both theories lead to the same prediction about how labor will be divided up within heterosexual couples' families, leading to a theoretical impasse.

The experiences of same-sex couples offer a natural experiment for distinguishing between the efficiency and gender norm theories of the sexual division of labor. If the desire for efficiency drives the division of labor, we would expect LGB people in same-sex couples to specialize in different kinds of tasks, just as people in heterosexual couples do. If gender norms determine the division of labor, we would expect two women or two men to divide up tasks much more similarly than do heterosexual couples. Indeed, economists have found that members of same-sex couples have much more similar levels of employment than do married heterosexual couples, implying much less specialization between home and workplace for LGB people. Studies by sociologists suggest that same-sex couples divide up housework more equally than different-sex couples as well. Overall, those patterns give support to the idea that gender norms help explain the observed sexual division of labor.

## The Economics of Discrimination

Although LGB families have received the most theoretical attention from economists, most published economic research has asked the question of whether—and why—LGB people's earnings differ from heterosexual people's earnings. Economists have studied employment discrimination for over half a century, and the economic approach to that subject has typically involved making detailed comparisons of the earnings of men and women, for instance, or of black workers and white workers. If workers have the same characteristics that are viewed as legitimate determinants of earnings, such as experience, skills, location, or education, then economists expect them to be paid similarly by employers. But if we see differences in earnings by race, sex, or sexual orientation among workers with the same productive characteristics, then economists typically conclude that discrimination must have occurred.

A growing set of studies over the last decade has compared earnings by sexual orientation separately for both men and women, beginning with M. V. Lee Badgett's 1995 article, "The Wage Effects of Sexual Orientation Discrimination." These studies have used the scanty relevant data from random samples, which has meant categorizing individuals by the sex of their sex partners (available in the General Social Survey) or by whether they have a same-sex unmarried partner (in the 1990 Census). Unfortunately, no existing large-sample data set contains information on self-identity, that is, whether respondents think of themselves as lesbian, gay, bisexual, or heterosexual. Therefore, existing datasets by necessity combine gay and bisexual men as well as lesbians and bisexual women in comparisons with otherwise similar heterosexuals.

These studies have found remarkably consistent patterns in comparing gay and bisexual men to straight men. After controlling for race, marital status, residential location, age, education, full-time work, and other relevant factors, economists have found that gay and bisexual men earn from 13 to 32 percent less than do heterosexual men in the United States. Findings in the comparisons for women are less consistent. Some studies find virtually no difference in the earnings of lesbians and bisexual women when compared to heterosexual women; other studies find a significant earnings advantage for lesbian and bisexual women of up to 27–30 percent. Given the sharp difference in findings by sex, economists have debated the reasons. One set of economists believes that discrimination explains the earnings difference for men since gay men earn less than otherwise similar heterosexual men. In this view, higher earnings for lesbians reflect earnings-enhancing characteristics of lesbians that cannot be easily measured, such as more direct experience or greater training than heterosexual women, many of whom expect to spend time out of the labor market while being supported by a husband. This school of thought also points to other studies in which lesbians report experiencing employment discrimination.

The other interpretation of the sexual orientation earnings patterns uses one of the theories of families discussed above. According to this view, since lesbians and gay men will partner with someone of the same sex, they acquire different skills (what economists call human capital) than do heterosexual men and women, and those differences in skills explain the earnings differences. Gay men earn less because they will not invest in as many work-related skills as will heterosexual men, who must be prepared to support a wife and children. Lesbians earn more because they acquire work-related skills to make up for the fact that they will not have a male partner who can provide for them.

Putting together all of the pieces of the puzzle suggests that each view is at least half right. Both sides agree that lesbians are likely to make different choices from heterosexual women, and studies confirm that lesbians work more weeks and more hours than do heterosexual women. However, we will need either better data or very different methodological approaches to study convincingly whether or not economic discrimination exists against lesbians.

The discrimination view of gay men's earnings disadvantage appears to have the clearly stronger hand than the family duty view, however. The existing studies show that gay men and heterosexual men appear to have a similar commitment to working in the labor market, and gay men actually tend to have more years of education on average than do heterosexual men. Overall, those facts suggest that gay men are just as serious about success in the labor market as heterosexual men, so it is unlikely that gay men's lower earnings result from having inferior work-related skills that derive from education and experience. Discrimination is the more likely cause of gay men's lower earnings.

## Other Directions

Aside from concerns related to family and employment, economists have taken up various other topics. Jeffrey Escoffier in 1975 was the first economist to think about the economic context for LGB workers' decisions about coming out in the workplace. Since then, Badgett has been the only other economist to investigate the factors influencing workplace disclosure decisions.

The influence of economic forces in the development of lesbian and gay desire and identity has occupied some economists' attention. Richard Cornwall has approached the social construction of desire from a highly theoretical and mathematical perspective. Julie Matthaei's historical work extends John D'Emilio's argument that the development of capitalism contributed greatly to the development of a gay identity. Matthaei shows how the sexual division of labor—in the context of both the family and occupational segregation—influenced gender and sexual identities. Some women found opportunities within a gender-segregated world to pursue relationships with other women, and as economic alternatives to marriage for women increased, so did the numbers and, eventually, the visibility of women living as lesbians. From a much more mainstream, essentialist perspective, Richard A. Posner has developed a theory connecting same-sex sexual behavior to individuals' choices made in the context of differing incentives. Other work still at early stages concerns the influence of sexual orientation on individuals' occupational position and on the economics of offering domestic partner benefits.

## Challenges

Although much fruitful economic research lies ahead, several challenges also stand in the way. There are relatively few out LGBT economists to lead the way and to pull heterosexual economists into this exciting subject area, and some young economists continue to worry that research on sexual orientation will stigmatize them. Further, many are in fields of economics that are far removed from issues of sexual orientation. Finally, and perhaps most problematically, economics is largely now a quantitative social science, and the dearth of large-scale data sets with questions on sexual orientation (not to mention gender identity) will seriously limit what economists can accomplish in the short run. In the long run, economists should be able to benefit from the efforts underway to develop new empirical methods and new sources of data that will further illuminate the economic lives of LGBT people.

## Bibliography

Badgett, M. V. Lee. *Money, Myths, and Change: The Economic Lives of Lesbians and Gay Men.* Chicago: University of Chicago Press, 2001.

———. "Discrimination Based on Sexual Orientation: A Review of the Literature in Economics and Beyond." In *Handbook on the Economics of Discrimination.* Edited by William Rodgers IV. Forthcoming.

Badgett, M. V. Lee, and Prue Hyman, eds. "Explorations in Lesbian, Gay, and Bisexual Economics." *Feminist Economics* 4, no. 2 (Summer 1998): 49–116.

Gluckman, Amy, and Betsy Reed, eds. *Homo Economics: Capitalism, Community, and Lesbian and Gay Life.* New York: Routledge, 1997.

Klawitter, Marieka, and Victor Flatt. "The Effects of State and Local Antidiscrimination Policies for Sexual Orientation." *Journal of Policy Analysis and Management* 17 (1998): 658–686.

McCloskey, Deirdre. *Crossing: A Memoir.* Chicago: University of Chicago Press, 1999.

Posner, Richard A. *Sex and Reason.* Cambridge, Mass.: Harvard University Press, 1992.

**M. V. Lee Badgett**

*See also* ADVERTISING; BOYCOTTS; BUSINESSES; CAPITALISM AND INDUSTRIALIZATION; DISCRIMINATION; EMPLOYMENT AND OCCUPATIONS; FAMILY ISSUES; LABOR MOVEMENTS AND LABOR UNIONS.

# EDUCATION

Issues concerning sexual orientation and gender expression have existed in U.S. schools ever since formal education first began in colonial America. Social norms and stereotypes regarding "appropriate" gender expression and "natural" sexual desires permeated school cultures via peer interactions (name-calling, role playing, dating) and student-teacher interactions (for example, casual references to spouses). Schools often sanctioned such messages (or at least failed to challenge them), both implicitly through silence and explicitly through policies of who should (or should not) be hired to teach, how students should (or should not) behave and dress, and what should (or should not) be included in the curriculum.

In the early 1900s, a small but increasing number of researchers of education examined sexual orientation and gender expression in schools, primarily in reference to the role of schools in promoting or failing to promote healthy or socially preferred desires and behaviors among young people. Early research on sexual orientation and gender expression in U.S. schools often characterized as pathological any deviation among students and faculty from the norms of heterosexuality and of appropriate masculinity for males and femininity for females. This was especially the case concerning teachers: women teachers (as well as their teaching of certain subjects) were blamed for emasculating male students, and homosexual teachers were feared for possibly "contaminating" otherwise heterosexual students.

Beginning in the 1970s, changes in the political consciousness of mainstream U.S. society, especially in the wake of multiple civil rights movements, shifted the ways that the field of educational research addressed sexual and gender differences.

## Normalcy and Identity Politics

The civil rights and women's movements of the 1960s created a climate of civil unrest that helped make possible two pivotal events for LGBT people in the United States: the 1969 LGBT riots at the Stonewall Inn in New York City and the 1973 decision by the American Psychological Association to declassify homosexuality as a mental illness. The insistence by both activists and the medical establishment that homosexuality should not be pathologized and that homosexuals should enjoy rights equal to those of heterosexuals fueled the growth of gay and lesbian studies in higher education in the 1970s. Gay and lesbian studies produced theories about the normalcy of same-sex desire, historical and anthropological research about same-sex desire in other cultures and eras, and psychological and sociological research about the experiences of gay and lesbian people (and sometimes bisexuals and transgenders) and the negative impact of homophobia in their lives.

Gay and lesbian studies did not simultaneously grow in the field of educational research. A few publications emerged in the 1970s, as did a growing body of feminist studies that would later significantly influence the study of sexual orientation. But it was not until the early 1980s that gay and lesbian studies in education began to proliferate, especially studies of schooling at the elementary and secondary levels and studies of masculinity and homophobia. Along with research on the experiences of gay and lesbian students and the different ways that homophobia manifested in schools, educational journals and books began including research on how the curriculum taught in schools perpetuated homophobia and how schools might revise curriculums to challenge stereotypes and myths about gay and lesbian people.

In the 1980s, the call to challenge homophobia by teaching students about gay and lesbian people coincided with a growing national and international epidemic, namely, the spread of HIV/AIDS. Although initially considered an African and Caribbean disease, the preponderance of infection among gay and bisexual men in the United States led many people both in and out of the medical profession to classify AIDS as a gay disease. An increasing number of schools began to teach about AIDS, and in doing so, found a politically safe way to teach about gay and sometimes lesbian and bisexual people, namely, as the population most affected by AIDS. Ironically, by doing so, schools no longer remained silent about gay and lesbian identities but were continuing to pathologize them by associating same-sex desire with illness. Health classes, particularly lessons on AIDS and sex education, soon became the most common places to

**Louie Crew.** A portrait of the English professor and activist. [Louie Crew]

teach about gay and lesbian people, and educational research, especially the field of curriculum studies, began focusing more attention on how to include or integrate gay and lesbian people and issues across the disciplines.

Of course, AIDS curriculum was not alone in characterizing LGBT people in problematic ways. Even educational research conducted by LGBT people came under fire from other LGBT people for failing to address differences among LGBT people (on the basis of, for example, sexual desires, gender identities, and racial and class backgrounds) and for presuming to know what it meant to be LGBT for all LGBT people. Similar internal tensions happened throughout the 1970s and 1980s among LGBT political and social organizations that witnessed the formation of many splinter groups that criticized the larger organizations for failing to address the experiences and needs of subpopulations of LGBT people, including bisexuals and transgenders, women, people of color, and other groups. As was happening in women's and civil rights movements across the United States, identity-based political organizing for LGBT people was under fire for operating in contradictory ways, namely, by challenging some forms of oppression and addressing certain populations while overlooking others.

The difficulties of getting educational research on LGBT issues published only compounded the problem. In the 1980s, most journals and book publishers had yet to publish any research on such topics, and few editors were openly supportive of doing so; few researchers could engage in this area of research without fear of retribution (loss of job, of benefits, of personal safety); and few resources (financial as well as collegial) were available to researchers and curriculum developers. A notable exception was the lesbian and gay special interest group of the American Educational Research Association, created in 1987. The publication of LGBT-related research required that researchers make difficult political choices about their topics, publication venues, and careers.

## "Queer" Studies in Education

A significant paradigm shift occurred in the late 1980s and early 1990s as postmodern and poststructural theories emerged in academia as alternatives to identity-based political theories and movements. The "posts" theories placed emphasis on the situatedness of identity and oppression, that is, on the ways that identity and oppression played out differently in different contexts, and on the ways that embracing differences or challenging oppression required different approaches, depending on the context. Applied to LGBT identities, the "posts" theories raised questions about what it meant to challenge the oppression of gays and lesbians when it was not clear what exactly those identities and oppressions were. Within this paradigm shift emerged "queer studies," a movement that turned its attention away from attempting to normalize gay and lesbian identities and more toward troubling the very meanings of "normal." Under examination and contestation were the conceptualizations of normalcy embraced by mainstream society as well as by LGBT communities.

Within the field of education, queer studies signaled several shifts in the 1990s: (1) from repressing homophobia to unearthing heteronormativity; (2) from LG to LGBTIQ; and (3) from inclusive curriculums to partial ones. In the first instance, much research from the 1980s and into the early 2000s focused on the dynamics of homophobia in schools and on the experiences of LGBT students. The emergence of queer studies, however, influenced more and more researchers to focus their analysis on the mechanisms that placed value on, normalized, and even regulated heterosexuality (especially certain forms of heterosexuality). This shift drew on Michel Foucault's classic book *The History of Sexuality* (published in

English in 1978), which argues that queerness or abnormality is not merely something that society has repressed—it is something that society needed and produced. After all, what was normal could not exist without something else being queer, which meant that reducing the marginalization of queer identities could not happen without disrupting the privileging of straight ones. Examining the production and regulation of certain kinds of heterosexual desire had already begun in the work of feminist thinkers who were examining ways that schools privileged and silenced different expressions of sexual desire among adolescent girls and boys. Queer studies in education drew on these studies of (hetero)sexuality, as well as on queer studies in education in Canada, which drew substantially on psychoanalytic theories of the surprising ways that sexual desire emerged in schools, even among youth, and even when educators presumed to contain it.

Just as queer studies problematized the notion that hetero identities were more valuable or natural than queer identities, so too did queer studies problematize the notion that certain queer identities (especially gay and lesbian ones) were more valuable or natural than others, including bisexual, transgender, intersexed, and questioning identities. Drawing on women's studies and ethnic studies, queer studies raised questions about the ways that even queer identities can normalize other identities, such as white, male, gender-appropriate, homo, middle-class, able-bodied, and English-speaking identities. "Gay," "lesbian," and other identities could mean different things with different bodies and in different contexts, and more researchers began to examine differences among LGBT students and faculty and the impact of their multiple identities on their experiences in school. For example, a range of quantitative and qualitative research on the intersections of race and sexuality appeared with increasing frequency in the 1990s, leading to the publication of the first book on race, sexuality, and education in 2001.

During the 1990s, research articles began appearing in increasing numbers of educational journals and books about ways that various school personnel could address LGBT students and homophobia in the school environment. These included articles on sports coaches, school counselors, administrators, and the general school climate. Book-length studies also appeared about educators themselves, including gay and lesbian schoolteachers and college faculty. Some articles examined the strengths, weaknesses, and successes and failures of various policy initiatives, including student gay-straight alliances on school campuses, safe-school policies (especially in the wake of costly lawsuits against school districts for failing to protect LGBT students from harassment and violence), and conservative backlashes (such as the backlash to the "Children of the Rainbow" curriculum in New York City in 1991, in part motivated by opposition to the inclusion of gay- and lesbian-headed families). But most common were publications centered on the study of curriculums (that is, on what is taught in schools), from problems of existing curriculums and materials to recommendations for curricular change in a range of subject matters, including social studies, English literature, health, art, drama, music, and the natural sciences. While some of these publications paralleled publications in the 1980s that offered solutions to the problem of exclusion and stereotypes in curriculums, others drew on queer theory to suggest that different approaches to curriculum revision have different strengths and weaknesses and that even inclusive curriculums can be problematic if they fail to raise questions about what it means to be LGBT or how homophobia and heteronormativity can play out differently for different groups in different contexts.

### New Directions

In the early 2000s, queer studies in education continued to raise questions about who was being addressed and what was being taught by schools and by research on schools. Educational researchers were conducting work on populations of queer students who had been overlooked by earlier research, including transgender students, disabled students, very young students, and student teachers. Researchers were conducting research on different subject matters (such as the technological sciences) and the developmental differences in how those subjects can be taught (for children versus adolescents versus adults). Researchers were even exploring alternatives to the frameworks that had been taken for granted in queer studies, including the "victimization" of LGBT youth (that focused on the harm experienced by youth rather than their resilience), relations among LGBT youth (versus between LGBT youth and heterosexual youth/teachers), and youth with unfixed identities (being queer in some contexts, straight in others, sometimes for political reasons, sometimes not). If educational researchers continue to embrace the impetus behind queer studies, the field of education can expect to continue to examine the limitations of what has already been produced, while exploring the changes made possible by frameworks, topics, and questions that have, until now, been deemed too queer to examine by the field of education.

### Bibliography

Blount, Jackie M. "Manly Men and Womanly Women: Deviance, Gender Role Polarization, and the Shift in Women's School Employment, 1900–1976." *Harvard Educational Review* 66 (1996): 318–338.

Epstein, Debbie, Sarah O'Flynn, and David Telford. "'Othering' Education: Sexualities, Silences, and Schooling." *Review of Research in Education* 25 (2001): 127–179.

Harbeck, Karen M., ed. *Coming Out of the Classroom Closet: Gay and Lesbian Students, Teachers, and Curricula.* Binghamton, N.Y.: Harrington Park Press, 1991.

Kumashiro, Kevin K., ed. *Troubling Intersections of Race and Sexuality: Queer Students of Color and Anti-Oppressive Education.* Lanham, Md.: Rowman and Littlefield, 2001.

Letts, William J., and James T. Sears, eds. *Queering Elementary Education: Advancing the Dialogue about Sexualities and Schooling.* Lanham, Md.: Rowman and Littlefield, 1999.

Lipkin, Arthur. *Understanding Homosexuality, Changing Schools: A Text for Teachers, Counselors, and Administrators.* Boulder, Colo.: Westview Press, 1999.

Pinar, William F., ed. *Queer Theory in Education.* Mahwah, N.J.: Lawrence Erlbaum Associates, 1998.

Unks, Gerald, ed. *The Gay Teen: Educational Practice and Theory for Lesbian, Gay, and Bisexual Adolescents.* New York: Routledge, 1995.

**Kevin K. Kumashiro**

*See also* GAY, LESBIAN, AND STRAIGHT EDUCATION NETWORK (GLSEN); EDUCATION LAW AND POLICY.

# EDUCATION LAW AND POLICY

## The Epidemic of Anti-LGBT Harassment in Schools

LGBT students, staff, and teachers have been abused, harassed, and discriminated against in schools across the United States. Students are "coming out"—acknowledging their sexuality or gender identity—at younger ages, and many school administrators are struggling to keep up with these cultural changes. LGBT youth, whether "out" or not, are in many instances rejected by family and friends and harassed and attacked by their peers and teachers in school. LGBT youth of color risk additional rejection by their ethnic community of origin, which can be essential to coping with an unequal, segregated, and still racist society. Children of LGBT parents are also commonly targeted and harassed. Meanwhile, though a substantial number of Americans believe in equal treatment for all people in the workplace, opposition to LGBT primary and secondary school teachers remains widespread and LGBT teachers continue to report numerous instances of employment discrimination.

Anti-LGBT prejudice, harassment, and violence are epidemic in the nation's schools. From elementary school through high school, "gay" is the epithet of choice to denote something bad, undesirable, or just different.

While all students can become targets of harassment for their perceived homosexuality or gender nonconformity, the nation's LGBT students and children of LBGT parents often suffer the worst abuse. Such abuse can have devastating effects on the children targeted, including higher rates of suicidal ideation and attempted suicide, higher truancy and drop-out rates, poor school performance, substance abuse, and running away from home. In a 1999 Massachusetts study, 49 percent of LBG students said they had considered suicide during the previous year. A 2001 Gay Lesbian and Straight Education Network survey found more than 80 percent of LGBT youth reported anti-LGBT verbal harassment within the past year; 40 percent said harassment occurred "frequently." Twenty percent of LGBT students reported physical assault because of their sexual orientation over the past year, while 10 percent reported being assaulted because of their gender identity or gender nonconformity. Nearly 70 percent felt unsafe in school because of their sexual orientation.

Despite these obstacles, LGBT youth often display amazing strength and resiliency. In many states, such as California and Massachusetts, they have organized to effect changes in policy to make schools safer. Youth and allied advocates have spearheaded successful intervention programs including nondiscrimination and anti-harassment policies, anti-homophobia initiatives, community and school-based support groups, adult mentors programs, positive curricula in the classroom, and teacher and staff training. Gay Straight Alliances (GSAs), which started in California, provide school-based locations where LGBT youth can safely discuss problems associated with prejudice against their sexual orientation or gender identity. A pilot study of the Massachusetts Safe Schools Program found that clear anti-discrimination policy statements, at both the state and local level, followed up by technical, legal and financial resources, and supported by key administrators, educators, community leaders, and student leaders are as important as (GSAs). While there are ethical reasons for making schools safer for LGBT students, there are also legal reasons: schools that fail to provide a safe environment to LGBT students are vulnerable to lawsuits that can incur financial liabilities. Jamie Nabozny was awarded $800,000 because teachers and administrators in his Wisconsin high school did not take action to stop the daily harassment and violence he experienced (*Nabozny v. Podlesny*, 1996).

## Nondiscrimination and Anti-Harassment Laws and Regulations

Since Wisconsin passed a law banning discrimination against LGB students in schools on the basis of sexual orientation in 1987, the District of Columbia and six other states have followed suit: California, Connecticut, Massachusetts, Minnesota, New Jersey, and Vermont. California, New Jersey, and Minnesota also prohibit discrimination on the basis of gender identity. In Minnesota, students in public and private schools are protected against discrimination on the basis of both sexual orientation and gender identity. In other states students are protected against sexual orientation discrimination only in the state's public schools. By cross-referencing its hate crimes statute, California also prohibits discrimination on the basis of "gender." A 2002 Washington state law also outlaws "anti-gay" harassment, but not "anti-gay" discrimination, in education.

Another way states ban discrimination is through regulations promulgated through the state department of education. The Pennsylvania and Rhode Island education departments outlaw sexual orientation discrimination. In states with no nondiscrimination or anti-harassment policies, municipalities can take matters into their own hands and amend school anti-harassment policies to include sexual orientation. North Olmstead, Ohio; Decatur, Georgia; and Lawrence, Kansas have done this.

## Safe Schools Initiatives

Massachusetts launched the first Safe Schools initiative in 1993, after the Governor's Commission on Gay and Lesbian Youth documented the homophobic climate pervasive in most of the state's schools. The Safe Schools Program seeks to fulfill four recommendations the Massachusetts Board of Education made in 1993:

- Develop policies that protect gay and lesbian students from harassment, violence, and discrimination.

- Offer school personnel training in violence prevention and suicide prevention.

- Offer school-based support groups for lesbian, gay, and heterosexual students.

- Provide school-based counseling for family members of lesbian and gay students.

The Massachusetts legislature appropriated funds to support the Safe Schools Program through the Departments of Education and Health and Human Services. Within a few years more than 140 schools across the state had GSAs, and many teachers and counselors were trained in how to deal with anti-LGB harassment and violence. Very quickly the program showed results. Laura Szalacha found that schools with GSAs, and schools that had undergone teacher and other staff training were more comfortable and affirming places for LGB youth.

Unfortunately, Republican Governor Jane Swift defunded the Mass. Safe Schools Program in 2002.

## Gay/Straight Alliances

The first Gay/Straight Alliance was started in Los Angeles in 1985 under the auspices of Project 10, so named because of the belief that LGB people comprise 10 percent of the population. GSAs are an important piece of the overall strategy to ensure that schools provide education in a safe and welcoming environment. They provide a frequently student-initiated organization for students and school staff to work toward ending anti-LGBT bias and homophobia in schools. They are also the most visible and widely adopted component of safer schools programs. Students are able to discuss the problems associated with social prejudice and make friends without hiding their sexual orientation and gender identity, which helps them develop social skills and self-esteem.

Although the Salt Lake City, Utah School Board tried to ban a GSA from meeting at East Side High School, a U.S. district court ruled that the 1984 Equal Access Act required that schools receiving federal funds let any voluntary, student-initiated club meet as long as other clubs are allowed to meet on campus.

Much work remains to be done regarding racial and gender diversity in GSAs. Often, even in racially diverse school districts, GSAs are disproportionately white and female. Some say it is harder for young men to attend GSAs because they may be at greater risk of harassment and physical attack from other young male peers if their participation is discovered. GSAs are also less often found in rural school districts.

A 2001 study by the California-based Gay-Straight Alliance Network found that 53 percent of LGBT students and allied straight youth of color with a GSA at their school said the group's membership did not reflect the racial diversity of the school. Nearly half (45 percent) said they did not feel comfortable going to the GSA at their school.

## LGBT Issues in Curricula

LGBT issues are still largely excluded from primary and secondary curricula, and children's stories that reference only straight relationships, curricula that teach girls to be feminine and boys to be masculine, and marriage, family education, and sex education classes oriented only to heteronormative relationships are still commonplace in the classroom. Laws such as the welfare reform law of 1996 have added new obstacles to getting LGBT curricula into classrooms. This recently reauthorized law promotes an

"Vote No on 6." This political ad warns, "You don't have to be gay to be fired!"—an example of the continual struggle to protect educators and LGBT students from discrimination and harassment through changes in laws and educational policies. [Gay and Lesbian Historical Society (GLHS)]

abstinence-only-until-marriage education policy that teaches that sex outside the context of marriage is intrinsically dangerous. Sine 1996 the federal government has spent $100 million a year on abstinence-only-until-marriage education. In 2002 President George Bush sought a one-third increase in funding for the program.

The often explicitly anti-LGBT and stigmatizing language of abstinence curricula can have a chilling effect on discussion of homosexuality and transgenderism in schools, including attempts to deal with incidents of anti-LGBT harassment. In reaction to a growth in sex education and anti-homophobia initiatives in the early 1990s, conservatives pushed "parents' rights" laws and parental notification laws in states across the United States, requiring teachers to provide advance written warning to parents prior to discussing homosexuality and other controversial topics in class. Parental notification laws followed by a few years the "no promo homo" laws enacted by many states in the late 1980s and early 1990s, which restrict any neutral or positive mention of homosexuality. South Carolina bans discussion of "alternative sexual lifestyles from heterosexual relationships including, but not limited to, homosexual relationships except in the context of instruction concerning sexually transmitted disease." Arizona law prohibits "instruction which: 1. Promotes a homosexual life-style. 2. Portrays homosexuality as a positive alternative life-style. 3. Suggests that some methods of sex are safe methods of homosexual sex." Alabama requires that any mention of homosexuality stress "that homosexuality is not a lifestyle acceptable to the general public and that homosexual conduct is a criminal offense under the laws of the state." And Texas law is almost identical to Alabama's statute. When taken together, these policies create a context that may have a chilling effect on open conversations about issues facing LGBT students and the children of LGBT parents, including issues of verbal and physical harassment. They may also preclude, as they are intended to, the incorporation of LGBT issues in social studies, literature, and health classes.

Despite the impediments that most states face in teaching LGBT material, state organizations such as the Massachusetts Governor's Commission on Gay and Lesbian Youth recommended the incorporation of gay and lesbian issues into curricula, such as including coverage of the gay rights movement in a social studies or contemporary history course. Some teachers are introducing the subject regardless of the legal barriers to LGBT curricula.

In GLSEN's 2001 national survey, 25 percent of LGBT youth reported that LGBT issues were taught in some of their classes. Usually the inclusion of LGBT issues in curricula occurred in history or social studies, English classes, and health classes. Nearly 80 percent said that the representation of LGBT topics were either somewhat positive or very positive. Fewer than a third of youth reported having inclusive textbooks in their classes, and about a third said they had LGBT resources in their libraries or internet access to LGBT community websites. Rural students were less likely to report that LGBT issues were taught in class or that LGBT issues were represented in textbooks or library books, or that LGBT resources were available via school library internet connections. The 2000 Child Internet Protection Act requires schools receiving federal funds for internet technology to install anti-pornography software that could prevent LGBT stu-

dents from accessing information on-line about LGBT community centers, social services, and social or political organizations. Many public libraries also have such anti-porn software, which can limit especially low-income LGBT youth's access to LGBT-related information.

## Teachers, Administrators, and Staff

Primary and secondary school teachers, administrators, and staff known to be LGBT have long experienced discrimination in hirings, promotions, and firings; some of the most visible anti-LGBT campaigns have focused on issues concerning LGBT teachers; and for decades a set of court battles have been waged by LGBT teachers over this issue. Nondiscrimination laws and clauses in teacher union contracts can make it easier for LGBT teachers to be out, thereby serving as role models for LGBT youth, and can also make it safer to teachers and school staff to intervene in cases of anti-LGBT harassment and violence. Data from the *Nuestras Voces* study of Latino gay and bisexual men from 1998 to1999 show that the presence of an adult gay role model while growing up increases self-esteem, lowers psychological distress and lessens the likelihood of engaging in risky sexual behaviors. Another study suggests that openly gay teachers may serve an important role in the development of students. However, as of 2003 it is legal in the majority of states to fire teachers, staff, and administrators on the basis of their sexual orientation or gender identity.

## The Anti-Gay Movement's Use of Education Issues in Ballot Campaigns

Since the first wave of anti-LGBT activism in the 1970s, issues of youth and education have been central. In the first nationally prominent anti-LGB initiative, in Miami in 1977, singer Anita Bryant vowed to "Save Our Children" from alleged homosexual recruitment by repealing the sexual orientation nondiscrimination law passed by Miami-Dade County earlier that year. Following Bryant's more than 2-to-1 victory, five anti-LGB ballot questions ensued across the United States in 1978. One, the Briggs Initiative on the California statewide ballot, would have barred open homosexuals from teaching in the state's public schools. But after the state's political establishment—including former governor Ronald Reagan, Governor Jerry Brown, and President Jimmy Carter— spoke out against the initiative, voters rejected Briggs. Anti-LGBT school initiatives continue, such as a 2000 initiative, rejected by Oregon voters, that would have banned any neutral or positive discussion of homosexuality in the state's public schools and colleges, including explicit HIV prevention education. Even as recently as the March 2003 Supreme Court hearing on a challenge to the Texas sodomy law, Chief Justice Rehnquist asked whether an equal protection finding would require municipalities to hire gay people as kindergarten teachers.

## Conclusion

Youth are the cutting edge of social change, and LGBT youth are coming out at younger ages. Schools are struggling to keep up. Eight states have adopted nondiscrimination or anti-harassment laws, as have many municipalities. Some districts have taken affirmative steps, conducting teacher and staff training and promoting GSAs. But education policy remains a key site of political struggle between the movement for LGBT equality and liberation and anti-LGBT forces.

### Bibliography

Chase, Bob. *Memorandum to National Education Association Board of Directors Re: Report of the NEA Task Force on Sexual Orientation.* Washington: National Education Association, 14 January 2002.

Diaz, Rafael, and George Ayala. *Social Discrimination and Health: The Case of Latino Gay Men and HIV Risk.* New York: Policy Institute of the National Gay and Lesbian Task Force, 2001.

Griffin, Pat and M.L. Ouellett. "Going Beyond Gay-Straight Alliances to Make Schools Safe for Lesbian, Gay, Bisexual and Transgender Students." *Angles,* 6(1). Amherst, MA: Institute for Gay and Lesbian Strategic Studies, 2002.

Kosciw, Joseph, and M.K. Cullen. *The 2001 National School Climate Survey: The School Related Experiences of Our Nation's Lesbian, Gay, Bisexual and Transgender Youth.* Washington: Gay, Lesbian and Straight Education Network, 2001.

Kumashiro, Kevin. *Troubling Intersections of Race and Sexuality: Queer Students of Color and Anti-Oppressive Education.* New York: Rowman and Littlefield, 2001.

Lambda Legal Defense and Education Fund. (1996, Nov.). "Case: *Nabozny v. Podlesny.*" 92 F.3rd 446 (7th Cir. 1996).

Lambda Legal Defense and Education Fund and Gay, Lesbian and Straight Education Network. *A Guide to Effective Statewide Laws/Policies: Preventing Discrimination Against LGBT Students in K-12 Schools.* New York, NY: Lambda and GLSEN, 2001.

Massachusetts Department of Education, *Youth Risk Behavior Survey,* 2000.

Miller, Neil. *Out of the Past: Gay and Lesbian History from 1869 to the Present.* New York: Vintage Books, 1995.

Rofes, Eric. "Young Adult Reflections on Having an Openly Gay Teacher During Early Adolescence." *Education and Urban Society,* 32(3). May 2000.

Ryan, Caitlin. *A Review of the Professional Literature and Research Needs for LGBT Youth of Color.* New York, NY: National Youth Advocacy Coalition, 2002.

Ryan, Caitlin and D. Futterman. *Lesbian & Gay Youth: Care and Counseling.* New York: Columbia University Press, 1998.

Schneider, M. E. and Owens, R. E. (2000). "Concern for Lesbian, Gay and Bisexual Kids: The Benefits for all Children." *Education & Urban Society,* 32(3): 349-68.

Szalacha, Laura. "Safe Schools Program for Gay and Lesbian Students," *Girls Coalition of Greater Boston Newsletter,* Fall 2001.

Varney, J.A. "Undressing the Normal: Community Efforts for Queer Asian and Asian American Youth." In Kumashiro, K. *Troubling Intersections of Race and Sexuality: Queer Students of Color and Anti-Oppressive Education.* New York: Rowman and Littlefield Publishers, 2001.

Yang, Alan. *From Wrongs to Rights: Public Opinion on Gay and Lesbian Americans Moves Toward Equality.* New York: Policy Institute of the National Gay and Lesbian Task Force, 1999.

**Sean Cahill**

*See also* ANTIDISCRIMINATION LAW AND POLICY; COLLEGES AND UNIVERSITIES; CRIME AND CRIMINALIZATION; EMPLOYMENT LAW AND POLICY; FEDERAL LAW AND POLICY.

**EHRHARDT, ANKE.** see MONEY, JOHN, AND ANKE EHRHARDT.

# EICHELBERGER, Ethyl (b. 17 July 1945; d. 12 August 1990), performer, playwright.

A central figure in the East Village scene in New York City during the 1980s, Ethyl Eichelberger was born James Roy Eichelberger in Pekin, Illinois. His stage debut was in his elementary school's production of *Hansel and Gretel.* He played the Wicked Witch in a pink yarn wig and black crepe paper dress made by his mother and claimed to have never recovered from the experience.

In high school Eichelberger emerged as an overachiever and drama queen and was cast in a major role in nearly each production. Eichelberger attended Knox College in nearby Galesburg, Illinois, where he portrayed the title roles in both *Hamlet* and *Oedipus Rex.* While at Knox he also directed a production of Jean Genet's *The Maids.* After two years at Knox, Eichelberger transferred to the American Academy of Dramatic Arts in New York City. Here, at the invitation of one of his classmates, he attended a rehearsal of Charles Ludlam and his newly formed Ridiculous Theatrical Company. Graduating from the Academy in 1967, he was asked to become part of the Ridiculous but instead became a member of the Trinity Repertory Company in Providence, Rhode Island. Here for the next seven years under the direction of

Adrian Hall, he became the company's lead character actor, portraying over thirty roles.

In 1972 Eichelberger abandoned his career at Trinity and took Ludlam up on his offer. Moving back to New York City, he became part of the Ridiculous and, to help support himself, a licensed hairdresser. Eichelberger acted in ten or more productions with the Ridiculous as well as styling wigs for many more. At this time he also had his full back tattooed and changed his first name to Ethyl. The new name was in homage to Barrymore, Merman, and Mertz, whom he called the great Ethels of theater; he employed the alternate spelling, however, for its gender ambiguity and petroleum-based chemical associations. The tattoo was an image of himself as an angel in drag.

Once with the Ridiculous, Eichelberger found himself yearning for more. He now began to write, produce, and perform his own plays. This body of some thirty solo and group performance pieces were based on the lives of great women of history, literature, and myth and include such works as *Phedre* (1972), *Medea* (1980), *Carlotta, Empress of Mexico* (1980), *Jocasta or Boy Crazy* (1982), *Lucrezia Borgia* (1982), *Lola Montez* (1982), and *Klytemnestra* (1985). These biographical, poetic miniplays about strong women who survived against all odds paralleled Eichelberger's experiences as a gay man.

Eichelberger performed these works in rotating repertory at spaces including the Pyramid Club, King Tut's Wah-Wah Hut, 8 B.C., Dixon Place, Gusto House, PS 122, and the Dance Theatre Workshop. Garnering a devoted cult following as well as high critical praise and accolades including an Obie Award, Eichelberger became a guiding spirit of the East Village scene. His work's gender play, mix of high and low culture, and grab bag aesthetic were typical of the era. His high octane performances might incorporate anything from accordion-accompanied songs to fire eating to fits of improvisation to cartwheels and splits. He would even perform his tattoo dance framed in a backless gown. Upon turning forty, Eichelberger, while continuing to perform female roles frequently, began to write a series of male roles for himself including *Leer* (1985), *Rip Van Winkle* (1986), and *The Tempest of Chim-Lee* (1987).

Beyond the fringe, Eichelberger also had a successful commercial theater career in productions from *The Comedy of Errors* at Lincoln Center in 1987 to a 1989 Broadway production of *Three Penny Opera* with Sting. He was also part of the cast of a children's TV show, *Encyclopedia,* produced by Home Box Office. His renown also allowed him to tour many of his plays nationwide and worldwide from England to Australia.

In 1990, two weeks after closing his last play, Eichelberger committed suicide. Diagnosed HIV positive several years before but never revealing his status to anyone until a few weeks before his death, and even then only to a handful of people, Eichelberger slit his wrists in a bathtub. His suicide is often conflated with artists who died of AIDS and stands in marked contrast to the "We Are Women Who Survive" theme song of his plays. At the time of Eichelberger's death, his impact on the performance scene was called "indisputable" by the *New York Times* and continues into the twenty-first century. His legend can also be felt in several novels, including Matthew Stadler's *The Sex Offender* (1994), Michael Cunningham's *Flesh and Blood* (1995), and Tom Spanbauer's *In the City of Shy Hunters* (2001), where he serves as the inspiration for fictional characters.

**Bibliography**

Eichelberger, Ethyl. "Nefert-iti." In *Extreme Exposure: An Anthology of Solo Performance Texts from the Twentieth Century.* Edited by Jo Bonney. New York: Theatre Communications Group, 2000.

Oxman, Steve. "Marzipan upon a Birthday Cake: An Interview with Ethyl Eichelberger." *Theatre* 21, no. 3 (Summer–Fall 1990): 66–73.

Smith, Ronn. "Ethyl Eichelberger." *Theater Crafts* 23, no. 1 (January 1989): 28–33, 51–52.

**Joe E. Jeffreys**

*See also* LUDLAM, CHARLES.

# ELECTORAL POLITICS

Visible participation in electoral politics was an element of the U.S. LGBT political movement from its early years in the 1960s and early 1970s. Shifts toward greater public acceptance of sexual diversity, increases in the visibility of sexual minorities in large cities, the mobilization of the religious right, and the political needs associated with the AIDS epidemic augmented the urgency and strategic plausibility of LGBT participation in electoral politics in the 1980s and 1990s.

Electoral engagement has taken several forms: mounting openly LGBT candidacies for public office; mobilizing LGBT-positive voters and donors; organizing activist groups and networks inside political parties; and countering anti-LGBT referenda and supporting positive ones. The unusually large number of electoral offices in the United States and the relative permeability of the major political parties created openings for LGBT involvement even at an early stage of political mobilization when the chances for serious impact on electoral outcomes were modest.

## Open Candidacies

In 1960 San Francisco drag performer José Sarria became the first openly LGBT person to seek electoral office, running unsuccessfully for the city's Board of Supervisors. This was an early example of seasoned activists using mainstream electoral processes to register protest and to provide vehicles for challenging discrimination and exclusion. Gay Activists Alliance veteran Jim Owles's 1973 run for a New York City Council seat followed that same tradition.

In 1974 Elaine Noble's election to the Massachusetts House of Representatives as the first openly LGBT candidate to hold office at the state level marked the beginning of a new phase in electoral politics. A year earlier, Nancy Wechsler and Jerry DeGrieck had come out as members of Ann Arbor's city council in Michigan. In the spring of 1974, Kathy Kozachenko won a seat on the same body after running as openly lesbian. Later that year, Minnesota State Senator Alan Spears came out as gay. In 1977 Harvey Milk was elected to local office, gaining a foothold for openly LGBT candidates in San Francisco that expanded in the decades following his 1978 assassination. It was only when Sherry Harris was elected to Seattle's City Council in 1991 that the first African American joined these growing ranks.

Gerry Studds became the first federal politician to come out in 1983. First elected in 1972 as a member of the U.S. House of Representatives from Massachusetts, he affirmed his homosexuality nine years later in the face of rebuke over an earlier sexual relationship. In 1987 Barney Frank came out as gay, having served in national office since 1981. Like Studds, Frank survived a "scandal" associated with his homosexuality and built unassailable majorities in his Massachusetts district. In the 1990s two Republican members of the House of Representatives (Steve Gunderson and Jim Kolbe) came out as gay. In 1998 Wisconsin's Tammy Baldwin became the first lesbian member of Congress and the first man or woman elected to federal office to be open about his or her homosexuality from the outset of a campaign.

In 1991, modeled on such women's movement organizations as EMILY's List, the LGBT Victory Fund was formed to support such candidacies. It raised and channeled donations to support the electoral races of viable candidates who were prepared to adopt assertive positions on issues related to sexual diversity. By the first years of the twenty-first century, there were over 225 openly LGBT politicians elected to office in the United States. This represented a small portion of the more than half million elected positions across the country and was still a phenomenon largely restricted to progressive regions or districts with high concentrations of LGBT voters, but it nonetheless represented a major gain in public recognition.

## Referenda

Activist engagement in electoral politics became inescapable as religious conservatives promoted referenda to strike down measures aimed at prohibiting discrimination based on sexual orientation. The first such instance followed the 1977 enactment of a nondiscrimination ordinance in Dade County, Florida, when Anita Bryant led a successful repeal campaign. The religious right, already mobilized by the 1973 U.S. Supreme Court decision on abortion (*Roe v. Wade*), now turned its attention to sexual "deviance." As a result, electoral cycles began to include recurrent threats to the rights of sexual minorities. In 1978, for example, California voters faced a referendum promoted by state representative John Briggs aimed at allowing school authorities to fire LGBT teachers, forcing large-scale defensive mobilization.

The 1980s witnessed several anti-LGBT referenda, many of them successful. The early 1990s saw religious conservatives mounting ambitious statewide campaigns in Oregon and Colorado to prohibit nondiscrimination measures from covering sexual orientation. Colorado's Amendment 2 was struck down by the U.S. Supreme Court in 1996, by which time the balance between losses and wins was shifting toward more favorable outcomes. But anti-LGBT initiatives have remained a fact of life across the country. This has forced sexual diversity activists to be vigilantly attentive to the electoral process and has served as a reminder to national organizations that state and local politics are crucial arenas worthy of their attention.

## Party Politics

Although U.S. party organizations are relatively weak compared to those of other countries, the opposition between Democrats and Republicans still dominates the electoral process. U.S. parties are relatively easy to enter, and many interest groups and social movement networks have organized inside them—often forming specialized Democratic and Republican "clubs." LGBT activists have operated visibly within the Democratic Party especially since the early 1970s, and in both major parties such work increased noticeably beginning in the 1980s. The influence of the religious right on the Republican Party from the 1970s onward increased the stakes for pro-LGBT activists on both sides of the partisan divide.

Such activists were more visible than ever on the Democratic side in the 1980 campaign, and the convention that year passed the party's first national resolution opposing anti-LGBT discrimination. The same convention also saw the name of openly gay African American Mel Boozer placed in nomination for the vice presidential slot on the Democratic ticket. The 1992 campaign broke new ground in the amount of organizing among sexual minorities and fundraising inside the party, and the extent to which candidates for the presidential nomination, including Bill Clinton, vied for the LGBT vote.

In many parts of the United States, however, there were significant minorities of Democratic politicians and voters opposed to any official recognition of sexual diversity, and as a result, the party as a whole was often cautious about taking assertively pro-LGBT positions. The conflagration and rout that resulted from the Clinton administration's 1993 attempt to lift the military ban prohibiting lesbians and gays from military service was a constant reminder of the risks associated with what was consistently viewed as a dangerously controversial issue. The persistence of anti-LGBT election campaigning, most often by Republicans, further solidified fears of appearing too pro-LGBT in many parts of the country.

LGBT organizing within the Republican Party began in earnest much later than in the Democratic Party and continued to encounter more internal resistance. The 1988 party convention saw growth in activist numbers, and two years later a number of local Republican clubs joined to form the Log Cabin Federation. In a party still so heavily influenced by the religious right, however, there were often heated struggles to obtain even elementary recognition. The conservative religious influence on the party persisted through the 1990s and into the current century, even in areas (like the Pacific Northwest) generally thought to have lower levels of religious fervor and conservatism than average.

National LGBT organizations became more active in partisan and electoral politics during the 1980s and 1990s. The National Gay and Lesbian Task Force (NGLTF) became a multipurpose national group in 1972 and supported a range of political initiatives that included work within the electoral mainstream. The Human Rights Campaign Fund or HRC (later "Fund" was dropped from the organization's name) was more resolutely focused on mainstream activism from its founding in 1980 and therefore deeply involved in partisan and electoral politics from the start. HRC sought to establish visibility for issues of sexual diversity at national party conventions, produced voting guides, and raised money for politicians who had provided at least some support for legislative initiatives, in addition to its extensive lobbying campaigns.

## Voters

The profile of electoral politics in the activist movement's agenda owes some of its growth to the emergence of big city neighborhoods identified with sexual diversity. They provided a base from which many openly LGBT candidacies took off and a draw to supportive politicians seeking endorsement within a constituency with relatively high voter turnouts.

LGBT constituencies, or at least those within them prepared to identify themselves as such, are significantly more progressive than the average American on a number of issues. Not surprisingly, in comparison to the general public, they are less supportive of traditional family values, more supportive of a woman's right to reproductive choice, more concerned about health care, and more in favor of a larger role for government.

In big city electoral contests, such constituencies are most often courted openly and persistently by progressive Democrats. LGBT activism inside the party reinforces the readiness of candidates to view sexual minority voting as important and to adopt pro-LGBT positions in their platforms. But in some urban areas and elsewhere, Democratic politicians' concern about straying too far left of center will produce circumspection on sexual diversity, especially after the primary process has secured their party's nomination and they must now face the larger electorate.

Republican candidates for office in areas with visible LGBT populations are often forced to fashion appeals to such voters, but they are regularly burdened with state and national party platforms at odds with voter opinion. Most Republican hopefuls, in fact, have to ensure the support of religious conservatives to gain their party's nomination. Some then attempt an awkward retreat to the middle once the nomination is in hand. Not surprisingly, self-identified LGBT voters are more than twice as likely to be Democrats as they are to be Republicans, even more so in urban areas.

## Tensions within the Movement

The commitment of activist energy and resources to electoral politics has created internal tensions. Many LGBT activists share with the general population the widely held resentment and cynicism about party politics and elections. The Clinton presidency sharpened internal debates on this front. The unprecedented access provided by that administration to movement representatives, combined with advances on AIDS and federal employment discrimination, convinced many activists that an investment in electoral politics reaped rewards. But for others, the failures associated with the struggle over the military ban led to new or intensified disillusionment with just such politics.

Involvement in electoral politics of course raises the profile of partisan divisions within the movement. Democratic and Republican activists are under pressure to display party loyalty, especially if they are to have any chance of access to the party's leadership. Those who are most intensely partisan are also likely to overstate the internal support they find for causes related to sexual diversity, further sharpening the party division. The tendency to focus attacks on LGBT activists in the opposing partisan camp is widespread, and especially among LGBT Republicans who see the entire LGBT movement as excessively supportive of the Democratic Party.

Internal differences are reinforced by the compromises that electoral politics entail. There are pressures on movement representatives to trim their demands or expectations to secure gains or prevent losses, and these pressures are felt most strongly by activists regularly operating inside mainstream institutions. The likelihood of differences of opinion with and isolation from other activists is strong. The sheer number of elections in the U.S. system means that any political movement seeking to place its issues before the public has to mobilize large forces and raise a great deal of money. Outcomes are hard to measure and dramatic political gains unlikely, so the wisdom of expending those kinds of movement resources on electoral politics is often challenged by activists.

Electoral politics also highlights differences in visibility and influence within the movement. A political system so driven by money makes electoral candidacy dependent on links to fundraising networks, which vary significantly across gender, class, and racial lines. Activist standing in that process or inside parties is enhanced by the appearance of respectability, professional expertise, and access to fundraising capacity. All of this contributes to the public face of electoral work remaining heavily male, Caucasian, upper-middle-class, and gay or lesbian rather than bisexual or transgender. Movement activists have been challenging those patterns, but struggle to do so within a political system that has deeply entrenched patterns of hierarchy and exclusion.

There is, however, no escape from electoral engagement. Abandoning the field expands the risk of significant political losses. Although religious and other conservatives have shared some of the disillusion experienced by sexual diversity activists about the cost/benefit ratios in electoral politics, they show no serious signs of abandoning the venture. The high stakes in U.S. partisan and electoral politics make LGBT involvement in them critical and inevitable.

### Bibliography

Bailey, Robert W. *Gay Politics, Urban Politics: Identity and Economics in the Urban Setting.* New York: Columbia University Press, 1999.

Rayside, David. *On the Fringe: Gays and Lesbians in Politics.* Ithaca, N.Y.: Cornell University Press, 1998.

Rimmerman, Craig A., Kenneth D. Wald, and Clyde Wilcox, eds. *The Politics of Gay Rights.* Chicago: University of Chicago Press, 2000.

Sharp, Elaine B., ed. *Culture Wars and Local Politics.* Lawrence: University Press of Kansas, 1999

Thompson, Mark, ed. *Long Road to Freedom: The Advocate History of the Gay and Lesbian Movement.* New York: St. Martin's Press, 1994.

Yeager, Ken. *Trailblazers: Profiles of America's Gay and Lesbian Elected Officials.* New York: Haworth Press, 1999.

**David Rayside**

*See also* ATLANTA; BOOZER, MELVIN; DEMOCRATIC PARTY; FEDERAL LAW AND POLICY; FRANK, BARNEY; HUMAN RIGHTS CAMPAIGN; KAMENU, FRANKLIN; LATINA AND LATINO LGBTQ ORGANIZATIONS AND PERIODICALS; MILK, HARVEY; NATIONAL GAY AND LESBIAN TASK FORCE (NGLTF); NEW RIGHT; NOBLE, ELAINE; POLITICAL SCANDALS; REPUBLICAN PARTY; SARRIA, JOSÉ.

# ELLIS, Ruth (b. 23 July 1899; d. 5 October 2000), activist, entrepreneur, printer, photographer.

Ruth Ellis often said that she was just an ordinary person. The centenarian believed that she had become famous because she was so old. Her experiences as an African American lesbian during a century of tremendous change often ran counter to the history of racism, sexism, and homophobia of the times. Her choice to share her life as an out lesbian senior offers an opportunity for a more critical understanding of U.S. history and serves as a reminder of the multitude of stories of ordinary LGBT people that remain untold.

Ruth Charlotte Ellis was born and raised in Springfield, Illinois. Her mother, Carrie Faro Ellis, died of a stroke when Ruth was twelve years old. The dominant influence in Ellis's early life was her father, Charles Ellis, the first African American postman in Springfield. He loved literature and music, and education was of the

339

utmost importance to him. Ruth and her brothers, Charles, Wellington, and Harry, all played musical instruments. The library in their home included the complete works of Shakespeare as well as many other authors and reference books.

Ellis attended predominantly white public schools. She grew up during a time when African Americans were not allowed the same social, cultural, and educational opportunities as white Americans. These limitations restricted the advancement of African Americans, yet Ellis graduated from Springfield High School in 1919, an unusual accomplishment for an African American woman at a time when only 16 percent of all Americans completed high school. After graduation, Ellis apprenticed with a printer and learned the trade. Her brother Harry, who was also thought to be gay, graduated from the medical school at the University of Illinois and became the first black doctor in Champaign-Urbana, Illinois.

Ellis never hid her sexual orientation. Her initial crush was on her high school gym teacher. Her father and brothers knew that she was a lesbian and accepted her. According to Ellis, she had it pretty easy being a lesbian. She said that she was never subjected to any cruel treatment.

Ellis met her life companion, Ceciline "Babe" Franklin, during her mid-thirties, in 1936; they were together for more than thirty-four years. In 1937 they moved to Detroit. Franklin worked as a cook and Ellis as a nanny until she found a printing job. The women took an unusual step for the time and became home owners. When her brother Harry died, Ellis used her inheritance to open Ellis and Franklin Printing. In 1946 Ruth Ellis became the first woman to own her own printing business in northwestern Detroit. According to Ellis, being gay did not hurt her business. Her primary customers were churches in the community. Later she added photography to her business. By reading books she taught herself how to shoot, develop, and hand-color black and white photographs.

From 1946 to 1971, Ellis's home was known as the Gay Spot. For many decades, midwestern African American gay men and lesbians found her home to be an alternative to the bar scene that discriminated against them. It was a refuge of sorts to African Americans who came out before the civil rights movement and the Stonewall Riots. Ellis offered lodging to black gay men newly arrived from the South and helped many of the young men and women through college. She also provided social services to others in the community. Ellis opened her home to battered women and their children and even gave her car to a large family because she felt they needed it more than she did. "We tried to help," recalled Ellis. "It wasn't much, because we didn't have much, but it helped them a little."

Ellis was seventy-nine when she began a new life as an activist and cherished elder in the LGBT community. It all began because Ellis decided to take a self-defense class. She took one look at her teacher, Jaye Spiro, and just knew she was a lesbian. When Spiro realized that Ellis was also lesbian, she introduced her to Detroit's white lesbian community. Soon LGBT people of all races from around the world began to embrace her. Suddenly, Ellis found herself dancing at lesbian bars, speaking to youth groups, holding workshops, and attending the Michigan Women's Music Festival, all the while advocating greater awareness of and support for seniors from younger members of the gay and lesbian community. "I'm just a common, ordinary person who has enjoyed life," Ellis commented. When asked about the recognition she received gracefully late in her life, she simply stated: "I am the oldest lesbian that they know." On 5 October 2000, Ruth Ellis passed away peacefully at home in her sleep. She was 101.

## Bibliography

Andrews, Nancy. *Family: A Portrait of Gay and Lesbian America*. San Francisco: HarperCollins, 1994.

Jewell, Terri. "Interview with Miss Ruth." In *Piece of My Heart: A Lesbian of Colour Anthology*. Edited by Makeda Silvera. Toronto: Sister Vision Press, 1991.

"Ruth Ellis: 1899–2000, a Celebration of Her Life." Available from http://www-lib.usc.edu/~retter/ruthmain.html.

"Sisters in the Life—Ruth Ellis." Available from http://www.sistersinthelife.com.

Thorpe, Rochella. "A House Where Queers Go: African American Lesbian Nightlife in Detroit, 1940–1975." In *Inventing Lesbian Cultures in America*. Edited by Ellen Lewin. Boston: Beacon Press, 1996.

**Yvonne Welbon**

# ELTINGE, Julian (b. 14 May 1881 or 1883; d. 7 March 1941), singer, actor.

Julian Eltinge (née William Julian Dalton) was the most famous and successful female impersonator on the American and international stage and screen from 1900 to 1930. Over his career, Eltinge published his own magazine, co-owned a self-named Broadway theater, and endorsed nationally advertised products including corsets, cold creams, cigars, and a bust-enhancing patent medicine.

Eltinge was born in Newtonville, Massachusetts, near Boston, to Joseph Dalton and Julia Edna (Baker) Dalton. His father's mining interest took the family to Butte, Montana, where he attended school. Eltinge returned to Boston when he was seventeen, becoming a dry goods salesman.

One story of the origins of Eltinge's career as a female impersonator points to his appearance at the age of ten in the annual revue of Boston cadets. His talent attracted the attention of theatrical agents, and he quickly began performing in minor productions around the United States. Eltinge appeared in more than thirty-eight stage shows, in which he was usually billed in two roles, one male and one female. His first success was in the 1904 musical comedy *Mr. Wix of Wickham,* and international acclaim followed a 1906 engagement at London's Palace Theatre. His debut on the New York stage was in 1907 at the Alhambra Theater in an act that included the skit "The Sampson Girl," a riff on the Gibson Girl, a willowy, ultrafeminine vision of American womanhood made popular by the illustrator Charles Dana Gibson. In 1908, he traveled with the blackface minstrelsy troupe of George M. Cohan and Sam Harris, playing the role of Salome. Eltinge's greatest success was the musical comedy *The Fascinating Widow,* which opened at New York's Liberty Theater in September 1911. The show ran for only six performances but toured until 1914. By 1912, Eltinge was the highest paid act in vaudeville, earning a weekly salary of $1,625. He then starred in *The Crinoline Girl,* which opened at New York's Knickerbocker Theater in March 1914, running for eighty-eight performances.

Eltinge's stage success drew the attention of Hollywood, and he appeared in seventeen films from 1914 to 1941, many adapted from his stage roles. Film editing maximized the effects of his portrayal of both male and female characters. In 1916 he starred with Rudolf Valentino in *The Isle of Love,* which was remade as the 1922 film *An Adventuress,* a project that started rumors of a secret romance with Valentino. While appearing in films, Eltinge also found time to write, cast, and produce vaudeville sketches for his Julian Eltinge Players.

Many audiences reportedly believed they were watching a woman until Eltinge removed his wig sometime during the show. He was five feet, nine inches tall, with brown hair and blue eyes, and his weight fluctuated between 185 and 210 pounds. A forty-inch waist was reduced to twenty-four through the tightly laced corsets he humorously referred to as "old ironsides." Eltinge's act was noted for its uncanny imitation of conventionally

feminine ways of walking, singing, speaking, and dancing. He obsessed over the smallest details of his performance, taking two hours to prepare. Although he once said, "It depends on where you put the paint, not how much you splash on," Eltinge used makeup to cover all exposed parts of his body to create the illusion of shorter, tapered fingers, a slimmer neck, and almond-shaped eyes. Many of Eltinge's reviewers indicated a general distaste for the genre but cited the relative inoffensiveness of his show. "Eltinge always appeared as a young woman of refinement, good breeding, education and 'class'—if wicked she was only a trifle so—just enough wickedness to serve as sauce" (Bulliet, pp. 266–267).

The success and acceptance of Eltinge's onstage presence might be explained by his maintenance of a conventionally masculine persona offstage. Photographs show him conservatively attired in suit and tie, sometimes carrying a tennis racket, and journalists made a point to note Eltinge's athletic figure, deep voice, and gentlemanly manner. Although not much is known about his love life, Eltinge reacted strongly, often violently, to anyone who suggested he was homosexual. His press agents were careful to publicize an obsession with boxing and horseback riding, and the press eagerly recounted his barroom brawls and fistfights with stagehands. He once claimed that he was uncomfortable with his career as a female impersonator and only reluctantly continued it for the money until his serious acting ability was recognized. The stark contrast between Eltinge's stage performance of ideal femininity and the bellicose masculinity of the "real" man behind it suggests he astutely sought to assure the public that his act did not represent a threat to prevailing notions of gender and sexuality.

Eltinge himself never married, and for the last years of his life lived with his mother on his ranch in southern California. He died of a cerebral hemorrhage at his apartment in New York City.

**Bibliography**

Bulliet, C. J. *Venus Castina: Famous Female Impersonators, Celestial and Human.* New York: Covici Friede, 1928.

"Julian Eltinge: A Dressing Room Marvel." *Variety* 42, no. 1 (11 December 1909): 28, 153.

Moore, F. Michael. *Drag! Male and Female Impersonators on Stage, Screen, and Television: An Illustrated World History.* Jefferson, N.C.: McFarland, 1994.

**Michael J. Murphy**

*See also* DRAG QUEENS AND KINGS.

# EMPLOYMENT AND OCCUPATIONS

For much of the twentieth century, coming out in most workplaces as a homosexual or transgender person would have been scandalous and dangerous. In many situations, it would have resulted in immediate dismissal and loss of economic livelihood, not to mention physical violence. By the twenty-first century, more people had come out at work, and some workplaces were even welcoming sexual and gender diversity—but not everywhere and not for everyone. Variations in the environment for sexual and gender minorities persist within and between occupations, regions of the country, and organizations.

## Historical Background

**Before 1969.** There have always been spaces where LGBT people gathered and were out, but until the late twentieth century, such spaces were often transient, dangerous, and hidden, and they rarely included the workplace. Still, in spite of the prohibitions directed at homosexuality and gender nonconformity, some occupations, workplaces, parts of the country, and historic periods were less repressive than others.

Occupational ghettos for gay men formed around activities that were stigmatized as appropriate only for women—work involving the serving of women or jobs requiring stereotypically female attributes. Workers in this category included nurses, hairdressers, makeup and haute-couture workers, restaurant waiters, figure skaters, dancers, and artists. Some LGBT people ran small businesses such as design stores, restaurants, and beauty parlors as a way to avoid repressive work environments. Lesbian job ghettos formed in characteristically male-dominated occupations such as security work, bus and truck driving, factory work, and physical education, and in some cases in female-dominated niches such as nursing.

There were a few settings and historic periods with unusual levels of LGBT acceptance or presence. Randy Shilts has described openly gay and effeminate men avoiding discharge from the U.S. military of the 1940s by entertaining the troops and catering parties for the senior officers. Leisa Meyer has documented the strong presence, despite repressive conditions, of lesbians in the U.S. military during World War II. Allan Bérubé has highlighted the presence of openly gay waiters, cooks, and attendants on the luxury liners and freighters traveling the Pacific Ocean from the 1930s to the 1950s, many of them members of the progressive Marine Cooks and Stewards Union. When these ships were superceded by air travel, many of the men dry-docked in San Francisco, helping to position that city as America's "gay capital."

There were also opportunities for unusual openness within the LGBT economy itself for bartenders, restaurant and hotel staff, and catering personnel. As well, some support for sexual and gender minorities existed within religious organizations offering isolated, single-sex environments for priests, nuns, and monks. There are also stories of fairly open LGBT workers in the film industry of Hollywood, Macy's department stores, and other settings, but they are told as anomalies. Other occupational enclaves may have existed, but they have not yet been uncovered by scholars.

**McCarthyism and homophobia.** During the McCarthy era in the 1950s, homosexuality and gender nonconformity were linked with security risks, and LGBT people, many of whom were viewed as potential spies and traitors, were purged from jobs and ostracized in society. Thousands of people were expelled from the military, hundreds were forced to resign from government positions, and countless others were fired from jobs on the grounds of being (or suspected as) LGBT.

The repressive environment of the 1950s and early 1960s, however, fostered increasing LGBT occupational activism. Homophile groups such as the Mattachine Society; One, Inc.; and the Daughters of Bilitis often discussed occupational and employment issues in their publications (*Mattachine Review, ONE,* and the *Ladder),* highlighted employment discrimination issues in their public demonstrations, and supported early courts cases related to anti-LGBT employment discrimination. Frank Kameny, who had been fired from his job as a map expert with the army in 1957, formed a Washington, D.C., chapter of the Mattachine Society to give advice, coordinate legal action, and organize protests for LGBT civil servants who had lost their jobs because of discrimination. Almost all of these cases, including Kameny's, were unsuccessful, but important foundations were laid for later victories.

**1969 to 1980.** At the time of the 1969 Stonewall Riots in New York City, LGBT people were formally barred from employment in the military, the civil service, most government agencies, and occupations such as teaching. There were no fair employment protections for LGBT people in any jurisdiction, and workplaces could discriminate against them with impunity when making hiring, firing, and promotion decisions. Because of blatant discrimination and the serious consequences of losing a job, workplace concerns became a larger focus for activists in the post-Stonewall period.

In 1969, the Homophile Action League (HAL) of Philadelphia undertook what was probably the first formal survey of workplace discrimination. Of five hundred major East Coast employers surveyed, only twenty responded and only Bantam Books indicated that sexual orientation was irrelevant when making employment and promotion decisions. In a 1970 newsletter, HAL set the tone for activism of the period by suggesting that "homosexuals were more in need of an employment counselor than a psychiatrist" and calling on members "to break down those statutory and traditional laws and customs which deny us equal employment opportunities." HAL called for mobilization through "meetings, pickets, boycotts, publicity, and every other means possible and necessary."

Established in 1973, the National Gay and Lesbian Task Force quickly focused on workplace discrimination, successfully lobbying the U.S. Civil Service Commission to allow homosexuals to work for government agencies. The Human Rights Campaign Fund (HRC), formed in 1980, soon thereafter created WorkNet to concentrate on occupational issues.

**The 1980s.** Nondiscrimination policies covering sexual orientation, same-sex relationship recognition, and the provision of domestic partner benefits continued as key activist issues through the 1980s. Activism prospered in larger and university-based cities, local governments, the health-care sector, and the rapidly developing technology sector. Amherst, Massachusetts; Champaign, Illinois; San Francisco; Ann Arbor, Michigan; Austin, Texas; Berkeley, California; and Urbana, Illinois, were among cities that included sexual orientation in workplace nondiscrimination policies by the early 1980s. Wisconsin became the first state to pass such a law in 1982. AT&T and IBM are credited with being the first major companies to add sexual orientation to their nondiscrimination policies, and Lotus is credited as the first large private-sector company to offer same-sex benefits programs. The spread of legal protections from the mid-1980s onward was bolstered by the impact of AIDS. The epidemic exposed new sources of discrimination and homophobia and highlighted the necessity of obtaining employer-based health benefits.

Nevertheless, the threat of being harassed, dismissed, or having a career derailed if one came out continued in many organizations. Some people adapted by gravitating to occupations, locations, and organizations perceived as "gay-friendly." Others adapted by compartmentalizing their work and nonwork life in a way unknown to most heterosexuals. James Woods's engaging study *The Corporate Closet* highlights the tactics used by professional gay men in the late 1980s to manage their sexual identity, including the fabrication of a false identity while at work.

**The 1990s.** Several high-profile cases in the early 1990s solidified the workplace as a site of and for activism. The 1991 firing of a cook at a Cracker Barrel restaurant because she was a lesbian, the on-the-job "gay-bashing" of a Detroit postal worker, and the intense harassment of Ron Woods after his homosexuality became known at a Chrysler plant in Michigan all sparked national protests. Fueling activism further was the 1993 announcement by three Oklahoma congressmen that they would never hire openly LGBT people, and the military's reassertion that the ban on gays and lesbians would continue. In 1992, for the first time in American history, sexual orientation discrimination at work erupted as a significant issue in the presidential elections. While Bill Clinton was actively courting the LGBT vote, promising to confront the military ban and enact antidiscrimination legislation, the presidential hopeful Ross Perot reaffirmed his stance that employers had the right to anti-LGBT bias.

Persistent activism related to employment discrimination yielded significant results in the 1990s, with more states and municipalities banning job discrimination on the basis of sexual orientation. In 1997, San Francisco passed its historic Equal Benefits Ordinance requiring organizations doing business with the city to provide health benefits to same-sex couples. The ordinance was adamantly opposed by corporations that were based elsewhere but conducted business in San Francisco. Companies such as Federal Express and United Airlines lodged legal challenges to the ordinance on the grounds that it attempted to regulate employment norms beyond the jurisdiction of San Francisco, but all were unsuccessful.

Some of the most dramatic developments were at the federal level. Once in power, Clinton capitulated on a promise to end the military ban, but in 1995 he issued an executive order barring discrimination based on sexual orientation in the granting of security clearances, and in 1998 he signed an executive order banning discrimination on the basis of sexual orientation throughout the federal civil service. Equally dramatic, after years of avoiding the issue, labor unions began to bargain for same-sex benefits coverage. Labor's support increased in 1997 with the endorsement of Pride at Work (a national association for LGBT labor) as a constituency group by the American Federation of Labor–Congress of Industrial Organizations (AFL–CIO).

## LGBT Employment and Occupational Groups

A particularly important development that began in the 1970s and accelerated in the 1980s and 1990s was the establishment of employment and occupational groups by LGBT people. These groups provided a forum for people to come out at work to a select few, network, and eventually exert pressure on employers.

Librarians and teachers were the first occupational group to organize formally around LGBT rights. The American Library Association's Task Force on Gay Liberation, created in 1970 and still active (in 2003 as the Gay, Lesbian, Bisexual and Transgender Roundtable), stands as the nation's first professional organization devoted to LGBT issues. In 1969, the California Federation of Teachers passed a resolution calling for an end to discrimination against gay and lesbian teachers, and the American Federation of Teachers passed a similar motion in 1970. By the mid-1970s, there were gay and lesbian teachers' associations in New York, Boston, San Francisco, and Los Angeles (subsequently expanded to deal with bisexual and transgender issues). As a measure of the hostility teachers faced even within their profession, the Lesbian and Gay Teachers Association of New York lobbied for three years before successfully placing an advertisement announcing the group in the New York State United Teachers Association newsletter.

College and university professors were next. A Gay and Lesbian Caucus of the Modern Language Association formed by 1974 and within a decade had around two hundred fifty members. The Committee on Lesbian and Gay History formed in 1979 and gained official recognition as an affiliate of the American Historical Association in 1982. Anthropologists, sociologists, and political scientists were also early organizers. These academic caucuses aimed to promote the study of sexuality in their respective fields, prevent discrimination within their professions, and facilitate broader communication among scholars. The Gay, Lesbian, and Bisexual Political Science Caucus of the American Political Science Association (APSA), for example, facilitated the preparation of a 1995 report on the status of lesbians and gays in the profession. The report became the basis for a series of recommendations related to increased recognition of sexual and gender diversity issues within and beyond the profession, all of which were approved by the APSA.

Doctors, psychiatrists, psychologists, and allied health-care professionals were also early to organize pressure and support groups around LGBT concerns. Following a campaign that in 1973 convinced the American Psychiatric Association (APA) to declassify homosexuality as a mental illness, the Caucus of Gay, Lesbian, and Bisexual members of the APA was established in the mid-1970s, and forced the APA to undertake a major review of its policies related to gays and lesbians in 1978. In 1985, the caucus became the Association of Gay and Lesbian Psychiatrists, a separate organization affiliated with the APA but not bound by its policies. The American Psychological Association established its Committee on

Lesbian, Gay, and Bisexual Concerns in 1980, and a year later the American Association of Physicians for Human Rights (later renamed the Gay and Lesbian Medical Association) was formed with a mandate inclusive of transgender issues.

**Large corporations and the federal government.** The first employee-based group focusing on equal rights for LGBT workers in a private-sector workplace was established in 1987 at AT&T's Denver operations, under the acronym LEAGUE (Lesbian, Bisexual, Gay, and Transgender United Employees). By 1992, LEAGUE had grown to fourteen chapters, organized an AT&T-wide conference, and was incorporating bisexual and transgender issues into its agenda as well. LGBT groups were formed at IBM, Xerox, Intel, Lucent, Dupont, Chevron, Shell, and Ford, among others. Among the earliest public-sector groups was the federal government workers' organization called GLOBE (Gay, Lesbian, Bisexual Employees), which spawned subgroups in various federal departments and agencies.

These groups typically began informally, enlarging their membership by word of mouth and advertisements in the LGBT press. Gradually, they became more formal and more assertive with employers. They focused on nondiscrimination provisions and equitable domestic partner benefits, then pushed for LGBT issues to be included in a wider range of activities such as diversity training programs and recruiting.

Developments at a relatively traditional company such as Ford provide a good example of the impact of an LGBT group. Ford GLOBE began in 1994, becoming an officially recognized employee resource group a year later. In 1998, it convinced Ford to include sexual orientation in its equal opportunity and affirmative action statement, a first for the automobile sector. By 1999, GLOBE had moved the company far enough along that it was listed on the Gay and Lesbian Values Index (later known as the HRC Corporate Equality Index). After the Big Three automakers announced that they would provide same-sex partner health-care benefits in 2000, arguably with Ford in the lead, GLOBE pushed the company to expand this to an even wider package of benefits, including legal planning for same-sex partners. GLOBE also worked with Ford to identify business possibilities in the LGBT marketplace. A similar relationship existed between IBM's EAGLE (Employee Alliance for Gay, Lesbian, Bisexual, and Transgender Empowerment) and the company for which its members worked.

HRC estimated that there were 282 LGBT employee groups in 2003. Groups existed to represent sexual and gender minorities within specific organizations, sectors, industries, and occupations. Examples included Digital Queers, National Gay Pilots Association, National Gay Journalists Association, Gay and Lesbian Prison and Correction Employees, National Organization of Gay and Lesbian Scientists and Technical Professionals, Gay and Lesbian Medical Association, and Harvard Gay and Lesbian Caucus.

Some groups have had more success than others. GALAXE (Gays and Lesbians at Xerox), for instance, has overseen the inclusion of gender identity in nondiscrimination policies at Xerox, whereas KOLAGE (Coca-Cola Lesbian and Gay Employees), the LGBT support group for Coca-Cola workers, remains an independent group, not endorsed by, sponsored by, or affiliated with the corporation. On its Web site in the early 2000s, KOLAGE envisioned "a global Coca-Cola system where lesbians and gays are ensured basic equal rights." Some groups, such as the one at Intel, eschewed a political mandate. Others, such as the one at Chrysler, formed with a very specific goal (benefit coverage) and then disbanded. The large majority of these groups, however, have been officially sanctioned and work in partnership with management, and many have evolved into broader-based "straight-gay-diversity" alliances.

## The Twenty-first Century

By the early twenty-first century, there had been unprecedented change. Surveys demonstrated that 75 percent of Americans believed that there should be laws to protect gays and lesbians from discrimination in job opportunities, that 70 percent believed health-care benefits should be available for same-sex domestic partners, and that 59 percent believed gays and lesbians should be allowed to serve openly in the military. There were openly LGBT politicians, doctors, lawyers, corporate executives, firefighters, police officers, secretaries, accountants, and athletes. Many occupational associations, including those for nurses, teachers, and doctors, had affirmed the right of members to be out at work and censured members who discriminated.

Sampling problems have so far precluded a reliable, large-scale survey of occupational decision-making by LGBT people. However, it is likely that when LGBT people make occupational choices, they make them not only on the basis of their skills, talents, and interests, but also by taking into account the steps that occupations and institutions have taken to ensure fair and equal treatment.

By March 2003, according to HRC, fourteen states and the District of Columbia had banned employment discrimination based on sexual orientation, and eight additional states had bans covering only the public sector. Minnesota, Rhode Island, and New Mexico also had provisions prohibiting discrimination on the basis of gender identity, and Connecticut, New Jersey, New York, Massachusetts, and Washington, D.C., had statutes read by courts as prohibiting discrimination against transgender people. HRC also estimated that nearly six thousand organizations offered domestic partner health benefits, pointing to Eastman Kodak, Xerox, Nike, and American Airlines as among the best.

**Continuing contradictions.** In spite of advances, many contradictions remained. Fifty-five percent of LGBT persons attested to facing discrimination in applying for or keeping a job. The majority of states and many cities and organizations still did not ban job discrimination on the basis of sexual orientation and/or gender identity. Perot Systems and ExxonMobil stood out as companies that had gone so far as to discontinue domestic partner programs, while Wal-Mart fell into a group of companies that did not resist legal change but were painfully slow to take affirming actions on their own. (Wal-Mart only added sexual orientation to its nondiscrimination policies in June 2003.) There was still no federal nondiscrimination legislation protecting Americans from being fired from their jobs for their sexual orientation or gender identity, and the military continued to discharge LGBT people for revealing that they were LGB.

The gains achieved have been largely confined to LGB people. Those who challenge gender, dress, or cosmetic norms continue to face an extremely hostile workplace environment. People living in rural locations, working for small businesses, or employed in market sectors such as retail, grocery enterprises, engineering, and construction are thought more likely to experience discrimination.

By pre-Stonewall standards, there has been a vast shift in the employment choices and occupational opportunities available to workers who want to be open about their sexual orientation and gender identity. Although many workplaces now tolerate differences, this has not necessarily altered longstanding, heterosexually biased organizational cultures. There are still far too few workplaces where sexual and gender minorities benefit, thrive, and prosper on an equal footing with their heterosexual and nontransgender counterparts.

### Bibliography

Badgett, Lee. *Money, Myths and Change: The Economic Lives of Lesbians and Gay Men.* Chicago: University of Chicago Press, 2001.

Conklin, Wendy. "Employee Resource Groups: A Foundation for Support and Change." *Diversity Factor* 9, no. 1 (fall 2000): 12–25.

Diamant, Louis, ed. *Homosexual Issues in the Workplace.* Washington, D.C.: Taylor and Francis, 1993.

Ellis, Alan, and Ellen Riggle, eds. *Sexual Identity on the Job: Issues and Services.* New York: Haworth Press, 1996.

Friskopp, Annette, and Sharon Silverstein. *Straight Jobs, Gay Lives: Gay and Lesbian Professionals, the Harvard Business School, and the American Workplace.* New York: Scribner, 1995.

Human Rights Campaign Foundation. "WorkNet." Available from http://www.hrc.org.

Hunt, Gerald, ed. *Laboring for Rights: Unions and Sexual Diversity across Nations.* Philadelphia: Temple University Press, 1999.

*Inside-OUT: A Report on the Experiences of Lesbians, Gays and Bisexuals in America and the Public's View on Issues and Policies Related to Sexual Orientation.* Menlo Park, Calif.: Henry Kaiser Family Foundation, 2001.

Meyer, Leisa D. *Creating G. I. Jane: Sexuality and Power in the Women's Army Corps during World War II.* New York: Columbia University Press, 1996.

Shilts, Randy. *Conduct Unbecoming: Gays and Lesbians in the U.S. Military: Vietnam to the Persian Gulf.* New York: St. Martin's Press, 1993.

Winfeld, Liz, and Susan Spielman, *Straight Talk about Gays in the Workplace.* 2d ed. New York: Harrington Park Press, 2001.

Woods, James. *The Corporate Closet: The Professional Lives of Gay Men in America.* New York: Free Press, 1993.

**Gerald Hunt**

**See also** ANTI-DISCRIMINATION LAW AND POLICY; ECONOMICS; KAMENY, FRANKLIN; MATTACHINE SOCIETY; MILITARY LAW AND POLICY.

# EMPLOYMENT LAW AND POLICY

Like most Americans, the vast majority of LGBT people in the United States work for a living. Employment for LGBT persons, however, has been fraught with problems. There have been bans explictly forbidding the employment of "homosexuals" and other sexual minorities, bans that were still in effect in the early 2000s in some parts of the U.S. government, the nation's largest employer. Even without overt prohibitions, discrimination against LGBT persons by public and private employers in hiring and other terms of employment has fostered legal activism aimed toward protecting members of the LGBT population. Litigation, legislative advocacy on the national, state, and local levels, and campaigns to influence members of

the government and the corporate world have been used as LGBT strategies, with mixed success.

## Government Employment

One of the most contentious employers for LGBT persons has been the U.S. military. The court-martialling of persons engaging in sodomy has been documented as early as the Revolutionary War. During World War II, military policy shifted toward discharge rather than criminal court-martial, although the type of discharge—which could have dramatic repercussions for future civilian employment—fluctuated. The most common discharge for homosexuality became the so-called Section Eight or "blue" (based on the color of the paper it was printed on) discharge, which occupied a "twilight zone" between honorable and dishonorable discharges and was generally understood to signal homosexuality.

Presently, the U.S. military retains one of the few explicit bans on the employment of homosexuals. Although this ban was mitigated somewhat under President Bill Clinton, who had originally proposed an abolition of the ban, the compromise "don't ask, don't tell, don't pursue" policy results in the loss of employment for a large number of LGBT persons, with most estimates placing the number at more than one thousand per year.

Outside of the military, other government employment has also been fraught with problems for LGBT persons because of the notion that "homosexuals" are security risks. In the McCarthy era of the 1950s, the government became obsessed not only with Communists but with "sexual perverts." In early 1950, the Undersecretary of State testified before a U.S. congressional committee that more than ninety employees of the State Department had been dismissed in the preceding three years for reasons of "moral turpitude," mostly related to homosexuality. Such testimony was not surprising given the fact that a congressional subcommittee had advised the State Department in 1947 about the extensive employment of homosexuals, a category of persons thought to be high security risks. After the hearing, other government agencies complied with congressional wishes that homosexuals be purged from government employment.

Soon after assuming office upon winning the presidential election of 1952, Dwight D. Eisenhower promulgated Executive Order 10450 relating to security requirements for government employment. The executive order specifically included "any criminal, infamous, dishonest, immoral, or notoriously disgraceful conduct" or "sexual perversion" as grounds for investigation and ultimately discharge. The congressional report and Eisenhower's executive order set the tone for a campaign against thousands of people, many of whom were not employed by the federal government. Given the national preoccupation with security during the cold war, many private companies with government contracts adopted Eisenhower's executive order as company policy. Further, the federal efforts were echoed in several states. Government employees, including those who were not involved in "security" such as teachers, professors, and staff at educational institutions, lost their jobs.

During this same decade the "homophile movement" began to organize to protest the ban on homosexuals in government employment. After numerous attempts and picketing, members of the Mattachine Society of Washington met with federal Civil Service Commission representatives on 8 September 1965, but the chairperson of the commission, John Macy, later wrote to justify the ban by stating that homosexual activity was criminalized and that the government needed to consider "the revulsion of other employees by homosexual conduct and the consequent disruption of service efficiency, the apprehension caused other employees of homosexual advances, solicitations or assaults, the unavoidable subjection of the sexual deviate to erotic stimulation through on-the-job use of common toilet, shower, and living facilities, the offense to members of the public who are required to deal with a known or admitted sexual deviate to transact Government business, the hazard that the prestige and authority of a Government position will be used to foster homosexual activity, particularly among the youth, and the use of Government funds and authority in furtherance of conduct offensive both to the mores and the law of our society" (Eskridge, "Challenging the Apartheid of the Closet," 1997, pp. 966–967).

In addition to organizational efforts, individuals brought lawsuits challenging their dismissals, often based upon allegations that their protections under the civil service system had been violated and often as part of a concerted effort to overturn the policies that prohibited the employment of LGBT persons. In cases such as *Anonymous v. Macy* (1968), *Norton v. Macy* (1969), *Scott v. Macy* (1965), *Schlegel v. United States* (1969), and *Adams v. Laird* (1969)—all of which reached federal appellate courts—the plaintiffs had varying degrees of success in convincing the courts that the ban on homosexuals in government employment was unjustified. Part of the plaintiffs' arguments rested upon the contention that their sexual conduct was a private matter unrelated to their employment. The facts as revealed in these cases demonstrate the draconian practices to which federal

officials resorted when investigating employees, including "arrangements" with local police officers and extensive interrogations. Perhaps because of the harsh practices the government was employing, courts gradually shifted toward finding that the government's terminations were unjustified under various civil service protections.

Unfortunately, some of this favorable precedent did not assist later LGBT litigants such as John Singer. Singer, employed as a clerk typist in a regional office of the Equal Employment Opportunity Commission, the federal agency charged with enforcing federal mandates against employment discrimination, was summoned to an investigative interview in 1972 to discuss his gay activism. Promptly fired for "immoral and notorious disgraceful conduct," Singer challenged his termination in the courts. However, in *Singer v. United States Service Commission* (1976), the federal appellate court accepted the government's argument that Singer was not terminated because of his status as a homosexual but because he "publicly flaunted his homosexual way of life." Although preceding it by many years, such a ruling is consistent with the "don't ask, don't tell" policy adopted by the U.S. military in the 1990s.

As of 2003, the employment of LGBT people in civilian nonsecurity positions was not subject to any ban; indeed, some federal policies prohibited sexual orientation discrimination in hiring for a number of these jobs. However, such civil service and employment rules fluctuate with changes in administrations, most notably through the president's issuance of executive orders.

In addition to the security concerns that dominated issues of public employment for LGBT persons, the possibility of interaction with children has raised governmental anxieties. Even when efforts to repeal public employment bans were successful in some localities, a blanket exclusion for those dealing with children, such as social workers, librarians, and school teachers, persisted. In 1967, a California appellate court in *Sarac v. State Board of Education* upheld the state board of education's revocation of Thomas Sarac's teacher's license for immoral and unprofessional conduct after Sarac was arrested for engaging in the sexual touching of another male (who happened to be an undercover police officer) on a public beach. The more successful litigation of Marc Morrison reached the California Supreme Court two years later. Yet the court in *Morrison v. State Board of Education* rested its decision on the unique nature of Morrison's "isolated incident" of a relationship of a "homosexual nature," which included no criminal activity such as sodomy, oral copulation, public solicitation of lewd acts, loitering near public toilets, or exhibitionism.

The court was careful to note that it did not, of course, hold that homosexuals must be permitted to teach in the public schools of California.

Marjorie Rowland, a high school guidance counselor in Montgomery County, Ohio, was not so fortunate. When she revealed her bisexuality to her secretary in 1974, the secretary promptly informed the school's principal. As a result, the school board did not renew Rowland's contract. Rowland sued on various grounds, including constitutional ones, and at trial a jury awarded her more than thirty thousand dollars in damages. The trial judge held that the school district's termination of Rowland violated her constitutional rights, specifically her first amendment right of free speech and her Fourteenth Amendment right to equal protection. The appellate court reversed in *Rowland v. Mad River Local School District* (1985), stating that Rowland's revelation of her sexuality was not "a matter of public concern" and thus did not merit First Amendment protection and that there was no Fourteenth Amendment protection because Rowland did not specifically prove that heterosexual school employees who revealed their sexual orientations would not have been terminated. The U.S. Supreme Court refused to hear the case, over the objection of several justices, implicitly validating employment discrimination against members of sexual minorities who revealed their sexual preferences.

## Private Employment

In 1964, the U.S. Congress passed the Civil Rights Act, still in effect, Title VII of which prohibits discrimination in employment based on race, color, religion, national origin, or sex. The courts have unanimously concluded that "sex" does not include sexual orientation. The courts have also concluded that a person who changes sex is also not protected. The first and still most often cited case for this proposition is *Ulane v. Eastern Airlines, Inc.* (1984), in which Kenneth Ulane was terminated from employment as a pilot after becoming female. The court ruled that Ulane was not being discriminated against based on sex, but based on "transsexuality."

Nevertheless, there are some specific avenues of protection from employment discrimination for LGBT persons available under Title VII. In *Price Waterhouse v. Hopkins* (1989), the Court ruled that the failure to promote a woman because she was not sufficiently feminine constituted sex discrimination, thus raising the possibility of arguments that gender identity discrimination is included in Title VII. And in *Oncale v. Sundowner Offshore Services, Inc.* (1998), the U.S. Supreme Court ruled that sexual harassment, which may be actionable as sex discrimination under Title VII, includes same-sex harassment. While this ruling obviously benefits many LGBT persons, it may also have a negative effect when LGBT supervisors or coworkers are accused of sexual harassment.

The passage of a federal law that would prohibit most public and private employers from discriminating against LGB persons has not yet occurred. The Employment Non-Discrimination Act was first introduced in Congress in 1994 and has been reintroduced every year since then. Even if passed, however, ENDA would have serious limitations since it does not encompass transgendered persons and includes an exemption for religious employers.

Thus, the most prominent protections for LGBT employees occur on the state and local level rather than the federal. Some states and numerous localities have amended their antidiscrimination laws to include sexual orientation. A handful of localities have amended even these laws to include, or to clarify the inclusion of, prohibitions against discrimination against transgendered persons or discrimination on the basis of gender identity.

The passage of local and state laws prohibiting discrimination against LGBT persons has not been uncontroversial. In Colorado, for example, voters succumbed to rhetoric that LGBT persons were being afforded "special rights" and in 1992 passed an amendment to the state constitution that prohibited the state or any of its agencies or subdivisions from enacting any law or policy "whereby homosexual, lesbian or bisexual orientation, conduct, practices or relationships shall constitute or otherwise be the basis of or entitle any person or class of persons to have or claim any minority status, quota preferences, protected status or claim of discrimination." This provision, known as Amendment Two, was immediately challenged by advocates for lesbian and gay organizations, joined by the cities of Aspen and Boulder. The case reached the U.S. Supreme Court in *Romer v. Evans* (1996), in which the Court held that the provision violated the equal protection clause of the Fourteenth Amendment. The Court held that a state could not put "homosexuals" into a "solitary class" and withdraw from them "but no others" the specific legal protections from injuries caused by discrimination.

An additional aspect of employment is the benefits that one receives from an employer. For LGBT employees, a legal marriage to their partner of choice may not be permitted or they may not have a legally cognizable relationship to children they consider part of their family. For these employees, part of the benefit package available to other employees may therefore be unattainable. Litigation on such issues has not been as successful as advocacy and lobbying. By the early 2000s, a large number of employers, both public and private, allowed persons meeting certain criteria to register their "domestic partners" or "children" and have their family members eligible for benefits such as health insurance.

Finally, not only are explicit bans and discrimination possible in the workplace, but so is an affirmative commitment to diversity. In 2003, the U.S. Supreme Court decided companion cases involving admission policies at the University of Michigan and upheld diversity as a constitutionally permissible interest. However, even when diversity has been accepted as a goal, the notion of workplace diversity has not always included LGBT persons within its ambit. At its most progressive, advocacy on behalf of the employment concerns of LGBT persons includes not only the elimination of the persistent ban on LGBT persons in the military and the prohibition of discrimination against persons on the basis of LGBT identities, but also the positive inclusion of LGBT persons in all workplaces.

At times, the exclusion of LGBT persons has been justified by the law's criminalization of LGBT sexual activity, but with the Supreme Court's 2003 decision in *Lawrence v. Texas,* such criminal laws are no longer constitutional. The Court's rhetoric in *Lawrence* that LGBT people are "entitled to respect for their private lives" and that the government "cannot demean their existence or control their destiny by making their private sexual conduct a crime" may translate into greater progress for LGBT persons in their working lives.

## Bibliography

Berube, Allan. *Coming Out under Fire: The History of Gay Men and Women in World War Two.* New York: The Free Press, 1997.

Currah, Paisley, and Minter, Shannon. "Unprincipled Exclusions: The Struggle to Achieve Judicial and Legislative Equality for Transgender People." *William and Mary Journal of Women and the Law* 7, no. 1 (2000): 37.

Eskridge, William N., Jr. "Challenging the Apartheid of the Closet: Establishing Conditions for Lesbian and Gay Intimacy, *Nomos,* and Citizenship, 1961–1981." *Hofstra Law Review* 25 (1997): 817.

———. *Gaylaw: Challenging the Apartheid of the Closet.* Cambridge, Mass.: Harvard University Press, 1999.

Johnson, David K. " 'Homosexual Citizens': Washington's Gay Community Confronts the Civil Service." *Washington History* 6, no. 2 (1994): 44–63.

Robson, Ruthann. *Sappho Goes to Law School.* New York: Columbia University Press, 1998.

**Ruthann Robson**

*See also* AMERICAN CIVIL LIBERTIES UNION (ACLU); ANTI-DISCRIMINATION LAW AND POLICY; DISCRIMINATION; EDUCATION LAW AND POLICY; EMPLOYMENT AND OCCUPATIONS; FEDERAL LAW AND POLICY; GOVERNMENT AND MILITARY WITCHHUNTS; HEALTH AND HEALTH CARE LAW AND POLICY; LABOR MOVEMENTS AND LABOR UNIONS; MILITARY LAW AND POLICY; NATIONAL GAY AND LESBIAN TASK FORCE (NGLTF); PROSTITUTION, HUSTLING, AND SEX WORK LAW AND POLICY.

# ENVIRONMENTAL AND ECOLOGY MOVEMENTS

In May 1987, deep ecologist Christopher Manes—under the pseudonym "Miss Ann Thropy"—published an inflammatory editorial in the *Earth First!* newsletter. Entitled "Population and AIDS," it argued that AIDS might be an appropriate and effective means to control the world's population: "if the AIDS epidemic didn't exist, radical environmentalists would have to invent it." Although environmentalists—including many Earth First!ers—were quick to condemn Manes's appalling reasoning; many otherwise green queers were forced to pause and take note. Here was a movement that could use arguments, apparently from "nature," to glorify a disease that was decimating the gay community (not to mention Africa and other parts of the world). Indeed, apparently "natural" arguments had been used since the late nineteenth century against LGBT people to pathologize their sex, gender, and sexuality; it was really not a surprise that environmentalist nature discourses might continue in a homophobic and transphobic vein.

Despite this dissonance, it is important to note that the history of the environmental movement is embedded in LGBT history. At one level, queers can point to environmental politics and see significant actors from LGBT culture, notably Henry David Thoreau and Rachel Carson. More profoundly, scholars have begun to investigate how ideas of nature and ecology are shaped by gender and sexuality. In the mid-nineteenth century, for example, pastoral ideas of nature played an important role in upper-class women's romantic friendships; nature represented a field of spiritual purity, linked to the qualities of moral virtue that were emphasized in the Victorian feminine ideals, which sheltered women's passionate friendships. This idea of nature as a place of virtue was strongly nostalgic—only with urbanization and industrialization were rural places "threatened." Thus, women's attachment to a declining pastoral nature placed them at the center of the constellation of conservative values associated with some of the earliest attempts at environmental preservation in the United States.

At the same time as pastoral nature signified a space of purity and femininity, wild nature stood as a heartily masculine realm. Although stories of the U.S. frontier include many male homosexual relationships, late-nineteenth-century recognition of the increasing "threat" to wild nature posed by settlement included a condemnation of the social values and rituals associated with urban life, especially effeminacy. In approximately the same period, homosexual male identity emerged as a primarily urban phenomenon, increasingly associated with camp and decadence. In specific opposition to this perceived feminization of male homoeroticism, some late-nineteenth and early-twentieth-century gay male literature (there are earlier glimpses in Thoreau) actively included a celebration of rural sexuality. Also drawing on pastoral ideas of nature, "rural rough" same-sex eroticism signified a renewed "natural" masculine virility.

Within the context of gendered sexual relationships articulated in the early years of nature preservation, it is not surprising to see distinct lesbian and gay relationships to the environmental movement in the post-Stonewall era. On the one hand, borrowing directly from Victorian ideas of gender, nature, purity, and virtue, lesbian separatists in the 1970s and 1980s founded rural communities devoted to sheltering women and the land from men and industrialism. Such themes were also present in lesbian utopian novels of the period, notably Sally Miller Gearhart's *The Wanderground* (1979). Some of these lesbian communities continue to exist. Although there are also rural gay men's intentional communities dating from the 1970s, by and large the mainstream U.S. gay male community has responded to nature with their own pastoral ideals in mind: a continuation and amplification of the idea of nature as a space of masculine sexual activity, ritualized in public parks and fetishized by Tom of Finland.

With the rise of environmental justice and ecofeminist politics in the 1980s and 1990s, which were oriented to exposing the racial and gendered dimensions of environmental degradation, new possibilities for queer ecological alliance have emerged. Specifically, these more socially critical environmental currents include an explicit orientation to uncovering the particular ways communities are affected by environmental problems. In this context, the destruction or alteration of a significant urban park or greenspace can be understood as a question of environmental justice for gay men who might depend on that space, and on a particular set of biotic features, for sexual activity. Along similar lines, lack of safe queer access to wilderness spaces points to the need for the kind of political alliance potentially inherent in gay

and lesbian groups within such organizations as the Sierra Club. More radically, social ecological and ecofeminist thinkers have argued that the forms of domination engendering sexist, racist, and homophobic violence are also responsible for violence against the earth. The oppression of some individuals' sexual identities and behaviors is part of a complex and destructive web of power relations that also includes strip mining and clear cutting. From this anti-oppression perspective, some "eco-queers" have challenged the increasing orientation of LGBT culture to lifestyle consumerism. They accuse festivities such as Pride Day of losing their radical ability to connect queer politics with other social issues amid a mainstream celebration of product-oriented queer culture.

Despite these promising links, there remains a rift between LGBT and environmental politics. Although the eco-queers' assertion of queer mainstreaming is certainly at play, one must also consider the environmental movement's continued problematic understanding of gender and sexuality in general. First, there is a persistent antisex flavor to Malthusian environmentalist assertions that the root problem of the environmental crisis is to be found in human population growth. While most environmentalists abhor Manes's misanthropy, many would not be averse to more voluntary (still racist) measures of population control. The idea of alternative sexualities and genders—or sexual pleasure and exuberance of any kind, for that matter—does not figure in this reductively heterosexist constellation. Second, most environmental politics continues to rely heavily for ecological knowledge on evolutionary biology. Although research has demonstrated convincingly that same-sex eroticism is plentiful and varied across the spectrum of nonhuman species, neo-Darwinian heterosexist understandings of reproductive fitness continue to influence ecology. For example, the widespread presence of same-sex eroticism or "transgender" behavior in animal populations has more than once been taken as a sign of environmentally caused behavioral pathology.

The newly emerging field of queer ecology seeks to challenge these assumptions, and to develop a better understanding of the social and political relations connecting environmental with LGBT issues.

## Bibliography

Bagemihl, Bruce. *Biological Exuberance: Animal Homosexuality and Natural Diversity*. New York: St. Martin's Press, 1999.

Gaard, Greta. "Toward a Queer Ecofeminism." *Hypatia* 12, no. 1 (Winter 1997): 114–137.

Ingram, Gordon Brent, Anne-Marie Bouthillette, and Yolanda Retter, eds. *Queers in Space: Communities, Public Places, Sites of Resistance.* Seattle Wash.: Bay Press, 1997.

Phillips, Richard, Diane West, and David Shuttleton, eds. *De-Centring Sexualities: Politics and Representation Beyond the Metropolis.* London: Routledge, 2000.

Sandilands, Catriona. "Lesbian Separatists and Ecological Experience: Notes Toward a Queer Ecology." *Organization and Environment*, 15, no. 2 (June 2002); 131-163.

**Catriona Sandilands**

*See also* CARSON, RACHEL; RADICAL FAERIES; WITTMAN, CARL.

# ERICKSON EDUCATIONAL FOUNDATION

The Erickson Educational Foundation (EEF) was a non-profit educational and philanthropic organization incorporated in Baton Rouge, Louisiana in 1964. The EEF was founded and funded by a wealthy female-to-male transsexual businessman, Reed Erickson, who held the sole voting membership. The EEF was active from 1964 to 1977, during which time it had offices in Baton Rouge and New York City. In 1977 Erickson retired the EEF and moved with his family to Mexico. The EEF picked up again from 1981 to 1984, then operating out of Erickson's home in Ojai, California. At various times the EEF also had mailing addresses in Mexico; Panama; El Paso, Texas; Los Angeles; and Phoenix, Arizona. The work of the EEF was done by Erickson, an executive director and a bookkeeper. The EEF ceased operations in 1984 due to the ill health of its founder, guiding light, and sole benefactor.

An early EEF brochure described the organization's goals as being to provide support in areas where human potential was limited by adverse conditions, or where the scope of research was too new or unconventional to receive support from mainstream sources. During its life, the EEF contributed both active leadership and millions of dollars of behind-the-scenes financial support to the early development of LGBT movements.

## The Erickson Educational Foundation and ONE

Shortly after the EEF's incorporation Reed Erickson, representing the foundation, contacted the offices of the Los Angeles homophile organization ONE, Inc., in response to a fund-raising mail campaign. A series of meetings and the phone calls between Erickson and W. Dorr Legg of ONE resulted in Erickson proposing and offering to finance the formation of the legally independent, nonpolitical, non-profit, and tax-exempt Institute for the Study of Human Resources (ISHR), which would enable Erickson and others to make tax-deductible donations to the educational work of ONE, Inc. The original acting directors of ISHR were Dorr Legg, Tony Reyes, and Don Slater, all three of whom had been among the founders of ONE. Erickson was named president and remained in the post until 1977, when the EEF temporarily suspended operations. According to its articles of incorporation, ISHR's purpose was to promote and encourage the study of male and female homosexuality and other types of human behavior. The EEF directly funded ISHR for fifteen years (1964–1976, 1980–1983), during which time between 70 and 80 percent of the ISHR's operating budget came from the EEF. In total, the ISHR recorded having received over $200,000 in direct grants from the EEF, aside from transfers of funds not recorded in surviving official documents but recalled by others. Although there were other donors to the ISHR and to ONE, it would not be an exaggeration to say that without the EEF's support many of ONE's activities, and perhaps even ONE itself, would not have been possible on the scale achieved with the benefit of the EEF's support.

The ISHR's educational programs, supported by the EEF and delivered through ONE, included nondegree courses, lectures, courses given offsite in cities beyond Los Angeles (where ONE had no offices), and the first graduate degrees in homophile studies ever granted in the United States. (In 1964 Deborah Coates received an M.A. degree and Michael Lombardi obtained a doctor of philosophy degree; in 1965 Paul Hardman obtained a doctor of philosophy degree.) Some of those whose work was supported by the ISHR and ONE included Vern L. Bullough, researcher and author of numerous texts on LGBT themes; Antony Grey, a key figure in promoting the liberal reforms urged by Britain's Wolfenden Report of 1957; Evelyn Hooker, author of the revolutionary 1957 research study *The Adjustment of the Male Overt Homosexual;* Laud Humphreys, author of *Tearoom Trade: Impersonal Sex in Public Places* (1975); Christopher Isherwood, widely acclaimed author; Christine Jorgensen, celebrated transsexual activist; and Virginia Prince, widely reputed to be the founder of transgender activism.

The EEF's contributions to the ISHR also supported the development of the Blanche M. Baker Memorial Library, which became one of the backbones of ONE Institute and Archives. The EEF also supported the research and publication of *An Annotated Bibliography of Homosexuality* (1976) and three other important books on human sexuality by Vern L. Bullough.

The EEF's single largest contribution to ONE was the 1983 $1.9 million purchase of two elegant mansions and numerous other buildings on a 3.5-acre downtown Los

Angeles property known as the Milbank Estate. Sadly, no sooner had the ink dried on the contract for the purchase when the relationship between the EEF and ONE began to unravel. Almost ten years of legal battles over ownership of the property left ONE facing possible ruin and effectively paralyzed most of the public operations of ONE. In 1992 the property was divided between Erickson's heirs and the ISHR, whose share was assessed at over $1 million. By 1997 the ISHR's part of the property had been sold and ONE's activities were largely transferred to locations owned by the University of Southern California.

## Support for Transgender Rights

When the EEF was created in 1964, transsexualism was little known to either professionals or the public. (The term transgender had not yet been coined by Virginia Prince.) One of the main functions of the EEF was to bring attention to this phenomena. Central to this work was Zelda Roth Suplee, EEF's executive director from 1967 to 1977, who was the public face of the organization during its most active years of operation.

The EEF supported in one way or another a large portion of the work done during the 1960s and 1970s by, for, and about transgender people in the United States. The EEF published an informative quarterly newsletter, produced an invaluable set of educational pamphlets, and developed and maintained an extensive referral list of service providers. The EEF funded many important beginning research efforts and was instrumental in organizing all of the earliest international conferences on transsexualism as well as bringing discussions about transsexualism to conferences of broader interest. The EEF sponsored innumerable educational public addresses on the topic of transsexualism for medical professionals, clergy, law enforcement officers, and university and college students. The EEF also sponsored educational films, radio and television appearances, and newspaper articles.

The importance of the EEF's quarterly newsletter (with a mailing list of 20,000), referral service, and pamphlet series would be hard to overemphasize. They were lifelines for transgender people for decades. During the 1970s and early 1980s, the only other literature available was a handful of not overly sympathetic and very hard-to-access professional publications. Most mental-health professionals and physicians considered transsexualism a perversion. Television talk-show appearances and documentaries were virtually nonexistent. The few organizations that did exist were mostly small, local, and clandestine. There was no Internet or email. The EEF served as *the* only national clearinghouse and informa-

tion source for transgender people, who wrote to the EEF from all over the United States asking for information about their feelings and for the names of doctors to whom they could turn for help.

The EEF responded to the needs of the transgender community by compiling a national referral list of psychologists, psychiatrists, physicians, and surgeons willing to help transgender people. The foundation maintained a hotline and welcomed people who visited the EEF offices. Between 1969 and 1974 the EEF produced a series of nine pamphlets that addressed various aspects of transsexualism in plain language. These pamphlets were reprinted and cherished well into the 1980s.

The EEF also donated hundreds of thousands of dollars to the support of key researchers studying transsexualism. The roster of the people who benefited from research grants from the EEF reads like a Who's Who of early transgender research. Among them were Harry Benjamin, Harold Christensen, Milton Edgerton, Anke Ehrhardt, Deborah Feinbloom, Norman Fisk, Roger Gorski, Richard Green, Donald Laub, Jon K. Meyer, John Money, Ira Pauly, Richard Pillard, June Reinisch, and Paul Walker.

In particular, the EEF supported the work of the father of transgender research, Harry Benjamin, through the Harry Benjamin Foundation, which enabled a group of physicians and researchers to convene at Benjamin's New York City offices during the mid-1960s. The conversations that took place at those meetings served as a birthing ground for the landmark books *Transsexualism and Sex Reassignment* (1969), edited by Money and Green, and *Man and Woman, Boy and Girl* (1972), edited by Money and Ehrhardt. The first university-based gender clinic in the United States, the Johns Hopkins Gender Identity Clinic (1965–1979), was conceived at those meetings and was partially funded by the EEF from 1967 to 1973.

Another invaluable contribution to transgender interests made by the EEF was the convening of the first (London, 1969), second (Elsinore, Denmark, 1971), and third (Dubrovnik, Yugoslavia, 1973) International Symposiums on Gender Identity, the first held solely to discuss transgender issues. A fourth symposium (Stanford University, 1975) was named for Harry Benjamin in honor of his ninetieth birthday. At the fifth symposium (Norfolk, Virginia, 1977), an urgent last-minute addition appeared at the front of the program announcing the demise of the EEF and calling for a special meeting to "brainstorm" about what to do to address the loss of "a vital force in the area of transsexualism" which "has been of inestimable value to the field" (Reed Erickson and the Erickson Educational Foundation at http://web.uvic.ca. ~123). It was at this meeting, called in direct response to the chasm left in the field of transsexualism by the withdrawal of the support of the EEF, that the Harry Benjamin International Gender Dysphoria Association was created. Erickson was made an honorary member.

Another of the EEF's major undertakings consisted of extensive public education and outreach that explained transsexualism to the public. The EEF had a cadre of dedicated speakers who visited colleges and universities, theological institutes, medical schools, nursing colleges, police academies, academic conferences, and government agencies. The EEF was featured on radio and television and in major print media such as *Look* magazine and *Dear Abby,* and produced educational films that were widely distributed and which literally defined the field by providing definitions of transsexualism and transvestism to 105 dictionaries and encyclopedias.

## Other Work

The EEF also provided assistance for investigations into parapsychology, religious experience, psychoenergetics, nondrug-induced altered states of consciousness, homeopathy, acupuncture, and nonmedical healing. Some of the projects that benefited from the EEF's largesse were Jean Houston's and Robert E. L. Masters's joint work on altered states of consciousness, Stanley Krippner's dream studies, John Lilly's research into dolphin–human communication, and the publication of the first edition of *A Course in Miracles* (1976).

## The Work Continues

In 1976 the EEF passed on many of its files to the Janus Information Facility under the direction of Dr. Paul Walker, who was director of the Gender Clinic of the University of Texas Medical Branch in Galveston, Texas. In 1986 the Janus Information Facility, in turn, passed on the EEF legacy to the care of J2CP Information Services under the direction of Joanna Clark (Sister Mary Elizabeth) and Jude Patton. In 1990, J2CP turned over the EEF files remaining in its possession to the American Educational Gender Information Service (AEGIS) under the direction of Dallas Denny. In 2000 AEGIS joined forces with others to form a new organization, Gender Education and Advocacy (GEA), which carries forward the work begun in 1964 by the EEF.

## Bibliography

Bullough, Vern L. et al. *An Annotated Bibliography of Homosexuality.* 2 vols. New York: Garland, 1976.

Devor, Holly. "Reed Erickson (1917–1992): How One Transsexed Man Supported ONE." In *Before Stonewall: Activists for Gay and Lesbian Rights in Historical Context.* Edited by Vern L. Bullough. New York: Harrington Park. 2002.

Foundation for Inner Peace. *A Course in Miracles.* New York: Foundation for Inner Peace. 1976.

Green, Richard, and John Money. *Transsexualism and Sex Reassignment.* Baltimore: Johns Hopkins University Press, 1969.

Hooker, Evelyn. "The Adjustment of the Male Overt Homosexual." *Journal of Projective Technique* 21 (1957): 18–31.

Humphreys, Laud. *Tearoom Trade: Impersonal Sex in Public Places.* Chicago: Aldine, 1970.

Money, John, and Anke A. Ehrhardt. *Man and Woman, Boy and Girl: The Differentiation and Dimorphism of Gender Identity from Conception to Maturity.* Baltimore: Johns Hopkins University Press, 1972.

"Reed Erickson and the Erickson Educational Foundation." Available from http://web.uvic.ca/~erick123.

**Aaron H. Devor**

***See also*** BENJAMIN, HARRY; ERICKSON, REED; HOMOPHILE MOVEMENT; HOOKER, EVELYN; INTERSEXUALS AND INTERSEXED PEOPLE; ISHERWOOD, CHRISTOPHER; JORGENSON, CHRISTINE; MONEY, JOHN, AND ANKE EHRHARDT; ONE INSTITUTE; PRINCE, VIRGINIA; TRANSGENDER ORGANIZATIONS AND PERIODICALS; TRANSSEXUALS, TRANSVESTITES, TRANSGENDER PEOPLE, AND CROSS-DRESSERS.

# ERICKSON, Reed (b. 13 October 1917; d. 3 January 1992), activist, philanthropist.

Reed Erickson, born Rita Alma Erickson, was a wealthy female-to-male transsexual man who helped create the medical, legal, and social support system through which transsexual people in the United States have addressed their unique needs from the 1960s forward. He was also a major financial contributor to the ONE Institute for Homophile Studies and to several nonmainstream causes such as research into interspecies communication, mental telepathy, hypnotic trances, and psychoactive botanical substances.

Born in El Paso, Texas, to a successful, geographically mobile, Jewish-German family of industrial entrepreneurs, Erickson grew up in Philadelphia and briefly attended Temple University. In the late 1930s the family relocated to Baton Rouge, Louisiana, where Erickson's father had transferred his lead-smelting business. Erickson completed his education at Louisiana State University, where he became the first female graduate of its school of mechanical engineering. He had a minor involvement in leftist politics in the later 1940s, reputedly buying communist party tracts and attending meetings of communist front organizations—activities that resulted in his being kept under surveillance by the Federal Bureau of Investigation until the 1970s.

Throughout the 1950s, Erickson lived as a lesbian and worked as an engineer, first in Philadelphia and San Francisco, and later in Baton Rouge. Erickson founded his own successful company, Southern Seating, which manufactured bleacher seats for baseball stadiums, in the early 1950s. After his father's death in 1962, Erickson inherited the family businesses, which he ran successfully until selling them to Arrow Electronics in 1969 for $5 million. Through shrewd oil and gas investments, Erickson eventually amassed a personal fortune of roughly $40 million.

In 1963 Erickson became a patient of Dr. Harry Benjamin, the pioneering advocate for transsexuals, and began hormonal masculinization. By 1965 he had undergone a hysterectomy in New York and mastectomies at Johns Hopkins University in Baltimore. A year earlier, in 1964, Erickson established the Erickson Educational Foundation (EEF); its stated goals were to "provide assistance and support in areas where human potential was limited by adverse physical, mental, or social conditions, or where the scope of research was too new, controversial or imaginative to receive traditionally oriented support" (Meyerowitz, p. 210). He used the foundation to reward the doctors and surgeons who had helped him achieve his personal goal of bodily transformation, and to support the cause of homosexual rights and his other, more esoteric, interests.

The first beneficiary of Erickson's largesse was the ONE Institute for Homophile Studies, an early offshoot of the Mattachine Society. In 1964 Erickson underwrote ONE's massive bibliographical research project, which was eventually published by Garland in 1976 as *An Annotated Bibliography of Homosexuality*. Over the years, Erickson provided more than $200,000 in cash support for ONE. He also owned the West Hollywood mansion where the ONE Institute was housed between 1984 and 1993.

Through the EEF, Erickson created the Harry Benjamin Foundation in 1964, which supported Benjamin's research into transsexuality, culminating in publication of his landmark monograph, *The Transsexual Phenomenon*, in 1966. The network of professional collaborations established through the work of the Benjamin Foundation eventually became formalized as the Harry Benjamin International Gender Dysphoria Association, which remains the professional association for medical and psychotherapeutic service providers working in the transgender field.

The EEF provided support for John Money of Johns Hopkins University, who worked to establish the first surgical sex-reassignment program in the United States in 1966, and who, with UCLA's Richard Green, compiled the first medical guidebook for transgender care, *Transsexualism and Sex-Reassignment*, in 1968. Erickson's philanthropy was also instrumental in helping establish the sex-reassignment program at Stanford University in 1968.

At the grassroots level, EEF supported the National Transsexual Counseling Unit (NTCU), the first U.S. transgender peer-support and referral service, which took shape in San Francisco in 1968 after two years of transgender-community work had produced several other short-lived precursor organizations. The EEF paid the rent for the NTCU's office and the salaries of its two peer counselors. The EEF also published a series of self-help pamphlets for transsexuals and their families that served into the 1980s as an initial source of information for many people whose lives were touched by transgender issues.

Sadly, Erickson's later life was marked by serious substance abuse problems. In the 1980s, he became a fugitive from felony drug charges in the United States, and until succumbing to bladder cancer and drug-induced dementia, lived out his later years in seclusion in his opulent compound, Love Joy Estates, in Mazatlan, Mexico.

## Bibliography

Devor, Aaron. "Reed Erickson and ONE: How One Transsexed Man Helped to Establish Homosexual Activism in the United States." Unpublished paper in the author's possession.

Meyerowitz, Joanne. *How Sex Changed: A History of Transsexuality in the United States*. Cambridge, Mass.: Harvard University Press, 2002.

**Susan Stryker**

*See also* BENJAMIN, HARRY; ERICKSON EDUCATIONAL FOUNDATION; MONEY, JOHN, AND ANKE EHRHARDT; ONE INSTITUTE; TRANSGENDER ORGANIZATIONS AND PERIODICALS; TRANSSEXUALS, TRANSVESTITES, TRANSGENDER PEOPLE, AND CROSS-DRESSERS.

# ESSENTIALISM AND CONSTRUCTIONISM

In the last three decades, two theoretical positions, essentialism and constructionism, have come to the fore in discussions of sex, gender, and sexuality in the United States. Essentialism (often referred to as biological essentialism) regards desires, behavioral predilections, and identities as the products of natural, fixed, and innate human characteristics. In contrast, constructionism (often referred to as social constructionism) emphasizes the social, cultural, political, and historical factors that produce and shape desires, acts, and identities.

Most people presume that most persons can be classified as heterosexual, homosexual, or bisexual and, furthermore, that a person's sexual desires neatly correspond with matching sexual behaviors, and that their desires and behaviors neatly correspond with a matching sexual identity. For example, a person who desires people of the same sex will engage in homosexual sex acts and will adopt a gay or lesbian identity. This conceptual model is essentialist. Essentialism also argues that today's sexual desires, behaviors, and identities have existed in the same basic form in all times and places. So, in this vein, an American gay man in the twenty-first century is virtually the same as a man who engaged in same-sex sexual acts in Greece thousands of years ago. Essentialists might recognize that the ability to act on one's desires and the ability to claim a sexual identity are affected by external circumstances, but they believe that there is a relatively fixed percentage of people (a minority) in all cultural contexts who are essentially LGB and that they can be clearly distinguished from people (a majority) who are essentially heterosexual. Sexuality, for the essentialist, is an unchangeable reality.

Constructionism argues that sexual desires, acts, and identities are bound by particular social, cultural, political, and historical contexts, and that these contexts produce, shape, and limit our experiences of sexuality. For example, socialization (the process of learning the rules of a particular social group), social control (the rewards and punishments associated with acceptable social behavior), and culture (a social group's set of established beliefs and practices) all influence sexuality. Constructionists emphasize that while some cultures classify people as heterosexual, homosexual, or bisexual, others do not. For example, in ancient Greece, the sex of one's partner was not of the utmost importance; whether one took the active or passive role in the sex act was. Cultural classification systems, constructionism argues, shape not only sexual identities but also sexual desires and acts, and so it can be anachronistic and ahistorical to refer to homosexual and heterosexual people in contexts in which these concepts did not exist. Constructionism also recognizes that desires, acts, and identities do not always line up as one might expect and highlights the differences, rather than the similarities, between sexual actors in the present and sexual actors in the past. Rather than assume that every culture has relatively fixed percentages of homosexual and heterosexual

people, constructionists believe that sexual desires, acts, and identities are constantly changing.

## Sexuality, Sex, Gender, and Gender Identity

The constructionist position so widely taken up in LGBT studies is frequently attributed to the work of the French theorist Michel Foucault. Foucault viewed sexuality as a discourse that was an expression of complex, dynamic power relations in society. In what has become a canonical text in LGBT studies, *The History of Sexuality,* Foucault set out to analyze the history of sexuality from ancient Greece to the modern era, and in so doing ended up providing a historical narrative about the formation of a modern homosexual identity. Taking a constructionist line, Foucault argued that homosexuality is necessarily a modern formation because, while there were previously same-sex sex acts, there was no corresponding category of identification based on these acts. The modern homosexual was fundamentally different from the earlier sodomite, according to Foucault, because the latter term referred to the sex act, while the former referred to a type of person with an identity defined by their desire for people of the same sex.

Feminist, queer, and transgender theory and scholarship necessitate the conceptualization of essentialism and constructionism, not only in terms of sexual orientation, but also in terms of sex, gender, and gender identity. For some essentialists, sex (male/female) and gender (masculinity/femininity) are both the products of innate biological factors. Those who argue for innate differences between lesbians and gay men often favor this model. A modified essentialist position posits that while males and females can be distinguished on the basis of sex in terms of essential biological traits, gender is socially constructed. This position has been used to interpret, for example, the history of butch lesbians and effeminate gay men. More radical constructionists, influenced by the existence of intersexed people and by the failure of biological frameworks to deal with people whose anatomy, DNA, hormones, and reproductive capacity do not correspond to normative expectations, argue that both sex and gender are socially constructed, or, put another way, that sex itself is gendered. Further elaborating on the complex relation between gender and sex, the historian Joanne Meyerowitz argues that for many transsexual people, gender identity (the sense of being male or female) is innate and essential, while bodies can be constructed. To capture this dimension of complexity and others, some scholars argue that it would be preferable to speak of sexes, genders, and sexualities in the plural rather than the singular.

Although essentialists and constructionists are often viewed as being at odds, the relationship between the two positions is more complicated than such a dichotomy would suggest. Most people hold some combination of essentialist and constructionist views. Constructionists cannot deny the popularity and influence of essentialist conceptions, and essentialists cannot deny that some aspects of sex, gender, and sexuality change over time.

## Homophobic and Antihomophobic Strategies

Debates about sexual identity, and homosexuality in particular, tend to be acutely polarized. This is due, in part, to the fact that such discussions often involve the crafting and implementation of laws and public policies and matters of religion and morality. Often central to these political, social, and intellectual disputes is the question of whether sexual orientation is socially constructed or biologically determined. However, both homophobic and antihomophobic advocates have employed essentialist and constructionist strategies and arguments.

A good example of this is illustrated in the debate over gay marriage. Arguments against gay marriage sometimes employ essentialist tactics in the contention that gay men are promiscuous by nature and therefore virtually incapable of monogamous relationships, a primary characteristic of marriage. The essentialist claim that homosexuality is an innate biological predisposition is also often used in the fight for gay and lesbian civil rights, including the fight for equal marriage rights. The crux of the LGB essentialist argument is that if homosexuality is not chosen but is assigned by nature, then homosexuals should be extended the rights and protections accorded to everyone.

Essentialist positions can also be found in both homophobic and antihomophobic arguments about the biological basis of homosexuality. Homophobic doctors have used essentialist arguments to justify surgery and hormonal treatment to "cure" people of their homosexuality, while antihomophobic scientists have used essentialist rhetoric to argue against attempts to cure homosexuals through psychotherapy. Meanwhile, constructionist arguments have also been used both for and against LGB interests. Homophobes sometimes argue that if homosexuality is a freely chosen sexual orientation (a notion that is sometimes conflated with constructionism), it is a vice that can and should be corrected. LGB constructionists counter that, given great historical and cross-cultural variability in sexual attitudes and practices, what needs correcting is not homosexuality but homophobia.

## The Instability of Sexual Constructs

Since most anti-LGBT arguments rely upon the alleged naturalness of heterosexuality and dominant gender norms, feminist, queer, and transgender scholars have attempted to show that dominant categories are themselves social constructs. A primary constructionist argument, for example, is that heterosexuality is also a historically contingent construction, although it is often believed to be an unproblematic, self-evident, and stable category that requires no explanation. Reflecting this notion, Jonathan Ned Katz has titled one of his books *The Invention of Heterosexuality*, which considers, among other subjects, the invention of the term "heterosexuality" in the late nineteenth century.

Although most queer scholars agree that heterosexuality is not, in fact, a stable, coherent category, one writer has been in the vanguard of arguing that homosexuality as a category is also unstable and incoherent. Critiquing the tendency to represent contemporary homosexuality as somehow self-evident and unproblematic, as opposed to its earlier configuration by scholars as fragmented and incoherent, Eve Kosofsky Sedgwick in *Epistemology of the Closet* draws attention to logical contradictions in the current conceptual models that constitute modern homosexuality. Sedgwick argues that the crisis of both defining homosexuality and heterosexuality is due in part to the contradictions between what she terms "minoritizing" and "universalizing" views and between what she calls "gender liminal" and "gender separatist" perspectives. According to Sedgwick, homosexuality is conceptualized as both an essential minority trait and as a universal human potential, and is simultaneously viewed both as a matter of gender transgression and gender differentiation. Sedgwick thus argues that there are fundamental contradictions at the heart of homosexuality and heterosexuality, and that there is no solid ground on which to choose between essentialist and constructionist models.

## Criticism of Constructionism and Essentialism

Constructionism has been criticized for being an academic theory not supported by most LGBT people in the United States in the early 2000s, who tend to believe that they were born LGBT. Critics also claim that constructionism, by raising questions about the coherence and legitimacy of LGBT categories, threatens effective LGBT foundations for political action, risks the infinite fragmentation of LGBT communities, and prevents effective coalition-building between LGBT constituencies. To counter this, the postcolonial theorist Gayatri Spivak suggests the deployment of "strategic essentialism." In effect, this refers to provisional and temporary uses of essentialism by those who do not necessarily accept the basic tenets of essentialism. Essentialism, meanwhile, has been criticized for policing the boundaries of LGBT communities, for failing to deal with historical, cross-cultural, and individual variability and fluidity, and for universalizing experiences, identities, and practices that differ on the basis of race, class, and other categories.

Even among constructionists, who held the dominant scholarly position in the early years of the twenty-first century (at least within the humanities and social sciences), there are major disagreements. Although most scholars argue that modern homosexual and heterosexual identities were initially constructed in the late nineteenth century, others believe that this occurred earlier or later. There is also general agreement among scholars that sexual identities are constructed, but there is less agreement about whether sexual desires and acts are influenced by society, culture, politics, and history. Scholars also disagree about whether sexualities have been constructed primarily by social elites (including scientific experts, religious leaders, and political authorities) or by ordinary people, and about the relative influence of straight and LGBT people in constructing sexes, genders, and sexualities. They also disagree about which social processes (capitalism, urbanization, commercialization, class relations, race relations, or gender relations, for example) have played the greatest roles in constructing sexualities.

At stake in many of these debates are not only the historical question of whether sexes, genders, and sexualities in the past were socially constructed, but the future question of whether today's sexes, genders, and sexualities should be reconstructed or deconstructed.

## Bibliography

Abelove, Henry, et al., eds. *The Lesbian and Gay Studies Reader.* New York: Routledge, 1993.

Butler, Judith. *Gender Trouble: Feminism and the Subversion of Identity.* New York: Routledge, 1990.

D'Emilio, John, and Estelle B. Freedman. *Intimate Matters: A History of Sexuality in America.* Chicago: University of Chicago Press, 1997.

Epstein, Steven. "Gay Politics, Ethnic Identity: The Limits of Social Constructionism." In *Forms of Desire: Sexual Orientation and the Social Construction Controversy.* Edited by Edward Stein. New York: Routledge, 1992.

Foucault, Michel. *The History of Sexuality: Volume One, An Introduction.* Translated by Robert Hurley. New York: Vintage Books, 1990.

Fuss, Diana. *Essentially Speaking: Feminism, Nature, and Difference.* New York: Routledge, 1990.

Jagose, Annamarie. *Queer Theory: An Introduction.* New York: New York University Press, 1996.

Katz, Jonathan Ned. *The Invention of Heterosexuality.* New York: Dutton Books, 1995.

Meyerowitz, Joanne J. *How Sex Changed: A History of Transsexuality in the United States.* Cambridge, Mass.: Harvard University Press, 2002.

Sedgwick, Eve Kosofsky. *Epistemology of the Closet.* Berkeley: University of California Press, 1990.

Weeks, Jeffrey. *Coming Out: Homosexual Politics in Britain from the Nineteenth Century to the Present.* New York: Quartet Books, 1977.

**Nichole Suzanne Prescott**

*See also* HISTORY; HOMOSEXUALITY AND HETEROSEXUALITY; LGBTQ STUDIES; QUEER THEORY AND QUEER STUDIES.

**EYDE, EDITH.** see BEN, LISA.

abcde**f**ghijklmnopqrstuvwxyz

# FAMILY ISSUES

Family issues have only sporadically garnered attention from scholars concerned with the life experience of LGBT people. Such scrutiny as has been directed toward matters of marriage (and other forms of union) and parenthood among these populations has tended to reflect developments in the legal or judicial arenas, frequently deriving from efforts to restrict or expand the familial rights of LGBT individuals rather than to understand the diverse forms of kinship-based connectedness such persons may forge. At the heart of these discussions have been questions of visibility and recognition: simply put, lesbians and gay men are conventionally elided from family units, assumed to be alienated from families of origin, incapable of forming families of procreation and unwilling to commit to long-term relationships with intimate partners. The tendency—both popular and scholarly—to conceptualize family in terms of biologically determined bonds, and as a set of naturally occurring, universal arrangements, has further marginalized efforts to understand LGBT families.

## Parenting Issues

Like many other areas of research on homosexuality, attention to family issues grew out of efforts to defend actual families whose survival or integrity was threatened. In the 1970s, several cases of lesbian mothers who had borne children within heterosexual marriages and who were faced with challenges to child custody burst onto the scene, most notably those of Jeanne Jullion in California, Mary Jo Risher in Texas, and Sandy Schuster and Madeleine Isaacson in Washington. Such cases, of course, represented only those situations in which the issue of homosexuality was publicly discussed in the course of litigation or became part of the legal record. In most instances, lesbian mothers quietly accommodated former husbands who threatened to sue for custody or challenged visitation rights: they often gave up child support, ceded jointly owned property, or simply avoided legal divorce proceedings to protect themselves and their families from judicial scrutiny. Lesbian mothers in this period were typically extremely secretive, avoiding any activity or association that would label them as homosexual or make their orientation visible to former husbands; identifying this population was further hampered by varying definitions of "lesbian" and overall lack of clarity about whether sexual orientation would necessarily prove to be a primary source of identity for most mothers who might be so labeled by others. Undertaking large-scale descriptive research on such a relatively invisible population, of course, was not feasible.

By the 1980s, however, lesbian motherhood took a decidedly different turn. Lesbians increasingly began to seek out motherhood through donor insemination or other methods, launching what some characterized as a virtual "baby boom." Some women sought out male friends as sperm donors, others used mainstream medical providers, and still others became pregnant through alternative medical institutions or by using intermediaries between themselves and anonymous sperm donors. At the same time, other lesbians became foster parents or adopted children through a variety of domestic and international mechanisms, both as couples and as single women. While lesbians had always been mothers, this

359

new wave of motherhood was open and public to an unprecedented degree; rather than seeking to keep a low profile and to thus avoid unwanted surveillance, increasing numbers of lesbian mothers began to proclaim themselves and to demand recognition and respect. The development of books for young readers like Lesléa Newman's *Heather Has Two Mommies* brought the issue into the educational domain as well, though the bitter controversies that accompanied some efforts to introduce the book into school systems indicated that families involving same-sex parents would continue to face struggles in their communities. While some jurisdictions have begun to regularly approve "second-parent" adoptions, that is, the extension of legal parenthood to two parents of the same sex, such arrangements are not routine, with dramatic differences between outcomes in urban and rural locales and between states. Some judges have ruled that sexual orientation is not a proper basis for determining the outcome of custody disputes, but since such determinations are carried out on a case-by-case basis, even the most positive rulings have no standing as legal precedent.

Gay fatherhood has been generally less visible to the general public, although the existence of men who had fathered children during heterosexual marriages has also emerged in contested custody and visitation cases. More recently, in efforts that parallel the lesbian "baby boom," gay men have sought to become fathers through adoption (domestic, private, and international), through surrogacy, and sometimes through shared-parenting arrangements with lesbians or other women who serve as biological mothers. While many of the obstacles gay men face when they seek parenthood are similar to those of lesbians, they also experience problems that derive from stereotyped images both of gay men and of men in general. Agencies that arrange adoptions tend to be more suspicious of men who desire parenthood, both because such desires run counter to gender expectations—that parenthood is a less urgent desire for men or less central to their personal identities—and because of deeply rooted images of gay men as child molesters. Many countries that regularly "export" children to the United States refuse to consider either gay male couples or single men (of any sexual orientation) as potential adoptive parents. Further, a number of states restrict adoption or foster parenting by lesbians or gay men in various ways; simply because of their gender, men are more likely than women to be singled out as "unsuitable" placements for children awaiting adoption or foster care. The paradox here is that as the existence of gay and lesbian parents has become more visible, a development that speaks to a growing sense of pride and legitimacy, visibility has also engendered political opposition and enmity. Nor is there any

consistency or obvious logic to the legal status of lesbian and gay parents. In Florida, for example, gays and lesbians can serve as foster parents and legal guardians of children, but are barred from adoption of these or other children. The presumption of the state is that "the best interests of the child" mandate adoptive placements with heterosexual married couples, despite the shortage of such families relative to the number of children awaiting adoption. One Florida challenge to these regulations was rejected in 2001; another case, brought by a Key West couple in 2003, is still being litigated. Efforts to limit LGBT access to either adoption or foster parenting have been prominently debated in various states throughout the 1980s and 1990s; results have been mixed and are subject to frequent legal challenges. Since objections to LGBT adoption and/or fostering often are grounded in state consensual sodomy laws that cast lesbians and gay men as criminals, some commentators have speculated that the Supreme Court's June 2003 ruling in *Lawrence v. Texas* on the Texas "homosexual conduct" law would invalidate such arguments.

Academic interest in lesbian-mother (and to a lesser extent, gay-father) families has tended to focus heavily on the psychological status of the children, both while they are growing up and in later years. Scholars in this field, mostly psychologists and psychiatrists, draw on a long tradition of studies of children from "broken homes," most of which have focused on outcomes, assuming the deviance of any families that vary from a heterosexual two-parent norm. Nonetheless, these studies, nearly all of which indicate that children of lesbian and gay parents do not differ as a group from those whose parents are presumed to be heterosexual, have provoked considerable debate, as some observers, from both pro-gay and antigay camps, are concerned that they imply that lesbians and gay men are no different from the general population. Among these are studies that have followed the children of gay and lesbian parents over long periods of time; these have indicated that these children are indistinguishable from other children once they reach adulthood. Other studies have depended on comparisons of children from lesbian or gay homes with children growing up in presumptively heterosexual single-parent environments; these have uniformly revealed few if any variations in terms of gender-related behavior, psychological health, or other variables.

The most useful of these psychological assessments have been longitudinal studies that examine the impact on children over a number of developmental stages. Fiona Tasker and Susan Golombok conducted one such project in Great Britain. Another major researcher in this field, Charlotte Patterson, has also examined some of the same areas of behavior and cognition, noting the complications involved in organizing such research considering that lesbian-mother families are not a unitary object of study: some women had children during previous heterosexual relationships, while others became mothers as lesbians; some were single, while others had partners. Beyond this, of course, lesbian-mother and gay-father families are diverse ethnically, economically, and culturally. Little is known, as well, about the domestic organization of lesbian-mother (or gay-father) families, or about the extent to which such families are embedded in larger kinship networks.

Bearing these uncertainties in mind, these researchers concluded that there were no meaningful differences between children born to heterosexual couples and those born (usually by means of donor insemination) to women who identified themselves as lesbian on measures of social competence, behavior problems, or sex role behavior, nor did the children display differences in cognitive functioning or behavioral adjustment. Such differences as were noted between children of heterosexual and lesbian parents appear mainly in the area of tolerating stress or openness to diversity. Considering the more general ambiguities that arise in categorizing families headed by heterosexual and homosexual parents as "different"—insofar as families of both types may share important socioeconomic, cultural, and psychological traits—it seems clear that outcome-oriented studies of children are unlikely to provide authoritative information on this issue.

Scholars who oppose the right of lesbians and gay men to be parents argue that these studies minimize the extent to which such children suffer from stigmatization among their peers; they further claim that same-sex parents are incapable of modeling normal adult behaviors for their children. At the same time, however, some scholars who fashion themselves as supporters of gay families (notably Judith Stacey and Timothy J. Biblarz) have maintained that studies emphasizing the similarities between children from gay and straight homes do not place enough emphasis on the ways in which gay and lesbian parenting may be superior to that of heterosexuals or may at least offer a distinctive or identifiably queer cultural environment. Their arguments hinge on a few studies that have suggested that children from lesbian and gay homes may show themselves to be more tolerant of nonnormative lifestyles and that they may engage in more sexual experimentation in later life. Because all of these studies are small and only a limited segment of the population of lesbian and gay parents, however, are ever sampled, such conclusions are speculative at best.

**Domestic Partnership.** Kathleen Burke (center) and Mary Louise Cervone, who is holding their two-year-old son, Daniel, are among the first thirty couples to get a Certificate of Life Partnership—granting them certain practical as well as symbolic rights—from Kevin E. Vaughan, executive director of the Philadelphia Commission on Human Relations, on 8 October 1998. [AP/Wide World Photos]

The legal issues facing gay and lesbian parents have fallen into a number of categories. As noted above, conflicts over the right of lesbians and gay men to foster or adopt children rage around the U.S., with each state setting its own policy and many decisions dependent on agency practices and precedents. Even among agencies that do permit lesbians and gay men to adopt, many only offer them children who are judged to be "hard to place," most often those who are non-white or mixed-race, older, and/or who suffer from mental or physical disabilities, giving heterosexual married couples preferential access to non-disabled Caucasian infants. Perhaps surprisingly, males are less coveted in the adoption market than females, possibly because of gender stereotypes of male children—particularly those who are not Caucasian—being more difficult to control. These policies have created a situation in which lesbians and gay men who adopt are implicitly considered "second best" families and are therefore offered "second best" children.

Although custody and visitation battles for formerly married gay and lesbian parents have become less prominent than they were in the 1970s and 1980s, these conflicts continue to surface and because of local policy variations and the wide discretion enjoyed by family court judges they continue to have unpredictable results. Since cases argued in family court are presumably judged as individual situations and thus not subject to legal precedent, even a more tolerant situation nationally may not translate into a positive outcome for individual parents. A noteworthy example of this was the Sharon Bottoms case in Virginia, a two year legal battle (1993–1995) in which a lesbian mother lost custody of her son to her mother (arguably a person who had proven her ability to raise a homosexual child). Ironically, several cases argued not long afterward in the same jurisdiction had different results, pointing to the idiosyncratic, individualized nature of all custody determinations.

In addition to research that aims to answer questions about the fitness of lesbian and gay parents, popular writing has begun to appear that speaks to the specific experience of LGBT parents or their children. A number of these works are overwhelmingly celebratory in tone. Some are drawn directly from personal experience, including memoirs that concern parenthood or same-sex marriage, and often focus on the hardships and obstacles encountered on the way to the final goal of family formation, while they also take pride in the ultimate achievement of these goals (examples: *The Velveteen Father* by Jesse Green; *The Kid* by Dan Savage; *You're Not From Around Here, Are You?* by Louise Blum; *Family Values* by Phyllis Burke; and from the perspective of children, *Out of the Ordinary* edited by Noelle Howey and Ellen Samuels). Scholarly studies that explore questions of family in the lives of lesbians and gay men include several ethnographic works: *Lesbian Mothers* by Ellen Lewin, *Families We Choose* by Kath Weston, and *One of the Children* by William Hawkeswood, as well as *Mommy Queerest* by the rhetorician Julie Thompson.

## Same-Sex Marriage and Domestic Partnership

Legal battles over parenthood are related on a number of levels to more recent struggles over same-sex marriage and domestic partnership. On one level, of course, parental rights are closely connected to marital status: if same-sex couples were permitted to marry, their claims for co-parenthood would proceed automatically from their marital status. To the extent that the right to marry defines the legitimacy and presumed durability of domestic arrangements, the absence of this right automatically situates same-sex couples in a radically different position from most potential or actual parents. Ironically, at the same time that growing numbers of same-sex couples are becoming more visible as parents, opponents of gay and lesbian marriage argue that procreation is the primary (or even sole) justification for marriage, and that

insofar as same-sex couples cannot reproduce "naturally," they ought not to be able to marry.

The recent attention given to same-sex marriage and domestic partnership rights rarely considers the fact that struggle for these entitlements—whether they are seen as primarily legal or cultural—is not wholly a new development. Probably most controversially, historian John Boswell argued in his book *Same-Sex Unions in Premodern Europe* that ceremonies celebrating same sex relationships were widespread in early Christian history and that the form of the modern wedding, in fact, draws on these earlier patterns. Jonathan Katz's *Gay American History* documents a number of instances in which a cross-dressing woman successfully passed as a man and was thus able to marry another woman. A number of accounts of Depression-era Harlem, for example, describe weddings of butch/femme couples in elaborate ceremonies; among cases that received extensive publicity was the wedding of lesbian blues singer Gladys Bentley to her white lover.

Other cases of passing women, such as that of the jazz musician Billy Tipton, who was only discovered to be anatomically female after her death, suggest ways in which transgendered individuals managed to negotiate the legal system in order to marry and raise families. Classification of these cases is often elusive, particularly when questions of chromosomal sex are pitted against transsexual technologies as they intersect with gender identity. In a 2000 case in Texas, for example, Jessica and Robin Wicks were issued a marriage license. Jessica had undergone a sex reassignment procedure to become female, and the couple identifies as lesbian. But in the eyes of the state, Jessica's chromosomal sex, male, is what entitled her to marry a woman, making the marriage a legal heterosexual union. According to a 1999 opinion issued by Texas's Fourth Court of Appeals in San Antonio, chromosomes, not sex-change operations or outward gender characteristics, determine a person's sex; even the Texas Conservative Coalition concurred with this opinion, since Jessica and Robin, regardless of their appearance and behavior, are considered "legally a man and a woman."

As far back as the early 1970s, gays and lesbians have challenged the legal restriction of marriage to opposite-sex partners. In 1970 the Reverend Troy Perry presided over a ceremony between two women, issuing a church marriage certificate that would have exempted the couple from obtaining a marriage license had they been a man and a woman. Other efforts to circumvent the law were subsequently undertaken in Minnesota (1971), Kentucky (1973), Boulder, Colorado (1975), Washington, D.C.

**Lesbian Wedding.** Two appropriately garbed women share a joyful moment in one of the many different kinds of commitment ceremonies that have taken place in various churches and nonreligious settings since the early 1970s. [AP/Wide World Photos]

(1990), and Ithaca, New York (1995). Decisions upholding the restrictions often cited biblical authority or invoked interpretations of "nature."

Even in the absence of a legal right to marry, same-sex couples have continued to celebrate their unions in ever more visible ceremonies, not only in large metropolitan areas with substantial LGBT populations but in rural areas and small towns throughout the U.S. Religious denominations differ in their openness to such rituals. The predominantly LGBT Metropolitan Community Church performs a ceremony called a "holy union"; clergy from the Unitarian Universalist Association, the United Church of Christ, and the Reform and Reconstructionist movements of Judaism have also demonstrated a willingness to perform such ceremonies. In other denominations, divisions over the issue have been heated. In 1999, for example, the United Methodist Church tried and suspended two ministers, Gregory Dell and Jimmy Creech, for performing same-sex weddings in different parts of the country. Similar heated debates have emerged among other mainline Protestant churches (along with conflicts over accepting lesbian and gay

clergy); efforts to challenge antigay stances in conservative Protestant churches, such as the Southern Baptists, have not been successful to date. The Roman Catholic Church has steadfastly refused to recognize same-sex unions, although its clergy sometimes officiate at ceremonies held in non-church locations.

Couples who hold commitment ceremonies often find that family and friends are not willing to participate. Unlike heterosexuals, as anthropologist Ellen Lewin has shown in *Recognizing Ourselves,* these couples nearly always bear the entire expense of their ceremonies, and rarely expect to receive the gifts and other indications of community approval that are routinely a dimension of weddings. Lack of support, however, does not seem to have dampened the desire for rituals of commitment; the increasing frequency of such ceremonies has spawned an industry of "how-to" books and businesses that provide wedding products such as rings and wedding cake ornaments suitable for same-sex couples.

With a surge of activism related to demands for marriage and domestic partnership, a host of authors from legal studies, philosophy, political science, cultural studies, and other fields have taken up questions of marriage and family, focusing primarily on arguments for and against legal recognition. Many of these works invoke personal experience in the service of proposing a course of action or a political initiative (examples: *What is Marriage For?* by E. J. Graff; *A Place at the Table* by Bruce Bawer). Yet others have sought to document arguments for and against family life; questions about same-sex marriage as a legitimate political goal have been particularly central for these authors (examples: Suzanne Sherman, ed., *Lesbian and Gay Marriage;* Gretchen Stiers, *From This Day Forward;* and Andrew Sullivan, ed., *Same-Sex Marriage: Pro and Con*). In many cases, these arguments have essentially reiterated the debates over accommodation and resistance that preoccupy LGBT communities and activists. The more fervently pro-marriage writers, particularly Andrew Sullivan and Bruce Bawer, have argued that the most important political struggle that LGBT people can undertake is the battle for marriage, and that all other rights hinge on achieving this goal.

A small number of new scholarship in the area of family are ethnographic, such as *Lesbian Mothers* and *Recognizing Ourselves* by Ellen Lewin; *Families We Choose* by Kath Weston; *No Place Like Home* by Christopher Carrington; and *One of the Children* by William Hawkeswood. Other works from philosophy, political science, rhetoric, and law have engaged with questions at a more speculative level, asking how the newly visible families of LGBT persons affect larger questions of civil rights for LGBT populations. These works are numerous, but include *The Morality of Gay Rights* by legal scholar Carlos Ball; *Sexual Justice* by philosopher Morris Kaplan; *Queer Family Values* by political scientist Valerie Lehr; *Sexual Strangers* by political scientist Shane Phelan; and *Legally Wed* by legal scholar Mark Strasser. Many of these authors are concerned with the ways in which family—conceptualized in terms of parenthood and/or marriage—signals citizenship and access to a kind of public legitimacy most clearly marked by the right to be "ordinary." *The Case for Same-Sex Marriage* by legal scholar William N. Eskridge, Jr., argues that marriage has the potential to "civilize" LGBT people by enhancing their ability to form enduring commitments. Others, particularly cultural studies scholar Michael Warner in *The Trouble with Normal,* have mounted critiques of the impulses that lead members of sexual minorities to "accommodate" seemingly mainstream values, urging a reinvigoration of "queer" sensibilities and an acceleration of resistance or subversion by LGBT persons and communities. These authors have often lamented the "normalizing" impulses that have accompanied greater visibility and acceptance, citing the influence of commercial interests and media in shaping

LGBT (examples: *All the Rage* by sociologist Suzanna Danuta Walters; *Selling Out* by human rights activist Alexandra Chasin).

Opinion is sharply divided in LGBT communities as well. Largely in response to grassroots efforts to achieve legal recognition, LGBT rights organizations such as the Lambda Legal Defense and Education Fund and the Freedom to Marry Project have taken up the cause of marriage and domestic partnership and launched test cases in a number of U.S. states. At the same time, some LGBT activists scorn marriage as an accommodationist goal, fatally corrupted by its historical association with patriarchy and (more recently) with consumption.

In the meantime, these arguments seem to have little direct effect on the contemporary movement to legalize same-sex marriage or to secure more limited rights via diverse mechanisms of domestic partnership. These struggles have been enacted in a number of judicial arenas, but also have emerged in the world of business, as increasing numbers of employers have begun to offer benefits to employees' domestic partners. At the same time, many municipalities and other governmental entities have also inaugurated domestic partnership registration. This mechanism is nearly always purely symbolic, though some locales may entitle registrants to a specific range of benefits such as health insurance, bereavement leave, and other rights associated with families.

Considerable controversy emerged in this area when the Supreme Court of Hawaii gave serious consideration to a measure that would have opened up legal marriage to same-sex couples (*Baehr v. Miike,* 1996). Legislative efforts to forestall this move led to the enactment of a more limited domestic partnership ordinance. At the same time, anti-gay sentiment in the U.S. Congress led to the passage of a paradoxically named measure, the Defense of Marriage Act (DOMA) in 1996, which gave states the right to refuse to recognize same-sex marriages enacted in other states and denied federal benefits to same-sex marital partners. The measure passed even though same-sex marriage had not yet been made legal anywhere in the United States, and despite the fact that it appeared to pose a conflict with the Constitution's provision for full faith and credit. Nonetheless, following a class-action suit in Vermont that began in 1997 (*Baker v. State*), a more robust version of domestic partner registration went into effect in that state in 2000, whereby same-sex couples who register for civil union gain access to some three hundred state benefits and privileges in the areas of inheritance, property transfers, medical decisions, workers' compensation, insurance, and state taxes previously available only to heterosexual married couples. As of this writing, however, these entitlements are only recognized in the state of Vermont and are not labeled "marriage," that term being reserved unequivocally for the union of a man and a woman. Though couples from outside Vermont can travel to the state to register for civil union, dissolution of such unions requires that at least one of the partners is a legal resident of the state. Civil union in Vermont has no bearing on federal tax policy or immigration rights. Other challenges to the definition of marriage are currently in process in Massachusetts and New Jersey.

Although efforts to recognize same-sex unions in the United States have produced equivocal, localized, and inconsistent results, the legal status of same-sex couples has been undergoing constant change in other countries, particularly in Western Europe. Beginning in 1989, when Denmark enacted a domestic partnership registration act, same-sex partners have had access to the same obligations and rights that heterosexual marriage bestows, with the significant exception of the rights associated with family formation, for example, adoption and artificial insemination. Subsequent to Denmark's legislation, the other Scandinavian countries (Norway, Sweden, and Iceland) followed with similar measures. In 1999, France created Pactes civils de solidarité (PACS), a sort of "marriage lite" available to both homosexual and heterosexual couples. Some similar rights have been extended to unmarried couples in the Catalonia region of Spain. As of 2002, same-sex couples in the Netherlands enjoy the same right to marry—including the right to call their unions "marriages"—as heterosexual couples, although the law does not offer gay and lesbian couples the same access to international adoption that other couples have. South Africa included protection against discrimination based on sexual orientation in its constitution in 1977, though the implications of that language for specific marital and family issues has yet to be determined.

Judicial efforts to extend specific rights to same-sex couples have had notable success in some other countries (including Israel, Hungary, and New Zealand), though ongoing cases have yet to be resolved as of this writing. In Canada, legislation that applies to common-law heterosexual marriages has been used as the starting point for demands for same-sex marriage. The landmark Ontario case, *M. v. H.* (1997), established the principle that same-sex spouses should have the same rights to support upon separating as heterosexuals and effectively nullified the heterosexual definition of "spouse." Most significant, as of this writing, for the situation of LGBT couples in the U.S. has been the June 2003 ruling by the Ontario appeals court that eliminates the restriction of marriage to het-

erosexual couples, along with the proposal by the Canadian prime minister that the new policy be extended to the entire nation. Because there are no citizenship or residency requirements for marriage in Canada, U.S. couples have begun to take advantage of the opportunity for legal marriage in Ontario, even though their marriages have no official standing in the United States.

The U.S. Supreme Court's 2003 decision in *Lawrence v. Texas*, which reversed the earlier *Bowers v. Hardwick* decision and struck down consensual sodomy laws across the nation, has been interpreted as providing a foundation for the legalization of same-sex marriage. Interestingly, many of the most insistent voices for such an interpretation have been those of vehemently anti-LGBT conservatives. Justice Antonin Scalia's dissent, for example, argues that the decision represents the Court's capitulation to "the so-called homosexual agenda," that it in effect has "taken sides in the culture war," and that other laws that aim to protect "order and morality," including those that now prohibit same-sex marriage, are jeopardized. Although the decision does not endorse same-sex marriage, Justice Anthony Kennedy's majority opinion noted that sodomy laws demeaned the existence of homosexual persons, "by making their private sexual conduct a crime." Other commentators have noted that without sodomy laws a primary justification for the denial of other civil entitlements—marriage and the right to adopt children among them—no longer can be invoked.

## Conclusion

As of this writing, LGBT families stand at the intersection of intense cultural, legal, and political controversy, both within LGBT communities and in the wider society. Intense debates continue among lesbians and gay men over "sameness" and "difference," whether fashioned as "accommodation" versus "resistance" or "normality" versus "queerness." Debates that surround lesbian and gay families—whether they focus on marriage, domestic partnership, parenting, adoption, or custody—thus reflect fundamental strains characteristic of LGBT politics. Are members of sexual and gender minorities fundamentally "the same" as other people, that is "normal," or can they lay claim to a profoundly "different" cultural position, that of queerness? And how can either of these positions provide the foundation for scholarship, activism, and community development?

At the same time, political developments in the U.S. and around the world have placed LGBT families in the spotlight. Policies that affect the status of LGBT people in marriage, domestic partnership, and as parents are in seemingly constant flux. The arena of family has become the battleground in which a host of other issues are being negotiated and in which redefinitions of legal status come to be understood in terms of fairness, citizenship, and personal dignity.

## Bibliography

Ball, Carlos A. *The Morality of Gay Rights: An Exploration in Political Philosophy*. New York and London: Routledge, 2003.

Bawer, Bruce. *A Place at the Table: The Gay Individual in American Society*. New York: Poseidon, 1993.

Blum, Louise A. *You're Not From Around Here, Are You?* Madison: University of Wisconsin Press, 2001.

Boswell, John. *Same-Sex Unions in Premodern Europe*. New York: Villard, 1994.

Burke, Phyllis. *Family Values: Two Moms and Their Son*. New York: Random House, 1993.

Carrington, Christopher. *No Place Like Home: Relationships and Family Life Among Lesbians and Gay Men*. Chicago and London: University of Chicago Press, 1999.

Chasin, Alexandra. *Selling Out: The Gay and Lesbian Movement Goes to Market*. New York: St. Martin's Press, 2000.

Chauncey, George. *Gay New York: Gender, Urban Culture, and the Making of the Gay Male World*. New York: Basic Books, 1994.

Eskridge, William N. *The Case for Same-Sex Marriage*. New York: Free Press, 1996.

Faderman, Lillian. *Odd Girls and Twilight Lovers: A History of Lesbian Life in Twentieth-Century America*. New York: Columbia University Press, 1991.

Graff, E.J. *What Is Marriage For?* Boston: Beacon Press, 1999.

Green, Jesse. *The Velveteen Father*. New York: Villard, 1999.

Hawkeswood, William. *One of the Children: Gay Black Men in Harlem*. Berkeley: University of California Press, 1996.

Howey, Noelle, and Ellen Samuels, eds. *Out of the Ordinary: Essays on Growing Up with Gay, Lesbian, and Transgender Parents*. New York: St. Martin's Press, 2000.

Johnson, Suzanne M., and Elizabeth O'Connor. *The Gay Baby Boom: The Psychology of Parenthood*. New York: New York University Press, 2002.

Kaplan, Morris B. *Sexual Justice: Democratic Citizenship and the Politics of Desire*. New York: Routledge, 1997.

Katz, Jonathan. *Gay American History: Lesbians and Gay Men in the U.S.A.: A Documentary Anthology*. New York: Crowell, 1976.

*Lawrence v. Texas*, 539 US ____, 123 S. Ct. 2472 (2003)

Lehr, Valerie. *Queer Family Values: Debunking the Myth of the Nuclear Family*. Philadelphia: Temple University Press, 1999.

Lewin, Ellen. *Lesbian Mothers: Accounts of Gender in American Culture*. Ithaca, N.Y.: Cornell University Press, 1993.

———. *Recognizing Ourselves: Ceremonies of Lesbian and Gay Commitment*. New York: Columbia University Press, 1998.

Middleton, Diane Wood. *Suits Me: The Double Life of Billy Tipton*. Boston: Houghton Mifflin, 1998.

Newman, Lesléa. *Heather Has Two Mommies*. Boston: Alyson Wonderland, 1989.

Patterson, Charlotte J. "The Family Lives of Children Born to Lesbian Mothers." In *Lesbian, Gay, and Bisexual Identities in Families: Psychological Perspectives*. Edited by Charlotte J. Patterson and Anthony R. D'Augelli. New York: Oxford University Press, 1998.

———. "Lesbian Mothers, Gay Fathers, and Their Children." In *Lesbian, Gay, and Bisexual Identities Over the Lifespan: Psychological Perspectives*. Edited by Anthony R. D'Augelli and Charlotte J. Patterson. New York: Oxford University Press, 1995.

Phelan, Shane. *Sexual Strangers: Gays, Lesbians, and Dilemmas of Citizenship*. Philadelphia: Temple University Press, 2001.

Polikoff, Nancy D. "We Will Get What We Ask For: Why Legalizing Gay and Lesbian Marriage Will Not 'Dismantle the Legal Structure of Gender in Every Marriage.'" *Virginia Law Review* 79:7 (1993): 1535–1550.

Savage, Dan. *The Kid (What Happened After My Boyfriend and I Decided to Go Get Pregnant): An Adoption Story*. New York: Dutton, 1999.

Sherman, Suzanne, ed. *Lesbian and Gay Marriage: Private Commitments, Public Ceremonies*. Philadelphia: Temple University Press, 1992.

Stacey, Judith, and Timothy J. Biblarz. "(How) Does the Sexual Orientation of Parents Matter?" *American Sociological Review* 66 (2001): 159–183.

Stiers, Gretchen A. *From This Day Forward: Commitment, Marriage, and Family in Lesbian and Gay Relationships*. New York: St. Martin's Press, 1999.

Strasser, Mark Philip. *Legally Wed: Same-Sex Marriage and the Constitution*. Ithaca, N.Y.: Cornell University Press, 1997.

Sullivan, Andrew. *Virtually Normal: An Argument about Homosexuality*. New York: Knopf, 1995.

Sullivan, Andrew, ed. *Same-Sex Marriage: Pro and Con: A Reader*. New York: Vintage, 1997.

Tasker, Fiona L., and Susan Golombok. *Growing Up in a Lesbian Family: Effects on Child Development*. New York and London: Guilford Press, 1997.

Thompson, Julie M. *Mommy Queerest*. Amherst: University of Massachusetts Press, 2002.

Walters, Suzanna Danuta. *All the Rage: The Story of Gay Visibility in America*. Chicago: University of Chicago Press, 2001.

Warner, Michael. *The Trouble With Normal: Sex, Politics, and the Ethics of Queer Life*. New York: Free Press, 1999.

Weston, Kath. *Families We Choose: Lesbians, Gays, Kinship*. New York: Columbia University Press, 1991.

Wolfson, Evan. "Crossing the Threshold: Equal Marriage Rights for Lesbians and Gay Men and the Intra-Community Critique." *New York Review of Law and Social Change* 21: 3 (1994–1995): 567–615.

**Ellen Lewin**

*See also* ECONOMICS; FAMILY LAW AND POLICY; JOHNSTON, JILL; MARRIAGE CEREMONIES AND WEDDINGS; PARENTS AND FRIENDS OF LESBIANS AND GAYS (PFLAG); SEX EDUCATION; WADDELL, TOM.

# FAMILY LAW AND POLICY

Demands that LGBT couples and LGBT people's relationships to children be recognized and treated equitably in U.S. law and policy date from the early 1970s, but they acquired prominence from the late 1980s onward. All levels of government regulate familial relationships, and courts have significant leeway within the bounds set by statute. This makes for jurisdictional fragmentation and great variation across states and localities in response to sexual and gender diversity.

## Relationship Regimes

Legal and policy regulation of intimate relationships extends far beyond family law. Rules on taxation, immigration, social insurance, health care decision making, inheritance, pensions, conflict of interest, and parenting create relationship regimes that privilege some family forms (that is, monogamous, nuclear, heterosexual, and reproductive families) over others. Restrictive definitions of family are heavily influenced by spiritual traditions, and religious conservatives have been at the forefront of opposition to extending familial recognition and rights to LGBT people and same-sex couples.

The regulation of heterosexual relationships has changed significantly over the last half century, and some of the openings created in what was once a more restrictive system have made room for gains by same-sex couples. One shift has been toward regarding marriage as a contract between two individuals, whose terms can be modified within broader bounds than before. This long-term change has included a loosening of rules on divorce.

Longer-term social and economic changes have increased the incidence of marital breakdown and of nonmarital cohabitation among heterosexuals. This has been accompanied by modest shifts toward recognizing de facto relationships, but only in a minority of states. In the United States, the distinction in law and public policy between marriage and any other status remains clear and substantively consequential, in contrast to some other industrialized countries (most notably Canada and Sweden). This is one of the factors explaining the early emergence in the United States of domestic partner registries aimed at same-sex couples alone and the prominence of marriage in the broader agenda of LGBT family activism.

## Relationship Recognition in Federal Law and Policy

Most family policy lies within the legal domain of the states, but more than two thousand references to family relationships are included in federal statutes—almost all of them exclusive of same-sex relationships. The Domestic Violence Act of 1994 included wording on abused partners in relationships that allowed subsequent interpretation to include same-sex couples. In 2002 Congress approved a bill that allowed (in limited circumstances) the domestic partners of public safety officers killed in the line of duty to receive a federal death benefit. This was inspired by the death on 11 September 2001 of New York City Fire Department chaplain Mychal Judge.

But losses have been more striking. The Defense of Marriage Act of 1996 allowed states to circumvent any gains in recognition of same-sex marriage and to stipulate that federal law governing spouses would be interpreted in heterosexual terms only. In the same year, a congressional measure designed to toughen barriers to illegal immigration effectively narrowed a small loophole through which some foreign partners of U.S. lesbians and gay men had come into the country.

With only modest exceptions, the majority of the U.S. Supreme Court has retained a general hostility to LGBT rights and a deference to states' rights over most of the period in which family-related claims have arisen. The prominence of state jurisdiction in areas affecting relationships means that the absence of progressive intervention by the Supreme Court leaves in place great variation in regime from state to state. As recently as 1986, its *Bowers v. Hardwick* ruling let stand state laws criminalizing homosexual behavior, which at the time still existed in about half of the states. This was an impediment to legal and policy change recognizing same-sex relationships, since LGB couples were presumed to engage in criminal activity.

The court's overturning of *Bowers* in its 2003 ruling in *Lawrence and Garner v. Texas* effectively did eliminate discriminatory state sodomy laws, and may boost relationship claims. However, even if the majority ruling's language was encouragingly broad, it was based on a privacy, and not an equality rights, argument, and it pointedly denied any direct link to same-sex recognition. The ruling will likely have positive but uneven effects.

## Relationship Recognition in State Law and Policy

The domain of state governments includes family law, estate law, a range of statutes granting decision-making authority to family members in the case of death or incapacity, and marriage. In only a few states have legislatures, governors, or courts taken significant and systematic steps to recognize same-sex relationships. Many more states than that (almost three-quarters) have moved in the opposite direction, enacting prohibitions on the recognition of same-sex marriage. Even the passage of basic nondiscrimination measures that include sexual orientation has been achieved in only a quarter of the states, and these have only unevenly and partially forced recognition of same-sex relationships.

The positive steps taken by state governments have usually been in the extension of family benefits to include same-sex partners of state employees. Massachusetts and Delaware extended health or other benefits for at least some such employees in 1992, and over the next ten years, nine other states, along with Washington, D.C., joined them. Change in Oregon was forced by a court challenge to an employee benefit plan that ended in a 1998 victory, leading to a statewide domestic partnership regime. Policy shifts beyond benefits for state employees have required court challenges. These have produced mixed results, but with several important victories registered in appeal courts (with precedent-setting impact).

In *Braschi v. Stahl Associates* (1989), Miguel Braschi won the right to remain in the New York apartment in which he and his deceased partner had lived, the court agreeing that they were "family" for inheritance purposes. In *In re Guardianship of Sharon Kowalski* (1991), an appeals court in Minnesota ended litigation that began after a 1983 car accident severely injured Sharon Kowalski, awarding guardianship to her partner Karen Thompson and describing their relationship as a "family of affinity." In *Vasquez v. Hawthorne* (2001), the state of Washington's Supreme Court ruled in favor of Frank Vasquez's claim that his partner's death without a will should be covered by state inheritance laws, on the grounds that their relationship was marriage-like.

Two dramatic victories were won in court challenges to restrictive marriage laws, the first in Hawaii *(Baehr v. Lewin* [1993]) and the second in Vermont *(Baker v. Vermont* [1994]). The first of these provoked a wave of "defense of marriage" bills. In 1998 a huge majority of voters in Hawaii effectively circumvented the court decision by adopting a constitutional amendment allowing for a strictly heterosexual definition of marriage. The state legislature enacted a consolation prize for same-sex claimants, a "reciprocal beneficiary" regime open to people not able to marry (including, for example, brothers and sisters). This was the first statewide domestic partnership legislation in the United States, and while it was modest in its scope, it did accord access to some health insurance coverage, some state employee benefits,

bereavement leave, hospital visitation rights, and inheritance rights. More profound change resulted from the 1999 court ruling by Vermont's Supreme Court that the exclusion of same-sex couples from marriage violated the state's constitution. This resulted in the legislative creation of a "civil union" system that sidestepped the symbolism attached to marriage itself but in other respects eliminated discrimination against gay and lesbian couples within state jurisdiction.

The California legislature has moved incrementally to recognize same-sex relationships, although in 2000 voters also approved an exclusionary measure on marriage itself. The state's domestic partnership registry is open to same-sex couples and includes provisions for relationship termination, health care decision making, sick leave to care for an ill partner, some social insurance and taxation benefits, and second-parent adoption (see below). There are a few other states, located in the Northeast, that seem close to enacting measures that accord at least some recognition to same-sex couples.

## Local Recognition of Same-Sex Relationships

The first governmental recognition of lesbian and gay relationships in the United States occurred at the local level, with the extension of employee benefits to the partners of municipal workers. In 1984 Berkeley, California, became the first to do so, and other college and university towns were among the pioneers. In 1988 Los Angeles was the first major city to extend such recognition, with Seattle and San Francisco following suit two and three years later. However, in over half of the states where cities or counties had established such benefit provisions, court actions were mounted challenging their jurisdictional right to do so. A few such challenges—for example, in Minneapolis and Boston—were successful. Also, referenda were frequently initiated to overturn such extensions, though by the turn of the century popular majorities were more likely to retain expansive benefit programs than reject them.

Some localities also created domestic partnership registries, although often they had little more than symbolic value. Starting in the late 1990s, a few cities sought to extend their leverage beyond the public sector in more substantively weighty fashion. Beginning in 1997 San Francisco's Equal Benefits Ordinance required that firms and nonprofit agencies doing business with the city provide equal benefit coverage for cohabiting couples, whether same-sex or heterosexual, and in all of such institutions' operations, not just those based in the city. Court challenges supported by a number of large corporations, including airlines, failed in 2001, by which time Los Angeles and Seattle had enacted similar measures.

**Adoption Rights.** Former foster parents Jon Holden and Michael Galluccio hold their newly adopted son, Adam Holden Galluccio, in Newark, New Jersey, on 17 December 1997, at the end of a long, successful court battle in the state for equal rights to adoption by same-sex couples. [AP/Wide World Photos]

By the end of 2001, almost half of the largest corporations in the United States had extended their own employee benefit plans to recognize same-sex partners (most of them also including de facto heterosexual couples for the first time). The vast majority of major universities and colleges had taken the same step by that time. While some of these changes were induced by legal or statutory change at the local or state level, others were the result of pressure from employee groups and labor unions, assisted by regional and national activist groups.

## Parenting Issues

Equity claims that raise the specter of lesbians and especially gay men in close contact with children are explosive, fueled by fears about sexual predation and childhood vulnerability. And yet parenting issues were among the first relationship issues to be raised by lesbians and gay men. From at least the 1970s, lesbian mothers were fighting openly for custody of children from earlier heterosexual relationships or defending themselves from the threat of losing custody. Pressure for change in parenting regimes intensified in the 1980s with the rapid growth in the number of gays and especially lesbians who had children as same-sex couples, or who aspired to. It also came from the prominence acquired by other relationship issues from the end of that decade on and the increased visibility of openly lesbian and gay couples.

Parenting claims in such areas as custody, adoption, foster care, and assisted reproduction lie within state jurisdiction, though individual courts have considerable room for maneuver. Custody disputes regularly appear before state and local courts, for example, and adoptions have to be approved in them. The particularly compelling circumstances of individual disputes or claims for second parent adoption in court have resulted in a surprising number of favorable rulings. Some of these decisions have been in states without much else in legislative or legal recognition of sexual and gender diversity.

On custody, there were favorable rulings in the 1970s (the first reportedly in 1967), but often they were accompanied by rules prohibiting cohabitation with a same-sex partner, or indeed any outward manifestations of homosexuality. By the 1980s most jurisdictions had adopted the "best interests of the child" standard in adjudicating disputes, in theory reducing the categorical exclusion of parenting claims by lesbians and gay men. An additional opening seemed to appear with *Palmore v. Sidoti*, a 1984 ruling by the U.S. Supreme Court on a race-related case, which stipulated that judges should not award custody on the basis of society's prejudice. Indeed, across that decade there were several important appeals court decisions that recognized lesbian or gay custody claims, most notably in West Coast states. But these shifts often coexisted with the continued application of closeting restrictions (obliging parents to keep partners away and in other ways to remain discreet about their homosexuality). There were also rulings by other courts that amounted to a categorical exclusion. In the 1990s there were startlingly negative appeals court rulings—often in southern states—aimed at shielding children from any exposure to homosexuality. And even in a decade marked by an overall shift to more equitable decisions on custody claims by lesbian and gay biological parents, the legal standing of nonbiological partners in same-sex relationships was rarely acknowledged. (This issue arose in access disputes involving now-separated same-sex partners.)

Adoption of children by lesbians and gay men, like custody, is not a new issue, since individuals have been legally able to adopt for a considerable time. From the late 1980s on, however, adoption claims have been more likely from same-sex couples seeking a formalization of rights and obligations for nonbiological parents through what are called second parent adoptions. An Alaska court granted what was probably the first such adoption in 1985, and many have followed it. On the other side of the ledger, there have been important appeals court rejections of such claims, even in states with otherwise positive records on sexual diversity (for example, California and Connecticut). There are also legislated or administrative bans on such adoptions in Florida, Utah, Mississippi, and Arkansas. About half of the states have seen little or no progress in recognizing adoption claims by lesbian or gay couples. But from the mid-1980s, favorable court judgments have been made in a striking array of states, including, for example, Tennessee in *In re Adoption of M. J. S.* (2000). In Vermont and Connecticut, second parent adoption was legislatively recognized in 1995 and 2000, respectively.

Positive outcomes for couples seeking the adoption of a child to whom neither partner is biologically related are much scarcer. They have been achieved through court rulings in Vermont, California, and New York. A favorable New Jersey verdict in *Holden and Galluccio v. New Jersey Department of Human Services* (1997) led to a change in state policy according equal treatment for homosexual and straight adoptive parents. By and large, however, there are immense legal barriers to "stranger" adoption, echoed in the placement policies of agencies and in rules established by countries (like China) that are the point of origin of many children adopted by U.S. couples.

Policy shifts in foster care are harder to chronicle. Few of the relevant agencies have taken significant steps to recognize sexual diversity among prospective foster parents. But chronic shortages of suitable homes for children and adolescents has meant that gay and lesbian cou-

ples have often been quietly given custody, especially of children who were otherwise difficult to place. A few states have had official policies (as with Arkansas); more have had informal rules prohibiting fostering by homosexuals. A few political and judicial challenges have been successful against such barriers (for example, forcing abandonment of Massachusetts's exclusionary policy in 1990, and allowing exceptions to Florida's prohibition on gay and lesbian fostering). Discrimination widely persists in the standards used to accept same-sex couples as foster parents and in the allocation of difficult foster children.

The development of facilities specializing in assisted reproduction has created new parenting options for many lesbians in particular. Most reproductive services in the United States are private and relatively unregulated. This means that clients have to bear the costs, creating effectively unequal access, and especially so because most insurance policies do not cover the costs. But it also means that services have emerged to address a growing market of same-sex couples, and some have mail-order operations that widen their geographic reach. Same-sex couples, of course, have to secure second parent adoption for the nonbiological parent even in the absence of a known donor, in contrast to the routine registration of parentage for married couples.

Gay male couples more seldom benefit from such openings, since they can secure biological parentage only through surrogate motherhood, with its extraordinary costs and not inconsiderable ethical dilemmas. Some states allow only married couples to enter into surrogacy arrangements, and it is not yet clear how many others would treat such arrangements as permanently voiding the biological mother's parental rights.

On parenting issues more broadly, even if stereotypes portray lesbians as not feminine enough, the fact that women are seen as more nurturant and child-centered than men creates some room for social acceptance of their parenting claims. The visibility and resources required to make parenting claims create class and race differences in the effective ability to pursue cases. Courts are also more receptive to claimants who conform to images of respectability and financial security. Such factors make claims from bisexuals (more likely to be seen as unstable in their relationships), and even more from transgender women and men, much more difficult to mount and to win.

## Cause and Effect

Change in relational and parental regimes have been effected most significantly in northeastern and West Coast states, along with Hawaii and the District of

Columbia. Most states have seen few or no steps toward recognizing lesbian and gay relationships, though within many there are municipalities and nongovernmental employers who have made changes within the limited policy terrain they control. Across the United States, steps toward equity have met fierce opposition and more than a few setbacks.

The pressure for change has come from activist networks and individuals, sometimes seeking court redress on their own, more often supported by equity-seeking groups. The national groups supportive of family policy claims include Lambda Legal Defense and Education Fund, the National Gay and Lesbian Task Force, and the Human Rights Campaign. Additional leverage has been provided by supportive allies, including organized labor, progressive religious groups, civil libertarians, and corporations recognizing the role of inclusive policies in attracting educated talent. Incremental change has come in part from courts faced not with a hypothetical argument about relationship recognition, but an existing well-functioning family arrangement, or a past one marked by tragic loss. Many second parent adoption claims are made by couples who can prove devotion to their children and who are not facing opposing arguments from directly involved parties.

Contributing subtly to a shift in climate over family policy is the ascendancy of anti-state and anti-welfare politics. Neo-liberalism emphasizes self-reliance and the obligations of family members to provide the kinds of material supports that otherwise would result in dependence on the public purse. This reinforces privatizing trends in family law and bolsters argumentation for same-sex family recognition. For example, opponents of state regulation could argue that cohabitation of any sort implies ongoing obligations on each partner to provide support to the more disadvantaged of the two, during the relationship and after separation, thereby lowering the potential drain on state resources.

The neo-liberal logic in favor of same-sex relationship recognition is weakened in the United States by the strength of social and religious conservatism. Republicans are still ready to campaign vigorously against the recognition of same-sex couples, with the support of the religious right and other conservative groups prepared to apply very considerable resources to recognition issues. Democrats are much more likely personally to support equity, but they are far from unanimous and regularly fear for their electoral futures if they press too hard. They also operate within complex political systems that easily produce stalemate.

Where law and policy do offer some recognition to LGBT families, there is still extensive statutory inequality, not least because of the absence of change at the federal level. There are also questions about the extent to which legal change is fully and equitably implemented by state officials, lower court judges, child-related agencies, medical personnel, funeral directors, insurance agents, human resource managers, and so on. Many LGBT people are not actually in a position to secure legal recognition, because of fears over disclosing their status. There are of course class, gender, and ethnic differences that influence the likelihood that such openness will be seen as safe. Claims are also easier to secure for those whose relationships most resemble traditional family structures, and for those whose social demographics conform to white middle-class norms.

There is a risk that legal shifts are being contained within heterosexual frameworks, sustaining discrimination against those whose intimate relationships do not fit easily within such models. But gains also contribute to the longer-term unsettling of the traditional family form brought on by the women's movement and by longer-term social and economic forces. They also increase the overall visibility of sexual and gender diversity and bring to the foreground the very fact of LGBT intimacy. The beneficiaries of change in any one policy area may not be broadly representative, and the extent of change is itself patchy and insecurely won. But those gains that have been won are of deep and broad importance.

## Bibliography

Bernstein, Mary, and Renate Reimann, eds. *Queer Families, Queer Politics: Challenging Culture and the State.* New York: Columbia University Press, 2001.

Cain, Patricia A. *Rainbow Rights: The Role of Lawyers and Courts in the Lesbian and Gay Civil Rights Movement.* Boulder, Colo.: Westview Press, 2000.

Dupuis, Martin. *Same-Sex Marriage, Legal Mobilization, and the Politics of Rights.* New York: Peter Lang, 2002.

Eskridge, William N., Jr. *Gaylaw: Challenging the Apartheid of the Closet.* Cambridge, Mass.: Harvard University Press, 1999.

Merin, Yuval. *Equality for Same-Sex Couples: The Legal Recognition of Gay Partnerships in Europe and the United States.* Chicago: University of Chicago Press, 2002.

**David Rayside**

*See also* ANTI-DISCRIMINATION LAW AND POLICY; COLORADO; DISCRIMINATION; FAMILY ISSUES; FEDERAL LAW AND POLICY; MARRIAGE CEREMONIES AND WEDDINGS.

# FASHION, STYLE, AND CLOTHING

Clothing, fashion, and other aspects of personal style have often held special significance in the lives of sexual minorities and gender variants. For queers and non-queers alike, fashion has been a means of creative exploration, self-expression, and group identification. It has also functioned as a social, economic, political, and cultural system for communicating (or hiding), among other things, one's social status, nationality, age, political beliefs, and ethnicity.

However, the close proximity of clothing to the surface of the body has often engaged it with issues of gender and sexuality and therefore makes it especially meaningful for queer folk. Outward appearance has long been the subject of social regulations enforcing sexual and gender norms, but also a favored place for articulating challenges to gender conformity and the very idea of sexual normality. Many queers have demonstrated a willingness to "play" with clothing and style in a manner often deemed threatening or subversive by social and cultural authorities.

The potentially dire, even life-threatening, consequences of such transgressions mean that the myriad stylizations composing queer fashionability have often represented perilous and profound political acts. Queers have used clothing and other elements of personal style to communicate sexual tastes and gender styles; to reform, augment, or minimize various parts of the body; to produce or heighten sexual desirability; and to visualize potentially invisible (and hide potentially visible) sexual and gender identities.

## The "Homosexuality" of Fashion

Histories and theories of fashion and clothing are riddled with homophobic generalizations about the inherent homosexuality of fashion. Based in the stereotype that all fashion designers are homosexual men and that all fashion is for heterosexual women, innumerable psychologists, psychoanalysts, and other social commentators have argued that the engine of the fashion industry's seasonal cycle was fashion designers' neurotic hatred of and obsessive identification with women. The close engagement of fashion, gender, and sexuality is evident in the longtime association of fashionable men and homosexuality, a trope based in codes of heterosexual masculinity.

Since at least the seventeenth century, any man who showed too great an interest in clothing, fashion, or other aspects of outer appearance was subject to charges of effeminacy, profligacy, or superficiality. Ephemeral fashion was considered the proper domain of "inconstant woman," and nattily attired men were regularly caricatured as fops, dandies, bucks, macaronis, exquisites, or swells, all terms indicating some departure from masculine gender norms and frequently implying sexual perversion or deviance.

The coupling of fashion and homosexuality continues today in the stereotype of the trendsetting and effortlessly fashionable gay man, often supplemented by a laundry list of mainstream styles and dressing practices that appear to have originated with gay men. By contrast, the fact that lesbians are also women has meant that their explorations of fashionable attire or other manipulations of physical appearance can be casually dismissed as a manifestation of, or a reaction against, stereotypes of femininity, which in the popular imagination is believed to be naturally drawn to fashion. Ultimately, the myth of the homosexuality of fashion facilitates the devaluing of gay and lesbian interrogations of clothing and personal style as techniques for liberation, arenas of self-expression, and crucial aspects of sex, gender, and sexual systems.

**Queer fashion production.** Nevertheless, the historical association of fashion and male homosexuality seems to have allowed a wide variety of men in the fashion and style industries more freedom to explore the realm of femininity, and has encouraged gay men in these industries to be more open about their sexuality. Like the fine and performing arts, the fashion world has attracted men whose creative talents might not be fully employed or realized in other lines of work. Richard Dyer has argued that gays are well prepared for work in the style industries through years of practice mastering their self-presentation and mimicking heterosexual norms as a means of survival within an often brutally homophobic society. In turn, the apparent prevalence of gay men in the needle trades has worked to reinforce the stereotype of homosexuality as essentially "artsy" and fashion forward.

*LGBT people in the fashion industry.* Gay male fashion designers are perhaps the most visible queer folk in the style industries, now and in the past. A number of famous couturiers were openly or not-so-openly homosexual or bisexual, including Christian Dior, Cristóbal Balenciaga, Yves Saint Laurent, Jean-Paul Gaultier, Giorgio Armani, Gianni Versace, Todd Oldham, Norman Hartnell, Halston, Rudi Gernreich, Willi Smith, and Calvin Klein. The top-flight designer Tom Ford, creative director of the Gucci Group, which includes the Yves Saint Laurent boutique, has been publicly open about his bisexuality. Contrary to stereotype, these designers exhibited wide variations in personal style and mannerisms, from the campy prima donna to the conventionally masculine.

Less visible, but at least as important, has been the presence of queer folk in the affiliated garment industries. Notable gay fashion photographers abound, but one might cite as examples George Platt Lynes's work in the 1930s and 1940s and the work of Herb Ritts and David LaChapelle in the 1980s and 1990s. Queers have also worked as makeup artists, hairdressers, and stylists for couture runway shows, fashion shoots, and celebrity fashion events. Others have influenced national style through their costume, hair, and makeup work in cinema and television production. The gay makeup artist Kevyn Aucoin reached celebrity status for his work on famous faces in the 1990s, authoring three books on the subject. Many queers work quietly behind the scenes (but not necessarily in the closet) in the fashion print media as graphic designers, stylists, and editors.

## History of Queer Fashion to the 1980s

**Before 1900.** Although the sheer diversity of gender and sex variant people over time makes it hazardous to assert any single queer style at a given moment, there have been a number of identifiably queer fashion trends. Some Native American tribes have longstanding traditions of transgender or *berdache* figures who used androgynous clothing to signal their two-spirited status. Court records and personal documents from as early as the colonial era indicate enduring interest in cross-dressing, both on the stage and in personal life. Often, this was temporary and humorous; other figures passed their entire lives dressed as the other sex, only to be discovered upon their death.

The increasingly industrialized production of clothing over the course of the nineteenth century allowed more Americans to explore the expressive and formative aspects of clothing and style goods. The theatrical and musical stage featured a number of famous cross-dressing troupes and performers (although usually with a comic edge), and playful cross-dressing was a common pastime among young men and women at home and school. A movement for the reform of women's dress emerged in the 1840s, proposing a more hygienic, comfortable hybrid of men's and women's clothes, akin to a shorter skirt over billowy pants.

By the end of the century, many women who rejected traditional roles or were associated with various suffrage, feminist, and reform movements favored a masculinized form of women's dress, simply tailored in dark colors with white linen. Near-hysterical commentators often explicitly attributed the personal style of these women to same-sex desire. At the fin-de-siècle, a few rare personal accounts and an increasing number of legal and scientific publications noted the complex personal aesthetics of "inverts."

Many metropolitan homosexual men expressed their gender and sexual dissonance and communicated their existence to others like them through custom tailored suits, boutonniere flowers (green carnations), neckties (green, later red), and a preference for bleached, highly styled hair and makeup. Female inverts variously sheared their hair, chewed tobacco, dressed in men's suits, and pursued traditional male occupations and other women as love interests.

**From 1900 to the 1980s.** The early twentieth century witnessed the rising popularity and increased presence of professional cross-dressing men in musical and dramatic roles in vaudeville and theater, a trend that culminated in the 1930s. Some queer men continued earlier trends of feminizing the details of a masculine wardrobe and demeanor; others adhered closely to gender conventions. New York City's "fairies" adopted some (but rarely all) of the elements of conventional female style, such as fastidiously tailored, brightly colored clothing, as well as rouge, mascara, and face powder. Other gay men were visible only through a specialized vocabulary and effeminate manner, while still others passed with ease among "normal" men.

Some LGBT's who belonged to homophile groups countered homophobic efforts to characterize sex and gender variants as deviant or marginal by pursuing a strategy of respectability. Central to this was the presentation of a more mainstream, gender-conforming appearance: women in skirts or dresses and men in suits and ties.

The middle decades of the century saw the emergence of lesbian communities marked by the ritualistic use of clothing and grooming in femme-butch roles. Butch lesbians adopted the work clothes and suits and ties of working and middle-class male attire, while their femme partners favored more conventionally feminine styles in hair, clothing, and accessories.

Needless to say, adherents of the 1960s counterculture, both LGBT and straight, did not care very much for mainstream fashion, embracing long hair, beads, and flamboyant clothing. Such costume was seen as transgressing gender boundaries: One often-heard complaint was that hippies wore their hair "like girls," and to be sure, there was no shortage of LGBTs who found the countercultural message of liberation personal as well as political.

*From the 1970s to the 1980s.* The era of gay liberation and lesbian feminism ushered in profound shifts in the queer use of clothing. The working-class attire of leather, blue jeans, and white t-shirts that had been evident in gay male communities at mid-century became the visually dominant gay male style in the 1970s and 1980s. Where gay men had tended to feminize conventional masculine fashion, now their short hair, beards and moustaches, leather bomber jackets, Adidas running shoes, aviator sunglasses, and plaid flannel shirts appeared to assert a masculinity historically denied them. A complex sartorial code using key chains or colored bandanas communicated gay men's sexual styles, preferences, and desires.

Some scholars view "clone style" as simply perpetuating traditional forms of heterosexual masculinity; others see it as paradoxically feminine in its presentation of the male body as a sexualized object of desire and display. It might also be seen as acknowledging the ways clothing and personal style have always served to gender and sexualize the body, even if this is habitually disavowed within codes of heterosexual masculine behavior.

At this time, a small group of gay liberationists argued for a more androgynous personal style, and "gender fucking" bearded men in dresses were a common feature at gay pride parades. But these were overshadowed and outnumbered by the votaries of clone style. The subsequent metropolitan disco culture attracted gay men in tight-fitting jeans, revealing t-shirts or tank tops, and running shoes, all designed to emphasize a sexualized and gym-styled gay male body.

Lesbian butch-femme style came under sharp criticism in the 1970s by lesbian feminists who misunderstood it as merely imitative of heterosexual sex-gender styles and roles. This was shaped by feminists' rejection of traditional feminine trappings in hair, clothing, and accessories as codifications of patriarchy's sexual objectification of women. The politics of lesbian feminism were encoded in a personal style featuring loose jeans or bib overalls, flannel shirts, no cosmetics, and little jewelry. Shaved heads, short hairstyles, and the long-in-back, short-in-front mullet were subsequently viewed as embodying the vestimentary tenets of lesbian feminism.

## History of Queer Fashion from the 1980s to the Early Twenty-first Century

The 1980s saw a thoughtful reconsideration of previous lesbian-feminist indictments of conventionally feminine styles. Many lesbians began to explore the potential pleasures and erotics of high-heels, makeup, and tight or revealing attire. Some began to revive mid-century femme-butch style, but in a more playful, less essentializing form, and commentators began to note the appearance of "lipstick lesbians," so-called for their preference for skimpy dresses, high heels, and makeup.

Meanwhile, a full-blown style and fashion industry courting the gay male consumer emerged in the 1980s and 1990s, complete with fashion and style magazines,

openly gay designers and advertising, and clothing, grooming, and lifestyle products. While gay male trends changed with dizzying speed, a lean, defined muscular body produced through strict diets, gym exercise, and illicit drugs; exhibited at "circuit" parties and metropolitan dance clubs; and covered by skin-tight clothing became increasingly fashionable. The ubiquity of this look in the gay media did not accurately reflect the plurality of queer styles at the end of the twentieth century.

The "queer moment" of the 1990s was accompanied by widespread adoption of gay pride fashions such as rainbow flags, pink triangles, and Don't Panic brand t-shirts with witty and sometimes confrontational slogans such as "Some of My Best Friends Are Straight." The flannel shirts and hirsute rotundity of bear style was increasingly evident, as was a widespread interest in more invasive modifications of the body through ritualistic scarification, innovative piercing, and tattoos.

**AIDStyle.** The normal invisibility of the HIV virus and its presence or absence in the human body has complicated the issue of personal sexual and gender style in the age of AIDS. The hollow-eyed, emaciated, Kaposi's sarcoma–lesioned AIDS "victim" emblematized the disease in the 1980s, and some viewed the subsequent fashionability of muscled bodies as a sign of gay men's desire to appear vital, healthy, and disease-free. Some people with AIDS sought a gym body as part of an overall health regimen and to cultivate an image of AIDS that countered prevalent media stereotypes. Some also publicized their HIV status through permanent tattoos inked on both normally visible and more intimate parts of the body.

In the late 1980s, members of the AIDS activist group ACT UP communicated their anger and commitment through a militant look composed of t-shirts and jeans, short hair, black leather jackets, and combat boots. Pink triangles on black backgrounds with the phrase "Action=Life, Silence=Death" were everywhere evident. The body image of those living with HIV/AIDS remained a hotly contested terrain, with advertisements for protease inhibitors criticized for unrealistic representations of life on AIDS medications, and some HIV-positive patients refusing certain medications associated with the appearance of lipodystrophy or "buffalo hump," a noticeable deposit of fat at the base of the neck.

The HIV/AIDS pandemic had disproportionate effects on fashion, design, and related industries due to their employment of so many gay and bisexual men. A number of high-profile fashion designers, photographers, and stylists have died of AIDS-related diseases, including Aucoin, Ritts, and Smith. Many industry charities were formed to raise money for safer-sex education and AIDS-related research and healthcare services; prominent examples include the California Fashion Industry Friends of AIDS Healthcare Foundation and the Design Industries Foundation Fighting AIDS (DIFFA). These and other regional AIDS charities regularly use runway fashion shows as fundraising events.

**Homoerotic fashion promotion** A number of queer theorists have speculated about the basically homosexual dynamic of mainstream advertisements, which use attractive models to induce the consuming desire of same-sex buyers. The effort to lure consumers into identifying with an invariably attractive, seductively arranged model of the same sex could never fully preclude that same consumer's objectification or attraction to that model. The most "heterosexual" of fashion ads are seemingly always available to an inadvertently or intentionally "homosexual" reception. In the early twentieth century, the apparently gay illustrator J. C. Leyendecker exploited these ambiguities in his ads for Arrow collars and shirts, often featuring Charles Beach, his longtime companion and probable lover.

In the 1980s and 1990s, many couturiers, fashion retailers, and magazines began to court LGB consumers through fashion photo layouts and advertisements whose ambiguity made them available for queer identification while remaining palatable to a mainstream audience. The designer Calvin Klein became famous in the 1970s for sensationalist ads promoting his line of jeans, but attained a new level of notoriety in the early 1980s for his men's underwear campaign. Appearing on oversized billboards in New York and Los Angeles, the ads featured an attractive male model wearing only a pair of the designer's "tighty-whities," and many critics reacted negativly to the sexual objectification and commodification of the male body, a longstanding taboo in the advertising industry. The inflationary sales effect of the controversy virtually guaranteed more such ads, and many competitors adopted a similar homoerotic appeal.

Some fashion companies such as 2(x)ist, Joe Boxer, Jocko, Benetton, Kenneth Cole, and Diesel Jeans directly courted gay male customers through ads in the gay press. Although not expressly homosexual, the clothier International Male/Undergear offered high-styled clothing and underwear through its West Hollywood store and its nearly pornographic mail-order catalogs. In the 1990s, the mall retailer Abercrombie and Fitch drew regular attention for the nude models and vaguely homoerotic situations in its print campaign and company "magalog."

Starting in the 1980s, fashion and other magazines began featuring expressly or ambiguously homoerotic imagery in their photo spreads. In 1993, *Vanity Fair* featured a Herb Ritts photograph of the supermodel Cindy Crawford shaving the lesbian singer k. d. lang on its cover, while "lesbian chic" was a term regularly used to describe the magazine's fashion photography. The transvestite model RuPaul was a regular on the catwalk and became the spokesperson for a number of fashion products, including M·A·C cosmetics. Yet as Danae Clark has argued, the fashion and style industry's courting of queer consumers should not be construed as evidence of the widespread acceptance of queerness: queer dollars are sought while queer lives, demands, and politics routinely go unacknowledged.

### Bibliography

Chauncey, George. *Gay New York: Gender, Urban Culture and the Making of the Gay Male World, 1890–1940.* New York: Basic Books, 1994.

Clark, Danae. "Commodity Lesbianism." *Camera Obscura* 25–26 (January–May 1991): 181–201.

Cole, Shaun. *"Don We Now Our Gay Apparel": Gay Men's Dress in the Twentieth Century.* Oxford and New York: Berg, 2000.

Dyer, Richard. *The Culture of Queers.* London: Routledge, 2002.

Edwards, Tim. *Men in the Mirror: Men's Fashion, Masculinity, and Consumer Society.* London: Cassell, 1997.

Halberstam, Judith. *Female Masculinity.* Durham: Duke University Press, 1998.

Kennedy, Elizabeth Lapovsky, and Madeline D. Davis. *Boots of Leather, Slippers of Gold: The History of a Lesbian Community.* New York: Routledge, 1993.

Levine, Martin P. *Gay Macho: The Life and Death of the Homosexual Clone.* New York: New York University Press, 1998.

Schuyf, Judith, "'Trousers with Flies!': The Clothing and Subculture of Lesbians." *Textile History* 24, no. 1 (1993): 61–73.

Stein, Arlene. "All Dressed Up, But No Place to Go? Style Wars and the New Lesbianism." *Out/Look* 1, no. 4 (winter 1989): 39–42.

**Michael J. Murphy**

***See also*** FEMMES AND BUTCHES; GYMS, FITNESS CLUBS, AND HEALTH CLUBS; HALL, THOMAS/THOMASINE; LYNES, GEORGE PLATT; PIERCINGS, TATTOOS, AND SCARS; RITTS, HERB; TRANSSEXUALS, TRANSVESTITES, TRANSGENDER PEOPLE, AND CROSS-DRESSERS.

# FEDERAL LAW AND POLICY

In the United States, most government policies relating to sexual and gender minorities have been debated and established by state and local governments. The federal government's interest in sexual and gender minorities has largely been limited to matters within its distinctive constitutional roles: movement of materials in the U. S. mail service and from abroad; immigration and citizenship; military and civilian employment; income tax rules and exemptions; and the expenditure of federal monies, especially on the arts and education. Before World War II, federal policy episodically suppressed discourse about sexual variation and excluded sexual minorities. After the war, the government engaged in a much more aggressive campaign to expose and persecute (as well as exclude) LGBT people as a predatory and dangerous group. After LGBT people openly resisted their persecution, most federal anti-LGBT policies collapsed, and later the U. S. Supreme Court started to protect these minorities against oppressive state laws. But just as sodomy laws and open censorship of sexual expression were being suppressed, new forms of anti-LGBT legislation, including "don't ask, don't tell" in the military and "no promo homo" laws such as the federal Defense of Marriage Act, took their place.

## Federal Suppression of Sexual "Degeneracy" and "Inversion," 1875–1945

Before World War II, there was no federal regulation of "homosexuality" or "homosexuals," as we understand the terms. But there were national rules insisting on gender and sexual conformity within arenas subject to federal jurisdiction. The purpose of the rules was to purge the body politic of any seductive discourse regarding nontraditional genders and sexualities.

**Censorship of Sexual Materials.** There was no general federal obscenity statute, but several laws sought to regulate obscene materials pursuant to national authority over the mails and commerce. The Comstock Act of 1872–73 prohibited the Post Office from mailing "[e]very obscene, lewd, lascivious, indecent, filthy, or vile article." The Tariff Acts of 1922 and 1930 prohibited the Customs Service from allowing "obscene" materials from coming into the United States from another country. These statutes had little if any effect on LGBT publications before World War I, as they were applied mainly against birth control materials. After World War I, homosexual and feminist themes became more common in Anglo-American literature and federal censors acted episodically to keep them out of the country. Although such important literary works as Marcel Proust's *A la recherche du temps perdu* (1913–1926) and Virginia Woolf's *Orlando* (1928), circulated in the United States without a federal peep, the authorities did seize other gay-friendly books, including Charles Henri Ford and Parker Tyler's *The Young and Evil* (1933), a campy depiction of "gay" life in Greenwich Village; Sir Richard Burton's 1886 edition of *The Arabian Nights*,

with its sexually suggestive closing essay; and *The Memoirs of Fanny Hill*, an eighteenth-century novel filled with episodes of sexual nonconformity. The Customs Service also suppressed importation of Radclyffe Hall's lesbian novel, *The Well of Loneliness*, when it was published in 1928 but later relented and allowed its importation (local authorities then seized the threatening novel). The Customs Service's censorship of ribald literature eventually came under fire as inconsistent with the First Amendment and Congress limited its authority in 1930, but this did not mark the end of Customs Service censorship of LGBT materials.

**Immigration.** From the beginning, national standards for immigration excluded sexual and gender nonconformists. The 1891 immigration law barred from entering the country prostitutes and their procurers; "persons suffering from a loathsome or a dangerous contagious disease"; and "persons who have been convicted of a felony or other infamous crime or misdemeanor involving moral turpitude." As the Commissioner-General of Immigration put it in 1909, "[n]othing can be more important than to keep out of the country the anarchistically and criminally inclined and the degenerate in sexual morality." The Immigration Act of 1917 carried over all prior exclusions and created a new one, for people suffering from "constitutional psychopathic inferiority." Congress added this category "to prevent the introduction into the country of strains of mental defect that may continue and multiply through succeeding generations," but the medical experts in the Public Health Service charged with enforcing the exclusion saw it as an instrument to exclude "sexual perverts" and others who "because of eccentric behavior, defective judgment, or abnormal impulses are in repeated conflict with social customs and constituted authorities."

**Military Exclusions.** In 1917, a Navy investigation of enlisted men at the Newport Naval Station exposed a subculture of "so-called moral degenerates whose pastime and pleasure is given to lewd purposes," including crossdressing and oral sex with townspeople as well as one another. The men were prosecuted because they were "inverts," people who were "morally degenerated." In the wake of this scandal, Congress and the War Department quietly updated the Articles of War in 1920–21 to criminalize the oral sex the sailors had been imprisoned for committing. (Only "attempted sodomy" had been a military crime in 1917, and the armed forces then defined sodomy as anal sex.) A subcommittee of the Senate Naval Affairs Committee in 1921 recommended "arbitrary and wholesale discharge" of any and all "suspected perverts."

Thus encouraged, the Army determined not only to discharge sodomites and inverts, but also, for the first time in its history, adopted a mechanism for screening them out in the first place. Army Regulation 40–105 (1921) announced that Army recruits would be examined and could be rejected for evidence of medical defects or diseases, including "degeneration" and "sexual perversion." The regulation also excluded recruits who showed signs of a "constitutional psychopathic state," including "sexual psychopathy," which made them "incapable of attaining a satisfactory adjustment to the average environment of civilized society." For a variety of reasons, few men were excluded from the armed forces under this rule. In 1940, when the United States reinstituted the draft, issues of exclusion reemerged. Psychiatrists persuaded the Selective Service to screen inductees for psychiatric as well as physical problems and, then, to include "homosexual proclivities" on the list of disqualifying "deviations." Largely because of manpower needs, however, of the millions of Americans inducted into the Army during the war, only four thousand to five thousand were explicitly rejected for "homosexuality."

As a large number of LGBT people were not detected by the porous gatekeepers, the armed forces developed policies for dealing with same-sex intimacy among soldiers. War Department Circular No. 3 (1944) directed separation but not court-martial for the "true or confirmed homosexual not deemed reclaimable." For the "reclaimable" homosexual whose misconduct was not aggravated by independent offenses such as rape, the policy was hospitalization and treatment. According to Allan Bérubé, more than four thousand sailors and five thousand soldiers were hospitalized and dismissed from service as "homosexuals" between 1941 and 1945. The new medical focus also established a basis for investigating and excluding lesbians. In the first modern "witchhunt," the War Department in 1944 purged the WAC training camp at Fort Oglethorpe of women who cross-dressed and displayed affection for other women.

## The Federal Anti-Homosexual Drive, 1946–61

By the end of World War II, the "homosexual" was an object of episodic federal concern. Within a few years, he (and occasionally she) had become a national obsession. Official federal policy remained essentially unchanged from the earlier period: "homosexuals and sex perverts," in the argot of the era, were not welcome to enter this country, work as civil servants or soldiers, or express themselves publicly. In the half-generation after the war, however, the federal government invested unprecedented resources to investigate, expose, and purge the body politic of such minorities.

**The Civil Service Witchhunts.** Responding to Republican charges that the civil service was filled with sexual as well as political subversives, the Democratic Truman administration between January 1947 and April 1950 investigated 192 cases of "sex perversion" in the federal civil service; most of the accused were discharged or resigned. In 1950, a subcommittee chaired by North Carolina U.S. Senator Clyde Hoey issued a report that made the case against having "homosexuals and other sex perverts" in the government. "The social stigma attached to sex perversion is so great that many perverts go to great lengths to conceal their perverted tendencies," making them easy prey for "gangs of blackmailers." According to the Hoey Subcommittee, "those who engage in overt acts of perversion lack the emotional stability of normal persons," and "indulgence in acts of sex perversion weakens the moral fiber of an individual to a degree that he is not suitable for a position of responsibility." Finally, "perverts will frequently attempt to entice normal individuals to engage in perverted practices. This is particularly true in the case of young and impressionable people who might come under the influence of a pervert. . . . One homosexual can pollute an entire office." This anti-homosexual fervor motivated federal agencies to adopt more explicitly anti-LGBT policies. The Civil Service Commission, for example, reinterpreted its regulation barring from federal employment people who engage in "immoral conduct" to include "homosexuality and other types of sex perversion" as "sufficient grounds for denying appointment to a Government position or for the removal of a person from the Federal service." In April 1953, President Eisenhower issued Executive Order 10405, which officially added "sexual perversion" as an official criterion for investigation and dismissal under the federal loyalty-security program. Thousands of alleged "homosexuals" were separated from the civil service under this rule—and many of those lost not only their jobs but also private employment opportunities because the Eisenhower administration denied security clearances to private as well as public employees who engaged in "immoral" conduct or "sex perversion."

At the same time federal legislators and administrators were studying ways to purge homosexuals inside the government, the U.S. Senate Judiciary Committee was drafting a broader law to keep more homosexuals out of the country. Senator Patrick McCarran redrafted the immigration law in 1950–52. A major goal of his bill was to exclude communists, anarchists, and other subversives. Reflecting fears that homosexuals were subversive, the McCarran bill excluded all "persons afflicted with psychopathic personality, or who are homosexuals or sex perverts." Upon the assurance of the Public Health Service that the term "psychopathic personality" was broad enough to "specify such types of pathologic behavior as homosexuality or sexual perversion," the Senate as well as House Judiciary Committees settled for an exclusion simply of "persons afflicted with psychopathic personality." The immigration service read the exclusion as targeting persons with records of consensual homosexual offenses.

**The Military Witchhunts.** During the same period, thousands of personnel were separated from the military. Departing from the War Department's earlier policy, the discharges were generally less-than-honorable "blue" discharges, thereby depriving these personnel of veterans benefits promised in the G.I. Bill of Rights and exposing them to discrimination in the private sector when the nature of the discharge was leaked by local boards. A 1949 Defense Department memorandum made mandatory the prompt separation of all "known homosexuals." They fell into three groups: Class I homosexuals, who engaged in coercive sex or sex with minors, were to be court-martialed; Class II homosexuals, who engaged in "one or more homosexual acts" or proposals or attempts "to perform an act of homosexuality," were to be court-martialed or allowed to resign under less-than-honorable (blue) conditions; Class III homosexuals, who "only exhibit, profess, or admit homosexual tendencies" but had not engaged in forbidden conduct, were to be retained or discharged (honorably or generally) depending upon the recommendation of a personnel board. Military policy directed not only that confirmed homosexuals be separated, but that they be sought out as well. Personnel were repeatedly questioned for clues to roust them from their closets, and undercover investigators sought out soldiers in homosexual bars, known male cruising areas, and women's softball teams. If military investigators had evidence (or just accusations) against one soldier, they often threatened that person with court-martial and unfavorable publicity unless he or she reported other names. All told, it is estimated that between two thousand to three thousand personnel were separated each year for that period, at a rate of one person separated each year for each one thousand serving in the armed forces and with a significantly higher rate of discharge for women than for men. These figures strongly understate the effect of the policy, as many personnel left the armed forces upon the slightest pressure, or even before investigators got to them.

**Anti-Homosexual Surveillance and Harassment.** In the 1930s, Federal Bureau of Investigation Director J. Edgar Hoover maintained files documenting the homosexuality of prominent federal officials. More extensive lists of suspected homosexuals were compiled by the armed forces

and local police forces. The Hoey Subcommittee charged the FBI to serve as a clearinghouse for all of this information and to channel it to the Civil Service Commission. The Bureau expanded its charge to include surveillance of homosexuals and their organizations and political activities, as well as investigations of people associating with known homosexuals. Once its agents had gathered the information, the FBI used it in various ways, including leaks to local officials and employers and interrogation to pry out the names of other homosexuals. Hoover's FBI was even more interested in homophile groups such as the Mattachine Society, One, Inc., and the Daughters of Bilitis (DOB). The FBI initiated an internal security investigation into the Mattachine Society in 1953 and started a more open-ended file on the Daughters of Bilitis in 1959. Although the FBI early on recognized that both Mattachine and the DOB were completely "law-abiding," FBI agents infiltrated both organizations, archived their declarations and publications, reported their meetings and activities, recruited informants, compiled lists of members whom they could identify, and speculated on their influence and future activities. On several occasions, FBI agents directly harassed and threatened Mattachine members because of their criticisms of Director Hoover.

During the same period, the U.S. Customs Service and Post Office were devoting unprecedented resources to monitoring and confiscating materials that were considered examples of "sexual perversion." Some of the materials were clearly literary in nature. The most famous, and resistant, example was Allen Ginsberg's raucously homoerotic poem *Howl*. Its second printing was confiscated at San Francisco's port as obscene. Although the publisher then came out with a domestic edition, hundreds of other LGBT-oriented materials were seized by Customs officials each year. The Post Office seized thousands of male physique magazines and other homoerotic materials that traveled domestically through the mail service. The Post Office and the Department of Justice also went after gay pen pal clubs and, in their most bizarre escapade, the exceedingly tame *One*.

In April 1954, Senator Alexander Wiley wrote the Postmaster General protesting the willingness of the Post Office to carry *One*, a magazine "devoted to the achievement of sexual perversion." In response, the Los Angeles Postmaster sent a copy of each issue of *One* to the central Post Office for evaluation under the Comstock Act. The Post Office determined that the October 1954 issue was obscene and lewd, based upon a poem, an advertisement, and an article, "Sappho Remembered," whose depiction of a lesbian's affection for a twenty-year-old "girl" was considered obscene because it was "lustfully stimulating to the average homosexual reader." Upon these findings, the Post Office determined the issue to be nonmailable and returned 600 copies to the sender. In *One, Inc. v. Olesen* (1958), the U.S. Supreme Court summarily invalidated this censorship as a violation of the First Amendment. The Court ruled in *Manual Enterprises v. Day* (1962) that the Post Office could not censor male physique magazines either. Notwithstanding these rulings, the Post Office, Customs Service, and FBI episodically seized LGBT erotica throughout the 1960s and 1970s and on occasion bullied gay publishers into self-censorship or even closing down their operations.

## Erosion of the Old Federal Exclusions and the Creation of New Ones, 1961–2003

Beginning with the early years of the homophile movement and increasingly after Frank Kameny's founding of the Mattachine Society of Washington (MSW) in 1961, LGBT people resisted their second-class status under federal law and policy. Most federal anti-LGBT exclusions were abandoned after LGBT people became politically mobilized in the wake of the Stonewall Riots (1969). But others (most notably the exclusion from the armed forces) have survived and remain the focus of struggles between LGBT rights activists and their opponents. The U.S. Supreme Court has recently become more protective of the rights of LGBT people, striking down a sweeping anti-LGBT state initiative in *Romer v. Evans* (1996) and consensual sodomy laws in *Lawrence v. Texas* (2003). At the same time, the other branches of the federal government have been relatively inactive in protecting LGBT people against violence and discrimination; this remains the province of state and local governments, whose protections have been uneven. Indeed, Congress and the President have pioneered new forms of anti-LGBT legislation, including a sweeping disavowal of same-sex marriages and other "no promo homo" laws.

**Demise of the Federal Civil Service and Immigration Exclusions.** The MSW's primary agenda was to end the exclusion of LGBT people from the civil service. Its strategy was to publicize the irrationality of the policy through protests and lawsuits. In 1966, the Civil Service Commission (CSC) explained its policy for the first time, indicating that it did not exclude "homosexuals" per se—only people who engaged in "overt" homosexual conduct that became public through an arrest or general knowledge. In *Norton v. Macy* (1969), Chief Judge David Bazelon of the D.C. Circuit overturned the discharge of a gay NASA budget analyst and admonished the agency to show a "nexus" between homosexual conduct and the requirements of the federal job. Decided the same week as

the Stonewall Riots, *Norton* encouraged the LGBT movement to move aggressively against the federal government. In 1973, the Society for Individual Rights in San Francisco brought a class-action lawsuit against the Commission and won an injunction against the anti-LGBT exclusion. On December 21, 1973, the CSC notified federal agencies that they could "not find a person unsuitable for Federal employment merely because that person is a homosexual or has engaged in homosexual acts" and could only dismiss such an employee where his "homosexual conduct affects job fitness—excluding from such consideration, however, unsubstantiated conclusions concerning possible embarrassment to the Federal service." In 1975, this instruction was formally codified in the Commission's rules for disqualification, which also dropped "immoral conduct" from the list of disqualifying conditions. Guidelines for "Infamous or Notoriously Disgraceful Conduct" were revised to the same effect, and the civil service statute was amended in 1978 to prohibit discrimination "on the basis of conduct which does not adversely affect the performance of the employee or applicant or the performance of others." In 1998, President Clinton issued Executive Order 13,087, adding sexual orientation to the list of prohibited basis for discrimination in federal employment.

At the same time the federal employment exclusion was falling, the Immigration and Naturalization Service (INS) was abandoning some of its anti-LGBT rules. Pressed by LGBT rights claims, medical experts, and adverse court rulings, the INS in 1976 announced that homosexuality was not a basis for denying citizenship. At the same time, however, the INS maintained that LGBT immigrants could be barred from entering (or deported after entering) the United States, because the Supreme Court had authoritatively construed the 1952 immigration law to that effect and the INS had no authority to craft a different policy. In 1979, however, the Public Health Service (PHS) announced that it would no longer certify LGBT people as afflicted with "psychopathic personality" or "sexual deviation" (terminology Congress added in 1965). Although PHS certification was technically required by statute before the INS could bar LGBT people from entry, the immigration authorities pretty much abandoned enforcement of the law after 1979, except in the rare case where immigrants announced their homosexuality. In 1990, Congress dropped the anti-LGBT exclusions when it redrafted the nation's immigration law.

**Military Exclusion: Standing Firm.** The armed forces' episodically enforced exclusion of LGBT people came under increasing fire in the 1960s and 1970s. Upholding the claims of openly gay Sergeant Leonard Matlovich and Ensign Vernon Berg, the D.C. Circuit in 1976 held that the discretionary-dismissal approach followed by the Air Force and Navy could not be invoked without giving reasons why certain personnel were being dismissed but not others. As in *Norton,* the court was requiring that there be a nexus between the disapproved conduct and legitimate state needs. In the wake of these decisions, more service personnel came out of their closets and successfully challenged their exclusion. The Carter Administration addressed the *Matlovich/Berg* problem by promulgating new regulations in 1980 that removed official discretion to allow openly LGBT personnel to serve in the armed forces. Immediately afterward, the Ninth Circuit in *Beller v. Middendorf* (1980) deferred to the executive department's judgment that the presence of sodomites or openly LGBT personnel would be disruptive of morale and unity cohesion. The Reagan administration enforced the new policy vigorously, through episodic witchhunts reminiscent of those in the 1950s. Nonetheless, LGBT personnel continued to come out of their military closets and bring constitutional lawsuits, some of which were successful, most not. In 1993, President Clinton announced that he intended to revoke the executive order embodying the anti-LGBT rules. Opposed by his own Joint Chiefs of Staff and U.S. Senator Sam Nunn, Clinton backed away from that announcement and instead supported a statute that barred from military service anyone who was openly LGBT or who engaged in a "homosexual act." Hundreds of women and men have been separated from the armed forces each year on the basis of this policy. Lawsuits seeking its invalidation have been unsuccessful, as of 2003. The Supreme Court's decision invalidating state sodomy laws in *Lawrence v. Texas* (2003) may require the federal government to revisit its criminalization of consensual sodomy in the Uniform Code of Military Justice (UCMJ). If the UCMJ's sodomy bar were revoked or invalidated, the 1993 statute excluding openly LGBT people from the armed forces would be more vulnerable, because a key defense of its exclusion is that LGBT people are presumptive "sodomites" and therefore violators of the UCMJ.

**New Federal Anti-LGBT Laws and Policies.** At the same time the federal government was abandoning most of its official anti-LGBT policies, state and local governments were adopting new laws affirmatively protecting LGBT people against private as well as public discrimination. On 14 May 1974, U. S. Representative Bella Abzug introduced a bill that would have protected against sexual-orientation discrimination in public and private workplaces, public accommodations, and housing. Although similar bills were introduced in every Congress after 1974, none even received a congressional hearing until the proposed Em-

ployment Non-Discrimination Act (ENDA) did in 1994. No bill even came to a vote on the floor of the House or Senate until the Senate considered ENDA in 1996. The only reason the Senate leadership agreed to bring ENDA up for a vote was to smooth the passage of the Defense of Marriage Act (DOMA). ENDA failed by one vote in the Senate, while DOMA sailed through both chambers by lopsided majorities. DOMA is the most anti-LGBT federal statute in American history, and by a wide margin. It authorizes states to refuse recognition to valid same-sex marriages and amends the U.S. Code to provide that the more than 1,000 provisions of federal law relating to "marriage" and "spouse" never be construed to apply to same-sex marriages and spouses. A dissenting opinion in the Supreme Court's decision in *Lawrence v. Texas* (2003) argued that the Court's LGB-friendly jurisprudence spelled the end of same-sex marriage bans in the United States. Like many dissenting opinions, this one overstated the effect of the majority's action, but in the event that a state recognizes same-sex marriage through its own legislative or judicial action, the constitutionality of DOMA would come into question. The most relevant authority would be *Romer v. Evans* (1996), where the Supreme Court ruled that a sweeping anti-LGBT initiative apparently motivated by animus against LGBT people violated the Equal Protection Clause. Similar arguments could be made against DOMA, although even pro-LGBT commentators caution that the Supreme Court would proceed cautiously in the arena of marriage.

As of 2003, there is no federal statute providing explicit protection for LGBT people against violence or discrimination. In 1990, Congress adopted a law requiring collection of data on hate crimes, including those against LGBT people, but the statute also provided that the law should not be applied to encourage or promote "homosexuality." This has been the newest face of anti-LGBT policies at the federal level. In addition to excluding openly LGBT people from the badge of citizenship represented by military service and the institution of marriage, federal policymakers express disrespect for homosexuality and transgenderism. LGBT people object that this represents a prejudice-based form of second-class citizenship. Traditionalists respond that this reflects a policy of "tolerance": Viewing homosexuality and transgenderism as an unfortunate condition, they maintain that LGBT people should be allowed most freedoms and job opportunities, but not given the full privileges of citizenship reserved for heterosexual and gender-normative Americans.

## Bibliography

**Statutory and Regulatory Materials**

Comstock Act, 17 Stat. 598 (1873).

Immigration Act of 1891, 26 Stat. 1084.

Immigration Act of 1917, 39 Stat. 874.

Act of June 4, 1920 (Articles of War), 41 Stat. 787.

Army Regulation 40–105, "Standards of Physical Examination for Entrance into the Regular Army, National Guard, and Organized Reserves" (1921).

Tariff Act of 1922 (amended 1930), 30 U.S.C. § 1305.

War Department Circular Letter No. 19, "Neuropsychiatric Examination of Applicants for Voluntary Enlistment and Selectees for Induction" (Mar. 12, 1941)

Army Regulation No. 615–368, "Enlisted Men: Discharge—Undesirable Traits of Character" (Jan. 1944, amended Apr. 1945).

Department of Defense, "Discharge of Homosexuals from the Armed Forces" (Oct. 11, 1949).

Subcommittee on Investigations of the Senate Committee on Expenditures in the Executive Departments, "Employment of Homosexuals and Other Sex Perverts in Government" (Dec. 15, 1950) (the Hoey Subcommittee Report).

McCarran-Walter Act, 66 Stat. 166 (1952).

Executive Order 10,405, 18 Fed. Reg. 2489 (April 1953).

Civil Service Reform Act of 1978, 92 Stat. 1114.

Memorandum from Julius Richmond, Surgeon General, to William Foege, CDC, Director (Aug. 2, 1979).

Hate Crimes Statistics Act, 104 Stat. 141 (1990).

Immigration Act of 1990, § 601(a), 104 Stat. 4978.

National Defense Authorization Act of 1994, § 546, codified at 10 U.S.C. § 654 (statutory codification of rule excluding openly LGBT people from the armed services).

Defense of Marriage Act, 110 Stat. 2419 (1996).

Executive Order 13,087 (May 29, 1998).

**Judicial Decisions**

One, Inc. v. Olesen, 355 U.S. 371 (1958) (per curiam).

Manual Enterprises, Inc. v. Day, 370 U.S. 478 (1962).

Norton v. Macy, 417 F.2d 1161 (D.C. Cir. 1969).

Beller v. Middendorf, 632 F.2d 788 (9th Cir. 1980).

Bowers v. Hardwick, 478 U.S. 186 (1986).

Romer v. Evans, 517 U.S. 620 (1996)

Lawrence v. Texas, 123 S. Ct. ___ (2003).

**Books and Articles**

Bérubé, Allan. *Coming Out Under Fire: The History of Gay Men and Women in World War II*. New York: Free Press, 1990.

D'Emilio, John. *Sexual Politics, Sexual Communities: The Making of a Homosexual Minority in the United States, 1940–1970*. Chicago: University of Chicago Press, 1983.

Eskridge, William N., Jr. *Gaylaw: Challenging the Apartheid of the Closet*. Cambridge, Mass.: Harvard University Press, 1999.

Eskridge, William N., and Nan Hunter. *Sexuality, Gender, and the Law*. New York: Foundation Press, 1997.

Faderman, Lillian. *Odd Girls and Twilight Lovers: A History of Lesbian Life in Twentieth-Century America*. New York: Columbia University Press, 1991.

Freedman, Estelle. "'Uncontrolled Desires': The Response to the Sexual Psychopath, 1920–1960." *Journal of American History* 74 (1987): 83–120.

Johnson, David K. "'Homosexual Citizens': Washington's Gay Community Confronts the Civil Service." *Washington History* (Fall–Winter 1994): 50–75.

Katz, Jonathan Ned. *Gay American History: Lesbians and Gay Men in the U.S.A.: A Documentary*. New York: Avon, 1976.

———. *Gay/Lesbian Almanac: A New Documentary*. New York: Harper & Row, 1983.

Koppelman, Andrew. *The Gay Rights Question in Contemporary American Law*. Chicago: University of Chicago Press, 2002.

Meyer, Leisa. *Creating G.I. Jane: Sexuality and Power in the Women's Army Corps during World War II*. New York: Columbia University Press, 1996.

Murdoch, Joyce, and Deb Price. *Courting Justice: Gay Men and Lesbians v. The Supreme Court*. New York: Basic Books, 2001.

Murphy, Lawrence. *Perverts by Official Order: The Campaign Against Homosexuals by the United States Navy*. New York: Harrington Park Press, 1988.

Rivera, Rhonda. "Our Straight-Laced Judges: The Legal Position of Homosexual Persons in the United States." *Hastings Law Journal*, 30 (1979): 799–932.

Shilts, Randy. *Conduct Unbecoming: Gays & Lesbians in the U.S. Military, Vietnam to the Persian Gulf*. New York: St. Martin's Press, 1993.

Stein, Marc. *City of Sisterly and Brotherly Loves: Lesbian and Gay Philadelphia, 1945–1972*. Chicago: University of Chicago Press, 2000.

**William N. Eskridge, Jr.**

*See also* AMERICAN CIVIL LIBERTIES UNION (ACLU); ANTI-DISCRIMINATION LAW AND POLICY; CENSORSHIP, OBSCENITY, AND PORNOGRAPHY LAW AND POLICY; COHN, ROY; CRIME AND CRIMINALIZATION; DEMOCRATIC PARTY; DISCRIMINATION; EDUCATION LAW AND POLICY; ELECTORAL POLITICS; EMPLOYMENT LAW AND POLICY; FAMILY LAW AND POLICY; GOVERNMENT AND MILITARY WITCHHUNTS; HATE CRIMES LAW AND POLICY; HEALTH AND HEALTH CARE LAW AND POLICY; HOOVER, J. EDGAR; IMMIGRATION, ASYLUM, AND DEPORTATION LAW AND POLICY; MILITARY LAW AND POLICY; POLICING AND POLICE; POLITICAL SCANDALS; PRIVACY AND PRIVACY RIGHTS; REPUBLICAN PARTY.

# FEMINISM

Broadly speaking, feminism refers to the notion that females and males are inherently equal but recognizes that structural and cultural forces damage, disadvantage, and disempower females in ways that leave them unequal to males. Feminist activism and feminist movements are collective efforts to improve the situations of women and girls. However, feminism is also built upon the idea that sex and gender intersect with other social hierarchies, including systems of sexual categorization. Ignoring intersecting hierarchies of class, race, sexuality, and other dimensions of difference in theorizing and practicing feminism serves only privileged women's interests (including the interests of straight women) and reinforces other social inequalities that disadvantage both women and men. Thus, in their efforts to challenge women's subordination, feminists have often addressed LGBT issues, promoting equality for LGBT people, offering queer perspectives on heterosexuality, and exploring intersections of race, class, and gender with sexuality. In many instances, feminists have challenged heterosexual dominance, but feminist activism has ranged from reproducing heteronormativity to offering a cultural and social vision fully inclusive of LGBT sexualities and genders.

In the last one hundred years, the term "feminism" has taken on varied and even contradictory meanings, and scholars have given significant attention to the question of what movements or actions count as "feminist." The meaning, focus, and application of the term "feminist" have also changed over time. In the United States, feminism has been used as the basis for movements in support of women's suffrage, women's rights, and women's emancipation, but it has also been used to argue for the destruction of the sex-gender system and the elimination of categories such as "male" and "female." It is instructive, then, to understand feminism not only as a belief about women's value in society and culture but also as a historical phenomenon. The word "feminism" (or féminisme) originated in late-nineteenth-century France and was imported into the United States in the 1910s, when it had very specific meanings related to women's emancipation. In U.S. history, feminism is often understood through a wave metaphor and has been defined in multiple ways to encompass the various ways in which women and their allies have sought female empowerment. In these waves of feminist activism women who can be viewed as lesbians have played central roles and feminists have grappled with issues related to LGBT sexualities and genders.

## The First Wave

The first wave of feminism began in 1848 with the Seneca Falls Convention. Women and men, many of whom maintained intimate same-sex relationships in the context of nineteenth-century values that placed women and men in "separate spheres," came together in Seneca Falls, New York, to discuss female education, legal equality, and social opportunity. At this meeting, they issued a Declaration of Sentiments, which offered their vision for change. As the women's movement developed, women's suffrage was embraced, but other issues, including sexual issues, also emerged as significant. Throughout the nineteenth century, heterosexual, monogamous marriage remained the most common and accepted type of sexual relationship in the United States. However, small groups of feminists began to offer alternatives to monogamous sexual relations, challenging marital sexuality, opening social and cultural doors to more options for sexual pleasure, and embracing a variety of transgressive relationships. Other feminists offered challenges to contemporary heteronormativity through sexual purity and moral reform campaigns.

Although first-wave feminists did not openly address same-sex sexuality, many within the movement developed "romantic friendships" and intense same-sex relationships. Various women involved in first-wave feminism embraced reform and suffrage activism not only as important work on behalf of women but also as a way to live independently of men and to forge relationships with women that today might be characterized as lesbian. Correspondence between women involved in the first wave of feminism suggests that many had intimate same-sex relationships and living arrangements. Susan B. Anthony, Anna Dickinson, Emily Gross, Frances Willard, Anna Gordon, Alice Stone Blackwell, Jane Addams, and many others built close relationships with other women. Although they rarely addressed questions and issues related to same-sex sexuality and may well have disavowed the label "lesbian" when it came into existence in the late nineteenth century, many lived their lives with other feminist women and pursued feminist causes, especially suffrage and reform efforts directed against "illicit" heterosexual relationships and "illegitimate" pregnancies.

***Free Love and Moral Reform.*** As the feminist movement developed in the nineteenth century, two divergent approaches emerged to address issues of sexual inequality and sexual freedom: free love and moral reform. The free love movement originated in nineteenth-century utopian communities, which attempted to establish perfect human societies, including perfect sexual and intimate relationships. While utopian communities varied widely in their sexual views, they commonly demonstrated concern about ways to regulate sexual impulses. For free love adherents, love and desire, rather than marriage and reproduction, should be the basis for sexual relationships, and they introduced a vital, queer critique that helped to deconstruct heteronormative dominance in U.S. society.

Free love's first major American proponent, Frances Wright, was a wealthy Scottish woman who immigrated permanently to the United States in 1825, after a two-year visit in 1818–1820. A freethinker who opposed slavery, organized religion, and marriage, Wright organized a utopian community in Nashoba, Tennessee, where devotees challenged conventional fears about interracial relations by bringing black and white people together. She believed that only racial integration would resolve racial strife and conflict in the United States, and the Nashoba community encouraged the formation of interracial sexual relationships, regardless of marital ties. In 1827, Wright argued that sexual passion was the "best source of human happiness." She was consequently vilified in the press, which suggests how deeply she threatened basic tenets of heterosexual, monogamous marriage. Other champions of free love included Mary Gove Nichols and Thomas Low Nichols, who published extensively on women's rights and birth control and founded a short-lived free love community, Memnonia, near Yellow Springs, Ohio. Mary Gove Nichols was also an advocate of dress reform, opposing the tight-laced corsets that were fashionable at the time. In their queer critiques of marriage and heteronormative sexuality, the Nichols claimed that marriage was a form of prostitution (since it involved the exchange of sex and reproductive services for material support), a claim that was echoed later in first and second wave feminism.

Free love reached a wider audience in the second half of the nineteenth century through the flamboyant Victoria Woodhull. Merging free love and free speech advocacy, Woodhull sought to challenge middle-class taboos on public discussions of sexuality while also combating the Comstock laws against the distribution and discussion of information about contraception. In speech and print she articulated a theory of sexual choice and advocated sexual passion as liberating, a message she promoted in her run for president of the United States in 1872. She was jailed for publishing stories of sexual affairs among members of the prominent social classes, most notably one between the Boston minister Henry Beecher Ward and parishioner Elizabeth Tilton. Her writings revealed how middle- and upper-class sexual ideologies of monogamous marriage contradicted their practices, an argument also made by critics of sexual abuse within slavery (including Sojourner Truth) and critics of racial lynching (including Ida B. Wells). Woodhull represents another example of how first-wave feminist activism raised important challenges to the cultural dominance of heteronormative sexuality, even if she and many other free love advocates did not openly embrace same-sex sexuality.

Moreover, by the early twentieth century free love ideas were influencing various bohemian radicals, social-ists, anarchists, and feminists (most notably Emma Goldman), many of whom embraced "mannish" dress, formed same-sex sexual partnerships, and defended LGB rights. They also influenced early twentieth-century radical, socialist, anarchist, and feminist campaigns for birth control, which helped to separate reproduction from pleasure in discourses and practices of sexuality.

Free love advocates offered radical sexual alternatives, and their ideas influenced later waves of feminist activism. However, public discussion and debate about sexuality in the nineteenth century, including discussion and debate by feminists, more commonly focused on moral reform and social purity. Male and female reformers were particularly concerned about the commercialization of sex, especially erotic literature, dance halls, and brothels. Entrepreneurs were increasingly trading in sexual fantasy and experience, especially in urban centers, and many working-class women were finding that sexual labor paid far better wages than other forms of work. While all of these "vices" raised the ire of social reformers, prostitution was the focus of attention.

In response to the "problem" of prostitution, many female reformers turned to politics, attempting to increase the regulation of sex and promote women's control over their bodies. In moral reform and social purity crusades, women expanded public discussions of sexuality, but often did so in ways that replicated heteronormative conceptions of men as sexual beasts and women as sexually pure. For many reformers sexuality itself was dangerous, a position with potentially negative consequences for LGBT people. In New York City, for example, the Female Moral Reform Society extended its assistance beyond the poor, widowed, and orphaned to the city's prostitutes. Rather than treat prostitutes as depraved and threatening, they sought to transform these "fallen women" into "true women" through conversion to Christianity. Although most prostitutes did not see themselves as "fallen" and did not aspire to live according to middle-class women's values, reformers' efforts persisted in part because such efforts permitted women to question men's authority and conduct as well as women's dependence on men.

After doctors in the American Medical Association (AMA) proposed to legalize and regulate prostitution in the late nineteenth century, the social purity movement emerged to counter this effort. By the 1890s the movement was firmly entrenched in the U.S. social and political landscape and contributed to public discussions of heterosexual sex beyond the privacy of marriage and the family. Rather than regulate prostitution, social purity activists sought to prevent women from turning to prostitution in the first place. They set up homes for girls working in cities, social clubs for young women to meet young men in "respectable" settings, and homes for single, pregnant girls and women. Social uplift campaigns, however, were tainted with condescension as reformers demanded that their clients adopt middle-class values of domesticity, temperance, and sexual propriety. Still, reformers did recognize that social inequalities of gender and class forced some women to sell their sexual services and they developed important arguments about the relationship between sexuality and inequality. In doing so they, like free love advocates, proposed a (hetero)sexual single standard for men and women.

Meanwhile, suffrage leaders Elizabeth Cady Stanton and Susan B. Anthony, feminists who embraced the cause of social purity, drew parallels between prostitution and marriage, suggesting that in both arrangements women traded sex for economic support. Marriage and divorce laws, they also argued, trapped women. Stanton called for more liberal divorce laws while Anthony advocated women's economic self-sufficiency. Other social purity advocates promoted "voluntary motherhood," or the right to say no to sex unless a woman wanted to become pregnant, preferring this strategy to other forms of contraception or abortion. Through rhetoric and action, feminists linked women's sexuality to broader political change.

At bottom, the social purity crusade and its feminist advocates sought not to oppose all sexuality but to control male sexuality and liberate female sexuality, while free love advocates sought to remove external constraints on love and sexuality. Although social purity was more palatable to middle-class Americans and feminists in particular, both approaches offered ways to unshackle women's sexuality. Still, many Americans opposed first wave feminists, in part because the pursuit of the vote was seen as potentially disruptive to a heteronormative gender order in which men supposedly represented women and children at the ballot box. Other first wave feminist campaigns were also seen as threatening because of the ways that they challenged patriarchal heterosexual dominance. Antifeminists criticized feminists by calling them unnatural mannish spinsters and intimated that they were lesbians. Sexologists, psychiatrists, and other scientific "experts" also linked feminism and lesbianism, attacking the former as a sign, symptom, and source of the latter. In this context, antilesbianism likely kept many feminists from discussing same-sex sexuality openly or from linking lesbianism with feminism.

## The Second Wave

The passage of the Nineteenth Amendment to the U.S. Constitution in 1920, which granted women the right to vote, brought about a decline of overt feminism. Liberating women's sexuality, an important component of first-wave feminism, emerged as a key idea in the second-wave. Arguing that "the personal is political," second wave feminists argued that such issues as rape, domestic violence, and economic dependence upon men had social causes and political solutions and were not merely personal problems confronted by individual women. While this phrase emerged during the second wave, it seems rather obvious in light of first wave feminists' attention to personal problems and political solutions. Building upon first wave challenges to the dominant heteronormative order, second wave feminists developed these challenges while also focusing more attention on same-sex sexualities.

Although feminism remained alive in the decades after 1920, the 1960s witnessed a revival of various social movements, including feminism. The civil rights, student, and antiwar movements contributed greatly to the resurgence of feminism in the 1960s and 1970s. Many women worked alongside men in pursuit of racial justice, equal rights, and world peace. Borrowing tactics, adapting ideas, and building upon networks in such organizations as the National Association for the Advancement of Colored People, the Student Nonviolent Coordinating Committee, and Students for a Democratic Society, many women embraced the greater goals of justice, equality, and liberation for all people.

Women made gains through the political system. In 1963, President John F. Kennedy signed into law the Equal Pay Act, which stated that employers could not pay women and men different wages for the same work. The following year, Congress passed the Civil Rights Act of 1964. Its Title VII outlawed workplace discrimination on the basis of "race, color, religion, sex, or national origin." It also provided a legal avenue of address by creating the Equal Employment Opportunity Commission (EEOC) to handle employee complaints.

Second wave feminism initially took organizational shape primarily around the work of the National Organization for Women (NOW), founded by Betty Friedan in 1966 by more than one hundred women interested in creating a feminist organization similar to the NAACP. NOW represented the interests and aspirations of liberal feminists, who were concerned with equality within existing social, political, and economic systems. Although a number of lesbians (including Pauli Murray) were active in NOW and other liberal feminist organizations, liberal feminism in the 1960s tended to downplay sexual issues (including abortion rights and lesbian rights), focusing instead on employment discrimination and lack of political representation.

In the late 1960s, NOW president Betty Friedan charged that lesbians constituted a "lavender menace" that would overtake the organization and the movement and damage the legitimacy of the movement in the public sphere. In the New York City chapter of NOW, young lesbians had suggested that lesbianism was a feminist issue, which antagonized many women in the local and national organization. While some lesbians, including Rita Mae Brown, left the organization of their own accord, others were purged from the organization. The media picked up on this and started "outing" lesbians in the movement or criticizing women in the movement for being gay or bisexual. When feminist Kate Millett acknowledged her bisexuality, for example, *Time* magazine (31 August 1970) wrote that it was "bound to discredit her as a spokeswoman for her cause, cast further doubt on her theories, and reinforce the views of those skeptics who routinely dismiss all liberationists as lesbians." In 1971, NOW endorsed the cause of lesbian rights, but the resolution resolved very little and tensions persisted between feminists and lesbians both in NOW and beyond.

Not based in NOW or radical feminist groups, the feminist fight for lesbian liberation in the 1960s and 1970s was also not based in the LGBT movement. Lesbians started organizing with gay men in the homophile movement during the 1950s. In 1955, Del Martin and Phyllis Lyon, lesbian partners, founded the Daughters of Bilitis (DOB) in San Francisco, and over the next decade, chapters were founded in large cities across the United States. The DOB was the first lesbian organization in the homophile movement and was established to address issues of political and cultural legitimacy as well as self-acceptance among lesbians. At times critical of the sexism of gay men in the homophile movement and in LGBT communities, in the late 1960s the DOB increasingly addressed feminist issues, including equal pay, on-the-job harassment, equal housing opportunities, and sexual freedom. The DOB, however, collapsed in the early 1970s. After the Stonewall Riots of 1969, some lesbians joined the radical gay liberation movement. Gay liberation borrowed heavily from the radical feminist movement that developed in the late 1960s and early 1970s, arguing that the oppression of homosexuals stemmed from a rigidly enforced sexist system of heterosexual supremacy that supported the primacy of the nuclear family and the reproduction of dichotomous sex roles. While many lesbians embraced gay liberation, they also felt that many men involved in the movement were antiwoman. In a landmark

1970 essay in the *Advocate*, Martin offered her farewell address to gay men and the gay movement, stating that gay men were more interested in sexual conquest than political advancement and legal equality. Her scathing critique drew attention to sexism in the gay movement as she charged that gay men expected lesbians to conform to heteronormative gender roles.

***Radical Feminism and Lesbian Feminism.*** Ultimately, feminism and lesbianism were more integrated into the radical women's liberation movement that developed in the late 1960s and 1970s than into any other movement. Many radical women who were passionate about equality, democracy, and social justice had found themselves devalued by men in the New Left, student, antiwar, and civil rights movements and had been expected to offer sexual services as evidence of their commitment to social revolution. In response, many women began to form radical women's liberation groups. While feminists from all walks of life connected women's personal dissatisfaction to broader social and political disadvantages, women's liberationists offered the earliest second wave critiques of the sexual system. Many radical women turned to consciousness-raising (CR) groups as a way to critique the sexual status quo and analyze the erotic as a vehicle for domination in American society. Through CR, feminists came to understand sexuality as an issue of power and politics. While such developments as the invention of the birth control pill offered women greater control over their own sexuality, some feminists offered strident critiques of sex in the United States. For example, rejecting the idea that women were designed sexually to please men, Anne Koedt—in her 1969 essay "The Myth of the Vaginal Orgasm"—challenged the Freudian notion that women could only achieve orgasm through vaginal penetration. Demolishing this myth had tremendous significance because it challenged the very foundation of heterosexual unions by suggesting that sexual pleasure was obtainable from either men or women. With heterosexuality understood as an option rather than a mandate, women raised new challenges to the sexual status quo.

In addition to issues related to political equality, second wave feminists addressed many issues related to sexuality. Through such landmark publications as *Our Bodies, Ourselves* (1971), they reclaimed knowledge of their bodies and promoted a feminist approach to health and sexuality. Feminists also attacked the sexual objectification of women and the reduction of women to little more than beings with sex appeal and reproductive organs. They also popularized the notion that rape was not a crime of sexual passion but instead was one of violence and power. Moreover, rape was committed not only by strangers, they observed, but also by acquaintances, friends, lovers, and spouses. Feminists also advocated reproductive freedom and control of fertility. In addition to promoting safe and effective birth control, they sought to dismantle the criminalization of abortion. In 1973, feminists succeeded in convincing the U.S. Supreme Court in *Roe v. Wade* to strike down laws banning abortions in the first six months of pregnancies.

Many lesbians flocked to the cause of women's emancipation, but they were not always accepted in feminist organizations. Even among self-identified radical women's groups, which sought to overthrow the oppressive patriarchal structures within which liberal feminists pursued equality, lesbians did not always find a happy home. While radical feminists offered thorough analyses of the ways in which U.S. society and culture oppressed women and while they focused attention on sexual matters, they typically did not advocate lesbianism as an alternative or as a solution and lesbians frequently felt alienated within radical feminist groups.

In this context, lesbians who had been involved in liberal feminism, radical feminism, and the LGBT movement and straight women who came out as lesbians in the context of feminist activism began to establish lesbian feminist groups in the early 1970s. Such groups as the Furies in Washington, D.C., and Radicalesbians in New York City were the first to articulate a radical feminist politics of lesbianism, arguing that mere acknowledgement of lesbian rights as women's rights denied the real oppression that lesbians faced and the politics of power that same-sex sexuality introduced into the women's movement. In 1970, Radicalesbians invented a new, political definition of what it meant to be a lesbian: "What is a lesbian? A lesbian is the rage of all women condensed to the point of explosion." Different from male homosexuality and certainly different from female heterosexuality, lesbianism, according to the Radicalesbians' manifesto, "The Woman-Identified Woman," was a source of political and cultural power. In separatist cells, groups, and communities, lesbian feminists suggested that lesbianism was the logical outcome of feminism, the ultimate expression of "the personal is political." In effect and sometimes in practice, they challenged all feminists to come out as lesbians. Over time, a dynamic lesbian feminist movement developed across the United States, having profound influence on LGBT politics and communities.

In time, lesbian feminism and the larger feminist movement developed competing and conflicting politics of sexuality. In the 1970s and 1980s, second wave feminists fought against sexual danger while also embracing sexual pleasure. Feminist analyses of rape, battering, and other forms of violence were central to the movement, but feminist sex radicals rejected the notion that some kinds of sexuality were more feminist than others. Resonant of the cultural conflict between free love advocates and moral reformists, a conflict emerged between "anti-sex" and "pro-sex" feminists, that is, women who emphasized the dangers of sex and those who focused on the pleasures of it. Lesbians were represented prominently on both sides of this conflict. In 1982 the feminist sex wars exploded at a Barnard College conference entitled "Toward a Politics of Sexuality." Some conveners and participants analyzed sexual pleasure as a source of female empowerment and embraced pornography, lesbian sadomasochism, and femme-butch lesbian identity as a way to "move toward pleasure, agency, and self-definition." Others, however, encouraged lesbianism in theory and practice because they saw heterosexuality as a vehicle for the continued oppression of women.

The most strident battle over sex emerged over the issue of pornography. Legal theorist Catharine MacKinnon conceptualized sexuality in pornography within a Marxist labor framework—that which is "most one's own, yet most taken away." Andrea Dworkin took this idea further, arguing that it is impossible to separate heterosexual intercourse from the social reality of male power. Essentially, the argument was that heterosexual intercourse constituted rape. Together, they developed a strategy to make pornography illegal as an infringement of women's civil rights. However, many feminists criticized this stance, suggesting that when feminists (including many who identified as lesbian feminists) attacked sex as the primary reason for women's second-class status, they were being prudish and refusing to acknowledge that sex could be empowering for women.

Other second wave feminists charged the movement with privileging white and middle-class women in defining and representing feminism. Women of color, including lesbians of color, played major roles in each branch of second wave feminism, but they were often alienated by the racism they encountered within the movement. Black lesbian feminist Anita Cornwell, who joined the women's movement in the late 1960s and wrote about her experiences in articles that were later anthologized in *Black Lesbian in White America* (1983), was among the first to offer a sustained criticism of racism in the women's movement. Audre Lorde and Barbara Smith soon offered even more influential antiracist arguments from the perspective of black lesbian feminists. From such critiques, a variety of feminisms emerged in the 1970s and 1980s. Socialist women argued that women's oppression was rooted in capitalism, which perpetuated a sex-based structure that disadvantaged women; they founded such organizations as Bread and Roses and Cell 16. Women of color developed a variety of distinct and influential feminisms. For example, the Combahee River Collective, which formed in 1977, was a group of black feminist lesbians who sought to combat racism, sexism, heterosexism, and class oppression as interlocking forces in U.S. society. Many women of color felt conflicted about feminism—they wanted to dismantle sexism in society, culture, and law, but they would not overlook white racism that disadvantaged people of color or abandoned men of their races for what they perceived to be white feminism. African American, Latina, Asian-Pacific, and Native American women developed feminisms based upon their inseparable experiences and identities as women and people of color.

Transgender people (and especially male to female transsexuals) also criticized feminism, some for failing to recognize them as women and some for reifying the male-female dichotomy in U.S. culture, politics, and society. For example, at the Michigan Womyn's Music Festival in 1994, trans persons were not allowed on the land because festival organizers enforced a policy of admitting only "womyn-born womyn." In response, trans people and allies formed Camp Trans across the street to draw attention to the anti-trans philosophy of the festival, and by extension, of feminism itself.

Second wave feminism thus can be criticized for failing to deal adequately with sexual difference, sexual pleasure, race, and transgenderism. But it can also be celebrated for opening up discussion of these issues and for inspiring the development of multiple feminisms that focus on precisely these matters.

## The Third Wave

In the early 1980s feminism was declared "dead" by the media and the United States moved into an era of antifeminist backlash, when feminists were routinely accused of being man-hating lesbians. Antifeminists caricatured and misrepresented feminism while also accusing feminists of going too far, alienating men, and causing a variety of social problems. In response, and insisting that feminism had never died, some women (most of them under thirty years of age) began articulating what they called third wave feminism. The term "third wave" stemmed from Rebecca Walker's founding in 1992 of the Third Wave Foundation, which launched a voter registration campaign that evolved into an organization inspiring feminist activism by women aged fifteen to thirty. While there is no clear split in terms of time between the second and third waves of feminism, third wave feminism is most often articulated by a younger generation of women and men reacting to critiques of second wave feminism leveled by women of color and pro-sex feminists.

Third wave feminists build upon various second wave critiques of feminism as white, straight, and middle class. They strive to come to terms with multiple bases of oppression in relation to multiple axes of identity, recognizing themselves (and people in general) as products of the contradictory definitions of and differences within feminism. Concerned with political issues and conservative, antifeminist political backlash, third wave feminists also address cultural issues of beauty, power, and pleasure—often reclaiming derogatory images, names, and acts (including dyke, girl, and bitch) and redefining them as empowering. They also build upon community-based institutions and cultural resources such as music to express themselves. For example, the early 1990s saw the rise of the Riot Grrl movement, comprised of women's bands and female singers who coupled images and accoutrements of girlhood, such as miniskirts and baby T-shirts, with images of masculinity, including combat boots and aggressive lyrics and song styles.

By emphasizing multiplicity and a lack of fixity in identities, proponents of third wave feminism embrace "queer" identities, encompassing lesbian, bisexual, and transgender identities but also reflecting the reality that sex, gender, and sexuality are fluid and evolving, which means that they can be changed and crossed. Many third wave feminists identify as "pro-sex" and often write positively about lust, sex, and sexuality. With their emphasis on personal narrative in writing and speaking, they see their feminism as one of everyday practice. Lesbian Avengers is an important example of this tradition. Founded in New York City in 1992, six experienced activists offered creative and dramatic tactics to draw attention to queer and feminist issues. As chapters were established across the United States, the Avengers confronted heteronormativity through such tactics as staging kiss-ins at local malls, conducting impromptu parades without permits, and passing out balloons with the slogan "ask about lesbian lives" to schoolchildren. Some third wave feminists have also embraced drag and gender performance as means of self-expression. Drag king troupes across the country reinterpret music and lyrics to reflect feminist awareness and critique of sex, sexuality, and the social construction of gender, and even convene yearly, beginning in 1999, at the International Drag King Conference hosted by Ohio State University in Columbus.

Whether challenging heteronormative practices and laws or openly debating same-sex sexuality, feminists in the United States have always grappled with issues of sex, gender, and sexuality. Feminists have not always agreed upon goals, strategies, and tactics, and the meanings of feminism have changed over time and been affected by race, class, and sexuality as well as by time period, political climate, and culture. In the United States, feminists—self-identified lesbians, women who can be viewed as lesbians, heterosexual women, transsexual persons, and others—have raised challenges to systems of sexual categorization and continue to build social movements to foment feminist change.

### Bibliography

Crow, Barbara, ed. *Radical Feminism: A Documentary History.* New York: New York University Press, 2000. Evans, Sara. *Tidal Wave: How Feminism Changed America At Century's End.* New York: Free Press, 2003. Hooks, Bell. *Feminist Theory: From Margin to Center.* Boston: South End Press., 1984.

**Stephanie Gilmore**

*See also* ADDAMS, JANE; LESBIAN FEMINISM; BROWN, RITA MAE; DALY, MARY; FULLER, MARGARET; GILMAN, CHARLOTTE PERKINS; GOLDMAN, EMMA; HOWE, MARIE JENNEY; MORGAN, ROBIN; RICH, ADRIENNE; SEX WARS; SEXISM AND MISOGYNY; SEXUAL REVOLUTIONS; SHAW, ANNA HOWARD; WILLARD, FRANCES; WOMEN'S STUDIES AND FEMINIST STUDIES; WOO, MERLE.

**FEMINIST STUDIES.** see WOMEN'S STUDIES AND FEMINIST STUDIES.

# FEMMES AND BUTCHES

In the United States, the origin of the terms femme and butch has been traced to working-class lesbian subcultures of the 1930s, 1940s, and 1950s. Popular knowledge would have it that a femme is the "woman" in a lesbian relationship, while her butch lover is the "man." However, many who have theorized, researched, and lived within these historical categories have effectively and passionately disputed such a crudely simplistic analysis. Multiple theorists and historians have argued that femmes and butches manipulated dominant cultural models of masculinity and femininity in order to create lesbian subcultures within harshly homophobic environments. Many scholars further argue that while femme and butch identifications did to some extent reproduce heterosexual roles, they simultaneously challenged dominant heterosexual gender constructions. Though the dominance of femme and butch subcultures faded with the rise of the gay liberation movement in the late 1960s and were frequently criticized by lesbian feminists during the 1970s, these persistent terms, and those who identify with them, show no sign of disappearing.

## Complex Erotic Statements

In *A Restricted Country*, Joan Nestle, a white, feminist, and decidedly femme historian, remembers that femme-butch relationships in the 1950s were complex erotic statements, both drawing on and transforming heterosexual models. Nestle describes the stance, dress, gesture, and loving of femme-butch relationships as deeply and authentically lesbian. In their oral history of a lesbian community in Buffalo, New York, Elizabeth Kennedy and Madeline Davis demonstrate that African American, European-American, and Native American femme and butch roles in middle-twentieth-century Buffalo differed from the hegemonic masculinity and femininity of the period. For example, according to the women interviewed by Kennedy and Davis, femme lesbians were central to the erotic system of femme/butch, often initiating and instructing their butch partners. Additionally, the femme's sexual pleasure was pivotal in this system. The ideal of the "stone butch," a woman who refused to be touched by her femme partner during sex, epitomized the centrality of femme pleasure. Kennedy and Davis further argue that femme and butch lesbians of the 1940s and 1950s manipulated dominant heterosexual constructs in order to organize a radically subversive and visible lesbian community. By providing a coded mechanism of communication between lesbians, femme/butch roles provided structure and safety during an extremely dangerous time to be a lesbian.

## Appearance and Roles During Sex

Kennedy and Davis identify the two crucial components of butch and femme identification as appearance and the role taken during sex. They record that butches generally wore pants, short hair, and sometimes attempted to conceal their breasts; femmes wore makeup, skirts, and dresses. However, Kennedy's and Davis's interviews suggest that physical presentation was not the deciding factor in butch or femme identification. Though not all narrators singled out one's role in sex as the ultimate definer of butch and femme, Kennedy and Davis argue that the sexual system in which butches always gave sexual pleasure and femmes always received it kept the structural system of working-class lesbian communities intact. As in any culture, there were exceptions to the rules, but these rules generally gave working-class lesbians a common sense of values and expectations.

Historian Rochelle Thorpe argues that the recent emphasis by lesbian historians upon bar culture has predisposed many lesbian historians to produce a specifically white lesbian history. In "A house where queers go," Thorpe presents a lesbian history of Detroit between

1940 and 1975, in which she focuses almost exclusively on the memories of black women. She emphasizes lesbian and gay house parties, where lesbians gathered, socialized, and danced together in private homes. Though Thorpe does not discuss femme and butch identifications in depth in "A house where queers go," her research complicates the bar-focused femme/butch histories presented by other scholars.

## African American Lesbian Bars

Thorpe does not mark African American lesbian bars as appearing until the 1970s. However, Ethel Sawyer's 1965 Master's thesis from Washington University documents an exclusively African American lesbian bar community in St. Louis during the 1960s. In this community, "feminine" lesbians were known as "fish," and "masculine" lesbians were known as "studs." Sawyer's work suggests that these identifications were most likely popular during previous decades. Parallel to the erotic dynamic of Buffalo femmes and butches, Sawyer records that fish pleasure was central to this erotic system, and that studs were expected to take the active role in sexual activity.

Kennedy and Davis report that most of the lesbian bars in Buffalo were shut down during the early 1960s, but that the spirit of these femme/butch communities created a foundation of resistance for the gay liberation movement of the late 1960s. By the 1970s lesbian feminism had taken the place of femme/butch as the most visible and public form of lesbianism. Writers Cherrie Moraga and Joan Nestle argue that lesbian feminism, drawing power from its predominantly white and middle-class base, actively criticized and shamed femme and butch lesbians.

## Lesbian Classism

Several historians argue strongly and convincingly that lesbian feminist classism is what caused the 1970s lesbian feminist rejection of femme/butch. For example, in her essay "Butches, Femmes, and Feminists," Elizabeth Smith argues that upwardly mobile lesbians have consistently rejected the specific working-class style of the butch/femme tradition. In *Sex and Sensibility,* historian Arlene Stein discusses a 1970s lesbian feminist who condemned femme/butch specifically because she felt that women who practiced femme/butch came from a working-class background. However, the stance of lesbian feminism throughout the 1970s was not based on class but, rather, on the assertion that femmes and butches reinscribed the values of heterosexist patriarchy.

During the 1980s, lesbian feminists whose roots lay in femme/butch communities began to speak out against lesbian feminist censure of femme and butch identifications. The reclamation of femme and butch during this time was part of a larger movement within lesbian and feminist communities known as the "sex wars." In *The Persistent Desire,* Joan Nestle marks 24 April 1982 as the public beginning of what would come to be known as the sex wars. On that day, hundreds of women attended the Scholar and the Feminist IX Conference held at Barnard College in New York City. The frequent denouncing of femme and butch identification, which Nestle witnessed at this conference through pamphlets, T-shirts, and panel discussions, motivated Nestle to begin her eloquent and prolific reclamation of 1950s femme and butch. Immediately following the landmark 1982 conference, a speak-out was held in Soho, in New York, where women whose sexual practices had been condemned at the conference were able to speak pieces. At this speak-out, lesbian feminists whose roots lay in the tradition of femme-butch began to form coalitions to speak out in defense of their sexual histories and preferences.

## Sex Radicals

On the side of femme and butch acceptance were women who called themselves "sex radicals," women who were also aligned with the anticensorship movement and the lesbian sadomasochist movement. Throughout the sex wars of the 1980s, sex radicals fought against what they saw as the "politically correct" and therefore asexual values of lesbian feminism. Sex radicals such as Susie Bright argued that the lesbian feminist movement of the 1970s had deeply internalized stereotypical norms of femininity as asexual, thereby scorning practices such as femme/butch, pornography, and sadomasochism, practices that were heavily identified with sexuality. Also during the sex wars, lesbian feminists such as Sheila Jeffreys retorted that pornography, femme and butch, and sadomasochism were harmful products of patriarchy that needed to be critiqued rather than embraced.

The vocal and written reclamation of femme/butch that began at the 1982 Barnard conference contributed to a phenomenon that Faderman calls "neo-butch/femme." Neo-butch/femme refers to the manifestation of femme and butch identities in lesbian communities from the 1980s to the present. Faderman writes that neo-butch/femme is characterized by a great deal more fluidity and play than was 1950s butch and femme. Femme and butch identities are now a choice for lesbians, but not a demand. Faderman points out that neo-femmes sometimes date other neo-femmes and that neo-butches sometimes date neo-butches. Such homo-genderal sexual relationships were strongly frowned upon during the 1950s, a point that Leslie Feinberg's novel *Stone Butch*

*Blues* illustrates through its depiction of two 1950s butches who felt compelled to hide their sexual attraction to one another.

Contributing to the popularity of contemporary femme and butch identifications are philosopher Judith Butler's critical observations of what she calls the performativity of gender, in both heterosexual gender roles and femme and butch gender roles. In her 1991 essay, "Imitation and Gender Insubordination," Butler deconstructs the popular notion of femmes and butches as imitative of heterosexual women and men. Butler writes that because all gender must be continuously learned and repeated in order to be presented as natural, femme and butch is no more an imitation of man and woman than man and woman is an imitation of femme and butch. In fact, Butler argues that heterosexuality, along with its gender roles, is in a constant process of imitating itself.

## Complicators of Femme and Butch Identities

Contemporary femme and butch identities have been complicated by the addition of the terms "bisexual" and "transgendered" to the lexicon of gay and lesbian communities and political movements. Clare Hemmings is a pioneering theorist who initiates a discussion of femme and butch in relation to bisexuality in her essay "Waiting for No Man: Bisexual Femme Subjectivity and Cultural Repudiation." Hemmings notes that, as a self-identified bisexual, she is frequently asked if bisexuals "do" femme/butch, whereas lesbians are more commonly described by these same people as "being" femme or butch. Hemmings draws on Butler's lucid deconstruction of femme and butch as imitating man and woman in order to deconstruct the concept of bisexual butch/femme as imitative of lesbian femme/butch.

The bisexual femme is an easily traceable historical subject, though little historical work has been dedicated to a project under the specific heading of "bisexual femme." Kennedy and Davis remark that they found more butches than femmes to interview for their project, because some of the femmes from the 1950s lesbian community they were studying had "gone straight." Bisexual theory instead suggests that, rather than changing sexual preferences from gay to straight, these femmes were, and are, open to both male and female sexual partners. In their discussion of Ethel Sawyer's 1965 dissertation, Laura Harris and Liz Crocker discuss that Sawyer presents fish as less dedicated to sexual expression than studs and that she cites evidence of fish who also had affairs with men. Crocker and Harris carefully add that there is an important distinction between chosen bisexual identity and socioeconomic reasons for maintaining a male partner.

While the femme as bisexual is certainly a historically traceable figure, this traceability also comes with the stereotype of the femme lesbian as *always* bisexual, a stereotype that sexologists historically attached to femme lesbians. The realities of both butch and femme sexualities need to be further complicated in relation to bisexuality: Some women identify as bisexual and femme, but others identify as femme and strictly lesbian. Some women identify as both butch and bisexual, though butch bisexuals are often rendered invisible by the same heterosexist and patriarchal models that render exclusively lesbian femmes as an impossibility.

## The Transgender Category

Transgenderism has also further complicated contemporary butch/femme. A transgendered man is one born with female or ambiguous genitalia, but who identifies as a man, and might therefore make use of hormones and/or surgery. A man who makes or plans on making a full physical transition is known as a transsexual, a subcategory of the broad umbrella term "transgender." As Nan Alamilla Boyd writes, the recent codifying of the terms transgender and transsexual has created historical conflict over whether to claim certain historical subjects as butch lesbians or as transgendered men.

In her article "Bodies in Motion: Lesbian and Transsexual Histories," Boyd presents compelling arguments for reclaiming historical figures such as Jack Garland (Babe Bean), Billy Tipton, and, more recently, Brandon Teena as transgendered, despite the fact that these historical figures had previously been claimed as butch lesbians or as women passing as men for economic reasons. Boyd's article clarifies that a female to male transgender identity, like a female bisexual identity, can be chosen rather than embodied simply for economic survival. Boyd also further complicates the narratives of Garland, Tipton, and Teena by addressing issues of racial and class-based passing, in addition to gender or biological sex "passing." By not eliminating the components of race and class from her analysis, Boyd makes it clear that no individual narrative can be reduced to a single identity, that history, identity, and subjectivity are far more complicated than any single lens is capable of revealing them to be.

The gray area between butch lesbians and female-to-male transsexuals is currently an area of heated debate. Judith Halberstam goes so far as to describe this debate as the "lesbian and ftm (female to male) border wars." In an attempt at finding commonality, Halberstam offers the category of "transgender butch" as an intermediary point between a woman who identifies as a butch lesbian and an individual who identifies as a transgendered man. A "transgender butch," according to Halberstam, is comfortable with a female body and a masculine presentation and does not identify with either biological sex. The "transgender butch" is just one point on Halberstam's "masculine continuum," a continuum that Halberstam offers in order to map the complex nuances of female masculinity and female-to-male masculinity.

Many of the 1950s butches interviewed by Kennedy and Davis fit into Halberstam's description of the "transgender butch," a masculine, female-bodied individual who identifies as neither man nor woman. Feinberg's *Stone Butch Blues* outlines the position of a transgender butch by creating a hero/ine who identifies as neither male nor female; Feinberg's hero/ine comes out as a butch lesbian in the 1950s, passes as a man during the 1970s, and returns to an intermediary "transgender butch" position in the 1990s. Feinberg's novel, like Boyd's essay on transsexual bodies and Halberstam's continuum, poignantly depicts the complications of gender, sex, and sexuality.

## Drag Kings

Another category that has complicated butch lesbian identity is the category of the drag king. A drag king is defined by Halberstam as a woman, femme, butch, or neither, who publicly performs masculinity as a form of entertainment. The drag king is a tradition born in lesbian and gay communities, similar to the male drag queen. Though many drag kings also identify as butch, Halberstam writes that she was surprised to see the extreme variation of day to day gender among the women who perform as drag kings. In "Mackdaddy, Superfly, Rapper: Gender, Race, and Masculinity in the Drag King Scene," Halberstam traces a history of drag king performances in the United States, particularly in the African American community. Though Halberstam notes that white women are starting to dominate the popular drag king circuit, she firmly grounds the roots of the drag king tradition in the cross-dressing female blues singers of the Harlem Renaissance, including Gladys Bentley, Ma Rainey, Bessie Smith, and Ethel Walters.

Halberstam's extensive work on female masculinity led her in 1998 to call for separate studies of butches and femmes. In "Between Butches," Halberstam points to unique butch traditions and experiences that radically differentiate butch experiences from the experiences of femmes. For instance, Halberstam points out that in the 1950s young butches were often "brought out" by an older butch, a tradition that is also portrayed in Feinberg's *Stone Butch Blues*. As part of this tradition, an older

butch referred to her protégée as a "baby butch." No similar tradition has been located in terms of femmes; there is no "baby femme."

As Halberstam begins a study of separate butch identity, other theorists and historians are at work constructing a uniquely femme history, unhinged from femme's attachment to butch. Leslea Newman's *The Femme Mystique* presents the "coming out" stories of femme lesbians. While Halberstam points out that butches face unique struggles in terms of a gender identity that does not correspond with the norms of dominant culture, Newman illustrates that femme lesbians often struggle with gender identities that do not correspond with norms and cultural expectations of the lesbian community. Butch is lesbianism's magical sign, according to Sally Munt in *Heroic Desire*, one of the few codes that connotes "lesbian" to heterosexual cultures. Many femme lesbians therefore first come out as butch lesbians, then come out a second time as femmes. Also unique to femme experience is the struggle for representation given the dominant society's masculinity/femininity hierarchy. Though femme and butch bisexuals and lesbians have clearly subverted and challenged this hierarchy throughout U.S. history, butch and femme lesbians and bisexuals can never absolutely separate themselves from dominant culture. Individual femme lesbian and bisexual identity draws on and alters dominant models of femininity, just as butch bisexual and lesbian identity manipulates dominant constructions of masculinity.

## Useful or Harmful?

Women have been identifying as femmes and butches since at least the middle of the twentieth century. Controversies have existed and still do exist as to the usefulness or harmfulness of these terms and the broadness of their applicability. Whether femmes and butches are lesbian or bisexual, transgender or not, stable or fluid, distinct or inseparable, the passion surrounding these discussions indicates that the exploration of these categories, both historical and theoretical, must continue.

### Bibliography

Boyd, Nan Alamilla. "Bodies in Motion: Lesbian and Transexual Histories." In *A Queer World: The Center for Lesbian and Gay Studies Reader.* Edited by Martin Duberman. New York and London: New York University Press, 1997.

Butler, Judith. "Imitation and Gender Insubordination." *The Lesbian and Gay Studies Reader.* Edited by Henry Abelove, Michele Ana Barale, and David M. Halperin. New York and London: Routledge, 1993.

Duggan, Lisa, and Nan D. Hunter. *Sex Wars: Sexual Dissent and Political Culture.* New York and London: Routledge, 1995.

Faderman, Lillian. *Odd Girls and Twilight Lovers.* New York: Penguin Books, 1992.

———. "The Return of Butch and Femme: A Phenomenon in Lesbian Sexuality of the 1980s and 1990s" *Journal of the History of Sexuality* 2, no. 4 (1992): 578–596.

Feinberg, Leslie. *Stone Butch Blues.* Ithaca, N.Y.: Firebrand Books, 1993.

Halberstam, Judith. "Mackdaddy, Superfly, Rapper: Gender, Race, and Masculinity in the Drag King Scene." *Social Text* 0, no. 52/53 (1997): 104–131.

———. "Transgender butch–butch/ftm border wars and the masculine continuum." *GLA-A Journal of Lesbian and Gay Studies* 4, no. 2 (1998): 287–310.

———. *Female Masculinity.* Durham and London: Duke University Press, 1998.

———. "Between Butches." In *Butch/Femme: Inside Lesbian Gender.* Edited by Sally R. Munt et al. London and Washington: Cassell, 1998.

Harris, Laura, and Elizabeth Crocker. *Femme: Feminists, Lesbians, and Bad Girls.* New York and London: Routledge, 1997.

Hemmings, Clare. "Waiting for No Man: Bisexual Femme Subjectivity and Cultural Repudiation." In *Butch/Femme: Inside Lesbian Gender.* Edited by Sally R. Munt et al. London and Washington: Cassell, 1998.

Hollibaugh, Amber, and Cherrie Moraga. "What We're Rollin' around in Bed with: Sexual Silences in Feminism: A Conversation toward Ending Them." In *The Persistent Desire: A Femme-Butch Reader.* Edited by Joan Nestle. Boston: Alyson, 1992.

Jeffreys, Sheila. "Butch and Femme: Now and Then." *Gossip* (Great Britain) 5: 65–95.

Kennedy, Elizabeth Lapovsky, and Madeline Davis. *Boots of Leather, Slippers of Gold.* Harmondsworth, Middlesex, England: Penguin Books, 1994.

Moraga, Cherrie. *Loving in the War Years.* Boston: South End Press, 1983.

Munt, Sally R. *Heroic Desire: Lesbian Identity and Cultural Space.* New York: New York University Press, 1998.

Nestle, Joan. *A Restricted Country: Essays and Short Fiction.* Ithaca, N.Y.: Firebrand Books, 1987.

Newman, Leslea. *The Femme Mystique.* Boston: Alyson, 1995.

Sawyer, Ethel. "A Study of a Public Lesbian Community." Master's thesis, Washington University, 1965.

Smith, Elizabeth. "Butches, Femme, and Feminists: The Politics of Lesbian Sexuality" *NWSA Journal* 3, no. 1 (1989): 398–421.

Stein, Arlene. *Sex and Sensibility: Stories of a Lesbian Generation.* Berkeley: University of California Press, 1997.

Thorpe, Rochelle. "A house where queers go?: African-American Lesbian Nightlife in Detroit, 1940–1975." In *Inventing Lesbian Cultures in America.* Boston: Beacon Press, 1996.

**Evalie Horner**

*See also* ARZNER, DOROTHY; BARS, CLUBS, AND RESTAURANTS; BISEXUALS; BUFFALO; DRAG QUEENS AND KINGS; GENDER AND SEX; LESBIAN FEMINISM; SEX WARS; TRANSSEXUALS, TRANSGENDER PEOPLE, TRANSVESTITES, AND CROSS-DRESSERS.

# FIERSTEIN, Harvey (b. 6 June 1954), playwright, performer.

Harvey Forbes Fierstein was born in Brooklyn, New York, and earned a B.F.A. degree from the Pratt Institute in New York City in 1973. By that time he had already established a reputation in New York City's gay clubs as a gravel-voiced, zaftig drag queen. Andy Warhol cast Fierstein as an asthmatic lesbian cleaning woman in his only play, *Pork,* produced at La Mama in 1971.

Around the same time, Fierstein began to write plays as vehicles for his own idiosyncratic performing style. His early works—*Freaky Pussy* (1973), *Flatbush* (1975), *Tosca,* and *Cannibals*—did not receive much attention outside of Greenwich Village. Fierstein began to be noticed, however, with the presentations of the three short plays that eventually would comprise *Torch Song Trilogy* (1981): *International Stud* (1978), *Fugue in a Nursery* (1979), and *Widows and Children First!* These plays, which were performed separately and together in various venues around Manhattan, demonstrate Fierstein's eclecticism as a writer. He was able to assimilate some of the techniques of experimental theater with the middle-class Jewish humor of Neil Simon and connect them both to gay liberation. While *International Stud* and *Fugue in a Nursery* are nonrealistic in form, in content they represent gay appropriations of popular mainstream domestic comedy.

In the trilogy, Arnold, a pudgy, gravel-voiced Brooklyn drag queen, falls in love with a man who is in denial about his homosexuality. *International Stud,* in which boy meets and loses boy, is presented as a series of monologues interspersed with torch songs. Only the final scene is conventionally dramatic. *Fugue in a Nursery,* which depicts the games played on a weekend in the country by Arnold, his former and new wives, and Arnold's beautiful, eighteen-year-old boyfriend, is set entirely in a giant bed in which the four characters enact scenes that take place around an upstate New York farm. The final play, *Widows and Children First!,* in which Arnold and his erstwhile lover finally reconcile and Arnold deals with both his mother and his adoptive son, is a conventional domestic drama. The message may be acceptance of gay men's unconventional domestic arrangements, but the domestic pattern established is actually the traditional nuclear family: a loving couple

*Torch Song Trilogy.* A performance of the 1981 trio of plays written by and starring Harvey Fierstein (third from left), who returned to Broadway with his book for the 1983 musical *La Cage aux Folles* and his featured role in the 2002 musical *Hairspray.* [The Kobal Collection]

and their child. It is this bridging of experimental technique, in-your-face gay politics, and mainstream family values that allowed the three-plus hours of *Torch Song Trilogy* (the collective name for the three plays) to run successfully on and off Broadway for almost three years between 1981 and 1984, and which made Fierstein a major Broadway figure as a performer and writer. The only weakness in the plays is a tendency on the part of the author and central character to enjoy the role of victim. Fierstein wrote and starred in a glossy film version of *Torch Song Trilogy,* released in 1988, which removed the play's structural innovations and emphasized its kinship to conventional romantic comedy.

Fierstein then wrote the book for the hit Broadway musical, *La Cage aux Folles* (produced in 1983, with music and lyrics by Jerry Herman), which ran at the Palace Theatre and on the road for over four years. Once again, he was able to turn a gay love story into popular commercial fare by emphasizing the commonality of the characters with their predominantly straight audience. Essentially, the musical is the story of a middle-aged married (gay) couple who must deal with their son's marriage. Jerry Herman's lyrics did more to insert the politics of gay liberation into the work than Fierstein's book, which was a fairly straightforward adaptation of the hit French film of the same name.

Fierstein was unable to capitalize on his early successes. *Safe Sex,* another trilogy, lasted only a week on Broadway in 1987. Again, two experimental plays are followed by a conventional domestic drama centering on a man who has lost his lover and a powerful female figure

(the lover's former wife). That play, *Tidy Endings,* was presented on television in 1988 and has been released on video. *Safe Sex* centered on the effect of AIDS on gay men's ability to make positive connections, but by the time the trilogy appeared on Broadway, there had been a number of successful, powerful plays about men with AIDS on and off Broadway (notably William M. Hoffman's *As Is* and Larry Kramer's *The Normal Heart,* both successfully produced in 1985) and also on television. *Safe Sex* seemed underdeveloped and too intimate for Broadway. Fierstein's last outing as a Broadway writer was as book writer for the notorious musical flop, *Legs Diamond* (produced in 1988, with music and lyrics by and starring Peter Allen).

By the time *Legs Diamond* opened and closed, Fierstein had built a Hollywood career as America's first openly gay celebrity who made a career creating and performing gay roles. He narrated a number of television shows on AIDS awareness and a documentary, *The Times of Harvey Milk* (1984), but also made a number of appearances on television sitcoms and in feature films like *Mrs. Doubtfire* (1993). While he also played nongay characters on television and in film, Fierstein is identified in the audience's mind with his earlier appearances as the tough but sentimental drag queen. In the more cynical, in-your-face era of *Will and Grace* and *Queer as Folk,* Fierstein's portrayals of sentimentality and victimization, which harks back to masochistic movie heroines played by Susan Hayward, seem to be vestiges of an earlier era of gay history. It is fitting that Fierstein made a sensational Broadway comeback, once again in drag, in Divine's role as the mother of the teenage heroine in the 2002 hit musical version of John Waters's 1988 film, *Hairspray*.

**Bibliography**

Clum, John M. *Still Acting Gay: Male Homosexuality in Modern Drama*. New York: St. Martin's Press, 2000.

De Johngh, Nicholas. *Not in Front of the Audience: Homosexuality on Stage*. London: Routledge, 1992.

Sinfield, Alan. *Gay and After*. London: Serpent's Tail, 1998.

———. *Out on Stage: Lesbian and Gay Theatre in the Twentieth Century*. New Haven, Conn.: Yale University Press, 1999.

**John M. Clum**

**See also** ACTORS AND ACTRESSES; COMEDY AND HUMOR; DRAG QUEENS AND KINGS; FILM; ICONS; MUSIC: BROADWAY AND MUSICAL THEATER; THEATER AND PERFORMANCE.

# FILM AND VIDEO

In *The Celluloid Closet*, his groundbreaking 1981 history of LGBT representation in film, Vito Russo draws attention to a 1895 Thomas Edison pre-Hollywood silent short film, *The Gay Brothers*, in which two men dance closely together while another man plays a violin. While we cannot call these two men gay simply because they are dancing together or because the film's title used the word, the Edison short depicts same-sex intimacy at the very beginning of filmmaking with apparent innocence and freedom. Hollywood's representation of same-sex coupling would never be so innocent or free. Still, 1920s Hollywood films included a diverse range of images and moral judgments, and this helped provoke a new level of censorship from the 1930s through the 1960s that reduced and complicated—but never eliminated—queer representation. Filmic representations were always constructed in a complex relationship with the discourses of sexologists, moralists, LGBT activists, and queer cultural workers. The number and diversity of queer characters and themes in films throughout the twentieth century belie the myth that LGBT films—or "positive images"—only emerged after the Stonewall Riots of 1969.

## The Early Twentieth Century

In the early part of the twentieth century, homosexuality and gender inversion (that is, effete men and mannish women) were linked in Hollywood films, vaudeville, and other popular forms of entertainment. This became the primary stereotype, paralleling the belief of many sexologists that homosexuality was only one part of a larger inversion of gender behavior, attitude, and appearance.

Since a lesbian was understood as a man stuck in a woman's body, and vice versa for gay men, they were often thought of as members of a third sex.

From the 1910s to the early 1930s, U.S. filmmakers and actors, including Charlie Chaplin and Stan Laurel, used various degrees of "gender inversion" in characters' mannerisms, costume, work, and other attributes to signify homosexuality. In silent comedies such as *Algie the Miner* (1912), Chaplin's *The Masquerader* (1914), and *A Florida Enchantment* (1914), the audience is led to laugh at the sissy male as this character interacts with conventional heterosexual, masculine men. After the comical interaction, the "abnormal" male (known popularly as "pansies," "nances," and "fairies" or by other words marking gender inversion) is either driven away from the social setting, beaten, or taught how to be manly and reclaim his male role in a traditional, two-sex society.

But while the "third sex" was seen commonly as an oddity and a butt of humor in this early period, some films provided moments of queer confidence and challenge to conventional gender and sexual roles. For instance, *A Florida Enchantment* shows the lead female character confidently assuming mannish characteristics and pursuing women. An equally subversive moment appears in Stan Laurel's short comedy classic *The Soilers* (1923). While the hero played by Laurel and the villain duke it out, a "sissy" cowboy appears, effeminately mincing and primping around them. After the fight, the queer cowboy blows a kiss to our hero, which the hero rejects. The effete cowboy then drops a flowerpot on the hero's head, leaving him woozy and confused and thus subverting the standard expectation that the queer will be punished.

In the last years of Prohibition, the number of queer images in Hollywood film increased dramatically. From musicals to gangster films to melodrama to exotic romances, queer was in. Numerous films featured "pansy" jokes or walk-ons where an effete gay man appeared for a brief comic moment. In Eddie Cantor's *Palmy Days* (1931), *The Sport Parade* (1932), and even Betty Boop cartoons, pansies were as plentiful as racial and ethnic stereotypes, which were standard features at the time. The actor Franklin Pangborn even made a living out of playing pansies in films such as *International House* (1933) and *Professional Sweetheart* (1933).

Hollywood enjoyed not just a pansy craze, but a sapphic one, illustrated most infamously by Marlene Dietrich's male drag performance and same-sex kiss in *Morocco* (1930) and Greta Garbo's mannish dress and same-sex kiss in *Queen Christina* (1933). Both female stars appeared in similar mannish dress offscreen. As their erotic and subversive kisses suggest, the sexual implications of women's assuming such poses were clear.

There were also many images of men in drag during this period. Some films teasingly placed heterosexual men in feminine disguise to escape danger or accomplish a goal. For instance, Eddie Cantor's character in *Palmy Days* (1931) avoids two gangsters by dressing in female disguise. Often male comic actors played women, as when Laurel and Oliver Hardy played their own wives in the comedy short *Twice Two* (1933). But Hollywood also occasionally portrayed men who chose to cross-dress for different reasons. In *The Circus Clown* (1934), a professional female impersonator in the circus sexually teases Joe E. Brown's small town character.

Even more astounding in films in this period, LGBT characters sometimes appeared in spaces marked as queer friendly. *Call Her Savage* (1932) includes a scene featuring a pansy duo dressed like chamber maids, singing about their desire for sailors before an audience evidently including both heterosexuals and homosexuals in a Greenwich Village basement café. Also, at this time, a number of directors and actors, including Dorothy Arzner, George Cukor, James Whale, and William Haines, were more open about their LGBT lives than would be possible later.

There were more horrible representations of homosexuality and transgenderism as well. By the late 1920s, many people were aware of the theoretical writings of Sigmund Freud and other psychoanalysts who challenged the model of "sexual inversion" by contending that homosexuality was not biologically inborn but was acquired through various deviations in "normal" psychosexual development toward heterosexual monogamy. This new theory shifted understanding from a biological model to a model of nurture, which suggested the possibility of correcting a person's "abnormal" gender and sexual behavior through parental, educational, and other institutional surveillance of and intervention into the rearing of a child. In the Hollywood films *Strange Interlude* (1932) and the more insidious *The Silver Cord* (1933), both based upon successful stage plays, mothers were blamed for the emasculation of their sons and for fostering their homosexuality. Gender inversion, mother love, and neurosis mark homosexuality in these films.

### The Hays Code Period

In the early 1930s, Catholic clergy and other moralists became outraged by the growing sexual license of Hollywood films and besieged the industry with threats of federal censorship and public boycotts. In response to this pressure, the Hollywood studios imposed their own censorship codes and empowered Will Hays and the Motion Picture Producers and Distributors of America (known unofficially as the Hays Office), of which he was president, to censor all films. In 1933, in one of his first moves toward strengthened regulation, Hays began censoring pictures with overt "pansy" characters. In 1934 the major Hollywood studios committed themselves through the Hays Code to banning "sex perversion or any inference to it" and began to advocate conservative gender roles, monogamy, and heterosexuality.

However, the representation of homosexuality and cross-dressing did not disappear during the Hays Code period (roughly from 1934 to 1968), as film scholars such as Richard Dyer, Andrea Weiss, and Steven Cohen have pointed out. Instead, representations became more coded through denigrating stereotypes. Homosexuality appeared as unnatural, comic, deviant, monstrous—and above all, as covert—until the 1960s, while cross-dressing appeared merely comic.

The characteristics of the pansy, for instance, continued to influence the screen personae of Bob Hope and Jerry Lewis, as well as secondary characters, such as those played by Franklin Pangborn. However, these characters were always played for laughs and never allowed explicitly to express homosexual desire. Male and female drag also appeared periodically. In *Sylvia Scarlett* (1935), Katharine Hepburn disguises herself as a young boy to escape France with her father. While this leads to some suggestive queer sexual subtext, all is righted once her sex is known. Another unusual film is *This Is the Army* (1943), in which World War II soldiers put on a professional touring musical show to raise morale. Many of the musical numbers feature soldiers in female drag. However, their masculinity and heterosexuality are salvaged at the end of the film when they march out of the theater to fight for freedom.

The dangerous queer became more prevalent during the Hays Code years. For instance, in the 1936 film *Dracula's Daughter,* the mannish vampire Countess Zaleska hypnotizes and feeds on young women. Alfred Hitchcock's 1948 film *Rope* features a witty, immaculately dressed, and psychopathically murderous male couple, modeled on the real world 1924 case of Nathan Leopold and Richard Loeb, who strangle a friend just to see if they can get away with it. In both cases, the filmmakers use gender inversion and Freudian references to invoke homosexuality and then associate it with psychopathic tendencies.

## Experimental Film before and after World War II

Although Hollywood films generally became more conservative in their representations of gender and sexuality during the Hays Code years, experimental filmmakers offered an alternative and often more sympathetic set of images. Even so, few experimental filmmakers explored queer sexuality before World War II. One exception is Melville Webber and James Sibley Watson Jr.'s *Lot in Sodom* (1933). While the film draws upon the biblical story of God's destruction of Sodom because of its sexual perversion, it depicts a captivatingly erotic and animated gay world and hints at the sexual pleasures experienced by the beautiful young male sodomites. The lives led by the dour Lot and his daughters seem uninteresting and uninviting in comparison.

After World War II, the number and diversity of depictions of male homosexuality and transgenderism grew dramatically in experimental film. Unlike *Lot in Sodom*'s use of literary motifs and Hollywood's use of stereotypical gender and psychoanalytic codes, Kenneth Anger's groundbreaking *Fireworks* (1947) used the filmmaker's own homosexual desires and experiences in 1940s queer Los Angeles for its inspiration and subject matter. While *Fireworks* was the most explicit gay experimental film made in the United States at that time, other filmmakers—including Gregory Markopoulos, Willard Maas, and Curtis Harrington—produced films that evoked homosexuality in more veiled ways—using, for instance, imagery, mythological characters such as Narcissus, and the tropes of Freudian psychoanalysis. Overt lesbian representation in experimental film was not seen at this time, as far as can be ascertained.

The number of experimental films with daring queer content proliferated in the 1960s, most of them adopting a playful and liberated attitude. Such films drew upon a wide range of influences, including personal experience, Hollywood and popular culture, Beat culture, and the all-male physique films of the 1950s. Two of the more influential films were Jack Smith's *Flaming Creatures* (1963) and Kenneth Anger's *Scorpio Rising* (1964). Smith's film celebrates a Hollywood "B" movie aesthetic with its playful, uninhibited transgender performances and exaggerated costumes and acting styles. By contrast, Anger's film voyeuristically submerges the viewer in homoerotic images of bike-boy culture and male adolescent drunkenness and play, making innovative, pre-MTV use of popular music and collage. The male nudity and lack of moral condemnation in both films shocked conservative society, and their screenings were often shut down by local legal authorities who confiscated the film prints.

Andy Warhol also made a number of influential experimental films during this period, including *Blow Job* (1963), *Tarzan and Jane Regained . . . Sort of* (1963), *Mario Banana* (1964), *Taylor Mead's Ass* (1965), and *Chelsea Girls* (1966). Warhol's films featured a cross-section of the queer underworld in New York City, including male hustlers, fairies, and drag queens and depicted both queer and straight sexual play. Warhol also featured eroticized male bodies in such films as *My Hustle* (1965), *Bike Boy* (1967), and the later Warhol-produced, Paul Morrissey–directed films starring Joe Dallesandro, including *Flesh* (1968) and *Trash* (1970). The latter films paralleled the rise of gay erotica in magazines and films such as Pat Rocco's gay male nudie shorts. Other influential avant-garde filmmakers from this period included Ken Jacobs (*Blonde Cobra*, 1962), Ron Rice (*The Flower Thief*, 1960, and *Chumlum*, 1964), and the Kuchar brothers (*I Was a Teenage Rumpot*, 1960, and *Sins of the Fleshapoids*, 1965).

## Hollywood in the 1950s and 1960s

In the 1950s and 1960s, Hollywood's representations of homosexuality and transgenderism were—compared to experimental film—limited and timid. But during the 1950s the industry did make a shift to more serious subject matter, including sexual and gender diversity. A variety of factors pushed Hollywood in this direction: economic competition from television and more sexually daring foreign films; the Kinsey reports and other medical literature detailing heterosexual and homosexual behavior in American society; the serious literary fiction and theatrical plays that were exploring more daring sexual material; and the declining power of the Hays Code.

In particular, Hollywood raised the issue of homosexuality in psychological and social problem films. *Caged* (1950) and *Tea and Sympathy* (1956), for instance, dramatized social concerns over homosexuality in U.S. society without quite naming them. But such explorations remained limited in the1950s, as witnessed by the censorship of homosexuality in the film adaptation of Tennessee Williams's *Cat on a Hot Tin Roof* (1958).

As the power of the censorship code waned in the 1960s, Hollywood films moved from subtextual to overt depictions and discussions of homosexuality. *The Children's Hour* (1961), for instance, explored the power of gossip when two young female schoolteachers, Martha Dobie (played by Shirley MacLaine) and Karen Wright (played by Audrey Hepburn), are accused of being lesbians. Near the end of the film, after the women have lost their school, Martha admits that she has desired Karen and feels "dirty" for having such feelings. Unable to handle her self-loathing, Martha commits suicide. Having

MacLaine's character openly admit her desire was a remarkable step, since under the Hays Code, films were never allowed to overtly name or represent same-sex desire. Equally groundbreaking was the 1962 film *Advise and Consent*, which also overtly tackled the issue and even included the first openly gay bar scene since the 1932 movie *Call Her Savage* (1932), although *Advise and Consent* too portrayed homosexuals as self-loathing.

As the 1960s progressed, however, Hollywood moved toward more openness and complexity in its representation of homosexuality in films such as *Lilith* (1964), *Inside Daisy Clover* (1965), and *Reflections in a Golden Eye* (1967). By the end of the decade, Hollywood had released *The Killing of Sister George* (1968) and was ready to release *The Boys in the Band* (1970), both based on successful stage plays and still two of the most searing and controversial dramatizations of homosexual themes ever released by Hollywood. *The Killing of Sister George* perpetuates the association of self-loathing and alcoholism with gay culture that was presented in earlier films, but it also provides a powerful portrait of a bold and unapologetic dyke called "George." *The Boys in the Band,* adapted by Mart Crowley from his stage play, likewise depicts a gay world saturated with self-loathing, psychoanalytic jargon, and alcoholism, but also portrays the rich social ties and camp humor of gay men and includes a range of gay social types, including the hustler, the fairy, the gay sportsman, the neurotic. These two films are views from inside the LGBT world, which is oppressed by mainstream conservative gender and sexual beliefs, but is also strong in its queer relationships and friendships.

## The 1970s

While *The Boys in the Band* was the best that Hollywood had to offer in 1970, queer experimental, independent, and documentary filmmakers brought their personal experiences of LGBT life, coming out stories, and LGBT politics into a post–Stonewall Riots queer film explosion. Lesbian filmmaker Jan Oxenberg ruminated on her childhood and her lesbian life in *Home Movie* (1972) and took on lesbian stereotypes in *A Comedy in Six Unnatural Acts* (1975). Lesbian feminist filmmaker Barbara Hammer challenged lesbians to celebrate their sexuality unapologetically and to create new visions of gender and sexuality in short films such as *Dyketactics* (1974) and *Women I Love* (1976).

The early 1970s was also a time when explicit gay male erotic experimental films and pornography began to be taken seriously in art film circles. For instance, gay male sexuality and the male erotic object were celebrated in Curt McDowell's *Confessions* (1971), *Ronnie* (1972),

and *Loads* (1980). Wakefield Poole's lyrical, pornographic *Boys in the Sand* (1971), starring Casey Donovan, received mainstream reviews. The Gage brothers' trilogy (*Kansas City Trucking Company,* 1976; *El Paso Wrecking Corporation,* 1977; and *L.A. Tool and Die,* 1979) combined expressions of an assertive gay pride with explicit depictions of men's sex with men (and occasionally with women), often using an experimental film approach.

LGBT filmmakers also made important documentaries during the 1970s that affirmed LGBT identity and community and challenged closeted LGBT people to come out and become politically active. Arthur Bressan's *Gay USA* (1977), for example, documented lesbian and gay pride marches in 1977 as a response to the anti-LGBT activism of Anita Bryant and other conservatives, while the Mariposa Film Group's *Word Is Out* (1977) depicted the diversity of lesbian and gay life by interviewing twenty-six lesbians and gay men.

In the 1970s, midnight features began to screen the queer films of John Waters, including *Pink Flamingos* (1972) and *Female Trouble* (1974), both of which starred Waters's drag diva Divine, and the cross-dressing, multisexual *Rocky Horror Picture Show* (1975), which eventually had phenomenal success. All three films attracted large LGBT and straight audiences. In addition, the rise of LGBT newspapers and magazines offered new publicity outlets for queer films. Furthermore, independent, documentary, and experimental LGBT filmmakers found a receptive and growing audience for their work on college campuses and especially through the establishment of gay and lesbian film festivals in major cities, including San Francisco, Chicago, and New York.

While this expansion of queer work was taking place in the 1970s, Hollywood often seemed to regress to the stereotypes of the Hays Code period. Hollywood made films, for instance, featuring murderous queers, such as the deadly transvestite in *Freebie and the Bean* (1974) and the psychopathic lesbian played by Elizabeth Ashley in *Windows* (1980). The pansy stereotype continued in films such as *The Choirboys* (1977), which features a cruising, mincing man with his pink poodle.

## The 1980s

However, two "event" films illustrate the growing attention given the subject of homosexuality in Hollywood films, though not always to the liking of LGBT viewers. William Friedkin's 1980 film *Cruising,* a film noir–like slasher film set in New York City's gay sadomasochism and leather subculture, led to LGBT protests, both when filming was taking place and at the premiere, by activists who worried that the film would only feed the growing anti-LGBT sentiment represented by Anita Bryant's crusade of 1977. Two years later Hollywood offered *Making Love* (1982), a melodramatic love triangle in which a wife finds out that her husband is having an affair with another man.

In the 1980s, however, a number of independent and mainstream films featuring more complex LGBT characters and themes broke out of the lesbian and gay festival circuit and into mainstream cinemas. In independent film, the most successful were director Donna Dietch's *Desert Hearts* (1985), a lesbian love story based upon a novel by Jane Rule, and writer-director Bill Sherwood's *Parting Glances* (1986), which features a young Steve Buscemi as a gay rock singer living with AIDS.

*Parting Glances* was only one of several gay films in this era to tackle the subject of AIDS, some in a confrontational voice and others using a more conventional, melodramatic narrative. Two important activist-based AIDS films were Arthur Bressan's 1985 feature *Buddies* and Marlon Riggs's 1989 experimental documentary *Tongues Untied*. In Bressan's two-person drama, one character becomes a "buddy" to an older man dying of AIDS. The experience of visiting and listening to the bedridden man turns the more naïve character into an activist. Riggs's *Tongues Untied* is a complex discourse on AIDS, homophobia, and racism from a gay African American man's perspective. Queer film lost important voices when the directors Sherwood, Bressan, and Riggs died of AIDS in the 1990s.

## The 1990s and Beyond

The AIDS melodrama proved to be the most successful vehicle for moving more complex and less stereotyped representations of LGBT people into the mainstream. *Longtime Companion* (1990) melodramatically shows a group of friends dealing with the effect of AIDS on both their close social circle and the larger gay world. With successful actors such as Campbell Scott, Bruce Davison (who was nominated for an Academy Award for his role), and Dermot Mulroney appearing in it, as Buscemi had in *Parting Glances*, the film showed other actors that they could play LGBT characters on screen without any setback to their careers. Better-known straight actors began to feel more comfortable taking on LGBT roles, most famously Tom Hanks in the courtroom AIDS melodrama *Philadelphia* (1993), directed by Jonathan Demme. *Philadelphia* is credited with taking gay characters and experiences into the multiplexes of mainstream America. For a grim story about a man who is fired from his law firm for being HIV positive and who then successfully

sues the firm before dying of AIDS-related diseases, *Philadelphia* was a phenomenal success at the box office and the Academy Awards, where Hanks won for best actor. With *Philadelphia*, Mike Nichols's *The Birdcage* (1996), and Kimberly Pierce's *Boys Don't Cry* (1999), Hollywood seemed to signal that the door was now open to LGBT representation in big-budget films.

Following in the successful footsteps of Dietch, Sherwood, Bressan, and Riggs, independent filmmakers in the 1990s continued to depict a much more diverse queer world than did Hollywood. Jennie Livingston's documentary *Paris Is Burning* (1990) portrayed the black and Latino drag ballroom scene in New York City, whose competitive ritual forms included voguing. Also in the 1990s, a group of well-made, provocative films by LGBT filmmakers signaled the birth of what became known as the new "queer cinema." Todd Haynes's *Poison* (1991), Tom Kalin's *Swoon* (1992), Gregg Araki's *The Living End* (1992), and Rose Troche's *Go Fish* (1994) marked a new level of visibility and success for LGBT filmmakers.

Outside of feature filmmaking, experimental and documentary film and video makers continued to break new ground in technique and subject matter. The important work of Su Friedrich, Cheryl Dunye, Sadie Benning, Greg Bordowitz, Tom Kalin, George Kuchar, Ellen Spiro, Yvonne Welbon, and others too numerous to list expanded and diversified the representation of queer identity, desire, and politics.

At the beginning of the twenty-first century, a number of successful films, both independent and mainstream, suggest that LGBT representation has expanded into a variety of genres, characters, and themes. Building on the art house and mainstream interest in queer characters and subject matter, films such as *Big Eden* (2000), *Hedwig and the Angry Inch* (2001), *Far from Heaven* (2002), and *The Hours* (2002) placed those characters and issues in dialogue with larger familial, social, political, economic, and cultural themes.

## Bibliography

Creekmur, Cory K., and Alexander Doty. *Out in Culture: Gay, Lesbian, and Queer Essays on Popular Culture.* Durham, N.C.: Duke University Press, 1995.

Dyer, Richard. *Now You See It: Studies on Lesbian and Gay Film.* New York: Routledge, 1990.

Gever, Martha, Pratibha Parmar, and John Greyson. *Queer Looks: Perspectives on Lesbian and Gay Film and Video.* New York: Routledge, 1993.

Hanson, Ellis, ed. *Out Takes: Essays on Queer Theory and Film.* Durham, N.C.: Duke University Press, 1999.

Murray, Raymond. *Images in the Dark: An Encyclopedia of Gay and Lesbian Film and Video.* New York: Plume, 1996.

Russo, Vito. *The Celluloid Closet: Homosexuality in the Movies.* New York: Harper and Row, 1981.

Tyler, Parker. *Screening the Sexes: Homosexuality in the Movies.* New York: Holt, Rinehart, 1972.

Waugh, Tom. *Hard to Imagine: Gay Male Eroticism in Photography and Film from Their Beginnings to Stonewall.* New York: Columbia University Press, 1996.

Weiss, Andrea. *Vampires and Violets: Lesbians in Film.* New York: Penguin, 1993.

White, Patricia. *Uninvited: Classical Hollywood Cinema and Lesbian Representability.* Bloomington: Indiana University Press, 1999.

**Ron Gregg**

*See also* ACTORS AND ACTRESSES; ANGER, KENNETH; ARZNER, DOROTHY; BERNSTEIN, LEONARD; CENSORSHIP, OBSCENITY, AND PORNOGRAPHY LAW AND POLICY; CUKOR, GEORGE; FILM AND VIDEO FESTIVALS; FILM AND VIDEO STUDIES; ICONS; KRAMER, LARRY; PORNOGRAPHY; RIGGS, MARLON; RULE, JANE; RUSSO, VITO; WARHOL, ANDY; WATERS, JOHN; WEBER, BRUCE; WILLIAMS, TENNESSEE.

# FILM AND VIDEO FESTIVALS

Politically organized around the concept of visibility, LGBT communities have looked to film and video as a vital arena of representation. After decades of erasure and distortion of queer desires and LGBT characters in Hollywood cinema, films and videos by, about, and, crucially, *for* LGBT people have in recent decades changed the picture irrevocably. Film and video festivals exhibiting such works emerged in cities with large LGBT populations, such as New York; London; San Francisco; Sydney, Australia; and Toronto, Canada, in the 1970s and 1980s. These festivals quickly became a central event on the queer cultural calendar, and the festival circuit grew to include smaller and geographically far-flung communities.

By 2003, approximately one hundred fifty LGBT film and video festivals existed worldwide, ranging in scope from short series to annual two-week events featuring hundreds of works from around the world. Most catered to LGBT audiences and the wider film-going public, but some also served film critics, distributors, and exhibitors. Certain events programmed exclusively lesbian work or work representing LGBT people of African descent; some festivals specialized in video or experimental film; and others featured work of interest to transgender people. This diversity reflects the fact that over the several decades of the existence of these festivals, the number and kinds of works available for exhibition have increased exponentially.

Film and video festivals enhance LGBT visibility in a number of ways. The diversity of representations and genres goes far beyond initial demands for "positive representations" of LGBT people. LGBT artists from all over the world, working in a variety of media and formats, receive unprecedented exposure. And the LGBT community is socially visible, as considerable audiences gather publicly in festival venues and the events receive significant press coverage. Film and video festivals have become arenas in which to debate such issues as the politicizing and commodification of LGBT identity; representations of violence and sexuality and their corresponding fantasies and realities; the politics of outing, identity, and nomenclature; and the risks and benefits of coalition and special interest politics. Like LGBT pride parades, festivals have become both public forum and holiday.

## Frameline

In the United States, the most influential and long-lived festival, the San Francisco International Lesbian and Gay Film Festival, is sponsored and presented by Frameline. Founded in 1977, Frameline has long been under the direction of Michael Lumpkin. Because of the concentration of LGBT people in San Francisco and the prominence of the festival's main venue, the historic Castro Theatre, in the center of the LGBT district, Frameline's annual festival is a citywide cultural event that also forms the heart of an international network of such festivals. During its history, the festival has provided a venue for numerous foreign films, including Alexandra von Grote's *November Moon* (1985), early works by Pedro Almodovar such as *What Did I Do to Deserve This?* (1985), and Derek Jarman's *Angelic Conversations* (1985), which did not find wide distribution. Frameline also provided a venue for sexually explicit materials, as well as for work of historical interest, including the Hollywood film *The Children's Hour* (1961), the archival treasure *Different from the Others* (1918), and the early activist film by Rosa von Praunheim, *It Is Not the Homosexual Who Is Perverse but the Society in Which He Lives* (1971). Also shown at Frameline were the increasing number of independently produced documentaries, shorts, narrative, and experimental works made in the context of the LGBT movement. These include the collectively produced *Word Is Out* (1978), and later award-winning documentaries, such as *Common Threads: Stories from the Quilt* (1989) and *The Celluloid Closet* (1995), by collective member Robert Epstein and his partner Jeffrey Freidman, as well as early independent features such as Bill Sherwood's

*Parting Glances* (1986). From the mid-1980s onward, the festival also featured works produced on video, many made in response to the AIDS epidemic, such as *Testing the Limits* (1987).

## New York Festivals

The NewFest in New York was founded in 1988 by lesbians involved with the annual LGBT pride celebration—an earlier New York Gay Film Festival was perceived as serving a mostly gay male audience—and developed a programming mix similar to that of Frameline and the Los Angeles Gay and Lesbian Media Festival and Conference, founded in 1982 and known since 1994 as Outfest. Like Frameline, the NewFest is held in June, and there is considerable cooperation among these nonprofit festivals in importing prints and sponsoring filmmaker appearances. Reflecting New York's important history of underground filmmaking, the city hosts, in November, MIX: The New York Lesbian and Gay Experimental Film Festival, founded in 1987 by the novelist and activist Sarah Schulman and the experimental filmmaker Jim Hubbard.

## The Festival Circuit

The growth of the festival circuit has responded to the astonishing amount of available programming, as well as to considerable and exciting work in LGBT film studies. Most events incorporate scholarly work through panels and presentations. Before his death from AIDS in 1991, the author and film historian Vito Russo hosted clip shows at the NewFest, harking back to the screenings he organized at a New York firehouse while researching his pioneering study of LGBT representation in film, *The Celluloid Closet* (1981). Lively debates on issues such as the mainstreaming of LGBT film, representations of race and ethnicity, pornography, and new media were generated at such forums. Notable for fostering critical and scholarly work, as well as networking among filmmakers and professionals, were conferences in conjunction with festivals in Amsterdam in 1991, and in San Francisco at Frameline's twenty-fifth anniversary event in 2001.

The histories of the festivals have also been shaped by wider changes in the media climate, which are in turn tied to political and cultural advances made by the LGBT community. At the 1992 Sundance Film Festival in Park City, Utah, a showcase for independent American cinema, a notable queer presence was addressed in a panel featuring the queer-film stalwart Derek Jarman and the emerging Pixelvision sensation Sadie Benning. A review of the event by the feminist scholar and critic B. Ruby Rich launched the term "New Queer Cinema" to designate a

critical mass of innovative independent feature films with box-office potential made by talented young queer auteurs. These include Todd Haynes's films *Poison* (1990) and *Far from Heaven* (2002), Jennie Livingston's *Paris Is Burning* (1990), Tom Kalin's *Swoon* (1991), and Gregg Araki's *The Living End* (1991). Central to the New Queer Cinema of the 1990s and later were the New York–based lesbian producer Christine Vachon and her company Killer Films, whose productions included *Go Fish* (1994), *Stonewall* (1995), *Boys Don't Cry* (1999), and *Hedwig and the Angry Inch* (2001).

The success of these films among critics and queer and independent film audiences, and the industry attention they have garnered, has fulfilled the promise of queer cinema fostered by the festivals, yet at the same time raised questions about the future of festivals. Early on, festival programmers faced the reluctance of distributors and filmmakers to exhibit at LGBT festivals for fear their films would be stigmatized. Now, similar commercial motives have created almost the opposite situation. Distributors no longer wait to showcase a film of interest to LGBT audiences in the relatively small LGBT festivals, since the market potential of the films has been tested positively enough to warrant mainstream release.

Nevertheless, LGBT festivals remain vital showcases for documentary, short, experimental, political, and otherwise noncommercial work, and they are of considerable sociological and theoretical interest. Festivals can be said to constitute what some have called a "counter public sphere," a public space in which representations, both commodified and challenging, are taken up, debated, and mobilized by a large and diverse community, one that is in part constituted by the events themselves.

## Bibliography

Olson, Jenni, ed. *Ultimate Guide to Lesbian and Gay Film and Video.* San Francisco: Serpent's Tail, 1996.

Russo, Vito. *The Celluloid Closet.* New York: Harper and Row, 1981.

White, Patricia, ed. "Queer Publicity: A Dossier on Lesbian and Gay Film Festivals." *GLQ* 5, no. 1 (1999): 73–93.

**Patricia White**

*See also* FILM AND VIDEO; FILM AND VIDEO STUDIES; RUSSO, VITO.

# FILM AND VIDEO STUDIES

In the United States, LGBT film and video studies began to take off in academic and popular circles in the 1970s. This was due to the greater mass visibility of LGBT issues;

the creation of academic programs and courses in fields such as LGBT studies, women's studies, and ethnic studies; and growth in the number of types of venue for showing film and video.

From the beginning, critical LGBT studies in film and video have been attuned to identifying homophobia in films and the film production industry. This has included criticism of the exclusion of LGBT directors, actors, and themes from Hollywood and independent films. There is also a strong tradition of criticism focused on the portrayal of LGBT characters or subjects in negative and stereotypical ways. Standard film narratives often portray LGBT characters as sexually deviant and violent, as in films such as *Basic Instinct* (1992). Many films rely on the destruction of LGBT characters who, even when portrayed in a positive light, are tragically killed off at the end of the film.

More recent "queer" film and video studies focus less on the portrayal of people with specific sexual identities or the securing of more opportunities for LGBT directors and actors. Rather, these studies emphasize the ways in which films produce deviance in relation to "heteronormativity"—socially constructed norms that link sexuality, race, gender, and class. However, all of these critical trends are important and they overlap, so they cannot readily be charted within a simple and linear history of development.

## Material Conditions

Understanding the material conditions of cinematic production and circulation has been important to all of these strands of LGBT criticism. LGBT film and video studies has addressed mainstream and Hollywood cinema productions; the more ambiguously funded "art house" genre, which often includes foreign and independent films; and experimental films that have been taken up by independent media distributors and shown in such venues as film festivals. The field has sought to complicate our understanding of these very different modes of production and circulation and the relationships between them. While suggesting the need to be attuned not just to aesthetics but also to the material conditions of a film's existence, LGBT cinema-studies scholars have also questioned any easy dichotomization of film practice as dominant or resistant and any easy division of films into commercial or artistic categories.

One example that illustrates this is the controversy over Marlon Riggs's work. Riggs produced several independent films about the intersections of gender, class, racism, and homophobia, particularly in relation to queer black men. His 1990 film *Tongues Untied: Black Men*

*Loving Black Men* came under attack by the conservative gatekeepers of the National Endowment for the Arts (NEA) when it aired on the Public Broadcasting System. It was held up as an example of the kind of "degraded" art that, the attackers argued, the NEA should not fund.

The controversy shows the extent to which ideas of "art" and "culture" are themselves influenced by homophobia and heteronormativity. That critics of Riggs saw queer content as equivalent to a lack of artistic and cultural merit suggests that we may want to question the use of such concepts as "art." Given this way in which notions of artistry and heteronormativity come to define each other, scholars have been attuned to the dangers of simply juxtaposing "artistic" modes of film production to Hollywood or mass media productions.

Just as importantly, the example illustrates the problems that LGBT film and video artists have faced in accessing traditional funding and distribution networks, and thus why venues such as film festivals have been so important to establishing LGBT cinema. Film and video festivals, which have provided a venue not only for films and videos but also for presentations of critical work and film clips by scholar-activists such as Vito Russo, Richard Dyer, and Gayatri Gopinath, have been significant in building LGBT audiences and constructing a critical language for LGBT film.

## Identification, Pleasure, and Spectatorship

In thinking about LGBT film studies, the question of what constitutes a queer film has often been raised. Is a film queer because of its content or because of who makes it, who appears in it, who views it, and how it is viewed? Does LGBT identity shape or get shaped by how films are viewed? Many cinema scholars emphasize the reception of film and assert the agency and ability of LGBT audiences to seek and produce pain and pleasure from cinema. In order to forward greater agency, scholars have sought to emphasize the reception of film and video rather than the production and circulation.

Focusing on the popularity of stars such as Marlene Dietrich, Judy Garland, and Tom Cruise with LGBT audiences, many scholars point out the creative acts of viewing that emphasize the homoerotic appeal of these figures and the ability of viewers to excavate and create pleasure from films that are not constructed from a queer-friendly point of view. For example, Tom Cruise's performances in many of his films, including his white brief-clad frolic in *Risky Business* and his sensual portrayal of the vampire Lestat, have been cited by many viewers as sources of homoerotic pleasure and identification, leading some to claim Cruise as a gay icon. Rather than suggest that LGBT viewers are simply duped by heteronormative narratives and points of view, these scholars have indicated that not all viewers see films identically and that spectatorship is socially differentiated. They emphasize that queerness can be both encoded in the text and serve as a method of decoding and reading. Additionally, they have argued that all viewing practices are gendered and sexualized, not just those that are specifically identified as LGBT.

LGBT film theory, therefore, seeks to understand how different spectator positions produced through the filmic apparatus (i.e., through camera angle, narrative, and point of view) and by the embodied social locations of individual viewers results in multiple modes of identification and viewing.

Cinema scholars have developed a variety of theories to describe the agency of the socially differentiated viewer. Laura Mulvey has argued that the female spectator of dominant films is forced to identify either with the dominant male protagonist or with the heterosexual masochistic female victim, options structured by the heterosexual male gaze or point of view that is created by the film. Feminist and LGBT studies scholars including Mulvey, Chris Straayer, and Teresa de Lauretis have refined this proposition to assign the spectator greater power in the viewing process, delineating the multiple ways (related, for example, to cross-gender, lesbian, and bisexual identifications) in which female and queer spectators can construct spectatorial positions. For example, focusing on films with cross-gender identifications such as *Mrs. Doubtfire*, *Tootsie*, and *Victor/Victoria*, Straayer suggests that many popular Hollywood films allow viewers shifting and multiple gender identifications that transgress fixed and static notions of gender and sexual identity.

Cultural and ethnic studies scholars such as Jacqueline Bobo, Michelle Wallace, and bell hooks have tried to mark the socially differentiated spectator who is distinguished by more than gender and sexuality. Wallace, for example, suggests that it is necessary "to view spectatorship as not only bisexual but also multiracial and multiethnic" (p. 264). In this manner, black and non-black viewers may have different experiences while watching Mammy (and Scarlett O'Hara) in *Gone With The Wind* or Madonna in *Truth or Dare*, with complex and contradictory processes of identification. As exemplified by the work of Riggs and Wallace, film and video studies has also been concerned with intersectionality, exploring the ways in which social categories such as sexuality, race, and gender interact with each other. Many feminist and LGBT film scholars explore complex and multiple spectator positions that pose the possibility of not only dominant

but also negotiated, contradictory, and oppositional identifications and viewing practices that account for the complex and shifting social locations of viewers.

## Representation

Representation has been a critical point of debate for LGBT studies scholars. It can be understood to refer to the visible presence of LGBT cultural producers, media critics, political figures, and even characters in mass media. LGBT presence is inevitably influenced by the lack of access to material and cultural resources. Many scholars have engaged in ongoing discussions about the usefulness of LGBT critical and cultural practices that emphasize the need for greater LGBT representation. They have been concerned with how to address the very real lack of representation while trying to understand power and privilege in a way that does not assume that representation is self-evident as a political solution.

Arguments critiquing the lack of LGBT representation and theorizing ways to increase LGBT representation are abundant. While such analyses continue to be important, many authors have usefully pointed to the problems with representation as a resistant critical and cultural practice. For example, are negative forms of representation better than no representation at all? Are "positive" representations primarily reflections of the normative in which transgression and difference are subdued into the acceptable and conforming? Additionally, does the idea of representation itself always presume a coherent, stable, and transparent subject and identity? Given the complexity of intersecting sexual, gender, class, and racial identities, some critics have pointed to the impossibility of ever achieving an adequate state of representation. Furthermore, authors such as Kobena Mercer have critiqued the "burden of representation" placed on cultural critics and producers with marginalized identities, pointing to the fact that this categorizes people according to their "level" of oppression and de-emphasizes the responsibility of those with privilege to produce resistant meanings.

Films have been taken up as a means to think through issues surrounding representation. *Paris Is Burning* (1990), a documentary made by a white, middle-class woman, Jennie Livingston, about lower-class people of color performing at drag balls, has been seen as exemplary in terms of the critical problems and questions it raises regarding representation. In what specific ways does the identity of a filmmaker shape a film's production, distribution, and reception? How do we talk about the agency of a director and the actors or subjects in a film? What does it mean to attempt to "give voice" to those who have been silenced?

Scholars have also discussed whether clear evidence of representational politics is necessary to qualify a film as properly queer. For example, K. Burdette argues that films such as Todd Haynes's *Superstar: The Karen Carpenter Story* (1987) may not be readily visible as queer films because they do not thematize easily recognizable queer issues, yet can be read as queer because they expose intersecting norms of sexuality, race, gender, and class and raise questions about the naturalness of such categories.

## Transnationalism

LGBT cinema studies has been indebted to the transnational circulation of actors, directors, and films from the very beginning. From work on the films of Hitchcock and Dietrich to research on those of Hanif Kureishi and Isaac Julien, U.S. queer film studies is clearly imbricated within transnational frameworks. The German film *Madchen in Uniform*, for example, is often heralded as the first lesbian film and has had significant impact on the understanding of U.S. LGBT cinema. One particularly important site of inquiry has been the impact of the transnational hegemony of Hollywood cinema on the globalization of sexuality and gender. For example, how does a film like *Go Fish* become iconic as a lesbian film globally; furthermore, what notions of lesbian identity and community does it disseminate?

Additionally, scholars have sought to understand the impact of transnational migration on LGBT cinema and on the nation in general. They examine how relations of power are depicted in affecting the lives of both Asian migrants and gay men (including Asian American ones) in films like Ang Lee's *The Wedding Banquet*. From the impact of German directors on Hollywood during World War II to the analyses of race by black filmmakers, LGBT studies scholarship has also pointed to the dangers of assuming national frameworks in the study of film, because such frameworks tend to simplify social differences. For example, Cheryl Dunye's hybrid-genre film *Watermelon Woman* stages a fake documentary to search for the missing history of a black woman actress of the 1930's; as it seeks to uncover this invented history, the film foregrounds the erasure and absence of black lesbians and desire in LGBT communities, histories, and cinema.

Since the 1980s, the production, circulation, and reception of films such as those by diasporic filmmakers Julien and Deepa Mehta have raised questions about our understandings of sexuality in relation to the category of the nation within a global context. Transnational films such as *Fire* often evoke different interpretations in different locations resulting in shifting understandings of sexual-

ity. *Fire*, for example, depicting the lives of two sisters-in-law living in New Delhi as they fall in love, created controversy and conflicting understandings of this same-sex desire as the film travelled among different audiences. As these filmmakers create different types of queer cinema, they disrupt narratives that pose U.S. LGBT sexualities as the global model. In other words, their films challenge models of sexuality and queerness that privilege Euro-American constructions of sexuality as normative within global contexts. By dismantling simple notions of LGBT culture as tied to a particular nation, ethnic and queer diasporas have complicated any idea of a singular national LGBT cinema.

Queer film theory's critique of the nation suggests the importance of film theory to queer studies in general. With its emphases on agency, representation, materiality, and power within globalization, Queer film theory significantly provokes conversations that are central to situating Queer Studies within a global context. Critical analyses of film, as a unique cultural form with a particular politics of production, sheds light on the need to be attuned to those troublesome foundational concepts (such as "sexuality" and "nation") that may creep into even careful analyses. Similarly, film studies has been a central theoretical location for thinking about how dominant cultural productions shape political claims in ways that need to be carefully examined; contain within them ruptures, tensions, and moments of resistance; and can be disrupted through various critical cultural practices.

## Bibliography

Bobo, Jacqueline. *Black Women as Cultural Readers.* New York: Columbia University Press, 1995.

Burdette, K. "Queer Readings/Queer Cinema: An Examination of the Early Work of Todd Haynes." *Velvet Light Trap* 41 (1998): 68–80.

Butler, Judith. *Bodies That Matter: On the Discursive Limits of "Sex."* New York: Routledge, 1993.

Cleto, Fabio, ed. *Camp: Queer Aesthetics and the Performing Subject. A Reader.* Ann Arbor: University of Michigan Press, 1999.

de Lauretis, Teresa. *Technologies of Gender: Essays on Theory, Film, and Fiction.* Bloomington: University of Indiana Press, 1989.

Doty, Alexander. *Flaming Classics: Queering the Film Canon.* New York: Routledge, 2000.

Dyer, Richard. *Gays in Film.* London: BFI, 1977.

———, ed. *The Culture of Queers.* London: Routledge, 2002.

Gopinath, Gayatri. "Nostalgia, Desire, Diaspora: South Asian Sexualities in Motion." *Positions* 5, no. 2 (1997): 455–477.

Halberstam, Judith. *Female Masculinity.* Durham: Duke University Press, 1998.

hooks, bell. *Black Looks: Race and Representation*. Boston: South End, 1992.

Mercer, Kobena. "Dark and Lovely Too: Black Gay Men in Independent Film." In *Queer Looks: Perspectives on Lesbian and Gay Film and Video*. Edited by Martha Gever, Pratibha Parmar, and John Greyson. New York: Routledge, 1993.

———. *Welcome To the Jungle: New Perspectives in Black Cultural Studies*. New York: Routledge, 1994.

Mulvey, Laura. "Visual Pleasure and Narrative Cinema." *Screen* 16, no. 1 (1975): 6–18.

Reddy, Chandan. "Home, Houses, Nonidentity: *Paris Is Burning*." In *Burning Down the House: Recycling Domesticity*. Edited by Rosemary Marangoly George. Boulder, Colo.: Westview, 1997.

Russo, Vito. *The Celluloid Closet: Homosexuality and the Movies*. New York: Harper, 1981.

Straayer, Chris. *Deviant Eyes, Deviant Bodies: Sexual Re-Orientations in Film and Video*. New York: Columbia University Press, 1996.

Wallace, Michele. "Race, Gender, and Psychoanalysis in Forties Films: *Lost Boundaries*, *Home of the Brave*, and *The Quiet One*." In *Black American Cinema*. Edited by Manthia Diawara. New York: Routledge, 1993.

**Danielle Bouchard and Jigna Desai**

*See also* FILM AND VIDEO; FILM AND VIDEO FESTIVALS; MEDIA STUDIES AND JOURNALISM; RUSSO, VITO.

# FLORIDA

Although the outline of the Florida peninsula was included on most European maps of the New World since the early 1500s, for most of its modern history the region was on the geographic and historical fringes of both North America and the Caribbean. With few natural resources, poor soil, long, shallow, barren coastlines and hot, humid insect-infested swamps, forests, and beaches, there was little to recommend the area. The state's contemporary history began when it was discovered in the late 1800s by the growing middle and upper classes from the industrial northeast and Midwest, seeking an escape from harsh northern winters. Florida's marginal character allowed the new invaders to reinvent the state in terms of their own fantasies and desires.

In short order, swamps were drained, native habitats destroyed, and palm trees and other foreign plants and creatures imported to create a tropical paradise—albeit a Christian, white, Anglo, middle-class paradise. Along with this physical transformation, Florida was symbolically reinvented as a site of exotic adventure for those wishing to escape established rules and regimes. Beneath the beguiling veneer, the reality was radically different.

From the beginning profiteering and shameless land speculation, racism and religious intolerance, labor exploitation, and environmental degradation shaped the daily life of those not living the tropical fantasy.

Yet, in spite of this darker reality, the magical quality of Florida still had a powerful allure. In particular, the warm, relaxed environs were a powerful draw to men and women whose erotic passions could not find easy expression elsewhere. Part of Florida's mystique was its promise as a place of sexual liminality and transformation. The state was the setting for the first U.S. fictional account of explicit lesbian sexual desire, the 1876 story "Felipe" by Constance Fenimore Woolson, about the passionate desires of a young girl for a visiting woman tourist. The first popular U.S. film representation of same-sex desires, the sixty-minute silent film "Florida Enchantment" (1914), told the story of a group of Florida vacationers who, upon eating magical seeds, were overcome with homosexual passions.

The particular tropical allure of South Florida was reflected in the construction of Vizcaya, a Mediterranean fantasy palace built on the shores of Biscayne Bay by James Deering in the early 1900s. Deering, the staid bachelor scion of a wealthy Chicago industrial family, moved to South Florida in the early 1900s. An early guest, the Anglo-American artist John Singer Sargent, whose sexuality was as obscure as Deering's, declared Vizcaya the equal of any Venetian doges' palace. The setting inspired him to paint a series of erotically charged male nudes, using the lush gardens as his backdrop and the black laborers working on the estate as his models. Further north in Boca Raton and Palm Beach, Addison Mizner, whose homosexuality was as closeted as his life was colorful, created what is South Florida's signature architectural style exploiting the pleasures of climate with a large touch of faux historical detail.

By the late 1930s, Miami had a thriving gay night life, with a number of bars catering to both local and visiting homosexuals. Particularly popular forms of entertainment were drag shows, which were advertised and reviewed in local newspapers. In 1939 the bar Club Jewel Box premiered a lavishly staged drag revue that quickly took on a life of its own as the "Jewel Box Revue," and became a national touring production, putting on shows in cities large and small until its demise in the late 1960s.

During World War II Miami became the largest training base for the U.S. Air Force, with tourist hotels serving as barracks. For many young men and women, both straight and homosexual, this introduction to South Florida enticed many to return after the war. With the introduction of air conditioning, extensive mosquito control, and the popularization of air travel, Florida became more than a winter vacation destination and the population exploded. At the beginning of World War II, Florida, with a population of nearly two million, was the least populated state in the Old Confederacy, with fewer people than Mississippi and Arkansas. Sixty years later it was the nation's fourth most populous state with over sixteen million people. Whatever unique cultural character it had as a state of the old South was quickly overwhelmed by the influx of new, nonsouthern residents.

Even as the year-round population of the state grew, tourism remained the most important component of its economy. South Florida, one of the state's major tourist destinations, maintained an easy attitude toward gambling, prostitution, and, during Prohibition, alcohol. In a similar vein, through the early 1950s, the city had an attitude of discreet tolerance toward homosexuals, viewing their presence as part of the varied beach scenes and night life. In the late 1940s and early 1950s, the Miami police had an explicit policy of not harassing those bars that catered to homosexuals, ostensibly to "keep a better watch on the deviants."

In the summer of 1954 this attitude changed drastically. Acting on the national moral panic over "sex crimes" and a more local desire by municipal progressives to clean up the city's image, Miami's mayor and the local media conducted an intense six-week campaign to close bars catering to homosexuals, using the "homosexual threat" to children as a key charge. After the campaign the bars quickly reopened; Miami, as a vacation destination, could ill afford a repressive moral climate. However, the larger goal of the campaign—to send a clear message that in Miami homosexuality was permitted, but highly stigmatized—succeeded.

This stigmatization of homosexuals in Florida was further intensified in the late 1950s and early 1960s with the investigations of the infamous "Johns Committee," a state legislative committee named after a reactionary North Florida legislator that conducted a six-year witch-hunt against homosexuals in the state's public universities and schools. Over two hundred public school teachers were questioned by the committee, and over one hundred college faculty and administrators and an unknown number of students were charged with homosexual activity and forced out of state universities. The committee was disbanded in 1965 when its abuses and excesses, including publishing photos of explicit homosexual sexual activity in its official report, outraged even conservative legislators.

In spite of a repressive climate, the homosexual community, particularly in South Florida, grew and flourished. For gay men, many activities centered on the bars, sexual cruising, private networks of parties, and social gatherings that served the wealthier tourists and resident members of the community. In contrast to other major urban homosexual centers like New York, Los Angeles, or San Francisco, which attracted the ambitious, talented, and career-oriented, Florida appealed to those seeking a less challenging environment. Attempts by Richard Inman, an early homosexual rights activist who had founded the Florida Mattachine Society in 1965, to organize local homosexuals politically and socially met with little success—his organization never had more than three members.

By the mid-1960s, Key West was identified nationally as a homosexual resort community. Miami was frequently listed in the national media in the list of major cities that had a large and active homosexual population. Responding to such attention, local media and public officials in Miami periodically reinvigorated their efforts to regulate and stigmatize homosexuality. In 1965, a local Miami television station produced an investigative report on Miami's male homosexual community with film of bathroom cruising and interviews with young hustlers. Local officers from the county vice squad lectured grade school students about the evils of homosexuality. Newspapers ran stories about young local boys recruited as hustlers, with wealthy homosexual tourists using local high school yearbooks as sexual catalogues. The local state attorney announced a major campaign against homosexuals around election time. Yet such repressive efforts were often more a matter of civic display than reality.

By the late 1960s, reflecting the changing national culture about sexual behavior and values, the attitude and climate of stigmatization and repression lessened. The local media reported more neutrally on the homosexual community. In the early 1970s, from the emerging national lesbian and gay post–Stonewall political consciousness a number of local organizations and community efforts emerged. In 1972, local activists successfully challenged a local Miami law that banned bars from serving homosexuals. The arrival of the national Democratic and Republican conventions in Miami that year prompted the city's first gay pride events organized by the local Gay Activists' Alliance. In 1973, transsexuals organized the Transsexual Action Organization based in Miami Beach and secured a promise of nonharassment from the city's police. In 1975, the police raided Club Miami, the bathhouse owned by Jack Campbell, owner of the national Clubs Baths chain and an activist in national gay politics. He filed suit against the city and received both a court injunction halting future raids and an apology from the police. In that fall's election, he ran for Miami-Dade County Commission as an openly gay candidate, receiving respectable media coverage, as well as nearly five thousand votes.

In other parts of the state there was both a growing and contested presence and visibility of a lesbian and gay community. In Pensacola, in the late 1960s, members of the community calling themselves the "Friends of Emma Jones" organized an annual beach party drawing people from north Florida, Alabama, and south Georgia. However, by the early 1970s, when the event was drawing over three thousand participants, local police and politicians started a major series of raids and community harassment campaigns to close down the celebration. Gay student organizations formed at the University of Florida, Florida Atlantic University, and Florida State University. In spite of periodic attempts by university officials and state legislators—including the passage of a state law later declared unconstitutional—to ban campus clubs, they thrived. In Tampa, local community members organized to protest police harassment and also to create a branch of the Metropolitan Community Church. In 1973, Barbara Grier and Donna McBride founded Naiad Press in Tallahassee, one of the oldest and most successful lesbian publishing houses. Key West, with its distinctive nineteenth-century American Caribbean style homes being converted into lush gay guesthouses, became the winter mecca of the international gay men's circuit.

In the summer of 1976 a small group of local Miami activists lobbied for the passage of a local ordinance banning discrimination on the basis of sexual preference. As over thirty other cities had similar ordinances, it was regarded as only mildly controversial. However, when the county commission passed it in January 1977, local Catholic and Protestant churches, joined by local activists from the newly emerging conservative right, conducted a vehement campaign to repeal it. With Anita Bryant, a singer, former beauty queen, and national media figure, as their chief public spokesperson, opponents of the ordinance resurrected old charges of homosexuals as child molesters and perverts. The ensuing campaign, reported extensively in the national press, represented the first major national media debate over the issue of gay rights. By a vote of 69 to 31 percent the ordinance was repealed. In response to the campaign the Florida legislature banned marriage and adoption by gay men and lesbians. Also citing the homosexual threat, the legislature voted down its expected ratification of the federal Equal Rights Amendment.

The Miami campaign was the first shot in the battle of religious and conservative forces against gay rights that would dominate sexual politics in the late twentieth century. It succeeded in energizing and mobilizing the national lesbian and gay community. For the local community in Miami the defeat proved demoralizing and community organizations and activities declined. Throughout Florida politically activism stagnated. In the years following the repeal, Broward County (Fort Lauderdale), twenty miles to the north of Miami, became the focal point of lesbian and gay life in South Florida.

One major element in the emerging lesbian and gay community in South Florida was the growing Latin lesbian and gay population. In the 1960s, thousands of middle-class Cubans moved into South Florida as political exiles from Castro's Cuba. Although a number were homosexual, because of the intense homophobia of Cuban culture they retained a highly closeted middle-class attitude about their sexuality and did not engage much in the growing lesbian and gay community. During the 1980 Mariel boat lift, however, Castro allowed a large number of Cubans, including men imprisoned for homosexuality, to leave, bringing to South Florida a large number of openly gay Cubans and giving the Latin homosexual community a greater visibility. In addition, in the 1980s many young Cubans and other Latin men and women who had come of age in the United States and whose sexual values were shaped by U.S. culture were beginning to emerge as a new voice in South Florida's lesbian and gay community. A distinctive gay, Cuban, urban culture grew, combining Cuban flair and style with Anglo-American emphasis on visibility, inclusion, and community organization.

If in the 1980s electoral activism was muted, the response to AIDS provided a focal point for community organizing and activism as many lesbian and gay men created support services for victims of AIDS and lobbied public officials for more money for the fight against AIDS. South Florida was one of the centers of the AIDS crisis. As a result of LGBT lobbying activities Florida passed state AIDS legislation that served as a national model for its privacy protections and prohibitions against discrimination against people with HIV and AIDS. Also in Miami, AIDS activists began organizing annual fundraising dances, including the White Party at Vizcaya—which, along with the Morning Party on Fire Island in New York, became precursors to the development of the circuit parties, the highly visible gay male celebrations of the 1990s.

Meanwhile lesbians and gay men were gaining visibility and recognition for the role they played in the revitalization of decaying urban areas in Miami, Fort Lauderdale, Tampa, Orlando, and West Palm Beach. Of particular note was the revitalization as an openly gay residential space of South Miami Beach, a blighted beach area of poor retirees and recent Latin immigrants This marginal neighborhood attracted many lesbians and gay men, particularly men with AIDS seeking a warmer climate. Also the beaches, the Art Deco architecture, and the growing Latin cultural influence attracted many international designers and modeling firms seeking inexpensive new venues. By the mid-1990s, South Beach was reborn as an international trendy resort destination noted for its broad beaches, exciting night life, sexually charged atmosphere, and expensive real estate.

The 1990s saw a return of political activism in Florida. Responding to efforts of local activists, Palm Beach County in January 1990 banned discrimination on the basis of sexual orientation in housing—the first gay rights measure successfully enacted in Florida. Over the next eight years more extensive measures were passed in Tampa and Hillsborough County in 1991, Miami Beach in 1992, Key West and Alachua County in 1993, West Palm Beach in 1994, Broward County (Fort Lauderdale) in 1995, Gainesville in 1995, and Palm Beach County and Sarasota in 2002. Such ordinances were often controversial and numerous attempts were made by groups on the religious right to repeal them. Unsuccessful attempts were made in Tampa (1992, 1995), West Palm Beach (1995), and Broward County (2002). Successful repeal efforts were launched in Alachua (1994) and Hillsborough (1995) counties. At the statewide level, the Florida chapter of the American Family Association in 1993 attempted to enact a Colorado-like state constitutional prohibition against local ordinances banning antigay discrimination. The wording for the proposed constitutional amendment was rejected by the Florida supreme court and no further attempt was made. However, this effort further mobilized local LGBT community efforts to pass and protect local ordinances and to create Equality Florida, a statewide political advocacy and educational organization.

In 1998 Miami-Dade County, site of the 1977 gay rights battle, again approved an antidiscrimination ordinance, prompting a four-year effort by the religious right to repeal it. This effort was defeated when voters in November 2002 upheld the ordinance by 53 to 47 percent. In contrast to 1977, the campaign was noteworthy for the broad and active support by community and elected leaders for the ordinance and the recognition of the economic importance and social position of the lesbian and gay community.

At the beginning of the twenty-first century, the state of Florida is still very much shaped by the fantasies and desires of those who come to the state, either as tourists, new residents, immigrants, or refugees. In South Florida, the most liberal part of the state, the lesbian and gay community is a recognized part of the larger political, social, and cultural community. The Miami community, with its large Latin lesbian and gay population, has a highly cosmopolitan trendy character and is the site of a number of major international circuit parties and cultural events such as a major Lesbian/Gay Film Festival. There is an increasing openness and visibility among South Florida black lesbians and gays with the creation of an LGBT African American church and local black gay pride events. The city's African American and growing Haitian communities strongly supported the 1998 ordinance.

In Broward County, the character of the community is shaped by the large influx of older lesbian and gay retirees from the northeast and the Midwest eager to build and participate in a growing, visible community. Efforts to create and support lesbian and gay businesses, churches and synagogues, and media, social, and cultural institutions, together with the election of lesbian and gay officials, are important reflections of community identity and involvement. At various times of the year, the large, but less-organized communities in the Tampa Bay area, Orlando, Pensacola, and Key West come alive around celebrations like Gay Days at Disney World in Orlando, Fantasy Fest in Key West, and Memorial Day Weekend in Pensacola.

The statewide political scene is dominated by the fiscally and socially conservative Republican Party and its supporters. A sodomy law is still on the books, and Governor Jeb Bush, running for reelection in 2002, strongly supported retaining the state ban on gay adoption. However, in a political first, the unsuccessful Democratic candidate, Bill McBride, a moderate north Florida corporate lawyer, openly campaigned for the vote of the lesbian and gay community. As in other states, it is evident that the growth and political and social progress of the lesbian and gay community at the local level cannot be ignored indefinitely at the statewide level.

## Bibliography

Arenas, Reinaldo. *Before Night Falls.* New York: Viking, 1993.

Arguelles, Lourdes, and B. Ruby Rich. "Homosexuality, Homophobia and Revolution: Notes toward an Understanding of the Cuban Lesbian and Gay Male Experience, Part I." *Signs* 9, no. 4 (Summer 1984): 683–699.

Brasell, R. Bruce. "A Seed for Change: The Engenderment of 'A Florida Enchantment.'" *Cinema Journal* 36, no. 4 (1997): 3–21.

Clendinen, Dudley, and Adam Nagourney. *Out for Good: The Struggle to Build a Gay Rights Movement in America.* New York: Simon and Schuster, 1999.

Fejes, Fred. "Murder, Perversion and Moral Panic: The 1954 Media Campaign Against Miami's Homosexuals and the Discourse of Civic Betterment." *The Journal of the History of Sexuality* 9, no. 3 (2000): 305–347.

Forrest, David W. "South Beach 'Paradise' and Reality." *The Gay and Lesbian Review* 9, no. 3 (May–June 2002): 24–29.

Patron, Eugene J., and David Forrest. "SoBe: The Making of a Gay Community." *The Gay and Lesbian Review* 7, no. 2 (April 2000): 28–33.

Rich, B. Ruby, and Lourdes Arguelles. "Homosexuality, Homophobia and Revolution: Notes toward an Understanding of the Cuban Lesbian and Gay Male Experience, Part II." *Signs* 11, no. 1 (Autumn 1985): 120–136.

Schnur, James A. "Closet Crusaders": The Johns Committee and Homophobia, 1956–1965." In *Carrin' On in the Lesbian and Gay South,* edited by John Howard. New York: New York University Press, 1997.

Sears, James T. *Lonely Hunters: An Oral History of Lesbian and Gay Southern Life, 1948–1968.* Boulder, Colo.: Westview Press, 1997.

Sears, James T. *Rebels, Rubyfruit, and Rhinestones: Queering Space in the Stonewall South.* New Brunswick, N.J.: Rutgers University Press, 2001.

Somerville, Siobhan B. "The Queer Career of Jim Crow: Racial and Sexual Transformation in Early Cinema." In *Queering the Color Line: Race and the Invention of Homosexuality in American Culture.* Durham, N.C.: Duke University Press, 2000.

Woolson, Constance Fenimore. "Felipe." *Lippincotts Magazine* (1876); reprint, *Rodman the Keeper* (1880). New York, AMS Press, 1971.

**Fred Fejes**

**See also** BISHOP, ELIZABETH; BROWN, RITA MAE; GOVERNMENT AND MILITARY WITCHHUNTS; GRIER, BARBARA; MORGAN, ROBIN; RADICALESBIANS; RESORTS.

# FORD, Charles Henri (b. 10 February 1908; d. 27 September 2002), writer, editor, visual artist.

Born Charles Henry Ford in Hazelhurst, Mississippi, in 1908, Ford first indulged in his life-long habit of reinventing himself by changing his middle name to Henri. His flair for such unusual self-dramatizing gambits was matched by an ambition so fierce that at seventeen he vowed to be famous within two years. Ford's elfin beauty drew the attention of traveling salesmen and maternal poetesses, and he learned early to ask his admirers for favors and then do whatever he pleased with anything he received. With $100 he cadged from one entranced salesman in 1929, he launched the literary journal *Blues:*

*A Magazine of New Rhythms.* Although the 1929–1930 life span of *Blues* produced only eight issues, Ford's spirited poetry (which combined modernism, camp, and homages to Walt Whitman), not to mention his cultivation of contributors like Ezra Pound and Gertrude Stein, paved the way in literary circles for his march toward fame.

In January 1930 Ford joined Parker Tyler, a coeditor of *Blues,* in New York City. Since Greenwich Village was then one of the only places in the United States where bohemianism and homosexuality intermingled freely, Ford found himself in both a sexual playground and the ideal university for his writing dreams. Around this time Ford also shaved five years off his age, adding the allure of seemingly extreme precocity to the evergreen appeal of boyish good looks. In such a milieu Ford was out, as if there were no other place to be. The adventures he shared with Tyler before he returned to Mississippi that summer would form the basis for *The Young and Evil* (1933), the novel that established him as the first gay novelist to celebrate guiltless sexual hedonism.

In May 1931 Ford sailed to Europe with the intention of finding a publisher for the novel and was soon in the Parisian thick of things, including the salon of Gertrude Stein and Alice B. Toklas. When Djuna Barnes arrived in distress later that year after a breakup with Thelma Wood and an emergency appendectomy, Ford made himself of service. Despite individually strong same-sex preferences, each turned out to be susceptible to the other's powerful sexual aura. Barnes was also professionally accommodating, recommending *The Young and Evil* to Jack Kahane, publisher of the Obelisk Press. And by taking Ford to a party in November she inadvertently facilitated his fateful first encounter with Russian painter Pavel Tchelitchev.

When the romance with Barnes soured, Ford traveled briefly with a Cuban heiress and then dropped in on Paul Bowles in Tangier. Inviting Barnes to visit in late 1932, he typed her manuscript for *Nightwood.* The time in Tangier was not Barnes's finest hour: she discovered that she was pregnant (not by Ford), rats invaded her luggage and ate her stockings, and Ford was so unseemly as to suggest raising the child together. Suffocated by her immediate prospects, Barnes fled to Paris for an abortion, and the unlikely affair with Ford was over.

Ford soon returned to Paris and took up with Tchelitchev again. Out of an almost maternal concern, Gertrude Stein cautioned Ford against Tchelitchev. Stein and Tchelitchev, once close, had had a falling out, and Stein regarded Ford as perhaps too naïve to spot what she saw as Tchelitchev's shortcomings (like his age and the fact that he was already partnered). That Ford not only ignored her advice but also maneuvered to oust Tchelitchev's then-partner cooled the once-warm Ford-Stein friendship.

In August 1933 *The Young and Evil* was published with blurbs from both Barnes and Stein. Its sexual frankness and insouciance created an immediate scandal. When five hundred copies appeared at British customs, they were seized and incinerated. Shipments bound for U.S. bookshops were repeatedly turned back at ports. Banned, burned, and accused of being too damned hot, the book made Ford as famous as he had ever wished to be.

The alliance with Tchelitchev ushered Ford into the inner sancta of the surrealists as well as the ballet esthetes who clustered around Lincoln Kirstein as he built the New York City Ballet. After the couple moved to the United States during the war years, Ford launched *View*, a literary journal that increased his profile as an ambassador for Surrealism and Existentialism. His brilliant editing of *View* between 1940 and 1947 produced coups like the first journal issue devoted entirely to Marcel Duchamp and the first appearances in English of the work of Jean Genet and Albert Camus.

After Tchelitchev's death in 1957, Ford expanded his artistic interests to collage and experimental film and released his film *Johnny Minotaur* in 1971. As if to ensure his standing as the epitome of unflagging creative vitality, an exhibit of his final collages opened in New York soon after his death in 2002. Titled "Alive and Kicking," it was one last dramatic flourish in a life full of them.

**Bibliography**

Dowell, James. "Charles Henri Ford Was There." *Gay and Lesbian Review* 8, no. 6 (November–December 2001): 32–34.

Field, Andrew. *Djuna: The Life and Times of Djuna Barnes*. New York: Putnam, 1983.

Ford, Charles Henri, ed. *View: Parade of the Avant-Garde: An Anthology of View Magazine (1940–1947)*. New York: Thunder's Mouth Press, 1991.

Ford, Charles Henri, and Parker Tyler. *The Young and Evil*. New York: Arno Press, 1975.

Smith, Roberta. "Charles Henri Ford, Ninety-Four, Prolific Poet, Artist and Editor." *New York Times* (30 September 2002), sec. B, p. 10.

Tillman, Lynne. Introduction to *Water from a Bucket: A Diary 1948–1957*, by Charles Henri Ford. New York: Turtle Point Press, 2001.

Tyler, Parker. *The Divine Comedy of Pavel Tchelitchev*. New York: Fleet, 1967.

**John McFarland**

*See also* BARNES, DJUNA; BOWLES, PAUL AND JANE; FILM AND VIDEO; KIRSTEIN, LINCOLN; LITERATURE.

# FORNES, Maria Irene (b. 14 May 1930), playwright.

Maria Irene Fornes, a Cuban American lesbian playwright, specializes in very visual works that often address issues relating to sexuality.

Born to schoolteacher Carmen Hismenia Collado and civil engineer Carlos Luís Fornes in Havana, Cuba, Fornes is the youngest of six children. Her childhood in politically unstable Cuba influenced her work by providing knowledge of life amid torture and violence. While his wife stayed at home to raise their offspring, Carlos Fornes struggled to make a living during the Great Depression. Fornes thereby also gained an early understanding of poverty, although her family's middle-class background in fact rendered them members of the privileged poor in Cuba.

The financial circumstances and free-spirited nature of the Fornes family meant that Fornes only sporadically attended Havana public schools. She completed the third through sixth grades. In 1945 she moved with her sisters and by then widowed mother to upper Manhattan in New York City and became a naturalized citizen six years later. She attended school in the United States long enough to perfect her spoken English.

Always a playwright more concerned with image than text, Fornes entered the art world as an abstract painter. Intending to make a living as an artist and to secure further art education, she moved to Europe for several years in the mid-1950s. In 1957 she left Paris for the United States to become a textile designer. Three years later, in 1960, Fornes began to write as a challenge to roommate Susan Sontag, the noted essayist and critic. Her subsequent works reflect a painterly sensitivity to the deployment of space as well as her trademark use of memorable images intended to garner audience attention.

After struggling as a painter and then briefly experimenting with short stories, Fornes found her niche in playwriting. Her first play, *La Viuda* (The Widow), was based on her translation of letters written to her Cuban great-grandfather by a cousin living in Spain. The play debuted in New York in 1961, was broadcast in Mexico, and won two writing awards. Unable to resist tweaking the play, Fornes did not include it in her first published anthology, *Promenade and Other Plays* (1987).

Fornes's first completely original work made her one of the pioneers of the avant-garde theater. *There! You*

*Died,* also known as *Tango Palace,* charts the existential struggles of two men in a master-slave relationship. The success of this 1963 play led Fornes to the Actors Studio to learn how to stage behaviors motivated by impulse and emotion rather than by conscious logic and cool rationality. Ultimately dissatisfied with Method acting, Fornes joined the breakaway Open Theatre (OT) in 1963. Anger at being ignored by the male head of OT led the increasingly feminist Fornes to join the avant-garde Judson Poets Theatre as a costume designer and playwright.

Although she has publicly acknowledged her lesbianism since at least the early 1970s, Fornes has shown reluctance to be identified as a lesbian dramatist. Although her plays often address sexuality, she does not want her sexual orientation to limit the reading of her work or to link her plays exclusively to the productions of more militant artists. Fornes uses drama to raise questions about the place of marginalized people in society, but does not make lesbianism the sole issue.

Fornes also shies away from the label of Latina playwright. She names Anton Chekhov, Eugène Ionesco, and Bertolt Brecht as her greatest influences rather than Latin American or Iberian dramatists. Her speech still bears an accent, and Fornes cites this characteristic as evidence of a retained Cuban sensibility, but she has additionally acknowledged that she thinks and writes in English. She has written a few plays in Spanish, including *La Viuda* and *Cap-a-Pie* (Head to Foot) in 1975. Only rarely do Fornes's plays contain specifically Latina or Latino characters.

While she steadfastly resists being typecast, Fornes has played a major role in the development of a uniquely Latin American style of drama. In 1981 Fornes founded the INTAR Hispanic Playwrights Lab in New York City with the special aim of mentoring and training Hispanic dramatists. Her protégés include noted lesbian Chicana playwright Cherrie Moraga. The works emanating from INTAR possess the distinct traits of Latin American literature: realism about social conditions and interpersonal relations combined with a respect for psychic and mystical events.

Although Fornes has won six Obie awards for distinguished playwrighting, she remains widely unknown. This anonymity is partly by choice. As an experimentalist who only repeats her penchant for unpredictability, Fornes creates works that are not as accessible as those of some of her peers. She continues to be content to hone her craft within the environs of Off-Broadway.

## Bibliography

Delgado, Maria M., and Caridad Svich, eds. *Conducting a Life: Reflections on the Theatre of Maria Irene Fornes.* Lyme, N.H.: Smith and Kraus, 1999.

Kent, Assunta Bartolomucci. *Maria Irene Fornes and Her Critics.* Westport, Conn.: Greenwood Press, 1996.

Moroff, Diane Lynn. *Fornes: Theater in the Present Tense.* Ann Arbor: University of Michigan Press, 1996.

**Caryn E. Neumann**

*See also* MORAGA, CHERRÍE; THEATER AND PERFORMANCE.

# FOSTER, Jeannette Howard
(b. 3 November 1895; d. 26 July 1981), writer and scholar.

Jeannette Howard Foster authored *Sex Variant Women in Literature: A Historical and Quantitative Study* (1956), a major seminal work that covers approximately 2600 years (600 BCE–1954) of literary images of female "sex variants" (a term Foster used for women who today would be called lesbian, bisexual, or transgendered).

Foster was born in Oak Park, Illinois. She attended Rockford College, where she received a B.S. degree in chemistry and engineering in 1918 and an M.A. degree in English and American literature in 1922. She went on to receive another B.S. in library science in 1932 from Emory University and a Ph.D. in library science from the University of Chicago in 1935. She was employed as a professor of library science and as a librarian at several major U.S. colleges and universities. Foster was the first librarian employed at Alfred Kinsey's Institute for Sex Research at Indiana University, where she worked from 1948 to 1952. Her tenure in this library gave her access to a wealth of material, both belletristic and psychiatric, which she utilized in *Sex Variant Women in Literature.*

Completed in 1955, the book was scheduled for publication by a university press in 1956. However, when Foster's editor died, his successor refused to honor the press's commitment to the book. Despairing that any publisher would undertake publication of a work as daring as hers, Foster decided to pay for publication with Vantage Press. In 1958 it was published in England by Frederick Muller. Although *Sex Variant Women in Literature* had fair library distribution in the 1950s, it was not until the 1970s, with the birth of a strong lesbian movement, that it found a large readership. In 1974 it was the third book to receive the American Library Association's Gay/Lesbian Book Award. It was republished by Diana Press, a lesbian-feminist publisher, in 1975, and then again by the lesbian publisher Naiad Press in 1985.

*Sex Variant Women in Literature* looks at images of "sex variants" not only in English and American literature, but also in French, German, and (to a lesser extent) Italian, Russian, Spanish, and Portuguese literature. (Foster read French and German; the other works were available in translation.) The book also contains an extensive bibliography of psychiatric publications on sex variant women, as well as a bibliography of works of fiction, drama, and poetry where sex variant females appear as primary or secondary characters.

Foster deserves particular credit for having conceived of such a bold project in the 1950s, a time when homosexuals were accused by McCarthyites of being a risk to national security. She was remarkably courageous for having published the book under her own name rather than a pseudonym, as other writers who dealt with lesbian subjects often did. She was careful, however, in her introduction to suggest that her interest in the subject of sex variant women was not necessarily personal. In her private life, Foster had a long-term relationship with Hazel Tolliver, a professor at Linwood College. In later years, the chair of the Linwood College Women's Physical Education Department, Dorothy "Dot" Ross, joined the household, and after retirement the three women moved to Pocohantas, Arkansas, where they bought a house together. Foster died in a nursing home in Pocohantas.

In the 1960s, when writing fiction and poetry for the *Ladder,* an early lesbian magazine, Foster employed a variety of pseudonyms, including Hilary Farr, Abigail Sanford, and Jan Addison. However, the books she published in the 1970s appeared under her own name, including her 1974 translation of Renée Vivien's French novel *A Woman Appeared to Me* (1904) and *Two Women: The Poetry of Jeannette Howard Foster and Valerie Taylor* (1976), which was expanded, revised, and republished in 1991 as *Two Women Revisited.* Among Foster's papers, which are housed in the Gay and Lesbian Center of the San Francisco Public Library, are various unpublished poems, short fiction, and novels, including "Home Is the Hunter" and "Death under Duress."

**Bibliography**

Foster, Jeannette Howard. *Sex Variant Women in Literature: A Historical and Quantitative Study* (1956). Tallahassee, Fla.: Naiad Press, 1985.

Jay, Karla. *Lavender Culture.* New York: Jove, 1979.

Kuda, Marie. "Jeannette Howard Foster." In *Gay and Lesbian Literature.* Edited by Sharon Malinowski. Detroit: St. James, 1996.

**Lillian Faderman**

*See also* GRIER, BARBARA; KINSEY, ALFRED C.; *LADDER,* LITERATURE: 1890–1969; LITERATURE: 1969–PRESENT; LITERARY CRITICISM AND THEORY; PUBLISHERS; TAYLOR, VALERIE.

# FRANK, Barney (b. 31 March 1910), U.S. representative.

In 1987 Barney Frank became the second member of the U.S. Congress to come out as gay. Frank's intelligence, wit, and legislative skill have gained him enthusiastic support in his Massachusetts home district and considerable standing in Congress. Though Frank has been a persistent advocate for lesbian and gay equality, the inherent complexities of American legislative politics and the power of socially conservative voices in Washington have made gains difficult to achieve.

Frank has exhibited a traditional liberal approach, believing in a positive and redistributive role for government and advocating programs designed to help the disadvantaged. He has also been a pragmatist on the "prudent" left of the Democratic Party and impatient with those who do not understand what he believes to be political realities.

Born in 1940, Frank was the child of Jewish, Roosevelt Democrat parents. His early interest in politics led to involvement in the civil rights activism of the early 1960s. While in graduate school at Harvard University, Frank more actively immersed himself in politics, working for Kevin White's Boston mayoralty bid in 1967, becoming the new mayor's chief of staff later that year, and moving into the Washington congressional office of Michael Harrington.

Frank's own electoral career began with a successful run for a seat in the Massachusetts House of Representatives in 1972. Within a year he was cosponsoring a LGB rights bill, but still was closeted. He remained so when, in 1974, Elaine Noble of Massachusetts became the country's first openly lesbian or gay elected politician to win a seat in a state legislature. Frank moved to Congress with a successful race in 1980, the election that put Ronald Reagan into the White House. His House district had progressive pockets, but also traditional small town areas to the south of the Boston suburbs. In 1983 fellow U.S. representative Gerry Studds (also from Massachusetts) became the first federal politician to publicly affirm his gay identity. This he did in response to impending publicity over an earlier affair with a congressional page. He was formally censured by legislative colleagues, but survived the next election.

**Barney Frank.** First elected to the U.S. House of Representatives in 1980, the liberal Massachusetts Democrat acknowledged seven years later that he is gay—only the second member of Congress to do so. [AP/Wide World Photos]

By the 1986 election, Frank had built seemingly unassailable majorities. Growing speculation in 1987 about Frank's sexuality prompted his coming out, which he did through an interview with the *Boston Globe* that appeared on its front page on 30 May. Frank survived the next election handily, and his already substantial track record shielded him from the commonplace characterization of openly LGB candidates for office as preoccupied by sexual orientation. The year 1989 brought controversy resulting from an earlier relationship with sometime hustler Steve Gobie. By the time of the 1990 election, however, Frank's standing among legislative colleagues and in his own district seemed largely to have recovered, and no election thereafter has posed a significant threat to his political career.

The 1992 election of Bill Clinton as president presented a different kind of challenge. LGB expectations for the new Democratic leader were exceptionally high, fueled by promises that included a commitment to lift the military ban that was directed at sexual minorities. That commitment withered under opposition fire, and Frank's efforts to salvage a small remnant of it in the spring of 1993 brought criticism from many activists. The episode starkly illustrated the contradictory roles played by an openly gay politician, expected on the one hand to respond to a social movement constituency and

on the other hand to retain effectiveness within the constraints of a legislative system. Frank has sometimes bristled at what he sees as unrealistic expectations, but has been a persistently central player in making occasional legislative gains in Washington and in defending against the regular threat of setback.

During the 1990s Republican U.S. representatives Steve Gunderson (in 1994) and Jim Kolbe (in 1996) came out as gay. Gunderson left Congress in 1997, as did Gerry Studds, but in 1998 Democrat Tammy Baldwin of Wisconsin won her race for the U.S. House of Representatives, the first openly lesbian candidate to do so. This was doubly remarkable in light of persistent male dominance in American legislative politics. By century's turn, the number of openly LGB elected politicians in the United States had passed two hundred, though the great majority were able to win races only in very progressive districts or those with large and visible sexual minority neighborhoods. Most of these politicians were male; only the tiniest fraction were other than Euro-American; and the transgendered were virtually invisible in electoral politics.

The ability of Barney Frank and these others to win and retain public office reveals the significance of openings to acceptance of sexual diversity. But the persistently small proportion of LGB politicians who are able to be fully out about their sexual orientation is also testament to the fragility of gains in a political system where religious conservatism remains influential and where anti-LGBT campaigning is still routine.

## Bibliography

Frank, Barney. *Speaking Frankly: What's Wrong with the Democrats and How to Fix It.* New York: Times Books/Random House, 1992.

Rayside, David. *On the Fringe: Gays and Lesbians in Politics.* Ithaca, N.Y.: Cornell University Press, 1998.

Rimmerman, Craig A., Kenneth D. Wald, and Clyde Wilcox, eds. *The Politics of Gay Rights.* Chicago: University of Chicago Press, 2000.

Yeager, Ken. *Trailblazers: Profiles of America's Gay and Lesbian Elected Officials.* New York: Haworth Press, 1999.

**David Rayside**

***See also*** DEMOCRATIC PARTY; ELECTORAL POLITICS; FEDERAL LAW AND POLICY; POLITICAL SCANDALS.

# FRIENDSHIP

Close, intimate, and frequently long-term same-sex friendships have existed throughout American history, yet they have often been invisible, forgotten, and ignored.

The same has been the case for other types of friendships in LGBT spheres. Today, the existence of these intense friendships—referred to, at times, as romantic friendship, Boston marriage, and passionate friendship—is well documented, but their meanings continue to be debated. Historians have often used letters, novels, diaries, poetry, fiction, and photographs to better understand such relationships. What they have found is that throughout American history, in fictional characterizations and in real-life friendships, many people were willing to espouse the intensity of their connections, sometimes openly, but more often through more cryptic codes.

Controversy has focused in particular on the ambiguous boundaries between homosocial and homoerotic friendships. Were intensely close same-sex friendships of the 1700s, 1800s, and early 1900s platonic or were they sexual relationships hidden behind a mask of friendship? Is it even appropriate to ask such a twentieth-century question, which often aims to label the sexual orientation of an individual who lived before such labels were constructed? How can we understand when and why same-sex intimate friendships, once valued by society, became illicit and even pathologized? These questions are in many ways current-day provocations pining for a dichotomous structure: Were they or weren't they? Did they or didn't they? Yet present-day definitions of sexual identity do not easily trace back to a past zeitgeist where terms, mores, and cultures differed from today's. As Carroll Smith-Rosenberg has argued in "The Female World of Love and Ritual" (1975), perhaps a more accurate analysis of same-sex friendships in historical context envisions a continuum of connections along which a fluid range of emotional and sexual intimacies existed. And insofar as GBT men have had historically significant friendships with LBT women, a comprehensive understanding of the history of LGBT friendships requires exploration of cross-sex and gender friendships as well. Whatever the experienced and expressed range of LGBT friendships, what is known is that they have been instrumental in the development of individual sexual identities, couple relationships, and LGBT communities in America.

## Colonial Friendships

From the creation of European colonies in the Americas, European American male friendships were often seen as the foundation of colonial life. Same-sex male friendships, often forged initially in the context of survival needs and later emphasized for the purpose of building society, were highly valued. Colonial women's friendships were not acknowledged to the same degree but served similar survival and social needs.

During the same period, Native American same-sex friendships were also highly valued. In the early 1700s, Joseph-François Lafitau, a French missionary, wrote about "special friendships" between same-sex Native Americans. These intense friendships were often lifelong partnerships equal in closeness and importance to relationships between blood relatives or spouses. In the mid-1800s, writing about a friendship between two Native American men, cross-country traveler Francis Parkman reflected: "If there be anything that deserves to be called romantic in the Indian character, it is to be sought for in friendships such as this which are common among many of the prairie tribes" (Katz, p. 457).

## Eighteen and Nineteenth Centuries

For women, same-sex friendships in the eighteenth and nineteenth centuries were often known as romantic or passionate friendships. These attachments were often intensely caring, devoted, and loving. By the latter part of the nineteenth century, the term "Boston marriage" was used to describe two women who had forgone marriage and lived together in a long-term monogamous relationship. The women involved were typically white, middle or upper class, financially independent, and feminist. According to Lillian Faderman's *Surpassing the Love of Men* (1981), in a time when women were considered asexual, such romantic friendships were often not only socially acceptable but valued and respected. Some historians, however, have pointed out that attitudes may have been less than idyllic, as a degree of disdain and disapproval existed toward women's same-sex romantic friendships.

Some middle- and upper-class white families supported their daughters living outside the family, with another woman, as practice for marriage. Not all women, however, wanted to leave these passionate friendships for marriage to a man. At the same time, the emergence of women's colleges provided for same-sex solidarity and the cultivation of close women's friendships (a phenomenon referred to as "smashing" or "chumming"). Education, moreover, meant expanded opportunities for self-sufficiency and options besides marriage.

The prominence of historical accounts of white middle- and upper-class women's romantic friendships does not mean that close same-sex friendships were limited to this stratum. Indeed, women of other races, ethnicities, and class levels also had strong female friendships, and although female friendships in this period were often segregated by race, ethnicity, and class, close friendships between white working-class women and black women did exist.

Well-known examples of romantic friendships in the nineteenth and early twentieth centuries included the poet Emily Dickinson and her future sister-in-law Susan Gilbert, women's movement leaders Susan B. Anthony and Elizabeth Cady Stanton, peace and reform activist Jane Addams and Mary Rozet Smith, poet Angelina Weld Grimké and Mamie Burrill, writer Willa Cather and Edith Lewis, college president M. Carey Thomas and her companions Mamie Gwinn and Mary Garrett, suffrage movement leader Ann Howard Shaw and Lucy Anthony, and Eleanor Roosevelt and journalist Lorena Hickok.

The characterization and categorization of particular women's friendships as sexual or asexual, self-conscious or innocent, has been fodder for many debates; reality likely falls on a continuum ranging from platonic friendships to sexual relationships. On this continuum, however, appropriate and proper conduct reigned over that of open expression. For those who had emotional and sexual relationships, deep friendships could provide an approved cover as long as they did not come across as critical of or challenges to marriage.

Romantic, close, and intimate friendships also existed for men in the eighteenth and nineteenth centuries. Younger intense male friendships in particular were acceptable as long as such fancies ended by adulthood, when men were supposed to turn their attention to marriage. Intimate and sexual friendships among men have also been documented in mining communities, cowboy cultures, frontier zones, seafaring groups, bachelor societies, and immigrant networks. John Watkins (2002) believes that distinctions between romantic friendships and homoerotic attachments were less absolute among men, yet as Victorian influences of the late nineteenth century called for more proper forms of homosocial connection and established stricter norms concerning sexual conduct, male friendships were affected. Men's friendships became subject to increased suspicion, paranoia, and homophobia. Even (as Gustav-Wrathall points out) Young Men's Christian Associations (YMCAs), places originally known for fostering male friendships, shifted to reflect more reserved gestures of friendship and became intolerant of any male connections that could be construed as homoerotic.

In the nineteenth century, male bonding via friendship was emphasized in fiction. Various authors cast indelible impressions of devoted male friendships founded on loyalty and trust. Examples include the platonic male friendship of Tom Sawyer and Huck Finn. Other works, however, were more suggestive in their homoerotic overtones; one notable example is Herman Melville's Ishmael and his interracial friendship with Queequeg. Some of these male authors themselves had intense, some would say homoerotic, friendships of their own. Melville and Nathaniel Hawthorne had an intense friendship, and Walt Whitman's many friendships and relationships with men were referenced in his writings, which espoused the virtues of male romantic friendships as the foundation for the revitalization of America.

## Early Twentieth Century

In the late nineteenth and early twentieth centuries, the construction of sexual identities based on sexual behaviors, emotional attractions, and gender characteristics by physicians, sexologists, and psychoanalysts brought an increased scrutiny of same-sex friendships. Sexologists such as Richard Von Krafft-Ebing, Cesare Lomroso, and Karl Westphal in the mid-to-late 1800s ushered in an era in which homosexuality was stigmatized and same-sex friendship was rendered suspect. By the early twentieth century, Havelock Ellis and Sigmund Freud had expanded on the negative characterization of homosexuality by describing the cause of aberration as "anomalies of nature" and "arrested development." Popular reception of their work led various social and cultural authorities to question and monitor same-sex friendships.

Descriptions of same-sex affection as "freakish," "inverted," "deviant," and "abnormal" replaced earlier accounts of same-sex friendships that described them in terms of virtue. Whether romantic friendships were sexual or not, the sexologists implicated inappropriate sexual intimacy in their descriptions of same-sex bonding in order to discredit these connections. In *A Desired Past* (1999), Leila Rupp writes that romantic friendships suffered the most from the new deviant labels of the sexologists. What had been considered innocent, loving friendships now had questionable overtones of homosexuality and all of the negative attributes that came with the new label.

Women's romantic friendships fell under even more scrutiny than men's as they became viewed as a potential threat to the status quo of patriarchal power. Uneasiness arose as more and more women chose to live in long-term friendships with other women rather than taking on the traditional roles of caregiving wife and mother. Sexologists were quick to denounce women's romantic friendships as pathological, pathetic, and perverse attempts to be like heterosexual couples.

The other threat women's friendships posed was in the solidarity that they offered women. Middle- and upper-class women formed political groups and asserted their power through such means as the suffrage movement. Sexologists attempted to quell such uprisings. For instance, Havelock Ellis regarded women's need for same-sex solidarity as a sign of female homosexuality, and since homosexuality was considered pathological, women who formed close associations were faced with the negative connotations and consequences of their actions. Nevertheless, it appears that expressions of same-sex physical affection between women such as holding hands and kissing remained more socially acceptable than similar expressions between men, leading some to argue that boundaries between homosocial and homoerotic relationships for women have remained more fluid than the comparable boundaries for men.

The sexologists did, in one way, offer a constructive framework. Their views reflected a shift in the late-nineteenth and early twentieth centuries from behavioral conceptions of homosexuality and bisexuality to conceptions of sexual identities and communities. Homosexual and bisexual individuals, often through forging friendships with other homosexuals and bisexuals, were now able to attach words and meanings to their sexualities. Urban subcultures in such cities as New York and San Francisco became the homosocial gateways for LGBT people to congregate as friends and to create LGBT communities. And friendships for LGBT individuals provided more than just people with whom one might socialize. The increasing disregard and disdain for LGBT individuals meant that LGBT friends played a variety of roles as emotional supporters, personal confidants, financial assistors, relationship counselors, roommates, workmates, and travel companions. Over time, LGBT friendships formed the basis for the development of vibrant LGBT communities in all parts of the country.

In the 1920s the country's zeitgeist challenged Victorian gender and sexual conservatism, embraced same-sex and cross-sex sexual experimentation, and launched what has been called the first sexual revolution. Popular writings added to the knowledge of LGBT identities by raising questions about the innocence of same-sex friendships. Works such as *The Well of Loneliness* (1928) by Radclyffe Hall and *The Sun Also Rises* (1926) by Ernest Hemingway brought attention to the tribulations and possibilities of same-sex friendships and love. In this and in subsequent decades, LGBT friends gathered in bars, clubs, restaurants, dance halls, amusement parks, theaters, drag balls, public parks, beaches, house parties, and other spaces. LGBT friendships were more common between people of the same class, ethnicity, race, religion, language, and sex, but friendships also crossed social boundaries in countless ways.

In the 1930s the Great Depression was accompanied in many contexts by increased hostility toward LGBT friendships and communities. With attention focused on family economic survival, many men and women who did not fit conventional gender and sexual norms experienced particularly intense financial and other difficulties. LGBT people still connected with friends in private bars, same-sex institutions, labor camps, and other locations, but public displays of LGBT affection were risky in a time that was disdainful of gender and sexual difference. Not all LGBT communities were affected in the same ways, however, as the San Francisco LGBT subculture appears to have grown during the 1930s, hobos and travelers formed new LGBT communities, and transsexuals began to form social networks that would later grow much more extensive.

## Midcentury

In the 1940s, World War II brought mixed experiences for LGBT friendships. Women who entered the workforce and the military during the war often counted on each other for support, as did women who remained at home, and many such women formed close, intimate, and affectionate bonds. Men, away from home in the military, in battle, and on leave, also supported each other through intense same-sex friendships and bonds. Wartime mobilization resulted in the extensive growth of LGBT friendship networks. After the war, returning LGBT soldiers and sailors moved into port cities such as New York and San Francisco and created expanded enclaves of LGBT friendship and community. In *Odd Girls and Twilight Lovers* (1991), Lillian Faderman states that more than ever before, knowledge about homosexuality during the post–World War II period increased and strengthened LGBT subcultures that were vital in the creation and maintenance of LGBT social support systems.

The end of the war, however, brought marked changes for LGBT people and their friends. Millions of men returned home, took jobs that had employed women, and expected women to return to their domestic responsibilities. In general, the Cold War climate laid a stress upon what were labeled traditional gender and sexual values. Not all women and men were willing to conform, as many had created close same-sex friendships, fallen in love, developed sexual partnerships, and participated in LGBT communities. But all people were pressured to conform, and many LGBT friendships suffered as a result. In a period in which homosexuals were labeled security risks, purged from the military, and barred from federal employment, same-sex friendships came under renewed suspicion. When U.S. senator Joseph McCarthy's hunt for political scapegoats was expanded to include gays and lesbians, scrutiny increased.

Many LGBT people responded to these campaigns by relying even more heavily on their bonds with other LGBT people, building and maintaining friendships and attempting to protect the small strides that had been made in the previous fifty years. As Trisha Franzen asserts in *Spinsters and Lesbians* (1996), "the collision between the permissive wartime climate and the postwar backlash forced lesbians and gay men into a greater self-consciousness as victims of a common oppression and fostered an increased community solidarity" (pp. 147–148). In the 1950s and 1960s, this manifested itself not only in bar- and home-based cultures, but also in the organized homophile movement that was established to fight for lesbian and gay rights. Building on preexisting LGBT friendships, homophile groups such as the Mattachine Society, ONE, and the Daughters of Bilitis further promoted the development of LGBT friendship networks, as did their magazines and newsletters. In this same period, the public celebrity of transsexual Christine Jorgensen helped encourage the growth of transsexual friendships.

The development of the gay liberation and lesbian feminist movements in the late 1960s and early 1970s affected LGBT friendships in significant ways. While the former strengthened bonds between men and the latter strengthened bonds between women, many cross-sex friendships suffered. For example, lesbians and gay men often had different political agendas; some lesbian feminists sought separation from all men, and new consciousness and criticism of gay male sexism caused rifts in LGBT friendship circles. Part of the fracture came about because of the representation of LGBT people in the media, which for the most part noticed gay men while ignoring lesbians, thereby creating tension between gay men and lesbians. In *City of Sisterly and Brotherly Loves* (2000), however, Marc Stein points out that cross-sex friendships between gay men and lesbians, even during the contested times of the lesbian separatist movement of the early 1970s, still remained strong because of shared sexual identities and experiences. And to whatever extent cross-sex LGBT friendships were weakened in the 1970s, they strengthened again in the 1980s when, in the context of the HIV/AIDS crisis, the significance of friendships between LGBT people often surpassed that of relationships within families.

## Late Twentieth and Early Twenty-First Centuries

It has been said that "the most commonly told relationship story among non-heterosexuals is one of friendship" (Weeks, Heaphy, and Donovan, p. 51). Indeed, various scholars examining the late twentieth and early twenty-first centuries have observed a prevailing friendship narrative among LGBT people that highlights the extraordinary and unique importance, function, and meaning of friendship in LGBT communities. LGBT friendships have been described as more important, more likely to be viewed as family, and more likely to include a history of sexual behavior, attraction, and/or relationship than their non-LGBT counterparts. Friendship's centrality for LGBT people is tied to homophobia, heterosexism, biphobia, and transphobia, which, despite much progress, continue as backdrops for LGBT identities and experiences. As Jeffrey Weeks, Brian Heaphy, and Catherine Donovan note, friendships "particularly flourish when overarching identities are fragmented in periods of rapid social change, or at turning points in people's lives, or when lives are lived at odds with social norms" (p. 51).

Various scholars have identified factors common to all types of friendships and several of unique significance to LGBT friendships. Available studies (mostly on lesbian and gay populations) indicate that friends provide LGBT people with profoundly important social, emotional, health, identity, relationship, and other types of supports. Most often emphasized is the central role of LGBT friendships in the development and maintenance of positive LGBT identities and relationships and in providing opportunities for LGBT people to be themselves. It is also often through friendships that LGBT identities and communities are constructed.

**Friends as Family.** LGBT friendships have been commonly referred to and experienced as family. As Peter M. Nardi explains in *Gay Men's Friendships* (1999), "within a society that values kinship institutions, friendships are more likely to be defined as family-like when individuals feel distant from, alienated from, or lacking in biogenetic family members" (p. 58). During the last decades of the twentieth century and the first few years of the twentieth-first, however, as more LGBT people gained acceptance from families of origin and created their own families with partners and children, fewer LGBTs have articulated the notion of friends as substitute family. Yet while some LGBT people have rejected this notion, others have used it as a means to challenge the institution of the family itself, including its emphasis on biological ties and heterosexuality. As Nardi suggests, "'Friends as family' . . . is a way of presenting a sense of coherence and solidity to the larger society, and perhaps of appropriating the 'family values' discourse invoked by those who oppose equal rights for gays and lesbians" (1999, p. 70).

"Friends as family" language also challenges the preeminence of sexual partners as opposed to friendships and communities based on shared personal and political commitments This language presents friendship as a better relational model to which to aspire. The inherent value of friendships is promoted with the language of "friends as family," which challenges "the inevitability or necessity of conventional family life" (Weeks, Heaphy, and Donovan, p. 53). Acknowledging that many LGBT peoples desire dyadic and child-focused families, Nardi and others—including Ellen Shumsky, Jacqueline Weinstock, and Kath Weston—argue that families of lovers and friends remain central in many LGBT lives.

A third meaning of "friends as family" has emerged out of this context; it focuses on extending rather than replacing or decentering the family. One frequent extension occurs through efforts to include ex-lovers (perhaps especially among lesbians). Some lesbians describe ex-lovers as similar to in-laws; "exes" come along as "a package deal" when new partner relationships are formed. Ex-lovers and friends become integral parts of the extended families of LGBT people with children.

**Blurred Boundaries between Friends and Lovers.** Research, clinical observations, and personal observations indicate a tendency among LGBT people to view friends and lovers as "two ends of a single continuum rather than as oppositional categories" (Weston, p. 120). For example, Nardi's research in "That's What Friends Are For" (1992) and elsewhere suggests that it is not uncommon for lesbians and gay men be at least minimally sexually attracted to and in love with their friends at some point in time. Personal stories also indicate that some lesbians and gay men can engage in sexual activity with friends and still remain friends. In "The Lesbian's Experience of Friendship" (1996), however, Jeanne L. Stanley reports that the most frequently mentioned concern of coupled lesbians in her focus groups was the potential threat of a romantic involvement with a friend. This is not surprising given that a common pattern by which lesbians become lovers is through friendship. Speaking from a lesbian feminist perspective, Sarah Lucia Hoagland argues in *Lesbian Ethics* (1988) that lesbians, in rejecting patriarchal constructions of love and desire, have "developed far more complex relationships than the distinction between friend and lover acknowledges" (p. 173).

While gay men also appear to experience blurred boundaries between friends and lovers and to have friends become lovers and lovers become friends, the pattern of movement may be reversed. In "Sex, Friendship, and Gender Roles among Gay Men" (1992), for example, Nardi suggests that sexual involvement may more frequently precede the development of a friendship for gay men, while for lesbians it may more frequently follow

from it. Sexual involvement may also serve as a driving force for the formation of close friendships between gay men, with attraction and sexual behavior more a part of the early stages of friendship formation (although sex is not limited to these stages). Despite the cultural belief that a good friendship will be ruined by sex, few of Nardi's research participants noted this occurring.

Sexual elements are likely present in heterosexuals' same-sex friendships but the context of heterosexism may restrict their expression. In *Gay Men's Friendships* (1999), Nardi suggests that gay men may be freer to express their erotic attractions with same-sex gay friends and in doing so actually subvert the cultural definition of masculinity at the same time as "reproducing the gendered sexual energy (instrumental, hierarchical) constitutive of hegemonic masculinity" (p. 85).

**Subtexts and Limitations to the Prevailing Narratives.** Lesbians and gay men have tended to form their closest friendships among other lesbians and gay men, respectively. For example, in Nardi's survey study —reported in his "Sex, Friendship, and Gender Roles among Gay Men" (1992), "That's What Friends Are For" (1992), and "Friendships in the Lives of Gay Men and Lesbians" (1994) with Dru Sherrod—82 percent of gay male respondents reported that their best friend was gay or bisexual while 76 percent of the lesbian respondents reported having a lesbian or bisexual best friend. The pattern of homosocial friendships among lesbians and gay men is not surprising; gendered experiences do produce different social worlds. Yet this pattern of homosocial friendships may also reinforce and replicate prevailing gender dynamics and the privileged status of gay men and lesbians in LGBT communities.

LGBT people do form friendships across sex, gender, and sexuality lines. For example, only 10 percent of the lesbian respondents in the National Lesbian Health Care Survey (1988) reported that all of their women friends were lesbians, and 78 percent reported having some close male friends, with only 9 percent of these women reporting that all of these males were gay. The gay men in Raymond M. Berger and D. Mallon's study "Social Support Networks of Gay Men" (1993) reported approximately three female members out of an average social network size of 8.5. Drawing on his study of relationships between lesbians and gay men in Philadelphia during the mid-twentieth century, Marc Stein argues for the need to challenge "the tendency to conceive of lesbians and gay men as either entirely distinct or completely conjoined" and that "lesbian and gay history, for better and for worse, has much to teach us about the past, present, and future of relationships between what we tendentiously call 'the sexes'" (p. 3).

Friendships across sex, gender, and sexuality lines offer particular challenges. Heterosexism, sexism, biphobia, and gender-related oppressions interfere with both the development and maintenance of these close friendships. Of particular concern is Paula Rust's finding in *Bisexuality and the Challenge to Lesbian Politics* (1995) that more than half of the 322 lesbians who responded to a questionnaire reported preferring other lesbians as friends and avoiding bisexual women as friends. Over 25 percent of the 45 bisexual respondents also reported a preference for lesbians as friends.

LGBT scholars have paid only limited attention to friendships involving bisexual and transgender individuals. Yet as Jacqueline S. Weinstock notes in "Lesbian, Gay, Bisexual, and Transgender Friendships in Adulthood" (1998), writings that examine bisexual and transgender experiences suggest a powerful role for friendships in supporting personal and community development and social justice politics.

While friendships across lines of race, ethnicity, class, age, and ability exist (and they present both challenges and benefits to those involved), LGBT peoples, like their non LGBT counterparts, tend to form friendships with people who have similar identities, experiences and characteristics. Insofar as multiple forms of oppression exist within LGBT communities, this tendency may reinforce as well as reflect prevailing power dynamics. As one example, the emphasis among LGBT people on "friends as family" may reflect and reinforce racism and classism through centering European American and middle-class conceptions of family.

## Conclusion

"Being queer gives us a chance to re-invent family, friendship, and community," states Urvashi Vaid in *Virtual Equality* (1995, p. 380). This "chance" emerged in part as a result of historically restricted access to family, friendship, and community. Yet LGBT peoples have responded by creating intimate friendships throughout American history and alternative models for relating as friends, lovers, and family, including blurring the lines between friends and lovers and creating "a variety of 'experiments in living' through which new patterns of commitment are being enacted in everyday life," as Weeks, Heaphy, and Donovan describe it in *Same Sex Intimacies* (2001, p. viii). They go on to note that

> The social changes we identify are affecting heterosexual and non-heterosexual lives alike, but they have a special resonance for those who are defined, and define themselves, as different. Underpinned by a widely accepted friendship ethic, women and

men who have rejected what we call the heterosexual assumption are creating ways of being that point to a more diverse culture of relationships than law and tradition have sanctioned. (p. viii)

Yet in the beginning of the twenty-first century, it remains to be seen how many of LGBT people's "experiments in living" will persist. Furthermore, insofar as LGBT friendships have been strongly influenced by the interactions of sexuality, sex, gender, race, ethnicity, class, ability, age, and religion, it also remains to be seen whether LGBT friendships and families will continue to replicate existing inequities and gender-related boundaries or whether they will come to challenge them.

## Bibliography

Becker, Carol S. *Unbroken Ties: Lesbian Ex-Lovers.* Boston: Alyson, 1988.

Berger, Raymond M., and D. Mallon. "Social Support Networks of Gay Men." *Journal of Sociology and Social Welfare* 20 (1993): 155–174.

Bradford, Judith, and Caitlin Ryan. *The National Lesbian Health Care Survey: Final Report.* Washington, D.C.: National Lesbian and Gay Health Foundation, 1988.

Card, Claudia. *Lesbian Choices.* New York: Columbia University Press, 1995.

Chauncey, George. "Christian Brotherhood or Sexual Perversion? Homosexual Identities and the Construction of Sexual Boundaries in the World War I Era." *Journal of Social History* 19, no. 1 (Winter 1985): 189–211.

Diggs, Marylynne. "Romantic Friends or a 'Different Race of Creatures'?: The Representation of Lesbian Pathology in Nineteenth-Century America." *Feminist Studies* 21 (1995): 317–340.

Faderman, Lillian. *Surpassing the Love of Men: Romantic Friendship and Love between Women from the Renaissance to the Present.* New York: Morrow, 1981.

———. *Odd Girls and Twilight Lovers: A History of Lesbian Life in Twentieth-Century America.* New York: Columbia University Press, 1991.

Fehr, Beverley. *Friendship Processes.* Thousand Oaks, Calif.: Sage, 1996.

Franzen, Trisha. *Spinsters and Lesbians: Independent Womanhood in the United States.* New York: New York University Press, 1996.

Gustav-Wrathall, John Donald. *Take the Young by the Hand: Same-Sex Relations and the YMCA.* Chicago: University of Chicago Press, 1998.

Hall, Ruth, and Suzanna Rose. "Friendships between African-American and White Lesbians." *Lesbian Friendships: For Ourselves and Each Other.* Edited by Jacqueline S. Weinstock and Esther D. Rothblum. New York: New York University Press, 1996.

Hoagland, Sarah Lucia. *Lesbian Ethics: Toward New Value.* Palo Alto, Calif.: Institute of Lesbian Studies, 1988.

Katz, Jonathan. Gay *American History: Lesbians and Gay Men in the U.S.A.* New York: Avon, 1976.

Kennedy, Elizabeth Lapovsky, and Madeline D. Davis. *Boots of Leather, Slippers of Gold: The History of a Lesbian Community.* New York: Routledge, 1993.

Kimmel, Douglas C. "The Families of Older Gay Men and Lesbians." *Generations* 17, no. 3 (Summer 1992): 37–38.

Kitzinger, Celia. "Toward a Politics of Lesbian Friendship." In *Lesbian Friendships: For Ourselves and Each Other.* Edited by Jacqueline S. Weinstock and Esther D. Rothblum. New York: New York University, 1996.

Kurdek, Lawrence A. "Perceived Social Support in Gays and Lesbians in Cohabiting Relationships." *Journal of Personality and Social Psychology* 54 (1988): 504–509.

Lehr, Valerie. *Queer Family Values: Debunking the Myth of the Nuclear Family.* Philadelphia: Temple University Press, 1999.

Macdonald, Barbara. *Look Me in the Eye: Old Women, Aging, and Ageism.* London: Women's Press, 1984.

Nardi, Peter M. "Alcohol Treatment and the Non-Traditional 'Family' Structures of Gays and Lesbians." *Journal of Alcohol and Drug Education* 27, no. 2 (Winter 1982): 83–89.

———. "Sex, Friendship, and Gender Roles among Gay Men. *Men's Friendships.* Edited by Peter M. Nardi. Newbury Park, Calif.: Sage, 1992.

———. "That's What Friends Are For: Friends as Family in the Gay and Lesbian Community. In *Modern Homosexualities: Fragments of Lesbian and Gay Experience.* Edited by Ken Plummer. New York: Routledge, 1992.

———. *Gay Men's Friendships: Invincible Communities.* Chicago: University of Chicago Press, 1999.

Nardi, Peter M., and Dru Sherrod. "Friendships in the Lives of Gay Men and Lesbians." *Journal of Social and Personal Relationships* 11, no. 2 (May 1994): 185–199.

Preston, John. *Friends and Lovers: Gay Men Write about the Families They Create.* New York: Dutton, 1995.

Price, Jammie. *Navigating Differences: Friendships between Gay and Straight Men.* New York: Haworth Press, 1999.

Raymond, Janice G. *A Passion for Friends: Toward a Philosophy of Female Affection.* Boston: Beacon Press, 1986.

Rose, Suzanna. "Heterosexism and the Study of Women's Romantic and Friend Relationships." *Journal of Social Issues* 56 (2000): 315–328.

Rose, Suzanna M., and Debbie Zand. "Lesbian Dating and Courtship from Young Adulthood to Midlife." In *Lesbian Love and Relationships.* Edited by Suzanna M. Rose. Binghamton, N.Y.: Harrington Park Press, 2002.

Rotundo, E. Anthony. "Romantic Friendship: Male Intimacy and Middle-Class Youth in the Northern United States, 1800–1900." *Journal of Social History* 23, no. 1 (Fall 1989): 1–25.

Rupp, Leila J. *A Desired Past: A Short History of Same-Sex Love in America.* Chicago: University of Chicago Press, 1999.

Rust, Paula C. *Bisexuality and the Challenge to Lesbian Politics: Sex, Loyalty, and Revolution.* New York: New York University Press, 1995.

Ryan, Caitlin, and Judith Bradford. "The National Lesbian Health Care Survey: An Overview." In *Psychological Perspectives on Lesbian and Gay Male Experiences.* Edited by Linda D. Garnets and Douglas C. Kimmel. New York: Columbia University Press, 1993.

Shumsky, Ellen. "Transforming the Ties That Bind: Lesbians, Lovers, and Chosen Family." In *Sexualities Lost and Found.* Edited by Edith Gould and Sandra Kiersky. Madison, Conn.: International Universities Press, 2001.

Smith-Rosenberg, Carroll. "The Female World of Love and Ritual: Relations between Women in Nineteenth-Century America." *Signs* 1, no. 1 (Autumn 1975): 1–29.

Stanley, Jeanne L. "The Lesbian's Experience of Friendship." In *Lesbian Friendships: For Ourselves and Each Other.* Edited by Jacqueline S. Weinstock and Esther D. Rothblum. New York: New York University Press, 1996.

———. "Young Sexual Minority Women's Perceptions on Cross-Generational Friendships with Lesbians." *Journal of Lesbian Studies* 6, no. 1 (2002): 139–148.

———. "Multiracial Sexual Minority Women: Understanding the Unique Aspects and Interactional Processes of Multiple Minority Identities." *Women and Therapy,* in press.

Stein, Marc. *City of Sisterly and Brotherly Loves: Lesbian and Gay Philadelphia, 1945– 1972.* Chicago: University of Chicago Press, 2000.

Stuart, Elizabeth. *Just Good Friends: Towards a Lesbian and Gay Theology of Relationships.* New York: Mowbray, 1995.

Tillmann-Healy, Lisa M. *Between Gay and Straight: Understanding Friendship across Sexual Orientation.* Walnut Creek, Calif.: AltaMira Press, 2001.

Vaid, Urvashi. *Virtual Equality: The Mainstreaming of Gay and Lesbian Liberation.* New York: Anchor, 1995.

Vetere, Victoria A. "The Role of Friendship in the Development and Maintenance of Lesbian Love Relationships." *Journal of Homosexuality* 8, no. 2 (1982): 51–65.

Watkins, John. "Romantic Friendship, Male." In *The Gay and Lesbian Literary Heritage: A Reader's Companion to the Writers and Their Works, from Antiquity to the Present.* New York: Routledge, 2002.

Weeks, Jeffrey, Brian Heaphy, and Catherine Donovan. *Same Sex Intimacies: Families of Choice and Other Life Experiments.* New York: Routledge, 2001.

Weinstock, Jacqueline S. "Lesbian, Gay, Bisexual, and Transgender Friendships in Adulthood: Review and Analysis." In *Lesbian, Gay, and Bisexual Identities in Families: Psychological Perspectives.* Edited by Charlotte J. Patterson and Anthony R. D'Augelli. New York: Oxford University Press, 1998.

———. "Lesbian Friendships at Midlife: Patterns and Possibilities for the Twenty-first Century." *Journal of Gay and Lesbian Social Services* 11 (2000): 1–32.

———. "Lesbian FLEX-ibility: Friend and/or Family Connections among Lesbian Ex-Lovers." In *Lesbian Ex-Lovers: The Really Long-Term Relationships.* Edited by Jacqueline S. Weinstock and Esther D. Rothblum. Binghamton, N.Y.: Harrington Park Press, in press.

Weinstock, Jacqueline S., and Esther D. Rothbaum, eds. *Lesbian Friendships: For Ourselves and Each Other.* New York: New York University Press, 1996.

———. *Lesbian Ex-Lovers: The Really Long-Term Relationship.* Binghamton, N.Y.: Harrington Park Press, in press.

Werking, Kathy. *We're Just Good Friends: Women and Men in Nonromantic Relationships.* New York: Guilford Press, 1997.

Weston, Kath. *Families We Choose: Lesbians, Gays, Kinship.* Rev. ed. New York: Columbia University Press, 1997.

**Jeanne L. Stanley, Jacqueline S. Weinstock**

*See also* COLONIAL AMERICA; HOMOEROTICISM AND HOMOSOCIALITY; NATIVE AMERICANS; ROMANTIC FRIENDSHIP AND BOSTON MARRIAGE; ROOSEVELT, ELEANOR, AND LORENA HICKOK.

# FUGATE, James Barr (b. 13 February 1922; d. 28 March 1995), writer.

Fugate was born in Texas (some sources say Oklahoma) and discovered his attraction to men with a fraternity brother while attending college. Following the Japanese attack on Pearl Harbor in 1941, he volunteered for service in the U.S. Navy and served until 1945.

After his discharge, he returned to university with the intention of completing a bachelor's degree in writing. During this time he learned of his fraternity friend's suicide in Oklahoma, an event that made life in the sheltered world of academia intolerable for him. In reaction, he left the campus world and moved to New York City, where he made a living as a writer of advertising copy for the new medium of television.

Fugate later returned to his home region to work as a laborer in the oil fields, where he gained practical knowledge of this all-male world that would give life to his later collection of seven stories titled *Derricks*, published in 1951. Volunteering for service during the Korean War as a reserve officer, he was posted to a naval base in Alaska and, unusually for the period, given an honorable discharge when his identity as the author of the gay-themed *Quatrefoil* and *Derricks* became known to his superiors.

This action led him to turn his talents to working and writing for the homophile movement, contributing pieces to the *Mattachine Review*, one of which attacked the then-prevalent notion that homosexuals molested children. After his discharge, he returned to his family in Kansas and became a newspaper reporter and photographer until the early 1970s, when he returned briefly to New York. He later took a job in the emergency room of a large hospital, from which he retired.

The work for which Fugate is most remembered is his groundbreaking novel of same-sex love in the military, *Quatrefoil*, which first appeared in print in 1950. Writing under the pseudonym of James Barr, the author broke sharply with then-established depictions of gay male characters, who were usually drawn as self-destructive and as lacking in a sense of honor and all other manly virtues. The lovers in *Quatrefoil* and the characters in *Derricks* exhibit none of these qualities and foreshadow the rebellion against stereotypic categories that would mark the literature of the gay-liberation era some two decades later. The distinctive name of the title of *Quatrefoil* would also become a part of the transmuted verbal folklore of the gay and lesbian community, as noted by the poet Judy Grahn in the preface to *Another Mother Tongue: Gay Words, Gay Worlds,* in which she recounts the tale of her first lover telling her that there was a word associated with being gay called "catafoil."

Fugate's frank account of the consequences to his military career of his identification as the author of a gay novel appeared in the *Mattachine Review* in the spring of 1955. This was one of the earliest personal statements on public record by a member of the U.S. military that describes the homophobia of military top brass, whose victims usually kept quiet about their experiences. It thus foreshadows E. Lawrence Gibson's *Get Off My Ship: Ensign Berg vs. the U.S. Navy* (1978) and the history of homophobic military policies compiled by Randy Shilts in *Conduct Unbecoming* (1993).

Fugate's emphasis on a balanced presentation of homosexuals as human beings possessing qualities that readers of any sexual orientation could identify with continued in his final two literary creations, a 1955 play titled *Game of Fools* (the first of an envisioned five-play cycle that was never finished) and the novel *The Occasional Man,* issued in 1966. By the time the latter was published, his moral position on homosexuality appears to have shifted somewhat, as noted by Hubert Kennedy in his review of Fugate's work. In *The Occasional Man,* Kennedy wrote, "the height of high-minded thinking for its protagonist is not to initiate anyone into homosexuality."

Taken together, *Quatrefoil* and *Derricks* can be seen as part of a body of gay literature that developed during the 1950s and was marked by realistic depictions of homosexuals as something other than immediately pathological. These and other works prepared the reading public, both gay and straight, for the revolution in gay male fiction that would begin in the 1970s.

## Bibliography

Fugate, James Barr. "Facing Friends in a Small Town." *Mattachine Review* 1, (January–February 1955): 9–12.

———. "Release from the Navy under Honorable Conditions." *Mattachine Review* 3, (May–June 1955): 6–9, 39–42.

Kennedy, Hubert. "*Quatrefoil* Broke New Ground." *Harvard Gay and Lesbian Review* (winter 1996): 22–24.

Ridinger, Robert B. Marks. "Barr, James." In *Gay and Lesbian Literature*. Edited by Tom Pendergast and Sara Pendergast. Detroit: St. James Press, 1998: 21–23.

**Robert B. Marks Ridinger**

*See also* PULP FICTION: GAY.

# FUKAYA, Michiyo (Michiyo Cornell) (b. 25 April 1953; d. 9 July 1987), writer, poet, activist.

Michiyo Fukaya was one of the earliest Asian American lesbian activists who spoke out and wrote about racism in the white lesbian and gay community and about heterosexism in the Asian American community. She had an impact on lesbian and gay rights for Asian Americans and others through her writings, readings, and participation in local organizing. She self-published a book of poems, *Lesbian Lyrics,* in 1981 and wrote articles, op-ed pieces, letters to the editor, and essays for various newspapers and journals including *Commonwoman* and *Azalea: A Third World Lesbian Magazine.* Hers is one of only a few voices from the late 1970s and 1980s by and about Asian American lesbians.

Fukaya was born in Japan and named Margaret Cornell by her parents; her father was a white U.S. soldier and her mother was Japanese. She had an older brother and two younger sisters. Fukaya described her mother as having few options in Japan after Fukaya's birth but to marry the military man with whom she already had two children. Fukaya's family left Japan in 1956 for southern Vermont, where her mother died of cancer in 1958. The loss of her mother at the age of four and the experience of being left in a physically and sexually abusive household with an alcoholic father and sadistic stepmother informed much of Fukaya's writings.

Fukaya's poetry and prose address the topics of incest, rape, racism, poverty, mother-daughter relationships, and biracial issues. As a biracial child in a white community in Vermont, she experienced racist taunts, physical assaults, and a lack of support from her family, schools, and teachers, who made her feel as if she, not the others, were the problem. Her schooling did not include any material on the history of Asians in the United States nor did it address the realities of biracial people. In her writing and speeches, Fukaya has talked about her Eurasian identity and her sense of alienation within both white and Asian cultures—including, for instance, the tension of being perceived as white by Asian Americans and as Asian by whites at the University of Massachusetts, Amherst, where she graduated with a B.A. in English literature in 1975. Beginning in her twenties, Fukaya changed her name a number of times in the process of trying to fashion and control her own identity. She first called herself Margaret Noshiko Cornell, then Michiyo Cornell, and finally settled on Michiyo Fukaya (her mother's name).

In 1979, during the first gay March on Washington, Fukaya represented the newly founded Asian American gay and lesbian collective that had formed at the first national Third World Lesbian and Gay Conference at Howard University. During the march rally at the Washington Monument, she gave a speech titled "Living in Asian America" that marks one of the earliest times when the issues faced by Asian American lesbians and gays were heard by a huge LGBT audience, both white and of color. Fukaya voiced her experience of living as a poor woman of color who faced the intersecting oppressions of racism, classism, heterosexism, and sexism. She urged people to recognize the shared and differing oppressions that united and divided third world lesbians and gays and straight people.

During the late 1970s, Fukaya moved to Burlington, Vermont, where she participated in an emerging and predominantly white lesbian and gay community. By the time of her arrival in Burlington, Fukaya had a daughter named Mayumi whose father was black. Being a poor, single lesbian mother of a multiracial child in a community of white lesbian feminists proved difficult. At various times Fukaya had bouts of depression and could not care for Mayumi, whose guardianship was taken on by white lesbian feminists within that community. In *A Fire Is Burning, It Is in Me*, an edited collection of Fukaya's writings and remembrances by those who knew her, many described the hardships wrought by her mental illness and the difficulty of surviving a life filled with anger, pain, and oppression. Within this context, Fukaya took her own life with a handgun and passed away on 9 July 1987, a few days after being taken off life support. In the poem "Poetry Class Umass/Amherst" in *Lesbian Lyrics*, Fukaya wrote,

i frighten myself
with my words.
if I speak too plainly,
too clearly,
i know i open myself
to death

## Bibliography

Cornell, Margaret Noshiko, "Living in Asian America: An Asian America Lesbian's Address before the Washington Monument." *Gay Insurgent* 6 (summer 1980): 16.

Cornell, Michiyo. "Poetry Class Umass/Amherst." In her *Lesbian Lyrics*. Self-published, 1981.

Shervington, Gwendolyn I. *A Fire Is Burning, It Is In Me: The Life and Writing of Michiyo Fukaya.* Norwich, Vt.: New Victoria, 1996.

Tsang, Daniel C. "Slicing Silence: Asian Progressives Come Out." In *Asian Americans: The Movement and the Moment.* Edited by Steve Louie and Glenn K. Omatsu. Los Angeles: UCLA Asian American Studies Center Press, 2001.

**Alice Y. Hom**

*See also* ASIAN; AMERICAN LGBTQ ORGANIZATIONS AND PERIODICALS, TSANG, DANIEL.

## FULLER, Margaret (b. 23 May 1810; d. 19 July 1850), feminist, writer, revolutionary.

Margaret Fuller was born into an upper-middle-class Puritan family in Cambridgeport, Massachusetts, and christened Sarah Margaret Fuller. Her mother, Margaret Crane Fuller (1789–1859), was a school teacher, who after her marriage led the life of a traditional wife and mother. Early on Sarah Margaret dropped her christening name, choosing to be known simply as Margaret. Her father, Timothy Fuller (1739–1835), was a politician who served in the Massachusetts legislature and as a member of the United States House of Representatives. Inheriting and fostering aspects of character and personality from both parents, Fuller developed as a sort of social and intellectual androgyne, throughout her life displaying in integration of both male and female traits.

Fuller was the first of nine children; six other siblings, of whom four brothers and one sister survived into adulthood, later completed the family. Positioned for some years, then, as the only child and recognized as gifted and self-willed, Margaret received her preliminary schooling from her father, who fixed his hopes for the future on her. Margaret learned Latin from the age of three, Greek at age ten, and then modern languages, including French and Italian. She later schooled herself in German in order to read Goethe, in whose work she developed a lifelong interest. A lonely child whose rigorous education excelled that of other female children, Margaret had difficulty fitting in with other girls her age. By age twelve, Margaret had determined that she was destined to be gifted, but ugly.

During her teenage years, her father enrolled her in several schools: Dr. Park's School in Boston, Miss Prescott's Boarding School in Groton, and Mr. Perkin's Cambridge Port School. But at these schools, finding no intellectual peers, Margaret became a social outcast, lacking the poise and social graces of the young women her age. Accordingly, she attached herself to sophisticated older women, initially to a British visitor, Ellen Kilshaw, whom she called her first friend, and later to older influential women, including Eliza Farrar, the wife of a Harvard professor of astronomy, who befriended her. (It was these associations, as well as her own fierce independence, that allowed a reputation of lesbianism to attach itself to Fuller's name, though that she took part in such a relationship—outside of the ordinary sort of passionate heterosocial friendships that were part of her educated, nineteenth-century milieu—has never been definitively proven.) Unable to attend university classes because of her sex, Margaret nonetheless found herself a peer with some of Harvard's finest male students. She was accorded honorary status by several of her confidantes in the Harvard undergraduate class of 1829 and the Divinity School class of 1833. When her father retired to Groton, Massachusetts, to attempt gentlemanly farming, Margaret reluctantly followed, leaving the stimulating intellectual milieu of Cambridge for the sanguine countryside.

In 1835, with the sudden death of her father, Margaret, now age twenty-five, became head of the household, assuming the responsibilities of educating her younger siblings and providing for her mother. Always self-reliant, but now calling on her Cambridge connections, she met and became a lifelong friend and correspondent of Ralph Waldo Emerson, a leading light of the Transcendentalist movement, a uniquely American strain of Romanticism that placed an emphasis on nature as a mirror of the self. Fuller enjoyed his writings, but challenged him because she thought his work did not adequately combine the realities of body/nature with spirit. Through Emerson she acquired a position teaching at Bronson Alcott's Transcendental experimental Temple School in Boston. There she conducted private lessons in German and Italian. After one year, when the school was faltering due in large part to Alcott's emphasis on learning through intuition and to his enrollment of a black child, Margaret moved to Hiram Fuller's Green Street School in Providence, Rhode Island. There she taught part-time for two years.

Family circumstances and her own desire to leave schoolroom teaching caused Margaret to relocate with her family to Jamaica Plain, Massachusetts, in 1839. There she served as head of household, teaching her younger brothers and sister, and initiating adult conversation classes for women in Boston and Cambridge. Largely because of these lectures Margaret Fuller's reputation as a feminist and as a Transcendentalist was established. During this same time, from July 1840 until July 1842, she served as the first editor of the *Dial*, the official organ of the Transcendental movement. She also traveled with Emerson to Brook Farm, the experimental community run under Transcendental principles. She and Emerson were too individualist to join the communal endeavor personally, though they supported it in theory. Through her ongoing study, her writing, and her work as editor of the *Dial*, Margaret became the lone female among the New England thinkers of her age, counting among her intellectual peers and intimate acquaintances not only Ralph Waldo Emerson and Bronson Alcott, but also Henry David Thoreau and William Ellery Channing (whom her sister, Ellen, later married). Completing her translation of the correspondence between Fraulein Gunderode and Bettina von Arnim and concluding her term as editor of the *Dial*, Margaret journeyed west, where many of her friends were establishing themselves. Accompanying James and Sarah Clarke, she traveled by wagon and boat through cities like Milwaukee and Chicago until she reached as far as Oregon.

The publication of her *Summer on the Lakes*, the fictive story of a gifted but alienated teenaged girl's experience at boarding school, attracted the attention of Horace Greeley, who subsequently offered Margaret a position as literary critic for the *New York Daily-Tribune*, of which he was editor. In moving to New York, Margaret expanded her feminist reputation and influence, publishing her most important work, *Woman in the Nineteenth Century*, an expanded version of "The Great Lawsuit: Man vs. Man, Women vs. Women," which she had published earlier in the *Dial*. Her circle of friends expanded internationally to include the British feminist Harriett Martineau and James Nathan, with whom she fell deeply in love. Continuing to publish numerous critical articles and book reviews, Margaret resigned her desk position at the *Tribune* in 1846 to fulfill a longtime dream. Acting as a foreign correspondent for the *Tribune*, she sailed for Europe, traveling first to England and Scotland and then to France with friends. During this part of her journey, she learned by post of James Nathan's engagement to a German woman. Her own hopes for marriage to James dashed, Margaret traveled on to Italy, where in Rome she met a young Italian nobleman, the Marchese Giovanni Angelo Ossoli, eleven years her junior. Ossoli was smitten with Margaret, who accepted his love. Because of the difficulties of differing religions and the political and personal issues involved, Margaret took up lodging outside

**Margaret Fuller.** The early-nineteenth-century feminist writer, Transcendentalist, and first editor of *Dial*, the movement's journal, she numbered Ralph Waldo Emerson and Henry David Thoreau among her friends and intellectual peers.

of Rome, and the couple kept their relationship a secret even from their families and closest associates. Whether they did, indeed, marry as they later said and, if so, when and where remain a mystery. However, in 1848 Margaret bore Giovanni a son, Angelo.

In February 1849, the Roman Republic was declared. During the siege of Rome by the French in the spring of that year, Ossoli was engaged fully in the revolution. Margaret, on being appointed director of a hospital and learning to care for the wounded, journeyed between Rome and a village, where she often left their son to the care of others for weeks at a time. Her dedicated hospital work with victims of the revolution earned her the reputation of a Roman Florence Nightingale. It also provided Margaret with the opportunity to combine her social theory with action. When it was clear that the revolution would fail, the Ossolis prepared to leave Italy for America. Margaret then wrote her mother and many of her friends concerning her marriage. After the fall of the republic, the Ossolis, having gone first to Florence, set sail for America. On the ill-fated voyage, first the ship's captain died, leaving the ship in the hands of willing, but inexperienced, hands. Then, on 19 July 1850, the ship foundered on a sandbar in a storm and Margaret, Giovanni, and their infant, Angelo, perished in the shipwreck just off Fire Island.

A feminist theorist and independent thinker, Margaret Fuller believed that women were equal to men and that they should be accorded every right and privilege accorded males in nineteenth-century American society. She depicted her beliefs, not only in her teachings, writings, relationships, and "conversations," but also, and most importantly, in the principles of feminism and revolution that she espoused.

### Bibliography

Beach, Seth Curtis. "Sarah Margaret Fuller Ossoli, 1810–1850," In *Daughters of the Puritans: A Group of Brief Biographies.* Freeport, N.Y.: Books for Libraries Press, Inc., 1967.

Brown, Arthur W. *Margaret Fuller.* New York: Twayne, 1964.

Spender, Dale. *Women of Ideas and What Men Have Done to Them.* Hammersmith, London: Pandora, 1992.

Stern, Madeleine B. *The Life of Margaret Fuller.* New York: Dutton, 1942.

Urbanski, Marie Mitchell Olsen. "Margaret Fuller: Feminist Writer and Revolutionary." In *Feminist Theorists: Three Centuries of Women's Intellectual Traditions,* edited by Dale Spender. London: Women's Press, 1983.

Watson, David. *Margaret Fuller: An American Romantic.* New York: St. Martin's Press, 1988.

**Lorine Getz**

*See also* FEMINISM.

# FURIES

The Furies developed a proud and uncompromising brand of lesbian feminism that resonated powerfully within the women's liberation movement, both in its hometown of Washington, D.C., and nationally. The Furies emerged in the early 1970s in a city with a thriving women's liberation movement that boasted the country's leading women's liberation newspaper, *off our backs.* However, in contrast to New York City's movement where lesbianism was broached well before the May 1970 Radicalesbian action, the D.C. women's liberation movement paid virtually no attention to it. In large part, this reflected the fact that radical feminists were the dominant voice in New York, whereas the D.C. movement remained very connected to the mainstream left and was much more comfortable blaming sexism on capitalism or imperialism, rather than on male dominance or men. D.C. women's liberationists, influenced by the efforts of the far-left group, the Weathermen, to eliminate vestiges of bourgeois sexuality, particularly marriage and mono-

gamy, were more intent on exploring nonmonogamy than lesbianism.

Several developments helped to change that point of view and to spark discussions of lesbianism in D.C., but of critical importance was the Black Panthers' Revolutionary People's Constitutional Convention (RPCC), which was held in Philadelphia in September 1970. It was there that D.C. feminists first encountered a number of New York Radicalesbians, among them the charismatic Rita Mae Brown and Martha Shelley. Shortly thereafter, the New York group dissolved, and Brown and another Radicalesbian, Cynthia Funk, relocated to D.C. The second RPCC was held in D.C. a little less than three months later, and once again a number of highly politicized lesbians, including poet Pat Parker, artist Wendy Cadden, poet Judy Grahn, and Nancy Adair, made a significant impression on some of the D.C. women. In the wake of the second RPCC, more D.C. women's liberationists, even some with long-standing allegiances to the left, became more curious about exploring the connections between feminism and lesbianism.

By the spring of 1971 two different groups were regularly meeting to discuss lesbianism. In May they merged and formed a working collective whose members included Charlotte Bunch, Joan Biren, Brown, Coletta Reid, Sharon Deevey, Ginny Berson, Helaine Harris, Lee Schwing, and Tasha Peterson. Nancy Myron and Jennifer Woodul were later asked to join the group. They called themselves "Those Women" because that was what many heterosexual feminists had taken to calling them. They changed their name to the Furies in January 1972 when they started publishing a newspaper by that name.

As their first action, the Furies decided to push the issue of lesbianism at a retreat for local women's liberation activists. At every workshop on the meeting's agenda, Furies hijacked the discussion and lectured the participants: if they were, in fact, serious about feminism, they would leave their husbands and boyfriends and come out. A full-scale verbal war ensued, and when the majority of women (including some lesbians) resisted their arguments, the Furies announced that they were no longer going to waste their time arguing the merits of lesbianism, they were leaving the women's movement. The Furies deployed the same logic, that the oppressed must organize outside of the earshot of the oppressor, which blacks had successively used with whites in the black freedom movement, and which women's liberationists had effectively used with men in the New Left. But this situation stood in marked contrast in that heterosexual feminists, unlike white civil-rights workers or New Leftists, could assume a new identity as lesbians and cast their lot with their more oppressed sisters—or so the Furies reasoned.

The Furies raised the issue of lesbianism in somewhat different terms than Radicalesbians had a year earlier. Both groups understood heterosexuality to be the linchpin in women's oppression, but while the New York group went out of its way to be conciliatory, the Furies adopted an antagonistic stance toward heterosexual feminists. Radicalesbians may have insinuated that lesbianism was the true feminist practice, but they had not accused heterosexual feminists of collaborating in their own (and other women's) oppression. The Furies viewed their lesbianism differently, as a way of ratcheting up the struggle against male supremacy. Women who came out, they reasoned, would no longer be dissuaded from fully resisting the system by the privileges accrued to them as heterosexual women. Lesbians would additionally destabilize capitalism because, in contrast to heterosexual women, they were generally not passive in the face of exploitive work conditions. The Furies made far more extravagant claims for lesbians than the Radicalesbians, who had only spoken vaguely of lesbianism's potential for creating a new consciousness among women. Many heterosexual feminists resented the way that the Furies defined lesbianism as the measure of one's feminism and heterosexuality as the measure of one's collaboration with the enemy. Some lesbians were also mistrustful of the Furies' interpretation of lesbianism, which seemed curiously disconnected from basic erotic desires and practices.

The Furies remained aloof from the larger D.C. women's movement, although they did organize a few educational and skills workshops, film screenings, and poetry readings. They restricted their theory workshop to lesbians, but advertised their skills workshops widely in alternative newspapers, the local women's center, black nationalist organizations, and laundromats in the predominantly black neighborhood where they lived. The skills workshops represented their attempt to empower women who were economically less privileged. Well-meaning though they were, the Furies did not always know very much about the manual skills they were teaching. One member recalls having to borrow books from the library to learn enough about electrical wiring to teach it.

The Furies had planned to connect a cadre of like-minded lesbians across the country, but this level of interaction never materialized. Nonetheless, through their newspaper, the Furies had a decided impact on the women's liberation movement. The Furies relished taking

**Furies.** Three of the women attending a meeting of the Furies working collective in the early 1970s sit on a futon on the living-room floor. [Joan E. Biren]

on movement pieties and shibboleths. They argued against the antileader line that was so prevalent in the women's movement at the time. They disagreed with women who argued that theory is "male" and should be avoided. And they took issue with those feminists who treated class differences as "man-made."

Among the Furies' most valuable contributions to second wave feminism was their effort to tackle the knotty problem of class differences among women. The Furies wrote about how class affects women's everyday interactions with one another and critiqued the practice of downward mobility among middle-class lesbians. They engaged in income pooling to help equalize members' financial situations, and they shared clothes, cars, and child-care duties. The Furies' thinking and writing on class could be reductive, as when they claimed that working-class women are more forthright and middle-class women more psychologically manipulative, but they nonetheless initiated a dialogue among women about an issue too long suppressed by the movement. One topic that was never on the table, however, was sex, which, according to one member, was simply assumed to be unproblematic for lesbians.

Although the Furies created a safe, albeit charged, space in which lesbians and feminists might discuss a number of critical issues, the group manufactured for itself a repressive environment in which internal dissent was quashed. Things came to a head when working-class women pushed for the expulsion of children from the collective on the grounds that as working-class women, they had spent their whole lives raising children and wanted nothing more to do with it. From that point on, a dynamic of internecine conflict developed. After the purge of several members, the group disbanded. The Furies lasted less than a year as a working collective, but several members continued to produce the group's newspaper until June 1973.

Reacting against the groups' insularity, a number of former members chose to work next on projects that reached out to lesbian and feminist communities. They were in the forefront of the mid-1970s movement to construct an alternative women's culture through the creation of record companies, publishing houses, schools, and credit unions. Ex-Furies members helped found Diana Press, Olivia Records, and Women in Distribution. In her capacity as a founding editor at the feminist journal *Quest,* Charlotte Bunch encouraged the development of such businesses, as did writer Rita Mae Brown in interviews and articles. Although the economic downturn of the 1970s and the difficulties women entrepreneurs faced ultimately did in most of their small businesses, the hope was that such ventures would not only lead to economic self-sufficiency for lesbians and feminists, but also to an expanded power base for the women's movement as its ideas and culture became more available to all women.

The Furies' redefinition of lesbianism as a political imperative helped to create a safe space for lesbians within the women's movement. Groups like the Furies that were unapologetically lesbian made it more possible for women to imagine themselves living independently of men. Their interest in addressing women's differences helped to lay the groundwork for more far-reaching discussions of difference in the 1980s. Yet in other ways, the Furies' conflation of lesbianism and feminism proved problematical as it encouraged some lesbians to subordinate their desires to the requirements of the movement. The pressure to conform to politically correct versions of sexuality that proscribed butch-femme or sadomasochistic practices helped to squelch frank discussions of sexuality within lesbian communities, and ultimately provoked a backlash in the 1980s as more and more lesbians began to "talk sex" honestly with one another, no matter how politically incorrect or "male-identified" their desires were perceived to be.

## Bibliography

Brown, Rita Mae. *A Plain Brown Rapper.* Baltimore: Diana Press, 1976.

Bunch, Charlotte. *Passionate Politics: Feminist Theory in Action, Essays, 1968–1986.* New York: St. Martin's Press, 1987.

Echols, Alice. *Daring to Be Bad: Radical Feminism in America, 1967–75.* Minneapolis: University of Minnesota Press, 1989.

Valk, Anne M. "Living a Feminist Lifestyle: The Intersection of Theory and Action in a Lesbian Feminist Collective." *Feminist Studies* 28, no. 2 (2002): 303–332.

**Alice Echols**

*See also* BROWN, RITA MAE; BUSINESSES; CLASS AND CLASS OPPRESSION; LESBIAN FEMINISM; OLIVIA RECORDS; RADICALESBIANS.

abcdef**g**hijklmnopqrstuvwxyz

# G

## GAY ACTIVISTS ALLIANCE

In the 1950s and the 1960s the politics of homosexuality was a modest, international effort dominated by leaders who emphasized similarities between homosexuals and heterosexuals. Then, the 1969 Stonewall Riots in Greenwich Village and their aftermath showed that impassioned community action could do more to advance freedom and equality.

During the last half of 1969 in Manhattan, radicals wanting to form alliances with existing revolutionary movements assembled a free-floating Gay Liberation Front (GLF). Leaders opting to focus on mobilizing a powerful sexual minority created a democratically structured Gay Activists Alliance (GAA, pronounced G, A, A). By devising new ways to embolden and to organize homosexuals, these rival groups with their spin-offs played a pivotal role in spawning the multifaceted LGBT movement that thrives today.

Both GLF and GAA encouraged activists in other locales to borrow their names and follow their leads. The Gay Activist Alliance formed a national LGB movement committee and dispatched its members to travel around the country helping others to start single-issue, democratically structured groups. These groups were locally based and independently run. Little research has been done on them. Most accounts of LGB political activity in the post-Stonewall years dwell on the influential founding group, which can be identified more precisely as GAA-New York.

Forging the way for GAA-New York were four young newcomers who had grown dissatisfied with the Gay Liberation Front. Jim Owles, a soft-spoken Midwesterner ousted from the Air Force for antiwar activity, objected that GLF's refusal to structure itself and its emphasis on consciousness-raising allowed strong members of the group to manipulate the weak. Marty Robinson, who had dropped out of Brooklyn College and become a countercultural carpenter, rebelled when GLFers showed no interest in the face-to-face challenges he considered essential to force politicians to speak out about LGB rights. Arthur Evans, whose free-thinking bent at Brown University had led him to graduate studies in philosophy at Columbia, joined a GLF study group on oppression, revolution, and liberation. But he concurred with his lover, Arthur Bell, director of publicity for children's books at Random House, that theorizing did little to improve well-being. Better to dramatize anti-LGB prejudice and discrimination in ways that would stir homosexuals to fend for themselves.

As in historic convocations of freedom-loving American revolutionaries held two centuries earlier, these 1960s-bred Founding Brothers brought different strengths to their politics. Robinson, with his personal confrontations, became a swift, self-righteous sword. Owles perfected his mastery of protest schemes. Evans mustered a compelling rhetorical voice. Bell was so skillful at publicizing their efforts that the *Village Voice* hired him to write a weekly column about the new LGB activism.

By combining bold moves, strong words, and passionately expressed anger with a sexy, sixties-style male charisma, this foursome and their followers gave homosexuality an unprecedented public face. As their headline-grabbing political theater became the toast of news-hungry Manhattan and beyond, the GAA swelled with fresh members who were convinced that homosexual liberation required something more—a vibrant new gay and lesbian culture.

## Institutionalizing an Uprising

The founders of GAA-New York believed that organization was the essential instrument for translating passions unleashed by the Stonewall riots into effective power. On 21 December 1969, they approved a constitution and by-laws. Introducing them was an eloquent preamble, written primarily by Evans, that wed politics to lifestyle. This preamble began, "WE AS LIBERATED HOMOSEXUAL ACTIVISTS demand the freedom for expression of our dignity and value as human beings through confrontation with and disarmament of all mechanisms which unjustly inhibit us: economic, social, and political."

This rhetoric of personal and political assertiveness in pursuit of homosexual freedom was original. So was the subsequent spelling out of demanded rights: "Before the public conscience, we demand an immediate end to all oppression of homosexuals and the immediate unconditional recognition of these basic rights:

"The right to our feelings . . . to feel attracted to the beauty of members of our own sex and to explore those feelings as truly our own . . .

"The right to love . . . to express our feelings in action . . . to make love with anyone, anyway, anytime, provided only that the action be freely chosen by all the persons concerned.

"The right to our own bodies . . . to treat and express our bodies as we will, to nurture them, to display them, to embellish them . . .

"The right to be persons . . . to express our individuality under the governance of laws justly made and executed."

Next came a specifying of tactical focus: "To secure these rights, we hereby institute the Gay Activists Alliance, which shall be completely and solely dedicated to their implementation and maintenance, repudiating at the same time violence (except for the right of self-defense) as unworthy of social protest, disdaining all ideologies, whether political or social, and forbearing alliance with any other organizations except for those whose concrete actions are likewise specifically dedicated."

Identifying GAA's strategic priority as community mobilization was a final way of acknowledging that power in a democracy stems ultimately from the consent and the contributions of concerned citizens. "It is, finally, to the imagination of oppressed homosexuals themselves that we commend consideration of these rights, upon whose actions alone depends all hope for the prospect of their lasting procurement." (This GAA constitution, and the other original documents quoted in this article, can be found in the GLBT archive listed in the bibliography.)

To make their group embody the participatory democracy it resolved to extend in society at large, GAA organized itself into committees and ran weekly membership meetings using *Robert's Rules of Order*. Decisions were made by majority rule. Members were required to pay dues and attend at least three general meetings every six months. Annual elections were held to choose five officers. Jim Owles, voted first president, presided over proliferating committees and packed meetings deftly enough to win a second term: By then he was twenty-four years old.

As its logo the group chose the Greek letter *lambda*, understood to be a symbol for wavelength in quantum physics. It was said to represent the dynamic energy that GAA would introduce to the politics of homosexuality.

## Theaters of Mobilization

During the euphoric first half of 1970, GAA-New York developed its signature tactic for, in the words of its constitution, confronting and disarming political "mechanisms which unjustly inhibit us." This tactic was dubbed "zapping." In order to force office-holders and candidates to take stands on legislation prohibiting job discrimination based on sexual orientation, for example, activists would infiltrate official public meetings and campaign events. One or two of them would interrupt routine proceedings by standing up or stepping forward to engage in some heated, in-your-face shouting of questions—"What do you think of employment rights for homosexuals, Mr. Mayor?" Ostentatiously, their associates would jot down uttered responses and brief observing reporters.

Since Mayor John Lindsay had done so much to help homosexuals during his first term, zapping him created a controversy that generated an enormous amount of publicity. Since getting publicity was one of their strategic priorities, GAA's zappers proceeded to target other prominent liberals, such as Democratic gubernatorial candidate Arthur Goldberg.

Symbolically speaking, a political "zap" required a scheme, a sword, a voice, and a pen (to produce dramatic first-person accounts for the burgeoning LGB press, in addition to standard publicity releases for mainstream media). The obvious agenda was to raise an issue of consequence. Its unspoken counterpart was to make news that would politicize and empower vast numbers of homosexuals who were believed to be fearful, inhibited, and apolitical because they had always felt politically powerless.

Early efforts to confront and disarm unjustly inhibiting "social" and "economic" mechanisms built upon the Stonewall precedent of impassioned protest. When the police interfered with locales in which homosexual men made sexual and social connections, they were challenged.

In February 1970, a GAA delegation confronted a local police inspector in New York about the dispatching of plainclothesmen to entrap patrons of the Continental Baths. A handout explained that the surest way to end such harassment lay in political organization. "The problem of the Continental is the problem of the bars, parks, etc. . . . We need representation, a body to make those in power sit up and listen and change the laws that constantly hammer that we're second rate citizens, when we're not."

Other political efforts ranged from marches and sit-ins to get-out-the-vote campaigns and lobbying. These, too, were spiced up with the theatrics perfected for "zaps." The month of March 1970 brought a police raid on an after-hours bar called the Snakepit. It resulted in 160 arrests for disorderly conduct as well as the impaling on a spiked fence of a Hispanic man trying to flee. GAA responded with a spirited rally in Sheridan Square followed by a boisterous march to the Charles Street precinct headquarters.

That summer, to show comparable concern about repeated arrests in the underclass hustling scenes populated by poor transvestites, among others, there was a determined trek to 42nd Street. Here GAAers were joined by radicalized lesbian feminists as well as members of GLF. Together they held an angry demonstration in Times Square.

All of these protest efforts were staged with a sensitivity for tone, performance, and politicizing impact borrowed from Broadway. But by 1971, the spotlight was shifting to GAAers who argued that liberation called for something more than political power. So-called cultural leaders wanted to promote more humane gay ways. They were out to construct a community that would be healthier, happier, more substantial, and more visible than the existing string of tryst-facilitating social networks and sex-laced subcultures.

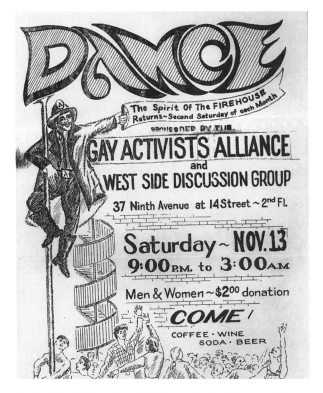

**Gay Activists Alliance.** The GAA, begun at about the same time as the more radical Gay Liberation Front, spread out around the country but is best known for its activities in New York, including events to promote "liberated gay culture." [Toby Marotta LGBT Archive/Photo by Carrie Marotta]

To raise what they called lifestyle issues, cultural leaders favored zapping culture-shaping institutions. In place of a sword and a voice, their schemes called for a whirl, a grin, and demonstrative affection, all designed to charm reporters into publicizing new possibilities for homosexual fulfillment.

When the city clerk threatened to ban "holy unions" being performed at a grassroots LGB church in Manhattan, cultural leaders saw an opening. Into his Municipal Building office popped robust public-school teacher Marc Rubin and his partner, Columbia graduate student Peter Fisher. They were accompanied by two other male couples and about thirty guests from GAA. All wore uniforms of the counterculture—brightly colored T-shirts with bell bottoms or jeans and, in many cases, long hair, headbands, and beads.

To upstage this public official's display of prejudice they threw a relaxed engagement party. While the affable hosts served coffee and doughnuts to members of his staff, their guests traipsed around the building inviting other office workers to join the celebration. The feted couples, holding hands, posed for photographs beside a large wedding cake. Atop it stood two sets of figurines, groom adoring groom, bride beaming at bride, icons personifying the frosted lambda and heart-enshrined endearment at their feet: "Gay Power to Gay Lovers." Photographs of this scene appeared in the 1971 Year in Pictures issue of *Life* magazine.

### Institutionalizing Lesbian Feminism

Within GAA-New York, the presence of lesbians did the most to highlight issues of lifestyle, culture, and community. Kay Tobin Lahusen had helped organize the group, and GAA attracted a handful of other talented women during its first year. Early in 1971, Nathalie Rockhill was named "chairman" of GAA's Community Relations Committee. Once "political leaders" accommodated "cultural leaders" by permitting them to organize "talk groups," Rockhill formed one to discuss making GAA more relevant to women.

But the floodgates to cultural innovation burst open in May of 1971, when GAA leased a vacant firehouse in SoHo to serve as its "community center." Now there was space for activities intended to build "liberated gay culture," beginning with sensibility-exploring dances, art work, research, and media presentations of various kinds. Following an International Lesbian Film Festival held at the end of 1971, GAA's membership voted not only to approve creation of a Lesbian Liberation Committee but also to strip its constitution and by-laws of their sexist language.

Before long, however, cultural leaders interested in personal growth, supportive ways of relating, and developing lesbian and gay culture expressed offense at the manipulation, backbiting, and compromises they found to be part and parcel of politics. And political leaders dismissed their critics for believing they could "dance their way to liberation."

A sign of changing times came when Jim Owles, at the end of his second term, was replaced by Rich Wandel, GAA's official photographer. Wandel described his leadership style as laissez faire. Most consequentially, the resulting frictions between men and women spurred the Lesbian Liberation Committee to incubate a reform-oriented philosophy of "lesbian feminism." In 1973, under the leadership of Jean O'Leary, this hybrid rationale for mobilizing lesbian women was institutionalized in a spin-off named Lesbian Feminist Liberation, Inc.

By this time activists of every stripe were leaving GAA-New York to form or to join groups that better reflected their individual political or cultural interests. As a pace-setter, GAA reached its end in the fall of 1973,

when Bruce Voeller, Wandel's successor as president, resigned and organized the National Gay Task Force.

### Well-Trained Leaders and Trailblazing Books

In its heyday, GAA-New York established affiliate groups in other boroughs of Manhattan and on Long Island. It promoted its model of a LGB-issues-only, democratically structured organization in correspondence, consultations, and conferences. It even dispatched teams of organizers to cities in the Midwest and the South.

Groups with GAA's name and agenda were started in several other locales, but the group's lasting influence was much more broadly based. Slowly but surely, GAA-New York's personal, political, and cultural innovations, down to routine public and private use of terms such as "liberated," "gay," "activist," "community," "zap," "action," "gay power," "gay culture," "lesbian," and "lesbian feminist" became popular new standards for LGB militancy. This change occurred partly because GAA-New York was well-promoted in the mainstream media with a steady stream of eye-catching publicity. But it was also because GAA gave rise to offshoot enterprises crafted by experienced alumni and alumnae. In addition to organizing well-structured lesbian and gay groups with specialized missions, former GAA-New York members wrote dozens of groundbreaking books that inspired others to follow their lead.

### Bibliography

Bell, Arthur. *Dancing the Gay Lib Blues: A Year in the Homosexual Liberation Movement.* New York: Simon & Schuster, 1971.

Fisher, Peter. *The Gay Mystique: The Myth and Reality of Male Homosexuality.* New York: Stein and Day, 1972.

Kantrowitz, Arnie. *Under the Rainbow: Growing Up Gay.* New York: Morrow, 1977.

Marotta, Toby. *The Politics of Homosexuality: How Lesbians and Gay Men Have Made Themselves a Political and Social Force in Modern America.* Boston: Houghton Mifflin, 1981.

———. GLBT Archive.

Russo, Vito. *The Celluloid Closet: Homosexuality in the Movies.* New York: Harper and Row, 1981.

Silverstein, Charles, and Edmund White. *The Joy of Gay Sex: An Intimate Guide for Gay Men to the Pleasure of a Gay Lifestyle.* New York: Crown Publishers, 1977.

Teal, Donn. *The Gay Militants.* New York: Stein and Day, 1971.

Tobin, Kay, and Randy Wicker. *The Gay Crusaders.* New York: Paperback Library, 1972.

Vida, Ginny, ed. *Our Right to Love: A Lesbian Resource Book.* Englewood Cliffs, N.J.: Prentice Hall, 1978.

**Toby Marotta**

See also BOOZER, MELVIN; GAY LIBERATION FRONT; GITTINGS, BARBARA, AND KAY TOBIN LAHUSEN; LESBIAN FEMINISM OWLES, JIM; STONEWALL RIOTS; TELEVISION.

**GAY AMERICAN INDIANS.** see NATIVE AMERICAN LGBTQ ORGANIZATIONS AND PUBLICATIONS.

# GAY AND LESBIAN ALLIANCE AGAINST DEFAMATION (GLAAD)

The Gay and Lesbian Alliance Against Defamation arose from frustration and turmoil within the gay movement surrounding media portrayal of the AIDS crisis. Earlier gay rights organizations had protested negative media depictions of homosexuals, but none had concentrated exclusively on the media until the founding of GLAAD. The organization began in the summer of 1985 when New York tabloids increasingly portrayed AIDS as a fitting punishment for homosexual behavior. The *New York Post* repeatedly referred to gay clubs as "AIDS dens" (11 September 1985, p. 35) and "sex dens" (26 October 1985, p. 1) and gay men as "desperate . . . without families" (12 November, 1985, p. 1). Editorial cartoons depicted "AIDS dragons" threatening children, perpetuating concern over the epidemic and fear of gays and lesbians.

An October 1985 article in the gay magazine *Christopher Street* called for a campaign aimed at media reform. In response, gay and lesbian activists gathered at the home of gay writer Darryl Yates Rist and established the Gay and Lesbian Anti-Defamation League, patterned on the Anti-Defamation League of B'nai B'rith. After B'nai B'rith objected to the name and threatened a lawsuit, however, the organization changed the name to the Gay and Lesbian Alliance Against Defamation or GLAAD.

The new organization began building a base of support at a "town meeting" in Greenwich Village on 14 November 1985, where nearly seven hundred gays and lesbians met to vent their anger over media handling of the AIDS crisis. GLAAD introduced itself to the media outside the offices of the *New York Post* two weeks later when some five hundred angry protesters picketed and hurled yellow rags at its entrance. Organizers cited twenty articles from the newspaper's editorial pages that associated gay men and lesbians with "every form of perversion known to man" (Darrell Yates Rist quoted by Freiberg, p. 16). GLAAD also protested *National Review* publisher William F. Buckley after his call for a mandatory tattoo to identify people with AIDS. Buckley later disavowed the proposal and acknowledged the successes of safe-sex campaigns to combat AIDS.

Though GLAAD made considerable inroads into the New York media establishment in the mid-1980s, the organization was virtually unknown elsewhere. In the spring of 1987 gay activist and lawyer Craig Davidson began transforming the organization into a professional media advocacy group that could confront homophobic depictions of gays on a broader scale. GLAAD established a central office and hired full-time staff. A year later it established a semi-independent Los Angeles office that focused on powerful executives in the motion picture industry. GLAAD envisioned a two-pronged approach: local affiliates would be organized to protest antigay media depictions and, at the same time, it would reward and encourage positive portrayals in film, television, radio, magazines, books, and music with annual achievement awards. From the beginning, GLAAD was dedicated to the fair and accurate media representation of LGBT people, as well as to providing accurate information to the media regarding the LGBT community and promoting LGBT visibility.

In New York City, membership quickly surged from five hundred to five thousand and GLAAD's mailing list swelled to ten thousand. A "phone tree" triggered a deluge of telephone calls, letters, and postcards aimed at offending outlets. A well-organized network of local chapters was established by 1993 to monitor media in New York, Los Angeles, Atlanta, Dallas, Denver, Kansas City, San Diego, San Francisco, and Washington, D.C., which provided GLAAD with a ready cadre of protesters who could react to the slightest media misstep.

One of the organization's earliest successes came in 1988 after comedian Bob Hope used the term "fag" on NBC's *Tonight Show*. Following angry objections from GLAAD, Hope agreed to produce a public service announcement condemning antigay violence. In addition, the organization published a *Media Guide to the Lesbian and Gay Community* to promote fair and accurate coverage in the news media. By 1992, GLAAD was seen as an effective force among media leaders. *Entertainment Weekly* listed it among the 100 "Most Powerful Entities in Hollywood." Two years later, the chapter structure was essentially disbanded in favor of a national organization headquartered in New York and Los Angeles.

By the late 1990s, GLAAD had evolved from the grassroots collection of volunteer activists that provided its foundation in 1985 into a professional, savvy media-advocacy organization. A series of directors led the organization through the mid-1990s until Joan Garry took the helm in 1997. A former executive at Showtime, Garry drew upon seventeen years in the entertainment industry to establish important connections with media heavyweights. Within four years, GLAAD's staff more than doubled and its annual budget rose to $4 million.

With its growth and continuing inroads into the mass media, critics inside and outside the gay community began to question whether its success would distract the organization from its activist roots. Scott Seomin, a former media relations director for *Entertainment Tonight* and E! Network, became its director of entertainment media in 1998, succeeding Chastity Bono, the lesbian daughter of singers Sonny and Cher, who became embroiled in a high-profile uproar over *Ellen*, network televison's first primetime program with an openly gay leading character. With Garry and Seomin at the helm, GLAAD's direction appeared to shift from the news media toward Hollywood's film and music industries.

As it entered the new millennium, GLAAD increasingly had to maintain its watchful stance with many of the powerful media outlets with whom it had relationships and was supposed to monitor. Concerns arose over its dependence on corporate contributions to fuel its burgeoning annual budget. An uproar erupted in 1997 when GLAAD accepted a $10,000 donation from Joseph Coors Brewing Company, a company with a long history of supporting right-wing organizations. Coors had been the target of a gay and lesbian boycott over the company's support of conservative, antigay causes. GLAAD's donor list also included such media heavyweights as NBC, CBS, *Time* magazine, Warner Brothers, and the music giant EMI.

The unified front among gay and lesbian media activists during the early stages of the AIDS crisis gave way a decade later to splintering and disharmony among LGBT activists in GLAAD's second decade. With its success in raising public consciousness about the negative media images that had haunted gays and lesbians for decades, GLAAD faced broader criticism over its mission and its strategies. The organization successfully challenged antigay talk show host Dr. Laura Schlesinger in 2001 by lobbying advertisers to drop the show, but critics were divided over its strategies. Gay writer Michelangelo Signorile, for example, questioned whether the organization failed to pursue its mission by not demanding that Paramount Television abandon the program before it hit the air. Other critics questioned whether the organization had trampled upon the talk show host's right to free speech by pressuring advertisers into silencing her. Gay writer Michael Bronski questioned whether GLAAD's strategies indicated that the organization had lost its way.

GLAAD's success and spectacular growth produced complicated conflicts over its mission, its strategies, and its future. The organization was called upon by the LGBT community to navigate tricky social and political issues arising from increased media visibility that GLAAD had helped perpetuate. As of 2003, it continues its demands for more positive LGBT media images, but it is hard pressed to insist on images that are exclusively positive. At the same time, the organization remains vigilant against active homophobia that often lurks beneath a thin veneer of corporate liberalism. As it moves forward, GLAAD grapples with the age-old debate: how the free speech of others should be limited as GLAAD protects its own freedom to speak for the LGBT community.

## Bibliography

Alwood, Edward. *Straight News: Gays, Lesbians and the News Media.* New York: Columbia University Press, 1996.

Bronski, Michael. "GLAAD—the Gay and Lesbian Alliance Against Defamation—Has Lost Its Way." *The [Boston] Phoenix*, 6–13 September 2001.

France, David. "Tuning Out Dr. Laura: Do the Fierce Protests against Her New TV Talk Show Violate the Shock Doc's First Amendment Rights?" *Newsweek*, 11 September 2000.

Freiberg, Peter. "Gays Protest NY Post Homophobia." *Advocate* 1 (December 1986): 16.

Gross, Larry. *Up From Invisibility: Lesbians, Gay Men, and the Media In America.* New York: Columbia University Press, 2001.

Kirk, Marshall, and Hunter Madsen. *After the Ball: How America Will Conquer Its Fear and Hatred of Gays in the 90's.* New York: Plume, 1989. *New York Post*, 11 September–12 November 1985.

**Edward M. Alwood**

*See also* AIDS AND PEOPLE WITH AIDS; COMMUNITY CENTERS; FILM AND VIDEO; HOMOPHOBIA AND HETEROSEXISM; RUSSO, VITO; TELEVISION.

**GAY AND LESBIAN INDEPENDENT SCHOOL TEACHERS' NETWORK.** see GAY, LESBIAN, AND STRAIGHT EDUCATION NETWORK (GLSEN).

## GAY COMMUNITY NEWS

*Gay Community News* (*GCN*), published as a weekly periodical in Boston from 1973 to 1992, was its era's most influential radical LGBT newspaper in the United States and a virtual training school for dozens of significant LGBT activists and writers. Founded as a locally-oriented mimeographed newsletter in the heyday of gay liberation and lesbian feminism, *GCN* quickly turned itself into a 16- to 24-page printed newspaper with a national and international reputation and readership. Over time, the newspaper committed itself not only to LGBT liberation but also to feminism, antiracism, multiculturalism, class transformation, prisoners' liberation, the fight against AIDS, and other leftist causes. These politics were reflected in many, though certainly not all, of its news stories, features, editorial columns, and letters to the editor. Often serving as a forum for dialogue between liberals and radicals in LGBT movements and communities, *GCN* proudly distanced itself from more conservative and more commercial LGBT publications, most especially the Los Angeles–based *Advocate.*

*GCN* prided itself on, and was supported by many of its readers because of, its coverage of controversial LGBT issues, diverse LGBT communities, and progressive social change movements. LGBT debates about pornography, sadomasochism, intergenerational sex, and relationship violence, for example, were all featured in the newspaper's pages. To a greater extent than most other LGBT newspapers, *GCN* included substantial coverage of (and significant contributions by) African American, Asian American, Native American, Latina/Latino, transgender, disabled, and working-class communities. And *GCN* embraced multi-issue leftist politics, making links between LGBT liberation and other progressive movements and providing critical coverage of what it considered mainstream, commercial, and assimilationist LGBT politics.

*GCN's* radicalism was also reflected in its unusual organizational structure. The paper was run as a non-hierarchical and democratic collective of staff members, who received equal (and always low) wages. Unlike most LGBT newspapers, which featured either exclusively female or predominantly male staff, *GCN* strove for gender parity and often had more female staff than male. While some regarded the Managing Editor (later the Coordinating Editor) as the first among equals, in theory and oftentimes in practice the person occupying this position had the same degree of power as did the typesetter, the office manager, the advertising staff, the art director, the staff writers, and the other editors. In turn, the staff was answerable to the *GCN* Membership, which consisted of all active volunteers (oftentimes numbering in the dozens), and a volunteer Board of Directors. In the early 1980s, *GCN's* structure became even more unusual when it was reorganized (primarily for tax and fund-raising purposes) as a nonprofit corporation, the Bromfield Street Educational Foundation, which also sponsored the Lesbian and Gay Prisoner Project and, later, the OutWrite conference of LGBT writers.

*GCN's* historical significance lies not only in its content and structure, but also in its role in inspiring and building an influential network of LGBT leaders, activists,

and writers. Former *GCN* staff members include Richard Burns (longtime director of the New York LGBT community center), Kevin Cathcart (who later headed Gay and Lesbian Advocates and Defenders and Lambda Legal Defense), Sue Hyde (who later directed the Privacy Project at the National Gay and Lesbian Task Force), Eric Rofes (who later headed the Shanti Project in San Francisco and the Los Angeles LGBT community center), and Urvashi Vaid (who later led the National Gay and Lesbian Task Force). Other *GCN* alumni include independent intellectual Michael Bronski, *Advocate* reporter Chris Bull, writer Amy Hoffman, writer Neil Miller, literary critic Chris Nealon, sociologist Cindy Patton, writer Elizabeth Pincus, writer Wickie Stamps, and historian Marc Stein.

Over the long term, *GCN* faced several major challenges that weakened its chances for survival. Operating in the increasingly conservative political environment of the 1970s and 1980s, *GCN* suffered a major setback when its offices, shared by the newspaper *Fag Rag* and the bookstore Glad Day, were destroyed by arson in 1982. *GCN* also faced increased local competition when a less unique but more commercially successful LGBT newspaper, *Bay Windows,* was founded in Boston (winning over most local LGBT advertisers), and when the *Advocate* increasingly came to be regarded as the main national LGBT periodical (helping it secure most national LGBT advertisers). *GCN* contributed to this particular problem by never quite abandoning its local Boston orientation, while also attempting to position itself as a newspaper with national reach. Perennial conflict among staff members and volunteers, invariably passionate about their politics and not inclined to be practical about compromises, damaged *GCN's* ability to survive in difficult times. Poor pay and long hours contributed to staff retention problems, while long-standing policies such as the one requiring staff collective approval for all editorials meant that the newspaper only rarely even attempted to publish editorials. Always dependent primarily on subscription rather than advertising income (a rarity in the LGBT newspaper world), *GCN* had a subscriber base that peaked at approximately 4,000 in the 1980s but then declined. In 1992 *GCN* suspended publication. It reappeared thereafter as an occasional newspaper or quarterly magazine, ceasing publication several years later. *GCN's* demise, occurring in the same general period that witnessed the end of Toronto's *Body Politic* and San Francisco's *Outlook* and the increased popularity of the *Advocate* and *Out,* signaled for many a conservative turn in LGBT communities, movements, and media and a narrowing of the LGBT political spectrum.

## Bibliography

Alwood, Edward. *Straight News: Gays, Lesbians, and the News Media.* New York: Columbia University Press, 1996.

Bronski, Michael. *Culture Clash: The Making of Gay Sensibility.* Boston: South End Press, 1984.

Bronski, Michael. *The Pleasure Principle: Sex, Backlash, and the Struggle for Gay Freedom.* New York: St. Martin's Press, 1998.

Hoffman, Amy. *Hospital Time.* Durham, N.C.: Duke University Press, 1997.

Marcus, Eric. *Making History: The Struggle for Gay and Lesbian Equal Rights, 1945–1990.* New York: HarperCollins, 1992.

Streitmatter, Rodger. *Unspeakable: The Rise of the Gay and Lesbian Press in America.* Boston: Faber and Faber, 1995.

Vaid, Urvashi. *Virtual Equality: The Mainstreaming of Gay and Lesbian Liberation.* New York: Anchor Books, 1995.

**Marc Stein**

*See also* BOSTON; NEWSPAPERS AND MAGAZINES.

# GAY, LESBIAN, AND STRAIGHT EDUCATION NETWORK (GLSEN)

Founded in 1990, the Gay, Lesbian, and Straight Education Network (GLSEN) became the largest and most visible organization working to end bias against LGBT people in U.S. schools. As of 2003, GLSEN has over thirty employees in three national offices (in New York, San Francisco, and Washington D.C.), over eighty community-based chapters, and over twelve hundred school-based gay/straight alliances.

## Expanding Scope

GLSEN, first established in Boston, was initially named the Gay and Lesbian Independent School Teachers' Network in Massachusetts. Kevin Jennings, then a high school social studies teacher, formed the volunteer support group in response to the pervasive isolation he perceived among gay and lesbian teachers. In 1991 the teachers renamed themselves the Gay and Lesbian School Teachers Network (GLSTN) and chose to broaden the scope of their work from supporting teachers to advocating for school reform.

One of the early successes of GLSTN involved collaborations with the newly elected Massachusetts governor, William Weld. In part to thank LGBT communities for their electoral support, Weld established a Commission on Gay and Lesbian Youth in 1992, charged with writing a set of recommendations to, among other things, address the disproportionately high rates of suicide and harm among LGBT youth. With significant involvement of GLSTN members, the Education Committee of the commission held hearings, conducted research, and produced a document, "Making Schools Safe for Gay and Lesbian Youth." In 1993 the Massachusetts Board of Education adopted its key recommendations, and GLSTN was hired to develop teacher training for Safe Schools for Gay and Lesbian Students, the first state-sponsored program in the United States aimed at ending homophobia in schools.

## Nationwide Outreach

In 1994 GLSTN became a nonprofit organization, hired Jennings as its executive director, and opened its first national office in New York City. To acknowledge the involvement of its heterosexual allies, it changed its name to the Gay, Lesbian, and Straight Teachers Network. In the years that followed, community-based chapters began forming and GLSTN became increasingly involved in struggles to change homophobic practices and policies throughout the United States.

In 1996 the struggle of Salt Lake City, Utah, students interested in forming gay/straight alliances (that is, student organizations dedicated to challenging anti-LGBT bias) gained national attention. Their school board, prohibited from discriminating against them, opted to end all extracurricular student organizations rather than permit the existence of student gay-straight alliances. GLSTN supported the students in their struggle against the school board. In 1997 GLSTN held its first national conference in Salt Lake City, drawing continued attention to this struggle. That same year, GLSTN changed its name to the Gay, Lesbian, and Straight Education Network (GLSEN), reflecting its ongoing evolution from supporting teachers to advocating for broader educational change.

To document the struggle in Utah as well as other historic struggles against homophobia, GLSEN co-produced a video in 1998 titled *Out of the Past: The Struggle for Gay and Lesbian Rights in America,* directed by Jeffrey Dupre. In 1997 GLSEN also began releasing annual Report Cards of school districts' protective and inclusive policies (or lack thereof), and, in 1998, School Climate Surveys based on data collected from students throughout the United States.

## Mainstreaming

In 1999 GLSEN helped to form a coalition of ten mainstream educational and mental health organizations (including the American Federation of Teachers and the American Psychological Association) that endorsed a publication called *Just the Facts about Sexual Orientation and Youth: A Primer for Principals, Educators, and School Personnel.* This publication, distributed to school administrators across the country, presented research that refuted the myths perpetuated by the growing number of therapies and ministries claiming to repair or transform a person's sexual orientation.

In 2000 GLSEN worked with community-based groups in Oregon to defeat a ballot initiative that would have prohibited any attempt to promote—with "promote" broadly construed—homosexuality in schools, including lessons on LGBT people and on challenging homophobia. To date, GLSEN has successfully lobbied for state legislation protecting LGBT students from discrimination and harassment in California, Connecticut, Massachusetts, Minnesota, New Jersey, Vermont, Washington state, and Wisconsin.

In 2001 GLSEN partnered with MTV to launch its Fight for Your Rights: Take a Stand Against Discrimination campaign, which was the largest-ever public education campaign against anti-LGBT bias. In 2002 GLSEN assisted the National Education Association, the nation's largest professional employee association, in adopting policies favoring the creation of schools that are safe and hospitable for LGBT students and employees. The same year GLSEN coordinated the seventh annual national Day of Silence protest in which over 150,000 students on over 1,700 campuses took a vow of silence to protest the silencing of LGBT people (see sidebar).

**Political Tensions**

According to its mission statement, GLSEN strives to ensure that each member of every school community is valued and respected, regardless of sexual orientation or gender identity and expression. The evolution of GLSEN's mission and work has not been free of criticism from both inside and outside the organization. In its early years, GLSEN's shift from supporting teachers to advocating for broader school change raised criticisms that it was abandoning teachers who had few other places, if any, to go for support. In the later 1990s, as GLSEN developed initiatives to support student leaders, a group of youth formed a Youth Empowerment Initiative within GLSEN to advocate for a bigger role by youth in the organization. As a result, GLSEN added young people to its board of directors and created a student organizing department.

The intersections of various social inequities have been another source of tension. GLSEN's mission statement has always acknowledged the adverse impact of racism in schools, but advocates have suggested that more needs to be done to address the parallels between racism and homophobia, as well as racism within LGBT com-

**cards handed out during GLSEN's 2002 day of silence:**

"Please understand my reasons for not speaking today. I support lesbian, gay, bisexual, and transgender rights. People who are silent today believe that laws and attitudes should be inclusive of people of all sexual orientations. The Day of Silence is to draw attention to those who have been silenced by hatred, oppression, and prejudice. Think about the voices you are not hearing. What can you do to end the silence?"

munities. Advocates have also suggested that more attention needs to be paid to the connections between homophobia and gender role conformity. Consequently, GLSEN added "gender identity/expression" to its mission statement in 2000. Advocates have even suggested that GLSEN needs to engage more actively in struggles that do not seem, on the surface, directly related to LGBT issues in education, such as other LGBT issues, other educational issues, and other social justice issues. These tensions should not be surprising, given the disagreement that exists even among educational researchers about what it means to challenge anti-LGBT bias in schools.

**Bibliography**

Gay, Lesbian, and Straight Education Network Website. http://www.glsen.org.

Jennings, Kevin, ed. *One Teacher in Ten: Gay and Lesbian Educators Tell Their Stories.* Boston: Alyson Publications, 1994.

                                    **Kevin K. Kumashiro**

*See also* EDUCATION; EDUCATION LAW AND POLICY; EMPLOYMENT LAW AND POLICY; SEX EDUCATION.

# GAY LIBERATION

The term "gay liberation" refers both to the type of LGBT politics that flourished in the late 1960s and early 1970s and to a form of LGBT politics that has persisted since that time. New York City's Gay Liberation Front (GLF), founded in 1969 in the immediate aftermath of the Stonewall Riots, was very much a gay liberation organization, but so too was Queer Nation, a group that burst into a frenzy of activity some thirty years after the birth of the GLF. This does not mean that gay liberation organizations have maintained a strongly rooted, historical sense of continuity. The connections between the first wave of gay liberation politics and the individuals and organizations that have followed in their wake are more often than not unwitting. Nonetheless, gay liberationists share some essential features. They were and are confrontational in tactics and rhetoric, suspicious of formal political remedies, and concerned with defining and building gay identity and community.

The original gay liberation movement—which lasted from the late 1960s to the early 1970s—resulted in quantitative and qualitative changes in LGBT politics. Gay liberation groups supplanted the homophile groups—such as the Mattachine Society and the Daughters of Bilitis (DOB)—that preceded them. Within a few short years of the advent of gay liberation, the social and political landscape was fundamentally altered. As late as 1969 there were only fifty homophile organizations; though active, their reach was limited. By the early 1970s there were literally hundreds of organizations with tens of thousands of active members. While demonstrations organized by homophile groups rarely had more than one hundred participants, thousands marched in 1970 to commemorate the Stonewall Riots, which had become a rallying symbol for the gay liberation movement. By the mid-1970s "gay pride" marches were held in most major American cities.

## LGBT Politics

The tone and rhetoric of LGBT politics was significantly altered by gay liberation activists. Unlike most homophiles, gay liberationists advocated public disclosure of one's sexual identity. "Coming out," a key term of gay liberationist LGBT culture, meant making a public statement that forcefully injected the personal into the political. Though not without vocal spokespersons, the homophile movement pursued change without significantly challenging the values of mainstream society. Homophiles sought equal access to the key institutions of American life. Gay liberationists sought to reconstruct, if not destroy, those very institutions; their goal was radical transformation, not amelioration.

In general, gay liberationists were dismissive or unaware of the work of homophile activists. Many of those who joined gay liberationist groups were new to LGBT politics. Those who were aware of the homophile groups saw them as painfully accommodationist. The Mattachine Society, for example, was called the "NAACP of our movement," a comparison that was not meant as a compliment. Like the NAACP, the homophiles were condemned for their willingness to pursue political change through the use of the courts and other formal institutions of power. In a 1969 article San Francisco activist Leo Laurence denounced local homophile activists as members of "good grey organization[s] . . . and as such an obstacle to the Gay Liberation Movement's construction of an alternative that truly serves and liberates its people" (Armstrong, p.64). Though not himself a young man at the time, Laurence's cutting metaphoric use of "grey" played to the era's celebration of all things youthful and sharply highlighted the generational tensions at work.

For their own part, many of the homophiles were unimpressed with the leftist rhetoric and radical pose of gay liberation activists. To them, the gay liberationist's willingness to embrace the whirlwind of late 1960s politics and culture seemed misguided at best. New York's *Mattachine Newsletter* claimed that during the Stonewall Riots "queens were almost outnumbered by Black Panthers, Yippies, Crazies, and young toughs from New Jersey. The exploiters had moved in and they were using the gay power movement for their own ends." The homophile activists feared that gay liberationists would undermine their hard work; that their sacrifices often went unrecognized was salt for the wound. Despite the uneasy relations between the two political generations, homophile activists provided critical resources that helped fuel the growth of gay liberation. New York's GLF, for instance, emerged from meetings that the Mattachine Society and Daughters of Bilitis helped organize.

Gay liberationists drew inspiration from the Black Power, second-wave feminist, and antiwar movements of the late 1960s and early 1970s. Much of the political discourse of gay liberation was lifted almost verbatim from the New Left. The sexual and gender politics generated by feminists were especially important in shaping the ideas of gay activists, but gay liberationists were inspired by many of the revolutionary currents raging through the country. A 1969 GLF manifesto, for example, proclaimed, "Babylon has forced us to commit ourselves to one thing—revolution!" Gay liberation was as much a rejection of contemporary liberal values as it was an attack on conservative homophobes. Martha Shelley, an active member of New York's GLF, railed against what she saw as the limitations of liberal tolerance. "Liberalism" she wrote, "isn't good enough for us." Gay liberationists rejected the idea that the goal of LGBT politics should be acceptance. They wanted fundamental change in American social, cultural, and political life.

Gay liberationists sought to link their struggles to those of other new social movement activists. In his oft-reprinted "A Gay Manifesto," published in 1970, Carl Wittman called for an alliance with "straights" working for radical change. Such an alliance, Wittman argued, was both tactically wise and made necessary by the complex web of affiliations that existed among sixties radicals.

"Many of us," he noted, "have mixed identities, and have ties with other liberation movements: women, blacks, other minority groups. We may also have taken on an identity which is vital to us: ecology, dope, ideology. And face it: we can't change Amerika alone." Gay liberation activists were visible at antiwar demonstrations, attended New Left conferences and gatherings where they sought to shape movement politics, and relied on contacts in the alternative press to disseminate manifestos to a broad audience. However, Wittman's hopes for a grand alliance were misplaced, wrecked by the homophobia of many putative allies. Despite a rocky relationship with straight activists, gay liberationists did make use of the social networks within the counterculture, New Left, and other new social movements to expand their reach and amplify their message.

## Gender Division

The gay liberation movement was also deeply split by divisions along gender lines. Membership in the GLF and other groups was dominated by men who in turn tended to dominate the political agenda. Debates over representation, goals, and group process became focal points for fights between gay men and lesbians. Most women who were active in gay liberation groups quickly gravitated to the rapidly growing women's movement and the developing lesbian feminist movement. Del Martin, a cofounder of the DOB, expressed many of these women's feelings in a scathing letter she wrote in 1970, entitled "If That's All There Is." This document captures the gender tensions and generational displacement that occurred within LGBT politics. In her statement Martin lambasts "the male chauvinists of the homophile movement," calling them "grandfathers" who "cling to their old ideas and their old values in a time that calls for radical change." But Martin also denounces gay liberationists who in their youthful zeal replicate the sins of their fathers. "Like the tired old men they berate," she wrote, "they have not come to grips with the gut issues. Until they do, *their* revolution cannot be ours." Though many LGBT activists continued to aspire to create a political movement that would accommodate both men and women, the gender splits of the early 1970s persisted throughout the decade. It was only the threat of the New Right—exemplified by the Moral Majority and Anita Bryant's Save Our Children crusade—and the deadly impact of HIV that reforged bridges that had been broken.

## Challenging Homophobia

Despite frequent calls for the overthrowing of "Amerika," most gay liberationist activity was not literally revolutionary. Activists worked on creating a visible gay culture and on challenging homophobic practices and ideas. They engaged in aggressive, theatrical, cultural politics, a testament to the influence of the tactics of the Yippies and other counterculture radicals. Tommi Avicolli-Mecca described the members of Philadelphia's GLF, which was modeled on the New York City group, as a "rowdy, radical bunch." Many of them—like Avicolli-Mecca, who came out while attending Temple University—were students and they used the university as a forum. The Philadelphia GLF ran a man for homecoming queen, made classroom presentations, and sponsored dances. The group "made headlines regularly because we were visible and defiant." The insistence on visibility, the challenge of authority, and the eagerness to transgress gender and sexual norms were all hallmarks of gay liberation politics. While the rhetoric of the period seems, from a distance, to be overblown and even hysterical, it may well have enabled and described the process of making public matters that had been carefully maintained in secrecy.

Gay liberation activists challenged various homophobic institutions and discourses. One of the key targets was the psychiatric definition of homosexuality as a sickness. In 1970 Chicago's GLF published a leaflet that attacked the heterosexism of the medical profession. The problem, GLF said, was not with the "patient" but with society: "A psychiatrist who allows a homosexual patient—who has been subject to a barrage of anti-homosexual sentiments his whole life—to continue in the belief that heterosexuality is superior to homosexuality, is the greatest obstacle to his patient's health and well-being." Avicolli-Mecca recalls that the Philadelphia GLF "succeeded in stopping the university from referring queer students to an aversion-therapy program at a local psychiatric institution where they were strapped with electrodes and zapped with electricity when shown pictures of naked men." Activists protested at the meetings of the American Psychiatric Association (APA), demanding that homosexuality be struck from the profession's *Diagnostic and Statistical Manual*. In 1973 the APA did just that; other health care associations followed suit. It should be noted that a number of former homophile activists, who had been working on challenging psychiatric definitions and treatment of LGBT people, were active in this process. Despite very real tensions and divisions between political generations in the LGBT movement, there were points of continuity.

## "Out of the Closet"

One of the fundamental shifts in LGBT politics and culture that gay liberation activists helped bring about was the rejection of the "double life" of secrecy and denial that had characterized much of LGBT life since World War II. "Out of the Closet and into the Streets" was the war cry of the new wave of political activism. Variations on the phrase "coming out" provided the title for anthologies, manifestos, and street demonstration slogans. While the homophile movement did not—for very good reasons—call on LGBT people to publicly disclose their sexual identity, gay liberationists made this act a cornerstone of their movement. The fact that gay liberationists were alienated from the political and cultural values of "Amerika" made this strategy available in a way that it had not been for the homophiles. The threat of being barred from public service jobs, being rejected for military service, or facing public disapproval was no longer effective. Activists who carried placards that read "Suck Cock to Beat the Draft" at antiwar rallies were not easily intimidated by the fear of disclosure and official sanction.

Until the late 1960s "coming out" implied acknowledging one's sexual desires and entering into the LGB world. But this knowledge was not to be shared outside the boundaries of this closely guarded, private realm. Gay liberationists rejected the public–private division that structured gay life. Like radical feminists they believed that the personal was political. Coming out was a political act that transformed what was characterized as a damaged personality trait into a positive social identity modeled on the idea of a gender or ethnic identity. This willful act of pride (note the persistence of the term "pride" in LGBT culture since the 1960s) functioned to build community and produce a transformation of social values. Community building through the declaration of sexual identity was one of the keys to gay liberation's success. It was a strategy that appealed to men and women who did not necessarily share the leftist politics of the more radical members of the movement. Gay liberation's embrace of identity politics unleashed an outpouring of passionate self-discovery and reinvention for hundreds of thousands of men and women.

## Decline of the Left

Ironically, the rapid expansion of a visible "out and proud" LGBT community helped to undermine the influence of the first wave of gay liberation activists. Unlike members of GLF, most gay men and women did not seek the overthrow of capitalism. And as the United States began to pull soldiers out of the Vietnam War, the antiwar movement and the radicalism it sustained ebbed. As the number of venues for gay men and lesbian's social and cultural expression expanded, the need to challenge society's rules and regulations diminished. The pleasures of the rapidly expanding LGBT world, typified by the emer-

gence of neighborhoods like the Castro in San Francisco, were a powerful lure; it was more fun to go to a bathhouse or a street fair than to attend a lengthy meeting—which is not to say that meetings were devoid of erotic possibilities. Increasingly, LGBT rights groups adopted the strategies and tactics of single-issue, civil rights organizations, with a focus on legal remedies and media activism aimed at the dominant cultural arbiters. This was an agenda that more closely resembled the homophile movements.

But gay liberation's emphasis on visibility and community building persists, marking a fundamental shift in LGBT political culture. And the oppositional spirit of the GLF did not completely disappear. Even "mainstream" organizations such as the National Lesbian and Gay Task Force went through periods in which, according to one-time Task Force member John D'Emilio, "marginality and outsider status" were celebrated "as values in themselves." The push to elect openly gay political candidates to office was a direct result of the transformation wrought in the late 1960s and early 1970s. The coming to office of Harvey Milk in San Francisco in 1978 was both a sign of integration and a sign that identity politics and the impulses of gay liberation continued to motivate people's political choices. According to his aide Anne Kronenberg, Milk was attempting to "shake up" the establishment—but he also found time to pass a pooper-scooper ordinance. Milk's career was tragically cut short; within a year of his election he was killed by a fellow supervisor. Like Stonewall, Milk has passed from history into legend. Milk is now an icon that shapes and helps fuel the persistent power of gay liberation.

## Bibliography

Armstrong, Elizabeth. *Forging Gay Identities: Organizing Sexuality in San Francisco, 1950–1994.* Chicago: University of Chicago Press, 2002.

Blasius, Mark, and Phelan Shane, eds. *We Are Everywhere: A Historical Sourcebook of Gay and Lesbian Politics.* New York: Routledge, 1997.

D'Emilio, John, *Sexual Politics, Sexual Communities: The Making of a Homosexual Minority in the United States, 1940–1970.* Chicago: University of Chicago Press, 1983.

———. *The World Turned: Essays on Gay History, Politics, and Culture.* Durham, N.C.: Duke University Press, 2002.

Duberman, Martin. *Stonewall.* New York: Dutton, 1993.

Humphreys, Laud. *Out of the Closets: The Sociology of Homosexual Liberation.* Englewood Cliffs, N.J.: Prentice Hall, 1972.

Kissack, Terence. "Freaking Fag Revolutionaries: New York's Gay Liberation Front, 1969–1971." *Radical History Review* 62 (Spring 1995): 104–105.

Leland, Winston, ed. *Out in the Castro: Desire, Promise, Activism.* San Francisco: Leyland, 2002.

Marotta, Toby. *The Politics of Homosexuality.* New York: Houghton Mifflin, 1981.

**Terence Kissack**

*See also* ANTIWAR, PACIFIST, AND PEACE MOVEMENTS; BISEXUALITY, BISEXUALS, AND BISEXUAL MOVEMENTS; GAY LIBERATION FRONT; HOMOPHILE MOVEMENT; LESBIAN FEMINISM; LYON, PHYLLIS, AND DEL MARTIN; MILK, HARVEY; NEW LEFT AND STUDENT MOVEMENTS; QUEER NATION; SEXUAL REVOLUTIONS; SHELLEY, MARTHA; STONEWALL RIOTS; THIRD WORLD GAY REVOLUTION; TSANG, DANIEL; WITTMAN, CARL.

# GAY LIBERATION FRONT

The first Gay Liberation Front (GLF) was formed in New York City in the aftermath of the Stonewall Riots in the summer of 1969. The organization's name was modeled on that of the National Liberation Front of South Vietnam and had obvious appeal to those men and women whose political commitments included opposition to the United States' war in Southeast Asia. GLF members saw themselves as part of "the movement," the loosely defined coalition of New Left, antiwar, liberation, and counterculture activists of the late 1960s and early 1970s. This expansive political vision linked the issue of sexual expression to the era's radical political agenda. "The current system," wrote one Front member in a 1970 flyer entitled "What is Gay Liberation," "denies us our basic humanity in much the same way as it is denied to blacks, women, and other oppressed minorities; the grounds are just as irrational. Therefore, our liberation is tied to the liberation of all peoples."

Within months of the New York group's founding GLF chapters sprang up in Chicago, Los Angeles, and Philadelphia and college towns such as Tallahassee, Austin, and Lawrence. Though the history of each of these groups varied—the Los Angeles group, for example, met at a bar called Satan's, while New York's GLF members tended to shun the city's bars—they shared in the general ethos of the original chapter. The GLF chapter that was founded in Lawrence in 1971 proclaimed in the first issue of the *Vortex*, its short-lived publication, that "We are being confronted by an uptight, authoritarian, racist, sexist Amerika. So the Gay Liberation Front joins other oppressed brothers and sisters of Amerika and the Third World to struggle against the nightmare and create one world of people living together."

New York's GLF marked a break with the politics and culture of the homophile organizations that preceded it. Though the homophile groups provided some support for the organizing efforts of the young radicals drawn to the Stonewall Riots, they, unlike the members of the GLF, did not see the riots in an unambiguously positive light. And they were wary of the revolutionary goals and language of the new activists. Kay Tobin Lahusen, who had been active in New York's chapter of the Daughters of Bilitis, recalled that she was "convinced that [the GLF] was a Communist or a New Left plot. I even made an effort to investigate these people for taking over our movement" (Marcus, p. 214). The cultural iconoclasm of GLF members, who were given to fervent denunciations of all things "Amerikan," proved unattractive to many homophile activists. The GLF combined socialist ideas of revolution, attacks on sexism, calls for sexual liberation, and celebration of the counterculture in equal parts; it was a heady but volatile brew.

In many locations GLF's membership was mixed, though weighted toward young white men. Philadelphia's Gay Liberation Front, in contrast to most other Fronts, was notably multiracial. The city's GLF played an important part in facilitating Front members' attendance at the Black Panther Party's Revolutionary Peoples Constitutional Convention, which was held in Philadelphia. According to New York members Karla Jay and Allen Young, "While many gay people from all walks of life came to the weekly meetings . . . the mainstay 'members' of the Gay Liberation Front . . . were street people, men and women in working-class jobs who had no great worries about career advancement, students, artists, unemployed hippies, and college educated Marxists subsisting in the New Left movement" (Jay and Young, pp. 33–34). New York's GLF seemed to have drawn more women than some of the other fronts. When Karla Jay was in Los Angeles, for example, she found "a lot fewer women at this GLF meeting than on the East Coast" (Jay, p. 177). Some of those drawn to the group had had little experience with gay culture. Bill Weaver recalls that he "came out" in the GLF and only after attending meetings did he venture into a gay bar. Some members, such as Martha Shelley, had been active in the homophile movement before coming into the GLF. Bob Kohler, who was in his early forties, was among the oldest of the group's members. The GLF brought together a fractious bunch of people divided along lines of ethnicity, ideology, gender, age, and life experience.

As a way to deal with diversity within the group, the GLF quickly evolved cells organized around shared interest or identity. Red Butterfly, according to its own 1970 publication "Gay Liberation," was "an association . . . of revolutionary socialists" that maintained that gay liberation was "linked to the class struggle." Red Butterfly, like many of the cells, published manifestos and circulated work that reflected its members' views. By 1970 the Radicalesbians, a women's group, and Third World Gay Revolution, an organization of people of color, were formed. In that same year, Ray "Sylvia" Rivera, Marsha Johnson, Dambi Lamour, and others formed the Street Transvestite Action Revolutionaries. The Flaming Faggots collective produced some of the early works of what would come to be known as "effeminism," a searing critique of gay male culture from a feminist perspective. The Aquarius Cell organized dances and communal dinners and published the *Gay Liberation Front Newsletter*. GLF dances were among the most popular of the group's events, bringing together Front members and men and women who sought a space in which homosexuality was celebrated and not simply tolerated.

A number of GLF's cells proved to be important in their own right. Radicalesbians, for example, produced "The Woman-Identified Woman," a manifesto of lesbian identity that was key in shaping the emerging discourse of lesbian feminism and lesbian separatism. The group organized one of the GLF's most famous actions, the "zap" of the second Congress to Unite Women in May 1970. Radicalesbians members took the stage, many wearing T-shirts bearing the phrase "lavender menace," to confront the issue of homophobia in the women's movement. Copies of "The Woman-Identified Woman" were distributed, spontaneous consciousness-raising groups formed, and the conference adopted a resolution that stated that "Women's liberation is a lesbian plot." The Radicalesbians zap of the conference was typical of the ludic political tactics of the GLF, which placed a premium on theatrical interventions meant to provoke and create attention. Although many women in the GLF gravitated to the increasingly separatist politics of the Radicalesbians, a number sought to maintain ties to the group—and to the idea of a multigendered politics—by forming the GLF Women's Caucus.

The GLF was a virtual propaganda machine. In addition to the efforts of the Aquarius group the June 28th cell published *Come Out!* "a newspaper by and for the gay community." The Gay Flames Collective published the work of group members, reprinted important texts such as Carl Wittman's "Gay Manifesto," and pressured the Liberation News Service, which fed the movement press, to carry work by gay liberationists. The GLF also worked to spread the word through consciousness-raising groups and other outreach efforts. Flaming Faggots member Jim Clifford claimed that his group started over fifty consciousness-raising groups in the New York City area. The

reach of the GLF extended well beyond the borders of Manhattan. A young man of fifteen who "felt utter and complete isolation and alienation" wrote *Come Out!* a letter after he came across a copy of the publication at a "peace center" in his town.

The political rhetoric and goals of the GLF alienated a number of those who attended meetings. Jim Owles criticized the "more radical than thou" tone of group meetings and accused Front leaders of "begging" their peers in the New Left, Black Power, and antiwar movements "for that same kind of acceptance they had accused some of the older homosexuals of wanting" (Teal, pp. 105–106). Ultimately a number of GLF members broke off to form the Gay Activists Alliance (GAA). Established in December of 1969, GAA meetings were run according to *Robert's Rules of Order*. GAA members rejected the idea of forging a broad progressive alliance. The group adopted bylaws that stated that the group "will not endorse, ally with, or otherwise support any political party, candidate for public office, and/or any organization not directly related to the homosexual cause" (Bell, p. 23). The GAA emerged as a single-issue interest group. It represented, in a sense, a return toward the homophile movement's agenda, albeit one transformed by an infusion of countercultural style and sexual politics.

Despite front members' repeated claims of solidarity with the Left, the issue of homosexuality was highly charged and proved problematic. Repeatedly the GLF found itself critiquing its supposed allies. In 1970, for example, members of the Flaming Faggots collective clashed with members of the Venceremos Brigades, whose members went to Cuba to experience life in a socialist country. Both groups had unwittingly rented the same space on the same night; the gaffe was not amicably resolved. Tensions on the subject of the Left's view of homosexuality were further exacerbated by the Cuban government's 1971 Declaration by the First National Congress on Education and Culture denouncing "the social pathological character of homosexual deviations." The fights around this issue proved to be particularly disillusioning for GLF members, such as Allen Young, who had done considerable work with the Venceremos Brigades and the issue of solidarity with Cuba. Though not all the Left supported Cuba and its policies, the issue was symbolic and led many in the GLF to disavow alliances with "the movement."

By late 1971 the GLF in New York had essentially collapsed. Most of the other GLFs across the country had equally short lives. The sharp political debates within the group, the rejection of practical political goals, and the homophobic environment in which the Front worked all contributed to the collapse. Despite its short life, the GLF proved enormously influential as a model and a catalyst for a new wave of political activists.

## Bibliography

Bailey, Beth. *Sex in the Heartland.* Cambridge, Mass.: Harvard University Press, 1991.

Bell, Arthur. *Dancing the Gay Lib Blues.* New York: Simon and Schuster, 1971.

Duberman, Martin. *Stonewall.* New York: Dutton, 1993.

Humphreys, Laud. *Out of the Closets: The Sociology of Homosexual Liberation.* Englewood Cliffs: Prentice Hall, 1972.

Jay, Karla. *Tales of the Lavender Menace: A Memoir of Liberation.* New York: Basic Books, 1999.

Jay, Karla, and Allen Young. *Out of the Closets: Voices of Gay Liberation.* New York: New York University, 1992.

Kissack, Terence. "Freaking Fag Revolutionaries: New York's Gay Liberation Front, 1969–1971." *Radical History Review* 62 (Spring 1995): 104–134.

Marcus, Eric. *Making History: The Struggle for Gay and Lesbian Equal Rights, 1945–1990.* New York: HarperPerennial, 1992.

Marotta, Toby. *The Politics of Homosexuality.* New York: Houghton and Mifflin, 1981.

Red Butterfly. "Gay Liberation." April 4, 1970. GLF File, Lesbian Herstory Archives.

Stein, Marc. *City of Sisterly and Brotherly Loves: Lesbian and Gay Philadelphia, 1945–1972.* Chicago: Chicago University Press, 2000.

Teal, Don. *The Gay Militants.* New York: Stein and Day, 1971.

"What is Gay Liberation," flyer, spring 1970. GLF File, Lesbian Herstory Archives, New York.

**Terence Kissack**

*See also* ANTIWAR, PACIFIST, AND PEACE MOVEMENTS; COMING OUT AND OUTING; GAY ACTIVISTS ALLIANCE; GAY LIBERATION; GITTINGS, BARBARA, AND KAY TOBIN LAHUSEN; HOMOPHILE MOVEMENT; KUROMIYA, KYOSHI; NEW LEFT AND STUDENT MOVEMENTS; RADICALESBIANS; RIVERA, SYLVIA; SHELLEY, MARTHA; STONEWALL RIOTS; THIRD WORLD GAY REVOLUTION; TSANG, DANIEL; WITTMAN, CARL.

**GAY MEN'S HEALTH CRISIS (GMHC).** see AIDS SERVICE ORGANIZATIONS.

# GENDER AND SEX

Gender and sex are social constructs associated with culturally and historically specific ideas about femininity-masculinity and femaleness-maleness. While gender and sex definitions and patterns vary significantly across cultural and historical contexts, they matter greatly in all human societies.

## From Sex to Gender

The term "sex" traditionally was used in ways that assumed that there is a correspondence between individuals' biological sex, their perception of themselves as female and feminine or male and masculine, and their social circumstances. Sex in this sense incorporates a wide range of phenomena ranging from the presence or absence of particular forms of genitalia to psychological dispositions. In the traditional view, all biological females, for example, perceive themselves as possessing similar female and feminine characteristics and are recognized socially as female and feminine. According to this conceptual framework, sex is biologically determined and immutable and all that is associated with that "fact" is a product of biological destiny. Moreover, there are fundamental anatomical differences between those we characterize as female and those we characterize as male; sex differences are associated with different reproductive capacities and social roles; and individuals perceive themselves as having masculine or feminine characteristics that correspond to normative cultural values. Conservative traditionalists believe that, in the absence of trouble, biological sex determines social gender in inevitable and desirable ways.

This deterministic position has been subject to harsh criticism, in part because it fails to take into account the influence of social, cultural, and historical factors. Because of racial or ethnic differences, for example, women of color and white women often conceptualize femininity in different ways. The traditional view also fails to acknowledge changes over time, ignores differences between cultures, treats femininity in men and masculinity in women as signs of trouble, and regards LGBT people as deviants. To mark the distinction between biological and social components, the term "gender" came into use in the mid-twentieth century to refer to the nonphysiological aspects of femininity and masculinity. For many proponents of this term, sex might be fixed, but gender is variable.

According to this view, while biological sex differences do matter, social influences have a significant effect in developing gender roles for males and females. Through the process of socialization, individuals learn gender roles and develop gender identities. In her influential paper "The Traffic in Women" (1975), anthropologist Gayle Rubin argues that each human society has a specific "sex/gender system" through which cultural understandings of gender organize and institutionalize sexual practices through marriage and kinship systems. These often translate into exchange systems where men are the givers and women are the gifts. Those who endorse the view that society constructs gender attack the conservatism of the biologically deterministic view, arguing that the latter legitimates power differentials by grounding gender differences in supposedly universal differences between females and males. To say that social inequities are grounded in "nature" limits the efficaciousness of raising voices of dissent to promote social change.

## Beyond Biological Sex and Social Gender

More recently, scholars and theorists have taken steps that challenge the notion that sex is biological and gender is social. Much feminist and queer theory seeks to destabilize the deterministic naturalism of sex and the dual-gender system. Judith Butler points out in *Gender Trouble* (1990) and *Bodies That Matter* (1993) that while there exists a corporeal, material aspect to human bodies, they are viewed and indeed experienced through a priori cultural lenses. In other words, sex is "always already" gendered and cultural understandings of gender precede sex rather than the other way around. According to this view, efforts to distinguish biologically between the sexes through references to body parts, reproductive capacities, or DNA invariably are based on conceptions of gender, these traditionally being the notion that men without penises are not really men and women without breasts or uteruses are not really women; the belief that prepubescent girls, postmenopausal women, and infertile and nonreproducing females are not really women; and the idea that people without XX or XY chromosomes are abnormal.

A second challenge comes from those who question the utility and applicability of concepts grounded in dual-sex, dual-gender systems. Anthropologists have long viewed gender as learned and have recognized the existence of cultures that transcend the Western male-female sex dichotomy and masculine-feminine gender dichotomy. Third and fourth gender systems are well documented in the ethnographic record. Furthermore, some argue that the parameters of male and female and femininity and masculinity are not mutually exclusive. This perspective holds that individuals possess both male and female and both masculine and feminine characteristics. As Anne Fausto-Sterling observes in *Sexing the Body* (2000), sex and gender need not be conceptualized in ways that suggest that more femininity means less masculinity and more masculinity means less femininity. Fausto-Sterling advocates instead the use of an orthogonal model of masculinity and femininity in which individuals may be high (or low) on both schemata.

Other challenges to the notion that sex is biological and gender is social have also emerged. Some scholars point out that the constellation of gender and sex attributes is not necessarily stable over the life course. And some trans theorists reverse the usual understanding of sex and gender by suggesting that while an individual's gender identity is relatively stable, sex is malleable (through modification of the body).

## Sex and Gender in Early America

Scholars in LGBT studies have examined gender and sex in a variety of contexts, including several key historical moments that have shaped current understandings. One such context is colonial America. According to the Christian views held by most European colonial settlers, sex differences between males and females reflect God's will. According to the Judeo-Christian origin myth, God's design for humanity incorporates a sex dichotomy. Genesis 1:27 states that God created male and female. This distinction became decisive when the first humans were cast out of the Garden of Eden. Although women and men were created in the equality, sameness, and perfection of God's image, the first woman was punished for transgression by being made to suffer pain in childbirth and required to be submissive to her husband, according to Genesis 3:16. Thus, the biblical creation account established for Western societies a schema with four distinct characteristics. First, there are two categories of persons: males and females. Second, these two sexes are distinguished by essential biological differences. Third, males and females will unite sexually and produce offspring. Fourth, the sex-gender order involves a social distinction based on status, with women expected to obey their male partners. By associating these features with God's creation and authority, these assumptions were normalized as immutable qualities of nature. Those who denied this order defied God's law.

When European travelers first came to North America and encountered indigenous cultures, many observed Native people who came to be called *berdaches*. The *berdaches* offended the sensibilities of the Christian colonizers, missionaries, and traders because they defied what these travelers thought should be the division of society into females and males. Many of these Native individuals—both biological males and biological females—engaged in economic activities typical of people of the opposite biological sex, cross-dressed, and took partners of the same biological sex. Of great concern to Christians was that these violations of God's will were not only recognized and accepted by members of indigenous communities but were also said to be sanctioned by supernatural powers, giving *berdaches* significant spiritual roles. Over time, pressures from both concerned Christians and the grand colonization project disrupted this once-venerable institution. Many Native Americans are now actively reclaiming their third and fourth gender heritage and self-identifying as Two-Spirit people to reflect their lack of fit in a dual-gender system imposed upon them by Europeans.

## Fairies, Clones, and Drag Queens

George Chauncey in *Gay New York* (1994) documents the existence of a vibrant gay male culture in the very heart of urban America in the early twentieth century. Like the *berdaches* of Native American societies, the effeminate male fairies and pansies of working-class New York City were members of a third gender defined not primarily on the basis of their sexual orientation or preference but rather on the basis of their variation from normative "masculine" deportment and dress. These fairies situated themselves in an intermediate but culturally relevant category outside of masculine-feminine dualism and participated in a system that allowed them to be recognized socially as members of a third gender. When assuming this gender role, the fairies were perceived as fundamentally different from other biological males who displayed "masculine" gender identities and roles. According to Chauncey, not only did fairies and pansies draw attention to themselves, but their difference was tolerated by working-class New Yorkers. Some working-class straight men felt perfectly comfortable having sex with fairies and pansies since it seemed normal for someone masculine to have sex with someone feminine. These third gender fairies and pansies created and occupied a gender category and social space that was both meaningful to and affirming of them.

A new type of gendered male emerged in many major American urban centers following the Stonewall Riots of 1969. In *Gay Macho* (1998), Martin P. Levine depicts the "gay male clone," arguing that between 1969 and the mid-1980s gay men in various American cities developed a "hypermasculine" gender role and identity. In doing so they rejected cultural assumptions that men who desire other men must also renounce their masculinity. Unlike the effeminate New York City fairies of decades before, the gay clone embraced many aspects of traditional masculinity. Gay clones displayed gym-toned bodies adorned in masculine dress and they played hard by dancing in discos and consuming copious amounts of drugs and alcohol. Consistent with the masculine ideal,

the gay clone flaunted a heightened sexual drive, continuously seeking sexual partners. Of course, the gay clone exhibited one fundamental difference: he sought sexual encounters not with women but with other men. For the gay clone, hot sex was gay sex, and promiscuous gay sex provided an opportunity to affirm the masculine ethos of males having and acting upon intrinsically strong sexual desires.

Both before and after Stonewall, drag queens (and more recently drag kings) have used performance to deconstruct conventional male-female sex and masculine-feminine gender dichotomies. When males dress as women and females dress as men, they challenge the notion that the performance of gender follows naturally and inevitably from the realities of sex. Esther Newton argues in *Mother Camp* (1972) that by "doing drag" individuals question the "naturalness" of their culture's normative sex and gender roles.

## Femmes and Butches

LGBT studies scholars have focused attention on not only the gay genders of fairies, clones, and drag queens but also the lesbian genders of femmes and butches. Since the early twentieth century, some American lesbians, particular working-class lesbians, have adopted femme/butch mannerisms and identities. Butch lesbians assume certain stereotypical "masculine" characteristics of dress and personality whereas femmes take on more conventional "feminine" displays of self. Most of the informants interviewed by Elizabeth Lapovsky Kennedy and Madeline D. Davis for *Boots of Leather, Slippers of Gold* (1993), their study of a working-class lesbian community in mid-twentieth-century Buffalo, New York, self-identified as butch or femme and paired off in femme/butch couples. Likewise, in her account of LGBT life in *Cherry Grove, Fire Island* (1993), Esther Newton noted similar patterns among women of the "young crowd" who arrived after World War II.

Some argue that the practice of imitating heteronormative gender roles condones a gender order that subjugates women and imposes heterosexist standards on LGBT people. The use of these gender and sexual categories is said to achieve a degree of tolerance at a high price: an agreement to resemble the normative gender and sexual order. This tacit agreement to conform imposes strict limits on the freedoms of nonheterosexuals because it situates the normative order as the ideal while recognizing that some individuals are incapable of achieving that goal. Rather than critiquing structures of inequality, these practices are said to affirm that which oppresses marginalized peoples.

Others assume a more accepting stance to femme/butch. Pointing to elements such as the butch's desire to sexually please her partner (which is not characteristic of normative masculinity) and the femme's greater earning power (which is not typical of straight women), Kennedy and Davis argue that butches and femmes do not imitate heterosexual roles but rather create distinct gender roles. In *Identities in the Lesbian World* (1978), Barbara Ponse views the use of conventional masculine and feminine characteristics as a form of role play, the specific forms of which vary across lesbians communities. Femme/butch may thus be considered as a way of creatively and playfully experimenting with different gender categories to suit the context and one's own interests. Rather than reinforcing the rigidity of a "natural" dual-gender system, such role play accentuates the plasticity of gender. As such, gender is recognized not as biologically determined but instead as socially accomplished.

### Changing Sex and Gender: The Intersexed and Transsexuals

Intersexuality and transsexuality present a significant challenge to those who espouse biologically deterministic and dichotomous views of sex. A surprisingly large number of individuals are intersexed. Fausto-Sterling estimates cautiously that 1.7 percent of American births result in babies with indistinct genitalia possessing features of both biological sexes. This suggests either that biology can be a cruel trickster or that the dual-sex system is itself not as "natural" as some would claim. The intersexed also present a formidable problem for Western physicians who seek to classify infants using the male-female dichotomy, preferably prior to leaving the hospital. Suzanne J. Kessler points out in *Lessons from the Intersexed* (1998) that sex assignment of sexually ambiguous newborns is based primarily on sociocultural rather than biological criteria.

As Joanne J. Meyerowitz explains in *How Sex Changed* (2002), while transsexual people are at birth classified according to their biological sex, there is a lack of concordance between their biological characteristics (their sex) and their sense of self as a cohesive gendered being (their gender identity). Technological advances in the twentieth century have provided American physicians with a variety of therapeutic measures, ranging from hormonal treatment to genital reassignment surgery, to offer their transsexual patients. At the same time, the popular media have raised public awareness of the issue of transsexuality. Beginning in the 1950s, when prestigious transsexuals such as Christine Jorgensen were featured in the news, individuals who have felt that their gender identity was inconsistent with their anatomical bodies have had a

way to classify their feelings and, more importantly, a community to turn to for help and support. Transsexual activists initially lobbied for access to new technologies to transform the malleable body so that it conformed to what they viewed as the constant, the individual's gender identity.

Over time it has become clear that many, perhaps most, transsexuals do not seek complete sex reassignment surgery. Today the transgender movement includes not only transsexuals but also cross-dressers, feminists, transvestites, LGB people, and anyone else who does not conform to the rigid, binary sex-gender system. Transgender activists push the limits of gender by exposing the artificiality of gender and sex as rigid constructs and by championing the legal rights of those of nonconventional sex and gender. Although some transsexuals and transgender people endorse elements of conventional sex and gender dichotomies, others radically destabilize these dichotomies.

### Beyond Sex and Gender

In *The Epistemology of the Closet* (1990), Eve Kosofsky Sedgwick challenges heterosexual-homosexual dualism, arguing that this binary opposition is reductionist in that it fails to capture all of the nuances and dimensions of sexuality. For Sedgwick, sexuality, like gender, must be viewed in historical and cultural contexts. Sexual distinctions are intertwined with different configurations of relations between the sexes, classes, races, and ethnicities. Systems of oppression thus operate not as isolated entities but rather are embedded in other aspects of the social fabric. Moreover, while some component of the social order may empower an individual, another element may function to oppress that same person. Sedgwick takes issue with an LGBT movement that is androcentric, Caucasian, middle-class, and European American. By destabilizing privilege, a new queer politics emerges. To embrace this movement one need not discard social conventions like sex, gender, and sexuality, but instead recognize that as social constructs there is no basis for assigning status to particular sexes, genders, and sexualities over others.

### Bibliography

Bornstein, Kate. *Gender Outlaw: On Men, Women, and the Rest of Us.* New York: Routledge, 1994.

Butler, Judith. *Gender Trouble: Feminism and the Subversion of Identity.* New York: Routledge, 1990.

———. *Bodies that Matter: On the Discursive Limits of "Sex."* New York: Routledge, 1993.

Califia, Pat. *Sex Changes: The Politics of Transgenderism.* San Francisco: Cleis Press, 1997.

Callender, Charles, and Lee M. Kochems. "The North American Berdache." *Current Anthropology* 24, no. 4 (1983): 443–470.

Chauncey, George. *Gay New York: Gender, Urban Culture, and the Makings of the Gay Male World, 1890–1940.* New York: Basic Books, 1994.

Cromwell, Jason. *Transmen and FTMs: Identities, Bodies, Genders, and Sexualities.* Urbana: University of Illinois Press, 1999.

Faderman, Lillian. *Odd Girls and Twilight Lovers: A History of Lesbian Life in Twentieth-Century America.* New York: Columbia University Press, 1991.

Fausto-Sterling, Anne. *Sexing the Body: Gender Politics and the Construction of Sexuality.* New York: Basic Books, 2000.

Fenstermaker, Sarah, and Candace West, eds. *Doing Gender, Doing Difference: Inequality, Power, and Institutional Change.* New York: Routledge, 2002.

Herdt, Gilbert H., ed. *Third Sex, Third Gender: Beyond Sexual Dimorphism in Culture and History.* New York: Zone Books, 1994.

Kennedy, Elizabeth Lapovsky, and Madeline D. Davis. *Boots of Leather, Slippers of Gold: The History of a Lesbian Community.* New York: Routledge, 1993.

Kessler, Suzanne J. *Lessons from the Intersexed.* New Brunswick, N.J.: Rutgers University Press, 1998.

Kintz, Linda. *Between Jesus and the Market: The Emotions That Matter in Right-Wing America.* Durham, N.C.: Duke University Press, 1997.

Lang, Sabine. *Men as Women, Women as Men: Changing Gender in Native American Culture.* Translated from the German by John L. Vantine. Austin, Tex..: University of Texas Press, 1998.

Levine, Martin P. *Gay Macho: The Life and Death of the Homosexual Clone.* Edited by Michael S. Kimmel. New York: New York University Press, 1998.

Lewin, Ellen, and William L. Leap, eds. *Out in Theory: The Emergence of Lesbian and Gay Anthropology.* Urbana: University of Illinois Press, 2002.

Meyerowitz, Joanne J. *How Sex Changed: A History of Transsexuality in the United States.* Cambridge, Mass.: Harvard University Press, 2002.

More, Kate, and Stephen Whittle, eds. *Reclaiming Genders: Transsexual Grammars at the Fin de Siècle.* London: Cassell, 1999.

Munt, Sally R., and Cherry Smyth, eds. *Butch/Femme: Inside Lesbian Gender.* London: Cassell, 1998.

Nestle, Joan. *A Restricted Country.* Ithaca, N.Y.: Firebrand Books, 1987.

Newton, Esther. *Mother Camp: Female Impersonators in America.* Englewood Cliffs, N.J.: Prentice-Hall, 1972.

Ortner, Sherry B., and Harriet Whitehead, eds. *Sexual Meanings: The Cultural Construction of Gender and Sexuality.* Cambridge, U.K.: Cambridge University Press, 1981.

Ponse, Barbara. *Identities in the Lesbian World: The Social Construction of Self.* Westport, Conn.: Greenwood Press, 1978.

Rich, Adrienne. "Compulsory Heterosexuality and Lesbian Existence." *Signs* 5, no. 4 (1980): 631–660.

Roscoe, Will. *Changing Ones: Third and Fourth Genders in Native North America.* New York: St. Martin's Press, 1998.

Rubin, Gayle. "The Traffic in Women: Notes on the Political Economy of Sex." In *Toward an Anthropology of Women.* Edited by Rayna R. Reiter. New York: Monthly Review Press, 1975.

——— "Of Catamites and Kings: Reflections on Butch, Gender, and Boundaries." In *The Persistent Desire: A Femme-Butch Reader.* Edited by Joan Nestle. Boston: Alyson Publications, 1992.

Rupp, Leila J., and Verta Taylor. *Drag Queens at the 801 Cabaret.* Chicago: University of Chicago Press, 2003.

Sedgwick, Eve Kosofsky. "Across Gender, Across Sexuality: Willa Cather and Others." *South Atlantic Quarterly* 88, no. 1 (Winter 1989): 53–72.

———. *Epistemology of the Closet.* Berkeley: University of California Press, 1990.

Smith-Rosenberg, Carroll. *Disorderly Conduct: Visions of Gender in Victorian America.* New York: Knopf, 1985.

Vance, Carole S., ed. *Pleasure and Danger: Exploring Female Sexuality.* Boston: Routledge and K. Paul, 1984.

**Bruce Freeman**

**See also** BISEXUALITY, BISEXUALS, AND BISEXUAL MOVEMENTS; DRAG QUEENS AND KINGS; FEMMES AND BUTCHES; HOMOSEXUALITY AND HETEROSEXUALITY; INTERSEXUALS AND INTERSEXED PEOPLE; LGBTQ STUDIES; QUEER THEORY AND QUEER STUDIES; SEXUAL ORIENTATION AND PREFERENCE; TRANSSEXUALS, TRANSVESTITES, TRANSGENDER PEOPLE, AND CROSS-DRESSERS; TWO-SPIRIT FEMALES; TWO-SPIRIT MALES; SEX ACTS.

**GENDER IMPERSONATION LAW AND POLICY.** see TRANSGENDER AND GENDER IMPERSONATION LAW AND POLICY.

# GENTRIFICATION

A term coined critically in 1964 by the British sociologist Ruth Glass, "gentrification" refers to a process begun in the 1950s whereby low-income and deteriorated inner-city neighborhoods, which had previously been abandoned by the middle classes in favor of suburbs, are regenerated by an influx of capital and higher-income, middle-class occupants. These occupants frequently purchase rather than rent residential properties and invest in restoring and improving the housing stock. The impact of this process usually displaces existing occupants, unable to afford the rising housing costs, and alters the character of a neighborhood.

Neil Smith suggests that a combination of factors accounts for gentrification, including economic restructuring, the breakdown of the patriarchal household, new employment patterns, changes in the availability of financing (including government subsidies as part of urban renewal projects), and the enormous influence of the feminist movement on social norms related to housing, employment, gender, and sexuality (p. 110).

## Gay Men as Gentrifiers

Although systemic gentrification began in the 1950s, the process is particularly associated with the 1960s and 1970s and, within LGBT communities, usually with white gay men. White males, both gay and straight, have been characterized as tending to command higher earning power than women in all sectors, as well as most Latino, African American, Asian American, Native American, and Pacific Islander men. When combined with their relative lack of dependents, white gay men have had economic advantages that made home ownership in low-income neighborhoods a possibility.

Existing LGBT ghettos did not necessarily gentrify, but adjacent residential neighborhoods tended to attract gay men seeking access to ghetto amenities, potential sexual partners, and safety in numbers. Their presence and their attempts to beautify and create identifiably gay space in their rented homes or apartments through a process of what Mickey Lauria and Lawrence Knopp term "incumbent upgrading" (p. 161), or what Stein calls "fagging it up" (p. 27), attracted more gay men as well as gay landlords or developers to a neighborhood. The rehabilitation of old housing stock by gay men and some lesbians was quite widespread, occurring on a significant scale in the Castro and the Mission Districts in San Francisco, South Beach in Miami, Capital Hill in Seattle, Marigny in New Orleans, and parts of Washington, D.C., Tampa, New York City, Jersey City, and other cities.

Manuel Castells (1983) argued that gentrification was a collective strategy by an oppressed community to secure housing in the face of homophobic discrimination, difficult market conditions, or both. This view has been challenged by Knopp, who in a series of articles put forward the most sustained analysis of gentrification by gay men. He suggests that gentrification is a complex process of social and geographical identity formation involving class, race, and sexuality in unpredictable ways. In an early theoretical article, he argued, with Lauria, that several contributing factors made gentrification possible. These included the existence of gay ghettos, which provided bases for political and economic power and community formation, the easing of penalties against gay

men as a result of widespread social change accelerated by the new social movements of the 1960s, and the concomitant decline of the nuclear family.

In a later case study of the Marigny neighborhood of New Orleans, gentrified through a process of gay male in-migration from the 1960s onwards, Knopp examines the role of individual middle-class gay men in actively promoting the district to other gay men. One motivating factor was gay men's discomfort with heterosexual family-oriented life in the region closest to their employer, the University of New Orleans. This discomfort, which prompted some gay men to seek alternative housing locations, corresponds with the argument by Castells and Karen Murphy that gay men are opposed to suburban values and thus favor inner-city residence.

Smith suggests that the argument that gentrification is a consumer-driven process, fuelled by disgruntled suburbanites now retracing their flight out of the city, lacks merit and fails to account for larger-scale factors such as economic and social restructuring. Knopp argues that gentrification is propelled by the desire of individual gay men to accumulate wealth, through speculation and development, as much as—or perhaps more than—conscious community development strategies of territorial control or a deliberate rejection of suburban life. He suggests that this contrast between individual and community goals generates tension over gentrification in and around LGBT ghettos.

## Gender and Gentrification

Lesbians were steady although far less visible contributors to the gentrification process. They were not as spatially concentrated in LGBT ghettos and nearby neighborhoods as gay men; instead, they were more likely to live scattered in low-income neighborhoods characterized by diverse household forms and some ethnic diversity. Professional women, particularly as their careers matured and they became more affluent, might buy houses in these areas and contribute to nascent general gentrification, rather than specifically gay gentrification. During the 1960s and 1970s, other women participated in the formation of lesbian-feminist communities. While they might collectively purchase a large building for communal living, it is unclear to what extent these communities affected the market value of properties around them.

The massive earnings differential between men and women began to slowly narrow during the 1960s, but proportionately fewer lesbians could afford to invest in property and profit from gentrification. They also lacked access to the male political and financial institutional networks that could benefit gay developers and individual gentrifiers. This in effect maintained and even exacerbated the economic disadvantage of lesbians and their social, economic, and political differences from gay men.

## Displacement

Since gentrification by definition leads to the displacement of the original class of occupants, it has had a bitterly contested history of pushing economically marginalized groups (oftentimes working class African Americans and Latinos) into ever poorer quality housing, a process that ultimately affects their health, well-being, and access to political and economic power. Gentrification by gay men and lesbians, however, seems to be atypical. Robert Bailey argues, on the basis of a close statistical analysis of contemporary gay and lesbian residential areas, that with a few exceptions, prior occupants have not been displaced in significant numbers and that lesbians and gay men may sustain housing markets that would otherwise fall victim to further disinvestment (p. 84). Indeed, it is the success of lower-income gay and lesbian gentrification that in some cases, as Tamar Rothenberg suggests, leads to *their* displacement over time by more affluent gay men and heterosexuals.

### Bibliography

Bailey, Robert W. *Gay Politics, Urban Politics: Identity and Economics in the Urban Setting.* New York: Columbia University Press, 1999.

Castells, Manuel. *The City and the Grassroots: A Cross-Cultural Theory of Urban Social Movements.* London: Edward Arnold, 1983.

Castells, Manuel, and Karen Murphy. "Cultural Identity and Urban Structure: The Spatial Organization of San Francisco's Gay Community." In *Urban Policy under Capitalism.* Edited by Norman I. Fainstein and Susan S. Fainstein. Beverly Hills, Calif.: Sage, 1982.

Knopp, Lawrence. "Gentrification and Gay Neighborhood Formation in New Orleans: A Case Study." In *Homo Economics: Capitalism, Community, and Lesbian and Gay Life.* Edited by Amy Gluckman and Betsy Reed. New York: Routledge, 1997.

Lauria, Mickey, and Lawrence Knopp. "Toward an Analysis of the Role of Gay Communities in the Urban Renaissance." *Urban Geography* 2 (April–June 1985): 152–169.

Rothenberg, Tamar. " 'And She Told Two Friends': Lesbians Creating Urban Social Space." In *Mapping Desire: Geographies of Sexualities.* Edited by David Bell and Gill Valentine. New York: Routledge, 1995.

Smith, Neil. *The New Urban Frontier: Gentrification and the Revanchist City.* New York: Routledge, 1996.

Stein, Marc. *City of Sisterly and Brotherly Loves: Lesbian and Gay Philadelphia, 1945–1972.* Chicago: University of Chicago Press, 2000.

**Liz Millward**

*See also* FLORIDA; GHETTOS AND NEIGHBORHOODS; NEW ORLEANS; NEW YORK CITY; SAN FRANCISCO; SEATTLE; URBAN, SUBURBAN, AND RURAL GEOGRAPHIES; WASHINGTON, D.C.

# GEOGRAPHY

Although sexual identities and practices are embodied and spatial, attention to LGBT spatialities is relatively new in the geographic literature. Some of the first work on sexuality and space emerged in the late 1970s and early 1980s as geographers sought to map and explain gay and lesbian communities in North American cities. The work of Manuel Castells, an urban sociologist, was particularly important in drawing geographers' attention to the spatial basis of gay identity and to the impact of gay communities on the urban fabric.

## The City

The focus on urban space in North America led to an emphasis on visible LGBT commercial and residential zones that were primarily populated by gay men. While some studies focused on the motivation for such clustering, others examined the role played by gays in urban gentrification. The neighborhoods of the Castro in San Francisco and Greenwich Village in New York City were nationally recognized, but geographers also drew attention to the important role gay men played in gentrifying the urban landscape in cities such as New Orleans and Seattle. The nature of these communities meant that the primary focus of this early work was communities of upper-middle and middle-class white gay men. Lesbian urban communities were initially neglected in the literature, reflecting early claims that men were inherently territorial and desired the visibility of spatially defined commercial districts while lesbians relied on less visible and less "ghettoized" networks.

By the early 1990s, however, geographers had produced a rich variety of studies suggesting that lesbians do create spatially concentrated communities. These local, but rarely highly commercial, territorial bases are often less visible to those "not in the know," as lesbians, like heterosexual women, tend to have less of the resources needed to own their own homes and businesses. Despite these barriers, spatial concentrations of lesbians create recognizable social spaces that serve perceived social needs and create zones of comfort. The attention to visible, permanent neighborhoods contributed to a neglect of bisexual and transsexual communities. Transsexuals were visible only in studies of sex work and prostitution, if at all. The same emphasis on the neighborhood led to studies of lesbian and gay spatialities that often erased sex from the analysis, a tendency that has been corrected by more recent, sex-positive research.

The focus on urban spaces also reflected a diffusionist bias that placed cities, specifically those with visible gay and lesbian neighborhoods, at the forefront of social change. It tended to reinforce straight/gay binaries and to focus on gays and lesbians to the exclusion of other non-straight-identified groups. While visible gay and lesbian enclaves can serve as symbols of safe havens and as a political base for organizing against antigay violence, they are not necessarily welcoming places for other sexual dissidents.

More recently, geographers have also noted the costs attached to the increased recognition of LGBT neighborhoods. While they may be important sites of cultural resistance, their very visibility can mark them as "hunting grounds" for LGBT-bashing expeditions. The safety to be openly LGBT does not necessarily mean freedom from violence. Moreover, the commodification and greater openness of LGBT space has in some instances made it a site of cosmopolitan consumption for non-LGBT-identified tourists, at times making these spaces seem "less safe," in addition to producing new forms of marginalization and exclusion.

The commercialization and greater legitimacy of public LGBT space has frequently coincided with mainstream LGBT activists' campaigns for more abstract rights, and the restriction of access to commercial spaces to those who can afford to consume them. This can be contrasted with the increasingly scarce "sites of sexual freedom" that transcend mainstream notions of the separation of public and private, incorporating both "public" and "private" activities into what most would think of as a public space. While a wealth of historical studies and microgeographies have shown that cruising and the use of outdoor spaces for public sex may create rich spatial networks, often invisible to the outsider, the core of LGBT community building has generally been associated with gentrification and a shift from the anonymous spaces of bars to more visible commercial and residential neighborhoods.

## Sexing Space

Most gays and lesbians spend little of their lives in these LGBT spaces, living instead in a "straight world" where LGBT spatialities may consist less of material landscapes and more of informal networks and identity. The everyday environments in which these take place are simultaneously produced as neutrally asexual and determinedly heterosexual. In the early 1990s, this recognition that repeated daily acts construct public space as naturally heterosexual generated a wave of research in the United States and Britain that interrogated the ways in which the performance of sexual identities constructs social landscapes. Building on the French philosopher Henri Lefebvre's argument that social relations both produce and are produced by space, geographers examined the multiple ways in which space is "heterosexed." Feminist geographers' insights regarding the performance of masculine and feminine gender identities noted the ways in which this binary performance marked the heterosexual nature of specific spaces.

The heterosexualized conversations, music, advertising, and interactions that take place in the street and in the home on a daily basis work together to produce a normality that is avowedly heterosexual. The naturalized norms of the street are more often enforced by the reactions of the "straight" passerby, which may lead to LGBT people feeling "out of place" in "normal" space. Space that appears asexual to heterosexuals who are unaware of their own performances of heterosexuality is clearly marked as straight for nonheterosexuals who police their own actions, often unconsciously.

The seeming hegemony of straight space, however, opens the door for acts that undermine its presumed existence and point out the existing contradictions that may already allow for glances and coded styles to create a relational gay space that goes unrecognized by those outside those spaces. Individuals can work to "queer" space by their everyday dress, presence, and actions, directly confronting unarticulated assumptions of heterosexuality. The success of these strategies, however, depends upon the audience, as the performance of identities will be read differently by different people in different places. A body that transgresses heteronormative sex-gender relations must "look like one" rather than merely "be one" to be recognized.

These random, individual acts may be more effective in confronting unarticulated assumptions of heterosexuality than the more carnivalesque atmosphere of gay pride marches, which, although very visible, are by their very nature contained in time and space. These large-scale, organized pride parades have become increasingly popular with tourists, both LGBT and straight, and are in some cases an important part of the urban economy. Like LGBT neighborhoods, the bounded nature of gay pride celebrations may actually reinforce the perceived heterosexuality of other spaces by creating a space in which dissident sexualities are seen to be contained. The increasingly commercialized nature of pride events contrasts with the political tactics of groups such as ACT UP, Queer Nation, and the Lesbian Avengers, which often use spatial tactics that appropriate mainstream cultural codes and symbols to disrupt the heterosexual nature of places such as shopping malls and restaurants.

While geographers have drawn attention to the heteronormative hegemony of everyday space, most work on sexuality within the discipline has continued to focus on deviant sexualities rather than heterosexuality itself. By the mid-1990s, the influence of queer theory led geographers to move beyond the study of lesbian and gay spatialities based on fixed categories and to begin to map bisexual and transsexual geographies in addition to acknowledging the fluidity of identities themselves. Despite this shift, geographic analysis continues to focus primarily on gays and lesbians (and even queer is often a stand-in for gay and lesbian), although the spatial turn in social and queer theory has led those outside the discipline to produce valuable contributions to the literature on the spatialities of other sexual dissidents.

## Complicating LGBT Space

Queer geography in the United States originally assumed a fixity that tended to privilege San Francisco as the "queer capital" and to perpetuate a queer identity based on the primarily urban gay communities located on the East and West Coasts of the United States. While there was important work done on lesbian and gay experiences in different regions of the United States, these were often read as local and particularized experiences, while the experiences of gay men and lesbians in New York and San Francisco were often universalized, suppressing regional differences and providing the platform for the "global gay." This universalizing tendency has, to some extent, been mitigated by the growing interest in rural geographies that arose in the mid-1990s, by work on the experiences of and constraints facing rural-urban migrants in the United States and Britain, and by Larry Knopp and Michael Brown's effort to "queer diffusion." Outside of geography, historians such as George Chauncey (1994) and Marc Stein (2000), with their respective studies of New York City and Philadelphia, have made important contributions to a more nuanced understanding of LGBT spatialities.

The creation of a gay niche market and the development of pink economies around gay and lesbian commercial entertainment zones led places to market themselves as "gay capitals" and "gay-friendly" places in order to attract LGBT tourists. Pride parades rooted in political protest evolved to become desirable tourist spectacles. Queer neighborhoods with a history of sexual dissidence have become commercialized zones of consumption, both

for LGBT and straight-identified visitors. Geographers have drawn attention to how these shifts have changed the nature of LGBT space, "watering down" its queerness and associated levels of comfort, generating fears of assimilation, and raising fears of exclusion based on race, income, age, and even looks.

Some of these same exclusions have been reproduced in the geographical literature. Linda Peake (1993) criticized early representations of gay neighborhoods and lesbian communities for a failure to give due attention to the heterogeneous race, class, and other relations that penetrate these spaces. Some authors of those early works have since taken into account the importance of these hierarchies and political economy in their research, as social and cultural geography as a whole has become more cognizant of the importance of power relations.

Racialized class-based identities and privileges, however, continue to pass unexamined in much of the geographic literature, although they are frequently acknowledged. While recognizing the need to forge alliances across identity categories, studies of the geographies of LGBT activism more often call attention to bridges built across sexual identities than across race and class. In a similar manner, and despite an increasing awareness of the complex nature of LGBT spatialities, globalization has frequently been represented as the transmission of images and information to the periphery, where activism and LGBT cultural landscapes were seen as shaped by interactions with the center.

While anthropologists, cultural studies scholars, and others have taken up the challenge of linking LGBT geographies to the processes of globalization, examining transnational communities and links to postcolonial and imperial formations, geographers have been slow to move beyond the study of local gay and lesbian communities. One area in which the role of capitalism and connections between communities and places has been made is that of tourism, where researchers working on LGBT identities and mobilities have begun to make important contributions (see Puar).

These questions are also explored in a 2002 issue of *Antipode: A Radical Journal of Geography*, edited by Heidi Nast, which broadly examines the circulation of images of a "white queer patriarchy," both in the media and in the academy itself. The collection of articles explicitly addresses the question of enfranchisement and the intersection of "race," gender, and class. The issue questions hierarchies of location and representation and demands an examination of the scales and sites of relations of power.

## New Directions

Geographers have produced a rich literature on the complex ways in which sexualities are produced and lived in particular places and spaces. Although much of the initial work done in the field was in the areas of urban, social, and cultural geography, important contributions have been made more recently in the areas of medical geography, particularly in work on AIDS, political geography (nationalism, sexuality, and sexual citizenship); and rural geographies. Originally focused on the neighborhood, the scale of analysis now extends from the body to the transnational and global. The discipline's emphasis on social and material landscapes is an important complement to social theory and queer theory. For instance, Michael Brown's *Closet Space* explores the relationship between the metaphorical and the material, in part to "address geographers' potent concerns over static metaphors of space" (p. 5).

Although some geographers utilize the categories of gay and lesbian without calling into question the ways in which these terms homogenize and exclude individual subjects, the field is increasingly employing a wide range of approaches that take into account the complicated intersection of sexuality with race, class, gender, and other relations. While some geographers such as Jon Binnie have critiqued the discipline for merely "adding in" gays and lesbians to existing forms of geographic analysis (and others have addressed the difficulty of coming out in the discipline and of having sexuality accepted as a legitimate field of study), issues of sexuality are increasingly, although by no means uniformly, addressed throughout various areas of the discipline. Finally, the inherently spatial links between sexuality, power, and knowledge means that work in geography will continue to enrich and be enriched by other disciplines.

## Bibliography

Beemyn, Brett, ed. *Creating a Place for Ourselves: Lesbian, Gay, and Bisexual Community Histories.* New York: Routledge, 1997.

Bell, David. "Bi-sexuality: A Place on the Margins." In *The Margins of the City.* Edited by Stephen Whittle. Aldershot, Hampshire, U.K.: Ashgate, 1994.

Bell, David, and Gill Valentine, eds. *Mapping Desires: Geographies of Sexualities.* New York: Routledge, 1995.

Binnie, Jon. "Coming Out of Geography: Towards a Queer Epistemology?" *Environment and Planning D: Society and Space* 15 (1997): 223–237.

Brown, Michael P. *Closet Space: Geographies of Metaphor from the Body to the Globe.* London and New York: Routledge, 2000.

Chauncey, George. *Gay New York: Gender, Urban Culture, and the Making of the Gay Male World, 1890–1940.* New York: HarperCollins, 1994.

Duncan, Nancy, ed. *Body Space: Destabilizing Geographies of Gender and Sexuality.* London and New York: Routledge, 1996.

Hemmings, Clare. *Bisexual Spaces: A Geography of Sexuality and Gender.* London and New York: Routledge, 2002.

Knopp, Larry. "Sexuality and Urban Space: Gay Male Identity Politics in the United States, the United Kingdom, and Australia." In *Cities of Difference.* Edited by Ruth Fincher and Janet Jacobs. New York and London: Guilford Press, 1998.

Knopp, Larry, and Michael Brown. "Queering Diffusion." *Environment and Planning D: Society and Space* 21 (2003): 409–424.

Namaste, Ki. "Genderbashing: Sexuality, Gender, and the Regulation of Public Space." *Environment and Planning D: Society and Space* 14 (1996): 221–240.

Nast, Heidi, ed. *Antipode: Special Issue—Queer Patriarchies, Queer Racisms, International* 34 (November 2002).

Peake, Linda. "'Race' and Sexuality: Challenging the Patriarchal Structuring of Urban Social Space." *Environment and Planning D: Society and Space* 11 (1993): 415–432.

Puar, Jasbir Kaur, ed. *GLQ: Special Issue—Queer Tourism: Geographies of Globalization* 8 (2002): 1–2.

Stein, Marc. *City of Sisterly and Brotherly Loves: Lesbian and Gay Philadelphia, 1945–1972.* Chicago: University of Chicago Press, 2000.

**Dereka Rushbrook**

*See also* GENTRIFICATION; GHETTOS AND NEIGHBORHOODS; RESORTS; URBAN, SUBURBAN, AND RURAL GEOGRAPHIES.

# GERBER, Henry (b. 29 June 1892; d. 31 December 1972), activist.

Henry Gerber was born in Bavaria, Germany, as Joseph Henry Dittmar. He immigrated to the United States with other family members when he was twenty-one, arriving at Ellis Island on 27 October 1913. They settled in the Chicago area. In January 1914 he enlisted in the U.S. Army. It appears that upon discharge he worked briefly for Montgomery Ward's. The United States entered World War I on 6 April 1917. That same year, Gerber was interned in a camp as an enemy alien because of his German citizenship.

Gerber reenlisted in the army in October 1919 and from 1920 to 1923 was stationed in Germany with the U.S. army of occupation. He worked as a printer and proofreader. During these years, he became aware of the flourishing German homosexual emancipation movement. He subscribed to several periodicals dedicated to the cause and visited Berlin, a hotbed of activity.

After leaving the army in mid-1923, Gerber returned to Chicago and began work as a U.S. Postal Service clerk. He felt compelled, however, to organize an association for homosexuals, similar to those he had witnessed in Berlin. The result was the Society for Human Rights in Chicago, which was incorporated by the State of Illinois on 10 December 1924. The society lasted less than a year. In July 1925, Al Meininger, its vice president, was arrested for disorderly conduct for having sex with another man. He revealed to authorities the names and addresses of Gerber, the society's secretary, and the Reverend John T. Graves, its president. Gerber and Graves were both arrested, but never charged with a specific crime. After three court appearances and an expenditure of $600 for attorneys' fees, Gerber's case was dismissed. The next month, he was fired from his job. Broken psychologically and financially by this ordeal, Gerber retreated to New York City and enlisted in the army for a third time on 13 October 1925. He worked as a proofreader for seventeen years until his discharge in 1942.

Gerber continued his agitation for the cause of homosexual emancipation, but turned instead to his typewriter as his chief ally in waging that campaign. In the late 1920s, he began writing articles, for example, for *Modern Thinker, Chanticleer,* and *American Mercury,* and letters to editors at such publications as the *Washington Times-Herald, Washington Post, American Freeman,* and *Writer's Digest.* He also sought out personal correspondents, in an effort to raise awareness of the dire position of the homosexual male in society. He read voraciously and kept a binder of articles on homosexuality. In 1930, he took over the year-old correspondence club Contacts from its founder, Merlin Wand. From 1930 to 1939, he produced a monthly sheet listing what today would be described as "personals," advertisements for people from across the country seeking pen pals. Californian Manual Boyfrank responded to Gerber's own 1939 ad, in which Gerber described himself as a lover of solitude, classical music, French films, and summer outdoors. The two began a correspondence that lasted almost a decade.

Gerber's views on homosexuality and his philosophy of life are revealed in his ongoing dialogue with Boyfrank. Gerber was a dour individual who despised most of his fellow human beings. Women, clerics, and politicians were three groups upon which he heaped particular vitriol. Gerber was a virulent misogynist and an ardent atheist. For him, the religious establishment conspired with politicians to reinforce the social order that oppressed

homosexual males. For Gerber, homosexuality was a natural form of birth control.

After his 1942 discharge from the army, Gerber took up residence at the U.S. Soldiers Home in Washington, D.C. He devoted his retirement years to research and writing about homosexuality. He wrote four books, including an autobiography, but none have survived. Gerber knew of the existence of the ONE Institute and the Mattachine Society, the 1950s homophile groups. He sent money and articles to both *ONE* magazine and the New York chapter of the Mattachine Society, but he avoided any major involvement with either group.

Gerber died of pneumonia on 31 December 1972 at the age of eighty. He is buried in the U.S. National Cemetery, adjacent to the U.S. Soldiers Home. He did not achieve his goal of liberating homosexual males from their social bondage—his vision was too radical for the time he lived in. But he was the first in this country to try, and for that the late James Kepner has called him the "grandfather of the American gay movement."

**Bibiography**

Katz, Jonathan Ned. "1940, January 27, Henry Gerber to Manuel Boyfrank: 'Our Proposed Movement Is of Great Social Value.'" In *Gay/Lesbian Almanac, A New Documentary.* New York: Harper and Row, 1983.

——. "1924–1925: The Chicago Society for Human Rights; 'To Combat the Public Prejudices.'" In *Gay American History: Lesbians and Gay Men in the U.S.A.* New York: Crowell, 1976.

Kepner, James, and Stephen O. Murray. "Henry Gerber (1895–1972): Grandfather of the American Gay Movement." In *Before Stonewall: Activists for Gay and Lesbian Rights in Historical Context.* Edited by Vern L. Bullough. New York: Harrington Park Press, 2002.

**Karen C. Sendziak**

*See also* SOCIETY FOR HUMAN RIGHTS.

# GHETTOS AND NEIGHBORHOODS

Ghettos were originally areas to which Jewish people were restricted in early modern European cities, but the term's meaning has expanded to encompass a wider range of urban forms. Sociologists and geographers define ghettos as urban areas with a concentration of residents belonging to, and institutions such as bars and restaurants catering to, a particular minority. The earlier sense of them as places of involuntary segregation no longer holds. In the United States until the late twentieth century, the term "ghetto" had a negative connotation. It was long associated with inner-city urban blight because African Americans were frequently limited to de facto ghettos through a combination of racism, "white flight" to the suburbs, and economic disadvantage. However, African American experiences of living in ghettos gave rise to an understanding of ghettos as positive places that could foster a sustaining community culture. In partially similar ways, some LGBT people have chosen to live in LGBT areas for a sense of community and support, and the meaning of the term "gay ghetto" has shifted over time toward positive self-identification rather than marginalization. The term may refer to a combination of residential, commercial, public, and political spaces. In the post-Stonewall era, gay ghettos are often associated with urban regeneration and processes of gentrification, though they have also displaced lower-income occupants, including some members of the LGBT community. Neighborhood is a less politically charged term, indicating a section of a city that has a preponderance of a particular community or identifiable subculture. Both terms indicate the existence of a spatial base for political power and for politicized, frequently contested, community identities.

It is difficult to speak of any LGBTQ ghetto prior to the historical development of an LGBT identity in the late nineteenth century, although each affects the possibility of the other. Thus, the extensive practice of male-male sexual activity in San Francisco during the gold rush era, for example, may have created specific and concentrated areas where men bonded, but these did not constitute gay ghettos. They may, however, have contributed to an image of San Francisco as sexually permissive, which in turn may have led to the development of LGBT identities and neighborhoods.

The development of distinctive and identifiable ghettos and neighborhoods where LGBT people could live, work, play, and find community was uneven. Class, race, sex and gender, economic cycles, and urban demographics all influenced the scope, extent, and geographical distribution of LGBT ghettos and neighborhoods. In addition, their forms, functions, and locations have shifted over time. For example, LGBT ghettos and neighborhoods were initially distinguished by low rates of property ownership, low incidence of families, and relative lack of wealth, but some of these characteristics have changed in some locations.

## Community Identity

Ghettos have been crucial in forming a sense of LGBT identity and providing the physical, visible location of LGBT economic, cultural, and political community. In his analysis of the gay community in San Francisco from the 1940s, Manuel Castells argues that ghettos underpin "the emergence of a social movement and its transformation into a political force through the spatial organization of a self-defined cultural community" (p. 138). To this extent the politicizing role of ghettos suggests that a neighborhood may be defined as LGBTQ if it is perceived to be one, even if it does not have predominantly lesbian and gay residents or institutions.

Castells makes the essentialist argument that gay men, as men, desire territorial control and actively take over a concentrated area of a city in order to stake political and economic claims to citizenship. He claims that lesbians, as women, are less interested in forming ghettos and more interested in developing networks that may be spatially dispersed. His view has been challenged by Sy Adler and Johanna Brenner, who argue that the relative inability of lesbians to form ghettos in which they control residential and business properties can be explained by economic and cultural restrictions on women's access to financing and space. These restrictions are further exacerbated for lesbians of color, and they apply as well to gay men of color. However, Marc Stein further challenges Castells by arguing that, at least in Philadelphia in the 1940s, 1950s, and 1960s, lesbians did develop spatial concentrations, although these took different forms from those developed by gay men. Most neighborhoods have had some degree of gender mixing in part because lesbians and gay men need a smattering of the opposite sex to act as heterosexual partners in the event of police raids. The distinction between men's and women's ability to form ghettos and neighborhoods has had an important impact on the development of ghettos and on the contours of the LGBT movement during the first decade of the twenty-first century.

## Changing Nature of Ghettos and Neighborhoods

Pre–World War II ghettos developed out of existing enclaves of nonconformity, vice, and low income. Two of the most famous were Greenwich Village and Harlem, both in New York City. Greenwich Village was a bohemian area that was attractive to artists and writers and that challenged heteronormativity and family life. An African American lesbian and gay culture flourished in Harlem during the 1920s and 1930s, closely linked to the vibrant Harlem Renaissance.

More identifiably LGBT ghettos were generally associated with white bar culture. The best known were in New York City and San Francisco, but many other cities, such as Buffalo, Detroit, and Philadelphia, had clusters of bars, parks, or streets that were considered gay or lesbian neighborhoods. Subject to discrimination and hostility, African Americans more often socialized in bars in heterosexually dominated African American neighborhoods. Drawing on the rich culture of African American urban social life, they also congregated in alternative semipublic spaces such as rent parties or buffet flats. Such spaces were located in individual homes and were not necessarily physically part of the LGBT ghetto.

Cherry Grove, Fire Island, was a summer resort frequented by elite gay men and women from the 1930s onward. It provides an example of a distinctive neighborhood with a specific function—recreation—rather than a ghetto.

The major expansion of the San Francisco ghetto, located in the Castro district, dates from World War II, when a critical mass of servicemen and women passed through the port of San Francisco in transit to and from the war in the Pacific. The war created the conditions for many to experience and develop LGBT identities. Once demobilized, many chose to stay in the city and develop a community there.

By the 1960s existing LGBT ghettos burgeoned and increased their political and cultural visibility in conjunction with the civil rights and women's liberation movements. In particular, the shift from interior locations, such as bars, to exterior locations, such as streets, signaled gay men's ability to exert increasing political and spatial control. The growth of West Hollywood is an example of this process. From the 1950s onward there were shifts toward gentrification propelled by gay men. Lesbian feminist influences in the 1970s increased lesbian visibility generally, but the rising living costs associated with gentrification decreased lesbian presence in ghettos.

Perhaps because of their spatial concentration, ghettos have never reflected the rich diversity of the entire LGBT community, which invariability extends beyond LGBT neighborhoods. Their visibility has made them seem to define the community, a status that has been challenged as not representative of the variety of LGBT perspectives, desires, and political projects. Nevertheless, LGBT ghettos and neighborhoods continue to play a major role in LGBT cultures.

### Bibliography

Adler, Sy, and Johanna Brenner. "Gender and Space: Lesbians and Gay Men in the City." *International Journal of Urban and Regional Research* 16 (1992): 24–34.

Castells, Manuel. *The City and the Grassroots: A Cross-Cultural Theory of Urban Social Movements*. London: Arnold, 1983.

Newton, Esther. *Cherry Grove, Fire Island: Sixty Years in America's First Gay and Lesbian Town*. Boston: Beacon Press, 1993.

Stein, Marc. *City of Sisterly and Brotherly Loves: Lesbian and Gay Philadelphia, 1945–1972*. Chicago: University of Chicago Press, 2000.

**Liz Millward**

*See also* GENTRIFICATION; URBAN, SUBURBAN, AND RURAL GEOGRAPHIES.

## GIDLOW, Elsa (b. 29 December 1898; d. 8 June 1986), writer, philosopher, and political activist.

A lifelong lesbian, Gidlow celebrated her love of women in clear, lyric poetry for more than sixty years. Born Elfie Gidlow in Hull, England, she immigrated with her family to the village of Tetreauville, Quebec, Canada, around 1904. At age fifteen, the family moved to Montreal and Gidlow began doing secretarial work for her father. When she was sixteen, she took a full-time office job to help with home finances and gain her freedom. Aware of her love of women from an early age, she shared her first sexual relationship with a woman at age eighteen.

Gidlow was primarily self-educated through reading that was later supplemented by friendships and travel. First published in the *Montreal Star,* she founded a writers' group in Montreal in 1917. In 1920 Gidlow moved to New York City, seeking a career in publishing. She became poetry editor (later associate editor until 1926) of *Pearson's Magazine,* an iconoclastic literary publication edited by the controversial English writer Frank Harris.

Gidlow published a book of her poetry, *On a Grey Thread,* in 1923; it is believed to be the first volume of poetry celebrating the love of women for women to have been published in North America. In 1924 in New York City, she found the life partner she had been seeking in Violet Winifred Leslie Henry-Anderson, called "Tommy." They moved to San Francisco in 1926 and remained together until Tommy died of lung cancer in 1935.

Through careful management of her earnings as a nursing magazine editor, Gidlow saved enough to spend a year in Paris, Berlin, and London in 1928 and 1929. While there she met author Radclyffe Hall, photographer Berenice Abbott, and lesbian sculptor Gwen LeGallienne. In 1934 Gidlow began supporting herself as a freelance journalist. In 1940 she purchased a disintegrating cabin that she named Madrona in Fairfax, Marin County, California. In the 1950s, she was accused of being a communist because of her activism: as part of the Fairfax Taxpayers' Association, she helped reveal graft in local government, causing the incumbents to lose office. The disgruntled former office holders caused Gidlow and others to be questioned—and found not guilty—by the Tenney Committee, a California version of the House Un-American Activities Committee. She also may have disturbed the authorities because of her mixed-race, African-born lover, Isabel Grenfell Quallo.

In 1954 Gidlow and others moved to an isolated farm near Muir Woods, north of San Francisco, which she named Druid Heights. Around her there gathered what Gidlow referred to as an "unintentional community" of free-thinking, spiritually inclined individuals pursuing organic gardening and independent projects. With Alan and Jano Watts, she co-founded the Society for Comparative Philosophy in 1962 with the goal of affirming a more contemplative way of life. She also experimented with LSD at this time.

Friendships were very dear to her and close friends included the Irish performance artist, poet, revolutionary, and scholar Ella Young; poets Robinson Jeffers and Kenneth Rexroth; poet Helen Hoyt; lesbian activists Del Martin and Phyllis Lyon; and writer-activist-publisher Celeste West. Gidlow joined the pioneering lesbian organization Daughters of Bilitis in the 1960s and through it made friendships and connections that would influence the rest of her life. By the mid-1970s she was a popular speaker at lesbian feminist events, where she read lesbian-themed poems.

Like many poets, Gidlow found self-publishing to be crucial to her writing career. Under the imprint of Druid Heights Books, she brought out her *Moods of Eros* in 1970 and co-published, with Booklegger Press, her *Ask No Man's Pardon: The Philosophical Significance of Being Lesbian* in 1975. Through second-wave feminism and Gidlow's involvement with West Coast lesbian feminist activities, her poetry reached an international audience. She was profiled in *The New Woman's Survival Sourcebook* (1975) and interviewed in the film and book *Word Is Out: Stories of Some of Our Lives,* both versions appearing in 1978. In 1976 the feminist publishing house, Diana Press, brought out a volume of her erotic poetry, *Sapphic Songs: Seventeen to Seventy.* Six years later she self-published a revised, expanded edition, *Sapphic Songs: Eighteen to Eighty.*

The author of poems, poetry dramas, and several unpublished novels, Gidlow supported herself through mainstream journalism. Her short stories, poems, and essays were published in the *Canadian Bookman, Pacific Weekly, Saturday Review, Heresies,* and elsewhere. Gay composer Lou Harrison, a longtime friend, set some of her poems and a playlet to music.

Gidlow had several long, loving relationships interspersed with periods of celibacy. These she wrote about in her autobiography, *Elsa, I Come With My Songs,* published in 1986, a few months before her death later that year. Her ashes are buried among the roots of her old apple tree at Druid Heights. Her papers are housed in San Francisco at the Gay, Lesbian, Bisexual, Transgender Historical Society.

### Bibliography

Adair, Nancy, and Casey Adair. *Word Is Out: Stories of Some of Our Lives.* San Francisco: New Glide Publications, 1978. Gildlow, interviewed on pp. 14–27, is identified only as "Elsa."

Gidlow, Elsa. *Sapphic Songs: Eighteen to Eighty.* Rev. ed. Mill Valley, Calif.: Druid Heights Books, 1982.

———. *Elsa, I Come With My Songs: The Autobiography of Elsa Gidlow.* San Francisco: Booklegger Press, 1986.

Rennie, Susan, and Kirsten Grimstad. *The New Woman's Survival Sourcebook.* New York: Knopf, 1975. See p. 115.

Tee A. Corinne

*See also* DAUGHTERS OF BILITIS; LYON, PHYLLIS, AND DEL MARTIN.

## GILMAN, Charlotte Perkins
(b. 3 July 1860; d. 17 August 1935), feminist, author, and activist.

Gilman was the author of more than two hundred short stories, several novels, and works of nonfiction, including "The Yellow Wallpaper" (1892), *Women and Economics* (1898), and *Herland* (1915). She was active in the women's movement and the labor movement and cofounded the Woman's Peace Party with Jane Addams in 1915. Her critique of the relations between the sexes established her as a leading theorist of the women's movement in the United States.

Gilman's fiction and nonfiction writing engaged with economic, social, and scientific debates over the "woman question" and argued that culture, not biology, forced women to be dependent upon men. Gilman's writing described the condition and treatment of women, while arguing for women's rights to vote, work, and express themselves sexually. Recent scholarship has investigated how Gilman's writing was primarily concerned with white women and has revealed that, although Gilman was engaged in numerous progressive causes, her writing had racist underpinnings.

Gilman was born Charlotte Anna Perkins in Hartford, Connecticut. Through her father, Frederick Beecher Perkins, she was related to the prominent Beecher family, which included Harriet Beecher Stowe, the author of the antislavery novel *Uncle Tom's Cabin.* Her father left his wife and family when Gilman was very young, and her mother, Mary Westcott Perkins, struggling with the demands of raising two children alone, starved her children emotionally.

Gilman's sexual relationships with men are well documented. She married the artist Charles Walter Stetson in 1884 at the age of twenty-four. With him, she had one daughter, Katharine. After giving birth to Katharine in 1885, Gilman suffered severe depression. In 1886, she was treated for hysteria by the noted alienist Silas Weir Mitchell. Gilman's best-known short story, "The Yellow Wallpaper," is based on her unhappy marriage and Mitchell's rest treatment. In 1888, Gilman separated from Stetson and moved to California, where she began to lecture and write prolifically on women's issues. She officially divorced Stetson in 1894 and married her cousin George Houghton Gilman in 1900.

Gilman's relationships with women have yet to be the subject of critical examination. However, there is strong evidence that, throughout her life, Gilman desired and had relationships with women that were both passionate and sexual. The most important same-sex friendship Gilman had in her adolescence was with Martha Lane (born Martha Luther) in Providence, Rhode Island. In 1881, the two formed an intimate relationship and they began exchanging passionate letters and exchanged identical bracelets to be worn as a bond of union. Gilman was devastated when her friend became engaged to Charles A. Lane. Available evidence only gives us Gilman's view on their relationship (as Lane's letters do not survive), yet her letters to Lane indicate an awareness of the transgressive nature of their relationship.

Gilman's relationship and correspondence with Grace Channing clarifies her feelings toward women and her earlier relationship with Lane. In 1885, when Channing became engaged to Gilman's ex-husband, Walter, Gilman expressed her own desire to marry Channing and understood this relationship as analogous to her relationship with Lane. To describe the nature of her desire for Channing, Gilman represented herself as a man trapped inside a woman's body, a representation that corresponded to theories of sexual inversion that were then being circulated to explain same-sex desire.

In 1891, Gilman moved to Oakland, California, where she had coinciding relationships with two women: the journalist Adeline Knapp and the feminist writer Harriet Howe. Both of these relationships were likely sexual. Gilman and Knapp met, declared their love for each other, moved into a room together, and began sharing a bed in 1891. An 1899 letter to her fiancé, George Hough-

ton Gilman, attests to the fact that Gilman saw her relationship with Knapp as both erotic and potentially scandalous, while displaying an awareness of sexual categories that would crystallize in the twentieth century. Evidence indicates that Gilman also had an affair with Howe, and it is believed that her relationship with Howe caused the bitter split between Gilman and Knapp in 1892.

Interpretations of Gilman's relationships with other women are informed by debates in historiography during the latter decades of the twentieth century about what meanings and labels should be ascribed to passionate and intimate relationships between women in the nineteenth century. Biographers and scholars have catalogued evidence indicating Gilman had same-sex sexual relationships but have favored the interpretation that Gilman was involved in sentimental friendships, or "Boston marriages." The one exception concerns Knapp; the possibility that she was Gilman's sexual partner is often cursorily acknowledged, usually with the caveat that we can never know whether their relationship was truly sexual. In short, biographers have explained away rather than explained the sexualized relationships between these women and have based their analysis on an understanding of sexual identities that rests upon the false and highly contested notions of a tidy divide between nineteenth-century presexual identities and twentieth-century sexual identities.

Although firm conclusions cannot be reached about the quality of Gilman's same-sex relationships, she was nevertheless aware of the evocative quality of her correspondence, for, as she wrote to Lane in August 1881: "Incidental thought, wouldn't these letters of mine be nuts for commentators! *If & if* of course, but how they would squabble over indistinct references and possible meanings!"

George Houghton Gilman died in 1934, and in 1935, Gilman was diagnosed with inoperable breast cancer at the age of seventy-five. She died in Pasadena, California, of a self-administered overdose of chloroform. In her suicide note, Gilman wrote, "I have preferred chloroform to cancer."

## Bibliography

Gilman, Charlotte Perkins. *The Living of Charlotte Perkins Gilman.* New York: D. Appleton Century, 1935.

———. *Herland.* New York: Pantheon Books, 1979.

———. *The Diaries of Charlotte Perkins Gilman.* Edited by Denise D. Knight. Charlottesville: University Press of Virginia, 1994.

———. *A Journey from Within: The Love Letters of Charlotte Perkins Gilman, 1897–1900.* Edited by Mary A. Hill. Lewisburg, Pa.: Bucknell University Press, 1995.

———. *The Yellow Wallpaper.* Edited by Dale M. Bauer. Boston: Bedford Books, 1998.

———. *Women and Economics: A Study of the Economic Relation between Men and Women as a Factor in Social Evolution.* Berkeley: University of California Press, 1998.

Gilman, Charlotte Perkins to Martha Lane, 13 August 1881. Correspondence 1879–1890, Rhode Island Historical Society.

Hill, Mary A. *Charlotte Perkins Gilman: The Making of a Radical Feminist, 1860–1896.* Philadelphia: Temple University Press, 1980.

Lane, Ann J. *To "Herland" and Beyond: The Life and Work of Charlotte Perkins Gilman.* New York: Pantheon Books, 1990.

**Gillian Frank**

*See also* ADDAMS, JANE; ANARCHISM, COMMUNISM, AND SOCIALISM; FEMINISM; LITERATURE.

# GINSBERG, Allen (b. 3 June 1926; d. 6 April 1997), poet, activist.

Irwin Allen Ginsberg was born in Newark, New Jersey. His father, Louis, was himself a moderately successful verse writer. Ginsberg's mother, Naomi—tough-minded and political, a consequence of growing up Jewish in western Russia during a time of pogroms—was a member of the local Communist Party chapter. This immersion in radical politics and verse profoundly influenced Ginsberg's life and work.

At school, the young Ginsberg was both apt and practical. Never athletic, he relied on his wits to survive. When bullies tormented him with anti-Semitic slurs, Ginsberg turned his considerable vocabulary against them and, somehow, managed to defuse disagreeable situations. His classmates nicknamed him "The Professor." He was a storyteller and an egoist, and he could talk about politics in a way that impressed even his teachers.

It was during these early years that Ginsberg grew aware of his own homosexuality. He developed a crush on a boy in his class. Later, he and his friends watched in rapture while one boy allowed another to kiss his penis. Throughout high school, Ginsberg continued to develop infatuations with classmates, though modesty and the nature of the times forced him to keep his passions hidden from others.

Ginsberg entered Columbia University in 1943 with the intention of becoming a labor lawyer. With his departure for college came the end of his mother and father's marriage. Their relationship had proven to be a miserable one, largely because of Naomi's declining sanity and paranoid fantasies. At school, Ginsberg was, at least for a time, a model student. The idea of studying under famous professors such as Lionel Trilling, Raymond Weaver, and Mark Van Doren amused and delighted him, and before long he found himself gravitating toward the study of the English language and literature in general. Ginsberg's interest in poetry grew. He fancied himself an unconventional thinker. Through his friend, Lucien Carr, Ginsberg was introduced to William Burroughs and ex-Columbia football player Jack Kerouac. It was during countless late-night conversations and arguments that Allen, Carr, and Kerouac began to shape their iconoclastic vision of the arts—a "New Vision" they called it—the underpinnings of what would eventually become the Beat Movement.

After Ginsberg's first year at Columbia, however, his unconventional life became more dangerous. Carr was arrested and convicted in a bizarre manslaughter case, after stabbing to death an apparently demented homosexual admirer. Ginsberg's reputation on campus got him into trouble with the school's administration. Much to his father's shame, he was upbraided for his carousing with Kerouac. His grades, as always, were excellent, but university administrators cautioned that more "respectable" behavior was expected of a Columbia student. Then in March 1945 Ginsberg was dismissed from the institution following a seemingly trivial incident now at least partly clouded by legend. To tempt a reluctant cleaning woman to clean his dorm room windows, Ginsberg scrawled obscenities into the dirt with his fingers. The cleaning woman reacted violently and accused Ginsberg of threatening her. It was the final offense in a long line of offenses, and Ginsberg was asked to go.

Now Ginsberg embarked on an "education" based on experience. He worked as a dishwasher, a clerk, and a spot-welder. He had sex with a young man he met at the Museum of Modern Art, his first such experience. With Kerouac, Burroughs, and, eventually, Neal Cassady, Ginsberg experimented with mind-altering substances. Still, from a critical point of view, his poetry was not yet very good. Indeed, much of it was quite bad, ill-formed, although with occasional flashes of brilliance. For inspiration, Ginsberg looked to the work of Walt Whitman, Percy Bysshe Shelley, William Blake, William Carlos Williams, and Christopher Smart. Ginsberg's loosely made poems (he called them his "bardic improvisations") relied heavily on the invocation of immediate experience, often that involving the consumption of hallucinogens, and were punctuated by graphic, sexually explicit, and sometimes disturbing imagery.

In 1948 Ginsberg decided to again pursue studies at Columbia, but further troubles followed quickly. In early 1949 Ginsberg was arrested for allowing street hustler Herbert Huncke to store stolen property in his apartment. To avoid time in jail, he cooperated with the Columbia administration, pled insanity, and spent more than eight months in the university's psychiatric institute. While there, he met the bohemian thinker Carl Solomon, another major influence and the person to whom Ginsberg's 1955 classic *Howl* is dedicated.

In 1954, following a short stint with a New York advertising agency, Ginsberg relocated to San Francisco, where a letter of introduction from his mentor, William Carlos Williams, gained him admittance to the local poetry scene. It was there that he began work on *Howl*, the long poem that would solidify his fame and his place at the core of the Beat Movement. That this Whitman-esque and scripturally charged poem's explicit depictions of public sex acts, many of them homosexual, as well as its attacks on the culture and institutions of postwar America, were vilified as obscene—leading to the arrest of the poem's publisher—only increased Ginsberg's celebrity. He was, rather suddenly, not merely a famous poet, but also a guru, a role he would maintain for the rest of his life. The subsequent publication of *Kaddish and Other Poems* (1961) and *Reality Sandwiches* (1963) served only to solidify this reputation.

Sometime before the publication of *Howl*, Ginsberg met and fell in love with Peter Orlovsky, and the two became life-long companions. Ginsberg could at last openly admit the feelings he had so long kept secret.

With one success came others. Ginsberg's work evolved, becoming both more political and more personal. Over the years, he was a regular at antiwar protests and antinuclear sit-ins. For many of his fans, Ginsberg was as much prophet as poet, an image Ginsberg encouraged by linking himself to William Blake and Walt Whitman. It was also to Whitman's sensual vision of the human experience that Ginsberg turned most often in defense of his homosexuality, which he addressed in his work with increasing ardor and frankness and which he clearly saw as intrinsic to his rejection of what he considered the dehumanizing values of his country. He was, of course, not without his serious critics. The poet and novelist James Dickey, for example, once disparaged his sometimes formless style by saying that it made poetry seem as though anyone could write it.

Despite this criticism, and despite those who found his open celebration of homosexuality distasteful, Ginsberg remained an important presence in various counter-

**Allen Ginsberg.** The influential Beat poet and counterculture activist, perhaps best known for his revolutionary poem *Howl* (1955), reads poetry in New York's Washington Square Park in celebration of a court decision against censorship. [AP/Wide World Photos]

culture movements in the United States for the rest of his life. In 1973 he received the National Book Award. In the mid-1970s he helped found the Jack Kerouac School of Disembodied Poetics at the Naropa Institute in Boulder, Colorado, where he taught poetry and Buddhist meditation. In 1985 his collected works were published.

Ginsberg died of liver cancer on 6 April 1997, approximately one week after being diagnosed.

### Bibliography

Caveney, Graham. *Screaming with Joy: The Life of Allen Ginsberg.* London: Bloomsbury, 1999.

Kramer, Jane. *Allen Ginsberg in America.* New York: Random House, 1969.

Miles, Barry. *Ginsberg: A Biography.* New York: Simon and Schuster, 1989.

Schumacher, Michael. *Darma Lion: A Critical Biography of Allen Ginsberg.* New York: St. Martin's, 1992.

**Laura M. Miller**

See also BEATS; BURROUGHS, WILLIAM; CENSORSHIP, OBSCENITY, AND PORNOGRAPHY LAW AND POLICY; LITERATURE; PULP FICTION: GAY; STONEWALL RIOTS; WHITMAN, WALT.

**GIRL SCOUTS.** see BOY SCOUTS AND GIRL SCOUTS.

# GITTINGS, Barbara (b. 31 July 1932),
activist and editor, and Kay TOBIN LAHUSEN
(b. 5 January 1930), activist, photographer, and author.

Barbara Gittings and Kay Lahusen have been a couple since 1961. They have devoted their lives to promoting LGB visibility, inclusiveness, and equality, and were present at many defining moments of the homophile and gay liberation movements. Each considers LGB activism her career, though they earned their living at various jobs.

Gittings was born in Vienna and raised in the United States and Canada. Lahusen was born in Cincinnati. As a writer and photographer, Lahusen used the pseudonym "Kay Tobin" in the 1960s and 1970s because, she said, people could not remember how to spell or pronounce Lahusen. Each first acknowledged her lesbianism while in college. Gittings turned to the Northwestern University library for information about homosexuality. The few books she found painted LGB people as miserable and mentally ill. Lahusen later looked up homosexuality in the archives of the *Christian Science Monitor*, where she worked. What little she found was filed under "Vice."

Prompted by the writer Donald Webster Cory, Gittings traveled to California in 1956 to meet leaders of the new homophile movement. While there, she met Del Martin and Phyllis Lyon, founders of the trailblazing Daughters of Bilitis (DOB). Two years later Gittings founded DOB–New York, considered the first lesbian organization in the eastern United States. Gittings and Lahusen met at a DOB picnic in 1961. The next year, Lahusen moved from Boston into Gittings's Philadelphia apartment.

### Developing a Gay and Lesbian Media Presence

From 1963 to 1966, Gittings and Lahusen co-edited DOB's national magazine, the *Ladder*, one of America's two most widely read LGB periodicals in that period. (Gittings was the official editor, but the two women worked closely together.) Lahusen, its principal photographer, calls herself "the first openly gay photojournalist." They took the *Ladder* in more daring directions than the previous editors. Gittings added the subtitle *A Lesbian Review* and Lahusen replaced the old line-drawing covers

with photographs of lesbians. Under their editorship, the *Ladder* aired controversies and debates of the day, concerning topics such as the movement's reliance on research on homosexuality to debunk the stigma of mental illness.

They participated in most of the early LGB pickets against governmental discrimination in the mid- to late 1960s. Venues included the Pentagon, the White House, and Independence Hall. Gittings began making radio and television appearances and was one of a handful of activists willing to address mainstream audiences at colleges, churches, and professional meetings. In 1970 she and Lilli Vincenz were the first lesbians to appear on the *Phil Donahue Show*. Gittings also read the news on WBAI-New York's groundbreaking radio series, *Homosexual News*.

In 1969 Lahusen moved temporarily to New York City, where she became a founding member of Gay Activists Alliance. She wrote and photographed for the newsweekly *Gay* and was principal author of the first book of biographies of LGB activists, *The Gay Crusaders* (1972). In the 1960s and 1970s, Lahusen worked at what is often considered the first self-identified LGB bookstore, the Oscar Wilde Memorial Bookshop in Greenwich Village. She also founded Gay Women's Alternative, a discussion group in New York City.

In 1970 Gittings joined the American Library Association's (ALA) new Task Force on Gay Liberation. As a non-librarian, she could take risks that career librarians could not. For instance, at the ALA's 1971 convention, she participated in a "Hug-a-Homosexual" kissing booth that captured mainstream media attention. Serving as leader of ALA's renamed Gay Task Force from 1971 to 1986, Gittings put on lively LGB-themed programs at ALA meetings, oversaw the annual Gay Book Award, and produced *A Gay Bibliography* and special-use LGB reading lists. Throughout, Lahusen added her own flair for activism and publicity to advance the campaign for inclusion of LGB materials.

### Other Forms of Activism

Gittings was among the half-dozen LGB activists who took on the American Psychiatric Association in 1971 and helped convince the organization to declassify homosexuality as a mental illness. Using negotiations, panel discussions, and confrontation tactics, Gittings, Lahusen, Franklin Kameny, and others pressed for constructive dialogue between mental health professionals and nonpatient LGB people.

**Leaders, Together.** In their more than four decades as a couple, Barbara Gittings (left) and Kay Tobin Lahusen have been career gay activists in a wide variety of ways, from editing and photojournalism to speeches and mentoring, along with major roles in numerous organizations. [B. Proud Photo]

In the 1970s Gittings was on the first boards of directors for the National Gay Task Force (later known as the National Gay and Lesbian Task Force) and the Gay Rights National Lobby. She also served on the Pennsylvania Council for Sexual Minorities, the first official government body devoted to LGB issues.

Both women remained busy, serving as advisers to numerous organizations and mentoring younger activists. Gittings has been a popular speaker at LGB and mainstream events, and has appeared in several documentaries. In 2001 the Free Library of Philadelphia unveiled its Barbara Gittings Gay/Lesbian Collection, a large circulating collection of books and audiovisual materials. That year, Gittings received from the Gay and Lesbian Alliance Against Defamation (GLAAD) its first Barbara Gittings Award, given for contributions to the development of gay and lesbian media.

In the early 2000s, Lahusen's photo exhibits on LGB activism have been displayed in Philadelphia, San Francisco, and Wilmington, Delaware. Her photos of 1960s and 1970s activism continue to appear in books, magazines, and documentaries.

**Bibliography**

Bullough, Vern L., ed. *Before Stonewall: Activists for Gay and Lesbian Rights in Historical Context.* Binghamton, N.Y.: Harrington Park Press, 2002.

Cain, Paul D. *Leading the Parade: Conversations with America's Most Influential Lesbians and Gay Men.* Lanham, Md.: Scarecrow Press, 2002.

D'Emilio, John. *Sexual Politics and Sexual Communities: The Making of a Homosexual Minority in the United States.* 2d ed. Chicago: University of Chicago Press, 1998.

Marcus, Eric. *Making Gay History: The Half-Century Fight for Lesbian and Gay Equal Rights.* New York: Perennial, 2002.

Stein, Marc. *City of Sisterly and Brotherly Loves: Lesbian and Gay Philadelphia, 1945–1972.* Chicago: University of Chicago Press, 2000.

**Steven Capsuto**

*See also* CORY, DONALD WEBSTER; DAUGHTERS OF BILITIS; GAY ACTIVISTS ALLIANCE; HOMOPHILE MOVEMENT; HOMOPHILE PRESS; *LADDER*; LYON, PHYLLIS, AND DEL MARTIN.

## GLENN (BONNER), Cleo
(b. 1930s; d. 1970s), activist

A strong, determined woman who took her responsibilities seriously, Cleo Glenn (Bonner) was president of the Daughters of Bilitis (DOB), the national lesbian organization, from 1963 to 1966. She was the first and only African American lesbian to lead the organization, and she helped steer it through a tumultuous, exciting period in its history. In 1960, two of DOB's founders, Phyllis Lyon and Del Martin, were invited to speak to a small, select gathering of lesbians in the San Francisco Bay area. Glenn was at the meeting, and she responded to their invitation to get involved. At this time Glenn worked at Pacific Bell, the local telephone company, and was raising a son. She was also in a committed lesbian relationship with a white woman. She chose the pseudonym "Glenn" in her work with DOB to protect herself and her family.

When Glenn joined DOB, she and her partner, Helen Cushman, took on the job of helping to implement DOB's Book and Record Service, which provided copies of publications and albums to members and subscribers. It was a tedious job that demanded accuracy and commitment, and Glenn and "Cush" shared the responsibilities. When the then-national president, Jaye "Shorty" Bell, resigned from her position in November 1963, Glenn became acting president. The next year, at DOB's national convention in New York City, she delivered the welcoming address and was elected president. She continued in that role until the 1966 national convention, held in San Francisco.

Glenn presided over a small organization that was expanding in many different directions at once, reaching thousands of women and men in the United States and around the world via its magazine, the *Ladder*. In this period DOB was starting to receive large quantities of mail and phone calls, media attention, and requests for information. Nascent internal tensions were also surfacing over issues as diverse as the organization's statement of purpose, its collaboration with researchers, the value of direct action tactics, and the content and tone of the monthly magazine. The development of chapters also meant the creation of a national structure and rules governing policy and practices, and DOB's leadership tried to maintain a balance between individual initiative and collective decision-making.

One of the most significant developments of the homophile movement took place while Glenn was national DOB president, and she was intimately involved in it. Glenn was one of the founding members of the Council on Religion and the Homosexual (CRH), which brought San Francisco homophile activists and religious leaders in 1964 for an historic and intense retreat. The retreat was the beginning of a groundbreaking coalition effort that led to the infamous New Year's Eve Ball of 1965. To raise money for the Council's activities and provide an opportunity to socialize together, CRH volunteers organized a public dance for members of religious and homophile communities to welcome in the new year. When the partygoers arrived at California Hall that night, however, they were greeted by rows of police officers, banks of bright lights, intimidating tactics, and intense scrutiny. The gay men and women in attendance were irritated but not surprised; the ministers and their wives were outraged. When the reactions turned angry, the police started making arrests, and hundreds of new allies to the homophile cause were created—including the local American Civil Liberties Union chapter, which helped with legal representation for those arrested.

In 1966, after the DOB national convention, Glenn left the organization. It is unclear why she so abruptly dropped out and what became of her in the intervening years. Lyon and Martin wonder if she had begun to feel the effects of the cancer that caused her death a few years later. They received a call from her partner when Glenn died.

Glenn is remembered as a dedicated, diligent worker who devoted herself to the administrative duties of a

growing lesbian organization at a crucial time in its development. She was one of a handful of women who were willing to complicate their personal lives and add to their professional responsibilities by acting on a passionate commitment to equality.

### Bibliography

Bullough, Vern, ed. *Before Stonewall: Activists for Gay and Lesbian Rights in Historical Context.* New York: Harrington Park Press, 2002.

The *Ladder*. 1963–1966.

**Marcia M. Gallo**

See also DAUGHTERS OF BILITIS; HOMOPHILE MOVEMENT DEMONSTRATIONS; *LADDER*; LYON, PHYLLIS, AND DEL MARTIN.

## GOLDMAN, Emma (b. 27 June 1869; d. 14 May 1940), anarchist.

Emma Goldman was born to a Jewish family in Kovno, Russia (later Lithuania), and immigrated to the United States in 1885. Having joined her sister in Rochester, New York, Goldman began working in local clothing factories and endured a brief and unhappy marriage. In 1889 she moved to New York City. It was during this tumultuous period that Goldman first encountered anarchist ideas. By the end of the 1890s, Goldman was a recognizable and increasingly respected figure in the anarchist movement. She expended enormous energy in promoting her views. In articles, books, lecture halls, and the pages of her journal, *Mother Earth*, she denounced the two-headed foe of capitalism and the state.

Goldman's concerns were not limited to the political and the economic. As an anarchist she sought the transformation of all social realms, including the sexual. The insistence on the rights of individuals to lead their lives according to their own desires and the belief that sexual expression was a positive force were at the heart of Goldman's sexual politics. "The sex organs," she wrote in 1899, "as well as all the other organs of the human body are the property of the individual possessing them, and that individual and no other must be the sole authority and judge over his or her own acts" (as quoted in S. D., p. 2). She spoke out against state-sanctioned marriage, ridiculed censorship of so-called obscene literature, advocated the legalization of birth control, denounced the nation's antimiscegenation laws, and defended the rights of homosexuals.

The arrest and imprisonment in Great Britain of writer Oscar Wilde in 1895 (for "gross indecency") was a key point in the development of Goldman's sexual politics. In her autobiography, *Living My Life*, Goldman tells of "the indignation I . . . felt at the conviction of Oscar Wilde." She did not suffer this indignation in silence. Ever ready to speak out, Goldman "pleaded [Wilde's] case against the miserable hypocrites who had sent him to his doom" (p. 269). Goldman continued to rise to his defense; in 1912 the *Denver Post* noted that in a lecture Goldman "glorified Wilde, and intimated that while society forgives the criminal, it never forgives the dreamer." In Goldman's eyes Wilde was a martyr, a critic of society whose willingness to expose how power operates resulted in his imprisonment, exile, and early death.

Goldman's interest in the politics of homosexuality was spurred by her personal relationships with gay men and lesbians. In 1914, for example, Goldman met and befriended Margaret Anderson and her lover, Harriet Dean. The two constituted a classic femme/butch relationship. Dean, according to Goldman, "was athletic, masculine-looking, reserved, and self-conscious. Margaret, on the contrary, was feminine in the extreme, constantly bubbling over with enthusiasm" (Goldman, p. 531). The pair were as smitten with Goldman as she was with them. For a period Anderson and Dean's journal, the *Little Review*, was filled with praise of anarchism. Goldman also had an intense relationship with a working-class woman named Almeda Sperry. Sperry met Goldman at one of her lectures. Though married, Sperry was passionately attracted to women, including, it seems, Goldman. Sperry wrote Goldman a series of remarkable letters that fairly burn with eroticism. It is unclear, however, to what extent—if at all—Goldman responded to Sperry's advances.

Goldman's lectures on homosexuality, which she delivered with increasing frequency from 1908 to 1917, were among the first sustained, clearly articulated, public defenses of same-sex love in the United States. Drawing on her political convictions, her personal experience, and her reading of sexology, Goldman recast homosexuality's status from that of a moral problem to evidence of the richness of sexual variation. Anna W., who attended a lecture in Washington, D.C., in 1915, thought the experience of hearing Goldman talk was transformative. "I do not hesitate to declare," Anna W. wrote,

> that every person who came to the lecture possessing contempt and disgust for homo-sexualists and who upheld the attitude of the authorities that those given to this particular form of sex expression should be hounded down and persecuted, went away with a broad and sympathetic understanding of the question and a conviction that in

**Emma Goldman.** Best known as an anarchist, she opposed regulation of the sexual realm as well, and was outspoken in defense of same-sex love. [**Library of Congress**]

matters of personal life, freedom should reign. (p. 517)

Gay men and lesbians who attended Goldman's talks shared Anna W.'s views. In her autobiography Goldman recalled that the "men and women who used to come to see me after my lectures on homosexuality" were fulsome in their thanks (Goldman, p. 555).

Goldman's political life in the United States ended with her arrest in 1917 for opposing America's entry into World War I. She spent two years in prison; upon her release she was deported to the newly created Soviet Union. Her hopes that Lenin's government would fulfill her lifelong hopes for revolutionary liberation were dashed by the communist's ruthless repression of any and all opposition. In 1921 Goldman left the USSR for a life of exile. She was permitted to return to the United States only once during these years and for only a brief time. Undaunted, Goldman struggled to keep her visionary politics alive. She died in 1940 while waiting to enter the United States and was brought to Chicago for burial.

Goldman was rediscovered in the late 1960s and 1970s. Her iconoclastic views found new audiences among sex and gender rebels of varied stripes. Goldman's face and words appeared on T-shirts, coffee mugs, and posters, and new editions of her writings were published. The Emma Goldman Papers Project of the University of California, Berkeley, is actively collecting materials that document Goldman's life and work.

**Bibliography**

Falk, Candace. *Love, Anarchy, and Emma Goldman.* New York: Holt, Rinehart, and Winston, 1984.

Goldman, Emma. *Living My Life.* Garden City, NJ: Garden City Publishing, 1934 [1931].

Haaland, Bonnie. *Emma Goldman: Sexuality and the Impurity of the State.* Montreal: Black Rose Books, 1993.

"Mild Comedy at the Tabor; Virile Talk at Woman's Club: Emma Goldman." *Denver Post,* April 22, 1912.

S. D. "Farewell." *Free Society* 13 (August 1899): 2.

W., Anna. "Emma Goldman in Washington." *Mother Earth,* May 1916, p. 516.

Wexler, Alice. *Emma Goldman: An Intimate Life.* New York: Pantheon Books, 1984.

**Terence Kissack**

*See also* ANARCHISM, COMMUNISM, AND SOCIALISM; ANDERSON, MARGARET, AND JANE HEAP; HOWE, MARIE JENNEY.

# GOODMAN, Paul (b. 11 September 1911; d. 2 August 1972), writer and activist.

During the 1960s, Goodman was a ubiquitous figure on college and university campuses, on alternative radio stations, and in the pages of a wide variety of popular periodicals. Goodman's fame during the 1960s was due in large part to his highly influential book *Growing Up Absurd,* a work that challenged dominant notions of education and delinquency by arguing that youth did not need regulation, discipline, and order, and that the regulatory system of education itself caused delinquency. Goodman was often accused of being a gadfly, an individual with too many interests. Indeed, Goodman did write on an enormous range of topics. Over the course of his life, he published novels, a collection of short stories, numerous volumes of poetry, plays, a work of criticism on Franz Kafka, a book on urban life and planning, two books of social criticism about education and youth, works on Gestalt therapy, and many, many articles. During the 1960s, his ideas became an important inspiration to the New Left, particularly the Students for a Democratic Society (SDS).

Born in New York City, Goodman was raised in the bohemian milieu of Greenwich Village. After receiving a B.A. from City College in 1931, Goodman moved to Chicago to pursue graduate work in literature. At the University of Chicago, Goodman clashed with administrators over his sexual conduct and lifestyle. Working as an instructor in the undergraduate college, Goodman had numerous sexual relationships with both students and nonstudents, behavior that alarmed college officials and ultimately resulted in his dismissal. This was not the last academic position Goodman lost because of his open and very public sexual behavior. Moving back to New York with his wife Sally and their three children, Goodman eked out a meager living as a writer and occasional teacher.

Goodman's book on delinquency, *Growing Up Absurd: Problems of Youth in the Organized System* (1960), arrived at the end of a decade that had seen a tremendous amount of debate and anxiety over the supposed problems of youth. Into this debate strode Goodman, who challenged dominant representations of delinquents by arguing that it was the exercise of authority over young people that was socially destructive and generative of delinquency. Under the current system, Goodman argued, young men (he was distressingly uninterested in the predicament of young women) had no real opportunity to learn, to enrich their lives, to grow and transform themselves. Education, he argued, was simply instrumental training for soul-deadening employment and not true instruction in skills and craft. For Goodman, delinquents were proto-anarchists, individuals resisting oppressive conformity and seeking through petty crime, vandalism, and truancy a way of surviving psychologically. What these delinquents had not yet found, but needed to find, were things of value, beauty, and worth with which they could build an alternative existence, community, and politics. In *Growing Up Absurd,* Goodman identified closely with his subject, even seeing himself as "a kind of juvenile delinquent." Writing in his diary/memoir *Five Years: Thoughts during a Useless Time* (1966), Goodman noted that "I move in a society so devoid of ordinary reality that I am continually stopping to teach good sense, to give help, to help out, as a young gangster might help an old lady across the street on his way to the stick up."

The historian John D'Emilio argues that Goodman's description of youth can be applied to the situation of homosexuals. In D'Emilio's reading, the two groups had a close affinity in the conformist culture of the 1950s. Both were social outcasts, forming marginal subcultures and living in fear of the police. Moreover, their participation and celebration of transgressive sexuality placed them outside the confines of respectable society. In fact, Goodman celebrated furtive and sweaty sexuality and same-sex erotics. In his poetry and fiction, as well as in *Five Years*, Goodman detailed his chance encounters, same-sex longings, and acts of public sexuality in clear defiance of the prohibitive Cold War chill. Such encounters were familiar terrain for Goodman, part of his practice of encounter, infinite possibility, and world making.

In his essays, Goodman became a critical voice for a more expressive sexual culture. During the 1950s, for example, Goodman wrote forcefully against forms of legal and cultural censorship. In the case of pornography, Goodman argued that the process of censorship and repression were of greater harm to society than the production and distribution of hard-core sexual material. For Goodman, the path of the censor, of policing, of trials and court rulings against pornography, was ultimately ineffectual because it did nothing to get at the root causes and the generator of demand for such material, which he saw as the repressive social environment.

Goodman's views on sexuality were steeped in the psychoanalytic traditions of Sigmund Freud and Wilhelm Reich. In particular, Reich's work on sexuality was central to Goodman's understanding of the operation of a repressive social system and the emergence of totalitarian regimes. The repression of sexual drive and bodily pleasures significantly contributed, in Goodman's view, to individual and collective alienation, to frustration and anger, which in time led to despair, violence, and militarism. Employing Reich's formula that a lack of sexual fulfillment resulted in tension, physical malady, and neurosis, Goodman sought to liberate sexuality as part of a larger anarchist political project, one designed to challenge what he saw as a pervasive system of repression and conformity. For Goodman, the repression of sexuality was symptomatic of other restraints on people's creativity—their ability to fashion their own workplace, to build communities of their choosing, and to pursue their own educational goals rather than those of capitalists and the State. Ultimately, Goodman became a major figure in the Gestalt psychology movement. Goodman died of a heart attack at his farm in New Hampshire.

Throughout the post–World War II decades, Goodman was one of the few public intellectuals whose poems, novels, and works of criticism dealt with questions of same-sex desire, longing, and intimacy. His tremendous appeal to young people during the 1960s and his importance to gay and lesbian liberation rested on his forceful challenge to the normative structures of the public and intimate lives of Americans and on the notion that people could emancipate themselves through therapy and experimentation.

**Bibliography**

D'Emilio, John D. *Sexual Politics, Sexual Community.* Chicago: University of Chicago Press, 1983.

Goodman, Paul. *Growing Up Absurd: Problems of Youth in the Organized System.* New York: Random House, 1960.

———. *Five Years: Thoughts during a Useless Time.* New York: Vintage Books, 1969.

David S. Churchill

*See also* ANARCHISM, COMMUNISM, AND SOCIALISM; NEW LEFT AND STUDENT MOVEMENTS.

# GOODSTEIN, David (b. 1932; d. 22 June 1985), businessman, publisher, activist.

Born in Denver, Colorado, Goodstein graduated from Cornell University and Columbia University School of Law. He began his career as a criminal defense attorney before turning to Wall Street, where he founded Compufund, a mutual fund that applied cutting-edge computer technology to analyzing stock trends. In his free time, he developed an unparalleled collection of Italian Baroque paintings, much of which he eventually contributed to the Andrew D. White Museum.

In 1971, Goodstein moved to San Francisco and was promptly fired from his job heading the investment department at a major bank when his employer discovered his homosexuality. Vowing revenge, he began using the fortune he had amassed to further an array of LGB rights causes, working in particular with the California Democratic Party, which he viewed as the most effective vehicle to further the goals of the movement. He also cofounded Concerned Voters of California, a statewide organization that opposed the 1978 "Briggs Initiative," which proposed to bar open gays and lesbians from the ranks of public school teachers. With an assist from then-governor Ronald W. Reagan, the ballot measure went down to defeat.

Goodstein played a leading role in the 1974 passage of California's consensual sex legislation, which decriminalized same-sex sodomy. In addition, he was among those responsible, some two years later, for the creation of the National Gay Rights Lobby, where he pioneered the prodigious fundraising that would later mark national LGBT politics.

In 1975, Goodstein purchased the *Advocate*, a 40,000-circulation gay and lesbian newsweekly based in Los Angeles, from Dick Michaels and Bill Rand. Goodstein began the arduous process of turning it into a national publication, giving it a magazine format and professionalizing its staff. Goodstein moved the magazine from Los Angeles to San Mateo, a suburb of San Francisco, in a symbolic effort to create distance between the magazine's editorial stance and what he termed "self-appointed gay leaders," who he charged had turned the magazine into their own personal soapbox.

Under Goodstein's direction, the magazine hired and featured the work of some of the best LGB reporters and editors in the country, including John Preston, Sasha Gregory-Lewis, Nathan Fain, George Whitmore, and Randy Shilts. Other prominent contributors were David Aiken, Arnie Kantrowitz, and Vito Russo. Goodstein took it upon himself to grill prominent politicians about LGB rights, interviewing Pete McCloskey, Percy Sutton, John Burton, Leo Ryan, and Edward Koch, among others. In the late 1970s and early 1980s, the magazine's aggressive reporting on the emergent Christian right proved prescient.

But Goodstein was also a lightning rod for criticism. Skeptical of his moderate politics and wealth, left-leaning activists accused him of abandoning the *Advocate*'s liberationist roots and turning it into a marketing vehicle for major advertisers. "The natural allies of David Goodstein are those who want a society based on everyone's conformity with affluent white male values," declared the publication *Gay Sunshine* in a typical denunciation.

Goodstein tangled repeatedly with the gay San Francisco politician Harvey Milk. He refused to endorse Milk's bid for the San Francisco board of supervisors on the grounds that Milk's earliest campaigns "did not speak out on gay rights and his campaign literature in past races did not even mention his being gay." Milk went on to become a beloved figure and broke down barriers to openly LGB elected officials.

In the early 1980s, critics ridiculed Goodstein for creating the "Advocate Experience," a spiritual self-help group inspired by his friend Werner Erhard, leader of the EST (Erhard Seminar Training) movement. Nevertheless, thousands of gay men and lesbians cycled through the coming-out program. Critics charged that Goodstein's interest in the cultlike EST distracted him from his magazine and softened his once-aggressive reporting standards.

AIDS activists took on the *Advocate* for ignoring the burgeoning epidemic except to deny any connection to the sexual lives of gay men. After coming under withering attacks from the AIDS activist Larry Kramer and others in the rival *New York Native,* and as several prominent editors succumbed to the disease, the magazine stepped up its AIDS coverage and encouraged readers to adopt safe-sex practices.

Despite the crossfire over his editorial strategy, by the time he died from complications related to bowel cancer in 1985, Goodstein had turned the *Advocate* into the largest circulation LGB news publication in the nation.

### Bibliography

Alwood, Edward. *Straight News: Gays, Lesbians, and the News Media,* New York: Columbia University Press, 1996.

Bull, Chris, ed. *Witness to Revolution: The "Advocate" Reports on Gay and Lesbian Politics, 1967–1999.* Los Angeles: Alyson, 1999.

Guide to the David Goodstein Papers (c. 1960–1985). Division of Rare and Manuscript Collections. Cornell University Library, Ithaca, New York. Available from http://rmc .library.cornell.edu/EAD/htmldocs/RMM07311.html.

Thompson, Mark, ed. *Long Road to Freedom: The "Advocate" History of the Gay and Lesbian Movement.* New York: St. Martin's Press, 1994.

**Chris Bull**

*See also* ADVOCATE; NEWSPAPERS AND MAGAZINES.

## GOVERNMENT AND MILITARY WITCHHUNTS

The history of repressive antigay policies in the United States military and government over the course of the twentieth century is inextricably connected to changing medical and criminal definitions of homosexuality and to the perception by psychiatrists of same-sex desire as antithetical to national security. During World War I, no formal mechanism for identifying or dealing with homosexuals existed within the armed forces, but by the 1940s and 1950s, as homosexuality increasingly became defined as a psychiatric rather than a criminal problem, it also came to be seen as a corrosive and contagious condition that could weaken the fighting power of the country and sap the moral resolve of a nation in the grip of a cold war against global communism. The explicit barring of gay men and lesbians from most federal government jobs was lifted in 1975 when the U.S. Civil Service Commission removed from its regulations the language related to sexual perversion. However, the mentality of purges trickled down to the state and local levels, with highly visible police roundups of homosexuals in parks, bars, and other public spaces, and even a statewide campaign to remove lesbian and gay professors and teachers in Florida. Purges also stood largely unchallenged and unchanged in the military, where through the early twenty-first century hundreds of lesbian and gay Americans continued to be discharged every year because of their sexual orientation. Throughout the century, there have been discernible periods in which the persecution of homosexuals in the military or in government institutions intensified and increased, often the result of other political or cultural anxieties that led to scapegoating. It is unquestionably important to examine these episodic bursts of antigay discrimination—the witchhunts against gay men and lesbians during both world wars and the post–World War II years. But in the context of the twentieth-century United States, they must be understood as part of a larger, systemic pattern of homophobia that helped determine policies and attitudes.

## World War I

Whereas the British army was court-martialing "sodomites" during World War I—even those who had distinguished themselves in battle and served as officers—the United States did not concern itself with such matters in any systematic way. In 1916, "assault with the intent to commit sodomy" became a felony and grounds for dismissal from the U.S. armed forces; three years later, sodomy (with or without assault) was written into military law as an offense punishable by court-martial. There is little evidence to document with any precision the number of people affected by this new policy. The most notorious instance of the growing awareness of homosexuality by American military leaders, however, occurred in Newport, Rhode Island, at the naval training station in 1919, after the end of the war. Here the navy dispatched a group of sailors to investigate the homosexual underground in the city and the involvement of enlisted men within it. The sailors went undercover—so deeply undercover, in fact, that they engaged in various sexual activities with other men in order to collect evidence against them. This campaign led to the arrest of twenty sailors and sixteen civilians. According to historian George Chauncey, the case went largely unnoticed until one of the accused, a local Episcopal minister, publicly condemned the navy's tactics, denied the charges, and brought the weight of the Episcopal church of Rhode Island to bear in the defense of the clergyman and the very principle of Christian brotherly love.

The end result was a Congressional investigation, not into "sex perverts" in the navy, but rather into the reasons why the navy would have assigned sailors to have sex with other men in the first place. (The answer, according to Chauncey, is that popular understandings of homosexual sex allowed for a greater variety of labels and identities, and that as long as sailors did not display effeminate characteristics or assume effeminate roles during sex, nobody—including naval officials—labeled them as perverts.) Chauncey uses this episode to explore the historical contours of sexual identity, class difference, and

definitions of homosexuality in the early twentieth century. But the incident in Newport also provides a striking illustration of the navy's relative uncertainty in addressing the question of homosexual behavior in its own ranks—indeed, its near refusal to see military personnel as deviants.

## World War II

A significant change occurred by the early 1940s with the advent of U.S. involvement in World War II as psychiatrists began in earnest to stake a claim for the authority to screen out mentally "unfit" volunteers, draftees, and enlisted men and women. They viewed homosexuality as a form or manifestation of mental illness that could threaten military morale and effectiveness; and they played a crucial role in shaping military procedures for identifying, removing, and treating lesbians and gay men. In previous decades, individuals could be court-martialed and imprisoned for individual sexual acts that were illegal, but World War II brought about an entirely new system of identifying homosexuals as a distinctive and damaged personality type.

Allan Bérubé's definitive study of the armed forces' treatment of lesbians and gay men during World War II, *Coming Out Under Fire,* carefully traces the path by which psychiatrists and mental health experts shaped ideas about homosexuality, and details the effects of these new policies as well as the varied responses of soldiers. The first to develop screening procedures for any signs of sexual deviation were the army, navy, and selective service system; these procedures were put in place in 1941, before the United States entered the war. Psychiatrists' twofold intentions, according to Bérubé, were to make the military more cost-effective by eliminating potential psychiatric patients who, once they joined the service, would become wards of the state later; and to bolster their own standing as invaluable experts within the medical profession. As well, many of the architects of the screening program (civilian psychiatrists hired by the military both to help devise the program and to train military physicians in the field of psychiatry) sought a more humane approach to the problem—by convincing military officials that lesbians and gay men were sick people who needed treatment rather than criminals who deserved punishment. Their original plans called for psychiatrists or military medical personnel who had taken a crash course in psychiatry to carry out the screening at local induction centers. But the exigencies of rapid, mass mobilization after Pearl Harbor allowed little time for such luxuries, and for the duration of the conflict it was largely up to local examiners to detect sex perverts in a matter of a few minutes per interview. All told, historians have estimated that roughly four to five thousand men (of the nearly eighteen million examined) were rejected on the grounds of homosexuality.

The armed forces also codified psychiatrists' proposals to treat homosexuals whose deviance became known while in the service as mentally ill. Now, instead of being sentenced to military prisons and being court-martialed, they were given a dishonorable discharge and a permanent stain on their military record—the stigma of a "section eight." Prisons and courts-martial were not replaced entirely, but the new policy did shift a significant burden away from the military's penal system and onto a growing bureaucracy of medical review boards and psychiatric hospitalization. It proved a boon to the psychiatric profession, as 2,400 physicians from the army and seven hundred from the navy (most of whom had no previous training in psychiatry) were now assigned the task of evaluating suspected or confessed homosexuals to determine how they would be treated. Historians have tallied the number of servicemen discharged for homosexuality during World War II as approximately nine thousand, though untold numbers were also likely discharged under other auspices or, conversely, intentionally misdiagnosed as "normal" in order to keep them in the service.

With such a wide-ranging and elaborate system in place, it is hardly surprising that military police and intelligence officers engaged in periodic roundups of homosexuals during the war. Whether following up on a hunch or a personal grudge, accusations or rumors lodged by a fellow soldier, or orders from commanding officers, they caught scores of lesbians and gay men who were trying to serve their country while passing as straight. As Bérubé has shown, it is impossible to pinpoint the frequency and location of the witchhunts, as well as the number of women and men targeted in each case. In spite of the shroud of secrecy covering these operations, however, some military records do reveal the inner workings of the antigay investigations and purges, and the rate at which homosexuals filled the "queer stockades" and were hospitalized and/or discharged are a testament to their effectiveness.

Women who joined the service were subject to psychiatric screening, though largely in name only. Still, the women who enlisted in the auxiliary branches of the army, navy, marines, and coast guard (more than 275,000 in all), were, as some historians have argued, even more closely scrutinized for signs of gender transgression and sexual deviance than their male counterparts. Historian Leisa Meyer has argued, however, that lesbians in the Women's Army Corps (WAC) were less likely to be discharged on the basis of homosexuality because the direc-

tor, Oveta Culp Hobby, and other leaders believed that public admission of lesbianism within the branch would threaten its reputation—and by extension the very concept of women serving in the armed forces. There were also rules against WACs fostering an atmosphere of suspicion, rumor-mongering, and gossip that would lead to witchhunts (another potential publicity nightmare for the corps). Still, during World War II there were occasional investigations and discharges of groups of lesbians; in the WAC, Fort Oglethorpe, Georgia, and Daytona Beach, Florida, were among the sites of the largest scale witchhunts aimed specifically at lesbians. Women, then, were not exempt from the new military discharge policies that treated homosexuality as mental illness and homosexuals as sex perverts, but they did experience the effects of the policies differently.

## Post–World War II Era

Immediately following the end of World War II, it became clear that military prohibitions against sex perverts were more than just a wartime measure; indeed, they continued to be upheld, and lesbians and gay men continued to be discharged. In 1949, the Department of Defense streamlined procedures for identifying and removing homosexuals, and all branches began following a uniform policy that led to two thousand service members being expelled annually. After 1947, as loyalty and national security became obsessive catch phrases in the federal government, a new sector of American society came under the microscope of the cold war state: federal government employees. Based largely on the armed forces' now firmly entrenched psychiatric construction of the homosexual as an unstable, emotionally immature, morally compromised, and sexually out-of-control personality type, the existence of sexual deviants in government came to be seen as a grave problem.

In December 1950, a subcommittee of the Senate Committee on Expenditures in the Executive Departments published a report dispassionately titled "Employment of Homosexuals and Other Sex Perverts in Government." Earlier that year, Under Secretary John Peurifoy had testified before the Senate Appropriations Committee that a majority of the ninety-one federal employees who had been fired for moral turpitude were homosexuals. Republicans such as Joe McCarthy of Wisconsin and Kenneth Wherry of Nebraska, and southern Democrats like Mississippi's James Eastland and Arkansas' John McClellan, seized upon the issue to attack President Harry Truman and to question his devotion to combating communism. The subcommittee concluded that homosexuals, as sex perverts who willingly and compulsively engaged in illegal and immoral acts, were inherently unsuited to the weighty responsibility of government service. Further, it provided a laundry list of homosexuals' defects: the "weakness of their moral fiber;" their susceptibility to blackmail; the fact that "the presence of a sex pervert in a Government agency tends to have a corrosive influence upon his fellow employees;" and the "tendency to gather other perverts" around them ("Employment of Homosexuals," pp. 4–5). The report also noted that between 1947 and 1950, 457 people who also happened to be government employees were arrested in Washington, D.C., in "sex perversion cases." No liaison existed between federal agencies and local police, but the subcommittee's report quickly remedied the situation. In 1951 an intensive sweep of the civil service occurred, resulting in an average of sixty dismissals (and countless resignations) per month. Two years later, Republican president Dwight D. Eisenhower signed an executive order that made sexual perversion a criterion for excluding individuals from federal employment as part of his expanded loyalty-security program. Historians have not yet tackled the daunting challenge of determining the precise racial and gender breakdown of the government witchhunts. Since white men made up a majority of federal employees, it is tempting to see them as the main targets of this repression. But black men as well as black and white women were ensnared in the government's net as well, and their stories remain to be told.

Taking a page from the federal government and the U.S. military, a state investigating committee in Florida carried out years of investigations into homosexual activity across the state, and in particular, among teachers. Originally one of several anticommunist committees formed by southern legislators as part of the massive resistance to the Supreme Court's *Brown* decisions of 1954 and 1955, the Florida Legislative Investigation Committee (FLIC) was created in 1956, but by 1959 had turned its attention away from suspected communists in the National Association for the Advancement of Colored People and to the "problem" of homosexual professors and teachers as a threat to young people and the state. For five years, the FLIC's chief investigator, with the cooperation of police officers, highway patrolmen, and school administrators, tracked down hundreds of suspected lesbians and gay men, subjected them to intensive questioning in which they were pressured into graphically describing the sex acts they had engaged in, and coerced them into naming names of other homosexuals and resigning from their jobs. In 1964, after years of investigations, the FLIC published a report of its findings, titled "Homosexuality and Citizenship in Florida." Intended as a means of informing citizens but also shocking them into a new consciousness about the gravity of the threat,

the booklet contained pornographic images—allegedly taken from male homosexuals in Miami during a police raid—of half-naked men kissing, of young boys in nude and seminude poses, and of a shirtless teenager bound and gagged. The firestorm of negative publicity made a laughingstock of the committee, which folded the following year.

For its part, the ban on gays in the military outlived the waning of any explicit association between homosexuality and national security risks and survived even the most modest attempts to alter it. In spite of the transition in the 1990s to a "don't ask, don't tell" plan—intended to be less, not more, draconian—the number of lesbians and gay men being discharged actually increased. Indeed, it was this policy that resulted in the expulsion of nine gay linguists/translators (seven of whom were studying Arabic) from the army in November 2002, at a time when the government was facing an alarming shortage of Arabic-speaking experts to assist in the global war against terrorism. Although the sort of antigay witchhunts conducted by the State Department in the 1950s or the state of Florida in the 1950s and 1960s gradually disappeared, the grip of homophobia on the armed forces proved fiercely tenacious. Though one enemy—communism—vanished and was replaced by the new menace of terrorism, the imagined threat posed by lesbians and gay men to the morale and combat readiness of the United States military ensured the continuation of witchhunts against them.

## Bibliography

Bérubé, Allan. *Coming Out Under Fire: The History of Gay Men and Women in World War II*. New York: The Free Press, 1990.

Braukman, Stacy. "'Nothing Else Matters but Sex': Cold War Narratives of Deviance and the Search for Lesbian Teachers in Florida, 1959–1963." *Feminist Studies* 27, no. 3 (Fall 2001): 553–575.

Chauncey, George. "Christian Brotherhood or Sexual Perversion? Homosexual Identities and the Construction of Sexual Boundaries in the World War One Era." *Journal of Social History* 9 (Winter 1985): 189–211.

D'Emilio, John. "The Homosexual Menace: The Politics of Sexuality in Cold War America." In *Passion and Power: Sexuality in History*. Edited by Kathy Peiss and Christina Simmons. Philadelphia: Temple University Press, 1989, pp. 226–240.

Faderman, Lillian. *Odd Girls and Twilight Lovers: A History of Lesbian Life in Twentieth-Century America*. New York: Penguin, 1991.

Meyer, Leisa D. *Creating GI Jane: Sexuality and Power in the Women's Army Corps During World War II*. New York: Columbia University Press, 1996.

Shilts, Randy. *Conduct Unbecoming: Gays and Lesbians in the U.S. Military.* New York: St. Martin's Press, 1993.

Smith, Geoffrey S. "National Security and Personal Isolation: Sex, Gender, and Disease in the Cold-War United States." *International History Review* 14 (1992): 307–337.

**Stacy Braukman**

*See also* COHN, ROY; EMPLOYMENT LAW AND POLICY; GRAHN, JUDY; HOOVER, J. EDGAR; MILITARY; MILITARY LAW AND POLICY; POLITICAL SCANDALS; ROBBINS, JEROME; WEBSTER, MARGARET.

# GRAHN, Judy (b. 28 July 1940), writer.

Judith Rae Grahn was born in Chicago and grew up in Las Cruces, New Mexico. Her father was a photographer's assistant and her mother was a cook. She attended six colleges before completing her bachelor of arts degree in 1984 at San Francisco State University. At age eighteen she eloped with her first woman lover, who introduced her to clandestine LGBT culture. Grahn entered the air force but was discharged at age twenty-one because she was a lesbian. In addition, her notes and letters were used by investigators against other lesbians in the military. Grahn subsequently moved to Washington, D.C., where she worked a series of jobs and in 1963 picketed the White House with the homophile Mattachine Society.

Using a pseudonym in the early 1960s, Grahn published an article in *Sexology* that argued that lesbians are "not sick," along with a few poems in *The Ladder*, the magazine of the Daughters of Bilitis. In 1964 she wrote "The Psychoanalysis of Edward the Dyke," a satirical prose poem about the attempts of a psychiatrist to cure the title character's lesbianism. Considering the poem too controversial to be publishable, Grahn did not print it until she had co-founded the Women's Press Collective in 1969. Along with Pat Parker, Alta, Susan Griffin, and others, Grahn was a leader of a burgeoning women's poetry movement in the San Francisco Bay Area in the late 1960s and early 1970s. Grahn belonged to the Gay Women's Liberation Group, an early lesbian feminist organization, and co-founded A Woman's Place, one of the first women's bookstores in the country.

In 1969 Grahn wrote the Common Woman poems, seven verse portraits of working women told with poignant attention to detail, illustrating each woman's simultaneous despair and gutsy resistance. These poems end with the promise that the common woman "will rise/and will become strong" (*Work of a Common Woman*, p. 73). Until published in *Edward the Dyke and Other Poems* (1971), they circulated through perform-

ance, publication in movement periodicals, and informal networks around the country.

*Edward the Dyke and Other Poems, She Who* (1972), and *A Woman Is Talking to Death* (1973) were published together as *The Work of a Common Woman* in 1978. *Edward the Dyke* exemplifies Grahn's project of transforming language and images of women, as in the opening lines:

I'm not a girl
I'm a hatchet
I'm not a hole
I'm a whole mountain. (p. 25)

The collection includes poems reclaiming objectified female sexuality, protesting the Vietnam War, centering on animal imagery (a trope developed in her 1988 novel *Mundane's World*), celebrating lesbian sexuality, and proclaiming ownership of the word "dyke."

The *She Who* poems are reminiscent of Gertrude Stein, whom Grahn discusses extensively in *The Highest Apple: Sappho and the Lesbian Poetic Tradition* (1985) and *Really Reading Gertrude Stein* (1989). The repetitions and rhythms invoke a recurring everywoman character, She Who, in poems such as "The enemies of She Who call her various names" and "She Who sits making a first fire." Interspersed are other poems about women's issues, including lesbianism, menstruation, and rape.

Grahn's most critically acclaimed poem is the long meditation on death and oppression, "A Woman Is Talking to Death," which considers the intersections of race, class, gender, and sexuality through vividly painted vignettes in which a wide array of people in need are portrayed as "so many of my lovers" left behind. The poem ends with Grahn's common vow to resist:

to my lovers I bequeath
the rest of my life
. . . . . . . . . . . . . . . . . . . .
your pot is so empty
death, ho death
you shall be poor. (pp. 130–131)

Grahn's epics *The Queen of Wands* (1982) and *The Queen of Swords* (1987, also performed as a stage play) transform Helen of Troy, recalling the work of H.D. In *The Queen of Wands* Helen travels from ancient Greece to Hollywood, spinning the myth of Spider Webster and emerging as the keeper of women's ancient knowledge. In *The Queen of Swords*, Helen reenacts the Sumerian myth of Inanna's descent into and triumphant return from the underworld, here figured as a lesbian bar.

encyclopedia of lesbian, gay, bisexual, and transgender **history in america**

Grahn's exploration of folklore, mythology, and what has been termed speculative archaeology inform her best-known prose work, *Another Mother Tongue: Gay Words, Gay World* (1984), in which Grahn chases down "the litany of words and phrases related to the forbidden subject of our way of being" (p. xii). She weaves a portrait of "Gay culture" as "extremely old" and "continuous . . . worldwide, and [possessing] tribal and spiritual roots" (p. xiv). Like her poetry, Grahn's prose is marked by humor and plays on language, examining and transforming words such as "common," "lover," and "dyke" until they render multiple meanings.

## Bibliography

Carruthers, Mary J. "The Re-Vision of the Muse: Adrienne Rich, Audre Lorde, Judy Grahn, Olga Broumas." *Hudson Review* 36 (1983): 293–322.

Constantine, Lynne, and Suzanne Scott. "Belles Lettres Interview." *Belles Lettres* 2, no. 4 (March–April 1987): 7–8.

Fisher, Delia. *Never-Ending Story: Re-Forming Hero in the Helen Epics of H.D. and Judy Grahn.* Diss., University of Oregon, 1997.

Garber, Linda. "Putting the Word *Dyke* on the Map: Judy Grahn." In her *Identity Poetics: Race, Class, and the Lesbian-Feminist Roots of Queer Theory.* New York: Columbia University Press, 2001.

Grahn, Judy. *The Work of a Common Woman: The Collected Poetry of Judy Grahn.* Oakland, Calif.: Diana Press, 1978.

———. *Another Mother Tongue: Gay Words, Gay Worlds.* Boston: Beacon Press, 1984.

Larkin, Joan. "Taking Risks: Underground Poets from the West Coast—Alta, Judy Grahn, Susan Griffin." *Ms.* 3, no. 11 (May 1975): 90–93.

Seajay, Carol. "The Women-In-Print Movement, Some Beginnings: An Interview with Judy Grahn." *Feminist Bookstore News* 13: 1 (May–June 1990): 19–25; *Feminist Bookstore News* 13, Summer Supplement (August 1990): 53–61; *Feminist Bookstore News* 13, no. 3 (September–October 1990): 35–43.

**Linda Garber**

*See also* ALLEN, PAULA GUNN; STEIN, GERTRUDE, AND ALICE B. TOKLAS.

# GRIER, Barbara (b. 4 November 1933), publisher and archivist.

Barbara Glycine Grier was born in Cincinnati, Ohio, and lived in several midwestern locales during her childhood. Grier's parents divorced when she was thirteen. Her mother, who "was able to withstand any kind of adversity, and was always funny, and up," probably most influenced her life (Grier, p. 73). Grier identified her lesbianism at age twelve, when she discovered she "wanted to jump on the bones of my girlfriend" (Grier, p. 72).

Grier's "love affair with lesbian publishing," as she put it, began at age sixteen, when she "began to collect every written word [she] could find having to do with lesbian lives" (Vida, p. 272). In *Happy Endings*, Grier describes how the task "began as a search, and then . . . became a dream, and then . . . became an obsession" (Brandt, p. 100). Interaction with lesbian bibliographer Jeannette Foster, whom Grier met in her twenties when both were living in Kansas City, further honed Grier's skills: "I had been dedicated before, but I became insane in a real serious way after that" (Brandt, p. 102).

Grier joined the lesbian organization Daughters of Bilitis (DOB) in 1957, shortly after she first saw an issue of its publication, the *Ladder.* She began as a correspondent, submitted several crisp essays, contributed "99 percent" of the book reviews, and became the *Ladder*'s last editor in 1968 "by default" because "no one else would take the job" (Cain, p. 148). When Grier assumed the helm, the *Ladder* counted perhaps 300 subscribers; four years later, subscriptions reached 3,800. Unfortunately, without sufficient advertisers, the *Ladder* "plateaued"; more subscribers simply meant more publication costs.

New DOB chapters began in several cities in 1969 and 1970. Soon Grier and DOB president Rita Laporte took control of the *Ladder* from DOB, turning it into "a very strongly women's liberation magazine" (*Happy Endings*, p. 104). As Grier put it, Laporte and her lover "picked up the magazine, and moved from San Francisco to outside greater Sparks, Nevada," while Grier herself helped direct things from Kansas City. She explains, "We 'stole' the magazine, but there was nothing to steal! . . . Because by that time DOB was nothing but the magazine. And when we went away, DOB died. Literally" (Cain, p. 149). In 1972 the publication, too, became defunct.

Meanwhile, in 1972 librarian Donna McBride fell in love with Grier, and Grier reciprocated, leaving Helen Bennett, her partner of twenty years, for McBride. Barbara calls that decision "the only thing in my life I've ever done that I really was agonized about" (Cain, p. 147). Happily, Grier and McBride remain together in a busy, loving partnership.

After the *Ladder* folded, Grier later wrote, Anyda Marchant and Muriel Crawford "came to me and [Donna], and proposed creating a lesbian/feminist publishing company." She continues, "They lent Donna and me $2,000 of their retirement funds as seed money. In 1973 the Naiad Press was born, with myself and Donna as managing partners" (Vida, p. 272). While Marchant (working under the pen name "Sarah Aldridge") envisioned a vanity press to publish her own works, Grier and McBride embraced a broader concept: a real publishing company.

Many lesbian feminist publishers began around that time, but most quickly folded. What set Naiad apart? According to Grier,

> "We survived through the most careful nurturing of our resources. And through fierce determination.
>
> We did not draw a dime of salary during Naiad's first nine years of existence; we funneled all of Naiad's income and all of our energy into establishing our publishing identity, into making the name Naiad Press synonymous with books by, for, and about lesbians." (Vida, pp. 272–273)

In 1994 Naiad had an in-house staff of eight and projected sales for that year of $1.8 million. In 1999 Grier, who is easing into semi-retirement, gave Kelly Smith, founder of Bella Books, the right to publish most (but not all) of Naiad's authors.

Meanwhile, after years of archiving, in 1992 Grier sent an eighteen-wheeler stuffed with LGBT miscellanea and "about fourteen thousand books" appraised at $400,000 to the San Francisco Public Library's James C. Hormel Gay and Lesbian Center. (She previously had sent myriad periodicals to West Hollywood's June Mazer Lesbian Collection.) Grier notes that "over 70 percent of [the books] were uncataloged in normal reference tools in the United States" and that "we have literally rescued really obscure stuff" (Cain, p. 152). She told Victoria Brownworth, "I feel so gratified that all that collecting and work has a place now, forever" (Bullough, p. 263).

In 1985 the Gay Academic Union, an organization devoted to the teaching of LGBT history, gave Grier its President's Award for Lifetime Service, and in 1992 Grier and McBride received a Lambda Literary Award for Publisher's Service. In addition, Naiad books have won six Lambda Literary Awards and an American Library Association Gay, Lesbian, Bisexual Book Award.

Grier has spent her "entire life determined to bring people to books and books to people" (Cain, p. 146). Her work has accomplished that.

### Bibliography

Brandt, Kate. *Happy Endings: Lesbian Writers Talk about Their Lives and Work.* Tallahassee, Fla.: Naiad, 1993.

Bullough, Vern L., ed. *Before Stonewall: Activists for Gay and Lesbian Rights in Historical Context.* New York: Harrington Park, 2002.

Cain, Paul D. *Leading the Parade: Conversations with America's Most Influential Lesbians and Gay Men.* Lanham, Md.: Scarecrow, 2002.

Grier, Barbara. Interview by Paul D. Cain. Unpublished transcript. 25 November 1994.

Vida, Ginny, ed. *The New Our Right to Love: A Lesbian Resource Book.* New York: Touchstone, 1996.

**Paul D. Cain**

*See also* DAUGHTERS OF BILITIS; FOSTER, JEANNETTE; HOMOPHILE PRESS; *LADDER*; PUBLISHERS.

# GRIMKÉ, Angelina Weld
**(b. 27 February 1880; d. 10 June 1958), poet, playwright.**

A prominent poet and playwright before and during the Harlem Renaissance, Angelina Weld Grimké faded into near obscurity soon thereafter, seemingly because of a struggle between her bisexuality, on the one hand, and black middle-class expectations and her father's dominating will, on the other. The extent to which she felt sexually thwarted is evident in her poetry, especially in the poems that she never tried to have published, and in a diary she kept briefly when she was in her twenties. Filled with images of longing, heartbreak, and death, these works offer a glimpse into the sense of despair and hopelessness that affected Grimké throughout much of her life and ultimately led her to give up writing altogether. Due to her limited literary output, Grimké has garnered less recognition than other Harlem Renaissance writers, but since the middle 1980s, she has received much needed critical attention, as scholars have recognized themes of same-sex desire in her work (although often ignoring her expressions of attraction to men).

As the daughter of one of the leading African American families of her time, Grimké's ability to act on her sexual feelings for both women and men was severely constrained. She was named in honor of her white great aunt, renowned abolitionist and women's rights advocate Angela Grimké Weld, who died the year before her grandniece was born, in 1880. Her father Archibald, a child of Weld's brother and one of his slaves, became a lawyer and was an important Democratic Party activist in the black community of Washington, D.C., and a leader of the National Association for the Advancement of Colored People (NAACP). Archibald Grimké married a socially prominent white woman, but the relationship ended several years after Angelina's birth, and by the time she was seven years old, Angelina was his sole responsibility.

Archibald demanded much of his only child, expecting her to distinguish herself and fulfill the Grimké legacy. She appears never to have measured up in his eyes, despite continually trying to please him, which included placing her relationship with her father above all others. She also strove to make him proud through excelling as a teacher at the prestigious M Street (later renamed the Dunbar) High School in Washington, D.C., and becoming recognized as a playwright and poet.

Grimké's 1916 play *Rachel*, her most famous work, was the first successfully staged drama written by an African American. The title character is a young black woman who decides to forego marriage and motherhood rather than bear children who would be subjected to lynching and other acts of race hatred. Lynching and the futility of having black children in a racist society were also the subjects of several of her short stories, two of which were published in Margaret Sanger's controversial *Birth Control Review*.

In contrast, Grimké's poetry rarely addressed racial themes, but instead focused on romantic desire and unrequited love. These love poems often use feminine imagery and metaphors to indicate the nature of her yearning. For example, one of her most well-known poems, "A Mona Lisa," begins: "I should like to creep / Through the long brown grasses / That are your lashes." Grimké left unpublished most of her love poetry, seemingly because many of these poems openly express desire for women. Less frequently, her published and unpublished writing addresses a male love interest, such as "Little Red Heart of Mine": "Unforgettable is the touch of his strong caressing hands / Piercing sweet the power of his lips . . . / The yearning of his eyes. / Hush! Hush! Little heart. It may never be."

Little is known about Grimké's romantic life. In the mid-1890s, she wrote two love letters to Mamie Edith Karne, a white classmate at Carleton Academy in Northfield, Minnesota, where Grimké was then attending school. She also kept a diary in her early twenties in which she chronicles her emotional anguish over a male love interest who fails to return her affections. When he does not respond to her love letters, she, like many of the protagonists in her fiction and drama, renounces marriage and motherhood, and forswears loving anyone in the future except her father.

After Archibald Grimké's death in 1930, Grimké became even more withdrawn. Without her father—the emotional center of her life—and unable to develop a close relationship with another woman or man, she suffered in isolation. She stopped submitting her poetry for publication and no longer wrote to many of her Harlem Renaissance friends. An apparent recluse for the remainder of her life, she died in 1958.

## Bibliography

Beemyn, Brett. "The New Negro Renaissance, A Bisexual Renaissance: The Lives and Works of Angelina Weld Grimké and Richard Bruce Nugent." In *Modern American Queer History*. Edited by Allida M. Black. Philadelphia: Temple University Press, 2001.

Grimké, Angelina Weld. Papers of Angelina Weld Grimké. Moorland-Spingarn Research Center, Howard University, Washington, D.C.

Herron, Carolivia, ed. *Selected Works of Angelina Weld Grimké*. New York: Oxford University Press, 1991.

Hull, Gloria T. *Color, Sex, and Poetry: Three Women Writers of the Harlem Renaissance*. Bloomington: Indiana University Press, 1987.

**Brett Beemyn**

*See also* HARLEM RENAISSANCE; LITERATURE.

# GUNN, Thom (b. 29 August 1929), poet.

Thom Gunn, born in Great Britain, is the son of Herbert Smith Gunn and Ann Charlotte Thomson. His father was a writer who became an editor at the *Daily Sketch*, a paper with a large circulation. His mother's Scottish family were nonconformists and had no love for the royal family. When Gunn was eight, his family settled in Hampstead, but his parents divorced soon after. Gunn remained close to his mother but not his father, who died in 1961. Gunn was an avid reader as a child, and his first attempt at writing came when his father gave him a dummy newspaper to fill in: the copy had been left out of the columns and Gunn happily supplied the text. He wrote his first novel at the age of twelve, at the request of his mother, while he and his brother were sequestered in a Hampshire school far from the shelling of London during World War II. When his mother died when Gunn was fifteen, he was taken in during vacations by two aunts.

Graduating from the University College School in London, Gunn spent two years in the British army, an experience that he claims was most influential in getting him out of an unrealistic dream world. His sense of literature had been formed to that point by a steady diet of nineteenth-century prose and poetry. In 1950 Gunn entered Cambridge University where he published his first book of poetry, *Fighting Terms*. Some of these early poems reflect Gunn's fascination with leather and motorcycles. Others, for example the "Allegory of the Wolf Boy," offer a veiled look at homosexuality. Still others, such as "Carnal Knowledge," seem gay to modern readers, although Gunn has insisted the poems were written to celebrate femininity. He credits the transformation in his poetry to several good Cambridge friends, including

**Thom Gunn.** The British poet's writings became increasingly explicit in their acknowledgment of his sexuality, including the AIDS-imbued collection *Man with Night Sweats* (1992). [Christopher Felver/corbis]

Mike Kitay, Tony White, and John Coleman. Kitay, an American, eventually became Gunn's lover. Winning a fellowship to Stanford University, Gunn moved to Palo Alto, California. His graduate studies were mentored by Yvor Winters, a premier poet whose style influenced Gunn's second volume of poetry, *Sense of Movement,* a volume that won both an Arts Council Award and the Somerset Maugham Award. It was in California that Gunn visited his first gay bar and the gay scene soon began to influence his writing overtly.

Leaving Stanford to teach for a year in San Antonio, Texas (where he could be near Kitay, who was living on an Air Force base there), Gunn missed the carefree atmosphere of northern California and hated Texas. He moved back to study at Stanford, but dropped out of graduate studies in 1958 to begin teaching at the University of California at Berkeley. In 1964 he lived for a short time in London where he worked with his brother on *Positives,* a book of photographs and verse. Missing California, he returned to Berkeley and found himself caught up in the drug culture, something that he considers to be the

biggest influence to that date on his creativity. Visits in particular to the Geysers, a spa in northern California, inspired important poems infused with the haze of drugs. "Moly," for example, relies heavily on drug images. Gunn gradually demonstrates in his poems a comfort with his homosexuality and drug involvement. Although his early poems only hint at his gay lifestyle, his middle and later poems explicitly acknowledge his sexuality. He survived the antiwar protests of the 1960s and early 1970s at Berkeley, but gave up his tenured position on the university faculty to move to New York City. He commuted to Princeton University in New Jersey where he taught for two years. In 1972 he returned to California where he still lives and teaches from time to time at Berkeley.

Outside of drugs, the most important social influence on Gunn's poetry is the crisis of AIDS. In 1992 he published the *Man with Night Sweats,* a collection that remains one of the most important poetic responses to the disease. It won for the poet the Lenore Marshall Poetry Prize. The book was the result of Gunn's seeing many of his friends die of AIDS. The disease informs every poem in the volume and affords the book a tight cohesiveness that many poets never achieve in a work. In 1993, when Gunn was awarded a MacArthur Fellowship, he published *Shelf Life,* nineteen essays about poets and poetry.

**Bibliography**

Gunn, Thom. *Collected Poems.* New York: Farrar, Straus, Giroux, 1994.

Hagstrom, Jack, and George Bixby. *Thom Gunn: A Bibliography 1940–1978.* London: Bertram Rota, 1979.

Klawitter, George. "Piety and the Agnostic Gay Poet: Thom Gunn's Biblical Homoerotics." In *Reclaiming the Sacred: The Bible in Gay and Lesbian Culture.* Edited by Raymond-Jean Frontain. Binghamton, N.Y.: Haworth, 1997.

Wood, Gregory. "Thom Gunn." In *Articulate Flesh: Male Homo-Eroticism and Modern Poetry.* New Haven, Conn.: Yale University Press, 1987.

**George Klawitter**

# GYMS, FITNESS CLUBS, AND HEALTH CLUBS

By the early twenty-first century, gyms, fitness clubs, and health clubs had frequently come to be associated with consumerism and commercialization in LGBT communities, but they were originally introduced into American life as part of a program of religious and social reform.

Because they were traditionally same-sex environments, and because they focused attention on physical appearance and strength, gyms, fitness clubs, and health clubs have been important sites for LGBT socializing and cruising, especially among gay men. Although the cultures centered in these institutions have often been associated with men, masculinity, and gender exclusion, lesbians have struggled against sexism in gyms, fitness clubs, and health clubs, as well as developed their own cultures within these spaces.

### Urbanization, Physical Culture, and the Rise of the Gymnasium

In the late nineteenth century, the growth of American cities led social reformers to worry that urban environments were not conducive to physical health and strength. Industrial civilization was thought to have generated a new set of physical and mental ailments, which many scholars associated with a "crisis of masculinity." The health and welfare of men became an increasing focus of concern as more people moved into crowded urban neighborhoods where they did not participate in agriculture or outdoor recreation. Between the Civil War and World War I, reformers built urban gymnasiums for the purpose of making physical exercise accessible to a broad spectrum of urban dwellers. Evangelical religious backers of "muscular Christianity" preached that spiritual reform should be fused with the physical development of the body.

Although some reformers advocated gymnastic training for women, many discouraged women from physical exertion because they believed it could threaten their supposedly delicate physical constitutions. Nonetheless, by the late nineteenth century, separate public and private gyms and other athletic facilities were accessible to increasing numbers of women. Some physical fitness advocates encouraged women to practice calisthenics, but women were often encouraged to build strength and stamina as an individual pursuit, rather than in competition with others. Some elite women had access to team sports, but as the historian Harvey Green put it, "collegiate sports for women were an experience of the few" (p. 228).

Meanwhile, late-nineteenth-century male commercial entrepreneurs began promoting physical fitness schemes and marketing images of muscular male bodies to the American public. Physical fitness advocates promoted male bodybuilding both as a spectator sport featuring "showmen," especially the wildly popular Eugene Sandow, and as an activity available to middle-class men in their own homes. Prominent bodybuilders sold dumbbells, weights, books, and photographs of themselves through pamphlets and magazines. Men who desired men and women who desired women were often drawn to these and other manifestations of the physical culture movement.

### Homosocial and Homoerotic Gym Cultures

Although many municipalities built public gymnasiums in the post–Civil War period, urban exercise facilities became especially associated with the Young Men's Christian Association (YMCA). John Donald Gustav-Wrathall has argued, "In order to shape men's physical and sexual development, the YMCA found it necessary to develop an enormous and costly physical plant, but also to create discourses and programs that focused on men's bodies. Both of these moves set the stage for the emergence of a flourishing same-sex sexual underground on YMCA premises" (pp. 156–157). By the 1920s, YMCAs were involved in several scandals involving same-sex sexual contacts and communities, and became widely associated with gay "cruising."

Physique pictorials and magazines, which played a central role in gay male visual and erotic culture in the early and mid-twentieth century, often positioned the subjects of their photographs in gyms and encouraged men to develop and desire the physical attributes pictured in these images. Some publishers oriented to the gay market used physique photos as "covers" for what were partially or essentially gay magazines, so as to circumvent postal censorship and antigay obscenity laws. In this period and later, gay male pornography often featured gym scenes. By emphasizing male beauty, gyms also helped circulate homoerotic imagery among non-gay-identified men. According to the sociologist Alan Klein, a hustler subculture still persists among heterosexually identified young male bodybuilders, who meet their clients in gyms.

Over the course of the twentieth century, lesbians began struggling to overcome sexism in gyms and fitness clubs and the cultural association between maleness and gym culture. Little scholarly research has been done on the history of lesbian gym cultures, but beginning in the late 1960s, lesbians shared with feminist activists an emphasis on the politics of women's bodies. In this period, some lesbian and feminist activists founded gym-based programs to train women in self-defense, in part to increase their power and confidence in the face of sexual harassment and assault.

Susan Stryker and Jim Van Buskirk document that in 1970, a San Francisco Bay Area group called Gay Women's Liberation held a demonstration opposing the exclusion of women from university karate classes. Later, this group picketed alongside heterosexual feminists at the headquarters of a television station that had broadcast an editorial opposing martial arts training for women. Thus, access to athletic facilities could serve as a point of convergence between lesbian and straight feminists who questioned women's exclusion from gyms and athletics. Partly as a result of these types of efforts, in 1972, the U.S. Congress passed Title IX of the Educational Amendments Act, which mandated equal access for women to federally funded school-based athletics.

## Urban LGBT Neighborhoods and Latter-Day Developments

In the post–World War II and then the post–Stonewall Riots eras, urban LGBT communities grew in size and visibility, and countless gay men used public and commercial gymnasiums as places to socialize with and cruise other men. The circulation of male physique magazines and gay pornography increased, and popular gay artists such as Tom of Finland depicted muscular men and their sexual adventures. In the mid-1970s, a highly masculine look known as the "clone" style, which appropriated clothing and mannerisms from working-class male culture, became popular among urban gay men. The clone style eroticized muscles and increased the social pressure on many gay men to work out in gyms or fitness clubs in order to obtain a muscular physique.

"Gym bodies" have been central to gay male culture since the 1970s. Lesbian gym culture has also grown, fueled in part by the influence of gay male gym culture and by the popularity of lesbian sports stars such as Martina Navratilova. The sociologist Martin Levine argues that the AIDS epidemic in the early 1980s heightened the erotic emphasis on muscularity among gay men, as men suffering from AIDS-related "wasting" cultivated a healthy, strong appearance by working out and in some cases taking anabolic steroids. Increased community activity in response to the AIDS epidemic probably accelerated the growth of businesses, including gyms, catering specifically to LGBT communities.

In the late 1980s and 1990s, significant controversies arose in some LGBT communities regarding the prestige of the "gym body." Some commentators argued that emphasis on going to the gym and becoming "buff" was a symptom of the shallowness, exclusivity, and sexism of gay male culture, and that lesbians should not follow this path. Others argued that gay gym culture challenged masculinity by making men's bodies into sexual objects; challenged homophobia by working against stereotypes of the effeminate gay man; and challenged sexual repression by providing gay men with social and sexual space. Similarly, lesbian proponents of gym cultures defended these cultures' potential for confronting sexist attitudes, heightening lesbian eroticism, and promoting lesbian health and strength.

The rise of LGBT gym cultures can be traced to U.S. health reform movements that accompanied late-nineteenth-century urbanization and industrialization, the same two social processes that contributed greatly to the formation of LGBT cultures. In the early twenty-first century, many urban LGBT neighborhoods had commercial gyms, fitness clubs, and health clubs with almost exclusively LGBT clienteles, and exercising and socializing in these spaces had become a very popular LGBT activity.

## Bibliography

Chauncey, George. *Gay New York: Gender, Urban Culture, and the Making of the Gay Male World, 1890–1940.* New York: Basic Books, 1994.

Green, Harvey. *Fit for America: Health, Fitness, Sport, and American Society.* New York: Pantheon, 1986.

Gustav-Wrathall, John Donald. *Take the Young Stranger By the Hand: Same-Sex Relations and the YMCA.* Chicago: University of Chicago Press, 1998.

Klein, Alan M. *Little Big Men: Bodybuilding Subculture and Gender Construction.* Albany: State University of New York Press, 1993.

Levine, Martin P. *Gay Macho: The Life and Death of the Homosexual Clone.* Edited by Michael Kimmel. New York: New York University Press, 1998.

Stryker, Susan, and Jim Van Buskirk. *Gay by the Bay: A History of Queer Culture in the San Francisco Bay Area.* San Francisco: Chronicle Books, 1996.

**Timothy Stewart-Winter**

*See also* BUSINESSES; PHYSICAL EDUCATION; SAME-SEX INSTITUTIONS; SPORTS.